1 MONTH OF
FREE
READING

at

www.ForgottenBooks.com

By purchasing this book you are eligible for one month membership to ForgottenBooks.com, giving you unlimited access to our entire collection of over 1,000,000 titles via our web site and mobile apps.

To claim your free month visit:
www.forgottenbooks.com/free976107

ISBN 978-0-260-84825-3
PIBN 10976107

TRANSACTIONS

OF THE

ROYAL
SCOTTISH ARBORICULTURAL SOCIETY.

A. W. BORTHWICK, D.Sc.,
HONORARY EDITOR.

ROBERT GALLOWAY, S.S.C.,
SECRETARY AND TREASURER.

VOL. XXVII.

STICKING IN A TREE · IT WILL BE GROWING · WHEN YE'RE SLEEPING · YE MAY BE AYE

EDINBURGH:
PRINTED FOR THE SOCIETY.
SOLD BY DOUGLAS & FOULIS, CASTLE STREET.
1913.

CONTENTS.

The Society does not hold itself responsible for the statements or views expressed by the authors of papers.

PAGE

1. The Development Commission and Forestry . . . 1

2. Experimental Forestry Area in Wales. By Fraser Story, University College, Bangor 19

3. Official Notifications:—1. Statement by the Development Commission in regard to State-aided Afforestation—2. Advisory Committee on Forestry for Scotland—3. Technical Advice for Private Owners 28

4. The Utilisation of Disused Pit-banks (with a Plate). By P. Murray Thomson, Whitehall Estate Office, Mealsgate 30

5. Observations on the Annual Increment of Spruce and Scots Pine (Third Article). By J. H. Milne-Home . . 34

6. Death Duties on Woods. By Robert Galloway, S.S.C. . 36

7. Continental Notes—France. By A. G. Hobart-Hampden . 41

8. On Protecting Young Spruce from Frost. By William Hall, Bilton, York 51

9 Some Uses of a Demonstration Forest in Forestry Education (with Plates). By J. F. Annand 54

10. Research Work and Educational Methods of the Forestry Departments and Forestry Schools in the United States and Canada in connection with the study of Timber and other Forest Products. Compiled from the Report of a visit by E. R. Burdon, M.A., to those countries . . 60

11 The Annual Excursion (with Plate). By Wm. Dawson, M.A., B.Sc. 67

12. Douglas Fir Plantation: Taymount Estate. By Frank Scott 77

13 The Arboretum 79

14. Nursery and Plantation Competition 85

15. Forestry Exhibition held in the Highland and Agricultural Society's Showyard at Cupar 102

Notes and Queries:—Deputation to the Chairman of the
     Board of Agriculture for Scotland in June last—Afforesta-
     tion at Talla—The Woodlands of Argyllshire—The Ardgoil
     Estate—The Effects of Light and Shade on Tree-Growth
     —The Uses of Douglas Fir Timber—Production of
     Timber in Great Britain—Appointments—The Action of
     Grass on Fruit Trees—Collection and Utilisation of
     Information for a Forest Survey—International Forest
     Congress at Paris—A Comparison between the Yields
     from Afforestation and Pasture Lands   .   .   .   104

International Memorial to Karl Gayer   114

Reviews and Notices of Books:—History of Forestry. By
     Bernhard E. Fernow. Revised and Enlarged Edition.
     516 pp., including Index. University Press, Toronto,
     1911   115

The Forest Trees of Britain. By the late Rev. C. A. Johns.
     10th Edition. Revised by Professor G. S. Boulger.
     Published by the Society for Promoting Christian Know-
     ledge. Price 6s. net   117

Flora and Sylva: A Monthly Review for Lovers of Gardens,
     Woodland Tree and Flower; New and rare Plants,
     Trees, Shrubs and Fruits; the Garden Beautiful, Home
     Woods and Home Landscape. Edited by and printed
     and published for W. Robinson, author of The English
     Flower Garden, and other works   118

The Story of our Trees. By Margaret M. Gregson. 16 pp.
     and 74 figures. University Press, Cambridge, 1912   .   118

The Care of Trees in Lawn, Street and Park: With a List
     of Trees and Shrubs for Decorative Use. By Bernhard
     E. Fernow, Dean of the Faculty of Forestry, University
     of Toronto. x+392 pp. including Index. Illustrated.
     New York: Henry Holt & Company, 1912   .   .   119

The Oak: Its Natural History, Antiquity, and Folk-lore.
     By Charles Mosley. 126 pp., with 8 Illustrations.
     Price 5s. London: Elliot Stock   120

16. Discussion on the Relation of Forestry to Agriculture and
     other Industries   121

17. Letter to the Board of Agriculture for Scotland   .   .   143

18. Development of Forestry in England. Reports by Advisory
     Committee   147

19. The Place of Forestry in the Economic Development of
     Scotland. By Sir John Stirling-Maxwell, Bart. .   .   161

PAGE

20. Some Lessons from the Recent Gales. By Sir Hugh Shaw Stewart, Bart. 172

21. The State Forests of Saxony. (With Illustrations.) By A. D. Hopkinson 174

22. Report on Speeches made at a meeting between Delegates representing the interests of Forestry in Scotland and the Scottish Railway Companies to discuss the Question of the Price of Sleepers manufactured from Home-Grown Timber as compared with that of those manufactured from Foreign Timber 188

23. A New Disease on the Larch in Scotland (with Plate). By A. W. Borthwick, D.Sc., Lecturer on Forest Botany, University of Edinburgh, and Malcolm Wilson, D.Sc., F.L.S., Lecturer on Mycology, University of Edinburgh . 198

24. Recent Publications on Swiss Forests. By W. S. Smith, Ph.D. 202

25. Notes of Silvicultural Interest (with Plate). By A. Murray . 206

26. The Use of Explosives in Forestry. By Dr Alexander Lauder 210

27. Continental Notes (Germany). By Bert. Ribbentrop, C.I.E. 212

28. The Prices of Home Timber 222

Notes and Queries:—The Rüping Process of Creosoting Timber—Afforestation at Vyrnwy—Deer Forests and Sporting Lands in Scotland—Royal Botanic Garden, Edinburgh: Proposed Guild—Testing of Forest Seeds—Appointments 235

Reviews and Notices of Books:—Illustrations of Conifers. Vol. III. By H. Clinton-Baker. Printed privately at Hertford, 1913 240

Planter's Note Book. By J. Woodward, Junr. *Gardener's Chronicle*, London, 1913. Price, 1s. . . . 241

Forest Conditions of Nova Scotia. By B. E. Fernow, LL.D., Dean of Faculty of Forestry, University of Toronto, assisted by C. D. Howe, Ph.D., and J. H. White. Commission of Conservation, Ottawa, 1912 . . 242

Obituary:—Lieut.-Col. F. Bailey, R.E., LL.D. (with Portrait) —The Late Mr John Grant Thomson—Mr John Methven 245

Proceedings of the Royal Scottish Arboricultural Society, 1913, with Appendices.

List of Members as at 21st June 1913.

TRANSACTIONS

OF THE

ROYAL

SCOTTISH ARBORICULTURAL SOCIETY.

VOL. XXVII.—PART I.

January 1913.

LIEUT.-COLONEL F. BAILEY, F.R.S.E.,
HONORARY EDITOR.

ROBERT GALLOWAY, S.S.C.,
SECRETARY AND TREASURER.

EDINBURGH:
PRINTED FOR THE SOCIETY.
SOLD BY DOUGLAS & FOULIS, CASTLE STREET.

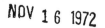

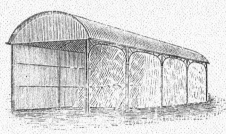
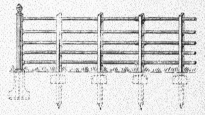

KEITH & CO.

ADVERTISING AGENTS

43 GEORGE STREET
EDINBURGH

ADVERTISEMENTS of every kind are received for insertion in the Daily, Weekly, and Monthly Publications throughout the United Kingdom.

Notices of Sequestration, Cessio, Dissolution of Partnership, Entail, etc., etc., for the Edinburgh and London Gazettes, are given special care and attention.

Legal Notices, Heirs Wanted, and all other Advertisements, are inserted in the Colonial and Foreign Newspapers.

Small Advertisements, such as Situations, Houses, and Apartments, Articles Wanted and For Sale, etc., etc., can be addressed to a No. at Keith & Co.'s Office, 43 George Street, Edinburgh, where the replies will be retained until called for, or, if desired, forwarded by Post. Parties in the country will find this a very convenient method of giving publicity to their requirements.

A SPECIALITY is made of ESTATE and AGRICULTURAL ADVERTISEMENTS, such as FARMS, MANSION HOUSES, etc., TO LET, ESTATES for SALE, AGRICULTURAL SHOWS, etc.

LAW and ESTATE AGENTS, FACTORS, TOWN CLERKS, CLERKS TO SCHOOL BOARDS, and other Officials may, with confidence, place their advertisements in the hands of the Firm.

One Copy of an Advertisement is sufficient to send for any number of newspapers; and the convenience of having only one advertising account instead of a number of advertising accounts is also a great saving of time and trouble.

Addressing of Envelopes with Accuracy and Despatch.

Telegrams—"PROMOTE," EDINBURGH.　　　　Telephone No. 316.

*a

The West of Scotland Agricultural College,

BLYTHSWOOD SQUARE, GLASGOW.

DEPARTMENT OF FORESTRY.

Day and Evening Classes, which provide a complete Course of Instruction in Forestry, qualifying (*pro tanto*) for the B.Sc. Degree of the University of Glasgow, for the Diploma of the Highland and Agricultural Society, and for the Certificate of the College, are held during the Winter Session (October to March) at the College.

A Special Summer Course for Foresters will be held at the College during the month of June.

Syllabus and particulars regarding these Classes and Prospectus of the general work of the College, including the Course for the Examination of the Surveyor's Institution, may be obtained free from the Secretary.

FOREST TREES, FRUIT TREES, SHRUBS, ROSES, &c.,

Grown in a most exposed situation on Heavy Soils, therefore the hardiest procurable.

Every Requisite for FOREST, FARM, and GARDEN.

Estimates for Planting by Contract furnished.

CATALOGUES ON APPLICATION.

W. & T. SAMSON, KILMARNOCK.

ESTABLISHED 1759.

JAMES JONES & SONS, LTD.,

LARBERT SAWMILLS,

LARBERT, N.B.

All kinds of HOME TIMBER in the Round or Sawn-up,

SUITABLE FOR

RAILWAYS, SHIPBUILDERS, COLLIERIES, CONTRACTORS, COACHBUILDERS, CARTWRIGHTS, &c., &c.

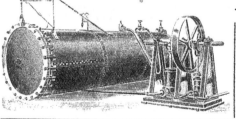
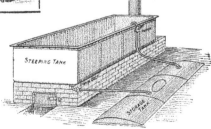

NOTICE.

WANTED TO PURCHASE.

Any of the following Parts of the *Transactions*, viz.:

Parts 1, 2, and 3 of Vol. I.

Parts 2 and 3   of Vol. III.

Parts 1 and 2   of Vol. IV.

Part 2   of Vol. V.

Part 2   of Vol. IX.

Part 1   of Vol. XII.

===

Apply to

—— THE SECRETARY, ——

19 CASTLE STREET, EDINBURGH.

Royal Scottish Arboricultural Society.

INSTITUTED 1854.

Patron—HIS MOST EXCELLENT MAJESTY THE KING.

Permission to assume the title "Royal" was granted by Her Majesty Queen Victoria in 1887.

OFFICE-BEARERS FOR 1912.

President.

SIR JOHN STIRLING-MAXWELL, Bart. of Pollok, Pollokshaws.

Vice-Presidents.

EUART FOTHRINGHAM of Murthly, Perthshire.
RT FORBES, Overseer, Kennet Estate Office, Alloa.
. W. BORTHWICK, D.Sc., 46 George Square, Edinburgh.

SYDNEY J. GAMMELL of Drumtochty, Countesswells House, Bieldside, Aberdeen.
CHAS. BUCHANAN, Overseer, Penicuik Estate, Penicuik.
The LORD LOVAT, D.S.O., Beaufort Castle, Beauly.

Council.

HON. LIFE MEMBER.

SIR KENNETH J. MACKENZIE, Bart. of Gairloch, 10 Moray Place, Edinburgh.

ORDINARY MEMBERS.

. MACDONALD, Overseer, Haystoun Estate, Woodbine ottage, Peebles.
ERT ALLAN, Factor, Polkemmet, Whitburn.
M SPIERS, Timber Merchant, Warriston Saw-Mills, Edinburgh.
ES COOK, Land Steward, Arniston, Gorebridge.
XANDER MITCHELL, Forester, Rosebery, Gorebridge.
ANDREW AGNEW, Bart., Lochnaw Castle, Stranraer.
NK SCOTT, Forester, Scone.
. LEVEN, Forester, Bowmont Forest, Roxburgh.
IN BROOM, Wood Merchant, Bathgate.
N F. ANNAND, Lecturer in Forestry, Armstrong College, Newcastle-upon-Tyne.
IN W. M'HATTIE, Superintendent of City Parks, City Chambers, Edinburgh.

BRODIE OF BRODIE, Brodie Castle, Forres.
WILLIAM DAWSON, M.A., B.Sc., Lecturer in Forestry, Marischal College, Aberdeen.
JOHN METHVEN, Nurseryman, 15 Princes Street, Edinburgh.
GILBERT BROWN, Wood Manager, Grantown-on-Spey.
WILLIAM DAVIDSON, Forester, Panmure, Carnoustie.
A. T. GILLANDERS, F.E.S., Forester, Park Cottage, Alnwick.
W. H. MASSIE, Nurseryman, 1 Waterloo Place, Edinburgh.
A. D. RICHARDSON, 6 Dalkeith Street, Joppa.
Captain ARCHIBALD STIRLING of Keir, Dunblane.
JAMES WHITTON, Superintendent of City Parks, City Chambers, Glasgow.

Hon. Editor.

LIEUT.-COLONEL F. BAILEY, LL.D., F.R.S.E., 7 Drummond Place, Edinburgh.

Auditor.

JOHN T. WATSON, 16 St Andrew Square, Edinburgh.

Hon. Secretary.

The RIGHT HON. R. C. MUNRO FERGUSON, M.P., Raith House, Kirkcaldy.

Secretary and Treasurer.

ROBERT GALLOWAY, S.S.C., 19 Castle Street, Edinburgh.

ABERDEEN BRANCH.

esident—A. FORBES IRVINE of Drum.
on. Secy.—GEORGE D. MASSIE, Solicitor, 147 Union Street, Aberdeen.

NORTHERN BRANCH.

President—BRODIE OF BRODIE.
Hon. Secy.—ALEX. FRASER, Solicitor, 63 Church Street, Inverness.

Hon. Consulting Officials.

nsulting Botanist.—ISAAC BAYLEY BALFOUR, LL.D, M.D., Sc.D., Professor of Botany, Royal Botanic Garden, Edinburgh.
nsulting Chemist.—ALEXANDER LAUDER, D.Sc., F.I C., 13 George Square, Edinburgh.
nsulting Cryptogamist.—A. W. BORTHWICK, D.Sc., Royal Botanic Garden, Edinburgh.

Consulting Entomologist. — ROBERT STEWART MACDOUGALL, M.A., D.Sc., Professor of Entomology, etc., 9 Dryden Place, Edinburgh.
Consulting Geologist.—R. CAMPBELL, M.A., B.Sc., Geological Laboratory, University of Edinburgh.
Consulting Meteorologist.—ANDREW WATT, M.A., F.R.S.E., Secretary Scottish Meteorological Society, 122 George Street, Edinburgh.

*

Former Presidents.

The following have held the office of President in past years, viz. :—

1854-56. JAMES BROWN, Wood Commissioner to the Earl of Seafield.
1857. The Right Hon. THE EARL OF DUCIE.
1858. The Right Hon. THE EARL OF STAIR.
1859. Sir JOHN HALL, Bart. of Dunglass.
1860. His Grace THE DUKE OF ATHOLL.
1861. JOHN I. CHALMERS of Aldbar.
1862. The Right Hon. THE EARL OF AIRLIE.
1863. The Right Hon. T. F. KENNEDY.
1864-71. ROBERT HUTCHISON of Carlowrie, F.R.S.E.
1872-73. HUGH CLEGHORN, M.D., LL.D., F.R.S.E., of Stravithie.
1874-75. Professor JOHN HUTTON BALFOUR, University of Edinburgh.
1876-78. The Right Hon. W. P. ADAM of Blair-adam, M.P.
1879-81. The Most Hon. THE MARQUIS OF LOTHIAN, K.T.

1882. Professor ALEXANDER DICKSON, Univ‹ of Edinburgh.
1883-85. HUGH CLEGHORN, M.D., LL.D., F.R. of Stravithie.
1886-87. The Right Hon. Sir HERBERT EUS MAXWELL, Bart. of Monreith.
1888-89. The Most Hon. THE MARQUI‹ LINLITHGOW.
1890-93. Professor BAYLEY BALFOUR, Univ‹ of Edinburgh.
1894-97. The Right Hon. R. C. MUNRO FERGI M.P.
1898. Colonel F. BAILEY, R.E.
1899-02. The Right Hon. THE EARL OF MANSF:
1903-06. W. STEUART FOTHRINGHAM of Murtl
1907-09. Sir KENNETH J. MACKENZIE, Bar Gairloch.

Membership.

THE Roll contains the names of over 1400 Members, comprising Landowners, Factors, Foresters, Nurserymen, Gardeners, Land Stewards, Wood Merchants, and others interested in Forestry, many of whom reside in England, Ireland, the British Colonies, and India.

Members are elected by the Council. The Terms of Subscription will be found on the back of the Form of Proposal for Membership which accompanies this Memorandum.

The Principal Objects of the Society,

and the nature of its work, will be gathered from the following paragraphs:—

Meetings.

The Society holds periodical Meetings for the transaction of business, the reading and discussion of Papers, the exhibition of new Inventions, specimens of Forest Products and other articles of special interest to the Members, and for the advancement of Forestry in all its branches. Meetings of the Council are held every alternate month, and at other times when business requires attention; and Committees of the Council meet frequently to arrange and carry out the work of the Society.

Prizes and Medals.

With the view of encouraging young Foresters to study, and to train themselves in habits of careful and accurate observation, the Society offers Annual Prizes and Medals for essays on practical subjects, and for inventions connected with appliances used in Forestry. Such awards have been granted continuously since 1855 up to the present time, and have yielded satisfactory results. Medals and Prizes are also awarded in connection with the Exhibitions and Competitions for Plantations and Estate Nurseries aftermentioned.

School of Forestry, Afforestation, Etc.

Being convinced of the necessity for bringing within the reach of young Foresters, and others interested in the Profession, a regular systematic course of Instruction, the Society, in 1882, strongly urged the creation of a British School of Forestry; and with a view of stimulating public interest in the matter, a Forestry Exhibition, chiefly organised by the Council, was held in Edinburgh in 1884.

In 1890, the Society instituted a Fund for the purpose of establishing a Chair of Forestry at the University of Edinburgh, and a sum of £584, 3s. 10d. has since been raised by the Society and handed over to the University. Aided by an annual subsidy from the Board of Agriculture, which the Society was mainly instrumental in obtaining, a Course of Lectures at the University has been delivered without interruption since 1889. The Society also drew up a Scheme for the Establishment of a State Model or Demonstration Forest for Scotland, which might serve not only for purposes of instruction but also as a Station for Research and Experiment, and as a Model Forest, by which Landowners and Foresters throughout the country might benefit. Copies of this Scheme were laid before the Departmental Committee on British Forestry, and in their Report the Committee recommended the establishment of a Demonstration Area and the provision of other educational facilities in Scotland.

The Government recently acquired the Estate of Inverliever in Argyllshire; and while this cannot be looked on as a Demonstration Forest, it is hoped that it may prove to be the first step in a scheme of afforestation by the State of unwooded lands in Scotland. Meantime Mr Munro Ferguson, M.P., for a part of whose woods at Raith a Working-Plan is in operation, has very kindly agreed to allow Students to visit them.

After the Development Act came into operation, the Council passed a Resolution urging that the Government should, as soon as possible, create a Board of Forestry, with an adequate representation of Scottish Forestry upon it, and an Office in Scotland, where the largest areas of land suitable for Afforestation are situated, which would provide Demonstration Forests and Forest Gardens, and otherwise assist the development of University and other Educational enterprise, and would carry out, as an essential preliminary to any great scheme of National Afforestation, a Survey of all areas throughout the country suitable for commercial planting. The Society's policy for the development of Forestry in Scotland has since been fully laid before the Development Commission. As a result of these representations, the Secretary for Scotland appointed a Committee to report regarding the acquisition and uses of a Demonstration Forest Area, and any further steps it is desirable to take in order to promote Silviculture in Scotland. The Committee reported in the beginning of this year, and the Society is now pressing the present Secretary for Scotland to give immediate effect to the Committee's recommendations, including the appointment of a Department of Forestry for Scotland promised by his predecessor.

The Society has also published a valuable Report on Afforestation —including a Survey of Glen Mor—prepared for it by Lord Lovat and Captain Stirling, which, it is hoped, may form the basis of the general Forest Survey advocated by the Society.

Excursions.

Since 1878 well-organised Excursions, numerously attended by Members of the Society, have been made annually to various parts of Scotland, England, Ireland, and the Continent. In 1895 a Tour extending over twelve days was made through the Forests of Northern Germany, in 1902 a Tour extending over seventeen days was made in Sweden, in 1904 the Forest School at Nancy and Forests in the north of France were visited, in 1909 a visit was undertaken to the Bavarian Forests, and it is now proposed to visit Switzerland during the ensuing summer. These Excursions enable Members whose occupations necessarily confine them chiefly to a single locality to study the conditions and methods prevailing elsewhere; and the Council propose to extend the Tours during the next few years to other parts of the Continent. They venture to express the hope that Landowners may be induced to afford facilities to their Foresters for participation in these Tours, the instructive nature of which renders them well worth the moderate expenditure of time and money that they involve.

Exhibitions.

A Forestry Exhibition is annually organised in connection with the Highland and Agricultural Society's Show, in which are exhibited specimens illustrating the rate of growth of trees, different kinds of wood, pit-wood and railway timber, insect pests and samples of the damage done by them, tools and implements, manufactured articles peculiar to the district where the Exhibition is held, and other objects of interest relating to Forestry. Prizes and Medals are also offered for Special Exhibits. In addition to the Annual Exhibition before referred to, large and important Forestry Sections organised by this Society were included in the Scottish National Exhibition held in Edinburgh in 1908, and in the Scottish Exhibition of National History, Art, and Industry, held in Glasgow in 1911.

Plantations and Estate Nurseries Competitions.

Prizes are now offered annually for the best Young Plantations and the best managed Estate Nurseries within the Show District of the Highland and Agricultural Society.

The *Society's Transactions.*

The *Transactions* of the Society, which extend to twenty-six volumes, are now published half-yearly in January and July, and are issued *gratis* to Members. A large number of the Prize Essays and other valuable Papers, and reports of the Annual Excursions, have appeared in them, and have thus become available to Students as well as to those actively engaged in the Profession of Forestry.

Honorary Consulting Officials.

Members have the privilege of obtaining information gratuitously upon subjects connected with Forestry from the Honorary Officials mentioned above.

Local Branches.

Local Branches have been established in Aberdeen and Inverness for the convenience of Members who reside in the districts surrounding these centres.

Local Secretaries.

The Society is represented throughout Scotland, England, and Ireland by the Local Secretaries whose names are given below. They are ready to afford any additional information that may be desired regarding the Conditions of Membership and the work of the Society.

Register of Estate Men.

A Register of men qualified in Forestry and in Forest and Estate Management is kept by the Society. Schedules of application and other particulars may be obtained from the Local Secretaries in the various districts, or direct from the Secretary. It is hoped that Proprietors and others requiring Estate men will avail themselves of the Society's Register.

Consulting Foresters.

The Secretary keeps a list of Consulting Foresters whose services are available to Members of the Society and others.

Correspondents.

The following have agreed to act as Correspondents residing abroad :—

Canada, . ROBERT BELL, I.S.O., M.D., LL.D., D.Sc.(Cantab.), etc., Chief Geologist to Government of Canada, Ottawa.

India, . . F. L. C. COWLEY BROWN, Principal, South Indian Forest College, Coimbatore, South India.

British East Africa, . EDWARD BATTISCOMBE, Assistant Conservator of Forests. Nigeri, *via* Naivasha, East Africa Protectorate.

United States of America, HUGH P. BAKER, Dean, New York State College of Forestry, Syracuse, N.Y.

Cape Colony, . W. NIMMO BROWN, M'Kenzie's Farm, Mowbray, P.O.

Western Australia, FRED MOON.

LOCAL SECRETARIES.

Counties. *Scotland.*

Aberdeen, . JOHN CLARK, Forester, Haddo House, Aberdeen.

JOHN MICHIE, M.V.O., Factor, Balmoral, Ballater.

Argyll, . . H. L. MACDONALD of Dunach, Oban.

Ayr, . . ANDREW D. PAGE, Overseer, Culzean Home Farm, Ayr.

A. B. ROBERTSON, Forester, The Dean, Kilmarnock.

Berwick, . WM. MILNE, Foulden Newton, Berwick-on-Tweed.

Bute, . . WM. INGLIS, Forester, Cladoch, Brodick.

JAMES KAY, retired Forester, Barone, Rothesay.

Clackmannan,. ROBERT FORBES, Estate Office, Kennet, Alloa.

Dumfries, . D. CRABBE, Forester, Byreburnfoot, Canonbie.

East Lothian, . W. S. CURR, Factor, Ninewar, Prestonkirk.

Fife, . . WM. GILCHRIST, Forester, Nursery Cottage, Mount Melville, St Andrews.

EDMUND SANG, Nurseryman, Kirkcaldy.

Forfar, . . JAMES CRABBE, retired Forester, Glamis.

Scotland.

Counties.	
Inverness,	. JAMES A. GOSSIP, Nurseryman, Inverness.
Kincardine,	. JOHN HART, Estates Office, Cowie, Stonehaven.
Kinross,	. JAMES TERRIS, Factor, Dullomuir, Blairadam.
Lanark, .	. JOHN DAVIDSON, Forester, Dalzell, Motherwell.
	JAMES WHITTON, Superintendent of Parks, City Chambers, Glasgow.
Moray, .	. D. SCOTT, Forester, Darnaway Castle, Forres.
Perth, .	. JOHN SCRIMGEOUR, Doune Lodge, Doune.
Ross, .	. JOHN J. R. MEIKLEJOHN, Factor, Novar, Evanton.
	Miss AMY FRANCES YULE, Tarradale House, Muir of Ord.
Roxburgh,	. JOHN LEISHMAN, Manager, Cavers Estate, Hawick.
	R. V. MATHER, Nurseryman, Kelso.
Sutherland,	. DONALD ROBERTSON, Forester, Dunrobin, Golspie.
Wigtown,	. JAMES HOGARTH, Forester, Culhorn, Stranraer.
	H. H. WALKER, Monreith Estate Office, Whauphill.

England.

Beds, .	. FRANCIS MITCHELL, Forester, Woburn.
Berks, .	. W. STORIE, Whitway House, Newbury.
Derby, .	. S. MACBEAN, Estate Office, Needwood Forest, Sudbury.
Devon, .	. JAMES BARRIE, Forester, Stevenstone Estate, Torrington.
Durham,	. JOHN F. ANNAND, Lecturer in Forestry, Armstrong College, Newcastle-upon-Tyne.
Hants, .	. W. R. BROWN, Forester, Park Cottage, Heckfield, Winchfield.
Herts, .	. JAMES BARTON, Forester, Hatfield.
	THOMAS SMITH, Overseer, Tring Park, Wigginton, Tring.
Kent, .	. R. W. COWPER, Gortanore, Sittingbourne.
Lancashire,	. D. C. HAMILTON, Forester, Knowsley, Prescot.
Leicester,	. JAMES MARTIN, The Reservoir, Knipton, Grantham.
Lincoln,	. W. B. HAVELOCK, The Nurseries, Brocklesby Park.
Middlesex,	. Professor BOULGER, 11 Onslow Road, Richmond Hill, London, S.W.
Notts, .	. WM. ELDER, Thoresby, Ollerton, Newark.
	W. MICHIE, Forester, Welbeck, Worksop.
	WILSON TOMLINSON, Forester, Clumber Park, Worksop.
Suffolk, .	. GEORGE HANNAH, The Folly, Ampton Park, Bury St Edmunds.
Surrey, .	. JOHN ALEXANDER, 24 Lawn Crescent, Kew Gardens.
Warwick,	. A. D. CHRISTIE, Hillside, Frederick Road, Selly Oak, Birmingham.
Wilts, .	. ANDREW BOA, Land Agent, Glenmore, The Avenue, Trowbridge.
York, .	. D. TAIT, Estate Bailiff, Owston Park, Doncaster.

Ireland.

Dublin, .	. A. C. FORBES, Department of Forestry, Board of Agriculture.
	JAMES WILSON, B.Sc., Royal College of Science, Dublin.
	ARCH. E. MOERAN, Lissadell, Stillorgan Park.
Galway,	. THOMAS ROBERTSON, Forester and Bailiff, Woodlawn.
King's County,	WM. HENDERSON, Forester, Clonad Cottage, Tullamore.
Tipperary,	. DAVID G. CROSS, Forester, Kylisk, Nenagh.
	ALEX. M'RAE, Forester, Dundrum.

Royal Scottish Arboricultural Society.

———•———

FORM OF PROPOSAL FOR MEMBERSHIP.

To be signed by the Candidate, his Proposer and Seconder, and returned to **ROBERT GALLOWAY**, S.S.C., *SECRETARY*, Royal Scottish Arboricultural Society, 19 Castle Street, Edinburgh.

Candidate's
- *Full Name,* ....
- *Designation, Degrees, etc.,* ....
- *Address,* . ...
- *Life, or Ordinary Member,* ....
- *Signature,* . . ..

Proposer's
- *Signature,* . . ..
- *Address,* . . ..

Seconder's
- *Signature,* . . ..
- *Address,* . . ..

[**CONDITIONS OF MEMBERSHIP**, see Over.

CONDITIONS OF MEMBERSHIP (excerpted from the Laws).

III. Any person interested in Forestry, and desirous of promoting the objects of the Society, is eligible for election as an *Ordinary* Member in one of the following Classes :—

1. Proprietors the valuation of whose land *exceeds* £500 per annum, and others, subscribing annually . . One Guinea.

2. Proprietors the valuation of whose land *does not exceed* £500 per annum, Factors, Nurserymen, Timber Merchants, and others, subscribing annually . . Half-a-Guinea.

3. Foresters, Gardeners, Land-Stewards, Tenant Farmers, and others, subscribing annually . . . Six Shillings.

4. Assistant-Foresters, Assistant-Gardeners, and others, subscribing annually . . . . . Four Shillings.

IV. **Subscriptions are due on the 1st of January in each year, and shall be payable in advance. A new Member's Subscription is due on the day of election unless otherwise provided, and he shall not be enrolled until he has paid his first Subscription.**

V. Members in arrear shall not receive the *Transactions*, and shall not be entitled to vote at any of the meetings of the Society. Any Member whose Annual Subscription remains unpaid for two years shall cease to be a Member of the Society, and no such Member shall be eligible for re-election till his arrears have been paid up.

VI. Any eligible person may become a *Life* Member of the Society, on payment, according to class, of the following sums :—

1. Large Proprietors of land, and others, . . . £10 10 0

2. Small Proprietors, Factors, Nurserymen, Timber Merchants, and others, ... 5 5 0

3. Foresters, Gardeners, Land-Stewards, Tenant Farmers, and others, ... 3 3 0

VII. Any *Ordinary* Member of Classes 1, 2, and 3, who has paid *Five* Annual Subscriptions, may become a *Life* Member on payment of *Two-thirds* of the sum payable by a *new* Life Member.

XII. Every Proposal for Membership shall be made in writing, and shall be signed by two Members of the Society as Proposer and Seconder, and delivered to the Secretary to be laid before the Council, which shall accept or otherwise deal with each Proposal as it may deem best in the interest of the Society. The Proposer and Seconder shall be responsible for payment of the new Member's first Subscription. The Council shall have power to decide the Class under which any Candidate for Membership shall be placed.

CONTENTS.

The Society does not hold itself responsible for the statements or views expressed by the authors of papers.

PAGE

1. The Development Commission and Forestry . . . 1

2. Experimental Forestry Area in Wales. By Fraser Story, University College, Bangor 19

3. Official Notifications:—1. Statement by the Development Commission in regard to State-aided Afforestation—2. Advisory Committee on Forestry for Scotland—3. Technical Advice for Private Owners 28

4. The Utilisation of Disused Pit-banks (with a Plate). By P. Murray Thomson, Whitehall Estate Office, Mealsgate 30

5. Observations on the Annual Increment of Spruce and Scots Pine (Third Article). By J. H. Milne-Home . . 34

6. Death Duties on Woods. By Robert Galloway, S.S.C. . 36

7. Continental Notes—France. By A. G. Hobart-Hampden . 41

8. On Protecting Young Spruce from Frost. By William Hall, Bilton, York 51

9. Some Uses of a Demonstration Forest in Forestry Education (with Plates). By J. F. Annand 54

10. Research Work and Educational Methods of the Forestry Departments and Forestry Schools in the United States and Canada in connection with the study of Timber and other Forest Products. Compiled from the Report of a visit by E. R. Burdon, M.A., to those countries . . 60

11. The Annual Excursion (with Plate). By Wm. Dawson, M.A., B.Sc. 67

12. Douglas Fir Plantation: Taymount Estate. By Frank Scott 77

13. The Arboretum 79

14. Nursery and Plantation Competition 85

15 Forestry Exhibition held in the Highland and Agricultural Society's Showyard at Cupar 102

PAGE

Notes and Queries:—Deputation to the Chairman of the Board of Agriculture for Scotland in June last—Afforestation at Talla—The Woodlands of Argyllshire—The Ardgoil Estate—The Effects of Light and Shade on Tree-Growth —The Uses of Douglas Fir Timber—Production of Timber in Great Britain—Appointments—The Action of Grass on Fruit Trees—Collection and Utilisation of Information for a Forest Survey—International Forest Congress at Paris—A Comparison between the Yields from Afforestation and Pasture Lands . . . 104

International Memorial to Karl Gayer 114

Reviews and Notices of Books:—History of Forestry. By Bernhard E. Fernow. Revised and Enlarged Edition. 516 pp., including Index. University Press, Toronto, 1911 115

The Forest Trees of Britain. By the late Rev. C. A. Johns. 10th Edition. Revised by Professor G. S. Boulger. Published by the Society for Promoting Christian Knowledge. Price 6s. net 117

Flora and Sylva: A Monthly Review for Lovers of Gardens, Woodland Tree and Flower; New and rare Plants, Trees, Shrubs and Fruits; the Garden Beautiful, Home Woods and Home Landscape. Edited by and printed and published for W. Robinson, author of *The English Flower Garden*, and other works 118

The Story of our Trees. By Margaret M. Gregson. 160 pp. and 74 figures. University Press, Cambridge, 1912 . 118

The Care of Trees in Lawn, Street and Park: With a List of Trees and Shrubs for Decorative Use. By Bernhard E. Fernow, Dean of the Faculty of Forestry, University of Toronto. x + 392 pp. including Index. Illustrated. New York: Henry Holt & Company, 1910 . . 119

The Oak: Its Natural History, Antiquity, and Folk-lore. By Charles Mosley. 126 pp., with 8 Illustrations. Price 5s. London: Elliot Stock 120

We regret to announce the death, on December 21, 1912, of Lieut.-Colonel F. Bailey, F.R.S.E., Honorary Editor of the " Transactions."

TRANSACTIONS

OF THE

ROYAL SCOTTISH ARBORICULTURAL SOCIETY.

1. The Development Commission and Forestry.

EXTRACTS FROM THE REPORT OF THE COMMISSIONERS FOR
THE YEAR ENDED THE 31ST OF MARCH 1912.

In regard to the General Position of the Commissioners and
the Principles of their Action, they say that from the provisions
of the Act establishing the Development Commission and
Development Fund three main results followed: first, that the
Commissioners themselves have no power to make grants or
loans from the Fund, but can only recommend expenditure
which needs to be authorised by the Government; secondly,
that they have no executive powers; thirdly, that they have no
formal and official cognizance of applications from bodies
other than Government Departments, and cannot report to
the Treasury on them until the applications have been examined
by and passed through the Departments concerned with their
subject-matter.

For various reasons, they think that it would be a mistake
to suppose that the schemes already put before them are an
adequate measure of the funds which should properly be
devoted to such purposes, among others, as afforestation.

The Commissioners consider that the improvement of inland
navigations, afforestation, the reclamation of land, fall into
the category of schemes which do not in principle differ from
ordinary business investments. They may be outside the usual
range of commercial enterprise, either because the time required
for their full fruition is too long, or because it is in practice
impossible to obtain for the individual investor a fair proportion
of the additional wealth which the country has gained through
the use of his capital. These objections do not apply to the
State, or apply only with reduced force; and they do not touch
the principle which the Commissioners have adopted, that such

schemes are cases for support by loan. From the later portion of this Report, it will be seen that far the greater portion of the expenditure from the Fund will be advanced by way of grant—necessarily, since the purposes to which the Commissioners have decided to allocate it are those of instruction, organisation and research. But it will also be seen that in the comparatively few cases where applications have been made for assistance to schemes expected ultimately to give a direct return, the Commissioners have held to the principle of loans.

They have not overlooked the question of the general state and prospects of employment, as affecting advances from the Development Fund. They are able again to congratulate themselves that these are at present good, and the advances made during the year are not such as to involve any large employment of labour at a very early date. In the important matter of afforestation they have stipulated that detailed schemes should provide for varying the extent of the operations in relation to the state of the labour market.

In their previous Report they stated that they propose to ensure, so far as it lies in their power, that the Fund shall not go into the pockets of private individuals. The Act itself gives no authority to make grants or loans either to individuals or to companies or associations of persons trading for profit. But the effect of this restriction is that sometimes the most direct way and simple method of giving effect to the purposes named in the Act is closed to the Commissioners. Afforestation might be sensibly assisted if it were open to them to recommend loans directly to private owners.

The existing law, however, prohibits the direct support of this kind of scheme from the Development Fund; and the Commissioners recognise the difficulties and dangers which Parliament had in mind when laying down this prohibition.

There is one further distinction which the Commissioners have tried to observe in their recommendations; but it is not one, they fear, which will commend itself in all quarters. The main purpose of the Development Fund is the development of certain industries, particularly agriculture (including forestry) and fisheries—which they understand to mean, principally, an increase in the production of those industries. Since the money available is limited, this object is not always identical with the development of some of the places where the industry is carried on. In the circumstances as they are, the Commissioners are bound to make a selection, and the criterion imposed on them by the Act is the development of the industry as a whole.

After the general remarks from which the above notes have been taken, the Commissioners proceed to deal in detail with each of the purposes mentioned in the Act, and we give in full the sections relating to Forestry.

FORESTRY.

(i.) *General.*

During the year 1911-12 the Commissioners received thirteen applications which fall mainly or entirely under this heading. It was not always made clear what was the exact amount of the advance desired; but so far as can be ascertained, the total of the advances for which application was made amounted to £114,780.[1] The Commissioners have recommended for the current year the grant of sums amounting to £15,460 : these are in some cases only the first instalments, and imply similar grants in future years, if funds are available.

The Commissioners stated in their previous Report[2] the main principles which they had formulated for their guidance in considering British schemes and applications in respect of forestry and afforestation. They may almost be reduced to one, viz., that education and the provision of technical advice are the best lines of advance for the immediate present. As the details of the Commissioners' action are stated below, they need not be set forth here; but it may be said that in accordance with this principle the Commissioners have recommended grants from the Development Fund of £500 a year in aid of technical advice and instruction at each of five centres in England and Wales—Oxford, Cambridge, Cirencester, Bangor and Newcastle; further grants amounting to £1200 a year in aid of research work; and a grant of £1000 for minor forestry experiments. All these grants are necessarily provisional, pending the establishment of a central demonstration area, where, in the Commissioners' opinion, a great—perhaps the principal—part

[1] These figures do not include several applications in which no sum was expressly mentioned.   [2] See vol. xxvi. p. 3.

of the State-aided educational and research work in forestry should be centred. The Commissioners think that such an area may be found among the existing Crown woods, in which case the heavy cost of acquiring a privately-owned forest would be avoided. At the end of the year this question *inter alia* was being considered by a Committee of the Board of Agriculture and Fisheries, on which the Development Commission was represented by Sir S. Eardley-Wilmot.

In Scotland the Commissioners have recommended considerable grants for the assistance of the Forestry School at Edinburgh; they trust that in administering them the University and the East of Scotland College of Agriculture will work in the spirit of harmony and co-operation which the Commissioners have endeavoured to help in promoting. But the main outstanding requirement of Scotch forestry education, as of English, is a demonstration area. The Commissioners stated last year their general views on this question, and explained that it was being considered in detail by a Committee appointed by the Secretary for Scotland. They have not yet received the definite proposals which the newly established Board of Agriculture for Scotland will no doubt formulate on considering the Committee's report.

Meanwhile the Commissioners see no reason why local authorities should not be assisted by loans on easy terms to afforest suitable land under their control, such as water catchment areas. They have already received a few schemes; but desiring to encourage local activity in this direction, they have recently issued a public notice, and drawn to it the special attention of some of the authorities who are known to control land not under wood. If this invitation produces a satisfactory response from the authorities, they hope that it may prove possible, at a comparatively small cost to the State, to add considerably to the afforested areas of the country, and, incidentally, to gain experience which may be of value to the State, to local authorities, and to private owners.

(ii.) *England and Wales.*

In the previous report, it was stated that the Commissioners had received at the close of their first year a memorandum from the Board of Agriculture and Fisheries outlining a comprehensive scheme of forestry for England and Wales, and that they were communicating with the Board on the subject. Under the scheme submitted grants would be required from the Development Fund, amounting during the next few years to about £200,000. The principal objects of the scheme were a national forest survey of England and Wales, experiments in existing woodlands (with the co-operation of the Royal English Arboricultural Society), the provision of experimental forests in different parts of the country, and grants to five existing teaching centres.

The Commissioners have already set forth their general views on the policy to be adopted for the development of forestry. On considering the Board's application in the light of those principles, they thought that it would probably save time and trouble if the questions raised were discussed personally between representatives of the Board and of the Commissioners. An interview took place between the Secretary to the Board and Sir S. Eardley-Wilmot, Chairman of the Commissioners' Forestry Committee; and the Commissioners subsequently intimated that they would be prepared, on receiving the details of the expenditure proposed during the next two years, to recommend a grant to the Board. At the same time, they asked that the Board should have regard to the opinions at which the Commissioners had arrived on the advice of their Forestry Committee, viz. :—

(a) That education, research, demonstration and survey are all part of one scheme for the furtherance of forestry as a national industry; a general survey not being an essential preliminary to that scheme but merely a part of the whole.

(b) That the value of a system of sample plots is recognised, but that the supervision of these experiments would be more efficiently carried out if entrusted to the subsidised institutions rather than to private societies.

(c) That the proposal for the early purchase of a demonstration area, to be used also as a centre for research, is approved, but that further similar purchases should be contingent on the progress made in State forestry.

(d) That the Commissioners agree with the policy of providing advisory officers at local centres, whose duties will be not only to advise individuals but to give instruction in elementary forestry, and also with the proposals to encourage provision for the higher technical education at one or at the most two centres; but research should be principally centred at the demonstration areas.

In the middle of July, the Commissioners received from the Board an estimate of the sum required for the development of forestry in England and Wales during the period from the 1st October 1911 to 31st March 1914. The estimate amounted in all to £95,000, of which £20,150 was required for grants to institutions for such purposes as advisory work, instruction, research, and forest gardens, and the remainder for other objects, mainly the purchase and equipment of a State forest. Of the total sum the Board estimated that about £2000 would be necessary in the current financial year, £20,000 in 1912-13, and the balance in 1913-14.

It will be convenient to set out in some detail the Commissioners' conclusions on this scheme.

(a) *Advisory Work.*—They agreed to recommend grants not exceeding £500 per annum for a period of three years, to cover salaries and travelling allowances at each of the five centres selected for this purpose. It was understood that two of these centres (Oxford and Cambridge) were to be equipped for higher education in forestry, and the other three (Bangor, Newcastle and Cirencester) for forestry education of a simpler kind. Such aid ought not to debar educational assistance from being concentrated in one or two localities where circumstances might indicate that it would ultimately prove more effective. As it seemed not impossible that Wales might be selected as affording the most suitable centres for demonstration and the development of State forestry, it might become essential to provide educational and other facilities nearer to the scene of action than are Oxford, Cambridge or Newcastle.

(b) *Instruction.*—With this proposed addition of another officer for advisory work to the staff of each of the five selected centres, they thought that it was unnecessary at present to consider any further grant in respect to forestry instruction at existing institutions. The demand for advice will not so suddenly increase as to employ the whole time of the new officers; and increased provision for instruction will therefore have been made temporarily at those five places.

(c) *Research.*—Pending the organisation of a national demonstration area, where they believe research should be principally centred, they agreed to recommend that research work should be assisted at Oxford and Cambridge by a grant to each University of £500 per annum for two years, to provide for the salary and expenses of a research officer. They were also disposed to view favourably the proposal to spend £200 per annum for two years on research work outside these two Universities, provided that it was carried out at Bangor, Newcastle or Cirencester. They were of opinion that the research grants should be conditional on the work being confined to investigations into the diseases of indigenous trees and the structure of indigenous timber, and to such exotics as have been proved or may be shown to be of commercial importance to the United Kingdom. They do not think that money should be granted from the Development Fund for investigations into the forest growth of other countries, whether temperate or tropical, for which it is believed separate provision is already made.

(d) *Forest Gardens and Demonstration Plantations.*—While

the Commissioners agreed that forest gardens would be an advantage to each of the educational institutions, they considered that, as a rule, an area of thirty acres would suffice in each case. They failed to see the need for demonstration plantations at the teaching centres, as such plantations provide no practical basis for the investigation of forest questions, and whatever need there may be for inquiries of this nature would be sufficiently met at a central demonstration area.

(e) *Buildings for Institutions.*—As regards financial assistance for new buildings at the educational centres, the Commissioners decided that they would prefer to consider each case on its merits rather than assent to a general principle that 50 per cent. of the cost should be met by the Development Fund.

(f) *State Demonstration Forests.*—The Commissioners concurred with the Board as to the necessity for demonstration forests, which they would prefer to see confined to one central area. In view of the importance of this question they suggested, following the precedent of Scotland, the appointment of a committee to ascertain the most suitable localities for demonstration forests, and to report, *inter alia*, on the respective advantages of adapting for these purposes existing Crown woodlands, or leasing or purchasing an area from local authorities or private owners.

(g) *Minor Forestry Experiments.*—The value of a system of sample plots was recognised by the Commissioners, but they thought that the educational advantages of such experiments would be more fully utilised if the control of the plots were vested in one or more of the five educational centres. In the event of the Board being able to arrange for such control, the Commissioners were prepared to recommend a grant of £1000 for the preparation and upkeep of sample plots.

(h) *Salaries and Expenses of Staff.*—The Commissioners suggested that the question of any considerable grant to the Board for this purpose should be deferred until forestry development in England and Wales is placed on more definite lines, and its scope becomes more apparent than at present. Meanwhile they were prepared to deal with an estimate of the additional administrative expenditure involved in carrying out the above proposals, to which they are willing to give immediate approval.

The expenditure required to carry into effect the proposals outlined above was estimated at £2900 for the remainder of the financial year 1911-12; and on the 13th October the Commissioners recommended the Treasury to make a grant to the Board up to this amount. They added that they were prepared, on application near the beginning of each financial year, to recommend further advances to the Board on the same lines; but they wished it to be understood that at the present stage the expenditure recommended was purely provisional, and that they did not bind themselves to recommend a continuance of the payments now proposed when once the selection of a demonstration area rendered further centralisation possible.

It will have been gathered that the Commissioners attach great importance to the practical measure which they have just mentioned, viz., the provision of a demonstration area for England and Wales. During the past year they have devoted much attention to this subject. From independent inquiries they had reason to believe that a suitable area could be obtained without a large initial expense; and, after considering a report of their Forestry Committee on the extent and administration of Crown Woods and Forests, the Commissioners instructed the Committee, "in view of the large area of Crown lands available, to pay special attention to their possible utilisation in connection with any forestry scheme submitted to the Commission."

During November, two members of the Commission (Sir S. Eardley-Wilmot and Mr Jones-Davies) visited the Forest of Dean and other Crown woodlands in the neighbourhood. From their report the Commissioners formed the opinion that strong reasons could be advanced for utilising the Forest of Dean as a State demonstration area, which would also serve as a centre for research, the education of woodmen, and the prosecution of special study by advanced students. No expenditure would be required for purchase or rental. The area might be made to serve not only for demonstrating the growth of the large majority of British timbers, but also as an object lesson in the conversion from one silvicultural system to another, and a standing proof of the effect of adverse prescriptive rights. The adjoining woods of Tintern, extending over some 4000 acres, would afford good examples of afforestation on poor soils and on elevations up to 1000 feet above sea-level. At no great distance are other areas in Wales which might well be taken up by the State on lease or otherwise; and thus the possibilities of afforestation might be illustrated, with funds saved from the purchase of land, for demonstration purposes.

These conclusions obviously superseded the Commissioners' previous opinion that a Committee should be formed to consider the acquisition of a demonstration area or areas. Towards the end of November, therefore, they communicated with the Board of Agriculture and Fisheries suggesting that it was unnecessary to proceed with the appointment of a Committee as originally proposed, and expressing their agreement with what they understood to be the Board's view, that an Advisory Committee should be appointed to frame and inaugurate a scheme for the administration of the Forests of Dean and Highmeadow as a demonstration area. On the 24th January, the Commissioners learnt semi-officially from the Board that they were appointing an Advisory Committee, of which Sir E. Stafford Howard had consented to act as Chairman, to consider among other matters

"the use of the Forest of Dean as a demonstration area."
Sir Sainthill Eardley-Wilmot was invited, and agreed, to serve
on the Advisory Committee, whose deliberations are now
proceeding.

Besides the application of the Board of Agriculture and
Fisheries, the Commissioners considered during the year the
following applications from local authorities for assistance in
promoting instruction and research in forestry :—

1. Denbigh County Council: £50 "for the purposes of
   forestry."
2. Oxfordshire County Council: Amount not stated.
   Forestry included in a general scheme for agricultural
   development.
3. Wilts County Council: £100 for inquiries, experiments
   and research.

It was decided that these applications could be sufficiently
covered by the comprehensive scheme of the Board of
Agriculture and Fisheries already made.

In addition, applications were received from the following
teaching centres in England and Wales :—

1. Cambridge University: £200 for temporary quarters for
   the School of Forestry.
2. Armstrong College, Newcastle-on-Tyne: £150—£200
   for a forestry lecture-room and museum.
3. University College of North Wales, Bangor: Amount
   not stated. For a forestry school, research station,
   and demonstration area.
4. Royal Agricultural College, Cirencester: £1000
   annually for research, instruction, and experiments
   in agriculture and forestry.
5. Oxford University (application made by the Board of
   Agriculture and Fisheries): £500 annually for aiding
   forestry instruction at the University.

The desired grant of £200 was recommended to Cambridge
University for temporary quarters to meet immediate needs,
pending the completion of the comprehensive scheme of the
Board of Agriculture and Fisheries. A grant of £200 was
recommended to Armstrong College for a new building to be
used for purposes of forestry lectures, and of a forestry museum
to be erected in Chopwell Woods, which are managed by the
College authorities under an agreement with H.M. Office of
Woods. The consideration was deferred of the application
of the University College of North Wales, Bangor, pending
the completion of the Board's scheme. The Commissioners
reported against the application of the Royal Agricultural
College, on the ground that the proposals were sufficiently
covered by schemes approved or under consideration. With
regard to the application made on behalf of Oxford University,

the Commissioners informed the Board of Agriculture and Fisheries that they found themselves unable to recede from their previous position, that having regard to the increase already made in the forestry staff at selected centres, including Oxford, they believed it to be unnecessary at present to recommend any further grant for forestry instruction at existing institutions.

The Commissioners have now set forth their action in regard to forestry research and instruction; but there is still one question of importance with which it is necessary to deal in some detail, viz., that of encouraging afforestation by local authorities.

Early in April the Commissioners were invited, on behalf of the Leeds City Council, to inspect the Corporation water-catchment areas in the Washburn Valley, of which several hundred acres had been afforested during the previous six years, chiefly by men selected from the ranks of the unemployed in Leeds. About the same time, the Commissioners received semi-official information that other local authorities contemplated seeking aid from the Development Fund in afforesting their water-catchment areas, or other suitable land which they possessed or proposed to purchase for the purpose. They therefore asked the Chairman of their Forestry Committee to report, after inspection, on the whole question of the afforestation of water-catchment areas. Sir Sainthill Eardley-Wilmot accordingly visited the Leeds watershed, and later (accompanied by Mr Jones-Davies) the principal watersheds of Wales. These comprised the catchment areas of the Corporation of Birmingham in the Elan Valley; Radnorshire; of Liverpool, at Lake Vyrnwy, Montgomeryshire; of Birkenhead in Denbighshire; of Cardiff and of Swansea in Brecknockshire; and of Pontypridd in Glamorganshire: at all of which places special facilities were afforded by the municipal officials, whose courtesy is gratefully acknowledged.

After considering the reports on the subject prepared for their information, the Commissioners came to the general conclusion that the water-catchment areas of local authorities provide considerable blocks of land which can be utilised for the development of forestry. The utilisation of these areas appears to them in the circumstances the course best calculated to enhance the value of the property, and to provide a fairly high and constant revenue in the future; and they think that the introduction of systematic forestry will confer a direct benefit upon the distant population dependent on the water by preserving and purifying the supply, and an indirect benefit on the immediate neighbourhood by the creation of new industries. For these reasons they were of opinion that the local authorities should be assisted by loans on easy terms to afforest their water-catchment areas, if the area afforested is large enough to provide permanent employment for a fairly considerable staff, and if the afforestation is carried out on a plan approved by the State.

Meanwhile the Commissioners were being urged to deal immediately with applications from local authorities for assistance in afforesting their watershed areas or other land in their possession, and for grants towards the purchase of land suitable for planting. The Board of Agriculture and Fisheries were preparing schemes by which, in the Board's opinion, the object of those applications would probably be met so far as might be considered desirable. But it appeared at least possible that for some time no general scheme would be ready which would enable the Commissioners to dispose of applications of this character, and it was thought likely that some of the municipalities concerned might desire to prepare a plan of operations against a possible increase of unemployment in their districts. The Commissioners felt, therefore, that they would not be justified in deferring any longer the consideration of local schemes, and in order to make clear their attitude towards applications from local authorities, the Commissioners decided at their meeting last March to issue a public notice of their views, to the effect that they will be prepared to consider applications from local authorities, or other responsible bodies, for assistance in the afforestation of water-catchment areas or other suitable areas under their control.[1]

At the end of the year, the Commissioners were considering applications from the following local authorities :—

(1) The Torquay Town Council, for an advance in aid of a scheme of afforestation on their water-catchment area at Dartmoor.

(2) The Carnarvonshire County Council, for a grant of £2830 for purposes of afforestation on their Madryn Castle estate.

(3) The Carmarthen County Council, for a grant of £4000 towards the cost of afforesting Crown and Common lands within the county.

Before they leave this subject, there is one point which they wish to make clear. In proposing that the extent of the afforestation work undertaken by the local authorities should vary according to its effect on unemployment, and should be arranged in relation to the state of the labour market and the aggregate demand for labour in the United Kingdom, the Commissioners do not contemplate that the authorities should utilise the services of unemployed casual labourers. They are not prepared to say that such a measure is compatible with good and economical forestry; if a local authority chooses to

---

[1] While this report was in preparation the Commissioners issued the public notice printed on p. 28.

adopt it, it must do so on its own responsibility. All that the Commissioners mean is that the afforestation schemes of the local authorities can and should be arranged so as to employ the largest number of men suitable for the work at the time when the aggregate demand for labour is at its lowest. The men employed by the authorities may be all skilled men, and not include one of the class popularly known as the "unemployed." The Commissioners hope that an increase in skilled employment at a time of stress will react beneficially on the market for unskilled labour; but they would hesitate to put forward any suggestions for economic development by afforestation on the basis that such labour must be used when and because it is unfortunately too abundant elsewhere. They believe that this policy is in accordance with the intentions of Parliament as expressed in the Development, etc., Act.

(iii.) *Scotland.*

At their April meeting the Commissioners had before them the application of the University of Edinburgh for grants in aid of forestry instruction. They decided to recommend that a grant, not exceeding £2000 spread over a period of five years, be made to the University for the establishment and maintenance of a forest garden on the following conditions :—

(*a*) That the garden shall be for the joint use of the students both at the University and at the Edinburgh and East of Scotland College of Agriculture.

(*b*) That the grant shall be expended under the supervision of a joint committee, composed of an equal number of representatives of the University Court and of the Board of Governors of the College.

It was also decided to inform the University that the Commissioners would be prepared to consider proposals embodying a reasonably complete scheme for the extension of the forestry museum and laboratory, and to consider an application for meeting the cost of increasing the staff of forestry instructors at the University, when a definite agreement had been reached with the College of Agriculture, such as would prevent duplication of work and expenditure in the two institutions.

This agreement was reached in August, with the co-operation of the Scotch Education Department. On the 27th September the Commissioners recommended, in addition to the previous advance of £2000 for the forest garden, that a grant amounting to £9000 be made to the University to be allocated in the following proportions for the purposes named :—

(1) £4500, being 50 per cent. of the estimated cost of erecting new buildings for forestry teaching, and of the expenditure required for a forestry museum, and for forestry laboratories, on condition that the remaining 50 per cent. be found by the University authorities.

(2) £2000 for equipment during the next five years, after which period the Commissioners will consider the question of renewing the grant.

(3) £2500 to meet for five years the cost of salary of an assistant lecturer, with demonstrators, on the understanding that such lecturer shall give whatever advice and assistance may be desired by persons interested in the practice of forestry : the renewal of the grant to be considered at the end of five years.

A further condition was imposed to the effect that the buildings, museum and laboratories shall be available for the joint use of students both at the University and the College.

In addition, however, to this kind of provision for forestry instruction at existing institutions, the Commissioners think that in Scotland, as in England and Wales, one of the main requirements is a suitable demonstration area. In 1910-11, they expressed their agreement in the opinion of the Scotch Education Department to that effect, and their concurrence with the proposal to appoint a Committee to consider the practical questions involved. In the spring of 1911, the Secretary for Scotland appointed the Committee. It was composed of Sir J. Stirling-Maxwell (Chairman), Lord Lovat, Mr Munro-Ferguson, Mr J. D. Sutherland, Sir John Fleming, and Mr R. H. N. Sellar. The terms of reference were as follows :—

(1) To report as to the selection of a suitable location for a demonstration forest area in Scotland ; the uses, present and prospective, to which such area may be put (including the use that may be made of it by the various forestry teaching centres in Scotland) ; the staff and equipment required for successful working ; the probable cost ; and the most suitable form of management.

(2) To report as to any further steps, following upon the acquisition of the said area, which, in the opinion of the Committee, it is desirable should be taken with a view to providing silviculture in Scotland, due regard being had to the interests of other rural industries.

No official proposals had been received by the end of the year.

(iv.) *Ireland.*

The Department of Agriculture and Technical Instruction for Ireland applied, on the 28th April, for grants to meet the salaries of additional staff to assist generally in their forestry work, and particularly in afforesting certain lands in South Ireland, for the acquisition of which the Commissioners recommended an advance of £25,000 in November 1910. The Commissioners did not think that forestry was sufficiently advanced in Ireland to justify them in meeting the whole of the Department's demands for increased staff, but they recommended, on the 21st August, an advance of such sum as might be required to defray that part of the following expenses which might become payable during the current financial year :—

Salary of a forestry officer to take charge of the Demonstration Forest and Research Institute .	£400–£600
Salary of a forestry officer to be employed in the preparation of working-plans . .	£300–£400
Salaries of temporary valuers . .	£200
Salary of a second division clerk . .	£70–£300
Salary of a surveying mapping clerk .	£90–£120
Salary of a typist	£50–£75
Travelling expenses	£250

Owing to the existence of grazing rights and to difficulties over boundary claims, the Department deemed it prudent to abandon negotiations for the purchase of about 3700 acres included in the scheme of afforestation approved by the Commissioners at the end of 1910. They informed the Commissioners of their decision on the 23rd February, and asked at the same time for authority to substitute other areas having about the same acreage. After considering a report on the proposed additional areas, prepared at their request by one of their members, Mr Ennis, the Commissioners, at their meeting on the 28th March, decided to approve negotiations for the purchase of two of these areas aggregating about 3150 acres.

In regard to certain smaller areas which the Department desired to acquire, the Commissioners came to the conclusion, from the evidence supplied by Mr Ennis's report, that while the eventual purchase of these areas may be desirable, the further consideration of the matter should be deferred until larger plots suitable for planting become available in the same localities.

At the same meeting, the Commissioners expressed their satisfaction that a policy is being followed in Ireland of concentrating afforestation areas in particular localities, and of linking up the lands available in these localities as far as possible.

In regard to the finance of the Development Fund in its relation to other similar funds, the Commissioners observe that the Agriculture (Scotland) Fund was established subsequent to the Development Fund by an Act passed only six months ago, and cannot therefore yet be exhausted. Its income will apparently be not less than £200,000 a year. It is applicable in Scotland to several of the most important purposes (*e.g.* forestry, agricultural research and agricultural instruction) to which the Development Fund can be applied. On these facts, if they stood alone, the Commissioners think that as a matter of principle the demands of Scotch agriculture and forestry should be met from the Scotch Fund so far as possible, before recourse is had to the Development Fund. If capital expenditure were necessary beyond what could be provided from the income of the former, the latter might reasonably lend money at a moderate rate of interest, but grants should not be expected from the central fund for purposes to which, *inter alia*, Parliament has devoted separate and special sums in one part of the United Kingdom, until those sums are exhausted. But in the particular case of the Agriculture (Scotland) Fund, the Commissioners are aware that the primary object of its establishment was the encouragement of small holdings, and, subject to Treasury approval, they would be prepared to agree that expenditure for that purpose should have priority over the other purposes to which the Fund can be applied. The practical result would be that such purposes would continue to be assisted from the Development Fund, and the question whether such advances should be regarded as grants or loans would be deferred until experience shows with some definiteness the probable amount required to meet the demands on the Scotch Fund in respect of small holdings.

The Commissioners have put these views before the Treasury and the Secretary for Scotland, but no decision has yet been reached.

On the Financial Estimate of the future position of the Development Fund, the Commissioners state that they have over—rather than under—estimated the demands upon the fund, and that they have included the advances already made. In regard to forestry and afforestation they say:—For the period till 1916, which must necessarily be in the main a period of forestry education and research (accompanied by assistance to local authorities undertaking the afforestation of areas under their control), they think that probably £350,000 will cover all the expenditure which can profitably be incurred.

Several of the schemes which the Commissioners have recommended, or propose to recommend, to the Treasury require to be continued for several years at least, and even permanently, if their full benefit is to be obtained. Any scheme on the matter of education is obviously of this character. They think that, after 31st March 1916, further assistance by Parliament will be required to keep in operation schemes previously sanctioned which ought not to be deprived of Government support. It would be a matter of regret to the Commissioners if aid could no longer be given from the Fund for such purposes, among others, as forestry education.

During 1911-12, the Commissioners have given their sanction and support to considerable schemes for forestry and other objects.

In forestry they have assisted in providing the indispensable basis of future developments by extending research, education, and the provision of technical advice. During the year now current they hope not only to give further support to the schemes already sanctioned, but also to consider and submit to the Treasury comprehensive schemes for the acquisition and administration of forestry demonstration areas in Great Britain.

APPLICATIONS OFFICIALLY RECEIVED BY THE DEVELOPMENT COMMISSIONERS DURING THE YEAR ENDED 31ST MARCH 1912.

Forestry.

Armstrong College, Newcastle-on-Tyne.

Amount applied for: Not stated.

In aid of: The extension of the work of the forestry department of the College.

Position on 31st March 1912.—Grant of £200 about to be recommended for new building in Chopwell Woods, to serve for purposes of a forestry museum and of forestry instruction. See p. 25 of Report.

Board of Agriculture and Fisheries.

Amount applied for: £95,000 for period 1st October 1911 to 31st March 1914.

In aid of: The development of forestry in England and Wales.

Position on 31st March 1912.—See pp. 22-24 of Report.

Cambridge University.

Applied for: £200.

In aid of: The provision of temporary quarters for the staff of the School of Forestry.

Position on 31st March 1912.—Grant of £200 recommended. See p. 25 of Report.

Carmarthenshire County Council.

Applied for: £4000.

In aid of: The development of afforestation.

Position on 31st March 1912.—See p. 27 of Report.

Carnarvonshire County Council.

Applied for: £2830.

In aid of: The development of forestry on the Madryn Estate.

Position on 31st March 1912.—See p. 27 of Report.

Denbigh County Council.

Applied for: £50.

In aid of forestry.

Position on 31st March 1912.—See p. 25 of Report.

Department of Agriculture and Technical Instruction for Ireland.

Amount applied for: Total sum not stated.

In aid of: Expenses of additional forestry staff.

Position on 31st March 1912.—Grant recommended. See pp. 28-29 of Report.

Edinburgh University.

Applied for: Capital sum, £386; annual grant, £332; museums and laboratories, £368 a year.

In aid of: The extension and improvement of the teaching of forestry in the University.

Position on 31*st March* 1912.—Grant, not exceeding £2000, spread over five years, recommended for the establishment and maintenance of a forest garden. See pp. 27-28 of Report.

Amount applied for: Total sum not stated.

In aid of: Forestry buildings and a forest garden for the purpose of extending forestry instruction in the University.

Position on 31*st March* 1912.—Grant of £9000 recommended (£4500 capital grant, £4500 spread over five years). In addition to the £2000 above. See pp. 27-28 of Report.

APPLICATIONS OFFICIALLY RECEIVED BY THE DEVELOPMENT COMMISSIONERS IN THE PREVIOUS YEAR ON WHICH ACTION HAS BEEN TAKEN DURING THE YEAR 1911-12.

Forestry.

BOARD OF AGRICULTURE AND FISHERIES:

Forestry in England and Wales . . Grant, £2900
(See pp. 22-24 of Report.)

CAMBRIDGE UNIVERSITY:

The provision of temporary quarters for the Staff of the School of Forestry . . Grant, £200
(See p. 25 of Report.)

DEPARTMENT OF AGRICULTURE AND TECHNICAL INSTRUCTION FOR IRELAND:

Forestry in Ireland . . { Grant, £1,360
{ Loan, £25,000
(See pp. 28-29 of Report.)

EDINBURGH UNIVERSITY:

The teaching of Forestry in the University Grant, £11,000
(See pp. 27-28 of Report.)

2. Experimental Forestry Area in Wales.

By FRASER STORY, University College, Bangor.

At a time when there is much talk of starting experimental areas and demonstration forests, it may be useful to describe what has been done in Wales.

Early in 1906 a private proprietor, Mr John Mahler, of Penissa Glyn, presented the freehold of fifty acres of land to the County Council of Denbighshire, with the object of establishing an experimental area in forestry. The only conditions which were attached to the gift were that the cost of planting should be borne by the County, and that the experiments should be carried out under the direction of the Forestry Department at Bangor.

In the spring of that year a forest nursery was formed, and in the following season planting operations were commenced. It was not considered desirable to carry out all the planting at one time, but the plots were gradually established during the next three seasons, so that while some of the sections show six years' growth, others contain plants of only half that age.

It should perhaps be explained that the area stands at an elevation varying from 950 to 1250 feet above sea-level, the top plots all but reaching the summit of the hill.

The natural vegetation consists largely of gorse, bracken and grass, with occasional patches of bramble. Here and there the rock comes to the surface. It will, therefore, be evident that ordinary hill land of the "mountain and heath" description has been chosen, and the treatment accorded to the young plants has also been such as might be given in ordinary cases of upland planting. The soil is a light weathered shale, overlying Silurian rock.

A narrow lane, connecting the small hamlet of Pontfadog with Oswestry, runs along the bottom of the area for some distance, so that visitors generally find it convenient to take the light railway from Chirk station to Pontfadog, and climb the hill from the latter point. As both Chirk and Oswestry are in Shropshire, it will be realised how near the area is to the English border.

About 116,000 trees have been planted, these being contained in thirty-one large plots ($1\frac{1}{4}$ acre in extent), ten small plots, and a shelter-belt (to the west and south). Paths 9 feet in width intersect the plots, and a ride 21 feet in breadth extends from the top to the bottom of the hill, dividing the area into two fairly equal parts. These dividing lines make inspection of the ground easy, prevent confusion as to the boundaries of the various plots, and will facilitate the removal of felled trees.

As to the expenditure upon planting, it will be readily understood that operations carried out on many small plots of different species are more costly than in cases where no subdivision is necessary. Among other things, the distance between the plants, regulating the number of trees per acre, had to be carefully measured, and occasional labourers had to be employed, as, of course, no regular staff could be maintained. For the planting of the 50 acres, including the cost of the plants and fencing, a sum of £386 has been expended.

Tests are being made with a view to finding out which species are most suitable for the class of ground experimented on, the rates of growth of each, the relative efficacy of various methods of planting, and the advantage of certain mixtures; while investigation is also being made into the effects of insect pests, fungus diseases, frost, wind, and so forth. Later on, thinning experiments will be made, and the volume of timber produced will be recorded. As the Chirk area is typical of a class of land very commonly found in Wales, it is hoped that some valuable lessons will be obtained, directly applicable to the surrounding country, while, with the growth of the movement elsewhere, comparative results will be available.

The general arrangement of the species in the larger plots will be seen from the following list :—

Plot 1. Sycamore, beech and oak. Plot 2. Ash and beech. Plot 3. European larch and beech. Plot 4. Douglas fir. Plot 5. Sitka spruce and Norway spruce. Plot 6. European larch. Plot 7. European larch and sycamore. Plot 8. European larch and Douglas fir. Plot 9. Japanese larch and Douglas fir. Plot 10. Corsican pine, Japanese larch and Sitka spruce. Plot 11. Scots pine, Japanese larch and Norway spruce. Plot 12. Norway spruce and silver fir. Plot 13. Scots pine and European larch. Plot 14. Norway spruce and European larch. Plot 15. Japanese larch. Plots 16 to 20. Scots pine, spruce and European larch—variously treated. Plot 21. Arborvitæ, Douglas fir, Norway spruce and European larch. Plot 22. European larch, silver fir and Scots pine.   Plot 23. European larch, silver fir and Scots pine.   Plot 24. European larch.   Plot 25. European larch. Plot 26. Norway spruce.   Plot 27. Corsican pine.   Plot 28. Scots pine.   Plot 29. Norway spruce.   Plot 30. Arbórvitæ.   Plot 31. Douglas fir.

It will be seen from the above that very few broad-leaved trees have been planted, the reason being, of course, that the elevation and character of the soil make the area more suitable for coniferous species.   On the whole, the broad-leaved trees have done badly.   At present, the beech is the only exception to the rule; the others may improve, however, after they have fairly established themselves.

The conifers which have grown most rapidly up to the present are the Douglas fir, European and Japanese larch.   One plot of Douglas fir, growing at over 1000 feet elevation, shows an average height of 8 ft. 6 ins., although only planted in 1907. The growth for the past three years has averaged 2 feet per annum.   As is usually the case with this species, there is considerable disparity in growth between the individual plants. The tallest young trees are already 12 feet in height, and quite a number have made growths of 4 feet in length during the past season.   While speaking of the Douglas fir, it may be said that it has been found best to use 3-year-old transplants, about 1 foot in height, rather than nursery stock of larger size.   For example, Douglas firs which had been standing side by side in the home nursery were planted on two adjoining plots.   In the one case, the trees were planted out after one year in the lines, but in the other case, after two years.   The former were 1 foot high when planted, and are now 8 ft. 6 ins.; the latter were 2 ft. 3 ins. high when planted, and are now 4 ft. 6 ins.   Attention may be drawn to the small number of deaths occurring among the Douglas firs, only 382 out of 12,175, an equivalent of 3 per cent., having been lost.   On one of the smaller plots, the Colorado Douglas fir is being tried alongside of the Oregon variety.   Up to the present the former has shown very slow growth, indeed it has not been easy to prevent weeds from smothering the trees; nor has the Fraser River variety proved superior in any way to the Oregon Douglas.

Common larch is being grown pure on three plots with a view to varied treatment at a later stage.   For example, heavy thinning and light thinning will be tested, and parts will be underplanted with shade-bearing species. On the other plots larch is mixed respectively with beech, sycamore, Douglas fir, Scots pine, Norway spruce and silver fir. In this way we hope to be able to judge of the behaviour of the tree under a variety of conditions.

The growth of the Japanese larch thus far compares favourably with that of the common species. One plot, consisting only of Japanese larch, stands at an elevation of 1100 feet. The plants were bought as 1-year-old seedlings, at a cost of 3s. 6d. per 1000. They were then 4 inches high; after standing two years in the home nursery they averaged 3 feet in height, when they were transferred to the hill ground. They now average 7 ft. 6 ins. and have a strong, healthy appearance, although no side shelter is afforded them.

On one of the most exposed plots on the area, the Japanese larch shows the following progression of growth :—

Size when planted in Spring 1907,	.	10 inches.
Size, December 1907,	.	1 foot.
,, 1908,	.	1 ft. 6 ins.
1909,	.	2 ft. 6 ins.
1910,	.	4 feet.
1911,	.	5 feet.
,, 1912,	.	6 ft. 9 ins.

One of the most promising species experimented with is the Sitka spruce. As with other spruces, some time elapses before the Sitka commences to make much in the way of height increase, so that measurements do not quite represent the development of the little trees. Their appearance, however, is most healthy, and they are evidently just commencing a period of robust growth. In one case, they are 1 ft. 6 ins. taller than the Norway spruce, with which they have been planted (3 ft. 6 ins. as against 2 feet).

A number of tests are being made with the Norway spruce. Rather better results have been obtained from spring than from autumn planting, and the keeping of the plants three years in the seed-bed before lining out has had a prejudicial effect. An attempt to use 2-year-old seedling spruces for hill planting, combining this with vertical notching, was not successful, owing to the failure of the small plants to struggle against the weeds. The best results have been obtained from 4-year-old transplants (2 years–2 years).

Scots pine plays a part in the composition of ten of the plots, and, on the whole, has grown satisfactorily up to the present. In addition, small numbers of plants of this species, grown from seeds procured from various countries, have been given a place on the area in order to test the influence of heredity.

Corsican pine has been made use of in several cases on account of its resistance to the effects of wind-storms at high elevations. As is well known, young plants of Corsican pine are very poorly provided with lateral roots ("fibre"), and are, therefore, apt to suffer when being planted out. It was found advantageous to use young plants that had been transplanted the previous season, and also to plant after the growing season had commenced. Some planted as late as the 8th of May, when they had already began to develop the leading shoot, grew better than any other.

One whole plot ($1\frac{1}{4}$ acre) is given over to the Pacific arborvitæ (*Thuya gigantea*). Unfortunately, a long period of dry weather, with east wind and frost, followed immediately upon the planting and caused a considerable number of deaths. The gaps, however, were filled with fresh plants, and now the plot is looking quite well. It is evident that this species is rather susceptible to such influences, but since establishing itself it has proved perfectly hardy.

The common silver fir has been planted on a few of the high-lying sections, as its deep-rooting qualities may come in useful there.

The smaller plots contain species which are perhaps less likely to become forest trees than those which have been mentioned above. They include such trees as the Servian spruce (*Picea Omorica*), American larch (*Larix microcarpa*), Lawson's cypress (*Chamæcyparis Lawsoniana*), Colorado Douglas fir, *Abies grandis*, *Abies nobilis*, *Abies concolor*, *Picea pungens*, and a few others.

The shelter-belt, which has already been alluded to, is composed of the quicker-growing, hardy, broad-leaved trees, interspersed with evergreen conifers, particularly pines. Briefly stated the arrangement is as follows:—To the outside, where the trees bear the brunt of the storm, are placed the mountain pine and white American spruce. Further in occur sycamore, Norway maple, hornbeam, birch, white alder, ash, rowan, Norway spruce, Corsican pine, Austrian pine, Scots pine and silver fir. The strip is 60 feet wide, and a planting distance of 6 feet has been adopted.

As to the experiments regarding methods of planting, the plots as a whole were planted by the method called "holing," the work being done with a heavy, narrow-bladed hoe, or mattock, followed by a trowel to aid in the insertion of the plants. Tests were, however, made with ordinary notching, and vertical notching. Under the holing system, gorse and other weeds were removed from a patch about 15 inches square before the soil was stirred with the mattock. The plants, therefore, made a better start, and this advantage has been maintained as compared with the notched-in plants. Common spade notching resulted in a greater number of deaths and entailed more expense in weeding. This, as well as the effect on height-growth, will be seen from the table given below.

SPECIES	Number of Deaths		Percentage of Deaths		Height when Planted		Height December 1912	
	Notching	Holing	Notching	Holing	Notching	Holing	Notching	Holing
					Ft. Ins.	Ft. Ins.	Ft. Ins.	Ft. Ins.
Larch . .	114	34	10·8	3·1	1 3	1 3	3 6	4 6
Scots pine .	34	9	3·1	·8	0 10	0 10	2 5	3 2
Spruce . .	18	5	1·6	·1	1 4	1 4	2 2	2 7

Vertical notching was carried out with a heavy iron wedge-shaped implement, and 2-year seedling plants were used. The ground is not really suitable for vertical notching, being too stony and the herbage too rough. Still excellent results have been obtained with the larch, and the Scots pine has done moderately well. The small plants of spruce have, however, been almost entirely crowded out by the grass and gorse. This result being anticipated, a planting distance of 3 feet, instead of the usual 4 feet, was resorted to, so that there is still a sufficient number of plants to the acre.

As rainfall has such an important influence on tree-growth, it was thought desirable to keep records at a point as close to the area as could be conveniently arranged. Daily observations have been taken since March 1907. Details are given below of the rainfall for each month from January 1908, onwards. The number of days on which rain fell is also given for the last three years.

	1908.	1909.	1910.	1911.
January	1·82	2·69	3·07	1·17
February	1·98	1·99	4·60	2·08
March	3·96	2·68	1 97	1·36
April	3·47	3·30	1·54	1·0
May	2·70	1·49	2·06	1·06
June	3·45	3 86	2·45	2·24
July	3·36	2·60	2·75	1·20
August	3·35	2 39	4·15	2·26
September	5·82	2·40	·32	3·79
October	3·87	5·22	3·39	3·32
November	2·83	·85	4·78	4·66
December	2·65	5·24	8·93	6·99
	39·26	34·71	40·01	31·13
Number of days on which rain fell	...	163	170	134

Pests so far have been well kept in check. Rabbits have been excluded with the help of the wire-netting fence which was erected at a cost of £80, 4s. 10d. This fence has been regularly inspected, a man being paid £3, 18s. od. annually for the work.

The larch woolly aphis made its appearance on some of the larches in 1910, and fears were entertained for the remainder of the trees. The affected plants were at once uprooted, however, carefully removed and burnt, and since then we have had no trouble, although, of course, it is quite likely that the insect will return.

Another aphis (*Chermes pini*) attacked the Scots pine rather badly during the summer of 1909. It did not actually kill more than one or two trees, but for a time it infested the stem and branches. The same tree also suffered from a leaf-attacking fungus (*Peridermium pini acicola*), but after the pines had fairly established themselves they were able to throw off the evil effects of both pests, and now present a healthy appearance. A small colony of pine sawfly was found on the Corsican pine, but the insects were easily destroyed and gave no further trouble. The beech trees in the year following planting were damaged to some extent by an aphis (*Phyllaphis fagi*) attacking the foliage. Nearly all the plants survived, and now seem to be quite clean. The spruce also has had its aphis pest in the shape of *Chermes abietis*. No injury worth mentioning has been done, however, but it may be mentioned that some galls were found on the Sitka spruce, as well as on the common species.

Of fungi, the disease that is dreaded most is, of course, the larch canker. Special efforts have, therefore, been made to prevent this fungus from obtaining a hold. Not only were all plants examined for signs of weakness or injury at the time of planting, and suspicious-looking plants rejected, but all the larch stakes and posts required for fencing were charred before use, in order to burn out any traces of disease from the bark. But in spite of all these precautions, individual plants here and there have been attacked. These have been uprooted and burnt, but the danger is always with us. It may be added that the soil and situation are most suitable for the healthy growth of the larch, and there are no trees of this species within at least half a mile of the area. A few plants, mostly Scots pine, have succumbed to *Agaricus melleus* and *Trametes radiciperda*.

The cleaning of plants has necessitated the expenditure of a good deal of labour, the gorse, bracken, etc., proving decidedly troublesome. Still, the cost has not exceeded £20 since the commencement—equivalent to an expenditure of about 2s. per acre per annum over the area planted. Maintenance charges, including the payment of a fire insurance premium and regular examination of the fences, come to an almost precisely similar sum, £19, 2s. 3d.

The carting of the plants to the hill from the railway station and home nursery added 1s. 3d. per 1000 to the cost. The expenses on plants which passed through the home nursery must be given as 8s. 4d. per 1000 for each time of transplanting. This sum is higher than it ought to be, owing to the fact that it includes all the original cost of forming and fencing the nursery, the ground having been previously under pasture and only used for a few years as a nursery. It includes expenditure on trenching, annual soil cultivation, transplanting, weeding, trimming of the roots, rent, etc., and is calculated upon the number of plants actually removed to the planting area, not upon the number originally lined out. If allowance is made for money received from the sale of surplus plants, the sum mentioned above would be reduced by more than half.

A total of 108,000 plants passed through the nursery, most of these being lined out as seedlings, and a few propagated from seed.

The cost of planting, most of which, as already stated, was done by the method known as "holing" or pitting, comes to 22s. 1od. per 1000 plants. In considering this figure, it must be borne in mind that experimental plots necessarily cost more to plant than an ordinary forest area.

It will be seen from the following table how many plants of each species have been planted, and the percentage of deaths in each case. The total casualty amounts to only 5 per cent. on the 116,000 trees planted. Of course, all the gaps which occurred have been carefully filled again, so that the plots are now completely stocked.

SPECIES	Number Planted	Percentage of Deaths
European larch	27,700	5·2
Norway spruce	20,020	·5
Scots pine	15,798	·8
Douglas fir	12,175	3·1
Japanese larch	7,604	4·5
Corsican pine	5,230	19·5
Beech	4,535	2·1
Pacific arborvitæ . . .	4,425	37·7
Silver fir	4,230	1·1
Sycamore	3,255	3·4
Sitka spruce	3,180	1·1
Ash	1,710	·2
Oak	1,130	49·0
Mountain pine	700	...
Birch.	690	...
Lawson's cypress . . .	670	34·3
Colorado Douglas fir . . .	600	...
Austrian pine	550	...
White American spruce . .	400	...
Abies grandis	374	10·7
Picea Omorica	350	...
Abies concolor	350	1·4
White alder	250	...
Mountain ash	125	...
Hornbeam	100	...
Canadian poplar	100	...
Norway maple	100	...
Larix microcarpa . . .	60	...
Fraser River Douglas fir .	60	...
Abies nobilis	50	...
Quercus rubra	25	...
Larix sibirica	22	...
Picea pungens	14	...
Pinus excelsa	12	...
Prunus serotina	5	...
Pinus Banksiana	4	...
Castanea crenata . . .	3	...
TOTALS	116,606	5·1

3. Official Notifications.

1. Statement by the Development Commission in regard to State-aided Afforestation.

The Development Commissioners, who for some time past have been in communication with the Government Departments concerned in regard to schemes of afforestation of a national character, have meanwhile drawn up the following statement for the guidance of Local Authorities who may contemplate applying for State-aid in carrying out schemes of afforestation on areas under their control :—

(1) The Development Commissioners will be prepared, pending the completion of any general schemes for this purpose by the English Board of Agriculture and Fisheries, and by the Departments of Agriculture in Scotland and Ireland, to consider applications, which, in the first instance, need not be in great detail, from Local Authorities or other responsible bodies, for assistance in the afforestation of water-catchment areas or other suitable areas under their control, with a view to ascertaining whether the schemes put forward are of public utility and likely to prove remunerative either directly or indirectly.

(2) The Commissioners consider it is important that such afforestation schemes as may be brought to their notice should be inquired into without delay in order to ascertain, by means of a flying survey, whether the above-mentioned conditions are likely to be fulfilled. They consider that any detailed scheme following thereon should provide, with due regard to economy and efficiency, for varying the extent of the operations prescribed from year to year, and that such variation should be governed by the effect of the afforestation works on employment, and should be arranged in relation to the state of the labour market and to the aggregate demand for labour in the United Kingdom, as reflected in the Board of Trade's index number of unemployment, or otherwise.

(3) Provided that approved schemes for afforestation are carried out in accordance with expert advice, and that the work is open at all times for inspection, and the areas made available, if required, for purposes of education, research and

demonstration, the Development Commissioners are prepared to recommend loans on the general principle that repayment commences so soon as the work becomes remunerative, or at some date to be fixed in reference to the method of afforestation to be followed in any particular case.

2. Advisory Committee on Forestry for Scotland.

The Secretary for Scotland has appointed a Committee to advise the Board of Agriculture for Scotland in matters relating to forestry.

The following gentlemen have accepted the invitation to serve on this Advisory Committee:—Mr John D. Sutherland (Chairman); The Right Hon. Lord Lovat, D.S.O.; The Right Hon. R. C. Munro Ferguson, M.P.; Sir John Stirling-Maxwell, Bart.; Sir W. S. Haldane; Mr J. M. Henderson, M.P.; Mr R. H. N. Sellar.

3. Technical Advice for Private Owners.

In connection with the grant from the Development Fund in respect of provision of technical advice in forestry, we understand that the whole of England and Wales has been divided into five districts, of which the following institutions are the advising centres, viz. :—

Newcastle-upon-Tyne	North of England.
Bangor	Cheshire, Salop and Wales, except Glamorgan.
Oxford	Part of Midlands and South of England.
Cambridge	Eastern Counties and part of Midlands.
Cirencester	South-west and West of England and Glamorgan.

Professor Story, who becomes Technical Adviser at the Bangor centre, retains his professorship, and Mr Thomson Thomson has been appointed assistant lecturer under him at the University College of North Wales.

Mr J. F. Annand, lecturer in forestry at the Armstrong College, Newcastle-upon-Tyne, and manager of the Crown woods at Chopwell, has been appointed Technical Adviser for the North of England ; and Mr J. M'Laren has been appointed assistant lecturer at the college. In addition to giving instruction in forestry to in-college students and to students in Chopwell woods, Mr M'Laren will give lectures and demonstrations at suitable centres in the North of England ; he will also assist in the management of Chopwell woods and other demonstration areas, and will generally assist the Adviser in Forestry in all branches of forestry work.

4. The Utilisation of Disused Pit-banks.

AN ACCOUNT OF THE PLANTING OF CHARLEY PIT-BANK, MEALSGATE, CUMBERLAND.

(*With a Plate.*)

By P. MURRAY THOMSON, Whitehall Estate Office, Mealsgate.

The present condition of the Charley Pit-bank, on the estate of Wm. Parkin Moore, Esq., Whitehall, Mealsgate, Cumberland, is an interesting and instructive example of what may be done, in some cases, to beautify and at the same time to utilise the unsightly refuse heaps which are left on the closing down of collieries. The pit-bank in question covers about 4 acres of ground, and the whole area now enclosed in connection with it, so as to permit of fairly straight fences, is about 6 acres. The height above sea-level is roughly 300 feet. The average annual rainfall is about 41 inches. The axis of the bank lies east and west, and the prevailing winds are from south-west to west. All the northern part of the bank is therefore fairly well protected from storms, and it is on that side that the most successful early planting has been done. More recently, the south and more exposed parts of the bank have been treated, and the results warrant continued planting.

The colliery was abandoned in July 1897, and as the bank is situated close to the main turnpike road, and within half a mile of Whitehall, Mr Parkin Moore was anxious to have it, if possible, greened over. With this object in view he had sweepings from the hay lofts, with the addition of rape seed, freely spread—rather than scattered—over the surface of the bank, for a number of years. The resulting grass has tended to bind the loose material of the bank, and the roots have helped in the disintegration of the surface.

Planting was commenced in the winter of 1898. Pits were made, and when the trees were planted one or two buckets of soil were put into each pit. There being no information available as to what kinds of trees might be successfully grown, it was determined to plant a mixture, and the result now affords a most interesting object lesson.

The trees and shrubs presently growing on the bank are:— larch (European), larch (Japanese), mountain pine, Scots pine, spruce, Austrian pine, oak, ash, beech, birch, sycamore, alder, elm, snowberry, cotoneaster, apple, rhododendron, spiræa, mahonia, privet, and a few Douglas firs and white alders planted in the spring of 1912. All of these show strong healthy growth, though canker appears on a few of the larches, and the alders show a tendency to produce seed on some comparatively young trees. The largest trees are larch, Scots pine and birch—the earliest planted of these standing from 18 to 24 feet high. The staff, in two of the accompanying illustrations, Figs. 1 and 2, is extended to its full length of 14 feet, and the photographs were taken with a view to illustrate the varied planting of the bank, with the free, straight growth of the trees, and to give a general impression of the results attained, rather than to show individual specimens of the tallest trees. Among the hardwoods, oak, ash, beech, sycamore and elm are not numerously represented, but what there are of them warrant their inclusion in any further planting that may be carried out.

For some years after the bank was first planted little was done in the way of filling up, except the using for that purpose of such plants as were left over after the planting on other parts of the estate was finished in each year. The bank may be termed the dumping ground, for a number of years, of what was left over. Whether trees would grow satisfactorily, and what would be best to use as the main crop, was uncertain. The result is that at the present time the growth on the bank is rather irregular both in age and density. Behind the trees in Fig. 2 lies a sheltered plateau lying on the north side of part of the highest ridge of the bank, on which the trees were so thin on the ground as to warrant the entire clearing and replanting of the area. As there were a quantity of well-rooted Scots pines five and six years old in the nursery, these were used for planting on the cleared plateau in February last. The addition of soil in the pits was then found to be unnecessary. The growth made in the first season ranges from 3 inches up to 15 inches; the average of the growths made by six trees in one line is 10 inches. When clearing this plateau for replanting, a number of young hardwoods were left from which to select specimens to be exhibited at the Society's forestry exhibition at Cupar in July 1912, or to be cut out later if this appeared to be necessary. Five oaks so left made an average growth, in 1912, of 2 feet; seven ash, an average growth of 20 inches; six beech, an average growth of 21 inches; and seven sycamore, an average growth of 12 inches.

Taking six trees of each of European larch, Scots pine and spruce growing on the bank, and comparing the growths made by these in each of the last four years with the growths made by the same kinds of trees of similar ages growing near, but not in pit-bank material, the average results in inches are as follows:—

	1909		1910		1911		1912	
	On bank	Not on bank	On bank	Not on bank	On bank	Not on bank	On bank	Not on bank
	Ins.	Ins.	Ins.	Ins.	Ins.	Ins.	Ins.	Ins.
[1] European larch early planted . . .	21½	...	23½	...	23	...	27½	...
Do. (end of Crowwood)	...	18	...	25	...	25	...	30
[2] European larch more recently planted .	14½	...	17½	...	21	...	27	...
Do. (end of Crowwood)	...	12	...	14½	...	17	...	23½
[2] Scots pine recently planted . . .	11	...	10½	...	15	...	20	...
Do. (Lowmill) . . .	...	12½	...	12	...	15	...	19
Spruce on sheltered plateau . . .	14½	...	17	...	15	...	16	...
Spruce on top of bank in exposed position	9½	...	10½	...	11½	...	15	...
Spruce to south of bank in exposed position . . .	...	11	...	12	...	13½	...	18½
Spruce to south of bank in a sheltered position . . .	...	21	...	26	...	26	...	26

The illustrations Nos. 4, 5 and 6 are photographs of the roots of trees lifted for exhibition to show the rooting of the plants. Extensive root action appears to be favoured by the free, loose material of the bank.

[1] The larches here measured are growing around those illustrated in Fig. 2.

[2] The larches and Scots pine here measured are growing on the steep bank illustrated in Fig. 3.

PLATE I.

FIG. 1.

FIG. 2.

FIG. 3.

[*To face p.* 32.

Birch

FIG. 4.

Ash   Oak

FIG. 5.

Spruce   ELM

FIG. 6.

No particular description of the character of the bank at the time it was abandoned and when planting was commenced has been kept, but comparison of the surface material with that taken from a foot below the surface shows that disintegration has gone on to a remarkable extent. At a very short distance below the surface, the material is caked into hard masses containing a considerable quantity of pyrites.

Part of another pit-bank on the estate was last year abandoned, and encouraged by the results attained on the Charley Pit-bank, Mr Parkin Moore is to have experiments carried out on this newer bank. The bank has been on fire for a number of years, and a large part of it is burned out. Examination shows that there are bands or strata in it which present a red burnt-brick appearance, and during the present summer it has been noticed that these parts are irregularly dotted over with vegetation, chiefly *Senecio viscosus*, while those parts of the bank which are of a finer, grey to black material have not naturally produced any plant life whatever. Rape seed sown on these two parts of the bank has produced much stronger plants in the red, rough material than in the finer, grey to black material. The capabilities of the two parts will be further tested.

DESCRIPTION OF ILLUSTRATIONS.

FIG. 1. Larch, birch and spruce in foreground, showing 9 years' growth in February 1912.

FIG. 2. Larch and Scots pine, showing 10 years' growth in February 1912, with younger larch and beech in foreground. The trees in this figure are growing behind the large Scots pine in the right background of Fig. 1.

FIG. 3. North side of steep part of bank with larch (European and Japanese), birch, Scots pine, etc., showing 6 and 7 years' growth in February 1912. Rhododendrons are growing near the top of this part of the bank. The large spruce to left of the illustration is the same tree as the spruce in the foreground of Fig. 1. Both photographs are taken from practically the same point and facing the same way—east. This figure illustrates what may be generally described as the second stage of planting on the bank, and Figures 1 and 2 the first stage.

FIG. 4. Root of birch.

FIG. 5. Root of { ash—to left.
                  { oak —to right.

FIG. 6. Root of { spruce—to left.
                  { elm—to right.

5. Observations on the Annual Increment of Spruce and Scots Pine (Third Article).

By J. H. MILNE-HOME.

The account of previous observations in 1910 and 1911 has been given in the *Transactions* (Vol. xxiv. p. 52 and Vol. xxvi. p. 160). The following tables summarise the results obtained in the growing season 1912. The percentage rates of growth have been calculated in the same manner as in previous years. n = the number of rings in the last inch of radial growth, and d = diameter of stem under bark.

Plantation	Species	No. of Trees observed	Average Circumference over Bark, 1st May 1912	Average increase in Circumference in inches during					Total	n	d	Percentage rate of growth
				May	June	July	Aug.	Sept.				
			Ins.								Ins.	
K	Scots Pine	5	20·50	·150	·100	·050	·012	·013	·325	16·8	5·55	4·41
K	Spruce	5	28·44	·050	·112	·150	·063	·037	·412	14·8	8·65	3·12
D	Spruce	5	22·69	·112	·238	·212	·113	·012	·687	9·1	6·92	6·35
I	Spruce	5	37·10	·100	·250	·175	·100	·012	·637	9·8	10·87	3·75
I	Scots Pine	5	33·12	·050	·125	·038	·075	...	·288	16·6	9·00	2·67
B	Spruce	5	23·10	·162	·062	·088	·063	·012	·387	16·2	7·25	3·41

The following figures for 1910 and 1911 were given previously, but are repeated for reference with the addition of the corresponding figures for 1912 :—

Year	Plantation	Species	Age	Estimated present growing Stock	Number of Stems per acre	Average Diameter	Mean annual Increment	Present °/₀ rate of Growth	Current annual Increment
				Cub. ft.			Cub. ft.		Cub. ft.
1910	K	Scots Pine	37	1200	710	6·2″	32½	4·24	51
	D	Spruce	32	1320	450	6·8″	41	6·95	91
	I	Spruce	40	2800	280	11·5″	70	4·16	116
	I	Scots Pine	40	1730	280	10·4″	43	4·27	67
1911	K	Scots Pine	38	1251	710	6·3″	34	4·75	59
	K	Spruce	38	2700	700	8·6″	71	3·29	89
	D	Spruce	33	1411	450	7·0″	43	6·58	93
	I	Spruce	41	2916	280	11·7″	71	3·54	103
	I	Scots Pine	41	1797	280	10·5″	44	2·59	46
1912	K	Scots Pine	39	1310	710	6·4″	34	4·41	58
	K	Spruce	39	2789	700	9·0″	71½	3·12	87
	D	Spruce	34	1504	450	7·2″	44	6·35	95
	I	Spruce	42	3019	280	11·8″	72	3·75	113
	I	Scots Pine	42	1843	280	10·5″	44	2·67	49

Reference was made, in dealing with last year's results, to the apparent effects of the unusual summer of 1911. An examination of the figures for 1912 shows that on fairly good soils the growth in the latter year has been on the whole better than in the drier and warmer season of 1911. Growth commenced early in 1912, the increment put on in May and June being considerable. The late summer growth was poor, and had practically ceased in August.

The second table, summarising the estimated growing stock and increment for three years, is now becoming of some practical value. It will be noticed that in all the woods under observation (with one exception) the current annual increment is still well above the mean annual increment. In other words, the most profitable felling age has not as yet been nearly reached. This, of course, is quite natural seeing that the oldest crop under observation is forty-two years. The exception mentioned is the Scots pine, Plantation I, where there is a close approximation between the mean annual increment and the current annual increment, probably due to want of proper canopy and other causes. Generally speaking, coniferous timber in this country is likely to yield the highest return at the age when the current and mean annual increments coincide. After this point has been passed, the increase in quality or price will not be sufficient to make up for the loss of bulk.

The results obtained over the three years' period are wonderfully consistent, as a detailed examination of the figures will show.

The rainfall during the growing season of 1912 was as under :—

			Inches.	No. of days on which rain fell.	Heaviest fall in 24 hours.
May	...	...	2·19	15	·47
June	...	...	5·18	26	·49
July	...	...	3·22	15	·50
August	...	...	5·95	23	·68
September	...	...	2·64	9	1·27
			19·18	88	
Same period 1911	...		16·38	73	
,, 1910	...		20·18	72	

6. Death Duties on Woods.

By ROBERT GALLOWAY, S.S.C.

Shortly after the passing of the Finance Act, 1910, there was published in the *Transactions* (pages 133-137 of Vol. XXIII.) a note on the death duties as affecting woods, with special reference to the changes made by that Act. The chief feature of the Act as regards woods was the establishment of the principle that the duties on them were not payable until the trees were cut down and converted into cash. This was certainly a great concession, but accompanying it there was the obligation to aggregate the value of the woods with the deceased's other estate, in order to ascertain the total value of the estate and the rate of duty payable. Aggregation had the effect, in many cases, of raising the rate of duty 1 per cent. or perhaps 2 per cent. or more according to the value of the woods. This increased rate was at once levied on the value of the other estate (without the woods), and the additional percentage thus really represented a duty immediately payable in respect of the woods. The trees when subsequently cut down also paid duty at the same increased rate as the other estate. Various other adverse criticisms were directed against the Act as affecting woods, and there gradually grew up a strong feeling of disappointment, which, in some cases, was so great as to cause proprietors who were formerly keen planters to suspend forestry operations on their estates, with the exception perhaps of the felling and converting into cash of such of their woods as were suitable for this purpose. Last year the Chancellor of the Exchequer promised to give the subject further consideration, and this year he accepted an amendment which was duly embodied in the Finance Act, 1912, as Section 9, and is as follows :—

"Where an estate, in respect of which Estate Duty is payable on the death of a person dying on or after the thirtieth day of April, nineteen hundred and nine, comprises land on which timber, trees, wood, or underwood are growing, the value of such timber, trees, wood, or underwood shall not be taken into account in estimating the principal value of the estate or the rate of Estate Duty, and Estate Duty shall not be payable thereon, but shall, at the rate due to the principal value of the estate be

payable on the net moneys (if any) after deducting all
necessary outgoings since the death of the deceased, which
may from time to time be received from the sale of timber,
trees, or wood when felled or cut during the period which
may elapse until the land, on the death of some other
person, again becomes liable or would but for this subsection have become liable to Estate Duty, and the owners
or trustees of such land shall account for and pay the
same accordingly as and when such moneys are received,
with interest at the rate of three per cent. per annum from
the date when such moneys are received.

"This section shall take effect in substitution for the
first paragraph of Subsection five of Section sixty-one of
the Finance (1909-10) Act, 1910, and that paragraph and
Section nineteen of the Finance Act, 1911, are hereby
repealed."

The remaining paragraphs of Subsection 5 of Section 61 of
the 1910 Act which are still in force, are as follows:—

"Provided that if at any time the timber, trees, or
wood are sold, either with or apart from the land on which
they are growing, the amount of Estate Duty on the
principal value thereof which, but for this subsection, would
have been payable on the death of the deceased, after
deducting the amount (if any) of Estate Duty paid in
respect of the timber, trees, or wood under this subsection
since that date, shall become payable.

"This subsection shall apply to Succession Duty
payable in respect of woodlands in like manner as it applies
to Estate Duty, except that nothing in this subsection shall
affect the rate of Succession Duty."

The rate of succession duty is not regulated by the amount of
the estate, but by "the degree of consanguinity existing between
the predecessor and the successor."

It will be seen from the foregoing that the main principle of
the 1910 Act has been maintained in the present Act, namely,
that death duties on the woods are not payable on the death of
the owner, but only as the trees are cut down and converted into
cash. The proviso is also maintained that where the land with
the woods, or the woods as a whole without the land, are sold,
the whole duty due on the "principal value" of the woods
becomes payable under deduction of any duty paid between the

date of death and the sale. That is to say, the duty must be paid by the seller out of the proceeds of the sale, as this burden cannot be transmitted with the woods to the purchaser. When this proviso was framed, the "principal value" of the woods meant the amount of the valuation of the woods as aggregated with the other estate, but as the value of the woods is not now aggregated with the other estate, a valuation would not now in ordinary course be required. If a valuation of the woods is not made as at the date of death, there may be difficulty in ascertaining the "principal value" of the woods on which duty would be at once payable in the event of this proviso coming into operation by reason of a sale taking place after an interval of years.

The principal changes effected by the new clause are :—

(*First*) That the value of the "timber, trees, wood or underwood" is not now to be taken into account in estimating the principal value of the deceased's estate or the rate of estate duty.

No valuation of these for the purposes mentioned is now necessary. In valuing estates on which timber, trees, wood and underwood are growing, each valuator may have his own method of procedure in giving effect to this concession, but a simple plan would be to take as a basis of valuation the rental of the estate as it appears in the Valuation Roll, always keeping in view Sec. 60 of the Finance (1909-10) Act, 1910, quoted in the note before referred to. This rental may include such entries as "plantations" or "woods," but these entries are misleading and really mean land occupied by plantations or woods. The annual value of the growing trees is not entered in the Valuation Roll any more than the value of other growing crops is. The woodlands are valued at the rent at which they might in their natural state reasonably be expected to let from year to year as pasture or grazing land, and the trees are therefore not taken into account. By adopting the rental in the Valuation Roll as a basis, the question of the value of the trees will not require to be dealt with.

(*Second*) That the rate of estate duty payable on the woods is now determined by the amount of the other estate without the addition of the woods. Formerly the duty was determined by the total of the other estate with the addition of the woods.

(*Third*) That "underwood," which is held by the Inland Revenue Authorities to mean "coppice and other quick-growing wood which is cut at frequent intervals, the root or stool remaining perfect to produce new shoots," does not now pay either estate duty or succession duty. It will be observed that the word " underwood " is omitted from the clause imposing the obligation to pay duty.

As the new clause applies to the estates of persons dying on or after 30th April 1909, it supersedes the nineteenth section of the Finance Act, 1911, which is accordingly repealed. A readjustment of the duties will be necessary where estates with woods have become liable to duty in the interval, and in respect of which any payment to account has been made.

The official interpretations of the words, "all necessary outgoings since the death of the deceased," have given much trouble and are still unsatisfactory. At first these outgoings were limited to the expenses of sale, felling and drawing out of the timber, and the restoring of fences, ditches, roads and gates injured by these operations. Later the expenses of replanting were included, provided these expenses were reasonable and were required to maintain the woods in the state in which they were at the time of the death. Both of these interpretations are inadequate, because their author has failed to give effect to the words, "since the death of the deceased." Felling and replanting may be separated from the date of death by a long interval of years, but there must have been necessary outgoings during that interval. The words should be held to cover the expenses of management and up-keep of the woods from the time of the death until they are converted into cash. The heir or trustee gets possession of the woods as " a going concern," and he pays duty on the net moneys (profit), if any, received by him after deducting all outgoings necessary to maintain this going concern, so that he in turn may pass it on to his successor, theoretically unimpaired in value. These outgoings would include all expenses of up-keep and management which a proprietor would naturally incur who managed his woods according to the best advice available to him. On most estates a separate account is kept in the estate books for woods, in which are entered on the one side, foresters' and workmen's wages, and all expenses of management and up-keep, and on the other, all sums received for the produce of the woods. This account, duly certified by some competent authority if required, could be used with advantage in connection with the settlement of the duties, but of course the expenses of forming new, *i.e.* additional plantations, would not be allowed as a deduction, because these plantations would not be liable to duty during the lifetime of the planter. The account should be balanced each year, and the duty should then be paid on any surplus at the rate fixed for the deceased's other estate. In the case of a deficit, this deficit would be carried forward to next year, and so on until there is a surplus on which duty would then be paid. This procedure would continue until the estate, on the death of some other person, again became liable in duty.

While there is no doubt that the new clause removes grievances from which numbers of estates might in course of time suffer severely, there is still room for further concessions. The recommendation of the Departmental Committee on Forestry in Scotland, "that there should be an amendment of the law affecting the taxation of woodlands to estate and succession duties whereby a private estate, approved for the purpose by the State, would be reckoned as a separate estate and possibly charged at a lower rate," might be given effect to at an early date. Meantime, with the exception of the rate of duty, the woods are now, as regards death duties, treated as a separate estate, but the rate of duty still payable is determined by the value of the deceased's other estate, and not by the value of the woods which, in most cases, is less than the value of the other estate. It may also be reasonably claimed that when State afforestation begins, these death duties on woods should be abolished so as to put the private owner of woods and the State on the same footing, and allow them to compete on equal terms.

The concessions that have been made are clearly intended to preserve the existing woods on private estates, and to discourage the practice of cutting down immature timber to meet death duties or other expenses. It is to be hoped that they will also have the further effect of inducing proprietors of woodlands not only to continue their operations as formerly, but to extend them and consequently to add to their woodland areas. Such additional plantations would of course escape duty during the lifetime of the planter, and after that would only pay duty when converted into cash in ordinary course of management after deducting "necessary outgoings."

7. Continental Notes—France.

By A. G. Hobart-Hampden.

I. The natural regeneration of the spruce, even at moderate altitudes, is extremely capricious, sometimes being so abundant as to be positively invasive, at others altogether lacking. At high altitudes it is extremely difficult, and M. Schaeffer, the head of the Working-Plans Branch in Haute Savoie, thinks there may be a connection between this and the apparent lowering of the upper limit of tree-growth. It is undoubted that the conifers have descended and supplanted the broad-leaved species. For one thing, the streams carry the seed down. In the Jura, Vosges, Pyrenees and Savoy this has happened. At the beginning of modern times the forest of Joux (near Pontarlier, it is believed?) was an oak forest, but it is now coniferous. M. Schaeffer suggests that what the spruce gains below it may be losing above, a sort of automatic law of migration. M. Moreillon, a Swiss forester, states that in the high Jura natural regeneration of the spruce is only found, either under branchy silver fir, where only about half as much snow falls as in the open, or on the stumps of trees that have been cut high, or upon the trunks of fallen trees, or, finally, upon hummocks of earth where the snow is less deep and whence it disappears quickly. Accordingly he thinks that the abundance and persistence of the snow is the cause of the difficulty in regeneration at these altitudes. At high altitudes the vegetable soil is often peaty, a condition very unfavourable to spruce seedlings. The resin in the fallen needles of conifer woods prevents their decomposition, and the incompleteness of the decomposition is the determining cause of the formation of peaty humus. This fact, it seems to me, is worthy of note by ourselves, since we often find ourselves engaged in the removal of old conifer woods having a bad soil of a peaty description, with a view to replanting the same area. One gathers that it might be well to allow a certain period to elapse between the felling and the replanting, so as to give time for the decomposition of the humus by exposure to sun and wind. Of course, doing this will give a start to the weeds, but this can be met by using large plants and clearing them afterwards from overgrowing weeds for a time.

M. Mathey, a conservator of forests, has also dealt with this subject in a most erudite discourse to the members of one of the French forest societies. It appears that the spruce comes down from exceedingly remote geological periods, and that it has been driven slowly southwards. The varieties most like the earliest spruce are now to be found in the Himalayas, in *Picea morinda* and *P. alba*. The European spruce has a great number of varieties, of which *Picea excelsa pendula* and *P. excelsa columnaris* stand at the extremes. The former takes the lower station, the latter the higher, and M. Mathey gives tables showing how much smaller is the projection of the crown of the columnar variety compared with that of the other, the ordinary spruce. This, he says, is due to adaptation to environment, enabling the tree growing in the high station to present as small a surface as possible to the strong winds of the mountain tops; also, the downward trend of the branches allows the snow to slip off easily. Whereas the spruce of the lower station grows densely and is a great shade-bearer, it is not so in the case of the other. But formerly, according to M. Mathey and others, there were broad-leaved species (especially the sycamore) on these heights, and their disappearance is leading to that of the spruce, which is receding downwards. The reason for the disappearance of the broad-leaved species is a contested point; M. Mathey says it is due to man and his flocks. Once the broad-leaved species are gone the struggle with the grasses and weeds is too much for the spruce. Also the lack of shade means the drying up of the soil, which kills the spruce seedlings. M. Mathey does not appear to agree altogether with M. Moreillon that the want of seedling growth is due to heavy and persistent snow. The spots where regeneration is found are those where there is a suitable germination bed, where the radicle can reach the mineral soil, and where the young plant is free from excessive competition with weeds and grass.

II. In the course of an article by M. Emile Mer upon quite a different subject we find mention of the extraordinary drying effect that spruce has upon the soil, and this is a very important point, for it must affect the growth of other species mixed with it if it occupies a large proportion of the space. It may be that species drawing their moisture from a deeper stratum than the surface stratum wherein the roots of the spruce are found could stand the mixture, but even so the spruce must be harmful to some extent, and in fact we know that the oak must not be mixed with spruce for this reason. The spruce is authoritatively stated to be a good tree to mix with many species, but except in more than ordinarily wet places (where it may be directly useful by removing the excess moisture) one would think that the statement must require some qualification, and that a further attentive study of the effect of spruce upon its neighbours would be worth while.

III. M. Huffel, the Nancy professor, quotes the results of a very interesting experiment in thinning spruce, made by Herr Schiffel in Austria. Four experimental areas, of nearly 200 acres each, were established for purposes of comparison in 1892. The altitude was something over 1800 feet; the ground level; the soil good and deep, over gneiss; the age about 80 years. Hitherto these areas had been moderately thinned, and Plot I was continued on the same lines. In 1893 Plots II, III and IV were thinned so as to reduce the basal area of the trees to 80 % of that of Plot I. In 1898 Plots II, III and IV were thinned so as to have basal areas of, respectively, 80 %, 65 % and 50 % of that of Plot I. Two years later Plot IV was so much damaged by the wind as to throw it out of the experiment. In 1903 a similar thinning was made in the other plots; and again in 1908. Then the data acquired were tabulated and considered, with the following results :—

1. One can, in a forest of the kind mentioned, reduce the volume of the standing timber by about a third by very heavy thinning without diminishing the production in volume.

2. These very heavy thinnings, far from spoiling the development in height, are, on the contrary, favourable to it.

3. These thinnings considerably augment the growth and the rate of increase in diameter and volume, so that by thinning heavily we obtain a return in material equal, or even superior, with a smaller uncut capital.

4. The thinning favours the growth of the medium stems.

M. Huffel says that had Herr Schiffel extended his calculations to the value of the production he would have seen that the influence of the thinning on the financial return is even greater than on the return in material. These results completely bear out those of a similar experiment made by M. Huffel himself in the Vosges. But M. Huffel adds a word of warning—we must be careful not to generalise too fast from experiments made in specially chosen spots; heavy thinnings, he says, are not possible save in really favourable conditions; ill-considered operations may be altogether harmful in dry, superficial and poor soils. Still these experiments are rather upsetting to one's ideas, more particularly in the matter of height-growth.

It may be that views about thinning are changing a little—in the direction of marking more freely. Even in the French school this is possible, for we find M. Pardé, a well-known forest officer, describing thinning in the forest of Hez Froidmont—and this a beech (with oak) forest, too—as follows:—" In the cleanings and thinnings the beech, and especially the promising oaks, are thoroughly freed (*fortement dégagés*). It is not rare for the thinnings in woods of about 50 years old to produce 50 steres (*i.e.* 1766 cubic feet) to the hectare (2·47 acres). Sometimes these woods look a little open after the operation, but the canopy soon closes, and the stems of the future, receiving air and light in sufficient quantity, develop with vigour." All that might happen and yet the operation might be wrong, for what we want is the maximum of wood production per acre, and not per individual stem; but it is curious to find a Frenchman quoting the above example with approval, apparently, when Boppe's definition of a good thinning, in conditions such as these, is one in which the after-appearance of the wood is not, to the casual observer, appreciably different to what it was before the operation. It is to be hoped these ideas may not be run away with and carry people too far. Only sample plots, observed for a long period of years, can really decide this most urgent matter. Could not the Royal Scottish Arboricultural Society start a Research Station for Scotland, and the Royal English Arboricultural Society one for England? There are endless questions of the utmost importance which can only be settled by scientific, and especially *permanent*, bodies.

IV. M. Jolyet continues his observations on the hardiness of certain species, more especially conifers. He remarks that it is the exceptional winters and summers one must consider, not the normal, and as the type of exceptional winter he takes 1879-80. I myself remember that, in that year near Nancy, the thermometer went down to − 14° F.; there was skating for six weeks; the temperature during December was only above freezing for half an hour on one day; water froze 4 inches in a night; and the plane trees in the public park of Nancy split with reports like pistol shots. For the type of exceptional

summer M. Jolyet takes 1911. His principal idea is to consider
how the conifers whose home is in the mountains, but which
everyone now plants at low altitudes, out of their true habitat,
can stand these excesses of climate. It is a valuable inquiry.
M. Jolyet has good means of observation, since he is in charge
of the arboretum at Nancy, and has many correspondents in
France, Belgium and Switzerland. He gives the palm of
resistance to drought to the Austrian pine, and after this to
the silver fir, a species supposed to want much rain; but his
observations have been carefully made. Unfortunately, while
good against drought the silver has a limited capacity for
standing winter frost, and of course it is very tender against
spring and autumn frosts. Fortunately for us, the winter frost
which kills it is never reached in Great Britain. It is true the
habitat of the silver runs to great altitudes, but though the cold
lasts longer there it is not more severe than at a lower level; on
the contrary, frost is more harmful in the dry air of the valleys
than in the moist air of the mountains. It can always be
remembered, too, that the atmospheric moisture in these islands
must be greater than on the Continent, a fact of importance to us,
for many species require moist air. The larch did not stand the
drought well in France (M. Jolyet is, probably, referring to east
or central France)—more especially the Japanese larch. My
own experience in the south part of the Midlands was that while
the Japanese made a very poor resistance to the drought of 1911
it was only occasionally that common larch suffered, except of
course when but recently planted; indeed it generally throve
grandly in the bright light—a light more resembling that which
the tree is accustomed to in its own habitat on the tops of the
mountains than is usual in England. So much indeed was this
the case as to impress upon me the conviction that it must be
advantageous to place larch on as bright aspects as possible. It
is true that it is said to suffer from late frosts in low land, because
of its early sprouting, and the aspects generally recommended
for it are not those I have been suggesting, but it is a fact that in
the situation I am thinking of, namely an exposed, gently sloping
place with a S.W. aspect, the growth was very vigorous, in most
cases, in 1911. The spruce, of course, stood the drought badly
in France. *Abies concolor* (a favourite with M. Jolyet) behaved
excellently, as also the Colorado Douglas. Both these also
stand extreme cold well—better than the Vancouver Douglas;

but here again the moisture of our climate is enough to render this Douglas safe here in regard to both extremes of temperature. The reason why *A. concolor* and the blue Douglas stand drought is to be found in the spreading nature of their roots, which can seek out water in any crevice. To the same cause M. Jolyet attributes the fact that *Robinia*, which generally wants depth in the soil, stood the drought so remarkably well. Lawson's cypress stood it fairly; the Nordmann fir and the *Pinus excelsa* did well; but the Weymouth not very well.

V. M. Salvador writes at length on exotics and other trees to be met with in the gardens of the Riviera, and considers which of them might advantageously be tried in the Alpes Maritimes under forest conditions. One may pick out a few of them which might, perhaps, judging from what M. Salvador says, do fairly well with us if placed in as bright and warm situations as we can give them. The intensity of the light is the point which, it seems to me, must be of so much importance with species coming from almost anywhere out of England. *Cupressus sempervirens* is a possible species; it is hardy, and its wood is very valuable. *Cupressus torulosa*, a Himalayan species growing at 9000 feet in its own home, has a very valuable wood, of a pink colour, but needs good soils, and is not very hardy. *Cedrus atlantica* will grow above 4000 feet in the Alpes Maritimes; it will grow on dry, oolitic soils, is hardy, and has a very valuable wood. *Cedrus deodara* is somewhat less hardy. M. Salvador considers it needs good soil. Like other Himalayan species, says M. Salvador, it fears winter frost somewhat, but it seems to stand it pretty well in England, and in its own habitat it has plenty of it. I should like to say that since its wood, in its own home, has such an absolutely superlative value, and since we know the tree will at least grow here, and the wood even retains its characteristic aromatic smell, it is at least probable that if grown with care as to situation the deodar may turn out to be valuable. It is said to have had its trial in England, but *has* it been tried in real *forest* conditions? I doubt it. I believe it should be planted in woods in small groups amongst other trees (as beech), and mixed with *Pinus excelsa* (*the* tree of all others with which it grows so well in the Himalayas), on a warm, bright aspect, on a decent soil, and, in order to put it in as natural conditions as possible, on a slope. M. Salvador mentions many other species, and of these *Pinus halepensis* and *P. pinaster* will grow to very considerable altitudes in that country, so they possibly might do here.

VI. I find in a French magazine what seems a useful note concerning the culture of exotics in Hesse, and extract the information given about the Sitka spruce. This species is said to be "but little affected by herbaceous vegetation or frosts, much employed at all altitudes for filling up blanks in woods, to associate well with broad-leaved species; at 530 metres (1738 feet), on compact soil, it exceeds in height, towards the twentieth year, the green Douglas and the spruce. Four stems of 26 years, on good sandstone soil, reached 12 metres (nearly 40 feet) in height, and 16 centimetres (6·3 inches) in diameter."

VII. The late Professor Fliche has left a book on the botany of the chalk lands of Champagne. This country contains practically no indigenous forest flora, nor was its bareness due to disforestation; it was bare for ages before planting was undertaken. There are now some artificial forests, chiefly of conifers planted far apart. The Scots pine, introduced in 1808, has definitely proved unsuitable; the Corsican suffers from cold; but the Austrian, introduced in 1845, is much better. At the same time, though M. Fliche appears to have thought rather well of the Austrian, he has a remark, in connection with the chemical condition of the soil, which seems to point the other way. He says that certain species that one is accustomed to consider as indifferent to the nature of the soil end by suffering and become anæmic, such as *Robinia*, the aspen, the oak (*sic*) and the Austrian pine. If, however, the last has done well since 1845 I think one may accept it as suitable, given at least a fair amount of top soil; and if beech were associated with it its success should be thoroughly assured. The matter is important, in view of the fact that England contains a great area of chalk downs that one may hope to see, some day, at least partially afforested. M. Fliche considers at length the reason for the bareness of these chalk lands of Champagne. He first dismisses the climate as being the hostile agent, and next the chemical condition of the soil, for he says that there are numerous facts which show that there is nothing incompatible between the existence of forest (omitting certain species definitely "calcifuge") and a strong proportion of lime in the soil. The physical condition is the fault—not through dryness, for although the surface dries up badly, a little way down the chalk will hold moisture well (and this is the cause of the success here of the alder); it is the compactness of chalky soils which is the difficulty. Where the top soil is thin the rapid drying of the surface is of course an important hostile factor, but, in view of what M. Fliche says, it should not be utterly impracticable to afforest a chalk down with a thin soil, if the surface soil were scraped together in mounds running in contour lines round the hillside and planted with a mixture of beech and Austrian pine.

VIII. In these Notes last year there was mention of *Robinia*, and now I find that a M. Vadas, a Hungarian, has written about it in his own country. It has been planted there with success since 1807. The author is evidently enthusiastic about it, and lays stress on its rapid growth, excellent wood, moderate demands in regard to soil, its extraordinary power of spreading by suckers and the extension of its roots, which make it so useful in fixing shifting sands; finally, the great number of uses to which it can be put. His ideal treatment appears to be as a high-forest with only a 50-year rotation, *Robinia* taking the upper stage, with plenty of room for the individual stems, and a shade-bearer as underwood. Although said to be unexacting as to soil, its growth is immensely better on a free soil with a warm climate, such as those required by vineyards and the Spanish chestnut. He gives some figures of growth of woods 32 years old, which are enlightening :—

	Good soil.	Medium soil.	Poor soil.
Number of stems . .	616	592	204
Volume in cubic metres . .	242	117	5
Mean height, metres . .	23·3	18·1	5·85
Mean diam. at chest height, metres	·229	·185	·025

IX. Weymouth pine is used to afforest marshy places in the Vosges. We find a description of a wood of 8¼ acres, said to be by no means the best in the neighbourhood, but just taken as an example. It is 46 years old, rather open, but contains 1276 trees, ranging from 7·8 inches to 23·6 inches diameter, of a volume of over 4000 cubic feet per acre. The value, including about £13 per acre as the estimated present value of the land, is now about £96 per acre. Before planting this marshy land was worth about £3, 5s. 0d. per acre, and produced practically nothing. Spruce appears to have been used with the Weymouth, but where it has not disappeared it is not half the size of the latter. In this instance the capital has functioned at 6 per cent., but another writer gives an example of a Weymouth plantation, grown in similar but even more difficult conditions, where the rate was at least $7\frac{1}{2}$ per cent.

X. M. Galland, having noticed when walking through compartments in course of exploitation that oak logs cut along the edges of roads always appeared to contain a large proportion of sapwood, made careful observations with a Pressler borer on numerous stems grown in similar situations, but varying only in the amount of light that reached—not their crowns but—their boles. The result bore out his casual observation. Thus, to quote only some of the cases out of many similar, the following examples may be taken :—

1. In a compartment of which the stock was coppice-with-standards, the standards being old and the underwood old enough to shade their boles completely, the mean thickness of the sapwood of six of the oaks was 15·42 mm.

2. In a compartment of high-forest under regeneration, with the oak reserves standing far apart and only seedlings on the ground, the mean thickness of the sapwood was 38·33 mm.

3. In a similar compartment it was 39·3 mm.

4. In a younger compartment, principally of oaks, fairly close, with the boles shaded by the neighbouring crowns, the figure was 18·6 mm.

5. In a compartment of very close-grown beech poles with some old oaks, their sapwood was 15·37 mm.

M. Galland then wished to ascertain the rate at which the sapwood increased with the admission of light to the boles. For this purpose he made observations in five compartments in sequence in a coppice-with-standards, and found that in two years the thickness of the sapwood was more than doubled. Thus :—

In a compartment of which the underwood was just cut, the sapwood of the standards was 14·3 mm.

Do. cut the previous year, the sapwood of the standards was 25·75 mm.

Do. cut two years before, the sapwood of the standards was 31·5 mm.

Do. cut three years before, the sapwood of the standards was 33 mm.

Do. cut four years before, the sapwood of the standards was 36·96 mm.

XI. In 1876, M. Carriére invented a clever and simple plan for dealing with relatively small ravines on bare hillsides, where torrents form and cause much damage below. This is known as "Garnissage," and it has been very successful. Having assured a firm bottom to the ravine with stones or lines of pegs, branches are laid heading up the ravine, the lower ends being stuck into the soil. On this are laid rough poles placed crisscross at about 45 degrees to the line of the ravine, the lower ends stuck into the banks. Finally, at right angles to the ravine, more poles are laid across and fixed to pegs driven into the banks. Wire is used liberally to tie these poles together. When finished the surface must be slightly concave. The rains and snows soon cover this garnissage with stones and soil, and it is then necessary to sow grasses and the seeds of bushy plants, to be followed by cuttings of willows and poplars, and plants of *Robinia*, alder and many other things. These are often afterwards cut back to make them bushy, or are layered. A further stage is to peg down branches higher up the slopes. The vegetation soon spreads.

XII. Of late years a new use for ash has sprung up, namely the manufacture of skis. Herr Janka, of the Research Station of Mariabrünn, has lately, writes M. Huffel, made a study of the matter, in order to ascertain which is the best ash-wood to employ. The special qualities of ash—elasticity, flexibility, hardness, resistance to crushing—are proportional to the density of the wood. An excess of moisture diminishes the hardness of ash and its resistance to crushing, but augments its flexibility and elasticity. To some extent we may judge merely by eye of the qualities of ash. The fact, already stated by Mathieu, that the breadth of the spring-wood of ash (as also of oak, elm and others of analogous structure) is constant, whereas the dense autumn-wood may vary in breadth, shows that the faster the growth (and larger the annual ring) the heavier the wood. It is the exact opposite with the conifers. While it is true that ash with a narrow annual ring, such as is grown in a crowded wood, has always a relatively inferior quality— another reason, by the way, for freeing the crowns of ash in a wood—it nevertheless does not follow (so the article states) that the trees that have grown quickest have always the densest wood, and it appears that wood grown moderately fast is the best for ski making. There is very great waste in this industry, for the fibres must not be cut, and only perfectly straight-grained wood, split out along the medullary rays, will do. Of course there must be nothing like a knot. Finally, only the sapwood is used, and the heartwood is rejected.

8. On Protecting Young Spruce from Frost.

By WILLIAM HALL, Bilton, York.

Great inconvenience and loss is frequently caused to young spruce plantations by frost, especially in late spring after the sap has begun to flow into the extremities of the branches. Spruce and a few other conifers suffer severely from such frosts; they are mostly met with on damp low-lying land which is sometimes difficult to drain, and generally on peaty soil, which in Yorkshire overlies a subsoil commonly known as quicksand.

The writer is desirous of explaining an experience obtained on this estate, in one of the above-mentioned hollows; although it happened by accident, and not by any plan or foresight, it proved very successful, and might be useful to anyone else working under similar conditions.

The facts of the case are that in 1905 about 6 acres of the Nova Scotia Wood were felled, and the following winter were thoroughly cleared out; the ground being replanted in February 1906. It might be advisable to explain here that owing to the low-lying, basin-like configuration of the ground, a very deep dyke about half a mile long had been cut at some previous time to drain this wood, which is intersected by smaller dykes, carried to all the wettest parts. As a rule there is no water in these dykes in summer; but in winter, owing to the fact that some of the surrounding arable land drains into the wood, and owing to its very level nature, the water becomes backed up, with the result that the lowest-lying part is kept very damp throughout the winter.

About two acres of a fringe round the outside of the plot, where the soil is stronger, were planted with larch and spruce in the proportion of about 3 to 1 respectively, and mixed with hardwoods, oak and ash, at about every 16 feet. The wet, low-lying part in the centre was planted entirely with spruce, mixed with alder, in place of oak and ash, as the ground was rather wet for these trees. The alders were planted in every third row, the rows being 4 feet apart, and were thus about 12 feet apart. They were planted simply because the soil suited them and not as a protection for the spruce, but, as it turned out, they have proved a splendid protection, as was seen shortly afterwards, when, about the end of April, a very severe frost scorched dozens of spruce round the outside of the wood, while those in the centre, which were protected by the alders, were practically unharmed. The alders were between 3 and 4 feet high when planted, and grew very rapidly, the situation and soil being suitable; and now, after having been planted six years, some of the best of them are from 12 to 15 feet in height, and measure nearly 12 inches in circumference. They have been constantly pruned, all the bottom branches being cut off every year, so as to give the spruce plenty of light and air space; and in another year's time it is intended to thin out the alders gradually by first taking out every alternate tree, and doing the same in each of the following years until all have been removed, when it is expected that the spruce will be past the stage in which they are most liable to get frozen.

It has been considered best to cut out all the alders as they are of very little commercial value, and the spruce is now wanted as game cover, while later on, when it comes to maturity, it will be required for estate purposes. Another reason for cutting out alders is that they make a very bad mixture, especially with spruce, for they grow very fast, overtopping the spruce very quickly, and they also throw out great numbers of side branches which spread out wide and would in course of time smother the spruce.

The plan here mentioned of protecting spruce by mixing them with alders is well worth bringing to the notice of all those interested in the growing of spruce. In this instance, the soil was suited to both species; but in some cases, where spruce is planted, the soil might be more suited to birch, and this species answers the purpose just as well as alder, especially where the situation is exposed to winds. Birch is more hardy and will thrive on poor soil. In some parts of the country birch grows naturally, and would only require thinning out to the required distance apart before planting with spruce, or it could be raised from seed by sowing broad-cast, which could be done at very small cost, and after a few years it would provide excellent shelter for the spruce.

A small exposed plantation on this estate has a considerable quantity of natural birch in one corner, and it is surprising to notice the better condition of the young plants which are sheltered by these trees, as compared with those which are not so sheltered.

Alders could be raised in the same manner, but are very easily grown from cuttings, which, on suitable soil, could be inserted in the same way as willow cuttings, just previous to planting with spruce; shoots of one year's growth are best for this purpose.

The damage done to spruce by severe frosts in late spring, and sometimes in early summer, is very annoying to foresters, besides resulting in a great loss, as very frequently the affected plants die altogether, while, should they live, they have a brown, scorched appearance for a long time afterwards; sometimes the young leading shoot will die and a side shoot take its place, and consequently the tree loses its commercial value. The best and most profitable way to treat frozen plants is to take them out at once, should the season be not too far advanced, and to fill up with ball plants of about the same size, if they can be procured; or should the season for planting be past, the first opportunity of putting in new plants should be taken in the following season.

The above experience is well worthy of the notice of foresters and others interested in the growing of spruce, for although it was obtained quite by accident it proved to be very successful, and is certainly worth a trial by others who have similar places to plant. The alder is a very suitable tree for the purpose, as it grows rapidly, and soon gets ahead of the spruce, allowing the lower branches to be lopped so as to let light and air to the spruce beneath it. Another point is that the side branches of the alder spread very rapidly, and afford protection to the spruce from frost and the scorching rays of the sun in summer; this benefit is proved by the healthy, dark green appearance of the young spruce underneath it, and by the rapid growth which they make after they are once fairly established.

9. Some Uses of a Demonstration Forest in Forestry Education.[1]

(*With Plates.*)

By J. F. ANNAND.

When we speak of forestry education we, obviously, do not refer merely to class-room teaching. Class-room and laboratory instruction are, of course, highly important and indeed quite indispensable. But one of the most essential conditions of success in the teaching of forestry is the provision of practical training ground; for forestry is nothing if not a practical subject.

If it is important for the future and the practising agriculturist to have the example of good farming before him, we can safely and confidently claim that it is even more important for the forester, who cannot hope to see the full effects of his labour during a natural life-time, to have the example of continuous good forestry practice before him. As every one connected with forestry knows, this practical example can be provided in Great Britain only by means of Demonstration or Example forests. It may be argued that in Continental states, where the most scientific forestry is practised, we do not as a rule find large tracts of forest land set aside especially for Demonstration purposes, and consequently that there is no need for it in our own case. But we have to remember that 50 per cent. of the forests, in the countries referred to, are managed and worked systematically, and more or less scientifically, on a large scale. The work is often undertaken by the State or by some large corporate body; and it is carried on, as a rule, as a great continuous commercial undertaking. Schemes of management have been in working order for many decades. No forest officer is given a position of such responsibility that he can even modify materially a working-scheme, until he has spent several years in the forests in some subordinate capacity. In fact, the forest manager receives his training in the actual forest which he is ultimately to control.

In Great Britain the case is entirely different. Here we have

[1] Compiled from notes of an address (with lantern slides) given at the Annual General Meeting of the Society, February 1911.

practically no State forests which have been made the objects of regular organisation for long periods of years.

Almost everything we have in the way of forests in Scotland is the result of private enterprise. Many of the landowners in Scotland have done great things for forestry, but they are always ready to admit, in fact are the first to admit, that for the purposes we have in view there is one great drawback; that is, that there is no guarantee for continuity of management. A private landowner, with the best intentions in the world, cannot give this guarantee. This cannot be gainsaid.

I think, also, we may accept it as a fact that whatever may be the case in the distant future, so far as concerns the present at any rate and the near future, the development and extension of forestry as an industry in this country must continue as now very largely in the hands of private owners. Hence the absolute necessity for having established a considerable number of organised forestry estates in suitable representative districts throughout the country, preferably perhaps under some State department, but certainly under some body where continuity of policy could be assured. Incidentally, these areas should provide the best practical training ground for the men who are largely to be responsible for the development and management both of existing woodlands and for the new planted forests, which we hope soon to see take practical shape.

The following notes on some of the educational uses which have been made of a small area of Crown woodland attached to Armstrong College, and also of private woodland areas in the same neighbourhood, may be of some interest to those specially concerned with similar matters in Scotland. The areas I propose to make a few remarks about are :—

    I. Forest Garden Plots at Cockle Park, Northumberland.

    II. The Crown Woods of Chopwell, Co. Durham (about 800 acres available and under a working-scheme).

    III. Some excellent private woodlands on Tyneside and in Cumberland.

Regarding the locality generally, it may be stated that satisfactory growth of the more valuable hardwoods is only to be found in the lower valleys and on the best soils; but many of the slopes in these valleys, which are too steep for field crops, give satisfactory results with ash, beech, sycamore and oak. On the soils usually available for the growth of timber the district generally is, however, one for conifers.

The forest garden plots were laid out by Dr Somerville of Oxford, about twelve years ago, and they now form a very valuable adjunct to the class-room for instruction in silviculture. The garden contains about twenty miniature forests, varying in size from half an acre to one acre.

The plots represent pure and mixed woods of various "light" and "shade" trees. Here the student can at once have a bird's-eye view, so to speak, of the earlier stages of many different kinds of forest, and of many of the results of various combinations and mixtures of species. It is hardly an exaggeration to say that without some such means of illustrating certain silvicultural principles, it is impossible to convey any proper conception of them to the mind of a student who has had no previous acquaintance with woods. These plots will now be supplemented by new and duplicate ones in the other Demonstration woods in Co. Durham, which are more accessible to the teaching centre.

While, individually, the Cockle Park plots are miniature forests, collectively they constitute a piece of woodland of considerable size. Situated as they are, also, close to woods of considerable extent, they will now provide material of very considerable value for the purposes of growth studies. Space does not permit of any of these questions being dealt with here.

CHOPWELL WOODS.

The woodland area at Chopwell, although not of sufficient extent to fulfil all the requirements of a school for practical training, can be used for most of the purposes to which a Demonstration forest can be put. The woods are worked as a commercial undertaking, but all the actual forestry operations are carried out by student workers under the guidance of a skilled foreman. The smallness of the area necessarily limits the number of such students. A working-scheme has been drawn up, and has been in operation for five years. The working students are young men qualifying to act as head foresters on estates, or for similar posts.   They receive class-room instruction at Armstrong College (six weeks at a time) in such subjects as botany, chemistry, entomology and geology of soils, and silviculture.   In the forest, during the summer, they get instruction in mensuration, chain surveying, forest mensuration, and other branches of forestry.

The Demonstration wood, from a variety of causes, is far from being in ideal condition, but it is typical of much of the wood-land in the district, and for this reason has a special value of its own; for the work of improvement now being undertaken is just the kind of work that most of the young men in training will be called upon to undertake.

The working-scheme is intended, ultimately, to lead up to conditions which will result in a continuous and regular yield of timber.   In the present condition of the woods this necessitates two main lines of action.   On the one hand, the most worthless and over-mature portions are being gradually cleared and replanted, while, on the other, works of improvement, such as thinning and underplanting, are being carried on in the younger and better portions so as to maintain a profitable annual increment there as long as possible.   These works provide favourable opportunities also for the study of such subjects as surveying, forest mensuration, etc. (see Plate II.).

Experimental Work.

Experimental plots are also being laid down annually to test the suitability of various species for underplanting, the advantages and disadvantages of various mixtures or pure woods, the effects of various degrees of density in planting, and so forth.   These experimental plots are arranged so as not to interfere with the main objects of the management of the woods. Experiments in selecting and testing tree seeds can also con-veniently be carried out in the tree nursery within the woods. As an example of this, several plots of Scots pine have been set out with plants raised from seeds collected from selected trees of different ages in Chopwell Woods and from other home localities.   It is to be feared that we are not making the best out of our native trees by the selection of seeds from good types, and there is still a wide field for investigation in these matters.

Supplementary Work in Private Woodlands.

As the woods under the immediate control of the college do not provide examples of all different stages and conditions of forest growth, they have to be supplemented, for demonstration purposes, by private woodlands in the vicinity, to which latter the landowners concerned have readily granted access. For these purposes the conifer tract on Tyneside is second to none in the country.

Plots have also been set out by Armstrong College for observation purposes in these woods. The following two examples show the nature of some of the growth studies which are being made. The observations were commenced by Mr A. C. Forbes six years ago, and re-measurements have been made from time to time since then, and other new plots taken up.

Extract from particulars of a Series of Measurements made in Observation Plots on Tyneside (Dipton Woods).

1	2	3	4	5	6		7	8	9			10	
					Number of Stems		Basal Area (quarter-girth measure) in each Plot	Volume of Timber in each Plot	Equal per acre			Thinnings removed at 35 years = per acre	
Date	No. of Plot	Area of Plot meas- ured	Age in years at time of Measurement	Average Height of Trees	in each Plot	= per acre			Volume	Mean Annual Production	Current Annual Incre- ment for past 5 years	Number of Stems	Volume
				Ft.			Sq. ft.	C. ft.	C. ft.	C. ft.	C. ft.		C. ft.
1905	I.	1 acre	1st measure- ment at 30 years	35	1073	1073	128·9	1718	1718	57	...	...	...
			2nd measure- ment at 35 years	38	930	930	147·3	2149	2149	61	86	143	112
1910	II.	¼ acre	1st measure- ment at 30 years	34	510	2040	32·6	420·6	1668	56	...	...	...
			2nd measure- ment at 35 years	37	450	1800	45·3	524·0	2096	60	85	240	100

NOTE.—The measurements are taken *over bark*. To make allowance for bark 11½ % or 12 % should be deducted from the volume figures given above.

PLATE II.

FIG. 1.—Section of larch with oak, birch, elm, etc. (winter condition), before improvement thinnings were made. Compare with Figs. 2 and 3. The picture was taken when there was snow on the ground and on the trees.

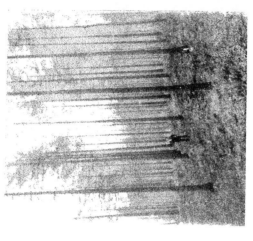

FIG. 2.—Section of larch wood immediately after improvement thinnings have been made for underplanting.

CHOPWELL WOODS.

FIG. 3.—Section of larch four years underplanted.

[*To face p.* 58

FIG. 4.—Scots pine crop, 35 years old   Number of stems per acre, 930. (For details of volume see Plot I. in table on p. 58.) Compare with Fig 5.

FIG. 5.—Scots pine crop, 35 years old.   Number of stems per acre, 1800. (For details of volume see Plot II. in table on p. 58.)

DIPTON WOODS

The examples given are intended to show the nature of some of the work which may be undertaken in Demonstration woods, and in the hope of inducing others to take up similar work. Other methods of making the measurements can of course be adopted, but the advantage of the quarter-girth method is that it is in daily use and best understood on estates where assistance may be obtained in keeping records. Apart from these considerations, Continental methods are to be preferred. An interesting point to be specially noted in connection with the plots selected, is that at thirty-five years of age the volume production in each case is about equal, notwithstanding that the number of stems per acre in one case is very much in excess of the other.

The quality of the timber may, however, be very different. A reference to Figs. 4 and 5 will make this apparent. The plots are situated near each other in nearly uniform conditions as regards soil, altitude and exposure. Space does not permit of full details being given of this branch of work, but one point may specially be noted with reference to thinnings (column 10 of table). The thinnings in the plots described were restricted almost entirely to the removal of suppressed (dead) trees. Many of the roots of those suppressed trees were dug up, and it was found that 80 per cent. of them had no proper root-system and that they had retained the bent, distorted shape which is sometimes produced through careless nursery treatment of the young plants, or, it may be, through careless planting. To what extent this may have resulted in actual loss of volume it is difficult to estimate. We may reasonably assume, however, that as the development of individuals in the crop has been retarded, this must also influence the mass. It may be argued that in any case these suppresseed stems would have to be removed as thinnings, but this may not necessarily be so. The largest plants in a batch of seedlings are most likely to have their roots damaged and distorted by careless handling in the nursery. It is conceivable therefore that the best and most vigorous growers may in this way be permanently crippled, and that a large loss in increment may result. If natural reproduction is impracticable (and as a rule it is), it is highly important to have careful handling of the trees in the nursery and in planting operations. Few species suffer so much from careless nursery treatment as Scots pine. In Plate III., Fig. 9, there is shown a portion of the stem and roots of a suppressed tree taken from one of the pine plots. If this root-system is compared with those in Figs. 6 and 7, it will at once be seen how great the difference is between it and those of a natural seedling or a carefully handled nursery plant.

As regards purely educational work in forestry, Example forests must also be the best means of reaching those already in charge of woodlands who have not had any opportunities of making a special study of scientific methods of dealing with woods, and who cannot take advantage of courses of instruction extending over lengthened periods, at teaching centres. For such a purpose several areas, even of moderate extent (if of easy access), in different parts of the country, would probably have more immediate influence in fostering good forestry than one or two large but comparatively inaccessible forests.

10. Research Work and Educational Methods of the Forestry Departments and Forestry Schools in the United States and Canada in connection with the study of Timber and other Forest Products.

Compiled from the Report of a Visit by E. R. BURDON, M.A., to those Countries.

The object of the journey, which was undertaken in accordance with a resolution of the Forestry Committee of the University of Cambridge, was to study the methods of research into the structure, properties and utilisation of timber employed in the United States and Canada, and the nature of the training given to forestry students in this branch of the subject.

PRODUCTS BRANCH OF THE UNITED STATES FOREST SERVICE.

The most important research work on timber in the United States is that which is being carried on by the Branch of Products of the Forest Service.

The main object of this branch is to develop more economical methods of utilising forest products generally, so as to eliminate the enormous waste which occurs not only in logging, but also in conversion into lumber and in manufacture.

In pursuance of this object the Products Branch endeavours

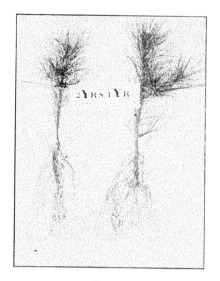

FIG. 7.
3-year-old Scots Pine properly transplanted
(British method).
Compare with Fig. 8.

FIG. 9.
Suppressed (dead) Tree taken from Pine Wood,
35 years planted, showing effect of improper
handling in Nursery after 35 years.
Compare root-system with those of Figs. 6, 7, 8.

SCOTS PINE TREES.

[To face p. 60.

to organise systematic scientific research and to disseminate information regarding the mechanical, physical and chemical properties of commercial woods and their products, the utilisation of forest products, the natural and artificial seasoning of wood, wood preservation, wood distillation, the production of paper pulp, naval stores and other chemical products. It also compiles statistics of production, consumption, prices and market conditions, investigates commercial methods of manufacture, of grading, and utilisation, and the possibilities of substitution of new species or other materials for woods which are becoming scarce, etc., etc. The range of the investigations of the Products Branch covers every industry which is in any way dependent on the forest for its raw material. The work is thus of the greatest economic value, and the results already obtained are doing more than almost any other agency to educate the timber trade at large in a proper appreciation of scientific forestry.

The organisation of the branch is as follows :

(*a*) The Forest Products Laboratory at Madison,

(*b*) The Office of Wood Utilisation at Chicago,

both co-ordinated under the direction of the chief of the branch who reports direct to Washington, D.C.

In addition to this the whole country is divided up into districts, and an officer of the Products Branch is stationed at a central point in each district, in order to enable the branch to keep in close touch with the principal timber associations and wood-using industries of each district.

Before the commencement of any research project, a working-plan as complete in detail as possible is insisted on. This working-plan is submitted by the head of the department concerned to a committee composed of all the heads of departments in the Products Branch. The need for the investigation, present knowledge of the subject, the proposed method of procedure, with plans of any instruments required, the probable cost, etc., etc., are all laid before the committee. The project after full discussion and criticism is revised and finally passed on by the chief of the branch for similar consideration by a committee composed of the heads of the Forest Service Departments at Washington, D.C.

Although this occasions some delay in beginning the work, the method has been found to be most satisfactory, since many points which would never have occurred to the originator of the project, but are capable of simultaneous solution, are brought forward. By this means not only is duplication of work saved, but the various departments of the Forest Service are kept in close touch with what is going on. Progress reports of research work are also handed in at intervals and considered in a similar manner, and a final report is also required before the project is considered completed.

THE FOREST PRODUCTS LABORATORY, MADISON.

The laboratory, which has an ample storage-yard of about two acres in extent, with sawmill, drying sheds and a woodworking shop, is organised into eight technical sections for experimental research, and one non-technical section which attends to general maintenance.

The technical sections are as follows:

1. Timber-testing.
2. Timber Physics.
3. Wood Preservation.
4. Wood Distillation.
5. Pulp and Paper.
6. Engineering (with Drafting Room).
7. Chemistry.
8. Pathology.

1. *Timber-testing Department.*—Here investigations are made into the mechanical properties of wood both before and after manufacture, or preservative treatment, or seasoning.

At present tests are being carried out on the different commercial woods of the United States with a view to determining their relative mechanical properties, *e.g.* strength, toughness, hardness, etc. A point wherein these tests differ from those generally made by engineers is that the specimens are collected from the forest, and the history of each, the conditions of soil and environment, etc., under which each was grown, are known. The structure of each specimen is noted from microscopic sections made in another department, and as sufficient data accumulate attempts will be made to correlate the structure with the mechanical and physical properties. It is hoped that this work may in time enable each species to be so graded according to structure and corresponding strength, that the factor of safety rendered necessary by the tables at present used by engineers, architects, etc., may be materially reduced. If by any means it is found possible to do this in such a manner that, by examination of the structure, an engineer may at once know within moderate limits the strength of a log, the work will be of immense value. But even apart from this the work will be of service by enabling consumers to readily find substitutes for woods which are becoming scarce.

Other tests are being made in this section to determine the effect which the treatment of wood under pressure in the process of preserving has on its mechanical properties.

The effects of different methods of seasoning on the mechanical properties are also investigated.

The equipment of this laboratory consists of—

    one 200,000 lbs. Riehlé testing machine ;
    one 100,000 lbs. Olsen   ,,   ,,
    three 30,000 lbs. Olsen   ,,   ,,
    one 60,000 inch pound Riehlé torsion testing machine ;
    one impact testing machine; and various machines for doing shop-repairs, grinding tools, etc.

Another piece of apparatus which is best described under this section, though it is actually set up in the Timber Physics Laboratory, is one which has been specially designed for determining the effect of dead loads on beams, the deflections of each beam being automatically recorded upon a revolving drum. The object of this research is to ascertain the relations that exist between the strength of a material as demonstrated by ordinary testing machines working at uniform speed, and its strength when placed under a constant stress or dead load.

2. *Timber Physics Department.*—In this section studies are made of the physical properties of wood and their relation to structure. These include determination of the specific gravity, specific heat, the effects of changes of temperature, pressure and moisture on the wood substance and general structure, etc. These researches have a special bearing on the artificial treatment of wood in the processes of seasoning, fire-proofing, preserving under pressure, etc., when it is important to know the effect of different pressures, the amount of heat required, the length of time different kinds of wood may be exposed to certain conditions, and so forth. The results of this work therefore

serve as a valuable check on the experiments of other departments.

This department possesses a complete equipment for preparing sections and photomicrographs of wood, and is making a collection of North American woods. The specimens are in the form of half-logs 4 feet long, with bark attached, cut so as to display the transverse, radial, tangential and obliquely tangential surfaces.

3. *Wood Preservation and* (8) *Pathology Departments.*—The wood of these two departments is so closely connected that it is simpler to describe them together. The Wood Preservation Laboratory contains a very complete equipment for testing the various problems of wood preservation by treating the wood with materials which increase its durability.

These problems may be divided broadly into two classes:

(*a*) Those dealing with the preservatives themselves, their effect on the wood and their efficiency in resisting fungi, insects and fire.

(*b*) Those concerned with the methods of forcing the preservative into the wood.

(*a*) In the study of the first of these problems the preservatives are analysed and fractionally distilled in the chemical laboratory. The efficiency of each preservative and its different fractions is then tested by subjecting woods treated with them to the action of wood-destroying fungi or animals, and noting their relative powers of resistance. The effects of weather on the preservative in the treated specimens are also investigated and taken into account in judging efficiency.

The efficiency of each preservative or of its fractional distillates is also tested by making culture media of wood-destroying fungi to which the preservatives are added in different percentage strengths. The extent to which the fungus succeeds in growing in such media affords an indication of the efficiency of the preservative.

Experiments of a similar kind on a larger scale are also being attempted in a fungus pit which has been specially constructed below the floor in one corner of the Wood Preservation Laboratory.

(*b*) The equipment for studying the second class of problems, viz., the methods of impregnating the woods with the different preservatives, is very complete. There are four sizes of pressure cylinders. An open tank is also provided in which the effect of soaking specimens in preservatives without pressure, as well as the degree of penetration obtainable by alternating applications of hot and cold preservative, can be investigated. Another piece of apparatus is specially designed for observing the course which the preservative takes through the wood elements when injected under pressure. Other problems, such as the loss of preservatives by evaporation at different temperatures, the relative inflammability of woods, etc., are being investigated with the help of ingenious pieces of apparatus designed for each problem. Piles which have been treated to test the possibility of preserving them against marine-boring animals have been sunk in the waters of the Gulf of Mexico and the Bay of San Francisco.

4. *Wood Distillation Department.*—In this laboratory studies are made of the products obtainable from different woods and of the most economical methods of extraction.

The work of this department is of high economic importance, for its main object is to find a profitable use for the enormous waste of material which occurs, not only in the forest in the shape of tops, branches and stumps, but also in the sawmills and factories, in the shape of slabs, ends, shavings and sawdust. Designs for an experimental plant to produce ethyl alcohol from sawdust are now being drawn up. Another line of investigation has been the commercial methods of collecting and refining turpentine, and the improved methods suggested are gradually being adopted by the trade.

5. *Pulp and Paper Department.*—The work here is mainly directed at present to the discovery of woods which can be substituted for spruce as a source of pulp in view of the rapid disappearance of the spruce forests. This involves studies of the methods by which ground wood-pulp can be obtained from species other than spruce; of the potentialities of different woods in the manufacture of chemical pulp; of the qualities of paper which can be made from various grades of sulphite, soda and ground wood-pulp; and of the possibilities of utilising various forms of forest and mill waste for the manufacture of pulp.

6. *Engineering Department.*—The work of this section, apart from the care of the machinery in the yard and building, consists in the designing of plant and apparatus. The discovery

of improved methods of working wood, or new applications for a given wood or wood product, is at once followed by the designing of apparatus which will enable the discovery to be put to commercial use.

7. *Chemistry Department.*—The work of this section is of course carried on in close collaboration with every other section. The main problems engaging its attention at present are the analysis and grading of commercial creosotes to determine their value as preservatives, and the analysis and grading of turpentines and rosins.

OFFICE OF WOOD UTILISATION, CHICAGO.

The main object here, as in the Products Laboratory, is to promote more economic utilisation of wood by elimination of waste in both forest and mill, but, as mentioned above, this Office only attempts the solution of problems which do not require the application of laboratory methods and can be solved by direct co-operation with lumbermen and manufacturers.

To achieve this a thorough knowledge of the timber business generally is essential, and detailed studies are being made of the wood-using industries of each State. These studies include statistics of production and consumption of lumber, the kinds of wood used, the source whence obtained, the product manufactured from each kind, and a variety of information as to market conditions, prices, etc. The work is carried on in co-operation with manufacturers, who are invited to supply the necessary information, and in most cases the States also lend the assistance of their Boards of Forestry, of Agriculture, of Labour, of Statistics, etc.

As a result of the knowledge acquired by these studies, covering as they do every important home wood-using industry, the Office is enabled to co-operate still more closely with manufacturers by giving valuable suggestions for the utilisation of material which would otherwise be regarded as waste. The Office is also ready to help manufacturers in the discovery of substitutes for species of trees which are becoming scarce.

FORESTRY SCHOOLS.

The forestry schools visited were those of Yale, Harvard, Michigan and Toronto Universities, which are recognised as being of the highest standard in North America. All of these are housed in temporary buildings which have been adapted for the purpose, and I was therefore unable to gain any ideas as to the most suitable type of building for a forestry school. None of them possesses a museum, nor is there even adequate accommodation for the collections of material necessary for class work.

The most pressing needs of the United States and Canada in connection with forestry at present lie in the better management of the woods and forests, and it is therefore natural to find that the work in their newly established forestry schools is almost entirely directed towards giving students a thorough training in the silvicultural side of forestry.

The study of Timber Physics, under which term I include all such studies as are undertaken at the Forest Products Laboratory, occupies quite a secondary position in the curricula of forestry schools, and except for microscopical studies of timber structure, no other research work is carried on.

II. The Annual Excursion.

(*With Plate.*)

By Wm Dawson, M.A., B.Sc.

The Society this year visited the north-eastern part of Scotland, and spent the week beginning June 24th in the valley of the Dee. The party was much larger than usual, there being nearly a hundred members present. The district visited is one of the best-wooded parts of Scotland, and includes places which have long been recognised as almost unique silviculturally. The old forest of Ballochbuie, in which the Excursion started, is almost the last remaining area of the native pine forests which once covered a large portion of the country, while Durris, at which it closed, is unique for the number and size of its exotic timber trees. The places visited between these extremes had, likewise, much to interest the silviculturist in the size and variety of their woodland areas. A point of interest is the fact that the Kirktown of Braemar, from which the Excursion started, stands at an elevation of about 1000 feet above sea-level —an elevation which for most parts of Scotland is recognised as beyond, or at the utmost limits of, the "timber line." Yet, in this particular district, trees of more than one species flourish at elevations many hundred feet higher. Practically all the time was spent in woods of a commercial kind, though most of the places visited afforded also great arboricultural interest. The estates visited had all very extensive woodland areas, mostly over 4000 acres each.

Special interest was lent by the fact that permission had graciously been granted to view the woods and policies of the Royal Residence at Balmoral.

On the afternoon of Monday, June 24th, the party assembled in Aberdeen, and the journey from there to Braemar was undertaken in the motor cars which accompanied the party throughout the tour. The headquarters on Monday and Tuesday were in the Fife Arms Hotel in Braemar, and for the remaining days in the Burnett Arms and other hotels in Banchory.

His Majesty the King was graciously pleased to entertain the members of the Society to luncheon at Balmoral. At the luncheon the President referred to the Royal estates as being models of good management. The King's woods afforded a model to other proprietors, and an object lesson to all his subjects. There were not only the old natural forests of Ballochbuie, but also extensive younger plantations perfectly stocked and in ideal order. He expressed the gratitude all felt to His Majesty for inviting them there, and for entertaining them that day. The following telegram was sent to His Majesty :—

" Sir John Stirling-Maxwell presents his humble duty to your Majesty and begs, on behalf of the Royal Scottish Arboricultural Society, to thank your Majesty for the kindness and hospitality with which its members, by your Majesty's command, have been received at Balmoral, and for the delightful and instructive days they have spent among your Majesty's thriving woods and plantations. The Society desires to assure your Majesty of its devoted loyalty, and prays that your Majesty and the Queen may continue to flourish like the pines in the Ballochbuie."

In the course of the next day the President received the following telegram from the King :—

"ROYAL YACHT CLUB, CARDIFF.

" To SIR JOHN STIRLING-MAXWELL.

" I thank you and the members of the Royal Scottish Arboricultural Society for kind telegram and good wishes for the Queen and myself, which it contains. I am delighted the Society enjoyed their visit to Balmoral.

" GEORGE R.I."

The Society was also hospitably received on the other estates visited.

Tuesday, June 25th.

BALLOCHBUIE.—The business of the Excursion started on Tuesday morning with a visit to the western portion of the old Ballochbuie Forest. This forest forms the centre of a very large area of woodland—an area which covers many square miles, stretching unbroken from Ballater on the east to considerably beyond Braemar on the west, a distance of more than twenty miles. The party was under the guidance of Mr John Michie, M.V.O., His Majesty's factor at Balmoral, who gave much interesting and valuable information, not only on the old wood alone, but on the general forestry of the district. The Forest of Ballochbuie is situated in a great hollow among the hills, the lowest elevation being nearly 1000 feet above sea-level, while the highest point at which good timber grows is about 1500 feet, though the trees persist up to 1800 feet. The forest consists of Scots pine alone, the remains of the old Caledonian Forest, true natives in their native habitat. Practically no cutting is done in the wood, but individual trees are removed when they die, and the oldest of these have been found to be nearly 300 years of age. Mr Michie gives the age of the oldest specimen at from 260 to 300 years, but the greater part of the area is occupied with trees somewhat younger. All the trees are big, and many of them are of vast size with tall, clean, full stems. On the lower ground, where the trees are biggest, one specimen was found to measure nearly 100 feet in height, and to girth 7 ft. 8 ins. at 5 feet from the ground. Even at higher elevations the size was great. Between 1200 feet and 1300 feet a number of trees were found to measure from 3 feet to 5 ft. 3 ins. in circumference at 5 feet from the ground, but in the same place a single tree girthed 11 ft. 10 ins. at 5 feet from the ground. Many of the trees contain over 100 cub. feet of timber, but some free-standing specimens contain between 200 and 300 cub. feet. As can be readily understood the stock is somewhat uneven; in places there is a fairly full stand while in others the crop is thin. In the lower ground a considerable area has been enclosed against deer. Within the fence natural regeneration took place, and on part of the ground a fairly full crop was secured.

The stocking of the area has now been completed by planting up gaps with seedlings raised from seed gathered from the old trees. Outside of the enclosed area few young trees are to be seen. The old trees are still producing fertile seed, a full crop being produced every four or five years.

Altogether Ballochbuie Forest is magnificent, and possesses a character entirely different from that of most Scottish woods. Its great age, the great size of its big trees, its vigour and vitality, and the general expression of strength, all go to make it distinctive. It is fortunate that it is being carefully preserved.

INVERCAULD.—In the afternoon the forests of Invercauld, which belong to Mr Farquharson, were visited. The Invercauld woods are adjacent to the Ballochbuie Forest, stretching to the north and to the west, forming part of the vast block of woodlands clothing this part of the valley. They consist, for the most part, of Scots pine though the specimens are considerably younger than those of Ballochbuie. Here too the Scots pine grows well at elevations up to 1400 or 1500 feet. A considerable amount of planting has taken place in recent years, and one noteworthy feature is the excellent growth of the spruce in the few clumps where it has been planted. The Invercauld woods extend to many thousands of acres, but the party had time to inspect only those near at hand. The trees near the house also afforded considerable interest. There are many good specimen conifers, and also an interesting group of *Picea alba* about 20 feet high. The party was under the guidance of Mr Andrew Smith, factor for the estates.

Returning from Invercauld, the party motored through Braemar and through the finely wooded country past Mar Lodge on to the Linn o' Dee. The members had thus a chance of seeing something of the nature and extent of the woodlands in the uppermost part of the valley. Special interest attaches to a very extensive area of thriving larch stretching along the hillside between Corriemulzie and Gley Ey, which attracted the attention of the party as it passed. The lowermost part of the wood stands at an elevation of 1200 feet, and it rises to an elevation of over 1800 feet. Even there the growth of the larch seems excellent, and it is obvious that planting could be carried to considerably higher elevation in this particular place. Between Inverey and the Linn o' Dee there are many magnificent spruce trees of great height.

Wednesday, June 26th.

BALLOCHBUIE, BALMORAL, ABERGELDIE, BIRKHALL.—The party was again met by Mr Michie in the morning at the Braemar end of the Balmoral estate, and, after passing through the western portion of Ballochbuie, a halt was made at the foot of Craig-deign in the eastern half of the forest. Craig-deign is a hill of about 1800 feet elevation, and the top of it is thus beyond the Scots fir "timber line" of the district. The effects of elevation on the growth of the tree were clearly seen—1500 feet being again about the highest limit at which useful timber grew. From the top of the hill some idea was obtained of the great areas of forest in the neighbourhood. Practically all the woodlands in view consisted of Scots pine, and most of it was either old or middle-aged.

The next area inspected was the large forest of natural timber known as Garmaddie Wood. Mr Michie places the age of the wood at from 100 to 130 years. It is certain that this wood, from its extent and character, stands unrivalled in the kingdom. The trees are all tall and exceedingly well grown, though the wood lies between the elevation of 1000 and 1250 feet. The wood is regular and the crop is full. In the thicker portions of the wood the trees vary from 10 to 20 cub. feet, and in the opener places where the individual trees have had more room they vary from 20 to 50 cub. feet.

The average crop amounts to considerably over 4000 cub. feet (q.g.) to the acre. The wood is in a very well-kept and tidy condition, and everywhere shows evidence of careful and skilful management. This wood, like all the other woods on the Balmoral estates, is intersected with an excellent system of well-made roads, which make every part of it accessible and thus facilitates management and control. Altogether the Garmaddie Wood is a most pleasing object, a model Scots pine wood. The timber of this and of the other woods, which was seen at the estate sawmill, is excellent in quality.

At Craig-gowan an entirely different aspect of forestry was seen. Craig-gowan is a hill of some 1300 feet elevation rising from the south side of the flat ground on which Balmoral Castle stands. Up to 1883 the part in question, with a N. and N.E. aspect, was covered with an irregular crop consisting mostly of birch. In that year operations were started, and efforts were made to secure a more complete cover of the ground without interfering with the existing birch trees. Now there exists on it considerable areas of very flourishing Douglas fir, while small pure plantations of *Pinus cembra, P. monticola, P. strobus*, spruce and several other species have been formed. There are also specimens of *Tsuga albertiana, Tsuga hookeriana, Abies nobilis, A. magnifica, A. grandis, Picea orientalis*, etc. The most striking picture was presented by the Douglas fir, which was flourishing in a most promising way. This is all the more remarkable in view of the elevation. Even at 1000 and 1200 feet the trees are growing well, and stand quite firm and storm fast.

This area affords a striking example of how a worthless and exhausted birch wood can be transformed into a useful as well as beautiful woodland, without disturbing the amenities in the least at any time ; it also shows clearly the advantages of utilising existing cover for establishing and rearing trees, which, without the cover, might only be reared with difficulty, or not reared at all.

In the gardens there are many well-grown conifers which were planted between 50 and 60 years ago. They include a Douglas fir, about 70 feet in height and 7 ft. 4 ins. in girth at 5 feet from the ground ; an *Abies Lowiana*, 50 feet in height ; *Abies magnifica*, 50 feet in height and 4 ft. 5 ins. in girth ; and *Abies grandis*, 60 feet high and 5 ft. 9 ins. in girth.

At Abergeldie Castle, which was visited in the afternoon, there are some very large silver firs. They seed themselves very readily. There are extensive areas of young Scots pine (30 to 50 years) near by, which are the most promising of the younger woods of the district. In the eastern portion of Abergeldie, through which the motors passed, there are extensive natural pine woods on Craig-na-baan and Craig-ghuibhais, all of which are equal to the standard of the natural wood already mentioned. At Birkhall, which was reached late in the afternoon, in addition to natural woods there are extensive areas of planted woods both of Scots pine and larch. Many of the old larches near the house are of great size. There are also extensive well-grown woods of larch and of pine, between 50 and 60 years old, at elevations of from 1200 to 1400 feet, in Glen Muick and on Craig of Knocks, and at other places.

Thursday, June 27th.

BALLOGIE.—The estate of Ballogie is situated on the south side of the Dee midway between Aboyne and Banchory. It is owned by Mr W. E. Nicol. The estate is very well wooded, having over 4000 acres of woodland. The woods consist largely of Scots pine which here also is very tall and well grown and is of excellent quality (see Plate IV.). There are woods of practically all ages. Mr Geo. Wyllie, who has had charge of these woods for nearly half a century, has kindly contributed the following notes on the visit:—

"As arranged, I met the members at Potarch. On the left-hand side of the Carlogie road, they could see a second crop of Scots fir trees which were planted 28 years ago, and, on the right-hand side of this road, on what is called the Darn Haugh, they could see some fine Scots pine and larch trees 90 years of age. Farther along this road we arrived at Balnacraig. Here I pointed out a fine old ash tree 200 years of age; its stem had a circumference of 15 ft. 8 ins. at 5 feet from the ground. Also, on the Cap of Balnacraig, a second crop of Scots pine and larch 7 years of age was pointed out, where some of the trees had made shoots of 20 inches this season.

"When we left Balnacraig, we came along the Pitsluggerty road until we arrived at Mr Robert Donaldson's sawmill, where the company had the opportunity of seeing the trees manufactured. We then examined the plantation of Scots fir, on the north side of Pitsluggerty road. Here I explained to the company that the trees were 28 years of age, and that this was the second crop of Scots fir growing on the same ground. My system was to commence planting as soon as I got the former crop cleared. But before doing so I had the ground "scriefed" —that is, a small portion of the surface (9 ins. x 12 ins.) is taken off at the spots where the young plants are to be placed. The plants used were Scots fir seedling twice transplanted, and they were planted at 4 feet apart. The year after planting, I had the ground examined and all failures made good. Nothing further has been done to this plantation, as I believe in leaving the Scots fir very much to thin themselves.

"We come next to the Inchbare plantation. Here a crop of Scots pine and larch was taken off this ground about 7 years ago. The present plants are 4 years planted. They consist of Scots fir, larch, Norway spruce, *Douglasii* and Menzies spruce. The trees are all planted in groups and are making good growths.

"In the old wood of Slidderybrae, which consists of Scots fir and larch 90 years of age, some of the members estimated that there would be at least 4000 cubic feet per acre in this plantation.

"Our next stop was at Midstrath Lodge, where the company saw some fine specimens of the *Picea nobilis, Abies nordmanniana,* and *Douglasii,* all 33 years planted. Some of them were 50 feet high.

"We then went along the main avenue, where the company were shown the following trees :—

"Scots pine—108 feet high (40½ feet clean stem), circumference of stem 11 ft. 7 ins. (at 5 feet up).

	Height.	Circumference.	Age.
Abies nobilis,	77 ft.	6 ft. 11 ins.	58 years.
Abies nordmanniana,	74 ,,	9 ft. 0 ins.	,,
Ps. Douglasii,	97 ,,	10 ft. 0 ins.	,,
Ps. Douglasii,	108 ,,	9 ft. 5 ins.	
Picea sitkaensis,	86 ,,	11 ft. 9 ins.	,,
Abies lasiocarpa,	74 ,,	5 ft. 10 ins.	50 years
Sequoia gigantea,	74 ,,	11 ft. 3 ins.	,,

All circumferences are measured at 5 feet from the ground."

FINZEAN.—The estate of Finzean, which marches with Ballogie, is the property of the Right Hon. Dr Farquharson. Perhaps the most interesting area is Easter Clune Wood, an area of about 200 acres of natural grown larch about 40 years of age. It had its origin in natural seeding and is entirely the result of chance. When the old wood which had previously occupied the ground had been cleared, it had so happened that the larch had been producing seed at the time. The breaking of the ground resultant on the felling and removing of the old trees had enabled the seedlings to get a hold, and the result to-day is a full crop of pure larch. This wood, unfortunately, like so many middle-aged woods in the neighbourhood, has suffered serious damage by attacks from squirrels. Very considerable financial loss has been sustained on this account.

Another remarkable wood is an area of pure Scots pine known as the "Laird's Walking-Sticks." The wood has always been full. In fact, at present when the trees are mature, there is over 250 to the acre. The crop is wonderfully regular, each tree

PLATE IV.

SCOTS PINE AT BALLOGIE.
(*Photo by C. Ronald Ritchie, Edinburgh.*)

Photo by]

LARCH AT FINZEAN.

[*Duncan, Banchory.*

To face p. 74.

Photo by]

[G. Ronald Ritchie, Edinburgh.

THE EXCURSION PARTY AT BALMORAL.

being tall, straight, clean and beautifully grown. The cubic contents of this area are much greater than that of any other area of Scots pine seen during the Excursion. Near at hand there are numbers of larches measuring over 100 feet in height and girthing up to 8 feet. There are also many good hard-woods including good specimens of *Juglans regia*.

General comment was made on the extent and excellence of the afforestable land in this neighbourhood. The valleys are very wide, and the levels are comparatively low, while the soil is ideal.

Mr F. J. Cochrane, factor for Dr Farquharson, and Mr Geo. Cocker, ground officer, conducted the party.

Friday, June 28th.

The concluding day of the Excursion was spent in the part of the valley of the Dee between Banchory and Aberdeen, and afforded a great variety of interest, including as it did visits to Silverbank Sawmills at Banchory, to Crathes and to Durris. At Silverbank Sawmills, which belong to Messrs A. and G. Paterson, Mr Donald Munro conducted the party. The visit afforded members an opportunity of seeing the quality of the timber they had been inspecting, in the growing condition, for the past three days. An exhibit of much interest and educational value was provided by Mr Munro, in a large selection of trees and boards showing the nature and the extent of the damage done by squirrels. The exhibits were such as to impress members with the seriousness of the matter.

CRATHES.—A short visit was paid to Crathes Castle, the residence of Sir Thos. Barnett, Bart., of Leys, where the party was under the guidance of Mr J. C. Dunbar, factor. Woods similar to those inspected on previous days were again seen. There are also many large specimen trees, singly and in groups. The special feature of the place is the magnificent yew hedges in and around the gardens. They are at least 12 feet high and from 10 to 12 feet thick. They are skilfully trimmed, and are still very vigorous and healthy. They were planted in 1596, at the time of the completion of the castle.

DURRIS.—The estate of Durris, belonging to Mr H. J. Baird, affords much of both silvicultural and arboricultural interest, so much in fact that the Society could only see a very small proportion of the woods and trees worth seeing, in the short time at their disposal. Mr E. Lees, factor, and Mr Stewart, head forester, acted as guides. The most interesting and instructive plantations seen were at Strathgyle. The larger of the woods, over 80 acres in extent, lies on the north and north-west slopes of the hillside at an elevation of from 700 to 800 feet. The soil for the most part consists of deep peat. Thirty-four years ago the area had been planted with a mixture of Scots pine, Norway spruce and Sitka spruce. The growth of the Sitka spruce, under the adverse conditions prevailing, has been wonderful. The other species have remained far behind, and merely serve as packing in what will ultimately be an almost pure Sitka spruce plantation. The Sitka spruces average over 50 feet in height, while some of the larger individuals contain from 16 to 18 cub. feet of timber. At a still higher elevation, about 900 feet, there is an area of 10 or 12 acres which had been planted at the same time as the last (1878) with Sitka spruce alone. It has been left unthinned. The consequence is that while the total cubic contents of the wood is large, none of the individual trees have any great bulk. The problem of thinning the wood now presents great difficulties. As a demonstration of the possibilities of the tree at high altitudes, these woods are invaluable. The object lesson was all the more striking, as between the two plantations there was to be seen Scots pine and some larch, all of which were wind-swept and broken down by snow.

The nurseries are extensive and are fully stocked with a variety of conifers, including Douglas fir, *Thuja plicata*, *Chamæcyparis lawsoniana*, European and Japanese larch, and many other exotic trees. All the seed sown in the nursery is collected on the estate.

The park is full of arboricultural interest. Two previous proprietors of the estate, Mr MacTair and Mr Young, were very keen planters, and both had collected trees from all quarters of the northern hemisphere. There is thus a great variety of conifers, and besides, most of them are very well developed. Some of the biggest and best include *Cupressus nutkaensis*, *Thuja plicata*, *Abies grandis* and *Pseudotsuga Douglasii*. One of the last-named, a tree of 72 years old, contains over 300 cubic feet of timber. It is 106 feet high and measures 12 feet in circumference at 5 feet from the ground.

12. Douglas Fir Plantation: Taymount Estate.

By Frank Scott.

As particulars of volume, etc., relating to this plantation have from time to time appeared in these *Transactions* (see Vols. xvii. p. 269, xviii. p. 200), the following measurements (see next page) taken in the middle of October last may be of some interest.

The following was the method adopted in taking the measurements. All the trees on the 9·69 acres of plantation were girthed at 5 feet from the ground. They were then classified according to this girth, and the girth of the average stems in each class was found by Weise's 40 per cent. rule. A number of trees of this girth in each class were measured, the timber-height being taken by hypsometer, and the mean girth by actual measurement. The timber-height was taken to 12 inches in girth over bark. In each class one average tree at least was measured in sections of 10 feet, and by this method, leaving out the average tree in Class 7, which showed an abnormal difference, the average increase was found to be 9·4 per cent.

Below is added the volume of blown timber removed in 1912, and a comparison made with the measurements of Dr Schlich taken in 1888.

	Volume by Square of Quarter-girth at half-height.	Established Volume in 10 feet Sections.	Absolute Volume up to 12 inches Girth.
Total Volume on 9·69 acres .	58,575	64,077	81,374
Average Volume per acre .	6,044	6,612	8,397
Blown timber removed 1912 per acre	145	158	200
	6,189	6,770	8,597
Volume, 1888 (Dr Schlich's) .	2,678	2,929	3,719
Total Increment per acre, 1888-1912	3,511	3,841	4,878
Aver. Annual ,, ,, 1888-1912	146	159	202
The Aver. Volume per tree is (1912)	40·5	44·3	56·2
The Form Factor calculated from the Average trees in each class . .	·41	·448	·568

The trees average about 90 feet in height, and are making annual growths of from 9 to 15 inches.

Class	No. of Trees	Range of Girths at 5 feet	Girth of Average Stems			Quarter-girth at half height		Height to 12 inches in Girth	Contents	Average Volume per Tree	Volume Quarter-girth.	Volume in 10 feet Sections.	Continental Measurement 10 feet Sections
			At 5 feet	No.	At half-height	Over Bark	Under Bark						
		Ins.	Ins.		Ins.	Ins.	Ins.	Feet		Cub. ft.	Cub. ft.	Cub. ft.	Cub. ft.
1	27	15-24	22	1	17¼	4 5/16	4	36	4·	4·2	113	123	156
				2	18	4½	4	40	4·4				
2	123	24-36	31½	1	23	5¾	5¼	49	9·3				
				2	23	5¾	5¼	42	8·				
				3	23½	5⅞	5½	48	10·	8·9	1·094	1,196	1,518
				4	21	5¼	4¾	53	8·3				
				5	23	5¾	5¼	47	8·9				
	340	36-48	45	1	30	7½	7	67	22·8				
				2	34	8½	8	62	27·5				
				3	33½	8⅜	7⅞	75	32·3	26·	8·840	9,670	12,280
				4	30	7½	7	73	24·8				
				5	29½	7⅜	7	67	22 8				
	513	48-60	55½	1	38	9½	9	64	36·				
				2	38	9½	9	78	43·8				
				3	38	9½	9	75	42·1	42·3	21·699	23,738	30,147
				4	39	9¾	9⅛	78	45·1				
				5	39	9¾	9⅛	77	44·6				
	360	60 72	66	1	44½	11⅛	10⅜	77	57·6				
				2	45½	11⅜	10⅝	81	63·5	57·3	20·628	22,567	28,660
				3	43½	10⅞	10⅛	79	56·2				
				4	42	10½	9⅞	82	55·5				
				5	41½	10⅜	9¾	82	54·1				
6	74	72-84	76½	1	53	13¼	12½	72	78·1				
				2	49½	12⅜	11⅝	81	76·	74·1	5·483	5,998	7,617
				3	48	12	11¼	80	70·3				
				4	48	12	11¼	82	72·				
7	6	84-96	} 96	1	54½	13⅝	12⅞	78	89·8	89·8	·718	785	996
8	2	96-99		1									
	1445								Total Volume		58·575	64,077	81,374

13. The Arboretum.

In the course of an address to the Dumfries and Galloway Natural History Society, delivered on the 17th March 1911, Mr W. H. Whellens, forester, Comlongon Nurseries, offered the following advice regarding the formation of an arboretum, which he suggested that every landed proprietor should possess.

Kind of Trees.—Spruces and silver firs should be introduced, for the foliage of some of the latter is magnificent. Take, for instance, *Picea nobilis* (or the noble silver fir) with its violet-tinted leaves, the silvery lines showing beneath; *P. Nordmanniana*, with pale green leaves; or *P. Pinsapo*, with its stiff prickly foliage. Others of the silver firs that are worth a place in the collection are *P. cephalonica*, *P. concolor*, *P. balsamea* (the Balm of Gilead fir), *P. grandis*, and, of course, our common silver fir, which, after all, is one of the noblest trees in this or any other country.

Many of these have varieties or sports of their own which are often obtainable.

The list of spruces is too long to give in full, even if I were able to do so, but some of the finest are the common Norway spruce, *Abies nigra* (the black American), *A. alba* (the white American), *A. Alcocquiana*, *A. Menziesii*, and *A. Smithiana*.

The two varieties of the Douglas fir, the Oregon or green and the Colorado or glaucous, are worthy of a place in any collection.

The pines are so numerous that want of space and time prevents my giving the names of more than a few of the better known ones. The Scots pine, the Austrian and Corsican pines (called the black pines), *Pinus cembra*, *P. Pinaster*, *P. strobus* and *Pinus insignis*, the last a beautiful tree, are examples.

The different varieties of the larch must have a place. There are the European, Japanese, Siberian, American, and a newer variety, the Occidental larch.

The cedars, *C. deodara*, the Cedar of Lebanon, and *C. atlantica*, with their varieties, cannot be overlooked.

Other coniferous trees that I may mention are the *Wellingtonia gigantea*, *Araucaria imbricata*, the Arborvitæ and its varieties, the many varieties of Cupressus, Cryptomeria, junipers, yews, Retinosporas, the maiden-hair tree, and countless others.

Specimens of most of our commoner hardwoods are to be seen dotted here and there over the country side, so that, perhaps, it would be unnecessary to put in the arboretum such trees as the oak, elm, ash, beech, etc., but there are many varieties of these species which might take the place of their better known relatives.

To mention a few of the oaks—there are the scarlet oak, Turkey oak, evergreen and holly oak, white American, red American, and the cork tree (*Quercus suber*). These all do well in this island, although I have not seen one of the last in Scotland. The acacias, the tulip tree, service tree, the willows, poplars and maples should all be represented.

The maples are numerous, but the eagle-clawed, the sugar maple, and the variegated varieties, *Acer negunda*, are worth mentioning.

I will not make a longer list, as long lists get monotonous, but reference to a standard work, such as Loudon's *Trees and Shrubs*, or any nurseryman's catalogue, will show what an endless variety of trees there is to pick from.

Soil.—I have given the list of trees without reference to soil or situation, but, in making the arboretum, the first thing to do is to find out the class of soil or soils. When these are known, then the different species can be selected to suit each soil. What suits one tree may be death to another, or at least the tree will never come to perfection if planted in a soil unsuited to its requirements. For instance, a Scots pine will grow on sandy soil, and become a fine tree in time, but it would be useless to plant an oak in sand and expect it to grow into a specimen tree.

Again, willows and poplars demand a moist soil, but others can grow on soil that seems to be almost devoid of moisture. These trees generally have strong tap-roots which go deep into the subsoil, and obtain their supply of moisture from it. In the space of a few yards even, we often find two different soils. We expect to find a deeper and better class of soil in the hollows than on the hillsides.

Most trees will do well in good deep soil, but only comparatively few will grow to any size on poor shallow soil. Some trees will not thrive where there is an excess of lime, others again will not come to perfection without it.

Climatic conditions play a great part in the selection of

species for different places. Frosty hollows should be avoided when planting most of the exotic trees, even though the soil may be quite suitable for their development. The common spruce, even, often suffers from frost. Early autumn and late spring frost cause thousands of pounds worth of damage every year. Therefore, in planting our miniature Kew Gardens, we must first of all find out the class of soil that we have to deal with; secondly, find out the hollows where frost is likely to do damage, and avoid them; thirdly, see what natural shelter can be obtained for the protecton of the less hardy species from the prevailing wind.

Shelter.—A wood or plantation, even if on an adjoining property, should be taken advantage of for this. In the absence of any such shelter from sharply rising ground, it would be necessary to plant a shelter-belt on the side from which the roughest winds come. This could be composed of beech, hornbeam, Austrian pine or Scots pine mixed. The trees forming the shelter-belt should be planted about 4 feet apart in the lines, the width of the belt being from 16 to 20 feet. This belt should preferably be formed a few years previous to the planting of the trees in the collection, so that it will be of sufficient height to protect these more valuable species.

Seed.—If the proprietor wished to rear his young trees from seed, the seed could be sown in the same year as the planting of the shelter-belt. This, although very interesting, entails a lot of work and care in tending the young seedlings, and, given a fair amount of success, the sower would have too many of each sort for his purpose, even with the smallest quantity of seed obtainable from the seedsmen. It would, I think, be more advisable to buy two or three good, healthy transplants of each variety, which had been lined out in the nursery at a distance suitable to the formation of well-formed specimen trees. I say two or three, because it is as well to have a second or third specimen handy in a temporary nursery in case of death.

Size of Plants.—The size of plants at certain ages will vary with the species. Plants from 2 to 3 feet high for conifers, and rather larger for deciduous trees, will be perhaps the best sizes to plant out. Larger trees are more difficult to move, and they will be longer in starting away in their new position. The plants should have good fibrous roots.

Classification of Soils.—To return to the subject of soils, I may class them thus:—Clays, loams, gravelly and sandy soils, chalky or calcareous, and peaty soils. To give a list of trees suited to each class of soil would take too much time, and it would be difficult to remember them all after having heard them. Sufficient it is to say that there is a long list for every soil, quite long enough at least to form a fair-sized arboretum. Webster's *Foresters' Diary* is a very useful book for helping one in this way.

Arrangement.—Another great point is the arrangement of the species. Some trees are fast growing from the start, for instance, the Oregon variety of Douglas fir, or the Japanese larch. Others, such as the silver fir, are slow growing in their early stages, but grow eventually to a great height. The trees should be divided into different classes, and planted in different groups, all the fast-growing ones together, and all the slower-growing ones together. It would be a pity to surround a silver fir with trees such as the Douglas fir and larch, as it would never be seen, even at a short distance, for many years, and it would appear as though there were a blank. I would suggest that the tallest and fastest growing trees be placed in the background, or in the centre of a group, with the others graduated down to the outside, with perhaps a border of flowering shrubs. Conifers and hardwoods could be judiciously mixed so as to make a good show of colour all the year round.

Distance apart.—As to the distance at which to place the trees apart, there can be no hard and fast rule. The smaller shrubs might be planted from 6 to 8 feet apart. A tree with a large spreading crown, such as the sycamore, would need from 24 to 36 feet of space, whereas a tree of the spruce tribe would be content with 18 to 20 feet.

In the early stages the intervals could be filled up with larch or birch, which would act as nurses to the more expensive trees, and should be cut out gradually as the latter spread their branches; or the spaces could be filled with flowering shrubs, which would also be cut out when they had served their purpose.

Time to Plant.—As to the time of year to plant, this again depends on the variety of tree. Most of our hardier trees can be planted with safety in the autumn, but the planting of the more delicate exotics should be deferred till the danger from spring frosts is past. Most foresters now plant such trees in

April or the beginning of May, so that they can have a better start in their new position.

Pitting.—The trees should all be planted in pits that have been opened some time before, to allow the soil to become broken up and sweetened by the action of frost. These pits should be large enough to admit of the roots being placed in a natural position all round the plant, not cramped and bent about to fit the hole. The soil at the bottom of the pits should be loosened down to a fair depth, and the tree planted not more than half an inch deeper than it stood in the nursery lines. This half-inch allows for a little subsidence of the soil. Trees planted too deeply never thrive. A stout stake should be driven in to support each tree, and to prevent the wind blowing it about, and thus letting air down to the roots to dry them.

Manuring.—In a close-grown plantation the trees provide their own food. As the sun cannot get in to dry the leaves, and so make them easily blown away by the winds, they die on the ground and rot, gradually forming a thick layer of humus, from which the trees draw a supply of nutriment. But when the trees are planted many yards apart (even when the spaces are filled with light-foliaged trees, such as the birch) the sun and wind have free access, and the leaves are blown away, thus depriving the trees of their natural food. This food should be replaced. The leaves can be raked together and mixed with road scrapings or any waste soil, or even the remains of a spent frame, and made into a compost. This should be left for at least two years before being applied, having been turned occasionally and sprinkled lightly with lime to hasten decomposition. Some of this might be added to the soil when the trees are first planted, and some might afterwards be used as a top-dressing. There is no need to supply a great quantity each year, but it should be dug in round the trees to the depth of 2 or 3 inches. This will help the trees considerably. Artificial manures, too, are often used. Basic slag, kainite and sulphate of ammonia are all good for the purpose, or if the soil be deficient in lime for the requirements of any particular tree, ground limestone could be applied.

Fencing.—If the park is grazed by sheep or cattle a fence would be a necessity round each group. This could be either of iron and wire, which is the least noticeable, or a rustic fence could be erected. Wire netting would have to be used if ground game were numerous.

Name-Plates—Record.—Each specimen should have a plate with its name and the date on which it was planted, and records of the yearly height, growth, girth, etc., of each tree should be kept. This would be valuable as well as interesting to a succeeding generation. Of course the planter of the arboretum would not see all the trees come to maturity, but he would have the pleasure of watching them grow from young transplants to sturdy young trees, and there is as much beauty in a tree of, say, thirty years as there is in one of one hundred and fifty. It is a different kind of beauty often, but is none the less pleasing.

There are many minor hobbies that could be taken up by young and old in connection with the arboretum—a collection of cones, for instance, or leaves, or insects which do damage to the different trees. The smaller the latter collection the better the owner should be pleased.

14. Nursery and Plantation Competition.

During the past year the Royal Scottish Arboricultural Society has added an important department to its sphere of activity by the inauguration of the above Competition, which was held for the first time in connection with the Society's Forestry Exhibition in the Highland and Agricultural Society's Show at Cupar.

This is an entirely new departure for the Society, and it was the first experiment of its kind to be tried in Scotland. The experiment was a distinct success, and the result will no doubt be that this Competition will become a permanent and important institution of the Society.

A circular was sent out by the Society inviting entries, as follows :—

NURSERIES.

Class   I. For the best managed Estate Nursery not exceeding 2 acres in extent—Prize, A Silver Medal.

Class II. For the best managed Estate Nursery exceeding 2 acres in extent—Prize, A Silver Medal.

PLANTATIONS.

Class   I. For the best young Plantation mainly of conifers not exceeding 25 years of age, and not less than 2 acres in extent. Confined to estates having less than 300 acres of woods—Prize, A Silver Medal.

Class II. For the best young Plantation mainly of conifers not exceeding 25 years of age, and not less than 5 acres in extent. Confined to estates having more than 300 acres of woods—Prize, A Silver Medal.

Class III. For the best young Plantation mainly of hardwoods not exceeding 35 years of age, and not less than 2 acres in extent—Prize, A Silver Medal.

In response to this circular, eighteen different estates entered altogether twenty-six subjects for competition. These were made up of eighteen plantations and eight nurseries.

The following list will show how these subjects were distributed in the various classes :—

1 NURSERIES.

Class I.

For the best managed Estate Nursery not exceeding 2 acres in extent.

1. The Marquis of Breadalbane, per Donald MacFarquhar, Kenmore.
2. { Edward Balfour, of Balbirnie, per James S. Reid, Forester.
   { James Younger, of Mount Melville, St Andrews, per W. Gilchrist.
3. William Bell, Head Forester, Balthayock, Perth.
4. Alex. Izat, Balliliesk, Rumbling Bridge, Dollar.

Class II.

For the best managed Estate Nursery exceeding 2 acres in extent.

1. The Duke of Atholl, per David Keir, Ladywell, Dunkeld.
2. Sir John Gilmour, Bart., of Montrave, per P. F. Cruickshanks, Factor.
3. The Earl of Mansfield, per Frank Scott, Jeaniebank, near Perth.

2. PLANTATIONS.

Class I.

For the best young Plantation mainly of conifers not exceeding 25 years of age, and not less than 2 acres in extent. Confined to estates having less than 300 acres of woods.

1. Colonel Purvis, Kinaldy, Stravithie. (Scots pine.)
2. { The Earl of Crawford, K.T., per G. R. Fortune, Balcarres.
3. {   (Scots pine.)
4. James Younger, of Mount Melville, St Andrews, per William Gilchrist. (Scots pine.)
5. { Alex. Izat, Balliliesk, Muckhart, Dollar.   } (Larch and
   {   ..   ,,   ,,   }   Scots pine.)
   {   ,,   ,,   ,,   }
6. James Younger, of Mount Melville, St Andrews, per William Gilchrist. (Douglas fir.)

7. { James Hogg, Forester, Stravithie, Fife. (Conifers.)
Colonel Purvis, Kinaldy, Stravithie. (Scots pine and larch.)
Captain Purvis, Gilmerton, Stravithie. (Conifers.)
Colonel E. R. Stewart Richardson, Ballathie, Stanley.
(Conifers.)

CLASS II.

For the best young Plantation mainly of conifers not exceeding
25 years of age, and not less than 5 acres in extent.
Confined to estates having more than 300 acres of woods.

1. J. S. Black, Balgowan House, Methven, per William Coupar.
(Menzies spruce and Colorado Douglas.)
2. The Rt. Hon. R. C. Munro Ferguson, M.P., per James
Grant, Raith Estate, Kirkcaldy. (Conifers.)
3. The Trustees of the Earl of Rosslyn, per George Prentice,
Factor, Dysart. (Conifers.)
4. { Edward Balfour of Balbirnie, per James S. Reid. (Conifers.)
The Earl of Mansfield, per Frank Scott, Jeaniebank.
(Conifers.)
5. Lord Ninian Crichton Stuart, M.P., Falkland. (Larch.)
6. Sir James H. Ramsay, Bart. of Bamff, Alyth. (Scots pine
and spruce.)

CLASS III.

For the best young Plantation mainly of hardwoods not
exceeding 35 years of age, and not less than 2 acres in
extent.

1. The Rt. Hon. R. C. Munro Ferguson, M P., per James
Grant, Raith Estate, Kirkcaldy. (Hardwoods.)

The conditions were that the whole plantation must be entered
if all of the same age, and the Judges were empowered to
withhold prizes in cases of insufficient merit. It is pleasing to
record that in none of the classes was a prize withheld; in fact, it
was felt by the Judges that prizes of merit might have been
added. As the remit stood the Judges were empowered to award
one prize only in each class, but, in the light of experience gained,
merit prizes should certainly be provided for. Among the entries
were many subjects which reflected great credit on both the
owner and the forester and which certainly deserved high
commendation, but, under the conditions previously stated, this

was unfortunately not provided for. It is hoped that in future provision will be made for merit, so that in addition to discovering the best, the Society may also be the means of locating and encouraging skill and enterprise of high merit, abundant evidence of which was to be seen in connection with the nursery and plantation management on the above-mentioned estates.

In the above list the various entries are arranged in order ot merit, those heading the list in each class being the prize winners. The object in classifying the subjects thus, especially the plantations, is that many of them will still be under 25 years of age the next time the Competition is held in this district, and it will, no doubt, be of some interest to compare the present relative order of merit with the then existing condition of the plantations. Of course, it is quite possible by that time the age-classes and conditions of competition may have been altered, so that the classification may be based on different data, but, nevertheless, no matter from what point of view the plantations are judged, that is, as regards age, size, treatment, general condition, general health and vigour of growth, the comparisons will be interesting and valuable.

In view of experience gained in connection with the recent Competition, the Judges would recommend that on the Nursery Schedule the exact area of the nursery should be stated, and that in the table provided for Nursery Statistics a column should be added for Judges' remarks opposite each entry. A similar table should be provided for seedlings, giving the area of seed-bed; quantity ot seed sown, source of seed, and time when sown.

In judging plantations there must always be great difficulty in finding common ground for comparison between a coniferous plantation of, say, 5 or 6 years of age and one of 18 or 23 years of age. The Judges would, therefore, further recommend that for conifers there should be three age-classes, as follows :—

Class   I. Coniferous plantations up to 10 years old.
Class II.   ,,   ,,   from 10 to 20 years old.
Class III.   ,,   ,,   from 20 to 40   ,,

A further grouping of plantations into pure plantations and mixed plantations would be desirable.

The Judges also recommend that prizes for merit should be awarded for those subjects which come above the average standard of excellence.

The expenses in connection with this Competition are considerable, but the result seems to justify the outlay; however, in future, it might be found advisable to institute a small entrance fee for each subject entered for competition.

ESTATE NURSERIES.

The home nursery is a comparatively new institution on many estates. The nurseries entered for this Competition may be taken as representing a fair average for estate nurseries generally in Scotland, and a glance at the list will show what an astonishingly large number and variety of young trees are raised in private nurseries.

In the great majority of cases, the location of these nurseries showed that such important points as soil, aspect, elevation, slope and surroundings had all been carefully considered in choosing the site. The internal division, of the areas chosen for the raising of plants, into seed-beds, transplanting lines, roads and footpaths showed also skill and forethought. The protection of the nurseries and plants by outside fences and hedges indicated in an unmistakable manner that our foresters have not much to learn in this department of their work.

The space allotted to the transplants in the nursery lines might have been in a few cases greater, especially in home nurseries where plenty of land is available and the quantity of produce is not limited or regulated by area, as it is in places where land is scarce and rents are high.

The artistic skill displayed in the embellishment of these home nurseries, by the judicious use of flowering herbs and shrubs, was a feature worthy of note. It must not be forgotten that the estate forester has often, as part of his duties, to attend to the arboricultural amenity of the property as well as to its silvicultural requirements. One is therefore not surprised to find many ornamental trees and shrubs in the home nursery, and these lend a distinct charm and additional interest to these places which might quite appropriately be called nursery gardens. From an æsthetic and utilitarian point of view, the home nursery has become a valuable adjunct to every well-managed estate, and might well be ranked along with the vegetable and flower garden in importance.

PARTICULARS OF NURSERIES.

Name of Estate	Total Area under Woodlands	Area of Nursery	Species	Transplanted in Nursery		
				Age	Numbers	Number of Times Transplanted
				Years		
Kenmore			Larch	3	30,000	Once.
			,,	2	15,000	,,
			Scots pine .	3	60,000	,,
			Swedish Scots pine	4	40,000	,,
			Scots pine .	4	40,000	,,
			Douglas fir .	3	20,000	,,
			Spruce . .	3	40,000	,,
			,,	5	5,000	,,
			Common birch	3	10,000	,,
			Mountain ash	3	9,000	,,
			Common beech	3	5,000	,,
			Purple beech	4	1,000	,, &c.
Balbirnie	2 000		Scots pine .	2	65,000	&c.
			Norway spruce	2	7,000	,, Twice.
			Picea sitchensis (Sitka spruce)	5	7,000	Once.
			Larix europea	2	2,000	,, &c.
			Abies Douglasii .	2	500	
			Larix occidentalis .	2	200	,, Once.
			Larix leptolepis .	5	16	&c.
			Oak . .	5-7	650	Twice.
			,,	9	40	Thrice.
			Beech . .	6-9	900	,,
			,, copper.	9	3	,,
			Ash . .		850	,,
			Plane . .		140	,, Twice.
			Silver birch .		200	
Mount Melville			Abies Douglasii .		3,500	Once.

Place					Species		No.	No.	Transplanted
Balshayock	I.	1,800	500		„ „ Spruce	.	5	3,400	Once.
					„ „	.	3	2,100	Twice.
					Picea nobilis	.	4	700	Once.
					Beech .	.	3	3,100	Twice.
					Poplar .	.	4	45	Thrice.
					Ash .	.	4	50	„
					Plane .	.	6	300	„
					Horse chestnut	.	6	17	„
						.	4	50	
					Abies Douglasii	.	3	10,500	Once.
					„ „	.	2	7,000	„
					European larch	.	2	3,000	„
					Scots pine .	.	2	12,500	„
					„ pine	.	3	4,000	„
					„ spruce	.	3	4,000	„
					N „ „ spruce	.	2	7,000	„
					Abies grandis	.	4	5,000	Twice.
					„ *lasiocarpo*	.	4	1,000	„
					„ *nobilis*	.	4	1,000	„
					Thuya lobbii .	.	4	500	„
					Plane .	.	3	400	Once.
					„	.	4	600	Twice.
					Common lilac	.	3	200	Once.
Balliliesk	I.	447	67	About ⅛	„ fir	.	3	1,000	Twice.
					„	.	2	3,000	Once.
					Scots pine	.	2	4,000	„ „
					„	.	3	8,000	„
					„	.	2	8,000	Once.
					„ Spruce fir	.	2	4,000	„ „
					„ Douglas fir	.	2	8,000	Twice.
					„	.	3	4,000	„
					„	.	2	500	Once.
					„	.	2	500	„
						.	3	220	„

PARTICULARS OF NURSERIES—*Continued.*

Name of Estate	Species	Transplanted in Nursery		
		Age	Numbers	Number of Times Transplanted
		Years		
Balliliesk— *Continued.*	Silver fir	2	400	Twice.
	Picea grandis	2	50	Once.
	,, *nobilis*	2	50	Twice.
	Pinus cembra	3	40	,,
	Corsican pine	2	200	,,
	... pine	2	200	,,
	Abies albertiana	3	16	,,
	...	3	14	Thrice.
	Bl... American spruce fir	4	50	Twice.
	...	3	37	,,
	Norway maple	3	100	,,
	Plane	3	100	,,
	Beech	2	300	Once.
	Oak	3	300	Twice.
	Ash	3	200	,,
	... chestnut	3	100	,,
	Spanish chestnut	4	40	Thrice.
	Oak	5	60	,,
	Hornbeam	3	50	Twice.
	Wych elm	3	25	,,
Dunkeld	Larch	2	00,000	Once.
	Spruce	2	50,000	,,
	Douglas	2	80,000	,,
	Lawson cypress	2	15,000	,,
	Albertiana	2	4,000	Twice.
	Beech	5	5,000	,,
	Sycamore	4	7,000	Twice.
	Chestnut	3	300	Once.

					Species	No.	Quantity	Times
Tomarave	11.	5,000	400	26	Japanese Larch	2	5,000	...
					„ „ Dgs fir, Oregon	2	10,000	...
					Scots pine, native	2	20,000	...
					Norway Spruce	2	30,000	...
					Sitka „	3	2,000	Once.
					Scots pine, native	3	10,000	...
					Norway Spruce	3	10,000	...
					Sika „	4	1,000	...
					Scots pine, native	4	1,200	...
					Norway Spruce	5	8,000	...
					Picea alba „	5	1,500	...
					Norway „	6	3,000	Twice.
					Dgs fir, Oregon	3	1,500	...
					Sycamore	3	2,250	...
					Birch	3	600	...
					Ash	4	500	Once.
					Sycamore	4	2,000	„
					Ash	4	30	Twice.
					Oak	6	30	Thrice.
					Beech	8	500	...
					Maple		48	
					Elm	3	40	
Scone		6,100			Scots pine	3	56,000	Once
					„ „	2	50,000	„
					Norway spruce	1	220,000	Once.
					„ „	3	34,000	„
					„ „	2	40,000	...
					Menzies spruce	1	27,000	Once.
					Thuya gigantea	3	13,500	Once.
					„ „	2	11,000	Twice.
					„ „	3	2,600	„
					Douglas fir (Colonial)	4	1,300	Once.
					„ „ (Pacific)	2	14,000	„
					Larix occidentalis	3	800	Twice.
					„ leptolepis	2	12,000	Once.
					Pinus laricio	3	300	„
					Abies grandis	2	10,000	„
							20,000	
							350	

PARTICULARS OF PLANTATIONS.

NAME OF ESTATE Description	Kinaldy. SCOTS PINE.	Balcarres. SCOTS PINE.	Balcarre SCOTS PIN
Area. Class	2·5 acres. I.	3 acres. I.	27 acres. I.
Soil .	Sandy clay.	Fairly good loam, wet.	West, half r east, good lo
Elevation . Rainfall Aspect Shelter	450 feet. About 35 inches. Slight slope to south. Sheltered by old trees on N.E. and south.	450 feet. Average 27 inches. South. From the north.	600 feet. Average 27 inc On top of hill. Quite exposed.
Previous occupation of land	Formerly cultivated, latterly pasture.	Grass.	Grass.
Rent of land adjoining the Plantation	15s. to 18s. per acre.	30s. per acre.	
Date of planting	Winter of 1890–91.	January 1904.	January 1904.
Cost per acre : (a) Fencing	Required on one side only ; wire fence.	£4, 11s. 1d.	£4, 11s. 1d.
(b) Draining (c) Planting, includ- ing beating up	Field drains remain. No beating up.	... Labour, £2, 6s. 11½d.; cost of planting, £1 per 1000.	... Labour, £2, 6s. cost of planti per 1000.
(d) Cleaning	None.	£2, cutting grass.	£1, 17s. 10d., grass.
(e) Soil cultivation or other outlay, if any	None.		..
Species planted and, if more than one, relative propor- tions of each	Scots pine only, with rows of birch next road.	Scots pine.	Scots pine.
Age of plants . Method of planting and number of plants used per acre	... Notched in ; 1200 to the acre.	3 years. Slitted ; 4790.	3 years. Slitted ; 4790 per acre.
Date of thinning, if any	Thinned once about 10 years after plant- ing.	None.	None.
Damage by fungi, insects, birds, rabbits, hares, squirrels, or other creatures	Not much damage ; protection having been given at first by rabbit netting.	Sawfly.	Pine sawfly rabbits.
Damage from other causes	Plants suffered at first from club root, but as the trees killed the grass the roots seemed to recover and develop.		

PARTICULARS OF PLANTATIONS.

Balliliesk. LARCH and SCOTS PINE. 6·34 acres. I.	Balliliesk. LARCH and SCOTS PINE. 7·99 acres. I.	Balliliesk. LARCH and SCOTS PINE. 7·75 acres. I.
Light and open.	Light and open.	Light and open.
650 to 750 feet. About 40 inches. South-east. None.	750 to 850 feet. About 40 inches. South-east. None.	750 to 850 feet. About 40 inches. South-east. None.
Grazing; hill sheep.	Grazing; hill sheep.	Grazing; hill sheep.
About 7s. 6d. per acre.	5s. per acre.	5s. per acre.
1901-02.	1902-03.	1903-04.
£7, 16s.	£8, 9s.	£7, 8s.
None. £22, 15s.	£2, 4s. £20, 19s.	£2, 2s. £25, 11s.
,,	,,	,,

N.B.—The cost given for (c), (d) and (e) is approximate. Great expense was incurred for several years in preventing the young trees being smothered and killed by grass. The plants used were 1-year 1-year, and were too small.

The plantations are in strips 250 to 300 feet wide, and the cost of fencing—a 7-wire iron fence—has accordingly been high. The fencing is also netted to try to protect them from rabbits.

Hardwoods, 14 feet apart. Larch and Scots pine equally, 3½ feet apart. A few spruce, in damp place.

1-year 1-year.
Hardwoods, pitted. Conifers, notched. About 3500 plants per acre.

None.

A grub did a good deal of damage to some of the Scots pine for 2 or 3 years after planting.

| | | Suffered a good deal from black game one season.
... |

PARTICULARS OF PLANTATIONS—*Continued.*

NAME OF ESTATE	Mount Melville.	Stravithie.	Kinaldy
Description	DOUGLAS FIR.	CONIFERS.	SCOTS PINE some LARC
Area	2 acres.	2¼ acres.	4·5 acres.
Class	ᵛ	I.	?
Soil	Clay.	Medium light, on freestone.	Moory loam.
Elevation	270 feet.	250 feet.	450 feet.
Rainfall	28 inches.	27 to 30 inches.	About 35 inches
Aspect	North.	North.	Slight slope to ?
Shelter	Stone dyke.	Row of large beech trees on north side.	By old timber or
Previous occupation of land	Trees—hardwoods.	Permanent pasture.	Scots pine.
Rent of land adjoining the Plantation	13s. per acre.	£1 per acre.	15s. to 18s. per
Date of planting	1906 (spring).	1900.	Winter of 1889–
Cost per acre:			
(a) Fencing		£8.	Stone dykes on sides, old wo fourth side.
(b) Draining	...	None.	A few cuts.
(c) Planting, including beating up	Not known.	£7 for plants and £2 making pits.	No beating up.
(d) Cleaning	£1, 5s. to date.	Nil.	None.
(e) Soil cultivation or other outlay, if any			None.
Species planted and, if more than one, relative proportions of each	Abies Douglasii.	Larch, Scots pine, Norway spruce, Austrian pine.	Scots pine, abo per cent.; about 20 per c
Age of plants	3 years.	2-year 2-year.	...
Method of planting and number of plants used per acre	Notched; 3000 trees per acre.	Pit planted; 4840; 3 feet apart.	Notched; 120C acre.
Date of thinning, if any		1911.	About 1901-2.
Damage by fungi, insects, birds, rabbits, hares, squirrels, or other creatures		Slight, by rabbits and over - hanging branches of beech trees.	Slight, by beetles and
Damage from other causes		None.	

PARTICULARS OF PLANTATIONS—*Continued.*

Kinaldi	Hilmerton.	Ballathie.	Balgowan.	Raith.
ts Prst Lat 4'5 acre	CONIFERS. 3 acres.	CONIFERS. 2 acres.	MENZIES SPRUCE and COLORADO DOUGLAS. About 5 acres.	CONIFERS. 72 acres.
	I.	I.	II.	II.
loam n clay and sand. eet. o		Light and stony, growing heather chiefly. About 220 feet.	Mossy. About 600 feet.	Shallow peaty on hard sandy 250 to 300 feet.
it 35 incl: hes.		About 20 inches.	25 inches.	About 29 inches.
		Chiefly south.	South.	North.
ld timber red N., E. and S. s pine.		Sheltered from north by old wood. Occasionally ploughed.	Fair. Under cultivation.	... Rough pasture.
to 18s. 15s. per acre		About 10s. per acre.	Say £1 per acre.	25s. per acre.
iter of 18 of 1906.		1891 or 1892.	1898.	1896.
ne dykes all; 27s. per		About £7, 10s.	Part of a large tract of land assigned to planting.	
ourth side ll; 6s. 8d. per		None.	1 main ditch on south side.	10s. per acre.
beating (men 2 weeks); 7s per acre.		About £6.	4 men for 12 days.	£4, 10s.
		Removal of dead branches.	None.	2s.
		None.	None.	None.
ots pine (3 to 1). Re- per cent ailer — beech, about 20 rd ash and oak, twice.		About two-thirds spruce and Scots pine, and the other third larch. 1½ years.	Half Colorado Douglas, half Menzies spruce. *Nobilis* used in filling up in a wet place. 7 years.	Scots pine and spr with a belt of h woods mixed spruce and S pine. 2 years.
otched: squares; 4000 acre.		Simply slit in at 4 feet apart or thereabout.	All pitted.	Notched; 6500; to 3 feet apart.
		None.		
light, od attacked by beet Larch in 1908 ect. Disease ppearing.		Slight damage done by rabbits.	Some insect damage on *nobilis* only.	
...			None.	

PARTICULARS OF PLANTATIONS—*Continued.*

NAME OF ESTATE .	**Dysart.** CONIFERS.	**Balbirnie.** CONIFERS.	**Lynedoch** CONIFERS.
Description . .			
Area	8 acres.	20 acres.	9·941 acres
Class . . .	II.	II.	II.
Soil	Moory clay, with sub-soil, sandy clay.	Moorland, peaty soil.	Sandy loam.
Elevation . . .	240 feet.	400 feet.	390–410 feet.
Rainfall . . .	36–40 inches.	30 inches.	30–35 inches.
Aspect . . .	North.	South.	Mostly south-ea
Shelter . . .	On south and west by wood.	Good.	By woods, exce south.
Previous occupation of land	Wood mixed.	Larch timber.	Crop of Scots pi larch.
Rent of land adjoining the Plantation	£1 per acre.	16s. per acre.	15s. per acre.
Date of planting .	Spring 1905.	1890.	1898.
Cost per acre :			
(a) Fencing . .	10s.	£1, 17s.	£2, 15s. (inc hedge).
(b) Draining . .	20s.	...	£1, 7s.
(c) Planting, including beating up	80s.	£3, 1s. 3d.	£3, 2s.
(d) Cleaning . .	10s.	None.	None.
(e) Soil cultivation or other outlay, if any	None.	None.	None.
Species planted and, if more than one, relative proportions of each	15,400 larch, 1600 beech, 1800 oak.	Scots pine, and a small proportion of spruce and larch.	Scots pine, 9 Japanese larc *Abies nobili* beech, on only, 1 %.
Age of plants . .	2-year 2-year and 18 m. hardwoods.	2-year 1-year.	3 years (2-year trans.).
Method of planting and number of plants used per acre		Notch system ; 4840 per acre.	T notching; 3(acre.
Date of thinning, if any		Dead and suppressed trees removed, May 1912.	Blown trees 1912.
Damage by fungi, insects, birds, rabbits, hares, squirrels, or other creatures	None. (Netted.)	Slight, by pigeons, rabbits and squirrels in the earlier stages.	Root fungus.
Damage from other Causes		Trifling.	Storm, 191 1911-12.

PARTICULARS OF PLANTATIONS—*Continued.*

Falkland. LARCH.	Bamff. SCOTS PINE and SPRUCE.	Raith. HARDWOODS.
40 acres. II.	11 acres. II.	2·413 acres. III.
ary loam.	Good coating of vegetable loam on Old Red Sandstone.	Peaty soil.
50 feet. onal. on.	600–660 feet. 25–30 inches. South-west.	331 feet. Average about 29 ins. Slight incline to the north.
n outh and west.	Sheltered from N. and E. by slope of ground.	..
n, Scots pine and suce.	Fir wood.	Timber, chiefly spruce.
l. per acre.	15s. per acre.	25s. per acre.
utnn and spring, 1 4–05; spring, 1 6; spring, 1907.	In successive breaks between 1895 and 1902.	1895–1896.
	Rabbit netting.	
ifult to ascertain th such exactss as to be of lue.	No draining done. Little beating up. Considerable. None.	... About £10.
European larch Japanese larch separate combment), strip of glas. larch, 1-year ar; all others ar 2-year. planting; 4840 acre.	No. 1 break Scots and spruce, the others all Scots pine. 2-year 1-year. Notched; 2700 per acre.	Blocks of about equal size of sycamore, Norway maple, ash, elm, poplar. 5 years when planted. Pitted; about 3000 per acre.
n	At various times as needed.	
by rabbits.	Much, by rabbits.	
	Very considerable, from broom having got in at first; spruce seemed to suffer most, but eventually did better than the Scots.	

MEASUREMENTS.

In the time at the disposal of the Judges, it was not possible to make many measurements. In some of the plantations, however, the girth measurement at 5 feet of six average trees was taken. The following table shows the figures :—

LYNEDOCH PLANTATION.

Girth at 5 feet of six average trees.

Scots pine . 10, 9, 12, 12, 9, 10 ins.
Jap. larch . 16, $21\frac{1}{4}$, $14\frac{1}{2}$, $22\frac{1}{2}$, 19, $28\frac{1}{2}$ „

BALGOWAN PLANTATION (Menzies and Colorado fir).

Girth at 5 feet of six average trees.

Menzies . . 18, 13, 16, 14, 19, 12 ins.
Colorado. . 16, 16, 20, 12, 18, 14 „

RAITH PLANTATIONS (Hardwoods).

Girth at 5 feet of six average trees.

Sycamore . $16\frac{1}{4}$, $13\frac{1}{4}$ $14\frac{3}{4}$, $12\frac{1}{2}$, $9\frac{3}{4}$, $12\frac{3}{4}$ ins.
Maple . . $13\frac{1}{2}$, $10\frac{1}{2}$, 14, 11, 10, 13 „
Elm . . . $16\frac{1}{4}$, $13\frac{1}{4}$, $11\frac{3}{4}$, $23\frac{1}{2}$, $15\frac{1}{4}$, 12 „
Ash . . . $9\frac{1}{2}$, 9, $12\frac{1}{2}$, $9\frac{1}{2}$, $13\frac{1}{4}$, $11\frac{1}{2}$ „
Poplar . . $15\frac{1}{2}$, 13, $9\frac{1}{2}$, $14\frac{1}{4}$, $11\frac{1}{2}$, 10 „
(Black Italian)

ROUGH PARK.

Scots pine . 10, 10, $10\frac{1}{4}$, $6\frac{3}{4}$, 9, 7 ins.

BALBIRNIE.

Girth at 5 feet of six average trees.

Scots pine $15\frac{1}{2}$, $18\frac{1}{4}$, 12, $11\frac{3}{4}$, $18\frac{1}{2}$, $14\frac{1}{2}$ ins. } Part had
„   18, $13\frac{1}{2}$, $14\frac{1}{2}$, $19\frac{1}{2}$, 18, $10\frac{3}{4}$ „ } been pruned.

BALCARRES.

Scots pine (Castle Park) . $7\frac{1}{2}$, $7\frac{1}{4}$, 5, 6, 5, $7\frac{1}{4}$ ins.
„ (Riris) . . . 5, 6, 7, $7\frac{1}{2}$, 5, 7 „

KINALDY (No. 1).

Scots pine . 15, 14, 18, 18, $14\frac{1}{2}$, $10\frac{1}{2}$ ins.

KINALDY (No. 2).

Larch . . 22, 20, 16, 22, 14½, 20 ins.
Scots pine . 15, 19, 17, 24, 15, 22 ,,

As so many details of the competing plantations in this year's Show district have already been brought together, it is felt that any further information concerning them would be very desirable.

If systematic measurements could be obtained at definite periods, for example, when each plantation reached the age of 10, 15 and 20 years, and if the results were published in the *Transactions* of the Society, a considerable amount of valuable statistics would soon be collected.

A schedule with instructions regarding the method of making the measurements could easily be drawn up, and this could be obtained by the various proprietors who were willing to co-operate. The printing of such statistics in the *Transactions* of the Society would not only form a permanent record of these plantations, but in time it would afford a valuable means of comparing the growth of one and the same species of tree in all parts of Scotland.

In conclusion, the Judges have to express their warmest thanks to the Secretary for the great amount of assistance he rendered them in their work.

To the proprietors and foresters of all the estates visited the thanks of the Judges are also due, for the kind and prompt way in which they made arrangements to suit the convenience of the Judges on the necessarily very short intimation of their intended visit.

A. W. BORTHWICK   } *Judges.*
G. U. MACDONALD

15. Forestry Exhibition held in the Highland and Agricultural Society's Showyard at Cupar.

The Royal Scottish Arboricultural Society held their annual exhibition in the showyard at Cupar, from 10th to 12th July 1912.

The newly-arranged division of the old classes for groups of specimens of timber into competitions for single species, was the means of bringing forward a large entry in most of the classes, one or two of them forming records.

The quality of many of the specimens exhibited was of a high order, and while the elimination of inferior specimens, sometimes unavoidably included in the old grouped-classes, was more satisfactory to the judges in one way, the uniformly high quality of the exhibits did not simplify their task. Among the specimens of timber of broad-leaved timber-trees, the ash from Falkland and the oak from Lockerbie House merit special mention.

In the local sections, where the grouping system still obtained, the classes did not fill well.

Among gates shown in working order there was keen competition, and here again the judges had a difficult task in deciding between the most outstanding of them. The class for gates for farm use brought forth a splendid entry, showing some fine timber and excellent workmanship. Mr James M'Hardy, Forglen, exhibited a good collection of specimens showing the good and bad effects of pruning when well and badly done respectively. In Class XXI. Mr Alex. Mitchell, Rosebery, exhibited a wire-reel, for which, though the judges did not consider it a marked improvement on the pattern now in use, they gave an award in consideration of the principle of the automatic brake attached to it. Among articles wholly or mainly made of wood, Mr Alex. Lowe, Lockerbie House, exhibited a large rustic bridge, which attracted much notice; and an exhibit from Scone, a beautiful door with standards made from Douglas fir, showed what can be done with timber of this species (see p. 106).

Among the articles brought together for exhibition only were the usual exhibits illustrating the rate of growth of trees, abnormal growths, different kinds of wood, methods of preservation, insects injurious to trees, collections of tools, working-plans and maps, photographs, etc. Among these the exhibit belonging to W. Parkin Moore, Esq., of Whitehall, Mealsgate, Cumberland, arranged by Mr P. Murray Thomson, factor, probably attracted more notice than any other single exhibit has done during the twelve years that the forestry exhibition has been organised It was composed of samples of the material forming an old pit-bank, that from the surface showing the herbage natural to it, and that from the under-lying layers giving an idea of the unpromising nature of the soil. Specimens of larch, Scots pine, beech, alder, birch, oak, spruce, etc., all grown on the pit-bank, were shown, as it were, *in situ*. The result would have been almost incredible had it not been for an excellent series of photographs which showed the rate of growth of the plantation as a whole, together with the comparative rate of growth of the several species.

The exhibit was of a highly educative nature, showing as it did what could be done not only in the way of beautifying blots in the landscape, but of turning them to good account by establishing crops of trees upon them. The judges considered that they were justified in recommending for this exhibit the highest award, a gold medal, and this opinion was evidently endorsed by most of the visitors to the exhibition. It is to be hoped that more may be learned of this interesting experiment.[1]

The exhibition, as a whole, compared well with the majority of those of former years, and it may fairly be said to have been above the average.

[1] *Vide* Mr P. Murray Thomson's illustrated paper at p. 30.

NOTES AND QUERIES.

DEPUTATION TO THE CHAIRMAN OF THE BOARD OF AGRICULTURE FOR SCOTLAND IN JUNE LAST.

The Society has been informed that consent to the publication of a detailed report of the proceedings at the reception of the Deputation would be contrary to official tradition.

AFFORESTATION AT TALLA.

We understand that the Edinburgh and District Water Trustees propose to afforest part of the Talla water-catchment area. According to a report of a meeting of the Trustees, which appeared in the *Scotsman,* Sir Sainthill Eardley-Wilmot and Sir William Haldane, two of the Development Commissioners, visited the area in September last, and as a result of their report the Commissioners state that they are prepared "to take a favourable view of an application from the Trustees for an advance from the Development Fund, by way of loan, to assist in afforesting the Talla catchment area." Mr Stebbing, lecturer on forestry at Edinburgh University, has, at the request of the Water Trustees, prepared a report upon the scheme, which includes proposals for the operations involved in the process of afforestation, and suggests that a beginning be made on a small scale, operations being begun during the present winter.

THE WOODLANDS OF ARGYLLSHIRE.

We understand that the Board of Agriculture for Scotland have issued a schedule of questions to proprietors of woodlands in Argyllshire, and that it is proposed, after particulars of the Argyllshire woods have been collected, to issue similar schedules to proprietors in other counties, so that in course of time a complete inventory of the woods of the country can be made.

The following are the questions contained in the Argyllshire schedule :—

1. Total area of estate woodlands (*excluding coppice woods and plantations under* 40 *years old*). 2. Predominating species. 3. Total area of coppice woods (if any). 4. Total area of plantations under 10 years old. 5. Predominating species. 6. Total area of plantations from 10 to 20 years old. 7. Predominating species. 8. Total area of plantations from 20 to 40 years old. 9. Predominating species. 10. Highest elevation of woodlands. 11. Do you plant an area annually, and if so, upon any definite system? 12. If there is a working-plan, please state by whom prepared. 13. Number of men engaged regularly in woods. 14. Foresters. 15. Labourers. 16. Number of men obtaining temporary employment. 17. Is further planting contemplated? 18. Any general remarks.

THE ARDGOIL ESTATE.

The Corporation of Glasgow has decided on carrying out a scheme of afforestation on the Loch Goil side of this estate, commencing in the neighbourhood of Lochgoilhead, where there are at present three areas covered with coppice and natural woods. These trees, though not of great commercial value, will supply much of the fencing material necessary for enclosing the young plantations. The three areas cover about 1100 acres. The slopes, though steep, have a good loamy soil well suited for tree culture. The present proposals give the general outline of a scheme of gradual afforestation, and the development of the estate as a place of resort for the citizens of Glasgow, and will therefore carry out the wishes of Lord Rowallan, the generous donor of the property. The scheme has been drawn up by Bailie Alston and Mr James Whitton, superintendent of the Corporation parks.

THE EFFECTS OF LIGHT AND SHADE ON TREE-GROWTH.

The article on the relation of light to tree-growth, which appeared in the July number of the Society's *Transactions*, is both interesting and suggestive, and opens up a subject which has had little attention even by those more immediately connected with forest management.

Those who had the fortune to attend the excursion to France some years ago, will remember the effects of light and shade on the growth of young oak forests, which was very apparent from the first stages of their growth. Instead of the young trees being thinned out, as probably would be done in Scotland, those that are ultimately to be thinned out are simply foreshortened by cutting 3 or 4 feet off the terminal shoot. By this means the trees which are to form the future crop are allowed light and air without exposing the main stems to excessive evaporation.

As a further illustration of the effects of light and shade on tree-growth, the following may be of interest :—

A number of years ago we had occasion to fill up some blanks in an old beech plantation, but, unfortunately, as too often happens, the plantation was infested with rabbits and roe deer, with the result that the young trees were being destroyed wholesale. After consideration, it was decided to surround the stems of the young trees with tall bracken, of which there was a plentiful supply near at hand.

The fronds of the bracken were inverted and placed on the surface of the ground, and the stems of the bracken tied round the stems of the young trees, which were upwards of 5 feet high. By this means they were not only effectively protected but the after results showed the effects of light and shade in a way little thought of. In the course of three or four years, the stems of the young beech covered with bracken had not only assumed a beautiful green bark, but had attained to about three times the diameter of the uncovered portion.

I need scarcely say that this illustrates the effects of light and shade in a very unexpected and remarkable manner, and shows very conclusively that however essential light and air may be for the growth of trees, it is quite possible to have too much sunlight, such as that caused by over-thinning, and exposing the stems of the trees to excessive evaporation and branch-production, with the ultimate loss of timber. Perhaps some one can give a little more information on the subject.   J. K.

The Uses of Douglas Fir Timber.

Several hundreds of Douglas firs having been blown down on the Scone estates in the gales of November 1911 and

April 1912, an opportunity has occurred for testing the value of its timber for estate purposes, and for offering it in the market.

The trees converted varied from forty to fifty-two years of age. Even at these ages the proportion of heartwood was found to be, on the average, about 70 per cent. of the total volume.

The timber converts something like spruce, keeping straight, even when long sizes are sawn, and it does not pinch the saw or spring from it. If carefully stacked, so that the surfaces are evenly exposed, it dries quickly, and is not liable to warp. When cut into boards $\frac{7}{8}$ in. thick, it was found, with open-air drying, that 1000 square feet weighed 24·6 cwts., as compared with 26·3 cwts. in spruce, and 29·8 cwts. in mature Scots pine.

Though left lying in the wood with the bark on for months, logs of this species have not the same tendency to become discoloured as larch and Scots pine have.

The timber is very durable, and in this respect equal to larch of the same age. A fence on Taymount Estate, erected with posts sawn from the thinnings taken from the Taymount Douglas wood in 1887, has just required renewal this year, having stood about twenty-five years. The posts were mostly broken at the ground surface, the part above being quite sound. The fence had received a coat of tar after erection, but the wood was otherwise untreated.

The clean, straight butts were converted into battens and boards for estate use. Second cuts were made into packing-case boards, or hutch boards for collieries; coarse upper cuts into railway sleepers, and these are now being accepted by one railway company. Though the latter only fetch the price of Scots pine, this outlet is a useful one, as most of the older Douglas fir in the country has been too openly grown, and in consequence the upper cuts are coarse and unfit for boarding.

A number of gates and gate posts have been made, and though, from the presence of larger knots, these may not be so strong as larch gates, they are first-class gates, and have the advantage of being much lighter.

A panelled door was also made, and for this purpose the timber was found to be quite suitable. No difficulty was experienced in dressing, fitting, or nailing the wood.

Three logs were sent to Sir John Fleming for his inspection, and were converted by him into 3 ins. × $\frac{5}{8}$ in. champhered linings. Sir John reported very favourably on the quality of the timber and expressed the opinion that, if grown on a long rotation, it would give good results for carpentry and joinery purposes. The linings are to be used for ceiling and inside wall linings, for which purpose the estate architect considers them well suited. FRANK SCOTT.

PRODUCTION OF TIMBER IN GREAT BRITAIN.

The Report of the Board of Agriculture and Fisheries, on inquiries made in connection with the Census of Production Act, 1906, contains information as to the area under woodland, and production of timber, in Great Britain in 1908.

A special return of the area of woodland was obtained in 1905, and the inquiry of 1908 was directed, in the first instance, to ascertaining what changes in area had occurred since that date. The schedules were, as far as possible, sent to the same persons as those by whom the returns in 1905 were made, the figures then returned by them being entered on the schedule with the request that they would supply the corresponding figures as at 4th June 1908. The total area under all woodland, and the area returned as plantations, *i.e.* land planted within the preceding ten years, are shown in the following table for both years :—

	ALL WOODLANDS		PLANTATIONS	
	1908	1905	1908	1905
	Acres	Acres	Acres	Acres
England . .	1,720,330	1,715,473	72,008	59,647
Wales . . .	186,723	184,361	11,355	8,629
Scotland . .	874,910	868,409	44,146	35,407
Great Britain . .	2,781,963	2,768,243	127,509	103.683

There were thus 2,782,000 acres of woodland in Great Britain in 1908, of which 128,000 acres were described as plantation. This represents an increase of 24,000 acres of plantation, the net increase in the total area of woodland in the three years being 14,000 acres.

The schedule also asked for particulars of the acreage of pure woods, distinguishing the kind of tree in each case, and of mixed woods whether of all coniferous, all broad-leaved, or of both together. The schedule further asked for the number, quantity in cubic feet, and value of trees felled or sold standing during twelve months, classified under the different headings. The acreage under the principal kinds of trees in England and Wales, Scotland, and Great Britain, respectively, was as follows:—

KINDS	England and Wales	Scotland	Great Britain
Coniferous woods—	Acres .	Acres	Acres
Scots pine	49,000	156,000	205,000
Larch	69,000	25,000	94,000
Spruce	1,000	8,000	9,000
Others and mixed . . .	135,000	293,000	428,000
Total	254,000	482,c00	736,000
Broad-leaved woods—			
Oak	130,000	9,000	139,000
Beech	25,000	1,000	26,000
Birch	1,000	10,000	11,000
Others and mixed . . .	476,000	75,000	551,000
Total	632,000	95,000	727,000
Mixed coniferous and broad-leaved woods	1,021,000.	298,000	1,319,000
Total acreage of woodland	1,907,000	875,000	2,782,000

The estimated production of timber in the twelve months ending June 1908, distinguishing the principal kinds, is shown in the following table :—

CROP	Trees felled for sale, or sold standing		
	Number	Quantity	Value
		Cubic feet	
Larch	560,000	3,709,000	£144,000
Scots Pine	441,000	3,895,000	81,000
Spruce and other coniferous trees	77,000	587,000	12,000
Oak	219,000	3,604,000	237,000
Beech	89,000	1,349,000	51,000
Ash	41,000	598,000	37,000
Elm	15,000	583,000	21,000
Birch, sycamore, chestnut, and other broad-leaved trees .	66,000	520,000	15,000
Total . . .	1,508,000	14,845,000	£598,000

The value of other wood sold or used at home, *e.g.* pit props, small thinnings, cord wood, faggots, bavins, etc., and the value of osiers sold, together make the total value of timber of all kinds sold or utilised during the year about £800,000.—*Journal of the Board of Agriculture* (By permission of the Controller of H.M. Stationery Office).

APPOINTMENTS.

Mr G. P. Gordon, a B.Sc. in Forestry and Agriculture, and a probationer for the Indian Forest Service, has been appointed Lecturer in Forestry, West of Scotland Agricultural College, in succession to Dr Nisbet.

Mr James W. Newton, B.Sc. (Agriculture and Forestry), has been appointed Forest Conservator to the Colonial Government, British East Africa.

THE ACTION OF GRASS ON FRUIT TREES.[1]

In this report an account is given of the experiments carried out during the past sixteen years on the effect of grass on fruit trees.

The conclusion arrived at is that the action is so deleterious that it arrests all growth, and often causes the death of the tree. In no cases has recovery been noticed, except where the roots began to extend beyond the grassed area. Trees which become grassed over gradually during the course of several years apparently accommodate themselves to the altering conditions, and suffer much less than when the grass is actually sown over their roots. It is suggested that it is partially due to this circumstance that the effect of grass in commercial orchards is often less than that on the experimental farm; differences in the nature of the soil have also an important effect, the evil effects of grass being much more noticeable on some soils than on others. The same effect is also seen in the case of trees which have become well established before the grass was sown.

In connection with apple trees, a point of practical interest

---

[1] *Thirteenth Report of the Woburn Experimental Fruit Farm*, by the Duke of Bedford, K.G., F.R.S., and Spencer U. Pickering, M.A., F.R.S., 1911.

is noted. In some soils where the effect produced is not great, grass might be advantageous from a commercial point of view, for the check given to the growth of the tree tends to increase its cropping, and grass affects the colouring matter of all parts of the tree, generally resulting in a high colouring of the fruit.

The authors are of opinion that forest trees are affected by grass in the same way as fruit trees, when the grass is sown immediately after planting. The only difference between their behaviour and that of the fruit trees was, that in the case of conifers planted in light soil, the effect was much less than with other trees, and some recovery occurred with them as time went on, instead of the effect becoming intensified.

Much experimental work has been carried out as to the cause of the deleterious effect of the grass. In particular, the action of grass as regards the aeration of the soil, and its effect on soil-moisture, food supply, and on the mechanical condition of the soil, were investigated but with negative results. Similarly the investigation of the bacterial conditions gave no help in the problem. Finally, it was concluded that the grass secretes a toxic substance during its growth, and a considerable amount of positive evidence is brought forward in support of this view. The experiments were carried out with trees growing in pots. It was found that such trees, when watered with the leachings obtained from trays containing grass growing in sand, flourished more than when water alone was supplied ; but when the trays were placed on the surface of the soil (or sand) in which the trees were growing, so that the washings from the grass reached the tree-roots with practically no exposure to the air, they then had a very deleterious effect, nearly, if not quite, as great as when the grass was grown above the roots of the trees in the ordinary way. The trays containing the grass were movable, and the sand in them, with the grass growing in it, was separated from the medium in which the trees were growing by the perforated iron bottoms of the trays and by a sheet of wire gauze ; moreover, the contact between the bottoms of the trays and the sand or soil beneath would be, at the best, very imperfect, so that it is impossible to explain the action of grass in such a case by the abstraction by the grass of anything from the soil (or sand) below the trays, and it must be due to the passage of something from the trays down to the trees. The experiments on this subject were numerous, and the grass-effect was uniformly shown in all of them; and, it should be mentioned, the trees without grass, with which the grassed trees were compared, were grown with trays of sand above their roots, so as to exclude the possibility of explaining the results by the mere presence of the trays.

The ready oxidisability of the toxic matter formed by grass into some substance which favours plant-growth, will explain the previously observed beneficial effect of grass-leachings in cases where these had been exposed to air, and also why soil taken from grass-grown ground should be more favourable to plant-growth than that from tilled ground.

ALEXANDER LAUDER.

COLLECTION AND UTILISATION OF INFORMATION FOR A FOREST SURVEY.[1]

The Board of Agriculture has published *Notes on Kerry Woods*, by Mr R. L. Robinson, illustrating methods of collecting and utilising information for a forest survey. The introductory section deals with the natural conditions of the locality—topography, climate, geology and soil. This is followed by a description of the methods of measurement, with details of the growth and quality of the timber of larch, Scots pine, spruce and some other species grown as pure crops or in mixture. In the third section, the author treats of the method of arriving at a basis for a survey, and the systematic method of conducting it. There are four appendices, relating respectively to Soil Analysis, Measurements of sample areas, Field Tables for spruce, and Soil Expectation Values for spruce. There are numerous photographic and diagrammatic illustrations.

INTERNATIONAL FOREST CONGRESS AT PARIS.

Under the patronage of the President of the Republic, the "Touring-Club de France" is organising a congress to be held in Paris from 16th to 20th June 1913, at which will be discussed questions relating to all the various branches of forestry, especially those which interest the private owner. A

---

[1] August 1912. Price 4d., post free, 64 pp.

programme of the work to be done may be seen in the Secretary's office. A detailed programme giving the work assigned to each day, including *fêtes*, receptions and excursions, will be issued later.

A Comparison Between the Yields from Afforestation and Pasture Lands.[1]

In this paper an account is given of the yield and financial returns of the Cantonal forest of Mont Chaubert. Part of this forest had originally formed the ancient park, and part had been pasture land. The forest consists almost entirely of silver fir and was planted about 1830. It was originally planted to afford shelter, and is favourably situated as regards fertility of soil and elevation.

A comparison between the financial results of the afforestation and the return from neighbouring properties, still under pasture, is of considerable interest.

	Forest.	Pasture.
Value per acre . . .	£127 9 0	£12 17 0
Income (gross) per acre .	3 4 3	0 12 10
„ (net) „ .	2 17 10	0 11 3

In order to avoid exaggeration the highest possible value was placed on the pasture; rentals being taken which are sometimes paid in the district, but which are occasionally too high to leave any profit to the lessee.

The above results show that in spite of early errors of management, such as too dense planting, insufficient thinning, and delay in starting thinning, the change from pasturage to forest has been highly successful.

The cost of the afforestation, including the capitalised value of the annual expenditure, works out at 760 francs per hectare (£12, 4s. per acre). The return on this is slightly over 6 per cent., and the author is of opinion that if the early mistakes in planting and management had been avoided, the return would have been 7 or even 8 per cent.

The author is firmly of the opinion that no species but silver fir would have given such good results in the afforestation of pasture land. ALEXANDER LAUDER.

[1] J. J. de Luze. "Comparaison entre le rendement du Reboisement et celui de Pâturages." *Aufforstung des Staates Waadt am Mont Chaubert; Schweizerische Zeitschrift für Forstwesen;* 62 J. n. 7-8; 205 *Bern* 1911.

International Memorial to Karl Gayer.

APPEAL.

Johann Karl Gayer, State Councillor and Professor of Silviculture and Forest Utilisation at the University of Munich, D.Œc., *honoris causa*, was born on the 15th October 1822, and died in Munich on the 1st March 1907, honoured and lamented by thousands of his pupils and friends, and by foresters throughout the world.

For over forty years Karl Gayer took an active and prominent part in the teaching of forestry : first at the Forestry School of Aschaffenburg, and subsequently (1878-1892) at the University of Munich, of which he was elected Rector, officiating during the period 1889-90. In 1880, in Munich, Karl Gayer first started his great propaganda on the silvicultural principles of the preservation of the natural productivity of the soil; principles which soon made his name and his teaching famous, and brought him pupils from all parts of Europe and America. He was decorated by Bavaria, Russia and Greece, and was made an honorary member of several forestry societies.

Apart from his work on silviculture, Karl Gayer's name is well known to all British foresters through his classic book on Forest Utilisation, which was translated into English by the late Professor W. R. Fisher.

The world of forestry owes a permanent deep debt of gratitude to Karl Gayer for his work in the advancement of silvicultural knowledge. A movement has been set on foot in Munich in this year, the 90th anniversary of Karl Gayer's birth, to perpetuate his memory by the erection of a monument over his grave. Yielding to the oft-expressed wishes of foresters throughout the world, it has been decided to give the memorial an international character, and it is thought that many British foresters may welcome this opportunity of joining in honouring the memory of a great forester.

Contributions may be sent direct to Geheim Ministerialrat Dr Kast, Munich, Bavaria; or to Dr A. W. Borthwick, 46 George Square, Edinburgh; or Professor W. Somerville, 12 Banbury Road, Oxford ; or A. M. F. Caccia, 19 Linton Road, Oxford.

REVIEWS AND NOTICES OF BOOKS.

History of Forestry. By BERNHARD E. FERNOW. Revised and
Enlarged Edition. 516 pp., including Index. University
Press, Toronto, 1911.

Dr Fernow always manages to make interesting whatever
he writes about, and his *History of Forestry* is no exception to
the rule. In it he has a subject which is itself most fascinating,
and it is made the most of in this important book. Much
need was felt for such a work, as the information could
otherwise be obtained only by patient search through many
books—chiefly German and French.

Although usually given little attention, few will deny the
usefulness of a study of history as it relates to the forest.
The fact is that forestry requires to be considered in this
way more than most subjects. We hope and believe that our
country has awakened to a new sense of its responsibilities
in regard to silviculture, but development in that direction is
only commencing, so that it behoves us to see how other
countries have advanced and to examine closely the lines of
progress. When this is done, it is wonderful how similar the
successive stages of evolution are seen to be in countries differing
fundamentally in other respects.

The forest history of Germany is taken by the author as a
kind of type or standard, and dealt with more fully than that
of other countries. In view of the leading position occupied
by Germany in all branches of forestry, this preference is
justifiable, besides which Germany is the only country provided
with an extensive literature on the subject. Dr Fernow follows
chiefly Schwappach's *Forst und Jagdgeschichte Deutschlands*
in this section of the book, but instead of making a division
into four periods three are considered, namely : (1) to the
end of the Middle Ages; (2) to the end of the eighteenth
century; and (3) the modern period.

The first of these is probably less interesting to English
readers than the later history, as it is largely concerned
with ancient conditions of ownership, the establishment of

"servitudes" and so forth. The feudal system became gradually weaker after the Middle Ages, and with industrial improvement forestry methods developed. By the end of the eighteenth century technical forestry was so well understood in Germany that it strikes one as strange that some of the knowledge did not reach England until almost exactly a hundred years later, and even then was not received with much enthusiasm. Although well advanced in forest organisation, administration, methods of management, education, and the practice of silviculture a century ago, Germany was just then beginning the great forward movement which has brought it to the forefront among the nations. Forest policy was then established, silvicultural principles founded on a scientific basis, and great advance made in every department of forest technology. This nineteenth century period is treated in masterly fashion by the author, who speaks from an intimate knowledge of the country and its conditions.

Austria and Hungary are taken separately—the account of the management of Austria's privately owned forests being particularly interesting. It shows among other things the far-reaching influence of legislation upon the treatment of forest areas. Switzerland comes under consideration next, and the evolution of its cantonal system of administration is traced. France is done justice to in a chapter which forms one-tenth part of the volume. After dealing with the development of forest proprietorship, policy and administration, the history of the great works of reclamation, for which France is so famous, is given in considerable detail, after which the successive stages by which the country has progressed in forestry education, literature, science and practice are described. This section has gained more than any other from the author's revision for the second edition.

Other parts of the book deal with the past and present condition of forestry in Russia, Scandinavia, the Balkan States and South-European countries, Great Britain and its Colonies, Japan, and the United States of America.

Some of Dr Fernow's pithy remarks on our countrymen and their attitude towards forestry may be quoted. They let us " see oorsels as ithers see us."

" Politically the Englishman is an individualist. . . .

Commercial and industrial enterprise rather than economic development appeal to him ; the practical issue of the day rather than demands of a future and systematic preparation for the same occupy his mind. He lacks, as Lord Rosebery points out, scientific method, and hence is wasteful. Moveover, he is conservative and self-satisfied beyond the citizens of any other nation ; hence if all the wisdom of the world point new ways, he will still cling to his accustomed ones. In the matter of having commissions appointed to investigate and report, and leaving things to continue in unsatisfactory condition, he reminds one of Spanish dilatoriness. These would appear to us the reasons for the difficulty which the would-be reformers experience in bringing about economic reforms."

It must be admitted that these words hit off the situation rather nicely. They may serve as an example of the forcible style in which the book is written. It is a work at once readable, accurate, concise and comprehensive. All who take a wide view of forestry, especially in its economic application, will read it both with pleasure and with profit.

F. S.

The Forest Trees of Britain. By the late Rev. C. A. JOHNS. 10th Edition. Revised by Professor G. S. BOULGER. Published by the Society for Promoting Christian Knowledge. Price 6s. net.

Two editions of this work, by different editors and publishers, have appeared within the past few months. We noticed one of these on p. 240 of our last volume.

The present edition comes from the original publishers, with a preface by Professor Boulger, in which he says, " With but a few verbal alterations, and some slight emendations rendered desirable by recent advances in our knowledge of the subject, it has been thought best to present the work much as Johns left it, though illustrated by a series of new and specially prepared plates." This edition is therefore practically a reprint, with all the original illustrations in addition to the beautiful new plates referred to above.

Flora and Sylva: A Monthly Review for Lovers of Gardens, Woodland Tree and Flower; New and rare Plants, Trees, Shrubs and Fruits; the Garden Beautiful, Home Woods and Home Landscape. Edited by and printed and published for W. ROBINSON, author of *The English Flower Garden,* and other works.

The author has very kindly presented to the Society's library the first three volumes of this work. The volumes are magnificent specimens of the paper-makers', printers', engravers', and colour printers' arts, and are a handsome monument to the author and all concerned in their upmake. The work originally appeared in monthly parts, but unfortunately it has now been discontinued because the subscribers to such an expensive publication, even although it was issued at less than cost price, were too few to warrant its continuance. This is not surprising in our age of cheapness, but is nevertheless very regrettable, because the mere mechanical production and handling of such a book, apart altogether from the intrinsic value of its contents, must have had an elevating effect on all concerned. The contents will appeal mostly to lovers of gardens and ornamental grounds, but there is a special series of articles on the greater trees of the Northern Forest, besides many others dealing with forestry subjects scattered throughout the volumes which are interesting to foresters and tree lovers. We record our grateful thanks to Mr Robinson for this very handsome donation to our library.   R. G.

The Story of our Trees. By MARGARET M. GREGSON. 160 pp. and 74 figures. University Press, Cambridge, 1912.

This book consists of twenty-four lessons on topics relating to trees, such as leaf-casting, winter buds and tree forms, how a tree lives, etc. It would be a useful guide to nature study relating to trees were it not that, as in so many of these books, too much is attempted to allow of strict accuracy. However, if the practical work, which includes visits to woods and timber yards, is followed with care, the teacher could convey the elements of tree-life. In some cases the practical exercises might be carried out on trees rather than on herbaceous plants: why study the bean in detail when the acorn is available? In the same way, the henbane is quoted as bearing millions of seeds, when willow seems quite as good; and sweet pea is figured as a type of fruit equally well exemplified by laburnum. Figure 7 is described as a pine cone but it is actually the spruce. The statement that on the heather-covered moors of Scotland "no trees will grow" owing to the cold winds is inaccurate, since many acres of these very moors do carry forest up to an altitude of 1500 feet or more. The lists of books, and firms who will supply lantern slides on trees, will be useful to many teachers.

The Care of Trees in Lawn, Street and Park: With a List of Trees and Shrubs for Decorative Use. By BERNHARD E. FERNOW, Dean of the Faculty of Forestry, University of Toronto. x + 392 pp. including Index. Illustrated. New York: Henry Holt & Company, 1910.

This is a good book, as was to be expected from the pen of so experienced and competent a master as is the author. It contains just the "information such as the owner of trees may be in search of." It is not a work on forestry. Its subject is the isolated tree wherever planted, whether for shade or ornament, and the aim of the book is to enlighten those who have trees under their care, so that their part as "Tree wardens"—the "expressive, dignified and honourable title" which the author coins—may be adequately performed.

The book opens with a lucid account of the essential points in the structure of trees, and in their method of life. In course of it, the relations to their environment and the recuperative capacity of trees are graphically sketched. To the ailments, however caused, that affect trees the author gives much space, and adds sound advice as to treatment. Tending of trees, pruning and planting are all dealt with succinctly and effectively. In the two hundred pages, making the first half of the book, that are devoted to this general account of the right basis for and of the right method in the care of trees, Mr Fernow has provided a guide for planters that is thoroughly sound in its information. It is written professedly for the amateur planter and for the custodian of town trees,—who is too often untrained,—not for the expert; yet the latter will find in it much that will remind him of principles. The author has been successful in the difficult task of conveying, in simple language that can be understood by anyone, those facts of science that govern the cultivation and preservation of trees.

The second half of the book is devoted to the choice of planting material, that is to say, it gives lists and short descriptions of desirable trees and shrubs; and also, under separate groupings, the names of trees and shrubs that have special features, whether individual as, for instance, coloured leaves, coloured fruits, or special adaptations suiting them to localities such as the seashore, exposed situations, wet soils and the like. This is well done, and it will appeal to many. It has, however, the defect of its time of appearance at a moment when the number of desirable trees and shrubs for cultivation is being increased manifold by the work of recent collectors in China—Wilson, Forrest, Purdom, Ward, and others—so that there are naturally missing from its pages many of the choicer sorts of recent introduction. But this a new edition will remedy.

It is no extravagant laudation to say that this is one of the most delightful and instructive books that has been written on a subject that gains daily in practical importance now that town planning has become an obsession of municipalities. Everyone interested in arboriculture should read the book.

I. B. B.

The Oak: Its Natural History, Antiquity and Folk-lore. By CHARLES MOSLEY. 126 pp., with 8 Illustrations. Price 5s. London: Elliot Stock.

This little book is not written for foresters, but for those of the general public who take an interest in trees. The opening chapter deals with the place of the oak amongst the other trees of the forest, its distribution, its influence on place names, and its other peculiarities. In the chapters which follow, the author discourses on the economic value of the oak, its enemies and parasites, historic and veteran oaks, mistletoe-oaks, the oak in myth, folk-lore and holy writ, and he concludes with a list of some of the more interesting species of oak. The book is enriched throughout by quotations in prose and verse from many authors.

TRANSACTIONS

OF THE

ROYAL
SCOTTISH ARBORICULTURAL SOCIETY.

VOL. XXVII.—PART II.

July 1913.

A. W. BORTHWICK, D.Sc.,
HONORARY EDITOR

ROBERT GALLOWAY, S.S.C.,
SECRETARY AND TREASURER.

STICKING IN A TREE IT WILL BE GROWING WHEN YE'RE SLEEPING YE MAY BE AYE

EDINBURGH:
PRINTED FOR THE SOCIETY.
SOLD BY DOUGLAS & FOULIS, CASTLE STREET.

to Non-Members, **3/-**

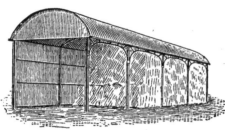
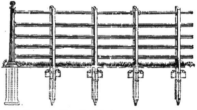

KEITH & CO.

ADVERTISING AGENTS

43 GEORGE STREET EDINBURGH

ADVERTISEMENTS of every kind are received for insertion in the Daily, Weekly, and Monthly Publications throughout the United Kingdom.

Notices of Sequestration, Cessio, Dissolution of Partnership, Entail, etc., etc., for the Edinburgh and London Gazettes, are given special care and attention.

Legal Notices, Heirs Wanted, and all other Advertisements, are inserted in the Colonial and Foreign Newspapers.

Small Advertisements, such as Situations, Houses, and Apartments, Articles Wanted and For Sale, etc., etc., can be addressed to a No. at Keith & Co.'s Office, 43 George Street, Edinburgh, where the replies will be retained until called for, or, if desired, forwarded by Post. Parties in the country will find this a very convenient method of giving publicity to their requirements.

A SPECIALITY is made of ESTATE and AGRICULTURAL ADVERTISEMENTS, such as FARMS, MANSION HOUSES, etc., TO LET, ESTATES for SALE, AGRICULTURAL SHOWS, etc.

LAW and ESTATE AGENTS, FACTORS, TOWN CLERKS, CLERKS TO SCHOOL BOARDS, and other Officials may, with confidence, place their advertisements in the hands of the Firm.

One Copy of an Advertisement is sufficient to send for any number of newspapers; and the convenience of having only one advertising account instead of a number of advertising accounts is also a great saving of time and trouble.

Addressing of Envelopes with Accuracy and Despatch.

Telegrams—"PROMOTE," EDINBURGH.   Telephone No. 316.

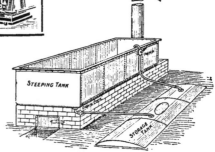

NOTICE.

WANTED TO PURCHASE.

Any of the following Parts of the *Transactions*, viz.:

Parts 1, 2, and 3 of Vol. I.
Parts 2 and 3 of Vol. III.
Parts 1 and 2 of Vol. IV.
Part 2 of Vol. V.
Part 2 of Vol. IX.
Part 1 of Vol. XII.

Apply to

—— THE SECRETARY, ——
19 CASTLE STREET, EDINBURGH.

OFFICE-BEARERS FOR 1913.

President.

CAPTAIN ARCHIBALD STIRLING of Keir, Dunblane.

Vice-Presidents.

WBORTHWICK, D Sc., 46 George Square, Edinburgh.

DEY J. GAMMELL of Drumtochty, Countesswells luse, Bieldside, Aberdeen.

? RD LOVAT, D.S.O., Beaufort Castle, Beauly.

CHAS BUCHANAN, Factor, Penicuik Estate, Penicuik

SIR ANDREW AGNEW, Bart., of Lochnaw, 10 Smith S Westminster.

W. STEUART FOTHRINGHAM of Murthly, Perthshii

Council.

HON. LIFE MEMBERS.

SIR KENNETH J. MACKENZIE, Bart. of Gairloch, 10 Moray Place, Edinburgh.
SIR JOHN STIRLING-MAXWELL, Bart. of Pollok, Pollokshaws.

ORDINARY MEMBERS.

EVEN, Forester, Bowmont Forest, Roxburgh.

BROOM, Wood Merchant, Bathgate.

. ANNAND, Lecturer in Forestry, Armstrong College, astle-upon-Tyne.

W. M'HATTIE, Superintendent of City Parks, City mbers, Edinburgh.

OF BRODIE, Brodie Castle, Forres.

M DAWSON, M.A., B.Sc., Reader in Forestry, bridge University.

* * * * * * * *

LLANDERS, F.E.S., Forester, Park Cottage, Aln-

WHITTON, Superintendent of City Parks, City abers, Glasgow.

M DAVIDSON, Forester, Panmure, Carnoustie.

W. H. MASSIE, Nurseryman, 1 Waterloo Place, Edint

GILBERT BROWN, Wood Manager, Grantown-on-Spe

GEORGE P. GORDON, B.Sc., Lecturer in Forestry, Scotland Agricultural College, 6 Blythswood S Glasgow.

A. D. RICHARDSON, 6 Dalkeith Street, Joppa.

ADAM SPIERS, Timber Merchant, Warriston Saw-Mills burgh.

ROBERT ALLAN, Factor, Polkemmet, Whitburn.

G. U MACDONALD, Overseer, Haystoun Estate, Wc Cottage, Peebles.

ALEXANDER MITCHELL, Forester, Rosebery, Gorebi

ROBERT FORBES, Overseer, Kennet Estate Office, Al

ALEXANDER J. MUNRO, Factor, 48 Castle Street burgh.

W. M. PRICE, Factor, Minto, Hawick.

Hon. Editor.

Dr A. W. BORTHWICK, 46 George Square, Edinburgh.

Auditor.

JOHN T. WATSON, 16 St Andrew Square, Edinburgh

Hon. Secretary.

The RIGHT HON. R. C. MUNRO FERGUSON, M.P., Raith House, Kirkcaldy.

Secretary and Treasurer.

ROBERT GALLOWAY, S.S.C., 19 Castle Street, Edinburgh.

ABERDEEN BRANCH.

—A. FORBES IRVINE of Drum.

Sy.—GEORGE D. MASSIE, Solicitor, 147 Union Street, Aberdeen.

NORTHERN BRANCH.

President—BRODIE OF BRODIE.

Hon. Secy.—ALEX. FRASER, Solicitor, 63 Church Inverness.

Hon. Consulting Officials.

g *Botanist.*—ISAAC BAYLEY BALFOUR, LL.D., Sc.D., Professor of Botany, Royal Botanic Garden, urgh.

g *Chemist.*—ALEXANDER LAUDER, D.Sc., F.I C., rge Square, Edinburgh.

g *Cryptogamist.*—A. W. BORTHWICK, D.Sc. rge Square, Edinburgh.

Consulting Entomologist. — ROBERT STEWART DOUGALL, M A., D.Sc., Professor of Entomology 9 Dryden Place, Edinburgh.

Consulting Geologist.—R. CAMPBELL, M.A., B.Sc. logical Laboratory, University of Edinburgh.

Consulting Meteorologist.—ANDREW WATT, M.A., F.I Secretary Scottish Meteorological Society, 122 Street, Edinburgh.

*

Former Presidents.

The following have held the office of President in past years, viz. :—

1854-56.	James Brown, Wood Commissioner to the Earl of Seafield.	1882.	Professor Alexander Dickson, Unive of Edinburgh.
1857.	The Right Hon. The Earl of Ducie.	1883-85.	Hugh Cleghorn, M.D., LL.D., F.R. of Stravithie.
1858.	The Right Hon. The Earl of Stair.		
1859.	Sir John Hall, Bart. of Dunglass.	1886-87.	The Right Hon. Sir Herbert Eus Maxwell, Bart. of Monreith.
1860.	His Grace The Duke of Atholl.		
1861.	John I. Chalmers of Aldbar.	1888-89.	The Most Hon. The Marquis Linlithgow.
1862.	The Right Hon. The Earl of Airlie		
1863.	The Right Hon. T. F. Kennedy.	1890-93.	Professor Bayley Balfour, Unive of Edinburgh.
1864-71.	Robert Hutchison of Carlowrie, F.R.S.E.		
1872-73.	Hugh Cleghorn, M D., LL.D., F.R.S.E., of Stravithie.	1894-97.	The Right Hon. R. C. Munro Fergu M.P.
1874-75.	Professor John Hutton Balfour, University of Edinburgh.	1898.	Colonel F Bailey, R.E.
		1899-02.	The Right Hon. The Earl of Mansf!
1876-78.	The Right Hon. W. P. Adam of Blairadam, M.P.	1903-06.	W. Steuart Fothringham of Murtl
		1907-09.	Sir Kenneth J. Mackenzie, Bar Gairloch.
1879-81.	The Most Hon. The Marquis of Lothian, K.T.	1910-12.	Sir John Stirling-Maxweil, Bar Pollok.

Membership.

THE Roll contains the names of over 1400 Members, comprising Landowners, Factors, Foresters, Nurserymen, Gardeners, Land Stewards, Wood Merchants, and others interested in Forestry, many of whom reside in England, Ireland, the British Colonies, and India.

Members are elected by the Council. The Terms of Subscription will be found on the back of the Form of Proposal for Membership which accompanies this Memorandum.

The Principal Objects of the Society,

and the nature of its work, will be gathered from the following paragraphs:—

Meetings.

The Society holds periodical Meetings for the transaction of business, the reading and discussion of Papers, the exhibition of new Inventions, specimens of Forest Products and other articles of special interest to the Members, and for the advancement of Forestry in all its branches. Meetings of the Council are held every alternate month, and at other times when business requires attention; and Committees of the Council meet frequently to arrange and carry out the work of the Society.

Prizes and Medals.

With the view of encouraging young Foresters to study, and to train themselves in habits of careful and accurate observation, the Society offers Annual Prizes and Medals for essays on practical subjects, and for inventions connected with appliances used in Forestry. Such awards have been granted continuously since 1855 up to the present time, and have yielded satisfactory results. Medals and Prizes are also awarded in connection with the Exhibitions and Competitions for Plantations and Estate Nurseries aftermentioned.

School of Forestry, Afforestation, Etc.

Being convinced of the necessity for bringing within the reach of young Foresters, and others interested in the Profession, a regular systematic course of Instruction, the Society, in 1882, strongly urged the creation of a British School of Forestry; and with a view of stimulating public interest in the matter, a Forestry Exhibition, chiefly organised by the Council, was held in Edinburgh in 1884.

In 1890, the Society instituted a Fund for the purpose of establishing a Chair of Forestry at the University of Edinburgh, and a sum of £584, 3s. 10d. has since been raised by the Society and handed over to the University. Aided by an annual subsidy from the Board of Agriculture, which the Society was mainly instrumental in obtaining, a Course of Lectures at the University has been delivered without interruption since 1889. The Society also drew up a Scheme for the Establishment of a State Model or Demonstration Forest for Scotland, which might serve not only for purposes of instruction but also as a Station for Research and Experiment, and as a Model Forest, by which Landowners and Foresters throughout the country might benefit. Copies of this Scheme were laid before the Departmental Committee on British Forestry, and in their Report the Committee recommended the establishment of a Demonstration Area and the provision of other educational facilities in Scotland.

The Government recently acquired the Estate of Inverliever in Argyllshire; and while this cannot be looked on as a Demonstration Forest, it is hoped that it may prove to be the first step in a scheme of afforestation by the State of unwooded lands in Scotland. Meantime Mr Munro Ferguson, M.P., for a part of whose woods at Raith a Working-Plan is in operation, has very kindly agreed to allow Students to visit them.

After the Development Act came into operation, the Council passed a Resolution urging that the Government should, as soon as possible, create a Board of Forestry, with an adequate representation of Scottish Forestry upon it, and an Office in Scotland, where the largest areas of land suitable for Afforestation are situated, which would provide Demonstration Forests and Forest Gardens, and otherwise assist the development of University and other Educational enterprise, and would carry out, as an essential preliminary to any great scheme of National Afforestation, a Survey of all areas throughout the country suitable for commercial planting. The Society's policy for the development of Forestry in Scotland has since been fully laid before the Development Commission. As a result of these representations, the Secretary for Scotland appointed a Committee to report regarding the acquisition and uses of a Demonstration Forest Area, and any further steps it is desirable to take in order to promote Silviculture in Scotland. The Committee reported in the beginning of last year, and the Society is pressing the Board of Agriculture for Scotland, being the Department now concerned with Scottish forestry, to give effect to the Committee's recommendations and to encourage the inception of schemes of afforestation. The Society has also published a valuable Report on Afforestation—including a Survey of Glen Mor—prepared for it by Lord Lovat and Captain Stirling, which, it is hoped, may form the basis of the general Forest Survey advocated by the Society.

Excursions.

Since 1878 well-organised Excursions, numerously attended by Members of the Society, have been made annually to various parts of Scotland, England, Ireland, and the Continent. In 1895 a Tour extending over twelve days was made through the Forests of Northern Germany, in 1902 a Tour extending over seventeen days was made in Sweden, in 1904 the Forest School at Nancy and Forests in the north of France were visited, in 1909 a visit was undertaken to the Bavarian Forests, and it is now proposed to visit Switzerland during the ensuing summer. These Excursions enable Members whose occupations necessarily confine them chiefly to a single locality to study the conditions and methods prevailing elsewhere; and the Council propose to extend the Tours during the next few years to other parts of the Continent. They venture to express the hope that Landowners may be induced to afford facilities to their Foresters for participation in these Tours, the instructive nature of which renders them well worth the moderate expenditure of time and money that they involve.

Exhibitions.

A Forestry Exhibition is annually organised in connection with the Highland and Agricultural Society's Show, in which are exhibited specimens illustrating the rate of growth of trees, different kinds of wood, pit-wood and railway timber, insect pests and samples of the damage done by them, tools and implements, manufactured articles peculiar to the district where the Exhibition is held, and other objects of interest relating to Forestry. Prizes and Medals are also offered for Special Exhibits. In addition to the Annual Exhibition before referred to, large and important Forestry Sections organised by this Society were included in the Scottish National Exhibition held in Edinburgh in 1908, and in the Scottish Exhibition of National History, Art, and Industry, held in Glasgow in 1911.

Plantations and Estate Nurseries Competitions.

Prizes are now offered annually for the best Young Plantations and the best managed Estate Nurseries within the Show District of the Highland and Agricultural Society.

The Society's Transactions.

The *Transactions* of the Society, which extend to twenty-seven volumes, are now published half-yearly in January and July, and are issued *gratis* to Members. A large number of the Prize Essays and other valuable Papers, and reports of the Annual Excursions, have appeared in them, and have thus become available to Students as well as to those actively engaged in the Profession of Forestry.

Honorary Consulting Officials.

Members have the privilege of obtaining information gratuitously upon subjects connected with Forestry from the Honorary Officials mentioned above.

Local Branches.

Local Branches have been established in Aberdeen and Inverness for the convenience of Members who reside in the districts surrounding these centres.

Local Secretaries.

The Society is represented throughout Scotland, England, and Ireland by the Local Secretaries whose names are given below. They are ready to afford any additional information that may be desired regarding the Conditions of Membership and the work of the Society.

Register of Estate Men.

A Register of men qualified in Forestry and in Forest and Estate Management is kept by the Society. Schedules of application and other particulars may be obtained from the Local Secretaries in the various districts, or direct from the Secretary. It is hoped that Proprietors and others requiring Estate men will avail themselves of the Society's Register.

Consulting Foresters.

The Secretary keeps a list of Consulting Foresters whose services are available to Members of the Society and others.

Correspondents.

The following have agreed to act as Correspondents residing abroad :—

Canada,	ROBERT BELL, I.S.O., M.D., LL.D., D.Sc.(Cantab.), F.R.S. of Ottawa, late Chief Geologist to Government of Canada, Ottawa.
India,	F. L. C. COWLEY BROWN, Principal, South Indian Forest College, Coimbatore, South India.
British East Africa,	EDWARD BATTISCOMBE, Assistant Conservator of Forests, Nigeri, *via* Naivasha, East Africa Protectorate.
United States of America,	HUGH P. BAKER, Dean, New York State College of Forestry, Syracuse, N.Y.
Cape Colony,	W. NIMMO BROWN, M'Kenzie's Farm, Mowbray, P.O.
Western Australia,	FRED MOON.

LOCAL SECRETARIES.

Counties.	*Scotland.*
Aberdeen,	JOHN CLARK, Forester, Haddo House, Aberdeen.
	JOHN MICHIE, M.V.O., Factor, Balmoral, Ballater.
Argyll,	H. L. MACDONALD of Dunach, Oban.
Ayr,	ANDREW D. PAGE, Overseer, Culzean Home Farm, Ayr.
	A. B. ROBERTSON, Forester, The Dean, Kilmarnock.
Berwick,	WM. MILNE, Foulden Newton, Berwick-on-Tweed.
Bute,	WM. INGLIS, Forester, Cladoch, Brodick.
	JAMES KAY, retired Forester, Barone, Rothesay.
Clackmannan,.	ROBERT FORBES, Estate Office, Kennet, Alloa.
Dumfries,	D. CRABBE, Forester, Byreburnfoot, Canonbie.
East Lothian,.	W. S. CURR, Factor, Ninewar, Prestonkirk.
Fife,	WM. GILCHRIST, Forester, Nursery Cottage, Mount Melville, St Andrews.
	EDMUND SANG, Nurseryman, Kirkcaldy.
Forfar,	JAMES CRABBE, retired Forester, Glamis.

Counties.		*Scotland.*
Inverness,	.	JAMES A. GOSSIP, Nurseryman, Inverness.
Kincardine,	.	JOHN HART, Estates Office, Cowie, Stonehaven.
Kinross,	.	JAMES TERRIS, Factor, Dullomuir, Blairadam.
Lanark, .	.	JOHN DAVIDSON, Forester, Dalzell, Motherwell.

JAMES WHITTON, Superintendent of Parks, City Chambers, Glasgow.

Moray,	.	.	D. SCOTT, Forester, Darnaway Castle, Forres.
Perth,	.	.	JOHN SCRIMGEOUR, Doune Lodge, Doune.
Ross,	.	.	JOHN J. R. MEIKLEJOHN, Foctor, Novar, Evanton.

Miss AMY FRANCES YULE, Tarradale House, Muir of Ord.

Roxburgh,	.	JOHN LEISHMAN, Manager, Cavers Estate, Hawick.

R. V. MATHER, Nurseryman, Kelso.

Sutherland,	.	DONALD ROBERTSON, Forester, Dunrobin, Golspie.
Wigtown,	.	JAMES HOGARTH, Forester, Culhorn, Stranraer.

H. H. WALKER, Monreith Estate Office, Whauphill.

England.

Beds,	.	.	FRANCIS MITCHELL, Forester, Woburn.
Berks,	.	.	W. STORIE, Whitway House, Newbury.
Derby,	.	.	S. MACBEAN, Estate Office, Needwood Forest, Sudbury.
Devon,	.	.	JAMES BARRIE, Forester, Stevenstone Estate, Torrington.
Durham,	.	.	JOHN F. ANNAND, Lecturer in Forestry, Armstrong College, Newcastle-upon-Tyne.
Hants,	.	.	W. R. BROWN, Forester, Park Cottage, Heckfield, Winchfield.
Herts,	.	.	JAMES BARTON, Forester, Hatfield.

THOMAS SMITH, Overseer, Tring Park, Wigginton, Tring.

Kent,	.	.	R. W. COWPER, Gortanore, Sittingbourne.
Lancashire,	.	D. C. HAMILTON, Forester, Knowsley, Prescot.
Leicester,	.	JAMES MARTIN, The Reservoir, Knipton, Grantham.
Lincoln,	.	W. B. HAVELOCK, The Nurseries, Brocklesby Park.
Middlesex,	.	Professor BOULGER, 11 Onslow Road, Richmond Hill, London, S.W.
Notts,	.	.	WM. ELDER, Thoresby, Ollerton, Newark.

W. MICHIE, Forester, Welbeck, Worksop.

WILSON TOMLINSON, Forester, Clumber Park, Worksop.

Suffolk,	.	GEORGE HANNAH, The Folly, Ampton Park, Bury St Edmunds.
Surrey,	.	JOHN ALEXANDER, 24 Lawn Crescent, Kew Gardens.
Warwick,	.	A. D. CHRISTIE, Hillside, Frederick Road, Selly Oak, Birmingham.
Wilts,	.	.	ANDREW BOA, Land Agent, Glenmore, The Avenue, Trowbridge.
York,	.	.	D. TAIT, Estate Bailiff, Owston Park, Doncaster.

Ireland.

Dublin,	.	.	A. C. FORBES, Department of Forestry, Board of Agriculture.

JAMES WILSON, B.Sc., Royal College of Science, Dublin.

ARCH. E. MOERAN, Lissadell, Stillorgan Park.

Galway,	.	THOMAS ROBERTSON, Forester and Bailiff, Woodlawn.
King's County,		WM. HENDERSON, Forester, Clonad Cottage, Tullamore.
Tipperary,	.	DAVID G. CROSS, Forester, Kylisk, Nenagh.

ALEX. M'RAE, Forester, Dundrum.

Royal Scottish Arboricultural Society.

FORM OF PROPOSAL FOR MEMBERSHIP.

To be signed by the Candidate, his Proposer and Seconder, and returned to **ROBERT GALLOWAY, S.S.C.,** *SECRETARY,* Royal Scottish Arboricultural Society, **19 Castle Street, Edinburgh.**

Candidate's
- *Full Name,* ....
- *Designation, Degrees, etc.,* ....
- *Address,* ....
- *Life, or Ordinary Member,* ....
- *Signature,* . . ..

Proposer's
- *Signature,* . . ..
- *Address,* . . ..

Seconder's
- *Signature,* . . ..
- *Address,* . . ..

[CONDITIONS OF MEMBERSHIP, see Over.

CONDITIONS OF MEMBERSHIP (excerpted from the Laws).

III. Any person interested in Forestry, and desirous of promoting the objects of the Society, is eligible for election as an *Ordinary* Member in one of the following Classes :—

1. Proprietors the valuation of whose land *exceeds* £500 per annum, and others, subscribing annually . . One Guinea.

2. Proprietors the valuation of whose land *does not exceed* £500 per annum, Factors, Nurserymen, Timber Merchants, and others, subscribing annually . . Half-a-Guinea.

3. Foresters, Gardeners, Land-Stewards, Tenant Farmers, and others, subscribing annually . . . Six Shillings.

4. Assistant-Foresters, Assistant-Gardeners, and others, subscribing annually . . . . . Four Shillings.

IV. Subscriptions are due on the 1st of January in each year, and shall be payable in advance. A new Member's Subscription is due on the day of election unless otherwise provided, and he shall not be enrolled until he has paid his first Subscription.

V. Members in arrear shall not receive the *Transactions*, and shall not be entitled to vote at any of the meetings of the Society. Any Member whose Annual Subscription remains unpaid for two years shall cease to be a Member of the Society, and no such Member shall be eligible for re-election till his arrears have been paid up.

VI. Any eligible person may become a *Life* Member of the Society, on payment, according to class, of the following sums :—

1. Large Proprietors of land, and others, . . . £10 10 0

2. Small Proprietors, Factors, Nurserymen, Timber Merchants, and others, ... 5 5 0

3. Foresters, Gardeners, Land-Stewards, Tenant Farmers, and others, ... 3 3 0

VII. Any *Ordinary* Member of Classes 1, 2, and 3, who has paid *Five* Annual Subscriptions, may become a *Life* Member on payment of *Two-thirds* of the sum payable by a *new* Life Member.

XII. Every Proposal for Membership shall be made in writing, and shall be signed by two Members of the Society as Proposer and Seconder, and delivered to the Secretary to be laid before the Council, which shall accept or otherwise deal with each Proposal as it may deem best in the interest of the Society. The Proposer and Seconder shall be responsible for payment of the new Member's first Subscription. The Council shall have power to decide the Class under which any Candidate for Membership shall be placed.

CONTENTS.

The Society does not hold itself responsible for the statements
or views expressed by the authors of papers.

PAGE

16. Discussion on the Relation of Forestry to Agriculture and
other Industries 121

17. Letter to the Board of Agriculture for Scotland . . 143

18. Development of Forestry in England. Reports by Advisory
Committee 147

19. The Place of Forestry in the Economic Development of
Scotland. By Sir John Stirling-Maxwell, Bart. . . 161

20. Some Lessons from the Recent Gales. By Sir Hugh Shaw
Stewart, Bart. 172

21. The State Forests of Saxony. (With Illustrations.) By
A. D. Hopkinson 174

22. Report on Speeches made at meeting between Delegates
representing the interests of Forestry in Scotland and the
Scottish Railway Companies to discuss the Question of the
Price of Sleepers manufactured from Home-Grown Timber
as compared with that of those manufactured from Foreign
Timber 188

23. A New Disease on the Larch in Scotland (with Plate).
By A. W. Borthwick, D.Sc., Lecturer on Forest Botany,
University of Edinburgh, and Malcolm Wilson, D.Sc.,
F.L.S., Lecturer on Mycology, University of Edinburgh . 198

24. Recent Publications on Swiss Forests. By W. S. Smith,
Ph.D. 202

25. Notes of Silvicultural Interest (with Plate). By A. Murray . 206

26. The Use of Explosives in Forestry. By Dr Alexander
Lauder 210

27. Continental Notes (Germany) By Bert. Ribbentrop, C.I.E. 212

28. The Prices of Home Timber 222

Notes and Queries:—The Rüping Process of Creosoting
Timber—Afforestation at Vyrnwy — Deer Forests and
Sporting Lands in Scotland—Royal Botanic Garden,
Edinburgh: Proposed Guild—Testing of Forest Seeds—
Appointments 235

PAGE

Reviews and Notices of Books :—Illustrations of Conifers.
   Vol. III. By H. Clinton-Baker.   Printed privately at
   Hertford, 1913   240

Planter's Note Book.   By J. Woodward, Junr.   *Gardener's
   Chronicle*, London, 1913.   Price, 1s.   .   .   .   241

Forest Conditions of Nova Scotia. By B. E. Fernow, LL.D.,
   Dean of Faculty of Forestry, University of Toronto,
   assisted by C. D. Howe, Ph D , and J. H. White.
   Commission of Conservation, Ottawa, 1912   .   .   242

Obituary :—Lieut.-Col. F. Bailey, R.E., LL.D. (with Portrait)
   —The Late Mr John Grant Thomson—Mr John Methven   244

Proceedings of the Royal Scottish Arboricultural Society, 1913,
   with Appendices.

List of Members as at 24th June 1913.

TRANSACTIONS

OF THE

ROYAL SCOTTISH ARBORICULTURAL SOCIETY.

16. Discussion on the Relation of Forestry to Agriculture and other Industries.

At the Annual General Meeting of the Society on 17th February, a discussion on the "Relation of Forestry to Agriculture and other Industries" was held in place of a formal address.

In opening the discussion, Mr Sydney J. Gammell of Drumtochty said:—"Mr Chairman and gentlemen, I trust that the members will not look upon this as a formal paper prepared to be read at a Philosophical Society, but as just the commencement of a discussion in which I hope a very large number of the members of the Society present will take part. This is a very large subject, and one which, I think, needs attention drawn to it, and I am very much flattered at being allowed to open the discussion and to make a public statement on a subject which I consider is important, and which at all events requires looking into. Now I do not think I need bother you by going into the various climatic conditions which are affected by the planting of trees. I wish to come at once to close grips with this subject, and to show how agriculture in particular is affected by the planting of woods themselves, and that various industries are created and an increased amount of labour is necessitated by the planting of these woods. This subject has been enlarged since it was first suggested in the Council, and has been made to include other industries as well as agriculture. I hope some other members will take up those other industries, as I intend to confine myself to the one question. Now, in order to get to that question we have first to ask ourselves what is the object of afforestation? I think I may put it shortly in this way—to utilise land which is at present either unutilised, or is not utilised to the best advantage. I wish, in the first place, to disabuse

people's minds entirely of the idea that land which is being now
profitably employed is to be taken from the present occupiers
and used for the purposes of forestry. . Nothing is further, I am
sure, from the idea of those who are guiding the destinies of
forestry in this country, and nothing is further from the views of
those who understand the subject. In the first place, let us take
the subject of agricultural land. There is no intention, and I
think it would be extremely unwise, from every point of view, to
take land which can be profitably employed in agriculture and
use it for the purposes of forestry. You do not get as large a
return from your land, and you do not get as much labour
employed upon your land, and these are the two points—the two
cardinal points—which must be kept firmly in view in the
discussion of this subject. But there is a great deal of land in
this country, some of it cultivated, some of it grazed, some of it
used for sport, some of it not used at all, which could very
profitably be employed, I maintain, for the purposes of silviculture, and it is to that land, and to that land alone, that we
must look for the enlargement of our forests.

"I will take the various classes which I have mentioned in order,
beginning with land which is at present under tillage, but not
under profitable tillage. I am sure every one in this room knows
the class of land to which I am referring. Part of it was taken in
when agriculture, for one reason or another, was in a more
profitable state than it is at present, and when larger returns
were got from the growing of crops. Some of that land at anyrate cannot be profitably cultivated now, and there are considerable areas of it. But it is not all of the same class. I think I
am right in saying that a good deal of it, if you take it in large
stretches, consists of portions of bad land and portions of good
land. Now it is one of the great points with regard to this
question of forestry that not only can you take the bad land—I
mean bad agriculturally—and use it for forestry to better
advantage than it is at present used for tillage, but you are not
obliged to plant up the small pockets of good land which occur
at varying distances through this bad land. Those can be
cultivated, and when properly sheltered by trees they can be
cultivated to considerably greater advantage than at present.
At present the question of shelter, the question of separat-
ing good land from bad, especially on the higher lands—
because most of the land I am speaking of is at higher

altitudes than the good agricultural land which we know in the best agricultural districts—lies at the root of this question of profitable occupation and tillage.

"Now let me go a little further, and take next the land which is at present grazed, and from that point of view I think we may look at it and see, in the first place, whether the occupation of land for grazing is more or less profitable on the whole than its use for the purpose of growing timber-trees; and, secondly, whether land under pasture employs more or less labour than land used under forest. This labour question is one of the most important. I seem to be reiterating it over and over again, but, believe me, it is one of the points which we must not allow to slip. We must keep it continually before our eyes when we are looking at this question. Now, of course, there are good grazing lands and there are bad. The grazing lands with which I personally have anything to do, and, of course, one can best speak with regard to one's individual experience, I find, do not bring in by any means high rents per acre. I do not think I should be understating it if I said that the average rental of hill grazing suitable for planting in the north-east of Scotland was not above a shilling per acre. Now surely we can make a profit of more than a shilling an acre from trees. As far as I have been able to go into the question, the resultant rental per acre for land of that class, judging from what could be and what has been grown in the past upon it, amounts to at anyrate four or five times that sum. You have therefore got the question of the better use of land which is at present not being utilised to the best advantage, and which I think I am right in maintaining can be utilised to better advantage.

"Then comes the question of labour. Forestry certainly employs considerably more labour than grazing. At what do you put the labour employed in grazing even if you add the temporary labour employed for shooting and subsidiary purposes? It does not amount to more than two or three persons at the outside per thousand acres. The average wages paid in the State Prussian forests is given in their return at about 11s. 4d. per acre per annum. I think in this country we can safely say that a forest under continuous conditions can absorb a supply of labour equalling a payment of about 10s. or so per acre per annum. From both points of view which is most profitable to the country? In the first place, you have at present, in certain instances at anyrate, capital being used in an unprofitable way.

That I would point out to you is not only an individual loss, it is also a national loss. We are not using our capital to increase the wealth of the country. We are not really producing anything; we are living upon our capital, and in that way depleting the wealth of the country, and using up the sources of the future development which we hope to see; and, further, we are not utilising the same amount of labour that we might do with regard to many of those waste places.

" From those two points of view I think we may look forward to an increase of our forest area which will certainly not be in any way detrimental to the agricultural interest. Not only will it not be detrimental, but it will be positively helpful, particularly to the outlying districts, in which this help will be greater than in those which are now more closely occupied. The great beauty of the relations which may exist, and I hope will exist, in this country between agriculture and forestry is the way in which the one will dovetail into the other, and the way in which the labour which is now not fully occupied upon agricultural land can be used profitably in the forest, and for which good wages can be paid. I refer particularly to the much vexed question that has been put forward before us so frequently, the question of small holdings. To my way of thinking forestry is the one way of solving this difficulty. You cannot put small holdings down in the country, in any portion of it with which I am acquainted, unless they are of such a size that they can no longer be called small, or, on the other hand, unless you provide labour to eke out the products of the holdings themselves. Now in this way forestry comes to our help. We can have, and would be glad to have, a great multiplication of these small holdings, because we (I am speaking now as a forester), in the first place, require the labour of the occupants, and they, on the other hand, require the wages which we give them.

" I can give you a personal experience with regard to this. I have a certain amount of land which is some distance from the sources of supply of labour. I tried in every way to get labourers to walk for two or two and a half miles to work for me in the woods. They did not like doing it, especially in the winter time, and I did not like it either, because they wasted half the day coming and going. I took a farm which happened to fall vacant—it was not a big one—and I split it and made it into two small holdings of about 10 acres each, crofts as we call them, though we have no crofters in the strict sense, as I am speaking of Aberdeenshire and Kincardineshire. I let these with the idea of utilising the labour in my woods. I have never regretted what I did. Although in itself it was not a profitable undertaking, because the capital expenditure was somewhat large, I maintain that in the long run even that capital expenditure will come back, and the tenants have not, I think, regretted having taken the crofts. I know perfectly well that they have improved their position ever since they came there, and it is simply because they are in the happy position of having work to do and wages to gain in the time when there is no work upon their holdings. I, on the other hand, am gaining because I get my workmen kept on the place, and I get the work done which I have undertaken. That I look to as one of the ways, I might almost say the main way, in which forestry is going to be beneficial to agriculture. Most of the forestry work, I need hardly say to such an audience as this, takes place in the winter time, when the work on the crofts or small holdings, or you may say almost on any farm, is more or less at a standstill. It is more, however, at a standstill upon small holdings than upon a farm. The amount of tillage to be done is small, and the amount of stock to be looked after small. The chief work of the small holder—I am speaking of holdings of 5 to 12 acres—is to get his crop put in, and that is only a matter of a few days, hours sometimes, while the tending of his stock is only a matter of a few minutes per day, and can often be done by his wife; therefore the work is spasmodic and not continuous, at anyrate in the winter time. Now the work in the woods is very largely wanted at that time, and for that reason they fit so well, the one works into the other, so that in every way they are profitable the one to the other.

"But let me go a little further. There is the question of subsidiary employment, there is the whole question of transport, the whole question of minor industries which spring from a forest being instituted in any particular place. One of the great difficulties in connection with small holdings considerably removed from larger neighbours is the question of tillage. Tillage requires the keeping of a horse or a stot, which latter I wonder is not more utilised by some as a means of cultivating the ground. One or two may club together and keep a horse between them. If some amount of haulage is required by the forest you will see how very much easier it is for those people to keep a horse profitably. The whole point which I wish to bring before you is that we must look at these matters from the point of view of things being profitably employed. It is no use keeping a horse at a loss; it is no use cultivating crops at a loss. What we want to do is to cultivate the ground so that it may be a profit to everybody concerned. Looking to the subsidiary industries which are bound to grow up, I do not hesitate to say that it can be so arranged that agriculture can be helped, and helped in no small degree, by the forestry which we hope will become one of the largest industries in this country.

"I do not wish to take up your time much longer because there are many others here who are equally well qualified to speak on this important subject. There is only one thing I would like to say and it is this—we must have forestry, in order to be profitable, in order to institute small holdings, in order to re-people many parts which are now too sparsely inhabited, we must have forestry upon a definite basis, we must have it continuous. I have heard it said in certain places that in very many of the planting operations a great deal of the labour employed was local, but notwithstanding this the population has gone down and that people are emigrating, people are going away—how are you therefore going to improve matters by forestry? I do not think that is the case where there has been a continuous system of forestry carried on not for five or ten years, but under a definite scheme which is intended to last for all time. That is what we want to see, and that is what we must have. The labour does not only take place in the planting; labour is wanted in the thinning, labour is wanted in the felling, and in the transport in the future. If you have a continuous scheme there will not be the complaint that people go away. They will look to the future and the wages that will some day come to them from labour in another form, while the crop is maturing. I do not think that it is going too far to say that the experiment has never been thoroughly tried in this country. We hope to see it tried, and I put it before you to-day as a reason why we should go forward.

"I have put a few things before you to show, as far as I can, that so far as I can see, so far from being hindersome, forestry will be helpful to agriculture. That is my belief, and that I believe is the wish of many people here. I put the matter before you to-day, and I would only ask in having opened this discussion, that the objections, and there must be objections, should be plainly stated now so that they may be dealt with. We do not want to have the whole thing on one side. I have opened the discussion, and I hope some one will take up the other side of this question in order that we may have a full and free discussion, and that we may show everybody what we consider is the best line to take with regard to this important subject."

Mr A. T. Gillanders, F.E.S., said :—" I would like to speak on one point, namely, planting shelter for stock. I do not wish to criticise the opinions and methods of anyone, but to give a candid expression of my own views. As regards shelter I am strongly in favour of it, because I believe that the future of this country is to a large extent as a stock country and therefore shelter is imperative. . But the relation of shelter-belt planting to correct forestry and the details of management are more complicated problems than appear on the surface. Hence my two points are—(1) the relation of shelter planting to good forestry, and (2) methods of management as regards the relation to forestry. Let us ask ourselves what is correct forestry ? To my mind good forestry is a continuity of some fixed method or system of cutting and planting according to the merits of each particular case, together with such elasticity as may adapt itself to unforeseen contingencies, as wind blows, etc. If the forester is to do good work he should know where cutting and planting are to take place five years hence, and so make every necessary preparation for the future. It is also the duty of the owner to acquiesce either in the opinions of his own forester or to solicit such practical advice as may confirm or amend his forester's views. In other words, having regard to contemporary thought, let the owner make sure that his forester is not an extreme faddist, because there are faddists even among foresters. Having thus settled a system, and feeling disposed to plant shelter from an agricultural point of view, the planting of such shelter should be carried out either as an 'extra,' or with such modifications as will not too far upset the present or prospective forestry of the estate. I venture to assert that this is a strong point, because shelter-belt forestry, as a general rule, will not pay from a commercial timber point of view. Hence the prospective letting value of the land must be carefully considered on the merits of each particular case. In other words, as regards economic management,

it is a doubtful point if shelter-belt planting should not
be entirely debited to 'improvements' and not to 'woods,'
because in the majority of cases the position precludes profitable
working. However, as this is a question of estate finance
outside the decision of the forester, I repeat my assertion that
coming as I do from a large stock country, I believe in the
principle of shelter planting.

"And now for my second point as regards methods. I
should say that in hilly countries of large areas the belts
should be of fair size, and not less than three or four chains
in width, and in length and shape according to the prevailing
winds, local storms, etc. And where one belt does not meet
the case, having regard to sheep 'raikes,' they may be in
groups overlapping and interlocking with each other so as to
give the maximum of unbroken shelter. As regards land more
valuable than hill land, very much narrower strips would, if
planted with the proper species, have a beneficial influence on
stock. As regards position and altitude opinions will obviously
differ; but my own opinion is that no fixed rule can be laid
down. The two questions to be considered are how to get the
maximum advantage with the minimum cost, and whether there
is a reasonable prospect of the natural pasture being amenable
to improvement or good enough to justify expenditure.

" In some cases the top of the hill may form a good position
for sheltering trees; in other cases it may be entirely unsuitable, as to plant on the summit of a hill where the land
is very poor is to court disaster from blown trees. While
the forester naturally covets good soil as a means of securing
success, the conditions of the case suggest a medium altitude,
always beginning with nature's shelter and then gradually increasing the good influences of shelter to the advantage of the
flockmaster. I would like to remark that in Belgium the bottom
of the hill, or some place with natural shelter, is always chosen
as a starting-point, and planting is then gradually continued
upwards from the established shelter. I have no wish to push
the idea that Belgian forestry is parallel with our shelter
planting. But even for the latter there is to my mind no harm
in reminding ourselves that it is far better to try to work
with nature rather than to attempt to fight her. In further
emphasis of this statement, let us remember that the conditions which exist in our hilly countries are such that the

soil varies greatly even within small areas. Thus an area of say 2 acres, may give good results on one half and utterly refuse to produce a single tree on the other half. Hence the need for giving great attention to the special characters of each area. As regards species for planting I would, as a general rule, suggest coniferous trees, though in some cases alder and birch would give good results. The coniferous trees I would suggest are white American spruce in large quantity, Sitka spruce, *Pinus uncinata* and *Pinus montana*, as an extreme outer fringe. I would not like to forget our own Scots pine, but black game and snow are against it; so that the species of spruce referred to might be better in many cases. The above brief notes apply to hill planting for shelter purely from a forester's point of view. I know full well that shelter-belt planting at fairly high altitudes on poor soil, and often with very doubtful prospects of success, is not a congenial enterprise to a forester. At the same time, the sister science of agriculture does often require his best skill and experience so that the improvement of the property, through the medium of his profession in all its diversified aspects, should ever be before him."

Mr John F. Annand, Armstrong College, Newcastle-on-Tyne, said:—"I may say that I was very much interested in Mr Gammell's speech, and I quite agree with practically everything that he said. Mr Gammell has ably treated the matter from the forester's or the timber-grower's point of view. At the same time we must look at the question, perhaps, from the farmer's standpoint as well as the forester's. Naturally it is in the growth of timber that we, as foresters, are specially interested. Unfortunately for us the farmer does not look at the matter from that point of view at all. The farmer, nevertheless, has a very big interest in forestry, inasmuch as the shelter derived from the woodlands surrounding his farm is very valuable not only to his stock, but it increases the yield of grass and field crops generally. I think farmers generally agree that this is so. But I doubt very much if we have ever had any actual experiments to show the full effects of shelter. I doubt if the results have ever been reduced to figures, that is to say, I think there is really need for systematic experiments on the actual effects and results of the shelter provided by woods. This is of very great direct interest to the stock-breeder, especially to the man who

winters his young cattle, as he very often does in the north of
England, in the open. It has become more and more apparent
to the farmer that if healthy cows for the supply of milk for
the large towns are to be reared, badly ventilated, overheated
byres do not constitute the best nursery for heifer calves and
young stock generally. It has been proved by experiments, on
a small scale at anyrate, that in the case of certain breeds (for
example, Galloways), with equivalent supplies of food, the actual
gain in live weight per head is greater in out-wintered young cattle
than in box or stall-fed ones, where there are plenty of shelter
woods for the pasture fields. Under such circumstances the stock
very seldom avail themselves of shelter sheds, and prefer to lie
out in the open fields. I think that this is a very important
matter—well worthy both of the attention and help of the
forester. I think it is generally admitted that tuberculosis
is of much rarer occurrence in cattle reared in the open than
with those animals reared under the 'coddling' system in often
very badly ventilated byres.

"'Selection' woods would probably solve the problem best
because they make for continuity of shelter. In those instances
where we cannot have 'selection' woods then we must periodically lay down new shelter-belts as occasion requires. I was
very much struck, in reading an old newspaper cutting from the
Scotsman which I came across the other day, with what Mr Elliot
of Clifton Park had to say about the effects of shelter. With your
permission I will read a very short extract from it. Mr Elliot
says that there is a proverbial saying amongst farmers that
'shelter is half meat'—that is to say that not only do you
get more grass within the influence of shelter but less pasture is
required because you have got warmer conditions for the stock.

"'It has been very partially recognised that the influence of
the shelter-belts of wood on crops, as well as on the growth and
especially the maintenance of grass in dry seasons, is of great
importance. It is most interesting to observe the decline or increase of grass as it is further away from or nearer to shelter.
In the case of a wind-swept haugh (flat) I lately measured the
height of the grasses, and they gradually, as regards their seeding
stems, fell from 6 feet in height to 5 ft. 8 ins. in the middle,
and 4 ft. 10 ins. at a distance of 70 yards from the shelter,
which consisted of a stone wall about 5 feet high. Two sides of
the shelter square were sheltered by the stone wall, the remaining

two sides (the ones most distant from the prevailing wind) being fenced with wire. The blades of the grass would be about one foot less than the seeding stems. The square was enclosed from a 2-year-old pasture, and was planted two years ago. The predominant grasses were those used in my mixture for this farm—tall-fescue, tall-oat-grass, and Cock's-foot. The bottom grass towards the sheltered end was, of course, much thicker than that at the unsheltered end of the enclosure. . . . If this amount of difference is perceptible with such a moderate degree of shelter, we can imagine what a difference would be made in production if shelter belts of trees became general. Their climatic effect as regards heat is far greater than one might be inclined to suppose, and I have been repeatedly struck with the very perceptible increase of warmth when passing into a zone under the influence of shelter-belts.'

"Then he goes on to say that the pasture within the shelter itself was very much better and richer than that outside the shelter. Very rightly he points out that if these results can be got with the very small amount of shelter accruing from a stone wall, you may expect to get very much better results on a large scale from having large and well laid out belts of shelter woods.

"At the present time, under the English Small Holdings Act, if County Authorities purchase areas of land for small holdings, which include woodlands, they have no power to deal with the latter as such. The ground must be devoted solely to small holdings. The trees must either be grubbed up and the ground reclaimed for tillage, or the woodlands will degenerate into poor, unprofitable pastures. Scotland may not be affected in the same way, but in England, if the system is not modified, much detached woodland in farming districts must ultimately disappear in this way, much to the detriment of the climate of the districts concerned and of the country generally."

Mr Scott Elliot said :—"There is no question whatever about the excellent effect of a shelter wood. Whether it is tree or grass, you favour the growth of that tree or that grass. I may mention a particular property in Wigtownshire where the proprietor 120 years ago planted a fringe of woods. It is the case that Wigtownshire is a particularly windy place. The trees on the outside edge never grew properly and were of a miserable character. If you go to this particular spot you can see the plantation on the hillside, which did not exactly go to the edge, but to within 200 or 300 yards of it. On that particular side the land was never touched, with the result that it is certainly not worth more than 2s. or 3s. per acre, while the grass within the sheltered area is worth £1 or 17s. per acre. I went over the ground and made every possible examination of it, and to my knowledge the result I have mentioned is due to the cumulative effect of this shelter acting for 120 years, and also what is a more important fact, that since you got the pasture up to a certain level of excellence you could feed upon it beasts supplied with cake and other artificial food, which improved the soil.

"There is one point I want to bring before the meeting, and it is this. I do not think that any of you who have not, as I have, tried to find your way along the boundary of Roxburgh and Dumfriesshire can have the very faintest conception of the amount of ground, in the south of Scotland especially, that is capable of cultivation. There are hundreds of thousands of acres in that part of Scotland running right across the hill country from the west of Wigtownshire and Ayrshire, right across the whole of Galloway, through Dumfriesshire and Roxburgh, and through the Lammermoors and the whole of that enormous district, land which certainly on the average is not rented at more than 2s. or 2s. 6d. per acre, and I do not suppose that this generation, or the generation that follows this generation, will ever manage to make a perceptible impression in the way of planting that enormous area. Still I do think that anybody to-day who begins in a small way to make an impression upon that enormous area, every man who is connected with this industry in any way whatever, is a public benefactor, and as soon as the British public begin to realise what it would mean to have the whole of this area covered with wood producing something like 6s. or 7s. per acre in the year, instead of something between 1s. 6d. and 2s. 6d., the encouragement from the public will be prompt and thorough; and as I think I could show, if I had time, there is at present even a perfectly good business reason for the promotion of forestry in Scotland. I do think that anybody nowadays who interests himself in a very small way in the protection and development of forestry is doing what is earnestly required and is really beginning a very great work which perhaps the great-grandchildren of the present generation will appreciate."

Mr J. H. Milne-Home, Canonbie, said:—"I was exceedingly interested to hear what Mr Gammell has said, especially the figures which he gave regarding the amount of labour which can be employed per acre in forestry work. I have worked out to some extent similar figures, and putting them side by side with those of Mr Gammell, they give almost identical results. 10s. to 12s. an acre is by no means an excessive amount to pay for labour in woods that are even moderately stocked. I include in this sum all ordinary work, fencing, draining, felling and hauling timber, planting, cleaning plants, nursery work, etc. I do not include the labour employed in the manufacture of timber after it reaches the railway or the saw-mill. That would add very largely to the bill.

"I think there is another point we should also try to keep in mind relating to this question so far as agriculture is concerned. The enthusiastic forester is very apt to want to plant any piece of ground he sees. I confess to having made a mistake in that direction myself. But you have also to look at the question from the farmer's point of view and the national point of view. I hope that in any large scheme that is pushed, either by County Councils or by the Board of Agriculture, every possible endeavour will be made to see that only land which is most suitable in the way of giving the largest increased return will be taken. You have land in the south of Scotland which is at present let for sheep grazing at a rate of from 2s. to 5s. per acre. It would be a very great pity, if the 2s. land is worth as much for afforestation as the 5s. land, to take anything but the former, for the reason that the 5s. land is producing more meat and wool at the present time than the lower-rented subject. What we want to get at is to make the country produce the greatest amount of wealth upon the land that we can, whether it is agricultural produce or whether it is timber. By taking the worst agricultural land you do least harm to the farmer and you decrease to the least possible extent the produce of food from that particular area. There is another thing which I think is often lost sight of. There is a great deal of land in the south of Scotland, in that area to which Mr Scott Elliot has referred, which is capable of being made into very fair second-class arable land. It is being let at present at 3s. or 4s. per acre. It is not steep, it is not very high, perhaps 400 feet to 600 feet above the level of the sea, but it requires buildings and fences, tile drainage, and the stones removed. You could, I think, make that land into fair second-class arable land, and you could possibly get a rent of 12s. per acre for it eventually. But you can only do this after a very large expenditure, of not less than £12 or £15 per acre, and it is very doubtful whether that money would be profitably spent unless it was obtainable at something like 2½ or 3 per cent. If you had to pay 5 per cent. it would not be possible to get an economic rent for that land, and I am inclined to think that such land would, in most cases, be better planted than turned into agricultural land, because the amount of capital you require to make it produce a gross return of say 30s. to 40s. per acre, which I think is not an unreasonable return for forestry, is very much less than the capital required to make it produce say £3 or £4 an acre from agriculture. In one case you have an initial capital outlay of £15, and in the other an initial capital outlay of about £4. From a national and an economic point of view it is desirable that at least a part of that class of land should be planted. There are some people who consider that it ought to be turned into agricultural land, and this might be done to some extent, but I think it would be a mistake if too much of such land were withheld from forestry, for which it is well suited."

Mr Gordon said :—" I was very interested to hear Mr Gammell take the view that the question of labour was of essential importance when considering the relation of forestry to agriculture. Personally I am of the opinion that a scheme of afforestation must in any country form the backbone of an economic system of small holdings, because of the amount and nature of the labour it supplies.

"We have many concrete examples of an almost ideal relationship existing between forest and croft-land in many parts of the continent of Europe. The crofter may be employed in the forest for six to eight months, and in such districts about half the total population may be largely dependent on the forest. The conditions of this employment are very favourable, since the crofters are in no way bound by contract with the forest authority, and are therefore able to give their holdings all the attention they require.

"Irrespective of the labour employed actually in forest operations there are other forms of labour which specially suit the small holder. For example, many of the crofters having perhaps two yoke of cows or oxen set up as small contractors, and find constant employment either in dragging timber in the forest or in transporting it to the nearest railway or waterway. The rearing of draught animals, principally cows and oxen, forms an important part of the business of the small holder in such regions.

"In addition, the forest industries of those districts, *e.g.* sawmilling, furniture-making, paper-pulp manufacturing, etc., absorb the labour not required for the forest and croft-land. Thus, that section of the community which in Scotland has either to emigrate or come into the large centres, is kept on the land. As a rule this section consists of the younger and more energetic members, who with riper experience invariably take up small plots of land, or return to the land altogether."

Mr H. M. Cadell of Grange, Bo'ness, said:—"There is one other aspect of the question which you might excuse me for calling attention to. It is not quite forestry, but it has got to do with forestry and agriculture, and there are a number of people here connected with the land. I have been looking into the question of the utilisation of peat mosses. There are a number of very good sites covered up with peat. A noble lord, who knew all about that in 1766, reclaimed 1800 acres of the Forth. I have written a book on the subject which will be published next week, and I have put forward a suggestion in that book. After making considerable inquiries into the subject, I find that one ton of peat contains 5s. worth of sulphate of ammonia. I had a sample examined by Messrs James Ross & Son, Philipstoun, and it was found that it contained 80 per cent. of water, but once the water is extracted the peat is three times as valuable as oil shale. It contains sulphate of ammonia, paraffin, coke, petrol, and in fact everything that ministers to human existence. Now there are a great many peat mosses in the country which might be cleared off, including the mosses of the Forth, and these mosses once cleared would produce splendid soil for forestry. There are about 2000 acres of mosses in the Forth, and these are far too good for forestry. But there are 10, 15, or 20 feet of moss which can be cleared off, and you could get that ground for 1s. an acre, making a profit in the clearing, and then you get the estate for planting trees for nothing.

That is an original idea which has suggested itself to me after considering the whole matter, and I just put it forward to the members of this Society as an important suggestion. At the present moment it just happens that this is an extremely opportune time, when the Government is going in for oil of high-flash point such as can be got by the distillation of peat just as well as from oil shale. So that you get a fortune by the peat once you get the water out of it, and you get the land under it for nothing. There are plenty of old lochs in the country which have been silted up over the edges, and the bottom of these lochs is not made up of mud, but it is made up of rich alluvial soil. There is an endless amount of possibilities for members of the Society who are interested in the growth of trees. It might be worth while for the Society to cultivate peat mosses. There is another point, and Mr Gammell stated that it was very important, and so it is, to have a local industry which gives employment to people in the summer time. Well, the cutting of these peats and the preparing of them for the retorts is the very thing they want. In the winter time they could not work at it because the peats are wet. This is one of those local industries which ought to be encouraged."

Mr George Leven, Bowmont Forest, Kelso, said :—" There is certainly need to deal with the point of shelter. Coming as I do from a part of the country that is naturally bare and exposed, the part that Mr Scott Elliot and Mr Milne-Home have referred to already, I know something of the benefit of shelter-belts. If you were to pass through a part of the Cheviot country at this moment you would see all the shepherds busy erecting bields. These, as a rule, are artificial, but where there is an abundance of sheltering belts of trees they are not required. The fact has also been referred to that shelter is half meat, and certainly in Mr Elliot's country of Clifton Park it has proved to be the case, because the local shelter they have provided by plantation has been the means of improving the grass and also of improving the stock. Mr Gammell also referred to small holdings. As has been shown, we find that small landholders require a certain amount of employment to fill in their time when they are not required on the holdings. While one class of small holder may be able to enter a holding that would occupy their full time, there are others who are quite prepared to take over a holding that would render it necessary to provide a certain amount of additional labour in order to fill in all the time they have at their disposal. I submit that unless the needs of this particular class are provided for, small holdings would not be possible unless all the small holders are placed in a position to find occupation to fill in all the time they have on their hands. There is another thing that ought to be borne in mind, and that is fruit-growing. We see, year by year, in the Blairgowrie and in other districts where strawberries and raspberries and small fruits are grown, that they have to introduce outside labour to a great extent. Some may say that it is a very desirable thing that people should be taken from the cities in this way and a healthy occupation given to them, but I also say these people ought never to have been in the town. Let us provide employment for them so that they may never have to leave their native glen. It has given me very great pleasure to listen to the ideas Mr Gammell has so ably propounded, and I think a great many of the points he has mentioned ought to be elaborated upon and impressed upon people, because I think there is a certain amount of prejudice throughout the country that requires to be removed. I know quite a number of farmers who are quite ready to admit that shelter is a very good thing—that it improves the stock and improves the crop—but they complain that on account of these very shelter belts they are unable to get their corn into the stack. I think that is one point which the forester should always bear in mind when he is preparing a shelter belt, that he should allow the sun at least to get scope for the purpose of ripening the crops. I have no doubt that if these little points are kept in mind they will tend a great deal to remove any prejudices that do exist.

Mr Gilbert Brown said:—" I have listened with very great interest to what has been said regarding the question under discussion. So much has been said not only to-day but for the past few years, and those who have spoken have dealt so fully with the subject that there is really nothing new to bring up. If I may be allowed, I will confine my few remarks to various conversations I have had with different farming men throughout the north of Scotland on this question of forestry. It has been hinted that in some agricultural communities forestry is viewed with some little aversion, but I must say, and I have talked the matter over with men in all grades of the farming world, I have found very little of this; in fact I have only found one real case of objection, and that was a sheep owner who had 7000 acres of grazing land, and was afraid that this would be entirely taken away. I explained to him that planting would not be carried out indiscriminately, but would be under a proper system, and that no large area belonging to one person would be taken and planted in one block, but would be divided into compartments and spread over a series of years. He considered that planting on that line would not affect existing conditions to any great extent.

"In so far as small land-holders are concerned I have not found one against any scheme of forestry; on the contrary, they say that forestry should go hand in hand with agriculture. I may say that I mentioned the fact to the Coast Erosion Commission who took some evidence in forestry some years ago, that on estates in the north of Scotland where numbers of crofters are employed in the woods department throughout the year, that these men say, and say emphatically, that the work they got in the woods helped them to lead comfortable lives, and that if it were not for this work they could not exist on their holdings. These men were so emphatic on this point five or six years ago that I feel sure they would be so still.

"In districts which are more or less treeless, the farmers have got it into their heads that a certain amount of tree planting would be beneficial to the district in general. I was asked the other day if I thought that it would be long before a planting scheme would begin. I replied that I did not think so. They appeared well pleased, and I was glad, therefore, that I told them such, even although I did so at the risk of telling a falsehood; but my conscience has been considerably eased since I heard Mr Sutherland's statement.

"It is really believed that woods have a greater effect in influencing the fertility of arable land than they get credit for. Many a farm in the higher lands of Scotland would not be worth cultivating if it were not for the shelter afforded from belts, strips and woods in the immediate vicinity. Evidence of this is not altogether wanting, crops growing well in a wooded part, while on soil at the same altitude, and of more or less the same nature, but in a treeless district, they are decidedly not so good, especially from a grain point of view.

"In some estates where the woods are, after a certain age, given over to the tenants for grazing and shelter for their farm stock for the payment of a small yearly rent, there is a great clamouring for this, even for a small corner, just for the shelter alone. I admit after a while they become lukewarm, and sometimes forget to pay any rent, but this is only in rare cases, and one has only to mention that the wood will be closed against farm stock to cause a fearful wail.

" I only mention these facts to show the general opinion held with regard to forestry, and this being more or less favourable there is no need to question the desirability of going on with any scheme."

Dr Borthwick said :—"There is no doubt in our minds that agriculture, whether it is practised on the large farm or small holding, can be more successfully carried out in connection with afforestation. In the highlands of Europe, wherever grazing lands exist, it has been found that a certain amount of protection forest is absolutely necessary to preserve the grazing area. Experience has shown that the destruction of the forest cover on those high grazing grounds has invariably led to the total destruction of the grazing lands themselves, and, unfortunately, the matter did not end there, but much damage was also done to the lower and more fertile lands through which the main rivers flow, on account of the liability of those rivers to become suddenly flooded. Very stringent laws are now in force regarding the maintenance of a proper balance between the area of protection forest and grazing land.

" We, in this country, have not seen the vast changes which undoubtedly must have occurred when the natural forest which clothed our hills was destroyed, but we have abundant examples in Southern France, Switzerland, the Tyrol, and also in America that wherever high grazing land exists a sufficient amount of forest cover is necessary for its preservation. My point is that in those countries it has been demonstrated beyond all doubt that, wherever the forest cover has been destroyed through ignorance or avarice, inestimable damage has been done to agricultural lands. If we wish to improve our present agricultural lands, and to extend their area, we must of necessity restore the balance which nature demands by re-establishing the forests which were destroyed in earlier times. If this were done, then great advantages would directly and indirectly follow to agricultural communities in the higher and lower ground, due to the beneficial climatic effect of the forests. That 'forests increase the rainfall' is a statement one frequently hears, and the fear is often expressed that if we were to extend the afforestation area we would make the country wetter. There is no need for that fear. It has not been definitely proved that afforestation increases the rainfall. It has, however, been definitely proved that afforestation regulates the drainage, it prevents excessive and destructive floods that damage the soil of crofts and farms on the low ground, while it improves the conditions for grazing in the higher ground. We are all of one mind in regard to the beneficial influence of shelter belts and the necessity for their establishment and maintenance on all well-cultivated farms in this country and elsewhere. We are all quite aware that on the prairie in Canada the value of forest shelter belts is well recognised, and, accordingly, efforts are being made to plant trees, and to form wood lots along with the farms. Of course we realise that the conditions are different in Canada from what they are in this country, but the guiding principles are practically the same.

" If we take a general survey of Europe and America, we find it has been proved in the past that afforestation in combination with agriculture improves the agricultural conditions. Canada and other progressive Colonies are rapidly going in for afforestation in connection with farming. Although we may have taken up the question late, still, it is better late than never.

"Mr Gammell invited criticism. He asked for arguments against the views he brought forward in opening this discussion, but he well knew that each statement he made was really an obvious truth, an axiom, and in my opinion it is not possible to bring sound arguments against what he said."

Mr A. D. Richardson, Edinburgh, said:—" There are just one or two points that I wish to refer to in connection with the discussion. Mr Scott Elliot and Mr Milne-Home have referred to land in the south of Scotland in Roxburghshire and Dumfriesshire. I have often wondered why more attention had not been paid to that tract as a field for afforestation. I think it is a magnificent field for afforestation. I think that Mr Milne-Home was right when he said that that land could probably be brought into agricultural condition, and could be made second-class arable land. But the expense of doing that would be enormous. I think what he says is true that it would be far better if it were put under timber. There are enormous tracts of land, all pretty low-lying land. I do not think that any of it will go more than 1000 feet above sea-level. I do not know the highest point in the Cheviot range, but I think most of it is below 1200 feet. There are no altitude difficulties. It is a part of the country which could be easily got at by means of railways and other means of transportation. That has not been very much referred to, but this part of the country is a field for forestry. I think it is one of the principal parts of Scotland from that point of view. Mr Leven referred to allotments and fruit-farming, and in connection with fruit-farming he alluded to the numbers of people who have to be taken to the fruit farms about Blairgowrie at a certain time of the year. It is very difficult to get sufficient people for that purpose. These people are only employed for a certain time, during the period that the fruit picking is on. It shows that there is a want of balance somewhere—that there should be something else to keep those people on the land at other times of the year. I think that forestry and farming, including fruit-farming and market-gardening, ought to go hand in hand, where they can possibly work together. It would be found, if that could be managed, that there would be sufficient employment for all classes, and plenty of people would be kept on the ground instead of being driven into the towns. With regard to high-class farming, I do not think forestry has very much to do with it. I think that high-class farming can only be carried on profitably as an economic thing in the better parts of the country, and probably on the outskirts of large cities. So far as forestry goes in connection with farming of that sort, I do not think forestry enters into it at all. I think what is wanted there is shelter belts. Now I do not think that shelter belts have anything to do with forestry at all. Shelter belts are merely for a certain purpose, and the trees are not intended to be—if they were grown as timber trees there would be no use for shelter. Mr Leven referred to another point in connection with those shelter belts. He said that farmers had protested against them, as in certain cases they prevented the crops getting the sun and thus prevented them from ripening. I think great mistakes have been made in laying out these shelter belts by running them east and west, and it is rather detrimental to growing crops when these belts do shut off the sun from them. A market-gardener or fruit-grower when he lays down fruit trees should run them north and south, so that his crops may get the full benefit of the sun. If shelter belts were run north and south there would be less objection to them. The haphazard way in which they have been laid down has created the prejudice against them among the farming class."

Mr William Dawson, Marischal College, Aberdeen, said :— " There are too many points to be touched upon in the discussion. The discussion was so well opened by Mr Gammell, who brought forward the chief economic views on forestry in such a clear way, that the rest was merely supplementary. I ask you to accord a hearty vote of thanks to Mr Gammell who has put himself to so much trouble in order to place the facts before us."

The Chairman—" I propose to give myself the pleasure of proposing a hearty vote of thanks to the other speakers. We have listened to some extremely interesting contributions to this discussion, and I am quite sure that when they are collected and printed—we have taken the precaution to have a verbatim report of every word that has been said—they will form a most interesting article for the pages of the *Transactions*. I wish you to give a hearty vote of thanks to the other speakers."

Mr Spiers—" I have very much pleasure in asking the meeting to accord a hearty vote of thanks to Captain Stirling of Keir for his conduct in the chair."

The Chairman—" I thank you very much for your kindness."

17. Letter to the Board of Agriculture for Scotland.

The following letter has been addressed by the President to the Chairman of the Board of Agriculture for Scotland :—

To the Chairman of the
Board of Agriculture for Scotland.

Sir,—The Council of the Royal Scottish Arboricultural Society observe with regret that another financial year has come to a close without any proposal for a considerable scheme of afforestation having been brought before the Development Commissioners. We do not for a moment suppose or suggest that a large scheme could have been matured in the time that has elapsed since the creation of the Board of Agriculture for Scotland; but it is, in our view, a matter for great regret, now that Scotland possesses a Public Department with special duties towards all rural industries, that no steps have been taken towards a great expansion of that rural industry, which is capable of its greatest development in those districts where employment is most needed by the people. The following answer to a question put by the Right Hon. R. Munro-Ferguson, M.P., in the House of Commons, deserves to be quoted at length :—

Mr Munro-Ferguson's Question No. 12.
Answered by Mr Robertson.

The advances from the Development Fund sanctioned for forestry purposes are—England and Wales, £18,435; Scotland, £11,150; Ireland, £28,050. The actual amounts issued from the Fund to date are £1800, £198 and £5365, respectively.

It is impossible to state the precise amount of the advances indicated as probable because they are frequently conditional on the satisfactory preparation of detailed estimates and schemes which are not yet available: but I am informed that the Commissioners have provisionally given it to be understood that they would, if necessary, support schemes for the provision of a certain number of experimental and demonstration forests in England and Wales, and would supply funds for the afforestation of about 15,000 acres in Ireland. As regards Scotland, the Commissioners have agreed to consider the provision of a demonstration area.

The Commissioners have also sanctioned certain grants for

education, research, advisory work, minor forestry experiments, and administrative expenses in England and Wales, which are estimated to cost hereafter about £5700 a year. They are now considering proposals from Scotland for similar purposes. They are also in negotiation with certain municipal authorities for the afforestation of water catchment areas under their control.

(*Thursday*, 17*th April* 1913—*Treasury.*)

From these figures it appears that Scotland, with a very much larger area of land suitable for afforestation than either England and Wales, or Ireland, has received in cash from the Development Fund little more than one-tenth of the sum received by England and less than one twenty-eighth of the sum received by Ireland, while the sums sanctioned are, in round figures, England and Wales, £18,000; Ireland, £28,000; and Scotland, £11,000. In the absence of a survey specially directed to ascertaining the amount of afforestable land in Great Britain, it is not possible to give even approximately accurate figures of the amount for each of the three countries—but for the purpose of comparing the above-mentioned sums, it may be confidently said that Scotland possesses at least as much land on which silviculture is likely to become the leading industry as is to be found in England and Wales and Ireland put together.

We earnestly hope that during the ensuing year the Board of Agriculture will do its utmost to obtain for Scotland a grant for afforestation in proportion to her silvicultural importance. We are well aware that the Development Commissioners are unable to advance money for any purpose until definite schemes have been brought before them, and it is no doubt to the want of a definite scheme that the great disparity in the advances to Scotland as compared with England and Ireland is mainly due.

We wish to urge on the Board of Agriculture the advisability of its taking every possible step to encourage the inception of a scheme of afforestation on a large scale. We have in our minds a larger scheme than any one individual or corporation would be able to undertake, we look forward to the establishment of a Forest Centre on a really considerable scale, believing that in no other way can afforestation be made to give the best results of which it is capable, both from a silvicultural and from a social and economical point of view.

We believe that the Board of Agriculture can put forward with authority the advantages of afforestation, and indicate suitable areas, leaving it to those interested to decide in each case whether a scheme of afforestation shall or shall not be adopted for the district.

The procedure which we suggest is as follows :—

1. That the Board of Agriculture through its Advisory Committee should select suitable Forest Centres.

2. That the Board of Agriculture should take steps to bring before the proprietors in each area the outline of a scheme, and invite their co-operation.

3. That the proprietors should meet to consider the proposals of the Board of Agriculture and the possibility of combined action.

We consider it of vital importance that the Board should be in a position to lay full information on the following points before those interested.

1. The terms of advance by the Development Commissioners, including a scheme of compensation for loss of rental and severance.

2. The extent of State control over expenditure and administration.

3. The action of the Board of Agriculture in assisting in the provision and equipment of small holdings in connection with the Forest Centre; such holdings to be created in definite connection with the Forest Centre.

We wish to lay all possible stress on the advantage of proceeding with one considerable scheme rather than by small sporadic efforts in different parts of the country. This advantage is particularly obvious in regard to the whole class of difficulties arising out of the disturbance of existing industries and interests, including compensation for loss of rent and for severance, as well as the problem of rateable values. When a considerable district is to be afforested as a whole, these difficulties can be minimised by arranging the planting in intermittent series, so as to interfere as little as possible with the existing uses of the land. But it is with regard to employment that the large area is most important. Small scattered areas may give considerable employment periodically, with long intervals during which little or no employment is given. Where the planting of a few hundred acres has been carried out in former years by individual proprietors in the Highlands, it is still remembered how for the three or four years that the planting lasted, every man, woman, and child in the glen was able to obtain employment during the planting season, and how much the employment was missed when it came to an end. Continuity of employment can only be secured by the afforestation of large areas, and this consideration is of vital importance in connection with schemes for increasing the number of small holdings and thereby attaching a larger population to the soil. In all districts suitable for silviculture afforestation should be made an integral part of the small holdings scheme, so as to secure for the existing population and the new small holders the benefit of regular employment at a time of year when employment is most difficult to obtain.

In making these suggestions it must not for a moment be supposed that we are losing sight of the great services which the Board of Agriculture is rendering to forestry in Scotland by its efforts on behalf of a Demonstration area and of silvicultural education generally. We believe that what is being done will be of the greatest possible benefit; at the same time we feel that the state of silvicultural knowledge in Scotland and the number of trained men available, fully warrant the adoption of practical afforestation on a large scale.

We have ventured to offer these suggestions in our capacity as Council of a society which has laboured long and earnestly on behalf of forestry in Scotland, and together with these suggestions we offer any services which it may be in our power to render in assisting to carry them out.

I am, Sir, your obedient Servant,

ARCHIBALD STIRLING.

12th May 1913.

18. Development of Forestry in England.

The English Advisory Committee on Forestry, appointed by Mr Runciman in February 1912, has recently issued several reports and memoranda of great importance for the development of forestry in England. These reports deal in a concise and at the same time in a thoroughly comprehensive and practical manner with the preliminary steps which must be taken in initiating a large scheme of forestry development. On this occasion the Committee was asked :—

1. To consider and advise upon proposals for a Forest Survey.

2. To draw up plans for experiments in silviculture and to report upon questions relating to the selection and laying out of forestal demonstration areas.

3. To advise as to the provision required for the instruction of woodmen.

We give in full the three reports on each of the above remits.

REPORT ON FIRST REFERENCE.

"1. The first of the three references submitted to us—'To consider and advise upon proposals for a Forestry Survey'—received our careful and detailed consideration at the three meetings of the Committee held respectively on March 19th, April 23rd, and May 20th.

"2. We understand that the proposals referred to are those contained in the Memorandum on the Development of Forestry submitted by the Board of Agriculture and Fisheries for consideration by the Development Commission.

"3. We have had before us, in addition, the following papers bearing directly or indirectly on the reference :—

Report of the Departmental Committee on Forestry in Scotland. [Cd. 6085.] Forest Survey of Glen Mor by Lord Lovat and Captain Stirling of Keir. Report on Kerry Woods by Mr R. L. Robinson. Memoranda by Sir Wm. Schlich, Sir S. Eardley-Wilmot, Professor Somerville, Mr Middleton, and the Secretary.

"4. We consider that the operations which are comprised in

[1] The following extracts from the Reports (price 6d.) are published by permission of the Controller of H.M. Stationery Office.

a complete Forestry Survey may be conveniently resolved into two component parts, viz. :—

(a) *A Preliminary Enquiry* or *Flying Survey* dealing with the location, in a broad way, of the land which is likely to prove suitable for afforestation purposes, *i.e.*, whether it would be more profitable to use for growing timber than to continue in its present condition or use.

(b) *A Minute Inquiry* or *Detailed Survey* to examine in detail any such suitable land.

"The object of the Preliminary Survey is to ascertain whether a *primâ facie* case exists for afforestation in a district, while the object of the Detailed Survey is to provide, for such specific areas as the Preliminary Survey may indicate, the data on which definite schemes of afforestation may be expeditiously and economically founded.

"5. We consider that surveys of both types are necessary as a preliminary step towards the inauguration of afforestation operations.

"6. From the evidence placed before the various Government enquiries which have dealt with forestry, and from our general knowledge of the distribution of relatively unproductive land in England and Wales, we recommend that the Preliminary Survey be restricted in the first instance to the following seven districts :—

I. South Wales. II. North Wales. III. Westmorland, Cumberland and Northumberland. IV. Kent, Surrey and Sussex. V. Berks, Hants, Wilts and Dorset. VI. Derby, Lancashire and the West Riding. VII. Lincoln, Norfolk, Suffolk and Essex.

"7. We recommend that the Board, in conducting these Preliminary Surveys, utilise to the fullest extent the knowledge which local landowners, agents and foresters possess, and we therefore suggest the formation of local committees to co-operate with the Board in making the requisite enquiries, and that the Royal English Arboricultural Society be invited to co-operate to this end.

"8. We recommend that the Preliminary Survey be started as soon as possible in districts I, III, IV, and VII, above.

"9. We recommend that, where the Preliminary Survey discloses a sufficient area in any district suitable for afforestation purposes, a Detailed Survey should follow to obtain the particulars necessary to justify the State in acquiring, if possible, an area for an Experimental Forest which should contain not less than 5000 acres, but not necessarily in one block.

"10. We recommend that the Detailed Survey be carried out by the Board, taking advantage of the assistance of, and employing temporarily where necessary, any capable local foresters who appear to be competent for the work.

"It will be necessary for the Board through their officers, in all cases, to check and amplify facts brought to their notice by committees and private individuals.

"11. We recommend that in conducting the Detailed Survey, regard should be had, as far as possible, to the growth of existing woods in the district. We consider, however, that owing to injudicious planting of species in unsuitable localities, and to subsequent mismanagement, mere estimates of the value of timber standing in such woods, will, in many cases, lead to an unfairly low valuation of the land for forestry purposes, and that due allowance should be made, in mapping the land, for any such unsatisfactory conditions where they occur.

"12. We recommend that in the Detailed Survey the land be mapped on the 6″ scale into several quality classes, indicating the probable productivity of the soil.

"We are doubtful, however, as to whether it would be to the public advantage to publish the maps when completed."

Mr Munro Ferguson adds the following note at the end of this report:—

"I am of opinion that £2000 is a sufficient sum to apply to survey work for the next two years, after which the expenditure could be reviewed in the light of experience."

REPORT ON SECOND REFERENCE.

"1. We have given the second of the three references submitted to us—'To draw up plans for experiments in silviculture, and to report upon questions relating to the selection and laying out of forestal demonstration areas'—very careful consideration.

"2. We have divided our Report into two sections, the first part dealing with the question of a Demonstration Area, and the second part with Forestry Experiments.

" I. *Demonstration Area.*—3. We consider that a Demonstration Area should be of such a character as to form—

- (*a*) An object lesson on the benefits arising out of systematic forest management and a centre for exhibiting accessory forest industries.
- (*b*) A practical training ground for forestry students.
- (*c*) A training ground for woodmen who wish to qualify as working foremen or head foresters.
- (*d*) One of the centres for the establishment of field experiments in silviculture.
- (*e*) One of the centres for the collection of statistics relating to forestry.

" 4. Such an area must of necessity be well wooded, and we use the term Demonstration Forest in that connection.

" 5. We recommend that Laboratory Research proceed principally at the existing teaching centres, but that opportunities for such work be also provided in the Demonstration Forest.

" 6. We consider that the Forest of Dean, with the adjoining Crown woods, is well suited to meet the requirements imposed by a Demonstration Forest, and we recommend accordingly that it be selected for the purpose.

" 7. With regard to local administrative control, we consider, as the ideal arrangement, that the whole of this Demonstration Forest should be in the sole charge of one fully trained man.

" 8. We recognise that it may be difficult to make the arrangement suggested in the last paragraph at once in the woods which are at present under the control of the Deputy Surveyor. In the meantime, it would be necessary to place some special portion of this Demonstration Forest, such as the High Meadow and Tintern Woods, from the beginning of operations under the management of a fully trained officer. It appears to us that the position is simplified by the fact that the President of the Board of Agriculture and Fisheries is also Commissioner of Woods in charge of the Forest of Dean, and of the adjoining woodlands; and that it may be possible for him also to devise a scheme for the use of the remaining area of these Crown woods, whereby the officer in charge of the Demonstration Forest should be placed in possession of all necessary information regarding their management, and have access to any part of them for the purposes of instruction and conducting approved experiments.

" 9. We recommend that if the arrangements referred to in

paragraph 8 be adopted, they should be regarded as only preparatory and leading up to the arrangement suggested in paragraph 7 above.

" 10. The question of buildings and equipment will depend upon which of the foregoing is adopted.

" II. *Forestry Experiments.*—11. We have had before us a memorandum submitted by the Board of Agriculture and Fisheries setting forth the general principles underlying the problems of forestry research and silvicultural experiment, and detailing methods by which these problems might be attacked.

" 12. We find ourselves in very close agreement with this memorandum, with the exception of the paragraphs dealing with the regeneration of woods. We have accordingly amended this section and we recommend that this memorandum, as amended, be adopted by the Board as a basis for action as occasion may arise.

" 13. We recommend that landowners be requested to give the Board of Agriculture and Fisheries the right to maintain plots of woodland for experimental purposes for a sufficient number of years certain, and under such conditions as will enable these experiments to be effectually carried out, and that the Royal English Arboricultural Society be invited to co-operate with the Board in obtaining the offer of such experimental plots from their members and others.

" 14. Such conditions might be roughly as follows :—

(a) The term should be, if possible, as long as may be required for the full duration of the experiment.

(b) The Board should have full control over the silvicultural operations (including due protection from ground game) on the plot during the whole period, should bear the expenses thereof, and should have the right for themselves and any persons authorised by them of ingress and regress at all reasonable times.

(c) The landlord should undertake to provide sufficient labour as and when required, for which he would be repaid by the Board ; all the proceeds to remain the property of the landlord.

(d) Rates and taxes to be paid by the landlord as before, but the Board to pay a lump sum down by way of acknowledgment for the use of the area during the term.

(*e*) The Board or the landlord may, at the end of any year, terminate the agreement, but in the event of any such action being taken by the landlord the latter shall refund to the Board the sum originally paid for the use of the area."

The following reservation is added by Mr Munro Ferguson :—

" I agree with paragraph 6, that the Forest of Dean with the adjoining Crown woods is well suited to meet the requirements imposed by a Demonstration Forest, and am of opinion, therefore, that the whole area should be removed from the control of the Deputy Surveyor and placed under a trained forest officer."

REPORT ON THIRD REFERENCE.

" 1. We have given the third reference submitted to us— ' To advise as to the provision required for the instruction of woodmen '—our careful consideration. We have had before us the opinions of the following lecturers in forestry :—Messrs Henry (Cambridge University), Fraser Story (University College of North Wales), Pritchard (Royal Agricultural College, Cirencester), and Annand (The Armstrong College, Newcastle-upon-Tyne), and Drs Nisbet (Glasgow University), and Borthwick (Edinburgh and East of Scotland Agricultural College).

" 2. As some confusion appears to exist as to the precise meaning of the word ' woodmen,' we prefer to use it to indicate the man whose occupation is only the manual labour connected with forestry operations.

" 3. The elementary education of the woodman as above defined is clearly a matter which rests with the local Education authorities, and should be provided by them.

" 4. We find that there is a growing demand for well-qualified working foremen and head foresters, and that should forestry become more popular in the country the demand will increase considerably.

" By a working foreman, we understand one who works with and directs a gang of woodmen, and by a head forester one who supervises the forestry operations within the area committed to his charge.

" It is to be hoped that if the local Education authorities provide educational facilities by continuation classes or otherwise, it may be possible to recruit 'working foremen' and 'head foresters' from the 'woodman' class.[1]

"5. We consider that the success of the management of the woods on estates depends very largely upon the practical efficiency of the working foreman or head forester employed.

"Owners of large woods are at present little disposed to employ permanently men who have received a technical training in forestry at one of the higher schools, and it must be assumed that in the near future at least the working foreman or head forester will remain the responsible person in charge. We understand that the Board of Agriculture and Fisheries are arranging that owners of woodlands shall be supplied with the best technical advice obtainable, but we feel, nevertheless, that the proper utilisation of such advice depends chiefly on the efficiency of the man in actual charge.

"6. At the present time the knowledge of forest management which those in charge possess cannot always be considered satisfactory. This arises from a number of causes, of which we consider that the chief are—

"(a) The low scale of pay attaching to the positions.

"It is not at all uncommon to find the details of management affecting many thousands of pounds' worth of growing timber entrusted to men receiving a wage but little above that of a labourer. There is consequently little to attract able men and no incentive towards improvement.

"(b) The lack of facilities for receiving instruction.

"Prior to the establishment of the Forest of Dean School in 1904, and later of the Chopwell Woods course, there were no organised schools for woodmen, and forestry instruction among this class consisted, with the exception of some local lecturers, chiefly in the accumulation of practical experience, the reading of periodicals devoted to arboriculture, and the stimulus of essay competitions promoted by the two arboricultural societies in Great Britain.

"7. At the present time the two establishments in the Forest of Dean and Chopwell Woods provide facilities for completing the training of about 14 men annually, and of these

[1] The number of persons in England and Wales returned as woodmen in the Census of 1901 was 12,035, while the area of woodland in 1908 was 1,907,000 acres. No distinction is made in the Census between the three classes referred to in paragraphs 2 and 4.

a number obtain forestry appointments in the Colonies. We consider that increased provision should be made for the training of men of this type.

"8. To provide this increase, we consider that the capacity of the above schools should be gradually extended. If, as appears probable, this extension should render the working of the woods in which the schools are situated more expensive, we consider that any such extra charge should be met by special grants made for the purpose of assisting forestry instruction.

"9. With the establishment of the Experimental Forests, to which we alluded in our report on the first reference submitted to us, further facilities will become available for giving practical instruction on certain sides of forestry work, and we can see no insuperable difficulties to arranging the courses at the Forest of Dean School and the Chopwell Woods on the one hand, and at the Experimental Forests on the other hand, so that any congestion at the schools may be relieved. The work at the one locality might conveniently supplement that at the other.

"10. We consider it desirable that it should be possible for boys who intend to become woodmen to find facilities for qualifying for the position of working foreman and eventually of head forester, and we recommend that the attendance at the courses of the type provided in the Forest of Dean or Chopwell Woods should be limited to those who can produce satisfactory evidence of having already gained considerable experience of the manual labour involved in forestry operations.

"11. We recommend that on leaving school at the age of 14-15 years, such boys should be apprenticed as woodmen on approved estates for a period of at least three years. At the end of this period the youths on production of certificates of conduct and health should go on to the Forest of Dean, the Chopwell, or other similar school, where special facilities should be provided for their further training.

"12. We recommend that the Education Committees of counties or groups of counties be invited to offer a limited number of scholarships to assist the most promising of those apprentices who might otherwise be unable to proceed to these woodmen's schools.

"13. We consider that the present course which is given at the Forest of Dean is very satisfactory. We recommend, however, that the entrance age be reduced to 19 years, and that the students be given greater opportunities for study, by reducing the hours of manual labour, but without reduction of the existing rates of wages.   As such a course would involve a further charge on the Forest, we recommend that this charge be made good by a grant under the head of Forestry Education.

"41. We recommend that one or two scholarships of a value of £50 be offered annually to enable the best of the students who have gone through a woodmen's school to proceed for one year to a centre for higher training.   If no courses are given at present which would prove entirely satisfactory for such continuation students, a suitable course could no doubt be arranged at some convenient centre.

"15. As supplementary to the above steps for the training of .woodmen, we consider that short courses of lectures at convenient centres have a distinct value.   The value of such lectures lies not only in the knowledge imparted, but also in the stimulus produced in those attending them.

"16. We therefore recommend that it should be arranged for short series of lectures in practical forestry to be given by the Board's advisory officers at convenient centres in different districts."

Four appendices are added.   The first is a memorandum by Sir W. Schlich on the organisation of the Demonstration Area for the purpose of practical instruction and experiments in silviculture.   We quote this appendix in full.

APPENDIX I.

MEMORANDUM ON THE ORGANISATION OF THE DEMONSTRATION AREA FOR THE PURPOSE OF PRACTICAL INSTRUCTION AND EXPERIMENTS IN SILVICULTURE.

"The Advisory Committee, at their sitting on 18th May 1912, defined the purposes of the Demonstration Forest as follows :—

(a) An object lesson on the benefits arising out of systematic forest management, including accessory forest industries.

(b) A practical training ground for forestry students.

(c) A training ground for woodmen.

(d) One of the centres for the establishment of field experiments in silviculture.

(e) One of the centres for the collection of statistics.

" To realise these objects it is necessary that—

(1) The officer in charge have full control over at least a portion of the Dean cum High Meadow Wood and Tintern Abbey Woods, where he can establish experiments in silviculture;

(2) He be brought into suitable official relationship with the Deputy Surveyor of the Dean, so as to organise the collection of statistics in any part of the forests, and to make the latter available for practical instruction purposes;

(3) All these forests be managed strictly in accordance with well-considered working-plans.

" The staff required, apart from the general administration of the woods, should comprise—

1 Director	on a salary of, say	£600	
1 Assistant Director	,, ,,	.	400
1 Clerk	,,	.	100
1 Head Forester	,,	.	100
General expenses . . .	,,	.	800
Total annual expenditure .	.	£2000	

" The capital outlay may be estimated as follows :—

1 House for the Director . .	say	£1,500	
1 ,, ,, Assistant Director .	,,	1,200	
1 ,, ,, Clerk . . .	,,	400	
1 ,, ,, Head Forester .	,,	400	
A building containing a mess-room, kitchen department and 10 single rooms for students . . .	,,	2,500	
A building containing a lecture room, museum, office, 2 rooms for the Director and Assistant Director	,,	3,000	
Furniture and equipment . .	,,	1,000	
Total . .	,,	£10,000	

"How far the accommodation may be met by existing buildings I cannot say. The Assistant Director would be in immediate charge of the training of woodmen, assisted by the Head Forester. Whether quarters for the woodmen under instruction would be required depends on the location of the establishment. Laboratory research on subjects such as botany and entomology should be done in connection with existing teaching centres."

Sir S. Eardley-Wilmot also contributes a memorandum on the organisation and cost of a Demonstration Area, in the course of which he says :—

" 1. It is of course admitted that demonstration, education and research are merely the means to an end, that of the development of forestry as a national industry: they form a basis for the systematic establishment of State 'Experimental Forests'; for State-aided afforestation by public bodies; and, it is hoped ultimately with the aid of legislation, for the formation of commercial forests by private individuals. Equally, of course, it is not desirable that other efforts towards the final objects in view should be postponed until arrangements for demonstration, education and research are completed; but it seems essential that Government should have, as soon as possible, a suitable centre where the best forestry methods should be displayed, where theories learnt in the schools may be studied in the field, and where opportunity would be afforded for the prosecution of practical enquiries into any special branch of forestry.

" 2. The organisation of an area which would efficiently serve the above purposes must necessarily be costly if the scheme is to be effective, and prove that Government is really desirous of reviving industrial forestry in the United Kingdom; but to make such an area the sole centre for research and education would be as inadvisable as it would be impossible; for the success of both education and research depends on the individual, and the individual will continue to resort to those localities where the exercise of his talents will have the fullest results. Yet the officers of the Demonstration Area should be provided with suitable facilities to carry on investigations and thereby continue to qualify themselves for their educational duties; and more particularly for such investigations as necessitate work in those forests which it is hoped may be ultimately so fully organised as to obviate the necessity of sending British students abroad for their practical training."

He then gives some valuable suggestions as to the organisation of the Crown Forests of Dean, High Meadow and Tintern for demonstration purposes. The constitution and organisation of the staff, together with the adaptation of the existing facilities in that particular centre, are carefully gone into. To make these Crown woods suitable for a demonstration area Sir S. Eardley-Wilmot estimates would entail in round figures an annual expenditure of £4500 and a capital expenditure of about £12,000 to £17,000.

Appendix III., entitled "Notes on Research and Experiments,' is by Mr R. L. Robinson. The writer shows in a convincing manner the urgent and vital necessity for research and experiment in the development of forestry. He points out in a clear and practical manner the lines along which investigation should at present proceed in connection with timber and seed research. We know next to nothing about the physical qualities of home-grown timbers, and for the bulk of our information we have to rely upon data which applies to timber grown in other countries. It may be said, however, that the Forestry Department at Cambridge is going ahead and attacking in a business-like fashion the problems of timber physics.

The following extract from this Appendix merely indicates one of the many important questions which still await *conclusive* demonstration in connection with timber research.

"Forestry would be receiving valuable service if it could be conclusively shown that Scots pine and spruce timbers of superior quality can be grown in this country. With certain classes of people who deal with forest products it now passes as proven that we cannot grow good timber of these species. The seller of timber naturally finds it difficult to dispute this assertion and is consequently at a disadvantage in doing business.

"Investigations abroad have shown that easily determined qualities such as specific gravity are an excellent measure of the relative strength of two pieces of timber of the same species. In an investigation of this kind the testing machine should play a secondary part only. The matter must be attacked in a more general way. The material which is being shipped into our ports should be sampled carefully according to its grade, and comparisons made with the converted home-grown material.

The basis of comparison should be suitability for the uses to which the material is actually put in practice."

Attention is called to the value and need of research in Forest Botany, Mycology and Entomology. In the part of the memorandum which deals with experimental work the question of experimental forestry and forest statistics is gone into in great detail.

Appendix IV. embodies a Memorandum on the Development of Forestry submitted by the Board of Agriculture and Fisheries for consideration of the Development Commission. The following useful synopsis which we quote in full will serve to give in a condensed form the general trend of the memorandum.

"The reasons for the present unsatisfactory condition of British Forestry are summarised. The reports of the Select Committee of 1885-87 [287], the Departmental Committee of 1902 [Cd. 1319], the Departmental Committee on Irish Forestry of 1907-08 [Cd. 4027] and the Coast Erosion Commission of 1908 [Cd. 4460] are referred to, and the chief conclusions indicated. It is shown that the general result of these public enquiries has found expression in the references to forestry occurring in the Development and Road Improvement Funds Act, 1909. It is urged that as a preliminary to the afforestation of land, and even to the 'setting up of a number of experimental forests on a large scale,' a forestry survey should be undertaken to determine the yield of timber which may reasonably be expected from the types of land considered suitable for afforestation, and to ascertain the approximate area of such land available for planting. While the survey is in progress it is proposed to arrange for experiments on existing woodlands through the Royal English Arboricultural Society and otherwise. It is also proposed to utilise so far as these may be available, the results of experiments carried out by private landowners. When accurate information is available, it is proposed that in districts containing much afforestable land typical areas should be secured for the purpose of establishing experimental forests and on these areas experiments in afforestation, as distinct from silviculture, should be carried out. It is proposed to make arrangements with five institutions for the provision of expert advice on subjects relating to forestry. Each institution will be asked to provide advice for the owners of woodlands within a definite area. Grants in aid of forestry instruction and of research are proposed."

The whole of the Memorandum and indeed the whole Report should be carefully studied by all Scottish foresters and others interested in the progress and development of forestry, as it is full of suggestions and replete with details of the highest importance for the promotion of this great national industry.

In connection with the Report Mr Munro Ferguson sends us the following note :—

The Advisory Committee's Report to the English Board or Agriculture on Training for Forestry and the provision of Demonstration Forests is of interest in more than one respect. To us it is mainly so in revealing the rapid progress of England as compared with Scotland. That, as matters stand, is inevitable. England has a first-rate department under a responsible minister, giving to it his whole time.

Scottish administration is congested in a one-man department at Dover House which, with its ring of local boards, has the control of the entire affairs of Scotland, a system which throughout its existence has failed to cope effectively with any single undertaking.

Comparing Scotland with England as regards training for silviculture—we find ourselves with nothing yet fixed as to any one of our main requirements. The official responsible for silviculture is the small holdings member of the Board of Agriculture; and, as if his energy was not already sufficiently engaged, not even a clerk is as yet allotted to the forestry section, although it was agreed nearly a year ago that such an appointment would be made.

A Forestry Department for Scotland remains non-existent. Apart from Mr Sutherland, no representative of the Government helps—though several hinder—in making provision for Demonstration Forest, Forest Garden and all other requirements for State Training for Forestry, and for State Afforestation. So that, while the administration gropes its way in the dark, and while the paramount national interest of silviculture, as affording the widest scope for additional skilled labour upon the land, is neglected—3000 emigrants leave the Clyde weekly.

R. MUNRO FERGUSON.

19. The Place of Forestry in the Economic Development of Scotland.[1]

By Sir John Stirling-Maxwell, Bart.

In a small and populous country like this forestry is essentially a highland industry. That does not mean that it is to be bounded by the line that guide books trace across the map of Scotland to warn the tourist when he passes from the clutch of the obstinate Saxon into that of the passionate Celt. The word highland is used here in its literal sense, and includes the great areas of uncultivated hills which occupy two-thirds of Scotland south of the Forth. The lowland country, subject to that deduction, is a meagre space. It is, in fact, confined to a fringe seldom 30 miles broad along the east coast, and a still narrower fringe on the west coast which extends only from the Clyde to the Solway. But within these narrow limits are enclosed most of the inhabitants and most of the wealth of Scotland. If you study the distribution of the existing woods, you will find that they stick pretty close to the cultivated country. The reason is that the woods have been planted or, if natural, enclosed and cared for out of the profits of agriculture and other lowland industries. In the Central and West Highlands, where trees flourish quite as well, woods are scarce because there has been no capital with which to plant them. Keep this in your mind; it is the root of the whole question. In the lowland fringe, with its rich soil and large population, little increase of the woodland area is to be expected or desired. True, the existing woods can be made much more productive than they are at present, but that is not our question. We may, therefore, confine our attention to the Highland districts where forestry has never had a look in, and never can have a look in unless the State comes to its aid, but where there are luckily woods enough to prove conclusively the worth of the great field which still lies undeveloped. It is the relation of forestry to agriculture in those districts that we have now to consider.

If anyone here thinks that there is, or can be, any conflict between the ploughman and the planter, let me beg him to put that idea out of his head at once. Agriculture comes first

[1] An Address delivered before the Aberdeen Branch of the Royal Scottish Arboricultural Society.

and forestry second, and any land which is good enough to repay cultivation by the plough or the spade is too good and too valuable for forestry. That is a fact which we need waste no time in discussing. The conflict, if there is a conflict at all, is between forestry and grazing. Grazing lies, as it were, between forestry and agriculture. Let us admit that there will always be land on the border line between grazing and forestry, whose ideal fate it may be difficult to decide. But let me add that no sane man would think of planting such land now. There is an ample field for forestry in the Highlands without touching land of that character at all. If that decision ever has to be taken, it will be taken not by us but by our grand-children, who will be in a position to judge whether afforestation does or does not bring with it the blessings which we anticipate. Let me, however, add by way of illustration, if not of prophecy, an observation from the little kingdom of Belgium, where agriculture in all its branches is as well understood and much better organised than it is here, and where the soil supports a much larger population. Not only have many Belgian villages planted their own common ground, but agricultural committees have petitioned the Government to drain and plant the moors belonging to the nation, and have even requested that the planting of waste ground should be made compulsory in every parish. After all, what is forestry but a branch of agriculture? Who hears of a conflict between cropping and grazing? Is the conflict between grazing and forestry any more real?

If we consider for a moment what we mean by rural develop-ment, we shall perceive what a mare's nest this supposed conflict is. We all want to increase the population of the Highlands, to people the now empty glens, to stem the excessive stream of emigration. It is in the light of this desire that every scheme of Highland development must be considered. We ask of every scheme how many people it will put on the land and induce to stay there, and by the answer to that question we judge it. It is a subject which can be argued in terms either of men or of money. It is in terms of men that I want to argue it now. Let us take the simplest case first. There are sheep farms in Scotland, especially in the West Highlands, which could be planted almost bodily and turned into splendid and profitable forests. A sheep farm employs one shepherd for about every 1000 acres and practically no other labour. The same ground under wood requires the services of at least one man for every 100 acres. In other words, it must employ ten men where the large sheep farm employs but one, without including the employment given by saw-mills or by any industries, such as the manufacture of wood-pulp or paper, which may establish themselves in the forest. If population be the criterion, there is really no comparison between these two methods of occupation.

Please do not suppose that under a scheme of afforestation every acre of the district afforested would be planted. We do not want to emulate the backwoods of America. Any ground, level and good enough for agriculture, would certainly be reserved for that purpose. Every forest must have a resident population on which it can draw for periodic labour—felling, roadmaking, carting, saw-milling, etc. This need can only be met by the establishment of groups of small landholders—these small landholders of whom we hear so much. I imagine that when afforestation comes, as it must sooner or later if common-sense prevails, the Highlands of Scotland will be very like the French district of the Vosges, to which they bear a strong physical resemblance. Instead of a bare glen with a shepherd's or a stalker's house every three or four miles, the hills and the side glens will be wooded. In the main valley there will be more cultivation than there is at present and many more houses, with here and there larger villages whose industries depend on timber. But you may say, "That is a charming picture, but why not have the small landholders without the woods and let them graze their sheep and cattle on the hills?" I reply by another question, to which I invite you to give an honest answer. Why does the lot of the small landholder appear so idyllic while that of the crofter is so uninviting? Is it not because the small landholder belongs to a golden future, while the crofter is wrestling with the hard facts of the present?

Parliament has made the crofter's tenure secure. It has given him a fair rent. If the small landholder is to be an economic being and not a mere creation of public charity, can he be very different? We are not speaking now of rich soils on the outskirts of large towns. There we may hope that the small landholder has a future solid as well as glittering. He may also thrive where he can wrest a harvest from the sea. But in the bulk of the Highlands, where soils are poor and markets distant, a dilemma confronts this individual, from which I can see no escape. If his holding is small, his life will be a very poor one unless he and his sons have some steady employment on which they can fall back. If you increase his holding to the size of a small farm and make him self-supporting, then in the nature of things there can be very few such holdings. Mark, please, that the afforested glens will have a much larger population than those devoted to grazing, even when these are divided among the largest possible number of smallholders. A sheep farm so divided can never support more than a few families, even if they devote their whole time to digging the arable ground and keep on the hills the heaviest stock of sheep and cattle which these can carry. Such division is not new. The system can be seen at work on the club farms which are found in some parts of Scotland; in one such case, which is fairly typical, 6,000 acres are divided into 23 holdings. But at best, this line of development has only a solitary and limited existence to offer. It affords no base for any kind of industrial development, nor does it invite easy communication with the outside world.

It is dangerous to generalise where the conditions are so variable, but it may be reckoned that 1000 acres, which would sustain only one or two families as part of a large sheep farm, might, if divided, sustain four or even five smaller tenants. The same area, if the arable land were devoted to small holdings of about 10 to 15 acres—not enough to support a family by themselves, but backed up with the certainty of healthy and well-paid employment in the woods in place of the precarious profits derived from a common grazing—would support a much larger and more prosperous population. The woods, as I have said, could not get on without a man to every 100 acres. That means double as many families as the divided sheep farm. Occasional labour and forest industries would employ at least as many as the regular work of the forest itself. This is a modest estimate compared with the figures which come to us from foreign countries, but it means that the woods would enable the population to be increased to four times what would be possible under a system of divided grazings, or about fifteen times the population of the same area used as an ordinary sheep farm. If you ask why a forest will support so many more people than the same area under grass, I can only reply because it puts the ground to a use many times more profitable. There are estates in the county of Aberdeen where the woods bring in a steady income of £1 an acre,[1] while the adjoining ground, just as fertile but unplanted, only brings in half a crown or less for pasture—pasture which has to be equipped with expensive buildings. In districts more remote it would be easy to name cases where the difference was even more marked. And these figures, please remember, tell only half the story. The woods which bring in a revenue of £1 an acre have already paid a wages bill equal to 10s. an acre, while the unplanted ground probably pays less than one-tenth of that amount in wages.

Those who live in forest communities in France and Germany enjoy a freedom and independence which accord well with the taste of this generation. Only the head foresters and forest guards and a few labourers are in the permanent service of the forest. The rest are their own masters. They work in the forest when they can—that is, when they are not busy cultivating their own holdings. The work of the forest, of which no branches except planting and nursery work are at any season urgent, is timed to suit them. The urgent work being light, is often done by women and children. Their holdings and their houses are usually their own property. Sometimes they work by the day, sometimes by contract. A father and his sons, or a man with his brothers, or an enterprising man with a group of friends, will undertake a definite piece of forest work, or the carting of forest produce. There is no reason why the thing should not work out in the same way in Scotland. Something very like it exists to-day in districts where forest work is undertaken by crofters, and it answers well. In reckoning the advantage to the State of such communities, it must be remembered that the life and the occupation in all its branches are as healthy as any to which human labour can be turned. It is impossible to imagine a better nursery of citizens. I do not think the same can be said of purely agricultural and pastoral communities in the Highlands. They are too poor. The life is healthy, but it is too narrow, and offers too few opportunities and too many spells of idleness.

Hitherto we have been considering the simple case where

[1] This does not include the orginal cost of creation. If that is deducted at compound interest the annual return per acre would probably not exceed 15s

whole sheep farms can be turned into small holdings and forests. Even without going outside this easy ground there is probably a large field for silviculture, especially now that the profits of sheep farming have fallen so low that it is difficult to get a tenant to take a sheep farm even at a half or a third of the old rent. But there are many parts of the Highlands in which the problem is more complicated. The chief complications arise, first, from sporting values, and secondly, from the existence of great areas of ground too high, too poor, and too exposed to plant, which, shorn of the adjacent wintering ground, have no value for any purpose whatever. These two difficulties are in many cases tangled together. Those who wish to see both questions thrashed out for a typical district should read the *Forest Survey of Glen Mor*, 1912, prepared by Lord Lovat and Captain Stirling of Keir for the Society, a work in which they had the assistance of lairds, factors, foresters, gamekeepers, forest experts, and actuaries—a singular report, because every one concerned put his best work into it for love.

I do not know what view you take of deer forests, but I suppose we should all agree that we have quite enough of them, and most people would be glad to see some of their area converted into the other kind of forest. Deer forests are so numerous simply because they secure a good rent without the outlay of much capital. My old friend, Mr George Malcolm, who speaks from a long experience of the Highlands, published a pamphlet last autumn, in which he maintained the double paradox that deer forests were economically sound, and that silviculture was economically unsound in the Highlands. It may be true, I believe it often is, that a deer forest employs more people than the same area under sheep. It certainly brings in a larger rent. From a purely parochial point of view, it may therefore claim to be economically sound; but from no other. It provides a healthy existence for a small group of people, but it produces nothing except a small quantity of venison, for which there is no demand. It causes money to change hands. A pack of cards can do that. I doubt whether it could be said of a single deer forest, however barren and remote, that it could serve no better purpose. One I happen to know well lies nearly all above the 1000-feet level, with a desperately bad soil and no wintering. Even there hundreds of acres can be profitably planted without diminishing the

sporting value, and they are being planted now. These plantations, even in their infancy, give more employment than the
whole of the rest of the estate. I am convinced that in many
deer forests—I was almost going to say in most deer forests—
there are areas which, if planted, and once yielding a regular
supply of timber, would bring in an income larger and steadier
than that which the whole subject brings at present. The same
is true of many a large sheep farm. If anyone wants a bird's-
eye view of the sort of ground available for this purpose, he
has only to travel from Helensburgh to Fort William by the
West Highland Railway. He will pass through nearly 100
miles of afforestable country, the only exception being the great
area of peat called the Moor of Rannoch, which lies between
Goreton and Loch Treig.

There may be a few deer forests which consist mainly of
plantable ground, but as a rule the greater part is too high and
exposed and poor for any purpose except summer grazing.
And so with many sheep farms. The height to which planting
can be profitably carried cannot be decided by any formula,
since shelter and soil are the determining features, rather than
mere elevation. It is certain, however, that there is little
plantable ground above 1500 feet, and that the bulk of the
best ground lies below 1000 feet. The value of the unplantable
high pastures depends entirely upon the adjacent ground
available for wintering. Now this is just the ground we want
to plant. The problem is how to plant it without rendering the
rest useless and without hopelessly upsetting the local budget,
which often depends mainly on the rates levied on sporting
rents. You will find, if you read the report to which I referred,
that two circumstances come to the rescue. The first is the
necessity of forming your plantations gradually, so that the
timber crops may ripen in succession and eventually give a
regular yield every year. If, for example, you intend to cut
the woods when they are 80 years old, you need not in the
first 20 years plant more than one quarter of the whole area
to be afforested. The second is the fact that a small area of
wooded ground is more valuable for wintering than a much
larger area of bare ground. Another lucky thing which
may be mentioned is that southern exposures are the best
for wintering sheep or deer, while northern exposures are
the best for growing trees. These fortunate circumstances

come to the rescue, and among them render a compromise possible.

Where, as in the case we considered just now, the whole waste ground of a farm or deer forest can be planted, the transition is quite simple. The stock of sheep or deer will be gradually reduced as the planting advances till there is none left and the woods take its place. But in the case with which we are now dealing, where there is a large hinterland to be devoted permanently to sheep and deer, the transition must be effected in what may be called a series of bounds. You must rapidly plant a large block, say, one-quarter or one-third of the whole area you mean to plant, and you must plant no more until that block is old enough to be opened for wintering. Then you enclose another, and so on, making sure that not more than one-third of the wintering is enclosed at any one time. Under this arrangement, which is too complicated to explain here in detail, but which is fully described in the above-mentioned report, the hinterland will still preserve its value for summer grazing, while the lower ground will not only still afford wintering, but will at the same time be put to the far more profitable use of growing timber. No opposition to a change of this kind need be expected from the owners of deer forests. Deer forests are spoken of as luxuries. To the rich tenants who hire them they are luxuries—a very sane and desirable kind of luxury, but still luxuries. To the owner they are more often the last resource of an impoverished estate. Many and many a deer forest has been unwillingly made under pressure of the fall in sheep rents and our extraordinary system of sheep valuation. In such cases the owner would welcome a change which will relieve both his conscience and his purse, and put his land to a use more economically sound. But the capital sunk in making plantations, however profitable, can bring in little or no return for the first 80 years. For an impoverished landlord such a speculation is out of the question.

In many cases, therefore, this reform can only be made with the assistance of the State. A joint arrangement under which the landlord will contribute the land and the State its credit—a business arrangement profitable to both parties—will not be found difficult to adjust. Where only part of the subject can be planted, this seems the best kind of arrangement, unless the owner can afford to plant it himself. But where the whole subject can be planted, I am convinced that the State would do best to purchase the estate out and out wherever it can do so, and create its own forest on its own ground. Continuous good management on a fixed plan is the alpha and omega of forestry, and the experience of other countries certainly tends to show that the State can provide this first essential better than any private proprietor. Of course, the State will only buy where it can buy at a reasonable price; but suitable estates are, as a matter of fact, continually changing hands at prices which will give a good profit to any purchaser who can afford to plant them and wait 80 years for a return on his money. This is a field of investment in which the State has no reason to fear competition. Now, a word as to the speed at which this change should be made. I am very impatient to make a beginning, but I am not at all impatient to see all the waste ground of Scotland planted up, nor do I want to see planting ventures scattered about promiscuously all over the country. I want to see a few carefully planned schemes started in carefully selected localities on a scale large enough to show the full advantages of forestry as the backbone of rural life in a hill country.

Its value in that respect is admitted in every country round us—in France and Germany and Belgium and Sweden,—but I admit it has still to be proved for Scotland. Let us, therefore, take two glens, such as we have in plenty on the west coast, containing nothing but a sheep farm or a shooting lodge and a few shepherds' or stalkers' houses. Let us plant one glen. Let us leave the other alone or develop it in any way you like without the aid of forestry. Then at the end of 50 or 80 years let our children compare them and see which glen is the happier, the more populous, and the more prosperous. I have no doubt myself about the result. I am also convinced that the change will be so rapid and so marked, when you import this great industry into a district which now has nothing to depend upon but wool and mutton, that long before 50 years are up you will find districts all over the Highlands petitioning to be afforested. This dream will not be realised in a moment. The new order cannot be in full swing for some 80 years, but this gradual extension is surely an advantage. You cannot plant people as you plant trees, and, after all, the progress is not so very slow. In the first or planting stage you will at least double the present population. In the next, when the young woods begin to require tending, men of a younger generation, who have been brought up in the place, will begin to be available, and the extension will go steadily on until the first crop is ready to cut and your forest population becomes complete.

Now in this paper I have purposely avoided figures, just as I have avoided the technical aspect of the subject, tempting though it is. My object was to concentrate on the broadest aspect of my case; but you are Aberdonians, and on two points at least will want some evidence beyond my mere statement. You will want to know whether forests do really employ so many people as I say, and you will want to know whether the State is likely to get a good return for the money it invests in afforestation. The only evidence I can, in the nature of the case, advance is drawn from other countries. First, as to employment, let me give you the details of a small German forest in the Spessart. They come to me first-hand from a friend who has recently been a student there. This forest extends to 10,000 acres, and attached to it are about 3000 acres of agricultural land. This area of 13,000 acres would, in the Highlands of Scotland, compose one small deer forest or a couple of fairly large sheep farms. We need not work out the comparison with the deer forest, because there are few, if any, deer forests which could be wholly planted, but let us compare it with sheep farms. As a couple of sheep farms it would support 2 tenants and, at most, 13 shepherds, or 15 families in all. Divided among a number of smaller tenants, it might, following our former calculations, support at most some 60 families. In Germany the population is as follows: the permanent staff of the forest consists of a head forester and clerk and 6 forest guards with 10 unskilled workmen; 25 other men find employment all the year round as contractors. There is thus permanent employment for 43 men. In addition to these, 80 woodcutters are employed for about six months, and 70 women and children are employed for about two months on nursery, planting, and other light work. There are also 260 men employed in forest industries. The forest with its industries is thus giving constant employment to 303 men besides the 80 men employed for six months and the 70 women and children occasionally employed. The total population of the area affected by the forest is 2500. It is calculated that

1520 of them are directly dependent on the forest. The remaining inhabitants are small tradesmen—saddlers, smiths, etc.—or people employed in small agricultural industries, and many of them are indirectly dependent upon the forest and the work it brings to the district.

For the profit the State is likely to make out of afforestation I will refer you to Belgium, a country which has many points of resemblance to ours. True, wages are lower in Belgium than in Scotland, but the value of land is much higher; in fact the deduction made for the capital value of forest land in Belgium is about double the price at which the Government could buy similar land in Scotland. This more than cancels the difference in wages. Mr Seebohm Rowntree, in his valuable book on *Land and Labour in Belgium*, has investigated this question. He is an ardent Radical, and may be taken as an impartial witness. He reckons that the Belgian Government obtains on the capital it has invested in forestry a return varying from 4·9 per cent. to 5·5 per cent. on different classes of soil. That is a modest return on a commercial venture, but it does not sum up all the national advantage which the State derives from forestry. I cannot put the point better than it is put in the words of the Belgian chief inspector of forests, whom the author quotes: "Ah, you English," said that official, "you always want to know, will it pay? In Belgium we look at the matter differently. We realise that the afforestation of waste lands affords an enormous amount of healthy work for the Belgian people, work required just when otherwise the men would be unemployed. We realise the importance of providing a large amount of home-grown timber, in view of the depletion of the world's timber supply, and we think, too, of the beneficial effects of forests, not only upon climate, but on the soil of the waste lands, to the great advantage of the country." "Surely," the author adds, "these considerations are important, and the British people may learn from the Belgians the great possibilities which lie in the afforestation of our enormous areas of uncultivated land."

20. Some Lessons from the Recent Gales.

By Sir HUGH SHAW STEWART, Bart.

The frequent and exceptionally severe gales which have ravaged the west and western centre of Scotland since November 1911 have provided practical foresters with plenty of food for thought as to the means of turning to the best account acres of blown and half-blown timber, and of freeing encumbered ground for the purpose of replanting with as little delay as possible. Their plans, no doubt, have long since matured and the work will, by now, be well on the way towards accomplishment, and so far as they are concerned the gales are things of the past.

But it will have been an ill wind indeed if estate owners do not profit by certain lessons to be derived from the devastation.

In the first place, some of us have heard of a considerable estate where all, or nearly all, the plantations of the last thirty years have been laid low. Obviously the mistake here has been in confining the planting of young trees to exposed lands.[1] In selecting planting ground it is, of course, advisable to study economy and to avoid devoting to timber land which might yield a higher profit under grazing or cultivation. On the other hand, a large estate requires an annual supply of timber for fences, gates, etc., and, in order to make sure of this, some portions of ground wholly or partially sheltered from prevailing storms should be devoted to the growth of timber for estate purposes. In the present instance there is bound to be a large gap in the supply of trees growing up to take the place of older timber, and before very long the estate will be forced for a number of years to purchase timber for estate purposes— an expensive and extravagant proceeding.

A still more impressive lesson is the importance of keeping in touch with the market and the wood-merchants.[2] This can only

---

[1] It is believed that on this estate much of the more sheltered woodland, instead of being cut and replanted systematically, has been at the mercy of roe-deer and rabbits.

[2] Landowners who have any difficulty in regard to this are advised to become members of the Landowners' Co-operative Forestry Association, 33 Queen Street, Edinburgh.

be done by cutting and selling every year, or at least every two years, such a proportion of timber over and above the necessary estate requirements as best suits the estate and the local demand.

In illustration of this I may refer to an estate where for the last decade, at any rate, a steady supply of ripe timber has been placed on the market, sometimes in different lots in one year. Thus several firms of wood-merchants have become familiar with the local facilities as to transit and the requisite lodging of their men and horses, and they have learned to what extent they can rely on the home staff for classifying and preparing the timber.

The home staff, moreover, has been constantly exercised in the best and most expeditious methods of preparing and grading the different kinds of timber, and in disposing it in such a manner as may best facilitate its removal.

The value of this procedure has been strikingly revealed by the recent gales, for no difficulty was experienced in obtaining offers for the various lots. It is true that owing to the congestion of the timber market a large portion of the blown trees[1] fetched only half price : on the other hand, some lots contained ripe trees of good quality which, because they had "amenity" value, never would have been cut. From an estate point of view these trees provided a real "windfall," and there was a strong demand for them, but it is certain that much of their value would have been lost if the home staff had not been regularly trained by an efficient head forester in the art of preparing timber for ready handling, and thereby presenting it to the market to the best advantage.

But it need not be supposed that it is only on large estates where an annual or biennial sale should be practised. I know of a little estate in central Scotland, where not more than three or four estate hands are employed, which for the past 38 years, to the writer's knowledge, has provided a small supply of properly prepared timber for market at regular intervals. The gales did not cause much trouble here, but such trees as were blown down were promptly prepared and readily disposed of to a merchant who, having purchased timber from this estate in the previous year, knew its quality.

[1] In one wood alone there were 3000 45-year-old larches which would have greatly increased in value had they stood for another fifteen years.

If estate owners condescend to profit by recent experiences they, or their successors, will not be taken by surprise by the next visitation of abnormal gales, but, on the contrary, will be ready to turn the results to the best account.

Those owners, on the other hand, who shut their eyes to obvious lessons will find themselves sooner or later in the position of a city merchant of my acquaintance who purchased an estate a number of years ago, regarding the trees on it as so many appendages, only to be removed, like furniture or table ornaments, at the will and pleasure of the owner. This worthy city man had never realised that trees, like other productions of nature aided by art, require continual attention and renewal. Accordingly, when the floods came and the winds blew and beat upon those trees, they fell—and great was the havoc of their fall. A neighbouring wood-merchant, called to the rescue, after surveying several acres of tangled branches and broken tree-trunks, was obliged to explain to my poor city friend —who abominates a bad bargain—that the labour and expense of clearing the ground would amount to more than the remaining sound timber would be worth. Thus, for want of skilled attention and foresight during the fat years, when the lean year came the owner found that he had lost not only his trees but also their money value.

21. The State Forests of Saxony.

(*With Illustrations.*)

By A. D. HOPKINSON.

Position.—The kingdom of Saxony lies on the western border of the German Empire, and is bounded on the south-west by Bohemia, while Prussia, Thuringia and Bavaria form the other neighbouring states.

. *Physical Features.*—Although flat and dry in the north, the eastern and southern parts of Saxony are hilly and even mountainous, and well watered by streams running down from the Erzgebirge—a range of mountains forming the chief physical feature of the country. It is on the well-watered hills forming the northern slope of the Erzgebirge that are situated the finest of the spruce forests, while towards the north, owing to the sandy nature of the soil, the Scots pine becomes the predominating forest-tree.

Climate. — The rainfall in Saxony varies considerably, being lowest towards the north-west and highest in the Erzgebirge. The wettest forest (*Revier*) is that of Altenburg, situated high in the Erzgebirge, which receives over 60 inches annually ; and the driest district is that around Leipzig, where a mean not more than 17 inches is recorded. In the chief spruce-growing area on the Erzgebirge the mean precipitation is 27-32 inches, which is none too high for the proper growth of this tree.

The mean summer temperature in the Erzgebirge is 55-57° F., which rises to 62-64° F. in the Elbe valley, where in winter about 30° F. is the average as compared with about 23° F. in the Erzgebirge.

Area of Woodlands. — Although the percentage of woodlands in Saxony is very nearly equal to the average of Germany taken as a whole, the acreage per head of population (1 for ·22 acres) works out lower than almost any other German state, owing to the dense population which its extensive and thriving industries are able to support. For all Germany there is on the average ·617 acres for every person. The area of woodland in Saxony is 949,739 acres, being 25·81 per cent. of the total area of the country ; whereas the collective woods of Germany amount to 33,569,793 acres, being 25·89 per cent. of the total area. Classified according to ownership, Saxony does not show any important divergences from the remainder of the Empire, except in having a somewhat higher percentage of State forests and a lower percentage of municipal woods. The comparative percentages are as follows :—

	Saxony	German Empire
State Forests . . .	45·2	31·7
Private Forests . . .	46·0	46·5
Crown Forests . . .	0·02	1·8
Municipal Forests . .	6·0	16·0
Association Forests . .	0·2	2·2
Institution Forests . .	2·6	1·5

The following table, which shows the percentages of woodland under different forms of management in Saxony and Germany as a whole, clearly demonstrates the greater preponderance of conifer woods in the former—

	Saxony	German Empire
Hardwoods—		
High Forest . . .	2·1	18·4
Selection Forest . . .	1·3	2·3
Coppice with Standards .	3·4	5·0
Coppice	4·5	6·8
TOTAL . .	11·3	32·5
Conifers—		
High Forest . . .	78·7	60·1
Selection Forest . . .	10·0	7·4
TOTAL . .	88·7	67·5

History.—Although the State forests only came into existence as such in 1831, being previous to that date the private property of the king, considerable strides had been made with their systematic management before they were handed over to the State. In 1831 King Antony declared the Royal *Kammergut* to be the property of the State, retaining however the hunting rights for his own exclusive use. In exchange for this sacrifice of revenue he was granted a " Civil List," which although since increased has not increased so rapidly as the returns which are obtained from the State forests ; and the bargain has turned out to be, from a financial point of view, a considerable loss to the reigning monarch.

The present king, although a very keen sportsman, is of course unable to shoot nearly all the stags and other deer which must be slain annually, and up till quite recently it was the practice for each *Forstmeister* to hunt and shoot in his own forest (*Revier*), except in those few which formed the particular hunting woods of the king. However, in 1912 this was changed, and all the game now goes to the State, the *Forstmeister* merely retaining the right to kill it.

The scientific management of the Saxon State forests may be said to date from the latter half of the eighteenth century, when *Oberforstmeister* von Lussberg made a very extensive survey of the woods (1764-1777). However, it was not until the arrival of Heinrich von Cotta in Saxony in 1811, when he was appointed *Forstrat* and director of the Forest Survey (*Forstvermessung*), that working-plans were systematically prepared. The great work that Cotta accomplished from that date until his death (1844) is unique in the annals of forestry, and made his name stand out peerless in the history of the science to which he devoted his life.

The result of this great forester's labours gave Saxony a start in scientific silviculture which, up to the present, no other country has been able to overtake; and the position the Saxon State forests now hold of being the most economically, and at the same time the most intensively, managed woods to be found, is directly traceable to the period when Cotta had charge of their management. The great degree of perfection in matters of detailed organisation which has now been reached is, of course, to a large extent the work of Cotta's successors, some of whom were his pupils; but the firm foundation of method which he laid for the administration and management of the State woods still remains intact.

Ever since the woods were taken over by the State in 1831, the policy of adding suitable areas by purchase has been pursued. Only land unsuitable for cultivation has been afforested, and, from 1831 to 1897, 77,454 acres were bought at an average price of £16 per acre. During the same period, however, 13,256 acres were sold, fetching on the average £32, 17s. The underlying idea in buying and selling was to round off the State woods, making them more compact and thus easier to administer. Small patches of wood situated at a considerable distance from an otherwise compact *Revier* were, if possible, disposed of, whereas tracts of wood or land suitable for wood found in or bordering on State forests and not State property were purchased to consolidate the forests. The high price received, on the average, for the land sold must have been due to the enormous strides which industry has made in Saxony during the last half century, and probably a number of towns have expanded so as to absorb parts of the forestry area for building purposes.

Administration.—There being no separate minister for agriculture in Saxony, the administration of the State woods is directly under the charge of the Minister of Finance. The *Finanzministerium*, as it is called, is divided up into three departments. Department I.—Rates and Taxes. Department II.—State lands, including forests, mines and State technical colleges, etc. Department III.—Railways and Post Office. The chief of the forestry section of Department II. is an *Oberlandsforstmeister* who is assisted by one *Oberforstrat*, one *Oberforstmeister*, and other junior officials.

Inspection.—For the purposes of inspection the State forests of Saxony are divided up into nine districts, each of which has a resident inspecting officer with the rank of *Oberforstmeister*. The total area of the State forests in Saxony is 445,380 acres, so that each inspector has about 49,486 acres under his charge divided up into twelve *Reviere*. This system is one of the three different systems of inspection found in Germany, and is called the "local *Forstmeister*" system, as the inspector is bound to reside within the area over which he has supervision. It has many points to recommend it, the chief being that, as the inspecting officer resides within the area, he has a better opportunity for organising the sale of timber and the close inspection of the woods. Again, it enables a less experienced *Forstmeister* to be put in charge of a forest *Revier*, as he is always able to refer to the *Oberforstmeister* of his district in cases of difficulty. The system found in Prussia—known as the Government *Forstmeister* system—differs from this, as in each Government there is a small council of two to three Government officials, one of whom is a forester, and they administer, besides other affairs, the forests in the district. In this case the *Oberforstmeister* has a considerably freer hand than in Saxony, the decentralised management being, of course, partly due to the very large area of Prussia as compared with Saxony. It probably suits the Prussian conditions better than the Saxon method would. In the case of Prussia the *Oberforstmeister* is responsible to the Minister of Agriculture, Lands and Forests. In countries where there is but little State-owned forest, the inspection is generally done from a Government Forestry Office; often under the Department of Agriculture, situated in the capital, which becomes the residence of the inspecting officers. Such a system is found in some of the smaller German states and in England.

Management.—The unit of administration is the *Revier* or forest range over which one *Forstmeister*, or *Oberförster* as he is called when first appointed, has charge. The average size

of the range differs in different parts of Germany. Those in
Prussia are the largest, being 9500 acres on the average; in
Baden and Bavaria they are nearly as large. In Saxony,
however, where intensity of management reaches its maximum
a range is, on the average, 3940 acres; but this is considered
by some authorities a somewhat small unit for the most
economic results. In Prussia, where the forests are very
large, there is a sub-division of the internal management work
which is not found in Saxony. The Prussian *Forstmeister* has
under him several—the number varies from about 3 to 8
according to the size of the woods—*Förster* (under foresters)
who are all ex-N.C.Os from a *Jäger* regiment. These are
generally good and reliable men, and have assigned to them
a certain section of the range, and they take charge of the
more or less routine part of the management of that particular
section. This is known as the "*Revier Förster*" system, and
is often found in large private woods as it is more economical
as regards highly trained officials. The plan adopted in
Saxony is known as the "*Oberförster*" system. Here the forest
officer or *Oberförster* (*Forstmeister*) looks after the details of
management himself, being, however, controlled fairly closely by
the inspecting officer (*Oberforstmeister*) to whom he must submit
estimates every year of the work, such as planting, cutting, roadmaking, etc., he proposes to undertake the next year, together
with a statement of the estimated cost. The inspecting officer
sends the combined estimates of the twelve *Reviere* in his
district to the Finance minister for his final sanction. Under
him the Saxon forest officer has, as a rule, one or more
under foresters, several forest guards, and the woodmen. The
under forester assists generally in the work of management,
usually doing, among other things, the routine book work, of
which there is a very considerable amount, owing to the somewhat complicated and very detailed way in which the accounts
are kept. To become an under forester in Saxony, the
candidate does not require any college training, merely being
apprenticed, as it were, to a forest officer for three years, after
which he must pass his first examination. Having passed this
he spends two more years doing practical work, then he is
again examined and, if successful, gets the title of "*Förster*" and
is entitled to a pension after so many years' service. Superior
woodmen are generally selected for the post of forest guards,

and they are, as a rule, changed from their native districts to new ones on being appointed, in order that they may carry more authority, according to the maxim that "familiarity breeds contempt."

The woodmen are divided into two classes, permanent woodmen and temporary woodmen. To become one of the former a man is required to do more than six months' work a year in the woods, and is required to pay towards his old age pension. Temporary woodmen are those that are more or less regularly taken on at certain periods when the permanent staff is not sufficient to undertake the work. There are some 500 of these and about 3800 permanent woodmen, which is, roughly speaking, taking both together, 1 man per 100 acres and 40 men to every range.

A feature of great importance in the administration of the Saxon State forests is the *Forsteinrichtungsanstalt* or Working-Plans Office, which is situated in Dresden. The duty of this department is to make and revise working-plans in the State woods, and in private woods, when asked, at a nominal charge. In the case of private estates that are entailed, the amount of timber to be cut, etc., every year is fixed exactly by the officers of the *Forsteinrichtungsanstalt*, which guards against an extravagant proprietor cutting more than the normal amount. The fact that the working-plans are made and revised by special officers, who have no other duty but to move from one range or *Revier* to another carrying on the work, is undoubtedly an advance upon the method usually employed in Prussia where the forest officer revises his own working-plan and submits the revision for approval to the inspecting officer. The continuity of plan and uniformity of method obtained by the Working-Plans Office in Dresden, which is so essential to the proper management of woodlands, is unequalled in other German States. Men working continually at the same work are bound to become more expert at it than men doing it, say, every five years, and the results are necessarily more uniform and consistent than when every *Forstmeister* drew up his own revision. However, the forest officer is not entirely ignored during the revision, his local experience being of the greatest assistance in many cases in deciding matters relating to planting, cutting, etc., and he is required to furnish the working-plans' officers with an estimate of what areas he thinks should be cut and planted in the next five years. If any serious difference of opinion should arise between them it is referred to a commission appointed to decide such questions. By this system of co-operation between the forest officer and the representatives of the *Forsteinrichtungsanstalt*, as it is in Saxony, a high degree of efficiency and continuity of policy is obtained without the danger of stereotyped regularity. As the objects of management differ according to the variations in the price of different sizes and kinds of timber, it is very desirable that the consequent regulations should be easily controlled and put into force without delay, and this is obviously more readily done by a central staff, such as the officers of the *Forsteinrichtungsanstalt*, than if every *Forstmeister* were allowed to interpret his instructions according to his own ideas.

Working-Plan.—The working-plan itself consists of two parts :

I. General Plan, II. Special Plan, both of which are kept in manuscript.

The contents of Part I. are roughly as follows :—

1. Total area of woods and area under trees, and so on.
2. Conditions of the locality, such as soil, situation, geological formation, etc.
3. Description of compartments according to—
    (*a*) Method of management (silvicultural system). (*b*) Species. (*c*) Age. (*d*) Quality of locality. (*e*) Amount of standing timber. (*f*) Situation.
4. All results of former management.
5. General directions for regulating the yield.
6. General directions for cutting and planting.
7. General outline of management, and other directions of a general kind, such as choice of species, methods of planting, etc.

In addition to this there are a number of tables showing—

(1) Normal and actual age-classes for the whole wood and for each "Working Section."
(2) Amount of each compartment on each of the five classes of soil.
(3) Areas on different geological formations.
(4) Normal and actual increments.
(5) Area and length of rotation of each "Working Section."

(6) Total amount of wood in the "Working Circle" and the number of cubic feet per acre on the average.

(7) Total normal annual yield and annual yield per acre, showing the amounts derived from clear cuttings and thinnings separately.

(8) Amount of average annual fellings classified according to class of wood and showing amount per acre.

Part II., the special plan, is renewed every ten years and is revised once between every renewal, generally in the middle of the period, but, in exceptional cases, sooner or later than five years after the renewal. Thus, a large windbreak or very extensive insect damage would immediately call for a revision at any time in order to cope with the altered conditions.

The special plan is divided as follows :—

A. Plan of cuttings. 1. Felling. 2. Thinning. 3. Cleaning.

B. Cultivation plan—planting, sowing, "beating up," etc.

C. Measures to be undertaken for the protection of the soil and young and old woods.

D. Plan of roadmaking.

E. Plan of draining and work required in connection with the banking up of streams (*Wasserbau*).

Once the renewal has been made the forest officer knows what areas have to be cut, thinned and planted in the next ten years, and he also knows what part of that must be done in the first five years; but he is generally allowed himself to choose the exact portions he will cut and plant each year. The necessity of revising the working-plan every five years is due to the rapidity with which conditions change as regards the state of the timber market, and the progress of the young plantations when affected by climatic extremes and pests.

The silvicultural year commences on the 1st October, both in Saxony and Prussia, which is a very convenient date as it neither comes in the middle of the cutting, as would the 1st January, nor does it come when planting is in progress. All matters relating to cutting and planting are reckoned according to the silvicultural year, whereas matters of finance are reckoned according to the ordinary year ending with the 31st December.

Forest Officer.—The position of forest officer in Saxony is no sinecure, there being a large amount of work both outside and indoors as well as a fair amount of responsibility attached to the post. Besides having control of some 4000 acres of woods the *Forstmeister* generally takes a very prominent part in local government, especially in thinly populated districts. While referring to the duties of the forest officer, it is necessary to point out that he has practically nothing to do with the financial side of the management, the work of the cashier and accountant being carried out by a separate office known as the *Forstkasse* or *Forstrentamt*, which has small branches distributed among the wooded districts. This office has charge of all the money accounts, payment of wages, receipts from timber sales, the arrangement of credit, and so on. Formerly these duties were performed by the *Forstmeister* himself, but it is certainly a far better arrangement to have a separate organisation for dealing with such matters, both from the point of view of the State and the *Forstmeister*. In certain respects the forest officer works in conjunction with the *Forstrentamt*, for example, when there is an auction sale of timber (nearly all the wood is disposed of in this manner) the forest officer must be present, although the sale is actually conducted by the *Forstrentamt* officials. He is there to answer questions as to the accessibility of the particular lots—wood-merchants often buying timber without first seeing it—and generally to supervise the sale, having the right to withdraw any lot which he thinks is not fetching a fair price. The system of book-keeping adopted in the Saxon forest service is somewhat complicated, but is simpler than that found in Prussia, where the *Forstmeister* is generally provided with a secretary. The Saxon forest officer is responsible for all accounts relating to the amount of timber felled and sold, and is required to fill in very detailed forms as to the quantity and kinds of timber and other products which his forest produces in the year. Anyone accustomed only to the manner in which the forest accounts are treated in this country can have but a poor idea of the labour entailed when these are properly kept, especially in the case of State woods. The making out of sale catalogues, the checking in the wood of every log felled, the marking of the trees to be taken out in the thinnings, and the close superintendence of the nursery work and planting are among the duties of a *Forstmeister* entailing a considerable amount of labour.

The " Revier."—The Forest Range or *Revier* (the area of

woods under one forest officer) is in Saxony as elsewhere, where scientific silviculture is practised, divided up into compartments and sub-compartments. The work of laying out the State woods was first seriously undertaken by Cotta. He personally supervised the compartment plan of a number of forests, and his influence lived long after he died. The principles he laid down can be traced in the plan of every range in Saxony. Nothing is easier than criticism, and the compartment plans of a number of Saxon woods are rather severely censured by present-day foresters. It is not so much the areas of the compartment that are taken exception to but rather their shape, especially in hilly country. We find, on looking at the compartment plan of an average Erzgebirge forest, that very little regard appears to have been paid to the contour lines, and we see rides running for miles over hill and valley in perfectly straight lines. This geometrical method of planning woods is now somewhat out of date so far as mountainous land is concerned, but when once a forest has been laid out the alteration of the main rides involves a great deal of trouble, and in cases where a road and ride coincide becomes almost a practical impossibility. Modern forest management teaches that too much importance should not be attached to compartments being rectangular in shape, and that more attention should be paid to convenience in working, and the persistent endeavour to unite roads and rides without unduly sacrificing the interests of either. The average compartment in Saxony varies from 50 to 75 acres which, for spruce woods, may be considered rather large. The length of the adjacent sides are roughly in the proportion of 1 : 2 or 3 or 1 : 2·5 on the average, which is quite a good shape (see Fig. 2). The assumption upon which nearly all the State forests have been laid out is that the chief provision to be made is for the safety of the woods from west and south-west winds, and for this reason we find all the main rides running from west or south-west to east or north-east. The longer sides of the compartments run at right angles to these directions, which means that the cross or "minor" rides run from north or north-west to south or south-east. The regulation width of main rides is 9 metres (about 29½ ft.), and that of the cross rides 4½ metres (about 14¾ ft.). The object of having the main rides so wide is to allow of the trees on the north and south sides of compartments becoming well clothed with branches

FIG. 1.—The face of a pure spruce cutting looking west, Tharandt Forest   Age 85.
Average height, 72 feet.   Contents, 6300 cubic feet (above 2·75 inches diameter).
Quality of soil, III   This *stand* was thinned on the old method and is consequently somewhat thicker than what is now considered ideal.   The crowns are
about one-third of the total height of the trees.

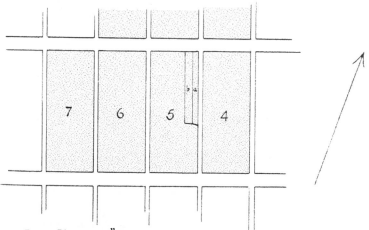

FIG. 2.—Diagram to illustrate the normal shape of the   compartment and
the direction of the rides with reference to the points   of the compass.
(The width of the rides is out of proportion for the sake of clearness.)

[*To face p.* 184

FIG. 3.—Part of a cutting series, compartment 20, Thurandt Forest, running roughly from east to west.

Section A = Pure spruce 25 years old. Section B = Pure spruce 25 years old. Section C = Pure spruce 5 years old. Section D = Silver fir and spruce 120 years old. Section E = Spruce 70 years old. Section F = Compartment 11. Section G = Compartment 12. Compartment 10 is to which sacrifices will be made spruce 120 years old. Section E = Spruce 70 years old. Section F = Compartment and also illustrates the extent to which sacrifices will be made

This photograph gives a good idea of the appearance of a cutting series in pure spruce. . . . . . not mature whereas those in Section D are at least thirty years es. The chief storm-winds undoubtedly come most frec ently om the west and south-west, and therefore much sho d be crificed in order to safeguard the woods from their tects, pecially when it is considered that spruce often forms most e entire crop. The obvious disadvantage, however, o plan- ng woods at the chief storms only is that the gales om other directions are no. provided against, and may often use very serious damage. Thus in Saxony d aded orm is not now from the south or south-west, but fro the rth and north-west, especially if it occurs when the owns are heavily laden with snow or ice. But as it is possible to shelter compartments from both north and west inds the predominating storm-wind must be provided a inst, d this we find very efficiently carried out in the Stat rests Saxony.

The direction of cutting is, of course, again the storm- nd, d is thus from east or north-east to south or south-west cording as the wood has been laid o, the face of the cutt gs ing always parallel or nearly so ith the cross rides.

The large number of small " Cutting Series " (Hiebzuge) fo d the State forests for s one of the most important d aracteristic featur of the woods in Saxony. Th sult of small " utting Series " is that the annual felling takes ace over numerous small areas scattered throug the wood, stead of in one or two large blocks. This is lvantageous om many points of view, especially for conifers d for a tree, ich as spruce, which is liable to suffer fr h frost and ought, it is particularly beneficial. The c ngs a also made ry narrow, not normally exceeding 60 t 70 yards in width, and e seldom finds a cleared area greate han 4 acres (see Fig. 2). he method of slicing narrow strip off the face of a number different " stands " (Bestände) s the direct opposite f the rench method of arranging c ttings, in which the ten ency to have, as it were, but on " Cutting Se s for the v hole Working Section " (Betriebsklasse) and concentrating the w le f the annual fellings in one place. The advantages, both silvi- ltural and æsthetic, of the Saxon method of numerous cuttings re so well known that it is hardly necessary to reiterate them all re. In a summer such as that of 1911, when a large number

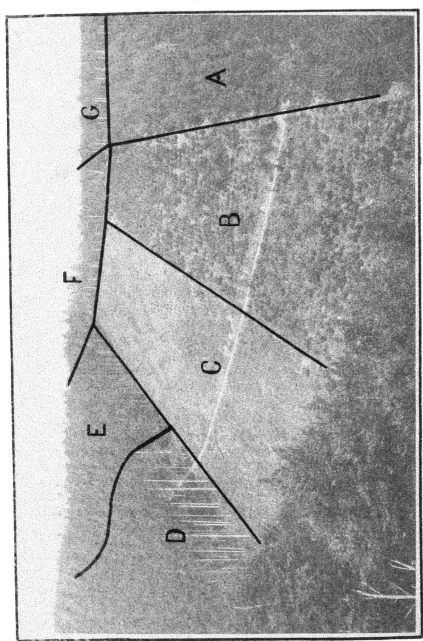

Fig. 4. Part of a cutting series, compartment 50, Tharandt Forest, running roughly from east to west.

Section A = Pure spruce 25 years old. Section B = Pure spruce 15 years old. Section C = Pure spruce 5 years old. Section D = Silver fir and
... ... years old. Section E = Spruce 70 years old. Section F = Compartment . Section G = Compartment

right down the stem, and thus forming more or less wind-fast trees. The chief storm-winds undoubtedly come most frequently from the west and south-west, and therefore much should be sacrificed in order to safeguard the woods from their effects, especially when it is considered that spruce often forms almost the entire crop. The obvious disadvantage, however, of planning woods to meet the chief storms only is that the gales from other directions are not provided against, and may often cause very serious damage. Thus in Saxony the most dreaded storm is not now from the south or south-west, but from the north and north-west, especially if it occurs when the tree-crowns are heavily laden with snow or ice. But as it is impossible to shelter compartments from both north and west winds the predominating storm-wind must be provided against, and this we find very efficiently carried out in the State forests of Saxony.

The direction of cutting is, of course, against the storm-wind, and is thus from east or north-east to south or south-west, according as the wood has been laid out, the face of the cuttings being always parallel or nearly so with the cross rides.

The large number of small "Cutting Series" (*Hiebzuge*) found in the State forests forms one of the most important and characteristic features of the woods in Saxony. The direct result of small "Cutting Series" is that the annual felling takes place over numerous small areas scattered through the wood, instead of in one or two large blocks. This is advantageous from many points of view, especially for conifers; and for a tree, such as spruce, which is liable to suffer from both frost and drought, it is particularly beneficial. The cuttings are also made very narrow, not normally exceeding 60 to 70 yards in width, and one seldom finds a cleared area greater than 4 acres (see Fig. 2). The method of slicing narrow strips off the face of a number of different "stands" (*Bestände*) is the direct opposite of the French method of arranging cuttings, in which the tendency is to have, as it were, but one "Cutting Series" for the whole "Working Section" (*Betriebsklasse*) and concentrating the whole of the annual fellings in one place. The advantages, both silvicultural and æsthetic, of the Saxon method of numerous cuttings are so well known that it is hardly necessary to reiterate them all here. In a summer such as that of 1911, when a large number of young trees died of drought, the great superiority of narrow cuttings became very evident as the percentage of deaths was always lowest on that part of the planted area which was to some extent shaded from the sun's rays during the afternoon by the old trees. Although it is unwise to allow the fundamental principles of management to be influenced greatly in order to make provision for exceptional circumstances, such as the drought of 1911, it is easily seen that Wagner's idea of north to south cuttings would have very great advantages even in spruce woods could it possibly be carried out. In Saxony, at any rate, north to south cuttings are out of the question on account of the wind dangers, but there is always a tendency to throw the cutting direction a little more round to the south in order to gain as much shelter for the young trees as possible. Before going further it would be well to point out that, so far as spruce is concerned, clear felling and planting is the rule and anything else is the exception. Natural regeneration has been repeatedly tried, and has proved consistently to be a failure owing chiefly to unfavourable conditions of soil and climate, although the spruce is, in any case, an unsatisfactory subject for this method of management. The short "Cutting Series," so characteristic of the Saxon woods, are not obtained without certain sacrifices in other respects, but we find these willingly undertaken in order to obtain and maintain the normal cutting series. Severances, for instance, have frequently to be made where large blocks of even or nearly even aged woods are met with. Again, in order that the "Cutting Series" may be carried right through uninterruptedly, some "stands" (*Bestände*) are often felled below the normal age, and others have to be left till they are considerably above it (see Fig. 3). The whole length of a "Cutting Series" varies, some extending only across one compartment and others extending over two, but longer ones are seldom found. "Cutting Series" do not often extend for the whole *length* of the compartment, although they normally would do so. In some cases there may not be more than eight or nine "stands" in one "Cutting Series," in which case fellings will not take place oftener than once every 10 years in that particular series. The general rule, however, for regulating how soon one felling is to follow another is that further felling should be postponed until the young plantation on the last area cut has got a good start. This may not take 10 years, but in Saxony it is seldom less than 5, and one of the greatest advantages of short "Cutting Series" is that you can leave the young plantations in the shelter of old woods for a considerable period without any difficulty in finding suitable places for the annual fellings. The formation of sub-compartments is generally based upon difference in age, species, or silvicultural method, in pure high forest, age being the only basis, and 10 years the lowest difference which may cause a separate sub-compartment. It is generally recognised now that the sub-division of compartments has been carried too far, and that the management has become too intensive in this particular respect, giving a large amount of extra work without equivalent return. Although there is no limit laid down many are not much larger than about half an acre, and it is not uncommon in indicating sub-compartments to go down to the letter "r" in the alphabet, whereas it is usually agreed that they should not, as a rule, be made smaller than one acre, or an acre and a quarter. Sub-compartments are only marked on the compartment maps and not in the woods. This tends at times to lead to confusion and might well be altered.

Another outstanding feature of forest management in Saxony is the care which is given to age-classes which are kept separate for each Working Section (*Betriebsklasse*). The classes run— I. 1-20, II. 21-40, III. 41-60, and so on, and every endeavour is made to keep them as nearly normal as possible, because the more normal they become the greater is the ease in providing a regular annual cut which in turn creates a more certain market, especially of small local buyers who are always to be encouraged. Taking the average rotation to be 80 years, the normal for the whole of the Saxon woods is—

I.	II.	III.	IV.	V.	VI.	Cleared Space.
24 %	25 %	25 %	25 %,	...	...	1 %

while

23 %	21 %	25 %		29 %		2 %

were the actual figures for 1909, which shows a remarkable uniformity only achieved, however, after 80 years or so of careful planning.

(To be continued.)

22. **Report on Speeches made at meeting between Delegates representing the interests of Forestry in Scotland and the Scottish Railway Companies, to discuss the Question of the Price of Sleepers manufactured from Home-Grown Timber, as compared with that of those manufactured from Foreign Timber.**

The Meeting took place at the Central Station Hotel, Glasgow, on Friday, 28th March 1913, at 2.30 P.M.

PRESENT—

Caledonian Railway Representatives.—Mr Wm. J. Chrystal, Director; Mr Donald A. Matheson, General Manager; Mr A. J. Easton, Stores Superintendent.

North British Railway Representatives. — Mr Andrew K. M'Cosh, Director; Mr J. Cathles, Secretary; Mr J. J. Smith, Stores Superintendent.

Glasgow and South-Western Railway Representatives.—Mr Melville, Engineer; Mr R. F. Harnson, Stores Superintendent.

Great North of Scotland Railway Representative.—Mr C. A. Thomson, Stores Superintendent.

Highland Railway Representatives —Mr R. M. Wilson, Chairman; Mr Charles Kennedy, Stores Superintendent.

Forestry Delegates.—Captain Stirling, Mr Sydney J. Gammell, Mr J. H. Milne Home, Dr Borthwick, Mr Frank Scott, Mr G. U. Macdonald, Mr A. Speirs, Mr John Broom, Mr T. B. Jones, Mr W. Wilson, Mr J. T. Garrioch, Mr Frank Sime, Mr Gilbert Brown.

In attendance also—Mr A. S. Leslie, Mr J. W. Douglas, Mr R. Galloway, Mr R. B. Fraser.

Mr CHRYSTAL of the Caledonian Railway Company having been appointed chairman of the meeting by the representatives of the railway companies, welcomed the delegates representing forestry interests, and intimated that all the Scottish railway companies were represented at the meeting.

Captain STIRLING, in introducing the deputation, thanked the Scottish railway companies for having consented to receive them, and stated that the deputation represented all the interests connected with home timber and specially those interested in the trade in home-grown railway sleepers. The deputation realised that the railway companies were not philanthropic institutions, and that it would be waste of time for them to ask the railway companies for concessions at the expense of the Shareholders unless they could offer something in return. What they asked for would not only be a benefit to the interests represented in the deputation, but also to the railway companies themselves. Captain Stirling explained that the three Societies who had sent delegates, in order of their seniority, were :—

1. The Royal Scottish Arboricultural Society, which represented all interests from the nursery to the saw-mill, and included in its membership landowners, nurserymen and timber merchants. The Society also dealt with the scientific and educational side of Forestry.

2. The Landowners' Co-operative Forestry Society, Limited, a society of comparatively recent origin, which had been in existence about three years; the membership consisted of landowners, the acreage of whose land under wood represented a large proportion of the whole of such acreage in Scotland.

3. The Home Timber Merchants' Association, which was formed to represent the larger interests of the home timber merchant.

Captain STIRLING also intimated that there were one or two representatives on the deputation who did not belong to any of the foregoing societies. Captain Stirling stated that he proposed to indicate briefly the various points with which the deputation would deal, and that he would leave the elaboration of these points to the delegates themselves, as they would be able to give first-hand information. He emphasised the point that the members who would speak knew the actual facts and had been all their lives in the timber trade. Captain Stirling raised the question of keeping a record of what took place at the meeting, and stated that the deputation were prepared to leave it to the railway companies to decide this point, but he expressed the hope that permission would be given to circulate a report of the meeting amongst the members of the societies represented. He suggested that the report should be submitted in draft to the railway companies for their approval.

Mr CHRYSTAL, in reply, stated that the railway companies would be glad to hear what the deputation had to say and that they would decide afterwards whether they approved of the report which it was proposed should be submitted to the members of the different societies. Captain Stirling agreed to the proposal and proceeded to refer to an agenda which had been drawn up of the points it was proposed to discuss, and stated that in this agenda certain figures were quoted, and asked whether it might be assumed that these figures were before the railway companies.

Mr CHRYSTAL, in replying to Captain Stirling, informed the deputation that the railway companies were in absolute ignorance of the reason for the deputation, that to a certain extent they understood it had to do with the afforestation of land in Scotland, and that the price paid by them for home timber had an indirect bearing on this point. He understood they had merely come to hear certain points which the deputation had to put before them.

Captain STIRLING remarked that he thought it was understood that the principal object was to lay before the railway companies the difference in the prices they were paying for home and foreign timber and to ask for a remedy. Captain Stirling then called upon Mr Sime to speak on the difference between Baltic and home timber prices.

Mr SIME pointed out that the present price of home sleepers was about 3s., and that Baltic sleepers of the same specification were being sold at 4s. 6d. and 4s. 7d., being a difference in price of about 1s. 6d. to 1s. 7d. per sleeper in favour of the foreign article. For the years 1909 and 1910 the difference was only about 5d. per sleeper, and he asked if the railway companies could state how this difference was accounted for. Mr Sime maintained that the Scots pine sleeper was better in quality than the Baltic sleeper, and gave as one of the reasons for this that the home-grown Scots pine sleeper is taken from root cuts, whereas the Baltic sleeper is taken from middle and top cuts. He explained that the railway companies in their own specification laid down that there must be only two sleepers cut from the block, and to get these two sleepers it was necessary for the Baltic merchants to go far up the tree with their cuts. Mr Sime expressed the view that the railway companies ought to know better than anyone else that the home-grown Scots pine sleeper was superior to the foreign.

Mr CHRYSTAL, in replying to Mr Sime, stated that the railway companies were giving the prices asked by the merchants, and that it was really a case of giving more for the foreign at present than less for the home. The probable reason for this was that they found that after buying all the available supply of home sleepers at the price asked they had to go abroad to meet their requirements, and pay the price asked for by the foreign merchant. He stated that if they could get them they would probably buy nothing but home - grown sleepers, but that apparently there was not a sufficient supply. He thought that the specification of the home sleeper was easier than that of the foreign, and he expressed his own personal opinion in emphatic terms to the effect that he considered Norway sleepers were much better than home - grown sleepers. Dealing with the general question before the meeting, Mr Chrystal said that he understood the question was one of re-afforestation in Scotland, and that this was at the back of the idea in getting better prices, and he expected that the deputation would make a very strong point of this question. He informed the deputation that he himself was a landowner, that he grew and sold timber, and realised how small its value was. As regards the question of the prices paid, he said that the railway companies, so far as his information went, bought as much home timber as they could get. He admitted that the prices were different, and stated that this was accounted for by the fact that the companies could not get a sufficient supply of home-grown sleepers. He supposed that the Scottish timber merchants and others got the best price they could for their timber, but he did not know how these prices were arranged. After the railway companies had bought as many home-grown sleepers as they could get they had to go abroad and purchase the balance at the prices quoted by the foreign merchants. He said that this year the railway companies were unfortunately in the position of having to pay more to the foreign merchants than previously, and he presumed this was the reason for the deputation waiting on them. He pointed out that the railway companies do not prefer to go abroad for their timber if they can buy it at home, and that he thought the Scots timber merchant gets better prices than the foreign merchant, seeing the specification of the Scots timber was, as he had already pointed out, easier. He further stated that he would, if offered Norway and home timber sleepers, everything else being equal, prefer the Norway.

Captain STIRLING thanked Mr Chrystal for his statement, which gave the deputation speakers a line to go on, and stated that the main point in the contentions of the deputation was that the prices have gone up for foreign sleepers, but not in the same proportion for home sleepers within recent date, that if the prices were compared five or six years ago it would be found that they were then almost identical, but that the foreign sleeper had been rising in price, although there had not been a corresponding rise in the price of home sleepers, and that the interests represented in the deputation would do everything possible to put both prices on a level. He then intimated that he would call upon two or three speakers able to deal with the question of the quality of the home-grown Scots pine and the question of supplies, and stated that the remarks of these delegates would go a long way towards dealing with the points raised by Mr Chrystal.

Mr TOM JONES, of Messrs James Jones & Sons, Ltd., Larbert, said he thought it right to tell the representatives of the railway companies exactly what was in his mind in speaking that day, and, to put it shortly, it was simply this :—

That he thought the railway companies of the United Kingdom on principle should give to the home timber merchants as good prices as they were giving to the foreign timber merchants, for timber of equal value for their purposes. At the present moment the home timber merchants were selling their sleepers at 3s. and 3s. 2d., and, in some cases, were paying a considerable amount of carriage to the depot of the railway company, whilst the foreign merchant was getting about 4s. 7d., or a difference roughly of about 1s. 5d. per sleeper. Whilst he was not prepared to prove that the home sleeper was superior to the foreign one, although he believed that to be the case, still the fact remained that the long experience of the railway companies themselves proved that the home sleeper was just as good as the foreign one. They were quite aware that they could not supply all the railway companies' wants, but that was no reason why they should not be able to supply what they had at as good prices as those given to the foreigners; and if the companies would give at the present time the same price for the home sleepers as for the foreign ones they would be surprised at the greatly increased supply they would get. Owing to the small price they were getting, it paid home timber merchants to put sleeper timber to other uses, but a price equivalent to the foreign sleeper would transfer a large portion of this timber into the sleeper market. He held that home timber merchants were giving to proprietors, in proportion to what they were getting themselves, as good prices as it was possible for them to give. In fact, those proprietors who had already made the test and sold their wood in the market had found that that was so. It was clear that the better price they got in the home market the better price they would be able to give to proprietors, and, in accordance with these better prices, so there would be greater encouragement to proprietors to go on planting more timber. As they were all doubtless aware afforestation on a large scale was held to be one of the most effective methods of keeping our people on the land. It was simply appalling to think that more people were annually leaving Scotland than were being born into it. It was clear also that if the railway companies adopted a wise broad policy in regard to home timber, and this resulted in the encouragement of afforestation, they themselves in the long-run would be great gainers, as a large portion of the cost of home timber was always represented by railway carriage. Besides, it was to their interests that their sources of supply should be as wide as possible, as in giving home timber of every kind fair play in the future they would be able to keep the foreigner much better in his place regarding his prices than they had been able to do in the past. Mr Jones finished up by appealing for a preference, just, indeed, as the Canadians gave the Mother Country a preference, but if they could not see their way to give a preference then they should at least give them equality and, if they did so, then not only would they be doing justice to the interests represented by the deputation, but they would be doing justice to the interests of the railway companies themselves. Mr Jones then exhibited a piece of home spruce which had been in the roof of a building at Larbert for twenty-five years and was still in perfect condition.

Dr Borthwick then spoke with regard to the durability of home-grown Scots pine, and stated that it had been tested up to the hilt in previous times. In experience it had been found that for structural work the lasting qualities were proved to be very great, that Scots pine compares extremely well with Baltic timber for joisting, etc., and that in many other departments its well-known qualities have been tested. He took up the point made by Mr Chrystal that Norway pine is more lasting than Scots pine, and disputed Mr Chrystal's contention. In support of the view held by himself he stated that Scots pine contained more resin, which is, in itself, a natural preservative, and that the conditions of soil and climate under which Scots pine is grown here, are equal to those under which the same tree is grown in Norway. He thought that future tests would show that Scots pine grown in Scotland is equal to, if not better than, that grown in Norway, and that experience already gained had shown the former to be extremely durable. He was quite sure that for sleepers Scots pine ought to do as well as imported timber. He informed the meeting that Prof. Myer, who had wide experience of continental forests, expressed the opinion that the Scots pine which he saw in Scotland was the finest he knew in Europe.

Mr SPEIRS, who has had considerable experience in the west coast, spoke with regard to supplies in that district, and stated that it was found to be extremely difficult to compete with the foreign timber merchant owing to the low rate paid for the home sleeper. He thought this was a pity seeing there was so much available timber being lost to the markets. He had carried out tests and found that home-grown sleepers would last longer than Baltic ones, and this was accounted for by the fact that Baltic trees were grown cleaner than ours and therefore they could go longer up the stem with their cuts. He maintained that it was only the question of cost which prevented a large quantity of timber being made available for the market from the west coast, and that an increase in the price would do away with this scarcity to some extent.

Mr M'COSH of the North British Railway Company said that to him it appeared as if the question was one of getting the timber to the market at a price, and he mentioned the difficulties there were in getting supplies from the home timber sellers. It seemed to him that if it could be arranged to supply big quantities of home-grown timber, there would be no difficulty in disposing of it at a good price and in competing on absolutely equal terms with the foreign sleeper. He said that if the foreign timber is not proved to be better than the home-grown timber, his company would certainly take all their sleepers from the home merchants, but, of course, they would have to get all they require.

Mr GILBERT BROWN then spoke as to the visible supply of Scots fir in the north. He said there was much timber in inaccessible places which could be brought down to the railway, and gave as his view that there was 600,000 to 800,000 sleepers visible and that if more remote lots were taken into consideration another 250,000 might be added to this estimate. The latter, owing to the high altitude in which they are growing and the consequent difficulty of transport, cannot, at the present rate offered for sleepers, be placed on the market. If, however, a slight rise in price could be got, they could be dealt with, and the benefits would not rest with the owners alone but also with the railway companies, as the timber is well matured and of splendid durability, and when cut up is more like pitch pine than ordinary Scots pine, and is altogether vastly superior to the quality of sleepers got from the Baltic.

Mr WILSON of Auchinleck dealt with the supplies which could be got from the west coast, Ayr, and the south-west of Scotland. He said that there was not a great deal of Scots pine suitable for sleepers in those districts, but that if a fair price was given a larger supply would certainly be available. In the meantime, the Glasgow and South-Western Railway did not use any home-grown sleepers and this was one of the reasons why he had not taken up the supplying of Scots pine sleepers. He used the Scots pine which he bought for other purposes, but would be prepared to use it for sleepers if the price showed a better profit. He also stated that, if the railway companies had any real sympathy with afforestation, there are many things which they could use home-grown timber for, which they did not at present do.

Mr WILSON of the Highland Railway had great sympathy with the objects of the deputation, but, from a business point of view, he said it could not be expected that the southern railway companies would pay more than they were bound to pay for home timber in the open market. The question of home and foreign sleepers did not really affect his company as they used only home-grown sleepers. He said that it seemed to him that one of the main points for the societies to consider was, whether they could deliver Scots pine sleepers at an equivalent or less price than foreign sleepers, and in sufficient quantities. Since Mr Brown had spoken he had made a small calculation which went to show that the 750,000 mentioned was a very small quantity compared with the consumption, and that if anything was to be done a business proposition must be put forward. He also emphasised the fact that it was apparently necessary to have a method of dealing centrally with the timber.

Mr M'COSH here stated that his company were on the look out just now for 250,000 sleepers and would purchase these from home merchants on the same terms as from foreign merchants. Mr Jones asked if they would give equal prices, and he also asked whether they would take the sleepers free on rail at any point on their system or would insist on deliveries at their depots. Mr M'Cosh did not commit himself definitely on these points.

Mr MILNE HOME spoke from personal experience of the supply which could be got from the South of Scotland, and said that they could not of course give as large supplies as the North or Centre of Scotland. At the same time this question was far more important to the South of Scotland than elsewhere, and if instead of the present price they could get a better price a very fair supply of sleepers could be got from the South of Scotland, whereas at present there were none at all being supplied as the timber was being used for other purposes.

Mr M'COSH stated that the railway companies were asking for home timber from time to time, and he appealed for organisation which would enable larger supplies to be made available.

Mr SYDNEY J. GAMMELL of Drumtochty was called upon by Captain Stirling to put the case before the railway companies' representatives in a concrete form. Mr Gammell stated that he did not think he could do more than consolidate the statements made by the other delegates after the exhaustive way the subject had been dealt with by them. He entirely endorsed what had been said by Captain Stirling, that any proposition must be made from a business point of view. The Societies represented did not pretend that it was possible for their members to supply all the railway sleepers required, but believed that there was a considerable quantity of home

Scots pine suitable for sleepers, and that with increased prices increased supplies would be available, which would exercise a steadying influence on the price of the Baltic sleeper. It was in the interests of the railway companies that encouragement in the form of increased prices should be given to the planting of extensive forests both by private and public enterprise, because such planting would do good to the country as a whole, and the railway companies would be bound to benefit by the increased prosperity of the country and the increased traffic which must follow it. He maintained that, quality for quality, the home producer should be put on an equal footing with the foreigner. He appreciated what had been said by Mr M'Cosh with regard to deliveries, and something might be done to meet this difficulty. With regard to the place where delivery should be given, he thought it would be good policy for the railway companies to take deliveries on any part of their system rather than at one point, as they would thereby get larger quantities, and that at any rate railway companies should carry the sleepers to their central depots at cost price. When considering the relative prices of the home and imported sleeper the question of freight had to be considered, but the difference in price did not correspond with the cost of carriage. What the Societies wanted was encouragement by increase in price, so that ultimately a large annual supply of home sleepers could be given. The railway companies must appreciate the business point of view of such a proposition, and he hoped that as a result of the views put forward by the deputation, the timber producers and suppliers would in future receive better prices, which would do good both to them and to the railway companies.

Mr CHRYSTAL, in replying to the whole points raised by the deputation, said he noticed there was a distinct difference in the position taken up by the merchants and growers, and that it was the work of the timber merchant to collect the supplies. His company sent out their specification and asked for offers, and the price was fixed by the merchants, not by the company. Mr Frank Scott took exception to the statement that the company did not fix the price, and Mr Chrystal, while recognising the reasonableness of Mr Scott's intervention, considered that he (Mr Chrystal) was entitled to make the statement he had made on this point. They took as many sleepers as they could get from the home timber merchants, and had to get the rest elsewhere at the lowest price they could. In concluding, Mr Chrystal promised that the railway companies would give due consideration to the whole matter as placed before them by the delegates.

Captain STIRLING then moved a vote of thanks to the Chairman and the Representatives of the railway companies, and stated that the deputation had not expected a definite reply then, but were glad to know that the railway companies would consider the case that had been put before them.

Note.—Since the date of the meeting several of the Scottish railway companies have agreed to buy sleepers of home-grown timber at the same price as foreign sleepers. It is hoped that in response to this concession an effort will be made by the timber trade to ensure a regular supply of sleepers of such a quality as will challenge comparison with the foreign article. The Landowners' Co-operative Forestry Society have already undertaken contracts for the supply of sleepers at 4/5 each delivered.

23. A New Disease on the Larch in Scotland.[1]

(*With Plate.*)

By A. W. BORTHWICK, D.Sc., Lecturer on Forest Botany, University of Edinburgh, and MALCOLM WILSON, D.Sc., F.L.S., Lecturer on Mycology, University of Edinburgh.

On the 22nd May 1912, Mr Donald Grant, forester to Sir John Stirling-Maxwell on his estate of Fersit in Inverness-shire, sent to one of us specimens of *Larix europæa* with a fungus disease on the leaves, which, he remarked, bore a striking resemblance to the pine leaf rust, *Peridermium pini f. acicola.*

An examination of the specimens in the laboratory leads to the conclusion that the fungus present must be provisionally included in *Peridermium*, a genus of the Uredineae, consisting of a number of species parasitic on Gymnosperms, of which only the æcidial stage is known. Klebahn,[2] in 1898, described a species of this genus parasitic on the larch, which he named

[1] Reproduced by permission from *Notes from the Royal Botanic Garden, Edinburgh*, March 1913.

[2] *Kulturversuche mit heteröcischen Rostpilzen,* Bericht vii. (1898). Zeitschr. f. Pflanzenkr., Bd. ix. 1899, p. 14.

Æcidium (*Peridermium*) *Laricis*,[1] and, although the form under discussion does not agree in all respects with Klebahn's description, the differences are too slight to justify the creation of a new species. In the same paper Klebahn shows that *Æcidium* (*Peridermium*) *Laricis* is the æcidial stage of *Melampsordium betulinum*.

As the occurrence of *Peridermium Laricis* has not been previously recorded in Scotland, the following information may prove of value to those interested in forestry. In his observations of the appearance of the fungus, Mr Grant found that the larch was attacked early in the season, and that the fungus was fully developed on leaves when they were about three weeks old. It is interesting to note that, in his subsequent observations, he found the branches had shed their diseased leaves by 30th July, and, in consequence, no further material was available for examination. This would indicate that the stage of the fungus upon the larch runs a rapid course, and may thus account to some extent for the fact that it has previously escaped observation.[2]

The fungus is almost always found on the under surface of the leaves but occasionally on the upper side. The æcidia are arranged in rows on one or both sides of the midrib, and are separated by short, irregular intervals (Figs. 1, 2, and 3, Pl. II.). The number of æcidia on each leaf is variable, but is usually 6–15. Each group of spores is enclosed by a delicate white protective covering, the pseudoperidium, which, at maturity, has the form of a cylinder, slightly flattened laterally and open at the upper end. The pseudoperidium varies from ·5–·7 mm. in height, ·5–·7 mm. long and ·3–·4 mm. wide. In the earlier stages it is closed, and then the cylindrical part is terminated by a bluntly conical upper portion (Fig. 1*b*). The ripe æcidiospores are set free by the irregular rupture of the apex of the pseudoperidium, and, in consequence, after dehiscence has taken place, this is terminated by a ragged or lacerate margin (Fig. 1*a*

---

[1] Arthur and Kern, in Bull. Torr. Bot. Club, vol. xxxiii. 1906, p. 403, definitely placed this species in the genus *Peridermium* ; the fungus is therefore described as *Peridermium Laricis* (Kleb.), Arth. et Kern, by Saccardo in the *Sylloge Fungorum*, vol. xxi. 1912.

[2] A re-examination of diseased larch leaves, sent by Mr Murray, forester at Murthly, Perthshire, in June 1911, shows that the fungus present is an early condition of *Peridermium Laricis*.

and Fig. 4). Occasionally two adjacent pseudoperidia become partially or completely fused together (Fig. 2). The wall of the pseudoperidium is one cell in thickness, the cells being rhomboidal or polygonal in shape and the walls finely verrucose (Fig. 7). The numerous spores are orange-yellow in colour and rather irregular in shape, ellipsoidal or polyhedral, about 16–22 μ in length and 14–18 μ broad. The spore wall is evenly verrucose, except a small area, which is smooth, and thinner than the remaining portions. Fig. 6 represents a spore in optical median section, and Fig. 5 in surface view. It will be seen that the outer part of the wall consists of a number of rods of material placed perpendicularly to the surface (Fig. 6). Before dehiscence takes place the spores are found arranged in chains at the base of the pseudoperidium ; when the latter ruptures they easily separate and escape from the opening at the upper end.

A fungus known as *Cæoma Laricis* bears a considerable resemblance to the form just described on the larch. *Cæoma Laricis* produces orange-yellow spots on the leaves, but is at once distinguished from *Peridermium Laricis* by the entire absence of the pseudoperidium, as well as by differences in the sculpturing of the spore wall. *Cæoma Laricis* has been shown by Klebahn and others to be the æcidial stage of six different species of *Melampsora*, in which the uredospore and teleutospore stages occur on various species of *Populus* and *Salix*.

Although no definite record of the occurrence of *Peridermium Laricis* in Great Britain or Ireland has been made [The attention of the authors has been recently called to a paper by Mr W. S. Jones on *Melampsoridium Betulinum* (*Quart. Journal of Forestry*, Vol. V., No. 2, p. 137), where he records the discovery of this disease in Bagley Wood, near Oxford, in 1911. We regret that, inadvertently, this important paper was overlooked. Dr Somerville informs us that the disease is very common in Ireland.], it is probable that Plowright,[1] in 1891, carried out experiments with this species. This investigator discovered a form of *Cæoma Laricis* near King's Lynn, the æcidiospores of which, when placed on *Betula alba* caused infection, and, in course of time, the uredospore and teleutospore stages of *Melampsora betulina* were produced. A subsequent infection of *Larix europæa* by the germinating teleutospores produced spermogonia only.

[1] *Einige Impfversuche mit Rostpilzen*, Zeitschr. f. Pflanzenkr., Bd. i. 1891, p. 130.

CIETY,

:come

of the

mboi-

(Fig.

r and

i-22 μ

verru-

an the

edian

at the

aterial

dehis-

at the

easily

lerable

Cæoma

out is

entire

in the

fferent

ospore

rmium

atten-

by Mr

scovery

I. We

looked.

mon in

out ex-

a form

which,

ourse of

only.

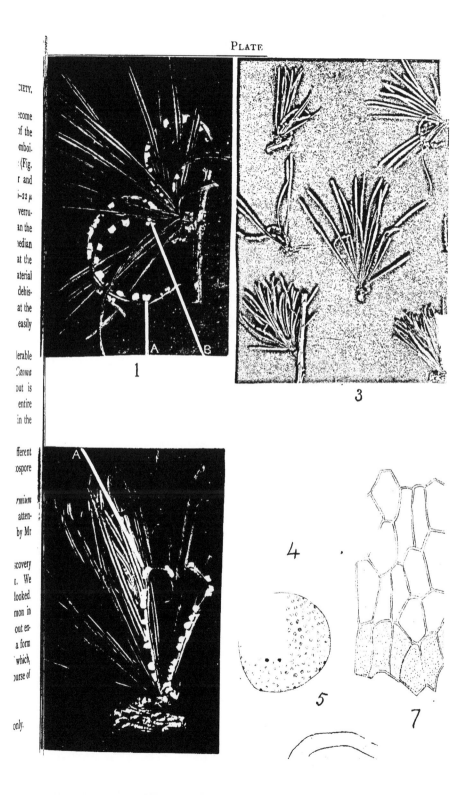

1

3

A

4

5

7

Klebahn,[1] by infection experiments commenced in 1896 in the neighbourhood of Hamburg, conclusively proved that *Peridermium Laricis* is the æcidial condition of *Melampsora betulina*. In his earlier experiments spermogonia were formed on *Larix europæa* as the result of infection by teleutospores from the birch, but in later investigations æcidia only were produced.

Melampsora betulina differs from the remaining species of the genus in the presence of a pseudoperidium enclosing the uredospore sorus. Klebahn has therefore instituted a new genus, *Melampsoridium*, for the reception of this species. The differences between the two genera are as follows :—

Melampsoridium : Æcidium of the *Peridermium* type. Uredospore sorus with a definite pseudoperidium.

Melampsora : Æcidium of the *Cæoma* type. Uredospore sorus surrounded by capitate hairs, but without a definite pseudoperidium.

The teleutospore sorus is similar in each genus.

Arthur and Kern include *Peridermium Laricis* in their list of North American species, since *Melampsoridium betulinum* is of common occurrence in that country ; the stage on the larch has not yet, however, been found in North America. Saccardo (*Sylloge Fungorum*, xxi.) records its occurrence in France and Germany.

The specimens of *Peridermium Laricis* obtained in Scotland differ in some respects from those described by Klebahn. Up to the present no spermogonia have been discovered ; it is possible, however, that these develop earlier than the æcidia, and have, in consequence, been overlooked. The colour of the pseudo-peridium is described by Klebahn as bright red-orange ("hell rötlich-orange"). In the Scottish specimens, in the early stages before the pseudoperidium had opened, the colour was pale yellow, and, after dehiscence, it became white.

Considering the abundance of *Melampsoridium betulinum* in this country, it is a remarkable fact that *Peridermium Laricis* is of such rare occurrence. Its resemblance to *Cæoma Laricis* may, however, partly explain the absence of previous records. It is possible that *Melampsoridium betulinum* really consists of several physiological species, and that *Peridermium Laricis* is only one of its æcidial forms; this supposition may explain the absence of records from North America. At present no information is

---

[1] *Loc. cit.* p. 198, and *Kulturversuche mit Rostpilzen*, Bericht viii. (1899), Jahrb, f. Wiss. Bot., Bd. xxxiv. 1900, p. 347.

available on this point, but it is proposed to carry out infection experiments to throw light on this and other questions in connection with the life history of the fungus.

DESCRIPTION OF PLATE II.

FIG. 1.—Photograph of twig of *Larix europæa* with diseased leaves : (*a*) pseudoperidium with lacerate margin ; (*b*) unopened pseudoperidium (× 4).

FIG. 2.—Photograph of twig of ditto, with fused pseudoperidia (× 4).

FIG. 3.—Photograph of twigs of ditto (about natural size).

FIG. 4.—A pseudoperidium showing lacerate margin (× about 50).

FIG. 5.—Spore in surface view (× 1000).

FIG. 6.—Spore in optical median section (× 1000).

FIG. 7.—Part of pseudoperidium ; the lower cells show the verrucose marking on the walls (× 220).

24. Recent Publications on Swiss Forests.

By W. S. SMITH, Ph.D.

The problem of afforestation requires, as most will admit, careful consideration of all conditions of the area, and it is well to regard what is being done in other countries. The members of the Society are to have this year the opportunity of seeing Swiss forestry, and several recent Swiss papers deal with forests. Two of the authors referred to below spent several weeks in Britain in 1911 and visited woodlands in all parts, so that they are in a position to make valuable comparisons.

Professor C. Schrœter of Zurich,[1] in comparing the vegetation of Britain and Switzerland, points out that in both countries man has had a great influence on the present condition of the woods. Both countries have below the tree limit a typical forest climate, so that the natural vegetation of the land, if left to itself to grow without restriction, would become forest and remain in this state with forest as a "climax plant formation." Exceptions to this rule occur on the salt marshes, shingle beaches, and moving sand dunes on our coasts, on certain shallow calcareous soils like the Chalk Downs, on many poor sandy soils, in wet marshes and peat bogs, and on the slipping banks along streams or below crags. Man has made extensive inroads on what were formerly great areas of forest. In Switzerland, out of every

[1] C. Schrœter in *New Phytologist*, xl., pp. 277-289, 1912.

100 square miles of original forest, only 21 per cent. is now under trees; the figures given for Britain are, England 5·3 per cent., Scotland 4·6, Wales 3·9, Ireland 1·5. That is, they are the least afforested lands in Europe. What woods are left in England are regarded as more natural and less altered than in Switzerland. This backward condition of English forestry is ascribed to the conservatism of the English landowner and the preponderance of sporting rights under private ownership. In Switzerland little original forest is left, and the woods are radically altered by a system of intensive forestry. The forests in the Middle Ages were used quite as much for grazing as for the production of timber; thus oak-woods were encouraged as they provided mast for herds of swine. Gradually, however, the increased demand for timber and the promotion of forestry have resulted in the closing of the forests against grazing animals, and the oak has been largely replaced by beech and spruce. In the most recent times, pure plantations of conifers have decreased, and there is a return to the establishment of mixed woods.

The greatest competitors of forest both in Switzerland and in Britain are grassland and moorland, because the climate and topography are favourable to these types of vegetation. The utilisation of these is, however, different in the two countries. The Swiss grasslands at lower levels are intensively manured and provide the chief forage for stock in winter; at higher altitudes the "Sennhütte" system of pasturing dairy cows and cattle on the high alpine meadows involves intensive grazing and encourages a valuable type of pasture, yielding large returns. In Britain cattle-grazing from the old hill-shielings has given place to the black-face sheep wandering at large over extensive areas, and this does not favour grassland to the same extent. Our uplands are thus much less productive; as grazing grounds their value is not high, but what grazing there is, combined with heather burning, has proved a most effective means of destroying all tree-seedlings on our moors.

One feature remarked by the Swiss writers is the lowness of the upper tree-limit in Britain. This comes about 2000 feet with Scots pine and birch on mountain masses like the Cairngorms, and is lower on the less elevated groups or on long hill-ranges. In Switzerland Scots pine rises to 4300 feet on the Northern Alps and to 7600 feet in the Puschlav area of the

Southern Alps. Birch attains to 5300 feet in the Northern Alps, and to 7000 feet in the Central Alps. Professor Schrœter discusses this question at some length. Even assuming that the present tree-limit in Britain is 1000 feet lower than is shown by tree-remains found in our peat, it is still far below the Swiss altitudes. This is an evidence of our oceanic climate, but it is also a result of the lower altitudes attained by even our highest mountains. If Ben Nevis (4400 feet) is compared with a summit in Switzerland of the same height (*e.g.* the Gabris), the following differences in climate are found on Ben Nevis: lower temperature in July and January, and in the mean annual, but a less marked variation throughout the year; a larger rainfall and much more fog and wind. As Schrœter says, "A study of meteorological figures conveys some idea of the foggy, rainy, snowy, stormy, and sunless oceanic climate of the Scottish Highlands." So far as statistics show, the upper limit of the birch in the Highlands coincides with a July temperature (10° Cent.) almost the same as is found towards its upper limit in Switzerland, but in the continental Swiss climate this temperature occurs at much higher elevations. One suggestion appeals to the Scottish forester: it might be well to investigate whether with the help of the larch, which flourishes so well in Scotland, the tree-limit in the Scottish Highlands might not be raised higher.

A paper by Dr Brockmann-Jerosch [1] also deals with the question of tree-limits, and although it is somewhat technical a short notice may indicate the line of argument. It is shown that the upper tree-limit cannot be determined by any one factor, such as rainfall, snowfall, or the average temperature of the year or of any particular month or period. The tree-limit depends more on the general climate as a whole, and this is determined for each locality by the physiography or lie of the land, in other words by what most foresters call exposure. Dr Brockmann's discussion refers to Switzerland, a continental area, but he shows by statistics that the northern and western parts of Switzerland are more oceanic than the central Alps. A continental climate with its hotter, drier summers and more intense winters, as seen in Siberia, is more favourable to tree-growth in this way that the tree-limit is farther north (*i.e.* nearer the pole) than in oceanic western Europe. So also a con-

[1] H. Brockmann-Jerosch in *Engler's Botan. Jahrbücher*, 49, pp. 19-43, 1903.

tinental climate favours a higher tree-line on the mountains. This is borne out in Scotland in that the tree-line on the Cairngorms and Deeside Highlands is higher than in the more oceanic Inverness and Argyll Highlands. An oceanic climate is, however, more favourable to a greater number of species of trees, and the visitor from the Continent is always struck by the flourishing condition of many foreign conifers (*Araucaria, Sequoia,* etc.) and such shrubs as rhododendron in Scotland (*e.g.* Dunkeld) and especially in the west of Ireland and Cornwall. On the other hand, the continental climate brings about a more rigid selection so that only a few species survive, but they are more robust and grow better than the same species in an oceanic climate.

Dr Ruebel's [1] paper contains a short sketch of the zones of vegetation in the Bernina district on which he has recently published a large memoir. The subalpine zone includes the forest belt, and it only is referred to here. Three types of forest are distinguished in this district. Larch in pure forest is somewhat rare, but it flourishes on ground along streams or on rock screes, always on newly made land where the larch finds the necessary light away from competition of other trees; the usual undergrowth is rough grass. The Cembran pine forest (Arvenwald) occurs on older soils and forms a denser forest with more humus; in deep shade there is no ground vegetation, but in opener parts juniper and bearberry (*Arctostaphylos*) occur. The Cembran pine invades the larch forest when the older larches become too dense and prevent regeneration by seedling larch; this shade does not, however, exclude the more shade-bearing Cembran pine. The pine forest (Föhrenwald) consists of the Engadine pine, a variety with a more pyramidal habit than the common Scots pine, and so better adapted to endure snow. The author regards the Engadine pine (*Pinus silvestris* var. *engadinensis*) as nearly allied to the native grey Scots pine of the Scottish Highlands. In the Swiss woods the cowberry (*Vaccinium vitis-idæus*) is one of the most abundant ground plants, just as it is in Rothiemurchus and the Speyside pine forests.

[1] E. Ruebel in *Engler's Botan. Jahrbücher*, 49, pp. 10-18, 1913.

25. Notes of Silvicultural Interest.

(*With Plate.*)

By A. MURRAY.

My principal object in compiling these notes is to lay before the members of the Society my experience in the cultivation of some of the newer conifers in regard to the production of commercial timber.

The most important of these is, I believe, the Japanese larch, grown from seed produced in this country. It is now over 20 years since the Japanese larch was introduced, so that many trees are bearing cones freely. The nursery treatment of this larch need not differ in any respect from that which is generally given to the European species. The only difficulty experienced at present is in obtaining adequate supplies of seed. This difficulty is much more pronounced when home-collected seed is required, but as time goes on this should become more plentiful.

It was during the autumn of 1904 that I collected the first cones produced on our Japanese larches,—and by sowing the seed from these in the spring of 1905 we got a crop of about 300 plants. These were planted out in the spring of 1908 as 3-year-old plants, after having been twice transplanted. The planting was done on the pitting system at 4-feet spaces. At this stage the plants were exceedingly fine, fully 3 feet high, and, in consequence of the transplanting, they possessed a mass of fibrous roots and were richly foliaged. In choosing a site for these plants, what is known as a frost hollow was selected, by way of experiment, in order to test their hardiness, and also to find out if they would remain free from disease in such a situation.

From the germination of the seed until now the plants have been exceedingly fast growers, surpassing both the native Japanese and the European larch, and they have kept free from damage by frost and from diseases of all kinds.

At the end of last growing season these 300 trees had an average height of fully 14 feet, with an average circumference at breast-height of $8\frac{3}{4}$ inches.

By some this larch is looked upon as a hybrid, and to a casual observer it does seem to resemble both the European and

PLATE III.

JAPANESE LARCH.

PLANTATION OF *TSUGA ALBERTIANA.*

[*To face p.* 206.

Japanese larch. The foliage and the cones (which these plants are now producing) are identical with the leptolepis, and the outward appearance and vigour of growth may be entirely due to climatic conditions; but it is very improbable that these plants are a cross between *Larix europæa* and *Larix leptolepis*, since, from observations made here, the flowering season of the two species does not seem to coincide.

We have now many thousands of these plants on this estate—all are fine growers, but those referred to are the only ones of their kind forming a pure crop, while it is believed that they are the oldest and largest of their kind. I do not think that planters will err in cultivating as many plants as possible from home-grown seed.

Alongside of these larches is a plantation of the Western Hemlock (*Tsuga albertiana*), which was formed in 1907, also with plants raised from home-collected seed. . The plants were put out when 4 years old, having been twice transplanted. The planting was done on the pitting method at 4 feet by 4 feet. The plants were then 30 to 36 inches high ; their average height now is about 11 feet, and the average circumference at 1 foot from the ground is $6\frac{1}{4}$ inches.

This tree is usually looked upon as being frost tender, but so far no damage has been done to it by frost, although the situation it occupies is quite open, and other species such as Douglas fir (*Thuja gigantia*) and Sitka spruce have all suffered.

Last winter was a very severe one in this particular place. The young trees were for some time completely covered with snow—only a mound appearing to mark where the largest of them were present. When the snow disappeared, however, the plants stood erect and no evil effects have followed. They are much more root-firm than the neighbouring Douglas firs, many of which, from their excessive mass of foliage, are bent over with the wind. The height-growth of the albertiana is much greater than that of the Douglas firs, but the diameter of the stem is about the same in both.

As in the case of the Japanese larch, albertiana seed is both scarce and dear, and the prices quoted in nurserymen's catalogues make the planting of this species as a forest tree prohibitive. On this estate we have many thousands, and beyond shading against the direct rays of the sun during germination, and giving overhead protection from frost during the first two winters, the mode of treatment differs but little from that of common nursery stock, and the cost of rearing is but little more.

It is to be noted that small birds are exceedingly fond of the seeds—red lead being of no use as a protection—consequently it is necessary to protect the beds with bird-proof netting as soon as they are sown.

The tree is of rapid growth and is sufficiently hardy to withstand an open exposure. The stem is always very straight, and the slender side branches and the flexible nature of the tree make it little liable to destruction by storms.

I believe that a plantation formed of this tree, pure or in mixture with the common larch—both being about equal in rate of growth — would help to prevent the spread of the larch disease. Unlike the common spruce the hemlock will not act as a nest for the chermes.

The durability[1] of the timber grown in this country is not known—it is harder and closer grained than the common spruce, while the rate of growth is much more rapid, and altogether the tree is worthy of cultivation on all situations suited to its growth.

A general method practised in rearing shade-bearing conifers in a frosty situation is to rear in advance a protective foregrowth of some hardy varieties—generally birch, but larch has also been tried in this way. An area of about 30 acres was cleared in 1904 of a fully matured crop of larch and oak. In 1907-8 most of the ground was planted with larch at 10 to 12 feet apart. In 1910 the spaces between were filled in with Douglas fir, a part being tried with *Cupressus Lawsoniana* and *Thuja gigantia*. It was expected by this means that the larch would have a sufficient ascendency over the Douglas firs, and that it would act as a nurse to these and also form a protection against damage by frost, while by such isolation the chances of spreading the larch disease would be less. All varieties have done exceedingly well, but from the fast-growing nature of the Douglas fir it looks as if these will soon overtop the larch. Perhaps the planting of the Douglas fir should have been deferred for a year or two longer.

[1] The *Canadian Forestry Journal*, vol. ix., No. 4, April 1913, p. 57, reports the "life" of railway sleepers as follows:—Cedar, 9 years; larch, 8 years; hemlock, 7 years; Douglas fir, 7 years; Jack pine and spruce, 6 years. Hon. Ed., *Transactions*.

Utilisation of scrub as nurse for frost-tender plants.—Whenever anything in the form of scrub naturally exists this is taken advantage of and thinned out as required, leaving the most suitable plants as a protection for the young crop until it is above the frost line.

Conversion of old oak coppice to coniferous high forest.—Through altered conditions the cultivation of oak coppice is no longer profitable, consequently these are thinned out and replaced with a shade-bearing coniferous crop. A sufficient number of the coppice-shoots are reserved to form a cover on the ground until the young crop is established, and are removed at periods of 4, 5 and 6 years after planting.

Semicircular planting spade.—Another matter of great importance is the method of planting. For several years past all planting has been done with the semicircular spade. The system is almost identical with that of pitting, while the expense is very little more than by the notch system. Experienced men can make in ordinary ground from 800 to 1200 holes in a day—two planters instead of one are, however, required to each spade. That is all the difference as regards time between this method and the barbarous notch system. The after-results do much more than compensate for the small extra expense. When the soil is of a poor or stiff retentive nature a little of a richer mixture can be introduced, thus giving the plant a start in life.

By this method the roots are put perpendicularly under the plant and are not one-sided and doubled up like a lot of golf clubs, as is generally the case in notch planting. Notched plants with such twisted and deformed roots generally become affected with either one or other of the root fungi, usually *Polyporus annosus.*

The method is of considerable importance, especially in forming margins and in planting exposed situations, as owing to the roots being perpendicular the plant develops evenly, and the roots anchor it to the soil on all sides alike. The young tree is also more easily planted erect, and is more firmly held in position.

Wind-proof margins.—Much care and judgment are necessary, not only in the planting, but also in the selection of species when forming margins. Many examples that meet the eye throughout the country indicate lack of judgment in planting and in the selection of suitable species, and the neglect of managing in such a manner as to encourage the trees to develop a mass of strong roots, together with strong side branches, forming a close barrier to the wind. If this matter was properly attended to destruction by gales would be reduced to a minimum.

Notwithstanding the large amount of damage done by recent gales and the large amount of timber suddenly thrown on the market, the demand and prices for timber, especially converted timber of all kinds, is on the increase, which alone should give encouragement to afforest all available waste ground.

26. The Use of Explosives in Forestry.

By DR ALEXANDER LAUDER.

The use of explosives for removing tree-stumps from the ground has been common for many years. Recently, however, the more extended use of explosives in connection with clearing the land for planting, root pruning, breaking up the subsoil to improve the drainage, as well as for agricultural purposes, has been recommended.

Whether the method is capable of this extended application depends not only on its efficiency but on its cost and its safety in the hands of ordinary workmen As far as the latter point is concerned there does not appear to be any danger if ordinary care and intelligence is exercised by those carrying out the work. With regard to cost, the following formula is suggested for calculating the cost of the explosive required to remove tree-stumps. For pine and fir trees the square of the girth in feet divided by 20 gives the approximate cost in shillings of the explosive required, *e.g.* for a tree 7 feet in girth $\frac{7 \times 7}{20} =$ 2s. 6d. approximately would be the cost of the explosive required. For deeply rooted trees, such as the oak or elm, the cost would be about double this. As regards the weight of explosive to be used, this may be calculated from the girth of the tree as follows :—

Pine stump, 5 feet in girth in light soil $\frac{5 \times 5}{3} = 8\frac{1}{3}$ ozs.

Oak stump, 4 feet in girth in very strong soil $\frac{4 \times 4}{1} = 16$ ozs.

The explosive in both cases is supposed to be gelignite. In the case of large stumps the main spreader roots must first be located and cut by exploding suitable charges underneath them. The method of blasting is to bore a hole either vertically or obliquely into the stump. The explosive is placed in the hole and carefully stemmed and fired by an ordinary or an electric fuse in the usual way.

For the purpose of clearing land of scrub or heavy undergrowth, it is recommended that holes 3 feet deep should be made in rows in the ground, the distance between the holes in each row being about 12 feet and the distance between the rows 10 feet. The holes in the adjacent rows are not placed opposite each other, but alternately, as indicated in the diagram:—

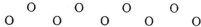

In each hole a single 2-oz. cartridge of "cheddite" is exploded. Where there are roots of heavier bushes the holes are made deeper and the amount of charge is increased. The explosion not only loosens the soil to such an extent that the scrub can easily be pulled up, but it also breaks and loosens the subsoil. For tree planting the hole should be from 3 to 4 feet in depth, and the charge 6 to 10 ozs. of "gelignite" or 7 to 12 ozs. of "cheddite." This should make a hole sufficiently large for planting the tree, or will loosen the soil so that it can easily be removed. The hole should be left for 24 hours before planting.

A demonstration of the method, as applied to the breaking up of the subsoil on land to be used for fruit culture, was recently given on land at the Hall of Aberuthven, belonging to the Blair Estates Company, by Messrs G. P. Berry and W. Bruce of the Edinburgh and East of Scotland College of Agriculture. Holes in rows were bored to the depth of about $2\frac{1}{2}$ feet. The distance between the holes was 9 feet and between the rows also 9 feet; 2 ozs. of cheddite were exploded in each hole. The demonstration was highly successful, the ground being cracked and fissured for a considerable distance round each hole A year or two must elapse before the full effect on the fertility of the land can be judged.

It is difficult to lay down any very definite rules as to the amount of explosive to be used, so much depends on the nature of the soil. The soil referred to above was a fairly heavy clay, and the distance between the holes and the depth was what was found most suitable for this particular kind of ground. These details would need to be determined by a few preliminary experiments in each case. The cost, including labour, worked out at about £6, 10s. per acre, but no doubt this could be materially reduced when larger areas were treated and the men became expert in making and charging the holes. A direct trial of the method for clearing scrub or heavy undergrowth is desirable and would furnish the necessary evidence as to the cost of the method.

27. Continental Notes—Germany.

By BERT. RIBBENTROP, C.I.E.

Prof. Dr R. Albert, after most laborious, intricate, and searching analysis and experiments, extending over several years, has finished his investigations of the soils of the heather regions of North-Western Germany, and is now engaged in summing up the results arrived at, more especially in regard to their practical application and utility in the afforestation of waste lands. The eminent explorer of the secrets of soils intends, however, to undertake, in the course of the coming summer, a further inspection and re-examination of numerous pattern areas and research plots, before publishing his summary. We may expect many interesting and original conclusions, some of which are, however, already foreshadowed in the reports before the profession.

The investigator finally and entirely does away with the opinion, till quite recently widely held, that the heather tracts of North-Western Germany were synonymous with sandy soils of low productive value, and shows that the development of heather growth is entirely due to climatic conditions, and is quite unconnected with the character of the soil; heavy loams and light sands produce heather within the heath regions, whereas outside their limits not even the poorest soils are heather clad, but are covered with inferior grasses and other low herbaceous growth. Dr Albert also explodes the equally widely spread misconception, that the soils in heather-covered areas are, almost without exception, bleached out in their upper layers, and rest on

seams of a ferruginous laterite formation (Ortstein), of varying
thickness and at varying depth.

This is not so. Even pure sandsoils, which can be proved to
have been covered with heather for hundreds of years, show no
signs of bleaching or of any indication of forming Ortstein.

Such phenomena are more or less local, and have taken place
whilst these regions were under forest, mostly in far-away times;
they occur, under certain conditions, even at present, where a
layer of dried peat humus, overgrown with bilberries, cranberries
and such like, has formed, in pure pine forests.[1] The mischief
can, however, be prevented, and in most cases even stopped in
its earlier stages, by underplanting the pine with beech or
other suitable deciduous species. In such cases, however, close
planting must be avoided, as a dense canopy would interfere
with the decomposition of the shed leaves and do more harm
than good, especially on inactive soils. It may be accepted
that wherever bleached-out soils and Ortstein are found under a
heather canopy, the present growth was not the cause thereof,
but only appeared when the previously existing forest had been
destroyed.

The belief in the almost general sterility of the heather regions
of North-Western Germany was an unjustifiable invention by
earlier writers, who rushed into print without looking below the
surface of the outwardly uniform, wide-stretching heather tracts.
It must be presumed that, by an unfortunate chance, they
pitched on an area to which their description would apply, and
that, misled by the outward uniformity of the picture before
them, they generalised, and presumed the same uniformity to
exist below the surface. It is a curious fact, however, that the
original assertion remained unchallenged for many years, and
that others, without further investigations, spent much time and
thought in searching for causes and reasons which would
explain the radical differences between the soils of the heather
tracts east and west of the Elbe, which all the time did not exist.

One of the most ingenious and audacious theories (they had
naturally all to be invented in the sanctum of the study) put
before a confiding public was, that the lands in North-Western
Germany were exposed to only one long uninterrupted glacial
period, in contrast to the areas farther east, where intermittent
glacial periods took place, and that this prolonged ice-covering

---

[1] A curious coincidence is the absence of worms in such deteriorating soils.

was quite sufficient to account for a more intense washing-out of the soils. However, this bladder is pricked by the recent progress in the geological surveys. It is already proved beyond doubt, that in the North-Western territories the deposits of at least two distinct glacial periods are in evidence, mostly separated by formations of interglacial character. There are thus practically no differences in the history or the composition of the deposits between the diluvium of the east and west of North Germany; any divergencies which may now exist have developed since vegetation and man took possession of the land.

Owing, to a great extent, to the accidents of agricultural tenure, belief in the old-fashioned theories regarding the inferiority of the heather-clad soils in North-Western Germany died slowly. Good bits of forests existed long ago, well-grown oak and pine trees surrounded most of the homesteads, and fields yielding satisfactory crops, chiefly of rye and potatoes, existed in the vicinity of the farms; those were considered oases, discovered ages ago in the desert of heather lands, and there was no incentive to search for and open out new fields.

The peasant proprietors, owning sometimes extensive areas, were satisfied with the yield of the limited acres under cultivation; it sufficed for their requirements. The cottager and labourer had no land to exploit. I lived in the Luneburger Heide at the time of the first awakening, nearly 50 years ago, and remember assisting in classifying lands as fit only for inferior sheep grazing, which are now covered with fine cereal crops.

When Dr Albert first visited the Luneburger Heide these changes were already in an advanced stage, thousands of acres of old heather lands were covered with smiling fields, and it was recognised and of late verified by the geologic-agronomical survey, still in progress, that heavy soils are as often hidden under the cover of heather as light ones, and that often extensive areas of *bona fide* loam soil exist. It was only necessary to lift the veil to discover that the better classes of soil formed the rule in these regions, and not rare exceptions as was assumed until recently.

The heather tracts of North-Western Germany extend to about 14,300,000 acres; of these nearly 200,000 acres are covered with forest, and 10,800,000 acres are used for agricultural purposes, fields and pasture.

The present waste lands aggregate, therefore, 3,300,000 acres, including 1,700,000 acres of moorlands and 1,600,000 acres of mineral soils; of the former about 500,000 acres have been classified as ultimately fit for agricultural purposes, and of the latter 600,000 to 700,000 acres have been set aside for afforestation, leaving about 900,000 acres for agricultural purposes.

It is only possible to realise the magnitude and character of Dr Albert's work by following his labours in some detail. He began his soil investigations in Ebstorf, a forest division which he considers to be one of the most instructive and most interesting in the whole heather area. Here are somewhat extensive areas which have been under forests for hundreds of years, afforestations of various ages, untouched heather waste, and intensively cultivated fields. Most of the North German species of trees are represented here, and the soils range from the heaviest loam to the lightest sand. Albert made his analysis (hundreds in each locality) at a depth of 0-10, 20-30, and 50-60 cm. in respect of clay, oxide of iron, lime, magnesia, soda, potash, phosphoric acid, and humus (Knop's method). He divided the soils into stones upwards of 2 mm.; sands down to 0·05 mm.; clay-bearing portions 0·05 down to 0·01 mm., and to finest dust below this. He also ascertained by Knop's method their power of absorption of nitrogen.

It would lead us too far to reprint even the summaries of his mechanical and chemical soil analyses, and these form but a portion of his work, which includes researches regarding the chemi-biological activity of the soils, their porosity and the water and air circulation within them. These experiments and analyses are, moreover, not confined to the Ebstorf division, but are spread over numerous centres in various parts of the heather regions.

With the knowledge of soils that Albert discloses before me, I marvel at the many mistakes we made in the cultivation of these lands, in several of which I assisted as a junior assistant some 48 to 50 years ago; but exact forest science has made enormous strides since then.

Albert made interesting investigations in Axstedt regarding the bleaching of the surface layers of poor inactive soil under dry peat, of which a 10-cm. thick bed had already formed in a 55-year-old *Pinus silvestris* forest, and calculated, on the basis of comparative analysis, that during this time 8100 kg. of clay, 5700 kg. oxide of iron, 900 kg. of calcium, and 300 kg. of phosphoric acid, have been washed down for each hectare. This is a valuable contribution towards the theory of the formation of Ortstein. The appearance of dry peat on soils inactive owing to the absence of lime, is encouraged by the cool and rainy climate of North-Western Germany, and constitutes the main danger to forests in these parts. Both deciduous forests and coniferous ones are affected thereby. How and to what extent this danger can be avoided and counteracted is best described in Edmann's admirable publications.[1]

To ascertain the bacterial life and activity in the soils was, till quite recently, a difficult and complicated process, requiring a special training and specially fitted-up laboratories. The time, labour, and cost involved in obtaining final results, though these were doubtless of high scientific value, were out of proportion to their practical utility in adjudging the general conditions of the soils under investigation. All this was changed by the genius of Remy, who elaborated a process by which certain chemical effects of the soil under analysis were ascertained, and from the results obtained direct conclusions of their bacterial activity were drawn.

Thus, to ascertain the power of decomposition possessed by any soil, Remy mixed a known quantity thereof, in solution, with a known quantity of a 1.5% solution of peptone. Keeping this mixture at a constant temperature, the amount of ammoniacal nitrogen separated in the same time limit gave the comparative activity, in this direction, of the bacteria in various soils.

This is, on the face of it, a very simple, rapid, cheap, and at the same time accurate process, a fact which has been proved by numerous experiments made not merely by Remy himself, but by many other eminent scientists.

The earlier elaborate researches gave, or pretended to give, the number and species of bacteria contained in a soil; whereas Remy's process deals only with the direct practical results of their work. The activity of the soil as regards fermentation, its power to form saltpetre, to bind or liberate nitrogen, can all be gauged by the same method, different reagents being used to suit each case.

It was evident to Albert that a process by which the

---

[1] *Die Heideaufforstung* (1904), and *Die Nord West Deutsche Heide in forstlicher Beziehung* (1907). J. Springer, Berlin.

productive condition of agricultural soils subject to frequent variations, due to annual manuring, changing of crops, etc., could at any time be accurately ascertained, would be even more applicable to the more constant forest soils.

It seemed, however, desirable to introduce for this purpose certain modifications and simplifications in the application of Remy's method, and Albert studied the problem for a season in the well-known forest plots at Eberswalde, in the vicinity of his central laboratories, before applying the method to the heather regions under investigation. He selected four pattern plots, and took in each, at two different spots, samples of the soil every month from April to October. He scraped the soil from the walls of freshly dug pits of 30 cm. depth directly into sterilised glasses fitted with glass stoppers, and conveyed these immediately to his laboratory. Here he put 300 grms. of each sample into sterilised sample glasses, and mixed them with 300 cub. cm. of sterilised water. After vigorously shaking the glasses for five minutes, the sand settled almost immediately at the bottom of the glasses, leaving the soil solution above it. This solution was carefully taken out with sterilised syphons and 5 cub. cm. of it, representing 5 gms. of soil, were then mixed with 10 cub. cm of a $1\cdot5$ % sterilised solution of peptone. This mixture was placed in test glasses within incubators in which a constant and even temperature of 25° centigrade (77° F.) was automatically maintained. After five days the quantity of separated ammonia was ascertained analytically.

Fifty-six different analyses were made during the summer; the results were entirely satisfactory, showing that the intensity of the power of decomposition ascertained by this method was in direct and close relation with the known conditions of the soil of the pattern area. The possibility of making at one and the same time a large number of such analyses, without any considerable increase of labour and time, is of special advantage as regards forest soil, which, as elucidated by Albert's experiments, are but rarely as uniform and homogeneous as the regularly worked up field soils. Dr Albert made many other experiments on Remy's principles in regard to the formation of saltpetre, the intensity of fermentation, etc., and found that all of them were closely bound up with the activity of the soil as regards decomposition. In his subsequent biological investigations he therefore restricted his quantative analysis to this and to the intensity of fermentation.

As regards saltpetre, which is really of very small importance in forest soils, he was satisfied with qualitative analysis, which as often as not gave negative results.

Whilst carrying on these biological researches he proceeded with investigations regarding the physical conditions of the soils, their porosity and behaviour towards moisture and air. The drying-up of the surface soil in the afforestation of old fields he found to be so extreme that the ground was frequently unable to supply any more moisture to the trees. It was at one time considered that this was the only cause of the dying of pine cultivations on such soils, but as the same drying-up happened, no doubt, to a somewhat less extent, on heather-covered afforestation areas, it was assumed that besides the drying-up of the soil some other reason existed for the large death rate.

Albert made, however, upwards of 1200 careful experiments in the Münster forest division alone, in regard to the conditions of moisture in soils under different cover. The results of these have now led him to the opinion that the early deaths and rapid opening out on Scots pine afforestation on all but *bona fide* forest soils, is in almost every case not merely partially but entirely due to want of moisture in the upper layers of the soil. The roots of the young pine, spreading out in the surface soil, consume the moisture therein in proportion to the density of the crop, till there is no longer sufficient to go round, and a large number dry up. Those that are left, having individually more water at their disposal, gradually adapt themselves to the conditions and send, by and by, roots deeper down into the soil. Where natural regeneration has taken place in exactly similar localities no deaths among the young trees are observed, clearly proving that the deaths in artificial afforestation are not due to anything in the soil itself. The healthy existence of a large number of closely packed trees of the same or similar species, resulting from artificial afforestation, is only conceivable on old *bona fide* forest soils where, by the rotting of old roots, channels have formed, leading into the strata below the immediate surface.

Albert was always sceptical in regard to the theory that the insufficiency of air in heather soils was one of the chief causes of the diseases and premature deaths in Scots pine afforestation; but it was put forward with such authority by P. Græbner, who, though not always reliable in his statements regarding the heather regions, found an increasing number of followers who could think of no other reason accounting for the mortality; and Albert felt thus compelled to make independent researches in this direction.

He had ascertained by numerous investigations on the various areas, that the porosity of the soils amounted to never less than 45 %, and that, unless lying within the zone of the natural water level, they cannot permanently retain more than 25 % of water, leaving, even when fully saturated, an open air space of not less than 25 %. Nowhere did he observe anything in the nature of the surface cover which could successfully resist the energy developed by the diffusion of gases, atmospheric pressure, the changes in temperature, evaporation, etc. Albert foresaw, however, that a further objection might be raised, viz., that in consequence of the stagnation of the air in the soil, it had lost its oxygen, and was solely or at least chiefly composed of nitrogen and carbonic acid gas, and had thereby become inactive and valueless. This objection, if raised, could be met only by direct analytical investigations of the air in the soil.

The chief, in fact the only real, difficulty connected with this investigation consisted in obtaining air from out of the interior of the soil, which could be guaranteed, and would be accepted as undiluted by the outer atmosphere. After many experiments and trials, Albert invented and constructed an instrument by which this difficult and delicate operation could be, and as a matter of fact was, successfully accomplished. The description of the instrument, its working, and the process of the subsequent analyses, cover nearly six pages of print, and we must content ourselves with the results he obtained. The average of a large number of analyses gave for air in the soil 19·79 % of oxygen, against 20·93 % in the outside air, and 0·246 % of carbonic acid, against 0·03 % in the open.

Albert's concluding investigation took place mainly in the Münster forest division, where the various methods adopted in the treatment of the very extensive areas afforested with Scots pine afford special object lessons. In addition to some older Scots pine afforestations, which are in a satisfactory condition, there are large areas broken up, during the closing years of last century, to a depth of 50 to 80 cm., by a steam-plough, others, where, at a somewhat later date, the soil was turned over by horse ploughs, about 35 c.m. deep, and finally, extensive 3- to 4-year-old pine afforestations on lands on which the heather had in the first instance been burned and peeled off. In this condition the soil had remained for a year and was then ploughed up to the depth of some 20 cm. All these areas were sown. It is probably too early to judge the various methods by present results; but, so far, the steam-plough culture is the least satisfactory, and that cultivated by the last-named method the best. The cos of the three different operations was 80s., 48s., and 38s. per hectare respectively. These soils Dr Albert ascertained by analysis to be of very uniform character throughout, both in regard to their physical construction and chemical components; they were for heather soil comparatively rich in lime. The humus conditions were analysed by Knop's method, by which only the already active part of the organic matter in the soil is ascertained. They were most satisfactory, and showed as much as 5 to 7 °/₀ of humus in the surface layers in all areas but those on which the steam plough had been at work. Here the humus averaged only 2·35 °/₀. Pine afforestation of the Münster land should present little difficulty in comparison with those of Eastern Prussia, where centuries of mishandling the soils have even been more effective than the steam-plough at Münster in removing the humus from the growing surface. The deep breaking-up and turning of the soil with the steam-plough has, besides the evils already mentioned, also destroyed the capillary activity of the soil, and the moisture lost by evaporation cannot be replaced by water, which may be contained in the lower strata. The principle of having the soil in a loose condition at the surface and closely packed below must be the leading guide for all heather soils, which mostly contain a considerable proportion of sand. No working up of the soils is very much preferable to a faulty one.

Albert considers that the spade and the hoe are the ideal tools for heather land cultivation and that they have, so far, not been replaced by any plough invented.

In other localities, especially where a cover of dry humus overlaid the soil, the Geist-Kaehler grubber, already described in previous issues, has done excellently well as compared with the hoe. It mixes the dry peat and other organic matters thoroughly with the surface soil, without, like the plough, covering it up.

Even on waste lands grown over with grasses and other small herbaceous plants, it proved superior. The soil was mixed with dead and living organic matter to a depth of about 30 cm. and was, after being sown with Scots pine seed, in spring 1911, subjected to treatment with somewhat heavy rollers. The seed germinated well, and the young plants resisted successfully the summer and autumn droughts of that year; where, however, the rolling had been intentionally omitted the results were similar to those under the comparative hoe culture.

The advantage of the rolled-grubber cultivation continued during the following year, as evidenced by the photos below of the yearlings of this (Fig. 1) and the cultivation with the hoe (Fig. 2) respectively.

FIG. 1.   FIG. 2.

These photos show clearly that the grubber plants have a much deeper and more rationally developed root formation, promising a greater power to resist in coming years the dreaded drying-up of the surface soil.

The grubber can also be advantageously used in the afforestation of clear fellings or even of selection fellings, wherever a wheeled vehicle can move about. It is not necessary to remove the root stocks, which the grubber surmounts as easily as projecting rocks. The difficulty in the use of the grubber comes in where dense undergrowth of berry-bearing shrubs and isolated heather clumps exist, as the long roots of these wind themselves round and round the roller. This difficulty has, however, been successfully surmounted by an ingeniously constructed cutter, the knives of which are pulled by horses or oxen through the ground, in two, or where required, three different directions. Heaps of pulled-up roots and other debris form, especially after the second and third cutting, and these must be spread out by hoe and pitchfork. The cost of this operation was, in the most difficult localities, about 27s. per hectare. The grubber worked well on areas thus prepared, at a cost of 33s. per hectare, but nevertheless small heaps of organic debris formed again in its wake. In order to secure a most perfect preparation of the ground, it was found necessary to pull these to pieces and to mix them with the soil, at a cost of about 30s. per hectare. As a matter of fact the whole cost of a most perfect preparation of the soil over a very difficult area of 10·8 hectare, in the forest division of Gross Bartel in East Prussia, averaged only 85s. per hectare. Both plantings and sowings, where the latter had been carefully trodden down, were entirely successful. The preliminary cutting and the working of the grubber destroy the whole system of the under-growth and grasses so thoroughly that no sign of their reappear-ance has been observed so far. This not only renders it cheap to keep the cultivation clear, but secures the whole of the moisture in the surface soil to the young pine.

28. The Prices of Home Timber.[1]

In accordance with the remit made to them on this subject by the General Committee on 15th January 1913, the Timber Sub-Committee have held several meetings. They have had before them a large amount of information regarding the prices at which home timber is sold in different parts of Scotland, both standing and in a manufactured state. They have also ascertained the prices at which foreign sawn timber of the usual commercial sizes is sold at the main ports of entry in Scotland. They have had the assistance, in their researches, of many prominent members of the timber trade to whom this report was submitted in draft and to whom the Committee

[1] A Report by the Timber Sub-Committee of the Landowners' Co-operative Forestry Society, Ltd., on remit to them by the General Committee as to general lines of policy to be pursued in view of the variation in prices between home and foreign timber, with the object of raising the prices of home timber.

desire to express their gratitude. They beg to submit their conclusions as follows :—

From 90 % to 95 % of the timber used in this country is imported. Home timber is therefore of secondary importance to the trade, and prices are ruled by the foreign rather than the home supply. The timber imports of the United Kingdom amounted in 1912 to more than 500,000,000 cubic feet (the value of which is estimated at £28,350,000). The main sources of supply are Russia, Sweden and Finland, but there are also very large imports from North America. The particulars regarding these imports may be found in the *Board of Trade Journal*, where quantities are given in "loads" of 50 cubic feet.

In the European markets the "St Petersburg" standard of 165 cubic feet is generally accepted for deals, battens and boards, and all prices and charges are based on this unit; for log timber, *i.e.*, square balks of some length, the measurement is by the "load" of 50 cubic feet or the standard of 150 cubic feet. American timber is usually dealt with by the "load" of 50 cubic feet or by the cubic foot. There are numerous other conventional measurements, such as the "cubic fathom," which need not be further referred to. Pitwood, and other similar material in the round, is commonly sold by the running or lineal foot, or by the 100 lineal feet. For purposes of comparison it is necessary to reduce all these rates to a price per cubic foot.

Foreign coniferous timber is not usually quoted by the name of the tree, the merchant's classification being "whitewood" and "redwood." These again are graded according to quality into three or sometimes five classes, and an additional class is described as "unsorted."

Foreign timber not only rules the market prices but also commands a much higher price than home timber of the same quality, as the following figures will show :—

Recent approximate quotations for east coast ports, for lengths up to 24 feet or 26 feet, taken from the *Timber Trades Journal* in February 1913, were as follows :—

Redwood—

Ins.	1sts.		2nds.		3rds.	
	Per Standard.	Cub. ft.	Standard.	Cub. ft.	Standard.	Cub. ft.
3 by 11	£18 10	2/3	£14 10	1/9	£12 0	1/5½
3 „ 9	15 0	1/10	13 0	1/7	12 0	1/5½
3 „ 7	12 15	1/6½	11 5	1/4½	10 5	1/3

Whitewood—

Ins.	1sts. Per Standard.	Cub. ft.	2nds. Standard.	Cub. ft.	3rds. Standard.	Cub. ft.
3 by 11	£14 10	1/9	£12 0	1/5½	£11 5	1/4½
3 ,, 9	12 10	1/6	11 10	1/5	10 15	1/3½
3 ,, 7	12 0	1/5½	11 0	1/4	10 0	1/2½

The following prices are taken from the invoice of a timber importer, a few months ago, before the recent sudden rise in prices. The prices include delivery, carriage free, at an inland station :—

		Feet	Inches	Price per running foot.	Price per cub. ft.
White deals	. .	24	3 by 9	3¾d.	1/8
,,	.	21	3 ,, 11	5d.	1/9·8
	.	20	2½ ,, 7	2⅛d.	1/5·4
,,	.	24	2 ,, 6	1½d.	1/6
,,	.	24	2 ,, 4	1d.	1/6
Red battens and deals	.	21	3 ,, 9	4¾d.	2/1
,, ,,	.	24	3 ,, 7	3⅛d.	1/9½
,, ,,	.	24	2½ ,, 6	2¼d.	1/7½

The 3 ins. by 11 ins. and 3 ins. by 9 ins. are of the best carpenter sizes of deals, and the other sizes are the best obtainable class of whitewood batten. The 3 ins. by 9 ins. and 3 ins. by 7 ins. red are of the best carpentry quality of deal, and the 2½ ins. by 6 ins. batten is the best roofing or sleeper quality. This timber is all Russian and Swedish. Generally speaking, therefore, it may be stated that best quality foreign timber of standard deal sizes for building or similar purposes costs from 1s. 2d. to 1s. 9d. per cubic foot for white, and from 1s. 3d. to 2s. 3d. for red. In log sizes the price is considerably higher.

Home timber of similar quality is worth about 11d. for white and 1s. or 1s. 1d. for red, free on rail—that is, little more than one-half of the rates current for foreign wood. Owing to the smallness of supply and the difficulties of organizing the trade so perfectly as that for foreign wood, it is scarcely to be expected that the price for home timber can be quite as high as the price for foreign timber of the same quality. There seems no reason, however, why at least 1s. 6d. should not be got for whitewood and 1s. 9d. for redwood. This last price is given for home-grown larch in the wagon trade, for sizes

7 ins. by 3 ins. and 7 ins. by $2\frac{1}{2}$ ins.[1]   The enormous difference which such prices would make on the price of standing timber is best shown by the following figures:—

	Whitewood.		Redwood.	
Sale price of sawn timber on rail .	11d.	1/6	1/1	1/9
Cost of manufacture, viz. :—				
Felling and cross-cutting, dragging and hauling, saw-mill charges, etc., per cub. ft.[2] . . .	6d.	6d.	6d.	6d.
Price of standing timber . .	5d.	1/-	7d.	1/3
Increase in price . . .	140 %		114 /o	

It must, of course, be understood that these figures relate only to 1st quality timber, and even the best standing crop must contain a certain proportion of 2nd and 3rd quality timber on which the increase in price would not be so great.

A single instance of a similar comparison between home and foreign timber may be quoted. The price of railway sleepers from home-grown Scots pine is 2s. 10d. to 3s. 2d. each, or about 1s. per cubic foot. The price of 2nd and 3rd quality foreign red, which is the corresponding grade, is 1s. 9d. to 1s. 6d. per cubic foot, making the cost per sleeper 5s. 3d. down to 4s. 6d. It is well known from the long experience of the Scottish railway companies that home-grown are quite as good as foreign-grown sleepers.

While the foregoing comparison illustrates the difference in current prices for home and foreign timber when both are utilised in the same markets, the situation is really far more serious than the mere figures would indicate, for in the principal industries in this country home timber is almost entirely excluded. Even in well-wooded country districts foreign wood is almost invariably used in buildings, except on large estates possessing private saw-mills. The result is that the chief industries to which timber is applied are those requiring only the cheapest class of timber, such as the manufacture of packing-

---

[1] In the wagon trade larch is held to be equivalent to foreign "redwood" of medium qualities.

[2] No allowance is made for wastage in sawdust, slabs, etc., in sawing, as this is allowed for by the method commonly adopted for the calculation of the cubic contents of timber in the round.

cases, fish-boxes, herring-barrels, and certain descriptions of colliery timbers (*e.g.* pit sleepers, pillar wood, etc.). It is often found that well-matured home timber of excellent quality which might compete on level terms with the best of foreign timber has to be manufactured for the foregoing purposes at a price which hardly pays the felling and sawing charges, and leaves little or nothing over to meet the cost of the timber in the round. The following represents a note of the prices which have had to be accepted recently by members of the Forestry Society.[1]

Pit Sleepers—Scots pine, spruce, or silver fir.

Size.	Price per 100.	Price per cubic foot.
3 ft. × 5 ins. × 2 ins.	12/9	9·20d.
3 ft. 3 ins. × 5 ins. × 2 ins.	14/-	9·31d.
3 ft. 6 ins. × 5 ins. × 2 ins.	15/6	9·56d.
3 ft. 9 ins. × 5 ins. × 2 ins.	17/9	10·22d.

Crowns—Scots pine, spruce, or silver fir.

Size.	Price each.	Price per cubic foot.
6 ft. × 6 ins. × 3 ins.	5d.	8·32d.
7 ft. × 7 ins. × 3½ ins.	7d.	7·35d.

Hutch Cleading—Larch and Scots fir.

Size.	Price per square yard. Larch.	Scots fir.	Price per cubic foot. Larch.	Scots fir.
⅞ in.	1/1½	9½d.	1/8.6	1/2·5
1 in.	1/3	10d.	1/8	1/1·3

Deals—Spruce.

Size.	Price each f.o.t. Glasgow.	Price per cubic ft. f.o.t. Glasgow.
10 ft. to 12 ft. × 10 ins. × 2½ ins.	1/10½ to 2/3	1/1

Boards—Spruce.

Size	Price per 1000 supfl. ft. f.o.t. Glasgow.	
12 ft. × 6 ins. to 14 ins. × ⅞ in.	75/-	1/0·5
12 ft. × 6 ins. to 14 ins. × ⅝ in.	55/-	1/2·1

All the above prices were subject to a broker's commission of 5 per cent.

[1] The prices per cubic foot are based on the assumption that the sleepers have a wane of 20 % off squared cubic contents, a very ample allowance.

It will be seen that the net price works out at the following approximate figures for home-grown manufactured timber:—

Scots pine, spruce and silver fir pit sleepers and crowns	8¾d. per cubic foot.	
Scots pine boards . .	1s. 2d. ,,	,,
Spruce deals .	1s. 1d. ,,	,,
Spruce boards .	1s. 1d. ,,	,,
Larch boards . .	1s. 8d. ,,	,,

Battens of a good length—up to 20 feet and 4 ins., 5 ins. and 6 ins. by 2 ins.—pay better than pit sleepers, making up to 1s. 1d. per cubic foot, and occasionally higher prices are obtained for longer lengths and special outlets, *e.g.*, deals up to 20 feet, for box-making, at 1s. 2d. without brokers' charges.

If the expenses of felling, dragging, sawing and consigning be taken at the modest estimate of 5d. per cubic foot for sleepers and 6d. per cubic foot for boards, the profits to be divided between landowner and timber merchant are approximately as follows:—

Scots pine, spruce and silver fir pit sleepers . .	3¾d. per cubic foot.	
Scots pine boards . .	0s. 8d. ,,	,,
Spruce deals and boards .	0s. 7d. ,,	,,
Larch boards . .	1s. 1d.[1] ,,	,,

It is not to be wondered at that in many cases even the best quality of Scots pine and spruce are unsaleable owing to their growing in remote districts, from which the cost of removal would exceed the ultimate market price.

It is a significant fact that the same consumers who are buying home timber at the foregoing prices are buying foreign timber of the same size and quality and for the same purposes at a price which would make it possible to realise the timber, even in the remotest parts of Scotland, at a handsome profit.

The foregoing remarks apply more particularly to the timber from Scots pine and spruce, which form the main bulk of the home supplies. The same principles apply, however, to other species. Larch being scarce and not subject to such severe foreign competition, usually makes a fairly good price. The hardwood market, which is an important one in the south of

[1] The cost of sawing larch is greater than that of sawing Scots pine and spruce—say 7d. per cubic foot.

Scotland, is in an unsatisfactory state, and might be much improved. This is partly due to the mixed nature of the crop in most plantations of broad-leaved trees and the high percentage of inferior timber.

The recent rise in the price of foreign timber has been not less than 25 per cent., but unfortunately, with the exception of Scots pine, which has risen 5 per cent. to 10 per cent., there has been no corresponding rise in the prices of home timber, which remain practically unaltered.

The following seem to be the chief causes of this :—

    1. Most architects expressly prohibit the use of home timber in their specifications.

    2. The foreign supply is large and fairly regular.

    3. The methodical system of conducting the trade in foreign timber.

It would be idle to pretend that this unsatisfactory state of affairs is not due to some extent to the superiority of foreign timber over the home product. Foreign timber is either produced in the virgin forest, where tree stems are often of great length and perfect cleanness, or in forests which have been under scientific management for generations; the immense size of these forests makes economic management easier and renders comparison with British woodlands impossible. Foreign timber also enjoys State protection, so that forestry is profitable and therefore commands capital and intelligence as a commercial concern. It should also be noted that wood pulping, which provides an outlet for the young and otherwise valueless thinnings of such timber as spruce, often contributes to the profitable management of the crop, as does the steady demand for firewood at good prices.

It may, however, be observed that of recent years the quality of foreign timber has not improved ; many of the finest sources of supply have been depleted and others equally good have not been brought in to replace them ; as a consequence many grades of timber which are now classed as 1sts and 2nds are only equal in quality to those classed as 2nds and 3rds ten years ago. This fact taken in conjunction with the general rise in price of foreign timber, intensified at present by the very large increase in freights, should now make it possible for home-grown timber to compete on more equal terms with the foreign importations.

We must add that not only is the foreign product, as a general rule, superior in quality to the home product, but the industry, by reason of its size and importance, has the advantage of thorough organization. The saw-milling business of Northern Europe and North-Western America and the merchants and brokers connected with the trade form highly organized bodies for the protection and advancement of their common interests. They conduct their business on up-to-date lines and deal in very large quantities. They are consequently in a position to gauge market requirements with great accuracy and to secure the highest possible prices. The supply of timber is not only large but also fairly regular, and the requirements of the various consumers, as to size, etc., are carefully studied. The timber is also carefully graded and each class is uniform in quality throughout. This is far from being the case with the home product.

The want of organization is more injurious to the home trade than any inferiority of quality that may exist. That this is so is proved by the fact that even those timbers such as oak and ash, in which we have an admitted superiority, do not command a ready sale, for often it is found that consumers are short of supplies while producers are unable to find a market for their produce, and owing to the same want of organization rather than to inherent defects of quality the reputation of home-grown coniferous timber is so bad that it is often prohibited by architects in their specifications.

Coniferous timber is mainly produced in the North of Scotland, but also in varying quantities in other parts of the United Kingdom. Hardwoods, especially oak, are very often the predominant crop in the South of Scotland and in England. Home timber of all kinds usually comes into the market in very irregular quantities, and at uncertain intervals. In some cases the lots offered are so small that it hardly pays a merchant to handle them ; the marketing of the timber where the woodland area is small presents a very grave difficulty, and one for which there is no ready or general remedy.

There are several reasons for this : haphazard management is the fundamental trouble : many owners and managers of considerable woodlands do not know approximately the area of ground under timber ; the financial embarrassment of estates and recurrent windfalls, added to this haphazard management, often contribute to cause disorganisation; so unprofitable on many estates has forestry proved in recent years that woods are often regarded as an expensive plaything and are maintained for ornamental and sporting purposes, the marketing of the forest products being a secondary consideration. By far the larger part of the timber is sold in the round to merchants, usually ·by private bargain. In too many cases no proper valuation is made, and even a proper measurement of the standing crop is sometimes omitted; there are cases where even the precaution of counting the trees is not adopted by the seller. This method of purchase would appear to be very favourable to the buyer, who can make some sort of profit without much trouble; and has helped to lower artificially the price of home timber, a process which is almost as injurious to the middleman as to the producer. Only a small amount is converted at saw-mills by the owners, and what is so converted is mainly for estate use. Very little is sold and no attempt is made to create a regular local market. Very few estate saw-mills are run on business lines, and in most cases no account is kept of the quantities and kinds of timber handled, nor is there any annual valuation of stock. Such a system is inefficient and unprofitable. It may safely be said that in most estate saw-mills a proper annual balance sheet could not be produced, and if it could it would show a considerable deficit.

To sum up—the exceedingly low prices current for home timber, standing or sawn, are mainly accounted for by—

1. A certain inferiority in some but not in all timbers, due to lack of proper silvicultural management.
2. The entire want of organisation which has hitherto existed among producers.
3. The lack of business methods and system in selling.
4. The mixed nature of many lots for sale, embracing some good and some bad trees; some species which the merchant wants, and other species which he does not want, but is nevertheless forced to take.
5. The irregularity and uncertainty of supplies.
6. The placing on the market of small lots which no timber merchant can handle economically.
7. The want of incentive to merchants who can buy the raw material cheap, to dispose of the timber at the highest market price procurable. Higher prices for standing

timber would force them to insist upon higher prices from the consumer.

8. Competition for contracts leading to excessive cutting of prices.

9. High railway rates.

The causes for the foregoing unsatisfactory condition of things have already been enumerated, and it only remains to examine two in detail :—

1. *Cutting of Rates.*—Whereas the foreign producer dictates his price to the consumer, the home timber merchant has to take what he is offered, and in competing for orders his only chance of securing business is to quote a lower rate than his fellow-merchants. This tends to encourage undercutting, and the margin of profit becomes so small that true competition is paralysed, and only those merchants best situated locally can buy standing timber at a profit.

The remedy lies in the hands of the landowners and the timber merchants conjointly. If the former firmly refused to sell their standing timber below its value, and if the latter resisted the temptation to undercut their trade competitors, and concentrated their powers of organisation upon the improvement of market conditions, the home timber trade might become a more profitable industry to all concerned.

2. *Cost of Railway Transport.*—This cause alone renders a large proportion of home timber unsaleable except at a loss. Only the most valuable kinds can be transported in bulk, and so the secondary lots have to be manufactured *in situ* by means of portable mills. In the case of conifers this system is quite satisfactory where the quantity is large, but it is impossible to deal with small lots in this way, and consequently they are wasted. In the case of hardwoods the position is more serious for it is difficult to manufacture hardwoods *in situ*, and they must be delivered to the merchant in the log. As a rule, the price for small consignments cannot be adjusted until after delivery, which places the producer at such a disadvantage that he does not care to take the risk of consigning. In consequence, the trade in home hardwoods has become stagnant, and though there is a keen demand for good home-grown oak, ash and sycamore, none of these species can be easily procured in the open market, and substitutes have to be imported from abroad at high prices.

The trade in low-priced forestry produce is practically killed by cost of transport. The following example may be quoted. A proprietor in Inverness-shire wished to sell several thousand tons of clean birch timber, with a view to replanting a large area with a more valuable timber crop. An order was obtained of 20s. per ton delivered in Dundee, the cost of cutting and putting on rail was estimated at 4s. per ton, but the railway rate of 15s. 10d. made it impossible to accept the offer, and the birch still remains standing.

In Scotland the railway rates vary according to the amount of competition, but on an average they probably amount to a little over 1d. per ton per mile, to which has to be added the terminal charges, which, on short journeys, often raise the total cost out of proportion to the value of the consignment. According to the figures given in Schlich's *Manual of Forestry*, the average cost of transport for timber in England is $2\frac{1}{2}$d. per ton per mile, but this is probably an over-estimate. The same authority quotes the following rates for continental railways :—

Belgium	.	.	·6 pence per ton per mile.
France	.	·7 ,,	,, ,.
Germany	.	·57 ,,	,, ,,

It will be seen from the foregoing statements that the present position is one which calls for immediate attention, and it only remains to consider what steps should be taken to improve the situation. The following suggestions are made with a view to discussion and criticism :—

1. The support of the home timber merchants should be enlisted, and their co-operation obtained in all efforts to raise the price of manufactured home timber. Even if they have to pay more for the standing timber, as they no doubt would, there would be a much larger margin available for profits both to the landowner and merchant.

2. The most paying markets in this country for foreign timber of standard sizes, such as can be produced by country mills without specially elaborate or expensive machinery, should be thoroughly investigated, and every endeavour made to introduce gradually home timber to the consumers who purchase in these markets. There are certain branches in the foreign

trade, such as that for plasterers' sawn laths, which do not offer any special inducement for competition. If deals and battens from home timber were cut into longer lengths than is at present customary, it might meet the demand in the building trade and result in better prices.

3. Supplies, even if not large, should be made as regular as possible to any consuming market, and the question of even quality and grading should receive much more attention so that a reputation for reliability may be earned.

4. Every possible effort should be made to induce proprietors not to sell timber below its proper value, and to have in the first place an accurate valuation made. If necessary and possible, timber should be held over for a year or so rather than sacrificed below its value.

5. Pressure should be brought to bear on architects not to exclude home timber from their specifications, if the quality is sufficiently good. The following form of specification would probably meet the case—"Only the best quality Foreign Redwood or Whitewood or Home-grown timber of equal quality to be used."

6. Home timber merchants should be encouraged to keep stocks of "seasoned" woods cut to the sizes required in the building trades, as architects will, of course, not allow "green" timber to be used. The question of seasoning is most important and will have to receive serious consideration.

7. In order to deal with mixed lots and also with the very small and practically unmarketable lots, it might be possible to establish a depot or a number of depots to which such lots might be consigned in a manufactured or semi-manufactured state, there to be classified and exposed for sale: if by degrees machinery could be provided at these depots for the conversion of this timber a solution might be found for one of the most baffling problems in the home timber trade.

8. Proprietors who have estate saw-mills should be urged to consider carefully the prices being obtained for sawn material. If such material is being sold locally at or below cost price, as is quite commonly the case, it

has a most unfavourable effect on the whole local market, and depresses the prices which can be obtained by the local timber merchants. The latter naturally cannot, under such circumstances, give the best prices for standing timber. Estate saw-mills should charge prices for sawn material very nearly as high as the prices prevailing for foreign timber, even if in doing so their sales are for the moment slightly restricted.

9. Either the Landowners' Co-operative Forestry Society or the Royal Scottish Arboricultural Society might, at the next Highland and Agricultural Society's Show, arrange for an exhibit of all the standard sizes of timber required by the building and other trades, exhibiting the home and foreign timber side by side, with relative prices. This might have a most valuable educative effect.

10. No summary would be complete that did not include a reminder that the future of the home trade depends in the long run on the careful and intelligent management of woodlands. In this all-important respect there is unfortunately no question that we lag far behind our foreign competitors.

Reported by :—

J. H. MILNE HOME (*Convener*).   WM. STEWART.
GRAHAM.   J. A. HOWISON CRAWFURD.
JOHN STIRLING-MAXWELL.   J. MACALPINE DOWNIE.
AUGUSTUS C. BAILLIE.   SYDNEY J. GAMMELL.

NOTES AND QUERIES.

The Rüping Process of Creosoting Timber.

The Controller of the Stores Department of the General Post Office, London (Mr G. Morgan, I.S.O.), has been good enough to inform the Editor that, for the purposes of experiment on a fairly large scale, his Department has recently arranged that, in those yards where the Post Office contractors have set up the necessary plant, all telegraph poles of the light and medium classes, together with those of the stout class which are 50 feet or upwards in length, will be treated by the Rüping process; but stout poles under 50 feet in length, which are used to carry the main trunk lines, will, for the present, continue to be treated by the old process.

The Rüpingising of timber has been widely practised both on the European continent and in America. The process was adopted in Germany some eight or nine years ago, and has been largely extended there, year by year, with all present appearance of efficacy. In the United Kingdom creosote oil is relatively cheap, and the economy in its use resulting from the newer process is therefore of less importance than it is in continental Europe and America.

Messrs Burt, Boulton & Haywood, Ltd., of Victoria Docks, London; Messrs Richard Wade, Sons & Company, of Hull; and Messrs Corry & Company, Belfast, are believed to be, at present, the only firms who have installed Rüpingising plant in their yards.

Messrs Wade have favoured the Editor with the following brief description of the process :—

"The Rüping process of creosoting consists in subjecting the timber to be preserved to an air pressure of 50 or 60 lbs., after it has been placed and sealed up in the impregnating cylinder. Then, *whilst maintaining the air pressure*, the creosote, at a temperature of about 100 to 140°, is admitted to the cylinder from an overhead storage tank, and the pressure is then increased to 70 or 80 or 100 lbs. (or whatever may be necessary according to the texture of the timber). After the desired pressure has been reached, it is taken off, either immediately or after a few minutes, and the oil is returned to the overhead tank. After this the impregnating cylinder is opened and the timber is found thoroughly penetrated by the creosote, but perfectly dry and clean, the air pressure inside the timber having opened up the pores of the wood to admit the oil, and having then driven out the superfluous oil from the interior of the pores of the timber and left only enough to impregnate the walls of the cells, which is quite sufficient for preserving them."

The aim is to saturate thoroughly the wood-fibre with the preserving liquid, without leaving any of it in the open spaces which these enclose, the result being that a smaller quantity of liquid is required than under the ordinary process. It is claimed that a deeper penetration is obtained, while the timber is left so clean and dry that it can be handled immediately after its removal from the cylinder, and can be painted after it has been in use for some time.

The advantages gained by the process are thus summarised :—

1. A thorough saturation of the whole of that portion of the timber which can be saturated by the preserving liquid.

2. The absorption of only so much liquid as is necessary to accomplish this.

3. The oozing and sweating of wood is completely prevented, the timber being dry and clean.

4. A great saving in cost without reducing the life of the timber.

The results of the process have been tested by Professor Baron von Tubeuf, of the Munich University, who has reported very favourably on it. Specimens of Rüpingised wood may now be seen at our Secretary's office, 19 Castle Street, Edinburgh.

Afforestation at Vyrnwy.

The afforestation of catchment areas around reservoirs is an undertaking of the highest importance, since the influence of the forest is such that not only is the quantity of available water increased, but the purity and regularity of supply are made more certain. Many large corporations[1] have already realised these

[1] See vol. xxiii., pt. I., January 1910, p. 22.

important facts, and in many districts great activity prevails in planting up catchment areas.

Among the great corporations which have gone in for the afforestation of its catchment areas, Liverpool has been actively engaged in such work for the last 10 years, and recently the City Council has confirmed a great scheme of afforestation for the Vyrnwy area, which has been agreed to after prolonged negotiation between the Water Committee of the city and the Development Commissioners. The Liverpool water engineer, assisted by the head foresters of Vyrnwy and of Rivington,[1] made a special survey of the area, and reported that 4680 acres of land at Vyrnwy were suitable for planting, and after subsequent correspondence with the Development Commissioners, the Liverpool Water Committee in a recent report state:—
" It will be seen that, in this final offer, the Commissioners have abandoned all their former proposals involving the payment of interest or compound interest, and that they simply propose to make a grant to the Corporation representing the full expenditure necessary for planting an area of approximately 5000 acres, on condition that, in return for the advance, the Corporation enter into an arrangement for the payment to the Development Fund of the value of one-half of the produce utilised or sold from the area afforested by means of the money advanced."

In connection with the above we understand that the terms proposed still await the approval of the Treasury.

DEER FORESTS AND SPORTING LANDS IN SCOTLAND.

A Parliamentary return (538), moved for by Mr Dundas White, and recently issued, gives particulars of all deer forests and lands exclusively devoted to sport in the various counties of Scotland as at the coming into operation of the Small Landholders (Scotland) Act, 1911, according to the valuation roll for the year 1911-12. Information was called for under the following headings:—County; name of deer forest or other subject; proprietor; total acreage; greatest altitude above

---

[1] Liverpool Corporation own two catchment areas, one of 1000 acres at Rivington, in S.-W. Lancashire, the other of 23,000 acres at Vyrnwy, in Montgomeryshire.

sea-level, in feet; least altitude above sea-level, in feet; acreage below 1000 feet; rental as in valuation roll; observations. The following is an official summary of the return :—

County.	Total Acreage.	Acreage below 1000 feet.	Rental as in Valuation Roll.		
			£	s.	d.
Aberdeen . . .	240,970	7,332	13,543	0	
Argyll . . .	392,754	35,691	15,094	0	
Ayr	954	954	144	0	
Banff . . .	74,540	240	4,535	0	
Bute . . .	4,967	2,238	315	0	
Caithness . . .	93,856	46,581	4,084	7	
Dumbarton . .	9,338	1,038	348	15	
Elgin . . .	10,140	7,140	390	0	8
Fife	1,193	1,193	30	0	
Forfar . . .	57,580	750	5,515	0	
Inverness . . .	1,081,172	142,426	65,311	0	
Kincardine . .	5,850	5,200	673	0	
Kirkcudbright . .	2,752	152	235	0	8
Lanark . . .	320	120	65		
Perth . . .	259,086	13,687	17,810	0	0
Renfrew . . .	95	95	50		
Ross and Cromarty .	927,854	65,191	40,845	0	0
Sutherland . .	436,323	270,190	14,800	0	0
Grand total	3,599,744	602,218	183,788	2	0

Appended to the detailed statistics are these notes :—

Following previous returns there are included in this return all deer forests and such other lands as are devoted exclusively to the sport of shooting.

Most of the information for this return has been obtained through the County Assessors from the proprietors or their agents, but in a number of cases particulars have been obtained from the Lands Valuation Department of the Inland Revenue. The acreages and altitudes entered are in very many cases merely estimated, and they cannot, therefore, be regarded as exact. Many of the deer forests are used for grazing some farm stock also, and in a number of cases they include considerable extents of woodland.

The above total area of 602,218 acres below 1000 feet is exclusive of the subjects of which the area below that level is not known. The total area of these excluded subjects is 1,136,887 acres.[1]

In many cases the rental includes other subjects.

ROYAL BOTANIC GARDEN, EDINBURGH: PROPOSED GUILD.

It will be of interest to all former members of the staff of the Royal Botanic Garden, many of whom are members of the Royal Scottish Arboricultural Society, to know that at an informal meeting which took place in spring at the Garden, a strong feeling was expressed in favour of establishing a Guild of past and present members of the staff. A temporary committee was formed to take the necessary steps in forwarding the movement. The committee will be glad if all old members of the staff will communicate their addresses either to the Head Gardener, Mr R. L. Harrow, or to the interim Secretary, Mr W. H. Morland, so that the list may be made as complete as possible. A circular containing the proposed rules will then be forwarded to them.

TESTING OF FOREST SEEDS.

The Board of Agriculture for Scotland have made arrangements whereby laboratory tests for purity and germination will be applied to forest seeds free of charge. Seeds for testing should be addressed to the Secretary to the Board, 29 St Andrew Square, Edinburgh. Small seeds should be sent in 1 oz. and large seeds in 3 oz. quantities.

APPOINTMENTS.

Mr Augustine Henry, Reader in Forestry at the University of Cambridge, has been appointed Professor of Forestry in the Royal College of Science, Dublin. Mr Henry is a Fellow of the

---

[1] A glance at the above figures will show how desirable and urgent is the need for further investigation. It is of the greatest importance to know what proportion of the 1,136,887 acres included in these deer forests lies below the 1000-feet level.

The Departmental Committee on Forestry, appointed by Lord Pentland in 1911, recommended, among their various proposals, that a flying survey should be made to gauge roughly the extent of the field for afforestation in Scotland. Until such a survey is completed, we are in ignorance as regards the extent of the available plantable area in this country. The above returns are in themselves very interesting, but for the foresters' purpose investigations must be carried out on different lines. A perusal of them will show how little is accurately known as regards the area available in Scotland for afforestation, or for any other purpose except the present one to which such land can be put.—HON. ED.

Linnæan Society and a Member of the Royal Irish Academy. His work in developing the Department of Forestry at Cambridge is well known to members of the Society. He was the first to hold the appointment of Reader in Forestry at Cambridge, and it is interesting to note that he is now the first to hold the Professorship at the Royal College for Ireland, which has only recently been established.

Mr William Dawson, M.A., B.Sc., Lecturer in Forestry at Aberdeen University, was offered and has accepted the appointment of Reader in Forestry at Cambridge. He studied forestry at the principal Forestry Schools in Germany, Austria, and France, and was appointed Lecturer in Forestry at Aberdeen six years ago. He was the first to hold this important appointment, and has been solely responsible for the development of the Department at Aberdeen. The transference of Mr Dawson to Cambridge is a great loss to Scottish forestry, and his absence will be keenly felt and regretted. At the same time we feel certain he takes with him the best wishes of all Scottish foresters, and especially of the members of this Society, for success in his new sphere of activity.

REVIEWS AND NOTICES OF BOOKS.

Illustrations of Conifers. Vol. III. By H. CLINTON-BAKER. Printed privately at Hertford, 1913.

The third volume of Mr H. Clinton-Baker's *Illustrations of Conifers* deals for the most part with the rarer genera, but also includes a few species of the less known pines, silver firs and spruces omitted in the previous volumes. Most of the plants described are little known in British gardens, though many of them are perfectly hardy and well deserving of cultivation, even in Scotland. Of the plants figured the writer grows successfully *Juniperus occidentalis, Jun. scopulorum, Jun. recurva, Prumnopitys elegans, Cephalotaxus drupacea* and *Fortunei,* two of the *Torreyas,* and several others in one of the coldest parts of Scotland; and doubtless many more would flourish in more favoured districts. To see fine specimens of many of the trees described in this volume, a visit would be necessary to such gardens as those of Rovelli Fratelli at Pallanza, on Lake

Maggiore, Mr Hanbury's garden at La Mortola, the ancient Botanic Garden at Montpellier, or best of all the exceedingly fine collection at Bussaco in Portugal, where the magnificent trees of *Cupressus Lusitanica* alone will repay the trouble of the long journey. In Cornwall and S.-W. Ireland one can see several of the *Athrotaxis* and more tender *Cupressus*, *Saxegothea conspicua*, and *Fitzroya Patagonica*, but we in Scotland cannot hope to succeed with many of these.

Of the very numerous new conifers introduced recently into cultivation by the successful botanical expeditions into Central and Western China by Mr E. H. Wilson, only two are here described, *Larix Potanini* and *Picea complanata*; both appear to be perfectly hardy in Scotland. We must hope that Mr Clinton-Baker will give us another volume with illustrations of the many new silver firs and spruces which Mr Wilson has found and which are now being described and named at the Arnold Arboretum.

The trouble involved in procuring specimens of so many rare species must have been very great, and Mr Clinton-Baker is to be congratulated on compiling a volume so instructive to the increasing number of those who take pleasure in the cultivation of conifers. Perhaps the most interesting description in the volume is that of *Fokienia Hodginsii*, the curious tree from Formosa, which seems to be a connecting link between Libocedrus and Cupressus. The frontispiece photograph of the gigantic *Cupressus Formosensis* will astonish even those who have seen the Sequoia forests of California.

F. R. S. BALFOUR.

Planter's Note Book. By J. WOODWARD, Jun. *Gardener's Chronicle*, London, 1913. Price 1/-

This little pocket-book is intended to give in handy form a much-to-be desired means of keeping accurate records of the planting of trees. While primarily intended for the purposes of an arboretum or for specimen trees, it might easily be adapted to the needs of the silviculturist.

The divisions and headings as given in the book are admirable for the purpose for which they are intended, and there .are useful spaces for the keeping of records of temperature, rainfall, etc. It is suggested that more space should be given :under these headings.

For the purposes of forestry records the main headings would need considerable modification and more space would be needed for the inclusion in the records of methods of planting, age of seedlings or transplants, source of origin of seed, the method and place of sowing and the subsequent treatment of the seedlings, as well as particulars of the locality in which they were planted. A column or columns for recording the cost of the forestry operations either per acre or per 1000 trees, and for amount of fellings and other income, would be useful, and if carefully posted at each stage of the plantation's history would be invaluable from the economic side of forestry. A useful index is incorporated in the book and should certainly be retained.

If the author can produce another note-book modified somewhat on these lines, I am sure its publication would be welcomed by all active silviculturists. S. J. GAMMELL.

Forest Conditions of Nova Scotia. By B. E. FERNOW, LL.D., Dean of Faculty of Forestry, University of Toronto, assisted by C. D. HOWE, Ph.D., and J. H. WHITE. Commission of Conservation, Ottawa, 1912.

This reconnaissance, as the authors prefer to call it, was made during the two summers of 1909 and 1910, with the object of obtaining definite knowledge regarding the conditions of timber supply in the province and of emphasising the need for more conservative management. The total cost, which was paid by the Provincial Government, did not exceed £1200, and the importance of the work accomplished for such a trifling sum can be realised when it is mentioned that it was found that fully two-thirds of the province consists of forest land yielding meantime an annual revenue of about £1,000,000, which is in danger of exhaustion within the next two decades. The authors made use of copies of the survey plans of the Government land grants, to which they transferred by means of symbols the information gathered in the course of their operations, and they now claim that these sheets represent probably the most detailed description of land conditions in existence for such a large territory (21,000 square miles) on the American Continent. The authors specially directed their attention to the following points:—the composition or type of forest: the degree of culling:

the extent of burnt areas: the condition of reproduction: the character of the barrens or relatively unproductive areas: the natural meadow lands: and the cleared lands. Studies on the rate of growth were also made which showed that the popular idea that spruce in Nova Scotia grows at an extraordinary rate is quite erroneous. To produce a red spruce tree 12 inches in diameter on the stump requires from 50 years for the most favoured trees to 170 for those which have been shaded for a long time; or in other words, 1 inch in diameter is formed in the best average cases in 6 or 7 years and in poorer conditions in 14 years. Amongst second growth the results are better, 1 inch being made in 5 years on old pastures and in 7 years in the forest.

Most of the land of the province has been sold to settlers, largely in small lots—only about 1·5 million acres remaining in the Crown. The result as regards the timbered areas is that less than half the area is owned in large holdings of 10,000 to 250,000 acres, while the remainder is owned in holdings which rarely exceed 1000 acres in extent. The Crown lands consist largely of barrens and semi-barrens, which, however, possess a present or prospective value sufficient to warrant careful investigation and conservative management.

A geological map and a map of forest distribution accompany the report. The latter map, which is divided into four sheets for the sake of convenience in handling, shows by means of colours and other markings the following divisions:—virgin forest, moderately culled, severely culled, and second growth. These again are subdivided into hardwood, mixed and coniferous forests. This map also shows the areas occupied by the barren, "fires," farms, and young growth. To one accustomed to home conditions the vast area coloured as "fires" is amazing.

The principal conifers are red spruce (*Picea rubra*), white spruce (*Picea canadensis*), balsam fir (*Abies balsamea*), and hemlock (*Tsuga canadensis*): while of the broad-leaf trees the principal are beech (*Fagus Americana*), sugar maple (*Acer saccharum*), yellow birch (*Betula lutea*), and paper or white birch (*Betula papyrifera*). In view of the enormous areas shown on the map as "fires," it is not surprising that the first recommendation of the authors is that existing means intended to combat this evil should be extended and perfected. Their second recommendation is the appointment of a technically educated provincial forester who would take charge of the forests—the potential value of which they estimate at something like £60,000,000—and who would advise and educate the public regarding methods of conserving and improving such an immense national asset. He would also conduct an investigation into the use and restoration of the barrens and carry out experimental forest-planting on suitable areas. They conclude their report by saying that, owing to the presence of an intelligent and well-distributed population, Nova Scotia is the most favourably circumstanced of all the portions of the Continent for the immediate inauguration of a definite practical forest policy. A valuable paper by Dr Howe on the distribution and reproduction of the forests in relation to underlying rocks and soils forms the second part of the report.   R. G.

OBITUARY.

Lieut.-Col. F. Bailey, R.E., LL.D.
(With Portrait.)

As was briefly announced in last issue our Colonel Bailey died on 21st December 1912, just before the issue of the January part of the *Transactions*, the preparation of which was almost entirely his work. The Society thus lost its Honorary Editor and one who had not only its interests but also those of forestry generally much at heart, as he had shown throughout long years of activity.

The son of an officer of the Royal Engineers, Colonel Bailey obtained his commission in that corps in 1859, and after passing through the School of Military Engineering, and serving as Adjutant at Aldershot for three years, embarked for India in 1864. He there served with the Bengal Sappers and Miners on the Bhutan Expedition of 1864-5, and obtained a medal for his services. In 1872 he was raised to the rank of Captain, was appointed Major in 1881, and obtained the rank of Lieutenant-Colonel in July 1887. His interest in forestry may be said to have dated from 1871, when he became attached to the Indian Forest Service. Shortly afterwards he was entrusted with the formation and superintendence of the Survey Branch of that Department, a position he continued to hold until 1884. In 1878 he was appointed a Conservator of Forests, and organised the Central Forest School at Dehra Dun, of

PLATE IV.

THE LATE COL. F. BAILEY, R.E., LL.D.

[To face p. 244.

which he was the first director. This appointment he held until 1884, in addition to that of Superintendent of Forest Surveys. When on furlough in England in 1884 he was appointed by the Secretary of State for India to the charge of the English students at the French Forest School at Nancy, and in acknowledgment of his services to the cause of forestry he was in 1887 awarded the cross for *Mérite agricole* by the French Government. On his return to India in 1887 he was appointed temporarily to the Conservatorship of the Punjab forests, and was shortly afterwards selected by the Government of India to act as Inspector-General of Forests. In 1890 he was a second time selected to fill the office of Inspector-General, but was prevented from taking up the appointment by a temporary illness, which obliged him to return to this country

Colonel Bailey had been elected a life member of the Royal Scottish Arboricultural Society in 1887, and on his return from India he took an active part in its work, and interested himself also greatly in the whole subject of forestry. The subject was at this time acquiring gradually increasing importance. A lecturership had been founded at the University in 1889, which was first held by Dr Wm. Somerville (now of Oxford). In 1890 Colonel Bailey succeeded to this post, which he held till 1907, when failing health made it necessary for him to retire. In 1893 he was elected a member of the Council of the Society, and was Convener of the *Transactions* Committee for many years, later becoming Editor of the *Transactions*. It was largely through his endeavours that the *Transactions* came to be issued half-yearly instead of annually, and he gave to his work as Editor an amount of attention which only those associated with him could fully appreciate. He laid especial stress upon punctuality of appearance, and this in itself involved an amount of continuous labour such as can best be realised by those who have attempted a like task. His tact, conscientiousness and exactness, no less than his wide knowledge of the subject, eminently fitted him for the post, and he neglected no opportunity of improving the standard of the journal, and of widening its scope, while at the same time keeping strictly in view the needs of the various interests represented in the ranks of the Society.

Colonel Bailey was President of the Society in 1898, and that year accompanied the members on the Annual Excursion, which was to the Forest of Dean. On the occasion of the Society's Jubilee in 1904 he was elected an Honorary Member, which is the highest honour in the gift of the Society. He was a member of the 1902 Departmental Committee on British Forestry, of which Mr Munro Ferguson was chairman, and rendered valuable assistance to Lord Lovat and Captain Stirling of Keir, in the drawing up of their report on the survey of Glen Mor. He also drew up a scheme for a demonstration area in Scotland.

The above notes have been chiefly confined to Colonel Bailey's activities in connection with forestry, but he was a man of wide interests and was connected with many scientific bodies in Edinburgh. Thus for twelve years he acted as Secretary to the Royal Scottish Geographical Society, and after his retirement in 1903 continued to work actively for that Society as a member of its Council. He was also a member of the Botanical Society of Edinburgh, of which at one time he acted as President, and a Fellow of the Royal Society of Edinburgh, as well as of the Royal Geographical Society of London. In recognition of his services, the University of Edinburgh conferred upon him the degree of LL.D., in July 1912.

The debt which the Society and the cause of forestry in Scotland owes to Colonel Bailey is indicated in the following remarks by Sir John Stirling-Maxwell, the retiring President of the Society, who, in the course of his speech at the Annual Meeting on 7th February 1913, said :—

"He was one of the oldest, and ablest, and to the very end one of the keenest and most useful among the heroes who have worked for Forestry in Scotland. When that great industry takes its proper place, as please God it soon will, in this country, I trust that his name will be remembered with the gratitude and honour which it deserves. During recent years Colonel Bailey's work has been confined to the *Transactions*, and illness has compelled him for the most part to work out of sight. To a Society like ours, a Society with scattered members, its published *Transactions* means nearly as much as mortar means to a wall. The excellent volumes which have issued from Colonel Bailey's study have not only served to hold us together, but they have also given direction to our movement, and they have won a place for themselves and for him in the forestry literature of Europe."

The Late Mr John Grant Thomson.

Mr John Grant Thomson, one of the original members of the Society, passed away on 30th March at his home, Mount Barker, Grantown-on-Spey. He was born at Petty in Inverness-shire on 13th February 1835, and when he was still a boy his father was appointed forester to the Earl of Stair at Culborn, near Stranraer. His first training in the work of woodlands was received in Wigtonshire. For short periods he was at Chopwell in Durham and at the Forest of Dean in Gloucestershire. In 1858 he was on the Abernethy district of the Strathspey estate, and from that date till his retirement in May 1909 he continued in the service of the Seafield family. In 1860 he was promoted to the wood-managership of the Strathspey estate, and in 1881 received also the wood-managership of the Glen Urquhart estate.

The outstanding feature of his management in the earlier period of his career was the extensive scale on which planting was carried on. This was during the lifetime of John, the seventh Earl (who died in 1881), and Ian Charles, the eighth Earl (who died in 1884). Millions upon millions of Scots pine plants were put into the ground and wide acres were covered with thriving plantations, and though this department of forest work ceased in 1884 the Strathspey woodlands retained their reputation. Special mention may be made of the success with which crops of Scots pine and larch have been obtained by natural regeneration in Curr, Skye, and other districts, from 1865 onwards.

The work done by Mr Grant Thomson in the management of the extensive woodlands under his charge as well as in the planting of large areas of hill-ground will remain the largest effort by any single individual in the cause of forestry in Great Britain during the whole course of the nineteenth century.

Mr Grant Thomson was very careful and zealous in the training of young foresters, and many of his pupils owe positions of trust to the skilled tuition and kindly interest of their chief.

On the formation of the Northern Branch of the Society in 1907, Mr Grant Thomson became its first president. The members of the parent Society have twice visited the forests under his management, and the fame of the Strathspey forests is such that, almost without exception, all the forestry experts of other countries who have visited Scotland have made a point of inspecting these famous woods.

For many years Mr Grant Thomson took a most active interest in all branches of the Society's work and was most faithful in his attendance at council and other meetings. On the occasion of the Society's Jubilee in 1904 he was elected to the Honorary Membership, which is the highest honour in the gift of the Society. His genial and helpful nature, and the punctuality with which he attended to every detail of his numerous engagements, deservedly earned for him the esteem and respect of a large circle of friends.

Mr John Methven.

By the death of Mr John Methven, which took place on 24th May, the Society has lost an old and much-respected member, and Scottish forestry an able and ardent supporter. Mr John Methven was the eldest son of Mr Thomas Methven, the founder of the firm of Thomas Methven & Sons, Nursery- and Seedsmen, Edinburgh, and joined the Society as far back as 1869. In 1883 he became a member of the Council, and in 1892 he was elected to the position of Vice-President. From the first he took a keen interest in the affairs of the Society, and spared no pains to promote its welfare. He served continuously on the Council till his death and sat on numerous Committees, including the Finance Committee, of which since 1900 he was Convener.

Mr Methven took great interest in the first Forestry Exhibition which was held in Edinburgh in 1884, and in connection with it he did much useful work as a member of the Executive Committee. He was also an office-bearer of the Royal Caledonian Horticultural Society, and took an active interest in its affairs and those of the Scottish Horticultural Society.

On account of his sound knowledge and long practical experience his advice was frequently sought on matters pertaining to the sciences of arboriculture and horticulture. Not many years ago he was asked to advise the Government as to the planting of trees on sandy areas at Barry to afford shelter to the military camping ground. In Mr John Methven, arboriculture and horticulture have lost an able supporter.

the Chancellor of the Exchequer, was the development of silviculture. For the first twelve months there was very little to report. Towards the end of the first year the Scottish Office decided to approach the Development Commissioners with a request for a grant for the development of silviculture in Scotland. He took that opportunity of saying how much reason they had to be grateful to Lord Pentland, the late Secretary for Scotland, who took the matter up, being convinced of its importance, and giving it, until he left Scotland, the best help he could. Lord Pentland appointed a Committee to make a scheme, and five of the seven members were members of the Society. That Committee presented a report, which had been published, and completed a scheme which he thought on the whole had won the approval of those who were interested in the subject in Scotland. Since then nothing had happened. A new Board of Agriculture had been appointed for Scotland. When it was first proposed, it was provided that one of the three members of the Board should have a special knowledge of the subject of forestry. Yielding to pressure later brought on, Lord Pentland, as he frankly stated, withdrew that provision, but gave a promise that instead he would appoint a Department in Forestry in connection with the new Board. That Department, he regretted to say, had not been appointed, although it was many months since that promise was given. The new Board of Agriculture had been in existence for some time, and one of its members, Mr Sutherland, was in every way qualified to deal with forestry, but since nothing had been done the Council of that Society approached it by a deputation, which was received by Sir Robert Wright and Mr Sutherland. The result from their point of view, he was bound to admit, was bitterly disappointing. But he would prefer to think, and he hoped that he might be right, that the remarkable speech which Sir Robert Wright made on that occasion was really only a masterpiece of official caution, and not, as some people, not without reason, thought at the time, a deliberate attempt to escape from the responsibility which Parliament had placed upon his Department. That was how matters stood at the present time. The delay which had taken place in the progress of the movement was not only irritating but actually harmful. The blame for the delay could not, he thought, be laid at the door of the Development Commissioners. On the contrary, that body showed signs of impatience. In the interval they had made a somewhat hasty grant to one of the teaching centres, a step which, in the absence of a complete scheme, had rather complicated matters, since the teaching centre that happened to be selected was, for the moment, over-clouded by controversies amongst the public bodies who controlled it. But the grant proved that the Commissioners had no intention of shirking their duty. The delay in the development of silviculture was probably due to the fact that the fashionable cure at the moment for rural development happened to be small holdings. Small holdings might succeed, and he hoped they would. In the Lowlands of Scotland, where the soil was rich, they might, and in the Highlands, where the fishing was good, he hoped they would succeed. It was certain, however, that in the inland Highland glens just as silviculture could not be introduced without small holdings, so small holdings could not be introduced without silviculture. He wished their members of Parliament had time to study these social and economic questions for themselves. If they were to look at what was going on in the highlands of Germany, France and Belgium, they would realise how impossible it was to bring back the population and prosperity to the Highland glens unless there was some profitable industry to back them up. They knew from experience that splendid timber could be grown in these glens, which were suitable for no other industry. It did seem strange that while other countries were making progress in this line of rural development, we who had the finest and largest field for it were doing nothing.

JUDGES' REPORT ON THE ESSAYS.

The SECRETARY gave in the Judges' Report as follows :—

1. On "Protecting Young Spruce from Frost." By WILLIAM HALL, Church Cottages, Bilton, York. Award— a Bronze Medal.

2. On "Soils." By W. H. WHELLENS, Comlongon Nursery, Ruthwell, Dumfriesshire. Award—a No. 2 Silver Medal.

The Meeting approved of the Report of the Judges, and thanked them for their services.

JUDGES' AWARDS ON EXHIBITS IN THE FORESTRY EXHIBITION AT CUPAR.

The SECRETARY read the Judges' awards which were as follows :—

Competition No. I.

Specimens of the Timber of Scots Pine (*Pinus sylvestris*).

1st Prize,	£1,	The Earl of Mansfield, *per* Frank Scott.
2nd ,,	15s.,	The Earl of Minto, *per* Francis Berry.
3rd ,,	10s.,	Sir John Gilmour, Bart., of Montrave, *per* P. F. Cruickshanks.

Competition No. II.

Specimens of the Timber of Norway Spruce (*Picea excelsa*).

1st Prize,	£1,	The Earl of Minto.
2nd ,,	15s.,	Lord Ninian Crichton Stuart.
3rd ,,	10s.,	The Earl of Mansfield.

Competition No. III.

Specimens of the Timber of Larch (*Larix europæa*).

1st Prize,	£1,	Captain Stirling of Keir.
2nd ,,	15s.,	The Earl of Minto.
3rd ,,	10s.,	C. Leaf Daniell, of Earlyvale.

Competition No. IV.

Specimens of the Timber of Ash (*Fraxinus excelsior*).

1st Prize,	£1,	Lord Ninian Crichton Stuart.
2nd ,,	15s.,	The Earl of Mansfield.
3rd ,,	10s.,	Captain Stirling of Keir.

Competition No. V.

Specimens of the Timber of Oak (*Quercus robur*).

1st Prize,	£1,	Alex. Lowe, Lockerbie House, Lockerbie.
2nd ,,	15s.,	Captain Stirling of Keir.
3rd ,,	10s.,	The Earl of Mansfield.

Competition No. VI.

Specimens of the Timber of Elm (*Ulmus montana*).

1st Prize,	£1,	Captain Stirling of Keir.
2nd ,,	15s.,	Lord Ninian Crichton Stuart.

Competition No. VII.

Specimens of the Timber of any three Coniferous Trees other than the above.

OPEN SECTION.

1st Prize,	£2, 10s.,	The Earl of Mansfield.
2nd ,,	£1, 10s.,	Captain Stirling of Keir.

LOCAL SECTION.

1st Prize,	£1,	Lord Ninian Crichton Stuart.
2nd ,,	15s.,	The Earl of Mansfield.

Competition No. VIII.

Specimens of the Timber of any three Broad-Leaved Timber Trees other than the above.

1st Prize, £2, 10s., Lord Ninian Crichton Stuart.
2nd ,, £1, 10s., The Earl of Mansfield.

Competition No. XI.

A Gate for Farm Use, manufactured from Home-grown Timber by the Exhibitor, who must be a Forester or Working Forester.

First. William Ritchie, Moss-side, Lynedoch.
A No. 2 Silver Medal.

Second. { Duncan M'Millan, Forester, Keir, Dunblane, and
Duncan M'Millan, Assistant Forester, Scone—equal.
Each a No. 3 Silver Medal.

Third. James Campbell, Assistant Forester, Mount Melville, St Andrews. A Bronze Medal.

Competition No. XII.

A Gate, manufactured from Home-grown Timber, which may be made by a tradesman, but must be designed and exhibited by a Member.

First. William Gilchrist, Mount Melville, St Andrews.
A No. 2 Silver Medal.

Second. William M'Hardy, Chancefield, Falkland.
A Bronze Medal.

Competition No. XIII.

A self-closing Wicket Gate, manufactured from Home-grown Timber.

First. The Earl of Mansfield, *per* Frank Scott.
A No. 2 Silver Medal.

Second. James Younger, of Mount Melville, *per* William Gilchrist. A No. 3 Silver Medal.

Competition No. XV.

A Full-sized Section of Rustic Fence.
James Younger of Mount Melville, *per* William Gilchrist. } Bronze Medal or 10s.

Competition No. XVII.

Specimens demonstrating the Beneficial Effects of Pruning when well done, and the Injurious Effects when badly done.

James M'Hardy, Forester, Forglen, Turriff . . . } A No. 2 Silver Medal or £2.

Competition No. XIX.

A Collection of Fungi injurious to Forest Trees and Shrubs.

Hugh R. Munro, Assistant Forester, Dalzell Home Farm, Motherwell . . } A No. 3 Silver Medal or £1.

Competition No. XXI.

Any useful invention or marked improvement of any of the Implements or Instruments used in Forestry.

A Wire Reel.

Alex. Mitchell, Rosebery, Gorebridge . . . . } A No. 3 Silver Medal *for the principle of the Brake.*

Competition No. XXII.

Any approved Article either wholly or mainly made of Wood.

(1) *A Rustic Bridge.*

Alex. Lowe, Lockerbie House, Lockerbie . . . . } A No. 1 Silver Medal.

(2) *A Door with Standards, etc., made of home-grown Douglas Fir.*

The Earl of Mansfield, *per* Frank Scott . . . . . } A No. 2 Silver Medal.

(3) *2 Plant Tubs, made of Oak and Larch, grown on the Minto Estates.*

Francis Berry, Forester, Minto, Hawick . . . . } A Bronze Medal.

ARTICLES FOR EXHIBITION ONLY.

For Articles brought forward for Exhibition only the Judges made the following Awards, namely: —

> Samples of Refuse of old Coal Pit-bank, with Specimens of Larch, Scots Pine, Beech, Alder, Birch, Oak, Spruce, etc., grown in it—and Photographs. W. Parkin Moore, of Whitehall, Cumberland, *per* P. Murray Thomson, Factor, a Gold Medal.

> Logs of Scots Pine and Douglas Fir, and battens of Scots Pine, Spruce, Douglas and Silver Fir. The Earl of Mansfield, *per* Frank Scott, a No. 2 Silver Medal.

> General Collection of Exhibits from the Balbirnie Estate. Edward Balfour, of Balbirnie, *per* J. S. Reid, a No. *2* Silver Medal.

> General Collection of Exhibits from the Raith Estate. Rt. Hon. R. C. Munro Ferguson, M.P., *per* James Grant, a No. 2 Silver Medal.

The Judges' awards and recommendations were unanimously approved of, and they were thanked for their labours. A vote of thanks was also accorded to the Highland and Agricultural Society for their donation to the prize money for the principal timber exhibits, and for giving the usual facilities for the Exhibition and the Meetings.

THE JUDGES' AWARDS IN THE NURSERY AND PLANTATION COMPETITION.[1]

(Restricted to the Cupar Show District.)

The SECRETARY read the awards of the Judges (Dr Borthwick and Mr G. U. Macdonald) as follows :—

NURSERIES.

CLASS I.

For the best managed Estate Nursery not exceeding two acres in extent.

> The Marquis of Breadalbane, *per* Donald MacFarquhar. A No. 1 Silver Medal.

[1] For further particulars as to entries in these competitions, see the Judges Report on page 85 of the *Transactions*.

Class II.

For the best managed Estate Nursery exceeding two acres in extent.

> The Duke of Atholl, *per* David Keir. A No. 1 Silver Medal.

PLANTATIONS.

Class I.

For the best young Plantation, mainly of conifers, not exceeding 25 years of age, and not less than 2 acres in extent. Confined to Estates having less than 300 acres of Woods.

> Colonel Purvis, Kinaldy, Stravithie. A No. 1 Silver Medal.

Class II.

For the best young Plantation, mainly of Conifers, not exceeding 25 years of age, and not less than 5 acres in extent. Confined to Estates having more than 300 acres of Woods.

> J. S. Black, Balgowan House, Methven, *per* W. Couper. A No. 1 Silver Medal.

Class III.

For the best young plantation, mainly of Hardwoods, not exceeding 35 years of age, and not less than two acres in extent.

> Rt. Hon. R. C. Munro Ferguson, M.P., Raith, *per* James S. Grant. A No. 1 Silver Medal.

Dr Borthwick, on behalf of Mr Macdonald and himself, said that eighteen Estates were entered in the Competition, and that the subjects which they had to examine embraced eight Nurseries and eighteen Plantations. As the area was a fairly large one, the work of judging had taken considerable time and involved considerable expense. He made various suggestions as to how the conditions of the Competition might be improved for the future.

The President thanked Dr Borthwick and Mr Macdonald for the work they had done, and for the suggestions they had been good enough to submit, which, no doubt, they would embody in their official report for the *Transactions*, and so make them available in connection with the revision of the regulations for next Competition.

EXCURSION.

Mr BUCHANAN, Convener of the Excursion Committee, reported that the Society had held a most successful Excursion on Deeside during the last week in June. He mentioned that the attendance on that occasion had been very much larger than usual, and that the privilege of inspecting Balmoral and the other estates visited had been highly appreciated by the Members. He intimated that the formal thanks of the Council had been conveyed to the various proprietors who had been good enough to open their grounds and woods to the Society's inspection.

The CONVENER also made sympathetic reference to the death of the Rev. J. S. Loutit, who had taken part in the Excursion, and mentioned that the Council had that day instructed the Secretary to send a letter of condolence to Mrs Loutit and family.

EXCURSION, 1913.

The PRESIDENT mentioned that the Council had agreed to recommend that the Society should visit Switzerland next year, and he asked the Members to express their views on this point, and as to a suitable date for the visit. In connection with the latter subject Mr Stebbing, Lecturer in Forestry in Edinburgh University, had suggested that the date should be about the end of July, so that his students might be able to take part in the Excursion. The President pointed out that the question of the date of such an Excursion must depend upon a considerable number of circumstances, and he suggested that the whole matter should be remitted back to the Council with powers. This was agreed to.

TRAVELLING BURSARIES.

The PRESIDENT reminded the Members that, as they had now agreed to visit Switzerland next year, the proposal to grant three bursaries of £10 each to Foresters to enable them to take part in the next Foreign tour would come into operation then, and that the conditions affecting those bursaries would now be adjusted for circulation amongst those members who had sent their names to the Secretary. He again intimated that if any who wished those particulars had not sent in their names, they should do so without delay.

Local Secretary for Argyll.

The meeting approved of the appointment by the Council of Mr H. L. Macdonald of Dunach, as Local Secretary for Argyll, in room of Mr John D. Sutherland, who had resigned on his appointment as a member of the Board of Agriculture for Scotland.

Dunn Memorial Fund.

The following resolution, passed by the Council on 3rd April 1912, was unanimously approved by the meeting :—"That the uninvested balance of the Dunn Memorial Fund, and the future Annual Income, be devoted to making additions to and improvements upon the Society's Library."

On the motion of Mr Robert Forbes, Vice-President, seconded by Mr James Watt, Carlisle, a cordial vote of thanks was accorded to the President for presiding.

Royal Scottish Arboricultural Society

Prizes Offered for Papers—1913.

The Council has decided to discontinue the Syllabus of specific subjects for which prizes are offered, and to award medals or their converted values for papers dealing with any branch of forestry. They hope that the new arrangement will not only serve to increase the number of papers submitted in competition, but will place at the Hon. Editor's disposal a large number of valuable papers suitable for publication in the *Transactions*.

In this connection they invite attention to the Hon. Editor's appeal for literary contributions, printed at p. 234 of Vol. xxvi., and from which an extract containing suggestions as to the class of papers which he would welcome is here given :—

"The subjects on which communications would be welcome are numberless, but a few of them may be mentioned by way of suggestion :—

> Nature of localities here found to be most suitable for forest crops of various species, including exotics.
>
> Species, including exotics, here found to be most suitable as forest crops in localities which are unfavourable from various causes, such as high elevation, exposure to cold or strong wind, frost, bog, etc.
>
> Cheap and successful methods of planting.
>
> Successful "direct" sowings.
>
> Successful natural regeneration.
>
> Successful treatment of crops up to middle age, especially with regard to mixed crops.
>
> Successful under-planting of crops of light-crowned species.
>
> Successful protection of nurseries and forest crops from injury by animals, birds, insects, fungi, weeds, smoke or meteoric phenomena (such as frost, wind, snow, etc.).

Successful use of mechanical appliances for the moving of timber.

Cheap and successful methods of increasing the durability of timber.

Cheap and successful methods of converting and seasoning timber.

Utilisation of waste wood (slabs, tops and branches, etc.).

But of course there are many other subjects.

As a rule, successful operations are more instructive than failures, but where the cause of non-success can be indicated with certainty, an account of such failure may be of much interest and value."

Conditions to which Writers must conform.

The Judges are empowered to fix the value of the Medals to be awarded according to the respective merits of the Essays.

All Essays, Reports, Models, or other Articles intended for Competition must be lodged with the Secretary not later than 10th May 1913. Each such Essay, Report, Model, or Article must bear a MOTTO, *and be accompanied by a sealed envelope bearing outside the* SAME MOTTO, *and containing a* CARD *with the* NAME, DESIGNATION, *and* ADDRESS *of the Competitor.*

Essays should be written on one side of the paper only; the left-hand quarter of each page should be left as a blank margin. The lines should not be crowded together.

Manuscripts for which medals have been awarded, or which have been wholly or partly reproduced in the Transactions, *become the property of the Society and are not returned to their authors.*

Judges cannot compete during their term of office.

Successful Competitors may have either the medals or their converted values, which are as follows:—Gold, £5 ; No. 1 Silver Gilt, £3 ; No. 2 Silver, £2 ; No. 3 Silver, £1 ; Bronze, 10s.

Royal Scottish Arboricultural Society.

Instituted 16th February 1854.

PATRON :

HIS MOST EXCELLENT MAJESTY THE KING.

PROCEEDINGS IN 1913.

THE ANNUAL MEETING.

The Sixtieth Annual General Meeting of the Royal Scottish Arboricultural Society was held in the Queen's Hall, 5 Queen Street, Edinburgh, on Friday, 7th February 1913, at 2.30 P.M. Sir JOHN STIRLING-MAXWELL, Bart., President of the Society, was Chairman, and there was a large attendance of Members.

APOLOGIES.

Apologies for absence were intimated from Lord Lovat, Lord Sinclair, the Right Hon. R. C. Munro Ferguson, M.P., Dr Nisbet, Sir Robert Buchanan Jardine, Bart., Captain Sprot, Sir Andrew Agnew, Bart., Messrs J. Grant Thomson, A. Mitchell, W. S. Curr, Jas. Johnston, W. Storie, Donald M'Lean, D. Scott, and Dr W. G. Smith.

MINUTES.

The SECRETARY submitted the Minutes of the General Meeting, held at Cupar on Thursday, 11th July last, which had already been printed and circulated along with the January *Transactions*, and these were approved and adopted.

REPORT BY THE COUNCIL.

The SECRETARY read the following Report by the Council :—

The Council is glad to be able to report that considerable progress has been made in the course of the year, although in some respects results have been disappointing.

a

Membership.

The Membership has been well maintained. At last Annual Meeting the number on the roll was 1411. In the course of the year 82 names have been added, but 49 have died or resigned and 28 have been removed through lapsing or other causes. The total number at this date is 1416. Amongst those who have been removed by death are:—Colonel Bailey, Hon. Editor of the *Transactions*, who was also an Hon. Member of the Society, and an Ex-President; Mr E. B. Nicholson, Advocate; Sir George Clerk of Penicuik; the Rev. J. S. Loutit; Mr John J. R. Meiklejohn, Novar; Mr John Watson, Timber Merchant; Major Farquharson of Corrachree, and Mr J. G. Cunningham.

Syllabus of Prizes.

The Syllabus for 1912 was issued as usual with the January part of the *Transactions* of that year. Twenty subjects were submitted for competition, but only two Essays were received. One of these was awarded a No. 2 Silver Medal, and the other a Bronze Medal.

The Council this year decided to discontinue the Syllabus of specific subjects, and to award medals for papers dealing with any branch of Forestry. A prize list was accordingly issued with the January *Transactions* this year inviting Members to send in papers, and indicating generally some of the subjects that might be dealt with. It is hoped that there will be a hearty response to this invitation.

Medals.

Two new reverse dies with the word "Royal" added to the name have now been obtained, and a new series of Medals will be struck from those dies, namely :—

From the small die :—A Gold Medal, a No. 3 Silver Medal, and a Bronze Medal.

From the large die :—A No. 1 Silver (Gilt) Medal, and a No. 2 Silver Medal.

Donors.

The thanks of the Society are due to the DIRECTORS of the Highland and Agricultural Society, who have again voted £20 to be expended on prizes for Exhibits of home-grown timber in their Show at Paisley. Thanks are also due to Mr A. F. MACKENZIE, Photographer, Birnam, for photographs of the "parent Larches" at Dunkeld, and the last of the Great Birnam Wood in 1906; and to Mr C. RONALD RITCHIE, W.S., for a photograph of the group of the Excursion party taken at Balmoral.

Editorship.

It was with great regret that the announcement was made in the January *Transactions* of the death, on 21st December last, of Colonel Bailey, Hon. Editor of the *Transactions*. Colonel Bailey, who had been ailing for a considerable time, gave intimation to the Council shortly before his death that he would be unable to continue his duties after the January part was issued. Unfortunately he did not survive to see that event. The *Transactions* Committee, who have considered the whole question of the Editorship, have recommended the appointment of Dr BORTHWICK as Hon. Editor, and he has agreed to accept office for a year.

Transactions.

It is still a matter for regret that a number of Members have again failed to obtain full advantage of the *Transactions* by forgetting to remit their subscriptions when due.

The Council has pleasure in stating that, through the good offices of Lord Balcarres, now the Earl of Crawford, who has kindly offered to give a handsome contribution towards the cost, a new and comprehensive Index to the *Transactions* has been prepared under the supervision of Dr Burgess of the University Library. The Index is now in manuscript and will be published in the course of the year.

Local Branches.

Reports from the Aberdeen Branch will be submitted in the course of the meeting. The Northern Branch has not been so vigorous and its reports have been delayed.

Exhibition at Cupar.

The usual Exhibition of Forestry was held in the Highland and Agricultural Society's Show, which took place this year at Cupar. The local Members of Committee, who took a great interest in the Exhibition, were:—Messrs J. S. REID, Balbirnie, WILLIAM GILCHRIST, Mount Melville, W. D. FERNIE, Balcarres, JAMES GRANT, Raith, GEORGE GAVIN, Falkland. There were in all 91 entries. An Exhibit of exceptional interest was that of Mr PARKIN MOORE, of Whitehall, Mealsgate, Cumberland, arranged by Mr P. MURRAY THOMSON, showing the results obtained from planting an old pit-bank. This Exhibit was awarded the Society's Gold Medal. An account of the Exhibition will be found on pages 102, 103 of the January *Transactions*. The Judges were:—Messrs GEORGE LEVEN, Bowmont Forest, WILLIAM DAVIDSON, Panmure, and ALEX. MORGAN, Timber Merchant, Crieff. Twenty-three money prizes were awarded, and nineteen medals. The detailed prize list was included in the "Proceedings" of the General Meeting appended to the January part of the *Transactions*. The Schedules in connection with next year's Exhibition, which is to be held at Paisley, have been issued. The Committee is considering a proposal that a Certificate should be given along with each Medal.

Nursery and Plantation Competition.

The first of what will probably become an annual competition in the Show District of the Highland and Agricultural Society was held last year. The district included Fife, Kinross, Clackmannan, the eastern part of Perthshire, and the western part of Forfarshire. Eighteen estates took part in the competition and twenty-six subjects were entered, namely—eighteen plantations and eight nurseries. The nurseries were divided into two classes, those over 2 acres and those under 2 acres in extent. The plantations were divided into three classes—Conifers, on estates having respectively more or less than 300 acres of woodlands and Hardwoods. The prize offered was a No. 1 Silver Medal in each of the classes. A detailed prize list will be found in the "Proceedings" of the General Meeting before referred to. The Judges were :—Dr BORTHWICK and Mr G. U. MACDONALD, Haystoun Estate, Peebles, whose report has been printed on page 85 of the *Transactions*. The conditions for this year were revised and additional classes of plantations made. In view of the expense of judging, an entry fee has also been instituted. This fee is 10s. 6d. for the first entry, whether plantation or nursery, and 5s. for each subsequent entry by the same competitor. Particulars have been issued to all Members, and entry forms may be obtained from the Secretary. The district embraces the counties of Argyll, Ayr, Bute, Lanark and Renfrew.

The Council.

Lord Balcarres, who was elected to the Council at last Annual Meeting, found it impossible, owing to his Parliamentary duties, to take up the office, and accordingly resigned. The Council thereupon elected Mr GILBERT BROWN, Manager of Seafield Woods, to the vacancy.

The Hon. Life Membership of the Council has been conferred on the retiring President, Sir JOHN STIRLING-MAXWELL, in consideration of his invaluable services as President for the past three years.

Annual Excursion.

The Excursion last year was held on Deeside, when Members had the privilege of inspecting the woods on Balmoral, Invercauld, Ballogie, Finzean, Crathes and Durris estates. On this occasion motors were hired for the whole Excursion, with very satisfactory results. Several Members gave great assistance in bringing their own motors. Ninety Members were present, but on the third day, when Balmoral was visited, the company was largely augmented by the addition of Members of the Aberdeen Branch, who attended on this day only. A telegram of thanks was despatched to the King from Balmoral, and a gracious reply was received from him. Formal thanks were also sent to the other Proprietors at the close of the Excursion. A full report of the Excursion, prepared by Mr DAWSON, will be found on page 67 of the *Transactions*. A suggestion has been submitted by Mr W. STORIE that Berkshire, and by Mr BOYD that Inverliever and District, should be kept in view for future Excursions. It will be seen from the notice calling this meeting that arrangements are being made for an Excursion in Switzerland, extending over ten days, in July next. It is hoped that Members who intend to take part in the Excursion will return their post-cards without delay so that the final arrangements may be completed as soon as possible.

The Council has decided to offer three bursaries of £10 each, to assist three Foresters to take part in this Excursion. Full particulars of these bursaries may be obtained from the Secretary, and applications should be lodged with him before the end of February, when the list will be closed.

General Meeting.

The General Meeting was held in the Showyard at Cupar on Thursday, 11th July 1912, when the reports of the various Judges on the Essays, on the Exhibits at the Exhibition, and on the Nursery and Plantation Competitions, were submitted. A full report of the proceedings is appended to the January part of the *Transactions*.

The Malcolm Dunn Memorial Fund.

This fund having now been devoted to the upkeep of the library, Messrs Elwes and Henry's great book on *The Trees of Great Britain and Ireland,* so far as issued, has been purchased at a cost of £20. Other two volumes of the work have still to be issued, which will absorb the further sum of £5, 5s.

Experiments with Railway Sleepers.

Some progress has been made with this matter during the year, and arrangements are being made to have other sets of sleepers laid down.

Death Duties.

The Council is glad to report that a further concession, as regards Death Duties on Woodlands, was made by the Budget of 1912. On the death of an owner, the value of the timber is not now added to his other estate for the purpose of ascertaining the rate of duty, but the duty is charged on the timber when cut, at the same rate as is charged on his other estate. The official interpretation of the words, "all necessary outgoings since the death of the deceased," is, however, still unsatisfactory. An article on the subject appears on page 36 of the *Transactions*.

The Development Commissioners' Second Report.

This report was issued in the course of the autumn, and the part which deals with Forestry has been reproduced in the *Transactions*, so that Members may be able to see what progress has been made by that body since the date of their previous report.

The Laws.

At last meeting a motion by Mr RICHARDSON, in which he proposed certain alterations on the Law relating to the election of Members of Council, was discussed and remitted to the Council for further consideration. The result will be intimated at a later stage of the proceedings.

Forestry in the West Highlands.

It having been brought to the Council's notice that considerable opposition to and prejudice against Forestry exists amongst crofters and others, a Committee has been appointed to consider the subject with the view of taking steps to remove this prejudice and opposition by convincing the people of the Western Highlands that Forestry would be a great boon to the districts where practised, as well as to the country generally. The subject is included in the discussion which is to take place at the close of the business part of the meeting.

International Congress of Agriculture.

The Tenth International Congress of Agriculture, which also includes Forestry, is to be held at Ghent from the 8th to 13th June. The Council hope to secure for the *Transactions* a report of the proceedings so far as these may be interesting to foresters.

International Forest Congress.

The International Forest Congress is to be held in Paris from the 16th to 20th June, and the Council is arranging for a representative to be present who will contribute a report of the proceedings for the *Transactions.*

Promised Department of Forestry.

At last Annual Meeting it was mentioned that Lord Pentland, the then Secretary for Scotland, had promised to establish a Department of Forestry which would be an integral part of the administration of the new Board of Agriculture for Scotland. Mr Mackinnon Wood, who succeeded Lord Pentland as Secretary for Scotland, was reminded by the Council of this promise and of the negotiations which had taken place with his predecessor on the subject. Meantime the report of the Departmental Committee on Scottish Forestry was laid before the Council, and was considered along with the reply received from the Secretary for Scotland, to the effect that the question of the administration of Forestry matters in Scotland was receiving his attention in consultation with the Board of Agriculture for Scotland, and that, as publicly announced, Mr Sutherland, Commissioner for Small-holdings, would meantime, under the direction of the Chairman, superintend the Forestry work of the Board. An interview with the Board to discuss these subjects having been granted, the meeting was held on 10th June. A short report of this meeting was printed in the *Transactions* of July last, page 202, but the Council was subsequently informed that the publication of the detailed report of the proceedings would be contrary to official tradition. At the General Meeting at Cupar, the President described the result of this meeting with the Board as "bitterly disappointing." Shortly afterwards, it was announced in Parliament that the Secretary for Scotland had appointed an Advisory Committee to advise the Board of Agriculture for Scotland in matters relating to Forestry. The Board has since advertised for an estate suitable for the purpose of forming a State Demonstration Forest Area, but, so far as known, such an estate has not yet been acquired, and nothing further has been made public as to the progress that has been made in connection with the promised Department of Forestry. The Board has, however, deputed Mr Sutherland to represent them at the Meeting to-day, in response to the Council's invitation addressed to the Board, and it is expected that he will make a statement with regard to the Board's Forest policy.

FINANCES.

The General Accounts were then submitted by Mr JOHN METHVEN, Convener of the Finance Committee, and the Dunn Memorial Fund and Excursion Fund Accounts by the SECRETARY, and were approved. (See Appendices A, B and C.)

REPORTS OF THE BRANCHES.

The SECRETARY read the reports from Aberdeen Branch (see Appendices D and E), and mentioned that the report of the Northern Branch had not yet been received.

On the motion of Mr WILLIAM DAWSON, the reports were adopted.

CHAIRMAN'S REMARKS.

The CHAIRMAN, in formally moving the adoption of the Council's report, said:—I do not think there is anything which I need call your special attention to. The Society has carried on its normal work. Its membership is slightly larger than it was at this time last year, and it is in as vigorous a condition as it has ever been. Its Membership is larger than it has ever been. This being the last time that I shall have the honour of addressing you as President, I should like to take the opportunity of thanking you all for the support which you have given me during my three years in the chair. No President has ever had more loyal and helpful colleagues than I have had in the Council of this Society. And one secret I have learned I should like to confide to you. It is that this Society owes more than perhaps it knows to three of its Members—its Honorary Secretary, its Secretary, and the Editor of the *Transactions*.

The death of the last-mentioned gentleman is a great blow to us. He was one of the oldest, and ablest, and to the very end one of the keenest and most useful among the heroes who have worked for forestry in Scotland. When that great industry takes its proper place, as please God it soon will, in this country, I trust that his name will be remembered with the gratitude and honour which it deserves. During recent years Colonel Bailey's work has been confined to the *Transactions*, and illness has compelled him for the most part to work out of sight. To a Society like ours, with its scattered Members, the published *Transactions* mean nearly as much as mortar means to a wall. The volumes which have issued from Colonel Bailey's study have not only served to hold us together, but have also given direction to our movement, and won a place for themselves and for him in the forestry literature of Europe.

The Honorary Secretary requires no testimonial from me. But it would be ungrateful indeed not to acknowledge the constant help which I have had from him during these three years. He has always been the guardian of the constitution of this Society, and we owe it more to him than to anyone else that those differences of occupation and interest and locality among our members, which might so easily have become a source of weakness, have, as a matter of fact, in our Society been a constant source of strength.

As for Mr Galloway, I can only say I have never met a secretary so efficient, or one with whom it is so delightful to work. With him a thing is no sooner decided than it is done, except when it is very urgent, and in such cases it is done first and decided afterwards. He simply does not know what red tape is.

The mention of red tape brings me naturally to our efforts of the last three years. We have made less progress than I hoped three years ago. But still a good deal has been done. Each year we have passed through a different phase, and with each new phase progress has become slower. In the first phase our Society had to choose a line for the development of silviculture. It fell to me to embody our ideas in a Memorandum, and I desire to record the fact that the policy laid down in that Memorandum was not only arrived at unanimously, but has never since been departed from. Nobody can say that we ask for one thing to-day and another to-morrow. The reason is that our views were the common-sense outcome of the experience and studies of our members and their predecessors during a great many years We also, since there was no one else to do it, made an attempt to tackle some of the greater difficulties of afforestation by means of a report drawn up for our Society by Lord Lovat and Captain Stirling, with the help of many others of our members. In this phase we moved steadily and fast until we came to the end of what a Society like ours can do in that line. In the next phase, a long and wearisome correspondence with various public departments led at last to the appointment, by the Secretary for Scotland, of a committee to consider and report on the policy which we had laid before him. It did consider and report, and our scheme was carried a little further, but at the expense of another twelve months. Then came the third phase, in which we are now moving, if we are moving—the appointment of the Board of Agriculture, with which forestry was very properly included, since they are branches of one great subject. Then came the welcome promise of a Department of Forestry, and the happy choice of Mr Sutherland to take charge of it. In my judgment, and I see in yours, no better choice could have been made. Then followed the appointment of an advisory committee, which includes several members of our Society.

At this point my narrative must cease, and I will leave it to Mr Sutherland, whom we welcome here to-day, to take up the tale. I may say that in his presence here begins to realise one of our fondest dreams. Here is at last a Department of Forestry for Scotland. Let me assure him and his colleagues on the Board of Agriculture that they may count on all the help that our 1400 members can give them. We must not shut our eyes to the difficulties that lie before us and before the Department of Forestry. We are in the toils of the serpent of red tape. In spite of our efforts to keep it free and independent, forestry is now entangled with a number of different departments, some of which in the nature of things çan know very little and perhaps do not care very much about the subject. We have not only to reckon with the Board of Agriculture, under which we have been, in my judgment, very wisely placed, but we have also to reckon with the Scottish Office, the Education Department, the Development Commission and the Treasury, and with a body of Members of Parliament who have unfortunately had little experience of the needs of country life. I hope that these gentlemen will at least take care that Scotland is fairly treated as compared with England and Ireland. At this moment the arrangements for the development of forestry are as a matter of fact further advanced in England and Ireland than they are in Scotland, a matter of some importance, not because we grudge our sister countries the honour of being first, but because they have got the pick of the few experts we possess in this subject. You will observe in the recent report of the Development Commissioners this ominous line—'no official proposals had been received from Scotland by the end of the year.' That was March of last year. I sincerely hope that that line will never appear in their report again. It is evident that this Society cannot for one moment afford to relax its efforts. I am not at all despondent. The ground is now cleared for an advance. I am confident that the Board of Agriculture has every intention to deal fairly with forestry. I am confident that the Development Commissioners have not forgotten, indeed their report shows as much, that forestry is one of the prime objects of the grant that they administer, and that Scotland is the most promising field for it. I find also reason for confidence in the fact, denied now by no one who has studied this question, that silviculture is the backbone of every flourishing highland community in Europe. This fact cannot much longer be disregarded by our politicians, nor can the blessings derived from forestry much longer be denied to the empty glens of Scotland.

The report was adopted.

ELECTION OF OFFICE-BEARERS.

Mr J. W. M'HATTIE, Superintendent of City Parks, Edinburgh, in moving Captain STIRLING of Keir be elected President of the Society, said that all the Members would be honoured in having Captain Stirling in the chair. He took great interest in forestry, scientific and practical, and would uphold the honour and dignity of this Society.

Mr JAMES WHITTON, Superintendent of City Parks, Glasgow, in seconding, said that the work Captain Stirling had already done was a good guarantee of what might be expected in the future. If the same enthusiasm and energy he had already shown were carried into his new duties, the affairs of the Society would flourish in the future as they had done in the past.

The motion was unanimously agreed to.

Sir JOHN STIRLING-MAXWELL, in leaving the chair, said :— Perhaps I may be allowed to say that your new President will bring quite as much zeal to our service as I have done, and I need not say that he will have the advantage of bringing much better wits. I hope you will give to him as kindly support as you have given to me.

Captain STIRLING, having taken the chair, said :—I thank you for the highest compliment which you could have paid to your late President, namely, to elect his brother to fill his place. I feel very strongly that that is the only claim that I have to your indulgence. If I had to find a reason for my election to this very honourable post, I certainly could not find it in my very brief period of service on the Council. I think if I had to find a reason for it, it is that in my election there may be a guarantee for a certain continuity of policy, and that I shall not have very far to go to ask for sound advice on your affairs. I think that the present moment is a most interesting one in the history of the Society, and that it is a very great honour, and also a very heavy responsibility, to be called upon to fill this chair. I am quite sure that I can count upon the support of the Council and of every member of this Society in my endeavours to carry out to the best of my abilities the duties which you have called upon me to perform.

The following were then elected to fill the other vacancies on the list of Office-Bearers, viz. :—Vice-Presidents—Sir ANDREW

AGNEW, Bart., and Mr W. STEUART FOTHRINGHAM, of Murthly. Councillors—Messrs ADAM SPIERS, ROBERT ALLAN, G. U. MACDONALD, ALEXANDER MITCHELL, ROBERT FORBES, ALEXANDER J. MUNRO, and W. M. PRICE.

Mr GEORGE P. GORDON, West of Scotland Agricultural College, was elected to fill the vacancy caused by the election of Captain Stirling to the Presidency. The Hon. Secretary, the Secretary and Treasurer, the Auditor, the Hon. Consulting Officials, Local Secretaries and Correspondents were re-elected. Dr A. W. BORTHWICK was elected Hon. Editor in succession to the late Colonel Bailey. (For full list of Office-Bearers, see Appendix F.)

Captain STIRLING said he had now the pleasure of introducing Mr John D. Sutherland, who was present as representing the Board of Agriculture for Scotland. He did not wish to go into the rather vexed question of the deputation to the Board of Agriculture last year, but he could not but refer to the disappointment which was felt by them when they were informed that no money was available for forestry purposes, because it was already ear-marked for small holdings. He asked them to give the warmest welcome to Mr Sutherland, because he was in the first place a firm believer in silviculture, and in the second place he came from a district which was very well suited for silviculture, and where he had had a very considerable experience.

Mr SUTHERLAND'S SPEECH.

Captain Stirling of Keir, Sir John Stirling-Maxwell and gentlemen, I would in the first instance beg to thank you for your very kind reception. I have all along been very much interested in forestry, and I hope that my interest in it will not lessen as the years go on. Before I make any official statement, I would like to say how much I feel that Sir John Stirling-Maxwell deserves every praise which you can bestow for the work which he has done for the Society. I know no one, and no member of the Society, who has done more for forestry than he has done. In all sorts of ways outside the Society, he also has done, to my knowledge, much useful work of great value to silviculture itself.

I much regret that it has been impossible for our Chairman,

Sir Robert Wright, to attend this meeting, and would offer you his apologies.

As you know, the functions of the Board of Agriculture for Scotland only came into operation ten months ago, and since that date there have been many matters other than forestry requiring immediate and urgent attention. It is almost unnecessary to say so, but the creation of a Government Department involves in the first instance a vast amount of organisation, and it takes time to achieve the output of work which should follow, after an establishment of the kind is in existence for some years.

Advisory Committee.

In connection with forestry, I may generally report that after the Board was formed it was decided by the Secretary for Scotland that it would be desirable to appoint a Committee to advise the Board and in the first instance to deal with the selection of a Demonstration Area, and also the erection of a Forestry School, both of which were specially recommended by the Departmental Committee which issued its report towards the end of 1911.

The Secretary for Scotland appointed an Advisory Committee in July 1912, and since then four meetings have been held, as also additional meetings of a special Sub-Committee.

Demonstration Area and School.

The first duty of the Committee, as already mentioned, was to aid in the selection of a Demonstration Area, and in this matter the Committee have found themselves in a dilemma. The Departmental Committee recommended that the School should be placed in the Demonstration Area, and that both should be at a point equally convenient of communication to all the existing teaching centres. The Committee's difficulty has been to find a suitable extent of land with woodlands and plantable ground for sale near the centre of Scotland, and they have been compelled to look elsewhere, but it is hoped that soon they will be able to make a definite selection for the consideration of the Board and of the Secretary for Scotland. Ultimately the Development Commissioners and the Treasury will have to be consulted, for the Board must look to the Development Commissioners for the funds to provide the Demonstration Forest, the School and its equipment.

Forestry Adviser for Scotland.

The Advisory Committee recommended that Mr John Nisbet should be appointed Forestry Adviser for Scotland, and, with the concurrence of the Board, this appointment was made in August of last year, and the Advisory Committee for the last five months have had the advantage of Dr Nisbet's advice in all the matters that have come under their consideration.

Advisory Officers.

Among other things, I should mention that the Board have determined to make a representation to the Development Commissioners of the urgent necessity for Advisory and Research Officers for Scotland. Five Advisory Officers have been allowed for England, and they more or less traverse their districts independently, working from different parts of the country. In Scotland it is proposed, however, that the work shall be directed from one centre, i.e., the Offices of the Board, in which the results will be tabulated and recorded, and this will ensure a definite and uniform policy, and one which, when promulgated with the advantage of the extensive knowledge of the unofficial members of the Advisory Committee, ought to have the support of your Society and of those interested in forestry.

Survey.

The Board felt that progress might be made in the direction of a general survey of Scotland, if it was possible to prepare plans showing the areas contained in elevations within which silviculture was practicable, and the first start in this direction has been made, and a map of one county has been completed. The areas are divided into three sections—the first being under 500 feet, the second from 500 to 1000 feet, and the third from 1000 to 1500 feet above sea-level. The Board propose gradually to have similar maps completed for each county in Scotland, and I am glad to say that they can be finished at comparatively small expense. These maps are intended to be of service in agricultural as well as silvicultural operations.

Correspondents.

The Board will, upon an early date, have a limited number of correspondents chosen in each of the " woodland " counties in Scotland. These correspondents will hold positions somewhat similar to those hitherto employed by the Board of Agriculture and Fisheries, and now by the Scottish Board of Agriculture, for reporting upon agricultural subjects. They will be required to make quarterly reports, and it is expected that these will contain a great deal of information which will aid in co-ordinating silvicultural work in Scotland.

Seed Testing.

Quite recently the Board have been able to arrange for the testing of forest-tree seeds for germination, and samples that are sent to the Secretary of the Board will be tested free of charge.

Well, gentlemen, I cannot claim that we have done very much, but I would remind you that ten months is not a long time for hatching not altogether the egg which Captain Stirling mentioned, but hatching something that will be of use to forestry in Scotland, and it is my hope at all events when we meet, as perhaps we will do next year, that we will have done something that will give you a little more satisfaction. I think it right to say that the Board fully realise the enormous amount that this Society has done for silviculture in Scotland. But for the Royal Scottish Arboricultural Society I am afraid Scottish woodlands would be in a poor plight to-day.

The CHAIRMAN.—It is now my duty to ask you to accord a hearty vote of thanks to Mr Sutherland for the statement which you have heard. We all know the great disability that all officials labour under when they have to make a public statement. They have to be very careful of their words, and to say perhaps a good deal less than they mean. But I am quite sure that through everything that has fallen from Mr Sutherland we recognise the spirit of one who has silviculture at heart and who intends to do his best for it. I am sure that I am expressing your wish as well as my own, when I say I hope that on many future occasions we shall have the pleasure of seeing Mr Sutherland here, and hearing year after year a report of the progress being made.

THE EXCURSION.

Mr CHARLES BUCHANAN, Convener of the Excursion Committee, gave in a report about the arrangements for the Excursion to Switzerland. He mentioned that a large number of Members had already sent their names to the Secretary in response to his invitation, and he hoped others would still come in. He expressed the Committee's indebtedness to the Foreign Office, to the British Minister at Berne, and to Dr Somerville and Mr G. P. Gordon, for the help given by them in connection with the arrangements. The Committee, he said, had offered three bursaries of £10 to assist working foresters to take part in this Excursion, and for these only four applications had been received. The list would not be closed, however, till the end of the month.

A MEMBER said that one of the reasons why some young foresters had not applied for bursaries might be that they had not been able to take part in any previous Excursion. A good many who might apply were disqualified by that condition.

The CHAIRMAN said that the point was being considered.

FORESTRY EXHIBITION AND COMPETITIONS IN CONNECTION WITH THE HIGHLAND AND AGRICULTURAL SOCIETY'S SHOW AT PAISLEY.

Mr ROBERT ALLAN, Polkemmet, Whitburn, said :—I have to report that the Highland and Agricultural Society's Show will be held at Paisley this year, and that the usual Forestry Exhibition will be held in connection with it. Last year the Society instituted a Nursery and Plantation Competition in the Show District, which is to be continued this year. The competition will be confined to the Counties of Argyll, Ayr, Bute, Lanark and Renfrew. Some little alteration has been made in the conditions of the Plantation competition as recommended by the judges of last year's competition, which the Committee hope will meet with the approval of those interested. The Committe hope that in the area of the Paisley Show they will have a large number of entries both for the Exhibition and the Nursery and Plantation Competitions.

Proposed Alteration of the Laws.

The CHAIRMAN.—The next item is a report on the proposed alteration of the Laws, which was remitted from this meeting last year. As the Council do not propose to submit any recommendation perhaps the best course would be for me to explain shortly what took place. The Committee of the Council to which this question was remitted met twice, and fully discussed it, and they finally, by a majority, adopted a compromise which was intended to meet the wishes of the proposer of the motion, Mr RICHARDSON. That compromise was not accepted by the mover of the motion and his seconder, and therefore it was thought better that nothing should be brought before the Council to-day. But it is, of course, quite competent for the mover of the original motion to bring forward his motion again.

Notices of Motion.

The SECRETARY.—I have a letter from Mr RICHARDSON repeating the notice of his motion as formerly made, so that the matter will come up for discussion at next Annual Meeting. I need not read the motion because it has already been printed in full and will be printed again when it comes up for discussion. Other two motions have been given notice of.

By Mr GAMMELL.—"That any Branch recognised by the parent Society and consisting of members of the Society subscribing to the funds of the Branch, shall have representation on the Council of the Society, consisting of the President of the Branch for the time being and one member of Council for the first fifty members of the Branch, and one extra member of Council for every additional completed fifty members, such member or members to be nominated by the members of the Branch in annual meeting, and that the rules of the Society shall be amended to that effect."

By Mr WM. GILCHRIST.—"That the annual business meeting of the Society extend over two days, the second day to take the form of a Conference for the discussion by members of subjects relating to arboriculture."

The CHAIRMAN.—These are three notices of motions that will come up for discussion next year.

b

Vote of Thanks to the Retiring President.

Mr GILBERT BROWN, Grantown-on-Spey, moved a vote of thanks to Sir John Stirling-Maxwell for his past services as President of the Society.

Sir JOHN STIRLING-MAXWELL.—I need scarcely say that I am very much obliged for the very kind way you have spoken of my work during the past three years on behalf of the Society. In working for the Society I never had any work which I enjoyed doing so much. I only wish that my efforts had produced rather more than they have done.

Discussion.

A discussion then took place on the relation of Forestry to Agriculture and other industries, which was opened by Mr Gammell of Drumtochty, and was taken part in by Mr A. T. Gillanders, Mr J. F. Annand, Mr G. F. Scott Elliot, Mr J. H. Milne Home, Mr G. P. Gordon, Colonel Cadell of Grange, Mr George Leven, Mr Gilbert Brown, Dr Borthwick and Mr A. D. Richardson.

Votes of thanks to Mr Gammell and the Chairman, proposed respectively by Mr WM. DAWSON and Mr A. SPEIRS, concluded the proceedings.

APPENDIX A.

ABSTRACT OF ACCOUNTS for Year ending 31st December 1912.

I.—CAPITAL.

CHARGE.

Funds at 31st December 1911,		£1822 18 4
£500 Caledonian Railway Company 4 per cent. Guaranteed Annuity Stock. No.		140 10 2
Dividends and Interest,		67 3 2
Transactions and Reports sold,		31 18 11
Income Tax Recovered,		3 19 4
Miscellaneous Receipt,		0 2 6
		£721 3 8

DISCHARGE.

1. Proportion of Life Members' Subscriptions transferred to Revenue,

Unexhausted: $\frac{4}{5}$ of Full Life Subscriptions, £948 8 9		£122 11 1
Rent of Room and Taxes for 1912, and rent for Annual Meeting,		£23 13 11
Auditor,		3 3 0
Hon. Editor's Assistant, £30; and Authors of German and French Notes for *Transactions*, £10,		40 0 0
Secretary and Treasurer,		125 0 0
Advertising, Insurance, and Premium on Secretary's Bond of Caution,		4 10 4
Cost of two obverse Metal dies,		5 0 0
Postages and Miscellaneous Outlays, viz.:—		
Postages of Parts I. and II. of Vol. XXVI. of *Transactions*, £32 5 9		
General Postages, Commissions on Cheques, Incidental expenses, and Petty Outlays, 49 2 6		81 8 3
		£282 15 6

8. Balance of Revenue carried to next year, subject to payment of cost, etc., of January *Transactions*, being sum at credit with National Bank of Scotland, Ltd., 136 18 10

£721 3 8

EDINBURGH, 20*th January* 1913.—I hereby certify that I have examined the Accounts of the Treasurer for the year to 31st December 1912, of which the above is an Abstract, and have found them correct. The Securities, representing the Funds as above, have also been exhibited to me.

JOHN T. WATSON, *Auditor*.

APPENDIX B.

ABSTRACT OF ACCOUNTS

IN CONNECTION WITH

THE MALCOLM DUNN MEMORIAL FUND, 1912.

RECEIPTS.

Balance in Bank at close of last Account . .	£27	2	0
Dividend on £100 3 per cent. Redeemable Stock of Edinburgh Corporation, payable at Whitsunday and Martinmas, 1912, £3, *less* Tax, 3s. 6d.	2	16	6
	£29	18	6

PAYMENTS.

Messrs Douglas & Foulis for Elwes' *Forest Trees of Britain*, 5 vols.	£20	0	0
County Directory of Scotland . .	0	15	0
	£20	15	0
Balance carried forward, being sum in National Bank of Scotland on Account Current . . .	£9	3	6

Note.—The Capital belonging to the Fund consists of £100 3 per cent. Redeemable Stock of Edinburgh Corporation.

EDINBURGH, *22nd January* 1913.—Examined and found correct. The Certificate by the Bank of above balance, and Edinburgh Corporation Stock Certificate, have been exhibited.

JOHN T. WATSON,
Auditor.

APPENDIX A.

ABSTRACT OF ACCOUNTS for Year ending 31st December 1912.

I.—CAPITAL.

CHARGE.

1. Funds at 31st December 1911, £1822 18 4

£500 Caledonian Railway Company 4 per cent. Guaranteed Annuity Stock, No. 2, at 101½, £507 10 0
£300 Caledonian Railway Company 4 per cent. Debenture Stock, at 109½, 328 15 0
£300 North British Railway Company 3 per cent. Debenture Stock, at 79½, 317 0 0
£300 North British Railway Company No. 1, 4 per cent. Preference Stock, at 102½,

Capital in hand uninvested (in National Bank of Scotland, Ltd.) 415 0 0

  14 13 4
£4732 18 4
  40 0 0
£4922 18 4

Furniture, etc., in Society's Room, 146 15 0
£126 9 0
  20 0 0

2. Life Members' Subscriptions transferred to Capital 146 15 0

New Members, £1 12 0
Ordinary Members by commutation,

£4978 13 4

DISCHARGE.

1. Proportion of Life Members' Subscriptions transferred to Revenue—
Unexhausted ⁴⁄₅ of Full Life Subscriptions, £722 11 1
⅕ of Commuted Subscriptions, 17 19 1
  £740 10 2

2. Decrease in value of Railway Stocks at 31st December 1912, 28 15 0

3. Funds, etc., at 31st December 1912,—
£500 Caledonian Railway Company 4 per cent. Guaranteed Annuity Stock, No. 2, at 101½,
£500 Caledonian Railway Company 4 per cent. Debenture Stock, at 101½, £508 15 0
£400 North British Railway Company 3 per cent. Debenture Stock, at 78½, 593 5 0
£400 North British Railway Company No. 1, 4 ½% Preference Stock, at 103½, 312 10 0
Capital in hand uninvested (in National Bank of Scotland, Ltd.) 402 0 0
  29 18 2
  40 0 0
£4789 8 2
  £4209 8 2

Furniture, etc., in Society's Room, say, £4978 13 4

II.—REVENUE.

CHARGE.

1. Balance in hand at 31st December 1911, £51 3 1

2. Ordinary Members' Subscriptions,
Arrears at 31st December 1911, £21 2 6
Add Arrears written off but since renewed, 1 12 0
  £22 14 6

Subscriptions for 1912, £486 1 0
Less Received in 1911, 8 6 6
  497 15 6

Subscriptions for 1913 received in 1912, 8 15 0
  £459 5 0

Deduct—
Cancelled or written off as irrecoverable, £12 0 6
Arrears at 31st December 1912, £22 0 6
  £472 0 6

Arrears at 31st December 1912, 32 15 0
  £426 6 6

Less Received but not appropriated, senders' names being unknown, 1 2 6
  £30 18 0

3. Proportion of Life Members' Subscriptions transferred from Capital, 140 10 2
4. Dividends and Interest, 67 8 2
5. Transactions and Reports sold, 31 18 11
6. Income Tax Recovered, 3 19 4
7. Miscellaneous Receipt, 0 2 6

DISCHARGE.

1. Printing, Stationery, etc.,—
Vol. XXVI. Part I. Transactions, £35 19 0
Authors' Reprints, 3 1 9
  £39 0 9
Vol. XXVI. Part II. of Trans., £104 2 7
Authors' Reprints, 2 18 0
  107 0 7

General Printing and Stationery, £71 9 9
Forestry Periodicals, Binding, etc., 3 18 5
  £196 1 4

Less Receipts for Advts. in Trans., 46 7 5

2. Prizes (Money, £24, 5s.; Medals, £23, 14s.) £292 8 9
  32 19 0
Less Donations from the Highland and Agricultural Society, for Prizes awarded for Home-Grown Timber exhibited at Inverness, £209 9 9
  £47 19 0

3. Forestry Exhibition at the Highland and Agricultural Society's Show at Cupar—
Printing, 90 0 0
Advertising, £11 15 0
Extra Tubing, Racks, etc., 8 6 0
Incidental Expenses, 8 19 4
  £7 19 0

4. Nursery and Plantation Competition in Show District—
Printing, £3 0 6
Advertising, 0 11 0
Judges' expenses, 17 8 7
  25 0 4

5. Index to Transactions—
Cost of preparing MS. of Index of Vols. I.–XXVI. preparatory to printing 21 0 3

6. Contribution to Aberdeen Branch, 13 0 0

7. Expenses of Management,—
Rent of Rooms and Taxes for 1912, and Hall for Annual Meeting, 5 0 0
Auditor, 582 15 6
Hon. Editor's Assistant £20; and Authors' Reprints, £30; and French Notes for Secretary and Treasurer, £23 13 11
Advertising, Insurance, and Premium on Secretary's Bond of Caution, 49 0 0
  125 0 0
Cost of two sheaves 4 10

APPENDIX B.

ABSTRACT OF ACCOUNTS

IN CONNECTION WITH

THE MALCOLM DUNN MEMORIAL FUND, 1912.

RECEIPTS.

Balance in Bank at close of last Account . .	£27	2	0
Dividend on £100 3 per cent. Redeemable Stock of Edinburgh Corporation, payable at Whitsunday and Martinmas, 1912, £3, *less* Tax, 3s. 6d.	2	16	6
	£29	18	6

PAYMENTS.

Messrs Douglas & Foulis for Elwes' *Forest Trees of Britain*, 5 vols.	£20	0	0				
County Directory of Scotland . .	0	15	0				
				£20	15	0	
Balance carried forward, being sum in National Bank of Scotland on Account Current . . .				£9	3	6

Note.—The Capital belonging to the Fund consists of £100 3 per cent. Redeemable Stock of Edinburgh Corporation.

EDINBURGH, 22nd *January* 1913.—Examined and found correct. The Certificate by the Bank of above balance, and Edinburgh Corporation Stock Certificate, have been exhibited.

JOHN T. WATSON,
Auditor.

APPENDIX C.

EXCURSION ACCOUNT.

Abstract of Accounts—Year 1912.

Balance brought from last Account	. . . . .		£60	19 10
Payments therefrom :—				
Auditor's Fee for 1911	£2 2 0			
Printing Programmes	2 2 6			
	———		4 4 6	
			56 15 4	

Excursion to Deeside.

Amount collected, *less* repaid	£430 2 1			
Paid :—				
Conveyance of Luggage . .	£ 10 3 4			
Hotel Bill at Braemar . . .	100 10 0			
,, ,, Potarch (Lunch) .	10 18 0			
,, ,, Banchory . .	88 5 0			
,, ,, Durris (Lunch) .	19 18 0			
Hire of Motors, 18 at £10 .	180 0 0			
Preliminary Expenses, Printing, Gratuities and Incidental Outlays . . .	20 12 2			
	——— £430 6 6			
		0 4 5		
Balance (subject to Auditor's Fee) carried forward to next year, being sum in National Bank of Scotland on Account Current		£56 10 11		

EDINBURGH, *22nd January* 1913.—Examined with Vouchers and Memorandum Book and found correct. Bank Certificate of above balance of £56, 10s. 11d. also exhibited. JOHN T. WATSON, *Auditor.*

APPENDIX D.

REPORT 1912.

The Committee beg to submit the Seventh Annual Report of the Branch.

The affairs of the Branch have been conducted on similar lines as in the preceding years.

The Membership of the Branch remains about the same as last year. Three new members have joined the Branch, but one or two have been lost on account of death and removal from the district. The Branch specially regrets the loss of the Rev. Mr Loutit, who died under such tragic circumstances.

During the year four meetings of the Branch have been held—on 9th December 1911, 30th March, 26th June, and 28th September 1912. At the Annual Meeting held in December, the Right Honourable Robert Farquharson, P.C., gave an address, the subject being "The Past, Present and Future of Forestry," in the course of which he touched on many points of interest to those interested in forestry. At the March meeting of the Branch, which was very largely attended, members and others were privileged to hear an address from Professor Somerville, Oxford, who chose as his subject "The Forests of North America," explaining particularly what is being done by the Governments of the United States and Canada in the development of forestry. On 26th June twenty-five members of the Branch joined the members of the Parent Society (whose Annual Excursion was held on Deeside from 24th to 28th June) in their visitation to the woods of Balmoral—the woods visited being Garmaddie, Invergelder and Craig Gowan, Balmoral Grounds and Abergeldie. The Branch party was heartily welcomed by Sir John Stirling-Maxwell, the President of the Society, and a very pleasant and instructive day was spent, His Majesty the King having been pleased to provide luncheon for the party, which was served in a marquee erected on the lawn near Balmoral Castle. The last meeting of the Branch for the year took the form of a visitation, on the invitation of the proprietors, to two of the local nurseries, namely, those of Messrs William Smith & Son at Burnside, and those of Messrs Ben Reid & Co. at Pinewood. The whole day was spent between the two places, which are both in the near vicinity of Aberdeen, and much of interest was seen and discussed both from an arboricultural and silvicultural point of view, and by both firms the company was hospitably entertained.

The Library recently installed for the Branch is now in full working order, and although it is not extensive most of the volumes are the most recent publications on the subject. The Committee would impress upon members the desirability of a more extensive use of the Library in the future.

The Committee have again to record their thanks to Professor Trail, and the University Authorities, for being allowed the use of the Botanical class-room for the meetings of the Branch.

ALEX. F. IRVINE,
President.

GEORGE D. MASSIE,
Honorary Secretary.

ABERDEEN, *December* 1912.

APPENDIX E.—ROYAL SCOTTISH ARBORICULTURAL SOCIETY (ABERDEEN BRANCH).

STATEMENT OF ACCOUNTS, Year 1912.

GENERAL ACCOUNT.

INCOME.					EXPENDITURE.			
Balance from last Account	£13	8	6		Printing	£1	5	3
Subscriptions from Members at 1s.	4	7	0		Advertising	1	11	0
Grant from Parent Society	5	0	0		Honorarium to Secretary for 1911	3	3	0
Savings Bank Interest	0	6	5		Postages and Incidental Outlay	2	4	11
					Balance carried to Abstract	14	17	9
	£23	1	11			£23	1	11

EXCURSION ACCOUNT.

Balance from last Account	£0	8	8		Printing	£0	10	0
Savings Bank Interest	0	0	3		Preliminary Expenses	0	9	3
Received from Members price of tickets	15	10	6		Hire of Motors	16	10	0
Balance carried to Abstract	1	19	10		Postages and Incidents	0	10	0
	£17	19	3			£17	19	3

LIBRARY ACCOUNT.

Balance at Debit of Account	£4	11	0½		Balance at Debit of last Account	£0	6	4
					Printing	1	15	0
					Books	1	19	2¼
					Postages and incidental Outlay	0	10	6
						£4	11	0¼

ABSTRACT.

Balance at Credit of General Account	£14	17	9
Balance at Debit of Excursion Account	£1	19	10	
Balance at Debit of Library Account	4	11	0½
	£6	10	10½
Balance at Credit of Branch	£8	6	10¼

ABERDEEN, *3rd December 1912.*—I have examined the foregoing Statement of Accounts, and have compared same with the vouchers, and find the same to be properly stated and vouched, the balance at the credit of the Branch being Eight pounds six shillings and tenpence halfpenny, which sum is deposited with the Aberdeen Savings Bank, per Savings Bank Book, No. C. 393, which I have also seen.

J. G. HOPKINSON.

APPENDIX F.

Office-Bearers for 1913 :—

PATRON.

His Majesty THE KING.

PRESIDENT.

Captain ARCHIBALD STIRLING of Keir, Dunblane.

VICE-PRESIDENTS.

A. W. BORTHWICK, D.Sc., 46 George Square, Edinburgh.

SYDNEY J. GAMMELL of Drumtochty, Countesswells House, Bieldside, Aberdeen.

The LORD LOVAT, D.S.O., Beaufort Castle, Beauly.

CHAS. BUCHANAN, Factor, Penicuik Estate, Penicuik.

Sir ANDREW AGNEW, Bart., of Lochnaw 10 Smith Square, Westminster.

W. STEUART FOTHRINGHAM of Murthly, Perthshire.

COUNCIL.

HON. LIFE MEMBERS.

Sir KENNETH J. MACKENZIE, Bart. of Gairloch, 10 Moray Place, Edinburgh

Sir JOHN STIRLING-MAXWELL, Bart. of Pollok, Pollokshaws.

ORDINARY MEMBERS.

GEO. LEVEN, Forester, Bowmont Forest, Roxburgh.

JOHN BROOM, Wood Merchant, Bathgate.

JOHN F. ANNAND, Lecturer in Forestry, Armstrong College, Newcastle-upon-Tyne.

JOHN W. M'HATTIE, Superintendent of City Parks, City Chambers, Edinburgh.

BRODIE OF BRODIE, Brodie Castle, Forres.

WILLIAM DAWSON, M.A., B.Sc., Lecturer in Forestry, Marischal College, Aberdeen.

JOHN METHVEN, Nurseryman, 15 Princes Street, Edinburgh.

A. T. GILLANDERS, F.E.S., Forester, Park Cottage, Alnwick.

JAMES WHITTON, Superintendent of City Parks, City Chambers, Glasgow.

WILLIAM DAVIDSON, Forester, Panmure, Carnoustie.

W. H. MASSIE, Nurseryman, 1 Waterloo Place, Edinburgh.

GILBERT BROWN, Wood Manager, Grantown-on-Spey.

GEORGE P. GORDON, B.Sc.,Lecturer in Forestry, West of Scotland Agricultural College, 6 Blythswood Square, Glasgow.

A. D. RICHARDSON, 6 Dalkeith Street, Joppa.

ADAM SPIERS, Timber Merchant, Warriston Saw-Mills, Edinburgh.

ROBERT ALLAN, Factor, Polkemmet, Whitburn.

G. U. MACDONALD, Overseer, Haystoun Estate, Woodbine Cottage, Peebles.

ALEXANDER MITCHELL, Forester, Rosebery, Gorebridge.

ROBERT FORBES, Overseer, Kennet Estate Office, Alloa.

ALEXANDER J. MUNRO, Factor, 48 Castle Street, Edinburgh.

W. M. PRICE, Factor, Minto, Hawick.

LOCAL SECRETARIES.

Counties.		*Scotland.*
Aberdeen,	.	JOHN CLARK, Forester, Haddo House, Aberdeen.
		JOHN MICHIE, M.V.O., Factor, Balmoral, Ballater.
Argyll,	.	H. L. MACDONALD of Dunach, Oban.
Ayr,	.	ANDREW D. PAGE, Overseer, Culzean Home Farm, Ayr.
		A. B. ROBERTSON, Forester, The Dean, Kilmarnock.
Berwick,	.	WM. MILNE, Foulden Newton, Berwick-on-Tweed.
Bute,	.	WM. INGLIS, Forester, Cladoch, Brodick.
		JAMES KAY, retired Forester, Barone, Rothesay.
Clackmannan,.		ROBERT FORBES, Estate Office, Kennet, Alloa.
Dumfries,	.	D. CRABBE, Forester, Byreburnfoot, Canonbie.
East Lothian,.		W. S. CURR, Factor, Ninewar, Prestonkirk.
Fife,	.	WM. GILCHRIST, Forester, Nursery Cottage, Mount Melville, St Andrews.
		EDMUND SANG, Nurseryman, Kirkcaldy.
Forfar,	.	JAMES CRABBE, retired Forester, Glamis.
Inverness,	..	JAMES A. GOSSIP, Nurseryman, Inverness.
Kincardine,	.	JOHN HART, Estates Office, Cowie, Stonehaven.
Kinross,	.	JAMES TERRIS, Factor, Dullomuir, Blairadam.
Lanark,.		JOHN DAVIDSON, Forester, Dalzell, Motherwell.
		JAMES WHITTON, Superintendent of Parks, City Chambers, Glasgow.
Moray,	.	D. SCOTT, Forester, Darnaway Castle, Forres.
Perth,	.	JOHN SCRIMGEOUR, Doune Lodge, Doune.
Ross,	.	JOHN J. R. MEIKLEJOHN, Factor, Novar, Evanton.
		Miss AMY FRANCES YULE, Tarradale House, Muir of Ord.
Roxburgh,	.	JOHN LEISHMAN, Manager, Cavers Estate, Hawick.
		R. V. MATHER, Nurseryman, Kelso.
Sutherland,	.	DONALD ROBERTSON, Forester, Dunrobin, Golspie.
Wigtown,	.	JAMES HOGARTH, Forester, Culhorn, Stranraer.
		H. H. WALKER, Monreith Estate Office, Whauphill.

England.

Beds,	.	FRANCIS MITCHELL, Forester, Woburn.
Berks,	.	W. STORIE, Whitway House, Newbury.
Derby,	.	S. MACBEAN, Estate Office, Needwood Forest, Sudbury.
Devon,	.	JAMES BARRIE, Forester, Stevenstone Estate, Torrington.
Durham,	.	JOHN F. ANNAND, Lecturer in Forestry, Armstrong College, Newcastle-upon-Tyne.
Hants,	.	W. R. BROWN, Forester, Park Cottage, Heckfield, Winchfield.
Herts,	.	JAMES BARTON, Forester, Hatfield.
		THOMAS SMITH, Overseer, Tring Park, Wigginton, Tring.
Kent,	.	R. W. COWPER, Gortanore, Sittingbourne.
Lancashire,	.	D. C. HAMILTON, Forester, Knowsley, Prescot.
Leicester,	.	JAMES MARTIN, The Reservoir, Knipton, Grantham.
Lincoln,	.	W. B. HAVELOCK, The Nurseries, Brocklesby Park.
Middlesex,	.	Professor BOULGER, 11 Onslow Road, Richmond Hill, London, S.W.

Counties.		*England.*

Notts, . . WM. ELDER, Thoresby, Ollerton, Newark.

W. MICHIE, Forester, Welbeck, Worksop.

WILSON TOMLINSON, Forester, Clumber Park, Worksop.

Suffolk, . . GEORGE HANNAH, The Folly, Ampton Park, Bury St Edmunds.

Surrey, . . JOHN ALEXANDER, 24 Lawn Crescent, Kew Gardens.

Warwick, . A. D. CHRISTIE, Hillside, Frederick Road, Selly Oak, Birmingham.

Wilts, . . ANDREW BOA, Land Agent, Glenmore, The Avenue, Trowbridge.

York, . . D. TAIT, Estate Bailiff, Owston Park, Doncaster.

Ireland.

Dublin, . . A. C. FORBES, Department of Forestry, Board of Agriculture.

JAMES WILSON, B.Sc., Royal College of Science, Dublin.

ARCH. E. MOERAN, Lissadell, Stillorgan Park.

Galway, . THOMAS ROBERTSON, Forester and Bailiff, Woodlawn.

King's County, WM. HENDERSON, Forester, Clonad Cottage, Tullamore.

Tipperary, . DAVID G. CROSS, Forester, Kylisk, Nenagh.

ALEX. M'RAE, Forester, Dundrum.

APPENDIX G.

Presentations to the Society's Library since the publication of last List in Volume XXVI. Part 2.

BOOKS.

1. *Complete Yield Tables for British Woodlands.* By P. T. Maw.
2. *Commission of Conservation, Canada :—*
    (1) *Report on Water Powers of Canada (with maps).*
    (2) *Report on Lands, Fisheries Game and Minerals, Canada.*
3. *The Country Gentleman's Estate Book,* 1912.
4. *New Zealand Official Year Book,* 1912.
5. *The Forest Trees of Britain.* By Rev. C. A. Johns. Revised by Prof. C. S. Boulger.
6. *Silviculture in the Tropics.* By A. F. Brown.
7. *The Story of our Trees.* By Margaret M. Gregson.
8. *Flora and Sylva,* 3 vols. By Wm. Robinson.
9. *Trees in Winter.* By A. F. Blakeslee, Ph.D., and Chester D. Jarvis, Ph.D.
10. *The Trees of Great Britain and Ireland.* By H. J. Elwes, F.R.S., and Augustine Henry, M.A. Vol. vi. (By purchase.)

GOVERNMENT AND STATE REPORTS.

11. *New York State College of Forestry Bulletins.*
12. *Pennsylvania State College Bulletins.*
13. *Illinois University Bulletins.*
14. U.S.A. Forest Service Bulletins :—
    (1) *Quebracho Wood and its Substitutes.*
    (2) *The Forests of Alaska.*
    (3) *Influence of Age and Condition of the Tree upon Seed Production in Western Yellow Pine.*
    (4) *Lightning in Relation to Forest Fires.*
    (5) *Possibilities of Western Pines as a Source of Naval Stores.*
    (6) *Condition of Experimental Chestnut Poles after 5 and 8 Years' Service.*
15 *Lloyd Library Bulletins.*
16. *Canada, Commission of Conservation, Second Annual Report.*
17. *India, Commercial Guide to its Forest Economic Products.*
18. *South Africa, Report of the Chief Conservator of Forests.*
19. Indian Forest Bulletins :—
    (1) *Memo. on the Oil Value of Sandal Woods from Madras.*
    (2) *Note on the Chemistry and Trade Forms of Lac.*
    (3) *Note on some Germination Tests with Sal Seed.*
    (4) *Note on the Resin Value of* Podophyllum Emodi.
    (5) *Bark-Boring Beetle attack in the Coniferous Forests of the Simla Catchment Area.*
    (6) *A Further Note on some Casuarina Insect Pests of Madras.*

(7) *The Bark-Eating and Root-Boring Beetles.*

(8) *Note on Calorimetric Tests of some Indian Woods.*

(9) *Catalogue of the Photographic Collection at the Forest Research Institute, Dehra Dun.*

20. *Indian Forest Records, vol. ii., part 4.*

21. Indian Forest Records :—

(1) Vol. ii., part 3. *The Silviculture of* Hardwickia Linata (*Anjan*) *and Notes of Sandal.*

Vol. ii., part 4. *Host Plants of the Sandal Tree.*

(2) Vol. iii., part 3. *Report on Investigation of Bamboo as Material for Production of Paper Pulp.*

(3) Vol. iii., part 4. *Note on the Preparation of Tannin Extracts.*

Vol. iv., parts 1, 2, 3, 4 and 5.

(4) *Note on the Distillation and Composition of Turpentine Oil, etc.*

(5) *On some New and Other Species of Hymenoptera in the Collections of the Zoological Branch of the Forest Research Institute, Dehra Dun.*

(6) *Useful Exotics in Indian Forests.*

(7) *On* Albezzia Lethamii.

(8) *Note on the Utilisation of Bamboo for the Manufacture of Paper Pulp.*

22. Indian Forest Memoirs :—Zoology Series, vol. ii., part 11.

23. New Zealand :—

(1) *Annual Report of Department of Lands,* 1910-1911.

(2) *Report on State Afforestation,* 1910-1911.

(3) *Report on Survey Operations,* 1910-1911.

(4) *Report on State Nurseries and Plantations,* 1911-1912.

24. *National Conservation Association Bulletins.*

25. *Development Commissioners' Second Report,* 31st *March* 1912.

26. *Scotland, Report of the Departmental Committee on Forestry,* 1912.

27. *Canada, Commission of Conservation, Third Annual Report,* 1912.

28. *Pennsylvania Department of Forestry Report,* 1910-1911.

29. *Report of H. M. Commissioners of Woods, Forests, etc.,* 27th *June* 1912.

30. *Madras Presidency, Report of Forest Department,* 1910-1911.

31. *British India, Statistics Relating to Forest Administration,* 1910-1911.

32. *Federated Malay States, Report on Forest Administration,* 1911.

33. *Malay Peninsula, Trees and Timbers of.* By A. M. Burn Murdoch, Conservator of Forests.

34. *Union of South Africa, Report of Chief Conservator of Forests,* 1911.

35. *South Australia, Report on State Forest Administration,* 1911-1912.

36. *Southern Nigeria, Report on Afforestation of Togo,* 1912.

37. Canadian Forestry Branch Bulletins :—

(1) *Pulpwood,* 1911.

(2) *Progress of Stream Measurements.*

(3) *Forest Products of Canada,* 1910.

(4) *Report on Timber Conditions around Lesser Slave Lake.*

(5) *Forest Products of Canada,* 1911. *Tight and Slack Cooperage.*

38. Canadian Department of Agriculture Bulletin :—

The Large Larch Saw-fly.

SOCIETIES' REPORTS AND TRANSACTIONS.

39. *Transactions of the Highland and Agricultural Society of Scotland,* vol. xxiv., 1912.
40. *Scientific Proceedings of the Royal Dublin Society,* vol. xiii., Nos. 12 to 23.
41. *Journal of the Board of Agriculture.*
42. *Journal of the Royal Agricultural Society of England,* 1911.
43. *Journal of Department of Agriculture and Technical Instruction for Ireland,* 1912.
44. *Journal of the Royal Horticultural Society.*
45. *Journal of the Royal Caledonian Horticultural Society.*
46.· *Transactions of the Foresters' and Gardeners' Society of Argyll,* vols iii. and iv.
47. *Transactions of the Nova Scotian Institute of Science.*
48. *Scientific Bulletin of the Royal Agricultural College, Cirencester.*
49. *Proceedings of the Society of American Foresters,* 1911.
50. *Journal of the Scottish Meteorological Society,* with two Reprints.
51. *Notes from the Royal Botanic Garden, Edinburgh.*
52. Royal Dublin Society:—
   (1) Vol. ii., No. 5, *Economic Proceedings.*
   (2) Nos. 24, 25, and 26 of vol. xiii., *Scientific Proceedings.*
53. *Kew Gardens Bulletin,* 1912.
54. Botanical Society of Edinburgh:—
   Transactions, parts 2 and 3 of vol. xxiv.
55. *Transactions of Perthshire Society of Natural Science,* vol. v., part 4.

REPRINTS AND MISCELLANEOUS.

56. *Farming and Forestry.* By J. F. Annand.
57. *Gold Coast Land Tenure.*
58. *Aarsberetning fra Net Norske Skogselskab,* 1911.
59. *L'Alpe.* Bologna.
60. *The Estate Magazine.*
61. *Tidskrift for Skogbrug.* Kristiania.
62. *Skogsvårdsföreningens Tidskrift.* Stockholm.
63. *The Indian Forester.* Allahabad.
64. *The Agricultural Economist.*
65. *Journal du Commerce des Bois.* Paris.
66. *Annual Report of the Delegates for Forestry, Oxford,* 1912.
67. *Planters' Notebook.* By Robert Woodward, jun.
68. *Forestry Quarterly.* New York. .
69. *Canadian Forestry Journal.*
70. *American Forestry.*
71. *Timber Trades Journal.*
72. *Timber News.*
73. *Revue des Eaux et Forêts.* Paris.   (By purchase.)
74. *Allgemeine Forst- und Jagd-Zeitung.* (,,   )
75. *Zeitschrift für Forst- und Jagdwesen.* (,,   )
76. *Bulletin de la Société Forestière de Franche Comté et Belfort.* (By purchase.)

Royal Scottish Arboricultural Society.

(INSTITUTED 16th FEBRUARY 1854.)

LIST OF MEMBERS, &c.

As at 24th June 1913.

PATRON.

HIS MOST EXCELLENT MAJESTY THE KING.

PRESIDENT.

Captain ARCHIBALD STIRLING of Keir.

FORMER PRESIDENTS.

YEAR.

1854–56	JAMES BROWN,	{ Deputy-Surveyor of the Royal Forest of Dean. { Wood Commissioner to the Earl of Seafield.

1857   THE EARL OF DUCIE.

1858   THE EARL OF STAIR.

1859   Sir JOHN HALL, Bart. of Dunglass.

1860   THE DUKE of ATHOLL.

1861   JOHN I. CHALMERS of Aldbar.

1862   THE EARL OF AIRLIE.

1863   The Right Hon. T. F. KENNEDY, P.C.

1864–71   ROBERT HUTCHISON of Carlowrie, F.R.S.E.

1872–73   HUGH CLEGHORN, M.D., LL.D., F.R.S.E., of Stravithie.

1874–75   JOHN HUTTON BALFOUR, M.D., M.A., F.R.SS. L. & E., Professor of Botany in the University of Edinburgh.

1876–78   The Right Hon. W. P. ADAM of Blairadam, M.P., P.C.

1879–81   THE MARQUESS OF LOTHIAN, K.T.

1882   ALEXANDER DICKSON, M.D., F.R.S.E., of Hartree, Regius Professor of Botany in the University of Edinburgh.

1883–85   HUGH CLEGHORN, M.D., LL.D., F.R.S.E., of Stravithie.

1886–87   The Right Hon. Sir HERBERT EUSTACE MAXWELL, Bart., P.C., of Monreith.

1888–89   THE MARQUESS OF LINLITHGOW, Hopetoun House, South Queensferry.

1890–93   ISAAC BAYLEY BALFOUR, M.D., Sc.D., F.R.S., Professor of Botany in the University of Edinburgh.

1894–97   The Right Hon. R. C. MUNRO FERGUSON, M.P., P.C.

1898   Colonel F. BAILEY, R.E.

1899–02   THE EARL OF MANSFIELD.

1903–06   W. STEUART FOTHRINGHAM of Murthly.

1907–09   Sir KENNETH J. MACKENZIE, Bart. of Gairloch.

1910–12   Sir JOHN STIRLING-MAXWELL, Bart. of Pollok.

HONORARY MEMBERS.

1907 CASTLETOWN, The Lord, of Upper Ossory, K.P., C.M.G., Granston Manor, Abbeyleix, Ireland.

1901 GAMBLE, J. Sykes, C.I.E., F.R.S., M.A., ex-Director of the Indian Forest School, Highfield, East Liss, Hants. (Also Life Member by Subscription.)

1911 GILLANDERS, A. T., F.E.S., Forester, Park Cottage, Alnwick, Northumberland. (Elected Ordinary Member in 1897.)

1905 HENRY, Auguste Edmond, Professor of Natural Science, etc., National Forest School, Nancy, France.

1886 JOHORE, The Sultan of, Johore, Malay Peninsula.

1904 KAY, James, Retired Wood Manager, Barone, Rothesay. (Elected Ordinary Member in 1867.)

1907 KUMÉ, Kinya, Chief of the Imperial Bureau of Forestry, Department of Agriculture and Commerce, Tokio, Japan.

1903 NILSON, Jägmästare Elis, Föreständare för Kolleberga skogsskola Ljungbyhed, Sweden.

1889 SARGENT, Professor C. S., Director of the Arnold Arboretum, Harvard College, Brookline, Massachusetts, U.S.A.

1889 SCHLICH, Sir William, K.C.I.E., Professor of Forestry, Oxford University.

1895 SCHWAPPACH, Dr Adam, Professor of Forestry, Eberswalde, Prussia.

1907 SIMMONDS, Frederick, M.V.O., 16 Abingdon Court, Kensington West.

1904 SOMERVILLE, Dr William, M.A., D.Sc., D.Œc., F.R.S.E., Professor of Rural Economy, Oxford. (Also Life Member by Subscription, 1889.)

1886 TAKEI, Morimasa, 58 Mikumicho, Ushima, Tokio, Japan.

HONORARY ASSOCIATE MEMBERS.

1903 BATTISCOMBE, Edward, Deputy Conservator of Forests, Nairobe, British East Africa.

1901 BRUCE, William, College of Agriculture, 13 George Square, Edinburgh.

1901 CROMBIE, T. Alexander, Forester, Estate Office, Longhirst, Morpeth.

1902 GILBERT, W. Matthews, The *Scotsman* Office, Edinburgh.

1902 SMITH, Fred., Highfield Mount, Brook Street, Macclesfield.

1901 STORY, Fraser, Professor of Forestry, University of North Wales, Bangor.

1901 USHER, Thomas, Courthill, Hawick.

LIFE AND ORDINARY MEMBERS.

C indicates Past or Present Member of Council.
M ,, Gold Medal.
m ,, Other Medal or Prize.
p ,, Author of paper published.
* ,, Life Member.
Italics indicate that present Address is unknown.

LAW V. Members in arrear shall not receive the *Transactions.* Any Member whose Annual Subscription remains unpaid for two years shall cease to be a Member of the Society, and no such Member shall be eligible for re-election till his arrears have been paid up.

Date of
Election.

1906 ... *ABERCROMBY, Sir George William, Forglen, Turriff.

1900 ... *ADAIR, David Rattray, S.S.C., 19 Castle Street, Edinburgh.

1907 ... *ADAIR, John Downie, Nurseryman, 75 Shandwick Place, Edinburgh.

1883 ... *ADAM, Sir Charles Elphinstone, Bart. of Blairadam, 5 New Square, Lincoln's Inn, London, W.C.

1913 ... ADAM, James, Assistant Forester, New Cottages, Dupplin, Perth.

1912 ... *ADAM, Thomas, F.S.I., J.P., Property Valuator, 27 Union Street, Glasgow.

1904 ... *ADAMS, Joseph Wm. Atkin, Resident Agent, Mill Hill, Middlesex.

1906 ... ADAMSON, John, Head Forester, Bell's Yew Green, Frant, Sussex.

1874 ... *ADDINGTON, The Lord, Addington Manor, Winslow. Bucks.

1913 ... *ADKIN, Benaiah Whitley, F.S.I., 82 Victoria Street, Westminster, London.

1904 *Cp* *AGNEW, Sir Andrew, Bart., 10 Smith Square, Westminster.

1903 ... AILSA, The Marquess of, Culzean Castle, Maybole.

1912 ... *AINSLIE, James Robert, Assistant Conservator of Forests, Ratnapura, Ceylon.

1906 ... AINSLIE, John, Factor, Stobo, Peeblesshire.

1902 .. AINSLIE, Thomas, Glenesk, Penicuik.

1908 ... AIRD, William, Mechanical Engineer, Woodend, Muirkirk, Ayrshire.

1902 ... AITCHISON, William, Assistant Forester, Weirburn Cottage, Grant's House.

1907 ... AITKEN, James, Overseer, Airth Estate, Larbert.

1905 ... ALEXANDER, Henry, Head Forester, Grimstone Estate, Gilling East, York.

1883 *p* *ALEXANDER, John A., 24 Lawn Crescent, Kew Gardens, Surrey.

1908 ... ALEXANDER, John, Nurseryman, 8 Chamberlain Road, Edinburgh.

1905 ... ALLAN, James, Forester, 6 Bostock Road, Middlewick, Cheshire.

1913 ... ALLAN, John Cameron, Assistant Forester, Mellerstain, Gordon, Berwickshire.

1903 *C* *ALLAN, Robert, F.S.I., F.H.R.S., Factor, Halfway House, Polkemmet, Whitburn.

4

Date of
Election.

1909 ... ALLISON, Thomas, Solicitor and Factor, Fort William.

1912 ... ALSTON, James, Merchant, 119 Virginia Street, Glasgow.

1910 .... AMOS, Frank, Surveyor and Auctioneer, The Parade, Canterbury.

1907 ... ANDERSON, James, 467 Cameron Avenue, Detroit, Mich., U.S.A.

1906 ... ANDERSON, Robert, Foreman Forester, Bowmont Forest, Roxburgh.

1901 ... *ANDERSON, Robert, Bailiff, Phœnix Park, Dublin.

1909 ... ANDERSON, Robert Lawson, Forester, Balgate, Kiltarlity, Beauly.

1887 Cmp ANNAND, John F., M.Sc., Lecturer in Forestry, Armstrong College, Newcastle-on-Tyne.

1903 ... ANSTRUTHER, Sir Ralph, Bart. of Balcaskie, Pittenweem.

1903 m ARCHIBALD, John Clark, Head Forester, Eden Hall, Langwathby, R.S.O., Cumberland.

1898 ... ARMSTRONG, Thos. J. A., Factor, Glenborrodale, Salen, Fort William.

1904 ... ARNOTT, William, Head Forester, Ardtornish Estate, Morvern, by Oban.

1883 m*ATHOLL, The Duke of, K.T., Blair Castle, Blair Atholl.

1913 ... AUCHTERLONIE, Alexander, Assistant Forester, 33 Weckley Kettering, Northants.

1860 ... AUSTIN & M'ASLAN, Nurserymen, 89 Mitchell Street, Glasgow.

1908 ... BAILLIE, Lieutenant-Colonel A. C., Factor, etc., Kirklands, Melrose.

1912 ... BAILLIE, Robert Richard Webster, Estate Agent, Lanfine, by Darvel.

1906 m*BAIRD, Henry Robert, D.L., J.P., Durris House, Drumoak, Aberdeen.

1896 ... *BAIRD, J. G. A., of Adamton, 89 Eaton Square, London, S.W.

1903 ... BAIRD, William Arthur, of Erskine, Glasgow.

1909 p*BALDEN, John, Estate Agent, Bywell Office, Stocksfield-on-Tyne.

1884 ... *BALFOUR OF BURLEIGH, The Right Hon. Lord, K.T., Kennet House, Alloa.

1900 ... *BALFOUR, Charles B., of Newton Don, Kelso.

1886 m*BALFOUR, Edward, of Balbirnie, Markinch, Fife.

1906 p BALFOUR, Frederick Robert Stephen, J.P., Dawyck, Stobo, Peeblesshire ; 39 Phillimore Gardens, Kensington, London, W.

1877 p*BALFOUR, Isaac Bayley, LL.D., Sc.D., M.D., F.L.S., Professor of Botany, Royal Botanic Garden, Edinburgh, Past President.

1912 ... *BALFOUR, Robert Frederick, Yr. of Balbirnie, Balbirnie, Markinch.

1892 ... BALLINGALL, Niel, Sweet Bank, Markinch, Fife.

1909 ... Baptie, William, Assistant Forester, Larachbeg, Lochaline, Morvern.

1904 ... *BARBOUR, George Freeland, of Bonskeid, Pitlochry.

1897 ... BARCLAY, Robert Leatham, Banker, 54 Lombard St., London, E.C.

1903 ... BARNES, Nicholas F., Head Gardener, Eaton Hall, Chester.

1909 ... BARR, D., James Service & Sons, Maxwelltown, Dumfries.

Date of
Election.
1907 ... BARR, John, Assistant Factor, Erskine, Bishopton. ..
1895 ... *BARRIE, James Alexander, Forester, Harlestone, Northampton.
1866 *Mp* *BARRIE, James, Forester, Stevenstone, Torrington, North Devon.
1877 *p* *BARRY, John W., of Fyling Hall, Fylingdales, Scarborough, Yorks.
1909 ... BARTON, Ebenezer Johnstone, Assistant Forester, Cruachan, Kilchrenan, Taynuilt.
1874 ... BARTON, James, Forester, Hatfield House, Herts.
1904 ... BARTON, James Robert, Factor, 3 Coates Crescent, Edinburgh.
1908 ... *BAXTER, Edward Gorrel, J.P., Teasses, Lower Largo, Fife.
1908 ... BAXTER, James, Gardener, Gorddinog, Llanfairfechan, Carnarvonshire.
1910 ... BAYLEY, James Francis, W.S., 4 Hill Street, Edinburgh.
1897 ... *BEGG, James, Rosslyne, Culter, by Aberdeen.
1883 ... *BELL, Andrew, Forester, Rothes, Elgin.
1898 ... BELL, David, Seed Merchant, Coburg Street, Leith.
1910 ... *BELL, Sir James, Bart., of Montgreenan, Kilmarnock.
1908 ... BELL, John R., Assistant Forester, Colstoun, Haddington.
1900 ... BELL, Robert, Land Steward, Baronscourt, Newtown-Stewart, Ireland.
1900 ... BELL, William, Forester, Balthayock, Perth.
1871 ... *BELL, William, of Gribdae, 37 Melbourne Grove, Dulwich, London, S.E.
1911 .. BENNETT, R. J., Savoy Park, Ayr.
1905 ... BENNETT, John, Forester and Acting Sub-Agent, Town's End, Wolverton, Basingstoke.
1913 ... BENNOCH, John, Forester, Newhousemill, East Kilbride.
1903 ... BENTINCK, Lord Henry, M.P., Underley Hall, Kirkby Lonsdale.
1904 ... *BERRY, Charles Walter, B.A., 11 Atholl Crescent, Edinburgh.
1889 *m* BERRY, Francis, Forester, Minto, Hawick.
1912 ... BERRY, William, Advocate and Landowner, of Tayfield, Newport, Fife.
1911 ... BETHELL, Slingsby Westbury, Blackford, Rothienorman.
1907 ... BEVERIDGE, James, Forester, Normanby, Doncaster.
1903 ... BINNING, The Lord, Mellerstain, Kelso.
1909 ... BISCOE, T. R., of Newton, Kingillie, Kirkhill R.S.O., Inverness-shire.
1897 ... *BLACK, Alexander, The Gardens, Carton, Maynooth, Co. Kildare.
1908 ... *BLACK, Florance William, of Kailzie, Peeblesshire.
1904 ... BLACK, John, Factor, Cortachy Castle, Kirriemuir.
1913 ... BLACK, Robert, Factor's Assistant, 66 Queen Street, Edinburgh.
1911 ... BLACK, William, Timber Merchant, 37 Clerk Street, Brechin.
1908 ... BLACKLAWS, John, Head Forester, Seafield Cottage, Portsoy.
1913 ... BLAIR, Alexander, Assistant Chief Valuer, 45 Hanover Street, Edinburgh.
1908 ... BLAIR, Charles, Glenfoot, Tillicoultry.
1910 ... BLAIR, Captain Hunter, R.N., of Blairquhan, Ayrshire.
1903 ... BLAIR, Thomas, Farmer, Hoprig Mains, Gladsmuir.

1872 ... Boa, Andrew, Estate Agent, Glenmore, The Avenue, Trowbridge.

1877 ... *Bolckow, C. F. H., of Brackenhoe, Kentisknowle, Torquay.

1892 ... Bond, Thomas, Forester, Lambton Park, Fence Houses, Durham.

1895 ... *Boord, W. Bertram, Land Agent, Bewerley, Pateley Bridge, Yorks.

1909 ... Booth, Miss Cary, 39 Mozartstrasse, Grosslichterfelde, Germany.

1898 *CMp*Borthwick, A. W., D.Sc., 46 George Square, Edinburgh, *Hon. Editor.*

1898 ... Borthwick, Francis J. G., W.S., 9 Hill Street, Edinburgh.

1908 ... *Borthwick, Henry, Borthwick Castle, Gorebridge.

1887 *Mp* Boulger, Professor G. S., 11 Onslow Road, Richmond Hill, London, S.W.

1912 ... Boyd, Alexander, Gardener, The Gardens, Ardgour, Argyllshire.

1883 *Cp* Boyd, John, Crown Forester's House, Ford, Argyll.

1897 ... Braid, J. B., Forester, Witley Court, Great Witley, Worcester.

1902 ... *Braid, William Wilson, 20 Esslemont Road, Craigmillar Park, Edinburgh.

1907 ... Breadalbane, The Marchioness of, Black Mount, Bridge of Orchy, Argyllshire.

1911 ... *Brebner, Robert F., Factor, Crecy House, Isle of Whithorn, Wigtownshire.

1910 ... Broadford, David, Forester, 189 Langley Old Hall, Langley, Huddersfield, Yorks.

1907 *Cp* Brodie, Ian, of Brodie, Brodie Castle, Forres.

1911 ..., *Brook, Charles, of Kinmount, Annan.

1900 *C* *Broom, John, Wood Merchant, Bathgate.

1900 ... *Brown, Charles, Factor, Kerse, Falkirk.

1911 ... Brown, Duncan, Foreman Forester, The Gardens, Birr Castle, King's Co., Ireland.

1910 *p* Brown, Francis Loftus Cowley Cowley-, Principal, South Indian Forest College, Coimbatore, S. India.

1904 ... Brown, George, Timber Merchant, Buckhaven Saw-mills, Buckhaven.

1900 *Cmp* *Brown, Gilbert, Wood Manager, Grantown, Strathspey.

1878 ... Brown, J. A. Harvie-, of Quarter, Dunipace House, Larbert.

1899 ... Brown, John, Forester, 65 Northgate, Peebles.

1896 ... *Brown, Rev. W. Wallace, Minister of Alness, Ross-shire.

1895 ... Brown, Walter R., Forester, Park Cottage, Heckfield, near Winchfield, Hants.

1900 ... Brown, William, Forester, Lissadell, Sligo, Ireland.

1905 ... Bruce, Alexander, Timber Merchant, 68 Gordon Street, Glasgow.

1907 ... Bruce, Charles, Assistant Forester, Beaumanor Park, Woodhouse, Loughborough, Leicestershire.

1901 ... Bruce, David, Overseer, Earnock Estate Office, Hillhouse, Hamilton.

1910 ... Bruce, David, M.A., LL.B., 141 West George Street, Glasgow.

1895 ... *Bruce, Peter, Manager, Achnacloich, Culnadalloch, by Connel.

1909 ... Brunton, James S., Forester, Hursley Park, near Winchester, Hants.

1904 ... BRUNTON, John, Head Forester, Langley Park, Norwich.

1907 ... *BRYDEN, Thomas, Nurseryman, Dennison Nurseries, Ayr.

1897 ... BRYDON, John, Seed Merchant and Nurseryman, Darlington, Co. Durham.

1879 m *BUCCLEUCH, The Duke of, K.T., Dalkeith Palace, Dalkeith.

1912 ... BUCHAN, Robert, Assistant Forester, North Lodge, Keithick, Coupar-Angus.

1879 C *BUCHANAN, Charles, Factor, Penicuik Estate, Penicuik.

1911 ... BUCHANAN, John Hamilton, of Leny (Callander), C.A., 8 York Place, Edinburgh.

1906 ... BURNETT, Sir Thomas, Bart., Crathes Castle, Crathes, N.B.

1909 ... BURNLEY-CAMPBELL, Colin N., 23 Melville Street, Edinburgh.

1909 ... BURN-MURDOCH, Alfred Maule, Conservator of Forests, Kuala Lumpur, Federated Malay States.

1911 ... BURROWS, Alfred John, Land Agent, 41 Bank Street, Ashford, Kent.

1910 ... BURTON, Richard Charles Fryer, District Forest Officer, George Town, Cape Province.

1904 ... BUTLER, Robert, Forester, Estate Office, Blenheim Palace, Woodstock, Oxfordshire.

1906 ... BUTLER, Walter James, Mellerstain Cottages, Gordon, Berwickshire.

1913 ... BUTTAR, Alexander, Blackfriars House, Perth.

1913 ... BUTTAR, Fernie Louden, Forestry Student, 7 Linkfield, Musselburgh.

1910 ... *BUTTER, Charles A. J., Cluniemore, Pitlochry.

1909 ... *BUXTON, Walter L., of Bolwich, Marsham, Norwich.

1909 ... *CACCIA, Anthony M., M.V.O., 19 Linton Road, Oxford.

1902 p *CADELL, Henry Moubray, of Grange and Banton, B.Sc., F.R.S.E., F.A.S., J.P., etc., Grange, Linlithgow.

1912 ... CAESAR, William, Solicitor, Bathgate.

1908 ... *CALDER, James Charles, of Ledlanet, Milnathort.

1912 ... CALDER, John Joseph, of Ardargie, Forgandenny.

1906 ... CALDERHEAD, William, Overseer, Eredine, Port Sonachan, Argyllshire.

1901 ... CAMERON, Alex., Balmina, Cookstown, Ireland.

1910 ... CAMERON, Angus, F.S.I., Factor, Seafield Estates Office, Elgin.

1908 ... CAMERON, Colin M., Factor, Balmakyle, Munlochy.

1907 ... CAMERON, Donald Walter, of Lochiel, Achnacarry, Spean Bridge.

1911 ... *Cameron, Duncan C., Assistant Forester, Damshot, Pollokshaws.*

1913 ... CAMERON, Grigor J., Assistant Forester, Lochgarten Cottage, Nethy Bridge.

1908 ... CAMERON, John, Forester, Isel Hall, Cockermouth, Cumberland.

1899 ... *CAMERON, John J., Norwood, Hamilton.

1904 ... CAMERON, Robert, Estate Office, Brinscall, nr. Chorley.

1912 ... CAMERON, Simon, Forester, Corrour, S.O., Inverness-shire.

Date of
Election.

1912 ... CAMPBELL, Adam, Factor's Assistant, Cromartie Estates, Kildary, Ross-shire.

1909 ... *Campbell, Alexander, Assistant Forester, Dalzell Farm, Motherwell.*

1895 ... CAMPBELL, Alexander, Land Steward, Rosemill Cottage, Strathmartin, by Dundee.

1899 ... CAMPBELL, Alexander, Tullymully, Dunkeld.

1904 ... CAMPBELL, David S., Forester, Middleton Hall, Belford, Northumberland.

1908 ... *Campbell, Donald, Assistant Forester, Homestall Cottage, Ashurstwood, Sussex.*

1897 ... *CAMPBELL, James Arthur, Arduaine, Lochgilphead, Argyllshire.

1900 ... CAMPBELL, James S., Forester, Ginsboro Hall, Ginsboro, Yorks.

1906 ... CAMPBELL, John, Land Steward, Forss Estates, Westfield, Thurso.

1911 ... *CAMPBELL, Keir Arthur, Student, Arduaine, Lochgilphead.

1908 ... CAMPBELL, Patrick William, of Auchairne, W.S., 25 Moray Place, Edinburgh.

1901 ... CAMPBELL, Peter Purdie, Factor, Lee and Carnwath Estates Office, Cartland, Lanark.

1908 ... CAMPBELL, Robert, B.Sc., Geological Laboratory, Edinburgh University.

1903 ... CANCH, Thomas Richard, B.Sc., P.A.S.I., 3 Greenbank Crescent, Morningside, Edinburgh.

1911 ... CANE, William, Assistant Forester, Brown's Lodge, Pembury, Tunbridge Wells.

1903 ... *CAPEL, James Carnegy Arbuthnott, of Ballnamon, 34 Roland Gardens, London, S.W.

1896 ... *CARMICHAEL, The Lord, Governor of Madras, India.

1908 ... CARMICHAEL, James Louis, younger of Arthurstone, Arthurstone, Meigle.

1906 ... CARNEGIE, James, of Stronvar, Balquhidder.

1907 ... CARNEGIE, Robert, Head Forester, Lime Walk Cottage, Rosehaugh, Avoch, Ross-shire.

1903 ... CARRUTHERS, Major Francis John, of Dormont, Lockerbie.

1898 ... *CARSON, David Simpson, C.A., 209 West George Street, Glasgow.

1907 ... CASSELLS, Andrew, Assistant Forester, Star, Markinch, Fife.

1904 ... CATHCART, Sir Reginald Gordon, Bart., Cluny Castle, Aberdeenshire.

1911 ... CAVERHILL, W. R., Factor, The Glen, Innerleithen.

1909 ... CHADWICK, James Melville, Findhorn House, Forres.

1906 ... *CHALCRAFT, George Barker, "Hillside," Gimingham, near North Walsham, Norfolk.

1911 ... CHALMERS, Frank, W.S., 13 Riselaw Road, Edinburgh.

1897 ... CHALMERS, James, Overseer, Gask, Auchterarder, Perthshire.

1898 ... CHALMERS, James, Overseer, Estate Office, Ballochmyle, Mauchline.

1904 ... CHALMERS, Robert W., Head Forester, Earlyvale, Eddleston, Peeblesshire.

Date of
Election.

1911 ... CHAPMAN, Alfred, Assistant Forester, Clumber Park, Worksop, Notts.

1892 ... CHAPMAN, Andrew, Factor, Dinwoodie Lodge, Lockerbie, Dumfriesshire.

1909 ... *Chapman, William, Foreman, Canonbie Saw-mill, Canonbie.*

1908 ... CHERMSIDE, Sir Herbert, Newstead Abbey, Nottingham.

1906 ... CHISHOLM, Alexander M'Kenzie, Clerk of Works, Dalkeith Park Dalkeith.

1909 ... CHISHOLM, George, Forester, Wishaw House, Wishaw.

1882 ... *CHOWLER, Christopher, Gamekeeper, Dalkeith Park, Dalkeith.

1884 ... CHRISTIE, Alex. D., Hillside, Frederick Road, Selly Oak, Birmingham.

1906 ... CHRISTIE, Charles, Factor, Estate Office, Strathdon.

1910 ... *Christie, James Sinton, Assistant Gardener, 50 Vicarage Road, Camberwell, London, S.E.*

1908 ... CHRISTIE, Miss Isabella Robertson, of Cowden, Dollar.

1906 ... CHRISTIE, Thomas, Nurseryman, Rosefield Nurseries, Forres.

1883 ... *CHRISTIE, William, Nurseryman, Fochabers.

1890 ... CLARK, Charles, Forester, Cawdor Castle, Nairn.

1902 ... CLARK, Francis Ion, Estate Office, Haddo House, Aberdeen.

1910 ... *Clark, George, Assistant Forester, Keiloch, Invercauld, Ballater.*

1910 ... CLARK, George, Forester, Crawfordton Estate, Thornhill.

1891 *Cp* CLARK, John, Forester, Kelly, Methlick, Aberdeen.

1906 ... CLARK, John, Forester, Almond Dell, Old Clapperton Hall, Midcalder.

1892 ... *CLARK, William, 66 Queen Street, Edinburgh.

1902 ... CLARK, William, Assistant, Minto Estates Office, Hawick.

1911 ... *Clarkson, Alexander G., Assistant Forester, Lindertis, Kirremuir.*

1911 ... CLERK RATTRAY, Colonel Burn, of Craighall Rattray, Blairgowrie.

1910 ... CLINTON-BAKER, Henry Wm., J.P., of Bayfordbury, Hertford.

1902 ... *CLINTON, The Lord, Fettercairn House, Fettercairn.

1906 ... CLYNE, James, Engineer, Knappach, Banchory.

1898 ... *COATS, Sir Thomas Glen, Bart., Ferguslie Park, Paisley.

1904 ... COBB, Herbert Mansfield, Land Agent, Higham, Rochester, Kent.

1913 ... COCHRAN, Francis James, of Balfour, 152 Union Street, Aberdeen.

1906 ... COCKER, Alexander Morrison, Nurseryman, Sunnypark Nursery, Aberdeen.

1904 ... *COKE, Hon. Richard, Weasenham, Swaffham.

1906 ... COLES, Walter G., Engineer, Board of Agriculture, 122 George Street, Edinburgh.

1908 ... COLSTON, William G., Estate Clerk, Rosemount, Lockerbie.

1908 ... COLTMAN, William Hew, J.P., B.A., Barrister, Blelack, Dinnet, Aberdeenshire.

1907 ... COMRIE, Patrick, Land Agent, Waterside, Dalry, Ayrshire.

1895 ... CONNOR, George A., Factor, Craigielaw, Longniddry.

1887 *C* *COOK, James, Land Steward, Arniston, Gorebridge, Midlothian.

1906 ... Cook, Melville Anderson, Assistant Forester, Glamis, Forfarshire.

1911 ... Cooper, George Mearns, Seedsman, 72 Guild Street, Aberdeen.

1911 ... Corbin, H. Hugh, B.Sc., Woods and Forests Dept., Adelaide, South Australia.

1911 ... *Corbin, John Christopher, Student, Louisville, Davidson's Mains.*

1904 ... Coupar, Charles, Manager, Barcaldine, Ledaig, Argyllshire.

1897 ... *Coupar, Wm., Overseer, Balgowan, Perthshire.

1912 ... Coutts, Duncan, Apprentice Forester, Royal Botanic Garden, Edinburgh.

1910 ... Coutts, James, Assistant Forester, Douglas Castle, Lanarkshire.

1908 ... Coutts, Wm., Forester, Gardener, and Ground Officer, Learney, Torphins, Aberdeen.

1908 ... *Cowan, Alexander, Valleyfield, Penicuik.

1876 ... *Cowan, Charles W., Dalhousie Castle, Bonnyrigg, Lasswade.

1892 ... *Cowan, George, 1 Gillsland Road, Edinburgh.

1908 ... Cowan, Henry Hargrave, Seafield Estates Office, Cullen.

1899 ... *Cowan, Robert, Mains of Househill, Nairn.

1901 ... *Cowan, Robert Craig, Eskhill, Inveresk.

1910 *m* Cowan, Robert, Head Forester, Hoddom Cross, Ecclefechan.

1912 ... Cowieson, Fred Davidson, Structural Engineer, 3 Charles Street, St Rollox, Glasgow.

1874 ... *Cowper, R. W., Gortanore, Sittingbourne, Kent.

1904 ... *Cox, Albert E., of Dungarthill, Dunkeld.

1904 ... *Cox, William Henry, of Snaigow, Murthly.

1900 ... Crabbe, Alfred, Forester, Glamis.

1875 *m* Crabbe, David, Forester, Byreburnfoot, Canonbie, Dumfriesshire.

1867 *C* Crabbe, James, Glamis.

1904 ... Craig, Alexander, Assistant Forester, Glamis.

1909 ... *Craig, Sir Archibald Gibson, Bart. of Riccarton, Currie.

1875 ... *Craig, Wm., M.D., C.M., F.R.S.E., 71 Bruntsfield Place, Edinburgh.

1913 ... Cramb, Daniel, Assistant Forester, Burnside Lodge, Dupplin Estate, Perth.

1903 ... Cranstoun, Charles Joseph Edmondstoune, of Corehouse, Lanark.

1908 ... *Craw, John Taylor, Factor and Farmer, Coldstream.

1908 ... *Crawford, The Earl of, Balcarres, Fife; 7 Audley Square, London, W.

1899 ... Crerar, David, Land Steward, Methven Castle, Perth.

1911 ... Crichton, Edward James, Wood Merchant's Clerk, Silverbank Sawmills, Banchory.

1903 ... Croll, John, of D. & W. Croll, Nurseryman, Dundee.

1900 ... *Crooks, James, Timber Merchant, Woodlands, Eccleston Park, Prescot.

1895 *Cmp* *Crozier, John D., Dept. of Forestry, Board of Agriculture, Dublin.

1910 ... Cruden, Lewis G., Forester, East Lodge, Brucklay, Aberdeenshire.

1907 ... Cruickshank, James, Farmer and Hotelkeeper, Port Erroll, Aberdeenshire.

1900 ... CUMMING, John H., Overseer, Royal Dublin Society, Ball's Bridge, Dublin.

1911 ... CUMMING, Thomas, Forester, Cluniemore Estate, Pitlochry.

1906 ... CUMMING, William, Nursery Foreman, Burnside Nurseries, Aberdeen.

1901 ... *CUNNINGHAM, Captain John, Leithen Lodge, Innerleithen.

1898 ... *CUNNINGHAM, George, Advocate, The Square, Kingsley Green, Haslemore, Surrey.

1909 ... CUNNINGHAM, Robert, Forester, Glenlogan, by Mauchline, Ayrshire.

1913 ... CURR, James, Estate Clerk, Ninewar, Prestonkirk.

1913 ... CURR, Thomas, Student, Ninewar, Prestonkirk.

1898 ... *CURR, W. S., Factor, Ninewar, Prestonkirk.

1907 ... CUTHBERTSON, Evan James, W.S., 12 Church Hill, Edinburgh.

1907 ... DALE, Robert, Forester, The Nursery, Sorn Castle, Ayrshire.

1867 ... *DALGLEISH, John I., of Westgrange, Brankston Grange, Bogside Station, Alloa.

1906 ... *DALGLEISH, Sir William Ogilvie, Bart., Errol Park, Errol.

1900 ... *DALHOUSIE, The Earl of, Brechin Castle, Forfarshire.

1908 ... DALKEITH, The Earl of, Eildon Hall, St Boswells.

1910 ... *DALLIMORE, William, Assistant, Royal Gardens, Kew, 43 Leyborne Park, Kew Gardens, Surrey.

1901 ... DALRYMPLE, Hon. Hew H., Lochinch, Castle Kennedy, Wigtownshire.

1906 ... *DALRYMPLE, The Lord, M.P., Lochinch, Stranraer.

1904 ... DALRYMPLE, The Right Hon. Sir Charles, Bart., P.C., of Newhailes, Musselburgh.

1905 ... DAVID, Albert E., Assistant Forester, Erlestoke, nr. Devizes, Wilts.

1912 ... DAVIDSON, George Alfred, Factor, Knockdow Estate Office, Toward.

1904 ... DAVIDSON, James, 12 South Charlotte Street, Edinburgh.

1892 mp DAVIDSON, John, Forester, Dalzell, Motherwell, Lanarkshire.

1908 ... DAVIDSON, Major Duncan Francis, Dess, Aberdeenshire.

1892 C *DAVIDSON, William, Forester, Panmure, Carnoustie.

1913 ... DAVIDSON, William Cameron, Estate Clerk, Seafield Estates Office, Cullen.

1901 ... DAVIE, George, Overseer, Balruddery Gardens, near Dundee.

1904 ... DAVIE, Thomas, Forester, Dunnotter Estate, Stonehaven.

1908 Cp *DAWSON, William, M.A., B.Sc.(Agr.), Reader in Forestry, Cambridge University.

1910 ... DEAS, James, Devon Cottage, Bonnyrigg.

1904 ... DENHOLM, John, Timber Merchant, Bo'ness.

1906 ... DEWAR, Alex., 12 Greenhill Park, Edinburgh.

1902 ... DEWAR, H. R., Forester, Beaufort Castle, Beauly.

1901 ... *DEWAR, Sir John A., Bart., M.P., Dupplin Castle, Perth.

1898 ... *DIGBY, The Right Hon. Baron, Minterne, Cerne, Dorsetshire.

1912 ... DODS, John Henry, Factor, Novar, Evanton, Ross-shire.

12

1903 ... *Don, Alex., Mikalongwe, Nyasaland.
1913 ... Donald, James A., Forester, Dupplin Estate, Perth.
1908 ... Doughty, James T. S., Solicitor and Factor, Ayton.
1896 ... *Douglas, Alex., Estate Bailiff's Office, Dean Road, Scarborough.
1882 ... Douglas, Captain Palmer, of Cavers, Hawick.
1903 ... Douglas, William G., Forester, Ingleborough Estate, Clapham, Yorks.
1911 ... Doull, Donald, M.A., A.R.C.Sc., High School, Kelso.
1903 ... Dow, Alexander, Forester, Bretby Park, Burton-on-Trent.
1898 *m* Dow, Thomas, Forester, Wakefield Lawn, Stony Stratford, Bucks.
1909 ... Drummond, A. Hay, of Cromlix, Dunblane.
1900 ... Drummond, Dudley W., Commissioner, Cawdor Estate Office, Carmarthen, South Wales.
1904 ... Drummond, William, Head Forester, Fairburn Estate, Muir of Ord, Ross-shire.
1862 ... Drummond & Sons, William, Nurserymen, Stirling.
1912 ... Drysdale, A. Leslie, Hartfell, Colinton.
1912 ... Drysdale, Alexander, Assistant Forester, Foresters' Cottages, Altyre, Forres.
1913 ... Drysdale, Robert, Foreman Forester, Novar Estate, Evanton, Ross-shire.
1909 ... Drysdale, Thomas, Land Steward, Estate Office, Auchinleck.
1908 ... Duchesne, M. C., Land Agent, Farnham Common, Slough, Bucks.
1909 ... *Duff, Alexander M., Land Steward and Farm Manager, Nine-wells, Snaigow, Murthly.
1912 ... Duff, James, Forester, Appin Estate, Appin, Argyll.
1907 ... Duff, John Wharton Wharton, of Orton and Barmuchity, Morayshire.
1903 ... Duff, Mrs M. M. Wharton-, of Orton, Morayshire.
1907 ... Duff, Thomas Gordon, of Drummuir and Park, Banffshire.
1907 ... Duguid, Charles, Head Forester, Philorth, Fraserburgh.
1910 ... Dunbar, John Christie Flockhart, Factor, Crathes Castle, Crathes.
1911 ... Duncan, Peter, Assistant Forester, The Lodge, Castle Toward, Toward, Argyllshire.
1910 ... Duncan, Robert, Forester, Kilmaronaig Cottage, Connel, Argyll.
1907 ... Dunglass, The Lord, Springhill, Coldstream.
1912 ... *Dunlop, Thomas, D.L., Shipowner, 70 Wellington Street, Glasgow.
1905 ... Dunstan, M. I. R., Principal of South-Eastern Agricultural College, Wye, Kent.
1902 ... *Durham, The Earl of, K.G., Lambton Castle, Durham.
1873 ... Durward, Robert, Estate Manager, Blelack, Logie-Coldstone, Dinnet, Aberdeenshire.
1912 ... Duthie, Edwin Charles, Nursery Assistant, Ewan Place, Countesswells Road, Aberdeen.
1900 ... Duthie, James A., of Benjamin Reid & Co., Nurserymen, Aberdeen.
1898 ... Eadson, Thomas G., Forester, Whaley, Mansfield.

Date of
Election.

1911 ... EASSON, Thomas S., W.S., 66 Queen Street, Edinburgh.

1906 ... EDGAR, James, Factor, Poltalloch Estate Office, Lochgilphead.

1885 ... EDINGTON, Francis, Overseer, Monk Coniston Park, Lancashire.

1904 .. EDMOND, James, Assistant, Wemyss Castle Estate Office, East Wemyss, Fife.

1899 *mp* EDWARDS, Alex. W. B., Forester, Thirlmere Estate, *via* Grasmere.

1912 ... EDWARDS, Johnston, Assistant Forester, Murthly, Perthshire.

1893 ... ELDER, William, Forester, Thoresby, Ollerton, Newark, Notts.

1902 ... ELLICE, Captain Edward Charles, Invergarry, and 48 Sloane Gardens, S.W.

1911 *p* ELLIOT, George F. Scott, Meadowhead, Liberton.

1899 ... *ELLISON, Francis B., Downesleigh, Shefford, Bedfordshire.

1904 ... *ELPHINSTONE, The Lord, Carberry Tower, Musselburgh.

1901 *p* ELWES, Henry John, F.R.S., of Colesborne, Cheltenham.

1901 ... ERSKINE, Richard Brittain, Oaklands, Trinity, Edinburgh.

1898 ... EWAN, Peter, Forester, Herbert Cottage, Ditchampton, Wilton, Salisbury.

1873 ... EWING, David, Forester, Strichen House, Aberdeen.

1906 ... FAICHNEY, John, Forester, Blythswood, Renfrew.

1906 ... FAIRBAIRN, John, Assistant Forester, Softlaw, Kelso.

1913 ... FALCONER, David, Foreman Forester, Achnacarry, Spean Bridge.

1912 ... FALCONER, James Grewar, Architect, 4 Cameron Square, Fort William.

1894 ... *FARQUHARSON, James, Forester, Ardgowan, Inverkip.

1911 ... FARQUHARSON, Right Hon. Robert, M.D., P.C., Finzean, Aboyne.

1900 *mp* FEAKS, Matthew, Forester, Lochiel Estate, Achnacarry.

1903 ... FENWICK, William, Factor, Darnaway Castle Estates Office, Earlsmill, Forres.

1908 ... FERGUSON, Donald, Joiner and Timber Merchant, Quarry Lane, Lennoxtown.

1900 ... *FERGUSON, James Alex., Arduith, Partickhill, Glasgow.

1910 *mp* FERGUSON, John, Forester, Brynllywarch Estate Office, Kerry, Montgomeryshire.

1888 *mp*FERGUSON, The Right Hon. R. C. Munro, M.P., P.C., LL.D., of Raith and Novar, Raith, Fife, *Hon. Secretary and Past President.*

1912 ... FERGUSSON, Donald Stewart, Dunfallandy, by Pitlochry.

1880 ... FERGUSSON, Sir James Ranken, Bart., Spitalhaugh, West Linton.

1908 ... FERNIE, Alexander, Forester, 14 Royston Terrace, Edinburgh.

1911 ... *FERNIE, William Duncan, Forester, Balcarres, Fife.

1907 ... *FERRIE, Thomas Young, Timber Merchant, 69 Buchanan St., Glasgow.

1901 ... *FINDLAY, John Ritchie, of Aberlour, Aberlour House, Aberlour.

1907 ... FISH, Andrew, Forester, Boghead, Kirkmuirhill, Lanarkshire.

1909 ... FISHER, Malcolm, Forester, Kenotin, Washington Mills, N.Y., U.S.A.

Date of
Election.

1869 ... FISHER, William, Estate Agent, Wentworth Castle, Barnsley, Yorkshire.

1902 ... *FITZWILLIAM, The Earl of, Wentworth, Rotherham.

1911 ... FLEAR, Edwin, Assistant Forester, Boughton, Newark, Notts.

1910 ... FLEMING, Archibald, Overseer, Culcreuch, Fintry, Stirlingshire.

1899 *p* FLEMING, Sir John, Timber Merchant, Albert Saw-mills, Aberdeen.

1906 ... *FLETCHER, J. Douglas, of Rosehaugh, Avoch, Ross-shire.

1911 ... FLETCHER, John A., Factor, Landale, Ardgour, Argyllshire.

1909 ... FLETCHER, John Sydney, 13 Braidburn Terrace, Edinburgh.

1910 ... FORBES, Alistair Hugh, Factor, The Foley, Rothesay.

1890 *Mp* FORBES, Arthur C., Department of Agriculture, Dublin.

1898 ... FORBES, James, Factor, Eallabus, Bridgend, Islay.

1896 ... *FORBES, James, The Gardens, Overtoun, Dumbartonshire.

1912 ... FORBES, John, Overseer, Cowden Home Farm, Dollar.

1878 *C* *FORBES, Robert, Estate Office, Kennet, Alloa.

1912 ... FORBES, Robert Guthrie, Forester, Cliffhouse, Gulworthy, Tavistock, Devon.

1873 *m* *FORBES, William, Estate Office, West Bilney Lodge, King's Lynn, Norfolk.

1869 *M* *FORGAN, James, Forester, 5 Belhelvie Terrace, Perth.

1892 ... FORGAN, James, Sunnybraes, Largo, Fife.

1912 ... FORSYTH, J. A., Assistant Forester, Panmure Cottage, Montrose.

1908 ... FORTESCUE, William Irvine, M.B.C.M., Kingcausie, Milltimber, Aberdeen.

1908 ... *FORTUNE, George R., Factor, Colinsburgh, Fife.

1897 *mp* *FOTHRINGHAM, W. Steuart, of Murthly, Perthshire, *Past President.*

1909 ... *FOULIS, Arch. Keith, Valuer, Inland Revenue, 5 Calder Street, Motherwell.

1908 ... FOWLER, Sir John Edward, Bart., Braemore, Garve.

1913 ... FRAIN, Peter, Assistant Forester, North Lodge, Dupplin, Perth.

1866 *Cmp* *FRANCE, Charles S., 13 Cairnfield Place, Aberdeen.

1901 ... *FRASER, Alexander, Solicitor and Factor, *Hon. Secretary and Treasurer, Northern Branch,* 63 Church Street, Inverness.

1908 ... FRASER, Charles James Roy, of Lochavich, Argyllshire.

1909 *m* FRASER, George, Assistant Forester, Midhope, S. Queensferry.

1892 ... *FRASER, George, Factor, Dalzell, Motherwell, Lanarkshire.

1902 ... *FRASER, George M., 13 Drumsheugh Gardens, Edinburgh.

1898 ... FRASER, James, Manager, Cahir Saw-mills, Cahir, Co. Tipperary.

1899 ... *FRASER, James, Factor, Fasque Estates Office, Fettercairn.

1911 ... FRASER, James, Student of Forestry, c/o Campbell, 12 Sylvan Place, Edinburgh.

1895 ... FRASER, J. C., Nurseryman, Comely Bank, Edinburgh.

1905 ... FRASER, John, Forester, The Little Hill, Leighton, Ironbridge R.S.O., Salop.

1913 ... FRASER, John, Assistant Factor, Raith Estate Office, Kirkcaldy.

1913 ... FRASER, John Cameron, Assistant Forester, Welldale, Douglas, Lanarkshire.

1901 ... FRASER, John M'Laren, of Invermay, Forgandenny, Perthshire.

1913 ... FRASER, Robert B., Assistant Secretary, Landowners' Co-operative Forestry Society, Ltd., 33 Queen Street, Edinburgh.

1907 ... FRASER, Robert S., Allangrange, Munlochy, Inverness; Ivy House, Comshall, Surrey.

1892 ... *FRASER, Simon, Land Agent, Hutton in the Forest, Penrith.

1907 ... *FRASER, Sweton, Forester, Gallovie, Kingussie.

1908 ... FRASER-TYTLER, James Francis, of Woodhouselee, Rosslyn.

1896 ... FRATER, John, Foreman Forester, Ardross Mains, Alness, Rossshire.

1907 ... FYFE, Harry Lessels, Assistant Forester, C.P.R., Forestry Dept., Maple Creek, Sask, Canada.

1906 ... *Fyffe, Robert, c/o Polytechnic Institute, Regent Street, London.*

1907 ... FYFFE, Robert B., Aden Estates Office, Old Deer.

1904 ... GALLOWAY, George, Quarrymaster, Roseangle, Wellbank, by Dundee.

1913 ... GALLOWAY, Robert Angus, Student, 1 Riselaw Road, Edinburgh.

1893 *p* *GALLOWAY, Robert, S.S.C., 19 Castle Street, Edinburgh, *Secretary and Treasurer.*

1909 *p*GAMBLE, J. Sykes, C.I.E., etc., Highfield, East Liss, Hants.

1896 *Cm* GAMMELL, Sydney James, of Drumtochty, Countesswells House, Bieldside, Aberdeen.

1910 ... *Gardinar, James, Assistant Forester, Forester's Bothy, Thirlmere, Grasmere.*

1909 ... *Gardiner, Francis Forsyth, Assistant Forester, Home Farm, Newmains, Douglas, Lanarkshire.*

1913 ... GARDINER, Frederick Crombie, Old Ballikinrain, Balfron.

1908 ... GARDINER, R., Mitchell Nursery, Coaldale, Alberta, Canada.

1908 ... GARDYNE, Lieutenant-Colonel Greenhill, of Finavon, Forfar.

1899 ... *GARRIOCH, John E., Factor, Lovat Estates, Beauly.

1907 ... *GARSON, James, W.S., Albyn Place, Edinburgh.

1903 ... *GASCOIGNE, Lieut.-Col. Richard French, D.S.O., Craignish Castle, Ardfern, Argyllshire.

1898 ... GAULD, William, Forester, Coombe Abbey, Binley, Coventry.

1902 ... GAVIN, George, Factor, Falkland Estate, Falkland.

1897 ... GELLATLY, Thomas, Forester, Hallyburton, Coupar Angus.

1912 ... GIBB, George Gibb Shirra, Farmer, Boon, Lauder.

1912 ... GIBB, Dr R. Shirra, M.B.C.M., D.P.H., F.H.A.S., Boon, Lauder.

1913 ... GIBSON, Gideon James, Tea Planter, Netherbyres, Ayton.

1903 ... GIBSON, William, Forester, Carnell, Hurlford, Ayrshire.

1905 ... GILBERT, Alexander, Assistant Forester, Midhope Castle, Hopetoun, South Queensferry.

Date of
Election.

1881 ... *GILCHRIST, Wm., Forester, Nursery Cottage, Mount Melville, St Andrews.

1913 ... GILL, Hugh Stowell Hope, C.A., Balerno Lodge, Balerno.

1897 *Cmp* GILLANDERS, A. T., F.E.S., Forester, Park Cottage, Alnwick, Northumberland.

1894 *m* GILLESPIE, James, Overseer, Garden, Arnprior, Port of Monteith.

1894 ... GILMOUR, Colonel Robert Gordon, of Craigmillar, The Inch, Midlothian.

1908 ... GLADSTONE, Hugh Steuart, F.Z.S., M.A., etc., Lannhall, Thornhill.

1900 ... *GLADSTONE, Sir John R., Bart. of Fasque, Laurencekirk.

1913 ... GLEN, James, Assistant Forester, Milton of Aberdalgie, Perth.

1891 *C* *GLENCONNAR, The Lord, The Glen, Innerleithen; 34 Queen Anne's Gate, London, S.W.

1901 ... *Godman, Hubert, Land Agent, Ginsborough, Yorkshire.

1913 ... *GOLD, William, Forester, Dellavaird, Auchinblae, Fordoun.

1913 ... GOLDRING, George, Assistant Forester, Wortley Hall, Wortley, Sheffield.

1909 ... GOODFELLOW, John, Forester, Faskally, Pitlochry.

1910 *Cp* GORDON, G. P., B.Sc., (Agric.), B.Sc. (For.), B.Sc. (Oxon.), Lecturer in Forestry, West of Scotland Agricultural College, Glasgow.

1911 ... GORDON, George, Timber Merchant, Aberdeen Saw-mills, Aberdeen.

1912 ... GORDON, Gregor, Assistant Forester, Tigerton, Menmuir, Brechin.

1912 ... GORDON, Seton, B.A., Auchintoil, Aboyne.

1868 ... *GOSSIP, James A., of Howden & Co., The Nurseries, Inverness.

1912 ... GOSSIP, William Murray, Knowsley, Inverness.

1897 ... *GOUGH, Reginald, Forester, Wykeham, York.

1912 ... *GOURLAY, William Balfour, B.A.(Cantab.), L.R.C.P. and S.(Ed.), Dawyck, Stobo.

1909 ... Gow, Alexander, Butt Field Cottage, Hatfield, Herts.

1897 ... Gow, Peter Douglas, Farmer, Bonaly, Colinton, Midlothian.

1897 ... Gow, Peter, Land Steward, Laggan, Ballantrae, Ayrshire.

1905 ... *Gow, Robert, Head Forester, Appin House, Argyllshire.*

1904 ... *GRAHAM, Anthony George Maxtone, of Cultoquhey, Crieff.

1907 ... *GRAHAM, Hugh Meldrum, Solicitor, Inverness.

1908 *m* GRAHAM, James, Marquis of, Brodick Castle, Arran (per George Laidler, Strabane, Brodick).

1910 ... GRAHAM, Robert Francis, M.A., Skipness, Argyll.

1905 ... *GRAHAM, William, Foreman Forester, St Ann's Cottage, Rae Hill, Lockerbie.

1909 ... GRAINGER, Henry Herbert Liddell, Ayton Castle, Ayton.

1887 ... *Grant, Alexander, Forester, Springfield, Kerry, Newtown, Montgomeryshire.*

1911 ... *GRANT, Captain Arthur, D.S.O., House of Monymusk, Aberdeen.

1867 ... GRANT, Donald, Forester, Drumin, Ballindalloch, Banffshire.

Date of
Election.

1908 ... GRANT, Donald, Forester, Fersit, Tulloch, Inverness-shire.
1904 *mp* GRANT, Ewan S., Head Forester, Priors Heath, Bedgebury Park, Goudhurst, Kent.
1908 ... GRANT, Iain Robert James Murray, of Glenmoriston, Inverness-shire.
1909 ... GRANT, James, Forester, Raith, Kirkcaldy.
1893 ... GRANT, John B., Forester, Downan, Glenlivet.
1874 ... *GRANT, John, Overseer, Daldowie, Glasgow.
1907 ... GRANT, Robert, Fernleigh, Birchington, Kent.
1908 ... GRANT, Sir John Macpherson, Bart., Ballindalloch Castle, Ballindalloch.
1913 ... GRANT, Robert, Assistant Forester, New Cottages, Dupplin, Perth.
1906 ... GRASSICK, William Henderson, Land Steward, Daviot Branch Asylum, Pitcaple, Aberdeenshire.
1912 ... GRAY, David, Foresters' Bothy, Kelburn Castle, Fairlie, Ayrshire.
1906 ... GRAY, David, Wheelwright, 371 Great Western Road, Aberdeen.
1907 ... GRAY, George, Forester, The Lodge, Eliock, Sanquhar, Dumfries-shire.
1908 ... *GRAY, James Lowrie, Farmer, Elginhaugh, Dalkeith.
1909 ... GRAY, James Ritchie, Wheelwright, 371 Great Western Road, Aberdeen.
1902 ... GRAY, Walter Oliver, Forester, Drimsynie, Lochgoilhead.
1901 ... GRAY, Major William Anstruther-, of Kilmany, Cupar, Fife.
1911 ... GREGORY, Charles, Gamekeeper-Forester, Granston Manor, Balla-colla, Queen's Co., Ireland.
1913 ... GREIG, Robert Blyth, (Hon.) M. Sc., Member of Board of Agriculture, 29 St Andrew Square, Edinburgh.
1898 ... GREY, The Right Hon. Sir Edward, Bart., K.G., M.P., P.C., of Falloden, Chathill, Northumberland.
1908 ... GRIEVE, J. W. A., Indian Forest Service, The Club, Darjeeling, Bengal.
1903 ... GRIFFITH, Sir Richard Waldie, of Hendersyde Park, Kelso.
1905 ... *GURNEY, Eustace, Sprowston Hall, Norwich.
1911 ... GUTHRIE, Charles, Assistant Forester, The Bothy, Pilsley, Bakewell, Derbyshire.

1911 ... HACKING, Thomas, B.Sc., etc., Agricultural College, Uckfield, Sussex.
1879 ... HADDINGTON, The Earl of, K.T., Tyninghame, Prestonkirk.
1910 ... HALDANE, David, Forester, Dalmeny Park, Edinburgh.
1900 *C* *HALDANE, Sir William S., of Foswell, W.S., 55 Melville Street, Edinburgh.
1905 *mp* HALL, Thomas, Superintendent of Public Park, 32 Colebrooke Street, Cambuslang.
1906 *mp* HALL, William, Head Forester, Church Cottages, Bilton, nr. York.
1897 ... *HALLIDAY, Geo., Timber Merchant, Rothesay.
1901 ... *HALLIDAY, John, Timber Merchant, Rothesay.

d

1911 ... HAMILTON, Alexander, Assistant Forester, Beaufort Woods, Kiltarlity, Beauly.

1907 ... HAMILTON, Andrew, Naval Architect, 9 Denman Drive, Newsham Park, Liverpool.

1908 ... HAMILTON, David R., 63 Cluny Gardens, Morningside, Edinburgh.

1882 ... *HAMILTON, Donald C., Forester, Knowsley, Prescot.

1899 ... *HAMILTON, The Lord, of Dalzell, Dalzell House, Motherwell.

1892 ... HANNAH, George, Overseer, Estate Office, Boynton, Bridlington.

1905 ... HANSON, Clarence Oldham, Deputy Conservator, Indian Forest Department, 3 Malvern Place, Cheltenham.

1913 m HANSON, Herbert S., Assistant Forester, Brinscall, Lancashire.

1907 ... HARBOTTLE, William, Forester, Bishop Burton, Beverley, Yorks.

1903 ... *HARDIE, David, Factor, Errol Park, Errol.

1880 ... *HARE, Colonel, Blairlogie, Stirling.

1896 ... *Harley, Andrew M., Forester, 5 Thayer Street, Manchester Square, London.

1908 m HARLOND, Henry, Park Forester, Sutton Coldfield, Warwickshire.

1911 ... HARRIER, James B., Forester, Innes House, Elgin.

1910 ... *HARRISON, Alexander, Apprentice C.A., 3 Napier Road, Edinburgh.

1905 ... HARROW, R. L., Head Gardener, Royal Botanic Garden, Edinburgh.

1897 ... HART, John, Factor, Mains of Cowie, Stonehaven, Kincardineshire.

1880 p *HAVELOCK, W. R., The Nurseries, Brocklesby Park, Lincolnshire.

1911 ... HARVEY, Andrew, Overseer, Rozelle, Ayr.

1911 ... HAWES, A. F., A.B., M.F., Experimental Station, Burlington, Vermont, U.S.A.

1911 ... HAWLEY, Ralph Chipman, A.B., M.F., Assistant Professor of Forestry, Yale Forest School, 360 Prospect Street, New Haven, Conn., U.S.A.

1908 ... *HAY, Athole Stanhope, of Marlefield, Roxburgh.

1892 C *HAY, John, Factor, Easter Dullatur House, Dullatur.

1904 m HAY, Sir Duncan Edwyn, Bart. of Haystoun, 42 Egerton Gardens, London, S.W.

1869 ... HAYMAN, John, Glentarff, Ringford, Kirkcudbrightshire.

1902 ... HAYNES, Edwin, Editor Timber Trades Journal, Cathedral House, 8-11 Paternoster Row, London, E.C.

1912 ... HEAVENER, Harvey Joseph, Forester, Woodstock, Inistioge, Co. Kilkenny.

1909 ... HECTOR, Thomas Gordon, c/o Messrs Bura & Evans, School Gardens, Shrewsbury.

1907 ... HENDERSON, John, Assistant Forester, Gateside, Balbirnie, Markinch.

1908 ... *HENDERSON, John G. B., W.S., Nether Parkley, Linlithgow.

1908 ... HENDERSON, R., Assistant Forester, 23 Brooklane Cottages, Chester.

1893 ... HENDERSON, R., 4 High Street, Penicuik, Midlothian.

1893 ... HENDERSON, William, Forester, Clonad Cottage, Tullamore, King's County.

1906 ... *HENDRICK, James, B.Sc., F.I.C., Marischal College, Aberdeen.

1898 ... HENDRY, James, 5 Thistle Street, Edinburgh.

1910 ... HENKEL, John Spurgeon, Assistant Conservator of Forests, Midland Conservancy, Knysna, Cape Colony.

1908 ... HENRY, Augustine, Professor, 5 Sandford Terrace, Ranelagh, Dublin.

1911 ... HENRY, George J., 66 Queen Street, Edinburgh.

1912 ... HENRY, Thomas, Assistant Forester, Bredisholm, Baillieston.

1901 ... *HEPBURN, Sir Archibald Buchan-, Bart. of Smeaton-Hepburn, Prestonkirk.

1913 ... HEPBURN, Robert Grant, Gardener, Culzean Castle, by Ayr.

1874 ... *HERBERT, H. A., of Muckross, Killarney, Co. Kerry, Ireland.

1884 ... *HEYWOOD, Arthur, Glevering Hall, Wickham Market, Suffolk.

1904 ... HILL, George, Assistant Forester, Fothringham, Forfar.

1904 ... *HILL, J. Smith, The Agricultural College, Aspatria.

1903 ... *HILL, Robert Wylie, of Balthayock, Perthshire.

1905 ... *HILLIER, Edwin L., F.R.H.S., Nurseryman and Landscape Gardener, Culross, Winchester.

1902 ... *HINCKES, Ralph Tichborne, J.P., D.L., Foxley, Hereford.

1907 ... HINDS, John, Forester, Stockeld Park, Wetherby, Yorks.

1895 ... HOARE, Sir Henry Hugh Arthur, Bart. of Stourhead, Bath.

1909 p HOBART-HAMPDEN, A. G., Indian Forest Service, Ferns, Great Hampden, Great Missenden.

1912 ... *HOG, Alan Welwood, Writer to the Signet, 4 South Learmonth Gardens, Edinburgh.

1908 ... *HOG, Steuart Bayley, B.A., Newliston, Kirkliston.

1866 ... HOGARTH, James, Forester, Culhorn, Stranraer, Wigtownshire.

1913 ... HOGG, David, Foreman Forester, South Lodge, Invermay, Forgandenny.

1913 ... HOGG, William H., Assistant Forester, Kinnordy, Kirriemuir.

1905 ... *HOLMS, John A., Formaken, Erskine, Renfrewshire.

1910 ... HOLZAPFEL, John William, B.Sc. and N.D.A., North Elswick Hall, Newcastle-on-Tyne.

1909 ... HONEYMAN, John A., Overseer, Kemback Estate, Cupar, Fife.

1902 ... *HOOD, Thomas, jun., Land Agent, Ras-el-Khalig, Egypt.

1908 ... *HOPE, Captain Thomas, of Bridge Castle, Westfield, Linlithgowshire.

1871 ... *HOPE, H. W., of Luffness, Drem, Haddingtonshire.

1912 p *HOPKINSON, Andrew Douglas, B.Sc.(Agr.), Lecturer in Forestry, Royal Agricultural College, Cirencester.

1907 ... HOPKINSON, James Garland, Factor, Drumtochty Estates Office, 11A Dee Street, Aberdeen.

1876 ... *HORSBURGH, John, 21 Dick Place, Edinburgh.

1908 ... Houston, Samuel, 17 Prince Edward Street, Crosshill, Glasgow.

1911 ... *HOWARD DE WALDEN, Baron, The Dean, Kilmarnock.

Date of
Election.

1902 ... HOWE, John Arnold, Overseer, Home Farm, Mount Stuart, Rothesay.

1905 ... HUDSON, W. F. A., M.A., Lecturer in Forestry, 2 Wollaston Road, Cambridge.

1913 ... HUNTER, Robert, Sawmiller, Eliock, Sanquhar, Dumfriesshire.

1913 ... Hutchins, David Ernest, Forest Service of India (ret.), Rectory Cottage, Ridley, Wrotham, Kent.

1905 ... HUTTON, George Kerse, Assistant Forester, Castle Kennedy, Wigtownshire.

1906 ... HUTTON, James, Head Forester, Glendye, Banchory.

1905 ... IMRIE, Charles, Assistant Forester, Balgove, Rossie, Montrose.

1910 ... IMRIE, George James, Forest Officer, Transvaal Conservancy, Government Nursery, Irene, Transvaal.

1901 ... IMRIE, James, Forester, Aberpergrom Estate, Glen-neath, Glamorganshire.

1884 ... *Inglis, Alex., Greenlaw Dean, Greenlaw, Berwickshire.

1908 ... *INGLIS, Alexander Wood, of Glencorse, Loganbank, Milton Bridge.

1904 ... *INGLIS, David, National Bank House, Pathhead, Kirkcaldy.

1911 ... Inglis, Frederick, Assistant Forester, Dalzell, Motherwell.

1910 ... INGLIS, Robert, Factor, Old Blair, Blair Atholl.

1891 m INGLIS, William, Forester, Brodick, Isle of Arran.

1912 ... INGLIS, W. G., 113 George Street, Edinburgh.

1913 ... INMAN, William, 11 Newbattle Terrace, Edinburgh.

1904 ... INNES, Alexander Berowald, of Raemoir and Dunnottar, Raemoir House, Banchory.

1895 ... INNES, Alexander, Forester, Drummuir, Keith.

1911 ... INNES, Robert, Assistant Forester, Dean Road, Kilmarnock.

1913 ... IRONSIDE, David, Forester, Lanfine Estate, Newmilns, Ayrshire.

1909 ... IRONSIDE, William, Solicitor, Royal Bank Buildings, Oban.

1906 ... *IRVINE, Alexander Forbes, J.P., B.A.(Oxon.), Drum Castle, Aberdeen.

1901 ... IRVINE, John, Forester, Colesborne, Cheltenham, Gloucestershire.

1906 ... IRVING, James Rae Anderson, Foreman Forester, Langholm Estate, Canonbie, Dumfriesshire.

1908 ... *IZAT, Alexander, C.I.E., Mem. Inst. C.E., Balliliesk, Muckhart, Perthshire.

1907 ... JACK, David, Assistant Forester, Kinnordy, Forfarshire.

1906 ... *JACKSON, George Erskine, B.A.(Oxon.), W.S., Kirkbuddo, Forfar.

1898 ... JAMIESON, James, Forester, Ynyslas, Llanarthney R.S.O., Carmarthenshire.

1896 ... JARDINE, Sir R. W. B., Bart. of Castlemilk, Lockerbie, Dumfriesshire.

1907 ... JERVOISE, Francis Henry Tristram, J.P., Herriard Park, Basingstoke.

1904 ... JOANNIDES, Pericles, Willesden, Sporting Club Station, Ramleh, Egypt.

1909 ... JOHNSTON, David T., Gardener, Dalmeny House Gardens, Edinburgh.

1910 ... JOHNSTON, Frank James, Nurseryman and Forester, Claycroft, Dalbeattie.

1911 ... JOHNSTON, George, Assistant Forester, Dean Road, Kilmarnock.

1901 *C* *JOHNSTON, James, F.S.I., Factor, Alloway Cottage, Ayr.

1883 ... *JOHNSTON, Robert, Forester, Bon Ryl Estate, Duns, Berwickshire.

1907 ... JOHNSTON, Robert, Forester, Dalkeith Park, Dalkeith.

1900 ... JOHNSTONE, William, Head Forester, Beil, Prestonkirk.

1907 ... *JOHNSTONE, Richard, Forester, The Glen, Innerleithen.

1911 ... JOLY DE LOTBINIERE, Major H. G., R.E., c/o Messrs Cox & Co., Army Bankers, Charing Cross, London.

1882 ... *JONAS, Henry, Land Agent and Surveyor, 23 Pall Mall, London, S.W.

1902 ... *JONAS, Robert Collier, Land Surveyor, 23 Pall Mall, London, S.W.

1903 ... JONES, Ireton Arthur, of Pennick & Co., Delgany Nurseries, Co. Wicklow.

1888 ... JONES, James, Wood Merchant, Larbert, Stirlingshire

1893 .... JONES, Thomas Bruce, Wood Merchant, Larbert.

1907 *p* *KAY, James, Nursery Station, Indian Head, Sask, Canada.

1867 *Cmp* KAY, James, Retired Wood Manager, Barone, Rothesay.

1909 ... KAY, John, Assistant Gardener, Grangemuir Lodge, Prestwick.

1911 ... KEAV, Robert Burton, Estate Overseer, Findon Cottage, Conon Bridge.

1896 ... KEIR, David, Forester, Ladywell, Dunkeld.

1906 ... KEIR, James S., Estate Manager, Borrodale, Arisaig.

1909 ... *KEITH, Marshall John, Factor, Brucklay Estates Office, Aberdour House, Fraserburgh.

1901 ... *KENNEDY, Frederick D. C.-Shaw-, Dyroch, Maybole.

1890 ... *KENNEDY, James, Doonholm; Ayr.

1912 ... KERR, John, Assistant Forester, Colenden, Stormontfield, nr. Perth.

1892 ... *KERR, John, Farmer, Barney Mains, Haddington.

1908 *m* *KERR, J. Ernest, of Harviestoun, Harviestoun, Dollar.

1913 ... KETTLES, Alexander, Assistant Forester, New Cottages, Dupplin, Perth.

1896 ... KETTLES, Robert, Assistant Forester, Craigend, Perth.

1910 ... *Khan, Allah Dád, District Forester, Fazilká, Ferozepur, Panjap, India.*

1894 ... KIDD, Wm., Forester, Harewood, Leeds.

1908 ... *KIMMETT, John, Forester, The Lodge, Glenstriven, Toward, Argyllshire.

1900 ... KING, David, Nurseryman, Osborne Nurseries, Murrayfield.

1910 .... KING, William, Gardener, Victoria Park, Whiteinch, Glasgow.

1906 ... *KINLOCH, Charles Y., of Gourdie, by Murthly.

1903 ... *KINNAIRD, The Master of, 10 St James Square, London.

1898 ... *KINROSS, John, Architect, 2 Abercromby Place, Edinburgh.

1902 ... *KIPPEN, William James, Advocate, B.A., LL.B., Westerton, Balloch, Dumbartonshire.

1910 ... KIRKPATRICK, James, Forester, Balbary, Meigle.

1898 ... KYLLACHY, The Hon. Lord, of Kyllachy, 6 Randolph Crescent, Edinburgh.

1911 ... LAIDLER, George, Strabane, Brodick.

1911 ... LAIRD, Eric P., of R. B. Laird, Dickson & Sons, Ltd., Nursery-men, 17 Frederick Street, Edinburgh.

1912 ... LAIRD, James M'Lean Dunn, Assistant Forester, The Cottages, Dupplin, Perthshire.

1911 ... LAIRD, William Pringle, Nurseryman, 20 High Street, Dundee.

1901 m *LAMB, Alexander, Overseer, Freeland, Forgandenny.

1910 ... LAMB, Everard Joseph, of Scotby House, Carlisle.

1894 ... *LAMINGTON, The Lord, G.C.M.G., Lamington, Lanarkshire.

1899 ... LAMOND, Alexander, Forester, Freeland, Forgandenny.

1905 ... *LAMONT, Norman, of Knockdow, Toward, Argyllshire.

1911 ... LANGE, Leopold Peter Harding, Superintendent of Plantations, c/o Conservator of Forests, Pretoria, Transvaal.

1906 ... *LANGLANDS, James H., Cunmont House, by Dundee.

1896 ... *LANSDOWNE, The Marquess of, K.G., 54 Berkeley Square, London, S.W.

1906 p LAUDER, Alexander, D.Sc., F.I.C., Edinburgh and East of Scot-land College of Agriculture, 13 George Square, Edinburgh.

1901 ... LAUDER, William, Steward, Summerhill House, Enfield, Co. Meath.

1897 ... LAURISTON, John, Forester, Newbridge Green, Upton-on-Severn, Worcestershire.

1913 ... LAW, Fred. W., M.A., B.Sc. (Agr.) Student, 13 Beaconsfield Place, Aberdeen.

1912 ... LAWSON, A. Anstruther, Ph.D., D.Sc., Lecturer in Botany, University of Glasgow.

1906 ... LAWSON, William, Assistant Factor, Cromartie Estates, Kildary, Ross-shire.

1902 ... LEARMONT, John, Nurseryman, Larchfield Nurseries, Dumfries.

1911 ... *LEATHER, Major Gerard F. T., Middleton Hall, Belford, Northumberland.

1904 ... LEES, D., of Pitscottie, Cupar, Fife.

1905 ... LEES, Ernest A. G., Factor, Durris Estate, by Aberdeen.

1909 ... LE FANU, Victor Charles, B.A., F.S.I., Estate Office, Bray, Co. Wicklow.

1909 ... LEGAT, Charles Edward, B.Sc.(Agric.), Chief of Forestry Division, Department of Agriculture, Transvaal, Pretoria.

1880 ... LEISHMAN, John, Manager, Cavers Estate, Hawick, Roxburgh-shire.

1909 ... LEITH, The Lord, of Fyvie, Fyvie Castle, Aberdeenshire.

1911 ... LESCHALLAS, Captain John Henry Pigé, Glenfinart, Ardentinny.

1908 ... LESLIE,' Archibald Stewart, W.S., 33 Queen Street, Edinburgh.

1868 ... *LESLIE, Charles P., of Castle-Leslie, Glaslough, Ireland.

1893 *Cmp*LEVEN, George, Forester, Bowmont Forest, Roxburgh.

1913 ... LEVEN, William, Assistant Forester, Old Scone, Perth.

1881 ... *LEYLAND, Christopher, Haggerston Castle, Beal, Northumberland.

1907 ... LINDSAY, Hugh, Head Forester, Torwoodlee Estate, Galashiels.

1909 ... *LINDSAY, John, Under Forester, Station Lodge, Brodie.

1879 ... LINDSAY, Robert, Kaimes Lodge, Murrayfield, Midlothian.

1907 ... LINDSAY, William, of Messrs J. & H. Lindsay, Ltd., Tourist Agents, 18 St Andrew Street, Edinburgh.

1909 ... LITTLE, Thomas, Assistant Forester, Burnside Cottage, Canonbie.

1913 ... LIVSEY, Edward, Under Forester, Leases Farm, Well, Bedale.

1913 ... LODGE, Charles William, Assistant Forester, New Cottages, Dupplin Estate, Perth.

1905 ... LOGAN, David, Factor, Saltoun, Pencaitland.

1908 ... *LOGAN, Douglas Campbell, Factor, Portbane, Kenmore, Aberfeldy.

1908 ... LOGUE, Hugh, Forester, Knockdow, Toward, Argyllshire..

1883 ... *LONEY, Peter, Estate Agent, 6 Carlton Street, Edinburgh.

1909 ... LONGMUIR, James, Assistant Forester, 12 Houghton Village, King's Lynn, Norfolk.

1911 ... LONGMUIR, James, jun., Forester, Houghton, King's Lynn, Norfolk.

1898 *Cp* *LOVAT, The Lord, C.B., D.S.O., Beaufort Castle, Beauly, Inverness.

1880 ... *Love, J. W., c/o Mrs Boyce, Byron Street, St Kilda, Victoria, South Australia.

1875 ... *LOVELACE, The Earl of, East Horsley Towers, Woking, Surrey.

1898 ... Low, James, Forester, Ballindalloch, Strathspey.

1900 ... *Low, William, B.Sc., of Balmakewan, Marykirk, Kincardineshire.

1912 ... *Low, William, of Blebo, Cupar, Fife.

1910 m LOWE, Alex., Forester, Lockerbie House, Lockerbie.

1912 ... LUKE, Nicol, Forester, Cairndow, via Inveraray.

1908 ... *LUMSDEN, George James, Aithernie, Lundin Links, Fife.

1891 ... *LUMSDEN, Hugh Gordon, of Clova, Lumsden, Aberdeenshire.

1900 ... LUMSDEN, Robert, jun., 11 Morningside Terrace, Edinburgh.

1908 ... LUNN, George, Forester, Invercauld, Ballater.

1875 ... *LUTTRELL, George F., of Dunster Castle, Taunton, Somersetshire.

1900 ... *LYELL, Sir Leonard, Bart. of Kinnordy, Kirriemuir.

1910 ... LYFORD-PIKE, James, B.Sc., 131 Warrender Park Road, Edinburgh.

1909 ... *LYLE, Alexander Park, of Glendelvine, Murthly.

1907 ... *M'AINSH, Duncan, Wood Merchant, Crieff.

1908 ... *M·Ainsh, R., Assistant Forester, Bowmont Forest, Roxburgh.

1911 ... M'ANDREW, Hamilton, Merchant, 7 Church Road, Ibrox, Govan.

1912 ... M'ARTHUR, Dr D. G., Aberfeldy.

Date of
Election.

1906   *m* MACALPINE-LENY, Major R. L., of Dalswinton, Ruanbeg, Kildare, Ireland.

1909   ... MACARTHUR, Alaster, Bank Agent, Inveraray.

1907   ... *M'BAIN, William, Forester, Estates Office, Drumnadrochit.

1892   *C* *MACBEAN, Simon, Land Steward, Estate Office, Needwood Forest, Sudbery, Derby.

1896   *m* *M'BEATH, David K., Factor, Benmore Estates Office, Kilmun.

1908   ... M'CALLUM, Alexander, Assistant Forester, Dunira Cottages, Comrie, Perthshire.

1908   ... M'CALLUM, D., Assistant Forester, Innerbuist Cottage, Stormontfield, Perth.

1894   ... M'CALLUM, Edward, Overseer, Kerse Estate, Falkirk.

1898   *p* M'CALLUM, James, Forester, Canford, Wimborne, Dorset.

1901   ...* M'CALLUM, Thomas W., Retired Ground Officer, Dailly, Ayrshire.

1911   ... M'CAW, Daniel, Forester, Thoresby Park, Ollerton, Notts.

1904   ... *M'Clellan, Frank C., Zanzibar Government Service, Pemba,* via *Zanzibar, East Africa.*

1870   ... *M'CORQUODALE, D. A., Carnoustie, Forfarshire.

1893   ... M'COUBRIE, M. S., Land Steward, Tullamore, King's County, Ireland.

1912   ... M'CUTCHEON, Robert, Forester, Whittingehame, Prestonkirk.

1904   ... MACDONALD, Alexander, Factor, Meggernie, Aberfeldy.

1912   ... MACDONALD, Arthur J., Assistant Forester, Chatsworth Institute, Edensor, nr. Bakewell, Derbyshire.

1912   ... M'DONALD, Donald, Foreman Forester, Garth, Balnald, Fortingal, Aberfeldy.

1901   ... MACDONALD, Mrs Eleanor E., The Manse, Swinton.

1893   *Cp* MACDONALD, George U., Overseer, Haystoun Estate, Woodbine Cottage, Peebles.

1908   ... MACDONALD, The Hon. Godfrey Evan Hugh, Factor, Macdonald Estates Office, Portree.

1900   ... *MACDONALD, Harry L., of Dunach, Oban.

1894   ... *MACDONALD, James, Forester, Kinnaird Castle, Brechin.

1903   ... *MACDONALD, James Farquharson, S.S.C. and N.P., Kilmuir, Linlithgow.

1895   ... MACDONALD, John, Forester, Skibo, Dornoch.

1908   ... M'DONALD, John, Forester, Ardgoil Estate, Lochgoilhead.

1908   ... MACDONALD, John Ronald M., of Largie, M.A., D.L., J.P., Largie Castle, Tayinloan, Kintyre.

1910   ... MACDONALD, John, Assistant Forester, Rose Cottage, Achnacarry, Spean Bridge.

1913   ... MACDONALD, William, Assistant Forester, New Cottages, Dupplin, Perth.

1907   ... *MACDONALD, T. Martin, of Barguillean, Taynuilt.

1906   ... MACDONALD, William Kid, Windmill House, Arbroath.

1904   ... M'DONALD, William Yeats, of Auquharney, Hatton, Aberdeenshire.

1913   ... M'DOUGALL, Hugh, Forester, Gentleshaw, Rugeley, Staffs

Date of
Election.

1907 ... *Macdougall, James, Assistant Forester, Perlethorpe, Thoresby Park, Ollerton, Newark, Notts.*

1895 mp *MacDougall, Professor Robert Stewart, M.A., D.Sc., 9 Dryden Place, Edinburgh.

1912 ... M'Dougall, William Cumming, Assistant Forester, Budby, Ollerton, Newark.

1884 ... *Macduff, Alex., of Bonhard, Perth.

1906 ... M'Ewan, James, Foreman Forester, Kingswood, Murthly.

1909 m M'Ewan, John, Assistant Forester, Castle Lachlan, Stralachlan, Greenock.

1908 ... M'Ewan, W., Assistant Forester, Drummond Cottage, Logie-almond, by Perth.

1909 ... *MacEwan, William, Assistant Forester, Garscube Estate, by Glasgow.*

1904 ... M'Ewan, Wm., Forester, Allangrange, Munlochy, Ross-shire.

1901 ... M'Ewen, Alexander, Overseer, Castle Lachlan, Stralachlan, Greenock.

1898 ... Macfadyen, Donald, Assistant Forester, Drumlanrig, Thornhill.

1907 ... Macfarlane, Archibald, Timber Merchant, Harbour Saw-mills, Paisley.

1910 ... MacFarquhar, Donald, Forester, Port Glas, Kenmore, Aberfeldy.

1904 ... *Macfie, John William, of Dreghorn, Rowton Hall, Chester.

1901 ... *M'Garva, Gilbert Ramsay, Factor, Rosehaugh Estate, Ross-shire.

1901 ... M'Ghie, John, Overseer, Kelburne Estate, Fairlie.

1901 ... *M'Gibbon, Donald, Forester, Rossie Estate, Inchture.

1904 ... M'Gibbon, R., Forester, Wentworth, Rotherham.

1908 ... M'Glashan, James, Forester, Belladrum, by Beauly.

1913 ... M'Glashan, John, Forester, Benmore, Kilmun, by Greenock.

1912 ... M'Glashan, Tom, Assistant Forester, Kingswood, Murthly.

1902 ... *MacGregor, Alasdair Ronald, Edinchip, Lochearnhead.

1902 m M'Gregor, Alexander, Forester, Abbeyleix, Queen's Co.

1908 ... *MacGregor, Alexander, Iron Merchant, Ravenswood, Dalmuir, Dumbartonshire.

1896 ... M'Gregor, Angus, Forester, Craigton, Butterstone, Dunkeld.

1899 ... M'Gregor, Archibald, Forest Office, Forestry Department, Nairobi, B.E.A.

1906 ... *MacGregor, Evan Malcolm, Factor, Ard Choille, Perth.

1912 ... MacGregor, James Gow, Land Steward, Duchal Estate, Kilmacolm.

1910 ... M'Gregor, John, Assistant Forester, Brucefield, Clackmannan.

1910 ... M'Gregor, John, Wood Merchant, Tam's Brig Saw-mills, Ayr.

1913 ... *MacGregor, Neil, Forester, Bridge of Dye, Banchory, Kincardineshire.

1905 m M'Hardy, James, Forester, Forglen, Turiff, Aberdeenshire.

1904 m M'Hardy, William, Forester, Chancefield, Falkland, Fife.

1901 C M'Hattie, John W., City Gardener, City Chambers, Edinburgh.

1894 ... M'Ilwraith, Wm., Forester, Hall Barn Estate, Beaconsfield, Bucks.

1907 ... M'INNES, William, Assistant Forester, Advie, Strathspey.

1905 ... M'INTOSH, Alexander, Foreman Forester, East Barkwith, Lincolnshire.

1911 ... M'INTOSH, Donald J., Assistant Forester, Faskally Cottage, Pitlochry.

1895 ... *Macintosh, D. L., The Gardens, Stronvar, Lochearnhead.*

1879 ... *M'INTOSH, Professor W. C., 2 Abbotsford Crescent, St Andrews.

1904 ... M'INTOSH, Robert, Forester, Cullentragh Cottage, Rathdrum, Co. Wicklow.

1885 ... *MacINTOSH, William, Fife Estates Office, Banff.

1901 ... MACINTOSH, William, Forester, New Chapel, Boncath R.S.O., South Wales.

1907 ... M'INTYRE, Charles, Forester, Inver, Dunkeld.

1912 ... MACINTYRE, Charles, Assistant Forester, Tomnaharrich, Fort William.

1910 ... *Macintyre, John Finlayson, Assistant Forester, The Gardens, Glencoe, Ballachullish (East).*

1908 ... MACINTYRE, Peter Brown, Findon Mains, Conon Bridge.

1911 ... M'INTYRE, Thomas Walker, Sorn Castle, Ayrshire.

1892 ... M'KAY, Allan, c/o Park & Co., Ltd., Timber Merchants, Fraserburgh.

1910 ... MACKAY, James Waite, Estate Office, Jervaulx Abbey,. Middleham, Yorks.

1865 ... MACKAY, John, Lauderdale Estate Office, Wyndhead, Lauder.

1908 ... M'KAY, Murdo, Forester, Castlecomer, Co. Kilkenny.

1887 ... *MACKAY, Peter, Forester and Overseer, Bargany Mains, Dailly, Ayrshire.

1907 ... MACKAY, William, Factor, Chisholm Estates, 19 Union Street, Inverness.

1900 ... M'KECHNIE, Angus, Head Forester, Apethorpe, Wansford, Northants.

1891 .. MACKENDRICK, James, Forester, Estate Office, Pallas, Loughrea, Co. Galway.

1908 ... MACKENZIE, A., Overseer, Old Place of Mochrum, Kirkcowan, Wigtownshire.

1908 ... MACKENZIE, Lieut.-Col. A. F., of Ord, Ord House,. Muir of Ord.

1867 ... MACKENZIE, Alex., Warriston Nursery, Inverleith Row, Edinburgh.

1909 ... MACKENZIE, Alex. James, Factor, 62 Academy Street, Inverness.

1907 ... MACKENZIE, Sir Arthur, Bart. of Coul, Strathpeffer.

1901 ... MACKENZIE, Charles, Factor, Clunes, Achnacarry, Spean Bridge.

1909 ... MACKENZIE, Charles J. S., Assistant Forester, Caberfeidh, Carr Bridge.

1908 ... M'KENZIE, Colin, Head Forester, Didlington Hall, Stoke, Ferry, Norfolk.

1901 ... M'KENZIE, Daniel, Forester, Wynyard Estate, Stockton-on-Tees.

Date of
Election.

1904 ... MACKENZIE, Major E. Walter Blunt, Castle Leod, Strathpeffer.

1908 ... MACKENZIE, Evan North Barton, Kilcoy Castle, Killearnan.

1908 ... MACKENZIE-GILLANDERS, Captain E. B., of Highfield, Muir of Ord.

1913 ... M'KENZIE, George, Estate Overseer, Douamou Castle, Co. Roscommon, Ireland.

1893 ... *MACKENZIE, James, Forester, Cullen House, Cullen.

1899 ... M'KENZIE, James, Wood Merchant, Carr Bridge, Invernessshire.

1897 ... MACKENZIE, John, Forester, Dalneich Cottage, Ardross, Alness, Ross-shire.

1907 ... MACKENZIE, John, jun., Factor, Dunvegan, Skye.

1913 ... M'KENZIE, Kenneth D., Assistant Forester, New Cottages, Dupplin, Perth.

1900 _p_ *MACKENZIE, Sir Kenneth John, Bart. of Gairloch, 10 Moray Place, Edinburgh, _Past President_.

1908 ... MACKENZIE, Nigel Banks, Factor, Fort William.

1908 ... MACKENZIE, Nigel Blair, Assistant Factor, Fort William.

1913 ... MACKENZIE, Robert, Assistant Forester, Achnacarry, Spean Bridge.

1913 ... MACKENZIE, Simon John, Assistant Forester, Chatsworth Institute, Edensor, nr. Bakewell, Derbyshire.

1907 ... MACKENZIE, Colonel Stewart, of Seaforth, Brahan Castle, Dingwall.

1911 ... MACKENZIE, Thomas, Factor, Craigard, Invergarry.

1907 ... MACKENZIE, W. Dalziel, Fawley Court, Henley-on-Thames.

1896 _p_ MACKENZIE, Wm., Forester, Novar, Evanton, Ross-shire.

1905 ... *M'KERCHAR, John, Bulb, Plant and Seed Merchant, 35 Giesbach Road, Upper Holloway, London, N.

1897 ... *_M'Kerrow, Robert, Manager, Carton, Maynooth, Co. Kildare._

1907 ... MACKEZZACK, George Ross, of Ardgye, Elgin.

1909 ... M'KIE, Henry B., Factor, Freeland, Erskine, Bishopton.

1898 ... *MACKINNON, A., The Gardens, Scone Palace, Perth.

1883 _C_ MACKINNON, George, The Gardens, Melville Castle, Lasswade.

1912 ... MACKINTOSH, Patrick Turner, Solicitor, 5 Albyn Place, Edinburgh.

1878 ... MACKINTOSH, The, of Mackintosh, Moy Hall, Inverness.

1905 .. *MACKINTOSH, W. E., Yr. of Kyllachy, 28 Royal Circus, Edinburgh.

1912 ... *MACKINTOSH, William R., Assistant Forester, Dyke, Forres.

1895 _C_ *MACLACHLAN, John, of Maclachlan, Castle Lachlan, Argyll.

1904 ... MACLAGGAN, George C. R., Forester, Hopetoun, S. Queensferry.

1908 ... M'LAREN, James, Chopwellwood House, Rowlands Gill, Co. Durham.

1879 ... *M'LAREN, John, 12 Findhorn Place, Edinburgh.

1909 ... MACLARTY, Alexander Sinclair, Forester, Glasserton, Whithorn, Wigtownshire.

1898 ... *_Maclean, Archibald Douglas, J.P., Harmony, Balerno._

Date of
Election.

1908 ... M'LEAN, Donald, 62 Craigmillar Park, Edinburgh.

1906 ... M'LEAN, James Smith, Forester, Douglas Castle, Lanarkshire.

1902 ... MACLEAN, Peter, Forester, Invergarry.

1912 ... M'LENNAN, Donald, Assistant Forester, Sand House, Maidens.

1909 ... *MacLennan, Murdo, Assistant Forester, c/o Mrs Riddles,* 12 *Rodney Street, Edinburgh.*

1912 ... MACLEOD, Donald, Assistant Forester, Raith Estate, Kirkcaldy.

1901 ... M'LEOD, Peter, Nurseryman, Perth.

1895 ... MACMILLAN, John D., Steward, Margam Park, Port Talbot, Wales.

1910 ... M'MORRAN, Peter, Assistant Forester, Dalzell, Motherwell.

1904 ... *M'NAB, David Borrie, Solicitor, Clydesdale Bank, Bothwell.

1909 ... M'Nair, Gregor, Overseer, Conaglen, Ardgour.

1913 ... M'NAUGHTON, Donald, Assistant Forester, New Cottages, Dupplin, Perth.

1903 ... M'NAUGHTON, John, Forester, Auchterarder House, Perth.

1911 ... *M'NEILE, Major John, Kippilaw, St Boswells.

1912 ... MACNIVEN, James, Forester, Bredisholm, Baillieston.

1910 ... M'PHERSON, Alexander, Tayness, Kilmartin, Lochgilphead.

1909 ... MACPHERSON, Duncan, Forester, Consall Hall, Stoke-on-Trent, Staffordshire.

1890 *mp* M'RAE, Alexander, Forester, Dundrum, Co. Tipperary.

1899 ... *MACRAE-GILSTRAP, Major John, of Ballimore, Otter Ferry, Argyllshire.

1900 ... M'RAE, Henry, Assistant Forester, Ufton, Southam, Rugby.

1908 ... MACRAE, Sir Colin G., W.S., 45 Moray Place, Edinburgh.

1906 *p* MACRAE, John, Forester, Highfield, Muir of Ord, Ross-shire.

1907 ... M'RAW, Donald, Manager, Strathgarve, Garve R.S.O.

1879 ... *MACRITCHIE, David, C.A., 4 Archibald Place, Edinburgh.

1895 *m* M'TAVISH, John, Assistant Forester, The Glen, Skelbo, Sutherland.

1905 ... M'VINNIE, Samuel, Forester, Skeagarvie, Rossmore Park, Monaghan.

1905 ... *MAITLAND, A. D. Steel, of Sauchie, etc., Sauchieburn, Stirling.

1908 ... MALCOLM, George, Factor, Fernie House, Fort William.

1880 ... *MALCOLM, Lieut.-Col. E. D., R.E., Achnamara, Lochgilphead.

1895 ... *MANN, Charles, Merchant, Lumsden, Aberdeenshire.

1909 ... *MANN, James, of Castlecraig, Dolphinton.

1911 ... MANNERS, Charles Robert, Civil Engineer and Estate Factor, 12 Lombard Street, Inverness.

1898 *Cm* *MANSFIELD, The Earl of, Scone Palace, Perth.

1896 ... MAR AND KELLIE, The Earl of, Alloa House, Alloa.

1895 ... *MARGERISON, Samuel, English Timber Merchant, Calverley, near Leeds.

1909 ... MARSDEN Reginald Edward, Director, Burma Forest School, Pyinmana, Burma, India.

1901 ... *MARSHALL, Archd. M'Lean, Chitcombe, Breda, Sussex.

1905 ... *MARSHALL, Henry Brown, of Rachan, Broughton.

Date of
Election.

1899 ... MARSHALL, John, Timber Merchant, etc., Maybole.

1893 ... MARSHALL, J. Z., Timber Merchant, 2 Dean Terrace, Bo'ness.

1907 ... MARSHALL, William, Assistant Forester, Dell Nursery, Nethy Bridge.

1910 _p_ MARTIN, Lieut-Col. Martin, Upper Ostaig, by Broadford, Isle of Skye.

1876 .... *MARTIN, James, Forester, Knipton, Grantham, Lincolnshire.

1911 ... MARTIN, Sir T. Carlaw, LL.D., Director, Royal Scottish Museum, Edinburgh.

1909 ... MASSIE, George Duncan, Solicitor (_Hon. Secretary, Aberdeen Branch_), 147 Union Street, Aberdeen.

1884 _C_ *MASSIE, W. H., of Dicksons & Co., 1 Waterloo Place, Edinburgh.

1907 ... MASSON, William, Forester, Meikleour, Perth.

1910 ... MASTERTON, James, Hedger and Assistant Forester, Kennet Cottages, Alloa.

1893 _C_ MATHER, R. V., of Laing & Mather, Nurserymen, Kelso.

1901 ... *MATTHEWS, Robert, Land Steward, Duncrub Park, Dunning.

1909 ... MAUDE, James, Timber Merchant, Hebden Bridge, Yorks.

1894 ... *MAUGHAN, John, Estate Agent, Jervaulx Abbey, Middleham R.S.O., Yorks.

1907 ... MAXTONE, James, Overseer, Strathallan, Machany, Perthshire.

1896 ... MAXTONE, John, Forester, Duff House, Banff.

1904 ... *MAXWELL, Aymer, Yr. of Monreith, Port William, Wigtownshire.

1891 ... MAXWELL, James, Forester and Overseer, Ruglen, Maybole.

1893 _Mmp_ *MAXWELL, Sir John Stirling-, Bart. of Pollok, Pollokshaws, _Past President._

1886 _p_ MAXWELL, The Right Hon. Sir Herbert E., Bart. of Monreith, Port William, Wigtownshire, _Past President._

1908 _p_ MAXWELL, Wellwood, of Kirkennan, Dalbeattie.

1908 ... MAXWELL, William James, Factor, Terregles Banks, Dumfries.

1905 _m_ MAXWELL, William Jardine Herries, of Munches, Dalbeattie.

1907 ... MEACHER, Sydney George, Land Agent, Marlee, Blairgowrie.

1906 ... MELDRUM, Thomas C., Nurseryman, Forfar.

1899 ... MELVILLE, David, The Gardens, Dunrobin Castle, Golspie.

1911 ... MELVIN, David, Foreman Forester, Stobhall Estate, Gillowhill, Coupar-Angus.

1901 ... MENZIES, James, Forester, Caledon Estate, Co. Tyrone.

1908 ... *MENZIES, William Dudgeon Graham, J.P., Hallyburton, Coupar-Angus.

1880 ... *MESHAM, Captain, Pontryffydd, Bodvari, Rhyl, Denbighshire.

1877 ... METHVEN, Henry, of Thomas Methven & Sons, 6 Frederick Street, Edinburgh.

1892 ... METHVEN, John, Viewforth, Kennoway, Fife.

1911 ... MICHIE, Henry M., Logan Estates Office, Chapel Rossan, Stranraer.

1881 _Cmp_ *MICHIE, John, M.V.O., Factor, Balmoral, Ballater, Aberdeenshire.

Date of
Election.

1893 ... MICHIE, William, Forester, Welbeck, Worksop, Notts.

1893 ... *MIDDLEMASS, Archibald, Forester, Tulliallan, Kincardine-on-Forth.

1905 ... MIDDLETON, James, Factor, Braehead House, Kilmarnock.

1910 ... MIDDLETON, James, Assistant Forester, Blythswood, Renfrew.

1905 ... *MILLAR, John, Timber Merchant, Greenhaugh Saw-mills, Govan.

1908 ... *MILLER, Robert E., Bonnycraig, Peebles.

1910 ... MILLIGAN, Alexander, Head Forester, 11 James Square, Biggar, Lanarkshire.

1913 ... MILLIGAN, David M. M., of Findrack, 20 Albyn Place, Aberdeen.

1910 ... MILLIGAN, J. A., Forester, Pippingford Park, Nutley, Sussex.

1899 ... MILNE, Alexander, Factor, Urie Estate Office, Stonehaven.

1902 ... MILNE, Alexander, Forester, Charboro' Park, Wareham, Dorset.

1903 ... MILNE, Colonel George, of Logie, Aberdeenshire.

1904 ... MILNE, Frederick, Assistant Forester, Nursery Cottage, Tarbrax, by Forfar.

1895 ... MILNE, James, Land Steward, Carstairs House, Carstairs.

1906 ... *MILNE, John, Forester, Bicton Estate, East Budleigh, Devon.

1899 ... MILNE, Ritchie, Assistant, Annandale Estate Office, Hillside, Lockerbie.

1898 ... *MILNE, Robert P., Spittal Mains, Berwick-on-Tweed.

1890 ... MILNE, William, Farmer, Foulden, Berwick-on-Tweed.

1902 ... MILNE, William, Forester, Huntly Hill, Stracathro, Brechin.

1906 ... MILNE, William, Nurseryman (Wm. Fell & Co., Ltd.), Hexham.

1901 ... MILNE-HOME, David William, of Wedderburn, Caldra, Duns.

1897 *p* *MILNE-HOME, J. Hepburn, Irvine House, Canonbie.

1909 ... *MIRRIELEES, Frederick Donald, B.A.Oxon., Goddards, Abinger Common, Dorking.

1904 *Cm* MITCHELL, Alexander, Forester, Rosebery, Gorebridge.

1913 ... MITCHELL, Andrew James, Assistant Factor and Architect, 12 Golden Square, Aberdeen.

1912 ... MITCHELL, Andrew W., 8 Queen's Terrace, Aberdeen.

1912 ... MITCHELL, Charles, of Pallinsburn, Cornhill-on-Tweed.

1898 ... MITCHELL, David, Forester, Drumtochty, Fordoun.

1882 *Mp* *MITCHELL, Francis, Forester, Woburn, Beds.

1904 ... MITCHELL, James, Organising Secretary for Technical Education to Fife County Council, County Buildings, Cupar, Fife.

1902 ... *MITCHELL, John, jun., Timber Merchant, Leith Walk Saw-mills, Leith.

1904 ... MITCHELL, John Irvine, M.A., Teacher, 4 Craighouse Terrace, Edinburgh.

1901 ... MITCHELL, William Geddes, Estate Agent, Doneraile, Co. Cork.

1903 *mp* MOERAN, Archibald E., Land Agent, etc., Lissadell, Stillorgan Park, Co. Dublin.

1902 ... MOFFAT, John, Head Forester, Boiden, Arden, N.B.

1909 ... MOFFAT, William, Forester, Castle Wemyss, Wemyss Bay.

1908 ... *MOISER, Cyril, P.A.S.I., Heworth Grange, York.

Date of
Election.

1895 ... *MONCREIFFE, Sir Robert D., Bart. of Moncreiffe, Perth.

1906 ... *MOON, John Laurence, Forest Ranger, Forestry Department, Nairobi, British East Africa.

1903 *m* MORAY, The Earl of, Darnaway Castle, Forres.

1897 ... *MORGAN, Alex., Timber Merchant, Crieff, Perthshire.

1899 ... *MORGAN, Andrew, Assistant Factor, Glamis.

1913 ... MORGAN, John, Assistant Forester, Innerbuist Cottage, Stormont. field, Perth.

1895 ... *MORGAN, Malcolm, Timber Merchant, Crieff, Perthshire.

1911 .... MORGAN, W. Dunlop, Forestry Student, 5 Hillside Street, Edinburgh.

1913 ... MORISON, A. C. F., of Bognie, Mountblairy, Turriff.

1907 ... MORRISON, Andrew, Estate Manager, Brodie Mains, Forres.

1911 ... MORRISON, David, Assistant Forester, Main Street, Sorn.

1895 ... MORRISON, Hew, LL.D., Librarian, Edinburgh Public Library.

1908 ... *MORRISON, Hugh, Little Ridge, Tisbury, Wilts.

1911 ... MORRISON, James, Factor for Forglen, 40 Low Street, Banff.

1908 ... MORRISON, John, Factor, Rhives, Golspie.

1903 ... MORRISON, William, Manufacturer, 61 Grant Street, St George Road, Glasgow.

1905 ... MORTON, Andrew, Forester, Stockstruther, Roxburgh.

1905 ... *MOTHERWELL, A. B., Writer, Airdrie.

1908 ... *MOUBRAY, John J., Naemoor, Rumbling Bridge.

1907 ... MOULTRIE, James, Foreman Forester, Denside, Durris, Drumoak, Aberdeenshire.

1908 ... MOWAT, George, Forester, Carmichael, Thankerton, Lanarkshire.

1906 ... MOWAT, John, Overseer, Hazelhead Estate, Aberdeen.

1890 ... MUIRHEAD, George, F.R.S.E., Commissioner, Speybank, Fochabers.

1912 ... *MUIRHEAD, Roland Eugene, Winona, Bridge of Weir.

1901 ... MULLIN, John, Forester, Eglinton Castle, Irvine.

1904 ... MUNRO, Alexander, Overseer, Invereshie, Kincraig.

1903 *C* MUNRO, Alexander J., 48 Castle Street, Edinburgh.

1912 ... MUNRO, Donald, Forester, Coul, Strathpeffer, Ross-shire.

1895 ... MUNRO, Donald, Forester, Holkham Hall, Norfolk.

1906 *p* MUNRO, Donald, Wood Merchant, Ravenswood, Banchory.

1911 ... MUNRO, Duncan H. Campbell, of Kenlochlaich, Appin, Argyll.

1908 ... MUNRO, George, M.B.C.M., Kerjord, Weisdale, Shetland.

1905 ... MUNRO, Sir Hector, Bart. of Foulis Castle, Evanton, Ross-shire.

1911 ... MUNRO, Hector, Assistant Forester, Cruachan, Kilchrenan, Taynuilt.

1909 *m* MUNRO, Hugh R., Assistant Forester, Blackwood Estate, Kirk-muirhill, Lanarkshire.

1902 ... *MUNRO, Sir Hugh Thomas, of Lindertis, Kirriemuir.

1910 ... *Munro, James Watson, B.Sc., Department of Forestry, Marischal College, Aberdeen.*

1907 *m Munro, John, Foreman Forester, Kingswood, Murthly.*

Date of
Election.

1907 ... MUNRO, John, Land Steward and Forester, The Lodge, Tarland, Aberdeenshire.

1911 ... MUNRO, William, Forester, Forest Department, Nairobi, British East Africa.

1909 ... MUNRO, William, Factor, Glenferness Estate Office, Nairn.

1909 ... *MURRAY, Major Alastair Bruce, of Polmaise, Stirling.

1892 mp *MURRAY, Alexander, Forester, Murtbly, Perthshire.

1900 ... MURRAY, George J. B., Forester, Holylee, Walkerburn.

1904 mp MURRAY, John M., Assistant Forester, Kingswood, Murthly.

1900 ... MURRAY, William, of Murraythwaite, Ecclefechan, Dumfriesshire.

1896 ... *MURRAY. William Hugh, W.S., 48 Castle Street, Edinburgh.

1899 ... *NAIRN, Sir Michael B., Bart. of Rankeillour, Manufacturer, Kirkcaldy.

1912 ... *NAIRN, Michael, of Pitcarmick, Dysart House, Dysart, Fife.

1904 ... NAIRN, Robert, Forester, Rowallan, Kilmarnock.

1907 ... NASH, William, Assistant Forester, Airdsmill, Muirkirk, Ayrshire.

1905 ... *NASMYTH, Norman, of Glenfarg, Glenfarg Lodge, Abernethy.

1909 ... *NAYLOR, John Murray, Laighton Hall, Welshpool.

1910 ... NEILSON, Walter Montgomerie, of Barcuple, Ringford.

1909 ... *NEISH, Edward William, Sheriff Substitute, Dundee.

1911 ... NELSON, Andrew S., Railway Carriage and Wagon Builder, 26 Huntly Gardens, Glasgow.

1893 ... NELSON, Robert, Assistant Forester, Hannahgate Cottage, Kinmount Estate, Cummertrees, Dumfriesshire.

1908 ... *NELSON, Thomas Arthur, of Achnacloich, Connel, Argyllshire.

1910 ... NEWTON, James Whittet, B.Sc., Assistant Conservator of Forests, Londiani, British East Africa.

1895 ... NICOL, James, Forester, Aird's Mill, Muirkirk, Ayrshire.

1912 ... *NICOL, Randall James, Ballogie, Aboyne, Aberdeenshire.

1906 ... NICOL, William, Forester, Cluny Castle, Ordhead, Aberdeenshire.

1903 ... *NICOL, William Edward, D.L., J.P., of Ballogie, Aboyne.

1909 ... NICOLL, William, Foreman Forester, Deer Park, Novar, Evanton, Ross-shire.

1901 ... NICOLL, William Peter, Bailiff to H.R.H. The Duchess of Albany, The Farm, Claremont, Esher, Surrey.

1912 ... NIELSEN, P., Seedsman, Jaglvej, 125tb, Copenhagen, L.

1893 p *NISBET, J., D.Œc., Royal Societies' Club, 63 St James Street, London, S.W.

1902 ... *Nisbet, Robert C., Farmer, Kingsknowe, Slateford.

1899 ... *NOBBS, Eric Arthur, B.Sc., Ph.D., Department of Agriculture, Salisbury, Rhodesia.

1899 ... NOBLE, Charles, Forester, Donibristle, Aberdour.

1904 ... NOBLE, Hugh C., Newhall Estate Office, Balblair, Invergordon.

1912 ... NORRIS, Henry E. Du C., Agent, Basildon Park, Reading.

1911 ... *OGILVIE, Fergus Menteith, of Barcaldine, Ledaig, Argyllshire.

1909 ... *OGILVIE, George Hamilton, Westlands, Broughty Ferry.

Date of
Election.

1911 ... OGILVIE, John, M.A., Solicitor, 13 Albert Square, Dundee.

1910 ... OGILVY, Mrs Mary Georgiana Constance N. Hamilton, of Biel, Prestonkirk.

1911 ... OGILVY, William, 58 Findhorn Place, Edinburgh.

1908 ... OGSTON, Alexander Milne, of Ardoe, near Aberdeen.

1908 ... *OGSTON, James, of Kildrummy, Kildrummy, Aberdeenshire.

1900 ... OLIPHANT, Joseph, Assistant Forester, Quarterbank, Abercairney, Crieff.

1909 ... OLIVER, Colonel William J., of Lochside, Kelso.

1894 ... *ORKNEY, William C., Surveyor's Office, Montrose Royal Asylum.

1899 ... *ORR-EWING, Sir Archibald Ernest, Bart., Ballikinrain Castle, Balfron.

1906 ... *ORR, George W., Hilston Park, Monmouth.

1906 ... ORR, Harry D., Timber Merchant, 21 Fairfield Road, Chesterfield.

1907 ... OSWALD, Major Julian, Portmore House, Church Street, Weybridge.

1902 ... OSWALD, Richard Alexander, of Auchincruive, Ayr.

1875 ... PAGE, Andrew Duncan, Land Steward, Culzean Home Farm, Ayr.

1911 ... PARK, James, Assistant Forester, Tower Cottage, Durris, Drumoak.

1908 ... PARK, Robert, Contractor, Hamilton Street, Motherwell.

1908 ... PATERSON, Alexander, Forester, Clifton Park, Kelso.

1900 ... PATERSON, George, Timber Merchant, Cliff House, Cults, Aberdeen.

1913 ... PATERSON, William George Rogerson, B.Sc., N.D.A. (Hons.), Principal of West of Scotland Agricultural College, 6 Blythswood Square, Glasgow.

1879 ... *PATON, Hugh, Nurseryman, Kilmarnock, Ayrshire.

1898 ... *PATON, Robert Johnston, Nurseryman, Kilmarnock.

1902 ... *PATON, Tom W., Nurseryman, Kilmarnock.

1908 ... PEARSON, Andrew, Commissioner, Littlecourt, Dorchester.

1897 ... PEARSON, James, Forester, Sessay, Thirsk, Yorks.

1899 mp PEARSON, James, Factor, Altyre Estates Office, Forres, N.B.

1909 ... *Peattie, William, Assistant Forester, The Nursery, Thirlmere, Grasmere.*

1912 ... PEFFERS, William, Sawmaker, Dovecote Street, Hawick.

1908 ... *PENTLAND, The Lord, Governor of Bengal, India.

1900 m *PERRINS, C. W. Dyson, of Ardross, Ardross Castle, Alness.

1904 ... PETERS, William, Assistant Forester, Gateside, Markinch, Fifeshire.

1897 ... *PHILIP, Alexander, Solicitor, Brechin, Forfarshire.

1895 ... *PHILIP, William Watt, Factor, Estate Office, Gigha, Argyllshire.

1912 ... PHILIPS, Charles, Assistant Forester, Balvaird, Kirkoswald.

1908 ... PHILLIPS, John, Nurseryman, Granton Road, Edinburgh.

1896 ... *PHILP, Henry, jun., Timber Merchant, Campbell Street, Dunfermline.

1896 .. *PHILP, John, Timber Merchant, Campbell Street, Dunfermline.

c

Date of
Election.

1896 ... *PITMAN, Archibald Robert Craufurd, W.S., 48 Castle Street, Edinburgh.

1910 ... PLENDERLEITH, Mungo Sinclair, Fire Insurance Superintendent, 102 St Vincent Street, Glasgow.

1902 ... PLUMMER, C. H. Scott, of Sunderland Hall, Selkirk.

1901 m POLLOCK, Alexander, Royal Rustic Builder, Tarbolton, Ayrshire.

1912 ... *PONSONBY, Thomas Brabazon, J.P., and D.L., Kilcooley Abbey, Thurles, Ireland.

1897 ... POOLE, Wm., Corn Exchange Buildings, Edinburgh.

1902 ... POPERT, E. P., 49 Britannia Square, Worcester.

1908 ... PORTEOUS, James, Solicitor and Factor, Coldstream.

1899 ... PORTEOUS, Colonel James, of Turfhills, Kinross.

1911 ... PORTEOUS, George, Overseer, Edmonstone Estate, Midlothian.

1912 ... PORTER, Donald Fraser, Bankell, Milngavie.

1910 ... PRENTICE, Andrew, Forester, Bank House, Worsley, near Manchester.

1896 ... PRENTICE, George, Strathore, Thornton.

1898 C *PRICE, W. M., Factor, Minto, Hawick.

1908 ... PRINGLE, James Lewis, of Torwoodlee, J.P., D.L., B.A., Torwoodlee, Galashiels.

1908 ... PRITCHARD, Henry A., Professor of Estate Management and Forestry, Royal Agricultural College, Cirencester.

1908 ... PROCTOR, John, Forester, West Grange, East Grange Station, Dunfermline.

1908 m *PURVIS, Colonel Alexander, St Andrews.

1907 ... PURVIS, George, Forester, Cowden Estate, Dollar.

1907 ... RAE, Frederick S., Tangkah Rubber Estates, Jasin, Malacca, Straits Settlement.

1907 ... RAE, Lewis, Foreman Forester, New Cottage, Dupplin, by Perth.

1876 C *RAE, William A., Factor, Murthly Castle, Perthshire.

1901 p *RAFFAN, Alexander, Forester, Bonskeid, Pitlochry.

1899 p RAFN, Johannes, Tree-Seed Merchant, Skovfrökontoret, Copenhagen, F.

1913 ... *RALPH, James Mackenzie, Bank Clerk, Lisnacree, Corstorphine.

1902 ... RALPH, William, I.S.O., Forrester Road, Corstorphine.

1897 ... RALSTON, A. Agnew, Factor, Philipstoun House, West Lothian.

1907 ... RALSTON, Charles W., Chamberlain on Dukedom of Queensberry, Dabton, Thornhill, Dumfriesshire.

1908 ... *RALSTON, Claude, Factor, Estates Office, Glamis.

1908 ... *RALSTON, Gavin, Factor, Glamis.

1910 ... *RAMSAY, Professor George Gilbert, LL.D., Drumire, Blairgowrie.

1907 ... RAMSAY, William, J.P., Longmorn House, Longmorn R.S.O.

1855 ... *RAMSDEN, Sir John, Bart., Byram Hall, Ferrybridge, Normanton.

1911 ... RANKINE, Professor John, of Bassendean, 23 Ainslie Place, Edinburgh.

1870 ... RATTRAY, Thos., Forester, Westonbirt House, Tetbury, Gloucestershire.

1909 ... RATTRAY, William, Wood Merchant, Tullylumb Terrace, Perth.

1908 ... REDPATH, John, Forester, Paxton, Berwick-on-Tweed.

1905 ... REID, Alexander T., Milldeans, Star, Markinch.

1901 ... REID, Hugh, Forester, Ashton Court, Long Ashton, near Bristol.

1909 ... REID, James, jun., Assistant Forester, Balbirnie, Milldeans, Markinch.

1894 ... REID, James S., Forester, Balbirnie, Markinch, Fife.

1913 ... REID, James T. M., Assistant Forester, Blackwood Kennels, Kirkmuirhill.

1911 ... REID, John, Assistant Forester, Foresters' Bothy, Pilsley, Bakewell, Derbyshire.

1910 ... *Reid, Peter, Assistant Forester, Cruachan, Kilchrenan, Argyll.*

1905 ... REID, Robert, Overseer, Kincairney, Dunkeld.

1903 ... REID, Robert Matelé, Thomanean, Milnathort.

1910 ... REIS, Gordon Stanley, B.Sc., Naga Timbool Estate, Post Bangoen Poerba, East Coast Sumatra, Dutch East Indies.

1901 ... RENNIE, Joseph, Overseer, Hillend, Possil, Maryhill.

1908 ... *RENSHAW, Charles Stephen Bine, B.A., Barochan, Houston.

1912 ... RENTON, James, F.S.I., Factor, Sunbank, Perth.

1910 ... RICHARD, James, Forester, Balnamoon, Brechin.

1873 *Cp* *RICHARDSON, Adam D., 6 Dalkeith Street, Joppa.

1910 ... RIGG, Patrick Home, of Tarvit, Cupar.

1907 ... RILLIE, Joseph, Assistant Forester, Acklam, Middlesbrough.

1892 ... RITCHIE, Alexander, Overseer, Brucehill, Cardross Estate, Port of Menteith.

1908 ... *RITCHIE, Charles Ronald, W.S., 37 Royal Terrace, Edinburgh.

1913 ... RITCHIE, Matthew Aitken, Assistant Forester, Owood, Woodhall Estate, Holytown.

1898 ... RITCHIE, Wm., Assistant Forester, New Inn Cottage, Stanley.

1906 ... RITCHIE, Wm. H., of Dunnottar House, Stonehaven.

1912 ... ROBB, Henry Grant, Forester, The Nursery, Knowsley, Prescot, Lancs.

1909 ... *ROBERTS, Alex. Fowler, of Fairnilee, Clovenfords, Galashiels.

1909 ... ROBERTSON, Alexander, Factor, Polmaise, Stirling.

1897 ... *ROBERTSON, A. Barnett, Forester, The Dean, Kilmarnock, Ayrshire.

1897 ... ROBERTSON, Andrew N., Forester, Westerlands, Graffam, Sussex.

1911 ... ROBERTSON, Andrew, Assistant Forester, Dean Road, Kilmarnock.

1911 ... ROBERTSON, Andrew Clark, Assistant Factor, 18 Manse Crescent, Stirling.

1899 ... ROBERTSON, Charles, Forester, Colstoun Old Mill, Gifford.

1911 ... ROBERTSON, Colin Halkett, Tebraw Rubber Estates, Johore, *via* Singapore.

1879 *mp* *ROBERTSON, Donald, Forester, Dunrobin, Golspie.

1907 ... *ROBERTSON, Edward Hercules, B.A., Advocate, Burnside, Forfar.

1896 ... ROBERTSON, George, Forester, Monreith Estate Office, Port William.

1908 ... ROBERTSON, George, Assistant Forester, Barcaldine, Ledaig, Argyllshire.

1910 ... *ROBERTSON, Henry Tod, Coalmaster, Meadowbank, Airdrie.

1900 ... ROBERTSON, James, Forester, Wortley Hall, Wortley, Sheffield.

1904 ... ROBERTSON, James, Forester, Cavens, Kirkbean, Dumfries.

1905 ... *ROBERTSON, James Morton, of Portmore, Portmore House, Eddleston.

1905 ... ROBERTSON, James W,. Head Gardener, Letham Grange and Fern, Arbroath.

1907 ... ROBERTSON, J. P., Forester, Edensor, Bakewell.

1905 ... *ROBERTSON, John, Factor, Panmure Estates Office, Carnoustie.

1896 ... ROBERTSON, John, Forester, Rynagoup, Dallas, Forres.

1909 ... ROBERTSON, John A., c/o Donald Robertson, Dunrobin, Golspie.

1895 ... ROBERTSON, Thomas, Forester, c/o Mrs Shaw, 5 Glenogle Road, Edinburgh.

1910 ... ROBERTSONWHITE, John Peregine, M.A., LL.B., Advocate in Aberdeen, 80 Union Street, Aberdeen.

1912 ... *ROBERTSON, William Hope, W.S., 8 Eton Terrace, Edinburgh.

1909 ... ROBINSON, Alfred Whitmore, Forester, Bamford, near Sheffield.

1912 ... ROBINSON, George, Forestry Inspector, Department of Agriculture, Dublin.

1910 ... ROBINSON, R. G., Department of Lands, State Forests Branch, Tapanui, Otago, N.Z.

1912 ... ROBINSON, R. L., Board of Agriculture, 4 Whitehall Place, London, S.W.

1890 ... *ROBINSON, William, Gravetye Manor, East Grinstead, Sussex.

1899 ... ROBSON, Alex., of Smith & Son, 18 Market Street, Aberdeen.

1901 ... ROBSON, Alexander, Head Gamekeeper, The Kennels, Culzean, Maybole.

1897 ... *ROBSON, Charles Durie, 66 Queen Street, Edinburgh.

1900 ... ROBSON, John, Forester, Sawmill Cottage, Baronscourt, Newtown Stewart, Ireland.

1893 *mp* RODGER, James, Forester, 82 Leinster Street, Athy, Co. Kildare.

1908 ... ROGERS, E. Percy, Estate Office, Stanage Park, Brampton Byran, Herefordshire.

1883 ... *ROLLO, The Master of, Duncrub Park, Dunning, Perthshire.

1872 ... *ROSEBERY, The Earl of, K.G., K.T., Dalmeny Park, Edinburgh.

1913 ... ROSE, William Duncan Ogilvie, M.A., Student, 11 Braidburn Crescent, Edinburgh.

1898 ... ROSS, Charles D. M., Factor, Abercairney, Crieff.

1905 ... ROSS, John S., Factor's Clerk, Monreith Estate Office, Wigtownshire.

1906 *m* *ROXBURGHE, The Duke of, K.T., Floors Castle, Kelso.

1903 ... RULE, John, Forester, Huntly.

1908 ... *RUSSELL, David, Silverburn, Leven.

Date of
Election.

1893 ... RUTHERFORD, James A., Land Agent, Highclere Park, Newbury, Berks.

1910 .. RUTHERFORD, James, Assistant Forester, Heckfield, Winchfield, Hants.

1870 ... RUTHERFORD, John, Forester, Linthaugh, Jedburgh, Roxburgh-shire.

1904 ... RUTHERFURD, Henry, Barrister-at-Law, Fairnington, Roxburgh.

1894 ... *SAMSON, David T., Factor, Seafield Estates Office, Cullen.

1875 ... SANG, Edmund, of E. Sang & Sons, Nurserymen, Kirkcaldy.

1906 ... *SANG, J. H., LL.B., W.S., Westbrook, Balerno.

1911 ... SCOTT, Alexander, Head Forester, Corsock, Dalbeattie.

1911 ... SCOTT, Crawford Allen, Factor, Killermont and Garscadden Estates Office, Bearsden.

1867 C *SCOTT, Daniel, Wood Manager, Darnaway, Forres.

1892 ... SCOTT, David, Overseer, Dumfries House, Cumnock, Ayrshire.

1901 Cp SCOTT, Frank, Forester, Jeaniebank, near Perth.

1911 ... SCOTT, George Ritchie, Farmer, Oxgang, Colinton.

1881 ... SCOTT, James, Forester, Wollaton Hall, Nottingham.

1907 ... *SCOTT, James Cospatrick, P.A.S.I., Yarrow Cottage, Poynder Place, Kelso.

1903 ... SCOTT, John, Forester, Annfield, Hartrigge, Jedburgh.

1908 ... SCOTT, John A., Forester, The Gardens, Knockbrex, Kirkcudbright.

1906 ... *SCOTT, John Henry Francis Kinnaird, of Gala, Gala House, Galashiels.

1913 ... SCOTT, William Lightbody, Assistant Forester, Braehead, Douglas, Lanarkshire.

1902 ... *SCRIMGEOUR, James, Horticulturist, Glasnevin College, Dublin.

1890 C *SCRIMGEOUR, John, Overseer, Doune Lodge, Doune.

1913 ... SELLAR, Robert Hunter Nicol, Agricultural Engineer, Huntly.

1912 ... SHAND, Ebenezer, Apprentice Forester, Haddo House, Aberdeen.

1897 m SHARPE, Thomas, Head Forester, Gordon Castle, Fochabers.

1904 ... SHAW, John, Factor, Kilmahew Estate Office, Cardross.

1913 ... SHAW, John, Forester, East Lodge, Castlemilk, Rutherglen.

1896 p *SHAW-STEWART, Sir Hugh, Bart., of Ardgowan, Greenock.

1904 ... *SHELLEY, Sir John Courtown Edward, Bart., Avington, Alres-ford, Hants.

1898 ... *SHEPPARD, Rev. H. A. Graham-, of Rednock, Port of Menteith, Stirling.

1907 ... *SHIACH, Gordon Reid, L.D.S., etc., Ardgilzean, Elgin.

1903 ... *SHIEL, James, Overseer, Abbey St Bathans, Grant's House.

1912 ... SHIELL, David Guthrie, Factor, Dalhousie Lodge, Edzell,

1911 ... SIM, Ernest James, Factor, Airthrey Estate Office, Bridge of Allan.

1911 ... SIM, James, District Forest Officer, King Williamstown, Cape Colony.

1905 ... SIM, John, Forester, Fernybrae, Cornhill, Banffshire.

1913 ... *SIME, Frank, Timber Merchant, Beauly.

1910 .... SIMPSON, Robert, Under Forester, Dean Road, Kilmarnock.

Date of
Election.

1912 ... SINCLAIR, John, Forester, Bluehouse, Bridgend, Islay.

1909 ... SINCLAIR, Magnus H., Seedsman, 156A Union Street, Aberdeen.

1906 *p* SINCLAIR, Robert, Board of Agriculture, Castletown, Caithness.

1908 ... SINCLAIR, The Lord, 55 Onslow Square, London, S.W.

1909 ... SINGER, George, Forester, Braidoun, Belmaduthy, Munlochy.

1900 ... SINGER, John G., Forester, Whitestone Cottage, Maybole.

1908 ... SKIMMING, Robert, Timber Merchant, Kirkinner.

1868 *CMp* SLATER, Andrew, War Department Estates Office, Tynemouth House, Rothbury, Northumberland.

1902 .. SMART, John, Merchant, 18 Leith Street, Edinburgh.

1893 ... *SMITH, Charles G., Factor, Haddo House, Aberdeen.

1906 ... SMITH, Douglas, P.A.S.I., Land Agent, Estate Office, Thwaite, Erpingham, Norwich.

1912 ... SMITH, F., Forester, Craigmyle Estate, Torphins, Aberdeenshire.

1911 ... *SMITH, George, Factor, Mount Hamilton, by Ayr.

1911 ... SMITH, Herbert, Assistant Forester, Home Farm, Wishaw Estate Wishaw, Lanarkshire.

1911 ... SMITH, James, Assistant Forester, Thoresby Park, Ollerton, Notts.

1901 ... SMITH, James, Forester, 1 Oxmantown Mall, Birr, King's County.

1908 ... SMITH, James, Nurseryman, Darley Dale Nurseries, near Matlock.

1908 ... SMITH, James, Assistant, Town Clerk's Office, Arbroath.

1906 ... SMITH, James Fraser, F.R.H.S., late Gardener, Barons Hotel, Auchnagatt.

1907 ... SMITH, Right Hon. James Parker, P.C., 20 Draycott Place, London, S.W.

1895 *m* SMITH, John, Cabinetmaker, 1 Eastgate, Peebles.

1907 ... *SMITH, J. Grant, Factor, Seafield Estates Office, Grantown-on-Spey.

1901 ... SMITH, Matthew, Manager for Dyer & Co., Peebles.

1908 ... SMITH, Robert, Factor, Cranstoun Riddell, Dalkeith.

1901 ... SMITH, Sydney, Factor, Drummuir Estates Office, Keith.

1895 ... *SMITH, Thomas, Overseer, The Nursery, Tring Park, Wigginton, Tring, Herts.

1896 ... SMITH, William, Forester, Camperdown, Lochee.

1899 ... SMITH, William, Overseer, Rothes Estate Office, Leslie, Fife.

1896 *p* *SMITH, William G., B.Sc., Ph.D., Lecturer on Biology, Edinburgh and East of Scotland College of Agriculture, George Square, Edinburgh.

1913 ... SMITH, W. J. Woodman, of Laithers, 12 Golden Square, Aberdeen.

1907 ... *SMITHSON, Harry S. C., of Inverernie, Daviot, Highland R.S.O.

1910 ... SMYLY, John George, B.A., Consulting Forester and Land Agent, 22 Earlsfort Terrace, Dublin.

1882 ... *SMYTHE, David M., of Methven Castle, Perth.

1907 ... SOMERSET, The Duke of, Maiden Bradley, Bath; 35 Grosvenor Square, W.

1906 ... SOMERVILLE, Hugh Christopher, 2 Fairhaven, Dalkeith.

1906 ... SOMERVILLE, Robert Anderson, Eastwoodbrae, Dalkeith.

Date of
Election.

1889 Cmp *SOMERVILLE, Dr William, M.A., D.Sc., D.Œc., F.R.S.E., Professor of Rural Economy, Oxford.

1904 ... SOUTAR, William, Forester, The Farm, Titsey Place, Limpsfield, Surrey.

1912 ... *SPEIRS, Robert Robson, Structural Engineer, Maxholme, Bearsden.

1910 ... SPENCE, James George, Forester, West Lodge, Vogrie, Gorebridge.

1898 ... SPENCE, William, Forester, Strathenery, Leslie.

1899 Cmp *SPIERS, Adam, Timber Merchant; Warriston Saw-mills, Edinburgh.

1883 ... *SPROT, Major Alexander, of Garnkirk, Chryston, Glasgow.

1911 ... *SPROT, Captain Mark, of Riddell, Lilliesleaf, Roxburghshire.

1909 ... *STAIR, The Earl of, Lochinch, Castle Kennedy.

1899 .... *STALKER, Wm. J., Nurseryman, Nairn.

1910 p*STEBBING, Edward Percy, Indian Forest Service, Lecturer in Forestry, Edinburgh University.

1911 ... STEPHEN, George, Forester, Castle Grant, Grantown.

1907 ... STEPHEN, John, Forester, Balliemore, Nethy Bridge.

1901 ... STEWART, Alistair D., Kinfauns Estates Office, Rockdale, Perth.

1897 ... STEWART, Charles, Forester, Nursery Cottage, Durris, Drumoak, Aberdeenshire.

1908 ... *STEWART, Charles, Achara, Duror of Appin, Argyll.

1907 m STEWART, David, Forester, Baunreigh Forestry Station, Mountrath, Queen's Co.

1909 ... STEWART, Sir David, of Banchory-Devenick, Banchory House, Banchory, Devenick.

1910 ... STEWART, Donald, Forester, The Lodge, Inverlochy Castle, Fort William.

1899 ... *STEWART, Duncan D., Factor, Ardenlea, Pitlochry.

1901 ... STEWART, James, Forester, Letham and Fern Estates, Fern, near Brechin.

1903 ... STEWART, John, Forester, Coltness Estate, Wishaw.

1909 ... STEWART, John M'Gregor, Assistant Forester, Saw-mill Cottage, Strathord, by Stanley.

1892 ... *STEWART, Sir Mark J. M'Taggart, Bart. of Southwick, Kirkcudbrightshire.

1908 ... STEWART, Colonel R. K., of Murdostoun, Murdostoun Castle, Lanarkshire.

1876 ... STEWART, Robert, Forester, Stonefield, Sunnyside, Tarbert, Lochfyne.

1910 ... STEWART, William, of Shambellie, Kirkcudbrightshire.

1904 Cmp *STIRLING, Captain Archibald, of Keir, Dunblane, *President*.

1907 m STIRLING, John Alexander, of Kippendavie, 4 Connaught Square, London, W.

1911 ... *STIRLING, Thomas Willing, of Muiravonside, Linlithgow.

1908 ... *STIRLING, William, D.L., J.P., of Fairburn, Muir of Ord.

1909 ... STOBART, Lionel Forrester, Harpur Ranch, Kamloops, B.C., Canada.

Date of
Election.

1909 ... *STODART, Charles, Farmer, Wintonhill, Pencaitland.

1897 ... STODDART, James, Valuator, Hillhead, Bonnyrigg.

1906 ... STODDART, James, jun., Joiner, Macondach, Bonnyrigg.

1893 ... STORIE, W., Whitway House, Newbury, Berks.

1908 ... STRATHEDEN and CAMPBELL, The Lord, Hartrigge, Jedburgh.

1908 .. *STRATHMORE AND KINGHORNE, The Earl of, Glamis Castle, Glamis.

1908 ... STUART, Alexander, Estates Office, Blair Drummond, Perthshire.

1910 ... STUART, George Morrison, Gardener, The Gardens, Forglen, Turriff.

1912 ... *STUART, Henry, Land Steward, Knoydart, Mallaig, Inverness-shire.

1911 ... STUART, Henry Campbell, Factor, Glen Caladh, Tighnabruaich.

1908 m STUART, Lord Ninian Edward Crichton, M.P., House of Falkland, Fife.

1902 ... STUNT, Walter Charles, Lorenden, Ospringe, Kent.

1880 ... *SUTHERLAND, Evan C., Highland Club, Inverness.

1907 ... SUTHERLAND, George, Assistant Forester and Saw-miller, Bowmont Forest, Roxburgh.

1883 ... *SUTHERLAND, The Duke of, K.G., Dunrobin Castle, Golspie.

1892 m *SUTHERLAND, John D., Member of Board of Agriculture, 29 St Andrew Square, Edinburgh.

1912 ... TAIT, Adam, of Wooplaw, Darnick, Braid Avenue, Edinburgh.

1869 mp TAIT, David, Overseer, Owston Park, Doncaster, Yorkshire.

1900 ... *TAIT, James, Westshiel, Penicuik.

1902 ... TAYLOR, John, Forester, Orchill Estate, by Braco, Perthshire.

1904 ... TAYLOR, Robert, Assistant Forester, Mosside Cottage, Almond-bank, Perth.

1905 ... TAYLOR, Robert, Forester, West Saline, Saline, Oakley.

1897 ... TAYLOR, William, Forester, Sandside, Kirkcudbright.

1905 ... TELFER, John, Forester, Basildon Park, Reading, Berks.

1911 ... *TENNANT, H. J., M.P., 33 Bruton Street, London, W.

1877 ... *TERRIS, James, Factor, Dullomuir, Blairadam, Kinross-shire

1911 ... THOMAS, David Gwilym, Forestry Student, 44 Lauriston Place, Edinburgh.

1908 ... THOMPSON, Archibald, Overseer, Auchindarroch, Lochgilphead.

1904 ... THOMPSON, Dugald, Forester, Kinnordy, Kirriemuir.

1911 ... *THOMSON, Alexander, of Burgie, Forres.

1893 C THOMSON, David W., Nurseryman, 113 George Street, Edinburgh.

1913 ... THOMSON, Herdman, Nurseryman, 113 George Street, Edinburgh.

1911 ... THOMSON, John, Forester, Kailzie, Peebles.

1902 p *THOMSON, Peter Murray, S.S.C., Cockbridge, Mealsgate, Cumberland.

1903 ... THOMSON, Robert, Foreman Forester, 57 Park Hill, Ampthill, Bedfordshire.

1901 ... *THOMSON, Spencer Campbell, of Eilean Shona, 10 Eglinton Crescent, Edinburgh.

Date of
Election.

1908 ... *THORBURN, Michael Grieve, D.L., etc., of Glenormiston, Innerleithen.

1911 ... THOW, William Keir, Assistant Forester, Pitcairngreen, Almond-
bauk, Perth.

1904 ... THREIPLAND, Captain W. Murray, Dryburgh Abbey, St Boswells.

1913 ... TIBBLE, Ernest Frank, Assistant Forester, South Lodge, Minto,
Hawick.

1906 ... TINDAL, Robert, Forester, Bellspool Cottages, Stobo.

1901 ... TIVENDALE, William D., Head Forester to Duke of Portland,
Burnhouse, Galston.

1871 ... *TOMLINSON, Wilson, Forester, Clumber Park, Worksop, Notts.

1912 ... *TORRANCE, James Watt, Timber Merchant, 11 Dundonald Road,
Glasgow.

1906 ... *TRAIL, James William Helenus, A.M., M.D., F.R.S., Professor
of Botany in University of Aberdeen, 71 High Street, Old
Aberdeen.

1903 ... *TULLIBARDINE, The Marquis of, D.S.O., Blair Castle, Blair
Atholl.

1903 ... TURNBULL, John, Forester, Forester's Lodge, Arbigland,
Dumfries.

1910 ... TWEEDIE, Alexander, Forester, etc., ʳGarth, Fortingal, Aberfeldy.

1883 ... UNDERWOOD, Henry E., Fornham, St Martin, Bury St Edmunds,
Suffolk.

1903 ... *UNWIN, Arthur Harold, D.Œc., Olokemeji, West͟ Province,
So. Nigeria.

1908 ... *URQUHART, Angus, Assistant Nursery and Seedsman, Inverness.

1907 ... URQUHART, Colonel Robert, Town Clerk, Forres.

1908 ... *USHER, Sir Robert, Bart. of Norton and Wells, Norton, Ratho
Station, Midlothian.

1908 ... VEITCH, Andrew, Seedsman and Nurseryman, Melrose.

1912 ... *VEITCH, Archibald, Chatlapore Tea Estate, Shamshernagar,
P.O., So. Sylhet, India.

1911 ... VEITCH, Robert, B.Sc., 7 Queen's Crescent, Edinburgh.

1912 ... *VESCI, The Viscount de, D.L., Abbeyleix, Ireland.

1911 ... WADDINGHAM, James Hart, Shambally, Cloghill, Co. Tipperary.

1903 ... WALDRON, Major Patrick John, East Haugh, Pitlochry.

1911 ... WALKER, Austine Harrington, Chemical Manufacturer, Richmond
House, Dullatur, Dumbartonshire.

1903 ... WALKER, Captain George Lawrie, of Crawfordton, Thornhill.

1894 ... WALKER, Henry H., Factor, Monreith, Port William, Wigtownshire.

1878 .... *WALKER, Colonel I. Campbell, Newlands, Camberley, Surrey.

1907 ... *WALKER, James, Wood Merchant, Inverness.

1906 ... *WALKER, John Steven, Yard Foreman, Saw-mills, Hurlford,
Ayrshire.

Date of
Election.

1906 ... *WALKER, Robert Williamson, C.E., Factor and Land Surveyor, 3 Golden Square, Aberdeen.

1903 ... WALLACE, Andrew, Saw-miller, 5 North Street, Freuchie.

1912 ... WALLACE, Andrew, Foreman Forester, Foresters' Cottages, Altyre, Forres.

1893 *m* WALLACE, David P., Forester, The Saw-mills, Filleigh, South Molton, N. Devon.

1912 ... WALLACE, John, Land Steward, Dunnikier Estate, Kirkcaldy.

1897 ... *WALLACE, John A. A., of Lochryan, Cairnryan, Stranraer.

1905 ... *WALLACE, Thomas Douglas, F.S.I., Hamilton Palace, Hamilton.

1899 ... WANDESFORDE, R. H., Prior of Castlecomer, Co. Kilkenny.

1909 ... WARING, Captain Walter, M.P., of Lennel, Coldstream.

1900 ... *WARWICK, Charles, Smiley Estate Office, Ailsa, Larne.

1901 ... WASON, Right Hon. Eugene, M.P., P.C., of Blair, Dailly, Ayrshire; 8 Sussex Gardens, Hyde Park, London.

1913 ... WATSON, Alexander S., Assistant Forester, New Cottages, Dupplin, Perth.

1901 ... WATSON, James, Manager, Moy Hall, Inverness-shire.

1893 ... *WATSON, John T., 6 Bruntsfield Gardens, Edinburgh.

1912 *p* WATT, Hugh Boyd, Secretary and Insurance Broker, 12 Great James Street, Bedford Row, London, W.C.

1872 ... WATT, James, J.P., of Little & Ballantyne, Nurserymen, Carlisle.

1893 ... WATT, James W., Knowefield Nurseries, Carlisle.

1911 ... WATT, Sidney, Forester, Pearsie, Kirriemuir.

1911 *m* WATT, William, Assistant Forester, Redstone, Darnaway.

1906 ... WEBSTER, Charles, Gardener and Forester, The Gardens, Gordon Castle, Fochabers.

1911 ... *WEBSTER, Sir Francis, Ashbrook, Arbroath.

1908 ... *WEDDERBURN, Ernest Maclagan, LL.B., W.S., F.R.S.E., Factor, 2 Glenfinlas Street, Edinburgh.

1911 ... WEIR, Andrew, Forestry Student, Doonhome, Colinton.

1908 ... *WEIR, William, of Kindonan, Adamton, Monkton, Ayrshire.

1891 ... *WELSH, James, of Dicksons & Co., 1 Waterloo Place, Edinburgh.

1913 ... WENSLEY, A., Forester, Grimsbury Castle, Hermitage, near Newbury, Berks.

1904 ... WENTWORTH-FITZWILLIAM, George Charles, of Milton, Peterborough.

1902 *mp* WHELLENS, W. Henry, Forester, Comlongon Nurseries, Ruthwell.

1898 ... *WHITE, J. Martin, Balruddery, near Dundee.

1895 ... WHITE, William, Farmer, Gortonlee, Lasswade.

1884 *C* *WHITTON, James, Superintendent of Parks, 249 George Street, Glasgow.

1899 ... *WHYTE, John D. B., Factor, Estate Office, Elveden, Suffolk.

1895 ... WIGHT, Alexander, Overseer, Thurston, Temple Mains, Innerwick.

1869 *p* *WILD, Albert Edward (Conservator of Forests, Darjeeling, India), c/o Henry S. King & Co., 65 Cornhill, London, E.C.

1883 ... WILKIE, Charles, Forester, Lennoxlove, Haddington.

1891 ... WILKIE, G., Architect, Hayfield, Peebles.

1902 ... WILKINSON, John, Factor, The Grange, Kirkcudbright.

1908 ... WILLIAMSON, James A., A.R.I.B.A., Public Works Office, City Chambers, Edinburgh.

1895 ... WILLIAMSON, John, Bank Agent, Loanhead, Midlothian.

1907 ... *WILLIAMSON, John, Joiner and Builder, Grangemouth.

1913 ... WILSON, Adam, Timber Merchant, Dailly, Ayrshire.

1907 *p* WILSON, Adam Frank, C.D.A.(Edin.), 164 Braid Road, Edinburgh.

1913 ... WILSON, Albert, Forester, Derwent Valley Water Board, Cliff View, Thornhill Hope, via Sheffield.

1907 ... WILSON, Andrew Robertson, M.A., M.D., Hopewell, Tarland, Aboyne ; and Trafford House, Liscard, Cheshire.

1898 ... *WILSON, David, Timber Merchant, Troon, Ayrshire.

1889 ... *WILSON, David, jun., of Carbeth, Killearn, Glasgow.

1908 ... WILSON, Edward Arthur, Rockingham, Edgbaston Park Road, Birmingham.

1907 ... WILSON, Ian Hall, Saw-mill Manager, Brodie Cottage, Brodie.

1900 ... WILSON, James, jun., Nurseryman, St Andrews.

1907 ... WILSON, James G., Assistant, 24 St Andrew Square, Edinburgh.

1910 ... *Wilson, John, Estate Steward, Brand's Mill, Dunbar.*

1902 ... WILSON, Sir John, Bart. of Airdrie.

1901 ... WILSON, John Currie, Factor, Tulliallan Estate Office, Kincardine-on-Forth.

1912 ... WILSON, John, Estate Agent, Egton Bridge, Yorks.

1912 ... *Wilson, Thomas, Assistant Forester, Matlock House, Baslow, Derbyshire.*

1903 ... WILSON, Thomas, Head Gardener, Glamis Castle, Glamis.

1899 ... WILSON, William, Timber Merchant, Auchenleck, Ayrshire.

1912 ... WINTON, Thomas, jun., Timber Merchant, 52 Seafield Road, Dundee.

1893 ... WISEMAN, Edward, Nurseryman, Elgin.

1895 ... WISEMAN, William, Nurseryman, Forres.

1911 ... WISHART, John, Ellangowan, Peebles.

1906 ... WOLFE, George, sen., J.P., Shovel Manufacturer, Millburn, Bathgate.

1909 ... WOOD, James, of Wallhouse, Torphichen.

1907 ... WOOD, Thomas, Forester, West Lodge, Durie, Leven, Fife.

1904 ... WORSFOLD, Edward Mowll, Land Agent, Market Square, Dover.

1904 ... *Wotherspoon, George, Factor, Cromartie Estate Office, Kildary, Ross-shire.*

1909 ... WRIGHT, John Moncrieff, of Kinmonth, Bridge of Earn.

1904 ... WRIGHT, Sir Robert Patrick, F.H.A.S., F.R.S.E., Chairman, Board of Agriculture, 29 St Andrew Square.

1868 ... WYLLIE, George, Ballogie, Aboyne, Aberdeenshire.

1906 ... WYLLIE, William, Seedsman, 18 Market Street, Aberdeen.

Date of
Election.

1908 ... *YEAMAN, Alexander, W.S., 32 Charlotte Square, Edinburgh.

1904 ... YOOL, Thomas, Factor, Ballindalloch Estates Office, Ballindalloch.

1905 ... YOUNG, John, Hedger, West Lodge, Corehouse, Lanark.

1907 ... YOUNG, John U., Cart Craigs, Pollokshaws.

1909 ... YOUNG, Peter, Assistant Forester, Lochend Cottage, Chapelhill, Methven.

1910 ... YOUNG, R. M., Nursery Manager, Cathcart Nurseries, Newlands, Glasgow.

1910 ... YOUNG, William George, Estate Clerk, Craigielaw, Longniddry.

1910 ... YOUNGER, Harry George, of Benmore, 21 Grosvenor Crescent, Edinburgh.

1912 *m* YOUNGER, James, of Mount Melville, St Andrews.

1899 ... *YULE, Miss Amy Frances, Tarradale House, Muir of Ord.

1911 .... YOUNG, James Weir, P.A.S.I., Land Surveyor, 198 West George Street, Glasgow.

TRANSACTIONS

OF THE

ROYAL
SCOTTISH ARBORICULTURAL SOCIETY.

A. W. BORTHWICK, D.Sc.,
HONORARY EDITOR.

ROBERT GALLOWAY, S.S.C.,
SECRETARY AND TREASURER.

VOL. XXVIII.

EDINBURGH:
PRINTED FOR THE SOCIETY.
SOLD BY DOUGLAS & FOULIS, CASTLE STREET.
1914

CONTENTS.

The Society does not hold itself responsible for the statements
or views expressed by the authors of papers.

PAGE

1. Deputation from the Society to the Right Hon. T. M'Kinnon
Wood, M.P., Secretary for Scotland—7th November 1913   1

2. The Development Commission and Forestry. Extracts from
the Report of the Commissioners for the year ended 31st
March 1913   14

3. The State Forests of Saxony (with Illustrations). (Continued from Vol. xxvii., p. 187.) By A. D. Hopkinson, B.Sc.   28

4. Some Vegetation Types at High Altitudes (with Illustrations). By G. P. Gordon, B.Sc.(Edin.), B Sc.(Oxon.)   .   46

5. Forestry at Home and Abroad. By A. W. Borthwick, D.Sc.   56

6. Continental Notes—France By A. G. Hobart-Hampden   .   60

7. The Formation of Plantations on Deep Peat (with Plate).
By Donald Grant   72

8. A Plan Adequate to Meet our Needs for Wood Timber   .   78

9. The Excursion to Switzerland (with Illustrations). By
G. P. Gordon, B.Sc.   83

10. The Forestry Exhibition at Paisley. By G. P. Gordon, B.Sc   97

11. Visit to German Forests by the Royal English Arboricultural
Society—1913. By A. T. Gillanders, F.E.S.   .   100

12. Timber Research Work at the Cambridge School of Forestry   105

13. Thuja gigantea and Douglas Fir in Mixture (with Plate).
By D. K. M'Beath   107

14. Nursery and Plantation Competition   110

Notes and Queries:—Witch's Broom on Pseudotsuga Doug-
lasii (with Plate)—Appointment of Chief Conservator of
Forests, South Africa—Protection of Scots Pine against
Black Game—Leaflet on the Large Brown Pine Weevil—
Tree-Growth in 1913—Forestry and the Anglo-American
Exposition—The Excursion to Switzerland   .   .   116

Reviews and Notices of Books:—The Forest of Dean. By
Arthur O. Cooke. With four Illustrations in Colour and
fifty-six in Black and White. Price 10s. 6d. net. London:
Constable & Co.   120

Albury Park Trees and Shrubs. 66+x pp. By A. Bruce
Jackson. London: West, Newman & Co., 1913 .   .   120

PAGE

15. Discussion on Forestry in Scotland, held at the Annual Business Meeting, Feb. 7, 1914 121

16. Summary of the Position of Scottish Forestry in regard to the Development Fund and the Agriculture (Scotland) Fund. [2nd February 1914.] By R. Galloway, S.S.C., Secretary of the Society 138

17. Report on Tour of Inspection of Woods and Afforestable Lands in Scotland, made by the Society's Foreign, Indian, Colonial and other Guests, in connection with the Celebration of the Diamond Jubilee, and also with Thirty-seventh Annual Excursion (with three Plates) . . . 154

18. The Conference and Dinner 179

19. The Right Hon. Sir Ronald Munro Ferguson, K.C.M.G., Hon. Secretary, 1898-1914 226

20. Mr Robert Galloway, S.S.C., Secretary and Treasurer (with Portrait) 229

21. Landowners' Co-operative Forestry Society . . . 231

22. Notes from Oak and Beech Forests in Denmark (with Plate). By W. G. Smith, B.Sc., Ph.D., Edinburgh and East of Scotland College of Agriculture 241

23. The Silvicultural Treatment of the Douglas Fir. By W. Steuart Fothringham 248

24. The Economic Disposal of Coniferous Timber (with Plate). By D. K. M'Beath 251

25. The Japanese Larch (Larix leptolepis). By Geo. Leven . 259

26. The Sitka Spruce in Ireland. By A. C. Forbes . . 264

Notes and Queries:—The Index—Scarcity of Pitwood— Forest Pests—The Oleoresins of some Western Pines— Prices and Supplies in the Timber Trade—Creosoting Tree Stumps against Pine Weevil—Japanese Larch— Notes re Acetone 266

Obituary:—Sir John Ramsden, Bart. 272

Proceedings of the Royal Scottish Arboricultural Society, 1914, with Appendices.

List of Members as at 1st September 1914.

General Index.

TRANSACTIONS

OF THE

ROYAL
SCOTTISH ARBORICULTURAL SOCIETY.

VOL. XXVIII.—PART I.

January 1914.

A. W. BORTHWICK, D Sc.,
HONORARY EDITOR

ROBERT GALLOWAY, S.S.C.,
SECRETARY AND TREASURER

EDINBURGH:
PRINTED FOR THE SOCIETY.
SOLD BY DOUGLAS & FOULIS, CASTLE STREET.

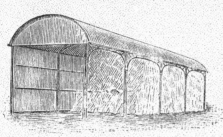
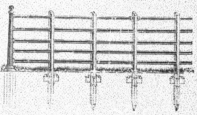

KEITH & CO.

ADVERTISING AGENTS

43 GEORGE STREET
EDINBURGH

ADVERTISEMENTS of every kind are received for insertion in the Daily, Weekly, and Monthly Publications throughout the United Kingdom.

Notices of Sequestration, Cessio, Dissolution of Partnership, Entail, etc., etc., for the Edinburgh and London Gazettes, are given special care and attention.

Legal Notices, Heirs Wanted, and all other Advertisements, are inserted in the Colonial and Foreign Newspapers.

Small Advertisements, such as Situations, Houses, and Apartments, Articles Wanted and For Sale, etc., etc., can be addressed to a No. at Keith & Co.'s Office, 43 George Street, Edinburgh, where the replies will be retained until called for, or, if desired, forwarded by Post. Parties in the country will find this a very convenient method of giving publicity to their requirements.

A SPECIALITY is made of ESTATE and AGRICULTURAL ADVERTISEMENTS, such as FARMS, MANSION HOUSES, etc., to LET, ESTATES for SALE, SALES OF TIMBER, AGRICULTURAL SHOWS, etc.

LAW and ESTATE AGENTS, FACTORS, TOWN CLERKS, CLERKS TO SCHOOL BOARDS, and other Officials may, with confidence, place their advertisements in the hands of the Firm.

One Copy of an Advertisement is sufficient to send for any number of newspapers; and the convenience of having only one advertising account instead of a number of advertising accounts is also a great saving of time and trouble.

Addressing of Envelopes with Accuracy and Despatch.

Telegrams—"PROMOTE," EDINBURGH.   Telephone No. 316.

The West of Scotland Agricultural College,

BLYTHSWOOD SQUARE, GLASGOW.

DEPARTMENT OF FORESTRY.

Day and Evening Classes, which provide a complete Course of Instruction in Forestry, qualifying (*pro tanto*) for the B.Sc. Degree of the University of Glasgow, for the Diploma of the Highland and Agricultural Society, and for the Certificate of the College, are held during the Winter Session (October to March) at the College.

Syllabus and particulars regarding these Classes and Prospectus of the general work of the College, including the Course for the Examination of the Surveyor's Institution, may be obtained free from the Secretary.

EDINBURGH AND EAST OF SCOTLAND COLLEGE OF AGRICULTURE

13 GEORGE SQUARE, EDINBURGH.

THE College is one of the Central Institutions administered by the Board of Agriculture for Scotland, and is intended to provide for Agricultural Education and Research in the Central and South-eastern Counties.

DAY CLASSES.

The Day Classes, in conjunction with certain University Classes, provide full courses of instruction in Agriculture, Forestry, Horticulture, and the Allied Sciences, and qualify for the College Diploma, the College Certificate in Horticulture, the Degrees of B.Sc. in Agriculture and B.Sc. in Forestry at the University of Edinburgh, and for other Examinations and Certificates in the Science and Practice of Agriculture.

SHORT COURSES AND EVENING CLASSES.

Short Courses in Agriculture and Forestry are given annually; and Evening Classes in Agriculture, Chemistry, Veterinary Science, Forestry, Horticulture, Botany, and Zoology are held during the Winter Session.

Particulars of Classes, and information as to Bursaries tenable at the College, will be found in the Calendar, which will be forwarded on application to the Secretary,

ALEXANDER M'CALLUM, M.A., LL.B.

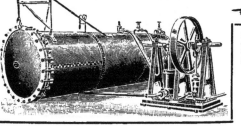

INSTITUTED 1854.

Patron—HIS MOST EXCELLENT MAJESTY THE KING.

Permission to assume the title "Royal' was granted by Her Majesty Queen Victoria in 1887.

OFFICE=BEARERS FOR 1913.

President.

CAPTAIN ARCHIBALD STIRLING of Keir, Dunblane.

Vice=Presidents.

BORTHWICK, D Sc , 46 George Square, Edinburgh.

DEY J. GAMMELL of Drumtochty, Countesswells use, Bieldside, Aberdeen

RD LOVAT, D S.O., Beaufort Castle, Beauly.

CHAS BUCHANAN, Factor, Penicuik Estate, Penicui

SIR ANDREW AGNEW, Bart., of Lochnaw, 10 Smith Westminster.

W. STEUART FOTHRINGHAM of Murthly, Perthsh

Council.

HON. LIFE MEMBERS.

SIR KENNETH J. MACKENZIE, Bart. of Gairloch, 10 Moray Place, Edinburgh.

SIR JOHN STIRLING-MAXWELL, Bart of Pollok, Pollokshaws.

ORDINARY MEMBERS.

LEVEN, Forester, Bowmont Forest, Roxburgh.

OF BROOM, Wood Merchant, Bathgate.

OF F. ANNAND, Lecturer in Forestry, Armstrong College, Newcastle-upon-Tyne.

OF W. M'HATTIE, Superintendent of City Parks, City Chambers, Edinburgh.

RIE OF BRODIE, Brodie Castle, Forres.

WILLIAM DAWSON, M.A., B.Sc , Reader in Forestry, Cambridge University.

* * * * * * * * *

A. GILLANDERS, F.E.S , Forester, Park Cottage, Alnick.

JAS WHITTON, Superintendent of City Parks, City Chambers, Glasgow.

WILLIAM DAVIDSON, Forester, Panmure, Carnoustie.

W. H. MASSIE, Nurseryman, 1 Waterloo Place, Edin

GILBERT BROWN, Wood Manager, Grantown-on-Sp

GEORGE P. GORDON, B.Sc., Lecturer in Forestry, Scotland Agricultural College, 6 Blythswood Glasgow.

A. D. RICHARDSON, 6 Dalkeith Street, Joppa.

ADAM SPIERS, Timber Merchant, Warriston Saw-Mil burgh.

ROBERT ALLAN, Factor, Polkemmet, Whitburn.

G. U. MACDONALD, Overseer, Haystoun Estate, W Cottage, Peebles.

ALEXANDER MITCHELL, Forester, Rosebery, Gorel

ROBERT FORBES, Overseer, Kennet Estate Office, A

ALEXANDER J. MUNRO, Factor, 48 Castle Stree burgh.

W. M. PRICE, Factor, Minto, Hawick.

Hon. Editor.

Dr A. W. BORTHWICK, 46 George Square, Edinburgh.

Auditor.

JOHN T. WATSON, 16 St Andrew Square, Edinburgh.

Hon. Secretary.

The RIGHT HON. R. C. MUNRO FERGUSON, M.P., Raith House, Kirkcaldy.

Secretary and Treasurer.

ROBERT GALLOWAY, S.S.C., 19 Castle Street, Edinburgh.

ABERDEEN BRANCH.

President—A. FORBES IRVINE of Drum.

Secy.—GEORGE D. MASSIE, Solicitor, 147 Union Street, Aberdeen.

NORTHERN BRANCH.

President—BRODIE OF BRODIE.

Hon. Secy.—ALEX. FRASER, Solicitor, 63 Church Inverness.

Hon. Consulting Officials.

Consulting Botanist.—ISAAC BAYLEY BALFOUR, LL.D., M.D., Sc.D., Professor of Botany, Royal Botanic Garden, Edinburgh.

Consulting Chemist.—ALEXANDER LAUDER, D Sc., F.I.C., 13 George Square, Edinburgh.

Consulting Cryptogamist.--A. W. BORTHWICK, D Sc., 46 George Square, Edinburgh.

Consulting Entomologist. — ROBERT STEWART DOUGALL, M.A., D.Sc., Professor of Entomolo 9 Dryden Place, Edinburgh.

Consulting Geologist.—R. CAMPBELL, M.A., B.S logical Laboratory, University of Edinburgh.

Consulting Meteorologist.—ANDREW WATT, M.A., F Secretary Scottish Meteorological Society, 122 Street, Edinburgh.

*

Former Presidents.

The following have held the office of President in past years, viz. : —

1854-56. JAMES BROWN, Wood Commissioner to the Earl of Seafield.
1857. The Right Hon. THE EARL OF DUCIE.
1858. The Right Hon. THE EARL OF STAIR.
1859. Sir JOHN HALL, Bart. of Dunglass.
1860. His Grace THE DUKE OF ATHOLL.
1861. JOHN I. CHALMERS of Aldbar.
1862. The Right Hon. THE EARL OF AIRLIE.
1863. The Right Hon. T. F. KENNEDY.
1864-71. ROBERT HUTCHISON of Carlowrie, F.R.S.E.
1872-73. HUGH CLEGHORN, M D., LL.D., F.R.S.E., of Stravithie.
1874-75. Professor JOHN HUTTON BALFOUR, University of Edinburgh.
1876-78. The Right Hon. W. P. ADAM of Blair-adam. M.P.
1879-81. The Most Hon. THE MARQUIS OF LOTHIAN, K.T.

1882. Professor ALEXANDER DICKSON, Uni of Edinburgh.
1883-85. HUGH CLEGHORN, M.D., LL.D., F. of Stravithie.
1886-87. The Right Hon. Sir HERBERT E MAXWELL, Bart. of Monreith.
1888-89. The Most Hon. THE MARQI LINLITHGOW.
1890-93. Professor BAYLEY BALFOUR, Un of Edinburgh.
1894-97. The Right Hon. R. C. MUNRO FE M.P.
1898. Colonel F. BAILEY, R.E.
1899-02. The Right Hon. THE EARL OF MAN
1903-06. W. STEUART FOTHRINGHAM of Mu
1907-09. Sir KENNETH J. MACKENZIE, I Gairloch.
1910-12. Sir JOHN STIRLING-MAXWELL, I Pollok.

Membership.

THE Roll contains the names of over 1400 Members, comprising Landowners, Factors, Foresters, Nurserymen, Gardeners, Land Stewards, Wood Merchants, and others interested in Forestry, many of whom reside in England, Ireland, the British Colonies, and India.

Members are elected by the Council. The Terms of Subscription will be found on the back of the Form of Proposal for Membership which accompanies this Memorandum.

The Principal Objects of the Society,

and the nature of its work, will be gathered from the following paragraphs:—

Meetings.

The Society holds periodical Meetings for the transaction of business, the reading and discussion of Papers, the exhibition of new Inventions, specimens of Forest Products and other articles of special interest to the Members, and for the advancement of Forestry in all its branches. Meetings of the Council are held every alternate month, and at other times when business requires attention; and Committees of the Council meet frequently to arrange and carry out the work of the Society.

Prizes and Medals.

With the view of encouraging young Foresters to study, and to train themselves in habits of careful and accurate observation, the Society offers Annual Prizes and Medals for essays on practical subjects, and for inventions connected with appliances used in Forestry. Such awards have been granted continuously since 1855 up to the present time, and have yielded satisfactory results. Medals and Prizes are also awarded in connection with the Exhibitions and Competitions for Plantations and Estate Nurseries aftermentioned.

School of Forestry, Afforestation, Etc.

Being convinced of the necessity for bringing within the reach of young Foresters, and others interested in the Profession, a regular systematic course of Instruction, the Society, in 1882, strongly urged the creation of a British School of Forestry; and with a view of stimulating public interest in the matter, a Forestry Exhibition, chiefly organised by the Council, was held in Edinburgh in 1884.

In 1890, the Society instituted a Fund for the purpose of establishing a Chair of Forestry at the University of Edinburgh, and a sum of £584, 3s. 10d. has since been raised by the Society and handed over to the University. Aided by an annual subsidy from the Board of Agriculture, which the Society was mainly instrumental in obtaining, a Course of Lectures at the University has been delivered without interruption since 1889. The Society also drew up a Scheme for the Establishment of a State Model or Demonstration Forest for Scotland, which might serve not only for purposes of instruction but also as a Station for Research and Experiment, and as a Model Forest, by which Landowners and Foresters throughout the country might benefit. Copies of this Scheme were laid before the Departmental Committee on British Forestry, and in their Report the Committee recommended the establishment of a Demonstration Area and the provision of other educational facilities in Scotland.

The Government recently acquired the Estate of Inverliever in Argyllshire; and while this cannot be looked on as a Demonstration Forest, it is hoped that it may prove to be the first step in a scheme of afforestation by the State of unwooded lands in Scotland. Meantime Mr Munro Ferguson, M.P., for a part of whose woods at Raith a Working-Plan is in operation, has very kindly agreed to allow Students to visit them.

After the Development Act came into operation, the Council passed a Resolution urging that the Government should, as soon as possible, create a Board of Forestry, with an adequate representation of Scottish Forestry upon it, and an Office in Scotland, where the largest areas of land suitable for Afforestation are situated, which would provide Demonstration Forests and Forest Gardens, and otherwise assist the development of University and other Educational enterprise, and would carry out, as an essential preliminary to any great scheme of National Afforestation, a Survey of all areas throughout the country suitable for commercial planting. The Society s policy for the development of Forestry in Scotland has since been fully laid before the Development Commission. As a result of these representations, the Secretary for Scotland appointed a Committee to report regarding the acquisition and uses of a Demonstration Forest Area, and any further steps it is desirable to take in order to promote Silviculture in Scotland. The Committee reported in the beginning of last year, and the Society is pressing the Board of Agriculture for Scotland, being the Department now concerned with Scottish forestry, to give effect to the Committee's recommendations and to encourage the inception of schemes of afforestation. The Society has also published a valuable Report on Afforestation—including a Survey of Glen Mor—prepared for it by Lord Lovat and Captain Stirling, which, it is hoped, may form the basis of the general Forest Survey advocated by the Society.

Excursions.

Since 1878 well-organised Excursions, numerously attended by Members of the Society, have been made annually to various parts of Scotland, England, Ireland, and the Continent. In 1895 a Tour extending over twelve days was made through the Forests of Northern Germany, in 1902 a Tour extending over seventeen days was made in Sweden, in 1904 the Forest School at Nancy and Forests in the north of France were visited, in 1909 a visit was undertaken to the Bavarian Forests, and during the past summer ten days were spent in the Forests of Switzerland. These Excursions enable Members whose occupations necessarily confine them chiefly to a single locality to study the conditions and methods prevailing elsewhere; and the Council propose to extend the Tours during the next few years to other parts of the Continent. They venture to express the hope that Landowners may be induced to afford facilities to their Foresters for participation in these Tours, the instructive nature of which renders them well worth the moderate expenditure of time and money that they involve.

Exhibitions.

A Forestry Exhibition is annually organised in connection with the Highland and Agricultural Society's Show, in which are exhibited specimens illustrating the rate of growth of trees, different kinds of wood, pit-wood and railway timber, insect pests and samples of the damage done by them, tools and implements, manufactured articles peculiar to the district where the Exhibition is held, and other objects of interest relating to Forestry. Prizes and Medals are also offered for Special Exhibits. In addition to the Annual Exhibition before referred to, large and important Forestry Sections organised by this Society were included in the Scottish National Exhibition held in Edinburgh in 1908, and in the Scottish Exhibition of National History, Art, and Industry, held in Glasgow in 1911.

Plantations and Estate Nurseries Competitions.

Prizes are now offered annually for the best Young Plantations and the best managed Estate Nurseries within the Show District of the Highland and Agricultural Society.

The Society's Transactions.

The *Transactions* of the Society, which extend to twenty-seven volumes, are now published half-yearly in January and July, and are issued *gratis* to Members. A large number of the Prize Essays and other valuable Papers, and reports of the Annual Excursions, have appeared in them, and have thus become available to Students as well as to those actively engaged in the Profession of Forestry.

Honorary Consulting Officials.

Members have the privilege of obtaining information gratuitously upon subjects connected with Forestry from the Honorary Officials mentioned above.

Local Branches.

Local Branches have been established in Aberdeen and Inverness for the convenience of Members who reside in the districts surrounding these centres.

Local Secretaries.

The Society is represented throughout Scotland, England, and Ireland by the Local Secretaries whose names are given below. They are ready to afford any additional information that may be desired regarding the Conditions of Membership and the work of the Society.

Register of Estate Men.

A Register of men qualified in Forestry and in Forest and Estate Management is kept by the Society. Schedules of application and other particulars may be obtained from the Local Secretaries in the various districts, or direct from the Secretary. It is hoped that Proprietors and others requiring Estate men will avail themselves of the Society's Register.

Consulting Foresters.

The Secretary keeps a list of Consulting Foresters whose services are available to Members of the Society and others.

Correspondents.

The following have agreed to act as Correspondents residing abroad :—

Canada, . ROBERT BELL, I.S.O., M D., LL.D., D.Sc.(Cantab.), F.R.S. of Ottawa, late Chief Geologist to Government of Canada, Ottawa.

India, . . F. L. C. COWLEY BROWN, Principal, South Indian Forest College, Coimbatore, South India.

British East ⎱ EDWARD BATTISCOMBE, Assistant Conservator of Forests, *Africa,* ⎰ Nigeri, *via* Naivasha, East Africa Protectorate.

United States ⎱ HUGH P. BAKER, Dean, New York State College of *of America,* ⎰ Forestry, Syracuse, N.Y.

Cape Colony, . W. NIMMO BROWN, M'Kenzie's Farm, Mowbiay, P.O.

Western Australia, FRED MOON.

LOCAL SECRETARIES.

Counties.	*Scotland*
Aberdeen,	. JOHN CLARK, Forester, Haddo House, Aberdeen.
	JOHN MICHIE, M.V.O., Factor, Balmoral, Ballater.
Argyll, .	. H. L. MACDONALD of Dunach, Oban.
Ayr, .	. ANDREW D. PAGE, Overseer, Culzean Home Farm, Ayr.
	A. B. ROBERTSON, Forester, The Dean, Kilmarnock.
Berwick,	. WM. MILNE, Foulden Newton, Berwick-on-Tweed.
Bute, .	. WM. INGLIS, Forester, Cladoch, Brodick.
	JAMES KAY, retired Forester, Barone, Rothesay.
Clackmannan,.	ROBERT FORBES, Estate Office, Kennet, Alloa.

Counties.		*Scotland.*
Dumfries,	.	D. CRABBE, Forester, Byreburnfoot, Canonbie.
East Lothian,	.	W. S. CURR, Factor, Ninewar, Prestonkirk.
Fife,	. .	WM. GILCHRIST, Forester, Nursery Cottage, Mount Melville, St Andrews.
		EDMUND SANG, Nurseryman, Kirkcaldy.
Forfar,	. .	JAMES CRABBE, retired Forester, Glamis.
Inverness,	.	JAMES A. GOSSIP, Nurseryman, Inverness.
Kincardine,	.	JOHN HART, Estates Office, Cowie, Stonehaven.
Kinross,	.	JAMES TERRIS, Factor, Dullomuir, Blairadam.
Lanark,	.	JOHN DAVIDSON, Forester, Dalzell, Motherwell.
		JAMES WHITTON, Superintendent of Parks, City Chambers, Glasgow.
Moray,	.	D. SCOTT, Forester, Darnaway Castle, Forres.
Perth,	.	JOHN SCRIMGEOUR, Doune Lodge, Doune.
Ross,	.	Miss AMY FRANCES YULE, Tarradale House, Muir of Ord.
Roxburgh,	.	JOHN LEISHMAN, Manager, Cavers Estate, Hawick.
		R. V. MATHER, Nurseryman, Kelso.
Sutherland,	.	DONALD ROBERTSON, Forester, Dunrobin, Golspie.
Wigtown,	.	JAMES HOGARTH, Forester, Culhorn, Stranraer.
		H. H. WALKER, Monreith Estate Office, Whauphill.

England.

Beds,	.	FRANCIS MITCHELL, Forester, Woburn.
Berks,	.	W. STORIE, Whitway House, Newbury.
Derby,	.	S. MACBEAN, Estate Office, Needwood Forest, Sudbury.
Devon,	.	JAMES BARRIE, Forester, Stevenstone Estate, Torrington.
Durham,	.	JOHN F. ANNAND, M.Sc., Lecturer in Forestry, Armstrong College, Newcastle-upon-Tyne.
Hants,	.	W. R. BROWN, Forester, Park Cottage, Heckfield, Winchfield.
Herts,	.	JAMES BARTON, Forester, Hatfield.
		THOMAS SMITH, Overseer, Tring Park, Wigginton, Tring.
Kent,	.	R. W. COWPER, Gortanore, Sittingbourne.
Lancashire,	.	D. C. HAMILTON, Forester, Knowsley, Prescot.
Leicester,	.	JAMES MARTIN, The Reservoir, Knipton, Grantham.
Lincoln,	.	W. B. HAVELOCK, The Nurseries, Brocklesby Park.
Middlesex,	.	Professor BOULGER, 11 Onslow Road, Richmond Hill, London, S.W.
Notts,	.	W. MICHIE, Forester, Welbeck, Worksop.
		WILSON TOMLINSON, Forester, Clumber Park, Worksop.
Surrey,	.	JOHN ALEXANDER, 24 Lawn Crescent, Kew Gardens.
Warwick,	.	A. D. CHRISTIE, Hillside, Frederick Road, Selly Oak, Birmingham.
Wilts,	.	ANDREW BOA, Land Agent, Glenmore, The Avenue, Trowbridge.
York,	.	D. TAIT, Estate Bailiff, Owston Park, Doncaster.
		GEORGE HANNAH, Estate Office, Boynton, Bridlington.

Ireland.

Dublin,	.	A. C. FORBES, Department of Forestry, Board of Agriculture.
		ARCH. E. MOERAN, Lissadell, Stillorgan Park.
King's County,		WM HENDERSON, Forester, Clonad Cottage, Tullamore.
Tipperary,	.	ALEX. M'RAE, Forester, Dundrum.

Royal Scottish Arboricultural Society.

FORM OF PROPOSAL FOR MEMBERSHIP.

To be signed by the Candidate, his Proposer and Seconder, and returned to **ROBERT GALLOWAY**, S.S.C., *SECRETARY*, Royal Scottish Arboricultural Society, 19 Castle Street, Edinburgh.

Candidate's
- *Full Name,* ....
- *Designation, Degrees, etc.,* ....
- *Address,* ....
- *Life, or Ordinary Member,* ....
- *Signature,* . . ..

Proposer's
- *Signature,* . . ..
- *Address,* . . ..

Seconder's
- *Signature,* . . ..
- *Address,* . . ..

[CONDITIONS OF MEMBERSHIP, see Over.

CONDITIONS OF MEMBERSHIP (excerpted from the Laws).

III. Any person interested in Forestry, and desirous of promoting the objects of the Society, is eligible for election as an *Ordinary* Member in one of the following Classes :—

1. Proprietors the valuation of whose land *exceeds* £500 per annum, and others, subscribing annually . . One Guinea.

2. Proprietors the valuation of whose land *does not exceed* £500 per annum, Factors, Nurserymen, Timber Merchants, and others, subscribing annually . . Half-a-Guinea.

3. Foresters, Gardeners, Land-Stewards, Tenant Farmers, and others, subscribing annually . . . Six Shillings.

4. Assistant-Foresters, Assistant-Gardeners, and others, subscribing annually . . . . . Four Shillings.

IV. Subscriptions are due on the 1st of January in each year, and shall be payable in advance. A new Member's Subscription is due on the day of election unless otherwise provided, and he shall not be enrolled until he has paid his first Subscription.

V. Members in arrear shall not receive the *Transactions*, and shall not be entitled to vote at any of the meetings of the Society. Any Member whose Annual Subscription remains unpaid for two years shall cease to be a Member of the Society, and no such Member shall be eligible for re-election till his arrears have been paid up.

VI. Any eligible person may become a *Life* Member of the Society, on payment, according to class, of the following sums :—

1. Large Proprietors of land, and others, ... £10 10 0

2. Small Proprietors, Factors, Nurserymen, Timber Merchants, and others, ... 5 5 0

3. Foresters, Gardeners, Land-Stewards, Tenant Farmers, and others, ... 3 3 0

VII. Any *Ordinary* Member of Classes 1, 2, and 3, who has paid *Five* Annual Subscriptions, may become a *Life* Member on payment of *Two-thirds* of the sum payable by a *new* Life Member.

XII. Every Proposal for Membership shall be made in writing, and shall be signed by two Members of the Society as Proposer and Seconder, and delivered to the Secretary to be laid before the Council, which shall accept or otherwise deal with each Proposal as it may deem best in the interest of the Society. The Proposer and Seconder shall be responsible for payment of the new Member's first Subscription. The Council shall have power to decide the Class under which any Candidate for Membership shall be placed.

NOTICE.

WANTED TO PURCHASE.

Any of the following Parts of the *Transactions*,
viz.:

Parts 1, 2, and 3 of Vol. I.
Parts 2 and 3   of Vol. III.
Parts 1 and 2   of Vol. IV.
Part 2   of Vol. V.
Part 2   of Vol. IX.
Part 1   of Vol. XII.

Apply to

—— THE SECRETARY, ——
19 CASTLE STREET, EDINBURGH.

NOTICES TO MEMBERS

SUBSCRIPTIONS

Annual Subscribers are reminded that subscriptions are payable on 1st January, and should be remitted now.

ESSAYS

A note of prizes offered is appended to this Part, and additional copies may be obtained from the Secretary.

ANNUAL MEETING

The date fixed for the Annual Meeting is Saturday, 7th February. The usual particulars will be sent later.

ROBERT GALLOWAY, S.S.C.,
Secretary and Treasurer.

19 CASTLE STREET,
EDINBURGH, *December 1913.*

CONTENTS.

The Society does not hold itself responsible for the statements
or views expressed by the authors of papers.

PAGE

1. Deputation from the Society to the Right Hon. T. M'Kinnon
   Wood. M.P.. Secretary for Scotland—7th November 1913   1

2. The Development Commission and Forestry. Extracts from
   the Report of the Commissioners for the year ended 31st
   March 1913   14

3. The State Forests of Saxony (with Illustrations . (Continued from Vol. xxvii., p. 187.) By A. D. Hopkinson. B.Sc.   28

4. Some Vegetation Types at High Altitudes (with Illustrations). By G. P. Gordon, B.Sc.(Edin.), B.Sc.(Oxon.) .   46

5. Forestry at Home and Abroad. By A. W. Borthwick, D.Sc.   56

6. Continental Notes—France. By A. G. Hobart-Hampden .   60

7. The Formation of Plantations on Deep Peat (with Plate).
   By Donald Grant   72

8. A Plan Adequate to Meet our Needs for Wood Timber .   78

9. The Excursion to Switzerland (with Illustrations). By
   G. P. Gordon, B.Sc.   83

10. The Forestry Exhibition at Paisley. By G. P. Gordon, B.Sc.   97

11. Visit to German Forests by the Royal English Arboricultural
    Society—1913. By A. T. Gillanders, F.E.S. . .   100

12. Timber Research Work at the Cambridge School of Forestry   105

13. *Thuja gigantea* and Douglas Fir in Mixture (with Plate).
    By D. K. M'Beath   107

14. Nursery and Plantation Competition   110

CONTENTS.

PAGE

Notes and Queries :—Witch's Broom on *Pseudotsuga Doug-lasii* (with Plate)—Appointment of Chief Conservator of Forests, South Africa—Protection of Scots Pine against Black Game—Leaflet on the Large Brown Pine Weevil— Tree-Growth in 1913—Forestry and the Anglo-American Exposition—The Excursion to Switzerland   .   . 116

Reviews and Notices of Books :—The Forest of Dean. By Arthur O. Cooke. With four Illustrations in Colour and fifty-six in Black and White. Price 10s. 6d. net. London : Constable & Co.   120

Albury Park Trees and Shrubs. 66 + x pp. By A. Bruce Jackson. London : West, Newman & Co., 1913 .   . 120

TRANSACTIONS

OF THE

ROYAL SCOTTISH ARBORICULTURAL SOCIETY.

1. Deputation from the Society to the Right Hon. T. M'Kinnon Wood, M.P., Secretary for Scotland —7th November 1913.

Mr M'Kinnon Wood, who was accompanied by Sir Robert Wright and Mr John D. Sutherland, members of the Board of Agriculture for Scotland, received the deputation within the offices of the Board, 29 St Andrew Square, Edinburgh. The following members of the Society formed the deputation:— Captain Stirling, President; The Right Hon. Sir Herbert Maxwell, Bart. of Monreith, ex-President; Dr A. W. Borthwick and Mr Charles Buchanan, Vice-Presidents; Messrs George Leven, John Broom, John W. M'Hattie, A. T. Gillanders, F.E S., William Davidson, G. P. Gordon, B.Sc., Adam Spiers, G. U. Macdonald, Alexander Mitchell and Robert Forbes, members of Council; and Robert Galloway, S.S.C., Secretary and Treasurer.

The President, in introducing the deputation, said:—"I am sure that every member of this deputation is grateful to you, Sir, for consenting to receive us to-day. We are very well aware of the immense amount of administrative and parliamentary work which falls to the share of the Secretary for Scotland, and there-fore, when approaching him with regard to a question which has not been brought very prominently before Parliament or before the country, we may hope that some of the views to be expressed by us may throw new light upon the subject. I cannot emphasise too strongly the non-political nature of our errand to-day. The Council of the Royal Scottish Arboricul-tural Society knows no politics. It is solely concerned with the interests and development of forestry in Scotland. Amongst the members of the Council are gentlemen who have taken, and are taking, active part in politics on different sides of the House of Commons, and I am sure that their presence here to-day has no connection whatever with any party considerations. It is as a matter of national importance that we wish to put the claims of afforestation before you to-day. The deputation consists of members of the Council of the Royal Scottish Arboricultural Society together with Sir Herbert Maxwell, a former President.

"I may, perhaps, be allowed to state briefly our claims as a Society to speak on behalf of forestry in Scotland.

"The Society, which was founded in 1854, has to-day a total of over 1400 members on its books, and includes amongst them those who are engaged in the production and manufacture of timber as well as those who have made a special study of the science of silviculture, so that the Society may justly claim to be the corporate expression of the needs and interests of Scottish forestry and its dependent industries. There is no need to go at length into the early history of the Society, its record is one of constant exertion towards two ends—first, to draw Scottish foresters together and enable them to compare and classify experience brought into the common stock; and second, to obtain from the State that recognition of and assistance for silviculture which almost every foreign State has long given to it as a great national asset, deserving of development at the hands of the Government. I may say, in passing, that the Society has been more successful in attaining the first object than the second. It has created a solid body of public opinion among Scottish foresters, and accumulated experience of the greatest possible practical value. With regard to State recognition or any active assistance in development, we are little better off in 1913 than were our predecessors in 1854. These are strong words. I hope to justify them when I come to the more recent history of our endeavours.

"In 1895 the Society made the first of a long series of tours in Continental forests, which have been of the greatest educational value, and have served, moreover, to bring the Society into close touch with the leading silviculturists of Europe. The Society has spent on these tours at home and abroad no less than £9600, the whole of that sum having been contributed by those who took part in them—the large majority of members attending being always practical foresters. Including these tours, with the sum spent on printing the *Transactions*, and other expenses, the Society has spent over £22,000 in all, directly in the interests of silviculture in Scotland. Next year, in celebration of its sixtieth anniversary, the Society intends to invite distinguished silviculturists from foreign countries and our colonies to be the guests of the Society in Scotland for ten days, and to take them to see our woods and districts suitable for afforestation.   Perhaps I may be allowed to run over briefly some of the milestones on the track of the Society in recent years :—

"In 1902 the Departmental Committee on Forestry (appointed largely at the instance of the Society) made its report recommending for Scotland the provision of a Demonstration Area.

"In 1904 the Council sent a resolution to the Board of Agriculture in London requesting that effect should be given to the recommendation of the Departmental Committee.

"In 1908 the estate of Inverliever was purchased by the Commissioner of Woods and Forests.   This estate, being destitute of woodlands, cannot for a long time to come serve the purpose of a demonstration area.   It is, in fact, valuable at present only as an example of afforestation of waste ground.

"In the same year was published the interim report of the Coast Erosion Commission with its colossal estimate of afforestable land.

"In 1909 a resolution was sent to the Government urging the appointment of a Board or Commission of Forestry charged with a survey of land suitable for silviculture, and (once more) the purchase of a demonstration area.

"The reception of a deputation by the Chancellor of the Exchequer, the establishment of the Development Commission, also in 1909, raised new hopes.   But in 1910 another resolution was sent to the Government again urging the importance of a Board of Forestry, demonstration areas, and a survey of afforestable land.   In the same year the Society undertook to make, at its own expense, a sample survey of a district suitable for afforestation, the result of which was published in 1911 as the Forest Survey of Glen Mor.

"To sum up the situation in a word, the attachment between the Board of Agriculture and Forestry is a platonic one, nothing comes of it.

"In 1911 a letter was addressed to the Secretary for Scotland asking that a Commissioner for Forestry should be appointed under the Small Landholders Bill.   The Minister in his reply, while refusing the request for a Commission under the Bill, promised in the event of the Bill becoming law, to establish, as an integral part of the Board of Agriculture for Scotland, a Department of Forestry for Scotland.

"This undertaking was welcomed by the Society—the only stipulation made by them was that the Department should be representative of those interested in silviculture, and that it should be endowed with a reasonable amount of independence and responsibility. A further letter from the Council to Lord Pentland defined their views on the constitution of the proposed Department.

"The circumstances under which Lord Pentland's promise of a Department came to be unfulfilled are better known to you, Sir, than they can be to us. We saw with deep disappointment the substitution of a Commissioner of Small Holdings with temporary charge of forestry for the promised Department—and we have had reason to regret the change.

"We recognise that an admirable appointment was made in the person of Mr Sutherland to the charge of the forestry side of the Board's work. His special knowledge of forestry as well as of all the economic and social conditions of the West Highlands made him particularly well fitted for the post. In what we have to say, it must be clearly understood that no single word of criticism is directed against Mr Sutherland or against his conception of his duties. We consider that a fatal mistake was made in tacking on forestry to his other duties as Commissioner for Small Holdings. This may, perhaps, seem a strange complaint in the face of what we shall have to say as to the intimate connection which should exist between afforestation and small holdings, but we cannot but feel that, through no fault of Mr Sutherland's, the small holdings side of his work has occupied his time and energy to the exclusion of forestry, and that the association of forestry with small holdings has, hitherto, been no part of the official policy of the Board of Agriculture.

"To resume the sequence of events:—In June 1912 a deputation of the Council waited on the Chairman of the Board of Agriculture for Scotland, to represent the needs of forestry and to ask that a share of the Board's grant should be spent on it. The reply received was that no part of the Board's grant could be expended on forestry, as it was already earmarked.

"I pass from an episode which caused us deep disappointment to another which gave us pleasure—the presence of Mr Sutherland as the representative of the Board at our General Meeting in February of the present year.

"Mr Sutherland gave us reason to hope that the long promised demonstration area would soon be definitely fixed upon. With that assurance we are content, and I have nothing to say on the demonstration area, except that though we cannot be expected to express an opinion on a report which we have not seen, we have all confidence in the judgment of the members of our Council who are serving on the Advisory Committee. We would urge strongly, however, that if the present negotiations should unhappily break down, the absence of a demonstration area shall not serve as an excuse for deferring progress in other directions. Mr Sutherland promised—or fore-shadowed—the appointment of advisory and research officers. We have since learnt that owing to a difference of opinion with the Development Commissioners as to the repayment of the salary of these officers, no appointment has been made.

"Mr Sutherland also told us that a survey was in preparation showing the areas contained within the limit of altitude at which silviculture is practicable. To borrow his description—the areas are divided into three sections, first, under 500 ft.; second, 500 to 1000 ft.; third, 1000 to 1500 ft.—and these maps are intended to be of service in agricultural as well as silvicultural operations. So far as Mr Sutherland's description goes, it is not easy to see, in this survey, anything which could not be accomplished by an intelligent child with the aid of a contour map and a penny paint-box. I hope that I am not unfair to the survey, but it appears to ignore the all-important considerations of soil and shelter. In the last sentence, the practised ear can detect the mewing of the agricultural cat inside the silvicultural bag. I cannot insist too strongly that these criticisms are not directed against Mr Sutherland, but against the impossible system under which he has to work.

"Therefore, Sir, we respectfully ask you to consider our demand for a Department of Forestry in connection with the Board of Agriculture for Scotland, with a separate grant for forestry purposes only. We are able to show ample justification for a separate Department and a separate grant in the work to be done. It will be shown by the speakers who are to follow me that—

(1) Large tracts of land well suited for afforestation exist in

Scotland, and that such land is purchasable on reasonable terms;

(2) Afforestation affords the only available means of giving more employment and wages to the existing population of the Highlands, and of enabling a larger population to live on the land;

(3) Intimate relationship should exist between afforestation and schemes for small holdings in the Highlands;

(4) Ample experience and a sufficiency of trained men can be found to justify afforestation on a large scale on carefully chosen areas."

Sir Herbert Maxwell said :—" My remarks bear entirely upon the amount of land, unsuitable for agriculture but capable of producing profitable timber, which exists in Scotland.

"The Central Highlands have been dealt with in a large measure by my friends Captain Stirling and Lord Lovat. As for the other parts of the Central Highlands I need only say that the forests of Deeside and Strathspey, and the mountains bordering the central parts of Strathspey, speak for themselves as to their capability for producing timber of the very highest quality. The part of Scotland with which I am more immediately familiar, with which I have a lifelong acquaintance, is the Southern Upland, extending from south of Ayrshire for about seventy miles, and with very few intervals—river valleys—as far east as Moffat and Hawick. The whole of that land is under pasture except the river valleys, and I have the greatest confidence in saying that that part of it which is under 1000 feet is capable of being brought under profitable forestry. I was asked indeed by the Office of Woods and Forests, about five years ago, to report upon an estate which was for sale at the time, and it was in the contemplation of the Office of Woods and Forests to purchase it for forestry purposes. I found that the whole of the ground, extending to between 8000 and 10,000 acres, except a very small proportion of moss, was most suitable for forestry purposes. The pasture rent was 5d. an acre, the sporting rent was 7d. an acre, and the whole area might have been purchased on that basis, say twenty-five years' purchase at 25s. an acre. The negotiations fell through. Estates in that part of the country have frequently changed hands of late years.

"If I may allude to that vast area offered by the Duke of Sutherland to the State, I am tolerably familiar with the greater part of it, and although no one can help recognising that a large proportion of it—moss lands and anything over, at that latitude, 800 feet—is quite unsuitable for forestry, or for any other purpose except game, still there does exist in that area considerable tracts where in some places trees are already growing vigorously, and in others I am sure that plantations would thrive. I would suggest that a very careful survey of the ground should be made to find out what portion is suitable for forestry.

" I have no doubt that you will meet in this country with a large body of public opinion adverse to forestry. We agriculturists are apt to look askance upon a crop, the rotation of which exceeds the span of a generation, and, indeed, in the case of some hardwoods, two or three generations—our imaginations are apt to be staggered by that.

" In view of the enormous importation of timber in this country, amounting to an annual value of over 26 millions, I submit it is not unreasonable that we should ask the Government to take into consideration such measures as would enable some part of that great industry to be brought to the doors of our own people, and so, with its subsidiary industries, to help to arrest the deplorable rural depopulation."

Mr Adam Spiers said :—" From the timber merchants' point of view, we find each year our supplies from the foreigner decreasing and the cost enormously increasing, and the supplies from our own country are very limited indeed. I am under the impression that we have not given the attention to the cultivation of hardwoods in the past that we might have done, or ought to have done, because we have no tree that we can get from foreign countries to take the place of many that grow so well in our own country, particularly ash, and the same thing applies to oak, elm and hickory.

" When we do set about demonstrations, I hope that we will not lose sight of the cultivation of hardwoods to a very much larger extent than we are doing at the moment, because in all the countries we have visited we have come across none that can grow a larger variety of hardwoods, and of equal quality to those grown in our own country."

Mr M'Kinnon Wood said :—" Mr Spiers says that we can cultivate hardwoods in Scotland profitably, and of the best quality that the trade would require. I should like some opinion, from the practical growers' point of view, whether you can profitably grow hardwoods on any large tracts in Scotland."

Mr Wm. Davidson said:—"I would say that on the lower land the hardwoods, especially ash and elm, could be grown with profit. For oak we do not generally get such a big price, but on the lower ground ash is very profitable, and also sycamore. We can get now for the very best quality of ash 2s. 6d. a foot."

Mr M'Kinnon Wood said:—"Would you consider it a satisfactory demonstration area which was practically given up to the cultivation of coniferous wood? Would it be satisfactory from the point of view of a place of education in forestry and a demonstration area?

Mr Davidson.—"I would say not. There should be high ground for conifers and low ground for hardwoods."

Mr M'Kinnon Wood.—"Captain Stirling laid stress on the purchase of a demonstration area."

. Captain Stirling.—"It seems to me that purchase would be infinitely more satisfactory than anything else, because I believe this demonstration area is intended to form a permanent home for a forest school."

Mr M'Kinnon Wood.—"That has been the view of the Advisory Committee. I may tell you they want to purchase an estate. They are afraid of a short lease."

Captain Stirling.—"My view is in favour of purchase."

Mr Gordon said:—"The contrast between one of our Highland glens and a glen in the Highlands of Europe is very marked indeed. We have in our typical Highland glen a stretch generally of indifferent pasture, with perhaps a dozen shepherds' cottages scattered along it. A similar continental glen supports a vigorous population of small holders. We find that it is the forest which maintains this population. It is thus not due to any greater advantage, either of soil or climate. I make that statement with detailed agricultural knowledge of the conditions in both countries—Germany and Scotland. The forest effects this by the employment which it affords. The nature of forest employment is specially well adapted to keep people on the land. First of all, it is permanent both in time and in place. The people, then, within its sphere of influence have security of employment and do not require to migrate. Secondly, the nature of the employment is very varied. You have people employed as wood-cutters, as saw-millers, as roadmakers. You have them also employed in various forest industries. You see then that this gives great scope for the people of a district. Thirdly, in winter, when other employment on the land is scarce, the forest demands a larger supply of labour, and this labour is highly paid. For example, a typical wood-cutter in Germany earns 4s. a day during five or six months of the winter. The following is a concrete example: a forest of 10,000 acres, with 3000 acres occupied by small holders attached. Such an area in the Highlands of Scotland would support at the most about 300. This area in question actually supports a population of 1500 in Germany. In 1907 81 per cent. of the persons employed in forestry were small holders. We see then that forestry forms the backbone of an economic system of small holdings. In 1907 the Prussian Government spent £200,000 in forests. In the same year the Bavarian Government spent £100,000.

"In this connection one should not lose sight of the fact that in forestry it is large areas which are truly economic, and this I may say is clearly demonstrated upon the Continent of Europe. The objection to small areas is that they do not give the same amount of employment, nor give the same permanency. They do not provide the same amount of timber, and the management of small areas is much more difficult and more costly.

"These few observations would seem to show that in any economic system of land holdings, especially when dealing with poor land, the forest is of prime importance."

Mr M'Hattie said :—" I think Mr Gordon pretty well touched on the question of the small holder ; but there has been a mistaken idea in the mind of the small holder himself in regard to forestry. The small holder has a fear that his land would be planted. The Society has always held that all land suitable for culture should be occupied for that purpose, and not planted. Being a Highland man I have always taken a great interest in these matters and have studied the question very fully, and there is no doubt at all that we would be able to utilise the small holder in the woods, both he and his horses. If the forest belonged to the Government and you had a continuity of policy, the crofter's security would be ample and he would therefore be able to get constant employment."

Mr M'Kinnon Wood.—" Are you suggesting that the Government should buy land ? "

Mr M'Hattie.—"Yes, because in forestry continuity of policy is absolutely imperative. This is no new idea. I might direct your attention to Perthshire, Ross-shire and Inverness-shire. There you have many hundreds of men who find suitable and constant work in afforestation. I should like you to bear in mind the strong feeling that it would keep the people on the land, to the advantage alike of the people and the nation."

Sir H. Maxwell.—"It is difficult for the private owners to provide sufficient salary for a trained forester on comparatively small areas."

Mr M'Hattie.—"I think even now you have splendid forests in this country for starting this operation, and the sooner it is started the better."

Dr Borthwick, in answer to a question by the Secretary for Scotland as to whether purchase or a lease would be best for a demonstration area, said that personally he thought purchase was preferable, but he would not go the length of saying that a lease was impossible. The one was preferable; the other was workable.

Mr M'Kinnon Wood.—"What length of lease would you desiderate?"

Dr Borthwick.—"From 100 to 120 years. I know this is not regarded as a business proposition."

Mr M'Kinnon Wood.—"Would you consider a 10 years' lease or a 20 years' lease?"

Dr Borthwick.—"Nothing like that would do."

Mr M'Kinnon Wood.—"Can you express any opinion about hardwoods?"

Dr Borthwick.—"I think hardwoods in the south and the Lowlands are of very great importance. In connection with large holdings and estates, a great quantity of useful and valuable ash and other hardwoods can be grown of a quality better than anything that can be imported."

Mr M'Kinnon Wood.—"Would you consider it a satisfactory demonstration area where there are practically no hardwoods?"

Dr Borthwick.—"No, I consider that, to be in every way satisfactory, it should contain hardwoods as well as conifers."[1]

Mr Macdonald said :—"We are fortunate in having at the

[1] An ideal area would contain both. If such an area is unobtainable, the best alternative would be to have a coniferous and a hardwood area, in different districts.—A. W. B.

present moment in Scotland a sufficient number of men, well trained in both theory and practice, who are perfectly able to carry on any form of afforestation scheme which may be agreed upon. We have on the Council of this Society many men who have devoted twenty years and more of their lives to the study and practice of this great subject, and are perfectly well able to carry out the work necessary on a demonstration area.

"I hold that there is no sufficient reason for hanging matters up until such time as there may be enough younger men. By the time trees that are planted now will reach the stage when they are ready for thinning and attending to in other ways, we have ample time to train men."

Mr M'Kinnon Wood said :—" Captain Stirling and gentlemen, I agree entirely with Captain Stirling—there is not the slightest vestige of politics connected with this question. It is a question of pure practical advantage to the country. I must congratulate the Society upon its forthcoming Diamond Jubilee, and I cannot help thinking that the proposal of the Society is an excellent one. I hope that the visit of the foreign delegates to Scotland will be an extremely successful one, and that something will be learnt from it.

"I don't know that there is occasion for the air of gloom and despair which seems to hang over the deputation, and which all their politeness hardly enables them to avoid expressing. It may be that you are little better off, as Captain Stirling said, but I think your prospects are better. I think the most practical thing for me to do is to tell you what I have done in this matter, and what the particular stage at which we have arrived exactly is, because the air of gloom which has reached you has been existing in other quarters all the time. It is a sort of perennial gloom and it does not depend upon circumstances.

"When I became Secretary for Scotland and took over the charge of agricultural affairs in Scotland, we had an important report from a Committee on Forestry which laid down certain general views and suggestions, but which did not precisely indicate what particular area ought to be bought as a demonstration area. I appointed an Advisory Committee to consider that question. Of course it would be impossible for the Board of Agriculture or for myself, as responsible Minister, who must answer to the House of Commons for the expenditure of funds, to give to any committee power to spend large sums of money, which indeed were beyond our resources, and which it was neither possible nor necessary to take from the Agriculture (Scotland) Fund. Well, that Committee had a task which they found difficult, of choosing a demonstration area. They considered the matter very carefully. They took the view which has been taken by the members of this deputation, that purchase was a more satisfactory thing than a lease. They had no choice of a lease for 100 or 120 years; the only possible leases were of very insignificant duration. They have been looking out for a place to purchase, and they have at last suggested the purchase of a property in Aberdeenshire, the property of Ballogie. Of course you know that among those interested in silviculture there are differences of opinion, and a little while ago a deputation representing the University of Edinburgh and the College of Agriculture waited upon me and made certain representations. They desired to have a demonstration area which was more centrally situated; objected that Ballogie was too far north; and they also raised the question that that particular forest consists of coniferous trees and that there are practically no hardwood trees there. At the same time they said that they had from a landlord in Perthshire a suggestion for dealing with an area there, of which I have not got exact particulars at the present moment. But, of course, I believe the Advisory. Committee would agree that if land were obtainable in a more central position it would be better. What they say is that they have not the offer of such land.

"With regard to this suggestion of land in Perthshire, which would not be open for purchase, but with regard to which different treatment was proposed, I am writing to the owner, asking him to put his proposal in a definite form, that it may be considered. I cannot say anything more about it.

"Now, you see, my position is this: that I have appointed an Advisory Committee and they have at last advised me. I have to consider representations from various parts of Scotland, and to consider what can be done; but no time has been lost. The Development Commissioners have sent an expert to view the property which is now offered, and no time is being lost in the matter. But you can see from what I have said that it is not an extremely simple matter, or a matter on which there is united opinion. I notice that no one here has any alternative to suggest of a forest that could be purchased.

"Now with regard to the money. The Development Commissioners, it has always been understood, are prepared to give money for forestry development in Scotland, as in England and Ireland; and I understand that, apart from this question of a demonstration area, they have under consideration a plan for assisting forestry which is nearly ready to be published, but which has not yet reached a form in which it can be put before me; so that I cannot discuss it. I want to show you that the matter has not been lost sight of or neglected.

" In its nature, it takes some time. We are providing a scheme that is to last a long time. We want to be careful to start on right lines. I think I have dealt with all the points you put to me. I should only like to thank you for the information and views you have put before me, which I will take into careful and respectful consideration."

Captain Stirling.—"We believe at the present time forestry has practically no staff under the Board of Agriculture, and it is quite incapable of dealing with such developments. We desire a separate State Department for dealing with forestry."

Mr M'Kinnon Wood.—"At the present time, if any landlord wants advice about afforestation we have Dr Nisbet who can advise him. I think you are quite right, Captain Stirling. When the Development Commissioners have made up their minds how they will supply money for this purpose of assisting forestry then will be the time to create a staff. I quite agree with you; there ought to be a Central Staff."

Mr Buchanan.—"Mr M'Kinnon Wood, I am sure we are very much indebted to you for the attention you have given to the deputation, and in the name of the Council and deputation I have to thank you for your kindness in meeting us here to-day, and to say that any assistance you may require from the Society hereafter in the work we have very much at heart, we will be very pleased to give you."

Mr M'Kinnon Wood.—"I am very much obliged to you, gentlemen. I am obliged to you for saying that if I want any information or guidance from you, you will allow me to come to you."

The deputation then withdrew.

2. The Development Commission and Forestry.

EXTRACTS FROM THE REPORT OF THE COMMISSIONERS FOR THE YEAR ENDED 31ST MARCH 1913.

(i.) *General.*

During the year 1912-13, the Commissioners received twelve applications which fall mainly or entirely under the heading of forestry; so far as can be ascertained the total of the advances for which application was made amounted to £50,442. The amount recommended during the year was £11,175.

In their last Report the Commissioners explained that the first object to which they were devoting their attention was the improvement of forestry education and the provision of technical advice. For this purpose they have made a grant of £5700 to the Board of Agriculture and Fisheries, to continue a scheme which provides instruction and advice at five centres in England and Wales (Oxford, Cambridge, Cirencester, Bangor, and Newcastle), and provides also for research work and minor forestry experiments. This grant is, however, only an interim measure, pending the establishment of a central demonstration area. A committee appointed by the Board of Agriculture has agreed in the view that such an area may be found among existing Crown woods; and the Commissioners will no doubt shortly receive from the Board detailed proposals for staff and equipment. It will then be necessary to consider how far the State-aided educational and research work in forestry should be centralised at the demonstration area; but, as it is clear that it cannot be confined to this area, the Commissioners have recommended grants of £2500 for a new forestry school at Cambridge, £1000 for a research laboratory at Oxford, and a small grant (in addition to a grant made last year) for a forestry museum and lecture room in Chopwell Woods, administered by Durham University.

They have not yet received definite proposals for a demonstration area in Scotland. They understand that this subject is still before the Committee appointed by the Secretary for Scotland some time ago. They have now before them an application from the Scotch Board of Agriculture for assistance towards a scheme for providing technical advice.

A total area of about 14,000 acres in Ireland has been

approved for purchase, if possible, out of the advance of £25,000 or £30,000 already sanctioned. The Department of Agriculture has submitted a working-plan for the first of the areas acquired.

As regards actual afforestation, it is necessary to say frankly that the amount of the Development Fund in relation to the claims upon it does not permit the Commissioners to contemplate afforestation upon any large scale, unless it is possible to draw also upon other funds. Excluding the purchase of land, it may be taken that £10 per acre is the minimum expenditure usually required before the planting operations begin to produce returns. As the total amount guaranteed to the Development Fund is £2,900,000 for numerous purposes, of which forestry is only one, it will be clear that the afforestation of even 100,000 acres solely from that Fund is scarcely feasible unless its resources are considerably augmented. In these circumstances, the Commissioners are compelled to restrict themselves at present to two lines of action. In the first place, they propose to assist the purchase and planting of what may be called experimental and demonstration areas, of perhaps 5000 acres each, in five or six different districts. One main object of this policy is to encourage private landowners to take up timber cultivation. Secondly, they propose, wherever possible, to make loans to local authorities already possessing suitable land, thereby economising the Fund and avoiding the financial strain of purchasing or leasing all land afforested. The Government Department concerned has already put before them proposals leading up to the first of these two measures; the steps taken on the second line of action are explained immediately below.

(ii.) *Afforestation by Local Authorities.*

During the early part of 1912 the Commissioners gave considerable attention to this subject. The obvious financial and economic advantages of promoting afforestation by local authorities have already been mentioned, and it is unnecessary to make more than a brief reference to the incidental benefits, such as greater purity of water supply and possible provision for periods of unemployment. After obtaining reports on several of the largest of the water-gathering grounds of the country and discussing the whole question with representatives of the Board of Agriculture and Fisheries, the Commissioners issued in July 1912 the following statement:—

"The Development Commissioners, who for some time past have been in communication with the Government Departments concerned in regard to schemes of afforestation of a national character, have meanwhile drawn up the following statement for the guidance of local authorities who may contemplate applying for State-aid in carrying out schemes of afforestation on areas under their control :—

" 1. The Development Commissioners will be prepared, pending the completion of any general schemes for this purpose by the English Board of Agriculture and Fisheries and by the Departments of Agriculture in Scotland and Ireland, to consider applications, which in the first instance need not be in great detail, from local authorities or other responsible bodies for assistance in the afforestation of water-catchment areas or other suitable areas under their control, with a view to ascertaining whether the schemes put forward are of public utility and likely to prove remunerative either directly or indirectly.

" 2. The Commissioners consider it is important that such afforestation schemes as may be brought to their notice should be inquired into without delay in order to ascertain, by means of a flying survey, whether the above-mentioned conditions are likely to be fulfilled. They consider that any detailed scheme following thereon should provide, with due regard to economy and efficiency, for varying the extent of the operations prescribed from year to year, and that such variation should be governed by the effect of the afforestation works on employment, and should be arranged in relation to the state of the labour market and to the aggregate demand for labour in the United Kingdom as reflected in the Board of Trade's index number of unemployment or otherwise.

" 3. Provided that approved schemes for afforestation are carried out in accordance with expert advice, and that the work is open at all times for inspection and the areas made available if required for purposes of education, research, and demonstration, the Development Commissioners are prepared to recommend loans on the general principle that repayment commences so soon as the work becomes remunerative or at some date to be fixed in reference to the method of afforestation to be followed in any particular case."

The publication of this statement has produced communications from several of the great municipalities, including Birmingham, Cardiff, Leeds, Liverpool, and Manchester, and negotiations with some of these authorities are now being conducted with a view to the framing of schemes of afforestation. Various difficulties have to be overcome before the schemes presented can become effective. In many cases the drawbacks of high elevation and poverty of soil are such that, in parts at least of the area, commercial forestry is almost hopeless: in other cases financial conditions, such as the loss of present rentals and reluctance to provide a share of expenditure without return over a long period, hamper the settlement of terms of loan. The Commissioners are in general prepared, if satisfied as to the suitability of a water-catchment area for economic afforestation, either to recommend the Treasury to assist a water authority in carrying out a practical scheme for this purpose by a loan from the Development Fund at 3 per cent. compound interest—the loan not to exceed £5 per acre afforested, and to be repaid with accumulated interest from the proceeds of the sale of timber grown on the lands afforested by means of the loan; or in the alternative to agree to a profit-sharing arrangement by which in return for loans at the rate of £5 per acre the Development Fund would receive a proportion of the price of the produce utilised or sold from the area afforested by means of such advances.

This latter basis of agreement has been preferred by the Liverpool City Council, with whom negotiations are furthest advanced. The City Council was informed in February that the Commissioners were prepared to recommend for the afforestation of, say, 5000 acres of the Corporation's water-catchment area at Lake Vyrnwy, in Montgomeryshire, advances at the rate of £5 per acre up to a limit of £25,000, provided that the Corporation would enter into an arrangement for the payment to the Development Fund of the price of one-half of the ultimate timber yield. The Waterworks Committee of the Liverpool City Council have accepted this proposal in principle, and have given instructions for the preparation of a detailed scheme.

Among other schemes, the Commissioners may mention in particular the application of the Torquay Town Council, on which they have agreed to approve a scheme that would ultimately provide for the planting of about 10,000 acres of Dartmoor; a proposal of the Bolton Town Council to afforest 6000 acres on their catchment areas at Belmont and Entwistle; and a proposal to afforest parts of the Dundee area at Lintrathen in Forfarshire, which has been inspected by representatives of the Commissioners and reported as suitable for the purpose. The Belfast water-catchment area has also been inspected by representatives of the Commission. A small loan has been made to the Edinburgh and District Water Trust for the experimental planting of about thirty acres on the Edinburgh water-gathering grounds in Peeblesshire; if the experiment is successful, it will promote the ultimate afforestation of considerable portions of the area.

The main conditions which the Commissioners think ought to accompany any advance to a local authority for the purpose of afforesting water-catchment areas, whether by means of loan or under a profit-sharing scheme, are as follows :—

(1) The local authority shall cause to be prepared a working-plan regulating the operations proposed in detail. The plan shall be submitted for approval to the Development Commissioners and the Government Department concerned (for England and Wales, the Board of Agriculture and Fisheries; for Scotland, the Board of Agriculture for Scotland; and for Ireland, the Department of Agriculture and Technical Instruction), who may require such modifications as seem to them desirable. No departure from its provisions after a working-plan is sanctioned shall be allowed without the approval of the Commissioners and the Government Department concerned.

(2) The working-plan shall provide, with due regard to economy and efficiency, for possible variations in the extent of the operations prescribed from year to year. In availing itself of such variations, the local authority shall be governed by the effect of the afforestation works on employment, and shall arrange the variations in relation to the state of the labour market and to the aggregate demand for labour in the United Kingdom, as reflected in the Board of Trade's index number of unemployment, or otherwise.

(3) The local authority shall keep such accounts of the expenditure on and revenue from the area as the Treasury or the Government Department concerned may require.

(4) If required by the Treasury, the Commissioners, or the Government Department concerned, the area shall be made available for purposes of research, education, and demonstration.

(5) The accounts, and the planting and other operations carried out on the area, shall be open at all times to inspection by representatives of the Commissioners or of the Government Department concerned.

(iii.) *England and Wales.*

A grant of £5700 was made to the Board of Agriculture and Fisheries for the financial year ending 31st March 1913, to enable the Department to continue forestry work inaugurated by means of the Development Fund in the previous year.

Of the total sum, £2500 goes to provide for the salaries and travelling expenses of an advisory officer at each of five centres—Oxford, Cambridge, Cirencester, Bangor, and Newcastle; £500 is granted to Oxford, £500 to Cambridge, and £200 to other institutions for research; £1000 is spent on minor forestry experiments conducted by means of sample plots, vested in and under the control of the five institutions which are the centres of educational and advisory work; and £1000 is required for administrative expenses. Pending the establishment of a central demonstration area, which will of course involve some reconsideration of the whole question of forestry education and research, the arrangements outlined above will perhaps be sufficient to meet immediate needs.

In January the Commissioners received the first reports of the Forestry Advisory Committee of the Board of Agriculture and Fisheries, together with an' application for an advance to give effect to the Committee's recommendation of a preliminary survey with a view to the creation of six or seven experimental forests of some 5000 acres. The Commissioners are willing to accept the proposal to acquire land for the formation of these forests; and at the end of the year were discussing with the Board the practical steps to be taken for the purpose. They had not received any application from the Board to give effect to the other recommendations of the Committee, viz., those relating to the utilisation of the Forest of Dean and adjoining woodlands as a central demonstration area, and to the provision or improvement of technical training for woodmen. Application will presumably be made as soon as the Board have reached a decision on these proposals.

Apart from the schemes submitted by the Board, several local authorities and teaching centres have applied for assistance to promote forestry instruction and research.

A grant of £2500 has been made to the University of Cambridge in aid of the erection and equipment of the Eastern portion of the School of Forestry, and the Commissioners will be prepared at a future date to recommend a further grant of £2000 if the accommodation provided by that part of the School becomes insufficient. A grant of £1000 has been made for a research laboratory at the Oxford School of Forestry; and a small grant of £85 (in addition to £200 previously sanctioned) for the completion of the forestry museum and lecture room in Chopwell Woods, used by the students of Armstrong College, Newcastle-on-Tyne.

For various reasons (generally because the objects of the scheme were already met so far as possible by previous grants from the Development Fund), the Commissioners have been unable to support applications from the University of Oxford, for a grant of £13,400 for research experiments, and advisory work; from the Town Council of Huddersfield, for £300 per annum to carry out a botanical survey of Yorkshire, which was represented to be a necessary preliminary to any large scheme of afforestation in the county; and from the University College of North Wales, Bangor, for a sum not stated in aid of instruction and research.

Besides applications for educational and research work in forestry, the Commissioners received during the year one or two applications for aid in the general work of afforestation.

To assist in its work of reclaiming and planting pit-mounds in the Black Country, the Midland Re-afforesting Association applied for a capital grant of £1947, and an annual maintenance grant of £30. The application was supported by a memorial from the Council of the Borough of Walsall. While sympathising with the Association's objects, the Commissioners could not see their way to depart from their policy of aiding only those schemes that promise to make for commercial forestry, and thus to develop the industry on business lines. They understand that the Association has undertaken to prepare a revised scheme in which closer attention will be given to the financial principles of commercial forestry. Meanwhile they have concurred in the proposal of the Board of Agriculture and Fisheries that, out of the £1000 a year received by the Board from the Development Fund for purposes of minor forestry experiments, a grant of £100 should be made to the Association. This grant will be utilised to place and maintain in order one of the most promising of the Association's existing plantations, with the object of ultimately obtaining experimental data which will be of use in considering any future schemes of afforestation in the Black Country.

Aid was also sought for two small schemes of afforestation submitted simultaneously by the Carnarvonshire County Council. The County Council desired a grant of £2830 for the purpose, under one scheme, of planting at a cost of £9, 4s. 10d. per acre some 260 acres on their recently acquired Madryn Castle Estate, and, under the second scheme, of felling and re-planting on the same estate some 55 acres at a cost of £7, 18s. 5d. per acre. As the Commissioners regard £5 per acre as a sufficient sum for planting, and are not prepared, save in exceptional cases, to recommend advances to local authorities at a higher rate, they were forced to the conclusion that the Carnarvonshire estimates, taken in conjunction with the limited area of land available for afforestation, would be prohibitive for purposes of commercial forestry.

(iv.) *Scotland.*

In September the Commissioners' Forestry Committee discussed forestry work in Scotland with some representatives of the Scotch Board of Agriculture. No application or scheme has yet been received from the Scottish authorities for the establishment of a central demonstration area in Scotland ; and the Commissioners understand that the whole question is still being considered by the Scotch Board of Agriculture.

They have intimated that, subject to the adjustment of the financial questions concerned with the Agriculture (Scotland) Fund, they will take a favourable view of an application for a grant towards the cost and equipment of an estate so far as relates to the educational and advisory functions of the proposed demonstration area, and for a loan, repayable on a terminable annuity basis, towards the cost of the estate so far as relates to its economic purposes.

The Secretary of the Royal Scottish Arboricultural Society forwarded in November a copy of a draft Memorandum and Articles of Association of an Afforestation and Development Trust, which contemplated the formation of a non-trading association with a view to assisting private landowners to afforest their estates by means of loans from the Development Fund. A decision on this proposal, which raises some important and difficult questions, was deferred until the Commissioners had consulted with the Scotch Board of Agriculture. The views of the Board have not yet been received.

An application from the Board of Agriculture for Scotland for a grant for the appointment of forestry survey and research officers was under consideration at the close of the period to which this Report relates.

(v.) *Ireland.*

In continuance of their policy of aiding afforestation in Ireland, the Commissioners during the year approved for purchase, as suitable for planting, five further areas to which their attention had been drawn by the Department of Agriculture and Technical Instruction. Together they comprise about 7000 acres, and bring up to 14,000 acres the amount of land which the Irish Department have been authorised to purchase if possible out of the advance of £25,000 or £30,000 already approved.

Certain difficulties of administration arose in connection with one of the areas approved for purchase. It adjoins existing woods acquired by the Department by means of the annual vote of £6000 borne on the Parliamentary Estimates to enable the Department to acquire the wooded residue of estates left on the hands of the Estates Commissioners of the Irish Land Commission. While the Development Commissioners thought it desirable that the two areas should be worked as one centre and by the same staff, they feared that in practice it might be found difficult to apportion the relative cost of administration between the Development Fund and the Parliamentary Vote. It seemed not improbable that similar difficulties of administration might arise in connection with other forestry areas in Ireland; and that much future inconvenience might be saved if arrangements for dealing with such cases were settled immediately by a conference of the Departments interested.

A conference was accordingly arranged, and took place on the 27th November, between representatives of the Department of Agriculture and Technical Instruction for Ireland, the Estates Commissioners of the Irish Land Commission, and the Development Commissioners. In the result the Development Commissioners agreed to defray from the Development Fund the whole cost of administration of forestry centres, whether acquired by means of the Fund or from the Parliamentary Votes.

The conference also considered the case of the smaller wooded plantations left on the hands of the Estates Commissioners, which the Irish Department are not disposed to purchase, on the ground that they are too small for purposes of commercial forestry. It was agreed that a scheme should be prepared jointly by the Department and the Estates Commissioners with a view to such woodlands being acquired by the County Councils concerned, on the understanding that the Development Commissioners, in accordance with a promise already given by them to the Irish Department, would be prepared to consider the question of recommending grants for maintenance.

The following month the first application arising out of the conference reached the Commissioners. It referred to the Baunreagh area of about 2000 acres on the Slievebloom range, which adjoins another area already acquired out of the Development Fund. The Commissioners recommended that the Department should be authorised to expend, out of the advance of £25,000 sanctioned in November 1910 for the acquisition of afforestable areas, the sum of £4111, 7s. in order to redeem the annuity now payable to the Irish Land Commission in respect to the Baunreagh area. They suggested at the same time that the Irish Department should be requested to utilise the amount thus set free from the Parliamentary Vote in the acquisition from the Estates Commissioners of such small isolated woodlands as it may be desirable to maintain, although they may not be adaptable to the purposes of commercial forestry.

One of the conditions attaching to the grants for the purchase of afforestable land in Ireland is that a working-plan shall be prepared for each area, prescribing for its treatment over the whole period necessary for its development, and shall be submitted for the consideration of the Commissioners at the time when application is made for further funds required for planting. The first working-plan reached the Commissioners in January, and related to the Ballyhoura area, in County Cork. The

Commissioners were doubtful whether the proposals embodied in it would eventually make for commercial forestry, and in view of the large sums involved in afforesting the lands already approved for purchase in Ireland, they felt it incumbent on them to propose a standard of management for this first scheme submitted, such as would form a basis for all future working-plans, and ensure a profitable return on the outlay. The principle adopted by the Commissioners is that to ensure remunerative forestry in Ireland the cost of afforestation, including the purchase of land, ought not to exceed an average sum of £12 per acre. At the end of the period covered by this Report, communications were proceeding with the Department.

In order to enable the Irish Department to cope with the additional work entailed by the various afforestation schemes supported out of the Development Fund, the Commissioners have recommended an advance of £1690, to meet during the forthcoming year the salaries and expenses of the central staff engaged by the Department on such schemes. The constitution and salaries of the staff were approved in the previous year.

In reply to an inquiry from the Irish Department whether they would be precluded from concluding negotiations for the acquisition of lands in cases where the mining rights are reserved from the sale, the Commissioners stated that they would be prepared to approve the purchase of such lands for tree-planting, provided that conditions are imposed securing to the Development Fund compensation sufficient to cover possible damage to land and timber.

The Treasury have directed, under section 2 (1) (c) of the Development and Road Improvement Funds Act, 1909, that all receipts arising out of forest lands purchased by means of the grant from the Development Fund shall be paid to the Treasury for the credit of the Fund.

FINANCE OF THE DEVELOPMENT FUND.

Last year the Commissioners explained their general view on the subject, viz., that where there are in existence separate public funds which can be applied within one part of the United Kingdom to some at least of the purposes to which the Development Fund is applicable, those separate funds should be exhausted before a demand is made on a fund common to the whole United Kingdom, and wider in its scope than the income of any single Department.

The practical point at issue was the question how far advances should be made for the present from the Development Fund to assist in Scotland schemes for purposes (such as forestry, agricultural research, and agricultural instruction) to which can be applied the newly established Agriculture (Scotland) Fund, with an income of some £200,000 a year. As a matter of general principle the Commissioners were of opinion that the demands of Scotch agriculture and forestry should be met from the Scotch Fund so far as possible, before recourse is had to the Development Fund; but recognising that the primary object of the Scotch Fund is the encouragement of small holdings, they have agreed that expenditure for that purpose may properly be regarded as having priority over the other purposes to which the Fund can be applied.

It is however at present a matter largely of estimates, and therefore of some uncertainty, what amount will be spent for land settlement in Scotland; and it has accordingly been arranged, with Treasury approval, that such schemes as the provision of new buildings and farms for the agricultural colleges, extension work at the colleges, and live stock improvement shall continue to be assisted from the Development Fund, and that about the end of the financial year 1915-16 (by which time there will be actual experience of the real demands on the Scotch Fund for land settlement) the Treasury shall decide whether such advances are to be regarded as grants or loans.

This arrangement does not cover advances for forestry purposes. The question of the terms' on which the Development Fund should provide money for these purposes will require to be settled separately on each application.

Forestry and Afforestation.—The requirements for this purpose are difficult to estimate, apart from the renewal of the annual grants of £5700 per annum for education, the provision of technical advice, and research. Considerable schemes are known to be now before the Government Departments concerned, but have not yet reached the Commissioners. They see no present reason to depart from their former estimate, that probably £350,000 will cover all the expenditure which can profitably be incurred by 1916. If it is found possible to obtain a suitable demonstration area or areas without purchase, the greater part of this sum will be available as a reserve to provide loans to local authorities for afforesting watershed areas under their control. The actual issue of any such loans will be spread over some 20 or 30 years, but it will obviously be necessary in such cases to earmark at once a sum sufficient to provide any funds which the Treasury on the Commissioners' recommendation may undertake to lend.

APPLICATIONS OFFICIALLY RECEIVED BY THE DEVELOPMENT
COMMISSIONERS DURING THE YEAR ENDED 31ST MARCH 1913.

Forestry.

Armstrong College (Newcastle-upon-Tyne).

Applied for: £85 to supplement a grant of £200 previously
recommended. In aid of the erection of a forestry
building in Chopwell Woods.

Position on 31st March 1913.—Additional grant of £85
recommended.

Board of Agriculture and Fisheries.

(1) Applied for: £5700 for the year 1912-13. In aid of forestry
research, advisory work, etc., in England and Wales.

Position on 31st March 1913.—Grant of £5700 recommended.

(2) Applied for: £5850 for the year 1913-14. In aid of the
development of forestry in England and Wales.

Position on 31st March 1913.—Under consideration.

Board of Agriculture for Scotland.

Applied for: £7500 spread over three years. In aid of the
appointment of forestry, survey and research officers
in Scotland.

Position on 31st March 1913.—Under consideration.

Cambridge University.

Applied for: £6000 capital, and £1900 per annum.
Amended application £2500. In aid of the erection
and equipment of the new University School of
Forestry.

Position on 31st March 1913.—Grant of £2500 recommended.

Department of Agriculture and Technical Instruction for Ireland.

Applied for: £6090 for the year 1913-14. In aid of (i.)
the working of three forest areas; and (ii.) payment
of central staff in connection with afforestation work.

Position on 31st March 1913 —Grant of £1690 recommended
in respect of (ii.). Decision deferred in respect of (i.).

Edinburgh and District Water Trustees.

Applied for: Not stated. In aid of experimental planting
on the catchment-area of the Talla water reservoir.

Position on 31st March 1913.—Under consideration.

Glasgow Distress Committee.

Applied for: £640. In aid of afforestation work at Palace-rigg.

Position on 31st March 1913.—Under consideration.

Huddersfield County Borough Council.

Applied for: £300 per annum. In aid of the extension of the botanical survey of Yorkshire now being done by the Biological Department of the Huddersfield Technical College.

Position on 31st March 1913.—Advance not recommended.

Midland Re-afforesting Association.

Applied for: Capital grant £1947, and annual grant of £30 for maintenance. In aid of afforestation works at Moseley, near Wolverhampton, and at Bentley Hall, near Walsall.

Position on 31st March 1913.—The Board of Agriculture and Fisheries propose to make a grant of £100 out of an advance recommended to them from the Development Fund for minor forestry experiments.

Oxford University.

(1) Applied for: £11,000 capital, and £2400 per annum. In aid of the University School of Forestry.

Position on 31st March 1913.—Advance not recommended.

(2) Applied for: £1000. In aid of a research laboratory at the University School of Forestry.

Position on 31st March 1913.—Grant of £1000 recommended.

APPLICATIONS OFFICIALLY RECEIVED BY THE DEVELOPMENT COMMISSIONERS PRIOR TO THE 1ST APRIL 1912 ON WHICH REPORTS WERE MADE TO THE TREASURY DURING THE YEAR ENDED 31ST MARCH 1913.

Forestry.

Armstrong College, Newcastle-on-Tyne.

Amount applied for: Not stated. In aid of the extension of the work of the Forestry Department of the College.

Position on 31st March 1913.—Grant of £200 recommended for new building in Chopwell Woods, to serve for purposes of a forestry museum and of forestry instruction.

Carnarvonshire County Council.

Applied for : £2830. In aid of the development of forestry on the Madryn Estate.

Position on 31st March 1913.—Advance not recommended.

Department of Agriculture and Technical Instruction for Ireland.

Amount applied for : Total sum not stated. In aid of expenses of additional forestry staff.

Position on 31st March 1913.—Grant recommended.

University College of North Wales, Bangor.

Amount applied for : Total sum not stated. In aid of the development of the work of the Forestry Department of the College.

Position on 31st March 1913.—Advance not recommended ; objects sufficiently met by the general scheme of the Board of Agriculture and Fisheries.

SCHEDULE OF GRANTS AND LOANS ACTUALLY RECOMMENDED TO THE TREASURY DURING THE YEAR ENDED THE 31ST MARCH 1913.

Forestry.

ARMSTRONG COLLEGE, NEWCASTLE-UPON-TYNE :	Grant
Erection of a forestry building in Chopwell Woods	£285
BOARD OF AGRICULTURE AND FISHERIES :	
Forestry in England and Wales .	£5700
CAMBRIDGE UNIVERSITY :	
School of Forestry at the University . .	£2500
DEPARTMENT OF AGRICULTURE AND TECHNICAL IN-STRUCTION FOR IRELAND :	
Forestry in Ireland . .	£1690
OXFORD UNIVERSITY :	
Research Laboratory at the Oxford School of Forestry	£1000
	£11,175

3. The State Forests of Saxony.

(*With Illustrations.*)

(*Continued from Vol. XXVII., p.* 187.)

By A. D. HOPKINSON.

Rotation.—Eighty years is about the average rotation for spruce in Saxony, but no hard and fast regulations are laid down that as soon as a wood reaches that age it must be cut and not before. Many considerations affect the age at which "stands" are cut, and tend to make it vary from the normal. Two of the chief of these are the production and maintenance of normal age-classes, and the uniformity of the "Cutting Series." If, for instance, a "stand" rather under the normal age comes in the middle of a cutting series, then it is generally cut in order that the regularity of the series may not be broken (see Fig. 3). The average rotation, eighty years, is the average economic rotation, and is obtained by calculating several soil expectation values for different rotations, and taking the maximum as being the most advantageous financial rotation. To obtain the necessary data accurately for working out the soil expectation values, a number of investigations were carried out to find both mass and worth increments in typical woods.

Regulation of Yield.—This subject takes us back to the days of Cotta, if we are to understand how the somewhat complex method at present in operation in Saxony arose. Cotta was a strong supporter of the "*Flächenfachwerk*" system, or system of determination of yield by area, whereas G. L. Hartig, his famous contemporary, strove energetically to introduce in Prussia the more complicated "*Massenfachwerk*," or system of determination of yield by volume. Neither of these have survived in their original forms, although the former has a much greater bearing on modern management than the latter. Latterly Cotta changed his views somewhat, and became a supporter of the system of determination of yield by combined area and volume, but area played always the more important part in his calculations, and the simple formula $a = \dfrac{A}{R}$ (where $a =$ annual area cut, $A =$ total area, and $R =$ rotation in years) remained the basis of his determination. Complicated inquiries into normal and actual increments were not at that time undertaken, and these factors played but a small part in the question of yield. Much more attention was paid to the actual condition of "stands" coming in the IV., V. and VI. age-classes, and these were carefully examined to ascertain whether forest per cent.[1] was up to standard.

Thus during the last eighty or ninety years a system has arisen called the "*Bestandswirtschaft*," founded upon the principle of a thorough examination of all the oldest "stands" (*Bestände*) in the forest, and the determination of how much can be cut without disturbing the age-classes if they are nearly normal, and if they are not so what rate of felling in the near future will bring them as near normal as possible. General rules as to what must be cut in the next period of ten years are given to form a basis upon which the forester can build his calculations. They instruct that the following areas are to be chosen in preference to others :—

I. Silvicultural necessities, *i.e.* all areas such as severances which are required to shorten "Cutting Series" and allow the formation of wind-proof edges, and so on.

II. All mature areas that show a lower "forest per cent." (*Weiserprozent*) than that laid down as the standard, in so far as it is possible to cut them without interfering with the normal course of "Cutting Series," or causing danger from wind by removing one "stand" sheltering another.

III. All areas which, although not mature, must be cut in order to meet the requirements of the "Cutting Series."

Thus if a 60-year-old "stand" of spruce was found closed in by a 120-year-old "stand" which it was decided to cut, the younger stand would be also felled for the sake of a regular cutting series in future. Although area is made the basis of yield calculations yet volume is not altogether neglected, and in every revision a forecast is made of the total amount of each class of wood (timber, faggots, etc.) which will be produced by the areas it has been decided to cut, and in determining the extent of the areas the quality of the locality and consequently the yield per acre is taken into account and allowed to exert its modifying influence.

[1] Schlich's *Manual of Forestry*, vol. iii. p. 187.

The work of determining the yield for the next decennial period is undertaken by the officers of the *Forsteinrichtungs-anstalt* in conjuction with the *Forstmeister* of the *Revier*. As a rule actual measurements are not made, the expected yield being estimated by the present volume of each "*Bestand*" as taken from the Saxon yield-tables multiplied by the "Quality of the Growing Stock,"[1] or the "*Vollertragsfaktor*," with the addition of the increments which will accrue in five years, this period being taken so as to obtain an average for the whole ten years, the exact position of each year's felling having not yet been decided upon. The very great uniformity of the spruce woods in Saxony, together with the accurate records that are kept of all fellings, make the work of estimation comparatively light. Very often, for instance, when cutting through a uniform block, the yield of the last felling, together with the estimated sum of the annual increments for the last eight or ten years, or whatever period will have elapsed since the date of the last cutting, is taken as the expected yield without further trouble. Although this system of estimating in almost every case, and doing away with actual calliper work, is criticised as being somewhat lacking in scientific exactitude, those who understand the peculiar conditions in Saxony, *i.e.* the great uniformity of the woods, the exact record of past yields, and the existence of permanent forest management officers who give their whole time to the work, recognise that it is the best and most economical method that could be devised.

The yield-tables just referred to are published by the Saxon Forest Service as a *Bonitierungs Tafel*, but are merely very simple yield-tables for spruce, silver fir, Scots pine, larch, beech, oak, alder and birch, giving nothing but the volumes produced by the different species on the five soil classes. They are used for calculating the "Growing Stock" or *Wirkliche Holzvorrat* in the decennial revision of the working-plans for all woods under forty years of age, those over that age are estimated in the manner to which allusion has already been made.

The *Forsteinrichtungsanstalt* also fix very arbitrarily the quality of the locality (*Standortsgüte*), this being also done alone by the estimation of its officers, and not according to the common practice by the average total height of the trees. The result of this method has been that, in order to avoid the

[1] Schlich's *Manual of Forestry*, vol. iii. p. 268.

risk of making the mean quality too high or too low, a great deal of the land is put into II. and III. which should be in I., IV. and V.

Of the maps used in connection with the working-plans the sub-compartment map (*Bestandeskarte*) is the most important. Its scale is 1 : 20,000, and each species occurring pure is represented by a different colour. Age-classes are shown by different shades of the same colour, the lightest being the youngest woods. Spruce is coloured black, and most of the Saxon maps appear chiefly composed of black in different degrees of density. The quality of the soil is indicated by a small number placed to the right of the sub-compartment letter; if lower than this it indicates that the age of the wood is in the first half of the age-class to which it belongs, and if higher that the wood in question belongs to the latter half of the age-class. Thus the age of any sub-compartment may be ascertained from the map to within ten years. This map is renewed for each revision of the working-plan, that is every ten years.

Finance, Accounts, etc.—A perusal of the summary of the annual accounts which appear in two parts[1] every year in the *Tharandter Forstliches Jahrbuch* gives a good idea of the thorough manner with which these are kept. Although to reproduce these here in full would serve no purpose, a few extracts may be of interest.

The exact area of the State forests for the end of the silvicultural year 1910-1911 was 445,380 acres, of which 426,722 acres were productive (actually producing timber— *Holzboden*) and 18,658 acres were non-productive (*Nichtholzboden*). There was during the year 29,559,000 cubic feet of wood over 7 cm. (2·7 ins.) at the smaller end (*Derbholz*) cut, being 68 cubic feet per productive acre, 85 per cent. of which was timber (*Nutzholz*) and the remainder firewood.

In addition 4,728,000 cubic feet of wood under 7 cm. at larger end (*Reissig*) was sold, of which 4,297,000 was firewood (*Brennreissig*) and the rest used for other purposes (*Nutzreissig*). Also 6,048,000 stacked cubic feet of root wood was sold.

The following mean prices of wood over 7 cm. at smaller

---

[1] "*Mitteilungen über die Ergebnisse der Kgl. Sächs. Staatsforstverwaltung*" and "*Die Reinertragsübersichten der Kgl. Sächs. Staatsforsten.*"

end show how the price of wood, especially that of "timber" is rising in Saxony.

1906	.	.	.	5·1d. per cubic feet.
1907	.	.	.	5·8d. ,, ,,
1908	.	.	.	6·1d. ,, ,,
1909	.	.	.	6·1d. ,, ,,
1910	.	.	.	6·2d. ,, ,,
1911	.	.	.	6·3d. ,, ,,

The total gross income was £829,378, or £1, 16s. 9d. per acre for the whole of the woodlands. The total expenses, including £7815 for the *Forsteinrichtungsanstalt,* amounted to £333,216, or 40 per cent. of the total income, which equals 14s. 9d. per acre. The expenses were made up of the following items :—

	£	£
Pay	86,791	
Lodging and other allowances . . .	11,804	
Buildings and repairs	10,635	
Sundry management costs . . .	36,769	
Total cost of management and administration (= 43·8 per cent. of total expenses and equals 6s. 6d. per acre of total area).	———	145,999
Planting, sowing, etc. (= 1s. per acre, net productive area).	21,397	
Care of young plantations (= 1·2d. per acre, net area).	2,194	
Repairing river banks, drainage, etc. (*Wasserbau*) (= 1·4d. per acre, net area).	2,583	
Road and bridge-making (= 1s. 8d. per acre, net area).	35,851	
Expenses on meadows within forests .	103	
Total cost of maintenance (= 19·1 per cent. of total expenses).	———	62,128
Research work	1,044	
Preparation of forest products for market felling, etc., of which £108,945 was for wood over 7 cm. (= ·883d. per cubic feet).	109,003	
Other working costs	15,042	
Total working costs (= 38 per cent. of total expenses).	———	125,089
Total expenses .		£333,216

besides which £8035 was paid for insurance of woodmen.

The total net income amounted to £496,162, or £1, 2s. 0d. per acre for the total area. The average net returns per acre for the previous five years were—

				£	s.	d.
1906	.	.	.	0	19	7
1907	.	.	.	1	3	11
1908	.	.	.	1	2	4
1909	.	.	.	1	0	5
1910	.	.	.	1	0	10

The most notable feature of these figures is the amount spent on roads and bridges, which, when it is considered that the Saxon State forests have been under good management for nearly a century, and consequently have always had a fair sum expended on transport facilities, must appear to many a very large sum. It shows very clearly, however, the very great importance of good roads or other means of transport if the greatest financial return is to be reaped. The net return of £1, 2s. per acre is also a very high figure when one considers the poor quality of the land from which the income is obtained—land which would probably not on the average let at more than a few shillings per acre for grazing purposes.

The summary of the net returns of the Saxon State forests for 1910 was published in 1912, and is of the usual detailed character, being divided into twenty columns with a line for each range (*Revier*). Each district is taken separately, and the sum of the figures for all the forest in the district is placed against the name of the district at the end of the list of component forests.

Taking one average range and one average district together with the totals for Saxony, an idea may be obtained as to what figures are given and as to their relative proportions. The forest of Grillenburg is familiar to most who have visited the woods of Saxony and may be fairly taken as an average, while that cannot be said of the Tharandt *Revier* which, although much better known, is by no means representative, on account of the fact that its expenses are materially increased in order to maintain and increase its unique educative value. The spruce forests of the Erzgebirge are characteristically represented in the district of Schwarzenburg, and this gives the results of practically pure spruce culture.

1	2	3	4	5	6	7	8	9	10
FOREST	Net wooded area	Normal annual yield of wood over 7 cm. at smaller end	Normal annual yield of "Timber," (i.e. Col. 3 less firewood)	Actual yield of wood over 7 cm. at smaller end	Actual yield of "Timber"	Per cent. of "Timber" in wood over 7 cm. at smaller end	Gross returns for wood	Gross returns for bye-products	Total gross returns
	Acres	Cub. ft.	Cub. ft.	Cub. ft.	Cub. ft.		£	£	£
Grillenburg .	3,974	296,520	247,100	313,428	276,610	88	8,095	14	8,10
Schwarzenburg (district) .	47,520	3,822,990	3,297,020 =86 %	3,689,061	3,297,443	89	111,330	115	111,44.
Saxon State Forests .	426,105	30,893,854	24,590,565 =80 %	30,533,264	25,668,712	84	784,863	5,890	790,75.

11	12	13	14	15	16	17	18	19	20
FOREST	Woodmen's Wages for felling, etc.	Planting, etc.	Other Working Expenses	Administration and Management	Total Expenses	Net Return	Net Return per acre	Net Return per cub. ft.	Forest Capital	Rate of Interest
£	£	£	£	£	£	£ s. d.	D.	£	%
Grillenburg .	964	674	218	1,092	2,948	5,161	1 6 3	3·9	250,330	2·0
Schwarzenburg (district) .	15,772	7,046	1,451	12,705	36,974	74,471	1 11 8	3·3	2,752,020	2·7
Saxon State Forests .	115,815	61,676	22,866	127,512	327,869	462,885	1 1 9	3·6	21,169,965	2·1

The most interesting of these figures are those which refer to the annual net income per acre and the interest upon capital. The return of £1, 1s. 9d. per acre appears at first sight a very high rent to receive for such poor land—too poor mostly for agricultural crops of any sort,—but it must be understood that only a small portion of this (about a quarter) is received as rent for the land pure and simple, the greater part of it being interest on the capital value of the growing stock upon the land. The average total capital per acre is £47, 6s., of which £11, 16s. 6d., or one quarter, may be taken as the land capital, and the remainder, £35, 9s. 6d., may be regarded as the capital value of the growing stock on the average, which gives 5s. 5¾d. as rent for the land, and 16s. 3¼d. as interest on growing stock capital. Thus the land capital is to the growing stock capital as 1 : 3, which is the normal proportions of these two for the Saxon State forests; but it is to be noticed that the proportions of these two forms of capital vary very considerably in other parts of Germany, many circumstances having a modifying influence. Variation in length of rotation and in the species has a very marked effect on the proportions of the two component parts of forest capital, and in a country such as Prussia, where Scots pine is grown on a long rotation, the proportion of the growing stock capital to the land or soil capital would probably very much exceed 3 : 1, although no figures are available. This proportion is, however, a very good guide for a conifer forest grown upon an economic rotation.

Although the interest, 2·19 %, is low it must be taken into consideration that the investment is exceedingly secure as long as the management remains in the hands of capable men, as there is every reason to suppose it will. Calamities of varying nature have from time to time threatened the Saxon State forests, but never has anything very serious befallen them. Wind storms, which used to be the much feared danger, are no longer regarded with such apprehension, owing to the methods which have been adopted so successfully to mitigate their effects. Large areas of pure conifer woods are, it is true, favourable to pests, but, again, the thorough mixing of the age classes within the forest has done much to prevent any pests becoming very destructive. But it will be pointed out that if three-quarters of the total capital, *i.e.*, that portion which represents the growing stock, were invested in an equally good security at 3½ %, which would be quite possible at present, it would bring in a greater annual return than is now being got from the whole capital locked up in the forests. Surely, then, it would appear wise, from a financial point of view alone, to clear the woods and reinvest the money at 3½ %, because then, even if the land fetched nothing when sold, the State would stand to gain. Such a line of argument is sometimes pursued by those whose object is to decry the financial aspect of forestry under the most favourable conditions, such as we see it in Saxony. The hypothesis upon which such an argument is based is, however, quite false in that the selling value and the expectation value of the woods only coincide in one particular case, and that is just when they are ready for the axe. Thus, supposing the age classes to be normal and the rotation one of eighty years, only one-eightieth of the woods could be sold at their silvicultural value, and it is, of course, the silvicultural value and not the value to the wood merchant which is put upon the growing stock. Thus we come to see that in forestry the growing stock capital and the land capital can only be separated in theory and not in practice. There are in addition many very important national economic reasons why this unconvertible capital, even with its low rate of interest, should not in any way be interfered with. The very existence of Saxony without her forests and her wood-utilizing industries is unthinkable.

This brings us to the vexed question of what is the correct amount of growing stock capital to invest in forest land in order to obtain the most desirable results. It is, perhaps, not so much a matter of the actual amount of capital which should be locked up in woods in order to produce the best financial returns, as this is capable of being worked out by calculation, but rather what is the object of forestry. Is forest land to be regarded, for example, as a mine which requires a certain amount of capital to develop it, and in which no more capital is invested than is consistent with its most economic development? or is it to be regarded as some auriferous reef the last ounce of which is to be exploited regardless of the capital outlay entailed? This comparison represents roughly the difference in the fundamental idea as to what is the object of forestry as understood by the Saxon and Prussian States respectively. The Saxon forester looks upon his forest land as a commercial concern and argues how is it possible to get the greatest return from the land together with a reasonable interest on the money it will require for its proper development, i.e. the growing stock capital. He wishes, in fact, to discover exactly what capital per acre is required to give the highest rate of interest on the combined capital of land and stock, and takes every means in his power consistent with good silviculture to reduce the stock capital (the land capital being fixed) in order that the rate of interest may reach a maximum. In other words, he manages his woods upon a strictly commercial basis. In Prussia, however, the State woods are regarded less as a business concern and more as a philanthropic organisation, the chief object of which is to supply the people with as much as possible of the particular kinds and sizes of timber they require, regardless of the cost of production. The fine old Scots pine forests of East Prussia, worked on a rotation of 120-150 years, the spruce woods of the Harz Mountains with their 100-120 years' rotation, and the many hardwood ranges scattered through Prussia managed on much the same lines, demonstrate clearly that no thought is paid to return on capital. To produce good timber and plenty of it appears to be the axiom of the Prussian forester, and he does not concern himself with soil expectation, or value calculations. The capital value of the Prussian forests is not officially published, but it probably averages considerably higher per acre than that of the Saxon woods in spite of the less intensive form of management, and the rate of interest which is yielded is generally estimated at under a half per cent. Although the Prussian Government will not countenance the open application of the *Bodenreinertrag* theory to their forests, yet there are not signs wanting to show that they are beginning slowly to recognise that their woods are vastly over capitalised, and everywhere there is a tendency to reduce rather than to lengthen the period of rotation. The *Bodenreinertrag*, it may be pointed out, means the net returns on the soil after paying interest on the working capital, whereas the *Waldreinertrag*, which is the foundation of the Prussian theory of forest management, is the return derived from the woods without any regard to the interest it may be capable of paying on the capital invested. The latter line of thought leads, of course, to one consideration only, and that is how large an annual income can be obtained from a forest, and is generally justified by the assertion that land is a monopoly, and therefore it is the duty of every owner, especially a State, to obtain the largest amount of produce possible without regard to the invested capital.

It has been necessary to refer to some other State besides Saxony in order to demonstrate the two chief ideas prevailing on the Continent, as regards this point, and Prussia makes the most convenient comparison, as the two States are directly opposed to each other on this particular question, and what appears to be an endless controversy is carried on in German forestry journals as to which party is right. As far as private landowners are concerned, there is every inducement to follow the Saxon plan and work upon a short rotation combined with heavy thinnings, especially towards the time of clear-felling. The recognition of the influence of thinnings upon soil expectation value and its culmination point has affected the degree of thinning to a marked extent in Saxony, and now considerably more wood is felled in this form than was formerly the case. There is also a silvicultural reason, quite apart from financial consideration, which favours opener woods, and that is the better decomposition of the " raw humus " which is so prevalent in the drier conifer forests of Saxony. It must, however, be understood that what is described in England as an open wood, would be referred to by Continental foresters as land with a few trees scattered over it.

Preponderance of Spruce.—The following list shows approximately the areas of high-forest covered by different species in the Saxon woods as a whole :—

Spruce . . .	518,370	acres.
Scots pine .	234,250	,,
Silver fir .	3,220	,,
Larch .	750	,,
Oak	5,050	,,
Birch, alder, and aspen .	3,600	,,
Beech and other hardwoods .	11,500	,,

These figures show the enormous preponderance of spruce over other species, the area under spruce being greater than under all other species together. It will also be noted here what a very unimportant part larch plays in the woods of Saxony. The reasons for the great predominance of spruce are not difficult to find. The chief one is the financial reason. Spruce undoubtedly gives a far better financial return than any other tree over a very large part of the wooded area, the dry sandy plains of the north forming the area where Scots pine not only grows better, but also, which is quite a different matter, gives a greater monetary yield. *The tree which grows best on a given piece of land is not always the most profitable tree, as the profit depends more upon the relative prices and the relative quantities of timber produced than upon the relative degrees of vitality of the trees concerned.* This is one of the most important lessons which a study of Saxon forestry teaches. In other words, do not plant the tree that grows best simply because it grows best, but plant the tree which will give permanently the greatest financial yield, that is the tree which will give the highest soil expectation value. This principle of economic silviculture we see being carried out all over Saxony, and especially in the Saxon State forests, where practically all (96·4 %) the woods are stocked with conifers, and only 3·6 % remain under hardwoods (2·1 % beech, 0·8 % oak, 0·7 % ash, alder, birch, and hornbeam).

Besides the economic reasons for the large preponderance of spruce over any other tree, there are, of course, the purely silvicultural reasons, which are, in short, the suitability of this species for the climate and soil of a large part of the Erzgebirge district—the most densely wooded part of Saxony. But little attention is now given to the question of hardwoods versus conifers, the latter being so obviously the more profitable in almost every case. The question of spruce versus other conifers, especially Scots pine, is not, however, so readily settled, and there exists at present a considerable divergence of opinion among prominent foresters in Saxony as to how far the cultivation of spruce should be allowed to replace that of pine. A distinct pine region and a distinct spruce region exist, in which there is no room for doubt as to which is the correct species. Between these two areas is a large extent of forest land upon which both spruce and pine will grow fairly well, and it is here that the difficulty arises in deciding which of the two is to be planted when an area has been cut. Practically speaking, everywhere where spruce is cut spruce is planted, and besides that a large extent of land formerly under pine has been converted into spruce wood, according to the government policy of favouring the species which gives the greatest financial return. Not in every case, however, has the conversion been a success with regard either to finance or silviculture, and now some reaction of opinion has set in against it, owing to the very poor results that have often enough been consequent on the introduction of pure spruce on dry sterile soil quite unsuited to meet its requirements. Those who still favour extending the spruce area almost regardless of the soil and climatic conditions, base their arguments upon "facts" which are briefly—(1) the price of the smaller sizes of spruce is considerably higher than the same sizes of Scots pine, and it can be never hoped to grow anything but comparatively small trees on such land; (2) spruce will produce more wood per acre, and yields a greater proportion of "timber" (*Nutzholz*) ; and (3) spruce is a better soil-protecting species than pine. The more modern school of foresters, led, so far as Saxony is concerned, by Prof. Borgmann of Tharandt, point out in their criticism of the "reckless introduction of spruce" that land which may, for example, only be class IV. spruce soil can very well be class III. pine soil, and that, consequently, the production of wood will be but little greater. Also they remind us that on poor soils a very large number of spruce develop rotten stems at an early period in the rotation, and again that in such places there is a very great tendency for the formation of " raw humus," which is particularly noxious to tree-growth, and which does not occur to such a marked degree in the pine woods. To these points they add the greater cost and uncertainty of spruce planting, and the extreme slowness with which the young trees form canopy under these circumstances, allowing in the meantime a dense growth of grass and other weeds to take place. This sums up shortly the differences of opinion between the spruce enthusiasts and those who recognise that, even although spruce has been, as it were, the making of the Saxon forests, yet its cultivation can be carried too far, and that before it is allowed to replace pine, the special circumstances of each case should be carefully considered.

Protection, etc.—The chief danger which threatens the Saxon forests lies in wind storms, as will be readily understood when it is considered what an important part spruce plays in their composition. Reference has already been made to the effect which the storm-wind has upon the cutting direction, and it is by cutting always against the wind that the greatest safety lies. The main rides are also purposely made wide (27 ft.), in order to allow of the formation of wind-fast edges to the "stands," which may later become exposed owing to the felling of a block on the other side of the ride. The cross rides used only to be made 6 ft. wide, but are now being made 13½ ft., in order that the trees or their edges may be allowed to become to a certain extent wind-fast; and whenever a severance is made it is put just to the windward of such a ride. Great care is also given to protection belts on the windward boundaries, and the instructions now in force are that they should be, in spruce forests, established from pure spruce planted close and but little thinned, the idea being to try to prevent the wind getting into the wood at all.

PLATE I.

FIG. 4.

Shows the predominance of pine over spruce on a sandy soil inclined to be dry.

FIG. 5.

Illustrates the manner in which split wood (on left) and bark are
stacked in yard lengths.

[To face p. 40.

Fig. 6.

Oberholz, Saxony. A private wood of Scots pine stripped by the Nun moth and killed. This wood was not grease-banded. The two oaks in the photograph were also stripped, but did not succumb.

Fig. 7.

The woodman's cottages in Saxony, as well as those of the agricultural labourer, are much larger buildings than those found in Scotland, there being nearly always two floors and often an attic above.

Before 1903 the instructions were just exactly the opposite, and trees in such belts were planted far apart and kept well thinned, with the result that strongly rooted well-branched trees were produced which were capable of standing an immense side pressure, but which allowed the effects of the storm to be felt farther into the wood. The planting of hardwoods in protective belts has not found favour. The present system of close planting is very severely criticised by many Saxon foresters, especially where the dangers of snow and wind are combined, as it is obvious that closely grown trees are more liable to injury in this case. Snow is also a danger that has to be reckoned with apart from wind, although the two are most destructive when combined, and the worst damage, so far as spruce woods are concerned, occurs when they are about 40 to 60 years old, as at this age the stems are generally splintered in breaking and a large amount of wood is rendered useless for anything except fuel. A considerable loss not unfrequently occurs in the upper parts of the Erzgebirge owing to rime and ice incrustation.

The ravages caused by red deer are not now so extensive as formerly, owing to the great reduction in the numbers allowed, but still a considerable number of trees are peeled and the proportion of rotten stems is thereby very materially increased. Spruce is in this case also the species which suffers most. In the King's special hunting forests a larger head of deer is kept, and special precautions are taken to prevent extensive damage. Fencing the deer out of young woods, hand-feeding and other palliatives are brought into use at a considerable cost, which is, however, borne by the Crown and is not a charge upon the forests. Hares and rabbits are comparatively scarce and cause but little trouble, and the same may be said of squirrels.

Bark beetles are kept well in check by clean woods and immediate barking of all felled timber. *Hylobius abietis* is occasionally troublesome, but the common practice of extracting stumps after felling prevents it becoming serious. There is, however, one insect which is dreaded in Saxony, and that is the Nun moth. The epidemic which broke out in Saxony in 1906, and which is now gradually dying out, was the first experience Saxon foresters had had of this pest on a large scale; but owing to a good system of inspection they were not taken unawares, as has occurred in other states. By counting the number of eggs on sample trees the authorities were enabled to forecast the rate at which the attack was growing in force, and were thus able to adopt preventive measures before it was too late. Whenever over 100 to 150 eggs were found on a spruce and over 150 to 200 on a pine grease-banding was undertaken, and this system, thoroughly carried through as it has been, has probably alone saved Saxony from what might easily have been a disaster as far as the forests were concerned. Probably few of the German States offer such a suitable breeding-ground for the Nun moth as Saxony, with its large extent of pure spruce forests; and it is undoubtedly a great achievement, worthy of the forest service, that their efforts in preventing a serious calamity have met with such success. Since the commencement of the attack (1904–6), which is now passing away, 50,000 acres have been completely grease-banded at a cost of about eight shillings per acre. Better and more economical methods have been devised for the application of the grease during this period, as special attention has been given to this detail, and at present the method generally adopted is "high banding," with the aid of 12 ft. ladders. The actual instrument now exclusively used for applying the grease is that invented by Max Janke, which is a great advance on any previous appliance, and the use of which has materially reduced the cost of the process. The instrument is light, handy and inexpensive, and can be worked with one hand, being thus particularly adapted for high banding which by its use can be carried out almost as cheaply as low banding formerly. The reason for this is partly that the bark on old trees is much smoother where the high band is applied and does not require, as a rule, to be scraped, which saves almost as much time as is required to manipulate the ladders. Of the eight shillings per acre which the process costs, five shillings go in labour at about fourpence per hour, and the remaining three shillings represent the cost of the grease which at ·82d. per lb. = 44 lbs. per acre.

The natural enemies and parasites of the Nun moth have helped considerably in suppressing the attack. Among these *Parasetigena segregata* took a leading place, but curiously enough it increased to such an extent in some *Reviere* that it became, unfortunately, itself the host of another parasite *Anthrax morio* (*Diptera*), which in no small degree checked its good work. The attack, which is now passing away, centred itself on certain spruce and pine woods in the dry flat country to the south-east of Leipzig. Since the outbreak started a great deal of research and experimental work has been carried on with reference to the larvæ of this moth and its diseases by Prof. Escherich in Tharandt, and the results have been both interesting from a scientific point of view and also useful in the practical work of fighting the pest.

Utilisation.—The dense population of Saxony (as compared with some other · timber - producing States in Germany) has the effect of facilitating the sale of wood to a very marked degree. A large and evenly distributed population renders local conversion and utilisation on a large scale possible, and this, by reducing the transport costs, means better returns for the forests. Such are the conditions in Saxony, and the favourable results are clearly reflected in the very flourishing state of the forest finances at present. But it must not be supposed that this degree of success is entirely the outcome of the enterprise of a hard-working and commercially-minded people. In no small degree is the result obtained due to proper methods of management entailing equal annual supplies of wood for the support of the industries concerned.

Before the facilities for transport which now exist came into being, the wood-converting industries, which are to be found in many cases right in the heart of the most densely wooded areas, were entirely dependent upon local supplies of raw material. Had not this raw material been obtainable in regular quantities annually, it is probable that many of the small factories which are now to be found amongst the forests would never have been started. Supposing, for instance, that a capitalist with £10,000 to invest wishes to start a wood-pulp factory, his first step is to find where he can obtain a sufficient regular supply of wood at a price which will render the undertaking profitable. He knows that the State forests are worked upon a regular system, and that every possible encouragement will be given by the Government for the establishment of a new industry, and the chances are he will select a central position among several State *Reviere* for his mill. First, however, he must ascertain from the past accounts of the forests concerned, that the amount of wood he requires, say 100,000 cubic feet, is annually put upon the market at a price, say 2½d. to 3d. per cubic foot on the average, which will allow a good margin for return on capital. This can only be done when woods are systematically·managed, and thus it can be seen that by conducting forests on rational lines and doing away with irregular fellings, an enormous impetus is given to local wood-converting industries. Local industry means local population, which in turn brings local wealth, which again is the cause of higher prices for wood and often gives rise to a market for certain hitherto unsaleable products.

However, when facilities for transport develop to such an extent as one finds them in Saxony, industries become less dependent upon local supplies of raw material, the limit of their development being no longer bounded by the extent of material available in the district and, as is often the case, they expand to such an extent that large imports from abroad are necessary to meet their demands. No better example of this could be found than the wood-pulp and cellulose factories of Saxony. Commencing by the conversion of local supplies only, they have grown into an enormous industry, importing wood to the extent of hundreds of thousands of tons annually, which they require, in addition to the supplies available at home, in order to keep pace with the demands for the converted product. A large proportion of the wood thus imported into Saxony is floated down the Elbe, in rafts, from Bohemia and is converted by the factories situated on the banks of the river.

Among the many and varied industries directly dependent upon the forests for their raw material is one which is particularly interesting, and that is the toy-making industry of the Erzgebirge. Here, in the heart of the mountains, one finds small villages, such as Seiffen and Heidelberg, given over entirely to the production of children's toys, and it is interesting to see over one of the factories and watch the processes by which the raw logs of spruce are turned into all sorts of wooden animals and other playthings. In some cases merely the roughest part of the work is done in the factory, the finishing off and painting being executed in the homes of the workers themselves, in which case the women and children take a large share in the labour.

Although very little is left of the *Eichenschälwald* (oak coppiced for bark), still a fair amount of spruce, which is cut in spring and early summer, can be profitably barked, five shillings being obtained per 35 stacked cubic feet, which only costs two shillings to strip.

—A single Scots pine left chiefly for
ient after a clear cutting—quite a
on practice in Saxony.

FIG. 9. — Well-grown Scots pine showing
clean stems and small crowns and giving a
high form factor.

. — Beech is always regenerated
lly where possible. The trees illus-
are anything but ideal mother trees.

FIG. 11.—A view of the famous Mauerhammer
ride—one of the first rides laid out by Cotta
when he came to Tharandt in 1811. It is
lined with silver birch, a common practice in
coniferous woods.

[To face p. 44

A considerable amount of the rougher and smaller classes of wood is sold as firewood directly to the consumers, and in the country districts this forms the chief fuel. Practically all the wood disposed of annually by the State forests is sold by auction sales, which are conducted by the *Forstmeister* and the *Forstrentamt* jointly. The sale is always advertised in the local papers, and likely buyers are supplied with catalogues in which every lot is recorded,—the position of the timber in the wood, the class as regards size and the exact contents being given. Every effort is made to sell timber as soon after felling as is practicable, so that there may not be an accumulation of felled wood scattered through the forest, and, besides, as the logs are measured by the woodmen immediately after felling, if left for any length of time, especially in summer, an undesirable discrepancy might occur between the catalogued size and the actual size at the time of sale. In special cases where it is difficult to obtain good prices for the larger classes of timber, a joint district sale is held, in which the best lots out of each component *Revier* are put up. This is done in order to attract large buyers who would perhaps not find sufficient timber of a particular size for their requirements in the sale of a single *Revier*.

Roads.—One particularly obvious factor amongst the different causes which contribute to the high prices gained for wood in Saxony, is the condition of the forest roads. Those who have not seen them will have difficulty in understanding fully what a vast amount of money has been laid out on these forest roads, and with what skill the work has been executed. Although the network of roads is not yet complete the accessibility of felled timber, even in the wildest parts of the Erzgebirge, is far better than is usually found in this country even on land suited to easy transport. As an object lesson upon the good return that money expended upon skilfully constructed forest roads is almost certain to yield, the State forests of Saxony stand out with remarkable clearness. Ordinary railways and light railways are also well developed, the latter especially being of great service to the forests, as they penetrate areas the population of which would not suffice to support the running costs of anything more than an economically managed narrow-gauge line.

It would be impossible to conclude this account of Saxon forestry, rough and imperfect though it is, without a word concerning the famous Tharandt Forest Academy which for more than a hundred years now has been one of the chief continental schools of scientific silviculture. Its renown is justly world-wide, and nearly every country in Europe, as well as America, Australia and Japan have, as a rule, representatives on the roll of students.

4. Some Vegetation Types at High Altitudes.

(*With Illustrations.*)

By G. P. GORDON, B.Sc.(Edin.), B.Sc.(Oxon.).

It is well known that under natural conditions the upper zones of tree-growth rarely, if ever, constitute normal forest, but rather form the all-important belts of protection-forest which make possible the economic development of forest and agri-cultural land at lower elevations. In order to investigate such vegetation types, it would seem advisable to select an area on which not only a large variety of types occurs, but where, in addition, a continuous succession of forest zones may be obtained, so that observations might be made at points where one forest type merges into another. With this end in view the district of Zernez, in the Engadin in north-east Switzerland, was fixed upon. The district is specially suitable because the floras of the Ober- and Unterengadin are there contiguous. It was therefore possible to observe the gradation from the forests of the Oberengadin, where larch is the dominant species, into the spruce forests of the Unterengadin. Further, the conditions in this area are such that observations may be made through a considerable range in altitude.

In addition to forming interesting plant associations, these forests afford many excellent examples of natural woodland types (Urwald). The contour of the country and the distribu-tion of these types would indicate that they have been free from all modifying influences, other than natural factors, and their present condition goes to confirm this. The entire absence of forests of broad-leaved trees is a striking feature of this district, and thus it forms a contrast with the highest tree zone in Scotland. It was only after traversing considerable areas that isolated specimens of birch (*Betula pubescens*), aspen (*Populus tremula*), and rowan (*Sorbus aucuparia*) were observed.

The localities in which observations were made include practically the whole of Val Cluoza and Valletta, Piz Quater Vals and Piz Murter, part of the Spöltal, and the watershed between Val dell Acqua and Val della Föglia. The total area has an altitudinal range of nearly 5532 feet, from 4832 feet at Zernez to 10,364 feet at Piz Quater Vals, the limit of tree vegetation being about 7700 feet. The configuration of the land is varied, and consists essentially of acute ridges extending to the snowline, the upper slopes of which are, for the most part, covered with loose frost-debris. In other parts these ridges constitute upland meadows. On the middle valley-slopes coarse gravel screes predominate, and these pass into block screes at lower levels. The valley bottoms are narrow and contain morainic material, while in the side valleys small glaciers occur.

The main physical features of the area are the two large valleys, Val Cluoza and Spöltal, which run parallel for some distance and join east of Zernez. These communicate with numerous side valleys which are usually short and steep. The rocks of the district consist of Dolomite and Muschelkalk beds resting on a floor of gneissic material. In places, for example at Clüz–Zernez, the underlying gneissic base is exposed and is there seen to consist of Augengneiss.

STEP-FORMATION (*Treppenbildung*).

In the area under consideration this formation is found at the limit of forest growth, and in fact of all other *closed* plant associations. At a higher elevation occurs the zone of alpine cushion-plants including *Androsace helvetica*, *Silene acaulis*, *Eritrichium nanum*, etc. *Papaver alpinum* also occurs here, together with a few species of lichen. The above plants, however, have quite a sporadic distribution, and cannot be said to form any definite association. Step-formation characterises the higher slopes of fine frost-debris, as also the wash-out channels, although in these it descends to a lower level. This would seem to indicate that while a certain stability of soil is necessary for the individuals which produce the steps, the formation is the pioneer on slopes lying at the angle of repose. Soil-creep combined with wind action· tends to make the formation a very open one and, in addition, to modify the individuals considerably. For example, where plants have established themselves on a ridge they assume crescentic, clipped forms, while on the steeper slopes the flat scrambling habit with spreading root-system, so typical of *Salix serpyllifolia* and *Azalea procumbens*, is characteristic. Other individuals of this association are *Arctostaphylos alpina, Daphne mezereum, Rosa alpina, Salix reticulata, Salix retusa, Dryas octopetala, Helianthemum vulgare* and *Globularia cordifolia*. A comparison of the above flora with that described by Dr Crampton [1] indicates striking differences. In the latter flora the dominant individuals are *Vaccinium myrtillus, Calluna vulgaris, Erica cinerea, Alchemilla alpina, Luzula silvatica, Empetrum nigrum, Azalea procumbens*. The only plant common to both is *Azalea procumbens*. As will be seen later, the flora referred to by Dr Crampton occurs at a lower elevation in association with mountain pine (*Pinus montana*) and larch (*Larix decidua*).

The evolution of step-formation is probably as follows:— One of the above-mentioned plants establishes itself on a frost-debris slope, and immediately the sliding debris begins to collect behind it. This causes a rise in level and at the same time a diminution in slope at that point, with the result that a miniature terrace is formed. The plant then by pressure from behind assumes a more or less vertical position, and, depending on the species and on the robustness of growth, it may develop so that the top is horizontal, while the lower part is almost vertical, thus forming a step (Pl. III. fig. 1). Such steps may be overwhelmed by falling debris during or after their formation and disappear. The formation is thus a shifting one, and as such its limits of occurrence cannot be definitely laid down, though in this locality it may range from 7000 feet to 8000 feet. As the lower limit of this formation is approached the association becomes more closed.

PINUS MONTANA (BUSH FORM) ASSOCIATION.

Descending through the above step-formation a change in the type of vegetation is observed, and mountain pine makes its appearance. As is seen from Pl. III. fig. 2, the latter at its upper limit is fairly open. Towards its lower limit, however,

[1] See *The Vegetation of Caithness considered in Relation to the Geology*, C. B. Crampton, M.B., C.M., 1911, pp. 43-46.

FIG. 2.

FIG. 4.

FIG. 6.

of figures, *see* text.

[*To face p.* 48.

FIG. 7.   FIG. 8.

FIG. 9.

For explanations of figures, *see* text

G. P. Gordon, photo.

it becomes almost completely closed. This association extends along the upper margin of tree-growth, where it forms the highest forest zone, and ascends to 7000 feet. It occurs typically as almost pure forest on the screes of the middle valley slopes, which are quite incapable of supporting any other species. Like the last association it descends considerably in the wash-out channels, and in these the trees tend to arch over the centre of the channel (Pl. III. fig. 3). It also occurs at comparatively low altitudes on moraines and gravel banks. Hence it would appear that soil conditions rather than climatic conditions are the main factors in its distribution. From the growth habit of the species its great value as forming protection-forest may be easily seen (Pl. III. fig. 4). As a result of the peculiar trailing habit, many of its branches are buried in snow for the greater part of the year. These are often attacked by the fungus *Herpotricha nigra*, which, by means of its mycelium, holds the trailing branches to the ground and forms a brown felt of hyphæ round the needles of erect branches. Practically the only species obtained in admixture in this association is spruce (*Picea excelsa*), and its occurrence is exceedingly rare.

The chief plant associates of the mountain pine are *Erica carnea, Daphne striata, Dryas octopetala, Calluna vulgaris, Arctostaphylos uva ursi, Juniperus nana, Vaccinium uliginosum, V. vitis idæa, V. myrtillus, Pirola secunda, Cotoneaster vulgaris,* etc. These, however, do not occur in the form of an undergrowth, since the low, branching habit of this form of mountain pine does not allow of any such development. They are to be found, therefore, forming the soil-covering of the many gaps which occur in the formation.

Perhaps one of the most interesting features of this type of forest is the suddenness with which it may give place to quite a new type. The main factors responsible for the change would seem to be a difference in depth and mechanical consistency of the soil. For example, Pl. III. fig. 5 shows in the foreground *Pinus montana* (bush form) forest changing abruptly into larch (*Larix europæa*) forest at the same altitude. The only explanation to be offered is that, where the larch occurs, the soil is deeper and not so loose as that on the scree slopes which bear the mountain pine formation. Another interesting case is seen in Pl. III. fig. 7, where the mountain pine (bush form) association gives place to a forest of erect varieties of mountain pine. Here again the difference is an increase in the depth of soil, combined with greater stability.

PINUS MONTANA (ERECT FORM) ASSOCIATION.

Following immediately on the last association, and forming with it the upper forest zone of the whole district, is the mountain pine (erect form) association. In general appearance it differs greatly from the last association, since it forms high-forest with an undergrowth. The individual trees have a height of over 30 feet, and, although the density of stocking is low, the quality of the stems is fairly good. A slight admixture of rowan (*Sorbus aucuparia*) is obtained in these forests. Species of juniper (*Juniperus communis* and *J. nana*) for the most part form the undergrowth, while *Erica carnea, Calluna vulgaris, Vaccinium myrtillus, V. vitis idæa, Dryas octopetala, Globularia cordifolia, Daphne mezereum, D. striata, Pirola secunda, Arctostaphylos uva ursi, Rhododendron hirsutum, Luzula silvatica, Poa alpina, Oxalis acetosella* complete the association, which is a practically closed one. This formation appears to be specially suited to the zone it occupies, constituting as it does the intermediate stage between the dwarf forest above and the high-forests of larch, Cembran pine, Scots pine and spruce at lower levels.

As regards general distribution the upper forest zone extends over large areas. Its outer margin assumes a very ragged appearance, particularly in the small valleys near the head of Val Cluoza, where the cold winds from the mountains limit its distribution in exposed places. The various forms of *Pinus montana* occupying this zone have been fully described by Dr S. E. Brunies.[1]

LARCH (*Larix europæa*) AND CEMBRAN PINE (*Pinus Cembra*) ASSOCIATION.

At a lower level the zone of larch and Cembran pine is entered upon. This is the highest belt of mixed coniferous forest in the district. It may, in parts, consist of practically pure larch forest, while elsewhere *Pinus Cembra* may predominate. Towards the upper limit of the formation, the canopy is even more open than that of the mountain pine

[1] *Die Flora des Ofengebietes*, Separatabdruck aus dem Jahresbericht der Naturforschenden Gesellschaft. Graubündens: Band xlviii, 1905-06, pp. 205-211.

(erect form) association. Small forest clearings occur in places, and are very characteristic of this class of forest, especially where larch is abundant (Pl. III. fig. 8). The undergrowth is very sparse and consists mainly of juniper (*Juniperus communis*). Approaching the lower limit *Pinus Cembra* is replaced by spruce (*Picea excelsa*) and Scots pine (*Pinus silvestris*), together with *Pinus silvestris* var. *Engadinensis*. Occasional specimens of the erect form of mountain pine also occur in this forest zone. Thus larch, spruce and Scots pine form the mixed coniferous forest of this region. The forests in the vicinity of Zernez form an excellent example of such a mixed forest.

The following broad-leaved species occur in the above association:—Aspen (*Populus tremula*), rowan (*Sorbus aucuparia*), *Sorbus Chamæmispilus*, and birch (*Betula pubescens*). In the undergrowth, juniper, barberry (*Berberis vulgaris*), *Lonicera nigra*, *L. cærulea*, and willow (*Salix cinerea*) make their appearance. The ground vegetation, which in the upper stretches of the zone has complete possession of the soil, has not such a robust development towards its lower limits owing to the presence of spruce. This ground flora consists chiefly of the following:—*Rhododendron hirsutum*, *Daphne striata*, *D. mezereum*, *Vaccinium vitis idæa*, *Pirola uniflora*, *P. media*, *Erica carnea*, *Calluna vulgaris*, *Melampyrum silvaticum*, *M. pratense*, *Linnæa borealis*, *Deschampsia cæspitosa*, *Sesleria cærulea*, etc.

Some of the tree types of the mixed coniferous forest association are of special interest, for example, *Pinus silvestris* var. *Engadinensis*, which is an important constituent of this forest zone. It differs in many respects from *Pinus silvestris* as we know it in Scotland. In growth habit it is tall and somewhat pyramidal, the side branches are comparatively slender, and the crown has no tendency to have a wide umbrella-like expansion. The crown is rather deeply set, and altogether of a loose, open nature, since the whorls of branches are widely spaced. As a result of this open formation of crown it suffers much less from snowbreak than the common variety. The red copper-colour of the bark of the crown branches, so characteristic of the common variety, extends practically to the foot of the tree in variety *Engadinensis*. The bark in quite old trees is neither so thick nor so much fissured as that of the common variety. The duramen even of large stems is light red to almost white.[1] There is in addition a marked difference in the cones—that of the variety *Engadinensis* is glossy with a dark ring on the apophysis round the base of the papilla. The cones also are not pendulous but horizontal.

The above description in many respects might apply equally well to the Schwarzwald (Black Forest) form of *Pinus silvestris* in Germany.

The larch (*Larix europæa*) of this association has an interesting growth habit. In these natural forests it has not the development in height-growth which is usually attained in a plantation. The stem is clothed almost to the ground with long slender branches, which are festooned with *Usnea barbata* and *Priologum barbatum*. The bark of the stem is often clothed with *Evernia vulpina*. The bark on the windward side is much thicker and redder in appearance. This is said to be due to the action of rain and snow driving against the stem. The cracks on the bark are consequently deepened on that side, and the following season a greater development of bark ensues. A feature of the larch in this area is the almost entire absence of larch disease (*Dasycypha Calycina*). At times, however, it suffers severely from the attack of *Steganoptycha pinicolana,* which occasionally causes complete defoliation. The timber of these larch forests shows a very large proportion of deep red heart-wood to sap-wood, with narrow uniformly-spaced annual rings indicative of healthy conditions and slow growth.

Pinus Cembra presents a marked contrast in habit to the last two types. It forms a compact, heavily-foliaged tree, which is strongly branched almost to the ground (Pl. III. fig. 8). The deep green foliage and sombre appearance gives it a good claim to the title of the "Cedar of the Alps." The development in height-growth would seem better than that of larch, while it has also a broader extension of crown. The short ovate, upright cone with thick seed scales and seeds in the form of light-brown, thick-shelled nuts; the five-needled sheaths; and the young shoots with a dense covering of felty brown hairs are prominent diagnostic characters of the species.

Spruce (*Picea excelsa*) in this forest zone does not show any abnormal development other than the pendulous habit of the smaller side branches and twigs, an adaptation common in all districts where the snowfall is heavy.

[1] *Die Flora des Ofengebietes.*

The foregoing types of forest form a natural succession which may be traced from Zernez along Val Cluoza and Valletta to Piz Quater Vals. The types forming the succession have undergone little or no modification, so that they give a fair sample of the original forest flora of the district. This natural sequence of forest is all the more interesting in that it is practically a pure coniferous one. Of the broad-leaved species which occur sporadically in it, birch (*Betula pubescens*) ascends highest, in the intermediate zones rowan (*Sorbus aucuparia*) is to be found, and in the lowest forest zone, aspen (*Populus tremula*) appears. A comparison of the above with forest zones in Scotland[1] shows considerable variation. In the first instance the individual species differ, while there are also fewer types in Scotland. As regards altitudinal distribution the Scottish forest zones have a more restricted range, and do not form any definite succession such as occurs in Val Cluoza and Valletta.

The forest succession in the Alps[2] is completed by the silver fir (*Abies pectinata*) and beech (*Fagus silvatica*) associations, the former following the mixed coniferous associations as a descent is made to lower altitudes. Such a succession shows clearly that different conditions of locality demand different species, and points to the importance of suiting the species to the locality in artificial cultivation.

GRAZING ASSOCIATIONS.

It is to be expected that where a natural succession of forest meets the agricultural land of the valleys, it will undergo modification. A very good example occurs in Valle di Livigno, a continuation of the Spöltal into the north of Italy. Valle di Livigno is a broad glaciated valley with a flat bottom, which is worked as meadow land. The only crops raised are grass and hay as fodder for cattle. The following plants constitute the meadow land association:—*Trisetum flavescens, Agrostis vulgaris, Phleum alpinum, Polygonum bistorta, Crepis grandiflora, Campanula Scheuchzeria, Rumex arifolius, Trifolium pratense, T. alpinum, Euphrasia minima, Nardus stricta, Anthoxanthum*

[1] See "Primitive Woodland and Plantation types in Scotland," G. P. Gordon, *Transactions of the Royal Scottish Arboricultural Society,* vol. xxiv., part ii., 1911, p. 174.

[2] See *'Fremdländliche Wald und Parkbäume für Europa,* Prof. Heinrich Mayr.

odoratum, *Viola tricolor*, *Lychnis alpina*, etc. This association extends to the bottom slope of the valley, where it meets and extends into larch forest (Pl. III. fig. 6). The density of stocking of the forest is very low, with the result that the meadow association completely covers the soil. The small chalet (Pl. III. fig. 6) indicates the centre from which grazing operations in the forest are carried on. This zone of open larch forest extends in a strip along both sides of the valley. The individual trees are almost of a park type, as each stem has ample room for development. The branches extend down to the ground and the trees are pyramidal in shape. The development in height-growth is poor, and evidences of natural regeneration are very rare.

Ascending to the middle valley slope where the ground is too steep for grazing cattle the type of forest changes, and an association of *Pinus Cembra* with some admixture of larch occurs (Pl. III. fig. 9). This formation is normal and corresponds to the description already given for the type.

At still higher elevations, up to over 7000 feet, and occupying all the land not under forest, occur the typical upland meadows of the Alps. These are managed on the chalet system, which is as follows:—In summer the cattle, sheep and goats are driven from the valleys to the upland meadows. The sheep and goats are put on the highest pastures, which are usually comparatively dry, while the cattle graze the lower and moister meadows. The milk of the cows and goats is manufactured into butter and cheese in the chalet. In autumn all the stock descends to the valleys. It is interesting to note that there are records that a similar system of grazing was formerly practised in certain districts of Scotland.

The primary effect of grazing on this association is to disturb the ecological equilibrium, since the cattle are selective in their feeding. Such a modification was clearly shown in the Bernina Pass where a grazed area was observed to adjoin an ungrazed area. In the moister parts of the cattle pastures, *e.g.* on plateaux and in slight depressions, etc., the land is worked into small hillocks (such as occur on alluvial land which is subject to flooding). The cattle construct a network of irregularly winding paths, which they always keep to, and so the ground forming the meshes of the network in time becomes much higher than the paths. The tops of these hillocks are comparatively dry, and often crowned with tufts of alpine rose

(*Rhododendron hirsutum*). The droppings of the cattle on these pastures encourage the growth of plants, so that a luxuriant rank growth is obtained in places.

Of the many representatives constituting this widespread association, the following examples may be mentioned :—*Carex nigra, C. sempervirens, Phleum alpinum, Poa alpina* var. *vivipara, Potentilla aurea, Viola calcarata, Pedicularis verticillata, Helianthemum alpestre, Veronica aphylla, Nardus stricta, Luzula lutea, Trifolium alpinum, Ranunculus montanus, R. pyrenaicus, Myosotis alpestris, Campanula barbata, Ligusticum mutellina, Euphrasia minima, Leontodon pyrenaicus, Festuca Halleri, Gentiana excisa, Crepis aurea,* etc.

SUMMARY.

The forest flora of the district under consideration may be grouped under several distinct associations, which arrange themselves into the following succession:—

1. Mountain pine (bush form). This forms a dwarf type of forest, which occupies the upper limits of tree-growth and occurs also in wash-out channels on the slopes. It has an irregular and somewhat restricted distribution.

2. Mountain pine (erect form). High-forest is produced at a lower level by the erect form of the mountain pine. In Val Cluoza its distribution is somewhat restricted, whereas in Spöltal it has the widest distribution of all the forest formations.

3. Larch and Cembran pine. A mixed forest type containing larch and *Pinus Cembra* succeeds the last association, and marks the beginning of mixed forests. The above two species occur at the upper limits of the zone, while larch alone descends to the lower limits, and is found there in association with spruce and Scots pine. These three species form the mixed forest type of the district. This association has the widest distribution of all.

4. Grazing forest (larch). This is a compromise between agricultural and forest land, and its distribution is restricted. It assumes a strip formation extending along the bottom valley slope and skirts the forest.

5. Forestry at Home and Abroad.

By A. W. BORTHWICK, D.Sc.

During the past few years some progress has been made towards the development of Scottish forestry, but that progress, it must be admitted, has been disappointingly slow. Undoubtedly the most important forward step made was the publication of the Glen Mor Survey Report by Lord Lovat and Captain Stirling. This pioneer and fundamental work leaves no room for doubt or even for hesitation, in accepting the statement, that, before the work of afforestation can be undertaken on a national scale, we must first know the extent of land available for that purpose. The prime importance of a general survey of the whole country is admitted by foresters of all grades and by all who know anything about the possibilities of forestry, but while much discussion is taking place about what are at the present time more or less irrelevant details, the main line of development is being lost sight of. The importance attached to survey work by eminent foresters in other countries, especially in America, is well illustrated by the following extract from *American Forestry* [1] :—

"The Secretary of Agriculture recently signed an agreement with the State of North Carolina for a co-operative study of forest conditions in the eastern Piedmont region. The work will be carried on by the Forest Service and by the State geological and economic survey with one-half of the cost paid by each.

"The study will determine the distribution and proportion of forest lands, and the relative value of lands for timber and for agriculture. It will take into account the present status of lumbering, the causes and effects of forest fires, and will recommend a system of fire protection and of forest planting.

"The study just arranged supplements two already completed in the more mountainous regions of the State. The first, a study of forest conditions in the Appalachians, has been published as a State report. A study of the forests of the western Piedmont region was completed recently, and the results are being prepared for publication. When the study of the eastern Piedmont region is finished, it is planned to proceed to a similar study of

---

[1] *American Forestry*, vol. xix., No. 8, p. 560.

the coàstal plain region, so that eventually the entire State will be covered by a forest survey."

This example, though taken at random, shows in a typical manner what America has done, what she is doing, and what she intends. to do. We beg to call special attention to the striking resemblance between the conclusions arrived at, after long experience, by Dr Fernow (see p. 78), who is one of America's greatest forestry experts, and the recommendations which have been advocated by this Society and carried into effect in such a masterly manner by the authors of the Glen Mor Survey Report.

As an appropriate illustration of the value of a flying survey of the whole country, attention may be called to the offer of a tract of land which was made by the Duke of Sutherland to the Government. The consideration of this offer was referred to the Development Commissioners, and it was refused by them. But how could they have possibly advised the Government adequately with regard to this offer when a proper survey had not been made of the land? As the matter stands at present, it is quite clear that our knowledge concerning the extent of the natural resources of our country as regards forestry and agricultural development is woefully deficient, and this even in a generation of educational and scientific enlightenment which prides itself upon its business capacity.

If we turn our attention to China, that country which has long been regarded as the most backward nation in forestry and other matters, we find that the new republic has established a department of agriculture and forestry, and bids fair in the near future to outstrip us in forestry development if our progress does not become a little more rapid. The following statement was made recently by a Chinese who is at present studying American methods of forestry [1] :—

" It is only since the republican form of Government has been established that China has awakened to the need of greater forest tracts, and this awakening is confined to the more progressive and better educated men and not to the great mass of people.

"The denuding of forest lands has been slow but steady, and the effects are now being felt keenly. Cutting timber has not

---

[1] *American Forestry*, vol. xix., No. 8, p. 560.

been a commercial enterprise, but has been done as the lumber has been needed for home and general use.

"It is not so many years ago that the scarcity was felt so keenly that bamboo, which grows rapidly, was selected for house building, furniture and other commodities. Brick, stone and mud are used for houses because there is not wood enough.

"There are fine forests in China yet, but they are inaccessible and comparatively useless in preventing floods. No man can hope to arouse the Chinese to the need of tree planting from a patriotic standpoint, but it can be done from the viewpoint of commercialism.

"Forestry will some day become one of the greatest fields of Government work in China. At present most of this work, the amount of which is hardly worth mentioning, is done by German foresters, but as fast as they can be educated Chinese will fill such positions as State foresters, superintendents, surveyors, rangers, clerks and timber experts. There are twenty-one provinces in China, each of which will have to have a head forester.

"The first work to be done will be the mapping of the entire country's forest area, a gigantic proposition, but one which the Government stands ready to undertake when trained men can be obtained. I hope to be in the field within the next three years."

Surely this indicates a rapid awakening on the part of China to the requirements of modern times.

Fortunately, Scotland is in some ways better off than China as regards the possibilities of forestry development. We have at least that spirit which prompts men to patriotic acts, among which tree planting is not the least.

The history of forestry development in most countries shows that the various governments have had to overcome a large amount of popular prejudice in their endeavours to protect the forest in the interests of the country as a whole. The former opposition to forest conservation and protection in Switzerland, by those interested in grazing rights, is typical of what has happened in other European countries, and even within our own shores examples in plenty could be given of the active hostility of those interested in grazing rights against the enclosure of parts of the Crown forests. In Canada the same lack of popular interest is felt. Apparently the man in the street does not know what forestry is, nor does he realise the enormous benefits which afforestation can confer.

In Scotland we have land in abundance suitable for tree-growth. The reports by Royal Commissions and inquiries otherwise made prove this statement to be an established fact, and, what is more, no one disputes it. This land, therefore, must be regarded as an undeveloped natural resource, but still no systematic attempt has as yet been made to take stock of its potential value as a national asset. Further, all are agreed that we have the men trained in scientific and practical forestry whose co-operation is necessary in making a survey of our plantable land. We have, therefore, at the present moment the land and the men capable of developing it. The first step in that development must be a flying survey of the whole country on the basis of the Glen Mor model. This view is strongly supported and backed up by the best brains in the country, but, unfortunately, no definite move has as yet been made to set in motion the machinery necessary for the making of such a survey, and still the puzzling question, Why this delay? remains unanswered.

We hear of schemes for forestry education, the provision of expert advice for foresters and forest proprietors, the establishment of demonstration areas, and the promotion of forest and allied industries. These are undoubtedly all very excellent things in themselves, but it would surely seem reasonable to expect that in view of further developments we should find out without delay the full extent to which afforestation is possible in Scotland. If this were once known definitely, then those in authority and responsible for the economic development of the country would be able to embark on forestry development schemes with a definite knowledge of the extent and value of the final results to which those schemes would lead. As the parts of an engine must be designed in proportion to each other and properly balanced, so must the organisation for forestry development be arranged and the subsequent operations carried out in their proper sequence.

The following paragraph, taken from the *Canadian Forestry Journal*, applies to the position of forestry in Canada [1]:—

"In taking stock of the forestry position, it is seen that there has been a good deal of activity along certain lines with

[1] *Canadian Forestry Journal*, vol. ix., No. 10, p. 145.

delay and hesitation along others. There is more machinery than ever before, more money being spent. The effort must now be to so balance the effort as to keep the cart behind the horse. What is needed is organisation, co-ordination, and the doing of first things first."

This might well have been written in regard to the present position of forestry in Scotland.

6. Continental Notes—France.

By A. G. HOBART-HAMPDEN.

I. As at home, so abroad, there is great discussion as to the advisability or otherwise of using seed from foreign countries. In particular the seed of Scots pine from Auvergne, where in that mild and regular climate seeding is profuse, has been very severely criticised in Germany, and M. Huffel has set himself to consider whether the criticism is justified. Possibly it began in trade rivalry, the French seed being very cheap, but foresters of note, from whom careful statements may be expected, have proved beyond doubt that the results of using foreign seed have often been most disastrous. Thus Dr Schwappach states that hundreds of acres of Scots pine grown from French seed have utterly failed at 10 to 15 years of age. Russian foresters have found that their plantations of Scots pine grown from German seed have failed at 20 to 30 years, and the Swedes have had a similar, and very marked, experience. Also in Prussia the French plants suffered badly from "leaf shedding." (*rouge, schütte*). At the same time the French plants have done well in Austria, Switzerland and Belgium. M. Huffel thinks that the cause of the disaster in Prussia may have been the habit of forwarding the cones from Auvergne before they are ripe (to prevent loss of seed in transit), and the consequent necessity of subjecting them on arrival to great heat.

Incidentally, M. Huffel writes in a most interesting way of the transmissibility of the characteristics of the various *races* of the Scots pine. This species ranges from Lapland to Spain, and varies, as M. Huffel says, as much as does a Lapp fisherman from a Basque mountaineer. He quotes many experiments showing that the seed of any variety, wherever sown, invariably produces young plants with the characteristics of its origin, but that these characteristics disappear gradually with time until the trees become precisely similar to the local race. Thus, at Les Barres, Scots pine grown from Russian seed still showed at 50 years of age signs of their origin, whereas at 80 to 90 years the difference had disappeared, and they resembled the local Scots pine. Again, at Nancy, Russian pines, 50 years old, while still showing some traces of their origin, have steadily and progressively grown more and more like the French pines.

M. Cannon, an old planter in Central France, writes of his experience with Scots pine seed. In 1871-72 he planted a large area—some 120 acres—4 feet by 4 feet, with plants from seed bought at Orleans, but coming probably from Alsace or Germany, since at that period other seed establishments within commercial distance did not exist. The success was great. In 1875 he planted as before, but the plantation suffered very much from a drought. Nevertheless this plantation is now quite good, and the point is that the stems are good even where they were accidentally thinned out by the drought. So, too, with the thinned parts of the 1871 plantation. Seeing this M. Cannon planted in 1881-82, at 5 feet by 5 feet, with plants raised from seed from Darmstadt. The result has been very bad. He thinks, then, that before 1870 the demand for Scots pine seed being slight only good seed from fine trees was used, but later, on the demand increasing very greatly, seed was obtained from all sorts and conditions of places and parent trees.

To know the origin, therefore, of the seed is of great importance, but what has gone before seems rather to show that so long as the seed itself is good, at a suitable condition of ripeness, from a strong parent, and properly handled in transit, the place from which it comes does not so much matter. That appears to me to be the inference, though it is not very definite.

II. M. Maire, Director of the forests of Eu and Aumale, in Normandy, noticed in the drought of 1911 very numerous instances of splitting, resembling frost-crack, among spruce of 20 to 30 years of age, and always on the most thriving stems. These particular spruce are growing at some 600 to 650 feet above sea-level, which is, of course, far below their natural habitat, and M. Maire hazards the suggestion that the damage was due to this fact, and if so that it is one argument the more against growing trees out of their proper *milieu*. Nevertheless he admits that the larch, as also the Scots and Corsican pines, growing with this spruce did not suffer; and it might be added that the silver fir is very successful in Normandy. However, if the larch did not happen to suffer from this particular trouble, though out of its habitat, it suffers from other things—canker for instance.

In this connection M. Guinier lays down that if the conditions of soil and climate allow recourse to a variety superior to the local variety by the rapidity of its growth, straightness of trunk, or any other advantageous character, we may employ this variety with profit, but we run the risk of seeing the introduced variety becoming modified more or less rapidly after the first generation. This agrees with M. Huffel above.

This matter of growing species out of their true habitat is really very important, yet somehow is very little considered. *Prima facie* it is of course unwise to employ species out of their own home, yet it may still be worth while to plant here, if they will grow,—even moderately—species which in their own home are unusually good, in the hope that they will at least give fair results.

III. M. Jolyet, of the Nancy Research Station, has an interesting note on Banks' pine. Its chief point is its great hardiness, for it can stand any amount of drought, and a very low temperature indeed (– 40° C.). It can accommodate itself to quite poor soils, both chemically and physically speaking. It prospers in even superficial calcareous soils, and might therefore, we should think, be used for planting up thin soils over chalk, where even the beech is stunted. It starts quickly, but does not attain great dimensions. The wood is said to be fairly good.

IV. M. Moreau states that he has found that the planting of lines of birch, with a north-south direction, at intervals in nurseries of broad-leaved species, has several advantages. First, since the birch is early in leaf and does not mind frost, it gives useful shelter against the rising sun, that special cause of damage when there is a spring frost; secondly, it gives shelter against the great heat in the dog-days, from 2 P.M. onwards; and thirdly,—a special point—it is useful in dealing with an invasion of cockchafers. The birch being early in leaf the cockchafers go first to it, and, therefore, all that has to be done is to shake the birch plants in the morning while the insects are still stupid with the cold, when they can be easily collected and destroyed. This tree, it appears, can itself survive attack from the grub in consequence of its faculty of throwing out rootlets just below the collar to replace those that have been eaten off. Cockchafers are indeed a tremendous curse when they swarm, which they do in cycles. They go for purposes of egg-laying to freshly turned earth, as in nurseries or fields, and some think, therefore, that nurseries should be made far inside a forest area.

V. It is often desired to introduce conifers into coppice-under-standards with the view of an eventual complete transformation into conifers. This has been done successfully on the first plateau of the Jura, among the coppices with somewhat shallow soil, and silver fir has been used. At this place the silver will not thrive with less than 24 inches of rain, nor below 500 metres (1640 feet), but obviously this altitude may be greatly reduced in higher latitudes. In the case in point, the method was to abandon at once the coppice method and to substitute for it thinnings at 10-year intervals, removing all the standards in the first thinning. This looks like eating up the capital rapidly, but circumstances might sometimes justify the proceeding. Were spruce or Douglas used the thinning would have to be heavier, while in the latter case the soil must not be shallow.

The matter is one of importance to us in Britain, because there are now so many coppices that have lost all value. M. Cuif, one of the Research officers at Nancy, is strongly in favour of the silver fir for this purpose. It can easily be brought into a thinned coppice—far more easily than other conifers. The process of removing the coppice should be gradual, because of the frost-tenderness of the silver. More than any other this species will stand the shade and cover of the coppice. After the plant has reached about 6 feet in height the spring frosts do not matter. M. Cuif says that the silver fir stands drought better than the spruce, and is perhaps the least touched by insects and fungi of all the conifers. One needs great patience, however, for the growth is dreadfully slow up to about 14 years of age, though after that the species goes ahead, and will produce more timber than any other European species (Schlich).

As an example of what may be done in substituting very good silver fir for bad coppice (which in this case meant also thin soil) M. Cuif quotes a plantation near Nancy. The place is very cold in winter and very hot in summer. The present crop comes from a sowing made in 1871 under the coppice standards, and all the old coppice has been gradually removed. The silver now numbers 2085 to the acre, measuring some 4255 cub. feet.; minimum girth at chest-height 5·1 inches, maximum 26·4 inches; height of stems 19 ft. 8 ins. to 46 feet; height of boles 13 feet to 23 feet; mean annual production during the last 40 years 105·8 cub. feet per acre.

VI. The Grand Duchy of Luxembourg is one of the best wooded countries of Europe. 32·2 % (205,907 acres) of the total area is under wood, but of this only 1593 belong to the State, 6422 to the Crown, and 125,728 to the communes and public establishments (whose woods, as elsewhere, are worked under State supervision). The south part of the Duchy is a plain; the north is mountainous (Ardennes), running up to some 1600 feet. Besides hardwoods (beech chiefly) there are the usual conifers (silver fir is scarce), but these have only been introduced since 1840. The latter are out of their true habitat, and though they grow rapidly (and have accordingly relatively inferior quality) they go off quickly from disease unless mixed with beech, when both longevity and quality improve. It has been found that among several exotic conifers tried only the green Douglas succeeds. This species is not exacting, and grows well wherever the spruce will grow. It resists spring frosts, drought and great cold well. In 1907 a spruce plantation on poor, sandy soil succumbed to drought, whereas an adjacent Douglas plantation stood it admirably. The species has been known to stand – 11° F. Hitherto the method of treatment (now changed) has been Selection with a 20-25-year cycle. As the crop was not touched in this interval this method has been harmful, because the young growth has been stifled by the upper stage.

But I think that had an Intermediate operation been prescribed which, while not being a regular regeneration felling, relieved congestion among the stems of the upper stage, and also cut back the stems whose crowns were growing out over existing groups of young growth, the system would not have been at all bad.

VII. The forests of Corsica cover 16 % of the island, and their area is 430,768 acres, or, deducting rocks and unproductive ground, 346,541 acres. Of this, 326,055 acres are worked by the Forest Service. The actual State forest area is only 115,673 acres. More than a third of the island is, apart from the forests, covered with scrub. The Holm oak (*Quercus ilex*) occupies 28 %, of the wooded area, the Corsican pine 25 %, the Maritime pine 23 %, the beech 12 %, the cork oak 3 %, and divers species 9 %. Government took up the subject in 1856, and began by tapping the Corsican pine for resin. This was commercially successful during the American war, but afterwards the trade fell to pieces. The out-turn was good, but there were no local workmen (*resiniers*), and those brought from the flat Landes did not like the steep ground and the loneliness. Tapping also does not suit the Corsican pine, and much damage has resulted from these early and crude workings. Of late years they have started, with apparent success, the tapping of the Maritime pine, which is the resin-producing pine of the Landes. They used to work the Corsican pine on the Uniform (or Successive fellings) method, and this is the method *par excellence* for pine forests, which regenerate themselves easily. It resulted in large areas clothed exclusively with young pine woods, which, when one of the numerous fires occurred, were destroyed—since the bark of young trees is not thick enough to resist—and there were then no means of restoring the regeneration. Accordingly they have fallen back on Selection, which is not so convenient for resin-tapping as the original method (with its concentration of work). A few standards—and but very few would probably be ample—left purposely scattered throughout the forest would, we think, meet the contingency, and allow of the application of the better method of treatment. Of course it is goats and fires that are the chief curse of the island.

VIII. It may have occurred to some that additional revenue might be made from our pine woods by tapping them for resin. The chief resin-yielding pine in Europe is the Maritime pine (*P. Pinaster*), and this tree, in the Landes, gives as much revenue from its resin as from its timber. To decide whether resin-tapping could be extended to other latitudes, with other pines, the Research Station at Nancy has made very careful experiments with the Scots and the Austrian pines, and the results have shown that commercial success would be very doubtful at that latitude (49° N.), and therefore, since heat seems to cause a more plentiful flow of resin, it would almost certainly not pay at home to undertake this work. The summer heat at Nancy is higher than in England. It is true that the price of turpentine and colophany (the components of resin) is nowadays rising, but it fluctuates, and therefore renders outlay on the construction of factories too risky.   Very occasionally, as during the American civil war, the prices obtained from the products of resin-tapping have been very high.   The Nancy experiments showed that the Austrian was a little better than the Scots for the production of resin, but the amount of resin per *quarre* (or groove made for the tapping) was only 12 to 13 oz. a year. The pine in the Landes produces from one to two litres (1 litre = 1·76 pint) per *quarre* per annum.

IX. M. Chancerel points out that whereas the fabrication of woodpulp for paper uses up immense quantities of timber, and the demand constantly increases, the pines, and especially the Scots and Maritime pines, are too full of resin to make good paper.   He suggests, therefore, that if the resin can be got rid of a very large addition to the supply of wood available will be made.   He says that the resin can be got rid of either by *dissolving* or by *neutralising* it.   For dissolving it he proposes, after rejecting several solvents that are dangerous or costly, the use of medicated (*dénaturé*) alcohol.   The alcohol is heated in a water-bath, and the vapour of the alcohol, when cooled and liquified, passes through the wood-fibre and back into the original vessel, carrying with it the resin (in the form of turpentine and colophany) and such other organic matters as are soluble in alcohol, but these are small in amount.   The wood is completely purged of resin.   The neutralising process is even simpler and cheaper. The turpentine is first removed by passing steam through the wood fibre, after which the fibre is boiled with a solution of soda, which neutralises all the acids present, as well as the colophany. To test this we may distil the fibre with alcohol, and if the alcohol dissolves nothing it is clear that the resin has been got rid of.

X. The French Parliament is discussing the placing of private woods under the surveillance of the State—not, it is thought, the forcible placing of them under the State, but whether private proprietors should be *at liberty* to obtain for their woods, to a greater or less extent, the assistance of the Government, as represented by its forest officers.   The object is, of course, to encourage afforestation, for the idea includes the formation of new woods as well as the maintenance o those in existence.   The subject is worthy of our consideration.   The first step has been made here by the appointment of advisory officers, but a great deal more could surely be done. In the first place, as things are at present, these advisory officers are given a difficult—even, sometimes, an invidious—task, for they are called in to prescribe for woods they have not previously known, and which they will probably not see again, and they seem to be situated as would be a doctor who has never seen his patient before, and is required to cure that patient with one prescription after one visit. Now the best forester in the world could not be certain of giving absolutely sure advice in such circumstances. The adviser needs to be permitted to watch his proposals in action for a certain period—say five years—in order that he may learn the *local* conditions, which are apt to vary greatly. A visit or two a year would be sufficient to show him how things were working out. It would probably be best to charge no fee for this, but the adviser should most decidedly be given the chance, not only to see whether the local conditions made it advisable for him to alter in any particular his original proposals, but also to see whether those proposals were understood in their execution. The necessity is not always fully realised of adhering strictly and steadily, and very patiently and persistently, to the prescriptions of a carefully thought-out scheme, if that scheme is to have a fair chance. Without this the advice will, it seems likely, lose more than half the value which it might have. In France the idea of assistance from State officers is not new—it is even, more or less unofficially, in practice. They have also one other advantage there that unfortunately cannot at once apply here—they have the *example* of the State forests. One hopes that some day there may also be State forests in the British Isles, and we may be perfectly sure, from the experience of other countries, that the true policy is to entrust to one energetic and wide-minded person (and *not* to a Board) the work of building up a Forest Department. Such a Department would go from strength to strength, and we should insensibly find ourselves making a practice of communicating with its officers. Thus—and, one is inclined to think, not otherwise—will forestry flourish, for the necessary *persistence* is perhaps only to be certainly attained in a State service.

XI. It may happen that members of our Society sometimes travel to Switzerland by way of Dijon and Lausanne. If so, and they would care to see the finest silver firs in France—perhaps in Europe—they might stop on the way and visit the

Forêt de Levier, which is some 20 kilometres from Pontarlier, on the highest plateau of the Jura. The forest of Levier is only one of many forests in that neighbourhood, but it is the most beautiful. Levier is a station up a branch line, which leaves the main line at Andelot, not far from Pontarlier. There is said to be an inn (the "hotel de l'Ours") to stay at in the village of Levier. This is the true home of the silver fir, most of the forest being at from 2300 feet to 2800 feet above the sea. The growth of the species is here quite grand, and the stems reach 130 feet (occasionally 150 feet) in height. The production is of course very high, and the regeneration very good where it escapes the brambles, which, however, are very prevalent. Silver fir constitutes 90 % of the crop, and 10 % is spruce, relatively recently introduced. But the spruce is not in its own station, and is only considered an auxiliary species, destined to be removed in the thinnings. Its presence has a happy effect on the regeneration of the silver. What they want is a certain mixture of beech as a soil-improver. The area of the forest is 6700 acres, and the enumeration made in 1904 showed 629,902 trees of from 31·5 inches (80 centimetres) to 15 ft. 9 ins. (4·8 metres) in girth at chest-height—that is, 93 stems to the acre; but note that all stems below $31\frac{1}{2}$ inches girth are omitted. The corresponding volume, from the same stems, was found to be just over 5800 cubic feet to the acre. The "possibility" has been fixed by the Working-Plans Service at 12 cubic metres per hectare (just over 171 cubic feet per acre) per annum.

XII. There has been great discussion lately concerning the sale of the forest of Eu, in Normandy. This forest belonged to the Orleans family, and it was proposed to sell it in the open market. This would have resulted in its complete devastation, in all probability, with dire effect on the local watercourses, and so forth. But the State has stepped in and acquired it by expropriation—that is, nine-tenths of the cost (and ownership) are to be the State's part, and one-tenth that of the Department. It is a big thing, for the forest is 25,000 acres in extent, and one can travel for 50 kilometres without leaving it.

XIII. The more inclement the climate, the more sterile the soil, the greater is the need for afforestation. This has been grasped of late years in a wonderful manner in Norway. There are, according to M. Perrin (in the *Bulletin trimestriel de Franche Comté et Belfort*), 14,820,000 acres under forest, and as much as 61,750,000 acres of unproductive land, in Norway. The treatment of the forest area leaves, it is believed, much to be desired, and in the waste country endless afforestation is possible and desirable, especially along the bare west coast. And for Norway the forest is the great asset. This having been perceived a society has, during the last dozen years, sprung up under the leadership of Axel Heiberg, and has spread itself over the whole of Norway. The Government has recognised its value, and assists it more and more each year. The constitution of the society appears to be rather complicated, but it is most effective. Besides extending forest knowledge in a variety of ways, it subscribes to afforestation work by private individuals and communes (which are not, in Norway, obliged to have their forests managed by the State), and although it must of course impose certain rules in regard to the spending of its subscriptions, more and more people come to it for assistance, both in advice and money. From its foundation to 1911 the society brought about the afforestation of between 54,000 and 55,000 acres with 88,000,000 plants and 4 tons of seed, and has drained over 32,000 acres with 2728 miles of ditches. Apart from these direct results is also the great effect produced, in a right direction, throughout the nation and on the Government.

XIV. The floods of the Seine, which caused such trouble in Paris in 1910, gave rise to a great deal of discussion, many holding that more forest was needed in the basin of the river, and others saying that forests were of little use. M. Viney, an Inspector of Forests, says that in point of fact the part of the basin of the Seine which lies above Paris (nearly 12,000,000 acres) is wooded to the extent of 4,200,000 acres nearly, and is certainly the best wooded basin in France. At the same time the cause of afforestation has been supported by bad arguments. There are plenty of good arguments for it, but it is a mistake to claim for it impossibilities. It can do a great deal, but it is not an absolute panacea. M. Viney traces with great ability the action of water on the soil, and that of forests in connection with it. It is recognised that near large forests the air is cooler in summer, and damper and nearer saturation point at all seasons, than in open country. The Research Station of Nancy has established that the rain water intercepted by the trees, and evaporated before reaching the ground, varies between 6 % when the leaf is off and 11 % in summer. Yet, after ten years of observations, it has been found that the forest soil receives 12 % more water than the open country. The water which reaches the forest soil is partly evaporated, partly transpired by the trees, partly retained by the trees (but this counts for very little), partly sinks in, and, in certain circumstances, in part flows over the surface. Direct evaporation is reduced to 35 % under the forest, as compared with open land, when litter is wanting, and to 12 % when it exists, the ground being screened from wind and sun, while the air is moister and cooler than outside, but these figures will vary according to the degree of humidity of the soil. Evaporation by the trees themselves (*i.e.* transpiration) varies according to the species, the heat, the light, and the intervals between the showers. It is immensely greater than direct evaporation, as is seen when plantations dry up marshy ground. According to Risler a field crop transpires 75 % of the rain that falls; a forest transpires a great deal less, and a young forest very much less than an old one; but, on the other hand, the forest goes far deeper for the water, and transpires throughout the period of vegetation. Höhnel states that birch and lime transpire 600 to 700 kilogrammes of water per kilo of leaves weighed in a dry state; beech, 400 to 500 kilos; oak, 200 to 300 kilos; and conifer, only 30 to 50 kilos. However, we should note, in passing, that this can scarcely apply to the spruce, for this species has a quite unusual power of drying up the soil. The water level descends far lower under forest than it does outside. M. Viney thinks that in the Seine basin above Paris, where the rainfall varies from 20 to 32 inches, 20 centimetres (or nearly 8 inches) is a fair estimate of the amount of water which reaches the rivers. The absorption of water varies according to the nature and depth of the soil, to the amount of water present in the soil at the time, to the slope, to the surface condition (grassy, cultivated, frozen, etc.), and, finally, to the duration and intensity of the rainfall. To study this phenomenon we must consider two things, the retaining capacity of the soil, and the rate at which it absorbs. The retaining capacity is reached when for every addition of water an equal amount runs away. After Meister, humus can take up 70 % of its own volume, garden soil the same, peat 64 %, and a lime soil 54 %. After

Ebermayer, moss retains 70 to 80 %. After Volny, turf retains half of the water a bare soil would allow to sink in. After Schloesing, a forest soil retains 42 %, or 10 % more than a limey clay soil. According to the German Research Stations 44 out of 100 millimetres of water falling on a forest soil will penetrate the upper layers, whereas with uncovered soil the figure would be 31. M. Viney therefore thinks that it would be reasonable to assume that an ordinary soil, 8 to 12 inches deep, covered by old coppice growth, would retain 2 inches more rain than waste land or bad pasture, which is the same as 500 cubic metres to the hectare (7149 cubic feet to the acre). The retaining capacity and the rate of absorption must go together, otherwise the water coming from a violent and continuous rain will pass off at once. Thus, a free gravel soil above rock will rapidly pass off the water along the top of the rock, and similarly a close-grained clay with a retaining capacity of 70 % will, after the surface is wetted, pass the water off the surface as does an impenetrable rock. The two qualities must go together if there is to be a properly regulated flow of water. And these two qualities are in fact found in the highest degree in a forest soil, with its sponge of humus, moss, etc., and its network of roots, which take the water down into the deep layers. Slopes of loose, unprotected soil are cut up by rain, the damage continually increasing, and spates and inundations result. Everything points to the necessity of checking the flow. Nothing does this like forest, which first prevents the dash of the rain on the surface, and then checks the flow by its spongy nature, while the roots hold the soil together. Still, it may be noted, even the best holding soil will sometimes reach its limit of saturation, and then the excess runs off the surface, so that even a forest soil cannot altogether stop floods.

Though the action of forests on floods is incontestable, and very marked, and much more so where the slopes are steep than in low country, yet, as said at the beginning, it is not fair to expect impossibilities from afforestation. Thus, whereas it was calculated that from the rainfall in November and December 1909 an excess of $4\frac{3}{4}$ inches of water ran into the Seine (not merely fell on the area), had as much as 400,000 hectares (988,000 acres) out of the 12,000,000 acres of the basin above Paris been afforested, in addition to the existing wooded area, this would only have absorbed 7064 million cubic feet (on the basis, as above demonstrated, of a 2-inch check), and this would have been but little when compared with the 6 milliards of tons of water which the excess represented over the area concerned (for a milliard equals 1000 millions).

We may mention certain figures giving an idea of the material carried down by floods. Thus, from the Pyrenees, in times of heavy flood, for every cubic metre of water in the Garonne there is 1½ kilo of mud, in the Neste 13 to 16 kilos, in the Agly up to 38 kilos; from the Alps, where matters are much worse, in the Glandon, 1 cubic metre of water will contain, in similar circumstances, 150 to 160 kilos, and the Isère has 123 kilos, which is equivalent, in 24 hours, to about 4,000,000 tons of silt for a flow of 380 cubic metres per second.

7. The Formation of Plantations on Deep Peat.

(*With Plate.*)

By DONALD GRANT.

The area on which the plantations have been established comprises part of the estate of Corrour in Inverness-shire. They occupy the stretch of land which extends from Loch Treig to the river Spean. The plantations assume the form of a strip, varying in width from 100 yards to 500 yards, extending along the West Highland Railway for two miles and a half, and following the course of the river Spean for one mile and a half. The boundaries consist of a deer fence along the inner limits of the plantations, while the railway and the river Spean form the outer boundaries. The land over the greater part of the planted area is peat, ranging from 3 to 10 inches in depth on the knolls and slopes, while it attains a depth of over 10 feet in the hollows and more level places. On gentle slopes where the peat does not exceed 10 inches in thickness the subsoil is a stiff clay with a small proportion of white sand, while on the knolls and steep slopes we find a loose gravel and sand which, to all appearance, has been deposited in glacial times. The whole surface is covered with a strong growth of herbage, the dominant plants of which are the following:—Heather (*Calluna vulgaris*), bog myrtle (*Myrica gale*), flying bent (*Molinia cærulea*), mat grass

(*Nardus stricta*); in addition to these, species of *Carex* and *Juncus*, cotton grass (*Eriophorum vaginatum*), species of orchids, and the dwarf willow are also met with. The elevation ranges from 700 feet to over 900 feet above sea-level. The aspect of the strip which extends along the railway ranges from south-west to north, and the strip along the river Spean from north to north-east. The whole area slopes towards the outer boundaries.

NATURE OF LAND.

With a view to tree planting the peat is divided into three classes, viz. :—First class, or the best quality for tree-growth ; second class, or the next best quality ; and third class, or the quality on which trees make least progress.

The first class peat, or best quality, is invariably deep, sometimes attaining a depth of 8 feet. It is very dark in colour, very porous, and holds a large quantity of water. It is very much easier cut with a spade, or any tool that may be used for draining it, than the second or third class. On it grow—*Molinia cærulea*, bog myrtle, some species of orchids, heather, and dwarf willow. The second class peat, or next best quality for tree planting, covers nearly two-thirds of the planted area. It is dark brown in colour and does not attain a great average depth, very often not more than 18 inches. It is more fibrous, tight, and holds much less water than the first class. On it grows a mixture of heather, mat grass, bog myrtle, and a species of *Carex*. The third class peat, or the most unsuitable quality for planting, is of a rather light brown colour, and varies from 3 inches to 8 feet in depth It is extremely tight, very fibrous, most difficult to cut, and holds less water than the first and second class. On it grow *Carex*, cotton grass, and a small proportion of heather.

It may be worth while to add the following observations, because they bear out some facts which I have stated regarding the qualities of peat for tree-growing :—The very best class of peat is found where birch had once grown freely, and where their stems are still to be found in a decayed state as deep as 3 feet below the surface. On the other hand, the very worst, or the most unsuitable class for tree-growth, is found where Scots pine grew. Here we find stumps of fairly large trees measuring 30 inches in diameter, with quite a large proportion of smaller stumps from 6 to 9 inches in diameter just immediately below the surface. A solid log of Scots pine was found last year about 2 feet below the surface. This tree was cut close to the root by a saw, and although we were able to count 115 annual rings, the diameter was only 15 inches.

PLANTATION TYPES.

The plantations are chiefly made of Sitka spruce (*Picea sitchensis*), Norway spruce (*Picea excelsa*), Scots pine (*Pinus silvestris*), Mountain pine (*Pinus montana* var. *uncinata*), with some *Picea Omorika* and *Picea Engelmannii.*

Sitka Spruce.—In March and April 1908 part of the enclosure which follows the course of the river Spean was planted with Sitka spruce. The peat was from 22 inches to 28 inches deep; this was not quite so deep as the average, and was the best quality or first class. A few weeks previous to planting some drains 18 inches deep with a proportional width were dug at a cost of 17s. per acre. The plants were notched at a distance of 3 ft. 3 ins. apart, and cost £1 per acre. The age of the plants was 2-year 1-year. They were bought from Germany at a very low price, and were planted straight out on their arrival. Some of the plants were so small that the grass had to be burned off the surface to allow of their being planted properly. In July 1908 the growth of grass threatened to smother some of the smaller plants, so that cutting had to be done, which cost 10s. per acre. The following summer some more grass had to be cut over the same area at a cost of 13s. 4d. per acre. The plants have now established themselves very well, and look very promising although they are still rather irregular in size. Beating up was considered unnecessary owing to the small number of deaths. In autumn 1908 another piece of the same enclosure was planted with Sitka spruce. The peat was on the whole rather shallow, and only in the hollows did it exceed 26 inches. It was second class quality. A few weeks previous to planting some drains were made 18 inches deep and 16 inches wide, at a cost of 13s. 4d. per acre. The plants were again got from Germany They were 2-year 1-year, and on their arrival in November they were immediately planted out.

In the beginning of the following summer it was observed that nearly all the plants had shed their leaves, and died. There are two reasons for this failure. In the first place, the peat had not been sufficiently drained, neither were the drains cut early enough to take away the excessive moisture; and secondly, the winter which followed planting was very severe. Later in summer it became evident that something should be done to replace the dead plants and to bring the land into a better state, by making more drains. The Belgian system of planting was suggested, and draining operations were at once begun, and completed before the end of November at a cost of £2, 6s. 8d. per acre. The drains were made at a distance of 6 feet apart, and were 18 inches wide and 10 inches deep. The inverted turfs were left to decay during the winter, and by the late spring they were in excellent condition for planting. The plants used were 3-year-old Norway spruce, raised in seed-beds at Pollok, and lined one year in the Fersit nursery. They were planted out in April. Two handfuls of coarse sand were put in along with the roots of each plant. Since then the plants have made steady progress; the death rate has hardly reached 1 %.

During the autumn of 1908 a strip 3 acres in extent, running along the railway side, had also been drained. The peat averaged 8 feet in depth, and was of first class quality. The Belgian method of draining had been employed at a cost of £2, 6s. 8d. per acre. The drains were cut 6 feet apart, 18 inches wide and 10 inches deep, and then this piece was left over till April 1909, when planting was begun on the inverted turf at a cost of 16s. 8d. per acre. The greater part of this was planted with 3-year-old Sitka spruce and the remainder with *Picea Omorika*. Both species were raised at Pollok, and lined one year in the Fersit nursery. At the beginning of autumn a close examination was made, and it was observed that all the plants had made a very short growth, but happily all were alive.

The following season they made a good vigorous growth and looked very well, again next summer they grew much better, but before the autumn came many of them got very yellow, owing to the fact that by this time the roots had made their way through the inverted turf, and penetrated the wet peat that had evidently not been sufficiently drained. Steps were at once taken to remove the excessive moisture, and the drains were dug to a depth of 20 inches at a cost of £2, 8s. per acre. The material from the drains was spread over the whole surface among the young trees, like a top dressing, and before the end of the following summer the effect of this deepening could easily be seen, while the trees grew more vigorously than before, and again assumed a robust green colour. In the summer and autumn of 1910 a large area towards the end of Loch Treig was drained. The peat varied in depth from 18 inches to 4 feet, and was mainly second class quality, the remainder being third class. The Belgian method of draining was at once decided on, and operations were immediately begun. Owing to the very wet nature of the land, and the difficulty of removing the excessive moisture, an improved method on the Belgian system of draining was carried out at a cost of £2, 5s. per acre. Drains were cut 11 feet apart, and 2 feet wide and 10 inches deep. Three rows of inverted turf were then placed between the drains about 2 ft. 8 ins. from centre to centre of each, then a further tramp was taken out of each drain to a depth of 22 inches, and placed on the side of each drain, making four rows of upturned peat for planting on instead of three rows as formally (Pl. IV. fig. 2). This method of draining had an early and striking effect on this very wet peat, for in the early spring the whole flat sank, and instead of the drains being 2 feet wide and 20 inches deep they were little over 16 inches either way. In the early part of May 1912 the whole area was planted chiefly with 3-year-old Sitka spruce. Groups of Scots pine, Mountain pine, Norway spruce, and Engelmann's spruce were also planted.

All these plants were raised at Pollok, and lined one year in the Fersit nursery, with the exception of the *Picea Engelmannii* which was obtained from Germany. With all the plants two handfuls of coarse sand, with a proportion of 15 to 1 basic slag mixed, were put in with their roots. The planting cost 16s. 8d. per acre. In autumn the planted area was inspected, and on the whole all the plants looked well, and altogether in very satisfactory condition. During the summer of this year the plants made still better progress, and they look very promising.

Norway Spruce.—Since 1907 fairly large areas of Norway spruce have been planted both along the river Spean and the railway side. The peat ranged from 8 inches to 5 feet deep. The quality of the peat was third class, with the exception of 2 acres first class. In 1909 the area along the river Spean was prepared by making a few ordinary drains on the very wet parts. Planting immediately followed draining in spring, the notching method being employed. The plants were 2-year 1-year, bought from Germany and planted straight out on their

PLATE IV.

FIG. 1.—A Demonstration of the Belgian system of Planting.

FIG. 2.—Improved Belgian system of Draining, with four rows of inverted turf.

arrival (in April). During the summer after planting all looked well, the plants making a short growth; but since then they have shed their leaves and now look quite hopeless. It is proposed now to replant Scots pine over the whole area, this being the only species that accommodates itself on third class quality of peat. Along the railway side large sections have been planted during the spring of 1911. The peat was very deep, averaging 7 feet, and all third class quality. During the summer of 1910 these sections were drained, Belgian system, at a cost of £2, 6s. 8d. per acre. Planting was begun about the end of April 1911; two handfuls of gravel, with a small proportion of basic slag mixed, were put in along with the roots of each plant. The plants were raised in Pollok nursery, and lined one year in the Fersit nursery. For two years they grew well, but now they look very unhealthy and many of them died during the past summer.

Scots Pine and Mountain Pine.—Scots pine has been more extensively planted on peat than any other species. We have limited its planting, as far as possible, to peat not exceeding 10 inches in depth; only in a few instances has it been planted on peat exceeding 20 inches in depth. The peat is divided into second and third class quality. Along the course of the river Spean, and also along the railway, large areas have since 1908 been notch-planted with 3-year-old Scots pine at 3 feet and 3 ft. 6 ins. apart. The depth of the peat on the slopes and knolls averaged only 4 inches, while it often attained 18 inches at the foot of a slope or on the level. Very few drains were made, and these only in the very wet places. Planting was always done during the spring. The plants were all raised at Pollok, and lined one year in Fersit nursery. Scots pine has been confined to peat limited in depth by inches, and has always done well, growing strong and healthy, but the progress of the plants is checked to a large extent for three years at least by the destructive black game. Mountain pine has been tried on a small scale only, and so far we can only place it on a level with Scots pine.

CONCLUSION.

The feasibility of establishing plantations on peat is demonstrated by the previous existence of trees on such areas. It is fairly evident that the most economic method of planting on land of this nature is the Belgian system. The modifications of this have had the effect of reducing the cost from £3, 3s. 4d. in 1910 to £2 per acre in 1913, not including price of plants. The species of trees which do most successfully on this land are Sitka spruce, Norway spruce, and Scots pine. The best species for peat of first class quality are Sitka and Norway spruce, while Scots pine and Mountain pine grow well also. But owing to their deeper root-system it is not advisable to plant the pines, because much more money would have to be spent on deepening drains during the first few years. The best species for peat of second class quality are Sitka spruce, Norway spruce, and Engelmann's spruce.

The species that accommodate themselves best on peat of third class quality are Scots pine and Mountain pine, while Sitka spruce and Norway spruce, *Picea alba*, *Picea Omorika*, and *Picea Engelmannii* will not grow on it even with the aid of artificial manure.

The best size of plants to use are 2-year 1-year, although 2-year seedlings of Scots pine also do quite well. 2-year 2-year spruce do quite as well as 2-year 1-year, but with the former more difficulty is caused by the larger roots which are more troublesome to plant properly. The best season for planting all these species is from March to May.

8. A Plan Adequate to Meet our Needs for Wood Timber.

An important address on the above subject was delivered by Dr B. E. Fernow to the Society for the Protection of New Hampshire Forests, on the 23rd July 1913.

A full report appears in the August issue of *American Forestry*, and the following excellent synopsis is given in the *Canadian Forestry Journal* of October last :—

Dr Fernow began by stating that there was probably now nobody who had not grasped the idea that the fundamental object of forestry was to reproduce the forest crop which we had used and, if possible, in better form. Looking over the United States there was little attempt at reproduction. The population was still growing, and, while a reduction in consumption, from the present 250 cub. feet per capita per year to something like the consumption of European countries was inevitable, this change would not be made readily.

Dr Fernow then quoted from the report of the National Conservation Commission to the effect that the cut was more than twice the annual growth and that there was then (1907) hardly thirty years' supply in sight, so there was no time for dilly-dallying.

He urged that fire protection and conservative logging would not meet the need, as these were concerned with the *utilisation* of the existing crop but did nothing to *insure* a new crop.

It was true that fire protection was essential to forestry, as no one would invest money with a high fire hazard; but fire protection had been so much improved of late years that the time was more propitious for pressing for reforestation.

Holding that, in spite of substitutes, timber would continue to be used and would continue to increase in price, and also that the natural regeneration method of timber reproduction would be found nearly as costly and far less effective than replanting, he wished to go on record as holding the opinion that "our future needs can not be satisfactorily and adequately provided for until we take recourse to planting operations on a large scale."

Within twenty years the United States would have reached the point where virgin timber, in which natural regeneration might still be practised, would be near its end. The country's needs must then be supplied chiefly from the so-called second growth and volunteer growth; and the area capable of restocking only by artificial means would have increased probably to 250,000,000 acres, over half the remaining forest soil. (Dr Fernow estimated that in 1907 the forest area of the United States was 580 million acres.) Then the people would be forced to plant whether they believed in that method or not.

It was useless to expect private enterprise to undertake this task owing to the long time element involved. The railways, needing a constant supply of ties, and paper companies, whose big plants were built with the idea of continuous forest supplies, might embark in tree planting, but Dr Fernow was afraid that for the rest they would have to abandon the idea of individual endeavour and learn that community interests must be attended to by the community. In the end only the State and the municipality could be expected to provide for a distant future. There were foolish notions abroad as to the distance of that future, and how long it took to grow a log tree. With most species in most localities nothing could be expected in less than 60 to 100 years.

He had no cut and dried plan for this except to set every State forester, State commission and forestry association thinking, to make them realise that their business was not only to conserve existing resources but to create new ones, and to recognise that this was a more serious matter than could be met by the distribution of a few thousand trees to private planters; that it required *systematic procedure on a large scale.*

Each State forester should make a canvass of his State to ascertain what lands could be left to private planting and what to municipal or State enterprise. He should work out a plan of State co-operation which might take the form, in the case of municipalities, besides furnishing plant material and advice, of pledging the State's superior credit for raising the necessary funds by bond issues for acquiring and reforesting waste lands, and in return securing supervisory power for the State. For New England municipal action was perhaps the most promising, although, in general, direct State control might be preferable.

Dr Fernow gave the following example to illustrate the method of procedure :—

"Let us assume that a town has bought 5000 acres of waste lands, which it could secure for say £3000, borrowing the money from the State at 3 %; the 5000 acres to be planted in a 25-year campaign; that is at the rate of 200 acres per year, at a cost of 32s. per acre; the annual outlay of £320 to be furnished by the State from year to year, when the interest charges will be £90 on the original investment and a series of interest payments of £9, 12s., increasing annually by £9, 12s. The loans will then, in the twenty-fifth year, have accumulated to £11,000 and the interest accumulations to £5374 or £215 per year, and the highest last annual charge to £330, amounts not difficult to raise. After the planting is finished, the annual interest charge remains stable at £330. Now each year 200 acres may be thinned and every five years the thinning repeated. A net result of 8s. per acre for the first thinning (at that time wood prices will be higher), 12s. for the second, and 14s. for every subsequent thinning would be a reasonable assumption. In other words, for the first five years after loans and planting have been completed the interest charges are met to the extent of £80, in the second quinquennium, to the extent of £140, and in the third quinquennium, a surplus begins to appear. Now arrangements for refunding the load may be made at once, or else merely interest may be continued to be paid out of returns for thinnings, the town receiving small incomes until the sixtieth year, when the first 200 acres may come to harvest yielding not less than £24,000 (likely much more at that time), wiping out the loan and leaving a very valuable property producing annual revenue.

"All that the State has done is to lend its credit, not one cent is given in charity, and the town has made no expenditure except for the care of the property.

"That these calculations are not chimerical may be learned from the experiences of France.

"Here the State reforested during the last century 200,000 acres of sand dunes at a cost of £400,000. Of this 75,000 acres were sold reimbursing the total cost of the 200,000 acres and £28,000 to boot, and leaving a property now valued at £2,000,000.

"In the Landes the State, municipality and private owners planted nearly 1,750,000 acres at a cost of £2,000,000, the value of the recovered properties being now placed at £20,000,000, based on their annual production.

"Some 200,000 acres of poor land, unhealthy useless waste, in La Sologne, was planted by a private association at a cost of £1 per acre. These lands, which fifty years ago could not be sold at 16s. per acre, now bring in over 12s. per acre annual revenue, being valued at £3,600,000.

"These are actual results achieved and not fancies or forecasts."

Dr Fernow went on to apply this to larger areas. In New England he estimated there were 5 million acres immediately ready for planting. This on a 25-year campaign would necessitate planting 200,000 acres per year. Some planting was now being done, but in the face of these figures did present work not look amateurish and inadequate?

Such an area (which is twice the forest area of Bavaria and Baden combined, producing £2,000,000) planted with white pine at £2 per acre and properly managed would produce annually its 2,000,000 M feet of lumber, worth even at present stumpage prices £4,000,000, and be an ample supply for any population that might then be located in New England.

Finally Dr Fernow applied his figures to the United States, and pointed out that now the Federal government was giving aid to reclamation schemes, good roads, waterways, etc., it would not be out of the way to include reforestation in this list.

In 1970, by which time the most advanced of the forests planted now would begin to mature, Dr Fernow estimated that the population of the United States would have become 225,000,000, and assuming that the per capita use of timber had decreased to that of England, 14 cub. feet per year, this would require the cut of close upon 1,000,000 acres per year of first-class forest, growing for 60 years at the rate of 400 feet B M per year. To keep up a continuous supply 60 million acres must be in that producing condition. The probability was that not less than 100 million acres would be required to satisfy all needs for wood material.

Since less than £4 per acre would be required for planting and interest account, an annual loan of £4,000,000 for sixty years—two dreadnoughts a year—would be ample provision. Dr Fernow's concluding summary of his plan was as follows:—

1. Each state to ascertain its quota of planting area, classified for systematic procedure in its recovery.

2. A co-operative financial arrangement by which municipalities may secure the credit of the State, and States the credit of the Federal government, for the purpose of acquiring and recovering their quota.

3. State planting to be done on a large scale.

" If I have not developed a very definite and adequate plan to meet our need for wood and timber in the future, I hope I have at least opened up a line of thought which may tend to its formulation."

9. The Excursion to Switzerland.[1]

(*With Illustrations.*)

By G. P. GORDON, B.Sc.(Edin. & Oxon.).

Through the medium of the Foreign Office the thirty-sixth annual excursion of the Society was organised to take place this year in Switzerland. Dr Coaz, Inspector-General of Forests for Switzerland, mapped out a comprehensive tour for the Society, and allotted three Federal Inspectors of Forests to conduct the party through its various stages. An extract of the official programme was made, a translation of which was in the hands of all the excursionists some time before leaving home.

The majority of the party travelled from Edinburgh to London on the evening of 10th July. The following morning, with increased numbers, the company proceeded via Folkestone and Boulogne to Paris, where the night was spent. The stage from Paris to Berne via Chaumont, Belfort and Basle occupied the greater part of the next day. During this part of the journey there was observed to be an almost complete absence of forest in the country traversed, the only tree which was at all in evidence being the poplar. This species does not form woods, but occurs as single standards along hedgerows, river banks and roads, and serves to break the monotony of an otherwise dull landscape. Beyond Belfort, however, when the region of the Vosges mountains was approached, the forest became dominant and extensive tracts of coniferous woods were passed through. We then arrived at the town of Basle, which forms the frontier station of Switzerland. After a short break here, the train was taken for Berne, where the headquarters of the Swiss Forest Department are found. Among those who received the members of the party at the station and accompanied them to the Hotel Bristol were Mr Clive, Dr Fankhauser, and Herr Schönenberger.

Sunday morning found us early astir, but in spite of that, time did not allow us to do full justice perhaps to the various points of vantage of the town of Berne. The town historically is intensely interesting, and even to-day has quite a mediæval appearance since much of the ancient part is well preserved. In addition, certain conditions are attached to the building of

[1] For the names of the gentlemen who took part in the Excursion, see page 119.

all new houses, so that they harmonise externally at least with their more venerable neighbours. The situation of the town is quite unique, as it is built upon a narrow tongue of land formed by a U-shaped bend of the river Aare, over which the old wooden bridge still stands. The combined effect is to give an impressive air of antiquity to the whole town.

Under the leadership of Dr Fankhauser and the city gardener, an inspection was made of the avenues which are so characteristic of the country in the vicinity of Berne. All the roads here have been converted into avenues by planting broad-leaved trees along either side at distances of from ten to twenty yards apart. The species usually planted are ash, elm, sycamore, chestnut, plane and walnut.

A return to the town was made by way of the Botanic Gardens, where Dr Fischer received us and demonstrated his very fine collection of Alpine plants. The Alpine Museum was next visited, where a description was given in English by Dr Nussbaum of the geological formations of the Alps.

In the course of the morning the President, Captain Stirling, had arrived, thus completing the party which now numbered sixty-six members.

From Berne on Sunday afternoon the company set out by train for Scherzligen on Lake Thun, from which point steamer was taken to Interlaken. The sail along the lake under ideal weather conditions showed to best advantage, perhaps, the natural grandeur of this part of the country. The deep blue waters of the glacier-fed lake contrasted sharply with the dark ridges fringing them, while in the distance the glistening Jungfrau complex formed a majestic horizon. The town of Interlaken, although low-lying, is very pretty, having a picturesque situation upon the neck of land between the two lakes of Thun and Brienz.

Mr Pulver and Mr Marti, the officials of the Department of Woods and Forests of the Canton, received the party here. Interlaken extended a kindly welcome to its visitors that evening, and the password "Écossais" gave free access to its various places of entertainment.

SCHYNIGE PLATTE.

The ascent of the Schynige Platte (6463 feet) was made early on Monday morning by mountain railway. This railway traverses forests of beech, ash and hazel, with a certain admixture of spruce. Towards the upper limits of the forests silver fir occurs, and extends to about 5200 feet. The forests here belong to the commune and are managed on a rotation of 100 years.

On reaching the summit perhaps one of the grandest views in Switzerland was obtained. A gigantic mountain range lay before us, extending from beyond Grindelwald to the Breithorn, and including among other peaks the Wetterhorn, Schreckhorn, Finsteraarhorn, Eiger, Mönch, Jungfrau and Grosshorn. After having breakfasted, the descent was commenced on foot in the direction of Grindelwald. During the first part of the route most of the country consisted of meadowland. Much of this had originally been forest, but the unrestricted grazing of cattle and especially of goats has quite depleted it. At present both meadowland and forest are under the same authority, so that grazing operations are properly controlled.

The typical Swiss chalet was very much in evidence in this region. The cattle are taken to these upland meadows in May and return to the valleys in September. While here the cows are brought in at 8 A.M. to be milked and again at 6 P.M., after which they are turned out for the night. In hot weather, however, they remain inside all day to escape the heat. The milk is made into butter and cheese in the chalet. In autumn the cattle return to the valleys in stages. During the months of November and December they again come up to the chalets, and are fed on the hay which is stored there. This obviates the necessity of transporting the hay from the high meadows down into the valleys.

The descent was continued via Iseltenalp to the protection works at Schiltriesete. Here some time ago a large landslide occurred which covered the main road at the foot of the slope. Evidence that the hillside was slipping was obtained from the fact that the trees commenced to lean down hill. These leaning stems were cut over, and retaining walls were built at the bottom of the slope. About twenty-five years ago a slip took place on another part of the area when the land was swept quite bare of vegetation. Retaining walls were again constructed, this time beginning at the top of the affected area, and the whole was planted with alder, willow and spruce. One of the walls examined showed a terraced construction, having been built in a series of large steps.

A short though somewhat steep climb brought the party to Sengg, from which point an excellent view was obtained of the opposite slope. The forest was again entered, and after about an hour's march a halt was made for lunch.

An inspection was afterwards made of the protection works at Rischbachriesete. Some thirty years ago this part of the Lütschenthal was bare of forest, and a start was made to re-afforest the area by controlling the springs. It was here that Dr Fankhauser first conceived the idea of erecting parallel walls in the form of terraces (Plate V. fig. 1). The walls were constructed by going down to the solid rock, getting a good foundation and upon that building a drystone dyke. These walls occur at intervals of 10 to 12 feet, and at this point upon a slope of 55 % to 66 %. These operations were begun at the foot of the slope and the work continued upwards. The land between the walls was planted with 4-year-old spruce and 3-year-old alder (*Alnus incana*). The species *Alnus incana* may be planted up to elevations of 1600 metres on southern aspects; at higher elevations green alder (*Alnus viridis*) is employed. The top canopy is established by those species, and they are later under-planted with beech or silver fir. The total cost of this protection work was £4400.

Early in the afternoon the small village of Burglauenen, in the Lütschenthal, was reached, whence train was taken for Interlaken. In the evening the party proceeded by steamer along Lake Brienz and, after an hour's journey, arrived in the old-world town of Brienz. Next morning the Brienzer Rothorn (7715 feet) was ascended by mountain railway. Unfortunately the weather had broken somewhat, so that the splendid panoramic view from the summit was not obtainable. The descent was made on foot, during which good opportunity was given to examine all the details in the extensive protection works of the Trachtbach. Formerly this stream was very difficult to control, since the grazing of cattle and goats had depleted the upper reaches of forest. In 1870 the lower part of the course was built up with protective masonry, but the first flood carried everything into the lake of Brienz. The community in 1880 decided to afforest the upper slopes of the gathering grounds of the river, and also to establish protection works in the side valleys. Accordingly the Forest Department drew up a plan of the work and an estimate of the cost which was submitted to Government and

PLATE V.

FIG. 1.—Wall protection works with afforestation of intervening land.   Trachtbach.

FIG. 3.—Wooden hurdles as protection works against avalanches.

FIG. 4.—Masonry protection works in stream-bed.　Trachtbach, Lake Brienz.

to the community. This was sanctioned—Government offering to contribute upwards of 50 % of the cost, the Canton of Berne providing 20 to 30 %, while the remainder was made up by the community. The community also undertook to maintain the works.

The Trachtbach rises at an elevation of 6068 feet, which is rather higher than the tree limit in this locality. The physical features of the valley show a series of gigantic steps. Operations were commenced at the top and the work gradually proceeded to the lower levels. A start was made by erecting parallel walls of stone, the ground between which was then planted with grass and trees. In the early stages of this work avalanches, which formed in the spring of the year, very often swept away the previous year's work. The mode of occurrence of these avalanches is well demonstrated in Plate V. fig. 2. The pasture which ultimately appeared on these upper slopes between the walls attracted the flocks of the peasants, with the result that these areas had to be rigorously enclosed. The tree species employed in the plantings were *Pinus Cembra*, Scots pine, larch, spruce, mountain pine and alder, and they were put in in very small groups. Experience has shown that at these high elevations groups are better able to stand up against snow than single trees, and by having an exposed surface between the groups the soil heats quicker under the action of the sun. Small nurseries were established as high up as possible in order to save transport and to acclimatise the young plants. *Pinus Cembra* has probably done best of all the species, as it has an extraordinary power of recovery from snow-break, bruising, etc. Direct sowings were tried in places but were not found to be successful. The grass was established partly by planting squares of turf and partly by collecting the seeds of the natural grasses and sowing them broadcast.

As the work progressed modifications of the original methods were made, the wall was discarded and gave place to a broad terrace (Plate VI. fig. 5). These terraces are simply broad drystone dykes which are topped with turfs. In localities where stones were scarce wooden hurdles were erected and small terraces of turf were built between (Plate V. fig. 3).

As lower elevations were approached an extensive drainage scheme became necessary. The waters from the melting snows accumulated at the bottom of the topmost large natural terrace, saturated the soil there and started a gigantic earth slide. Drains were therefore cut at this point and the water was led into a central reservoir ; from this it was taken through cement pipes to the edge of the next natural step, at the foot of which similar works were established. In the lower reaches of the valley the waters of the Trachtbach are in two channels, and just before they meet there is a last barrier. This is in the form of a natural weir, which retains any large debris that may have reached this point. The river-bed has in several places been specially protected to prevent washing-out taking place (Plate V. fig. 4). From the point where the waters join, the river-bed takes the form of a large open aqueduct which extends right into the lake.

The extensive and varied nature of this protection work is perhaps best seen from Plate VI. fig. 5. In addition, the effectiveness of the work is also very striking and an excellent opportunity was afforded of testing this. Prior to the first visit to the Trachtbach no rain had fallen. During the next night, however, a heavy thunderstorm occurred, and on visiting the Trachtbach in the morning it was found that the volume of water in the stream was practically the same.

The work is maintained by a staff of ten men who start operations in April and work until September. Planting is commenced at the lower elevations, as the land there is earlier clear of snow. The forests on the area are managed on the Selection system. The timber is used for fuel, for paper pulp manufacture, and the small material for props.

After the descent from the Rothorn a visit was made to a wood-carving factory in the town of Brienz. This establishment furnishes an excellent example of an important forest industry. On inquiry it was found that all the employees were small-holders, thirty of whom were employed permanently while 120 were employed on piece-work in their homes.

In the evening at dinner Mr Pulver officially welcomed the party to the Canton Berne, and expressed regret that the visit was of such short duration. Captain Stirling in replying expressed our high appreciation of the kindness we had received since entering the Canton, especially at the hands of Dr Fankhauser and Mr Pulver. Later in the evening a small local orchestra entertained us with folk-songs, yodles, and with selections upon the alpine horn. A reel, a sword dance and selections on the bag-pipes were contributed by members of our party.

A departure was made from Brienz on Wednesday morning by train over the Brünig Pass to Lucerne. The scenery on this part of the journey is typically Alpine, and represents one of the most picturesque parts of Switzerland. Lucerne was reached by midday and, after lunch, under the leadership of Mr Bühler, a tour was made through the town. Lucerne occupies a beautiful position at the end of the lake of the same name, and is flanked by the two peaks Pilatus and the Rigi Kulm. The journey to Zürich was completed in the evening.

SIHLWALD.

The programme for the next day comprised a visit to the famous town forest of Zürich, the Sihlwald. This forest is perhaps unique in having been under systematic management for probably a longer period than any other forest in the world. Forstmeister Dr Meister joined the party in Zürich and train was taken to Sihlbrugg. The railway extends to the head of the valley of the river Sihl and skirts the forest all the way. During the journey Dr Meister described the general nature of the forest area.

The land is mountainous, being characterised by steep slopes which alternate with more or less level terraces. The elevation above sea-level varies from 16,007 feet in the valley to 3087 feet on the top of the ridge. The hill-slopes are cut up by over twenty mountain torrents, which rush down during the rains with such violence as to necessitate the construction of costly protection works to prevent erosion taking place on a large scale. The climate is temperate with an annual rainfall of 59 inches. The snow-fall is heavy, and this forms the greatest danger to the forest, since heavy falls occur in autumn before the trees are stripped of leaves. Early and late frosts are common although no great damage is done by them. The forest because of its sheltered position does not suffer from storms. The geological formation is a Tertiary fresh-water sandstone giving rise to a soil of the nature of a sandy loam which is deep and fertile.

Growing stock.—The forest is a mixed one with 85 % broad-leaved species and 15 % coniferous species. Of the broad-leaved trees beech constitutes 85 % of the crop, ash and maple about 14 %, while elm and hornbeam, etc., form about 1 %. Among the conifers spruce predominates, while silver fir, larch and Scots pine form the other species. It is interesting to note that the conifers are mainly confined to the right bank of the Sihl where the soil is inferior to that of the left bank. All the species have very good height-growth, beech especially yielding very tall stems of good quality timber.

Management.—This forest has been treated as high-forest for over 1000 years, and has been under regular management since the thirteenth century. The proportion between the broad-leaved species and the conifers has varied from time to time. The aim of the present management is to increase the percentage of conifers, and thus establish equal proportions of both conifers and hardwoods.

The areas are for the most part regenerated naturally under the Shelter Wood Compartment system, the regeneration period of the broad-leaved species being about 7 years, while that of the conifers is about 15 years. The thinnings lead on to "preparatory fellings" which are followed in about 3 years' time by "seed fellings"; the "final fellings" are then carried out after an interval of about 7 years. The direction of felling is not in any way influenced by prevailing winds, so that cuttings proceed from north to south and south to north in the two working-sections into which the forest is divided. It is thought that by increasing the regeneration period from 7 to 15 years or more, and adopting the group system of regeneration where possible, conifers will be favoured and the mixture will be more efficiently controlled.

In the spring after "final fellings" have been made, the felled area is cleared of timber and any young growth injured in the operation is removed. During the second year spruce is planted in groups and larch singly in the young crop. The planting material is taken from small nurseries when 4 years old and is put out at distances of 4 feet apart. The first regular cleaning is made in the 8-year-old wood, and consists in the removal of bad stems and weeds (poplars and willows), and of freeing some of the valuable species. There is a second cleaning made 5 years later, which consists in the removal of stems overgrowing and suppressing the planted conifers, and of such of the other stems as may have been injured by snow. These operations lead on to the first of the real thinnings which take

FIG. 5.—-Terraced walls as protection works in the gathering ground of the Trachtbach.

FIG. 6.—Loaded trucks on the permanent tramway
in the Sihlwald.

[To face p. 90.

FIG. 7.—Sledge road and loaded sledge in the Sihlwald.

FIG. 8.—Sledges for the transport of firewood. Sihlwald.

place in the
following obj
remove the c
The thinning
at intervals o
decade up t
the final yie
so as to obt
in order to le
The fores
Oberesihlwal
Untersihlwa
The annu
according to
yield =
a =
The real in
The yield

i.e.
Transport.
entirely by
adopted. T
streams, and
and mainten
chief method
1. The P
a distance
mill. It is
firewood.
per running
5¼ feet broa
degrees. T
106 feet ra
them down,
(Plate VI. f
2. Sledge
bringing fire
the tramway
branches a

place in the 18-year-old wood. These are carried out with the following objects in view :—(1) to favour the conifers; (2) to remove the cankered and unhealthy stems; (3) to realise revenue. The thinnings recur at intetvals of 5 years up to the age of 30, at intervals of 7 years between the ages of 30 and 50, and every decade up to 70 years, after which the produce is included in the final yield. Thinnings are thus made early and frequent so as to obtain large girth classes as soon as possible, and in order to lessen the damage done by snow.

The forest is divided into two working - sections — the Oberesihlwald, which has a rotation of 90 years, and the Unteresihlwald, which is managed on a rotation of 110 years.

The annual possibility or yield of the forest is calculated according to Heyer's method, viz.—

$$\text{yield} = \text{real increment} + \frac{\text{real growing stock} - \text{normal G. S.}}{a}$$
$$a = \text{rotation.}$$

The real increment $\quad = 6219$ f.m. pro ha. and year.
The yield thus calculated $= 6630$ f.m. per year.
Thinnings $= 2250$ f.m. per year.
Total $= 8880$ f.m. per year on 1000 ha.
i.e. per ha. 8·9 f.m. $= 124·6$ cub. ft. per acre per annum.

Transport.—The transport of the forest produce is carried out entirely by the forest staff, and a large variety of methods is adopted. The locality is so irregular in contour, so cut up by streams, and so liable to erosion that the cost of road construction and maintenance would be prohibitive. The following are the chief methods of transport employed :—

1. The Permanent Tramway.—This traverses the forest for a distance of some 5 miles, and leads directly to the saw-mill. It is employed in the transport both of timber and firewood. The gauge is 24 inches with rail weight of 28 lbs. per running metre ($3\frac{1}{4}$ feet). The road on which it is laid is $5\frac{1}{3}$ feet broad and has a gradient which ranges from 3 to 7 degrees. The curves on the track vary from 49 feet radii to 106 feet radii. The momentum of the loaded trucks carries them down, the speed being controlled by powerful back brakes (Plate VI. fig. 6). The empty trucks are pulled up by oxen.

2. Sledge Road.—This provides a very effective method of bringing firewood down short slopes to depots on the line of the tramway. The sledge track is built with slender beech branches about 5 feet long, which are laid across any path

or road at distances of about a yard apart, and are kept in position by pegs driven into the ground at their ends. The total cost of construction is about a penny per yard. The sledges are taken down by men who control them by means of a pole fastened to one side of the sledge (Plate VI. fig. 7). The sledges after they reach the depot are unloaded, and are then carried up on the shoulders of the men (Plate VI. fig. 8).

3. Wooden Slide.—At Sihlbrugg a transportable wooden slide for firewood was seen in operation. It had a total length of 650 feet, and was constructed from two boards fitted to form a wide V about 2 feet across the top. The slide was made in 20-feet sections, each section being supported on four V-shaped trusses. This slide is only employed in the transport of firewood, and upwards of 7060 cubic feet may be taken down in a day.

Protection works.—Owing to the loose nature of the soil, the heavy rainfall, and the declivity of the land, the forest area is liable to suffer great damage from erosion. Accordingly it is found necessary to erect weirs in the beds of most of the streams. Plate VII. fig. 9 shows a cheap and effective method of protecting such a bed from erosion.

The walk through the forest from Sihlbrugg to Sihlwald occupied the greater part of the morning. At the Restauration von Sihlwald the company was entertained to lunch by Dr Meister and Mr Tuchschmidt, who represented the Corporation of Zürich. After lunch an inspection was made of the various methods and the machinery employed in the forest depot in the conversion of timber. Here an extensive plant for the impregnation of telegraph poles with copper sulphate was examined. A machine for the manufacture and bundling of firewood was also seen. In addition to band and circular saws there are "polishing" machines, "shaping" machines, and "copying" machines for the manufacture of tool handles. Perhaps one of the most interesting machines is seen in Plate VII. fig. 10, which illustrates the manufacture of wood wool from small spruce and silver fir timber. It was unfortunate that time did not allow of a longer examination being made of the various forms into which the timber is converted here.

. The effect of the intensive form of management practised in the Sihlwald is seen in the returns obtained from the forest, which in 1910-11 were 23s. per acre.

PLATE VII.

FIG. 9.—Timber protection works in stream-bed in the Sihlwald.

FIG. 10.—Wood Wool Machine in Sihlwald.

[To face p. 92.

WINTERTHUR.

Eschenberg Forest.

The town forest of Winterthur lies some miles to the north-east of the town of Zürich. The forest covers an area of some 30,000 acres. The geological formation is similar to that of the Sihlwald district and gives rise to the same deep, sandy, loamy soil. The annual precipitation of this locality is about 40 inches.

Growing stock.—Unlike the Sihlwald this forest consists almost entirely of the coniferous species spruce and silver fir. There is no definite succession of cutting series, but fellings are made in groups, as a result of which there is considerable variety in the forest. Here conifers have replaced the original hardwoods, since they were found to pay better.

Management.—The old system was one of "clear cutting" in high-forest, and there is still an area of 1500 acres of high-forest which is worked on a rotation of 100 years. The ordinary rotation of the greater part of the forest is 120 to 140 years. The management is being directed at present to produce (1) the highest possible volume per acre, (2) the highest possible money return. The regeneration period varies from 20 to 30 years. As the result of the "group" system of regeneration the soil has been greatly improved in its productive capacity. In addition valuable "light increment" is put on by the stems of the oldest "age-class," since they occupy more or less isolated positions. The total increment in some of these classes may amount to as much as 238 cubic feet per acre. Thinnings require to be very carefully carried out as a dense weed-growth occurs on the ground. Operations are not conducted over large areas, and all thinnings are made very light.

The regeneration of the forest is proceeded with in the following manner:—In crops which are about 75 years of age "light fellings" are commenced, as a result of which a crop of brambles immediately appears on the ground. These are cut over and rooted out at once, the latter operation helping to prepare the soil for seed. Full seed years of spruce occur here only at intervals of from 8 to 10 years, but a certain quantity is obtained every year and this is relied upon for regeneration purposes. The "light fellings" are made partly in groups, or in "Horsts," or in strips. In each case silver fir forms the nucleus of the group, and, under the influence of side light, spruce comes in and forms a girdle round the outside. The origins of these groups are usually small patches of "advance growth." Regeneration operations are conducted over a whole compartment at one time, and except for keeping the canopy closed on the west side the groups are not arranged in any definite manner. In this respect Dr Arnold, who has charge of this forest division, is not a disciple of Wagner. Each compartment is regenerated usually within two periods. Cleanings are commenced in the young crop before the mother-trees are removed.

Returns.—During the past 50 years the revenue of this forest has steadily risen, largely as the result of the completion of a splendid road system. The net return per acre and year 50 years ago was 23s., to-day this amounts to 50s. The increase has not been obtained by trenching upon capital, since there is a larger growing stock to-day than there was formerly. The current annual increment per acre is 98 cubic feet, while the final yield is 89·3 cubic feet per acre.

Before returning to the town of Winterthur for lunch, a visit was paid to a very old crop of spruce and silver fir in which some of the stems were 180 to 200 years of age, 150 feet high, and contained upwards of 700 cub. feet. In the afternoon the party made a short tour, under the guidance of Dr Arnold, in the Lindberg Forest. The return journey to Zürich was made in the evening.

ZÜRICH and ADLISBERG.

In the company of Dr Schinz and the city gardener an inspection was made, on Saturday morning, of the gardens and specimen trees, etc., at the Alpenquai. A very varied and interesting collection of trees has been established here. Later a visit was paid to the Botanic Gardens.

In the afternoon, under the leadership of Professor Engler, the party was conducted over the Forest Research Garden at Adlisberg. The objects of maintaining the garden are as follows :—(1) to supply the plants used in forestry, (2) to study the early stages of the life histories of trees, (3) to supply material for experiment in the forest, (4) to supply material for the School of Forestry. The garden is 3⅛ acres in extent, and occupies a small plateau which overlooks the town of Zürich. Careful meteorological records are kept in the garden, and in addition

there is a duplicate station in the forest. The experiments are
largely concerned with the relationship between the source of
seed and the nature of the tree produced. A detailed account
of the experiments which are being conducted here is to be
found in the proceedings of the Swiss *Centralanstalt für das
forstliche Versuchswesen.*

The official programme for Sunday was somewhat altered, and
the departure from Zürich for Chur was postponed until the
afternoon.

CHUR.

Oberthor Forest.

On Monday Mr Enderlin and Mr Meier conducted a tour
through the forests of the Oberthor, which clothe the steep slopes
behind the town of Chur. These forests are chiefly coniferous,
consisting of some 4500 acres of spruce, silver fir, and a few Scots
pine. The spruce is dominant in the upper parts, while more
silver fir occurs towards the valley bottom. Conifers constitute
95 % of the stock of the forest, while broad-leaved species make up
the remaining 5 %. The broad-leaved species consist of beech,
sycamore and ash. Originally the only means of transport here
were earth slides, which did considerable damage to the timber,
and also caused a great deal of erosion to take place. These
have now been discarded, as a good road system was planned
and carried out 10 years ago. This divides the hill slope into a
series of parallel strips (Etagen), along the lower edges of which
run the contour roads. In each strip the timber is slid down for
short distances until the road is reached.

The old method of regeneration was by producing gaps in the
canopy artificially. The method now employed is to take advantage of any natural gaps, thin out the trees on their edges, and
in this way obtain groups of young growth. Early thinnings are
made in order to regulate the mixture and to get the proper
proportions of the different species. Throughout the rotation
the best trees are favoured in all thinnings. As thinnings are
proceeded with, light gets in and patches of "advance growth"
appear and form the nuclei of the groups. There is only about
5 % to 6 % of beech in the forest at present, and the management is striving to increase this.

The prices of timber in this locality are fairly good, spruce
fetching up to 1s. 0$\frac{1}{4}$d. per cubic foot on rail, Scots pine 1s. 4d.

per cubic foot, and silver fir 9d. to 10d. per cubic foot. The permanent forest staff here consists of about 50 men, while in summer 150 hands may be employed. The average wage is 3s. 2d. to 4s. 5d. per day, the foreman getting 1s. per day extra. The annual wage bill may amount to £4800. Here a forest nursery was seen with large numbers of young plants, chiefly spruce.

A return was made to Chur for lunch, and in the afternoon a visit was made to Landquart, which is situated some 7 miles from Chur, where an inspection was made of a paper-pulp mill.

THE ENGADIN.

Next morning Dr J. Coaz assumed the leadership, and it would be indeed difficult to have had a more venerable leader, as he was in his 92nd year. An early start was made by special train for the Engadin. The route taken was by Ems, Thusis, Tiëfenkastel, Bergün to Pontresina and St Moritz. The scenery of this part surpassed anything in the earlier part of the tour. At Muottas Muraigl the main line was left and the mountain railway taken to the summit, from which a very fine panoramic view was obtained. The grand Bernina complex lay directly to the south, while to the west Celerina, St Moritz, Silvaplana and Sils with their respective lakes were seen. The descent was made in the direction of Pontresina. The route led past the Schafberg, which is the largest protection work in Switzerland. This lies directly behind the town of Pontresina, and was begun in 1890. The total cost of the work when complete will be over £16,000. The lower slopes of this area are clothed with fine old forests of larch and Cembran pine; some of the larch stems which were measured had a girth at breast-height of over 10 feet.

From Pontresina train was taken to St Moritz, where after lunch a short visit was paid to the larch and Cembran pine forests lying behind the town. In the evening a return was made by train to Thusis.

On Wednesday morning, which was the last day of the tour, an inspection was made of the protection works which have been constructed in the lower reaches of the river Nolla, another of those turbulent streams which are found so difficult and costly to control.

After this the party drove for several miles up the steep Via Mala, as far as the second bridge. The land here, although very steep in nature and poor in character, is capable of yielding forests which are considered worth putting under definite management. The grandeur of the gigantic gorge was much appreciated.

The return was made by coach to Thusis, whence the party set out for Zürich in the evening. From Zürich they travelled to Brussels via Basle, visited the Exhibition at Ghent, and returned to London by way of Ostend and Dover.

10. The Forestry Exhibition at Paisley.

By G. P. GORDON, B.Sc.

The annual Forestry Exhibition organised by the Society was held this year at Paisley, in connection with the Highland and Agricultural Society's Show there. The large stand placed at the disposal of the Society occupied a prominent position, which served to show to advantage the large variety of articles forming the exhibit.

Section I.—Timber. This section—taken as a whole—was one of outstanding merit. The classes were well filled and contained material which for size and quality left little to be desired. In the competitive section the entries in the hardwood classes were of an exceptionally high standard, so that they formed the main feature of the section. Among the coniferous timbers the general standard was slightly lower, except in the case of the larch class, which was quite unique both for the number of entries and for the very high quality of the timber. The material in the Scots pine class was somewhat inferior in quality to that in the other coniferous classes. The local classes were well represented, and in these the high standard was maintained.

Among the timbers for exhibition, in addition to several well-arranged collections of hand specimens, a very interesting exhibit was sent by the Landowners' Co-operative Society.

For the purposes of this exhibit the Landowners' Co-operative Forestry Society purchased from one of its members a quantity of manufactured timber at the current prices ruling for home-grown and home-sawn timber. It then purchased, through a timber-importing firm, a similar quantity of foreign timber of exactly the same specifications. Except for the fact that the home-grown timber was classed as Scots pine and spruce while the foreign timber was classed as redwood and whitewood, there was practically no difference between the two lots; in individual cases the home-grown timber appeared to be of better quality than the foreign timber and *vice versa*. The various specimens were placed side by side, and bore descriptive cards with particulars for comparison. The following difference in prices were shown :—

	PRICE PER PIECE.		PRICE PER CUBIC FOOT.	
	Home Grown.	Foreign.	Home Grown.	Foreign.
1.	2/10½	3/4½	1/5	1/8
2.	2/4	3/2¼	1/2	1/7
3.	3/2½	3/9	1/5½	1/8
4.	2/7½	3/6½	1/2½	1/7
5.	4/2½	4/8¼	1/6	1/8
6.	3/6	4/5¼	1/3	1/7
7.	3/9½	5/7½	1/1½	1/8
8.	1/–	1/6	1/–	1/6
9.	1/6	2/7½	1/–	1/9
10.	1/2	2/0¼	1/8	2/9
11.	–/10½	1/6	1/8	2/9
12.	1/1	1/10½	1/3¾	2/3
13.	–/7½	1/10½	1/3¼	2/3
14.	–/10¾	1/5	1/2	1/10
15.	–/5¾	–/10	1/1¾	2/–
16.	–/7½	–/7½	2/0½	2/–
17.	–/8½	1/3	1/5	2/6
18.	–/8	1/1¾	1/5	2/6
19.	5/8	9/4½	1/6	2/6

Two large specimens of Douglas fir timber in the round added greatly to the interest of this section. The specimen from Argyllshire showed a greater height-growth and a greater volume per acre for its age than the specimen from Perthshire. The latter, however, was superior in quality, as it was cleaner and showed slower growth than the former specimen.

Section II.—Converted Material. The gates entered for competition and exhibition in the various classes formed a large and popular exhibit, as they demonstrated some very good timber and excellent workmanship. The judging of this exhibit presented some difficulty ; in the first place, because there were several good gates with very little to choose between, and secondly, because some of the gates had not been made strictly according to the specifications contained in Clauses XI., XII., and XIII. of the competition schedule. The judges were therefore forced, rather unwillingly, to disqualify some of the entries in these classes.

Some very artistic examples of rustic work were shown under this section, in the form of porches, seats, and arbours, etc. In addition, a tree-lifting machine manufactured from timber poles was exhibited.

Section III.—Museum Specimens. The large variety of hand specimens, photographs, models and collections of objects of forest importance was a feature of great interest, not only to the general public but also to the proprietor of woodlands and to the forester. The high educational value of such an exhibit should not be underestimated, since it functions as an excellent demonstration of the various tree and timber diseases, insect pests, forms of damage by game, methods of pruning, etc., etc.

In this section the judges were much impressed with the collective exhibits of Mr J. G. Singer, which were of such a nature and arranged in such a manner as to merit the high award they received.

Messrs Austin & M'Aslan very kindly supplied pot plants and greenery, which added greatly to the appearance of the stand.

Conclusions.—In the opinion of the judges the exhibition maintained the high standard of previous years. As it was held in close proximity to one of the largest timber-consuming cities in the world, it served the very useful purpose of arousing the interest of large numbers of people who visited the showyard. While the entries were fairly representative the judges noted that, in spite of the large quantities of blown-timber in the West of Scotland, the number of entries from Dumbartonshire and Argyllshire were very few.

It was observed also that in the timber classes more importance had evidently been paid to the size than to the quality of the timber. In the class for field gates the judges recommend that a minimum length should be specified in the schedule, as a gate which is less than ten to ten and a half feet in length is of little value for general use.

The judges desire to express their appreciation of the valuable assistance rendered by the local committee.

Judges.—Mr Boyd, Inverliever; Mr M'Gregor, Ayr; Mr Gordon, Glasgow.

11. Visit to German Forests by the Royal English Arboricultural Society—1913.

By A. T. GILLANDERS.

The annual excursion of this Society was held in Germany from the 8th to the 20th of September, and a more instructive and pleasant trip it is impossible to imagine. The President, Sir William Schlich, acted as guide. Sir William is a native of Hesse Darmstadt, and in his younger days he was a student of forestry in this district, and has re-visited it in company with his students for the past twenty-five years. The party, which numbered 90 in all, was made up as follows:—17 landowners, 13 land agents, 31 foresters, 6 instructors in forestry, 9 members of the Home and Indian Civil Service, 10 wood merchants, 3 forestry students, and 1 doctor of medicine who acted as honorary medical adviser. The first night was spent at Frankfort on the Main.

On the following morning, the 10th September, a visit was made to the Mitteldick Forest, which belongs to the Grand Ducal House of Hesse Darmstadt. The forest is situated on a level plain near Frankfort and extends to 3763 acres. The soil is of tertiary formation and is of a sandy nature, changing here and there to gravel, and is very poor in mineral food constituents, especially lime. Sections of the soil were cut at intervals to show its quality. In examining these sections, the party were much interested in the large numbers of a species of *Geotrupes* or dor beetle, which congregated on the exterior of the pit.

The forest is composed of both pure and mixed woods, grown only as high-forest. The villagers, as in many other parts of Germany, have special grazing rights and liberty to remove waste wood. The general crop was composed of—oak, 46 %, occupying 1730 acres of total area ; Scots pine, 26 % = 975 acres ; beech, birch and alder, 24 % = 901 acres ; spruce, 4 % = 156 acres, making a total of 3762 acres. The rotations provided for in the working-plan are—oak, 160 years ; Scots pine and beech, 120 years ; spruce, 100 years. Wherever possible natural regeneration is encouraged, but where surface conditions are not favourable for natural regeneration, artificial cultivation is adopted. The acorns of the oak (sessile preferred) are sown in rows 1 metre (3 ft. 3 ins.) apart, which averages 600 lbs. of seed per acre. Beech is also added. The soil is first broken up by means of a specially constructed disc plough, which rises easily over strong roots and other solid obstructions. This plough is followed by a suitably formed grubber which still further stirs up the soil, and thus a good seed bed is formed. To protect the oak fairly tall birches are planted between the rows. Another implement used in "wounding" the soil for the reception of seed was shown. It works much in the same way as a heavy Cambridge roller, such as is used in this country, and makes seed beds for species, generally other than oak.

This proved a very interesting day. Perhaps the most valuable lesson to be learned was the way in which a poor soil can be utilised, provided a mulch of humus is formed, by a soil-improving species such as beech. Everywhere the obvious advantages of a sustained system of management based on sound silvicultural principles was recognised.

On the following day a visit was paid to the Frankfort Town forest, the general features of which had been described in a lantern lecture given the previous evening by the Oberförster. The forest consists chiefly of oak and beech. As far as possible it is laid out in park form, and thus serves the double purpose of providing profit to the city and pleasure for the inhabitants. Bird life is everywhere encouraged by the provision of nesting-boxes, food-trays and drinking fountains for the "feathered songsters of the grove." In fact, bird sanctuaries are created ; but, compared with our home conditions, we find that the country shows an entire absence of hedges and hedgerow trees, which attract our feathered friends more into the open sunshine where they love to revel.

The two following days were spent in the Spessart, but as some of the ground was the same as that which our Society visited four years ago, it is unnecessary to give a report on it.

On Sunday, 14th September, the party left Frankfort at 8 A.M., and journeyed towards the Black Forest, reaching Forbach station at 3 o'clock in the afternoon. Then followed a drive to Schönmünzach. The weather was lovely, and the journey through interesting, cultivated valleys with high mountains in the distance, clothed to the summit with gigantic trees, gave one a grand impression of flourishing agriculture coupled with skilful forestry.

On Monday morning a walk through the Schifferschafts Forest from 8 A.M. till 1 P.M., with a rest in the afternoon, formed the programme for the day. The term Schifferschafts means a company of timber floaters, and at one time such a company owned the forest area of 12,400 acres. Now, however, one-half is owned by the Baden state. The woods are, for the most part, on steep slopes, varying in elevation from 1000 to 3000 feet. The annual rainfall is 70 inches. Up to about 2300 feet the underlying rock is granite, and above this bunter sandstone of lower, middle and upper formation. On both formations the soil has a tendency to be acid in reaction, which is rather detrimental to natural regeneration. To help to counteract this and to improve the surface conditions a small quantity of beech is added. Thus the crop as a whole is composed of 95% conifers (silver and spruce fir), and 5% beech. The rotation extends to 120 years. Natural regeneration is carried out very gradually. Regeneration is commenced at the top of the wood, to prevent the necessity of fallen timber being dragged through the young growth. Natural regeneration is effected by the group or strip method, though the selection method is also practised; the cuttings take place at intervals of about ten years.

On the following day the Schönmünzach State Forest was visited. As the morning was rather wet the party drove in brakes to the forest, a few miles distant. During the drive the party was much impressed with the splendid condition of the fine metalled roads in the forest. The whole forest area is divided into compartments, all carefully numbered. In this forest, as elsewhere, when there is a conspicuous difference in age between two adjacent compartments, a broad severance cutting is made between them. The trees of the younger compartment which border on the severance cutting have thus a chance to become gradually more storm proof before the older compartment is clear felled.

The strip system of natural regeneration is practised in this forest, thus contrasting with the combined strip and group system witnessed in the forest previously visited. The silver fir can stand more shade than spruce, and it can be regenerated under a denser canopy than most trees. It is, therefore, not unusual to find on certain favourable spots, small groups of fore-growth appearing before the regeneration cuttings have begun. If these groups of advance growth occur in suitable places and give promise of good growth in the future, they are left to shelter the subsequent regeneration from wind, because it is asserted that a young crop of uneven age is more storm proof than one of even age.

The correct method of natural regeneration in strips is carried out in something like the following way :—The strips as far as possible should run from north-east to south-west. A commencement is made at the outer north-east edge, where a strip 50 yards in breadth is heavily thinned, by the removal of about one-third of the trees upon it. Within 3 to 5 years another third of the crop is removed, and simultaneously a second strip of 50 yards breadth is thinned to the extent of one-third of its whole stand. After a further period of 3 to 5 years, the whole of the remaining trees of the first attacked strip are removed, and another third of the second strip is taken out, while a third strip is attacked and one-third of its crop removed. Within the forest there are a certain number of similarly managed compartments, so that every year's total cutting produces approximately the same number of cubic feet.

On 16th September the party left Schönmünzach and proceeded in motors to Freudenstadt, a little town overlooking a lovely valley lying between two mountain ranges which are covered with trees. Next forenoon the party drove to the Freudenstadt Forest, and in the afternoon the Steinwald State Forest was visited. Both of these forests were of a similar composition to those already visited, namely spruce and silver fir, but there was considerable variation in the management as regards cutting and natural regeneration. Again we saw large crops of timber; in fact, we were now impressed with the immensity and density of the timber stands, and the large volume of felled material lying ready for removal.

On the 18th we visited the Pfalzgrafenweiler State Forest. Hitherto we had seen wonderful crops of timber, but this day, which was the last, presented the finest crops we had seen. The very last wood we visited was said to be one of the finest crops of silver fir in Germany. It was 175 years of age and had a volume of about 8000 cubic feet per acre. Some of the trees which had been felled measured 132 feet in length and 12 inches quarter-girth at the smaller end. The total length of the trees was about 160 feet. The outstanding features of interest seen this day were the strip system of natural regeneration, already described, the pruning or removal of "wolf" trees in the advance growth, the importance of thinning at the proper age, instead of sacrificing volume growth to growth in length by the hitherto prevalent method of deferred thinning. Another method of thinning was seen which consisted in ear-marking, so to speak, about double the number of stems required for the final crop, and thus having one-half for reserve. We also saw systematic planting much like our own, to make good the injury caused by roe deer to the natural regeneration.

The tour was a complete success. We saw many well-managed and excellent crops, which presented a very different picture from our own. But it must be remembered that the conditions in our country are such that we cannot transplant the German methods here. We must recollect that we saw State forests in Germany, while ours are Estate forests in which such things as, for example, a 300 years' rotation is out of the question.

Opinions will obviously differ when we come to generalise on the net educational value of the tour. To the mind of the writer it showed what could be done by continued and systematic management under highly skilled foresters. The crops inspected were perfect in type of tree, density, and volume per acre. The foresters knew with great precision the volume and value of their crops. A fixed volume is cut annually in each district, and so purchasers can rely upon getting a fixed quantity. The foresters can conjure with their woods as regards natural regeneration. Further, timber transport is carefully provided for. As a result of good roads, with a gradual descent, two oxen can take a load of 200 to 250 cubic feet in one waggon,—impossible, says the English waggoner! Destructive insects were kept in check as a result of systematically peeling felled timber. Further, it may be noted that the workmen are woodmen in winter and small holders in summer. Last, but by no means least, in every case the woods returned a handsome profit per acre.

12. Timber Research Work at the Cambridge School of Forestry.

At the beginning of last year, a temporary grant of £500 for two years from the Board of Agriculture and Fisheries was made to the Cambridge Forestry School, to enable research work in British timber to be instituted. Mr Russell Burdon and Mr A. P. Long were appointed by the Cambridge Forestry Committee to be Investigator and Assistant Investigator respectively, and the following scheme of work, which we have taken from the Annual Report of the School, just received, was drawn up:—

1. A comparative study of home-grown pine and spruce with imported timber of the same classes, with the object of ascertaining to what extent British-grown timber of these genera is capable of substitution for the foreign.

2. Inquiries as to the capabilities of home-grown timber for use as pit-props, railway sleepers, paving blocks, telegraph poles, building timber, etc.

3. Special studies as to the utilisation of elm, maple, poplar and chestnut with a view to the possible extension of the use of these timbers.

4. A survey of the wood-using industries of the Eastern counties, paying special attention to the kinds, qualities and sizes of timber required.

Two interim Progress Reports, and a Bulletin on Scots pine woods at Woburn, Bedfordshire, have already been published, and a perusal of these shows that work is being energetically organised in regard to the first two items on the above scheme. An inquiry into the production and utilisation of pine timber has been commenced, and Messrs Burdon and Long are at work on the collection of specimens from various districts in the United Kingdom. The method of collecting is to select pine woods where the trees have been grown under proper silvicultural conditions, and then, after measuring up a sample plot, to fell one or two trees which represent the mean. In this way they obtain average trees according to measurement.

The specimens of pine timber to be seen at every forestry show are of course specially selected, and are no guide as to the general run of the timber from that particular district. The collection of timber being made at Cambridge should, when complete, be most interesting, as it will fairly represent the average obtainable at different ages, from different districts and under different silvicultural conditions. The whole of the timber from these sample trees is being taken to Cambridge and, after it has been examined and compared with foreign grades, it will be employed for various experiments in utilisation.

The measurements taken in the ordinary course of selecting the timber are being published in a series of bulletins which, it is hoped, may ultimately assist in the preparation of yield tables. These bulletins contain full descriptions of each sample plot measured, with tables giving the soil analysis, the yield per acre, details and measurements of the sample trees, stem analyses, and the amount of converted material obtained, etc. The first bulletin on Scots pine at Woburn, Bedfordshire, has appeared; a second on Scots pine at King's Lynn is in the press; and a third on Corsican pine at Highclere, Hants, is in preparation.

In the second Progress Report, the influence of the work which Mr Burdon saw in progress during his visit to the United States two years ago is evident, and we are glad to read of the plans being made for experiments on the utilisation of British woods on a semi-commercial scale. Such experiments should be of considerable assistance in extending the use of British timbers. As soon as the School obtains the necessary support to enable the work to be started, it is proposed to test the comparative value of different British woods for sleepers, paving blocks and building timbers, and at the same time the comparative value of different processes of preservation. A small experiment in this direction has been started at the request of the Great Northern Railway Company, who have also spontaneously offered the School facilities for carrying out tests on their line on a much larger scale. Mr Collins, City Engineer for Norwich, has also, with the approval of the City Council, offered similar facilities for testing different woods for paving blocks, and several firms connected with timber preservation have expressed a wish to co-operate in these experiments. The semi-commercial scale on which the work is being planned is seen in the fact that, for each species to be tested, at least 400 to 500 sleepers and 18,000 to 20,000 paving blocks will be required, even if only six different processes of preservation are employed.

Another direction in which the Cambridge School of Forestry is trying to promote interest in British woods is through technical schools, where students are given instruction in woodwork. By the distribution of hand specimens of different woods, and of leaflets giving elementary information about the trees and the structure and uses of the timber, it is hoped that interest may be aroused and an impetus given to the revival of woodland industries. From a prospectus of the Central School of Arts and Crafts in London, which came into our hands, we see that a commencement in this direction has been made by Mr Burdon, who is delivering a course of lectures there.

The development of work on these lines should materially assist the progress of British forestry, and it is to be earnestly hoped that the support required to carry out all these plans will be forthcoming.

13. Thuja Gigantea and Douglas Fir in Mixture.

(*With Plate.*)

By D. K. M'BEATH.

Claudy House Wood Plantation, Gairletter, on the estate of Benmore, Argyllshire, was planted during the autumn of 1876 and spring of 1877 with a mixture of Douglas fir, *Thuja gigantea* and a few larch. The plantation is about 5 acres in extent, although unfortunately about 3 acres of it have now been blown. It is situated on the north-west shore of Loch Long, with an easterly exposure, rising from an elevation of 12 feet above sea-level to that of 130 feet, and is fully exposed to the severe gales of the west coast. The locality is a moist one, having an average annual rainfall of about 100 inches.

As regards the geological formation of the district, the "base" consists of a mass of hard, impervious rock composed of various kinds of schists. From Dunoon northwards the rocks are chiefly mica-schists and schistose grits, which are traversed by numerous dykes of lava rocks. While in places the overlying soil is heavy and wet, the soil of the plantation is morainic in character, being somewhat light, pervious and of moderate depth.

Formation.—An enclosure was made with a post and wire fence to protect the plantation agaist the inroads of farm stock, at a cost of 7d. per yard. The surrounding land is let at 5s. per acre for agricultural purposes. In 1876 this area was partly covered with the natural oak woodland of the locality, which consisted of about 15 standards per acre with wide-spreading crowns, the intervening gaps being occupied by small oak scrub. The scrub was cut out, the remaining standards were left for shelter, and were underplanted with a mixture of Douglas fir, *Thuja gigantea* and a very few larch. The plants were notched in about 4 feet apart; the sizes of plants used were 2-year seedlings and 2-year 1-year transplants. The two species were planted alternately, equal proportions of each being used, while a few larch were planted along the exposed edges. On the north-west side, where the soil was wet, surface drains were cut at an average cost of 2s. 6d. per 100 yards.

Treatment.—From the evidence of partly decayed stumps, it would seem that a partial thinning had been made about twenty years ago; unfortunately, however, no actual records of the value of this thinning are obtainable. The old crop of standard oaks was sold by private bargain in the year 1905, when considerable damage was done to the young crop by their fall and removal. A number of the Douglas firs were injured and broken, and large gaps were thus left in the young wood. In addition, the removal of these old trees left the plantation exposed for the wind to obtain an entrance. As a result of this a portion was blown in the November gale of 1911, while the remainder was levelled by another gale in 1912.

Normal condition.—Two years ago the plantation was fully stocked, the trees standing from 4 to 9 feet apart. The average height-growth of the Douglas fir was about 70 feet, while that of the *Thuja* was about 60 feet. The stems of the Douglas fir showed natural pruning up to two-thirds of their height (see Plate VIII. fig. 1), the average annual increment per stem being ·6 cubic feet, and that of the *Thuja* ·3 cubic feet. The forest floor has a covering of 2 to 3 inches of humus. It is evident that this cleaning effect has been largely due to the occurrence of *Thuja* in single mixture with the Douglas. In the year 1911 there was a full seed year of both species. The trees all show healthy development, there being no signs of insect pests or fungus disease.

The stems number on the average about 890 per acre, one-half of that number being of pole size while the remainder are of timber size and consist of equal numbers of Douglas fir and

Thuja. The volume of timber per acre, according to quarter-girth measurement to 5 inches diameter, deducting 1 inch for bark, is as follows:—Douglas fir, 5000 cubic feet per acre ; and *Thuja gigantea*, 2430 cubic feet per acre. This gives the high total of 7430 cubic feet per acre.

Existing condition.—At present the plantation is in the hands of the wood cutters, who are employed in preparing the timber for market, on contract at 2½d. per tree. The stems present some considerable difficulty in their removal, as they are lying six or seven deep and are badly crossed. The gales of 1911 and 1912 were from the north-west, so that the stems lie with their crowns down hill in a south-easterly direction. A number were broken across by the force of the storm. As the work of cleaning goes on large numbers of Douglas fir and *Thuja* seedlings are found growing under the cover of the blown trees. Many of these will be destroyed during the operations of removal, but it is hoped that a full crop of young growth will establish itself in the future. Rabbits have obtained an entrance and destroyed a certain number of seedlings, but it is proposed to erect a rabbit-proof fence round the regeneration area.

Transport and uses.—The plantation is situated within a few yards of a good road which runs along the foreshore. The stems will be cross-cut into the desired lengths in the wood, and will afterwards be hauled by horse on to the foreshore, where they will be stored until there is sufficient to make a boat-load. It is possible that an opening for poles 50 to 60 feet long, with a diameter of 6 inches at the small end, will be obtained in the Clyde ship-building yards. The probable price for such timber would be about 15s. per pole. Failing this market there is a good demand for it for pit-wood at 5d. per cubic foot, lying in the wood, for material over 8 inches on the side. The small trees and tops may be sold for 1½d. per lineal foot cut off root, and snedded.

Conclusions.—Thus it would appear that Douglas fir grown in single mixture with *Thuja* is superior in quality to Douglas that has been grown pure. Up to the 36th year the *Thuja* is only 10 feet less in height-growth than the Douglas, and does not up to this age suffer from suppression. The stems of the *Thuja* in this plantation, are almost perfectly cylindrical, and do not show the fluted appearance typical of stems grown in the open. Under this unexpectedly short rotation the Douglas fir attains a maximum height of 85 feet, with a clean bole of 60 to 70 feet (see Plate VIII. fig. 1). The great volume per acre of marketable timber produced by a plantation of this type, coupled with the relatively good prices obtainable, should make this a valuable mixture. The facility with which this mixture may be naturally regenerated adds greatly to its intrinsic worth. The prospective uses to which the timber may be put, even under a short rotation, tend to show that this mixture is a profitable one to grow in suitable localities.

In addition where ship-building yards form available markets, the towing or rafting of long poles would cut down the water transit to a minimum. The presence of *Thuja* on the edges of this plantation affords useful shelter, as the crowns extend practically to the ground level (see Plate VIII. fig. 2).

14. Nursery and Plantation Competition.

The Nursery and Plantation Competition was conducted broadly on the same lines as last year. One or two alterations in details were made as a result of the Judges' recommendations, but the main object of the competition remains unaltered. The subjoined extract from the schedule which was sent to proprietors within the competition area, *i.e.*, the counties of Argyll, Ayr, Bute, Lanark and Renfrew, will show these minor alterations :—

"The Society invites entries in the following competitions. The necessary entry forms may be obtained from the secretary.

"*Nurseries.*—Class I.—For the best managed estate nursery not exceeding 2 acres in extent (Prize, A Silver Medal). Class II.— For the best managed estate nursery exceeding 2 acres in extent (Prize, A Silver Medal).

"*Plantations.*—Class I.—For the best young plantation mainly of conifers not exceeding 10 years of age, and not less than 2 acres in extent. Confined to estates having less than 300 acres of woods (Prize, A Silver Medal). Class II.—For the best young plantation mainly of conifers exceeding 10 years and not exceeding 20 years (Prize, A Silver Medal). Class III.—For the best young plantation mainly of conifers exceeding 20 years and not exceeding 40 years (Prize, A Silver Medal). Class IV.— For the best young plantation mainly of conifers not exceeding

PLATE VIII.

FIG. 1.—Douglas fir and *Thuja gigantea*, 36 years old.
Height of Douglas fir, 85 feet, with clean bole of 60-70 feet.

FIG. 2.—*Thuja gigantea* as shelter tree on the margin of the plantation.

[*To face p.* 110.

10 years of age, and not less than 5 acres in extent. Confined to estates having more than 300 acres of woods (Prize, A Silver Medal). Class V.—For the best young plantation mainly of conifers exceeding 10 years and not exceeding 20 years (Prize, A Silver Medal). Class VI.—For the best young plantation . mainly of conifers exceeding 20 years and not exceeding 40 years (Prize, A Silver Medal). Class VII.—For the best young plantation mainly of hardwoods not exceeding 35 years of age, and not less than 2 acres in extent (Prize, A Silver Medal).

"*Conditions.*—1. Each competitor must pay an entry fee of 10s. 6d. for his first entry and an additional 5s. for each subsequent entry. 2. The whole plantation must be entered if all of the same age. 3. The Judges will be empowered to withhold prizes in cases of insufficient merit. They will also be empowered to award a Bronze Medal for those subjects which are not prize winners but are above the average standard of excellence."

The entries taken as a whole were of a high order of merit, and the Judges found it necessary to recommend special and merit prizes, as a glance at the prize list[1] will show.

A significant fact, and one to which attention must be called, was that there were no entries in Class VII. for hardwood plantations.

Ten subjects were entered by six estates. These were made up of three nurseries—two in Class II. and one in Class I.—and seven plantations.

Sir James Bell, Bart., Montgreenan, entered three plantations which had been formed on previously uncultivated boggy peat. The conspicuous success which has attended the methods employed to bring such an area under tree-growth was such that the Judges found it necessary to put this entry into a class by itself, as it was so wholly unique in character that there was nothing to compare it with. Mr Bogie, land steward, Montgreenan, under whose supervision the planting operations were carried out, has kindly supplied the following account of the methods he employed :—

"AFFORESTATION AT MONTGREENAN ON MOSS LANDS.

"Operations in connection with the scheme of afforestation at Montgreenan were begun on 3rd January 1910, when a start

[1] See "Proceedings," p. 38.

was made with the draining of the land. This work was not completed till the middle of May, but by the early days of April it was in a sufficiently forward state to enable planting to be proceeded with. The German system of planting was followed, and for that purpose a German spade called the Spiralborer was used.

"The process was as follows :—Two small turfs were taken off the surface, about 2 inches thick. Other two of equal thickness were then taken out close by, and the four pieces all placed together at one side of the hole. Another spading was then taken out about 6 inches deep and placed at the other side of the hole, which measured 8 inches deep by 6 inches in diameter. The turf and soil were left lying on the surface for eight days to dry, which removes the acid, and a quarter lb. of unburned ground limestone was added to the soil at each hole, which was then ready for the planters. Before planting, the roots of each tree were dipped in a solution composed of 1 gallon of farm liquid manure to 6 gallons of water, and in order to make the mixture thick some clay was added. One of the turfs was then placed at the bottom of the hole, and when the tree was put in special precaution was taken against the burying of the roots too deeply. On an average the roots were planted 3 inches from the surface. After the hole was filled in with soil mixed with lime or slag, the three remaining turfs were placed on the top and pressed lightly round the plant. As the locality is high and exposed to northeast winds, it was considered expedient to provide a little protection by placing a large turf at the side of each tree. The advantage of this procedure was seen in August, when a careful examination showed that very few deaths had taken place and that very fine growths were formed.

"The trees had also the benefit of heather protection. The work of planting was carried out in the following rotation :—1. Drainers; 2. hole-borers; 3. boys adding lime to soil; 4. tree planters (women); 5. turf placers. When planting was completed a minute inspection was made in order to ascertain if any of the trees had got loosened by the strong winds.

"The work was finished towards the end of May. Altogether 472,000 trees were planted. These were equally divided between Scots pine and Norway spruce. The distance between each tree was about 3 ft. 9 ins. As will be seen from the following tables each plantation was divided into sections, the soil of which was treated in three different ways :—

Plantation (No. 1).

West side of Glasgow road .	Area, about 20 acres.
Distance between drains . .	20 feet.
Depth of drains . . .	3 feet.
Width of drains . . .	20 inches.
Section No. 1	Ground limestone.
,, ,, 2	Basic slag.
,, ,, 3	Ground limestone.

Plantation (No. 2).

North side of Glasgow road and west side of large ride . .	Area, about 70 acres.
Distance between drains . .	15 feet.
Depth of drains . . .	3 feet.
Width of drains . . .	20 inches.
Section No. 4	Ground limestone.
,, ,, 5	Basic slag.
,, ,, 6	Ground limestone.
,, ,, 7	Basic slag.
,, ,, 8	Ground limestone.
,, ,, 9 . . .	Basic slag.
,, ,, 10	Ground limestone.
,, ,, 11 (North side large ride)	Ground limestone.

Plantation (No. 3).

Auchentiber Moss . . .	Area, about 70 acres.
Distance between drains . .	18 feet.
Depth of drains . . .	3 feet.
Width of drains . . .	20 inches.
Section No. 12	Ground limestone.
,, ,, 13	Loam.
,, ,, 14	Ground limestone.
,, ,, 15	Loam.

" During planting, which lasted six weeks, we employed a large number of people—upwards of 100. They came from all parts of the district, and also from Irvine, Kilwinning and Dalry. At that time there seemed to be a lot of people out of work and they were thankful to get employment here."

In a recent communication Mr Bogie informs us that measurements made in November showed that the growth during this year was from 6 to 18 inches.

At Mount-Stuart, in the Island of Bute, the fine plantations of Japanese larch deserve special mention, and Mr Howe, overseer, Mount-Stuart, has been good enough to send the following account of these interesting plantations :—

"Carn Bann Plantation, Bute Estate.

"This plantation was planted during February and finished 6th March 1908. It extends to 20 acres—18 acres of which are pure Japanese larch. Two acres on top of the hill are planted with Scots pine for shelter from the west winds. The trees when planted were 2-year 1-year seedlings, and notch-planted in straight rows 4 feet apart. The average height of trees in the plantation at present is 12 feet with 6½ inches circumference 2 feet from the ground. The plantation has a south-east exposure and rises from 200 feet at bottom of plantation to 250 feet at top above sea-level. The soil is a free sandy loam on top of rock, and carried a crop of beech before the present trees were planted.

"With the exception of having to fence it against rabbits and roe deer when planted, it has not cost anything. No filling up was necessary. The cost of cutting bracken is the only expense since planting, and amounts to the wage of a man for one day in each of the first two years. Should the plantation continue to grow as well as it is doing just now, in two years' time it will require a light thinning, as I observe the bottom branches are being suppressed already. The plantation on the whole is very healthy. I can safely say there is not a diseased tree in it.

"Culivine Plantation, Bute Estate (see Plate IX.).

"This plantation is 10 acres in extent, 5 of which are pure Japanese larch and 5 acres pure European larch, with only an 18-foot roadway dividing them. The area was planted in February 1905; it has a southerly exposure and rises 300 feet above sea-level. The soil is a deep, rich loam on top of clay. The Japanese larch was planted 4 feet apart and the native larch 3½ feet. Fencing was necessary against rabbits and roe deer. The average height of the trees in the Japanese section

PLATE IX.

Japanese (left) and European (right) larches in Culivine Plantation, Bute.   The plants are of the same age.

[*To face p* 114.

Witch's Broom on *Pseudotsuga Douglasii*.

is 19 feet, and 9½ inches in girth 2 feet from the ground. The plantation will require a light thinning this winter as the under branches are already dead, and a good few of the smaller trees might be removed to allow the others to develop. The native larch has a height of 10½ feet with a circumference of 5½ inches and is growing well, but will not require any thinning for some time yet. I may say it is a beautiful sight to stand on the 18-foot roadway and compare the two sections. One can scarcely realise that they were planted in the same year and month with 2-year 1-year seedlings. It appears to me the climate of Bute suits the Japanese larch, and also the Douglas fir, for we planted 20 acres of *Douglasii* during last year with very few failures."

The Glenstriven larch plantations are particularly fine, and indicate the splendid capacity of the district to produce larch of the finest quality, when the plantations are tended by skilful hands.

It is interesting to compare the growth of the European larch in Bute and Arran. At both Mount-Stuart and Brodick, these plantations have received every attention and treatment that skill and knowledge can bestow, but the "locality" in Bute seems to be more favourable for the growth of larch. This point would well repay a careful comparative investigation or detailed survey of these two—apparently in every other way similar—localities.

The Culzean Nursery—the only one entered in Class II.—was extremely interesting not only on account of the number of different species it contained, but because in it was demonstrated, in a very striking manner, the large variety of plants which can be used for hedging purposes. The two nurseries of Class I. were each excellent examples of well laid out and cared for home "tree gardens." Without exception these three nurseries were being conducted on sound economic lines, and the high state of excellence in which they were maintained reflects the greatest credit on their owners and those responsible for their management.

A. W. Borthwick }
G. U. Macdonald } *Judges.*

NOTES AND QUERIES.

WITCH'S BROOM ON PSEUDOTSUGA DOUGLASII.

(With Plate.)

The photograph on the back of Plate IX. shows a remarkable growth, a " Witch's Broom " found hanging from a Douglas fir. It is a very perfect specimen, and measures 8 inches in diameter and 6 inches deep, the small stem by which it is attached to a branch being 7 inches long and only $\frac{3}{16}$ of an inch in diameter. Its total weight when found was 1 lb. Witch's Broom on *Douglasii* is believed to be the result of mite attack.

JAMES M'CALLUM.

APPOINTMENT OF CHIEF CONSERVATOR OF FORESTS, SOUTH ·AFRICA.

One of the most important forest appointments of recent times has lately been filled in South Africa. Mr J. Storr-Lister has recently retired, and Mr Charles Legat has been appointed in his place.

The Chief Conservator of Forests, South Africa, has under .his direction the Conservators of the various Colonies which have been united to form the Union of South Africa, viz., Cape Colony, with four Conservators or their equivalents ; and one Conservator each for Natal, the Orange Free State, and the Transvaal.

Mr Legat has for some years been Conservator of the Transvaal. Immediately after the war Lord Milner obtained expert advice, and a Conservator for the Transvaal was resolved on. It was first proposed to obtain a forest officer from India ; but that not proving feasible at the time, Mr Legat, who was already in the Transvaal in a junior capacity, was appointed Conservator. The results have amply justified this selection ; and the Premier, with that sense of fairness and knowledge of a good officer which have given General Botha his influence in South Africa, has now made the present appointment.

Charles Legat is a B.Sc. of Edinburgh, and had his forest training under the late Colonel F. Bailey. He has passed some time in the German forests, and has toured in the sub-tropical forests of the south of France, which form a most instructive study for a South African forest officer. He went out to the forest department of Cape Colony in a junior capacity some sixteen years ago, and rose by merit until he was selected to go to the Transvaal after the Boer war.

It will be recalled that although the area of the indigenous forest of South Africa is comparatively small (only some half-million acres all told), an important work is being performed in the formation of extensive plantations of exotic trees. These exotics are carefully selected as regards climatic suitability, and are hardier and grow faster than the native trees. Some £150,000 is spent yearly on South African forestry, of which over one-third is at present returned as revenue. The young plantations of exotic trees are already yielding, from thinnings only, more revenue than the indigenous forest.

PROTECTION OF SCOTS PINE AGAINST BLACK GAME.

During last winter when there was a lot of snow, black game did a considerable amount of damage by eating the buds of newly planted Scots pine, and it occurred to the forester that some sort of dressing might save the remainder. Two dressings were tried, Smearoleum and a dressing made up at home which consisted of one part of Archangel tar to two parts of tallow fat boiled together. Only the terminal leading buds were dressed, and the result in both cases was the same; those buds which had been dressed were left alone, though the buds on the side shoots were eaten as much as before, but the effect of the Smearoleum was that the buds did not open or grow when the spring came, while those dressed with the home-made mixture grew well and have continued to do so. The method of applying the dressing consisted in dropping a little on the leading bud from a paint-brush. After a little practice the men employed got over a great number of plants in a day; it was found that a man could do about 5000 in a day. The dressing will have to be applied again on the new leading bud until the plants have reached a size sufficient to make them safe from black game. This year I propose to apply the preparation in the nursery before planting out, and expect to save time.   W. STEUART FOTHRINGHAM.

LEAFLET ON THE LARGE BROWN PINE WEEVIL.

An important leaflet (No. 8) has been recently issued by the Board of Agriculture, dealing with the large brown pine weevil (*Hylobius abietis*, L.). In this leaflet an excellent description of the weevil and of its life-history is given, while the plants attacked, the damage done, together with preventive and remedial measures are dealt with in a thoroughly practical manner. The beautifully reproduced photographs of the insect at work are of outstanding merit.

Every forester should procure a copy of the leaflet, which may be obtained free of charge and post free on application to the Secretary, Board of Agriculture for Scotland, 29 St Andrew Square, Edinburgh. Letters of application so addressed need not be stamped.

TREE-GROWTH IN 1913.

The year 1913 has been remarkable for plant-growth, and trees are no exception to the rule. In the south of England we had an unusually showery spring and early summer, followed by some weeks of extreme heat, then showers all through the autumn and early winter. This combination of circumstances tended to produce growths above the average.

The following are measurements taken in the plantations and nursery on the Canford estate :—

Conifers.

Larix europæa, .	3 ft.	10½ ins.	.	Planted in spring 1911.	
,, *leptolepis*, .	2 ,,	4 ,,	.	,,	., ,,
Pseudotsuga Douglasii,	3 ,,	9 ,,	.	,,	
Pinus Pinaster, .	3 ,,	4 ,,	.	,,	,,
,, *silvestris*, .	2 ,,	6 ,,	.	,,	,, 1909.
,, *insignis*, .	3 ,,	5 ,,	.	,,	,, 1912.

Hardwoods.

Hazel coppice, 1 year old,	.	.	.	.	6 ft.	8 ins.	
Beech, young hedge,	.	.	.	.	2 ,,	10 ,,	
Hornbeam, old hedge,	.	.	.	.	4 ,,	10 ,,	
White thorn, young hedge,	.	.	.	.	5 ,,	2 ,,	
Horse chestnut, in nursery,	.	.	.	.	4 ,,	8 ,,	

The European larch are still growing (25th Nov.), but the Japanese have ripened off.

JAMES M'CALLUM.

FORESTRY AND THE ANGLO-AMERICAN EXPOSITION.

The Anglo-American Exhibition, to be held at Shepherd's Bush during the present year (1914), has for its object the celebration in a fitting manner of the hundred years of peace and progress between the English-speaking peoples since the treaty of Ghent in 1814, and will contain sections devoted to horticulture, arboriculture and forestry. The forestry department is now engaging the special attention of a committee of experts, and it is believed that the scheme proposed will ensure an adequate representation of the varied aspects of this great industry. A special forestry conference in connection with the exposition is to be held in August.

THE EXCURSION TO SWITZERLAND.

The following are the names of the gentlemen who took part in this Excursion (see Report, p. 83) :—

B. W. Adkin, Westminster; J. H. Alexander, Kew Gardens; Frank Amos, Canterbury; J. F. Annand, M.Sc., Armstrong College, Newcastle (*Councillor*) ; T. Blair, Hoprig Mains, East Lothian; A. W. Borthwick, D.Sc. (*Vice-President* and *Hon. (Editor*; John Broom, Bathgate (*Councillor*); Gilbert Brown, Grantown-on-Spey (*Councillor*) ; Charles Buchanan (*Vice-President*) ; James Clyne, Banchory; R. W. Cowper, Sittingbourne, Kent; John D. Crozier, Dublin; James Curr, Prestonkirk; Tom Curr, Prestonkirk; W. S. Curr, Prestonkirk; Robert Dale, Sorn, Mauchline; W. Dallimore, Kew Gardens; Wm. Dawson, B.Sc., Cambridge (*Councillor*); J. A. Donald, Dupplin, Perth; A. C. Forbes, Avondale; R. Forbes, Kennet (*Councillor*); R. B. Fraser, Edinburgh; R. Galloway (*Secretary and Treasurer*); R. Angus Galloway, Edinburgh; Sydney J. Gammell, of Drumtochty (*Vice-President*); Wm. Gold, Dellavaird; G. P. Gordon, B.Sc., Glasgow (*Councillor*); Donald ˉGrant, Fersit; James Grant, Raith; James L. Gray, Dalkeith; David Hardie, Errol; H. J. Heavener, Inistioge, Ireland; Professor Henry, Dublin; A. D. Hopkinson, B.Sc., Cirencester; John Kerr, East Lothian; David King, Edinburgh; Major Leather, of Middleton Hall; George Leven, Bowmont Forest (*Councillor*); D. A. M'Corquodale, Carnoustie; Alex. MacGregor, Dalmuir; John M'Kerchar, London; R. V. Mather, Kelso; David

Mitchell, Drumtochty; Alex. Morgan, Crieff; A. B. Motherwell, Airdrie; George Mowat, Carmichael; Donald Munro, Banchory; J. Lyford Pike, B.Sc., Edinburgh; J. M. Ralph, Corstorphine; W. Ralph, Corstorphine; George Robertson, Monreith; H. T. Robertson, Airdrie; Wm. D. O. Rose, M.A., Edinburgh; The Earl of Rosse, Birr Castle, King's County; James Smith, Birr; Frank Sime, Beauly; John G. Singer, Culzean; Professor Somerville, Oxford; Adam Spiers, Edinburgh (*Councillor*); Thomson Spiers, Edinburgh; Capt. Stirling, of Keir (*President*); Walter C. Stunt, Lorenden, Kent; D. P. Wallace, North Devon; W. H. Whellens, Comlongon; James G. Wilson, Edinburgh; George Wolfe, Bathgate.

REVIEWS AND NOTICES OF BOOKS.

The Forest of Dean. By ARTHUR O. COOKE. With four Illustrations in colour and fifty-six in black and white. Price 10s. 6d. net. London : Constable & Co.

This is an excellent guide for the tourist. Even the experienced forester may find interesting passages in it, but he will be disappointed if he expects to find it a treatise on forestry. The author makes no pretensions to deal with that subject unless incidentally. Anyone wishing a quiet but interesting holiday could not do better than take up his quarters in the historic Speech House (which is now a very good hotel), and spend the days at his disposal in following the many attractive routes in the forest and neighbourhood sketched out in this book.

Albury Park Trees and Shrubs. 66 + x pp. By A. BRUCE JACKSON. London : West, Newman & Co. 1913.

In our issue of July 1911 (Vol. xxiv., p. 236) we noticed the same author's catalogue of hardy trees and shrubs at Syon House, owned by the Duke of Northumberland. The present work is a similar catalogue of the trees and shrubs at Albury Park in Surrey, which belongs to the same owner. In the present case the compiler has enhanced the value of his work by giving references to well-known works on trees where a detailed account and a drawing or photograph of the species under notice can be found. The catalogue is printed for private distribution only.

Royal Scottish Arboricultural Society.

Instituted 16th February 1854.

PATRON:

HIS MOST EXCELLENT MAJESTY THE KING.

PROCEEDINGS IN 1913.—*Continued.*

THE GENERAL MEETING.

The General Meeting of the Society was held in the Show Yard at Paisley, on Wednesday, 9th July 1913, at 3 P.M. Captain STIRLING, President of the Society, was Chairman, and there was a large attendance of members.

MINUTES.

The CHAIRMAN mentioned that the Minutes of the Annual Meeting had been printed and circulated with the *Transactions*, and that it was proposed to hold them as read. This was agreed to.

APOLOGIES.

Apologies for absence were intimated from Sir John Stirling-Maxwell; Sir Kenneth Mackenzie; the Rt. Hon. R. C. Munro Ferguson, M.P., *Hon. Secretary;* Lord Balfour of Burleigh; Mr Gammell; Sir Arthur Mackenzie; Colonel Stewart Mackenzie; Dr Nisbet; Mr John Mackenzie, Dunvegan; Mr Davidson, Panmure; and Mr Leven, Bowmont Forest.

CHAIRMAN'S REMARKS.

In opening his remarks the CHAIRMAN made suitable reference to the death of Mr John Methven, Member of Council and Convener of the Finance Committee, and mentioned that a wreath had been sent to the funeral and a letter of condolence to his relatives. In the course of his further remarks the President said that

a

there was little progress to report since the Annual Meeting, and that there was no visible progress except what was due to the efforts of the Society itself and kindred societies. He referred to the Deputation to the Railway Companies which was taken part in by this Society, the Landowners' Forestry Co-operative Society and the Timber Merchants' Association, and mentioned that the Deputation had been more successful than they had anticipated—more favourable terms having since been made with the Railway Companies with regard to the price of home-grown sleepers. He was sorry that no response had yet been received to the letter sent by the Council to the Chairman of the Board of Agriculture for Scotland urging the Board to make progress with afforestation, but he believed the Board was carefully considering the suggestions that had been made, and he was hopeful that something would be done. The Council would continue to do what it could to advance the cause of afforestation. He believed that the best hope of progress was in taking steps to procure the afforestation, under suitable management, of a large area, by the joint action of proprietors and the State, and he was hopeful that something of this nature would be carried out before very long.

Judges' Report on the Essays.

The Secretary gave in the awards of the Judges on the Essays received in Competition as follows :—

1. "Cleaning Young Trees." By Alex. S. MacLarty, Head Forester, Glasserton, Whithorn, Wigtownshire. Award—a No. 3 Silver Medal.

2. "Notes of Silvicultural Interest." By W. H. Whellens, Head Forester, Thoresby Park, Ollerton, Notts. Award—a Bronze Medal.

3. "A Visit to Bordeaux and the Landes." By "Pinaster." No Award.

4. "The Utilisation of Waste Wood." By "Scots Pine." No Award.

5. "Pruning." By "Erica." No Award.

6. "Successful Methods of Converting and Seasoning Timber." By "Arboretum." No Award.

Exhibition at Paisley.

The Secretary also gave in the awards of the Judges in the Exhibition Competitions as follows :—

Competition No. I.

Specimens of the Timber of Scots Pine (*Pinus sylvestris*).

1st Prize, £1, Alex. Lowe, Forester, Lockerbie House, Lockerbie.

2nd „ 15s., The Marquis of Bute, *per* John A. Howe, Forester.

3rd „ 10s., H. G. Younger of Benmore, *per* John M'Glashan, Forester.

Competition No. II.

Specimens of the Timber of Norway Spruce (*Picea excelsa*).

1st Prize, £1, Sir John A. Dewar, Bt., of Dupplin.

2nd „ 15s., Sir Hugh Shaw-Stewart, Bt., of Ardgowan.

3rd „ 10s., The Earl of Minto.

Competition No. III.

Specimens of the Timber of Larch (*Larix europæa*).

1st Prize, £1, Sir Hugh Shaw-Stewart, Bt., of Ardgowan.

2nd „ 15s., The Marquis of Bute.

3rd „ 10s., The Earl of Minto.

Competition No. IV.

Specimens of the Timber of Ash (*Fraxinus excelsior*).

1st Prize, £1, The Marquis of Bute.

2nd „ 15s., Do.

3rd „ 10s., Captain Stirling of Keir.

Competition No. V.

Specimens of the Timber of Oak (*Quercus robur*).

1st Prize, £1, The Marquis of Bute.

2nd „ 15s., Alex. Lowe, Forester, Lockerbie House.

3rd „ 10s., Captain Stirling of Keir.

Competition No. VI.

Specimens of the Timber of Elm (*Ulmus montana*).

1st Prize, £1, The Marquis of Bute.
2nd „ 15s., Captain Stirling of Keir.
3rd „ 10s., Sir Hugh Shaw-Stewart, Bt., of Ardgowan.

Competition No. VII.

Specimens of the Timber of any three Coniferous Trees other than the above.

A. OPEN SECTION.

1st Prize, £2, 10s., The Marquis of Bute.
   (*Cupressus macrocarpa*, *Abies nobilis* and Common Silver Fir.)

2nd Prize, £1, 10s., Captain Stirling of Keir.
   (Corsican Pine, *Abies nobilis* and Douglas Fir.)

B. LOCAL SECTION.

2nd Prize, 15s., The Marquis of Bute.
   (*Abies nobilis*, Douglas Fir and Common Silver Fir.)

Competition No. VIII.

Specimens of the Timber of any three Broad-Leaved Timber Trees other than the above.

A. OPEN SECTION.

1st Prize, £2, 10s., The Marquis of Bute.
   (Turkey Oak, Sycamore and Spanish Chestnut.)

2nd Prize, £1, 10s., Sir John A. Dewar, Bt., of Dupplin.
   (Canadian Poplar, Beech and Spanish Chestnut.)

3rd Prize, £1, Sir Hugh Shaw-Stewart, Bt., of Ardgowan.
   (Beech, Elm (*Ulmus campestris*) and Sycamore.)

B. LOCAL SECTION.

1st Prize, £1, The Marquis of Bute.
   (Beech, Sycamore and Spanish Chestnut.)

Competition No. XI.

A Gate for Farm Use, manufactured from Home-grown Timber by the Exhibitor, who must be a Forester or a Working Forester.

First. Duncan M'Millan, Forester, Keir. No. 2 Silver Medal.
Second John G. Singer, Forester, Culzean. No. 3 Silver Medal.
Third. Lewis S. Rae, Foreman Forester, Dupplin.
Bronze Medal.

Competition No. XII.

A Gate, manufactured from Home-grown Timber, which may be made by a tradesman, but must be designed and exhibited by a Member.

First J. A. Donald, Forester, Dupplin. No. 1 Silver Medal.

Competition No. XIII.

A self-closing Wicket Gate, manufactured from Home-grown Timber.

First. John M'Glashan, Forester, Benmore.
No. 3 Silver Medal.

Competition No. XVIII.

Specimens of Stems illustrating the Effects of Dense and Thin Crops in Branch Suppression and quality of Timber.

John G. Singer, Forester, Culzean. Bronze Medal.

Competition No. XIX.

A collection of Fungi injurious to Forest Trees and Shrubs.

George Fraser, Midhope, Hopetoun. No. 2 Silver Medal.

Competition No. XXI.

Any useful invention or marked improvement on any of the Implements or Instruments used in Forestry.

Thos. Armstrong, Eden Hall Estate, Langwathby. Bronze Medal for Wire-winding Machine for winding Lacing Wire on to Spindles, with Photographs illustrating old and new methods.

Competition No. XXII.

Any approved Article of British manufacture either wholly or mainly made of Wood grown in the United Kingdom.

> Alex. Lowe, Forester, Lockerbie House. No. 2 Silver Medal for a Rustic arch with gate.

> Alex. Pollock, Royal Rustic Builder, Tarbolton. No. 3 Silver Medal for two larch and oak plant-tubs and an oak seat, made of wood grown on the banks of Ayr.

In addition to the foregoing awards the Judges recommended that a No. 1 Silver Medal should be awarded to Mr JOHN G. SINGER, Forester, Culzean, for the general collection of exhibits brought by him to the Exhibition.

The Judges' awards were unanimously agreed to.

The Marquis of Graham asked if it would be competent to exhibit, in successive years, boards which had already taken a prize. It was pointed out that there was no rule against this, and that it would be quite competent to exhibit the boards until they were beaten by better ones.

Judges' Awards in the Nursery and Plantation Competition.[1]

(Restricted to the Paisley Show District.)

Dr BORTHWICK, in giving in the Report of this Competition, on behalf of Mr G. U. Macdonald and himself, mentioned that six Estates had taken part in the Competition, and that three Nurseries and nine Plantations, making twelve subjects in all, had been entered. He reported that, with the approval of the Council, the Judges had agreed to recommend that in the case of the Glenstriven plantations which would each receive a No. 1 Silver Medal, a Gold Medal should be offered ; in the case of the Bute plantations, a Gold Medal should also be offered in place of the No. 1 Silver Medal and the Bronze Medal which would otherwise be given ; and that in the case of the Brodick plantations a No. 1 Silver Medal should be offered in place of two Bronze Medals.

The meeting approved of these recommendations.

[1] For further particulars as to entries in these Competitions, see the Judges' Report on page 110 of the *Transactions.*

The prizes awarded were as follows:—

NURSERIES.

Class I.

The best managed Estate Nursery not exceeding two acres in extent.

> R. Dale, Forester, Sorn Castle, Mauchline. A No. 1 Silver Medal.

Class II.

The best managed Estate Nursery exceeding two acres in extent.

> John G. Singer, Forester, Culzean, Maybole. A No. 1 Silver Medal.
>
> Wm. Inglis, Forester, Brodick, Arran. A Bronze Medal.

PLANTATIONS.

Class I.

For the best young Plantation, mainly of Conifers, not exceeding 10 years of age, and not less than 2 acres in extent. Confined to Estates having less than 300 acres of Woods.

> Sir James Bell, Bart., of Montgreenan—3 Entries. A No. 1 Silver Medal.

Class II.

For the best young Plantation, mainly of Conifers, exceeding 10 years and not exceeding 20 years of age, and not less than 2 acres in extent. Confined to Estates having less than 300 acres of Woods.

> The Proprietors of Glenstriven, *per* John Kimmett, Forester. A No. 1 Silver Medal.

Class III.

For the best young Plantation, mainly of Conifers, exceeding 20 years and not exceeding 40 years of age, and not less than 2 acres in extent. Confined to Estates having less than 300 acres of Woods.

> The Proprietors of Glenstriven, *per* John Kimmett, Forester. A No. 1 Silver Medal.

Class IV.

For the best young Plantation, mainly of Conifers, not exceeding 10 years of age, and not less than 5 acres in extent. Confined to Estates having more than 300 acres of Woods.

The Marquis of Bute, *per* John A. Howe, Forester— 2 Entries. A Gold Medal for the combined plantations.

The Marquis of Graham, *per* Wm. Inglis, Forester— 2 Entries. A No. 1 Silver Medal for the combined plantations.

Society's Diamond Jubilee.

The President mentioned that the Diamond Jubilee of the Society would take place in February of next year, and said that a Committee was considering how this event might be suitably celebrated. The Committee would welcome any suggestions from members. Mr James Watt, Carlisle, suggested that subscriptions should be asked to provide a President's badge, which could be handed down to succeeding Presidents. He proposed that the badge should be secured before the Annual Meeting, and should be presented then to the present President. He said he would be glad to be one of the subscribers. Mr James Johnstone, Ayr, suggested a dinner. Mr M'Hattie suggested that a Diamond Jubilee Medal should be struck, to be awarded from time to time for special services rendered to Forestry. These proposals were all seconded, and it was agreed to remit them to the Council for consideration. Mr Watt, however, asked that his proposal should be sent to the Council to be carried out.

Excursion to Switzerland.

The Secretary reported that all the arrangements in connection with the Excursion had been completed, and that the party, which numbered about seventy, would start from Edinburgh the following evening. He expressed the indebtedness of the Committee to the British Minister in Berne and the Secretary to the Legation, and to Dr Coaz, head of the Swiss Forest Department, and his staff, who had been kind enough to prepare a programme for the tour and to secure the necessary accommodation.

Excursion 1914.

The PRESIDENT mentioned that the Council had been considering a locality for the Excursion for next year, and had unanimously agreed to recommend the West of Scotland, including Inverliever and Poltalloch. He invited other suggestions, but the meeting concurred in the Council's recommendation.

Development of Afforestation.

The CHAIRMAN said that on this subject he had nothing further to add to what he had referred to in his opening remarks, but he would welcome any suggestions that members might care to make. Sir Herbert Maxwell said he would like to draw attention to the unfortunate practice that prevailed, in planting Spruce and Larch on the same ground. He referred to an article in the *Gardener's Chronicle* of that week, by Dr Henry, upon the Spruce louse, which showed conclusively that it was a great mistake to plant these two trees together, and he recommended that this practice should be discontinued.

Votes of Thanks.

Votes of thanks were awarded to the Judges; to the Exhibition Committee; to the Highland and Agricultural Society for their vote to the Prize Fund, for the provision made by them for the Exhibition, and for the accommodation for the meeting; and to the Chairman for presiding.

Royal Scottish Arboricultural Society

Prizes Offered for Papers—1914.

The Council has decided to discontinue the Syllabus of specific subjects for which prizes are offered, and to award medals or their converted values for papers dealing with any branch of forestry. They hope that the new arrangement will not only serve to increase the number of papers submitted in competition, but will place at the Hon. Editor's disposal a large number of valuable papers suitable for publication in the *Transactions*.

In this connection they invite attention to the late Hon. Editor's appeal for literary contributions, printed at p. 234 of Vol. xxvi., from which an extract containing suggestions as to the class of papers which would be welcomed is here given :—

"The subjects on which communications would be welcome are numberless, but a few of them may be mentioned by way of suggestion :—

Nature of localities here found to be most suitable for forest crops of various species, including exotics.

Species, including exotics, here found to be most suitable as forest crops in localities which are unfavourable from various causes, such as high elevation, exposure to cold or strong wind, frost, bog, etc.

Cheap and successful methods of planting.

Successful "direct" sowings.

Successful natural regeneration.

Successful treatment of crops up to middle age, especially with regard to mixed crops.

Successful under-planting of crops of light-crowned species.

Successful protection of nurseries and forest crops from injury by animals, birds, insects, fungi, weeds, smoke or meteoric phenomena (such as frost, wind, snow, etc.).

Successful use of mechanical appliances for the moving of timber.

Cheap and successful methods of increasing the durability of timber.

Cheap and successful methods of converting and seasoning timber.

Utilisation of waste wood (slabs, tops and branches, etc.).

But of course there are many other subjects.

As a rule, successful operations are more instructive than failures, but where the cause of non-success can be indicated with certainty, an account of such failure may be of much interest and value."

Conditions to which Writers must conform.

The Judges are empowered to fix the value of the Medals to be awarded according to the respective merits of the Essays.

All Essays, Reports, Models, or other Articles intended for Competition must be lodged with the Secretary not later than 9th May 1914. Each such Essay, Report, Model, or Article must bear a MOTTO, *and be accompanied by a sealed envelope bearing outside the* SAME MOTTO, *and containing a* CARD *with the* NAME, DESIGNATION, *and* ADDRESS *of the Competitor.*

Essays should be written on one side of the paper only; the left-hand quarter of each page should be left as a blank margin. The lines should not be crowded together.

Manuscripts for which medals have been awarded, or which have been wholly or partly reproduced in the Transactions, *become the property of the Society and are not returned to their authors.*

Judges cannot compete during their term of office.

Successful Competitors may have either the medals or their converted values, which are as follows:— Gold, £5 ; No. 1 Silver Gilt, £3 ; No. 2 Silver, £2 ; No. 3 Silver, £1 : Bronze, 10s.

PART.

TRANSACTIONS

OF THE

ROYAL
SCOTTISH ARBORICULTURAL SOCIETY.

VOL. XXVIII.—PART II.

1914.

A. W. BORTHWICK, D.Sc.,
HONORARY EDITOR.

ROBERT GALLOWAY, S.S.C.,
SECRETARY AND TREASURER

STICKING IN A TREE — IT WILL BE GROWING — WHEN YE'RE SLEEPING — YE MAY BE AYE

EDINBURGH:
PRINTED FOR THE SOCIETY.
SOLD BY DOUGLAS & FOULIS, CASTLE STREET.

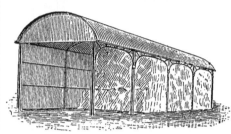
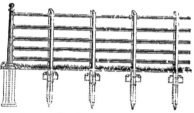

KEITH & CO.

ADVERTISING AGENTS

43 GEORGE STREET EDINBURGH

ADVERTISEMENTS of every kind are received for insertion in the Daily, Weekly, and Monthly Publications throughout the United Kingdom.

Notices of Sequestration, Cessio, Dissolution of Partnership, Entail, etc., etc., for the Edinburgh and London Gazettes, are given special care and attention.

Legal Notices, Heirs Wanted, and all other Advertisements, are inserted in the Colonial and Foreign Newspapers.

Small Advertisements, such as Situations, Houses, and Apartments, Articles Wanted and For Sale, etc., etc., can be addressed to a No. at Keith & Co.'s Office, 43 George Street, Edinburgh, where the replies will be retained until called for, or, if desired, forwarded by Post. Parties in the country will find this a very convenient method of giving publicity to their requirements.

A SPECIALITY is made of ESTATE and AGRICULTURAL ADVERTISEMENTS, such as FARMS, MANSION HOUSES, etc., to LET, ESTATES for SALE, SALES OF TIMBER, AGRICULTURAL SHOWS, etc.

LAW and ESTATE AGENTS, FACTORS, TOWN CLERKS, CLERKS TO SCHOOL BOARDS, and other Officials may, with confidence, place their advertisements in the hands of the Firm.

One Copy of an Advertisement is sufficient to send for any number of newspapers; and the convenience of having only one advertising account instead of a number of advertising accounts is also a great saving of time and trouble.

Addressing of Envelopes with Accuracy and Despatch.

Telegrams—"PROMOTE," EDINBURGH.   Telephone No. 316.

The West of Scotland Agricultural College,

BLYTHSWOOD SQUARE, GLASGOW.

DEPARTMENT OF FORESTRY.

Day and Evening Classes, which provide a complete Course of Instruction in Forestry, qualifying (*pro tanto*) for the B.Sc. Degree of the University of Glasgow, for the Diploma of the Highland and Agricultural Society, and for the Certificate of the College, are held during the Winter Session (October to March) at the College.

Syllabus and particulars regarding these Classes and Prospectus of the general work of the College, including the Course for the Examination of the Surveyor's Institution, may be obtained free from the Secretary.

EDINBURGH AND EAST OF SCOTLAND COLLEGE OF AGRICULTURE

13 GEORGE SQUARE, EDINBURGH.

THE College is one of the Central Institutions administered by the Board of Agriculture for Scotland, and is intended to provide for Agricultural Education and Research in the Central and South-eastern Counties.

DAY CLASSES.

The Day Classes, in conjunction with certain University Classes, provide full courses of instruction in Agriculture, Forestry, Horticulture, and the Allied Sciences, and qualify for the College Diploma, the College Certificate in Horticulture, the Degrees of B.Sc. in Agriculture and B.Sc. in Forestry at the University of Edinburgh, and for other Examinations and Certificates in the Science and Practice of Agriculture.

SHORT COURSES AND EVENING CLASSES.

Short Courses in Agriculture and Forestry are given annually; and Evening Classes in Agriculture, Chemistry, Veterinary Science, Forestry, Horticulture, Botany, and Zoology are held during the Winter Session.

Particulars of Classes, and information as to Bursaries tenable at the College, will be found in the Calendar, which will be forwarded on application to the Secretary,

ALEXANDER M'CALLUM, M.A., LL.B.

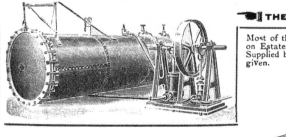

NOTICE.

WANTED TO PURCHASE.

Any of the following Parts of the *Transactions*
viz. :

Parts 1, 2, and 3 of Vol. I.
Parts 2 and 3 of Vol. III.
Parts 1 and 2 of Vol. IV.
Part 2 of Vol. V.
Part 2 of Vol. IX.
Part 1 of Vol. XII.

Apply to

—— THE SECRETARY, ——
19 CASTLE STREET, EDINBURGH.

CONTENTS.

The Society does not hold itself responsible for the statements or views expressed by the authors of papers.

PAGE

15. Discussion on Forestry in Scotland, held at the Annual Business Meeting, Feb. 7, 1914 121

16. Summary of the Position of Scottish Forestry in regard to the Development Fund and the Agriculture (Scotland) Fund. [2nd February 1914.] By R. Galloway, S.S.C., Secretary of the Society 138

17. Report on Tour of Inspection of Woods and Afforestable Lands in Scotland, made by the Society's Foreign, Indian, Colonial and other Guests, in connection with the Celebration of the Diamond Jubilee, and also with Thirty-seventh Annual Excursion (with three Plates) . . . 154

18. The Conference and Dinner 179

19. The Right Hon. Sir Ronald Munro Ferguson, K.C.M.G., Hon. Secretary, 1898-1914 226

20. Mr Robert Galloway, S.S.C., Secretary and Treasurer (with Portrait) 229

21. Landowners' Co-operative Forestry Society . . . 231

22. Notes from Oak and Beech Forests in Denmark (with Plate). By W. G. Smith, B.Sc., Ph.D., Edinburgh and East of Scotland College of Agriculture 241

23. The Silvicultural Treatment of the Douglas Fir. By W. Steuart Fothringham 248

24. The Economic Disposal of Coniferous Timber (with Plate). By D. K. M'Beath 251

25. The Japanese Larch (*Larix leptolepis*). By Geo. Leven . 259

26. The Sitka Spruce in Ireland. By A. C. Forbes . . 264

CONTENTS.

PAGE

Notes and Queries:—The Index—Scarcity of Pitwood—
Forest Pests—The Oleoresins of some Western Pines—
Prices and Supplies in the Timber Trade—Creosoting
Tree Stumps against Pine Weevil—Japanese Larch—
Notes re Acetone 266

Obituary:—Sir John Ramsden, Bart. 272

Proceedings of the Royal Scottish Arboricultural Society, 1914,
with Appendices.

List of Members as at 1st September 1914.

General Index.

INSTITUTED 1854.

Patron—HIS MOST EXCELLENT MAJESTY THE KING.

Permission to assume the title "Royal" was granted by Her Majesty Queen Victoria in 1887.

OFFICE-BEARERS FOR 1914.

President.

CAPTAIN ARCHIBALD STIRLING of Keir, Dunblane.

Vice=Presidents.

LORD LOVAT, D.S.O., Beaufort Castle, Beauly.

HA BUCHANAN, Factor, Penicuik Estate, Penicuik.

ANDREW AGNEW, Bart., of Lochnaw, 10 Smith Square, Westminster.

STUART FOTHRINGHAM of Murthly, Perthshire.

SYDNEY J. GAMMELL of Drumtochty, Count House, Bieldside, Aberdeen.

JOHN F. ANNAND, M.Sc., Lecturer in Forestry, Art College, Newcastle-upon-Tyne.

Council.

HON. LIFE MEMBERS.

SIR KENNETH J. MACKENZIE, Bart. of Gairloch, 10 Moray Place, Edinburgh.

SIR JOHN STIRLING-MAXWELL, Bart. of Pollok, Pollokshaws.

ORDINARY MEMBERS.

GILLANDERS, F.E.S , Forester, Park Cottage, Alnwick.

M WHITTON, Superintendent of City Parks, City Chambers, Glasgow.

WILLIAM DAVIDSON, Forester, Panmure, Carnoustie.

MASSIE, Nurseryman, 1 Waterloo Place, Edinburgh.

ROBERT BROWN, Wood Manager, Grantown-on-Spey.

O. E P. GORDON, B.Sc., Lecturer in Forestry, West of Scotland Agricultural College, 6 Blythswood Square, Glasgow.

RICHARDSON, 6 Dalkeith Street Joppa.

SPIERS, Timber Merchant, Warriston Saw-Mills, Edinburgh.

B T ALLAN, Factor, Polkemmet, Whitburn.

MACDONALD, Overseer, Haystoun Estate, Woodbine Cottage, Peebles.

ALEXANDER MITCHELL, Forester, Rosebery, Gorel

ROBERT FORBES, Overseer, Kennet Estate Office, A

ALEXANDER J. MUNRO, Factor, 48 Castle Street burgh.

W. M. PRICE, Factor, Minto, Hawick.

GEORGE LEVEN, Forester, Bowmont Forest, Re

JOHN W. M'HATTIE, Superintendent of City Par Chambers, Edinburgh.

JOHN BROOM, Wood Merchant, Bathgate.

ALEXANDER MURRAY, Forester, Kingswood, Mur

J. H. MILNE HOME, Irvine House, Canonbie.

DAVID W. THOMSON, Nurseryman, 133 George Edinburgh.

JOHN A. HOWE, Overseer, Home Farm, Moun Rothesay.

EXTRA MEMBER—PRESIDENT OF ABERDEEN BRANCH.

Hon. Editor.

Dr A. W. BORTHWICK, 46 George Square, Edinburgh.

Auditor.

JOHN T. WATSON, 16 St Andrew Square, Edinburgh.

Hon. Secretary.

SIR JOHN STIRLING-MAXWELL, Bart. of Pollok, Pollokshaws.

Secretary and Treasurer.

ROBERT GALLOWAY, S.S.C., 19 Castle Street, Edinburgh.

ABERDEEN BRANCH.

President—A. FORBES IRVINE of Drum.

Secy.—GEORGE D. MASSIE, Solicitor, 147 Union Street, Aberdeen.

NORTHERN BRANCH.

President—BRODIE OF BRODIE.

Hon. Secy.—ALEX. FRASER, Solicitor, 63 Church Inverness.

Hon. Consulting Officials.

Consulting Botanist.—ISAAC BAYLEY BALFOUR, LL.D., D., Sc.D., Professor of Botany, Royal Botanic Garden, Edinburgh.

Consulting Chemist.—ALEXANDER LAUDER, D Sc., F.I.C., George Square, Edinburgh.

Consulting Cryptogamist.—A. W. BORTHWICK, D.Sc., George Square, Edinburgh.

Consulting Entomologist. — ROBERT STEWART DOUGALL, M.A., D.Sc., Professor of Entomolo 9 Dryden Place, Edinburgh.

Consulting Geologist.—R. CAMPBELL, M.A., D.Sc logical Laboratory, University of Edinburgh.

Consulting Meteorologist.—ANDREW WATT, M.A., F Secretary Scottish Meteorological Society, 122 Street, Edinburgh.

Former Presidents.

The following have held the office of President in past years, viz. :—

1854-56. JAMES BROWN, Wood Commissioner to the Earl of Seafield.
1857. The Right Hon. THE EARL OF DUCIE.
1858. The Right Hon. THE EARL OF STAIR.
1859. Sir JOHN HALL, Bart. of Dunglass.
1860. His Grace THE DUKE OF ATHOLL.
1861. JOHN I. CHALMERS of Aldbar.
1862. The Right Hon. THE EARL OF AIRLIE.
1863. The Right Hon. T. F. KENNEDY.
1864-71. ROBERT HUTCHISON of Carlowrie, F.R.S.E.
1872-73. HUGH CLEGHORN, M.D., LL.D., F.R.S.E., of Stravithie.
1874-75. Professor JOHN HUTTON BALFOUR, University of Edinburgh.
1876-78. The Right Hon. W. P. ADAM of Blairadam.
1879-81. The Most Hon. THE MARQUIS OF LOTHIAN, K.T.

1882. Professor ALEXANDER DICKSON, Univ of Edinburgh.
1883-85. HUGH CLEGHORN, M.D., LL.D., F.R. of Stravithie.
1886-87. The Right Hon. Sir HERBERT EUₜ MAXWELL, Bart. of Monreith.
1888-89. The Most Hon. THE MARQUI LINLITHGOW.
1890-93. Professor BAYLEY BALFOUR, Univ of Edinburgh.
1894-97. The Right Hon. Sir RONALD C. Ⅴ FERGUSON, K.C.M.G.
1898. Colonel F. BAILEY, R.E.
1899-02. The Right Hon. THE EARL OF MANSI
1903-06. W. STEUART FOTHRINGHAM of Murₜ
1907-09. Sir KENNETH J. MACKENZIE, Baₜ Gairloch.
1910-12. Sir JOHN STIRLING-MAXWELL, Bₜ Pollok.

Membership.

THE Roll contains the names of over 1450 Members, comprising Landowners, Factors, Foresters, Nurserymen, Gardeners, Land Stewards, Wood Merchants, and others interested in Forestry, many of whom reside in England, Ireland, the British Colonies, and India.

Members are elected by the Council. The Terms of Subscription will be found on the back of the Form of Proposal for Membership which accompanies this Memorandum.

The Principal Objects of the Society,

and the nature of its work, will be gathered from the following paragraphs:—

Meetings.

The Society holds periodical Meetings for the transaction of business, the reading and discussion of Papers, the exhibition of new Inventions, specimens of Forest Products and other articles of special interest to the Members, and for the advancement of Forestry in all its branches. Meetings of the Council are held every alternate month, and at other times when business requires attention; and Committees of the Council meet frequently to arrange and carry out the work of the Society.

Prizes and Medals.

With the view of encouraging young Foresters to study, and to train themselves in habits of careful and accurate observation, the Society offers Annual Prizes and Medals for essays on practical subjects, and for inventions connected with appliances used in Forestry. Such awards have been granted continuously since 1855 up to the present time, and have yielded satisfactory results. Medals and Prizes are also awarded in connection with the Exhibitions and Competitions for Plantations and Estate Nurseries aftermentioned.

School of Forestry, Afforestation, Etc.

In 1882 the Society strongly urged the creation of a British School of Forestry; and with a view of stimulating public interest in the matter, a Forestry Exhibition, chiefly organised by the Council, was held in Edinburgh in 1884.

In 1890, the Society instituted a Fund for the purpose of establishing a Chair of Forestry at the University of Edinburgh, and a sum of £584, 3s. 10d. has since been raised by the Society and handed over to the University. Aided by an annual subsidy from the Board of Agriculture, which the Society was mainly instrumental in obtaining, a Course of Lectures at the University has been delivered without interruption since 1889. The Society also drew up a Scheme for the Establishment of a State Model or Demonstration Forest for Scotland, which might serve not only for purposes of instruction but also as a Station for Research and Experiment, and as a Model Forest, by which Landowners and Foresters throughout the country might benefit. Copies of this Scheme were laid before the Departmental Committee on British Forestry, and in their Report the Committee recommended the establishment of a Demonstration Area and the provision of other educational facilities in Scotland.

The Government recently acquired the Estate of Inverliever in Argyllshire; and while this cannot be looked on as a Demonstration Forest, it is hoped that it may prove to be the first step in a scheme of afforestation by the State of unwooded lands in Scotland. Meantime Sir Ronald Munro Ferguson, for a part of whose woods at Raith a Working-Plan is in operation, very kindly allows Students to visit them.

After the Development Act came into operation, the Council passed a Resolution urging that the Government should create a Board of Forestry, with an Office in Scotland, where the largest areas of land suitable for Afforestation are situated, which would provide Demonstration Forests and Forest Gardens, and would carry out, as an essential preliminary to any great scheme of National Afforestation, a Survey of all areas throughout the country suitable for commercial planting. The Society's policy for the development of Forestry in Scotland has since been fully laid before the Development Commission. As a result of these representations, the Secretary for Scotland appointed a Committee to report regarding the acquisition and uses of a Demonstration Forest Area, and any further steps it is desirable to take in order to promote Silviculture in Scotland. The Committee reported in the beginning of last year, and the Society is pressing the Board of Agriculture for Scotland, being the Department now concerned with Scottish forestry, to give effect to the Committee's recommendations and to encourage the inception of schemes of afforestation. The Society has also published a valuable Report on Afforestation—including a Survey of Glen Mor—prepared for it by Lord Lovat and Captain Stirling, which, it is hoped, may form the basis of the general Forest Survey advocated by the Society.

Resolutions in favour of the acquisition of part of Ballogie, on

Deeside, and Supplementary Areas in other districts for Demonstration purposes, and of the creation of a Department of Forestry for Scotland with a separate annual grant, were passed at last Annual Meeting and sent to the Ministers and Government Departments concerned, and to all the Scottish Members of Parliament.

Excursions.

Since 1878 well-organised Excursions, numerously attended by Members of the Society, have been made annually to various parts of Scotland, England, Ireland, and the Continent. In 1895 a Tour extending over twelve days was made through the Forests of Northern Germany, in 1902 a Tour extending over seventeen days was made in Sweden, in 1904 the Forest School at Nancy and Forests in the north of France were visited, in 1909 a visit was undertaken to the Bavarian Forests, and during the past summer ten days were spent in the Forests of Switzerland. These Excursions enable Members whose occupations necessarily confine them chiefly to a single locality to study the conditions and methods prevailing elsewhere; and the Council propose to extend the Tours during the next few years to other parts of the Continent. They venture to express the hope that Landowners may be induced to afford facilities to their Foresters for participation in these Tours, the instructive nature of which renders them well worth the moderate expenditure of time and money that they involve.

Exhibitions.

A Forestry Exhibition is annually organised in connection with the Highland and Agricultural Society's Show, in which are exhibited specimens illustrating the rate of growth of trees, different kinds of wood, pit-wood and railway timber, insect pests and samples of the damage done by them, tools and implements, manufactured articles peculiar to the district where the Exhibition is held, and other objects of interest relating to Forestry. Prizes and Medals are also offered for Special Exhibits. In addition to the Annual Exhibition before referred to, large and important Forestry Sections organised by this Society were included in the Scottish National Exhibition held in Edinburgh in 1908, and in the Scottish Exhibition of National History, Art, and Industry, held in Glasgow in 1911.

Plantations and Estate Nurseries Competitions.

Prizes are now offered annually for the best Young Plantations and the best managed Estate Nurseries within the Show District of the Highland and Agricultural Society.

The Society's Transactions.

The *Transactions* of the Society, which extend to twenty-seven volumes, are now published half-yearly in January and July, and are issued *gratis* to Members. A large number of the Prize Essays and other valuable Papers, and reports of the Annual Excursions, have appeared in them, and have thus become available to Students as well as to those actively engaged in the Profession of Forestry.

Honorary Consulting Officials.

Members have the privilege of obtaining information gratuitously upon subjects connected with Forestry from the Honorary Officials mentioned above.

Local Branches.

Local Branches have been established in Aberdeen and Inverness for the convenience of Members who reside in the districts surrounding these centres.

Local Secretaries.

The Society is represented throughout Scotland, England, and Ireland by the Local Secretaries whose names are given below. They are ready to afford any additional information that may be desired regarding the Conditions of Membership and the work of the Society.

Register of Estate Men.

A Register of men qualified in Forestry and in Forest and Estate Management is kept by the Society. Schedules of application and other particulars may be obtained from the Local Secretaries in the various districts, or direct from the Secretary. It is hoped that Proprietors and others requiring Estate men will avail themselves of the Society's Register.

Consulting Foresters.

The Secretary keeps a list of Consulting Foresters whose services are available to Members of the Society and others.

Correspondents.

The following have agreed to act as Correspondents residing abroad :—

Canada, . ROBERT BELL, I.S.O., M.D., LL.D., D.Sc.(Cantab.), F.R.S. of Ottawa, late Chief Geologist to Government of Canada, Ottawa.

India, . . F. L. C. COWLEY BROWN, Principal, South Indian Forest College, Coimbatore, South India.

British East } EDWARD BATTISCOMBE, Assistant Conservator of Forests,
Africa, . } Nigeri, *via* Naivasha, East Africa Protectorate.

United States } HUGH P. BAKER, Dean, New York State College of
of America, } Forestry, Syracuse, N.Y.

Cape Colony, . W. NIMMO BROWN, M'Kenzie's Farm, Mowbray, P.O.

Western Australia, FRED MOON.

LOCAL SECRETARIES.

Counties.	Scotland.

Aberdeen, . JOHN CLARK, Forester, Haddo House, Aberdeen.
JOHN MICHIE, M.V.O., Factor, Balmoral, Ballater.

Argyll, . . H. L. MACDONALD of Dunach, Oban.

Ayr, . . ANDREW D. PAGE, Overseer, Culzean Home Farm, Ayr.
A. B. ROBERTSON, Forester, The Dean, Kilmarnock.

Berwick, . WM. MILNE, Foulden Newton, Berwick-on-Tweed.

Bute, . . WM. INGLIS, Forester, Cladoch, Brodick.
JAMES KAY, retired Forester, Barone, Rothesay.

Clackmannan, . ROBERT FORBES, Estate Office, Kennet, Alloa.

Counties.		*Scotland.*
Dumfries,	.	D. CRABBE, Forester, Byreburnfoot, Canonbie.
East Lothian,	.	W. S. CURR, Factor, Ninewar, Prestonkirk.
Fife,	. .	WM. GILCHRIST, Forester, Nursery Cottage, Mount Melville, St Andrews.
		EDMUND SANG, Nurseryman, Kirkcaldy.
Forfar,	. .	JAMES CRABBE, retired Forester, Glamis.
Inverness,	.	JAMES A. GOSSIP, Nurseryman, Inverness.
Kincardine,	.	JOHN HART, Estates Office, Cowie, Stonehaven.
Kinross,	.	JAMES TERRIS, Factor, Dullomuir, Blairadam.
Lanark,	. .	JOHN DAVIDSON, Forester, Dalzell, Motherwell.
		JAMES WHITTON, Superintendent of Parks, City Chambers, Glasgow.
Moray,	. .	D. SCOTT, Forester, Darnaway Castle, Forres.
Perth,	. .	JOHN SCRIMGEOUR, Doune Lodge, Doune.
Ross,	. .	Miss AMY FRANCES YULE, Tarradale House, Muir of Ord.
Roxburgh,	.	JOHN LEISHMAN, Manager, Cavers-Estate, Hawick.
		R. V. MATHER, Nurseryman, Kelso.
Sutherland,	.	DONALD ROBERTSON, Forester, Dunrobin, Golspie.
Wigtown,	.	JAMES HOGARTH, Forester, Culhorn, Stranraer.
		H. H. WALKER, Monreith Estate Office, Whauphill.

England.

Beds,	. .	FRANCIS MITCHELL, Forester, Woburn.
Berks,	. .	W. STORIE, Whitway House, Newbury.
Derby,	. .	S. MACBEAN, Estate Office, Needwood Forest, Sudbury.
Devon,	. .	JAMES BARRIE, Forester, Stevenstone Estate, Torrington.
Durham,	.	JOHN F. ANNAND, M.Sc., Lecturer in Forestry, Armstrong College, Newcastle-upon-Tyne.
Hants,	. .	W. R. BROWN, Forester, Park Cottage, Heckfield, Winchfield.
Herts,	. .	JAMES BARTON, Forester, Hatfield.
		THOMAS SMITH, Overseer, Tring Park, Wigginton, Tring.
Kent,	. .	R. W. COWPER, Gortanore, Sittingbourne.
Lancashire,	.	D. C. HAMILTON, Forester, Knowsley, Prescot.
Leicester,	.	JAMES MARTIN, The Reservoir, Knipton, Grantham.
Lincoln,	.	W. B. HAVELOCK, The Nurseries, Brocklesby Park.
Middlesex,	.	Professor BOULGER, 11 Onslow Road, Richmond Hill, London, S.W.
Notts,	. .	W. MICHIE, Forester, Welbeck, Worksop.
		WILSON TOMLINSON, Forester, Clumber Park, Worksop.
Surrey,	. .	JOHN ALEXANDER, 24 Lawn Crescent, Kew Gardens.
Warwick,	.	A. D. CHRISTIE, Hillside, Frederick Road, Selly Oak, Birmingham.
Wilts,	. .	ANDREW BOA, Land Agent, Glenmore, The Avenue, Trowbridge.
York,	. .	GEORGE HANNAH, Estate Office, Boynton, Bridlington.

Ireland.

Dublin,	. .	A. C. FORBES, Department of Forestry, Board of Agriculture.
		ARCH. E. MOERAN, Lissadell, Stillorgan Park.
King's County,		WM. HENDERSON, Forester, Clonad Cottage, Tullamore.
Tipperary,	.	ALEX. M'RAE, Forester, Dundrum.

ɣal Scottish Arboricultural Society.

———◆•◆•▼———

FORM OF PROPOSAL FOR MEMBERSHIP.

signed by the Candidate, his Proposer and Seconder, and returned
;o ROBERT GALLOWAY, S.S.C., *SECRETARY*, Royal Scottish
Arboricultural Society, 19 Castle Street, Edinburgh.

Full Name, ...

Designation,
 Degrees, etc., ...

Address, ...

Life, or Ordinary Member, ...

Signature, ...

Signature, ...

Address, ...

Signature, ...

Address, ...

[CONDITIONS OF MEMBERSHIP, see Over.

CONDITIONS OF MEMBERSHIP (excerpted from the Laws).

III. Any person interested in Forestry, and desirous of promoting the objects of the Society, is eligible for election as an *Ordinary* Member in one of the following Classes :—

1. Proprietors the valuation of whose land *exceeds* £500 per annum, and others, subscribing annually . . One Guinea.

2. Proprietors the valuation of whose land *does not exceed* £500 per annum, Factors, Nurserymen, Timber Merchants, and others, subscribing annually . . Half-a-Guinea.

3. Foresters, Gardeners, Land-Stewards, Tenant Farmers, and others, subscribing annually . . . Six Shillings.

4. Assistant-Foresters, Assistant-Gardeners, and others, subscribing annually . . . . . Four Shillings.

IV. Subscriptions are due on the 1st of January in each year, and shall be payable in advance. A new Member's Subscription is due on the day of election unless otherwise provided, and he shall not be enrolled until he has paid his first Subscription.

V. Members in arrear shall not receive the *Transactions*, and shall not be entitled to vote at any of the meetings of the Society. Any Member whose Annual Subscription remains unpaid for two years shall cease to be a Member of the Society, and no such Member shall be eligible for re-election till his arrears have been paid up.

VI. Any eligible person may become a *Life* Member of the Society, on payment, according to class, of the following sums :—

1. Large Proprietors of land, and others, . . . £10 10 0

2. Small Proprietors, Factors, Nurserymen, Timber Merchants, and others, ... 5 5 0

3. Foresters, Gardeners, Land-Stewards, Tenant Farmers, and others, ... 3 3 0

VII. Any *Ordinary* Member of Classes 1, 2, and 3, who has paid *Five* Annual Subscriptions, may become a *Life* Member on payment of *Two-thirds* of the sum payable by a *new* Life Member.

XII. Every Proposal for Membership shall be made in writing, and shall be signed by two Members of the Society as Proposer and Seconder, and delivered to the Secretary to be laid before the Council, which shall accept or otherwise deal with each Proposal as it may deem best in the interest of the Society. The Proposer and Seconder shall be responsible for payment of the new Member's first Subscription. The Council shall have power to decide the Class under which any Candidate for Membership shall be placed.

Royal Scottish Arboricultural Society (1854-1914).

DIAMOND JUBILEE OVERSEA GUESTS AT BENMORE, 9th JULY 1914.

K. A. CARLSON,   J. CZALLINGER,   C. BJÖRKBOM,   J. H. JAGER GERLINGS,   A. M. CACCIA,   R. H. CAMPBELL,   R. G. ROBINSON,
So. Africa.   Hungary.   Sweden.   Holland.   Italy.

TRANSACTIONS

OF THE

ROYAL SCOTTISH ARBORICULTURAL SOCIETY.

15. Discussion on Forestry in Scotland.

HELD AT THE ANNUAL BUSINESS MEETING, FEB. 7, 1914.

The sixty-first Annual Business Meeting of the Society was held on the 7th of February last. In order to give the members who might attend the General Meeting the whole day to devote to the affairs of the Society, the Council had met on the previous day and disposed of its business. A full report of the sitting in the forenoon will be found in the " Proceedings " at the end of this issue. In the afternoon an important discussion was held on the " Progress of Forestry Development in Scotland," and two important resolutions were passed.

In his opening remarks the Chairman referred to a correspondence which had taken place between Mr Galloway and the Development Commissioners on the subject of the formation of a company, not trading for profit, which might be the medium through which funds for afforestation purposes might be advanced by the Commissioners. He then went on to say that the latest pronouncement of the Development Commissioners, conveyed in a letter dated 14th January from the Secretary to Mr Galloway, deserved very careful attention, and said,

" I will read an extract :—

" ' With reference to my letter of the 17th November last and previous correspondence, I am directed by the Development Commissioners to inform you that they have now been advised that the terms of the Development and Road Improvement Funds Act, 1909, do not permit of a scheme under which an advance would be made from the Development Fund to a Government Department or a Company or Association of persons not trading for profit, such advance to be employed by the Department or Company in loans to private individuals for the encouragement of afforestation.'

"The effect of this decision is to debar individual landowners from taking part in any scheme of afforestation except on the condition, which must be prohibitive to all but a very small minority, of meeting the whole of the initial cost from their private resources.

"We cannot suppose that the decision has been arrived at without mature consideration, or without consulting the highest legal authority in interpretation of the Act of Parliament constituting the Development Fund, and therefore what I shall have to say must be regarded not as criticism of the action of the Commissioners, but rather of the limited powers conferred upon them by Parliament.

"This said, we are free to point out the very unfortunate results of the decision.

"In the first place, we may doubt the power of the Development Commissioners to prevent private individuals from benefiting by the advances made from the Fund for other purposes, such as, for example, the improvement of the breed of horses or of cattle ; indeed if the improvement is to benefit the country at all, it must begin by conferring a private advantage on the breeders of stock. It is difficult to see the difference in principle between a benefit from the Development Fund to a stock breeder, and an advance for planting expenses to a landowner—except, perhaps, that the stock breeder gets his benefit here and now, and that the planter must wait for thirty or forty years for any return.

"We are driven to the conclusion that the Act under which the Commissioners hold their powers, discriminates against afforestation as compared with the improvement of stock, and that appears to me to be a very unfortunate state of affairs, which our Society should do its best to alter.

"Let us consider for a moment the effect of this notice, that ' No landowner need apply,' on the future of afforestation.

"There are two axioms which will command the assent of most of those who have given special consideration to the problem of introducing a large scheme of afforestation into Scotland. (1) That such a scheme must accommodate itself to existing interests and local conditions, and (2) that it must be as comprehensive as possible.

"That is to say, the scheme must aim at making willing helpers of those who are affected by it, and with this end in view, it must give just and fair compensation for any temporary or permanent loss which it may cause to existing interests, and the first object being to get the land under trees, economically and in accordance with the provisions of a regular plan, it must not reject any available means towards that end.

"Now to obtain a block of 20,000 to 30,000 acres of afforestable land in the Highlands, a number of different individuals and interests must be dealt with, and in every case the land suitable for afforestation will have a special value as wintering for a wide extent of ground only suitable for summer grazing, grouse shooting or deer forest. Even in those cases in which a single large estate is concerned, the special circumstances of the different holdings will require special consideration, and in the commoner cases in which several estates are affected, some landowners may be willing to let or to sell, and others, while unwilling or unable to part with the land, might agree to plant under a regular scheme provided that the cost was advanced by the State.

"It must not be forgotten that in many cases afforestation would be accomplished at the least possible cost to the State by the payment of the landowners' out-of-pocket expenses, and fair compensation for loss of rent. Except the compensation, every sixpence advanced by the State would go directly into planting, and therefore any definite sum available would bring more land under trees in a given time than could be afforested under sale or lease. The one condition implied in this method is that there should be effective supervision by the State. This condition, again, implies the existence of a Department of Forestry, which is the first indispensable step towards any real progress in afforestation.

"Under proper supervision I believe that a scheme of advances to individual landowners would be of the greatest value as one means towards the end of afforestation, and the one under which afforestation could be carried out at the lowest cost to the State and with the minimum of friction, and therefore I learn with the greatest regret that the Development Commissioners are debarred by Act of Parliament from considering it. It is earnestly to be hoped that the Commissioners will obtain an extension of their powers sufficient to cover advances to individuals who wish to take part in afforestation.

"I pass on to the suggestion made by the Commissioners in their letter of a method which they would consider, subject to a favourable opinion of the legal authorities.

" Here we see the Commissioners in a new light. Hitherto they have been well-wishers to afforestation bound by the restrictions of the Act; now they give us some indication of what might be their constructive policy if they were free to adopt it, and on this constructive attitude I think it may be assumed fairly that they invite our criticism. I will give you their own words from the letter of the Secretary of the Commissioners to Mr Galloway :—

" ' The Commissioners would be prepared to submit to the legal authorities the question whether the terms of the Act permit of an advance to a Government Department or a Company or Association of persons not trading for profit, for the execution of a rather different scheme, viz., that the Department or Company should itself hold or acquire control of land for afforestation by means of an advance from the Development Fund—the owner of the land and his heirs standing out of the rent of the land (if any) during the afforestation, but receiving an agreed proportion of the proceeds of the afforestation as they accrue.'

" ' The owner of the land and his heirs standing out of the rent (if any).' These are the words: what are we to make of them? Is this a sparkle of bureaucratic wit, or is it the sober and serious belief of the Commissioners that there exist in Scotland tracts of land which could be profitably afforested yet producing to-day no rent whatever?

" If the suggestion is serious, I am afraid it is not likely to find much favour with owners of afforestable land. It requires the owner to give the use of his land, to forego his rent, and offers no inducement beyond an agreed proportion of the eventual return—if any—as the Commissioners might have been expected to say.

" The Commissioners do not mention the proportion, but the rate has really very little bearing on the proposal; even if it were 99·9 per cent. few landowners could afford to accept the terms.

" The loss to the landowner and his tenants caused by the enclosure for afforestation of the natural wintering belonging to sheep farms and deer forests is entirely ignored by this suggestion. It is true that by a well-devised working-plan this loss could be kept down to the minimum, both by attention to the order of planting of the various blocks, and by opening the first planted blocks as soon as they were safe from damage. Still, even with the most skilful plan a substantial loss of rent during the development period must be anticipated and provided for.

"The proposal of the Commissioners as it stands is one that no ordinarily prudent landowner could consider on his own account, and one that trustees could not consider.

"The plan suggested is one that could only be applied on a scale so small as to have no importance at all in any large scheme of afforestation. It would be confined to those cases in which the landowner is actually receiving no rent for the land to be planted, in practice to areas at present under woodland for which the landowner is receiving no grazing rent.

"It is not for me to seek to probe into the minds of those who have put forward a proposal so manifestly inadequate. I see nothing to be gained from an expedition into the region of hazard and conjecture, which might lead us perilously close to the barren desert of party politics, a forbidden land—and happily so—to our Society.

"While advocates of afforestation are bound to criticise adversely proposals which seem to them incapable of wide application in practice, we are also bound to insist strongly on the conditions essential to success.

"Even at the risk of repeating myself, I would once more insist on the necessity (1) of a careful study of existing economic conditions, and the adjustment of the scheme so as to cause a minimum of disturbance, while giving full compensation for unavoidable loss of rent; (2) an earnest endeavour to bring about co-operation between all classes and interests affected in a scheme that will in the long run benefit the district, but must in its early days cause a certain amount of dislocation and friction.

"There is no royal road to afforestation, nor do I for a moment believe in or advocate any such heroic measure as wholesale purchase of land by the State.

"While it cannot be denied that there may be instances in which State purchases may play a useful part in afforestation, my belief is that these instances will be few and limited in practice to those areas, rare in Scotland, which are capable of being planted as a whole, and that the great bulk of afforestation must be achieved by the State and individuals working in co-operation either as partners or under a lease, and that the terms and conditions under which afforestation will proceed must be of the most flexible nature and adjusted with due regard for the variable local requirements.

"To those who share my belief, the letter of the Secretary of the Development Commissioners offers very cold comfort. It indicates that our ideals are very far from being understood, and that in their place some rigid uniform system seems to be here as ever the ideal of the bureaucratic mind.

"For the time we must be content with stating our beliefs and our readiness to give reasons for them if they are required.

"In conclusion, I would say a word to those who may have thought that I have dwelt too much on a single aspect of the question of afforestation, that of the landowners' share in it. I hold no brief for the landowners, nor do I for one moment claim the high honour of being able to speak on their behalf, but this I say without fear of contradiction, that the question of afforestation in Scotland is in the main a landowners' question. Practically everything that has been done for forestry in Scotland in the past, and that is much more than some adverse critics would care to admit, has been the work of the landowners. I do not believe that the lairds of to-day are at all behind their predecessors in their will to work for the development of the natural resources of Scotland, and do not doubt that schemes of afforestation founded on a wise consideration of the best interests of the country as a whole, and on full and fair compensation for any unavoidable disturbance of existing interests, will find willing support from the owners of the soil."

The Chairman then said :—"In order to get some results from the meeting this afternoon, we shall propose certain resolutions. I think it would be a good thing if the Secretary were to read the proposed resolutions now, before we enter upon the discussion."

The Secretary then read the following resolutions :—

1. *Resolution* re *Demonstration Areas.*

"The members of the Royal Scottish Arboricultural Society, in Annual Meeting assembled, desire to express their satisfaction at the announcement made by the Secretary for Scotland to their deputation recently received by him, that the Advisory Committee on Forestry to the Board of Agriculture for Scotland had recommended the purchase of Ballogie estate on Deeside as a demonstration area, and to urge the Government to acquire that estate without further delay.

"They also desire to urge the Government to select and purchase, as soon as possible, supplementary areas in other districts of Scotland for further demonstrations areas.

"At the same time they desire to express their great disappointment that the promised Advisory and Research Officers have not been appointed, and to ask that these appointments be now made."

2. *Resolution* re *Department of Forestry in connection with the Board of Agriculture for Scotland.*

"The members of the Royal Scottish Arboricultural Society, in Annual Meeting assembled, beg to remind the Government of the promise made by Lord Pentland, when Secretary for Scotland, and repeated by the present Secretary for Scotland, that a Department of Forestry would be created in connection with the Board of Agriculture for Scotland, and to request that this promise be now given effect to; and in view of the obstacles raised by the Board of Agriculture and the Development Commissioners to making reasonable provision out of the funds under their control for forestry in Scotland, they beg to ask that the new Department of Forestry be provided with a separate annual grant adequate for this purpose."

The Secretary added that it was proposed that these resolutions should be sent to the Secretary for Scotland, the Board of Agriculture for Scotland, the Development Commissioners, the Treasury, and the Chancellor of the Exchequer.

The Chairman said:—"It would be of great interest to the Society if some one associated with Ballogie would say a few words on that subject. I think my brother is probably the only member of the Advisory Committee in the room, and I am quite sure he will give us an account of what has been done with regard to that area."

Sir John Stirling-Maxwell said:—"I did not come here prepared to say anything, but as I happen to be the only member of the Advisory Committee here, I will say a word. I had hoped that Mr Munro Ferguson would have been here. He could have spoken to you with far fuller knowledge and mastery of the question than I can, because he has from the very beginning studied these things, and he knows them from the earliest time.

I need not discuss the question whether a demonstration area is desirable or not, because that is a matter upon which our Society made up its mind many years ago, and the fact that the question of a demonstration area is being considered by the Government is entirely due to the Society's suggestion that it was desirable. There was a Committee appointed, as you may remember, about three years ago of which I was chairman as then President of your Society. It was desired to form a scheme for education and development in forestry, and we were requested, not I think in our public remit, but privately, to endeavour to select a suitable area for demonstration purposes, and to make a recommendation privately on that subject to the Secretary for Scotland. Until we began to look for a suitable area I do not think any of us had realised how very difficult it would be to find one. We heard some witnesses in that Committee—some of them I am glad to say are here. None of them was able to help us to an area which was both suitable and obtainable. The Committee made one or two recommendations. They were confidential, and I must not enter into them on this occasion. We made certain recommendations, and afterwards, when the Advisory Committee was appointed in connection with the new Board of Agriculture for Scotland, they again were asked to make a recommendation. The area recommended is part of the estate of Ballogie and part of the adjoining estate of Finzean in Aberdeenshire. It is of course subject to the criticism that it is not in the centre of Scotland, and not equally convenient, as an ideal area would be, to each of our three teaching centres. That difficulty was one which we have had to face from the beginning, simply from the fact that a suitable area was not to be found in the right spot. What we want is an area close to Perth. We started thinking that would be the ideal site, and I think still that would be the best. But in the upshot it proved that no area thereabouts is available—unless the Government is going to find some way of taking it by compulsion—which any of the owners are prepared to put at our disposal except in a tentative way for a few years.

"Now—and this is really the only other point I have to mention —if we are to be satisfied with a demonstration area of so many acres of ground covered with trees or not covered with trees, it can be obtained anywhere. But our recommendation has been made throughout on the assumption that it is not worth while to have an area at all unless it fulfils two conditions. First, that it should be so well stocked with wood as to be within the first few years a forest in being, fit to demonstrate every department of forestry—the cutting of crops in regular rotation and their transport and utilisation, forest management and book-keeping, and practical forestry in all the various stages. Our desire is to see all these things in a position to be studied in practice at the earliest moment. This means a ready-made forest, and that is what is so difficult to get. That was one of our conditions. The other was that the Government should not embark on the expense of such an undertaking unless it could obtain complete control of the area for a long period. We did not lay down purchase as the only possible method, but when we were asked, as we have been asked very often, whether a lease would do, we have always said in that case it must be a very long lease, because the value of the place would be much greater at the end of a hundred years than now, the value consisting largely in its accumulated records. For the first few years, as forestry is in Scotland at present, it would be of great value for the demonstration of practical work, but when forestry is in better order in Scotland, as we hope it may be in fifty or sixty years, the value of the area will lie mainly in its records, and in what it has been able to do towards building up the science of Scottish forestry. In these circumstances, determined to have something of which we could get continuous management, and determined to have something which would be of value at the outset, we were driven to the selection of this area in Aberdeenshire which is fully stocked with woods on a considerable scale, and of the various age-classes of which a working forest must consist. The trees are almost entirely conifers. Admittedly that is a disadvantage. It would have been better to have had hardwoods also, but beyond any doubt conifers come first in Scotland, and must come first partly because they give an earlier return, and partly because the demand in this country for coniferous wood is far greater than for hardwood.

" It seems that there would have been less criticism of this proposal if the area selected had not been nearer the one teaching centre than the other two. The fact of Aberdeen being near to Ballogie has been a great drawback with people who feel keenly about the claims of the rival Institutions. Let me say this, that no question of rivalry between the teaching centres has ever occurred to the minds of any of us who have been concerned with the selection of the area. We have been concerned with nothing but the quality of the area itself, and perhaps I may say that we believe, and I think we have made out a good case for saying so, that the increased journey to Aberdeen is not really the drawback which at first sight it may seem. The school for apprentices, which there must be in connection with the area, will be established there, and presumably the students will be there for a period of not less than two years. To them it will not make much difference whether the journey is an hour more or less. It will make all the difference whether they are studying something worth studying. For other students who will do most of their work at the University as they do now with their professors, the journey will not be very serious. They won't go to the forest for a day. They will go for periods of three to six weeks, and they need not grudge an hour more or less in the train if it is to take them to a place where their studies can be prosecuted to better advantage. Finally, I would say that in the great country of France,—where forestry has been studied for a longer continuous period than in any other country—they are content to have their forestry school almost on the frontier at Nancy. They have it there because they are within reach of woods of all kinds. The distance from Bordeaux and the west of France to Nancy is very much greater than any distance we can travel in Scotland. I cannot help thinking that an arrangement which is wise in France may be wise in Scotland. The support of this Society at this time to this proposal, if you agree to give it, would be of the greatest possible value, because, as I say, the proposal has its critics, and the weight of your opinion will go a long way to decide whether the matter is carried through or not."

The Chairman said :—" This question of the purchase of Ballogie has been urged on the Secretary for Scotland by the Council. We were not at that time in possession of the Advisory Committee's report. However, we can only say that those members of our Society who were acting on the Advisory Committee felt every confidence in their report. Now that the thing has been made public, I think that a recommendation from the Annual Meeting of the Society will have much more weight than any opinion which the Council were able to give on the occasion of their interview with Mr M'Kinnon Wood.

So I hope the resolution, which I will ask Mr Galloway to read again, will be unanimously adopted. But in the meantime we shall be delighted to hear any views on the subject from individual members of the Society."

The Secretary again read the first resolution.

Mr Sydney Gammell, Drumtochty, said :—" I have been able to see something of the work of the Advisory Committee, and have taken a great interest in all they have been doing all along, and I think I cannot do better, in proposing acceptance of this resolution to this meeting, than express my entire approval that this Society should endorse most heartily the finding of a Committee in whom they can have such absolute trust. We may have our individual ideas as to the suitability of one area or another, possibly from geographical position, possibly from some ideas which may be entirely our own and which may concern ourselves or concern any particular schemes with which we have been closely associated, but I think when we get a report like this by such a Committee, it is very necessary that we should do all in our power to carry through what they propose and get something done for the advancement of forestry in Scotland, which is really what we are here to promote. I have great pleasure in moving acceptance of the resolution read by Mr Galloway to this meeting, and I hope it will be carried unanimously."

The Chairman said :—"The resolution requires a seconder, and I think it would give it all the more force if the seconder were to come from some part of Scotland remote from Aberdeen."

Colonel Martin Martin said :—"I have very great pleasure in seconding the motion, particularly as I come from a very remote quarter as regards Aberdeen—from the Isle of Skye. I know that the Government pretend to consider the question of the Western crofter. Still, travelling down from Skye, I could see at every railway station the attractions offered by the Colonies to take the crofter away from his country. "Come to Canada" and "Send your sons to Australia" were posted all over the line. That, gentlemen, is what our crofters are doing now. They are leaving the country, and one cannot wonder at it. Many of them say to me, "The croft only offers a home; it does not offer a living." That is the position. The only way the croft may offer a living is with the assistance that may be given by occasional employment in forestry, and that is why we on the West coast are so anxious to see forestry advanced.

"Had it been possible that an area could have been found in the West we should have welcomed it, but we know perfectly well that is impossible, and that such an area as has been found at Ballogie cannot be found in any part of the Western counties. Therefore I think I am justified in saying that all in the West would cordially agree to plump for the area which has been so carefully selected."

The Chairman said:—"Is there any amendment to the resolution which has been moved and seconded? I think we may take it that it is unanimously carried."

The Secretary thereafter read the second resolution again (see p. 127).

The Chairman said:—" This second resolution follows very closely what has been urged by this Society for the past two or three years. It also takes up what was said by the deputation to Mr M'Kinnon Wood about six weeks ago. No doubt there must be amongst those who attended that deputation some who could say a few words on the subject of what was said at that deputation and the reception which they received, which I may say at once was in every way a satisfactory one, so far as the Secretary for Scotland was concerned. I think is would be a very good thing if any member of that deputation would say a few words to us."

Dr Borthwick said:—" I think this resolution is quite as important as the first one, and deserves our strongest support. On our recent visit to the Secretary for Scotland it was quite apparent to us that he was extremely sympathetic, and had thought carefully about the questions relating to forestry and forestry development in Scotland. One of the points we endeavoured to impress on him was the urgent necessity for the creation of a Department for Forestry. We pointed out that Mr Sutherland was already overburdened with work, and that no mortal man could deal adequately with the overwhelming duties of his office, which were sufficiently numerous and important to justify the establishment of a special Department. One cannot help being struck by the fact that while England and Ireland and Wales have been making rapid progress, Scotland, comparatively speaking, has been making no progress at all. This is in a large measure, no doubt, due to the fact that we have as yet no properly constituted forest authority. In the last report which was issued by the Development Commissioners, we learn that there is only some £350,000 available for purposes of afforestation from the funds that are presently at the disposal of the Commissioners, and in looking over schemes for other parts of Great Britain and Ireland which have been sanctioned or partly sanctioned, it would seem that by the time our turn comes there will be absolutely nothing left. Areas are suggested in various places in England—five or six—each one of them in itself quite as large and expensive at any rate as Ballogie. It is quite possible that these areas will be sanctioned in addition to the Forest of Dean School, while in Scotland we sit still and say nothing. Even when a place like Ballogie, which is eminently suitable, has been found, it is being shelved while the funds available for forestry development are being used up elsewhere. It is time this Society, in addition to the endeavours it has made in the past, now began to press for immediate action. We have lost much valuable time, and the more time we lose the more difficult will it become to make up the lost ground which should have been covered. It is, however, pleasing to think that the deputation which the Scottish Secretary received so sympathetically, went a long way towards furthering the interests of forestry in Scotland. I feel certain that every forester, and every member who is present at this meeting, will heartily join in strongly supporting the resolution. The matter is urgent, and it is very desirable that we should have a separate Department of Forestry in Scotland, a strong separate Department of Forestry which can look after forestry affairs in this country which require immediate and serious attention."

Mr George Leven, Roxburgh, said:—" Might I be allowed to second what has been said by Dr Borthwick. I feel that there are many other points that Dr Borthwick might have brought forward in advocating this Forestry Department of the Board of Agriculture. There is one thing apparently that has been overlooked—the fact that an independent Board of Agriculture has been given to us in Scotland, which has, among other things, to deal with forestry. Now, if we had still been under the British Board of Agriculture we would probably have been served as a province. We find that England has been divided into five or six provinces, each one with a staff attached to it, all working under a Department of Forestry. If we go across to the sister Isle, we find that they have a very strong Department and also an excellent staff. There is no part of this United Kingdom more favourably adapted for afforestation than our own. We may assure ourselves that if forestry is to develop at all that it will be on land that is suited to conifers in the first place, and of such land we have abundance. I hope this resolution will have a certain amount of effect with the powers that be, coming as it does from this large and important Society, and supported with all the force of this General Meeting, I think that it may not be neglected. We are representative of all who are interested in forestry, not only from the landlords' point of view, not only from the factors' point of view, not only from the foresters' point of view, but even from the national point of view. We are quite representative of the whole of Scotland, and I think it ought to go forth that we make a decided call upon the powers that be to do something now."

Mr Adam Spiers, timber merchant, Edinburgh, said :—" As one present at the deputation to the Secretary for Scotland, I must say that we were very courteously received, but beyond that we have got very little further. Is there any doubt in the minds of our Parliamentarians that we can grow timber in Scotland? It looks as if there were so. We in Scotland have fed England with foresters for twenty or thirty years, possibly longer ; we have done the same to Ireland ; we have filled her teaching institutions with teachers, and here we are in Scotland with every facility for growing timber of the best quality and yet we are starved. We have got to take a lesson from our friends over in Ireland, and make plenty of noise until we get what we want. Until we have made up our minds to that we will never get any further forward. As far as we can see there is very little hope of getting any of this Development Fund for forestry, at least for a considerable time. The timber imported into this country has risen 20, 30, ay 40 per cent. within the last very few years, and there is no prospect of these prices ever going back. Why? It is simply because the timber cannot be got. If a home timber man was to contract for a supply of home timber, he would have to run throughout the whole length and breadth of the land before he could get supplies, and every fifty miles he passed he would find plenty of land capable of growing timber, with not a tree upon it. I think we have entirely ourselves to blame. Our representatives in Parliament are not doing anything like their duty. The question of afforestation is certainly not a vote-catching one, and I believe that has a great deal to do with the way it has been neglected. We only want the Government to give us the money, and we will find the land and the men, and we will demonstrate to the world what Scotland can do. There is not a country in the world that has done less for afforestation than our own. This is a disgrace to Scotsmen."

Mr H. M. Cadell of Grange, Linlithgow, said :—" I have been over in Canada lately, and I travelled from Nova Scotia to Klondyke. It has been said in Canada that half of the people who govern Canada come from Scotland. Instead of staying at home and energetically developing their own resources, they go abroad and show their native capacity. Those who develop Canadian resources get a lot of assistance from the Government, and we ought to kick until we get more encouragement and help in afforestation and the development of our resources at home. We should not sit down humbly and quietly as we do like decent, honest, and well-behaved people, and submissively let Ireland and England get all the plums. Look at the amount we contribute to the Imperial revenue in comparison with Ireland. Nobody in Scotland is any good at asking boldly. If our ancestors had behaved like this there would never have been any Bannockburn at all. " Ye have not because ye ask not" is a text that we are too apt to forget on this side of the Tweed.

" In the Island of Raasay a large seam of ironstone has lately been discovered and is now being worked, and if this new local industry develops it may require a good deal of coniferous timber. Our coal is getting exhausted and will become permanently dearer, so that we should also turn our attention to the growing of trees that will make good fuel in the future, such as beech. We should find out the best places and grow different kinds of trees and not confine attention to conifers entirely, as they have less fuel value than hardwoods, and may as time goes on not be needed so much for colliery purposes."

The Chairman said :—"This resolution has been moved,

seconded, and supported. I do not know whether there is any amendment to it."

The resolution was adopted.

The Chairman said :—" Copies will be sent to the Secretary of the Board of Agriculture, the Secretary of the Development Commissioners, the Right Hon. D. Lloyd George, M.P., the Secretary to the Treasury, and the Right Hon. T. M'Kinnon Wood, and I hope some attention will be paid to them."

Mr Sydney Gammell said :—" Let us also send them to the Prime Minister, who is head of the Government, charged with the development of the country, and member for a Scottish constituency."

Mr Robert Forbes, Kennet, suggested that they should be sent to the Scottish Members of Parliament.

The Chairman said :—" I am afraid we should find a great deal of deplorable ignorance on this subject, and the resolutions would have very little to say to them. I think it would be far better if they could have a reasoned statement on the subject in some form, and I think anything of that sort which could be printed in a form that it could be sent round to every member for a Scottish constituency would be a very good thing indeed. Of course we are entirely in the hands of the meeting with regard to that."

Sir John Stirling-Maxwell suggested that whatever was to be sent might be sent soon.

Mr H. M. Caddell said :—" A great many of the Members of Parliament in Scotland are Englishmen. I would send it to those Members of Parliament in Scotland who are Scotsmen."

Dr Borthwick thought they should send in addition to the resolutions a reasoned statement.

The Chairman said :—" That could be done. I think it is very desirable that there should be no delay in sending the actual resolutions to the officials who are from the nature of their office supposed to understand them. I certainly feel with regard to the wider application to the Members of Parliament generally that there should be a covering letter enclosed, and if it is the wish that such should be prepared I should be most happy to refer something of that sort to the Council, and let the Council send such a letter on behalf of the Society to every Scottish Member of Parliament together with the resolutions."

The Chairman further said :—" We have an interesting

resolution from the Northern Branch, which was dealt with by the Council. I would like to take this opportunity of explaining to you how that resolution was dealt with by the Council."

The resolution was then read by the Secretary. It was in the following terms :—

1. "That in the interests of forestry in the country it is urgent that provision should be made without delay for the formation of a separate Department in connection with the Board of Agriculture for Scotland, charged with the special duty of advancing the interests of silviculture in Scotland."

2. "That the meeting strongly advise the extreme advisability, in the interests of the Highlands at large, of considering from the point of view of forestry the value of the lands offered by the Duke of Sutherland to His Majesty's Government, in order to secure that the land offered by his Grace should be reported upon with the object of finding out its value from a silvicultural point of view; and it was the view of the Branch that the successful establishment of small holdings lay in the provision of work for small holders, and that this work could best be provided by the establishment of forests either by the State or by private individuals with the encouragement of the State."

The Chairman said :—"That resolution embodies what has been the view of the Society all along. Before receiving that resolution they had already decided to take the action of inquiring what the Board of Agriculture for Scotland had done, or what it proposed to do, with regard to this offer of land by the Duke of Sutherland ; and they also at the same time took the opportunity of pointing out that if the survey which has been constantly urged by this Society on the Government had been carried out, that they would have had all the facts at their disposal the moment such an offer came before them. They would only have had to look at their map and see what waste land there was. With regard to the survey, the reason they gave against it was that such a survey would very speedily be out of date. That may be true in certain respects, such as deer forests, but we pointed out that such a map did not require details. We required, in the first place, a map which would show the altitudes, and which would give the quality of the land with regard to the possibility of afforestation. We hope to obtain an answer from the Board of Agriculture as to what steps they actually took in ascertaining the value of the land, and I can only say that when the Council obtain an answer from the Board of Agriculture—which is not always a very rapid process —they will submit to the Northern Branch an account of the answer which they receive."

The Chairman continuing, said :—" Mr Galloway has secured very valuable figures as to the actual sums which have been expended under the Development Commission in grants for afforestation in recent years, and we are proposing to print those figures in the *Transactions* so that they will become accessible to all the members" (see p. 148).

On the motion of Mr Buchanan a hearty vote of thanks was accorded to the Chairman for presiding, which terminated the meeting.

16. Summary of the Position of Scottish Forestry in regard to the Development Fund and the Agriculture (Scotland) Fund. [*2nd February* 1914.]

By R. GALLOWAY, S.S.C., Secretary of the Society.

The Development Fund was created by the Development and Road Improvement Act, 1909, dated 3rd December of that year and entitled—An Act to promote the economic development of the United Kingdom and the improvement of the roads therein. The improvement of roads is however entrusted to a separate Road Board who receive a special grant called the Road Improvement Grant, and have therefore no interest in the Development Fund; consequently this part of the Act need not be further referred to here.

The Development Fund at present consists of £500,000 charged on and issued out of the Consolidated Fund for five years, in addition to any other sums that may be specially voted by Parliament. In 1910-11 a special vote of £400,000 was added to the Fund, bringing up the total to £2,900,000.

It is unnecessary to detail fully all the purposes to which the

Fund may be applied, but speaking generally they are— AGRICULTURE and RURAL INDUSTRIES, FORESTRY, RECLAMATION and DRAINAGE, RURAL TRANSPORT (except roads), HARBOURS, INLAND NAVIGATION, FISHERIES and OTHER PURPOSES calculated to promote the economic development of the United Kingdom.

Forestry in the Act includes (1) the conducting of inquiries, experiments and research for the purpose of promoting forestry, and the teaching of methods of afforestation; (2) the purchase and planting of land found after inquiry to be suitable for afforestation.

The Commissioners were originally five in number, but by the amendment Act of 1910 the number was increased to eight. The period of service is ten years, and one member retires every year but may be reappointed. The first Commissioners were appointed by Royal Warrant on 12th May 1910, and at 31st March 1913, the close of the Commissioners' financial year, their names were as follows :—Lord Richard Cavendish (*Chairman*); Mr Vaughan Nash, C.V.O., C.B (*Vice-Chairman*); Sir S. Eardley-Wilmot, K.C.I.E.; Mr H. Jones-Davies; Mr M. A. Ennis; Sir William Haldane; Mr A. D. Hall, F.R.S.; Mr Sidney Webb, L.L.B.

Two of the Commissioners may receive salaries not exceeding in the aggregate £3000 per annum.

The bodies that can apply for advances are a Government Department or a Public Authority, University, College, School, or Institution, or an Association of persons or Company not trading for profit, applying through a Government Department. Thus applications from individuals cannot be considered.

Money may be advanced from the Fund either by way of grant or by way of loan, or partly in one way and partly in the other, and upon such conditions as the Commissioners may think best. The Commissioners' duty is to consider and report to the Treasury on applications referred to them. They have no power to make grants or loans—only to recommend them. They have no executive powers, that is to say, they cannot carry out any schemes themselves.

Where an advance is made for any purpose which involves the acquisition of land, such land can be acquired and held by the recipient of the advance, and powers may be obtained if necessary to acquire it compulsorily.

The Commissioners have to submit an annual report to the

Treasury, which must be laid before Parliament annually by the Treasury.

Such is a brief outline of the constitution of the Development Fund, and of the powers of the Development Commissioners.

Three reports have been issued, carrying the Commissioners' operations down to 31st March 1913, and from these the following particulars have been abstracted.

During the first year of their operations, the Commissioners formulated the following principles for their own guidance in considering British schemes of forestry :—

(a) That the first requirement for forestry development is effective education in forestry at suitable centres, regulated by organised research and demonstration.

(b) That no scheme of State afforestation on a large scale can be considered until investigation has shown where State forests might be economically and remuneratively provided (regard being had to the interests of other rural industries), and until a trained body of foresters becomes available.

(c) That for the present, applications for grants for the above purposes should include provision for the creation and maintenance of such staff as may be necessary to give practical advice and assistance to those who desire to undertake afforestation, or to develop existing afforested areas.

After visiting Ireland, the Commissioners concluded that State afforestation on a small scale might be started in that country at once owing to the following special circumstances :—

(a) That Ireland has only 1·5 per cent. of its total area under wood.

(b) That a system of peasant proprietorship has been adopted in Ireland, by which the land is being divided into properties much too small ever to admit of successful silviculture by the individual owners.

(c) That there are now special opportunities to acquire available areas for afforestation purposes which are not likely to occur again.

At the same time they laid down other general principles applicable to Irish schemes which it is unnecessary to repeat.

The Scotch Education Department, which was in charge of forestry education in Scotland in 1910, sent in applications for advances on behalf of the three agricultural colleges for various experimental areas, forest gardens, and nurseries, and also from the University of Edinburgh for a grant towards forestry instruction, and at the same time pointed out the urgent need of a Demonstration Forest, and indicated a proposal to appoint a Committee to report on the subject. The Commissioners approved of the Committee, and the Committee's report was issued in December 1911.

The Society also submitted a representation to the Commissioners, dated 10th September 1910, pointing out that the preliminary steps the Council considered essential to the orderly development of forestry were :—

1. A Survey.
2. A Demonstration Forest with Forest School attached ; and
3. Forest Gardens for the Agricultural Colleges.

The Commissioners in replying to this representation stated that a national survey would, in their opinion, quickly fall out of date, and that while they were favourably impressed with the Forest Survey of Glen Mor, published by the Society, which they regarded as valuable pioneer work, they had decided to postpone the question of recommending assistance from the Development Fund for such surveys until the Demonstration Area had been established, when the staff and students there could deal with the subject.

At the close of their financial year, 31st March 1911, they summed up the position thus :—

In regard to England and Wales, the Commissioners have just received a comprehensive scheme from the Board of Agriculture and Fisheries.

In regard to Scotland, they have agreed to the provision of a Central Demonstration Area—for the acquisition of which preliminary steps are being taken—and of a forestry school in connection with it ; and also to the provision of small forest gardens for the local use of the agricultural colleges.

In regard to Ireland, they have agreed to advances of £25,000 or £30,000 for the purchase of land, and to further advances as soon as formal and definite applications are made under the Act ; for additions to staff, and for the maintenance and management of small woodlands in the hands of County Councils.

In the following year, that is, to 31st March 1912, the Commissioners received altogether thirteen applications, and the following grants were recommended :—

England.—To the Board of Agriculture and Fisheries a grant at the rate of £5700 per annum for the following purposes, viz.:—£500 for technical advice and instruction at each of five centres, namely, Oxford, Cambridge, Cirencester, Bangor and Newcastle; £500 each to Oxford and Cambridge, and £200 to other centres for research; £1000 for minor forestry experiments, and £1000 for administration expenses.

Various applications from County Councils for small grants were held to be covered by these larger sums.

A grant of £200 was also made to Cambridge University for temporary accommodation for the staff of the forestry school, and a similar sum—£200—to Newcastle for a forestry building in Chopwell woods.

The Commissioners also suggested that the Forest of Dean and High Meadow woods might be utilised as a Demonstration Area.

Scotland.—In Scotland the Commissioners recommended a grant of £2000 spread over five years, for the establishment and maintenance of a forest garden for the joint use of the University and the Edinburgh and East of Scotland College of Agriculture, to be expended under the supervision of a joint committee composed of an equal number of representatives of the University Court, and of the Board of Governors of the College.

A grant of £9000 was also recommended to be made to the University for the following purposes :—£4500—being 50 per cent. of the cost of new buildings for forestry teaching; £2000 for equipment during five years; £2500 to meet, for five years, the salaries of an Assistant Lecturer, and an Adviser in Forestry with demonstrators.

These grants were made on the understanding that the buildings, etc., were to be available for the joint use of university and college students.

Ireland.—A grant of £1360 rising to £1945 was recommended for salaries of additional staff required in connection with the Department of Agriculture's forestry operations.

For the year to 31st March 1913, the Commissioners continued the grant of £5700 to the Board of Agriculture in *England* for the purposes previously approved; gave also £2500 for a new forestry school at Cambridge, £1000 for a research laboratory at Oxford, and £85 further to Newcastle for the building in Chopwell woods. In addition, the Commissioners said they were willing to accept the Board's proposal to acquire land for the formation of six or seven experimental forests of some 5000 acres each, and at the end of the year were discussing with the Board the practical steps to be taken for the purpose.

Scotland.—As regards Scotland, the Commissioners said that no application or scheme had yet been received from the Scottish authorities for the establishment of a Central Demonstration Area for Scotland, and that they had intimated, subject to the adjustment of the financial questions concerned with the Agriculture (Scotland) Fund referred to below, that they would take a favourable view of an application for a *grant* for cost and equipment of an estate so far as relates to the educational and advisory functions of a Demonstration Area, and for a *loan* repayable on a terminable annuity basis towards the cost so far as relates to its economic purposes.

An application from the Board of Agriculture for Scotland for a grant of £7500 for three years for Survey and Research Officers was under consideration at the close of the financial year.

Ireland.—The purchase of various areas making up an acreage of 14,000 acres was carried out from the loan of £25,000 to £30,000 previously recommended.

Local Authorities.—In 1912 the Development Commissioners issued a circular to Local Authorities and other responsible bodies, intimating that the Commission was prepared to consider applications from such bodies for assistance in the afforestation of water-catchment areas or other suitable areas under their control, with a view to ascertaining whether the schemes put forward were of public utility and likely to prove remunerative, either directly or indirectly. The Commission proposed to ascertain, by means of a survey, whether the above conditions were likely to be fulfilled in schemes submitted. They thought that schemes should, with due regard to economy and efficiency provide for varying the extent of the operations from year to year, and have also regard to the question of employment. It was stated as conditions, that the schemes put forward by public authorities must be carried out in accordance with expert advice, be open to inspection at all times, and be available for education, research and demonstration ; and in the event of these conditions being complied with the Commissioners were prepared to recommend loans on the general principle that repayment commences as soon as the work becomes remunerative, or at some date to be fixed with reference to the method of afforestation to be followed in any particular case.

In response to this invitation communications were received from a number of the large municipalities, including Birmingham, Cardiff, Leeds, Liverpool and Manchester, and negotiations were proceeding with them. The terms offered by the Commission were,—loans not to exceed £5 per acre, at 3 per cent. interest, to be repaid, with accumulated interest, from the proceeds ; or alternatively, a profit-sharing arrangement would be made by which the Development Fund would receive a proportion of the price of the produce.

An arrangement has been arrived at with Liverpool City Council that 5000 acres at Lake Vyrnwy in Montgomeryshire shall·be afforested by means of an advance from the Fund—the loan being limited to £5 per acre = £25,000, the Fund receiving the price of one-half of the ultimate timber yield. A detailed scheme is being prepared.

Other schemes from public bodies in England are being considered, as well as small schemes from Edinburgh and Dundee Water Trusts and Glasgow Distress Committee. In the case of Edinburgh, a loan of £150 has been authorised for experimental planting at Talla.

Cost of Administering Schemes.—The cost of administering schemes financed from the Development Fund was raised both in England and Ireland, and the Treasury held that grants made from the Fund should cover all consequential expenditure, both for staff and other purposes. In Ireland the Commissioners have further agreed to defray from the Development Fund the whole cost of administration of forestry centres, whether acquired by means of the Fund or from the Parliamentary votes.

The Commissioners' Powers.— As has been already mentioned the Commissioners have no executive powers. If therefore they wished or agreed to spend money on a scheme, they could not spend ·it themselves, but would have to entrust it to some suitable body, and they have pointed out in their reports that a suitable body is not always available. They are also debarred by the terms of the Act from making grants or loans to private individuals or to companies trading for profit. The Commissioners were of opinion that one consequence of these restrictions was that few schemes have been submitted for some of the important purposes mentioned in the Act, including afforestation. They suggested that this difficulty might be overcome by the formation of suitable National Associations (not trading for profit) which might receive and administer advances from the Fund. On 25th November 1912, the draft Constitution of a non-profit company was prepared and submitted to the Commissioners for consideration. The Constitution submitted provides all the executive powers that the Commissioners lack, so that the company could assist, or carry out, any scheme that the Development Commissioners could advance money for.

It was, a few weeks ago, intimated by the Commissioners that they had been advised by the Legal Authorities that no loans could be given even by this means to private owners for the encouragement of afforestation. The question as to whether they have power to recommend money for schemes to be carried out on a co-operative basis by the proposed company is now engaging the attention of the Legal Authorities.[1]

Finances of the Development Fund—(Relation to other Funds).— The Commissioners point out that there are several funds in existence which can be applied to purposes for which the Development Fund is also applicable, and the question has arisen as to whether these other funds must be exhausted before any claim can be made on the Development Fund. The case which has caused most difficulty is the Agriculture (Scotland) Fund, with an annual income of about £200,000, which was created in 1911, about two years later than the Development Fund. This Scottish fund is applicable to forestry amongst other purposes, and the question is, Can the Development Commissioners advance money for this purpose in Scotland so long as the income of this fund is unexhausted? It is recognised, however, that the primary object of this fund is the encouragement of small holdings, and the Commissioners say they are prepared to agree, subject to the approval of the Treasury, that expenditure for small holdings should have priority over other purposes to which the Scottish fund could

[1] It is understood that an affirmative reply has now been received.

be applied. In these circumstances the Commissioners say the question of the terms on which the Development Fund should provide money for forestry purposes in Scotland will require to be settled separately on each application. As already mentioned the application for a grant for survey and research officers is under consideration, and the price of the promised Demonstration Area is offered partly by way of grant and partly by way of loan.

Estimate of Future Position of the Development Fund.—In estimating the future expenditure and funds available for particular purposes, the Commissioners stated in their second report that for the period to 1916, £350,000 would be sufficient for forestry, and they adhere to this estimate in their third and last issued report. This sum, they say, will not permit of afforestation upon any large scale, as it is scarcely sufficient to deal effectively with 100,000 acres, unless other funds are available. They accordingly propose to restrict themselves to two lines of action—

1. The purchase and planting of experimental and demonstration areas of perhaps 5000 acres each, in five or six different districts; and

2. Providing loans to Local Authorities already possessing suitable land.

The first of these proposals is evidently the scheme submitted by the Board of Agriculture and Fisheries before referred to, and these areas will therefore be situated wholly in England, as the Commissioners go on to say that the Government Department concerned has already put before them proposals leading up to the first of these two measures.

England has already secured, free of cost, in the Crown Forest of Dean, a large and very suitable demonstration area, and these five or six areas will be additional experimental areas for that country.

The second proposal will also affect England more than Scotland, seeing that the watershed areas in England are much more numerous than those in Scotland.

Loans to Local Authorities for the afforestation of their areas will not be all required at once, but the Commissioners say that it will be necessary to earmark a sufficient sum to meet the loans recommended.

BOARD OF AGRICULTURE FOR SCOTLAND.

This Board was constituted by the Small Holders (Scotland) Act, 1911, which came into operation on 1st April 1912. It consists of three members, viz. :

Sir Robert Wright (*Chairman*); Mr R. B. Greig; and Mr John D. Sutherland, Commissioner for Small Holdings and Chairman of the Advisory Committee on Forestry.

The Board is charged with the general duty of promoting the interests of agriculture, forestry, and other rural industries in Scotland, and has control of the Agriculture (Scotland) Fund before referred to, which is to be applied for the purpose of facilitating the constitution of new landholders' holdings, the enlargement of landholders' holdings, etc., and for the purpose of exercising the other powers and duties conferred on, or transferred to, the Board, in accordance with schemes to be approved of by the Secretary for Scotland.

After allowing a reasonable interval of time to elapse from the date of the Board's appointment, the Council of the Society urged the Board to create the Department of Forestry in connection with the Board which was promised by Lord Pentland while Secretary for Scotland, and to give effect to the report of the Departmental Committee on Scottish Forestry before referred to. A conference afterwards took place between the Board and the Council, when these matters were discussed. The Chairman of the Board pointed out that the Board had no funds available for forestry, as the whole of the fund at their disposal would be required for small holdings. The Board and the Council, he said, must therefore look to the Development Fund for the necessary money. The position of matters was considered by the Council to be very unsatisfactory, and they appealed to the Secretary for Scotland, who, on 7th November last, received the Council, accompanied by Sir Herbert Maxwell, a former president, in the chambers of the Board.

The President repeated the Council's demand for the promised Department of Forestry in connection with the Board, and asked that it should be provided with a separate grant for forestry purposes only. Sir Herbert Maxwell submitted facts to show that there were large tracts of suitable land purchasable on reasonable terms, and other speakers pointed out that ample experience and a sufficiency of trained men were available to carry out schemes of afforestation, and that such schemes would involve the creation of small holdings and would provide more work and wages in the Highlands than any other industry.

In his reply, the Secretary for Scotland informed the deputation that the Board's Advisory Committee on Forestry had recommended the purchase of Ballogie on Deeside as a Demonstration Forest, and elicited from the deputation the view that this estate would be a very suitable area for conifers, but would require to be supplemented by an area elsewhere to demonstrate the cultivation of hardwoods, which several members had shown was also very important.

With regard to money, Mr M'Kinnon Wood said it had always been understood that the Development Commissioners were prepared to give money for forestry development in Scotland as in England and Ireland.

In answer to the President, who reminded him of the need for a separate Department, Mr M'Kinnon Wood said: "When the Development Commissioners have made up their minds how they will supply money for this purpose of assisting forestry, then will be the time to create a staff. I quite agree with you; there ought to be a central staff."

The matter of the provision of money therefore appears to be still unsettled, and until a satisfactory settlement is arrived at, there can be no Demonstration Area, no Department of Forestry, and no real progress in afforestation.

DEVELOPMENT FUND.

Abstract of Expenditure on Forestry as at 31st March 1913.
(Taken from the Commissioners' Third Report.)

Total Grants recommended by the Commissioners . £26,635
Total Loans ,, ,, ,, £25,000–30,000
Allocation of Grants:

England and Wales . .	£12,585
Scotland	11,000
Ireland	3,050
	£26,635

Allocation of Loans:

England	*Nil*
Scotland	*Nil*
Ireland	£25,000–30,000

DETAILS OF ABOVE GRANTS.

England.

CAMBRIDGE UNIVERSITY:

Temporary provision for staff of School
of Forestry £200
School of Forestry 2,500

£2,700

OXFORD UNIVERSITY:

Research Laboratory at School of Forestry . 1,000

ARMSTRONG COLLEGE, NEWCASTLE:

Forestry building in Chopwell Woods. . . 285

BOARD OF AGRICULTURE AND FISHERIES:

Advisory research and experimental
work—proportion for year to 31st
March 1912 . . . . £2,900
Advisory officers at five
centres . . . £2,500
Research—
Oxford . £500
Cambridge . 500
Other places 200
———— 1,200
Minor forestry experiments
at five centres . . 1,000
Administration expenses . 1,000
———— 5,700
————
8,600

Ireland (to 31st March 1912).

Salary of Forestry Officer for Demon-
stration Forests and Research
Institute £400– 600
,, Forestry Officer for Working-plans 300– 400
,, Temporary Valuers . . . 200– 200
,, Second Division Clerk . . 70– 300
,, Surveying and Mapping Clerk . 90– 120
,, Typist 50– 75
Travelling expenses 250– 250
————————
£1,360–1,945

Carry forward . . . £12,585

Brought forward   £12,585

(*To 31st March* 1913.)

Salaries, etc., as above . . .	1,690	
	————	
		3,050
		————
		15,635

Scotland.

EDINBURGH UNIVERSITY :

Forest Garden and Agriculture College
—five years £2,000

EDINBURGH UNIVERSITY :

Building for joint use of University and College	£4,500		
Equipment	2,000		
Salary of Assistant Lecturer and Adviser with Demonstrators for five years	2,500		
	————	9,000	
		————	11,000

Total to 31st March 1913   £26,635

Note.—These figures were brought down to 17th April by Mr Robertson, in answer to Mr Munro Ferguson's question in the House of Commons, as follows :—

England . . .	£18,435
Scotland . . .	11,150
Ireland . . .	3,050
	————
	£32,635

being an increase of £6000.

England . . .	£5,850
Scotland . . .	150

This increase probably consists of annual grant to Board of Agriculture, £5700, with the additional £150, and the loan of £150 to Edinburgh Water Trust for experimental planting at Talla.

EQUIPMENTS IN THE THREE COUNTRIES FOR THE DEVELOPMENT OF FORESTRY.

England.

Five Advisory Officers at £500 . .	£2,500
Research Officers	1,200
Experimental work	1,000
	———
	4,700

Forestry Staff at Board of Agriculture:

Superintending Inspector .	£500– 700
Three Inspectors at £300–400	900–1,200
One Assistant Inspector . .	150– 250
One Clerk	200– 500
.. . . . .	70– 300
	———————
	£1,820–2,950

1,820

£6,520–7,650

The whole of the £4700 and £1000 of the £1820 is paid out of the Development Fund = £5700 per annum meantime— the above exclusive of the teaching staffs at the various centres.

Ireland.

Professor of Forestry	£500– 600
Chief Forestry Inspector . . .	500– 600
Two Assistant Forestry Inspectors .	600– 800
Superintendent—Avondale Forestry Station	200 & Board, &c.
Working Foresters—eleven at £75–150	825–1,650

Note.—About £2000 of this expenditure and of the general clerical staff of the departments is paid out of the Development Fund.

It appears that the Irish Board are also in receipt of £6000 per annum from Parliament, to enable them to preserve existing woods or estates passing through the Estate Commissioners' hands. They have further received a loan of £25,000 free of interest for thirty years from the Development Fund as mentioned elsewhere.

The total expenditure of the Department on Forestry for the ten years, from 1902 to 1912, appears to have been £49,047, of which £34,878 was received from the Endowment Fund—£13,696 from the Parliamentary Vote, and £6000 p.a., and £473 from the Development Fund.

(See Statement prepared by the Irish Department of Agriculture, etc.)

Scotland.

Salaries of Assistant Lecturer and Adviser and Demonstrators in Edinburgh University—per annum .	£500
Forestry Adviser to the Board of Agriculture, p.a. .	400
A second class Clerk £70-£300 has now been authorised	70
	£970

The £500 is paid out of the Development Fund, and the £470 out of the Board of Agriculture's own grant.

The above is exclusive of the teaching staffs at the university and college, except the ones mentioned.

How the Development Fund stood at 31st March 1913.

Total Fund to 1915-1916	£2,900,000
Made up thus—	
Sum provided by the Act £500,000 for five years .	£2,500,000
Sum voted by Parliament 1910-11	400,000
Advances recommended to 31st March 1913 .	£725,988

Apportioned thus—

	Grants.	Loans.
Agriculture and Rural Industries	£448,756	
Forestry	26,635	£25,000
Harbours	105,825	71,100
Inland Navigation . . .		19,500
Fisheries	20,172	9,000
	£601,388	£124,600
Total . £725,988		

Estimated additional advances to 1916.

Agriculture, etc.—

Research and Instruction	£850,000
Rural Industries	130,000
Horses and live stock breeding . . .	400,000
Co-operation	60,000
Forestry and Afforestation	350,000
Harbours	450,000
Fisheries	100,000
	£2,340,000

Nothing is included in this amount for inland navigation, reclamation and drainage, which the Commissioners say should be dealt with. Thus there may be a balance unexpended (allowing for interest) of £1,000,000, or perhaps only £500,000.

The annual sum needed after that year to continue schemes started, which ought to be permanent, will be about £250,000.

17. Report on Tour of Inspection of Woods and Afforestable Lands in Scotland.

MADE BY THE SOCIETY'S FOREIGN, INDIAN, COLONIAL AND OTHER GUESTS, IN CONNECTION WITH THE CELEBRATION OF THE DIAMOND JUBILEE, AND ALSO WITH THIRTY-SEVENTH ANNUAL EXCURSION.

(With Three Plates.)

On the 16th of February last, the Royal Scottish Arboricultural Society reached the sixtieth anniversary of its foundation. The Diamond Jubilee Celebrations which were arranged and carried out to commemorate that important event took the form of a tour of inspection of woods and afforestable lands in Scotland, to which were invited representative foresters from all parts of the world. The meeting lasted from 27th June to 10th July, during which time a very comprehensive programme was carried through. On the 10th of July, a Conference on forestry was held, at which the Foreign, Indian and Colonial representative foresters had an opportunity of stating their views in regard to the suitability of Scotland for afforestation. Their unanimous pronouncement on that occasion, which was entirely in favour of afforestation, is probably the most authoritative, and therefore the most valuable, statement which has ever been made with regard to Scottish forestry. A reception and dinner in the evening brought the celebrations to a close.

The tour was started at Perth, on the morning of the 29th June. Most of the Foreign and Colonial representatives had spent the week-end as the guests of Captain Stirling of Keir, Sir John Dewar of Dupplin, and W. Steuart Fothringham, Esq. of Murthly. Motor cars were in waiting to take the party on its tour of inspection. The first place to be visited was the Lynedoch Old Pleasure Grounds, where were seen the first two Douglas firs to be brought into this country. As plants they were sent with others by David Douglas, and were planted in 1834. The larger tree now contains 573 qr.-girth cubic feet over bark. The total height is 115 feet. Most of the young Douglas trees on Lord Mansfield's estates were raised from seed obtained from these trees.

The next stage reached was the Drumcairn Plantation, which consists of conifers and broad-leaved species, in pure and mixed trial plots, of 12-13 years old. The plots inspected were as follows: — 1. *Abies nobilis;* 2. Lawson's Cypress; 3. Sycamore; 4. Sycamore with Japanese larch; 5. Norway spruce; 6. European larch; 7. Japanese larch. Much interest was aroused by this interesting demonstration, where, among many other points of interest, it was noticed that the growth of the sycamore in this place was on the whole unsatisfactory, except in the plot where it was mixed with Japanese larch.

The Drumveigh Plantation, aged 15–16 years, which consists of Scots pine with Japanese larch, and Norway spruce with Japanese larch, was next seen, after which Longhill Woods and portable sawmill were visited. The wood consists of Scots pine, spruce and larch, varying in age from 60 to 115 years. Much damage was done to this wood by the gales of 1911 and 1912. At the portable sawmill large Scots pine were being converted into railway sleepers and boards; smaller Scots pine into pit crowns, small sleepers and pillar-wood; spruce into boards and rickers; and larch into planks, hutch boards, fencing materials, etc.

The motor cars were re-entered and headed for the picturesque village of Stanley, where, on the invitation of the Earl of Mansfield, the party were entertained to lunch. Thereafter the Taymount Douglas fir plantation was inspected. This plantation, which has an area of 9·69 acres in all, was planted in 1860 with Douglas fir and larch at the rate of 1210 plants per acre, 303 being Douglas fir and 907 European larch. The whole of the larch was cut out by 1880, as it had become very much diseased. In 1887, 600 to 700 stems were removed. In 1888, the stems were pruned to a height of 15 to 20 feet. In 1896, the pruning was continued to a height of 30 feet. In 1897, damage was done by wind at the north end. In 1912-13, blown and dead trees amounting to 106 stems were removed. The average number of stems per acre is 143, with a volume of stems per acre of 6276 feet. The delegates were much impressed with this plantation.

From the Taymount Plantation the party proceeded to Murthly, where the nursery at Kingswood was shown, and here methods of improved nursery management in regard to sowing and transplanting were demonstrated. The sawmill was passed on the way to the Byres Wood, and sawn examples of well-grown Douglas were seen. The creosoting tank was also inspected. In the Byres Wood the substitution of coniferous timber crops for old-oak-coppice is being carried out, the species used being Douglas, *Albertiana*, *Thuja plicata*, and *Cupressus Nootkatensis*; the ages vary from 1 to 8 years. From the Byres Wood the party proceeded to the Ringwood, and were shown a plantation of pure Douglas 14 years old and already lightly thinned. The forestry museum and policies near the Castle were next visited. The museum is entirely local, and contains only specimens of timber, fungoid and insect pests found on the estate.

The night was spent at the Birnam Hotel.

Next morning, 30th June, the party proceeded *via* the Perth-Dunkeld Road to Bee Cottage. The plantations visited were, one of pure Douglas fir 8 years old, and experimental plots of *Albertiana*, *Thuja plicata*, and the supposed hybrid between the European and the Japanese larch. The Douglas fir plantation was found to be in a flourishing condition and was much admired, while the experimental plots aroused keen interest. From an educational point of view nothing could be finer. Many silvicultural problems of fundamental importance are here elucidated. The immunity of the *Albertiana* from snow damage was well illustrated. The trees, which now average 12 feet in height, were last winter laid flat on the ground, and all that indicated their presence was the mounds of snow which covered them. An attempt was made to release as many as possible, but when the snow melted, every stem regained its perpendicular position, and there is now not the slightest trace of snow bending visible in the whole plantation. The experimental plot of *Thuja* and Douglas fir is doing well, but it would appear that the *Thuja* will ultimately be suppressed by the Douglas. The hybrid larches planted in 1908 now average about 20 feet in height, and show every sign of continued vigour of growth.

At Rohallion, seed and potting boxes made of Douglas fir wood were seen. These boxes have been in use for 10 years, and the wood is still in good preservation. In the vicinity of Rohallion Lodge was shown a plantation of larch planted at wide intervals, and filled up after a lapse of 5 years with Douglas fir and other species.

The party then ascended the shoulder of the hill to Allan's Bridge, from which a magnificent view of a wide stretch of country was obtained, and later they walked through the fine old larch plantation on Birnam Hill. The trees are 80 years old, of great height and good stem form, with sound timber of first-rate quality.

After lunch at Birnam the party proceeded per motor through the Dunkeld woods *via* Cally Lodge as far as the Glack Dam. On the way to the Glack good old larch and spruce, planted 1820-30, were seen. The greater part of this wood is not worked commercially, but kept for æsthetic purposes. After arriving at the Glack, the party proceeded to Loch Ordie, passing on the way through a large area of good larch (altitude 1000 to 1500 ft.); some of this wood is now being cut and manufactured at a sawmill which was passed on the way. After leaving Loch Ordie the party motored to Dunkeld House *via* Dowally sawmill. On the way were seen plantations of the European, the Japanese, and the hybrid larch. After passing Dunkeld House, a plantation of fine larch mixed with beech was seen, also large silver firs, and the parent larch.

On Wednesday, 1st July, a start was made from Birnam at 8 A.M., and the route taken was *via* Blairgowrie and the Devil's Elbow to Braemar, which was reached after a very pleasant journey, on which much plantable land was seen.

Mar is one of the oldest, if not the oldest, deer forest in Scotland. The woods on the estate, apart from the natural forest, vary in age from about 30 to 120 years. They were planted solely for shelter to the deer, which is necessary in a rigorous climate, and have been managed since with that object in view. Commercially, timber is of little value at Mar, as the cost of haulage would in many cases be more than the value of the timber. The planted woods are solely composed of pine and larch, and what remains of the natural forest is, of course, pine.

The party motored along past the Linn of Dee and a few miles beyond it into Glendee. Good examples of larch growing at high elevations were seen on the way. Returning from Glendee, they went in the direction of the Derry—where one or two younger plantations were inspected—and thereafter they proceeded past Mar Lodge on the north bank of the Dee to the Fife Arms, where, on the invitation of H.R.H. the Princess Royal, the party were entertained to lunch.

Braemar was left at 2 P.M., and the afternoon was devoted to an inspection of such parts of the Old Ballochbuie Forest,

Garmaddie Wood, Craig-gowan and Balmoral grounds as could be overtaken in the time at the party's disposal.

Nowhere can finer specimens of the native Scots pine be seen than those in the Old Ballochbuie Forest, and nowhere can better managed or more thriving plantations be found than those at Balmoral.

The *Pinus cembra* planted to commemorate the visit of the Society in 1887 had grown well, and was in a healthy and flourishing condition. After tea, which His Majesty was graciously pleased to · provide in the Castle, the following telegram was sent to His Majesty :—

" SIR WILLIAM CARRINGTON,
    " Buckingham Palace.

" Please convey to the King grateful thanks of Royal Scottish Arboricultural Society, and Foreign, Indian and Colonial guests, for His Majesty's great kindness and hospitality shown to them at Balmoral.   ARCHD. STIRLING, *President.*"

After a most instructive and enjoyable day the party arrived at Ballater, where the night was spent.

Next morning, 2nd July, the party set out for Ballogie, and were met at the Lodge by the proprietor, Mr Nicol, and his forester, Mr Wylie. They then drove through the main avenue past Marywell to Sawmiller's Croft. On the way many fine trees were seen, among which a group of old Scots pine claimed special attention and was greatly admired.

A tour of inspection was then made through Craigmore Wood, over Slithery Brae and past Hunter's Lodge, down to Carlogie. The plantations seen *en route* were found to be in capital order, and the general opinion expressed was that they are so well stocked and the age-classes are so well balanced and distributed, that on this area it would be quite possible to carry out all practical operations in forestry from the earliest stages to the final felling. At Carlogie, as elsewhere on Ballogie, it was abundantly manifest that natural regeneration could be practised on a large scale. At Balnacraig some fine old specimens of ash and walnut trees were seen. After lunch at Potarch, a temporary sawmill was visited, where timber is being converted into lengths for fish boxes, herring barrel staves and pit sleepers. The wood was carefully examined, and found to be of the finest quality and fit for any purpose for which coniferous timber may be used. It cannot be denied that our timber markets are not well organised, and here is an example of what might be called bad economy, in so far as first-class timber, through lack of general organisation on the part of buyers and sellers of wood, has to be used for purposes for which timber of inferior quality would do equally well.

On leaving Potarch the party motored to the Corsedardar Stone, where they were met by Dr Robert Farquharson of Finzean. A 30-year-old plantation of Scots pine was first inspected. This plantation extends up to an elevation of 1000 feet. Considerable damage is being done by squirrels. The woods in the vicinity of Finzean House were greatly admired; here were seen fine *Albertianas*, *Abies nobilis*, and magnificent old larches, over 100 feet high, among a general matrix of beech.

Dr Farquharson entertained the party to tea, after which a visit was made to the "Laird's Walking Sticks," a splendid plantation of Scots pine about 120 years old and averaging about 85 feet in height. A start was then made for Durris *via* Strachan. An interesting example of oak underplanted with Douglas fir was inspected on the way, and the problems connected therewith were discussed. The afternoon was now far advanced, and as time was limited, the party made straight for Strathgyle to inspect the famous Menzies spruce plantation. This plantation, which is at an altitude of 700 to 900 feet, extends to 83 acres, and was planted in 1878 as a mixed wood of Menzies spruce, Scots pine and Norway spruce; the two latter species have been suppressed by the phenomenally good growth of the Menzies spruce. This plantation met with the general admiration of the Foreign and Colonial delegates.

The company then journeyed to Aberdeen, where the night was spent.

On the following morning a start was made for Orton, where the party were met by Mr and Mrs Wharton Duff. On the Smithy Hill a fine stand of larch and Scots pine 82 years old was seen, and passing along the Black Hill the various sections of Scots pine, larch, spruce and beech, pure and in mixture, were generally admired. The soil was pronounced by experts to be of the best quality for tree-growth. From carefully kept records the remarkable fact has been demonstrated that the Scots pine, of 100 to 120 years old, have increased more in diameter during the last 10 years than they did in the previous 20 years. The trees attain a great height and develop splendid cylindrical stem form. The larch, Scots pine and spruce grow magnificently at Orton, and the timber produced is of the finest quality.

After the party had been hospitably entertained to lunch by Mr and Mrs Wharton Duff, the tour was continued to the Strathspey Woods.

STRATHSPEY.—The woods on the Strathspey Estate are situated at altitudes ranging from 600 feet to 1600 feet.

The soil for most part is of a shallow and light nature overlying rock or pan. The superficial accumulations on the level ground of this district consist principally of gravelly and sandy till, and this also may be said in a less degree of the higher ground, while small alluvial flats occur along the valleys.

The woods are purely coniferous, the main crop consisting of Scots pine with a small percentage of larch and spruce. The shallow nature of the soil, combined with the prevalence of early and late frosts, makes it a little difficult to deal with conifers other than those mentioned, unless as under-plants. ·

Natural regeneration of both Scots pine and larch occurs all over the estate to a greater or less degree according to soil conditions, etc. The treatment of all woods from their younger stages upward bears relation to the general methods of silviculture, but the woods from about 18 years of age are generally grazed by sheep or cattle. When woods have reached the end of the rotation, they are thinned gradually and treated more or less under the compartment or selection system. The preparatory stage comprises several thinnings, and although it varies according to exposure and the condition of the crop, there are generally three cuttings or thinnings, then seeding stage and final felling. The period over which these stages may extend depends upon the forest conditions,—in some cases it is short, the young plants showing quite early; in others it extends to 10 years and over. A commencement is made by removing all inferior trees, or trees not suited for the main purpose or object in view. The point aimed at is to leave trees with narrow crowns, long clean boles, and having a healthy appearance, thus fostering strong fresh shoots and ensuring a plentiful supply of healthy seed. Briefly, the procedure with a crop of say 200 trees to the acre is as follows:—First thinning, 100 trees are removed; second thinning, 50 trees; third thinning, 35 trees;

thus 15 trees are left as seeding trees, which are removed when the area is more or less re-stocked.   This method has been found to work well here, and has the advantage of not only allowing the seeding trees to develop shoots sufficient to produce healthy seed, but also there is little or no danger from wind-blows.

After the Scots pine woods here begin to open up naturally, or are opened up artificially, admitting light and air, the ground is very quickly covered with heather and moss, which if not disturbed would render self-seeding impossible, or at least of little consequence.   In order to combat this as far as possible the woods are grazed heavily and closely by farm stock,—thus the heather is to a certain extent kept in check and the mossy surface disturbed and broken up.   The breaking up of the surface for the reception of seed could be done by workmen, but this would add considerably to the expense, and as almost the same benefit can be got by pasturing, that method is adopted here.   At the seeding stage all sheep and cattle are removed.

Although the selection and compartment system is always applied here, evidence is not wanting that the strip system would be successful in some cases.

Tominourd Plantation.—The area of this plantation is 1031 acres, and it rises in altitude from 620 feet to 1350 feet.   Up to 1000 feet the crop grew well, but beyond that elevation the trees fell off considerably.   The north side to the extent of 520 acres has been recently felled or cleared of old trees, the crop then being an equal mixture of Scots pine and larch.   The fellings extended over a period of 17 years.   To begin with, larch came up a pure crop where the herbage was mainly heather, but latterly the percentage has increased in favour of Scots pine.   On grassy surfaces self-seeding was not so perfect, especially on the lower levels, and artificial planting had to be resorted to in order to make the crop complete.   The young natural larch here is almost completely free from disease, and although in places the plantation is so thick and close as almost to exclude light and air, the plants remain immune.   Larch aphis (*Chermes laricis*) attacks the crop occasionally, but so far has not acted as a serious check.   So long as the larch remains healthy it will be left to form a pure crop, but if it begins to show signs of disease it will be immediately thinned out and underplanted.   The main point here was the area of pure larch produced by natural regeneration.

Upper Tomvaich Plantation.—This area is divided into two compartments—(1) containing 267 acres, and (2) 36 acres. (1) The crop consists of Scots pine of about 90 years of age, with a few larch trees, standing to the number of about 40 trees to 50 trees to the acre. A number have been marked for sale, but about 15 trees have been left to the acre as seeding trees. (2) This area consists of Scots pine standards with an under-crop of natural plants. This part was fenced against sheep a number of years ago, only cattle and horses being allowed access. Young plants have come up well and show what might be expected from the larger area.

Lower Tomvaich Plantation.—This wood has an area of 208 acres, divided as follows :—(1) 200 acres of Scots pine and larch standards, (2) 8 acres of old Scots pine with an undercrop of natural Scots pine and larch. The large area is to be thinned out and left to fill up naturally, farm stock being excluded. Until a few years ago, these 8 acres formed part of the same area. When fenced off against farm stock natural plants came up freely, which shows pretty conclusively what might be expected from the adjoining area. The standards have been left too long, but are to be removed next year. Meantime the area is a pretty picture, and shows well the result of the system adopted.

Policies of Castle Grant.—On the right is Drumdunan Wood —250 acres—consisting of a pure crop of Scots pine reared naturally. A number of old standards are left on the drive side to form a wind-screen and shelter to the young crop. These trees show the nature of the previous crop.

Milton and Old Grantown Woods also form part of the policies, and carry a crop of Scots pine about 140 years of age. The trees have long clean boles and a limited branch area. The woods in their younger stages were very carefully thinned, and records show that for a long number of years only dead trees were taken out, which no doubt accounts for the clean nature of the stems. The highest of the trees measuring from the top of the leader is 109 feet, and many have clean boles up to 70 feet and 80 feet. From old records it appears that the plants for this wood were carried from Abernethy Nursery, a distance of 6 miles, on panniers strapped on the backs of ponies, and that they were of a larger size than is now generally employed in planting, consequently they were all pitted.

Lower Lynmacgregor Wood.—This wood contains a more or less pure Scots pine crop, and was planted 62 years ago. No thinnings of any consequence have been taken out beyond dead and completely suppressed trees. In some parts it was noticed that a light thinning was now necessary. This plantation was shown as a specimen of the planted woods.

The night was spent in Grantown, and next morning, Saturday, 4th July, Curr Plantation was visited. This plantation extends to 260 acres, and contains a natural crop mainly of Scots pine with a few larch. The trees are of various sizes and ages, the oldest being about 35 years of age, but the difference is small as the plants come up with surprising regularity. There is very little space entirely bare of trees, and generally speaking the whole area is fully stocked. Naturally the trees form thickets in spots specially favourable to the germination of seed, but in these parts a few of the strongest have gone ahead and formed dominant stems which suppress those not able to keep abreast. Thinning in some parts is now absolutely necessary. The soil is of an open tilly nature, admirably suited for the reception of seed and the growing of Scots pine and larch, especially the former. The old timber in this wood, which is only about 1 mile from the estate sawmill, is used for estate purposes, the trees being taken out as the young plants come up. This is the method from which the best results have been obtained in the way of a natural crop. It is scarcely to be expected, that with ordinary and regular thinnings, each taking a few months in stated years, the same satisfactory result would be obtained. A few old trees remain which show the nature of the old crop.

Balnagown Wood.—This wood has an acreage of 73 acres, and a crop of Scots pine standards, with an undercrop of natural plants. The number of standards per acre varies according to the condition of the undercrop. In this wood also the old timber is manufactured at the estate sawmill, and accordingly the management is similar to that followed in the case of the Curr Plantation, and somewhat different from the management generally followed. The mother trees are being taken out as the young crop comes up, none being removed until the latter is complete. This method is giving here a close and complete crop.

The soil in this wood is of exceptionally poor quality, viz., a thin, poor, gravelly soil, with a little peat or rough humus. That the soil is poor in this case is evident from the appearance of the old crop, and from that of the smallest of the natural plants. It appears, however, that once the young crop has attained the age of about 7 years, the growths are much stronger, and the plants assume a more vigorous appearance. Judging from the specimens of the old crop left, it is very doubtful if it would pay to spend money in planting here, but as re-stocking is done naturally and therefore without expense, the chances of profit are more favourable than they otherwise would have been.

Abernethy Forest.—As this area forms part of the deer forest, everything is left to work out naturally, nothing whatever being done to assist the new crop. So far this has been secured in a somewhat more or less complete form, and thus the wood contains trees of all ages coming up together. The branch system of the young trees here, when grown openly, is not of the same rough nature as in the case of those trees grown at the lower levels of the country, so that trees of different ages grow together without causing each other any serious damage. All that is done by way of management is to remove the old trees when they have fostered a new crop.

A number of the trees that formed part of this forest are still to be seen, but those left are somewhat rough and branchy. The timber of these trees is of the best quality, of exceptional durability, and stands exposure to extreme weather well.

Proceeding to Aviemore Railway Station, where the motors were dismissed, the party took train for Dingwall, *via* Inverness.

NOVAR.—In the afternoon and evening a short visit was made to the Novar Woods. Motors were in waiting to convey the party to Inchcholtair, where larch underplanted with *Abies grandis* was seen. Afterwards Crosshills was visited, where larch underplanted with various conifers was inspected; and on the way back to the station experimental plots and beech of natural regeneration under oak were noticed in passing.

The experiments in underplanting aroused extraordinary interest, as few of the party had previously had an opportunity of inspecting such well devised and successful experiments in the cultivation of the larch. Much regret was expressed that the time available for the inspection was so short. On the return of the party to Inverness, a cablegram of thanks was sent to Sir Ronald Munro Ferguson at Melbourne.

The party arrived in Inverness at 9.30 P.M., where the week-end was spent. A few of the delegates remained at Novar, as the guests of Sir Ronald Munro Ferguson and his brother Mr Hector Munro Ferguson, and the factor Mr Dods.

GLEN MOR.—On Monday, 6th July, the party assembled at Muirtown Pier, on the Caledonian Canal, at 7.45 A.M, and left by steamer at 8 A.M. for Oban. In the course of the sail down the canal, the members had an opportunity of seeing the area of 60,300 acres dealt with by Lord Lovat and Captain Stirling in their "Forest Survey of Glen Mor," which was published by the Society in 1911.

In the preface to this report, the Council of the Society says that the report establishes the following propositions :—

1. That it is possible to create forests in the Highlands, even in districts where the economic conditions appear most adverse, without seriously impairing existing sources of wealth.

2. That afforested areas will, even in the early stages of the movement, gain greatly in employment and population.

3. That the actual work of planting can and ought to be cautiously begun as soon as the progress of the survey justifies the selection of definite areas.

Several members of the party were able to give explanations regarding this area and the problems dealt with in the report.

Oban was reached at 7.5 P.M., where the night was spent.

ANNUAL EXCURSION.

The members who took part in the annual Excursion assembled at Oban on Monday evening, 6th July, where they were joined by the Society's Diamond Jubilee guests.

On Tuesday, 7th July, the combined party left Oban by train, at 7.30 A.M., *via* Taynuilt and the Pass of Brander for Loch Awe Station. MacBrayne's steamer "Loch Awe" conveyed them down the loch to New York Pier.

In the course of the sail a good view of the country on both sides of the loch was obtained, and some patches of good woodland and much land covered by natural scrub, birch, oak, alder and ash were noticed, which gave a general idea of the possibilities of the country from a forestry point of view.

INVERLIEVER ESTATE.[1] (Area 12,628 acres.)

The estate was purchased by the Commissioners of Woods in 1907 for the purpose of conducting an afforestation scheme on a large scale.

The first cost of the estate was £25,115 : the redemption of fixed charges has since amounted to £2417, and the payments for acclimatisation values of sheep stock to £4024, making a total of £31,556.

A further payment of small amount for acclimatisation value will have to be made on the termination of the existing tenancies.

GENERAL DESCRIPTION.—The estate is situated at the west end of Loch Awe, on which it has a frontage of about $8\frac{1}{2}$ miles. The loch lies at an elevation of about 120 feet above sea-level, while the highest point on the estate is about 1450 feet. The rocks are mapped by the Geological Survey into two main types: *Schists* (epidiorite, hornblendic, chloritic and talcose), and *Grits* (greywackés, quartzite, and quartz schist). There are also a number of intrusive dykes of basalt and dolorite. The route followed by the Society lay almost wholly on the schists.

The soil changes rapidly from place to place; on the steeper slopes it is generally a yellowish loam of good depth, on the gentle slopes there is everywhere a tendency for peat to form, and on badly drained sites this formation goes down to a depth of several feet. The whole area has been heavily glaciated, generally in a direction parallel with the loch, with the result that the ground on the upper slopes is very broken. What were formerly numerous small glacial lakes are now the sites of peat bogs.

At the north end of the property, near New York Pier, and again near Ford, there are some fluvio-glacial deposits.

The sea is only four miles distant from the western boundary of the estate, but a certain amount of shelter is derived from the intervening high land. Apart from the persistent winds the climate is mild and well suited to tree-growth. The rainfall varies from 70 to 96 inches per annum, the snowfall is light and does not lie

---

[1] These notes on Inverliever Estate were supplied by the Office of Woods, etc.

long.   Winter frosts are of short duration and are not severe. Late spring and early autumn frosts are frequent.   The following meteorological data were collected at Ford for the year 1913 :—

Months	RAINFALL			TEMPERATURE			No. of Days 31 Degrees or lower	Total Degrees of Frost
	Inches	Dry Days	Average Max.	Max. Re-corded	Average Min.	Min Re-corded		
			Degrees	Deg.	Degrees	Deg.	Days	Degrees
January .	7·28	10	40·4	49	33	20	9	51
February .	4·22	11	45	51	33·7	20	10	59
March .	10·11	6	46·7	57	32·8	16	8	48
April . .	5·82	9	59·9	61	35	24	5	18
May . .	6·96	8	59·16	70·5	40	30	1	2
June . .	4·19	9	66	77	45·3	36·5	...	...
July . .	1·88	20	65·61	79	44·5	32	...	...
August .	3·49	17	69	77	44	33	...	...
September	3·56	16	62·4	70	44	34	...	...
October .	5·41	11	55·03	65	40·64	25	4	15
November	12·03	2	49·6	57	38·4	26	3	12
December	8·35	7	43·76	57	33·3	16	11	86
Totals .	73·30	126	Average 55.2		38.7	...	51	291

In general, the conditions obtaining on this estate are not unrepresentative of very large areas of rough grazing land along the west coast of Scotland.

UTILISATION AT TIME OF PURCHASE.— At the time of purchase the estate was divided into four farms, carrying the stock indicated below.

Name of Farm	Approximate area	Sheep	Rental per annum
	Acres		
Salachry . .	635	300	£66
Torran . .	2,800	1,900	190
Arichamish . .	4,900	2,700	150
Barmaddy & Cruachan	4,000	1,750	190
Totals,	12,335	6,650	£596

Torran Farm carried in addition some twenty to thirty cattle.

There were also some 200 acres of scrub (oak, ash and birch) of little value, and about 80 acres of plantations.

Considerable outlay has been necessary on the buildings

which were on the estate at the time of purchase. Up to the 31st March 1914, approximately, £2495 was spent in repairs and improvements to houses and buildings let with the farms and shootings, and in erecting two new cottages. This is exclusive of outlay on buildings used for forestry purposes.

AFFORESTATION OPERATIONS—*Nursery.*—In the summer of 1908, 8¾ acres of land at Ford were fenced off to form a nursery, and in the following spring plants were lined out and seed sown in 2½ acres of it. The nursery was subsequently extended to the total of 8¾ acres. The soil, which is light and gravelly, has gradually been worked into condition. The want of a good supply of farmyard manure has been felt, but guano and artificial manures have been used with fair success.

Planting.—At the time of purchase the lease of Arichamish Farm was falling in, and it was judged advisable to begin planting operations at the east end of that farm. The method employed was to fence off a block containing roughly 400 acres, and subsequently to cut off successive strips of about 150 acres each by a temporary fence running more or less at right angles to the loch. In this way the ground was grazed up to the time of resumption for planting. The permanent fencing has been exclusively iron and wire with hare and rabbit netting. For temporary fencing iron standards and wire have also been used, but with a sheep netting only. The greater part of the planting has been done with the half-round planting spade. The only exceptions were in 1909–1910 when the plants were notched in, and later when a rocky face was planted with the planting arrow, and some small lots of large-sized plants were pitted. The bulk of the plants have been 2-yr. 2-yr., but some 2-yr. 1-yr. and a few 2-yr.-seedlings have been used as well.

The areas actually planted from year to year are as follows :—

Year	Area planted	Total number of plants used for planting and beating up
1909-10	190	674,000
1910-11	169	664,100
1911-12	187	509,600
1912-13	178	445,900
1913-14	150	346,600
Total,	874	2,640,200

Of the total number of trees planted out, 1,474,100 were lifted from the nursery at Ford, while the remaining 1,166,100 were purchased from nurserymen in this country. Of the plants raised in the nursery a small proportion only have been purchased from nurserymen abroad, the remainder being obtained from seed or from British nurserymen. It is hoped that now the nursery is in full working order, practically all the plants required will be raised direct from seed.

In the initial stages a good deal of Scots pine was planted on the upper slopes, but subsequently the use of this tree was abandoned, both on account of its unsuitability for the conditions and because of the damage done to it by black game. In general the better soils have been planted with larch and Douglas fir, according to exposure, with a limited quantity of silver fir and beech. The bulk of the ground, however, is only suited to spruce, and both the Sitka and common spruces have been largely employed. The common spruce is, of course, very slow in establishing itself, and it is difficult to say at this stage how it will grow on the upper slopes. Much of the early planting was experimental in nature, particularly that relating to the planting of peat on upturned turfs.

The first plantings were made in blocks of about 150 acres, which were treated as units for accounting purposes. The present system is to divide each block into compartments, bounded by natural topographical features or by permanent roads, and not exceeding about 30 acres in extent.

It is proposed in future to leave unplanted all ground of a doubtful nature, and for this purpose a detailed mapping of the soil is being carried on as opportunity permits. About 1200 acres of plantable land have been mapped out on Barmaddy and Cruachan Farms in this way, and it is hoped that by the time the planting of that area has been completed, sufficient data will be available to decide on the value of those large areas which in the existing state of knowledge are of doubtful nature.

SMALL HOLDINGS.—The area of land on the estate which is adapted for the use of small holdings is strictly limited, but it is being scheduled for that purpose as planting proceeds.

The policy which the Crown is following in this respect is to equip small holdings as they are wanted, and as they can be placed to the advantage of the holder himself. The rapid multiplication of small holders is prevented, first, by the fact that considerable capital was sunk in bothy accommodation, in the first instance, in order to push on with planting operations; and secondly, by the fact that there was very little ground in the immediate neighbourhood of planting operations suitable for the purpose. The absence of good roads through the estate renders it imperative that workmen should live in the neighbourhood of planting operations.

The following buildings have been erected and were occupied at the end of 1912-13:—Bothy at Cruachan; two cottages at Ford (occupied by nurseryman and handyman); cottage at Ford (converted into nursery bothy); cottage at Kilmaha (occupied by trapper).

EXPENDITURE.—The chief items of expenditure directly applicable to afforestation operations to 31st March 1914, are as follows:—

New Works.

Purchase of seeds and plants	£1434
Preparation of ground and planting . . .	1814
Fencing	919
Drainage	435
Erection and improvement of houses and buildings	3078

General Maintenance.

Killing vermin	£186
Repairs to houses and buildings	265
Machinery and implements	280
Bothy caretakers and upkeep	613
Preparation of produce for sale	182

LABOUR AFFORDED BY AFFORESTATION OPERATIONS.[1]—The question of the amount of labour absorbed by afforestation operations on an estate of this kind is of particular interest at the present time. It is estimated that in 1908 when the property was used almost solely for grazing and game, a total of 6800 days' male labour was expended on it. For 1912-13, the total is estimated at 11,000 days, representing an increase of 62 per cent. The latter is exclusive of time spent on the construction of new buildings. It may be assumed that the amount of employment will increase slowly until the time for thinning the young plantations arrives, when a considerable increase should take place.

[1] For more complete details see Report of the Forestry Branches, Board of Agriculture and Fisheries, and Office of Woods, for 1912-13.

ITINERARY.

The party left the steamer at New York Pier and passed on the left a mixed coniferous wood (larch, silver and Douglas fir, Scots pine, etc.) about 35 years old. Traces of the storm of 1911 were visible. The excellent growth of silver fir was a feature of considerable silvicultural interest. Silver firs have been measured on the estate with a height of 75 feet at 35 years' growth.

Proceeding along the road or track, the ground which is to be planted in 1914-15 was passed through. After leaving the iron and wood structure erected for accommodating workmen, the ground to be planted in 1915-16 was traversed, and there was seen an example of the best quality of planting land. Just before the men's bothy was reached and for some distance after it had been passed, a good general view was obtained of the higher land to the right of the road; thereafter the view was more restricted.

At the bothy a coloured plan showing the plantable land on Barmaddy and Cruachan was displayed. After a walk of about 2 miles from the pier, the oldest part of the new plantations was reached (planted 1909-10). On leaving the road, groups of Douglas and larch were seen on the left; passing on, larch was seen on both sides, and then a group of Douglas and Sitka spruce extending right across the path; farther on, more Douglas and Sitka spruce were seen on the left hand with larch on the right, and then a small group of silver fir with Sitka spruce and common spruce in damp places was noticed.

On passing over the ridge, a group of silver fir was seen doing very well on the steep face, and shortly afterwards plants a year younger were reached; below the path a group of very healthy spruce was seen adjoining an old ash wood, and right and left of the path a group of Douglas fir; while, after passing along the bottom of the steep bank, the workmen's cottages were passed on the left; to the right on the bank are some promising larch.

It was proposed to conduct the party to the higher ground to inspect a number of plots planted on upturned turf, but as time would not permit, the party passed on, through grazing ground as yet unplanted, to Arichamish Farm. Here a number of chars-à-bancs were in waiting, and these were used to convey the party from place to place during the remainder of the tour. During the later part of the walk and the motor-ride, some of the best planting ground was passed.

Some effects of the wind-storm of 1911 were observed in the mixed coniferous wood to the right of the road after passing Arichamish farm-house.

On reaching Ford a halt was made for a walk through the nursery. Unfortunately the seedlings and young plants had been very badly damaged by frost on the morning of 24th May last.

POLTALLOCH.—Leaving the nursery at Ford at 1.20 P.M. the party proceeded to Poltalloch. Upper Largie Plantation, extending to about 18 acres, was first noticed. It was clean-cut and replanted in 1907 with European larch and spruce rides. Behind this plantation lies one of the estate nurseries, formerly the mansion-house garden, previous to the present mansion-house being built. A little farther on, and on the left, was seen an attempt at cheap cottage building, the constructive timbers of which are entirely native spruce and larch, creosoted by the immersion process. Auchavaan Wood was next to be noticed. It extends to about 87 acres and was planted in 1838, mostly with European larch. Three sections of this wood were badly damaged by the Tay Bridge gale, and afterwards replanted.

Poltalloch was reached about 2 o'clock, where the party were received and hospitably entertained to luncheon by Colonel Malcolm. After an inspection of the splendid gardens and fine policies had been made the party motored back to Oban where the night was again spent.

The following day, 8th July, was entirely occupied by a motor trip from Oban to Dunoon *via* Lochgilphead, Inveraray (where lunch was served), Loch Fyne, Strachur and Loch Eck. At Cairnbaan, Craiglass Wood (22 acres—planted 1876) was inspected, in which a clump of Douglas fir showing abnormal growth as compared with the other species planted was noticed. At Inveraray some very fine specimens of old and remarkable silver firs and Scots pine were seen, while at Ardkinglas one among a number of fine old silver firs was measured and found to girth $21\frac{1}{2}$ feet.

All were delighted with the drive, in spite of the fact that the road led for miles and miles through treeless tracts of country, in every way well adapted for tree-growth and the attendant benefits of afforestation. After contemplating such a landscape for hours great enthusiasm was aroused by the first glimpse of

PLATE XI.

A' CRUACH BEFORE PLANTING.   Note the rocky face.

[*To face p.* 172

PLATE XII.

A' CRUACH 32 YEARS AFTER PLANTING WITH DOUGLAS FIR.

the Benmore Woods, which clothe the steep and lofty slopes of the glen to their ultimate summits. Here was a proof to demonstration of the possibilities for afforestation of the wide stretches of bare country previously traversed.

Dunoon was safely reached, and here the night was spent. On the kind invitation of Mr Younger, a number of the party spent the night at Benmore.

On Thursday, 9th July, a start from Dunoon was made, about 9 A.M., for Benmore. This estate extends along Loch Long for about 3 miles to Strone Point, from which it continues along the eastern shores of the Holy Loch and the slopes of the Echig Valley to Loch Eck. The remainder of the estate occupies a position to the west of Loch Eck and lies between it and the Masson Valley. On the estate there are some 2000 acres of woodlands between 30 and 40 years of age, in addition to some 200 acres of natural oak and birch scrub. These occur in scattered blocks and separate enclosures, some of them a few feet above sea-level while others rise to a height of 1200 feet. The dominant species comprising the woodlands are larch, Douglas fir, Scots pine, spruce and *Thuja gigantea*. In addition a large variety of exotic conifers have been planted in small groups throughout the plantation.

Cruach Wood. (Sample Plot).—The sample plot is 1 chain in width at its base, and extends for 2 chains up the hill-side. It lies at an elevation of about 500 feet above sea-level, and is situated on a steep slope with an eastern exposure. It consists of a practically pure crop of Douglas fir, which is now 35 years of age. At the time of planting the ground was described as being steep, undulating and rocky. The surface soil was a sandy peat, with heather on the ridges and the tops of rocks, while the intervening hollows were of an open, sandy and gravelly nature. The subsoil consisted of clay-slate and quartz-rock which occurred in alternating layers. By the kind permission of Mr Younger of Benmore, we are able to reproduce two very interesting photographs, Plates XI. and XII. Plate XI. shows the general features of the Cruach before planting, while Plate XII. shows the same hillside from a slightly different aspect 35 years after planting. The soil is now greatly improved by the *humus* formed from the rich annual fall of foliage, but the peaty nature of the ground is still very apparent in many places. The age of the plants at the time of planting is said to have been " 2-year seedlings, twice and thrice transplanted," and the planting method adopted seems probably to have been a rough form of pitting. The hillside is so steep that the planters are said to have been obliged to kneel on the ground while planting, to avoid slipping down the hill.

In default of exact measurements and stem-analysis, it may be taken that the mean of the percentages of the current annual growth in girth and growth in height will give a fairly correct estimate of the percentage of current annual growth in cubic contents. In such case it would be 5 per cent., and with the present volume of 3255 cubic feet per acre, the increment for the year 1912 may be estimated at 5 per cent. of this, or 162¾ cubic feet, making a total of 3417 cubic feet when the plantation will have completed its thirty-fourth year of growth. This shows an average annual increment of 100½ cubic feet (square of quarter-girth measurement and with full bark allowance deducted).

Nursery.—An area of about 4 acres was broken in last year to form a nursery. The soil seems well suited for the raising of seedlings, as it is naturally drained by a gravelly subsoil. In the spring of the year breaks were laid out 30 by 40 yards, in which the following plants were lined out:—100,000 1-year seedling larch, 100,000 1-year seedling silver fir, 50,000 2-year seedling silver fir, 20,000 1-year seedling Douglas fir, 110,000 2-year seedling *Thuja gigantea*. Sowing operations were delayed until 18th May on account of wet weather, when 10 seed-beds were laid off and the following seeds sown:—100 lbs. Douglas fir (which was purchased direct from America), 30 lbs. *Cupressus Lawsoniana* (home seed), 11 lbs. Norway spruce, 1 lb. Sitka spruce, and small quantities of birch and alder. It is intended to utilise these seedlings mainly for underplanting larch and Scots pine.

Japanese Larch.—At Puck's Glen, on the lower ground, two strips of Japanese larch have been successfully established. These are now 9 years of age, and range from 14 to 18 feet high. It is interesting to note that it has been found impossible to establish European larch on this land on account of disease.

Natural Regeneration Plots.—On the lee side of Rashfield Wood two small areas were enclosed about four years ago with the idea of obtaining natural regeneration. These plots were found to contain a fair crop of *Thuja* seedlings.

At Kilmun the party were entertained to lunch by the kind invitation of Mr Younger. In returning thanks to Mr Younger for his hospitality Sir John Stirling-Maxwell said that Benmore was one of the most striking places visited during the whole excursion. In replying Mr Younger said that from personal experience, he saw no reason why the whole of the glen for miles above the Cruach should not be afforested, nor, indeed, why all barren places in Scotland should not be planted, thereby giving employment to a vastly increased population.

Gairletter Plantation.—This is situated on the north-east shore of Loch Long with an easterly exposure, and rises from sea-level to about 130 feet. Before it was blown down two years ago the plantation was fully stocked, the trees standing 4 to 9 feet apart. The average height of the Douglas fir was about 70 feet, while that of the *Thuja* was about 60 feet. The stems of the Douglas fir showed natural pruning up to two-thirds of their height. The average annual increment per stem was about ·6 cubic feet for Douglas fir, and for *Thuja* about ·3 cubic feet. The stems numbered on the average about 890 per acre, half of that number being of pole size while the remainder were of timber size. There were about equal numbers of Douglas and *Thuja*. The volume of timber per acre, according to quarter-girth measurement (deducting 1 inch for bark), was as follows:—Douglas fir 5000 cubic feet, and *Thuja* 2430 cubic feet. This gives the high total of 7430 cubic feet per acre.

The following interesting statement, showing approximate cost of and receipts from one acre, was supplied:—

Expenditure.

Cost of formation with 3 per cent. compound interest thereon, £5 at 35 years	£13	15	0
Loss of rent as a grazing, at 5s. per year	15	2	6
Management, maintenance, rates and taxes, 4s. per year	12	2	0
Cost of cutting off root and weeding	20	0	0
	£60	19	6

Receipts.

From 3 acres—
8 boat loads, of 75 tons each, at
12s. per ton, £360 = £120
for 1 acre . . . £120 0 0
1500 fence posts, at 5d. each,
£31, 5s. = £10, 8s. 4d. for
1 acre . . . £ 10 8 4
————————— £130 8 4

Apparent Profit . . . £69 8 10

Thereafter the estate of Glenfinart was visited. The wooded part of this estate occupies a position surrounding Glenfinart Bay on the eastern shore of Loch Long. The dominant species of tree is larch, ranging in age from a few years up to 90 years. In addition there is a certain proportion of fine old Scots pine, and occasional specimens of exotic conifers. The hardwoods consist mainly of beech, sycamore, oak and birch scrub.

Scots Pine Woods.—On the hillsides overlooking Glenfinart House the remains of extensive Scots pine plantations were seen. These contain fine specimens of Scots pine, some of which have a cubical content of over 80 feet.

Laggandrishaig Plantation.—This is a thriving young plantation of about 60 acres consisting of a mixture of larch, Scots pine and spruce. It takes the form of a belt running along the loch side, and is bounded all the way by the road. It was established seven years ago on a cleared area, upon which, after draining, 2-year seedlings were notched about 2 ft. 6 ins. apart.

This concluded the annual Excursion. The party returned to Dunoon in time to allow the members to leave for their destinations by the afternoon steamers. The Society's Jubilee guests returned to Edinburgh, where headquarters were established in the North British Station Hotel. The following very pleasant and interesting programme for the forenoon of Friday, 10th July, had been arranged by the Corporation of Edinburgh and was duly carried out. At 9.30 A.M., the party left the North British Station Hotel for a motor-run to Queensferry and the Forth Bridge. The interest in the Forth Bridge was enhanced by the fact that the Royal train with His Majesty on board was the first seen by the party to pass over the huge structure. The motor-drive was continued *via* Hopetoun House to Saughton Park, where the rose garden was inspected and greatly admired. Thereafter the Castle, St Giles and Parliament House were visited, after which the party were received and cordially welcomed by the Lord Provost in the City Chambers, where they were hospitably entertained to lunch by the Corporation.

The following are the names of those who took part in the Excursion :—

Captain Archibald Stirling of Keir, *President.*
Sir John Stirling-Maxwell, Bart. of Pollok, *Hon. Secretary.*

DIAMOND JUBILEE GUESTS.

REPRESENTATIVES OF FOREIGN GOVERNMENTS.—*Denmark*—Dr P. E. Müller. *France*—Monsieur L. Pardé, Inspector of Waters and Forests at Beauvais. *Holland*—Monsieur J. H. Jager Gerlings, Inspector of the Government Forestry Administration at Breda. *Hungary*—Mr John Czillinger, the Royal Hungarian Inspector of Forests. *Russia*—Actual Councillor of State Monsieur S. J. Rauner, Vice-Director of the Corps of Foresters. *Sweden*—Mr Carl Björkbom, Inspector of Forests.

REPRESENTATIVES OF INDIAN AND COLONIAL GOVERNMENTS.—*India*—Mr A. M. Caccia, M.V.O., Director of Indian Forest Studies. *Canada*—Mr R. H. Campbell, Director of Forestry. *New Zealand*—Mr R. G. Robinson, Superintending Nurseryman for South Island. *South Africa*—Mr K. A. Carlson, Conservator of Forests, Orange Free State Conservancy.

HOME REPRESENTATIVES.—*England*—Professor Somerville, Oxford University ; Mr William Dawson, Cambridge University ; Mr H. J. Elwes of Colesborne. *Wales*—Professor Fraser Story, University College, Bangor. *Ireland*—Professor Augustine Henry, Dublin ; Mr A. C. Forbes, Chief Inspector of Forestry, Dublin. *Scotland*—Mr John D. Sutherland, Member of the Board of Agriculture ; Dr John Nisbet, Forestry Adviser to the Board of Agriculture ; Mr E. P. Stebbing, Edinburgh University ; Mr George P. Gordon, B.Sc., West of Scotland Agricultural College ; Mr P. Leslie, B.Sc., North of Scotland Agricultural College ; W. Steuart Fothringham, Esq. of Murthly (*Vice-President*) ; Sydney J. Gammell, Esq. of Drumtochty (*Vice-President*) ; Dr A. W. Borthwick (*Hon. Editor of "Transactions"*) ; Mr Charles Buchanan, Convener of Excursion Committee ; Mr Robert Galloway, S.S.C. (*Secretary and Treasurer*).

LIST OF EXCURSIONISTS.—Thomas Adam, Glasgow ; B. W.

Adkin, Westminster; B. C. Adkin, Cambridge University; John H. Alexander, Edinburgh; Robert Allan, Polkemmet (*Councillor*); R. L. Anderson, Beaufort; J. F. Annand, Armstrong College (*Vice-President*); C. W. Berry, Edinburgh; Thomas Bond, Lambton Park; John Boyd, Inverliever; John Broom, Bathgate (*Councillor*); Gilbert Brown, Grantown-on-Spey (*Councillor*); Wm. Brown, Comlongon, Ruthwell; H. M. Cadell of Grange, Linlithgow; Lt.-Col. J. M. Cadell, Foxhall, Kirkliston; D. S. Campbell, Middleton, Northumberland; James Clyne, Banchory; R. W. Cowper, Gortanore, Sittingbourne; T. Alex. Crombie, Longhirst, Morpeth; James Curr, Ninewar, Prestonkirk; W. S. Curr, Ninewar, Prestonkirk; Robt. Dale, Sorn, Mauchline; Henry Dalziel, Edinburgh; G. A. Davidson, Knockdow, Toward; J. A. Donald, Dupplin, Perth; J. A. Duthie, Aberdeen; Robt. Forbes, Kennet (*Councillor*); Angus Galloway, Edinburgh; G. G. Shirra Gibb, Boon, Lauder; Robert Shirra Gibb, Boon, Lauder; Donald Grant, Corrour; James L. Gray, Dalkeith; James B. Harrier, Elginshill, Elgin; W. Henderson, Tullamore, King's Co.; Fred. Shaw Kennedy, Kirkmichael, Maybole; Major Leather of Middleton Hall, Northumberland; Hugh Logue, Knockdow, Toward; Lord Lyell of Kinnordy; D. K. M'Beath, Benmore; R. M'Cutcheon, Whittinghame, East Lothian; Allan Macdonald, Benmore; H. L. Macdonald of Dunach, Oban; John M'Gregor, Ayr; Neil MacGregor, Bridge of Dye, Banchory; J. W. Mackay, Jervaulx Abbey, Yorks; John M'Kerchar, London; Donald Macpherson, East of Scotland College; Alex. M'Rae, Dundrum, Co. Tipperary; D. M'Millan, Keir, Dunblane; R. V. Mather, Kelso; Wellwood Maxwell, of Kirkennan; Thomas C. Meldrum, Forfar; J. H. Milne Home, Canonbie (*Councillor*); A. E. Moeran, Blackrock, Co. Dublin; Alex. Morgan, Crieff; A. B. Motherwell, Airdrie; Donald Munro, Banchory; Charles Petley, Canterbury; J. Lyford Pike, Edinburgh; J. M. Ralph, Corstorphine; W. Ralph, Corstorphine; Geo. Robertson, Monreith; R. L. Robinson, Office of Woods, etc., London; W. D. O. Rose, Edinburgh; John Rule, Huntly; George R. Scott, Oxgang, Colinton; James Shiel, Abbey St Bathans; John T. Smith, Edinburgh; Adam Spiers, Edinburgh (*Councillor*); David Spraggon, Benmore; Thomas Stark, Holker, Lancs; Robert Tindal, Stobo; J. H. Waddingham, Grimsby; James Watt, Carlisle; James William Watt, Carlisle; Wm. Wilson, Auchinleck; Major Waldron, Pitlochry.

18. The Conference and Dinner.

The President presided over a full attendance at the Conference, which was held after lunch (p. 177) in the Goold Hall, St Andrew Square.

The Chairman said:—"It is my duty, as President of the Royal Scottish Arboricultural Society, to offer a very hearty welcome to the representatives of the Forest Administrations of foreign countries, of India, and of the British dominions beyond the seas, whose presence here to-day lends to our meeting unusual importance and interest. I could wish for the sake of my hearers that this grave duty and high honour were in abler hands—but at least in undertaking it I am acutely conscious of its importance and my responsibility.

"First, it is fitting that we should express to our guests our appreciation of the very kind reception given by their respective Governments to our request that they would send representatives of their Forest Administrations to our Sixtieth Anniversary. Their Governments might have said to us :—'You are a private Society without any official standing in your own country, and, therefore, we cannot be officially represented at your festival,' and if they had said so, we could have had no just cause of complaint. But their Governments have taken a larger and more generous view, possibly in the knowledge that we possess the patronage of our King, and that in the absence of any State Department of Forestry for Scotland this Society has laboured for many years at work which, in their own countries, is carried out by the State. I am sure that all the foreign, English and Colonial representatives will understand how very welcome to us, as a Society, is the recognition of which their presence here to-day is the happy token.

"There is no need to dwell on the blessings of the state of peace which makes such meetings as this possible, or on the infinite good to international relations which comes of these opportunities. But it is not only as witnesses of our recognition, and as messengers of peace and goodwill that we welcome you to-day. Our warmest welcome to you is from foresters to brother foresters—a greeting between men bound in the strong ties of common interests and enthusiasms, between kindred spirits which no difference of race and language can keep apart.

"It is now my duty to ask the meeting to approve of the election as Honorary Members of the Society of those whose names are to be found on the printed paper in your hands. It may be true that nothing that we can do can add anything to the honours of those distinguished silviculturists who are our guests. But I would ask them to remember that our Honorary Membership is the only distinction in silviculture which Scotland has to bestow, and one that always has been, and I hope always will be, jealously guarded. In reading the names, I must explain that those of our foreign guests, following the established custom in Great Britain, are printed in the alphabetical order of the countries represented by them.

"The first country is Denmark, represented by Dr P. E. Müller. In Dr Müller, the accident of the alphabet has given to the foreign representatives a doyen whom any assembly of foresters might be proud to choose for that position. France is represented by M. Pardé, Inspector of Waters and Forests, Beauvais, who is not only distinguished as a forester, but as a dendrologist of European reputation. Holland is represented by M. J. H. Jager Gerlings, Inspector of the Government Forestry Administration at Breda, who represents a country known to us best perhaps for its dairy industry and flower culture; and yet Holland is very much alive to the duty of placing under silviculture all the ground which is not available nor suited for any higher economic purposes. Hungary is represented by Mr Johann Czillinger, Royal Hungarian Inspector of Forests, who comes to us from a country where the relatively large proportion of woods belonging to private owners presents some features of similarity to our own country. Russia is represented by Actual Councillor of State M. S. J. Rauner, Vice-Director of the Corps of Foresters, who is engaged in afforestation work in an empire which already possesses, I believe, the largest area of trees of any country in the world. Sweden is represented by Mr Carl Björkbom, Inspector of Forests, who is an expert in the tending of forests of spruce and Scots pine, which are precisely two of the most important forest trees in Scotland.

"Then, besides these who are elected as foreign Honorary Members, there is the second list of those to be elected as Home and Colonial Honorary Members. The first name is that of the Right Honourable Sir Ronald Munro Ferguson, K.C.M.G., Governor-General of the Commonwealth of Australia. I am sure if there is one man whom we all wish to be with us if he could, it is he. The next name is that of Mr Ř. H. Campbell, Director of Forestry, Canada. Canada, though possessing enormous resources in timber, has already decided to have a forest service, which we have not yet discovered in Scotland. Next there is the Right Honourable Sir Herbert E. Maxwell, Bart. of Monreith. I am extremely sorry not to see him here to-day, when we could have congratulated him personally, but the honour which the Society has done him is, I am sure you will agree, a very well-deserved honour. He has been one of the pioneers in writing, speaking and lecturing on the subject of afforestation. The last name, but by no means the least, is that of Dr John Nisbet, Forestry Adviser to the Board of Agriculture for Scotland, who, I think, by the very able books which he has written on the subject, was the first man to arouse any very wide spirit of interest in scientific silviculture in Scotland. I take it you approve, by acclamation, of the election of these gentlemen as Honorary Members.

" Perhaps you will allow me, as an introduction to the Conference, to explain briefly the mind of the Council in arranging for the celebration of the Sixtieth Anniversary of this Society.

" When Foreign Governments, India and the Dominions had consented that their Forest Administrations should be represented at a silvicultural tour in Scotland, the Council had to consider how the time available could best be spent with a view to the attainment of a certain definite object. That object has been two-fold,—first, to show our guests existing crops of trees in Scotland, and, so far as our experience goes, the soil and situation most favourable to each species under local conditions. Second, to show that there is a large extent of land, now bringing in a very low return from grazing and shooting rents, which is capable of growing as good crops of trees as any which have been seen on our tour.

" Probably the first half of our object has been attained more completely than the second. Naturally, the greater part of our time was spent in showing to our guests silvicultural results already obtained—since, of course, they are the all-important foundation on which a constructive policy must be based. For that very reason the earlier part of our tour may have caused our guests to form opinions altogether too favourable to the existing state of silviculture in Scotland. Indeed, some of them said to us—'You have told us that in your country silviculture is very much in need of assistance and development, and you have shown us little else but well-wooded valleys and thriving plantations.'

"Possibly the latter part of the tour has changed their views; if not, we must ask them to take it from us that we have only shown them a small fraction of the promising field for afforestation now lying waste. In pursuit of our object, we have shown to our guests as much of Scotland as perhaps it is possible to show in a twelve days' tour.

"It has been a one-sided tour turned towards silviculture and silvicultural possibilities alone. We have resisted with iron virtue every by-path leading to the tempting regions of art and industry, of history and romance. And I think we have our reward in having gained for our guests—and incidentally for ourselves—a connected series of impressions of the object of our study which may be compared to a cinematograph film. No one, so far as I know, but ourselves, has taken such a rapid and comprehensive survey of Scottish silviculture and its possibilities. That by itself is a valuable experience, but it sinks into insignificance beside the privilege which we have enjoyed of making it in a company representing, as may be said without exaggeration, the silvicultural theory and practice of all the world.

"It is not possible that such a temporary association can fail to bear permanently useful fruit—it is for us to record and tabulate and compare the experience gained. The benefit to Scottish forestry will be great, even looking to existing conditions, and far greater looking to future possibilities. For I think that besides the Scotland of the latter part of our tour, the Scotland of bare and rain-swept hills, of scanty patches of cultivation and infrequent houses, our guests will carry away with them the picture of another and a different Scotland.

"The scientific imagination, working from known data, can pass over as of no account the lapse of time required to bring to perfection the fruits of a well-ordered plan, and can show us the lower slopes of the hills no longer bare but forest-clad, the hill streams harnessed for industrial service, and thriving villages in place of lonely crofts. That this is no vain dream we can call expert testimony from all the world to prove.

"I have now to ask our guests to give us the advantage of hearing some of the impressions which they have received of Scotland as a field for silviculture. It will also be of the greatest interest to us to hear something of the various methods by which silviculture is encouraged by the Governments of the countries which they represent. I have, in the first instance, to call upon Dr Müller."

Dr Müller said :—" Mr President and Gentlemen, in expressing my warmest thanks to the President for the kind words he has been good enough to address to me as the Danish delegate, I have the honour to inform you that my government was much gratified to receive your kind invitation to send a representative to the sixtieth anniversary of this illustrious Society. To the courtesy of this invitation to my country has been added the great honour of including its representative among the Honorary Members of the Royal Scottish Arboricultural Society. For both courtesies I wish to offer my warmest thanks, and to assure you that I am delighted to be connected with your celebrated Society in this way.

"In compliance with the request for an expression of our joint opinion as delegates of other governments on the subject of afforestation in Scotland, we have thought it best to embody this in a written statement, which I have now much pleasure, Mr President, in handing to you."

The Chairman then read the resolution, which is as follows :—

"From what we have had the opportunity of seeing of the soils and woodlands of Scotland, and from what is known of the climatic conditions, we are of opinion that the country lends itself admirably to afforestation. Under such natural conditions, afforestation can be undertaken on a large scale, and we think that the Society should receive that active support of the nation which is necessary to bring this about."

M. Pardé, speaking in French, said :—" I thank you very sincerely for the great honour you have just conferred on me, in electing me an Honorary Member of the Royal Scottish Arboricultural Society. I know quite well that this distinction is given to me, more on account of my being a delegate of France than because of the modest forester I am. I am not the less sensible of it, and wish to express to you my very sincere gratitude. Your President, Captain Stirling, has expressed the desire that I should tell you the impressions left on me by the beautiful and interesting trip I have just made in your pleasant company, and

I take advantage of his invitation. Generally speaking, except in high situations and those situations near the sea which are too much exposed to the wind, the climate of Scotland, judging from its beautiful vegetation and the very satisfactory growth of the conifers, seems to be very suitable for the culture of the resinous species. Except the parts of ground which are too rocky or too shallow and peaty, in which experiments have still to be made, the soil in Scotland, generally speaking, appears to be suitable for silviculture, provided that you put the various kinds of trees in the places where they will find suitable conditions. An estimate should be made out of the parts of ground to be planted, and a scheme for the planting of these lands should be made, taking into consideration the various local conditions, such as sport and pasturage (that could be permitted under certain regulations, such as under old larch trees), questions connected with labour, etc. A centre should be created for forestry instruction and forestry research; the estate of Ballogie seems to be well suited for this. The State should purchase lands which would be replanted to serve as an example, and also, of course, a Forest Administration should be established, the officers of which should be at the disposal of the private landowners to give them advice and assistance. Encouragement should be given to the private landowners by example, advice, and especially by delivering to them gratuitously plants, the use of which would be easier to supervise than grants of money. Plans should be made for the management of the forests, and especially of plantable lands. As far as possible, mixed woods should be made by groups, and Scots pine and broad-leaved trees should be included in these mixtures. Planting should be less close, thus diminishing the cost of planting, and especially that of thinning, which, in Scotland, is difficult and costly. Thinning should be done, where seen to be necessary for the improvement of the woods, even though it be costly. Those are the opinions I can give, but very timidly, because I cannot pretend to know your beautiful country well after having made an excursion through it for some days only."

M. J. H. Jager Gerlings said:—"I have to thank the Society for electing me an Honorary Member. The days I have spent in Scotland have been of great interest to me, and I assure you I shall never forget them, or the great hospitality which your Society has extended. Regarding the suitability of Scotland for afforestation, you have already heard that our opinion is that it is very good."

Herr Czillinger said :—"I thank you for the honour you have. conferred on me and my country in electing me an Honorary Member, and I have to convey the best wishes of my country to you on the occasion of your Diamond Jubilee. When I look back on the pleasant days I have had, and the striking scenes I have contemplated, it seems to me that all these beautiful plantations and valuable experiments during the last few decades have been made with the greatest skill and the most careful selection of the proper places. I think that the establishment and development of national economic afforestation in Scotland is closely associated with the work of this Society. During the last sixty years, under difficult conditions, this Society has struggled on. It has many arboriculturists among its members who are keenly interested in afforestation, and there must be a successful future in store for it. I sincerely trust that the noble ideals of the Society may soon be realised, and that the beautiful Highlands may before long be covered with noble forests."

M. S. J. Rauner said :—"My first duty is to thank you for the honour you have conferred upon me in electing me an Honorary Member of your Society. I will do all I can to assist as a member of your Society. All our experience and investigations will be at your service. I should like to say something about the impressions I have received. When I left Russia, I never expected to see so many interesting things in forestry as I have seen in your country. Russia is a forest country, and you can see the different conditions of tree-growth in the mountains, the flat lands and the steppes. I have never known such a suitable climate for woodlands as you have here in Scotland. Every day you have to thank the Lord that He has given you such a country, where the conditions are so favourable and the climate so suitable for growing trees. I saw some Douglas firs, the ages of which were only 80 years. On the Continent, such growths could never be attained even at 100 or 120 years, so that you can grow crops in Scotland at a lower rotation than we can. The common Scots pine is grown at a rotation of 120 years in our country. Nearer to the western part, which is more accessible to the market, everything grown at 80 years is the same size as everything at 60 years in this country, so that you have a preference of 20 years. You have ascertained which trees are most suitable for growing in Scotland. I am not speaking of the common Scots pine, but of the larch and the Douglas fir. So that if you only continue to work along the lines advocated by your Society together with the experience you have in raising very fine crops, your nation will be greatly benefited."

Mr Carl Björkbom said:—"In expressing gratitude for the honour conferred on me by being elected an Honorary Member of your Society, I beg at the same time to thank you for the invitation extended to my native country, Sweden, to send a representative to take part in the rejoicings on the occasion of your Diamond Jubilee. I offer you my heartiest congratulations on its attainment. I am convinced that the great interest in forestry taken by this Society will always carry it forward, and will result in a great harvest. I am sure greater interest in forestry and the increasing activity in afforestation in the country will prove a great reward for your labours. The inhabitants of Scotland will yet be much indebted to you for what you have done and will do for afforestation in Scotland."

Mr R. H. Campbell said:—"I do not know that I can give you information such as has been given you by the representatives from foreign countries, because in Canada we have not advanced in many phases of forestry as much as you have, but I am glad indeed to have the opportunity of thanking the members of the Royal Scottish Arboricultural Society for the honour they have done me in electing me one of their Honorary Members. I count it a very great honour to have a connection with anything Scottish at any time, and a particularly high honour to have such a connection with the Royal Scottish Arboricultural Society. You have expressed your appreciation of the action of the Government of Canada in sending a repre_sentative to this Diamond Jubilee Celebration and of the interest it takes in forestry, and I may say that I think your remarks were justified, because we have found in Canada that there is a very keen sympathy by the heads of the Government in the works of the 'Forestry Society' and in works of forestry throughout the Dominion. Both the previous Premier, Sir Wilfred Laurier, and the present Premier, the Right Honourable R. L. Borden, have taken a deep and personal interest in the development of forestry in Canada. This was particularly exemplified by Sir Wilfred Laurier in 1906, when he called a Conference in Ottawa over his own signature as Premier of the

Dominion, and the Convention held then was one of the greatest things we have had to help the Forest Administration in Canada. The present Premier at this time has under consideration the question of calling another Convention. We have, of course, a different question in Canada from the question as it faces you here, and one thing that does strike us very much at first is the extent to which the matter is considered from a private point of view here, in contrast to the way in which it is considered almost entirely from the public point of view in Canada. The forests are in the hands of the Government, and perhaps that is one reason why that view is taken, but, at the same time, the Government in assisting forestry work has not confined itself to its own lands or to its own special interests.

" I may just mention the three special ways in which forestry has been assisted or taken up by the Government. In the first place, I would mention that the Dominion Government makes an annual grant to the Canadian Forestry Association to assist it in carrying on its work. I do not know whether you have induced the British Government to do that for the Royal Scottish Arboricultural Society; but I know this, that you are just as deserving of that support as the Canadian Association is, and I think more so, because of your longer existence and the longer time you have been struggling with this great problem, which is a very difficult one everywhere. In the second place, we are giving some assistance to private owners who are living out in the prairie districts. We have taken up that phase of assistance to private owners first, because it was a most pressing one. As you know, we have extensive tracts of land in the west, prairies where for miles you do not see a tree growing. Here and there is an isolated home on these prairies, absolutely unsheltered, bare and uninviting-looking, and the Government came to the conclusion that it was its province and duty to do something to provide shelter for these people round their homes, and to give them a supply of wood. As a matter of fact, the Government at the present time is maintaining a large forest nursery at Saskatchewan, and is giving trees without charge to the farmers in the Western Provinces in order to assist them in this work. Thirdly, we are doing some work in assisting private owners by giving advice. We have at the present time one man on our staff whose special duty it is to assist private owners by looking over their properties and giving advice in regard to the management. We intend to extend that work somehow, and though I do not know how much it will be extended, the policy has been adopted, and it is intended that it shall be developed. As regards the question of silviculture, Canada is hardly in a position to say very much to Scotland. One of the things that impressed me very much, on coming to Scotland, was to find the extent to which Scotsmen had looked abroad and tried experiments with introduced species, and I was quite pleased to find that among the species which you considered as very suitable ones here, are the Douglas fir and Sitka spruce. Both of these are growing in British Columbia, Canada, and they are there considered very satisfactory. They make good growth in a climate similar in many respects to yours, that is to say, a soft climate with a good deal of moisture. The timber produced is very fine, and I see no reason why the same result should not be obtained in Scotland. I should like to say in closing that in our work in forestry in Canada, we have been very much indebted to a large number of Scotsmen. I do not suppose you care to have them go away, but I must say that travelling round the old district of Argyll, I felt rather sad at heart myself to see so many desolate glens, although I suppose some of my ancestors are responsible for some of the desolation. We have a number of young men from Scotland who are assisting us in our forestry work in Canada."

Dr John Nisbet said:—"I have to thank you very heartily for the great honour you have done me in electing me an Honorary Member of your Society. I feel the honour is very much enhanced by my name being placed in the list along with such illustrious Scotsmen as the Right Honourable Sir Ronald Munro Ferguson and the Right Honourable Sir Herbert E. Maxwell. Those who know the history of Scottish forestry for the last thirty years must remember that Sir Herbert Maxwell, who was President of this Society from 1886 to 1888, took an active part in the Parliamentary Committee on silviculture from 1885 to 1887, that delivered in August 1887 a very good report, which, if it had been acted upon to a far greater extent than it was, would have placed Scotland in a better position regarding silviculture than it occupies to-day. Sir Ronald Munro Ferguson was also President from 1894 to 1897, and it does not require any words of mine to bring to your recollection the great services he has done for the cause of afforestation, both in the House of

Commons and outside the House. In a letter that I received from him very shortly before he went to Australia he said as follows—'Keep the flag flying. I really think we are near the end of our long lane, through the wilderness, at last. Well, we have done our best. It is far the best bond in which I have ever found myself in public life.' As yet, I do not know that Sir Ronald's mantle has fallen upon any Honourable Member in the House of Commons, but I hope he will soon have a younger successor who will have his love for afforestation. I have sometimes heard members of the Society say that slow progress is being made in the advance of forestry in Scotland. As you know, all large buildings need strong foundations, and although the foundations now being laid are perhaps being slowly laid, I feel sure they are being well and firmly laid; and the superstructure to be put on them afterwards may be much larger than it could have been if the foundations had not been so severely tested. I have been privileged to be present at all the meetings of the Advisory Committee, and I should like to express to the members of the Society my great admiration for the wonderful care and the tranquil patience with which the Chairman and members of Committee consider every phase of the question of forestry. It is my earnest prayer that if I am privileged to do anything more for forestry in Scotland, I may be given the health, strength, energy and ability to do good work for it, and that the work throughout Scotland may conduce very largely to the comfort, content, health and happiness of all those connected with or affected by it in any way."

Mr Robinson, New Zealand, said :—" In the first place, I have had very much pleasure in being associated during the past eleven days with so many gentlemen distinguished in forestry science, and am also proud to represent New Zealand at this Conference. It is not my desire, or perhaps yours, that I should attempt to tender information in regard to advanced forestry in New Zealand, particularly as our work is merely in its initial stages. During our tour, however, I have explained some of our methods to those desiring such information, and perhaps the following few condensed notes taken during the tour will show you in what direction I have been specially impressed. Taking it generally, under existing conditions, there is a very large tract of country through which we travelled which appears to be eminently suitable for the production of commercially valuable timber, and it would be in the combined interests of the State and people generally if such land, which at present evidently returns only a comparatively small revenue, were planted. Afforestation work not only provides healthy occupation, but the presence of trees in any locality, amongst other tendencies, has an ameliorating effect on the climate. The planting of trees, therefore, ought surely to receive due recommendation by the State. Existing conditions in New Zealand almost coincide with those of this country, and, therefore, I feel sure your plantations would at least compare favourably with those in the Dominion, except, perhaps, in the semi-tropical places, where the annual development is marked. I do not believe in planting spruces in large blocks, owing to the disastrous effects of wind on such shallow-rooted trees. I believe a partial remedy for that would be in planting some deeper-rooted trees in groups round about, so as to provide shelter for the spruce. This method of forming forests should be more extensively adopted, and full information relative to the matter should be widely distributed amongst estate owners. It is generally recognised that the proportion of forestry enthusiasts in most communities is small, and although your Society has undoubtedly the means of diffusing expert knowledge freely and assisting worthy students to attain that knowledge, doubtless your attempts are spoilt by agriculturists placing more value on agriculture than on silviculture. The Government should have a demonstration area which would be an instrument in raising forest management throughout the country to a still higher standard. It appears to me that the State should exercise greater activity by securing and subsequently planting suitable areas in several localities within reasonable distance from rail and water communication. The distribution to private persons and public bodies of State-grown trees at growing-cost price might also be the means of extending artificial forests. The under-planting at Novar was a revelation in how to combat disease and make provision for a second crop. It also showed the enduring capabilities up to a certain age of the species introduced. The question is whether this system will maintain such a measure of success in places where only a small rainfall is recorded. I can only say the tour has been an educational treat for me, and I heartily thank you for the extreme kindness and consideration that has been extended to me. It will not be

very difficult for me in the future to understand why a native of
your country is so proud of ' Bonnie Scotland.'"

Lord Lovat said:—"When I was asked to speak at this
Conference, I had not the least idea that I should be in the
unfortunate position of being the first speaker. I had hoped
we might have had at this, probably the most important Conference of foresters that has ever been held under the ægis of
the Royal Scottish Arboricultural Society, a statement, at all
events, if not a policy of goodwill from either the Secretary of
State for Scotland or the Chairman of the Board of Agriculture.
No doubt, the Secretary of State for Scotland is not able to be
with us on this occasion, but I must say I do very much regret
that we have not the honour of hearing to-day a statement
from the Chairman of the Board of Agriculture. I would like,
in the few remarks I propose to make, to point out exactly
to the foreign representatives what is the inner meaning of
this Jubilee of the Royal Scottish Arboricultural Society. I
think I could define it in a word by saying that it means sixty
years of private endeavour and sixty years of organised inactivity
on the part of the State. On the subject of private enterprise, I
will only say that you gentlemen must be aware, as you have no
doubt been told by every practical forester, many of whom have
been round on tour with you, that the work you have seen,
which I hope you consider is good work, has been done by
private enterprise and by private enterprise only. Forestry,
like all institutions which require continuity run by private
enterprise, suffers from the intermittent expenditure which has
to be made over the various woods which you have seen.
There cannot be a single mature wood that you have visited
which in course of its growth upwards has not passed through
some period when the estate may have been embarrassed, or
the proprietor has been in his minority, or when there has
been some other reason why silviculture has not been given
the attention it required. We have no laws in this country
by which the State aids afforestation in return for a certain
measure of control, and, therefore, everything is done just
according as each individual wishes. The result is most unfortunate for forestry generally. The million acres of woods are
in some places like the woods in my neighbourhood which John
Grant Thomson was asked to admire, and regarding which he
said—'They're nae woods.' That is so much for private enter-

prise, which, though it may have produced a rugged effect, still has produced one million acres of woods in Scotland, and brought men to work there, and to that extent prevented rural depopulation. Next, the question of this organised official indifference is what I wish to emphasise. In this country when there is a certain movement in the State in favour of any particular thing, whether Tariff Reform or bi-metalism or any other difficult subject, the habit is to pursue some particular line. At elections, politicians speak with very guarded enthusiasm on the subject which it is their policy to support. As soon as they get into Parliament, however, they appoint a Committee on which possibly there is a large number of members with as many different ideas as possible, and after some years some legislation is adopted which in the end, if members are hostile, is killed in the administration. That is what happens to forestry. We have had Committees; I doubt if there is on the first three benches in this room any one gentleman who has not sat on one Commission after another and Departmental Committee after Departmental Committee. Finally, we had two bills which we hoped were going to do something for forestry. I am not making a political oration, but am condemning both Governments. While condemning the Tory Government, I condemn this Government, because, while the Tory Government did nothing, this present Government promised to do something, but has done as little as the last Government. That is fair criticism. We have had a Development Commission from which we hoped for very large things. In that Development Commission forestry was mentioned. In the House of Lords I put forward certain recommendations, many of which have been embodied in the speech made just now by the representative of France. These, however, were cut out. They said it was no good putting these recommendations in, and that if conditions were put in, it would hamper rather than help. In the Small-holders Act, at one time we had a representative appointed for forestry, but he was cut out, and the lack of interest in forestry is what you see to-day. What has happened since these millions of pounds have been set aside for development in Great Britain? This money has been devoted to development of small holdings. England, it is true, has got a demonstration area, but we have none in Scotland. Speaking as a member of the Advisory Committee, and with a knowledge

of what I am saying, I believe we are just as far away from
having a demonstration area in Scotland as we have been at
any period of our history.

"Then, there is the question of forest officers. It is true
we have Dr Nisbet as adviser, but we have no other, though
England has her forest officers. The question of survey has
already been taken up in England. Our survey, except what
has been done by this Society itself, is still in the realms of
what is to be. I need not go through the list of what has
been done elsewhere than in Scotland. When I say nothing
has been done I have forgotten one thing. It is said the
mountains once laboured and brought forth a mouse. The
Scottish Board of Agriculture has laboured and has produced a
beetle. Beyond the appointment of a few officials, and beyond
a few sovereigns being sent to local correspondents who have
no one to report to, the only action that has been taken is the
action of the people. I see no reason why a representative of
the Government or a representative of the Board of Agriculture
should not be here to justify their position. To-day we have to
rely on private work, the work of individuals, to accomplish
what we do in forestry, while the work of the Boards and of the
Governments is nil. I do not think we need put it better.
There are six points on which we are agreed, and which are
identical with the points that the foreign and colonial representatives and others have made. That is important, because it
has been very often urged against us by politicians that they do
what we want, but that we do not know what we want. I
venture to say that the delay has had two effects; it has
hardened us against politicians, but it has also united us in our
opinions as to what should be done. We know that a demonstration area is necessary; that forest officers are absolutely
essential for our guidance in the woods that are now growing
up; that nothing can be effectively done in Scotland until we
have a survey. It is true we have a flying survey showing what
land it is possible to plant, so that instead of generalities we can
get to facts. We also know that assistance for private or
corporate effort must be given in some shape or form until the
Government comes forward with large measures and large funds.
We also believe that there has been a great collection of facts. I
am sure the gentlemen who have been on the tour, and who have
seen our Scottish forestry and the many experiments we have

made in forestry, will say that we require such experiments as much as they are required in any research work, and that we must have a demonstration area. We require all the intelligence in this room collected together, so that it may be of advantage to the whole nation. I venture to think there is not a single man here who does not on broad lines subscribe to every one of these points that I have put forward. We may have these silly little difficulties as to the particular place where this demonstration area is to be, or there may be some foolish points as to how the money is to be advanced, or minor points concerning education or policy, but these are small matters. On the big points, we foresters of Scotland are agreed absolutely and entirely, and I am glad to see our opinions are held by the experts who are visiting this country on this occasion.

"If we are agreed, and if private enterprise so far as we can see has reached its limit, and I fear, speaking as a proprietor with some knowledge, that it is much more likely to go backward in the future rather than forward for reasons I need not mention at the present time, we must see what action we are going to take; and I would venture to say in speaking on the subject of a constructive policy and of how we are to advance forestry in Scotland, there is one method which stands out alone. What we have to do is to educate our politicians and show them the driving force which exists behind this movement in the country, and, of course, the advantages which it offers to the rural dwellers of the whole of Scotland. I think we have been apt to neglect in the past the question of this education of our politicians. You all know the story told at the time of the passing of one of these many Landholders Acts that we have in Scotland. One gentleman came out of Committee and asked someone outside to tell him what was the 'rotation of crops' that was being discussed in Committee. We have had exactly the same thing in regard to our Forestry Committee. We have a great deal of work to do in order to bring up our average representative to anything approaching the knowledge of each gentleman present to-day. As foresters we must press home these points. The driving force of forestry lies in the certainty that it is the cheapest, most effective and most permanent method of getting the population back to the soil. I am sorry the Chairman of the Board of Agriculture is not here to-day, because I wanted to ask him one or two pertinent questions in regard to the matter of cost. We have yet, as you know, only had the first report of the Board of Agriculture, and we have not had the financial statement. I do not make a statement, but will give you what I believe, and it is that when we get hold of the statement of the increased number of individuals resident on an agricultural farm, that is the number of families by which you will be able to increase the existing families on an agricultural farm, they will work out at a cost to the State at something between £800 and £5000 per family. I wish, first of all, to qualify my statement by saying that I am a supporter in principle of small holdings, and that I believe forestry can never interfere with agricultural land. I would never plant an agricultural acre. I believe, moreover, that on the West Coast forestry is almost impossible on account of the wind and the proximity to the sea, so that small holding work must always go on there. Regarding the increase of population and the work of settlement on the land, there are other methods which can be carried out at a cheaper rate than those adopted, and which can go along with arboriculture.

" It is easier to put the matter in a concrete form than to give an absolute statement of fact. I have seen no departmental documents, and I am speaking from constructive views. Regarding the retention of some of these farms, there have been sums up to £15,000 and nearly £20,000 expended, and if you take the difference between the farmer who has to go and the agricultural workers who have to go, and the number of small holders placed on the soil, the difference in certain cases will work out as high as £5000 per additional family. If I am more than £400 or £500 out in my estimate, I shall be extremely surprised. On the other hand, I believe you can make settlements, and very often will make settlements in the future, as low as perhaps £800 per family. Taking the mean, let us imagine for a moment that upon the mainland the average division of an agricultural farm will cost you a plusage of £2500 for a family. We shall know if that is so in a year. If you expended £2500 in planting, you would plant at the rate which is generally recognised, and which is certainly not higher than £5 an acre, including fences, so that for that sum you would plant 500 acres. Accordingly, right away we can hope to settle more families with forestry; we get nearly five times the people for the money expended that you will get if it is spent agriculturally. I do not believe it is ever right to plant agricultural land. On the West Coast, where trees will not grow, we cannot meantime improve the present conditions, but in the Highlands of Scotland, where the configuration of the land is such that the glens are narrow and the amount of agricultural land is extremely limited, if you wish to get a residential population on the soil there, forestry, and forestry alone, is the best and cheapest way. I will only say a word about this method. Forestry is specially adapted to our Highland glens where most of our land exists, because there it works in with the crops. People are able to get a few weeks' work with early potatoes, and they get the crops in, and they also have the seasonal employment that the shooting and tourists and others afford, so that practically a man getting 18s. or 20s. a week, with a croft as well, is better off, and I contend this in the face of any argument, than the corresponding workman in the town with up to 30s. That is my opinion based not only on personal observation, but also on such well-known books of the Fabian Society as '20s. a week,' and books on slumming conditions. I have no hesitation in expressing the opinion that a 20s. croft man is better off than a town man with 30s., as well as being a better inhabitant and a more stalwart representative of the British Isles. Just a word more on the subject of permanency. The employment given by forestry is not artificial employment which alteration in fashion and prices may kill. Every year the woods will require more and more work, and at the producing stage you can eventually get down your number of men to two or possibly three regularly employed per 100 acres. I ask you to consider this point, and each one in his own position to endeavour to thrust this on our politicians, so that we may have some chance of pushing forward a policy on the broad lines of which I believe every man here is united. There is just one objection which I know does rank heavily with politicians of a certain class. That is the idea that the landlord will be benefited. Now, that is enough in certain ranks to banish the idea, whether the subject is good or bad. May I put these two arguments before you, which I think are almost final. One is, that the poor landlord at best will only receive the result of the work at the end of thirty years, when most of us will be dead, and then, if he received it in thirty years' time, surely you could obtain such Parliamentary powers that you could tie up advances in such a way that the landlord does not make undue profit. If you have a profit in thirty years, and Parliament makes it impossible for you to get undue profit, that should set aside this ludicrous objection. If there is a desire to tie up methods of purchase in such a way that the landlord shall not immediately benefit, so long as he is not put in a worse position, I shall give that movement my support. I do hope that the weighty words which the distinguished representatives from other countries have said regarding the advantages accruing to the population by methods of afforestation, and the suitability of our soil, will be put on record in our Society's report, and that a copy of that report be sent with the compliments of the Society to every single Member of our Parliament."

The Chairman said:—"We have the advantage of having amongst us to-day two representatives of official bodies. There is Sir William Haldane, representing the Development Commission, and also Mr Sutherland, representing the Board of Agriculture for Scotland. Before going further, I should like to ask either of these gentlemen if they have anything to say."

Sir William Haldane said:—"I came here to listen, not to speak. We in the Development Commission are not a talking body; we confer in private. We do not appear much in public, and it is quite unusual for me to address such a meeting as this on the topics with which we deal. Although I came here entirely unprepared to make any statement, I should like to say I have been listening to this most interesting speech from Lord Lovat, and that I am sorry I did not hear the earlier speeches as I could not get here sooner, owing to other engagements. Although I do not always see eye to eye in all things with Lord Lovat, I am very glad to find myself in complete agreement with most things he has said to us this afternoon. Of course, I do not refer to the domestic matters of which he spoke. I do not think the Development Commission came in for very much criticism, but other Departments apparently did, and the representative of the Board of Agriculture is here and will be able to speak for the Board, so I do not need to make any reference to that matter. Lord Lovat did make some reference to the Development Commission. We are a body, as you know, which is not supplied with any Executive. We have to deal with applications for financial assistance as they come to us. I see we are referred to as a much abused body. I do not think we are so very much abused, at any rate it does not come much to our notice. We have often to say 'No' to people who come. Sometimes they bring what we know are very dear fads of theirs, and often we have seriously to alter schemes brought to us, whether by Departments or by bodies of philanthropic people, but we find that our efforts seem to be well received, and I do not think we have had any need to complain of the attitude of the public. As regards the matter to which Lord Lovat referred, of assistance to private owners from such funds as the Development Funds, I can say the Development Commission is entirely in sympathy with any such proposal. I think the most important part of his speech was with reference to what might be done in assisting private proprietors in planting their suitable, plantable land. If the proposal is brought before us in any definite shape, I can assure you it will receive most careful and friendly consideration. We have already discussed these matters with Mr Galloway, the most able and excellent Secretary to the Royal Scottish Arboricultural Society, and he knows the Development Commission are prepared to give what I believe would be substantial aid to private owners in Scotland, in planting up their suitable lands. I do not think I need say more than this, that the door is open. If you come to us through the Board of Agriculture, we shall be delighted to consider any proposal for the setting aside of such funds as we can set aside for the purpose of planting in Scotland, or if you prefer to go through some suitable Society, with, no doubt, the full approval of the Board of Agriculture, we shall equally be prepared to do what we can for the afforestation of Scotland."

The Chairman said:—"I am sure you will all be delighted to hear the very guarded statement of the Chairman of the Forestry Committee of the Development Commission. Of course, this question is absolutely and entirely a question of terms. I cannot say too strongly that it is on the terms that any such proposal must stand or fall, and, therefore, any such vague proposals of assistance as have been offered us to-day, until translated into black and white terms, are of very little value to us. I do not wish in the least degree to say that in a carping spirit, but only this spring, terms were offered to us of a wholly unsatisfactory nature, and there is nothing we have heard now to make us think that these terms are altered or improved. If it were so, every one would rejoice, but till we get these terms in black and white, we would consider it too previous to offer any gratitude for them. I have now to ask Mr Sutherland, representing the Board of Agriculture, if he has anything to add."

Mr Sutherland said :—" I feel, from what Lord Lovat has said, that you did not expect me to come here to-day to speak on behalf of the Board of Agriculture. I really came in my private capacity, and I had no intention whatsoever of addressing you. It so happens, however, that the Chairman of the Board, in consequence of other engagements, has not been able to be present, and I think it is my duty to express to you his regret, and at the same time to say that I am quite certain if he had had any conception that forestry was going to be mixed up with small holdings, he would have been here on this occasion, and would probably have defended the Board against Lord Lovat. I would like to say, as you have criticised to some extent the work of the Board in forestry, that you are a Society of at least sixty years' standing, and that the Board is only a child of about two years, and I think that as old and judicious people you ought not at once to begin and whip your own offspring, for, after all, you were the people who made Scotland think it was necessary, at all events to have a Board in which there should be one person who would give some consideration to the work of forestry. I do feel satisfied, however, in what we have heard to-day, that Scotland is the proper place for afforestation. I did not require, I am sure, to be convinced by anything that our guests and friends have said, because after two or three short sojourns in Europe, and after giving a good deal of study to the subject, I was sure that our Scottish Highlands were better, and in many cases a long way better, than many parts of Europe for growing conifers. I am satisfied we can grow them quickly and grow them to profit, and I am perfectly certain we can compete in dimensions, at all events in larch, pine and spruce, with any other country in the world. I also know that we have enormous tracts available and bare that can be used for forestry more profitably and better than for any other purpose. I would like to join you in welcoming our guests here. Unfortunately, I was unable to accompany you all over the tour, but for the time during which I had that privilege, I felt that instruction was to be got at every turn—whether it came from our learned friends from the Continent, or from our colleagues in the Colonies, it was the same useful, helpful criticism and advice. I do not think I ought, in the dual capacity of Small Holdings Commissioner and an indifferent adept in forestry, to say anything about the cost of small holdings. That will all be duly made public in the reports to Parliament, and when they do come out, then I hope my Chairman will be able to come and discuss the matter with Lord Lovat."

The Chairman said :—" In thanking Mr Sutherland for his remarks, I should also like to take this opportunity of thanking the Board of Agriculture for the way in which they assisted us in making possible the tour which we have just given to the foreign representatives. I am sure the whole Society is most grateful to the Board of Agriculture for their very practical assistance in this matter. In regard to other matters which Mr Sutherland has mentioned, I can only say I look forward with anticipation to the day when the Board of Agriculture shall create the first small holding in Scotland in connection with afforestation. That day is still to come. I do not know whether Dr Somerville has anything to add?"

Dr Somerville said :—" As you know, I have done my little in the earlier stages in the development of forestry to help it on, and like you I sometimes feel disposed to despond. I suppose, however, that the historian of the subject, half a century or so ahead of us, may find that all the little pushes that each of us has given to the cart have been the means of getting it along to some appreciable extent. No doubt, this Society and its members individually have laboured hard in the face of great discouragements, and I could name men whom you see here, and, unfortunately, I could name those that I do not see here, who have given of their best, cheerfully and ungrudgingly, to the service of what we believe to be one of the main industrial and economic questions in Scotland."

The Chairman said :—" I do not think we could do better than adopt as our resolution the latter part of the resolution which has been come to by the foreign representatives, as follows :— ' That it is the finding of this meeting that afforestation can be undertaken on a large scale, and the meeting is of opinion that the Society should receive that active support of the nation which is necessary to bring this about.' For the word ' nation ' I should propose to substitute the word ' State.' "

Mr S. J. Gammell said :—" I should like to suggest one other alteration in the resolution. Our foreign friends have all along been too complimentary to us, and I would suggest that we are hardly entitled to pass a resolution that our Society should receive the support of the State. The expression "Society" was put into the resolution out of kindness to ourselves, and is a compliment we hardly deserve."

The Chairman said:—"That is quite right. I should have left out the word 'Society' and put in 'afforestation' instead."

Mr Gammell said:—"I should like most heartily to support the resolution as it stands now, and I may possibly be allowed to say a word. I feel the position is to a certain extent due to the fact that all our politics have got very much either into one party or another. I was very glad to hear Lord Lovat in his remarks divide his criticisms most fairly between the present Government and the one which preceded it. It has always been a great treat to find in a Society like this that we never allow our private political opinions to interfere with our pressing forward the cause of afforestation in the country. So long as we maintain that attitude to politics, it will be better for afforestation in Scotland and better for the Society itself. We must realise that in order to get anything done, we must press our proposals on the Government of the day, so that they may be put forward for the acceptance of the nation and be crowned with success. We maintain that our case is a good one, and I think we are right in so maintaining. We can show them in every way that it is not a leap in the dark, and I think the encouragement we have to-day received from our foreign friends on the same lines strengthens us in our contention. In order to give point to what I have been saying in regard to the future of this policy, I should like to add some concrete example of what can be done in the matter of small holdings. It is *the* thing which dovetails into forestry in a way no one can understand, unless he has actual experience of it. I have done it myself on my own land for the purposes of keeping labour, and it has been an advantage to me, and I think I am justified in saying it has also been an advantage to the tenants of the small holdings. An ounce of practice is worth a ton of theory, and if we can bring that home to the Government of the day, no matter what their politics, we shall have taken an important step in bringing about what we in this Society desire to see accomplished in this country.".

Sir John Stirling-Maxwell said:—"At the time when the Society did me the honour of making me President, I could scarcely have believed that we should have made so little advance in Scotland as we have made in these four years. At that time, we were in great hope that a period of advance was beginning, and at the risk of seeming for the moment disloyal to the political party to which I belong, I must honestly say we were receiving from the Liberal Government a measure of encouragement which we never received from a Government of the other complexion. When I remember that this Society really gathers up into its membership practically all the experience of forestry which exists in Scotland, and that as a result of that experience it has tabulated in a perfectly distinct way the proposals necessary for the advance of silviculture, I cannot help feeling that the Scotsmen who in official life represent the country in this matter, whether in Departments or in the Development Commission, have wonderfully little to show for any efforts they may have made on their side. We heard to-day of the open door of the Development Commission. Well, I know that door, and it is a very peculiar piece of furniture. It does undoubtedly stand open, and inside there is a beautiful silence and a beautiful abstention from action of any kind so far as we are concerned. When we approach that open door with any practical proposal, it is invariably slammed in our faces. Of the proposals which this Society has drafted and sent through the Advisory Committee and the Board of Agriculture to the Development Commission, not one has so far been allowed to enter in at that door. They have had no reception except the slamming of it."

Sir William Haldane :—" Question !"

Sir John Stirling-Maxwell, continuing, said :—" I do not wish to speak in a bitter spirit. I admire Lord Lovat for having spoken apart from the party spirit. There may be many roads upon which we may proceed in quest of what we have in view. What we complain of is, that there seems to be no disposition on the part of those in office to advance in any direction. If they do not accept our proposals, it is now 'up to them' to make some proposal and let us know on what lines they are prepared to encourage some advance. I have nothing more to add, but merely wish to say if there has been any tinge of bitterness in any word I have said, I hope it may be unwritten."

Mr J. F. Macdonald said :—" I thought Lord Lovat was a little hasty in dismissing the Western Isles. Why do we not grow the sycamore and the alder there? Both are first-rate trees, and both will grow well in the Western Isles."

Lord Lovat:—"I believe they will grow in the Western Isles. I planted a section there myself, but the wind-swept outer islands will never grow trees."

Mr H. Rutherford said:—"You have been extremely indulgent and fair in giving every opportunity to speak on this occasion, but some of us feel there is a need for a little fresh air, and we have dinner in one and a half hours' time. Our foreign visitors would be distressed if we had not an appetite by then, so I think the Conference might close."

The Chairman:—"I have little doubt the remarks we have listened to have been much enjoyed by all present. I will now put the Resolution as follows:—

'That it is the finding of this meeting that afforestation can be undertaken on a large scale, and the meeting is of opinion that it should receive that active support of the State which is necessary to bring it about.'

I take it the motion is unanimously carried. This completes our business."

A vote of thanks was accorded to Captain Stirling for presiding, and the proceedings terminated.

THE DINNER.

The Diamond Jubilee celebrations were brought to a conclusion in the evening by a dinner in the North British Station Hotel. About one hundred gentlemen were present, and the chair was occupied by Captain Stirling of Keir.

The Chairman said:—"In proposing the health of His Majesty the King, I cannot do better than read a message which was despatched to His Majesty by the Society, and the answer received from His Majesty. The following telegram was sent this morning:—

'The Members of the Royal Scottish Arboricultural Society present their humble duty to your Majesty as their patron on the occasion of the sixtieth anniversary of the formation of the Society, and desire to assure your Majesty of their loyalty and affection. The representatives of your Majesty's Indian Empire and of the

Dominions of Canada, New Zealand and South Africa desire to be associated with this message. The representatives of Denmark, France, Holland, Hungary, Russia and Sweden, at present the guests of the Society, also desire to convey to your Majesty an expression of their admiration and esteem.'

"I have received the following answer :— `

'As patron of the Royal Scottish Arboricultural Society, the King has received with much satisfaction the loyal message from its members, and desires me to offer his congratulations on this auspicious occasion in the life of the Society. Will you also convey to the representatives of India, Canada, New Zealand and South Africa, as well as to your foreign guests, His Majesty's best thanks for the kind sentiments communicated in your telegram. CLIVE WIGRAM.'

"I now give you the toast of His Majesty the King."

The other loyal toasts were also given from the Chair.

Mr Sydney J. Gammell, in proposing "The Houses of Parliament," said :—"I rise with very great pleasure to propose the toast of 'The Houses of Parliament,' which stands in my name, and I do so with a certain amount of diffidence, as I feel that I am not competent to deal with so important a toast in the manner in which it deserves to be dealt with, and I must particularly ask these gentlemen who have honoured us with their presence as the representatives of foreign countries not to take what I may say with regard to the Houses of Parliament, as too strictly in accordance with the actual state of affairs, because I do not feel that I am competent to do justice to the subject. My first regret, and I fear it must be a regret in proposing this toast, is that we have so few representatives of our Houses of Parliament present with us to-night. I am sure that if they had been here, and particularly if they had been at the Conference which we held this afternoon, they could not have failed to have been impressed by the weighty words which fell from those who have honoured us with their presence, and who are more competent to speak on forestry subjects than any of us here. But I know there are party exigencies and other questions which are more to the front than forestry at this particular moment. That is also one of my regrets, because I do feel it is very sad

that so great a subject, a subject so fraught with importance to
the country at large, to those of our population who have to
gain their living in the country districts, should sometimes at any
rate be sacrificed to party exigencies and put to a cetain extent
upon the shelf. This is so important a subject that it really
deserves considerably more consideration than the Houses of
our Legislature have apparently been able to give to it up to the
present time. We who have not the honour of being at any
rate intimately connected with the Government of the country
by being Members of either of the august Houses that sit at
Westminster, sometimes think that the party exigencies play too
strong a part from what we see at any rate in the newspapers.
We have the feeling that it is more important sometimes to score
a party point, or to say something which is to the party
advantage, than to press forward measures which are not
immediately before the electorate, and which the electorate
do not understand. We heard this afternoon that one of the
things which our Society had to keep in the forefront of its
programme was the education of our legislators, and I think I
might add to that that we ought also to keep in the forefront of
our programme the education of the electorate. There are a
great many people, especially the large bodies of the electorate
who live in the city and suburban districts, who really do not
know, and who do not realise the importance of forestry not
only to the country districts but indirectly to themselves. It is
to their interest, even looking upon it from a most materialistic
and selfish point of view, that our country population should be
kept in the country. We maintain, and are prepared to maintain,
and to a very large extent are prepared to prove, that forestry
would do this for the country and for the people. Now,
'Development' is a word about which we have heard a great
deal, and we have been told that our duty is to develop our own
country. Nothing truer was ever said. I do not propose to
enter for one moment into anything which converges upon
party politics in any sense whatever. This afternoon any blame
which was attached to the Government was impartially distributed
between both political parties in, I am sure, quite equal shares,
and it is very proper that all matters of that kind should be kept
absolutely apart from the object we have in view. Our personal
opinions we are entitled to maintain, but there is a saying which
says, 'Let difference of opinion never alter friendship,' and I am

sure that is a motto which we can keep before us, and never allow our individual political opinions to interfere in the slightest degree with our wish to press forward an industry which is undoubtedly for the benefit of the country, whichever political party may eventually bring it into force. But when we see large sums of money voted for development not only in this country, but for other countries, we ask why a fair share should not be devoted for the development of forestry in Scotland. I fear there may be in the political exigencies which affect both parties quite impartially, the necessity of playing a little bit to the gallery and of putting forward schemes which will bring votes to the political party which puts them forward. It is our duty to educate not only the legislature, but also the electorate, in order that going hand-in-hand we may see a large develop-ment of forestry in this country, which, when once it has come, I have not the slightest doubt will entirely substantiate the argu-ments we have put forward in its favour. I need not detain you longer in proposing this toast. I have great pleasure in associating with it the name of Lord Lovat, a more capable and enthusiastic forester than whom there is none to be found in the whole of Scotland. I give you 'The Houses of Parliament,' coupled with the name of Lord Lovat."

Lord Lovat, replying, said:—" I have addressed you at such disgraceful length this afternoon, that my reply shall be very brief, and, so far as I am capable, to the point. The allusion which Mr Gammell has made regarding our Members to-night must, I think, be accepted as due to the exigencies of the moment rather than to their wish, because I certainly know a great number of the Members of my House wished to be here, and Members of the other House equally wished to be present. To reply to this toast at the present moment, without getting into the realms of party politics, would be impossible. We can only hope that at this great crisis Members of both Houses will be well advised and will carry out their duties faithfully to the country as a whole. We have probably never been, certainly not in our time, at a crisis more anxious and more fraught with danger, and we can only hope that both Houses will, as Mr Gammell has so suit-ably expressed, put their duties before their own personal feelings, and loyalty to the country before their loyalty to party. I turn from this side of the question with great readiness to the question of the relation of both Houses to the subject of silviculture generally. I do hope, as Mr Gammell has said, and as I endeavoured to say this afternoon, that we shall slowly and surely build up a greater interest in both Houses in this great subject of forestry. Nothing has impressed me more, and I feel, with proper and careful presentation of the facts, nothing will in the future impress the general public more than the words which have fallen from our distinguished visitors to-day. The general public is quite accustomed to hear what I might almost describe as the firebrands who go about the country and try to stimulate interest in both Houses on this particular subject, and because they are always on the one subject are sometimes regarded as cranks. These people who look upon the efforts of the advocates of afforestation as the work of cranks will receive rather a shock when they find that distinguished representatives from the whole Continent of Europe come here and tell us our soil is magnificent—which we know—and tell us our climate is first-rate—which we very much doubt—and tell us that the growth of our trees is even quicker than what obtains in many suitable soils abroad. This re-echoes exactly what we have been told in the past by Sir William Schlich and others, who tell us that the increment of our trees in certain parts of Scotland undoubtedly passes what they have met with abroad. When we have these facts presented to us, and when we know the population is drifting more and more rapidly into the towns, and the subject of rural depopulation is a really live subject which every Scotsman who calls himself a Scotsman wishes to face, I am sure, armed with these facts and the remarks of experts from all over the Continent of Europe, we can place with even more resolution than before the facts of our case before all political parties. I believe the strength of the movement is not going to lie to any great extent with people like myself, who have the misfortune to possess a great extent of territory, but its strength will come from you gentlemen who have looked at this matter closely, and have a greater knowledge than any of us can pretend to have. If each one, in his own sphere of action, puts the facts forward and tells what he believes to be the possibilities of forestry, not for any particular rank, but for the general public in the country, then when the time for action comes we may have the backing of the country behind us as we must eventually have. I thank you for drinking the health of the Houses of Parliament, and for the kind way Mr Gammell proposed the toast."

The Chairman said :—" In the absence of the Lord Provost of Edinburgh, which we all regret very much, I think we will pass over the next toast for the present. The Lord Provost told me he might be very late, but he would use his best endeavours to be here to-night, and, therefore, I suggest we should leave this toast over for the present in case he is able to come later. I, therefore, call upon Dr Somerville, in the absence of Sir William Schlich, to propose the toast of the Royal Scottish Arboricultural Society."

Dr Somerville said :—" I am sure that I only express your regret when I state mine, that my distinguished colleague, Sir William Schlich, has not seen his way to be present on this important and record-making occasion. I saw Sir William at the end of last week, and at that time he thought he might not be able to join in the tour, but he certainly did not indicate that it was probable he would not be present at this gathering ; and I can only say that I sincerely trust there is no very special reason for his absence, beyond what some or many of us are suffering from, a slight attack of advancing years. Needless to say, there are more reasons than one why I should have wished Sir William to be present to-night, but, after all, a great toast speaks for itself. I had the honour ten years ago of saying a few words in proposing a similar toast, and if I had had time between the intimation that Sir William could not be here and the present moment, I might have revived my recollection of what I said on that occasion, trusting to defective memories to let it pass off, as it were, as a new production. But not having had time, and also not having had a copy of the *Transactions*, I have to fall back on what you may call original matter. My connection, of course, with the Society does not extend over sixty years, but still I joined about the year 1889, and, although many of you can claim a longer acquaintance with the Society, some of you, I may venture to say, have had a shorter connection therewith. In the earlier years of my connection with the Society, I think I was brought more intimately into contact with it than recently. This is not my desire, but my misfortune. When one drifts southwards, it is natural one gets a little out of touch with events in the north, and although I think, on the whole, that you have a more interesting and eventful time than we in the south, the English Arboricultural Society endeavours, just as you endeavour, to stimulate interest in the subject and advance the business. We do not, however, have those pleasant *tête-à-têtes* with those in the high places that you have, although I recollect in my earlier association with this Society, that an opportunity of interviewing the various Presidents of the Board of Agriculture as they used to come north to the Annual Autumn Conferences, was never missed. How early these interviews began I do not know, but I have very distinct recollections of taking part in deputations that waited on Mr Chaplin, to begin with, and Mr Long, and later on Lord Onslow was not allowed to escape, and possibly Sir Ailwyn Fellowes, but that is more recent history, in which I did not participate. These Annual Meetings with the Presidents became almost monotonous in their similarity. We met one of these Presidents one year, and he came back the next, then the next, and then a new President came on, and we were enthusiastic to see that he was impressed. He received us as a new man seeking new ideas receives people, and he appeared to be interested, and I remember well how our hearts rose when, at the end of an interview, he would say, 'Now, then, gentlemen, you will kindly put all that in writing and send it to me.' In my innocence, I imagined getting things on paper, and getting them sent by request, was almost a certain way of securing a thing. I have grown older and wiser since those days, and I now know these requests are very much the same as those we hear of to-day in connection with Royal Commissions, Departmental Committees, etc., which are just a delicate way of giving a decent burial. These meetings took place with the Presidents of the Agricultural Board in London, and I suppose our importunity began to tell in the end, because, as you know, the Presidents of the Board of Agriculture escaped finally by cutting Scotland adrift from the English Board. Whether the importunity of the Royal Scottish Arboricultural Society had anything to do with the severance of that Board I know not, but at anyrate it effected a means of escape for the Presidents of the Board of Agriculture, who are no longer button-holed, because the necessity of coming to Scotland is past. Now, the toast I have the honour of proposing is, of course, the health of the Royal Scottish Arboricultural Society, and when one talks of health, one thinks of diagnosis and one asks oneself whether in effect there is any great necessity to inquiry into the health of this old and honourable Society. I have not even had time to get figures from Mr Galloway, but, if I had, I cannot fail to believe that these figures would have shown substantial and continuous and persistent progress, and I may almost venture to guess, or almost venture to say, on my own authority without figures, that the Society was never in a stronger position financially and numerically than it is at the present time. The secret of the strength and vigour and robustness and, I hope, permanency of the Society comes from various sources. You have in Scotland an extraordinary valuable asset, as it seems to me, in what one might call the intelligent, reasoned support of landowners, who are convinced of the intrinsic merit of the subject of afforestation. When you find owners of land, men who give their mind to the improvement of the social and economic conditions of the countryside, neglecting no opportunity of instructing themselves as to the importance of forestry, and urging the claims of forestry on the Government and coming to meetings of this kind, and maintaining that in their estimation forestry is the one available and possible instrument of rural amelioration in large parts of the Highlands, such testimony as that has enormous value in the development of the subject. That, I consider, is one of your valuable assets—the support you get from men most directly and practically and to a large extent economically interested in the subject. Then you get other support, the support of the kind of person I am, not altogether unprejudiced, and perhaps in their own way attempting to be as unbiased as they can, though, of course, they are not altogether beyond criticism. But to-day we have had further support. I think we have had more direct and definite recognition by the Town Council and Corporation of Edinburgh than we have ever had before. I do not recollect that we have ever been entertained in the City Chambers of this old Corporation as we have been entertained to-day. That sort of thing counts, and helps to get the subject forward. I suppose you will all agree with me that besides what you may call the technical development of forestry, what most of us have tried to do is to get the subject known through improved education in the widest sense of the word. That is to say, from the earliest stages we have recognised that definite and systematic education of the young foresters is likely in the end to advance the subject. We have gone, as you know, on many tours abroad, five, at least, to foreign countries, and, therefore, we have tapped what we may call the fountain-heads of forestal knowledge. This year, when we could not go abroad, we bring the fountain-heads to our own country and tap them. When Mahomet cannot go to his mountain, he fetches the mountain to himself, and I am bound to say as a member of the Royal Scottish Arboricultural Society, that, in this instance, the action in respect to these gentlemen was a positive stroke of genius. I have not a doubt that in what will be the comparatively near future, this departure from custom will bear a rich and glorious harvest. With these remarks I give you, in all cordiality and speaking as a member of your great kindred Society south of the Border, the toast of the Royal Scottish Arboricultural Society, long life, increased vigour and improved usefulness."

The Lord Provost of Edinburgh entered the room at this stage, amid applause.

The Chairman said:—"You will all be very glad to see that the Lord Provost of Edinburgh has been as good as his word and has joined us.

"It is now my duty to respond to the toast which has been so ably proposed on very short notice by Dr Somerville. More fortunate than Dr Somerville, I had the opportunity of reading the remarks which he made ten years ago on a similar occasion, and I can tell him that I do not think he has on this occasion gone over more than a single inch of the same ground, that inch being the part of his speech devoted to the necessity of education. It is becoming a custom for Dr Somerville to propose this toast on the occasions of our Jubilees, and I hope he may be here to propose the next, for I suppose we are entitled to another Jubilee on our seventy-fifth year. I should like to express, on behalf of the Society, very great regret that Sir William Schlich, the President of the Royal English Arbori-cultural Society, has not been able to be present to-night. I am sure you would wish me, on your behalf, to send him a telegram expressing our regret at his absence.

"When I found that I should be in the position of having to return thanks for this toast, I naturally looked up the proceedings of ten years ago. The task which has fallen to me is an easier one than that which Mr Fothringham had ten years ago, the period under review being ten years instead of fifty years, as it was at that time. Mr Fothringham said then very truly, that this Society had outgrown both its

name and its motto, and that its chief concern was then no
longer arboriculture, still less the haphazard sticking in of trees,
but the formation of woods In the ten years that have passed,
the Society has continued to grow in stature. Its horizon has
widened, and now we are no longer content with the care of
such woods as we have, but we are chiefly concerned with
obtaining for silviculture in Scotland that recognition and
position which it holds in nearly every civilised country in the
world. I will not go over the domestic history of the Society
in recent years. That is only too well known to most of us,
particularly to those who had the misfortune of listening to the
history of the Society which was poured into the more or less
sympathetic ears of the Secretary of Scotland, not very long
ago. Out of consideration for them, if for nothing else, I
would say no more on that subject, but, so far as external events
go, the past ten years have been a period of hope and, I am
afraid I must add, of disappointment. The one single real
benefit we have to chronicle is the removal from growing timber
of that taxation for death duties purposes which never should
have been imposed upon it. During that time, there has been
the creation of the Board of Agriculture for Scotland, with an
official for forestry purposes, the creation of the Development
Commission, with special funds for the encouragement of
agricultural industry, and a special Committee for forestry,
and the acquisition by the Crown of 12,000 acres in Argyllshire
for afforestation, also the appointment of an Advisory Committee
by the Board of Agriculture, on which Scottish silviculture was
well represented by members of this Society who had the fullest
trust of the Society. All these things led us to suppose that
better times were at hand. It is difficult, however, to see that
we have derived much benefit from these changes. Ten years
ago, the necessity for a demonstration area was already recognised
in the Committee. The Advisory Committee of the Board of
Agriculture, which I mentioned just now, reported some time
since, I think it is getting on for two years, that a suitable
area had been found. It was afterwards announced
to us that money for the purchase of this area would
be included in the estimates. Since that time months
have passed, the purchase has not been completed, and
we understand the option given on the property has been
allowed to lapse. If we turn to the ground acquired for afforesta-

tion at Inverliever, what do we find? After an occupation of
seven years in a district singularly fitted for the creation of
small holdings, where scores of acres of old arable land at a low
elevation are to be found, on a property administered by the
State, not one single small holding has been formed. Instead
of attaching to the soil good houses and small holdings for
foresters and their families, the State has deliberately built
bothies and employs casual labour. We are entitled to
inquire what the Board of Agriculture has been about. It
has been busy creating small holdings in other parts of Scotland,
often where outside employment for the holders is very
problematic. Here, where the conditions are admirable, and
where regular employment for eighteen or twenty workmen is
ensured, not a thing has been done. Gentlemen, I do not
seek to lay the blame for these things at any man's door. I
have little doubt that it is the system that is to blame more
than any one individual. But what shall we say of the
system under which such absurdities are possible?

"Let us turn now from these disheartening failures to our own
work and ideals. This afternoon we have heard from men
peculiarly qualified to give opinions of weight that silviculture in
Scotland is an asset to national prosperity which has been little
developed. For its proper development three things are needed—
the knowledge to plan, the skill to execute and the money to pay.
Without the last, the two first can effect little or nothing. With
regard to knowledge, Scotland has been striving for some time
past to qualify herself, and it must be owned with regret that
at the present moment the supply of knowledge is fully equal
to the demand—indeed we have lost from Scotland highly
trained men, because we have not the appointments to offer
which would enable us to keep them. Skill is relatively better
off, being kept alive in existing woods, but, with an increased
area under wood, the demand for skilled men would be much
greater than it is to-day. Money or capital is really the difficulty.
Forestry is no less unsuitable as an investment for mortal men
than agriculture would be if it took one hundred years to grow
a turnip. Limited liability companies, even if they have a
potential and corporate immortality, are composed of mortal
shareholders not wholly indifferent to dividends. We cannot
look to private or corporate parties to provide funds for this
development. It is the State which can take the long views which

justify afforestation, and the State alone, which can afford the expenses. The State has everything ready to its hand to assist silviculture in the initial work in the form of the Development Commission. It is no secret perhaps that the Commission have for long been considering the question of State aid for afforestation, and that in England and Ireland considerable grants have already been made. Let me urge respectfully upon the Commissioners, and I am glad to see one here to-night, that in the opinion of this Society the time for action in Scotland has arrived. Let them lay before us the terms upon which they are prepared to assist afforestation, and so long as these terms are founded upon a knowledge of the conditions and the needs of Scotland, and upon just dealing between man and man, they are sure of a good reception from us.

"One other word I would say to the Commissioners, with a great sense of responsibility and with all respect. In this great national purpose there is room for all who are willing to work, and, therefore, let the Commissioners see to it that they do not reject for any unworthy reason the help and advice of those who are best able to help and advise them. Possibly the Development Commission is not an ideal body for dealing with a great national object like afforestation. It will probably surprise our guests to learn that afforestation is dependent for any doles it may receive upon a body of which only one member has had any silvicultural training, and that that member has had no practical experience in Scotland; further, that silviculture has to cómpete not only with the legitimate claims of agriculture and kindred industries, but with any number of schemes and devices which may be brought before the Commissioners. Therefore, there is a danger of silviculture being regarded by the Commissioners not as a great national industry, but as one crank amongst many other cranks. The Society demands for Scotland what almost every country possesses—a State Forest Department with separate funds for silviculture and silviculture alone. This we believe is the first step towards real progress, and we shall continue to advocate it with increased conviction of its necessity. This is neither the time nor the place for detailed study of a complete scheme of afforestation, but I venture to lay before you four elementary conditions which seem to be indispensable for the success of any scheme. They are: (1) The scheme must be conciliatory, that is, it must avoid expensive lawsuits and unnecessary compensation; (2) It must take full account of existing industries and means of employment, rentals and burdens, and while disturbing these conditions as little as possible, it must provide full compensation for unavoidable disturbance; (3) Its operations must be grouped round suitable forest centres, having special regard to the necessity of attaching to the soil, by well-considered small holdings schemes, the labour which will be required for afforestation; (4) The last condition must follow the others if they are to receive proper weight, and it is that the scheme must be economically and definitely sound. These conditions are perhaps of the nature of truisms. That cannot be denied for a moment, but they are truisms which cannot be neglected with impunity. They are the result of such thought as I have been able to give to the subject, and of much conversation and consultation with others more qualified than myself to give opinions. It may seem sometimes to us that our advocacy of afforestation is a very thankless, and often a hopeless task, and when we are apt to think so, we should remember the words of a poet who knew and loved Scotland well, words whose inspiration seems to have been drawn from that rocky and deeply indented coast which we visited so lately—

> ' For while the tired waves vainly breaking,
> Seem here no painful inch to gain,
> Far back, through creeks and inlets making,
> Comes silent, flooding in, the main.'

It may be that the tide which has set so strongly against us is even now on the turn. If it be so, I cannot wish for this Society any more useful or more congenial task than that of guiding the flood into the channels which knowledge and experience indicate as leading to success. I thank you very much for the kind way in which you have received this toast."

Mr Buchanan said:—" The toast which has been put in my hands is that of 'The Lord Provost, Magistrates and Town Council of the City of Edinburgh.' I am sure we are very much indebted to them for their kindness to us to-day. We have visited some of Edinburgh's old historic buildings, as well as its pleasant parks and gardens, and all our foreign and Colonial guests were very much interested in what they saw. I am sure the present Lord Provost and Magistrates are the right men in the right place. They have looked after the interests of the town, and there is no city that I know of that has more beauty than the city of Edinburgh. The roses in Saughton Park to-day were the admiration of all the gentlemen who visited that place. The cultivation of roses may not be arboriculture, but still it shows that the beauties of the city are looked after, and we all admire the work of Mr M'Hattie in laying out that Park. I understand the Lord Provost and Magistrates have now a large area of 6000 acres, and they have already begun to plant. Their interest in afforestation work will increase, and I hope their efforts will be a great success. Without saying more, I ask you to drink to the Lord Provost and Magistrates of Edinburgh."

Lord Provost Inches said :—" I deem it a very great honour to be here to-night, although I came late. Let me explain and apologise for my lateness. I had a very important engagement, one which I could not in any way get rid of, and in fact I did not wish to get rid of it. It was virtually a command, and as soon as I could get away, I have come away, and I am here as early as I possibly could get. I am sure you will sympathise with me, seeing it was a call of duty. I must thank Mr Buchanan for his good opinion of the Lord Provost, Magistrates and Town Council of Edinburgh, and for the nice manner in which he expressed that good opinion. We try to do our very best. We know we have a very important charge committed to us, and I assure you we do our best to work up to it. We have an ancient and historic city, one full of romance, and its prestige must be maintained in the very best manner. I am very glad to know that this Society has come here this year, and I hope that what you have seen has been appreciated. I feel that the Town Council of Edinburgh does a good deal in the way of floriculture, and your appreciation, especially of the roses in Saughton, is very gratifying to me. I was one of those who had something to do at first with Mr M'Hattie, one of the most able gardeners. I do not know whether he is an arboriculturist or not, for we have never asked him to grow trees, but we have asked him to grow roses, and he has done it to perfection. I know Mr M'Hattie holds a high position in this Society, and I am sure the members will find no gentleman more willing to communicate what he knows and give advice in any way than Mr M'Hattie. He is in my opinion the most able official we have in the city; and I hope he will long continue to be so. Now, gentlemen, I do not think it necessary for me to say more than that I very much appreciate your very kind invitation to be here to-night, and your appreciation of the welcome that we have given you to-day. If you meet in Edinburgh on the next Jubilee Celebrations, I am sure the Lord Provost of the day will be glad to welcome you."

The Chairman said:—"I have to call on Dr Borthwick to propose a toast which I think should have been printed in larger type, the toast of 'Our Guests.'"

Dr Borthwick said:—"I rise with great pleasure to propose this important toast. Our guests have come from all parts of the world, and they have made a thorough inspection of Scotland. Our honoured guests are men who in their own countries occupy high and distinguished positions as scientists and foresters, and they have been chosen by their respective countries to represent them at our Diamond Jubilee. They have given us their opinion regarding forestry conditions in Scotland, and also as regards the possible future developments of Scottish forestry. That opinion has been extremely favourable, and will go far to promote the development of forestry in this country. We regret that one or two countries found it impossible to send representatives on the present occasion, but they have sent their congratulations to the Society on the occasion of its Diamond Jubilee, and cordial wishes for its continued prosperity. From time to time, distinguished foresters from France, Germany, Sweden, America and Japan have visited Scotland and pronounced very favourable opinions as regards her future forestry possibilities. This Society, which is the oldest arboricultural society in the Empire, is celebrating its Diamond Jubilee, and it is absolutely certain, and therefore quite safe to say, that on no previous occasion has there ever been assembled at one time in this country a company of foresters so distinguished as our foreign guests. I can safely say that we have represented here the highest talent and knowledge which the world can produce. Our honoured guests, in addition to bringing a vast amount of skill and scientific knowledge, which they have freely imparted to us, are also most excellent linguists. We have had no difficulty in exchanging ideas with them in our own language, and that has been very valuable to us, because we have all been able to converse with our guests, and thereby to learn a great amount of new and useful knowledge, as well as having confirmed ideas and opinions which we previously held. As Editor of the *Transactions*, I am very pleased to say that we have promises from our guests of articles and papers on forestry subjects, which I am sure will be most useful to us.

"We have to-day added to the strength of our membership. We have now on our list of Honorary Members a number of new names distinguished in the world of forestry. The Society has not confined itself to one part of the country. It has local secretaries in different parts of Scotland, England, Ireland, the Colonies and the Continent. It has become quite cosmopolitan. The membership, which is large, has now spread itself over most parts of the world. We are in close touch with absent members who are constantly sending us the result of their experience in the form of articles for our *Transactions*, and it is very interesting to anyone who goes over the back numbers of the *Transactions*, because he can almost see the different stages of forestry development through which the various countries and Colonies have passed and are passing. Some are more advanced than others. I am afraid we possibly bring up the rear. Still, as regards silviculture, we are told by our guests that there is very little or nothing to criticise in our methods. As has been said to-night already, knowledge and skill are available at present, also the soil and climate—everything but the necessary help from the State. Our friends and guests have told us that they consider that Scotland is in every way admirably adapted for afforestation. I referred to distinguished foreign foresters who have visited Scotland in former times, and I cannot let this subject pass without referring, as I am sure the whole Society would wish me to do, with great regret to the loss we have sustained in the recent decease of Mr Nilson, who on several occasions came to this country from Sweden and gave us valuable advice about our forests and forest management. He also contributed valuable articles to our *Transactions*, and acted as our guide when we visited his own interesting country. Professor H. Mayr has also passed away, and his loss was deeply regretted by this Society. When we were in Bavaria, he acted as our guide and showed us the different kinds of forest and systems of forest management which exist in that country, where forests have long been managed on scientific lines. He also visited us in Scotland, and admired the possibilities of our country for tree-growth and afforestation. We deeply regret the loss of these two distinguished foresters, but as time goes on, we are always adding to the strength of the Society, and never has it been so strong in members and Honorary Members as it is at the present moment. I hope the day is not far distant when some of the great Continental forestry societies will find it worth while to visit us, and that we shall be able to show them a rising forest industry based on the lines advocated by our Society. It is by the meeting of kindred spirits and the exchanging of ideas that progress is made. It is not necessary for me to mention individually our distinguished foreign guests, but it is well within the limit to say that there is no forest condition in Europe but is understood by one or other of our guests—from north, south, east and west. Our Indian and Colonial friends bring to us the result of their experience and knowledge from other parts of the world. When we have our complete records written up, I am perfectly sure that the work of the Society during the year of its Diamond Jubilee will have gone as far as and further than any other development which this Society has promoted or achieved. It is a great honour to have these new names on our list of Honorary Members, and I have much pleasure in proposing the toast of 'Our Guests.' We regret parting with them. We wish them a successful journey to their different homes, and hope to meet them again at some future time. I have much pleasure in asking you to drink heartily to the health of our distinguished foreign, Indian, Colonial and home guests, associated with the names of Dr P. E. Müller, Denmark, and Mr R. H. Campbell, Canada."

Dr Muller then addressed the gathering in French, as follows :—

" Mr President, My Lords and Gentlemen, in my capacity as senior representative of the foreign delegates, there falls to me the honour of expressing to our hosts our warm gratitude for the unforgettable days which we have passed in your ancient and beautiful land. In renewing the congratulations already presented by us on the occasion of the sixtieth anniversary of your august Society, I beg you to believe, gentlemen, that your guests will always keep in their hearts the memory alike of the cordial hospitality which has been offered to us here, and of the beautiful and impressive scenery of Scotland. With these pleasant memories will always be associated admiration for your venerable Society, which devotes itself to the enrichment and embellishment of your fatherland, and above all to the afforestation of the Highlands—a task worthy indeed of Scottish energy. Accept, gentlemen, for all our heartiest thanks!"

M. Pardé, speaking in French, said:—"My Lord Provost and Gentlemen,—My ignorance of the English language, of which I am really ashamed, compels me to express myself in French; I beg you to excuse me, and in order to merit your pardon I will be very brief. I only wish to tell you how much I have enjoyed the time which I have passed in your company in visiting your country, examining your woods and seeing your trees. Your country, gentlemen, is superb; your lakes and mountains possess a beauty, derived from their dark-blue tint, which I have seen nowhere else. Your woods, also, have a great deal of artistic beauty; indeed, in opposition to what is too often seen in France, it sometimes seems as though you had considered their æsthetic beauties rather than their financial returns. As to the trees, one may say that Scotland is a veritable museum; native and exotic species are represented in many places by magnificent specimens whose perfect health and great size I have much admired. You love trees, gentlemen, and that is the first requisite for a forester. The days which I have just passed with you will always remain fixed in my memory as the most agreeable and interesting of my life. In the name of my colleagues, the delegates for foreign countries, as well as on my own account, I wish to express to you our very deep gratitude for your hospitality, which you must allow me to call 'Scottish,' because in my own country this word expresses hospitality of the widest and most cordial character. I also wish to thank most sincerely the Lord Provost and the Municipal Councillors of Edinburgh, one of the most beautiful cities in all Europe, for the hearty reception given us this morning. I drink to the prosperity of Edinburgh, which combines the interest of an ancient city with all the beauties of a modern town. I also drink to the prosperity of the Royal Scottish Arboricultural Society, which ought to be a most precious auxiliary to the ·Government in the afforestation of the waste lands of Scotland, a work which will increase the riches and beauty of the country; to your President, Captain Stirling, to Sir John Stirling-Maxwell, and to the members of Council, who have shown for us an unique friendship. You will also allow me, gentlemen, in the name of my colleagues and myself, to thank your Secretary, Mr Galloway, who throughout the excursion took such pains to

carry out the difficult task of satisfying us all. Finally, gentlemen, I drink to you all, and to you all I say 'I thank you,' and
as I hope to see you again, *au revoir.* I sincerely hope that
most of you will come and visit the forests of France, where I
shall always be happy to see and to guide you."

Mr R. H. Campbell said:—"I feel very much at this moment
like imitating the example which some people say was set
by my Highland ancestor of disappearing under the table
instead of appearing above it, and it was absolutely the same
feeling that affected him that affects me, namely, modesty. It
would make a person feel very modest indeed to be called upon
to address an audience in the capital of Scotland, this ancient
capital which represents Scotland in miniature by its great
buildings, its old and solid architecture, its beauty, its romance
and its history. These things perhaps do not impress the Scotsman as much as they do the man who is away from Scotland
and ever looks back upon it; or comes to it for the first time,
after having heard many old tales of Scotland from those who
left it years before; for the love that a Scotsman has for his
country is no less in the Scotsman who goes abroad and his
descendants than in the Scotsman who remains at home.
Perhaps, in a way, it may be even a stronger feeling, for the
love is sometimes enhanced by distance, and the man who is far
away abroad looks back in an ideal fashion to the land he has
left behind.

> ' From the lone shieling in the misty island
> The years divide us, and the waste of seas,
> But still the heart is Highland,
> And seems to see the Hebrides.'

These sentiments are in the heart of every Scotsman on the
other side, whether their recollection is Highland or Lowland.
It makes me feel rather diffident, too, when I consider that I am
representing such a great country as the Dominion of Canada,
a vast extent of country undeveloped, without any great history
as yet, but making history every day.

> ' Ours is not a land of story,
> Ours is not a land of glory.'

"We have no long line of bards and sages looking down on
us through the ages, but we are trying to build up one of the
component parts of the British Empire. There is beating in the
heart of every Canadian citizen a feeling that he is very proud

of, namely, that he is not only a Canadian citizen, but that he is a citizen of the British Empire. I must not forget, however, in speaking for Canada, that I am also given the further duty of speaking for the other dominions of the Empire, and I am very ready to take the responsibility of returning thanks for the other parts of the Empire. I do not know that I would be prepared to take responsibility for the representatives of the other dominions in every respect; but I think in this respect I am prepared to take absolutely full responsibility, and to express their thanks to the Royal Scottish Arboricultural Society for the kind invitation and for the thoughtfulness which dictated the invitation, and for the splendid way in which we have been entertained since we have come to the old land. We have heard much of the beauty of Scotland, but I think every one of us will carry away from here a still stronger impression of the beauties of old Scotland. I am sure that I am expressing the sentiments of the other Colonial representatives, for they have so expressed themselves quite openly and strongly already.

" We have a very important work in this forestry work, and although it is new to us in these new countries, we can still appreciate some of the difficulties which the Royal Scottish Arboricultural Society has had to face in trying to develop forestry in this country, and in fact we can understand it very much better now, having come to Scotland and seen something of it at closer range. When we look around we begin to recognise that the difficulties here are of very much the same character essentially as the difficulties we have to face. You have referred, Mr President, to a suggestion that possibly the Royal Scottish Arboricultural Society had outgrown its name. Well, we found a little difficulty at first when we started the Canadian Forestry Association in having that name, which unfortunately in our country, was not a distinctive name, because we had there several benefit societies which had adopted the name of forestry. We have the Ancient Order of Foresters, and the Independent Order of Foresters, and when Mr Stewart, my predecessor in office, was trying to work up a little interest and to get the support of Forestry Associations, he approached a prominent gentleman, I can not be sure, but I think he was a member of Parliament, and said something to him about forestry, and wanted to get his support. There is a distinguished man of Indian blood at the head of the forestry

movement, Dr Baunitigha, and the gentleman upon whom
Mr Stewart called suggested to him that this forester would be
in town in a few days, and the matter had better be put before
him, as he was an important man in forestry! So you see the
area of ignorance we had to work upon was quite as extensive,
and perhaps as dense as it is in some quarters of the old land.
But the light is breaking. I do not wish, however, to be understood to be attempting to say that the Parliamentarians have
not assisted us and given their support, but there are
Parliamentarians and Parliamentarians. I happened to meet one
leading Parliamentarian of the Dominion when we were within a
short time of having one of our annual conventions, and I spoke
to him about it and asked him if he would attend the meetings to
be held while Parliament was sitting. " Oh," he said, " I do not
think I will attend. I think that is just a sort of a 'fad.' " I
had the extreme pleasure two years afterwards of attending a
large convention of the Forestry Association in one of the
Provinces at which a large dinner was given, and to hear this
distinguished Parliamentarian, in a very good speech indeed,
explain what a great and important matter forestry was, and
what a deep and personal interest he took in it.

"Therefore, although there are many discouragements and
difficulties from time to time in trying to develop and
encourage this work, there are still signs of progress and very
evident signs of progress in the Dominions. The coming
together here of the representatives of the Dominions may
possibly be, to some extent, a help to you, but it has certainly
been a help to us and greatly encouraged us. It has shown us that
we are not alone in the struggle against difficulties and problems,
because we find that here men are struggling with the same
problems, and have been struggling for sixty years, while we
have only been at it for ten or twelve years, and we have a long
distance to go before we can catch up on the Scottish Society.
But I think that the fact of the Dominions taking up the
question of forestry is strong evidence of advancing civilisation
in those far-off regions. I think the attitude in regard to forestry
indicates this, because the view of the forester is not the view of
the moment. It is the long view, the view that does not consider
only to-day or even to-morrow, but considers the years to come and
the future generations as well as the present generation, and the
fact that that thought is getting into the minds of the people of the

Dominions is evidence that they are realising that the Dominions must be established on a permanent basis, that our industries and our development must not be haphazard and based on the exigencies of the moment, but that we must lay clear and far-sighted plans that look to the future and that will make for the development of our own countries, and, making for the development of our own countries, will make for the development of the Empire. There are two things that perhaps have struck me particularly in coming to Scotland and seeing the situation in regard to forestry here. One of them I referred to particularly this afternoon, and that is the different attitude taken by the Government towards forestry in our country to that which at present is apparently taken towards it in Scotland. In our country the Government has made the first move, and it has found some difficulty in getting private persons to follow its lead. In this country, the order seems to be reversed. For instance, we find that here it is the private person who is making experiments in regard to species of trees suitable for growing in Scotland. In Canada it was the Government that took up that work, and in fact, if the Government had not experimented quite thoroughly with different species of trees, in the Western Provinces, before they took up tree planting on farms under the supervision of the branch I represent, we would not have had the knowledge to make that enterprise the success it has been. I know Scotsmen are modest and do not like to have themselves or their fellow countrymen praised up too much, but I may say that branch of the work is practically in the hands of Scotsmen from the chief downwards. Another thing which has struck me in connection with the view taken here is the fact that you are counting on forestry to increase the population in the country. The difficulty that we run up against in Canada is the fact that when we wanted to hold land for forestry purposes we were almost denounced, in fact, were denounced sometimes, or at least it felt a good deal like that when they 'got talking' of trying to prevent population by taking lands for forestry that ought to be used for agricultural development. It has been very interesting to me in going about Scotland to see the situation and talk to members of your Society and understand their views of the situation, that development of forestry does not mean decreasing the population but increasing the population and prosperity in the country. I can go home and preach that doctrine in Canada with a great deal more confidence and heart than I could do before I came over on this occasion. Now, I do not want to detain you longer. I can only again express for myself and for the other delegates from the Dominions, and I think I speak for India too, our appreciation of the invitation we received and of the splendid reception and treatment we have received since we came. We would wish to include also our thanks to the Lord Provost of Edinburgh and the Council, for the splendid entertainment which they gave us to-day, and the opportunity of seeing some of the sights of this city, which has well been described as the most beautiful city in the world."

The Chairman said :—" I have now to call on M. Rauner, Russia, to propose the last toast."

M. Rauner said :—" I have been sent by the Ministry of Agriculture in Russia, to be the representative of the Russian Government at the celebration of your Diamond Jubilee. All that I have seen on this tour has been done by private enterprise. We Russians are accustomed to think that all that is done by your great people is done well, at the right time, and is always a success. Of course this hard work that is accomplished by your Society is done because all the members of the Society possess that remarkable energy, high scientific knowledge and love for forestry, which is possessed by your President. The Russian Imperial Minister of Agriculture sends you his congratulations on this occasion, and expresses his best wishes for the future. I am further asked by the Ministry to request you to accept this piece of plate in memory of this occasion. Allow me to drink to the health of your President, our Chairman."

The toast was then enthusiastically drunk, the gathering uprising and singing—" For he's a jolly good Fellow."

The Chairman said :—" I have to thank M. Rauner from the very bottom of my heart for the very kind words in which he has proposed this toast. I have also to thank him, and through him the Imperial Government of Russia, for this very magnificent present which they have made to the Society, in the form of a Quaich. The Imperial Government has given to the Society what I think is the first and only piece of plate which it possesses. I am sure that it will be highly prized and long kept—as long as the Society endures, and that I hope, is for ever—in memory of this occasion. I would ask Monsieur Rauner to express to his Government our most grateful thanks for the very handsome present which he has brought us on this occasion. Time is getting on, and we have all to catch trains, but I cannot come to the end of what has been a very delightful fortnight without the greatest regret, and without wishing that the many pleasant acquaintances which have been formed here may be destined to be taken up again in the future, either here or in the countries and Dominions represented by our guests."

The proceedings were then brought to a close by the singing of "Auld Lang Syne" and "God Save the King."

19. The Right Hon. Sir Ronald Munro Ferguson, K.C.M.G., Hon. Secretary, 1898-1914.

The resignation of Sir Ronald Munro Ferguson at last Annual Meeting of the Society came as a great surprise, particularly to members of Council with whom he had been conferring on the business of the Society the previous afternoon ; but when it was known that the reason for the resignation was his selection by the King for the honourable position of Governor-General of Australia, the surprise and disappointment gave place to gratification and congratulation.

To give any adequate account of the work of Sir Ronald in the interests of forestry would involve the preparation of a history of the Society for the past twenty years, as no one was more intimately connected with all the various movements that were initiated and developed during that period than he was   While it would be out of place to attempt to do this in the present article, a few of the leading facts must be briefly referred to.

It would, perhaps, be difficult to find a time when he was not interested in forestry, but the first public recognition of such interest appears to have been his appointment as a member of the Select Committee of 1887. Two years later he became a member of the Society, and began to take an active personal interest in its affairs. He became a Vice-President in 1890, and served as President from 1894 to the beginning of 1898. On his retirement from that position, he was elected to the new office of Honorary Secretary, a post which he held with great benefit to the Society and forestry, and with much acceptance to his colleagues in the management of the Society's affairs, till his appointment by His Majesty to the honourable position already alluded to.

Sir Ronald believed that example was more effective than precept. While some were pointing out that Scottish foresters were lacking in knowledge of scientific methods, he suggested that instead of confining the Society's annual excursions to home woods, occasional visits should be made abroad, and he mentioned Germany as a suitable and easily accessible country where correct silvicultural methods could be studied. The suggestion was immediately acted on, and the excursion to Prussia in 1895 was carried out with most gratifying results. It is hardly possible to exaggerate the importance to forestry of this visit, but it may be confidently said that from that date Scottish forestry, which for a time appears to have been languishing somewhat, made a great forward movement which has since been carefully fostered and maintained.

Again, when there was much talk about the need for systematic management, continuity of policy and such matters, he had a working-plan drawn up for the woodlands on his Raith estate. This plan, which was published in 1898, is understood to have been the first regular working-plan put into operation in this country. A similar working-plan for his Novar woods was prepared and published two years later. His experiments in underplanting at Novar were a revelation to the Society's Foreign and Colonial guests, when they had the opportunity of inspecting them during their recent tour in Scotland.

Again, when there was a call for facilities to enable students to take advantage of the higher education in forestry which was available at Edinburgh University, he instituted at his own expense what was known as the Raith Bursary of £30 per annum, which was awarded each year to a young forester selected on the recommendation of a small committee of the Council and the then Lecturer on Forestry. This bursary he continued for three years.

In connection with the frequent deputations of the Society to Ministers and Departments, and the preparation of the numerous Resolutions passed by the Council and the Society, Sir Ronald always took a leading part; and it was on his suggestion that Mr Hanbury, then Minister of Agriculture, appointed the Departmental Committee on British Forestry with Sir Ronald as chairman, which issued its Report in 1902 He gave valuable evidence before the Irish Departmental Committee on Forestry in 1907, and was a member of the Departmental Committee on Scottish Forestry which the Secretary for Scotland appointed in 1912. He was also a member of the Advisory Committee on Forestry, appointed during the following year by the Board of Agriculture for Scotland.

Sir Ronald's contributions to the *Transactions* of the Society included his Presidential Addresses and other speeches, as well as papers specially written on various forestry subjects.

In addition to all these special efforts, he was faithful in his attendance at Council, Committee and General Meetings of the Society when his Parliamentary duties made this possible, and he was always ready with helpful counsel and advice when difficult or delicate positions had to be considered and dealt with. It was with great gratification that members heard that the Council had resolved to offer the highest honour at the Society's disposal to Sir Ronald on the occasion of the Society's Diamond Jubilee, and of the names submitted for election to the Honorary Membership at the Conference in Edinburgh, on 10th July last, none received a heartier welcome than his.

In resigning his official connection with the Society, he gave an indication that he believed his work for forestry here was only interrupted; and it is hoped that when his term of office in Australia expires, and he resumes his place at home, he will give the Society the opportunity of welcoming him back to its counsels.

PLATE XIII.

MR ROBERT GALLOWAY, S.S.C.,
Secretary and Treasurer.

20. Mr Robert Galloway, S.S.C., Secretary and Treasurer.

(*With Portrait.*)

The Royal Scottish Arboricultural Society has never been, at any period in its sixty years' existence, in a more flourishing condition than it is in at the present time, and in a very large measure its success is due to the fact that it has, in Mr Robert Galloway, a Secretary who, in addition to his immense power of organisation, devotes untiring energy and great enthusiasm to his arduous and many-sided duties. Only those who have been brought more closely into contact with the Secretary can realise the extent, difficulty, and very often delicate nature of the work involved in the discharge of his duties. In addition to his many other good qualities, Mr Galloway possesses a great amount of real tact and skill in conducting affairs to the entire satisfaction of all concerned. The slightest murmur of dissatisfaction with his work is never heard in the Society.

Mr Galloway became *interim* Secretary in 1895, when the tide in the affairs of the Society was at a somewhat low ebb, but since his term of office began the tide has turned, and it has ever since flowed steadily towards prosperity.

It was in 1895, the first year Mr Galloway was in office, that the first foreign excursion was organised and successfully carried through. In that year Prussia was visited, and nothing could have been more satisfactory than the business-like way in which the tour was arranged. Since then Sweden (1902), France (1904), Bavaria (1909), Switzerland (1913), have been visited, and it must be admitted that nothing has tended more to broaden the views of silviculturists in this country than those foreign excursions, which have been so well organised and so successfully accomplished, thanks principally to the energy and ability of our Secretary. The home excursions have been equally well managed. The fact that the annual excursion is now such a popular and important event in the affairs of the Society, is due to the admirable way in which arrangements are made by our indefatigable Secretary for the comfort and convenience of all. The educative and economic value of those carefully planned excursions cannot well be over-estimated. The annual forestry exhibition and competitions held in connection with the Highland and Agricultural Society's Show were started during Mr Galloway's tenure of office, and here again his organising skill and devoted energy has made this phase of the Society's activities the success it is to-day. The exhibits in connection with the National Exhibitions at Edinburgh in 1908, and Glasgow in 1911, also owed their success to his efforts.

Recently a very comprehensive and business-like scheme for the formation of a company to promote forestry in all its branches was drawn up by Mr Galloway, and submitted to the Development Commissioners. Unfortunately the putting into operation of this scheme has been delayed, but on all sides this scheme is regarded as the basis of future developments.

Last, but not least, to Mr Galloway is due the entire credit for the conception and organisation of the recent Diamond Jubilee celebrations which were so successfully carried out. This was by far the most important and comprehensive forestry meeting and tour which has ever taken place in Scotland, yet not one detail in the entire arrangement was neglected, with the result that not a single hitch occurred in the entire programme, and Mr Galloway well deserved the manifold expressions of appreciation which he received for his work. In regard to his capacity as treasurer one need only refer to the sound financial condition of the Society.

From the moment Mr Galloway undertook the duties he so faithfully discharges, the affairs of the Society have prospered and its activities have increased. Our Secretary has a sound knowledge of forestry, and takes a keen interest in all that helps to forestry development. He is proud of the Society, and the Society is proud of him.

21. Landowners' Co-operative Forestry Society.

1. Speech Delivered at the Annual General Meeting by Sir John Stirling-Maxwell, Bart., Chairman.

The Reports show an advance in every direction, which reflects great credit on Mr Leslie and his staff and on our committees. The success of our undertaking cannot be entirely gauged by its financial results, but it is dependent, like other undertakings, on finance, and it is important to know that our financial position shows steady improvement. We shall not be satisfied till our trading account is self-supporting. Up to now it has had to borrow from the subscriptions, which ought to be free for other purposes, but this necessity will disappear with an increased turnover. This year the turnover has increased by 170 per cent., from £4000 to over £10,000, and Mr Leslie reckons that when it reaches the figure of £25,000, which it may easily do this year, the trading account will be self-supporting. The main thing to note is that as the business expands the profit is increasing more rapidly than the expenses. In the year under review the profit increased by 130 per cent., the expenses of management by 52 per cent. The business has now reached a point where the committee has found it necessary to abandon the provisional arrangement under which Mr Leslie has provided the office staff at a fixed sum, and the Society will henceforth have its own staff. This will entail no change in the personnel, in which we have been extremely fortunate. Before leaving the question of the trading account, I should like to point out that many of our members make no use of the Society. In some societies no members are so valuable as those who pay their subscriptions and ask no questions. This is not one of them. I believe some members refrain from employing the Society from a feeling that their small sales or purchases will give more trouble than they are worth. They forget that transactions which give a great deal of trouble to a private individual or his estate office give scarcely any trouble here where all the year's information is at hand, and where business is transacted by those who have daily experience of precisely similar transactions. This is where the advantage of co-operation comes in. The more our business increases the more our position is strengthened, with advantage both for our own members and, I may add, for those with whom we are dealing. No member need therefore scruple to entrust business to us or to ask for advice and quotations. On the other hand, members who are content to sell timber, as some do, for less than its value are not only losing money (which is their own affair) but are also undoing the work of the Society. .

This brings me to the wider objects of our Society, which aims not only at the assistance of individual members but also at the revival of an industry which on nineteen estates out of twenty is worked at a loss when it might be worked at a profit. It is not a simple case of protecting ourselves from robbery. I remember pointing out when the Society was first started that we could not make a greater mistake than that of regarding the timber merchant and the nurseryman as our natural enemies. They are really our natural allies. When an industry is at a low ebb and utterly disorganised, as forestry is in this country, every one engaged in it suffers. Every one is suspicious of the other, but we all suffer together. In other countries, where forestry is better organised, not only does the producer of timber make good profits, but the nurseryman and the timber merchant also do a thriving and necessary business. The baffling uncertainty which now overclouds all their operations is happily absent. The reorganisation of an industry is a very slow business, but even in these three years, and working on a modest scale, we have been able to prove that it is not only possible for the producer of timber to make a better bargain with the nurseryman and the timber merchant than he had usually done, but to make a bargain which is more profitable to both sides. One-sided co-operation is not likely to lead to much in a big and complicated business like this. The conferences which have been held regarding the prices of home timber as compared with those of imported timber, and especially of railway sleepers, prove beyond a doubt that co-operation between the producer of timber and the timber merchant will be profitable to both, and will lead to a great deal of business being done where now none is done at all.

It is pitiful to think how much timber in Scotland is felled in a hurry and sold below its value to merchants who scarcely know what to do with it.   The secretary gives in his report a typical example where two offers were received for one lot of timber—an offer of £800 and another of £2000.   If the offer of £800 had been accepted, as such offers frequently are, the owner would obviously have lost £1200.   Yet it is more than doubtful whether the purchaser at £800 would have made a larger profit than the purchaser at £2000.   On the contrary, experience shows that the timber merchant who knows what he is buying, how to handle it, and place it to the best advantage, is the man who both makes the best offer and secures for himself the best profit   In this difficult business knowledge and organisation count for as much as the raw material which proprietors grow and merchants harvest and sell.

In one point, surely a very elementary one, and typical of the chaotic state of the home timber market, this Society has been of great service both to sellers and purchasers of timber. This is in measuring and classifying timber offered for sale by our members.   It seems scarcely credible that anyone can propose to sell a crop of which he knows neither the quantity nor the value, but this is quite a common occurrence in forestry, even on large and otherwise well-managed estates.   It is no paradox, but a statement of fact, to say that by the mere process of measuring or classifying timber exposed for sale by our members this Society has been able greatly to increase its value.   Since it has become known that the measurements made by this Society are accurate and trustworthy, timber merchants have readily admitted the advantage, from their point of view, of dealing with clients who know what they have to sell, and have been willing to reduce the margin which they are usually obliged to allow for the disappointment caused by inaccurate estimates.   We have much reason to thank our Travelling Forester, James Grant, for his services in this respect.

I cannot conclude these remarks without pointing out that the thanks of members are particularly due to members who have served on the Nursery and Timber Committees, especially to Mr Gammell and Mr Milne Home, the chairmen of these committees.   Just as the trading business of the Society depends mainly upon Mr Leslie and his staff, so the realisation of the Society's larger aims depends mainly upon the work of these two important committees.

2. REPORT OF SECRETARY.

The work of the Society during 1913 has been continued on the same lines as in the previous year, but in many respects the conditions have improved. This has been especially marked in the case of sales of standing timber. In 1912 it was very difficult to find markets, but in 1913 the glut of blown timber had begun to work off, while trade prosperity combined with increased freights on foreign supplies gave an impetus to prices for manufactured timber, and this was reflected in the demand for standing trees.

The Society has continued the system, referred to in last year's report, of making a careful preliminary valuation before offering members' timber for sale. The former practice of selling on the strength of a rough estimate of value has been completely discarded. I would emphasise the importance of this preliminary valuation, for not only does it enable the proprietor to judge as to the offers received, but it has the still more important effect of improving those offers. As a rule, timber merchants have not time to make an exhaustive valuation, and in offering for standing timber they have to allow a margin for possible error, especially as the numbers and sizes of the trees are never guaranteed by the proprietor. If, however, they know that every tree has been separately counted and classified according to a recognised system, they can afford to reduce this margin for error and increase their offer accordingly ; indeed, in many cases they will adopt the Society's valuation as a basis for their offer even though no guarantee is given. It is gratifying to report that timber merchants have accepted without question the Society's *bona fides* in the matter of valuations, and no question has ever arisen with regard to the accuracy either of the count or the classification. In this way the Society has been of assistance to the buyer as well as to the seller, thus securing the benefits of co-operation in its best form. But in thus obtaining the confidence of timber merchants the Society has assumed a responsibility to the timber merchants themselves, and it is necessary that this confidence should not be shaken. The Society must see that buyers as well as sellers receive fair treatment, and in particular that all offers are treated as confidential ; they must spare no pains to make the particulars as accurate as possible ; they must be prepared if necessary to discuss the details of their valuations, and to modify them if on investigation they are found to be inaccurate. The Society is fortunate in having the services of a forester whose knowledge and experience enable them to draw up valuations which will stand the test of criticism. As an illustration of the accuracy with which it is possible to value standing trees, it may be mentioned that out of the eight principal lots sold since the beginning of 1913 the combined valuations amounted to £9817, and the actual accepted offers amounted to £10,007, a difference of only two per cent. The total amount of these offers do not appear in the accounts, because in many cases the price is payable by future instalments.

An important feature in connection with sale by valuation is that by this means the market for manufactured timber is strengthened. The best class of merchant is always ready and willing to give fair value for standing timber, because he will not offer for anything which he cannot dispose of to the consumer at a profit. There exists, however, another class of merchant whose trade connections are more limited. Such a man can only afford to buy if he can buy below the market price, and he uses his advantage for the purpose of underselling the legitimate trader. His own profit may be less than the legitimate trader would have made if he had bought for the full market price, or he may even lose on the transaction, but the harm he does to the market is greater than any loss he may suffer himself, for not only does the proprietor get an inadequate price for his produce, but the legitimate trader is handicapped owing to the market being flooded with cheap timber. Thus the paradox is explained that if standing timber were never sold below its value, the timber merchant would benefit as well as the proprietor. The remedy lies in the hands of the proprietors rather than in that of the merchants, for the latter cannot be expected to "buy in" lots which they do not require merely to prevent their being thrown upon the market at bargain prices, but proprietors can very easily ascertain the value of what they have to offer, and can refuse to sell below that value. The system of advertising timber for sale and accepting the highest offer is founded on the fallacy that the highest offer must necessarily be the true market value; in actual fact it may not be more than half the market value, and it will pay a proprietor to wait for a year or even more if the result produces a substantial improvement in the price. But merchants must endeavour to co-operate with proprietors in this respect, and if a lot has to be withdrawn because no adequate offer has been received the Society will inform its principal trade supporters and invite them to negotiate on the basis of a mutual valuation.

In illustration of the inadequate prices offered by merchants who hoped to pick up cheap lots, I may mention a case which was reported to me where only two offers were received : the higher offer was £2000 and the lower was £800. Had the higher offer not been received the proprietor would have accepted the offer of £800 under the impression that that was the market value of the lot.

In order that combination and co-operation may be properly secured, it is necessary that the Society should be truly representative of the landowners of Scotland. At present a certain number have declined to join because their estate management is so good that they do not require the assistance of their fellow landowners, but they do not seem to consider that their fellow landowners may require their assistance ; their experience will be valuable, and the mere fact of their names appearing among the list of members will strengthen the hands of the Society in any combined action that may be necessary.

It may be objected that if the Society limits its dealings only to the so-called legitimate traders the smaller buyers will be squeezed out, competition will be reduced, and the larger merchants will be tempted to combine against proprietors in a movement for the reduction of prices. There is no likelihood of such a result ; the small buyer will not be squeezed out, only the buyer, be he large or small, who buys below market price, and the competition of such a buyer is destructive competition, and should be got rid of in the interests of healthy trade. Combination among merchants for the reduction of prices may be attempted, but it is not likely to succeed, for proprietors can afford to play the waiting game better than merchants; it costs nothing to allow a tree to remain standing for a few years, but an idle staff and a silent mill are not things to be regarded with equanimity. The fact is, proprietors and merchants are mutually dependent upon one another, and any combination by one class to bring undue pressure upon the other will result in loss to both. A fair arrangement seems to be for the timber merchants to settle the basis of valuation.

for each class of timber, then for proprietors to sell at that value and not less.

During 1913 the Society has given much attention to the present unsatisfactory condition of the market for home timber, and in this they have been assisted by the leading timber merchants. Owing to the causes already referred to the price of home timber has been allowed to fall below its intrinsic value as compared to that of foreign timber. A report upon the subject was drawn up by the Timber Committee and circulated among the members; from this report it was shown that for manufactured Scots pine and spruce, the prices ranged from 11 per cent. to 77 per cent. less than for manufactured foreign timber from the same species of tree. This is partly accounted for by the fact that the foreigner controls the trade in the larger sizes of battens and deals used for construction, a department in which the home timber merchant cannot meantime compete with him; this, however, is not a complete explanation, for even in those classes of manufactured timber which can be equally well made of home and foreign timber (*e.g.* railway sleepers), the prices ruling for the home-grown article are far lower than for the corresponding article of foreign manufacture. The true remedy for this state of things lies in standardising the price of standing timber by the method already indicated, but concurrently with this movement something might de done by drawing the attention of merchants to the need for combined action for improving the prices of manufactured home timber. The Society is presently in negotiation with the railway companies with a view to obtaining a fair price for home sleepers; the negotiations have not reached a definite conclusion, but it is believed that in course of time a satisfactory compromise will be arrived at. The position of the market for colliery timber is even more serious than that for railway sleepers; the trade in Scots pine and spruce pitwood has been captured by the foreigner, and it is feared will not be recovered under present trade conditions; but with regard to manufactured articles such as pit sleepers, crowns, hutch cleading, etc., which are mainly supplied by home timber merchants, the remedy lies in the hands of the merchants themselves, for the present prices are so low that it would not pay the foreigner to compete against them.

There is only one branch of the timber trade in which we need not fear foreign competition; I refer to larch. No larch timber is imported from abroad, if we except Siberian larch, which does not possess the valuable properties of the home-grown wood. We have therefore a virtual monopoly, and the price is not likely to fall to any appreciable extent unless the tree is planted on too extensive a scale, and this is not likely, for it is only in certain well-defined districts that larch will flourish. Larch pitwood is probably the most profitable crop that can be grown in our woods, and it has the great advantage of a short rotation.

Compared with Scots pine and larch the importance of other coniferous timber grown in this country is insignificant. Spruce rarely comes into the market, and when it does, it is usually so rough that it cannot be sold at a profit. Some foresters doubt whether it can be grown clean in our climate, but at least the attempt might be made, for spruce of good quality would be a móre valuable crop than Scots pine. Douglas fir and Menzies spruce have not yet established themselves as marketable timber, but they are being planted in such large quantities that a use will unquestionably be found for them by the time they reach maturity. It is important that members should bear in mind that no coniferous timber, however good its quality, can be profitably sold unless grown in large lots. Railway rates are so high that the lower-priced timbers must be manufactured on the ground, and the cost of installing a sawmill makes it impossible to deal thus with small lots. Even larch shows only a narrow margin of profit if it has to be consigned in bulk. When small quantities of coniferous timber are grown on adjoining properties, an attempt should be made to market them as one lot, so as to make it worth while for a buyer to erect a sawmill. The Society is adopting this policy where practicable.

With regard to hardwoods, the market depends entirely upon quality; oak, ash, sycamore, elm command a good price if sound, clean, and of the proper dimensions; even beech can be profitably sold if it be sufficiently good, and there is a prospect that the demand for beech may improve. Sycamore and oak is most valuable when of large size. Ash, on the other hand, need not be large, and many proprietors make the mistake of allowing their ash to continue standing until long past its best.

The market for hardwoods differs from that for conifers in respect that hardwoods are not usually manufactured on the ground, but are delivered in the log, and this makes it possible to dispose of small lots provided the proprietor can arrange for felling and putting on rail.   But it will be seen that one result of incurring the outlay of consigning is to emphasise the difference between good and bad quality; a valuable log may pay the cost of transport ten times over, while inferior timber may hardly show a profit after delivery.

Very few hardwoods are being planted, and members who are able to grow ash and sycamore would be well advised to plant these species more extensively.   Beech is sometimes grown in a mixture with larch with a view to improving the larch crop, and in such cases might prove to be a valuable secondary crop, though it is doubtful whether at present prices beech by itself can be regarded as a profitable crop.

The planting season of autumn 1913 and spring 1914 has been marked by an increased demand; the following plants have been sold to members :—

Larch .	650,000
Douglas fir . .	356,650
Menzies spruce .	313,200
Scots pine . .	236,750
Japanese larch .	168,700
Willows . .	112,900
Norway spruce . .	64,200
Thuja gigantea .	44,750
Corsican pine .	33,850
Beech . .	25,200
Silver fir . .	22,000
Sycamore . .	10,950
Ash .	7,500
Maple .	6,600
Austrian pine .	5,000
Various . . .	50,100
Making a total of . .	2,108,350

The approximate value of the plants sold was £1270.   Of the foregoing plants 1,340,300 were obtained from home nurserymen, 25,000 from foreign nurserymen, 493,050 from members' nurseries, and 250,000 from the Society's own stock of 2-year seedlings.   The figures show a large reduction in plants obtained from abroad and an increase in plants supplied by members.

Where members gave their orders at the beginning of the planting season, these orders were met out of stocks selected by the Nursery Committee, and gave unqualified satisfaction, but many orders were received too late to be supplied out of the selected stocks, and it was found difficult to meet the demand either as regards quantity, quality, or price. Members are urged to give their orders early if they wish to obtain good plants.

It has been thought that the development of the trade in members' plants may be prejudicial to nurserymen. This does not appear to be the case; in fact, a large proportion of the plants sold for members were sold to nurserymen to make up their stocks. So long as nurserymen grow good plants they must remain the principal source of supply, and every encouragement should be given to them by the Society. Nurserymen are showing a tendency to be more particular as to the quality of the plants they grow, and the prices of nursery stock are becoming more standardised.

The following tendencies are to be noted :—

1. An increase in the demand for larch and Douglas fir.
2. A decrease in the demand for Scots pine.
3. A further decrease in the demand for hardwoods from 97,000 to 39,000, representing 1 hardwood for every 55 conifers

22. Notes from Oak and Beech Forests in Denmark.

(*With Plate.*)

By W. G. SMITH, B.Sc., Ph.D.,
Edinburgh and East of Scotland College of Agriculture.

The following notes were taken in the summer of 1913, during a series of excursions in Denmark under the guidance of Professor Warming and other Danish botanists.   One day the leader was Dr P. E. Müller, the veteran Danish forester, one of the guests invited by the Royal Scottish Arboricultural Society to visit forests in Scotland this year.   These notes have reference to a long series of investigations made by Dr Müller, and published in Danish periodicals, the earlier ones so long ago as 1878, so that this short communication may also serve to make members better acquainted with the work of one of the ablest of European foresters.   Some of the facts have already appeared in the English edition of Professor Warming's *Œcology of Plants* (1909), but these are somewhat dispersed throughout the book, and without direct observations in the forests one missed their importance to forestry.   Another short statement is included in *Descriptive Notes on Denmark*, a pamphlet issued to members of the International Botanical Association in 1913.   But we are most directly indebted to the leaders of the excursion in Denmark for their demonstrations on the spot, and in our own language.   The notes also form an addition to some observations—"The Vegetation of Woods,"—which appeared in this Journal in 1911.

The points may be best presented by first giving notes on woods seen, then we shall consider the wider questions raised in the papers of Dr Müller.

Near Copenhagen an example of good beech forest was visited (June 28), and it showed the following features:—The beech was tall and clean on the stem, and regeneration by young trees of all ages was in progress.   The canopy was open enough to allow of a ground-vegetation very characteristic of the older, open, good beech forests.   The plants included wood anemone, wood sorrel (*Oxalis*), woodruff (*Asperula*), nightshade (*Circæa*), oak fern, wood grasses (*Milium* and *Melica*), etc. A feature was that each of these plants formed large patches,

although in places they were more or less blended. The
absence of a mossy carpet was also a special characteristic.
This vegetation, as pointed out by Dr Müller, is an indication
of "muld" or mild humus, and the soil when examined in the
hand was seen to be grey but humous and particularly free and
crumbly, so that when you squeezed it and then opened the hand
the soil fell apart freely, and did not stick together or adhere
to the hand. The same kind of soil was seen again last August
in North Yorkshire in a wood with well-grown beech and an
undergrowth not unlike the Danish forest.

This ground-vegetation is not limited to beech forest, for in
a large oak wood in the south of Seeland (the island on which
Copenhagen stands) we noted (June 30)—oak (*Quercus pedun-
culata*), beech with numerous seedlings, elm (*Ulmus montana*),
maple (*Acer campestre*), hazel, hawthorn, with a rich ground-
vegetation which included the plants given above, also dog's
mercury (*Mercurialis*), primrose and oxlip, etc.

Referring back to the woods near Copenhagen (June 28),
in the course of the day a type of inferior beech forest was
demonstrated. The trees were neither tall nor straight, and
many of them were branched low on the stem, or several stems
arose from one root. There was no sign of natural regeneration, and the ground-vegetation consisted largely of species
recognised by P. E. Müller as characteristic of beech or oak
forest on acid humus (see Warming's *Œcology*, p. 333), such as the
fine-leaved wavy hair grass (*Aira flexuosa*), yellow cow-wheat
(*Melampyrum*) and winter-green (*Trientalis*), all common
enough in the woods of the Tay valley, Speyside, and Deeside.
The mossy carpet covering the ground was pointed out as
another indicator of raw humus. There was a marked
absence of anemone, woodruff and the broader-leaved wood
grasses. A somewhat similar condition of beech and oak
woods in East Jutland was seen two days before (June 26), with
a stronger representation of such plants as birch, rowan,
heather, blaeberry (*Vaccinium*), tormentil (*Potentilla*) and heath
bedstraw (*Galium saxatile*). The resemblance to many of our
own woods is evident.

Some of Dr Müller's experiments on the effect of lime in
improving these impoverished soils were seen in the woods
near Copenhagen. These soils are no longer profitable for
beech, and have to be planted with Scots pine and spruce.

PLATE XIV.

The effect of lime on beech (see text).

[*To face p.* 243.

The effect of lime is seen in the illustration (Plate XIV.),[1] which has the further interest that it includes the authors. The plots were laid down (May 5, 1905) in the forest (Rude Skov) within a wire-netting enclosure. The area was part of a beech forest 120 to 150 years old, and the soil had deteriorated into "mor" or acid humus. The enclosure contains four plots each about 4 sq. yards. Plot 1 (left-back plot) had the soil dug over one spade deep so that some of the mineral soil below the 2-inch coat of "mor" was brought up; when seen in June 1913 it was mainly covered with sheep's sorrel (*Rumex acetosella*), a sign of need of lime, while the beeches were few in number and small. Plot 2 (left-front) was also dug over, and received a dressing of about $2\frac{3}{4}$ cwts. per acre of burnt limestone ; this carried much the same number of beech, but larger in size, while the ground-vegetation was mainly wavy hair grass. Plot 3 (right-front), dressed with about $13\frac{1}{2}$ cwts. per acre of the same lime, carried (in 1913) a fair covering of beech varying in height up to about 3 feet high, but the presence of moss and winter-green in the plot indicated that the acid humus was not quite eradicated. Plot 4, dressed with about 68 cwts. of lime per acre, carried a full covering of beech about 5 feet high. Referring to the paper quoted, more details are available. The seeds sown on May 5 (1905) germinated quicker on plot 4, which carried (June 12) 140 seedlings as compared with under 20 on each of the other plots. At the end of June there was a more uniform germination, but plot 4 carried the larger plants. During the growing season 1905, germination continued till each plot carried several hundred seedlings, and the plots without lime and with $2\frac{3}{4}$ cwts. were even fresher looking than those with the larger amounts. The following summer, the under-limed plots (1 and 2) showed signs of falling off, until in July 1908 the number of living beech in each plot was— plot 1, 4·3 p. cent.; pl. 2, 16 p. c.; pl. 3, 61 p. c.; pl. 4, 93 p. c. During these three years larvæ, green fly and fungi had been at work, but the $13\frac{1}{2}$ cwts. of lime plot for some reason suffered worse than the others. One thing was evident that $2\frac{3}{4}$ cwts. of lime per acre was little better than no lime, and in both plots the soil had felted together again into raw humus. On the two

[1] Reproduced by permission from *Studier over Skov- og Hedejord*, III., by P. E. Muller and Fr. Weis, 1913 ; on the left Dr Muller in a cloak, on the right Prof. Weis. Photograph taken Sept. 16, 1911.

plots (3 and 4) with heavier liming the soil was loose and free like mild humus. At the time when the photograph (Plate XIV.) was taken the number and size of beech plants were as follows :—

Plot 1, no lime,   3 plants, average height $6\frac{1}{4}$ inches.

,, 2, $2\frac{3}{4}$ cwts. lime, 3 ,,   ,,   10   ,,

,, 3, $13\frac{1}{2}$,,   33 ,,   ,, $13\frac{1}{2}$

,, 4, 68   ·   ,,   143 ,,   ,, $22\frac{1}{2}$,,

Other experiments, including one on a larger scale, have confirmed the results just described. They also showed that an excessive amount of lime may be injurious on these acid humus soils, so that before beginning on a large scale it would be well to test the requirements of any particular area by a preliminary series of experiments.

The effect of the lime in these cases is not due to its direct action on the plant, but to its influence on the soil, and it is in the study of this that P. E. Müller has done much important work. The studies were made in Denmark, but as is indicated in the notes on woods, the general climate, soils and vegetation of Denmark are sufficiently like those of Britain to allow of useful comparison.

The remains of plants and animals in drier soils, away from marshes and bogs, are decomposed more or less completely and converted into various sorts of humous soils. One of the extreme types is "muld," mild humus or vegetable mould. Another type is raw humus, acid humus or the Danish "mor." These two types, "muld" and "mor" (using the Danish names), show very different characters, but between the extremes there exist all degrees of transitional soils.

"'Muld,'" in Dr Müller's own words, "consists of the mineral soil in intimate mixture with remains of plants and animals in various degrees of decomposition. The mixing is carried on in nature mainly by animals, especially earthworms. The organic refuse is quickly decomposed (in woods, as a rule, in the course of a year), and the decomposition is effected mainly by bacteria, which by energetic fermentation of cellulose and sub-division of the peptones rapidly brings the constituents of the refuse into circulation again. The nitrogenous compounds are decomposed with development of nitric acid. The natural 'muld' soil has a gritty structure and is loose, so that it is easily permeable by air and water; it reacts neutral or faintly acid or faintly alkaline. The vegetation of higher plants on this soil varies according to the warmth and light of the place, the moisture of the soil, and its content of available mineral matter." This soil, when not too deeply shaded, carries a varied vegetation like that already given for a good beech and oak forest. A full list of species will be found in Warming's *Œcology of Plants* (p. 332).

"Mor" is formed when the organic refuse accumulates as a coating above the mineral soil, the animal life being absent or for various reasons unable to carry on the mixing of soil and humus with sufficient energy. Fungi play a prominent part in the conversion of the organic refuse on the surface of the soil into humus, while bacteria play a minor part. Decomposition proceeds slowly, extending often over many decades, and during this process large quantities of humic acids (colloidal, non-absorptive, saturated humus bodies) are developed. On being carried down into the soil by rain water, these "acids" withdraw from the upper soil-layers a large quantity of soluble mineral matter (salts of iron and lime, alkaline bases, etc.), leaving the upper soil-layers leached and poor, but depositing the absorbed mineral matter at some distance below the surface, often in the form of hard-pan. The uppermost humus layer or "mor" varies, sometimes loose, sometimes felted together, but the leached layer of soil under the "mor" is always close and dense. The hard-pan layer also varies from a loose earthy texture to a hard stony crust impenetrable by roots of plants; in this latter condition it consists of grains of soil fused together by colloidal, humic compounds. A "mor" soil is always strongly acid. The soil-bacteria are greatly reduced in number, and have little power to decompose cellulose and to break up the peptones, and do not lead to development of nitric acid. In older deposits of "mor," the nitrogen is so locked up that the plants are starved as regards nitrogen compounds. Almost every species growing on "mor" has mycorhiza (fungus-roots), in which the lower organism is the main agent in acquiring nitrogenous compounds for the roots of the higher plant. The part played by these mycorhiza in supplying the mountain pine (*Pinus montana*) with atmospheric nitrogen is one of P. E. Müller's important contributions to the problem of afforestation of sandy heaths. Other workers have demonstrated the utility of mycorhiza in heather and other Ericaceæ, crowberry (*Empetrum*), and other species characteristic of "mor."

It has also been pointed out by P. E. Müller that the dominant plant association has a considerable influence on the development of "mor" and "muld" respectively. The Ericaceæ (heather, bell-heaths (*Erica*), and blaeberry, with other species of *Vaccinium*) prepare the way for malignant "mor," that is their presence, as on our grouse-moors, gradually destroys the utility of the soil for afforestation. The worst form is where heather, crowberry, and grey crackling lichens cover the ground. Where heather occurs with a covering of mosses, there is still some formation of nitrates and a better chance for trees, especially conifers and birch.

Beech, especially on dry sandy soils, favours the formation of "mor," and may convert a "muld" soil into a more or less pronounced "mor" within a single generation. This is the case illustrated in the examples of woods given above. The soil gradually becomes impoverished so that the natural regeneration of beech is prevented. This is quite distinct from the prevention of regeneration by rabbits, which might take place on a "muld" soil. Spruce and firs (species of *Picea* and *Abies*) are not so favourable for the formation of "mor." Oak and other deciduous trees with open canopy are those which best encourage and preserve the "muld" soil.

A sequence of forest periods is now recognised in Northern Europe, and this has had a great influence on the humous conditions of the soil. At the close of the glacial period the land became covered with a vegetation of low arctic plants, whose remains have recently been fully demonstrated by F. J. Lewis in Scotland. As the climatic conditions improved trees such as birch and aspen arrived, and these prepared the way for extensive pine forests; remains of birch and pine are also well known in Scottish peat-bogs, even at high altitudes. Then a segregation begins. On the soils naturally poor, or impoverished by exposure to wind and rain, or where tree-growth is checked by grazing animals and by burning the heather and old grass, the pine and birch woods have gone, and heather or a grassy vegetation has replaced them. But on the deeper and less wasted soils, oak followed the pine. The open canopy and other conditions of oak forest are all in favour of that series of processes which promote "muld" formation, and this, the best of forest soils, was made and preserved so long as oak forest retained its place. Enclosure of land for agriculture has almost exterminated the old oak forest in Northern Europe, because in it the earlier settlers found the better soils, shelter, and other conditions favourable to their needs. Another rival of the oak appeared when the beech gradually migrated northwards into the oak forests. This stage of the natural sequence cannot be followed out in Scotland where the beech is only a planted tree, so that we again quote P. E. Müller :—

"The old Jutlandic oak woods on sandy soil have in many places been able to withstand the invasion of the heath (heather, etc), and have preserved the 'muld' character of the soil for thousands of years, for they must be regarded as the direct descendants of the extensive oak woods of the post-glacial period before the late immigration of the beech. Even in historical times the woods in East Jutland have been such oak woods with 'muld,' into which the beech has migrated. Now the oak has quite disappeared as a plant association from these woods, and the chief natural tree is the beech which in its ascendency has transformed the 'muld' of the soil into 'mor,' and thus produced a condition in the humus soil which will probably no longer permit the beech wood to renew itself without the interference of man."

The influence of oak wood in accumulating and preserving the better class of humus may not be quite evident under Scottish conditions. Our native oak woods are generally coppice, whereas the reference above is to old oak forests, of which the Spessart in Bavaria is an example often referred to in works on forestry. Oak coppice, on the other hand, does not usually preserve the humus as "muld." The periodic cutting of coppice leaves the soil exposed to sun, wind and weather, so that the "muld" is destroyed. In extreme cases the soil may be exposed, and becomes crusted or loose, according to its nature. Sometimes the humus persists, but it is in the form of "mor," and the ground-vegetation includes those species indicative of raw humus. The woods in the Tay valley, for example, show all stages from "muld" through "mor" to bare soil. The same is the case in English oak woods, and in *Types of British Vegetation* (1911, . Cambridge Press) the gradual change of the ground-vegetation incidental to repeated coppicing has been recently described.

23. The Silvicultural Treatment of the Douglas Fir.

By W. STEUART FOTHRINGHAM.

I am led to make the following notes by the perusal of some accounts of Douglas fir plantations which have appeared in the *Journal of the Board of Agriculture* during 1913.

Five plantations are very carefully described, and the conditions under which they have been raised are given in great detail, also the measurements of the selected areas and volumes of timber. In all these accounts great volumes of timber per tree and per acre are recorded, but unfortunately nothing is said about the quality of the timber, I do not mean the strength or durability, but the presence or absence of side branches and consequently of knots.

All the plantations described appear to have been planted at wide intervals, which would seem to suggest a lack of sufficient plants at the time of their formation, a consideration that need not now be taken into account, as there is plenty of seed to be got in all parts of the country, and it is no more expensive to raise than any other seed. Where the plantations were not of pure Douglas that tree seems to have suppressed its nurses at an early age.

In describing the Taymount plantation, the writer says that 303 Douglas firs were planted to the acre with about three times as many larch, but the larch soon fell victims to disease; and at Llandinam the system of mixing the Douglas with the larch seems to have been followed with the same result, for the writer records that the larch all disappeared at an early age. In both cases the larch was of probably no value.

At Cochwillan the selected area contained, at the age of fifty-eight, only a little more than 100 trees to the acre, which cannot be looked upon as a full crop, and no history is given of any previous thinnings or of any mixture.

At Tortworth the trees are reported to have been planted at 10 to 15 feet apart, and at Dunster at 10 feet apart.

All these plantations give somewhat similar results, viz., large volume of timber per tree and per acre, but nothing is reported about the quality of the timber, and the question arises whether the best silvicultural methods have been adopted and the best financial results secured.

I have two small plantations here which I am taking into account in making these notes. In one, the Douglas was mixed with spruce and planted in about equal numbers at 6 feet apart; in the other, pure Douglas was planted at 3½ feet. Both these plantations are too young—14 and 18 years old respectively— to give very definite results, but they are old enough to be instructive. In the first, the result has been the practical suppression of the spruce but a great growth of Douglas of a rather branchy nature, the lower branches have been killed off but should have been killed off sooner; in the other, the trees have been too much drawn up, and a considerable thinning has had to be undertaken, and the thinnings are of no value.

After considering the above, I have come to the conclusion that the Douglas will produce the best results when planted in a pure plantation. The light-demanding larch appears to be killed out by want of light before it is of any value, and the shade-bearing spruce does not start into height-growth soon enough to hold its own. The Douglas in a suitable locality grows so fast that nothing can live with it.

The conditions suitable to the growth of the Douglas fir are well known to most foresters—there must be sufficient depth of soil and permeable subsoil to admit of a good root-formation or else the tree develops a root-system similar to that of the spruce, all on the surface, and is then easily blown down. The leading shoot is apt to be soft and easily broken by the wind. The tree will bear a considerable amount of shade, especially side shade. When the soil and subsoil admit of the formation of a good root-system the tree is not easily blown down, and when the height-growth is not too rapid the leading shoot is not so easily broken.

Having found a situation that is sheltered from the strongest winds, which are not necessarily the prevalent winds, and with a sufficient depth of soil, the next question that arises is at what distance to plant the trees, and all the other questions that arise in economic forestry are involved. The labour and cost of plants increase with the density of the plantations, and the value of the thinnings and the cost of thinning have to be taken into account. If too many trees are planted the cost of making the plantation is increased, the thinnings have to be made earlier, and they are probably of no value; if too few trees are planted the result is branchy timber and no thinnings, but expense in pruning, as at Taymount, and probably other places if an attempt has been made to get timber results.

I can only give my own experience, which is that a distance of $4\frac{1}{2}$ to 5 feet is the most economical distance at which to plant Douglas, and I arrive at this conclusion because I have found that when planted at 6 feet mixed with spruce the trees have grown too branchy, and when planted pure at $3\frac{1}{2}$ feet they have been too much drawn up.

From my own experience I think the following results may be expected:—Douglas planted on a proper woodland soil, not a garden soil, at $4\frac{1}{2}$ to 5 feet apart will cover the ground and kill off the lower branches before they have grown too strong, and at the same time develop sufficient crowns to keep them in vigorous health. Such a plantation might be left to take care of itself for about twenty years, when the thinnings would be of some value for pit props, being 4 inches or possibly 6 inches in diameter at 12 feet. Probably half the trees would have to be taken out at that time and the plantation left to take care of itself for ten or fifteen years, when half the remainder would probably have to be removed leaving the rest for the final timber crop. The second thinning might be expected to be of a size that would be suitable for fencing posts, pit sleepers, box making, and so forth. The final crop might be expected at about seventy to eighty years of age, and would be useful for railway sleepers, boarding, and all constructional purposes.

24. The Economic Disposal of Coniferous Timber.

(*With Plate.*)

By D. K. M'BEATH.

Considering the long period of time which elapses between the formation and harvesting of timber crops, there has always been an element of uncertainty as to the future profits from plantings. One of the reasons for this state of affairs is that mature woods are often left until they are "blown" or attacked by root rot, as a result of which the timber only fetches a fraction of its real value. Again, crops sometimes remain standing longer than the financial rotation would justify, *i.e.* they reach a stage when the current mean annual increment is less in value than the interest on the invested capital.

Timber merchants also are considerably handicapped by the restrictions imposed in connection with the working and removal of timber. On estates where game is reared the woods are closed to timber merchants during the shooting and nesting periods, which times are best suited for the felling and extraction of timber. Further, proprietors invariably specify that the timber shall be cleared within a comparatively short period of time. This necessitates the timber merchant converting before he has a market, transporting the material further than would otherwise be necessary, and storing it in a highly rented timber yard. Purchasers also may require to transport timber in the round, thereby paying carriage on much waste material in addition to entailing extra handling and storage.

Perhaps the most important reason, however, is that in this country timber crops are not put on to the market in the most economic manner. The usual method employed is for the forester to make an ocular estimate of the volume and value of the wood. The timber merchant thereafter, usually in company with the forester, makes a similar ocular estimate, and the valuation is arrived at by the two parties coming to a compromise. It is now generally admitted that the error limit of such ocular estimates may be as much as 50 per cent. The following is an instance of how far such a valuation may be out. Recently a leading firm of home timber merchants offered for an excellent lot of standing timber a little more than half what was actually realised for it. In this particular case a loss of nearly

£500 was avoided by making a preliminary survey of the wood. As the following description shows this consists of actually measuring the timber in the wood by making use of sample trees as indicators of its true volume. The extra cost involved in the survey is negligible as compared with the gain.

Survey of Woods.

Before profitably disposing of standing timber it is absolutely necessary to make a detailed survey of the crop. The best method of procedure is as follows :—Strips one chain wide are taken in hand along the greatest length of the wood, in these every tree is callipered at breast-height and marked on either side with chalk. For this it has been found that two men suffice for callipering with one man booking, he in addition keeping the line of the strip. The trees are entered according to species and are arranged in inch diameter-classes, *i.e.* trees between 9½ and 10½-inch diameter are classed as 10-inch trees, trees between 10½ and 11½-inch as 11-inch trees, and so on. The height of each diameter-class is also ascertained by measuring a few of the average trees in it with a hypsometer. When callipering, in each inch class, a tree having as nearly as possible the diameter and height of its class is marked for felling. These trees represent the average stems of the various inch classes, and for identification should have their diameters painted upon them.

The average trees are then felled and ringed in the middle for measurement at half their length, this being usually determined by the diameters 6, 7 or 9 inches at the small end. The stems are ringed and girthed in order to arrive at the bark allowance, which is adjusted for every third inch class. The diameters mentioned above depend on the dimensions of the timber, for example, heavy timber is usually sold down to 9-inch diameter, medium to 7-inch diameter, and light timber to 6-inch diameter. The saleable contents of these trees are then accurately obtained by means of quarter-girth measurement.

The volumes of the sample trees are booked separately and multiplied by the number of trees of the same species in each class. In this way the volume of the several species in the wood is ascertained, and therefore by addition the volume of the whole wood.

Further, the facilities for extracting timber should be noted in order that they may be specified in the notices of sale.

APPROXIMATE SURVEY.

In cases of valuation of extensive woodlands for purposes of transfer or for rating, other than on the solum value, where the greatest accuracy is not necessary, since the volume of the woodlands alters year by year, it has been found by experience that this method of approximate survey is the most suitable. It entails the callipering of all trees in the wood and arranging them according to species and diameter-classes. The basal area corresponding to each diameter is obtained, these are totalled and divided by the number of trees of each species, which gives the average basal area of the individual of each species. From these the average diameters are obtained, and trees having these diameters are selected as being the average sample trees of their species. These are felled and a stem analysis made of them by cutting into 10 feet sections. By this means, in addition to obtaining the exact volume of the stems, the current mean annual increment, as well as the periodic increment are ascertained, which latter would be available for quinquennial valuation purposes. Further, the grower would be in a position to determine the financial rotation of his crops.

From the above measurements the volume of timber in the whole wood may be ascertained by multiplying the contents of each sample tree by the number of trees of their respective species and by adding the results. This enables a producer, by sacrificing a minimum number of trees, to arrive at the value of his woods, and to set a reserve price upon them. He is then in a position to offer his woods at a time when they are most valuable and when market conditions are most favourable.

ASSORTMENT OF TIMBER.

Following upon the survey of woods a careful study of both local and distant markets should be made, in order that the timber may be assorted in the most advantageous manner possible. This would entail a knowledge of the dimensions for which there was a good demand, and also of the uses to which the timber might be put.

The number of stems and the volume of timber in each inch

class are already known from the survey of the standing wood, and the material in each is assorted according to species into the following classes:—"Heavy Timber," "Medium Timber," "Pit Wood," and "Stobwood." The first class, namely *heavy timber*, comprises in the case of larch stems of 12 inches and over (quarter-girth measurement) for which a price of 1s. per cubic foot may be obtained in the wood; Scots pine 12 inches and over (quarter-girth measurement) fetches roughly half the price of larch; spruce and silver fir of the same dimensions may realise 6d. per cubic foot. *Medium timber, i.e.* stems over 8 and under 12 inches on the side constitute the second class. For larch of this class 10d. per cubic foot is a fair price, while Scots pine and spruce realise on the average 4d. per cubic foot. A third assortment, classed as *pit wood*, is composed of timber having dimensions below that of the last class down to 3 inches diameter at the small end. This is usually sold by weight or per 100 running feet, and the following are the average prices for such material. In the case of larch there is a steady demand for 5-inch material (peeled), which may fetch a price of 30s. per ton. Perhaps the best method, however, of selling this class of material is by the 100 running feet, which may contain from 5 to 7 stems. The following are fair average prices in the West for unpeeled larch and Scots pine.

Larch.

Length.	Diameter.	Price per 100 running feet.
14 feet and upwards	7 inches	24s.
20 ,, ,,	6 ,,	16s. 8d.
18 to 20 feet	5	12s. 6d.
16 ,, 18 ,,	4	7s. 6d.
15 feet and upwards	3 ,,	3s.

Scots Pine.

Length.	Diameter.	Price per 100 running feet.
20 feet and upwards	7 inches	12s.
18 to 20 feet	6 ,,	10s.
18 ,, 20 ,,	5	6s.
16 ,, 18 ,,	4 ,,	3s. 6d.

In the above cases the purchaser does all haulage and carting.

PLATE XV.

FIG. 1.—Larch widely grown.

FIG. 2.—Larch closely grown in group.

Photo by G. P. Gordon.]

[*To face p.* 255.

For the last assortment, namely *stobwood*, there is a very good demand, especially for larch. This material consists of young poles taken from thinnings and tops of the older trees. These are cut into lengths of 5, $5\frac{1}{2}$, 6 and sometimes $6\frac{1}{2}$ feet for fencing posts, and realise from 5d. to 7d. each. The usual practice is to peel the stobs made from thinnings, and to quarter the tops of large stems in the sawmill.

In the process of assorting larch timber, special cases arise in connection with the material over 8 inches on the side. For example, the diameter limits 6, 7 and 9 inches at the small end, already referred to, are fixed in order to maintain the quarter-girth measure—so that a widely-grown tree having a fair taper when measured out to a 3-inch top may be an inch less on the quarter-girth than when taken out to a 6-inch top. As a result of this the volume and therefore price would be greatly reduced in the individual tree and in the wood.

Another case arises when comparing stems which have been widely grown with close-grown material. In the former case the trees are of the type as shown in Plate XV., A. Fig. 1, where they are seen to be slightly rougher and not so cylindrical as stems more closely grown (Plate XV., B. Fig. 2). In addition there are fewer trees per acre, although probably there is a greater volume of saleable timber. A crop in this condition allows of grazing, which in the wood represented in Fig. 1 actually brought in a rental of 10s. per acre per annum, the land before planting being let as a sheep-grazing at 6d. per acre per annum. Fig. 1 shows that such a plantation can be profitably underplanted. On the other hand, stems of the type B. Fig. 2 are lighter, more full bodied and form denser crops than the types already described. They produce altogether a better quality of timber, although as a result of the present market conditions they realise less per tree and per cubic foot. The fact should not be overlooked that woods grown close have not the same value for grazing or for underplanting.

A further point to note is that the cost of felling and logging is considerably more in the case of dense crops, in proportion to the total volume of timber per acre, than in the case of more widely-grown ones. The following example, which is taken from actual measurements and sales, indicates the difference both in volume and in price between the above two types of stems :—

Stem A.

A is a tree 12¼ inches, quarter-girth measurement, grown in the open.

A is 72 feet high at 9 inches diameter, and is of the same age and grown in the same locality as B.

A being over 12 inches on the side realises 1s. per cubic foot.

$$\text{Therefore A} = \frac{(12\frac{1}{4})^2}{144} \times 72 = 75\cdot03 \text{ cubic feet}$$

at 1s. per cubic foot = £3, 15s. 0¼d.

Stem B.

B is a tree 10 ins., qr.-girth measurement, grown in close canopy.

B is 73 feet high at 9 inches diameter, age and conditions of growth being the same as in the case of A.

B being under 12 ins. on the side realises 10d. per cub. foot.

$$\text{Therefore B} = \frac{(10)^2}{144} \times 73 = 50\cdot7 \text{ cubic feet}$$

at 10d. per cubic foot = £2, 2s. 3d.

Thus it is seen that the stem of type A contains 24·33 cubic feet more timber than a stem of type B, and is worth £1, 12s. 9¼d. more per tree than a tree of type B. The difference per acre in different woods of the two types would be infinitely greater.

OFFERING FOR SALE.

In connection with this, the question of conditions of sale arises first. It is therefore necessary to specify where the timber is offered, where the various lots are situated, the distance from a good road, railway station and consuming centre. In addition the species and number of trees are given together with their dimensions, *i.e.* length and diameter at small end as well as cubical contents. Further, all trees over 12 inches on the side are classed and lotted as *heavy timber;* trees over 8 and under 12 inches quarter-girth measurement as *medium timber;* trees under 8 inches quarter-girth measurement as *pit wood.*

As a rule there are certain obligations incumbent upon the timber merchant, for example, sites for sawing machinery for the conversion of timber are chosen subject to the consent of the grower. All operations require to be completed within a certain time. Compensation is paid for all unnecessary damage to fences, gates and shrubs, etc., and the tyres of all wood waggons and carts are required to be at least 4 inches wide.

Offers are then invited either by public tender, *i.e.* by advertising in newspapers and journals or by private tender, *i.e.* notifying selected timber merchants of the conditions of sale. In certain cases also timber is put into the market and sold by public auction.

When timber merchants receive this notice they usually come and inspect the material. As a preliminary to inspection they make inquiries regarding the supply of local labour, the local rate of wages, housing and stabling accommodation, etc.

Up to the present their method of surveying the timber has been purely by ocular estimate, which as shown before may be as much as 50 per cent. under estimated. It is often difficult to obtain the full value for timber when offered for sale on account of merchants refusing to encroach upon each other's territory. Another reason is that timber is sometimes offered for sale when the market is glutted through windfalls. The vendor should therefore know the prices which prevail in the principal distant markets as well as those in the local markets.

Measurement Allowances.

The allowances claimed by timber merchants are somewhat varied in nature. The usual bark allowance is 1 inch in 12 inches quarter-girth, rising half an inch in every 3 inches of increase in quarter-girth. This however is by no means strictly adhered to ; for example, recently 2 inches was claimed as bark allowance for Douglas fir, when on actual measurement under bark half an inch was found to be the real allowance. Timber less than 6, 7 and 9 inches diameter is classed as tops and claimed free by the timber merchant. Some time ago an offer was received for larch in which timber down to 12 inches was to be measured, the remainder of the tree to be classed as a top and to go free.

When stems are pumped the method of procedure is to estimate the length of log affected, which part is deducted from the total length so that the quarter-girth is taken higher on the trees. The purchaser then has the affected part free, in spite of the fact that it may have a greater value than the first section of equal length above the centre of the tree. Due allowances are also claimed for wind-shaken and splintered wood.

ACCEPTANCE OF OFFERS.

On the date fixed for offers to be submitted they are examined, and the highest offer should naturally be accepted. Sometimes however merchants make a higher offer than the timber is worth to them in the hope of getting larger allowances in measurement, or with a view to excluding outside competition so that they may negotiate future sales privately.

SUMMARY AND CONCLUSIONS.

The foregoing observations would seem to indicate that at the present time growers of timber in this country do not market their crops at the most opportune time nor in an economic manner. The purchasers of timber are unfortunately severely handicapped in their handling and marketing of the material by the unfair and needless restrictions imposed upon them by the growers. As a result of this they naturally offer less than the true value of the timber.

Experience has shown that preparatory to selling timber, for the benefit of all parties concerned, a survey of the crop should be made. Such a survey may take the form either of a detailed investigation or of an approximate one. This leads on naturally to the grading of the material, so that the timber is exposed for sale in a way which is best suited to the various requirements of the market. Observations go to support the contention that at present in the home market quality of timber ranks only second to large dimensions. The explanation of this is not very apparent, but the result is it may be more profitable to-day to grow coarse timber of large size than good quality material. This would seem to indicate, especially in the case of larch, that the planting distance should be extended to say not less than 6 feet and the thinnings made fairly heavy. As regards offering timber for sale, it would appear that sale by private bargain is the best method, while sale by auction is not to be recommended. On many estates at present the questions of obtaining local labour and of housing imported labour are serious problems for both grower and purchaser. Cases are known in which offers had been made and accepted for timber, but eventually the purchasers were forced to ask for an extension of the time limit, or to be relieved of the bargain, on account of their inability to find labour. Finally, as regards bark allowance, although this has become a recognised thing in the timber trade, in reality all trees should be measured over bark and no allowance made.

25. The Japanese Larch (*Larix leptolepis*).

By GEO. LEVEN.

"Will the Japanese larch ever have the same value as the European larch?" This question is often asked by people who profess to know little or nothing about forestry matters, and as often they get an answer that leaves the matter in doubt.

The above question prompts another of a speculative nature: "What is meant by 'value' as used above?" In a commercial sense, 60 cubic feet of the timber of the Japanese larch may, or may not, be of the same value as 60 cubic feet of the timber of the European larch, while, in a silvicultural sense, the former may be many times the value of the latter. The "value," in the popular sense, of the timber of the European larch has been estimated per cubic foot, in comparison with, say, spruce and Scots pine, or, according to the point of view, as regards durability, forgetful of the restricted area on which it can be grown well and with profit. The fact that spruce may yield three times as many cubic feet as the European larch on an equal area is also often lost sight of.

It is not intended here to give a definite answer to the first question above, even if that could be done at the present stage in the growth of the Japanese larch in Britain, but rather to consider the far more important point as to what position the Japanese larch is likely to hold in British silviculture in the near future. Within recent years the demand for the seed of this species has increased to a great extent, notwithstanding uncertainty as to the tree's ultimate value as timber. This in itself points to the direction in which opinion is veering, but probably, as in all other things, there is a fashion in things silvicultural. Considerable disappointment is felt in years when " crop failed " describes, in the seed lists, the result of a bad seed year. It is to be hoped that the uncertain supply will not lead to the introduction of seed from other sources to the detriment of the character of the true *leptolepis* as imported here from Japan, for, undoubtedly, it has suffered enough already through the demand for seedlings leading, to a certain extent, to forcing by means of artificial manure, in order to have them of a size large enough to transplant after one season's growth.

In a good rooting medium this method of producing rapidly a good-sized plant may have little or no bad effect on the after life of the tree, but indiscriminate forcing on all classes of soil is bound to tell sooner or later on the stamina of the plant. Numerous cases of 1-year seedlings and of 1-year 1-year transplants with bad leaders have been seen and heard of within recent years, and there is more than a suspicion abroad that undue forcing, among other evils, prolongs the growing season and does not allow of the proper ripening of the shoot. One redeeming feature of the tree lies in its ability readily to form a new leader and straighten itself up quickly, even in the first growing season, after losing the original shoot. A "pious opinion" as to what constitutes a good seedling would be out of place in an article such as this, but, undoubtedly, a sturdy, medium-sized plant with abundance of "fibre" is superior to a lanky overgrown one.

Rapidity of growth in this country is an acknowledged characteristic of this species, at least in its earlier life, and this must be taken into account in deciding the age at which it is most advantageous to plant the tree in its permanent position. This quality ought also, to a certain extent, to decide as to the position in which it should be planted. Indiscriminate planting of the European larch has taught us a lesson that ought not to be forgotten, and it is to be hoped that this knowledge will lead to better results in the case of the Japanese larch. We are told that its habitat is Central Japan, and that it attains to its best at about 2000 feet elevation. This fact ought to decide against planting it in soils and situations, near sea-level for instance, where it flourishes and grows apace, certainly, but where, from analogy, we are justified in concluding that it cannot attain to its best development. The earlier specimens planted in this country were looked upon as tender exotics, and were given situations where climate, soil, etc., combined to produce prodigious growths that could not be maintained for any lengthened period. The leading shoot, stimulated beyond the normal, could not stand erect, and this may have given rise to the impression that its leaders rambled about a good deal. The more or less sudden culmination of growth of the Japanese larch has probably also given rise to the idea that the European species overtakes it in later life, but until the Japanese species has been grown under proper silvicultural conditions for a lengthened period in this country, it would not be advisable to assume that this idea is correct.

That the Japanese species exhibits a number of characteristics, absent in the case of the European species, is now being realised where comparatively large numbers have been planted. While it is a light-demander like its relative, it is not so intolerant of shade, especially as regards the side branches. This quality will allow of its being planted much closer on the ground, in fact it clearly indicates that such treatment would be advantageous in order to curtail the gross growth of branches that results from open planting of this species, or planting in admixture with thin-foliaged species. The expense has told against pure planting on a large scale, but where it has been done the prospects are good in many respects. It is too early yet to consider if under-planting will even be necessary, but it is almost certain that a considerably larger number of stems per acre will stand to the end of the rotation than is possible in the case of its relative. No mixture seems to fit in with it in its early years, and the enormous amount of foliage it produces seems to fit it for growing as a pure crop, the fall of needles certainly acting not only as a soil preserver but as a soil improver, the layer of rich humus acting as a water absorber and as a medium through which myriad rootlets run. It possesses the undoubted quality of being a drought resister, one that fits it for planting in many soils and situations given up to probably less suitable species or carrying no crop of trees. It seems to thrive on light, warm soils equally as well as on moist, cool soils, and does not object to moorish ground.

It is perfectly hardy, in the sense of being able to withstand any degree of frost usual to our winters, but, as might be taken for granted, it is not suited any more, probably, than its relative, for planting in "frost holes." Late frosts affect it to a certain extent, but only on spots with an impervious subsoil, positions that but few species can exist in, let alone thrive. It is comparatively late in developing its shoots, when its haste in flushing its spur-leaves is taken into account. This is a most marked feature, for while the foliage appears so early that it invariably gets "browned," more or less, by late frosts, and does not seem to suffer therefrom, as already stated, the development of the shoot hangs fire to such an extent that one might almost fancy the terminal bud was dormant. It thus escapes all but excessively late frosts, such as those of June 13th, 14th and 15th, 1911, when very few trees escaped injury in some degree. Even in extreme cases it has been observed that only young trees suffer to any extent, and then nothing occurs approaching to the damage done to the European larch. An extremely short growing period seems to suffice for it, its shoots maturing long before its relative has ceased growing.

It cannot be said that the Japanese species is entirely immune from the larch disease, but this is not to be wondered at when the situations it has been planted in are taken into account. Where proper silvicultural conditions obtain there is evidence of the saprophytic *Peziza*, but this is comparatively harmless. Several examples of the parasitic form have been observed during the last few years in some of the wetter parts of Scotland, and in other positions favourable to the disease, but there has been no recorded epidemic. Systematic examination of many acres of both pure and mixed plantations has resulted in not a single example of disease being observed, where anything like proper conditions exist.

The insect enemies of this species do not appear to be either numerous or formidable, its general vigour evidently repelling to a great extent the attentions of the larch mining moth and the larch aphis; while specimens of the European species growing side by side with it have been observed to be badly attacked by both of these pests. A number of twigs on side branches of the Japanese species were observed in each of the last three years to have been attacked by the insect *Argyresthia lævigatella*, but the general health of no single tree of this species was in the least impaired, while numerous specimens of its European relative, of the same age and growing within a few yards of it, were almost completely destroyed. The leading shoots of the European species were in many instances attacked, while the leading shoots of the Japanese larch remained immune. The European larch had certainly been very much weakened by the larch disease, but it formed a remarkable contrast and spoke volumes in favour of the Japanese larch.

It is not contended that the facts noted above warrant the assumption that the Japanese larch is to revolutionise British silviculture, and that it should take the place of other species of proved value, but they at least give justification for an optimistic view being taken of its possibilities. Observations and opinions recently recorded in the *Transactions* differ in some degree from, and in one or two instances appear to be diametrically opposed to, the above, but the consensus of practical opinion bears them out.[1]

Note of Measurements of Japanese Larch.

The following measurements have been noted at 500–600 feet above sea-level :—

> 1-year seedlings, height (above ground),   4 ins.
> 2　,,　　　,,　　　　　　　,,　　17 ,,
> 1-year 1-year transplanted　　,,　　11 ,,
> 1　,,　2　,,　　　,,　　　　23 ,,
> 2　,,　1　,,　　　,,　　　,,　　27 ,,

Pure plantation, four years' growth since planting out (200 feet above sea-level) :—

> Height of four specimens—10 ft. 5 ins., 10 ft. 10 ins., 11 ft. 0 ins., 11 ft. 8 ins.

Pure plantation, seven years' growth since planting out :—

> Height, 14 ft. 0 ins., girth over bark at breast-height, $7\frac{1}{2}$ ins.
> ,,　14 ,, 3 ,,　　　　　　　　　8　,,
> ,,　14 ,, 3 ,,　　　　　　　　$8\frac{1}{2}$,
> ,,　15 ,, 0 ,,　　　,,　　　,,　　8 ,

Pure plantation, nine years' growth since planting out :—

> Height, 18 ft. 0 ins., girth over bark at breast-height, $11\frac{1}{2}$ ins.
> ,,　19 ,, 0 ,,　　　,,　　　,,　　$10\frac{1}{2}$,,
> ,,　19 ,, 0 ,,　　　　　　　　　11　,
> ,,　21 ,, 6 ,,　　　　　　　　　13　,
> ,,　21 ,, 9 ,,　　　　　　　　　$11\frac{1}{2}$,
> ,,　22 ,, 0 ,,　　　　　　　　　11　,

[1] [In the present state of our knowledge concerning the silvicultural characteristics of the Japanese larch in this country, it may be well to keep in mind that this species, like all others, is bound to vary according to soil, climate, altitude and exposure.

In the meantime, we have no reason to doubt the accuracy of the "observations" or the correctness of the "opinions" expressed by our different contributors. More data, such as those so ably supplied by Mr Leven, are required before it would be safe to draw general conclusions.—HON. ED., *Trans.*]

Mixed plantation (Scots pine, European larch, spruce and Japanese larch), Japanese larch dominant, sixteen years' growth since planting out :—

Height, 31 ft. 2 ins., girth over bark at breast-height, 1 ft. 8½ ins.

,,	31 ,, 8 ,,	..	,,	2 ,,	0½ ,,
,,	32 ,, 2 ,,			1 ,, 10	,,
,,	36 ,, 2 ,,			2 ,, 2	
,,	36 ,, 8 ,,			1 ,, 8 ,,
,,	37 ,, 4 ,,			2 ,, 0½ ,,

26. The Sitka Spruce in Ireland.

By A. C. FORBES.

The value of Sitka spruce for planting on the exposed sites and wet soils which occupy so large a proportion of the surface of Ireland can scarcely be overestimated. Short of actually submerged ground, no degree of moisture appears to be too much for this species, and it bears the salt-laden winds of the Atlantic as well as, if not better than, any tree capable of growing in the low summer temperatures which characterise this part of the United Kingdom. While common spruce will bear wet ground, it cannot thrive in very exposed places. Corsican and Austrian pines stand wind well, but dislike wet soils for any length of time, and before the introduction of the Sitka spruce it was difficult to find a conifer which could give a satisfactory return on many sites with which the planter has to deal along the western seaboard of Ireland or Scotland. *Pinus insignis* and *Pinus maritima* have been planted more or less generally during the last fifty years, and leave little to be desired as regards rate of growth and resistence to exposure ; but the branches of the former cannot stand against gales unless planted in thick masses, while the stems of the latter are invariably crooked and curved at the base. Sitka spruce possesses neither of those defects, its branches being seldom broken or damaged, while a leaning or crooked stem is practically unknown. Another disad-vantage attaching to the two pines is the difficulty in transplanting them successfully on exposed ground after they have attained a foot or more in height, while small plants are difficult to keep clear of weeds and grass. Sitka spruce, on the other hand, can be transplanted with perfect safety when from 3 to 4 feet in height, although sizes varying from 1 to 3 feet can usually be used in any class of soil—the advantage of large plants being greater freedom from spring frost damage, and injury from rabbits.

The seedlings, being exceptionally slow in growth during the first two years, are difficult to handle, and the best results are usually obtained from thin-seeding and leaving the seedlings in the seed-beds for two or occasionally three years, or until they have reached a height of 6 inches. If transplanted into nursery lines then, they will be fit for planting out at any time after the second year from the seed-bed, according to the situation of the land to be planted and the surface vegetation it carries.

The only serious enemy of the Sitka spruce hitherto observed in Ireland is a species of aphis, apparently identical with the one found on the common spruce, and usually known as *Aphis abietina*, Walker. In the winter of 1912-13 Sitka spruce all over Ireland were attacked by this insect, and it looked at one time as if permanent injury might result from the attack. The aphides were first noticed about November scattered over the needles, and during the winter they increased considerably in numbers until the whole of the shoots of many trees were covered with the pest. The effect on the needles was not noticed particularly until the following February or March, when they acquired a sickly mottled appearance and fell off in large numbers, some trees being quite bare before the new growth commenced at the end of April. The effect upon the summer growth varied a good deal, vigorous trees apparently being little the worse, while weakly individuals made little growth, and an occasional one died altogether. Soil and situation, however, had no great influence upon the attack, plants growing in moist and deep loam suffering almost as much as those in poorer soils, although the final effect upon the former was naturally less. By the end of April few traces of aphides could be seen, although the young needles of 1913 were not entirely free. A great feature of the attack, however, lies in its continuing during the winter and early spring months, with a certain amount of multiplication from November to March.

In the present year, 1913-14, few traces of the insect have been seen, and it is evident that no serious injury has been done. To what this immunity is due it is difficult to say. Both winters were equally mild, and until the life-history of the aphis has been thoroughly worked out, its economic importance with regard to this valuable timber tree must remain undecided.

NOTES AND QUERIES.

THE INDEX.

Owing to the initiative and generosity of the Earl of Crawford we are able to publish in the present issue a detailed index of the *Transactions* for the past sixty years. This will greatly increase the value of the past issues by rendering their subject-matter more readily available for reference. The index appears at a very appropriate time in the history of the Society, as it shows in a striking way the remarkable activity which has prevailed in the Society concerning all phases of forestry for the past sixty years.

The Society is under a deep debt of gratitude to the Earl of Crawford for this generous gift, which will be of great use and practical value to the Society, and to all those interested in forestry and forestry literature.

SCARCITY OF PITWOOD.

In consequence of the war imports of pitwood have ceased, and supplies must now be got from home woods if the collieries are to be kept going. Conferences between Colliery Owners and Timber Merchants have been held at the Board of Agriculture, at which the Society and the Landowners' Co-operative Society were represented, and committees are now endeavouring to simplify specifications and fix suitable prices, and to obtain information regarding available supplies of material and labour where the latter is scarce. The Board has also conferred with the Railway Companies with the view of securing a reduction in railway rates. Members who may have pitwood available should send their names to the Secretary, who will gladly forward further particulars when these are ready.

FOREST PESTS.

THE GREEN SPRUCE APHIS (*Aphis abietina*, Walker). Reference is made elsewhere, in Mr A. C. Forbes's article (p. 265), to this aphis. It is known both in England and in Ireland as an occasionally harmful species on the genus *Picea*. It has proved most harmful on Sitka spruce. I am anxious that the distribution of this aphis in Scotland should be worked out, and for this purpose would welcome examples of aphis found on *Picea excelsa* or any of the other species of spruce. The best way in which to send the specimens would be to place some shoots containing the aphis in a cleaned out mustard or cocoa tin.

THE LARGE LARCH SAWFLY (*Nematus erichsoni*). This is one of the insect enemies scheduled by the Board of Agriculture and Fisheries. Its distribution in Scotland is not well known. Our Scottish foresters could settle this matter in a season. The caterpillars of this sawfly are found only on *Larix*. I would willingly send a specimen of the caterpillar to any of the members of the Society who have opportunity of making observations on larch. The caterpillar is easily recognised by the following characters:—Head, black. Body, grey-green. Legs, twenty in number; the front six black, the others grey-green. The caterpillars should be looked for in July and August. Any records received will be duly chronicled in the *Transactions*.

R. STEWART MACDOUGALL.

THE OLEORESINS OF SOME WESTERN PINES.

The shortage in the supply of the better qualities of turpentine in recent years, and the steadily increasing demand, has naturally directed attention to the possibility of increasing the sources of supply at present available.

In the Forest Service *Bulletin*, 119, 1913, an account is given of such an investigation carried out by the Forest Products branch of the U.S. Department of Agriculture.

Owing to the rapid decrease in the supply of Longleaf pine and Cuban pine, experiments were carried out to see if the various species of western pine yielded a turpentine of commercial value. The following species were examined:—Western yellow pine (*Pinus ponderosa*, Laws.), grown in Arizona; western yellow pine, Digger pine (*Pinus Sabiniana*, Dougl.); lodgepole pine (*Pinus contorta*, Laud.); and sugar pine (*Pinus Lambertiana*, Dougl.), grown in the Sierra National Forest in California; and Piñon pine (*Pinus edulis*, Engelm.), from the Montezuma Forest, Colorado.

The trees were tapped by the "cup system" and the samples

of oleoresin conveyed to the laboratory for examination. The crude resin was distilled with steam, and the amount of turpentine and rosin which it contained determined by the usual methods. Of the various turpentines examined that from the western yellow pine (Arizona) agrees most closely in its composition and properties with ordinary turpentine. The oil from the Californian yellow pine differs more in composition from ordinary turpentine, but it is suggested that both the California and Arizona turpentine could be used in the place of ordinary turpentine. Further tests of their behaviour in actual practice will be necessary before this statement can be accepted. The product from the Piñon pine resembles ordinary turpentine, but has an unpleasant smell, which is not entirely removed by distillation. The volatile oil from the Digger pine does not at all resemble turpentine, but consists largely of a hydrocarbon (Heptane), a normal constituent of petroleum. While it cannot take the place of turpentine, it is suggested that it might be used as a solvent. The yield of crude resin from the sugar and lodgepole pines is so small that their turpentines will hardly become commercial products.

ALEX. LAUDER.

Prices and Supplies in the Timber Trade.

From the fortieth annual special issue of the Timber Trades *Journal* we learn that the wood trade was generally of a more remunerative character than had been experienced for several years past, and that the optimistic references to the present year's prospects betoken a confidence in the stability of prices.

The chief feature of the present moment is the course of the white wood market. The demand for pulp wood is increasing at such a rate that the price of white wood approximately equals that of red wood, and, as the demand will still further increase, white wood must appreciate still more in value in the near future.

From an article on the "Development of wood pulp production," we get some insight into the enormous quantity of timber used in the production of pulp in Sweden in 1911.

To obtain the 896,650 standards of sawn and planed wood shipped from Sweden in that year about 280,000,000 cubic feet of raw material was required. For the production of the

576,200 tons of chemical, and the 147,800 tons of mechanical pulp shipped from Sweden in the same year no less than 150,000,000 cubic feet were required, or over fifty-three per cent. of the quantity needed for the saw-mill industry. If (the article goes on to say) it is borne in mind that the sawn and planed white wood shipped is only about forty per cent. of the whole sawn and planed wood manufactured, and that to produce this only about 112,000,000 cubic feet in form of logs was required, whereas more than this cubic quantity of raw white wood was required to provide the mechanical and sulphite wood pulp produced, the rise in the value of sawn and planed white wood is easily explainable. It may, in fact, safely be asserted that the requirements of the mechanical and sulphite pulp works now dominate the white wood market, and not the saw-mills, more especially in the narrow sizes. Further, the means of production in the pulp trade are continually being augmented, whereas the contrary is the case with the saw-mills.

How the pulp trade has undermined the prop and pitwood trade is seen from the following—"In 1890, for example, the shipment of props from Sweden (almost exclusively to Great Britain) amounted to 176,458 standards; in 1900 it reached 324,514 standards, but gradually dropped after that until in 1911 the shipment only amounted to 151,839 standards." Evidently it has been the demand of the pulp mills that has been at the bottom of this reduction.

The bulk of the prop trade will be done by Russia and Finland in the near future.

The article concludes with a plea for the afforestation of waste lands in Scotland in the following terms :—In view of the fact that in the naturally reproduced forests of Scandinavia, Canada, and Newfoundland, the cubic quantity of wood on a given area is not even one-third of what the planted woods of Scotland contain, according to the assertion of one who had many years' practical experience of saw-milling in each of these countries, it seems certain that most of the waste lands of the United Kingdom would now pay well for re-afforestation if this can be effected for not exceeding £4 per acre. This has been done in many cases in Scotland, at all events, and the subject ought to be pressed forward without delay. There can be little doubt that there will be a serious dearth of wood in Norway and Sweden before many years are passed, and it will be risky relying altogether on Russia and Finland for the supply of building and mining timber.   GEO. U. MACDONALD.

CREOSOTING TREE STUMPS AGAINST PINE WEEVIL.

It may be of interest to members of the Society to learn of our method at Dawyck of combating pine weevil, from which in past years we have suffered severely. We formerly barked the stumps of felled trees in the area to be replanted and found this fairly satisfactory, but we now creosote the stumps, and so far this has been entirely successful.

Three years ago we felled 100 acres of wood, which consisted for the most part of larch but contained considerable numbers of silver fir, Scots pine, and *Pinus montana*. The wood was very thin, and the stumps to be treated numbered about 6000. We heated the creosote on the ground and poured it hot on each stump, being careful that the sap-wood should be well soaked. As the stumps were green we found that they absorbed the liquid very freely. The cost of the operation was small. 360 gallons of creosote were used, costing 4½d. per gallon delivered at Stobo Station; carting, say 18s.; one man's labour for five weeks, say £6; the total cost thus amounting to £13, 3s., or a trifle over ½d. per stump.

We have scarcely found one pine weevil in the whole area since, and have satisfied ourselves of the efficacy of our method. The fact that the life of the stumps is somewhat prolonged is of no consequence.   F. R. S. BALFOUR.

JAPANESE LARCH.

In view of the promising manner in which the Japanese larch has been growing during the past fifteen years or so since its introduction to this country as a forest tree, it is becoming of increasing interest and importance that we should have, if possible, more definite information regarding its native habit, especially in regard to the length of time it takes to reach maturity.

The account given of this tree by Messrs Elwes and Henry, though full of interest, is somewhat lacking in definite details. Mr Elwes, when visiting Japan, "saw no larches felled, and was therefore unable to count the rings." Now that we have experience of the vigour of its growth, we have learned that it ought to be planted "pure"; but during the failure of seed in recent successive seasons it sometimes became necessary to "beat up" with the European variety, and in thinning and pruning plantations the problem sometimes arises and will arise more frequently as growth increases—If a choice has to be made of either European or Japanese, which should be sacrificed? The European larch is subject to disease; but though the Japanese is (here, at any rate) free from disease, its very extravagance of growth seems to foretell a too early maturity for it to compete with its rival in height and diameter and value as timber. Moreover, some of us, aware that the tree was in its experimental stages, did not feel safe in trusting to a "pure" planting, and (wrongly, as we now know) planted it "mixed." Thus the problem is becoming increasingly imminent as regards individual young trees, whether or not to destroy the adjacent Japanese larches, and so save the slower-growing European.

Can any reader supply details as to its native habit, so that we may be guided more clearly?

HUGH SHAW-STEWART,
ARDGOWAN.

NOTES RE ACETONE.

Acetone, so much used in the manufacture of smokeless powder, can be obtained from different sources, but the main supply comes from the dry distillation of acetate of lime, and this in its turn comes from the dry distillation of wood.

According to the kind of wood used and its dryness, the amount necessary to produce a final quantity of 1 ton of acetone varies between 34 and 70 tons. It is very difficult to get exact figures as to the amount of acetone used in this country, as it is sometimes imported as such both from the Continent and from America, and is also manufactured in this country from acetate of lime imported from the same sources. But as acetate of lime is also used in large quantities for making other products than acetone, its importation cannot be taken as a guide. I understand, however, that the demand is under 5000 tons per annum. This would entail a supply of wood of 170,000 to 350,000 tons of wood per annum.

It would, in my opinion, add greatly to the security of this country in time of war if they could count on a small supply of acetone (say 500 tons per annum) made from raw materials, none of which required to be imported, whereas just now *all the finished acetone, or the raw material,* requires to be imported and stands the risk of capture on the seas in time of war.

W. D. ASHTON BOST.

OBITUARY.

SIR JOHN RAMSDEN, BART.

We regret to record the death of Sir John Ramsden, Bart., which took place at his Buckinghamshire seat, Bulstrode Park, Gerrards Cross, on the 16th of April last. The deceased baronet was the oldest member of the Royal Scottish Arboricultural Society, having joined in the year 1855. He succeeded his grandfather in 1839, and entered into possession of the Ramsden estate on coming of age. The town of Huddersfield was built on the Ramsden estate, and for three centuries the family has been closely associated with this important centre of industry. Sir John entered Parliament at the age of twenty-two, and represented various constituencies for a period of twenty-four years. At one time he held the position as Under Secretary for war, under Lord Palmerston.

In 1871 he entered into possession of the estate of Ardverikie, on the shores of Loch Laggan, where, on the 29th of June 1910, he received and entertained the Society during the Lochaber excursion. On that occasion the members of the Society were privileged to see a splendid example of what can be done by extensive planting at altitudes between 800 and 2000 feet, where an area of 10,400 acres had been planted since 1873.

The operations involved in this extensive scheme of afforestation gave employment to eighty men, from the year 1872 to the year 1890. Since the latter date a staff of forty men has been kept in steady employment. For the first few years an average of two million trees, chiefly Scots pine, was planted. Scotland, and especially the Royal Scottish Arboricultural Society, will not easily forget the deep debt of gratitude it owes to Sir John Ramsden, whose broad-minded enterprise and pioneer work will be a lasting tribute to his memory.

Royal Scottish Arboricultural Society.

Instituted 16th February 1854.

PATRON:

HIS MOST EXCELLENT MAJESTY THE KING.

PROCEEDINGS IN 1914.

THE ANNUAL MEETING.

The Sixty-first Annual Business Meeting of the Royal Scottish Arboricultural Society was held in the Goold Hall, 5 St Andrew Square, Edinburgh, on Saturday, 7th February 1914, at 11 A.M. Captain ARCHIBALD STIRLING of Keir, President, in the Chair. There was a large number of members present, including Mr John D. Sutherland who represented the Board of Agriculture at the meeting.

APOLOGIES.

Apologies for absence were intimated from the Rt. Hon. R. C. Munro Ferguson, M.P.; Sir Andrew Agnew; Dr John Nisbet; and Messrs W. Steuart Fothringham, Robert Usher, J. F. Annand, A. T. Gillanders, James Kay, and others.

MINUTES.

The Minutes of the General Meeting held at Paisley on 9th July last, which had been printed and circulated amongst the members, were approved.

ELECTION OF HONORARY MEMBER.

The CHAIRMAN said: "The first business on the paper is the election of Dr J. Coaz, Inspector-General of Forests in Switzerland, as an Honorary Member of the Society. I am quite sure all of those members who took part in the tour of Switzerland last year recognise the extraordinary trouble and care which had been taken by the Swiss authorities in arranging the tour for the Society, and it was thought a very fitting mark of gratitude on behalf of the Society that we should award the greatest honour which it is in our power to bestow, that is our honorary membership, on Dr Coaz, the venerable—and I may call him venerable, for his age, I believe, is over 90 — Inspector-General of Forests for Switzerland. I have great pleasure in proposing that " The proposal was carried with acclamation.

REPORT BY THE COUNCIL.

The SECRETARY read the Council's Report, as follows :—

Membership.

As usual the membership has fluctuated considerably in the course of the year, but shows again a slight increase. The number reported at last Annual Meeting was 1416. There have been added to the Roll in the course of the year 103 names, but 94 have been removed either on account of death, resignation, lapsing or other cause, and the total number at this date is 1425. Amongst those removed by death were Mr Thomas Ogilvie ; Mr H. J. Younger of Benmore ; Mr J. Grant Thomson; Mr James Donaldson ; Mr John Methven; Mr Trotter of Bush ; Lord Avebury ; the Duke of Sutherland ; Mr George Malcolm ; Mr Weir of Kildonan ; Mr Robert Lindsay ; Mr J. W. Hope of Luffness ; Sir W. O. Dalgleish, Bart.

Essays.

In response to a notice issued with the January *Transactions* of last year inviting members to send in papers for competition, six papers were received and submitted to the Judges. Two only of these were awarded medals—the other four being below the standard expected. Certificates were issued along with the medals. An invitation in a similar form has been issued with this year's *Transactions*, and it is earnestly hoped that there will be a larger number of papers of a higher standard submitted in the course of the year.

Donors.

The thanks of the Society are again due to the DIRECTORS of the Highland and Agricultural Society, for voting £20 to be expended in prizes for exhibits of home-grown timber in their Show at Hawick. Hearty thanks are also due to Dr J.

Coaz, Inspector-General of Forests for Switzerland, for presenting to the Library eleven volumes on Forestry, as detailed in the usual List appended.

Editorship.

Dr Borthwick has acted as Hon. Editor during the year with much acceptance. He was able to arrange with Dr Marion I. Newbigin—who assisted Colonel Bailey—to continue to act in that capacity, and he also secured the continued co-operation of Mr A. G. Hobart Hampden and Mr Bert Ribbentrop in connection with the preparation of the French and German notes respectively.

Transactions.

There are still a number of members who unfortunately fail to obtain full advantage of the *Transactions* by omitting to forward their subscriptions at the proper time. It would be a great advantage to the Society if this list could be reduced.

It is proposed that the detailed Index to the *Transactions* issued during the past sixty years should be published in the course of the current year.

Local Branches.

The reports from the Aberdeen and Northern Branches will be submitted in the course of the meeting.

Exhibition at Paisley.

The annual Exhibition of Forestry within the Highland Society's Showyard was held at Paisley last year. The local members of Committee, who contributed largely to the success of the Exhibition, were Messrs G. P. Gordon, Whitton, Singer, Farquharson, J. Forbes, Young and Bryden, and they were very efficiently helped by Mr Samuel Houston, who was very kindly lent as Attendant by the Glasgow Corporation It will be remembered that Mr Houston was in charge of the Society's Forestry Section at the recent National Exhibition in Glasgow, a duty which he carried out to the entire satisfaction of the Exhibition Committee. The catalogue contained 92 entries in all—62 of these being articles in competition and 30 articles for exhibition only. An exhibit which attracted much attention was that provided by the Landowners' Co-operative Forestry Society of home and foreign manufactured timber with relative prices. The report of the Exhibition, written by Mr G. P. Gordon, will be found on page 97 of the January part of the *Transactions*. The Judges were Mr John Boyd, Inverliever, Mr John M'Gregor, Ayr, and Mr G. P.

GORDON, Glasgow. Twenty-three money prizes and eleven medals were awarded. The prize list is included in the "Proceedings" of the General Meeting appended to the January part of the *Transactions*. The Schedules for the next Exhibition, which is to be held at Hawick, have been issued.

For the first time a Certificate, signed by the President and the Secretary, was issued to all prize winners along with the money prizes and medals.

Nursery and Plantation Competitions.

The second of these competitions was held within the Highland and Agricultural Society's Show District last year, which included the counties of Argyll, Ayr, Bute, Lanark and Renfrew. The number of entries was smaller than in 1912, and consisted of three nurseries and nine plantations making twelve in all. On this occasion the plantations were divided into seven classes—three being for conifers not exceeding 10, 20 and 40 years of age respectively, and not less than 2 acres in extent, confined to estates having less than 300 acres of woods; and three for conifers in similar age-classes, not less than 5 acres in extent confined to estates having more than 300 acres of woods; and the last being for plantations mainly of hardwoods not exceeding 35 years of age, and not less than 2 acres in extent. The prize offered in each class was a Silver Medal. A detailed list of the awards will be found in the "Proceedings" appended to the January part of the *Transactions*, and from this it will be seen that eight medals were awarded. A full report by Dr BORTHWICK and Mr G. U. MACDONALD, who again acted as Judges, is printed on page 110 of the *Transactions*. Particulars for this year's Plantation competition have been issued to all members, and entry forms can now be obtained from the Secretary. This year's district embraces the counties of Berwick, Peebles, Roxburgh and Selkirk.

General Meeting.

The General Meeting was held in the Showyard at Paisley, on 9th July 1913, when the reports of the Judges on the Essays, Exhibits at the Exhibition, and the Nursery and Plantation Competitions, were submitted. A report of the proceedings will be found appended to the January part of the *Transactions*.

Annual Excursion.

The Excursion last year was held in Switzerland, being the fifth occasion on which the Society has made a tour abroad. As usual the preliminary arrangements were made through the Foreign Office, and subsequently negotiations were carried on direct with the British Embassy in Berne, through whom a programme, prepared by Dr Coaz, Inspector-General of Forests for Switzerland, was obtained. The Swiss Forestry Department also very kindly secured hotel accommodation and made other arrangements for the party. About sixty-six members took part in the Excursion. The programme was divided into two parts so as to permit of members, who could not stay the whole time, breaking off at the end of the first week, but very few took advantage of this arrangement. The whole arrangements made by the Swiss authorities were excellently planned, and were much more economically carried out than had been expected, with the result that a very substantial balance will be added to the Excursion Fund, and will be dealt with in connection with the Diamond Jubilee celebrations, as explained below. Owing to some outstanding questions with the Continental Railway Companies the accounts are not yet closed, but they will be submitted to the Auditor in the usual way as soon as possible. The party left Edinburgh for London on Thursday, 10th July, and travelled *via* Folkestone and Boulogne, Paris and Bâle, and made the return journey by Brussels, Ghent, Ostend and Dover, reaching London on the night of Thursday, 25th July, and Edinburgh the following morning. On the return of the party, the thanks of the Society were duly conveyed to the Swiss Forestry authorities and other officials, both directly and through the Foreign Office. Thanks were also conveyed to the British Minister in Berne and the British Consul in Zurich, both of whom rendered the members great service. A detailed account of the Excursion, written by Mr G. P. Gordon, appears in the January *Transactions*. As mentioned in last annual report, the Council decided to offer three bursaries of £10 each, to enable three Foresters to take part in the Excursion. For these bursaries six applications were received, and the Committee finally selected the following :— Mr George Mowat, Mr W. H. Whellens, and Mr J. G. Singer. These three duly attended the Excursion, and submitted satisfactory reports upon it, which are being circulated amongst the members of the Committee.

Malcolm Dunn Memorial Fund.

The two remaining volumes, being the sixth and seventh, of *The Trees of Great Britain and Ireland*, price £5, 5s., and also a copy of Messrs Bartholomew's *Survey Atlas of Scotland*, price £2, 12s. 6d., have been purchased and added to the Library during the year. It is now proposed that the former work should be suitably bound, with the plates inserted in the appropriate places in the letterpress, at a cost of about 14s. per volume.

Library.

The usual list of additions to the Library will be found at the end of the "Proceedings."

Forestry Congresses at Paris and Ghent.

The Society was duly represented at these Conferences, and the Official Reports of the Paris Congress have been received and added to the Library.

Deputation to Railway Companies.

A deputation, consisting of members of this Society, of the Landowners' Co-operative Forestry Society, and of the Timber Merchants' Association, waited, by arrangement, upon representatives of the Scottish Railway Companies, in Glasgow, on Friday, 28th April last, and discussed with them the question of the prices of home-grown railway timber, and pointed out the grievance under which growers of timber in this country suffered by obtaining a smaller price for their home-grown railway timber than the Railway Companies were paying for foreign railway timber of the same quality. A detailed report of this Conference was printed on page 188 of vol. xxvii. of the *Transactions.* Although the Railway Companies made no formal promise of alteration in their policy, more favourable terms have since been offered by Railway Companies for home-grown railway timber.

Development Commissioners' Third Report.

This report was issued in the autumn, and the part dealing with Forestry has been reproduced in the January *Transactions.*

Forestry in the West Highlands.

This Committee met in the course of the past year, and considered a number of suggestions as to how interest in Forestry might be aroused, and prejudice in the West Highlands removed. It was generally recognised that this could best be done with the co-operation of the officials of the three Agricultural colleges with such active support as the members of the Society could give in formulating schemes of operations.

Forestry Examinations.

The advisability of arranging for an examination in Forestry for working foresters, and for the further provision of education for working foresters, was considered by the Council, and a

Committee, with Dr BORTHWICK as Convener, has been appointed to consider the whole question, and to report.

Society's Diamond Jubilee.

As members are aware the Society's Diamond Jubilee took place on 16th February. The Council considered carefully the various suggestions which were submitted by members with the view of celebrating this event in a suitable manner, and they finally decided as follows :—

1st. That the lists of Home and Foreign Honorary Members should be filled up, and that the Honorary Membership should be conferred on Dr J. Coaz, Inspector-General of the Swiss Forest Service, at the earliest opportunity.

2nd. That the Society should invite, through the Foreign, Colonial and India Offices, representative foreign and Colonial foresters from the following countries :—France Prussia, Bavaria, Switzerland, Sweden, Norway, Denmark, Italy, Belgium, Russia, Austria, Hungary, Holland, India, United States, Canada, Japan, Australia, New Zealand and South Africa. It is proposed that these Foresters should be the guests of the Society for about a fortnight, beginning Saturday, 27th June, and that during that time they should have an opportunity of seeing some of the best examples of our existing woodlands, and also some of our bare hills and glens, which may be found capable of being profitably afforested. An outline of a tour has been drawn up which includes—Scone, Murthly and Atholl, in *Perthshire*; Mar, Balmoral, Ballogie, Finzean and Durris, in *Deeside*; Cullen and Grantown, in *Speyside*; and *Glen Mor*. The party will then join the Society's usual Annual Excursion, which will embrace Inverliever, Poltalloch, and other places in the West of Scotland. The proceedings will terminate in Edinburgh with a Reception, Conference, and Dinner. It is expected that the Corporations of Edinburgh and Glasgow will entertain the guests. These proposals have been submitted to the Government Offices concerned, and already several nominations of foreign representatives have been received. The expense of this tour will heavily tax the resources of the Society, but the Council believe that they will find sufficient funds available for the purpose by drawing partly upon the Society's uninvested balance and upon the balance of the Excursion Fund before referred to. Several members of the Society have kindly agreed to take the foreign representatives as their private guests for the two week-ends embraced in the time, and also to give assistance by lending motor cars and otherwise.

It is also proposed to have various special articles of an appropriate nature published in the *Transactions*.

8

Promised Department of Forestry.
Development of Forestry.

In their last report the Council pointed out that no Demonstration Forest had yet been purchased, and the promised Department of Forestry had not been created. At that meeting Mr Sutherland made a statement on behalf of the Board of Agriculture, in which he said that the Board's Advisory Committee was searching for a Demonstration Area; that Dr Nisbet had been appointed Forestry Adviser to the Board; that the Board proposed to appoint Advisory and Research Officers and Correspondents and to continue a Survey they had begun, and to create a seed-testing establishment. As no further progress had been reported, the Council, on 12th May, addressed the letter to the Board of Agriculture, which was printed in the July *Transactions* of last year. It will be remembered that that letter began by expressing regret that no proposals for carrying out a considerable scheme of afforestation had been put forward by the Board; that Scotland had so far received a most inadequate share of money from the Development Fund as compared with England and Ireland; and went on to urge the Board to encourage a large scheme in preference to smaller ones, and to point out the steps which the Board might take towards this end. The letter concluded by offering such assistance as the Society was able to give. When this letter was under the consideration of the Council, the Secretary pointed out that the difficulty of promoting private schemes of afforestation by Government money lay in the fact that the Development Commissioners had no power under their Act to advance money to private owners. He said he had submitted to the Development Commissioners the constitution of a small non-profit company which was intended to overcome this difficulty, and to provide the machinery for carrying out any schemes of development which the Commissioners could advance money to promote. This draft had been submitted by the Commissioners to the Board of Agriculture who have expressed general approval of it, and he was then hopeful that it would be also approved by the Treasury. He pointed out that while the Council and the Society would incur no responsibility in connection with the Company, it was desirable that it should be worked in close association with the Society. The Council gave their general approval to the scheme. At the General Meeting in Paisley, the President mentioned that no reply had been received from the Board since the Society's letter, and he again urged the need for a large scheme by joint action of proprietors and the State. On 10th October a reply was received from the Board of Agriculture to the effect that until the Advisory Committee's report was considered, and the Board had been able to make arrangements for the appointment of Advisory and Research Officers, and had selected a Demonstration Area and created a Forest School, they could not deal adequately with the question of schemes of afforestation, but that they would always be glad to consider any representations offered by the Society on all matters relating to forestry. This reply was considered unsatisfactory, and a further communication was sent to the Board pointing out that the position as regards forestry seemed to be worse than it was six months previously, and that the Society itself knew that expert advisers were available and could be obtained, so that there need be no further delay on that account. A deputation, consisting of the Council with the addition of Sir Herbert Maxwell, an ex-President of the Society, was afterwards received by the Secretary for Scotland in the offices of the Board of Agriculture for Scotland, 29 St Andrew Square, Edinburgh, when these matters were discussed. The full proceedings of the deputation are printed in the January *Transactions*. Since then a letter has been received from the Board of Agriculture saying that they have nothing to add to what was said by the Secretary for Scotland in reply to the Society's deputation, but that they welcomed the Society's offer of co-operation in any schemes of afforestation which might be forthcoming in the future.

Motions.

The Council appointed a Committee to consider the motions which are on the agenda for discussion at this meeting, and after receiving the Committee's report, the whole question was very fully discussed, when the following decisions were arrived at:—

1. As to Mr RICHARDSON's motion : That the proposed changes on the Laws were unnecessary, and should not be made.

2. As to Mr GAMMELL's motion : That the President of each effective Branch with not less than fifty members should be *ex officio* an additional member of the Council.

3. As to Mr GILCHRIST's motion : That the whole day should be devoted to the Annual Meeting—the forenoon for business, and the afternoon for conference ; and that it was unnecessary to pass a formal motion on the subject.

The report was adopted.

FINANCES.

The Abstract of Accounts, which had been printed and circulated amongst the members previous to the meeting, was formally submitted by Mr M'HATTIE, Convener of the Finance Committee. In moving the adoption of the accounts, Mr M'Hattie urged that each member should endeavour to secure one new member in the course of the year. He pointed out that it was only by a powerful membership that the work of the Society could be effectively carried on, and the present members had to be depended upon to secure new members to fill up the gaps.

The SECRETARY submitted the Dunn Memorial Account, which showed a credit balance of revenue at the end of the year of £4, 16s. 6d.

With regard to the Excursion Account the Secretary said that, as explained in the Council's report, this account had not yet been closed, but as soon as the outstanding claims had been adjusted and the necessary entries made, the accounts would be submitted to the Auditor and appended to the " Proceedings" in the usual way. The Secretary again referred to the proposal to expend part of the surplus in connection with the Diamond Jubilee celebrations, as explained in the Council's report. The various accounts were approved of. (See Appendices A, B and C.)

REPORTS OF THE BRANCHES.

The SECRETARY read the reports from Aberdeen and Inverness Branches, which were adopted. (See Appendices D, E and F.)

CHAIRMAN'S REMARKS.

The CHAIRMAN said :—" The remarks I have to make will be brief, because we have a discussion this afternoon in which the larger questions dealing with progress generally may, I think, be better discussed. So I propose to leave till this afternoon the greater part of what I have to say about the actual progress of afforestation since the last Annual Meeting of this Society. There is one thing, however, on which every member would like me to say something. I am quite sure every member would read with great pleasure the announcement in this morning's *Scotsman*. I am quite sure that you would wish me to take this the very earliest opportunity of offering our most hearty congratulations to our Honorary Secretary, Mr Munro Ferguson, on the very high and distinguished office to which he has been appointed by His Majesty the King. I think our congratulations may be rather saddened, though they cannot be made less sincere and hearty, by the reflection that we as a Society lose what Australia is going to gain, and the loss to this Society is a very heavy one. No one who has any acquaintance with its affairs can doubt that Mr Munro Ferguson has done more than probably any one individual on behalf of this Society. Whether it is by the example he set as a landowner in showing the best possible practice in his own woods, whether in his place in Parliament, or as a member of Committees and Commissions, Mr Munro Ferguson has worked without ceasing to try to put forestry into the position which it ought to occupy among the industries of this country. I am quite sure that you will all join with me in wishing to the new Governor-General and Lady Helen Munro Ferguson a safe journey to Australia, a happy and prosperous tenure of office, and a safe return to this country.

"Turning for one moment to the report read by the Secretary, on the whole we can congratulate ourselves on a sound position The membership shows a slight increase, and as Mr M'Hattie has said it is quite to be expected we have not yet reached the limit of our expansion. Year by year more interest is taken in afforestation, and that fact, I think, ought to bring us fresh members. We ought not to be content with our present membership. We should aim at obtaining more, and I hope this year, when the Society will be thoroughly advertised by the fact of its Diamond Jubilee celebrations, we shall be successful in increasing our membership even above the high figure at which it stands at present.

"On the events of the year there is really very little to say. What I have to say as to the negotiations with the Government Departments I shall leave entirely to the afternoon. I would refer for one moment to the joint deputation which was sent early in the year from this Society and the Landowners' Co-operative Forestry Society to the railway companies with regard to the prices for timber used for railway sleepers. We did not receive at the time any great promises, but that deputation has had an undoubted result. Better prices are actually being given for sleepers than in the past, and I think we ought to be very glad indeed that our representations have had such good effect. This question is one really for timber merchants and for proprietors to tackle together. Their interests are absolutely one and the same. As long as you get owners selling below the proper value of timber, you will get timber merchants putting in offers below cost price for railway sleepers and for other purposes. We have got by joint action to determine that timber shall not be put on the market at a lower price than that at which it can be grown. I feel quite sure that we are moving in that direction, and I hope that this year still further progress will be made in consolidating the position of timber merchants with regard to this great and important question.

"I have only one other word to say to you just now, and that is with regard to Mr Sutherland's presence here to-day. He will, I hope, be able to attend our discussion this afternoon as well as our meeting this morning, and I am quite sure that the members of this Society will recognise most fully the efforts which Mr Sutherland has made on behalf of forestry in this country. Though the progress he has to report may not be as great as he would wish it to be, we are quite certain that the result is not due to any want of good-will on his part, and I am quite sure that this Society will give him as ever the most hearty possible welcome. I won't detain you longer."

ELECTION OF OFFICE-BEARERS.

Dr BORTHWICK, Edinburgh, moved the re-election of Captain Stirling as President, and this was unanimously approved.

Captain STIRLING said :—"I thank you for the honour. I can only say I am conscious of falling far short of possessing the qualities which your Chairman should have in the present most strenuous time for this Society. I can only assure you that I shall do the best I can in the office to which you have been good enough to re-elect me."

Mr SYDNEY J. GAMMELL of Drumtochty and Mr JOHN F. ANNAND, M.Sc., Lecturer in Forestry, Armstrong College, were elected Vice-Presidents; Messrs GEORGE LEVEN, J. W. M'HATTIE, JOHN BROOM, ALEXANDER MURRAY, Forester, Murthly, J. H. MILNE HOME, Irvine House, Canonbie, DAVID W. THOMSON, Edinburgh, and J. A. HOWE, Overseer, Rothesay, were elected Councillors.

The SECRETARY read the following letter addressed to him by Mr Munro Ferguson, Hon. Secretary :—

RAITH, KIRKCALDY,
6th February 1914.

DEAR MR GALLOWAY,—

I must ask you to place my resignation as Honorary Secretary of the Royal Scottish Arboricultural Society before the Council, and convey my sincere regret at having to demit the office with which I have so long been honoured. From the first day that

I found myself in the chair, in most lively circumstances, until that most important and unanimous meeting of Council from which we have just separated to-day, I look back over a long space of time filled with good, useful work, and unclouded by one single regret. We have been as a band of brothers, associated in a cause of vital interest to Scotland, and if I leave you now it is in sight of our objective. We have had to deal with ignorance, prejudice and indifference, and that for the most part in high places, where it is as yet by no means, even now, extinct. But we are sure of our ground. We feel we have the country behind us, and we know that when so much has been done by the Government where it is least required, Scotland cannot be long neglected. We have fought a good fight together, and victory must soon be yours. I regret that pressure on my time prevents me attending your meeting to-morrow. I shall also regret to miss all the interesting events of our "Diamond" celebration. I beg you to convey to the President, and Council, and members, and accept for yourself my heartfelt gratitude for continuous kindness. There is no happier recollection that I shall carry with me than that of my association with the foresters of Scotland.

Always yours truly,

R. MUNRO FERGUSON.

It was remitted to the President and Secretary to frame a suitable answer on behalf of the Society, and the following was subsequently sent :—

The Royal Scottish Arboricultural Society, while receiving with the greatest regret the resignation of the Honorary Secretary, wishes to offer most hearty congratulations to the Right Hon. R. Munro Ferguson on his appointment by His Majesty the King to the high office of Governor-General of Australia.

The Society welcomes this opportunity of recording its appreciation of the great services which Mr Munro Ferguson has rendered, both to the Society and to forestry in Scotland generally, not only in the discharge of his duties as Honorary Secretary to the Society, but also by his example as a land-owner in making his woods a model of silvicultural practice, by his constant exertion in his place in Parliament, and by his invaluable services as a member of Royal Commissions and Committees.

The Society offers to the new Governor-General of Australia and to Lady Helen Munro Ferguson the warmest good wishes for their voyage and their tenure of office, and for their safe and happy return to Scotland.

ARCH. STIRLING, *President.*

R. GALLOWAY, *Secretary.*

Mr Munro Ferguson's reply was as follows :—

RAITH, KIRKCALDY,
12th February 1914.

R. GALLOWAY, Esq., S.S.C.,
19 CASTLE STREET, EDINBURGH.

DEAR MR GALLOWAY,—

I have to acknowledge receipt of your letter enclosing excerpt from Minutes of Annual Meeting of the Royal Scottish Arboricultural Society, the terms of which I much appreciate. I thank the Society for its generous recognition of anything I have been able to do for it and for forestry generally, and I hope that that work is not even now at an end.

And believe me,

Yours truly,

R. MUNRO FERGUSON.

Mr CHARLES BUCHANAN, Factor, Penicuik, said: "We all feel that Mr Munro Ferguson has done a great deal of good to our cause, and we are very sorry to part with him. I would suggest that Sir John Stirling-Maxwell, who has been our President, should be asked to take his place as Honorary Secretary. I know of no other gentleman connected with the Society who has done more for it, or who has more energy to follow Mr Munro Ferguson in this position."

Mr W. H. MASSIE, Edinburgh, seconded the proposal and expressed the hope that Sir John would accept office.

Sir JOHN STIRLING-MAXWELL said: "Mr Buchanan would have been as kind as he usually is if he had warned me of this proposal. It comes to me as quite new, and though I have to consider it on the spur of the moment, I think if you consider I can be of any use to you in that capacity I shall be very glad to serve."

The Secretary and Treasurer, the Hon. Editor, the Auditor, the Hon. Consulting Scientists and the Local Secretaries were all re-elected. (For full list see Appendix G.)

DIAMOND JUBILEE.

The SECRETARY, in referring to the proposals in the Council's Report regarding the Diamond Jubilee celebrations, said that the PRESIDENT had kindly intimated that he was prepared to give two prizes, of 15 guineas in all, for certain papers on subjects to be written by foresters on a subject which would be formally intimated later.

Dr Borthwick said that the subject chosen was "The Natural Regeneration of Conifers, including Exotics, with Details of the Previous Crop," which would give every forester and every man of experience something to write about. The conditions had yet to be adjusted, but would be intimated in the notice calling the meeting in the summer.

Excursion in West of Scotland.

The Secretary mentioned that at the General Meeting held at Paisley in July last, it was decided that the next Annual Excursion would be in the West of Scotland. Invitations from Col. Malcolm, of Poltalloch, to visit his estate, and from Mr Runciman, President of the Board of Agriculture and Fisheries, to visit Inverliever, had already been received and accepted. If time permitted other places would be visited. It was proposed that this excursion should form part of the tour which is to be arranged for the Society's foreign and colonial guests, and that both parties should meet in the West of Scotland for the last two or three days. After the Excursion, a Reception and Conference, followed by a Dinner, would be held in the evening, which members would have an opportunity of attending.

Annual Forestry Exhibition and Plantation and Nursery Competition.

Mr Allan drew attention to the schedules which had been issued in connection with the Exhibition which is to be held in Hawick this year, and expressed the hope that there would be a much larger number of entries than last year. He further referred to the Competition for estate nurseries and plantations within the Show District, and mentioned that entry forms could be obtained from the Secretary.

Development of Afforestation.

The Chairman said: "I think this is a very fitting juncture at which Mr Sutherland might be asked to make a few remarks to the Society."

Mr SUTHERLAND said: "Captain Stirling and gentlemen, I have come here to-day, as you know, to represent the Board of Agriculture, and I must admit I thought that probably before you asked me to say anything I would have heard some criticism of the Board and the various Departments interested, and that I might have been able to answer some of them. But apparently that opportunity is not to be my privilege. I would like to say, however, in connection with the proposed demonstration area about which you have all heard a good deal, that, as Mr M'Kinnon Wood intimated to the deputation which he received some time ago, the Advisory Committee have selected an area in Aberdeenshire. The Board of Agriculture and the Secretary for Scotland have forwarded, with their own recommendation, the report of the Advisory Committee to the Treasury, and the Treasury in turn will pass it on to the Development Commissioners. I am glad to say that the favourable opinion of the area has been fortified by an expression of entire approval by our friend Dr Borthwick, by Mr John Nisbet, the Board's expert adviser in forestry; by Mr Gordon of the Glasgow College; and also, last but not least, by Mr Dawson, who was so long associated with forestry in Aberdeen, but who to our regret has now gone to England. I can only hope—and I suppose that you also will share that hope—that the recommendation of the Board and of the Advisory Committee, fortified as it is by the opinions of all these gentlemen, will have the favourable opinion of the Development Commissioners. You of course know that the Board, in so far as a big investment of that kind is concerned, is absolutely helpless, and that we must look to the Development Commissioners for the necessary funds.

"Last year I said something about Advisory and Research Officers. I regret to say that until now we have not been able to make any appointments. It is outwith my sphere to say anything further than to assure you that it is the Board's endeavour as soon as possible to have these appointments made. Last year also—and this at all events is one small item of progress—I mentioned that it was our intention to elect correspondents to collect information in all the various counties of Scotland that would be of use in finally compiling statistics in connection with forestry. Well, these correspondents I hope will be appointed within the next two months, and I am sure, judging by the amount of useful detail that we have received on the agricultural side from men in a similar capacity, that what we do get from these correspondents will be found equally useful.

" I earnestly hope that the celebration of the Diamond Jubilee will be in every way successful. I do not think you could have conceived a better method of celebrating it, and I know our friend Mr Galloway, who is always full of enthusiasm and interest in the work, will do everything to assure these guests a very hearty welcome. In connection with the Diamond Jubilee, I am glad to be able to tell you that the Board decided the other day to give a grant to the Society for the purpose. This grant is, I think, historical in respect that it is probably the first money that has ever passed into the coffers of the Arboricultural Society from any Government Department. I only hope that it will be the forerunner of other assistance that I cannot of course myself foreshadow."

The Chairman said : " As we have a discussion this afternoon practically devoted to this, I don't propose that we should discuss it further at present. I would only wish in your name to thank Mr Sutherland for what he has said. He has told us that the gift is a historic one, that this is the first time that we have seen the colour of the Board of Agriculture's money, but I cannot, even while thanking him, fail to point out that although we have received a promise, the amount which we are to receive was, I think, not stated. This, I am sure, will be remedied before long. You all know how difficult it is for a Government official to come here and say much about the work of his own office. I think we must all make as much allowance as possible for that when listening to a responsible representative who is here to speak for a Government Department. And of course what we find in what Mr Sutherland has said is no doubt more in the nature of what he hopes may take place in the future than of what has actually been done. That I think we shall see very clearly when we come to the afternoon's discussion. We shall, I think, in the course of that discussion, have occasion to pass severe criticisms on what has actually taken place. I wish, however, to say that in any hard things which may be said this afternoon there is not one personal word directed at Mr Sutherland. I hope we shall all keep that most clearly in our minds."

Motions to be Disposed of.

Mr Richardson formally submitted the following motion standing in his name for the purpose of altering Rule XIV. regarding the election and term of service of members of Council.

(a) "To delete the words 'one of the retiring Vice-Presidents, and four of the retiring Councillors,' in the second clause of the second sentence; and

(b) "To insert the following as the third sentence of the Law—'One of the retiring Vice-Presidents or one of the retiring Councillors may be elected as President, and two or more of the retiring Councillors may be elected as Vice-Presidents; but none of the retiring Vice-Presidents or retiring Councillors shall be eligible for re-election till after the expiry of one year."

Mr Price seconded. Mr M'Hattie moved the previous question, and Mr Whitton seconded. A discussion followed which was taken part in by Messrs R. V. Mather, C. S. France and J. Scrimgeour, who all supported Mr Richardson's motion. The President explained the compromise that had been offered by the Council but had been refused by Mr Richardson, namely, that two only of the retiring Councillors should be eligible for re-election instead of four as at present. Mr Massie said that the Council had not been satisfied that there was any strong feeling among the members of the Society in favour of such an alteration as that indicated in Mr Richardson's motion, but he felt sure the Council would now see that there was such a feeling, and he hoped they would act accordingly. Sir John Stirling-Maxwell supported the Council's compromise, and Mr H. M. Cadell thereupon moved as an amendment that the Council's compromise be adopted. Colonel Purvis seconded. Mr M'Hattie having withdrawn his amendment, a vote was taken between the amendment and the motion when it was found that 32 had voted for each. The President said that although the vote had left matters as they were, it was evident that a large number of those present at the meeting were in favour of some change, and he thought the Council might consider the adoption of the procedure provided by Rule XVIII.

Mr Gammell's motion regarding the representation of

Branches upon the Council of this Society was next proposed and seconded.

> "That any Branch recognised by the parent Society and consisting of members of the Society subscribing to the funds of the Branch, shall have representation on the Council of the Society, consisting of the President of the Branch for the time being and one member of Council for the first fifty members of the Branch, and one extra member of Council for every additional completed fifty members, such member or members to be nominated by the members of the Branch in annual meeting, and that the rules of the Society shall be amended to that effect."

After discussion an amended Resolution to the following effect was adopted, namely :—

> "That any effective Branch recognised by the parent Society and consisting of not less than fifty members of the Society subscribing to the funds of the Branch, shall be represented on the Council of Society by an extra or additional member of Council, who shall be the President of the Branch for the time being, or other member elected by the members of the Branch at their annual meeting, and that the rules of the Society be hereby altered accordingly."

Mr GILCHRIST mentioned that he was quite satisfied with what the Council proposed in their report as to his motion, and he accordingly withdrew it.

DISCUSSION.

(For a report of the President's address and the discussion which followed, and for the resolutions which were passed and sent to Ministers and Departments and Scottish members of Parliament, see p. 121 of the *Transactions*, vol. xxviii.).

APPENDIX A.

ABSTRACT OF ACCOUNTS

IN CONNECTION WITH

THE MALCOLM DUNN MEMORIAL FUND, 1913.

RECEIPTS.

Balance in Bank at close of last Account . .	£9	3	6
Dividend on £100 3 per cent. Redeemable Stock of Edinburgh Corporation, payable at Whitsunday and Martinmas, 1913, £3, *less* Income Tax, 3s. 6d.	2	16	6
Repayment of Income Tax for four years to November 1912	0	14	0
	£12	14	0

PAYMENTS.

Messrs Douglas & Foulis for Elwes' *Forest Trees of Britain*, vols. vi. and vii.	£5	5	0			
Survey Atlas of Scotland . .	2	12	6			
				£7	17	6
Balance carried forward, being sum in National Bank of Scotland on Account Current . . .				£4	16	6

Note.—The Capital belonging to the Fund consists of £100 3 per cent. Redeemable Stock of Edinburgh Corporation.

EDINBURGH, 19*th January* 1914.—Examined and found correct. The Certificate by the Bank of above balance, and Edinburgh Corporation Stock Certificate, have been exhibited.

JOHN T. WATSON,
Auditor.

APPENDIX B.

ABSTRACT OF ACCOUNTS for Year ending 31st December 1913

I.—CAPITAL.

CHARGE.

1.—To Capital, [December 1912]	.	140 14 4
4. Dividends and Interest,	.	69 0 3
5. *Transactions* and Reports sold,	.	11 17 9
6. Income Tax Recovered,	.	3 19 4
7. Scottish Exhibition of Natural History, etc., 1911.— Donation from Glasgow Corporation to meet the Society's Expenses in connection with the Forestry Section	.	150 0 0
		£938 7 6

DISCHARGE.

for Annual Meeting,	.	£24 11 1
Auditor,	.	3 3 0
Hon. Editor's Assistant, £30 ; and Authors of German and French Notes for *Transactions*, £10,	.	40 0 0
Secretary and Treasurer,	.	125 0 0
Advertising, Insurance, and Premium on Secretary's Bond of Caution,	.	4 8 3
Councillors' Railway Fares and Luncheons	.	12 4 11
Postages and Miscellaneous Outlays, viz.: Postages of Parts I. and II. of Vol. XXVII. of *Transactions*, £32 1 6		
General Postages, Commissions on Cheques, and Petty Outlays, . £42 11 5		74 12 11
		£284 0 2
9. Balance of Revenue carried to next year, subject to payment of cost, etc., of January *Transactions*,	.	343 17 10
		£938 7 6

Note.—Balance of Revenue as above £343 17 10
Less Balance at debit of Capital as above, 40 2 2

At credit of National Bank of Scotland, Ltd., £303 15 8

EDINBURGH, 19*th January* 1914.—I hereby certify that I have examined the Accounts of the Treasurer for the year to 31st December 1913, of which the above is an Abstract, and have found them correct. The Securities, representing the Funds as above, have also been exhibited to me.

JOHN T. WATSON, *Auditor.*

APPENDIX B.

ABSTRACT OF ACCOUNTS for Year ending 31st December 1913

I.—CAPITAL.

CHARGE.

1. Funds at 31st December 1912:

		£	s.	d.
£500 Caledonian Railway Company 4 per cent. Guaranteed Annuity Stock, No. 2, at 100¾,		503	15	0
£500 Caledonian Railway Company 4 per cent. Debenture Stock, at 104¼,		521	5	0
£400 North British Railway Company 3 per cent. Debenture Stock, at 78¼,		312	10	0
£400 North British Railway Company No. 1, 4 per cent. Preference Stock, at 100½,				
Capital in hand uninvested (in National Bank of Scotland, Ltd.)		402	0	0

	£	s.	d.
	29	18	2
	40	0	0
	£1809	8	2

Furniture, etc., in Society's Room, £65 2 0 ... 70 14 0

2. Life Members' Subscriptions in 1913,
Members,
New Members, Ordinary Members by commutation, £65 2 0, 5 19 6

£1880 2 2

DISCHARGE.

1. Proportion of Life Members' Subscriptions transferred to Revenue, £130 10 8

			£	s.	d.
(Overcharged.)					
Servants,	£99 19 0				
⁴⁄₁₅ of Full Life Subscriptions,	14 14 4				
⁵⁄₁₅ of Commuted Subscriptions,	17 3			79	12

2. Decrease in value of Railway Stocks at 31st December 1913, 79 12

3. Funds, etc., at 31st December 1913:—

	£	s.	d.
£500 Caledonian Railway Company 4 per cent. Guaranteed Annuity Stock, No. 2, at 94½,	472	10	0
£500 Caledonian Railway Company 4 per cent. Debenture Stock, at 100⅜,	501	17	6
£400 North British Railway Company 3 per cent. Debenture Stock, at 74¼,	297	10	0
£400 North British Railway Company, No. 1, 4 per cent. Preference Stock, at 97,	388	0	0

	£	s.	d.
Furniture, etc., in Society's Room, say,	£1659	17	6
	40	0	0
	£1699	17	6
Less Balance at Debit of Capital	40	2	2

£1659 15 4

£1880 2 2

II.—REVENUE.

CHARGE.

		£	s.	d.
1. Balance in hand at 31st December 1912,		£136	18	10
2. Ordinary Members' Subscriptions:				
Arrears at 31st December 1912,	£29 0 6	45	17	0

		£	s.	d.
Less Received, but not appropriated, senders' names being unknown,	1 2 6			
Add Arrears written off but since received,	£30 18 0			
	2 14 0	£32 12 0		
Subscriptions for 1913,	£435 16 6			
Less Received in 1912,	8 15 0	427 1 6		
Subscriptions for 1914 received in 1913,		9 19 0		

£460 12 6

Deduct—		£	s.	d.
Cancelled or written off as irrecoverable at 31st December 1913,	£15 8 6			
Less Received, but not appropriated, as above,	1 2 6	£14 6 0		
Arrears at 31st December 1913,	£20 9 6	34 15 6		

£425 17 0

	£	s.	d.
3. Proportion of Life Members' Subscriptions transferred from Capital,			
4. Dividends and Interest,	140 14 4		
5. Transactions and Reports sold,	60 0 3		
6. Income,			

DISCHARGE.

				£	s.	d.
1. Printing, Stationery, etc.,—						
Vol. XXVII. Part I. Trans.,	£97 12 0					
	2 12 6	£100 4 6				
Vol. XXVII. Part II. of Trans.,	£113 13 7					
Authors' Reprints,	1 15 6	115 9 1				
				£231	19	5
General Printing and Stationery, £47 8 6						
Forestry Periodicals, Binding, etc., 3 8 2		£315	13	7		

| Less Receipts for Advts. in Trans., | | £200 | 10 | 3 | | |
| | | 34 | 10 | 10 | £231 | 19 | 5 |

			£	s.	d.
2. Prizes (Money, £34, 5s.; Medals, £21, 15s.)					
Less Donation from the Highland and Agricultural Society, for Prizes awarded for Home-Grown Timber exhibited at Inverness,		£45	18	0
3. Forestry Exhibition at the Highland and Agricultural Society's Show at Paisley,		50	0	0
Printing, £8 16 0					
Advertising, 0 18 0					
Extra Tabling, Racks, etc., 2 16 6					
Incidental Expenses, 9 4 11		115	18	0
4. Nursery and Plantation Competition in Shaw District—					
Printing,					
Judges' expenses,		21	15	5

| Less Entry Money received | £45 0 6 | | | |
| | 12 9 2 | £18 9 8 | | |

		£	s.	d.
5. Contributions to Aberdeen Branch	£18 9 8			
Contribution to Dr Gayer's International Memorial Fund,	4 13 0	13	16	6
6.		5	0	0
7. Fee to Reporter,				
8. Expenses of Management,—				
Rent of Room and Taxes for 1913, and Hall for Annual Meeting,	7 0 0	7	0	0
Auditor,	0 0 0			
Hon. Editor's Assistant,	£34 11 1			

APPENDIX C.

EXCURSION ACCOUNT.

Abstract of Accounts—Year 1913.

Balance brought from last Account	. . . . .		£56 10 11
Deduct—Auditor's Fee for 1912 . . . £2 2 0			
Three Bursaries of £10 each for Swiss Tour 30 0 0		32 2 0	
			24 8 11

Amount collected for Common Purse (including £14, 11s. for Accident Insurance Premiums) £1081 11 6

Paid :—

Railway Tickets (Home and Continental) . . . £385 13 10			
Less repaid . . 9 4 11			
	376 8 11		
Local Railways and Hiring . 76 15 2			
Hotels in Paris, Berne, Interlaken, Brienz, Zurich, Chur, Thusis. Brussels . . . 373 11 8			
Lunches and Refreshments . 42 9 0			
Printing 6 19 0			
Accident Insurance Premiums . 14 11 0			
Gratuities, Carriage of Luggage and Incidental Outlays . . 27 7 1			
		£918 1 10	
			163 9 8

Balance carried forward to next year, being sum in National Bank of Scotland, viz. :—

(1) On Deposit Receipt £150 0 0			
(2) On Current Account . . . 37 18 7			
			£187 18 7

EDINBURGH, *20th March* 1914.—Examined with Vouchers and Memorandum Book and found correct. Bank Deposit Receipt and Certificate of above balance on Current Account, together £187, 18s. 7d. stg., have been exhibited.

JOHN T. WATSON,
Auditor.

APPENDIX D.

Royal Scottish Arboricultural Society (Aberdeen Branch).

REPORT 1913.

The Committee beg to submit the Eighth Annual Report of the Branch.

The affairs of the Branch have been conducted on similar lines as in the preceding years.

The Membership of the Branch is 122. Sixteen new members have joined the Branch during the year, but one or two names have been deleted from the list of members through having left the district, failure to pay subscriptions, and other causes. The Branch has lost the active services of Mr William Dawson, M.A., B.Sc., formerly Lecturer on Forestry at Aberdeen, who was a member of Committee, and who was recently appointed Reader in Forestry in the University of Cambridge.

The four quarterly meetings of the Branch were held on 14th December 1912, 17th May, 9th August, and 17th October 1913. At the Annual Meeting held in December consideration of the Report of Lord Lovat and Captain Stirling of Keir, on "Afforestation in Scotland" in reference to the Forest Survey of Glen Mor, was taken up, the subject being opened by Mr Sydney J. Gammell, of Drumtochty, and various aspects of the Report were discussed at some length by him, and by Professor Hendrick, Mr Dawson, and others.

The meetings held in May and August took the form of excursions to the Woods of Drum, owned by Mr A. F. Irvine, the President of the Branch, and to the Cullen Woods. On both occasions much of interest to Arboriculturists was seen and discussed, and on both occasions the party were hospitably entertained to luncheon by Mr Irvine, and by the Seafield Trustees. It has been found that these and previous excursions have proved very beneficial to members of the Branch, and they have been largely taken advantage of, there having been an average attendance of about forty on each occasion. At the final meeting for the year, held in October, an open discussion on "A Comparison of Home and Foreign Timber" took place. This meeting was held on a Friday afternoon as an experiment, but it was found that the attendance was not so good as has been experienced with meetings on Saturday afternoons, when they have usually been held.

The Committee have again to record their thanks to Professor Trail, and the University Authorities, for the use of the Botanical class-room for the meetings of the Branch.

ALEX. F. IRVINE,
President.

GEORGE D. MASSIE,
Honorary Secretary.

ABERDEEN, *December* 1913.

APPENDIX E.—ROYAL SCOTTISH ARBORICULTURAL SOCIETY (ABERDEEN BRANCH).

STATEMENT OF ACCOUNTS, Year 1913.

GENERAL ACCOUNT.

INCOME.	£ s. d.	EXPENDITURE.	£ s. d.
Balance at credit of last Account	£14 17 9	Printing	£1 3 6
Subscriptions from Members at 1s.	5 4 0	Advertising	1 13 6
Savings Bank Interest	0 4 2	Honorarium to Secretary for 1912	3 3 0
Grant from Parent Society	5 0 0	Postages and Incidental Outlay	2 7 6
		Transferred to Excursion Account	1 19 10
		,, Library Account	6 11 0½
		Balance carried to Abstract	8 7 6½
	£25 5 11		£25 5 11

EXCURSION ACCOUNT.

	£ s. d.		£ s. d.
Transferred from General Account	£1 19 10	Balance at Debit of last Account	£1 19 10
Received from 23 Members for driving at Cullen	3 9 0	Printing	0 13 0
Balance at Debit carried to Abstract	1 3 8	Driving at Cullen	2 14 0
		Postages and Incidents	1 5 8
	£6 12 6		£6 12 6

LIBRARY ACCOUNT.

	£ s. d.		£ s. d.
Transferred from General Account to meet Balance	£4 11 0½	Balance at Debit of last Account	£4 11 0½
Do. to meet Current Expenditure	2 0 0	Balance at Credit carried to Abstract	2 0 0
	£6 11 0½		£6 11 0½

ABSTRACT.

	£ s. d.
Balance at Credit of General Account	£8 7 6½
Balance at Credit of Library Account	2 0 0
	10 7 6½
Balance at Debit of Excursion Account	1 3 8
Balance at Credit of Branch per Savings Bank Pass Book No. 393	£9 3 10½

ABERDEEN, *10th December* 1913.—I have examined the foregoing Statement of Accounts, and have compared same with the vouchers, and find the same properly stated and vouched, the balance at the credit of the Branch being Nine pounds three shillings and tenpence halfpenny, which sum is deposited with the Aberdeen Savings Bank, per Savings Bank Book, No. 393, which I have also seen.

J. G. HOPKINSON.

APPENDIX F.

ROYAL SCOTTISH ARBORICULTURAL SOCIETY (NORTHERN BRANCH).

REPORT TO 31st DECEMBER 1913.

The Committee beg to report that since last meeting of the Branch it has not been found possible to arrange for the excursions and lectures which had hitherto formed the principal work of the Branch. The work up to date has therefore, to a large extent, been at a stand-still, but a renewed effort is being made to revive interest in Forestry matters in the north, and the Committee hope that by next year a programme of work will have been overtaken and some good done in the way of increasing knowledge in Forestry work in the District covered by the Branch.

A statement of the accounts for 3 years to 31st December 1913 is appended, showing the sum of £15, 19s. 9½d. at the credit of the Branch as at the end of the year.

For the Council,

ALEX. FRASER,
Hon. Secretary and Treasurer,
Northern Branch.

INVERNESS, *3rd January* 1914.

Statement of Accounts for three years ending 31st December 1913.

RECEIPTS.

	£	s.	d.
Balance from Last Account	£17	7	6½
Subscriptions	1	0	0
Copy of Glen Mor Report	0	3	0
Grant from Parent Society	5	0	0
Bank Interest	0	5	7
	£23	16	1½

EXPENDITURE.

	£	s.	d.
Printing	£1	11	6
Expenses in connection with Inverness Show .	5	14	10
Postages and Incidental Outlay	0	10	0
	£7	16	4

Balance at Credit of Branch at 31st December 1913—

	£	s.	d.			
Sum in Treasurer's hands .	£2	6	10½			
Sum in Bank . . .	13	12	11			
				15	19	9½
				£23	16	1½

APPENDIX G.

Office-Bearers for 1914 :—

PATRON.

His Majesty THE KING.

PRESIDENT.

Captain ARCHIBALD STIRLING of Keir, Dunblane.

VICE-PRESIDENTS.

THE LORD LOVAT, D.S.O., Beaufort Castle, Beauly.

CHAS. BUCHANAN, Factor, Penicuik Estate, Penicuik.

Sir ANDREW AGNEW, Bart. of Lochnaw, 10 Smith Square, Westminster.

W. STEUART FOTHRINGHAM of Murthly, Perthshire.

SYDNEY J. GAMMELL of Drumtochty, Countesswells House, Bieldside, Aberdeen.

JOHN F. ANNAND, M.Sc., Lecturer in Forestry, Armstrong College, Newcastle-upon-Tyne.

COUNCIL.

HON. LIFE MEMBERS.

Sir KENNETH J. MACKENZIE, Bart. of Gairloch, 10 Moray Place, Edinburgh.

Sir JOHN STIRLING-MAXWELL, Bart. of Pollok, Pollokshaws.

ORDINARY MEMBERS.

A. T. GILLANDERS, F.E.S., Forester, Park Cottage, Alnwick.

JAMES WHITTON, Superintendent of City Parks, City Chambers, Glasgow.

WILLIAM DAVIDSON, Forester, Panmure, Carnoustie.

W. H. MASSIE, Nurseryman, 1 Waterloo Place, Edinburgh.

GILBERT BROWN, Wood Manager, Grantown-on-Spey.

GEORGE P. GORDON, B.Sc., Lecturer in Forestry, West of Scotland Agricultural College, 6 Blythswood Square, Glasgow.

A. D. RICHARDSON, 6 Dalkeith Street, Joppa.

ADAM SPIERS, Timber Merchant, Warriston Saw-Mills, Edinburgh.

ROBERT ALLAN, Factor, Polkemmet, Whitburn.

G. U. MACDONALD, Overseer, Haystoun Estate, Woodbine Cottage, Peebles.

ALEXANDER MITCHELL, Forester, Rosebery, Gorebridge.

ROBERT FORBES, Overseer, Kennet Estate Office, Alloa.

ALEXANDER J. MUNRO, Factor, 48 Castle Street, Edinburgh.

W. M. PRICE, Factor, Minto, Hawick.

GEO. LEVEN, Forester, Bowmont Forest, Roxburgh.

JOHN W. M'HATTIE, Superintendent of City Parks, City Chambers, Edinburgh.

JOHN BROOM, Wood Merchant, Bathgate.

ALEXANDER MURRAY, Forester, Kingswood, Murthly.

J. H. MILNE HOME, Irvine House, Canonbie.

DAVID W. THOMSON, Nurseryman, 133 George Street, Edinburgh.

JOHN A. HOWE, Overseer, Home Farm, Mount-Stuart, Rothesay.

Extra Member—PRESIDENT OF ABERDEEN BRANCH.

LOCAL SECRETARIES.

Counties.		*Scotland.*
Aberdeen,	.	JOHN CLARK, Forester, Haddo House, Aberdeen.
		JOHN MICHIE, M.V.O., Factor, Balmoral, Ballater.
Argyll,	.	H. L. MACDONALD of Dunach, Oban.
Ayr,	.	ANDREW D. PAGE, Overseer, Culzean Home Farm, Ayr.
		A. B. ROBERTSON, Forester, The Dean, Kilmarnock.
Berwick,	.	WM. MILNE, Foulden Newton, Berwick-on-Tweed.
Bute,	.	WM. INGLIS, Forester, Cladoch, Brodick.
		JAMES KAY, retired Forester, Barone, Rothesay.
Clackmannan,.		ROBERT FORBES, Estate Office, Kennet, Alloa.
Dumfries,	.	D. CRABBE, Forester, Byreburnfoot, Canonbie.
East Lothian,	.	W. S. CURR, Factor, Ninewar, Prestonkirk.
Fife,	.	WM. GILCHRIST, Forester, Nursery Cottage, Mount Melville, St Andrews.
		EDMUND SANG, Nurseryman, Kirkcaldy.
Forfar,	.	JAMES CRABBE, retired Forester, Glamis.
Inverness,	.	JAMES A. GOSSIP, Nurseryman, Inverness.
Kincardine,	.	JOHN HART, Estates Office, Cowie, Stonehaven.
Kinross,	.	JAMES TERRIS, Factor, Dullomuir, Blairadam.
Lanark,.	.	JOHN DAVIDSON, Forester, Dalzell, Motherwell.
		JAMES WHITTON, Superintendent of Parks, City Chambers, Glasgow.
Moray,	.	D. SCOTT, Forester, Darnaway Castle, Forres.
Perth,	.	JOHN SCRIMGEOUR, Doune Lodge, Doune.
Ross,	.	Miss AMY FRANCES YULE, Tarradale House, Muir of Ord.
Roxburgh,	.	JOHN LEISHMAN, Manager, Cavers Estate, Hawick.
		R. V. MATHER, Nurseryman, Kelso.
Sutherland,	.	DONALD ROBERTSON, Forester, Dunrobin, Golspie.
Wigtown,	.	JAMES HOGARTH, Forester, Culhorn, Stranraer.
		H. H. WALKER, Monreith Estate Office, Whauphill.

England.

Beds,	.	FRANCIS MITCHELL, Forester, Woburn.
Berks,	.	W. STORIE, Whitway House, Newbury.
Derby,	.	S. MACBEAN, Estate Office, Needwood Forest, Sudbury.
Devon,	.	JAMES BARRIE, Forester, Stevenstone Estate, Torrington.
Durham,	.	JOHN F. ANNAND, M.Sc., Lecturer in Forestry, Armstrong College, Newcastle-upon-Tyne.
Hants,	.	W. R. BROWN, Forester, Park Cottage, Heckfield, Winchfield.
Herts,	.	JAMES BARTON, Forester, Hatfield.
		THOMAS SMITH, Overseer, Tring Park, Wigginton, Tring.
Kent,	.	R. W. COWPER, Gortanore, Sittingbourne.
Lancashire,	.	D. C. HAMILTON, Forester, Knowsley, Prescot.
Leicester,	.	JAMES MARTIN, The Reservoir, Knipton, Grantham.
Lincoln,	.	W. B. HAVELOCK, The Nurseries, Brocklesby Park.
Middlesex,	.	Professor BOULGER, 11 Onslow Road, Richmond Hill, London, S.W.

Counties.	*England.*

Notts, . . W. MICHIE, Forester, Welbeck, Worksop.
WILSON TOMLINSON, Forester, Clumber Park, Worksop.
Surrey, . . JOHN ALEXANDER, 24 Lawn Crescent, Kew Gardens.
Warwick, . A. D. CHRISTIE, Hillside, Frederick Road, Selly Oak, Birmingham.
Wilts, . . ANDREW BOA, Land Agent, Glenmore, The Avenue, Trowbridge.
York, . . GEORGE HANNAH, Estate Office, Boynton, Bridlington.

Ireland.

Dublin, . . A. C. FORBES, Department of Forestry, Board of Agriculture
ARCH. E. MOERAN, Lissadell, Stillorgan Park.
King's County, WM. HENDERSON, Forester, Clonad Cottage, Tullamore.
Tipperary, . ALEX. M'RAE, Forester, Dundrum.

APPENDIX H.

Additions to the Library since the publication of the List in Volume XXVII. Part 2.

BOOKS.

1. *A Handbook of Forestry.* By W. F. A. Hudson, M.A.
2. *New Zealand Official Year Book,* 1912-1913.
3. *Illustrations of Conifers,* vol. iii. By H. Clinton-Baker.
4. *The Forest of Dean.* By Arthur O. Cooke.
5. *The Truth about the West African Land Question.* By Caseby Hayford, 1913.
6. *Die Stadtwaldungen von Zürich. Von Ulrich Meister.* (By purchase.)
7. *Catalogue of Hardy Trees and Shrubs growing at Albury Park, Surrey.* Compiled by A. Bruce Jackson, 1913.
8. Presented by Dr Coaz, Superintendent of Forestry, Switzerland :—
    (1) *Baum & Waldbilder aus der Schweiz,* 1-3 Serie.
    (2) *Schweizerische Forststatistik,* 2 and 3 Lieferung.
    (3) *Erhebungen über die Verbreitung der wildwachsenden Holzarten in der Schweiz.*
    (4) *Ein Besuch im Val Searl.*
    5) *Ueber das Auftreten des grauen Lärchenwicklers.*
    (6) *Die Lawinen in den Schweizer-Alpen.*
    (7) *Der Lawinenschaden in Schweiz. Hochgebirge im Winter und Frühjahr* 1887 *and* 1888.
    (8) *Der Schneeschaden vom* 28/29 *September* 1885 *in den Waldungen der Schweiz.*
    (9) *Der Frost schaden des Winters* 1879/80 *und des Spätfrostes vom* 19/20 *Mai* 1880.
    (10) *Die Stürme vom* 20 *Januar,* 25 *Juni und* 5 *November* 1879.
    (11) *Statistik und Verbau der Lawine in den Schweizer-Alpen.*

GOVERNMENT AND STATE REPORTS.

9. Scotland.—*Return of Particulars of all Deer Forests and Lands exclusively devoted to Sport,* 29*th January* 1913.
10. England.—*Report of Advisory Committee on Forestry in England,* 1912.
11. Ireland.—*Scientific Proceedings of Royal Dublin Society, December* 1912, *February and March* 1913.
12. India, Forest Bulletins :—
    (1) No. 13. *Note on Ligno Protector as a possible means of preventing Timber from Splitting while Seasoning.* By R. S. Pearson.
    (2) No. 14. *A Further Note on the relative strength of Natural and Plantation grown Teak in Burma.* By R. S. Pearson.
    (3) No. 15. *Note on the Technical Properties of Timber.* By R. S. Pearson.
    (4) No. 16. *Note on Gumhar.* By A. Rodgers, I.F.S.
    (5) No. 17. *Note on Bija Sal or Vengai.* ,,

(6) No. 18. *Note on Sain or Saj.* By A. Rodgers, I.F.S.

(7) ,, 19. *Note on Benteak or Nana Wood.* ,,

(8) ,, 20. *Note on Sándan.* ,,

(9) ,, 21. *Note on Dhaura or Bakli.* ,,

(10) ,, 22. *Note on the Causes and Effects of the Drought of 1907 and 1908 on the Sál Forests of the United Provinces.* By R. S. Troup, F.C.H.

13. Indian Forest Records. Vol. v., parts 1-3.

14. Indian Forest Memoirs. Vol. i., part 3, vol. ii., part 2.

   (1) *Statistics of Forest Administration*, 1911-12.

   (2) *Report of Forest Department of Madras*, 1911-12.

15. Canada :—

   (1) *Report of Director of Forestry*, 1912, *with Map and Plans.*

   (2) *Forest Conditions of Nova Scotia.* By B. E. Fernow, issued by the Commission of Conservation, 1912.

   (3) *Sea Fisheries of Eastern Canada.* Do.

   (4) *The Canadian Oyster.* Do.

   (5) *Mine Rescue Work in Canada* Do.

   (6) *Epidemics of Typhoid Fever in City of Ottawa.*

   (7) *Forest Conditions in the Rocky Mountains Forest Reserve.* By F. W. Dwight, M.I.

   (8) *Report of the Forest Branch of British Columbia*, 1912.

   (9) *Preservative Treatment of Fence Posts.* Circular No. 6 of Forestry Branch.

   (10) Forest Products :—

   Lumber, &c. Bulletin 34.

   Poles and Cross Ties. Bulletin 35.

   Wood-using Industries of Ontario. Bulletin 36.

   (11) Forest Products, 1912 :—

   Lumber, Square Timber, Lath and Shingles. Bulletin 40.

   Pulpwood. Bulletin 38.

   Poles and Cross Ties. Bulletin 39.

16. U.S.A. :—

   (1) *Examination of Oleo Resins.* Bulletin 19.

   (2) *Forest Preservation and National Prosperity.* Circular 35.

   (3) *Greenheart.* Circular 211.

   (4) *Circassian Walnut.* Circular 212.

   (5) *The Use Book, a Manual for Users of the National Forests.*

   (6) *The Grinding of Spruce for Mechanical Pulp.* Bulletin 127.

   (7) *Wood-Using Industries of New York.* By J. T. Harris, U.S. Forest Service.

   (8) *Cottonwood in Mississippi Valley.* Bulletin No. 24, Department of Agriculture.

17. New Zealand :—

   (1) *Report on State Nurseries and Plantations*, 1911-12 and 1912-13.

   (2) *Report on Land Survey.* ,, ,,

   (3) *Report on Survey Operations.* ,,

   (4) *Report of Royal Commission on Forestry*, 1913.

18. South Australia :—*Report on State Forest Administration*, 1912-1913.

19. Great Britain :—*Report of Commissioners of Woods, 27th June* 1913.
20. Philippine Islands :—*Report of Director of Forestry, 30th June* 1913.
21. Federated Malay States :—*Report of Forest Administration*, 1912.

SOCIETIES' AND INSTITUTIONS' REPORTS AND TRANSACTIONS.

22. Scotland :—
    (1) *Transactions of the Highland and Agricultural Society*, 5 series, vol. 25, 1913.
    (2) *Transactions of Botanical Society*, vol. 26, parts 1 and 2.
    (3) Royal Botanic Garden, Edinburgh :—*Notes from March and October* 1913.
    (4) Natural History Society of Glasgow :—*The Glasgow Naturalist*, vol. iv., Nos. 3 and 4 ; vol. v., Nos. 1-4 ; vol. vi., No. 1.
23. England :—
    (1) *Journal of Royal Agricultural Society*, vol. 73.
    (2) *Kew Gardens* Bulletin. 1913.
24. Ireland :—
    (1) *Scientific Proceedings of the Royal Dublin Society*, vol. xiii. (N.S.), Nos. 38 and 39, Title and Index ; vol xiv. (N.S.), Nos. 1-7.
    (2) *Economic Proceedings*, vol. ii., No. 6, *Injurious Insects in Ireland*, 1912.
25. Canada :—
    (1) *Transactions of Nova Scotian Institute of Science*, vol. xii., part 4.
    (2) *Reports of Canadian Forestry Association*, 1912 *and* 1913.
26. U.S.A. :—
    (1) *Reports of Smithsonian Institution*, 1911 *and* 1912.
    (2) *Lloyd Library, Bibliography relating to Floras of North America and West Indies*, 1913.
    (3) *Yale Forest School, Prolonging the Cut of Southern Pine.* Bulletin 2.
    (4) *A Working-Plan for the Woodlands of the New Huron Water Company.* By Ralph C. Hawley, 1913.
27. Italy :—*International Institute of Agriculture Monthly Bulletin, Economic and Social Intelligence, February, March, July and September* 1913.

REPRINTS AND MISCELLANEOUS.

28. *A Brief History of the Arboriculture of the New Forest, Hampshire.* By the Hon. G. Lascelles, Deputy Surveyor, 1st August 1913.
29. France :—*Reports of International Forestry Congress,* 1913.
30. *Crataegus in New York.* By C. S. Sargent, 1913.
31. *L'Alpe.* Bologna.
32. *The Estate Magazine.*
33. *Tidskrift for Skogbrug.* Kristiania.
34. *Skogsvårdsföreningens Tidskrift.* Stockholm.
35. *The Indian Forester.* Allahabad.
36. *The Agricultural Economist.*
37. *Journal du Commerce des Bois.* Paris.
38. *Planters' Notebook.*

39. *Forestry Quarterly.* New York.

40. *Canadian Forestry Journal.*

41. *American Forestry.*

42. *Timber Trades Journal.*

43. *Timber News.*

44. *Revue des Eaux et Forêts.* Paris. (By purchase.)

45. *Allgemeine Forst- und Jagd-Zeitung.* (,,)

46. *Zeitschrift für Forst- und Jagdwesen.* (,,)

47. *Bulletin de la Société Forestière de Franche Comté et Belfort.* (By purchase.)

Royal Scottish Arboricultural Society.

(INSTITUTED 16th FEBRUARY 1854.)

LIST OF MEMBERS, &c.

As at 1st September 1914.

- - - - - - - - -

PATRON.

HIS MOST EXCELLENT MAJESTY THE KING.

- - - - - - - - -

PRESIDENT.

Captain ARCHIBALD STIRLING of Keir.

FORMER PRESIDENTS.

YEAR.

1854–56	JAMES BROWN, { Deputy-Surveyor of the Royal Forest of Dean. { Wood Commissioner to the Earl of Seafield.
1857	THE EARL OF DUCIE.
1858	THE EARL OF STAIR.
1859	Sir JOHN HALL, Bart. of Dunglass.
1860	THE DUKE of ATHOLL.
1861	JOHN I. CHALMERS of Aldbar.
1862	THE EARL OF AIRLIE.
1863	The Right Hon. T. F. KENNEDY, P.C.
1864–71	ROBERT HUTCHISON of Carlowrie, F.R.S.E.
1872–73	HUGH CLEGHORN, M.D., LL.D., F.R.S.E., of Stravithie.
1874–75	JOHN HUTTON BALFOUR, M.D., M.A., F.R.SS. L. & E., Professor of Botany in the University of Edinburgh.
1876–78	The Right Hon. W. P. ADAM of Blairadam, M.P., P.C.
1879–81	THE MARQUESS OF LOTHIAN, K.T.
1882	ALEXANDER DICKSON, M.D., F.R.S.E., of Hartree, Regius Professor of Botany in the University of Edinburgh.
1883–85	HUGH CLEGHORN, M.D., LL.D., F.R.S.E., of Stravithie.
1886–87	The Right Hon. Sir HERBERT EUSTACE MAXWELL, Bart., P.C., of Monreith.
1888–89	THE MARQUESS OF LINLITHGOW, Hopetoun House, South Queensferry.
1890–93	ISAAC BAYLEY BALFOUR, M.D., Sc.D., F.R.S., Professor of Botany in the University of Edinburgh.
1894–97	The Right Hon. Sir RONALD MUNRO FERGUSON, K.C.M.G., P.C.
1898	Colonel F. BAILEY, R.E.
1899–02	THE EARL OF MANSFIELD.
1903–06	W. STEUART FOTHRINGHAM of Murthly.
1907–09	Sir KENNETH J. MACKENZIE, Bart. of Gairloch.
1910–12	Sir JOHN STIRLING-MAXWELL, Bart. of Pollok.

d

HONORARY MEMBERS.

Date of
Election.

1914 BJÖRKBOM, Carl, Inspector of Forests, Halsingborg, Sweden.

1914 CAMPBELL, R. H., Director of Forestry, Department of the Interior, Ottawa, Canada.

1907 CASTLETOWN, The Lord, of Upper Ossory, K.P., C.M.G., Granston Manor, Abbeyleix, Ireland.

1914 COAZ, Dr J., Ex-Inspector General of Forests, Bern, Switzerland.

1914 CZILLINGER, Johann, Royal Hungarian Inspector of Forests, Alkotmany, u6, Budapest v. Hungary.

1914 FERGUSON, The Right Hon. Sir Ronald Munro, K.C.M.G., Governor-General of the Commonwealth of Australia. (Also Life Member by Subscription.)

1901 GAMBLE, J. Sykes, C.I.E., F.R.S., M.A., ex-Director of the Indian Forest School, Highfield, East Liss, Hants. (Also Life Member by Subscription.)

1914 GERLINGS, J. H. Jager, Inspector of the Government Forestry Administration at Breda, Holland.

1911 GILLANDERS, A. T., F.E.S., Forester, Park Cottage, Alnwick, Northumberland. (Elected Ordinary Member in 1897.)

1905 HENRY, Auguste Edmond, Professor of Natural Science, etc., National Forest School, Nancy, France.

1886 JOHORE, The Sultan of, Johore, Malay Peninsula.

1904 KAY, James, Retired Wood Manager, Barone, Rothesay. (Elected Ordinary Member in 1867.)

1907 KUMÉ, Kinya, Chief of the Imperial Bureau of Forestry, Department of Agriculture and Commerce, Tokio, Japan.

1914 MAXWELL, The Right Hon. Sir Herbert E., Bt. of Monreith, Wigtownshire. (Elected Ordinary Member in 1886.)

1914 MÜLLER, Dr P. E., Vestervoldgade, 109, Copenhagen, Denmark.

1914 NISBET, Dr John, Forestry Adviser to the Board of Agriculture for Scotland, Edinburgh. (Also Life Member by Subscription.)

1914 PARDÉ, Léon, Inspector of Waters and Forests, Beauvais, France.

1914 RAUNER, S. J., Actual Councillor of State and Vice-Director of the Corps of Foresters, Ministry of Agriculture, Petrograd, Russia.

1889 SARGENT, Professor C. S., Director of the Arnold Arboretum, Harvard College, Brookline, Massachusetts, U.S.A.

1889 SCHLICH, Sir William, K.C.I.E., Professor of Forestry, Oxford University.

1895 SCHWAPPACH, Dr Adam, Professor of Forestry, Eberswalde, Prussia.

1907 SIMMONDS, Frederick, M.V.O., 16 Abingdon Court, Kensington West.

1904 SOMERVILLE, Dr William, M.A., D.Sc., D.Œc., F.R.S.E., Professor of Rural Economy, Oxford. (Also Life Member by Subscription.)

1886 TAKEI, Morimasa, 58 Mikumicho, Ushima, Tokio, Japan.

HONORARY ASSOCIATE MEMBERS.

Date of
Election.

1903 BATTISCOMBE, Edward, Deputy Conservator of Forests, Nairobe, British East Africa.

1901 BRUCE, William, College of Agriculture, 13 George Square, Edinburgh.

1901 CROMBIE, T. Alexander, Forester, Estate Office, Longhirst, Morpeth.

1902 GILBERT, W. Matthews, The *Scotsman* Office, Edinburgh.

1902 SMITH, Fred., Highfield Mount, Brook Street, Macclesfield.

1901 *p* STORY, Fraser, Professor of Forestry, University of North Wales, Bangor.

1901 USHER, Thomas, Courthill, Hawick.

LIFE AND ORDINARY MEMBERS.

C indicates Past or Present Member of Council.
M   ,,   Gold Medal.
m   ,,   Other Medal or Prize.
p   ,,   Author of paper published.
*   ,,   Life Member.
Italics indicate that present Address is unknown.

LAW V. Members in arrear shall not receive the *Transactions.* Any Member whose Annual Subscription remains unpaid for two years shall cease to be a Member of the Society, and no such Member shall be eligible for re-election till his arrears have been paid up.

Date of
Election.

1906 ... *ABERCROMBY, Sir George William, Forglen, Turriff.

1900 ... *ADAIR, David Rattray, S.S.C., 19 Castle Street, Edinburgh.

1907 ... *ADAIR, John Downie, Nurseryman, 75 Shandwick Place, Edinburgh.

1883 ... *ADAM, Sir Charles Elphinstone, Bart. of Blairadam, 5 New Square, Lincoln's Inn, London, W.C.

1913 ... ADAM, James, Assistant Forester, New Cottages. Dupplin, Perth.

1912 ... *ADAM, Thomas, F.S.I., J.P., Property Valuator, 27 Union Street, Glasgow.

1904 ... *ADAMS, Joseph Wm. Atkin, Resident Agent, Mill Hill, Middlesex.

1906 ... ADAMSON, John, Head Forester, Bell's Yew Green, Frant, Sussex.

1874 ... *ADDINGTON, The Lord, Addington Manor, Winslow, Bucks.

1913 ... *ADKIN, Benaiah Whitley, F.S.I., 82 Victoria Street, Westminster, London.

1914 ... *ADKIN, Benaiah Colson, Forestry Student, Emmanuel College, Cambridge.

1904 *Cp* *AGNEW, Sir Andrew, Bart., 10 Smith Square, Westminster.

1903 ... AILSA, The Marquess of, Culzean Castle, Maybole.

1912 ... *AINSLIE, James Robert, Assistant Conservator of Forests, Ura Division, Hapatale, Ceylon.

1906 ... AINSLIE, John, Factor, Stobo, Peeblesshire.

1902 .. AINSLIE, Thomas, Glenosk, Penicuik.

1908 ... AIRD, William. Mechanical Engineer, Woodend, Muirkirk, Ayrshire.

1902 ... AITCHISON, William, Assistant Forester, Weirburn Cottage, Grant's House.

1914 ... AITKEN, George, Assistant Forester, The Cottages, Bruckley Castle, Aberdeenshire.

1907 ... AITKEN, James, Overseer, Airth Estate, Larbert.

1914 ... *AITON, Robert Scott, Sub-Factor, Estate Office, Lennel, Coldstream.

1905 ... ALEXANDER, Henry, Head Forester, Grimstone Estate, Gilling East, York.

1883 p *ALEXANDER, John A., 24 Lawn Crescent, Kew Gardens, Surrey.

1908 ... *ALEXANDER, John, Nurseryman, 1 Waterloo Place, Edinburgh.

1905 ... ALLAN, James, Forester, 6 Bostock Road, Middlewick, Cheshire.

1913 ... ALLAN, John Cameron, Assistant Forester, Mellerstain, Gordon, Berwickshire.

1903 C *ALLAN, Robert, F.S.I., F.H.A.S., Factor, Halfway House, Polkemmet, Whitburn.

1909 ... ALLISON, Thomas, Solicitor and Factor, Fort William.

1912 ... ALSTON, James, Merchant, 119 Virginia Street, Glasgow.

1910 .... AMOS, Frank, Surveyor and Auctioneer, The Parade, Canterbury.

1901 ... *ANDERSON, Robert, Bailiff, Phœnix Park, Dublin.

1909 ... ANDERSON, Robert Lawson, Forester, Balgate, Kiltarlity. Beauly.

1914 ... ANDERSON, Sir Kenneth Skelton, K.C.M.G., Stamford House, Wimbledon Common, London, S.W.

1914 ... ANDERSON, Thomas, M.A., B.Sc., Staff Director, Seed Testing Station, Board of Agriculture, 29 St Andrew Square, Edinburgh.

1887 Cmp ANNAND, John F., M.Sc., Lecturer in Forestry, Armstrong College, Newcastle-on-Tyne.

1903 ... ANSTRUTHER, Sir Ralph, Bart. of Balcaskie, Pittenweem.

1903 m ARCHIBALD, John Clark, Head Forester, Eden Hall, Langwathby, R.S.O., Cumberland.

1898 ... ARMSTRONG, Thos. J. A., Factor, Glenborrodale, Salen, Fort William.

1904 ... ARNOTT, William, Head Forester, Ardtornish Estate, Morvern, by Oban.

1883 m *ATHOLL, The Duke of, K.T., Blair Castle, Blair Atholl.

1913 ... AUCHTERLONIE, Alexander, Assistant Forester, 33 Weekley Kettering, Northants.

1860 ... AUSTIN & M'ASLAN, Nurserymen, 89 Mitchell Street, Glasgow.

1908 ... BAILLIE, Lieutenant-Colonel A. C., Factor, etc., Kirklands, Melrose.

1912 ... BAILLIE, Robert Richard Webster, Estate Agent, Lanfine, Newmilns.

Date of
Election.

1906   *m* *BAIRD, Henry Robert, D.L., J.P., Durris House, Drumoak, Aberdeen.

1896   ... *BAIRD, J. G. A., of Adamton, 89 Eaton Square, London, S.W.

1914   .. BAIRD, Sir David, Bart. of Newbyth, New Club, Edinburgh.

1903   ... BAIRD, William Arthur, of Erskine, Glasgow.

1913   ... BAKER, William, Assistant Forester, Pitcox Lodge, Biel, Dunbar.

1909   *p* *BALDEN, John, Estate Agent, Bywell Office, Stocksfield-on-Tyne.

1884   ... *BALFOUR OF BURLEIGH, The Right Hon. Lord, K.T., Kennet House, Alloa.

1900   ... *BALFOUR, Charles B., of Newton Don, Kelso.

1886   *m**BALFOUR, Edward, of Balbirnie, Markinch, Fife.

1906   *Mp* BALFOUR, Frederick Robert Stephen, J.P., Dawyck, Stobo, Peeblesshire ; 39 Phillimore Gardens, Kensington, London, W.

1877   *Cp* *BALFOUR, Isaac Bayley, LL.D., Sc.D., M.D., F.L.S , Professor of Botany, Royal Botanic Garden, Edinburgh, *Past President.*

1912   ... *BALFOUR, Robert Frederick, Yr. of Balbirnie, Balbirnie, Markinch.

1892   ... BALLINGALL, Niel, Sweet Bank, Markinch, Fife.

1904   ... *BARBOUR, George Freeland, of Bonskeid, Pitlochry.

1897   ... BARCLAY, Robert Leatham, Banker, 54 Lombard St., London, E.C.

1908   ... BARNES, Nicholas F., Head Gardener, Eaton Hall, Chester.

1909   ... BARR, D., James Service & Sons, Maxwelltown, Dumfries.

1895   ... *BARRIE, James Alexander, Forester, Harlestone, Northampton.

1866   *Mp* *BARRIE, James, Forester, Stevenstone, Torrington, North Devon.

1877   *p* *BARRY, John W., of Fyling Hall, Fylingdales, Scarborough, Yorks.

1874   ... BARTON, James, Forester, Upper Tofts, Kirkton, Hawick.

1904   ... BARTON, James Robert, Factor, 3 Coates Crescent, Edinburgh.

1908   ... *BAXTER, Edward Gorrel, J.P., Teasses, Lower Largo, Fife.

1908   ... BAXTER, James, Gardener, Gorddinog, Llanfairfechan, Carnarvon-shire.

1910   ... BAYLEY, James Francis, W.S., 4 Hill Street, Edinburgh.

1897   ... *BEGG, James, Rosslyne, Culter, by Aberdeen.

1883   ... *BELL, Andrew, Forester, Rothes, Elgin.

1898   ... BELL, David, Seed Merchant, Coburg Street, Leith.

1910   *m* *BELL, Sir James, Bart., of Montgreenan, Kilmarnock.

1908   ... BELL, John R., Assistant Forester, Colstoun, Haddington.

1900   ... BELL, Robert, Land Steward, Baronscourt, Newtown-Stewart, Ireland.

1900   ... BELL, William, Forester, Balthayock, Perth.

1871   ... *BELL, William, of Gribdae, 37 Melbourne Grove, Dulwich, London, S.E.

1914   ... BELL, Wm., Assistant Forester, Old Mill, Cuckney, Mansfield, Notts.

1911   .. BENNETT, Col. R. J., Savoy Park, Ayr.

1913   ... BENNOCH, John, Forester, Newhousemill, East Kilbride.

1903   ... BENTINCK, Lord Henry, M.P., Underley Hall, Kirkby Lonsdale.

1904 ... *BERRY, Charles Walter, B.A., 11 Atholl Crescent, Edinburgh.

1914 ... BERRY, Edmund, Danish Consul General for Scotland. 7 Belgrave Place, Edinburgh.

1889 *m* BERRY, Francis, Forester, Minto, Hawick.

1914 ... BERRY, George Andrew, M.B., LL.D., 31 Drumsheugh Gardens, Edinburgh.

1912 ... BERRY, William, Advocate and Landowner, of Tayfield, Newport, Fife.

1911 ... BETHELL, Slingsby Westbury, Blackford, Rothienorman.

1907 ... BEVERIDGE, James, Forester, Normanby, Doncaster.

1903 ... BINNING, The Lord, Mellerstain, Kelso.

1909 ... BISCOE, T. R., of Newton, Kingillie, Kirkhill R.S.O., Inverness-shire.

1897 ... *BLACK, Alexander, The Gardens, Carton, Maynooth, Co. Kildare.

1908 ... *BLACK, Florance William, of Kailzie, Peeblesshire.

1904 ... BLACK, John, Factor, Cortachy Castle, Kirriemuir.

1913 ... BLACK, Robert, Factor's Assistant, 66 Queen Street, Edinburgh.

1911 ... BLACK, William, Timber Merchant, 37 Clerk Street, Brechin.

1908 ... BLACKLAWS, John, Head Forester, Seafield Cottage, Portsoy.

1913 ... BLAIR, Alexander, Chief Valuer, 9 Wemyss Place, Edinburgh.

1908 ... BLAIR, Charles, Glenfoot, Tillicoultry.

1910 ... BLAIR, Captain Hunter, R.N., of Blairquhan, Ayrshire.

1903 ... BLAIR, Thomas, Farmer, Hoprig Mains, Gladsmuir.

1872 ... BOA, Andrew, Estate Agent, Glenmore, The Avenue, Trowbridge.

1877 ... *BOLCKOW, C. F. H., of Brackenhoe, Kentisknowle, Torquay.

1892 ... BOND, Thomas, Forester, Lambton Park, Fence Houses, Durham.

1895 ... *BOORD, W. Bertram, Land Agent, Bewerley, Pateley Bridge, Yorks.

1909 ... BOOTH, Miss Cary, 26 Calandrellestrasse, Lankwitz, Berlin.

1898 *CMp**BORTHWICK, A. W., D.Sc., 46 George Square, Edinburgh, *Hon. Editor.*

1898 ... BORTHWICK, Francis J. G., W.S., 9 Hill Street, Edinburgh.

1908 ... *BORTHWICK, Henry, Borthwick Castle, Gorebridge.

1887 *Mp* BOULGER, Professor G. S., 11 Onslow Road, Richmond Hill, London, S.W.

1912 ... BOYD, Alexander, Gardener, The Gardens, Ardgour, Argyllshire.

1883 *Cp* BOYD, John, Crown Forester's House, Ford, Kilmartin, Argyll.

1897 ... BRAID, J. B., Forester, Witley Court, Great Witley, Worcester.

1902 ... *BRAID, William Wilson, 20 Esslemont Road, Craigmillar Park, Edinburgh.

1907 ... BREADALBANE, The Marchioness of, Black Mount, Bridge of Orchy, Argyllshire.

1911 ... *BREBNER, Robert F., Factor, Crecy House, Isle of Whithorn, Wigtownshire.

1910 ... BROADFOOT, David, Forester, 185 Langley Old Hall, Langley, Huddersfield, Yorks.

1907 *Cp* BRODIE Ian, of Brodie, Brodie Castle, Forres.

1911 ... *BROOK. Charles, of Kinmount, Annan.

1900 *C* *BROOM, John, Wood Merchant, Bathgate.

1900 ... *BROWN, Charles, Factor, Kerse, Falkirk.

1911 ... BROWN, Duncan, Foreman Forester, The Gardens, Birr Castle, King's Co., Ireland.

1910 *p* BROWN, Francis Loftus Cowley Cowley-, Principal, South Indian Forest College, Coimbatore, S. India.

1904 ... BROWN, George, Timber Merchant, Buckhaven Saw-mills, Buckhaven.

1900 *Cmp* *BROWN, Gilbert, Wood Manager, Grantown, Strathspey.

1878 ... BROWN, J. A. Harvie-, of Quarter, Dunipace House, Larbert.

1899 ... BROWN, John, Overseer, Isel Hall, Cockermouth.

1896 ... *BROWN, Rev. W. Wallace, Minister of Alness, Ross-shire.

1895 ... BROWN, Walter R., Forester, Park Cottage, Heckfield, near Winchfield, Hants.

1900 ... BROWN, William, Forester, Comlongon Nursery, Ruthwell, R.S.O.

1905 ... BRUCE, Alexander, Timber Merchant, 68 Gordon Street, Glasgow.

1907 ... BRUCE, Charles, Assistant Forester, Beaumanor Park, Woodhouse, Loughborough, Leicestershire.

1901 ... BRUCE, David, Overseer, Earnock Estate Office, Hillhouse, Hamilton.

1910 ... BRUCE, David, M.A., LL.B., 141 West George Street, Glasgow.

1895 ... *BRUCE, Peter, Manager, Achnacloich, Culnadalloch, by Connel.

1909 ... BRUNTON, James S., Forester, Hursley Park, near Winchester, Hants.

1907 ... *BRYDEN, Thomas, Nurseryman, Dennison Nurseries, Ayr.

1897 ... BRYDON, John, Seed Merchant and Nurseryman, Darlington, Co. Durham.

1879 *m* *BUCCLEUCH, The Duke of, K.T., Dalkeith Palace, Dalkeith.

1879 *C* *BUCHANAN, Charles, Factor, Penicuik Estate, Penicuik.

1911 ... BUCHANAN, John Hamilton, of Leny (Callander), **C.A.**, 8 York Place, Edinburgh.

1914 ... *BURDON, Edward Russell, M.A., J.P., F.L.S., Ikenhilde, Royston, Herts.

1906 ... BURNETT, Sir Thomas, Bart., Crathes Castle, Crathes, N.B.

1909 ... BURNLEY-CAMPBELL, Colin N., Ormidale, Colintrave.

1914 ... BURROWS, Frank Herbert, Land Agent and Valuer, 41 Bank Street, Ashford, Kent.

1910 ... BURTON, Richard Charles Fryer, Conservator of Forests, Pietermaritzburg, Natal.

1904 ... BUTLER, Robert, Forester, Estate Office, Blenheim Palace, Woodstock, Oxfordshire.

1906 ... BUTLER, Walter James, Mellerstain Cottages, Gordon, Berwickshire.

1913 ... *BUTTAR, Alexander, Blackfriars House Perth.

1913 ... BUTTAR, Fernie Louden, Forestry Student, 7 Linkfield, Musselburgh.

Date of
Election.

1910 ... *BUTTER, Charles A. J., Cluniemore, Pitlochry.

1909 ... *BUXTON, Walter L., of Bolwich, Marsham, Norwich.

1909 ... *CACCIA, Anthony M., M.V.O., 19 Linton Road, Oxford.

1902 *p* *CADELL, Henry Moubray, of Grange and Banton, B.Sc.,
F.R.S E., F.A.S., J.P., etc., Grange, Linlithgow.

1914 ... CADELL, John Macfarlane, M.B., Lt.-Col., Indian Medical
Service (Ret.), Foxhall, Kirkliston.

1912 ... CAESAR, William, Solicitor, Bathgate.

1913 ... CAIRNS, John, Seedsman, 89 Mitchell Street, Glasgow.

1908 ... *CALDER, James Charles, of Ledlanet, Milnathort.

1912 ... CALDER, John Joseph, of Ardargie, Forgandenny.

1906 ... CALDERHEAD, William, Overseer, Eredine, Port Sonachan, Argyllshire.

1901 ... CAMERON, Alex., Balmina, Cookstown, Ireland.

1910 ... CAMERON, Angus, F.S.I., Factor, Seafield Estates Office, Elgin.

1907 ... CAMERON, Donald Walter, of Lochiel, Achnacarry, Spean
Bridge.

1913 ... CAMERON, Grigor J., Assistant Forester, Lochgarten Cottage,
Nethy Bridge.

1908 ... *Cameron, John, Forester, Isel Hall, Cockermouth, Cumberland.*

1899 ... *CAMERON, John J., Norwood, Hamilton.

1904 ... CAMERON, Robert, Estate Office, Brinscall, nr. Chorley.

1912 ... CAMERON, Simon, Forester, Corrour, S.O., Inverness-shire.

1912 ... CAMPBELL, Adam, Sub-Factor Cromartie Estates, Kildary,
Ross-shire.

1895 ... CAMPBELL, Alexander, Land Steward, Rosemill Cottage, Strathmartin, by Dundee.

1899 ... CAMPBELL, Alexander, Tullymully, Dunkeld.

1904 ... CAMPBELL, David S., Forester, Middleton Hall, Belford,
Northumberland.

1914 ... CAMPBELL, George, Assistant Forester, Barcaldine, Ledaig.

1897 ... *CAMPBELL, James Arthur, Arduaine, Lochgilphead, Argyllshire.

1900 ... CAMPBELL, James S., Forester, Gisboro Hall, Gisboro, Yorks.

1906 ... CAMPBELL, John, Land Steward, Forss Estates, Westfield,
Thurso.

1911 ... *CAMPBELL, Keir Arthur, Student, Arduaine, Lochgilphead.

1914 ... CAMPBELL, Kenneth, Assistant Forester, Groan Cottages, Logic-
almond by Methven.

1908 ... CAMPBELL, Patrick William, of Auchairne, W.S., 25 Moray
Place, Edinburgh.

1901 ... CAMPBELL, Peter Purdie, Factor, Lee and Carnwath Estates
Office, Cartland, Lanark.

1908 ... CAMPBELL, Robert, M.A., D.Sc., Geological Laboratory, Edinburgh University.

1914 ... CAMPBELL, Thomas, Forester, Forest Department, Nairobi,
British East Africa.

Date of
Election.

1903 ... CANCH, Thomas Richard, B.Sc., P.A.S.I., 3 Greenbank Crescent Morningside, Edinburgh.

1911 ... CANE, William, Assistant Forester, Brown's Lodge, Pembury, Tunbridge Wells.

1903 ... *CAPEL, James Carnegy Arbuthnott, of Ballnamon, 34 Roland Gardens, London. S.W.

1896 ... *CARMICHAEL, The Lord, Governor of Madras, India.

1908 ... CARMICHAEL, James Louis, younger of Arthurstone, Arthurstone, Meigle.

1906 ... CARNEGIE, James, of Strouvar, Balquhidder.

1907 ... CARNEGIE, Robert, Head Forester, Woodside, Balnillo, Dun, Montrose.

1914 ... CARNEGY, Caesar, Assistant Forester, Torbain, Raith, Kirkcaldy.

1903 ... CARRUTHERS, Major Francis John, of Dormont, Lockerbie.

1898 ... *CARSON, David Simpson, C.A., 209 West George Street, Glasgow.

1904 ... CATHCART, Sir Reginald Gordon, Bart., Cluny Castle, Aberdeenshire.

1911 ... CAVERHILL, W. R., Factor, The Glen, Innerleithen.

1909 ... *CHADWICK, James Melville, Findhorn House, Forres.

1906 *CHALCRAFT, George Barker, "Hillside," Gimingham, near North Walsham, Norfolk.

1911 ... CHALMERS, Frank, W.S., 13 Riselaw Road, Edinburgh.

1897 ... CHALMERS, James, Overseer, Gask, Auchterarder, Perthshire.

1904 ... CHALMERS, Robert W., Head Forester, Earlyvale, Eddleston, Peeblesshire.

1911 ... CHAPMAN, Alfred, Assistant Forester, Clumber Park, Worksop, Notts.

1892 ... CHAPMAN, Andrew, Factor, Dinwoodie Lodge, Lockerbie, Dumfriesshire.

1914 ... CHAPPLOW, John Nelson, Assistant Forester. Harewood. Leeds.

1908 ... CHERMSIDE, Sir Herbert, Newstead Abbey, Nottingham.

1906 ... CHISHOLM, Alexander M'Kenzie, Clerk of Works, Dalkeith Park, Dalkeith.

1909 ... CHISHOLM, George, Forester, Wishaw House, Wishaw.

1882 ... *CHOWLER, Christopher, Gamekeeper, Dalkeith Park, Dalkeith.

1884 ... CHRISTIE, Alex. D., Hillside, Castle Road, Warley, Birmingham.

1906 ... CHRISTIE, Charles, Factor, Estate Office, Strathdon.

1910 ... Christie, James Sinton, Superintendent of Parks, Town Hall. Camberwell, S.E.

1908 ... CHRISTIE, Miss Isabella Robertson, of Cowden, Dollar.

1906 ... CHRISTIE, Thomas, Nurseryman, Rosefield Nurseries, Forres.

1883 ... *CHRISTIE, William, Nurseryman, Fochabers.

1890 ... CLARK, Charles, Forester, Cawdor Castle, Nairn.

1902 ... CLARK, Francis Ion, Estate Office, Haddo House, Aberdeen.

1910 ... CLARK, George, Forester, Crawfordton Estate, Thornhill.

Date of
Election.

1891 *Cp* CLARK, John, Forester, Kelly, Methlick, Aberdeen.

1906 ... CLARK, John, Forester, Almond Dell, Old Clapperton Hall, Midcalder.

1892 ... *CLARK, William, 66 Queen Street, Edinburgh.

1902 ... CLARK, William, Factor, Dunglass Estate Office, Co'path.

1914 ... CLARK, William, Assistant Forester, Bourtrees, Fairlie, Ayrshire.

1914 ... *CLARKE, Ian Anderson, M.A., B.Sc., Student of Forestry, 7 Chanonry, Aberdeen.

1911 ... CLERK RATTRAY, Colonel Burn, of Craighall Rattray, Blairgowrie.

1914 ... CLERK, Sir George James Robert, Bart., of Penicuik, Midlothian.

1910 ... CLINTON-BAKER, Henry Wm., J.P., of Bayfordbury, Hertford.

1902 ... *CLINTON, The Lord, Fettercairn House, Fettercairn.

1906 ... CLYNE, James, Engineer, Knappach, Banchory.

1898 ... *COATS, Sir Thomas Glen, Bart., Ferguslie Park, Paisley.

1904 ... COBB, Herbert Mansfield, Land Agent, Higham, Rochester, Kent.

1913 ... COCHRAN, Francis James, of Balfour, 152 Union Street, Aberdeen.

1906 ... COCKER, Alexander Morrison, Nurseryman, 130 Union Street, Aberdeen.

1904 ... *COKE, Hon. Richard, 14 Tedworth Square, London, S.W.

1914 ... COLAM, Rosslyn Leigh, Factor, C.D.A., Galloway Estates Office, Newton Stewart.

1906 ... COLES, Walter G., Engineer, Board of Agriculture, 122 George Street, Edinburgh.

1879 ... *COLQUHOUN, Andrew, Yew Bank, Luss.

1908 ... COLSTON, William G., Estate Clerk, Rosemount, Lockerbie.

1908 ... COLTMAN, William Hew, J.P., B.A., Barrister, Blelack, Dinnet, Aberdeenshire.

1907 ... COMRIE, Patrick, Land Agent, Waterside, Dalry, Ayrshire.

1895 ... CONNOR, George A., Factor, Craigielaw, Longniddry.

1887 *C* *COOK, James, Land Steward, Arniston, Gorebridge, Midlothian.

1906 ... COOK, Melville Anderson, Assistant Forester, Glamis, Forfarshire.

1914 ... COOK, James, Shipowner, Enfield, Cults.

1904 ... COUPAR, Charles, Manager, Barcaldine, Ledaig, Argyllshire.

1914 ... COUPAR, James, Assistant Forester, East Lodge, Ballechin, Ballinluig.

1897 ... *COUPAR, Wm., Overseer, Balgowan, Perthshire.

1912 ... COUTTS, Duncan, Apprentice Forester, Royal Botanic Garden, Edinburgh.

1910 ... *Coutts, James, Assistant Forester. Douglas Castle, Lanarkshire.*

1908 ... *COWAN, Alexander, Valleyfield, Penicuik.

1876 ... *COWAN, Charles W., Dalhousie Castle, Bonnyrigg, Lasswade.

1892 ... *COWAN, George, 1 Gillsland Road, Edinburgh.

1908 ... COWAN, Henry Hargrave, Seafield Estates Office, Cullen.

1899 ... *COWAN, Robert, Mains of Househill, Nairn.

1901 ... *COWAN, Robert Craig, Eskhill, Inveresk.

Date of
Election.

1910　　*m* Cowan, Robert, Head Forester, Hoddom Cross, Ecclefechan.

1912　...　Cowieson, Fred Davidson, Structural Engineer, 3 Charles Street, St Rollox, Glasgow.

1874　...　*Cowper, R. W., Gortanore, Sittingbourne. Kent.

1904　...　*Cox, Albert E., of Dungarthill, Dunkeld.

1904　...　*Cox, William Henry, of Snaigow, Murthly.

1900　...　Crabbe, Alfred, Forester, Glamis.

1875　　*m* Crabbe, David, Forester, Byreburnfoot, Canonbie, Dumfriesshire.

1904　...　Craig, Alexander, Assistant Forester, Glamis.

1909　...　*Craig, Sir Archibald Gibson, Bart. of Riccarton, Currie.

1875　...　*Craig, Wm., M.D., C.M., F.R.S.E., 71 Bruntsfield Place, Edinburgh.

1913　...　Cramb, Daniel, Assistant Forester. Burnside Lodge, Dupplin Estate, Perth.

1903　...　Cranstoun, Charles Joseph Edmondstoune, of Corehouse, Lanark.

1908　...　*Craw, John Taylor, Factor and Farmer, Coldstream.

1908　...　*Crawford, The Earl of, Balcarres, Fife ; 7 Audley Square, London, W.

1899　...　Crerar, David, Land Steward, Methven Castle, Perth.

1911　...　Crichton, Edward James, Wood Merchant's Clerk, Silverbank Sawmills, Banchory.

1914　.....　Critchley, Edgar Godsell, Solicitor. 29 High Street, Inverness.

1903　...　Croll, John, of D. & W. Croll, Nurseryman, Dundee.

1900　...　*Crooks, James, Timber Merchant, Woodlands, Eccleston Park, Prescot.

1895 *Cmp* *Crozier, John D., Dept. of Forestry, Board of Agriculture, Dublin.

1910　...　Cruden, Lewis G., Forester, East Lodge, Brucklay, Aberdeenshire.

1907　...　Cruickshank, James, Farmer and Hotelkeeper, Port Erroll, Aberdeenshire.

1914　...　Culton, Walter R., Foreman Forester, Benmore, Kilmun.

1900　...　Cumming, John H., Overseer, Royal Dublin Society, Ball's Bridge, Dublin.

1911　...　Cumming, Thomas, Forester, Cluniemore Estate, Pitlochry.

1906　...　Cumming, William, Nursery Foreman, Burnside Nurseries, Aberdeen.

1901　...　*Cunningham, Captain John, Leithen Lodge, Innerleithen.

1898　...　*Cunningham, George, Advocate, The Square, Kingsley Green, Haslemore, Surrey.

1909　...　Cunningham, Robert, Forester, Glenlogan, by Mauchline, Ayrshire.

1913　...　Curr. James, Estate Clerk, Ninewar, Prestonkirk.

1913　...　Curr, Thomas. Student, Ninewar, Prestonkirk.

1898　...　*Curr, W. S., Factor, Ninewar, Prestonkirk.

1907　...　*Cuthbertson, Evan James, W.S., 12 Church Hill, Edinburgh.

1907　　*m* Dale, Robert, Forester, The Nursery, Sorn Castle, Ayrshire.

Date of
Election.

1867 ... *DALGLEISH, John I., of Westgrange, Brankston Grange, Bogside Station, Alloa.

1900 ... *DALHOUSIE, The Earl of, Brechin Castle, Forfarshire.

1908 ... DALKEITH, The Earl of, Eildon Hall, St Boswells.

1910 ... *DALLIMORE, William, Assistant, Royal Gardens, Kew, 43 Leyborne Park, Kew Gardens, Surrey.

1901 ... DALRYMPLE, Hon. Hew H., Lochinch, Castle Kennedy, Wigtownshire.

1906 ... *DALRYMPLE, The Lord, M.P., Lochinch, Stranraer.

1904 ... DALRYMPLE, The Right Hon. Sir Charles, Bart., P.C., of Newhailes, Musselburgh ; 97 Onslow Square, London, S.W.

1914 ... DALYELL, Sir J. B Wilkie, Bart., of Binns, Linlithgow.

1914 ... DALZIEL, Henry, Forester, Eliock Lodge, Sanquhar.

1905 ... DAVID, Albert E., Assistant Forester, Erlestoke, nr. Devizes, Wilts.

1912 ... DAVIDSON, George Alfred, Factor, Knockdow Estate Office, Toward.

1904 ... DAVIDSON, James, 12 South Charlotte Street, Edinburgh.

1913 ... DAVIDSON, James Stewart, Cairnlee, Bieldside.

1892 mp DAVIDSON, John, Forester, Dalzell, Motherwell, Lanarkshire.

1908 ... *DAVIDSON, Major Duncan Francis, Dess, Aberdeenshire.

1892 C *DAVIDSON, William, Forester, Panmure, Carnoustie.

1913 ... DAVIDSON, William Cameron, Estate Clerk, Seafield Estates Office, Cullen.

1913 ... DAVIDSON, William, Clerk of Works, The Square, Ellon.

1901 ... DAVIE, George, Overseer, Balruddery Gardens, near Dundee.

1904 ... *Davie, Thomas, Forester, Dunnotter Estate, Stonehaven.*

1908 Cp *DAWSON, William, M.A., B.Sc.(Agr.), Reader in Forestry, Cambridge University.

1904 ... DENHOLM, John, Timber Merchant, Bo'ness.

1906 ... DEWAR, Alex., 12 Greenhill Park, Edinburgh.

1902 ... DEWAR, H. R., Forester, Beaufort Castle, Beauly.

1901 m *DEWAR, Sir John A., Bart., M.P., Dupplin Castle, Perth.

1898 ... *DIGBY, The Right Hon. Baron, Minterne, Cerne, Dorsetshire.

1912 ... DODS, John Henry, Factor, Novar, Evanton, Ross-shire.

1903 ... *DON, Alex., Mikalongwe, Nyasaland.

1913 m DONALD, James A., Forester, Dupplin Estate, Perth.

1908 ... DOUGHTY, James T. S., Solicitor and Factor, Ayton.

1896 ... *DOUGLAS, Alex.. Estate Bailiff's Office, Dean Road, Scarborough.

1882 m DOUGLAS, Captain Palmer, of Cavers, Hawick.

1903 ... DOUGLAS, William G., Forester, Ingleborough Estate, Clapham, Yorks.

1911 ... DOULL, Donald, M.A., A.R.C.Sc., High School, Kelso.

1903 ... DOW, Alexander, Forester, Bretby Park, Burton-on-Trent.

1898 m DOW, Thomas, Forester, Wakefield Lawn, Stony Stratford, Bucks.

1914 ... DOWIE, Stuart, Forester, Muirend, Madderty, Crieff.

1909 ... DRUMMOND, A. Hay, of Cromlix, Dunblane.

1900 ... DRUMMOND, Dudley W., Commissioner, Cawdor Estate Office, Carmarthen, South Wales.

Date of
Election.

1904 ... DRUMMOND, William, Head Forester, Fairburn Estate, Muir of Ord, Ross-shire.

1862 ... DRUMMOND & SONS, William, Nurserymen. Stirling.

1912 ... DRYSDALE, A. Leslie, Hartfell, Colinton.

1912 ... DRYSDALE, Alexander. Assistant Forester, Parkend, Lydney, Glos.

1913 ... DRYSDALE, Robert, Foreman Forester, Novar Estate, Evanton, Ross-shire.

1909 ... DRYSDALE, Thomas, Land Steward, Estate Office, Auchinleck.

1908 ... DUCHESNE, M. C., Land Agent, Farnham Common, Slough, Bucks.

1909 ... *DUFF, Alexander M., Land Steward and Farm Manager, Ninewells, Snaigow, Murthly.

1914 ... *DUFF, Captain L. Gordon, Yr. of Drummuir and Park, Park House, Cornhill, Banffshire.

1912 ... DUFF, James, Forester, c/o Mrs Maxwell, Balboughty, Perth.

1907 ... DUFF, John Wharton Wharton, of Orton and Barmuchity, Morayshire.

1903 ... DUFF, Mrs M. M. Wharton-, of Orton, Morayshire.

1907 ... DUFF, Thomas Gordon, of Drummuir and Park, Banffshire.

1907 ... DUGUID, Charles, Head Forester, Philorth, Fraserburgh.

1910 ... DUNBAR, John Christie Flockhart, Factor, Crathes Castle, Crathes.

1911 ... DUNCAN, Peter, Assistant Forester, The Lodge, Castle Toward, Toward, Argyllshire.

1910 ... DUNCAN, Robert, Forester, Cloan, Auchterarder.

1907 ... DUNGLASS, The Lord, Springhill, Coldstream.

1912 ... *DUNLOP, Thomas, D.L., Shipowner, 70 Wellington Street, Glasgow.

1905 ... DUNSTAN, M. I. R., Principal of South-Eastern Agricultural College, Wye, Kent.

1902 ... *DURHAM, The Earl of, K.G., Lambton Castle, Durham.

1873 ... DURWARD, Robert, Estate Manager, Blelack, Logie-Coldstone, Dinnet, Aberdeenshire.

1912 ... DUTHIE, Edwin Charles, Nursery Assistant, Ewan Place, Countesswells Road, Aberdeen.

1900 ... DUTHIE, James A., of Benjamin Reid & Co., Nurserymen, Aberdeen.

1898 ... EADSON, Thomas G., Forester, Whaley, Mansfield.

1911 ... EASSON, Thomas S., W.S., 66 Queen Street, Edinburgh.

1906 ... EDGAR, James, Factor, Poltalloch Estate Office, Kilmartin, Argyll.

1885 ... EDINGTON, Francis, Overseer, Monk Coniston Park, Lancashire.

1904 m EDMOND, James, Assistant, Wemyss Castle Estate Office, East Wemyss, File.

1914 m EDMOND, William A., Foreman Joiner, Farm Lodge, Floors Castle, Kelso.

1899 mp EDWARDS, Alex. W. B., Forester, Thirlmere Estate, via Grasmere.

1912 ... EDWARDS, Johnston, Assistant Forester, Pollok Estate, Pollokshaws.

Date of
Election.

1914 ... EDWARDS, J. H., Advocate, of Edmond and Ledingham, Golden Square, Aberdeen.

1893 ... ELDER, William, Forester, Leny Estate, Callander.

1902 ... ELLICE, Captain Edward Charles, Invergarry, and 48 Sloane Gardens, S.W.

1899 ... *ELLISON, Francis B., Downesleigh, Shefford, Bedfordshire.

1904 ... *ELPHINSTONE, The Lord, Carberry Tower, Musselburgh.

1901 *p* ELWES, Henry John, F.R.S., of Colesborne, Cheltenham.

1901 ... ERSKINE, Richard Brittain, Oaklands, Trinity, Edinburgh.

1898 ... EWAN, Peter, Forester, Herbert Cottage, Ditchampton, Wilton, Salisbury.

1873 ... EWING, David, Forester, Strichen House, Aberdeen.

1906 ... FAICHNEY, John, Forester, Blythswood, Renfrew.

1914 ... FAIRWEATHER, James, Assistant Factor, Bute Estate Office, Bute.

1913 ... FALCONER, David, Forester, Ballechin, Perthshire.

1912 ... FALCONER, James Grewar, Architect, 4 Cameron Square, Fort William.

1894 ... *FARQUHARSON, James, Forester, Ardgowan, Inverkip.

1911 ... FARQUHARSON, Right Hon. Robert, M.D., P.C., Finzean, Aboyne.

1900 *mp* FEAKS, Matthew, Forester, Lochiel Estate, Achnacarry.

1903 ... FENWICK, William, Factor, Darnaway Castle Estates Office, Earlsmill, Forres.

1900 ... *FERGUSON, James Alex., Ardnith, Partickhill, Glasgow.

1910 *mp* FERGUSON, John, Forester, New Road, Newtown, Montgomeryshire.

1888 *Cmp**FERGUSON, The Right Hon. Sir Ronald Munro, K.C.M.G., P.C., LL.D., of Raith and Novar, Governor-General of Australia, *Past President.*

1912 ... FERGUSSON, Donald Stewart, Dunfallandy, by Pitlochry.

1880 ... FERGUSSON, Sir James Ranken, Bart., Spitalhaugh, West Linton.

1908 ... FERNIE, Alexander, Forester, Dunnotter Estate, Stonehaven.

1911 ... *FERNIE, William Duncan, Forester, Balcarres, Fife.

1907 ... *FERRIE, Thomas Young, Timber Merchant, 69 Buchanan St., Glasgow.

1914 ... FINLAY, James, Foreman Forester, Kingswood, Murthly.

1901 ... *FINDLAY, John Ritchie, of Aberlour, Aberlour House, Aberlour.

1907 *m* FISH, Andrew, Forester, Ladywell Cottage, Kinneil Estate, Bo'ness.

1909 ... FISHER, Malcolm, Forester, Kenotin, Washington Mills, N.Y., U.S.A.

1869 ... FISHER, William, Estate Agent, Wentworth Castle, Barnsley, Yorkshire.

1902 ... *FITZWILLIAM, The Earl of, Wentworth, Rotherham.

1914 ... FLAHERTY, Ewen C., Assistant Forester, Royal Botanic Garden, Edinburgh.

1910 ... FLEMING, Archibald, Overseer, Culcreuch, Fintry, Stirlingshire.

1899   *p* FLEMING, Sir John, Timber Merchant, Albert Saw-mills, Aberdeen.

1906   ...   *FLETCHER, J. Douglas, of Rosehaugh, Avoch, Ross-shire.

1911   ...   FLETCHER, John A., Factor, Landale, Ardgour, Argyllshire.

1909   ...   FLETCHER, John Sydney, 13 Braidburn Terrace, Edinburgh.

1910   ...   FORBES, Alistair Hugh, Factor, The Foley, Rothesay.

1890   *Mp* *FORBES, Arthur C., Department of Agriculture, Dublin.

1898   ...   FORBES, James, Factor, Eallabus, Bridgend, Islay.

1896   ...   *FORBES, James, Ivy Bank, Taunock Drive, Milngavie.

1912   ...   FORBES, John, Overseer, Cowden Home Farm, Dollar.

1878   *C* *FORBES, Robert, Estate Office, Kennet, Alloa.

1912   ...   FORBES, Robert Guthrie, Forester, Cliffhouse, Gulworthy, Tavistock, Devon.

1873   *m* *FORBES. William, Estate Office, West Bilney Lodge, King's Lynn, Norfolk.

1869   *CM* *FORGAN, James, Forester, 5 Belhelvie Terrace, Perth.

1892   ...   FORGAN, James, Sunnybraes, Largo, Fife.

1912   ...   FORSYTH, J. A., Assistant Forester, Panmure Cottage, Montrose.

1908   ...   FORTESCUE, William Irvine, M.B.C.M., Kingcausie, Milltimber, Aberdeen.

1908   ...   *FORTUNE, George R., Factor, Colinsburgh, Fife.

1897   *Cmp* *FOTHRINGHAM, W. Steuart, of Murthly, Perthshire, *Past President.*

1909   ...   *FOULIS, Arch. Keith, Valuer, Inland Revenue, 5 Calder Street, Motherwell.

1913   ...   FOWLER, George Ballantyne, Assistant Forester, Benmore, Kilmun, Greenock.

1908   ...   FOWLER, Sir John Edward, Bart., Braemore, Garve.

1913   ...   FOWLER, William Shaw, Inland Revenue Valuer, 57 Airlie Gardens, Hyndland, Glasgow.

1913   ...   FRAIN, Peter, Assistant Forester, North Lodge, Dupplin, Perth.

1866   *Cmp* *FRANCE, Charles S., 13 Cairnfield Place, Aberdeen.

1901   ...   *FRASER, Alexander, Solicitor and Factor, *Hon. Secretary and Treasurer, Northern Branch,* 63 Church Street, Inverness.

1914   ...   FRASER, Alexander, Assistant Forester, Croftcat Cottage, Grandtully.

1909   *m* FRASER, George, Assistant Forester, Midhope, S. Queensferry.

1892   ...   *FRASER, George, Factor, Dalzell, Motherwell, Lanarkshire.

1902   ...   *FRASER, George M., 13 Drumsheugh Gardens, Edinburgh.

1898   ...   FRASER, James, Manager, Cahir Saw-mills, Cahir, Co. Tipperary.

1899   ...   *FRASER, James, Factor, Fasque Estates Office, Fettercairn.

1911   ...   FRASER, James, Student of Forestry, Station Road, Dingwall.

1895   ...   FRASER, J. C., Nurseryman, Comely Bank, Edinburgh.

1905   ...   FRASER, John, Forester, The Little Hill, Leighton, Ironbridge R.S.O., Salop.

1913   ...   FRASER, John, Factor, Dormont Grange, Lockerbie.

1913 ... FRASER, John Cameron, Assistant Forester, Innerbuist Cottage, Stormontfield, Perth.

1901 ... FRASER, John M'Laren, of Invermay, Forgandenny, Perth-shire.

1914 ... FRASER-MACKENZIE, Evelyn Robert Leopold, Allangrange, Munlochy.

1913 ... FRASER, Robert B., Assistant Secretary, Landowners' Co-operative Forestry Society, Ltd., 33 Queen Street, Edinburgh.

1907 ... FRASER, Robert S., Allangrange, Munlochy, Inverness; Ivy House, Comshall, Surrey.

1892 ... *FRASER, Simon, Land Agent, Hutton in the Forest, Penrith.

1907 ... *FRASER, Sweton, Forester, Gallovie, Kingussie.

1913 ... FRASER, Thomas, Assistant Forester, North Lodge, Dupplin, Perth.

1908 ... FRASER-TYTLER, James Francis, of Woodhouselee, 22 Young Street, Edinburgh.

1896 ... FRATER, John, Foreman Forester, Ardross Mains, Alness, Ross-shire.

1907 ... FYFE, Harry Lessels, Assistant Forester, C.P.R., Forestry Dept., Maple Creek, Sask, Canada.

1907 ... FYFFE, Robert B., Aden Estates Office, Old Deer.

1904 ... GALLOWAY, George, Quarrymaster, Roseangle, Wellbank, by Dundee.

1913 ... GALLOWAY, Robert Angus, 1 Riselaw Road, Edinburgh.

1893 p *GALLOWAY, Robert, S.S.C., 19 Castle Street, Edinburgh, *Secretary and Treasurer.*

1909 p*GAMBLE, J. Sykes, C.I.E., etc., Highfield, East Liss, Hants.

1896 Cm *GAMMELL, Sydney James, of Drumtochty, Countesswells House, Bieldside, Aberdeen.

1913 ... GARDINER, Frederick Crombie, Old Ballikinrain, Balfron.

1908 ... GARDINER, R., Mitchell Nursery, Coaldale, Alberta, Canada.

1908 ... GARDYNE, Lieutenant-Colonel Greenhill, of Finavon, Forfar.

1899 ... *GARRIOCH, John E., Factor, Lovat Estates, Beauly.

1907 ... *GARSON, James, W.S., Albyn Place, Edinburgh.

1903 ... *GASCOIGNE, Lieut.-Col. Richard French, D.S.O., Craignish Castle, Ardfern, Argyllshire.

1898 ... GAULD, William, Forester, Coombe Abbey, Binley, Coventry.

1902 ... GAVIN, George, Factor, Falkland Estate, Falkland.

1897 ... GELLATLY, Thomas, Forester, Hallyburton, Coupar Angus.

1912 ... GIBB, George Gibb Shirra, Farmer, Boon, Lauder.

1912 ... GIBB, Dr R. Shirra, M.B.C.M., D.P.H., F.H.A.S., Boon, Lauder.

1913 ... GIBSON, Gideon James, Tea Planter, Academy House, Coldstream.

1903 ... GIBSON, William, Forester, Carnell, Hurlford, Ayrshire.

1905 ... GILBERT, Alexander, Assistant Forester, Midhope Castle, Hopetoun, South Queensferry.

1881   *m* *GILCHRIST, Wm., Forester, Nursery Cottage, Mount Melville, St Andrews.

1897   *Cmp* GILLANDERS, A. T., F.E.S., Forester, Park Cottage, Alnwick, Northumberland.

1894   *m* GILLESPIE, James, Overseer, Garden, Arnprior, Port of Monteith.

1894   ... GILMOUR, Colonel Robert Gordon, of Craigmillar, The Inch, Midlothian.

1908   ... GLADSTONE, Hugh Steuart, F.Z.S., M.A., etc., Lannhall, Thornhill.

1900   ... *GLADSTONE, Sir John R., Bart. of Fasque, Laurencekirk.

1913   ... GLEN, James, Assistant Forester, Milton of Aberdalgie, Perth.

1891   *C* *GLENCONNER, The Lord, The Glen, Innerleithen; 34 Queen Anne's Gate, London, S.W.

1901   ... **Godman, Hubert, Land Agent, Ginsborough, Yorkshire.*

1914   ... GODMAN, Hubert, Land Steward, The Hollins, Ingleby Cross, Northallerton.

1913   ... *GOLD, William, Forester, Dellavaird, Auchinblae, Fordoun.

1913   ... GOLDRING, George, Assistant Forester, Wortley Hall, Wortley, Sheffield.

1909   ... GOODFELLOW, John, Forester, Faskally, Pitlochry.

1910   *Cp* *GORDON, G. P., B.Sc. (Agric.), B.Sc. (For.), B.Sc. (Oxon.), Lecturer in Forestry, West of Scotland Agricultural College, Glasgow.

1911   ... GORDON, George, Timber Merchant, Aberdeen Saw-mills, Aberdeen.

1912   ... GORDON, Gregor, Assistant Forester, Tigerton, Menmuir, Brechin.

1914   ... GORDON. Robert, Bank Agent, Ellon.

1912   ... GORDON, Seton, B.A., Auchintoil, Aboyne.

1868   ... *GOSSIP, James A., of Howden & Co., The Nurseries, Inverness.

1912   ... GOSSIP, William Murray, Knowsley, Inverness.

1897   ... *GOUGH, Reginald, Forester, Wykeham, York.

1912   ... *GOURLAY, William Balfour, B.A.(Cantab.), L.R.C.P. and S.(Ed.), Dawyck, Stobo.

1909   ... Gow, Alexander, Butt Field Cottage, Hatfield, Herts.

1897   ... Gow, Peter, Land Steward, Laggan, Ballantrae, Ayrshire.

1904   ... *GRAHAM, Anthony George Maxtone, of Cultoquhey, Crieff.

1907   ... *GRAHAM, Hugh Meldrum, Solicitor, Inverness.

1908   *m* GRAHAM, James, Marquis of, Brodick Castle, Arran (per George Laidler, Strabane, Brodick).

1910   ... GRAHAM, Robert Francis, M.A., Skipness, Argyll.

1905   ... *GRAHAM, William, Foreman Forester, Kinross House, Kinross.

1909   ... GRAINGER, Henry Herbert Liddell, Ayton Castle, Ayton.

1887   ... Grant, Alexander, Forester, Fyershill Lodge, Ardsley, near Barnsley.

1911   ... *GRANT, Captain Arthur, D.S.O., House of Monymusk, Aberdeen.

1867   ... GRANT, Donald, Forester, Drumin, Ballindalloch, Banffshire.

1908   *p* GRANT, Donald, Forester, Fersit, Tulloch, Inverness-shire.

e

Date of
Election.

1904 *mp* GRANT, Ewan S., Head Forester, Priors Heath, Bedgebury Park, Goudhurst, Kent.

1908 ... GRANT, Iain Robert James Murray, of Glenmoriston, Inverness-shire.

1913 ... GRANT, James, Factor, Mortonhall, Midlothian.

1909 ... GRANT, James, Forester, Raith, Kirkcaldy.

1893 ... GRANT, John B., Forester, Downan, Glenlivet.

1874 ... *GRANT, John, Overseer, Daldowie, Glasgow.

1907 ... GRANT, Robert, Fernleigh, Birchington, Kent.

1908 ... GRANT, Sir John Macpherson, Bart., Ballindalloch Castle, Ballindalloch.

1913· ... GRANT, Robert, Assistant Forester, New Cottage, Dupplin, Perth.

1906 ... GRASSICK, William Henderson, Land Steward, Rankeillor Mains, Home Farm, Springfield, Fife.

1912 ... *Gray, David, Foresters' Bothy. Kelburn Castle, Fairlie, Ayrshire.*

1906 ... GRAY, David, Wheelwright, 175 Holborn Street, Aberdeen.

1907 ... GRAY, George, Sawmill Manager, Coburn House, Drymen.

1908 ... *GRAY, James Lowrie, Farmer, Elginhaugh, Dalkeith.

1909 ... GRAY, James Ritchie, Wheelwright, 371 Great Western Road, Aberdeen.

1902 ... GRAY, Walter Oliver, Forester, Drimsynie, Lochgoilhead.

1901 ... GRAY, Major William Anstruther-, of Kilmany, Cupar, Fife.

1911 ... GREGORY, Charles, Gamekeeper-Forester, Granston Manor, Balla-colla, Queen's Co., Ireland.

1913 ... GREIG, Robert Blyth, (Hon.) M. Sc., L.L.D., Member of Board of Agriculture, 29 St Andrew Square, Edinburgh.

1898 ... GREY, The Right Hon. Sir Edward, Bart., K.G., M.P., P.C., of Falloden, Chathill, Northumberland.

1913 ... GRIEVE, James, Farmer, Rumbletonlaw, Greenlaw.

1908 ... GRIEVE, J. W. A., D. C. Forests, Rajabhatkhowa, E.B.S. Railway, India.

1903 ... GRIFFITH, Sir Richard Waldie, of Hendersyde Park, Kelso.

1905 ... *GURNEY, Eustace, Sprowston Hall, Norwich.

1911 ... GUTHRIE, Charles, Assistant Forester, The Biggins, Keir Estate, Dunblane.

1911 ... HACKING, Thomas, M.Sc., etc., Education Offices, 33 Bowling Green Street, Leicester.

1879 ... HADDINGTON, The Earl of, K.T., Tyninghame, Prestonkirk.

1910 ... HALDANE, David, Forester, Dalmeny Park, Edinburgh.

1900 *C* *HALDANE, Sir William S., of Foswell, W.S., 55 Melville Street, Edinburgh.

1905 *mp* HALL, Thomas, Superintendent of Public Park, 2 Vicarland Road, Cambuslang.

1906 *mp* HALL, William, Head Forester, Church Cottages, Bilton, nr. York.

1897 ... *HALLIDAY, Geo., Timber Merchant, Rothesay.

1901 ... *HALLIDAY, John, Timber Merchant, Rothesay.

1911 ... HAMILTON, Alexander, Assistant Forester, Bargany Mains, Dailly, Ayrshire.

1907 ... *HAMILTON, Andrew, Naval Architect, 9 Denman Drive, Newsham Park, Liverpool.

1882 ... *HAMILTON, Donald C., Forester, Knowsley, Prescot.

1899 ... *HAMILTON, The Lord, of Dalzell, Dalzell House, Motherwell.

1892 ... HANNAH, George, Overseer, Estate Office, Boynton, Bridlington.

1905 ... HANSON, Clarence Oldham, Deputy Conservator, Indian Forest Department, 3 Malvern Place, Cheltenham.

1913 m HANSON, Herbert S., Assistant Forester, School Lane, Brinscall, Lancashire.

1907 ... HARBOTTLE, William, Forester, Bishop Burton, Beverley, Yorks.

1903 ... *HARDIE, David, Factor, Errol Park, Errol.

1880 ... *Hare, Colonel, Blairlogie, Stirling,

1896 ... *Harley, Andrew M., Forester, 5 Thayer Street, Manchester Square, London.

1908 m HARLOND, Henry, Park Forester, Sutton Coldfield, Warwickshire.

1911 ... HARRIER, James B., Forester, Innes House, Elgin.

1910 ... *HARRISON, Alexander, Apprentice C.A., 3 Napier Road, Edinburgh.

1905 ... HARROW, R. L., Head Gardener, Royal Botanic Garden, Edinburgh.

1897 ... HART, John, Factor, Mains of Cowie, Stonehaven, Kincardineshire.

1880 p *HAVELOCK, W. B., The Nurseries, Brocklesby Park, Lincolnshire.

1911 ... HARVEY, Andrew, Overseer, Rozelle, Ayr.

1911 ... HAWES, A. F., A.B., M.F., Experimental Station, Burlington, Vermont, U.S.A.

1908 ... *HAY, Athole Stanhope, of Marlefield, Roxburgh.

1892 C *HAY, John, Factor, Easter Dullatur House, Dullatur.

1913 ... HAY, Malcolm V., of Seaton, Seaton House, Aberdeen.

1904 m HAY, Sir Duncan Edwyn, Bart. of Haystoun, 42 Egerton Gardens, London, S.W.

1869 ... HAYMAN, John, Glentartff, Ringford, Kirkcudbrightshire.

1902 ... HAYNES, Edwin, Editor Timber Trades Journal, Cathedral House, 8-11 Paternoster Row, London, E.C.

1914 ... HEALY, Thomas, Assistant Forester, Donamon Castle, Roscommon, Ireland.

1912 ... HEAVENER, Harvey Joseph, Forester, Woodstock, Inistioge, Co. Kilkenny.

1909 ... HECTOR, Thomas Gordon, c/o Messrs Burd & Evans, School Gardens, Shrewsbury.

1914 ... HENDERSON, George, Assistant Forester, Colstoun House, Haddington.

1907 ... HENDERSON, John, Assistant Forester, Gateside, Balbirnic, Markinch.

1908 ... *HENDERSON, John G. B., W.S., Nether Parkley, Linlithgow.

1914 ... HENDERSON, John, Factor, Annandale Estates Office, Moffat.

1908 ... HENDERSON, R., Assistant Forester, Cross Street, Scone, Perth.

1893 ... *HENDERSON, R., 4 High Street, Penicuik, Midlothian.

1914 ... HENDERSON, William, Assistant Forester, Benmore, Kilmun.

1893 ... HENDERSON, William, Forester, Clonad Cottage, Tullamore, King's County.

1906 ... *HENDRICK, James, B.Sc., F.I.C., Marischal College, Aberdeen.

1898 ... HENDRY, James, 5 Thistle Street, Edinburgh.

1910 ... HENKEL, John Spurgeon, Assistant Conservator of Forests, Midland Conservancy, Knysna, Cape Colony.

1908 ... HENRY, Augustine, Professor, 5 Sandford Terrace, Ranelagh, Dublin.

1911 ... HENRY, George J., 66 Queen Street, Edinburgh.

1912 ... *Henry, Thomas, Assistant Forester, Bredisholm, Baillieston.*

1901 ... *HEPBURN, Sir Archibald Buchan-, Bart. of Smeaton-Hepburn, Prestonkirk.

1913 ... HEPBURN, Robert Grant, Gardener, Culzean Castle, by Ayr.

1874 ... *HERBERT, H. A., of Muckross, Killarney, Co. Kerry, Ireland.

1884 ... *HEYWOOD, Arthur, Glevering Hall, Wickham Market, Suffolk.

1914 ... HIGHGATE, Hugh, Blairmore House, Blairmore.

1904 ... HILL, George, Assistant Forester, Fothringham, Forfar.

1904 ... *HILL, J. Smith, The Agricultural College, Aspatria.

1903 ... *HILL, Robert Wylie, of Balthayock, Perthshire.

1905 ... *HILLIER, Edwin L., F.R.H.S., Nurseryman and Landscape Gardener, Culross, Winchester.

1902 ... *HINCKES, Ralph Tichborne, J.P., D.L., Foxley, Hereford.

1907 ... HINDS, John, Forester, Stockeld Park, Wetherby, Yorks.

1895 ... HOARE, Sir Henry Hugh Arthur, Bart. of Stourhead, Bath.

1909 *p* HOBART-HAMPDEN, A. G., Indian Forest Service, Ferns, Great Hampden, Great Missenden.

1912 ... *HOG, Alan Welwood, Writer to the Signet, 4 South Learmonth Gardens, Edinburgh.

1908 ... *HOG, Steuart Bayley, B.A., Newliston, Kirkliston.

1866 ... HOGARTH, James, Forester, Culhorn, Stranraer, Wigtownshire.

1913 ... HOGG, David, Foreman Forester, Deer Park, Novar, Evanton, Ross-shire.

1913 ... *Hogg, William, H., Head Forester, Broomhall, Alyth.*

1905 ... *HOLMS, John A., Formaken, Erskine, Renfrewshire.

1910 ... HOLZAPFEL, John William, B.Sc. and N.D.A., Kenton Estate, Nawasha, British East Africa.

1909 ... HONEYMAN, John A., Overseer, Kemback Estate, Cupar, Fife.

1902 ... *HOOD, Thomas, jun., Land Agent, Ras-el-Khalig, Egypt.

1908 ... *HOPE, Captain Thomas, of Bridge Castle, Westfield, Linlithgow-shire.

1912 *p* *HOPKINSON, Andrew Douglas, B.Sc.(Agr.), Lecturer in Forestry, Royal Agricultural College, Cirencester.

1907 ... HOPKINSON, James Garland, Factor, Drumtochty Estates Office, 11A Dee Street, Aberdeen.

1876 ... *HORSBURGH, John, 21 Dick Place, Edinburgh.

Date of
Election.

1908 ... Houston, Samuel, 17 Prince Edward Street, Crosshill, Glasgow.

1911 ... *HOWARD DE WALDEN, Baron, The Dean, Kilmarnock.

1902 C HOWE, John Arnold, Overseer, Home Farm, Mount Stuart, Rothesay.

1914 ... HUNTER-ARUNDELL, H. W. F., of Barjarg, Thornhill, Dumfries-shire.

1913 ... HUNTER, Robert, Sawmiller, Hall Bank Head, Featherstone, Halfwhirtle, Northumberland.

1913 ... Hutchins, David Ernest, Forest Service of India (ret.), Medo House, Cobham, Kent.

1905 ... HUTTON, George Kerse, Assistant Forester, Castle Kennedy, Wigtownshire.

1905 ... IMRIE, Charles, Assistant Forester, Balgove, Rossie, Montrose.

1910 ... *IMRIE, George James, Forest Officer, Groenkloof, c/o Forest Dept., Union Buildings, Pretoria.

1901 ... IMRIE, James, Forester, Aberpergrom Estate, Glen-neath, Glamor-ganshire.

1884 ... *Inglis, Alex., Greenlaw Dean, Greenlaw, Berwickshire.

1908 ... *INGLIS, Alexander Wood, of Glencorse, Loganbank, Milton Bridge.

1904 ... *INGLIS, David, National Bank House, Pathhead, Kirkcaldy.

1910 ... INGLIS, Robert, Factor, Old Blair, Blair Atholl.

1891 m INGLIS, William, Forester, Brodick, Isle of Arran.

1912 ... INGLIS, W. G., 113 George Street, Edinburgh.

1913 ... INMAN, William, 11 Newbattle Terrace, Edinburgh.

1904 ... INNES, Alexander Berowald, of Raemoir and Dunnottar, Raemoir House, Banchory.

1895 ... INNES, Alexander, Forester, Drummuir, Keith.

1914 .. INNES, George Pirrie, Head Forester, Burleywell Cottage, Lockerbie.

1911 ... INNES, Robert, Assistant Forester, Dean Road, Kilmarnock.

1914 ... IRONSIDE, Arch. Jennings, M.A., Student, 1 Alma Terrace, Laurencekirk.

1913 ... IRONSIDE, David, Forester, Lanfine Estate, Newmilns, Ayrshire.

1909 ... IRONSIDE, William, Solicitor, Royal Bank Buildings, Oban.

1906 C *IRVINE, Alexander Forbes, J.P., B.A.(Oxon.), Drum Castle, Aberdeen.

1901 ... IRVINE, John, Forester, Colesborne, Cheltenham, Gloucestershire.

1906 ... IRVING, James Rae Anderson, Foreman Forester, Langholm Estate, Canonbie, Dumfriesshire.

1908 .. *IZAT, Alexander, C.I.E., Mem. Inst. C.E., Balliliesk, Muckhart, Perthshire.

1907 ... JACK, David, Assistant Forester, c/o Mrs White, The Park, Guildtown, Perthshire..

1906 ... *JACKSON, George Erskine, B.A.(Oxon.), W.S., Kirkbuddo, Forfar.

1898 ... JAMIESON, James, Forester, Ynyslas, Llanarthney R.S.O., Car-marthenshire.

1896 ... JARDINE, Sir R. W. B., Bart. of Castlemilk, Lockerbie, Dumfriesshire.

1907 ... JERVOISE, Francis Henry Tristram, J.P., Herriard Park, Basingstoke.

1904 ... JOANNIDES, Pericles, Willesden, Sporting Club Station, Ramleh,
Egypt.

1909 ... JOHNSTON, David T., Gardener, Dalmeny House Gardens, Edinburgh.

1910 ... JOHNSTON, Frank James Nurseryman and Forester, Claycroft,
Dalbeattie.

1911 ... JOHNSTON, George, Assistant Forester, Dean Road, Kilmarnock.

1901 C *JOHNSTON, James, F.S.I., Factor, Alloway Cottage, Ayr.

1883 ... *JOHNSTON, Robert, Forester, Bon Ryl Estate, Duns, Berwickshire.

1907 ... JOHNSTON, Robert, Forester, Dalkeith Park, Dalkeith.

1900 ... JOHNSTONE, William, Head Forester, Beil, Prestonkirk.

1907 ... *JOHNSTONE, Richard, Forester, The Glen, Innerleithen.

1911 ... JOLY DE LOTBINIERE, Major H. G., R.E., c/o Messrs Cox & Co.,
Army Bankers, Charing Cross, London.

1882 ... *JONAS, Henry, Land Agent and Surveyor, 23 Pall Mall, London,
S.W.

1902 ... *JONAS, Robert Collier, Land Surveyor, 23 Pall Mall, London, S.W.

1903 ... JONES, Ireton Arthur, of Pennick & Co., Delgany Nurseries,
Co. Wicklow.

1888 ... JONES, James, Wood Merchant, Larbert, Stirlingshire.

1893 .... JONES, Thomas Bruce, Wood Merchant, Larbert.

1907 p *KAY, James, Nursery Station, Indian Head, Sask, Canada.

1867 Cmp KAY, James, Retired Wood Manager, Barone, Rothesay.

1909 ... KAY, John, Assistant Gardener, Grangemuir Lodge, Prestwick.

1896 ... KEIR, David, Forester, Ladywell, Dunkeld.

1906 ... KEIR, James S., Estate Manager, Borrodale, Arisaig.

1909 ... *KEITH, Marshall John, Factor, Brucklay Estates Office, Aberdour
House, Fraserburgh.

1901 ... *KENNEDY, Frederick D. C.-Shaw-, Dyroch, Maybole.

1890 ... *KENNEDY, James, Doonholm, Ayr.

1914 ... KENNEDY, James Beckett, Assistant Forester, Welldale Cottage,
Douglas, Lanarkshire.

1914 ... KENNY, Peter, Assistant Forester, Donamou Castle, Roscommon.

1912 ... KERR, John, Assistant Forester, Douglasfield Sawmill, Murthly.

1892 ... *KERR, John, Farmer, Barney Mains, Haddington.

1908 m *KERR, J. Ernest, of Harviestoun, Harviestoun, Dollar.

1913 ... KETTLES, Alexander, Assistant Forester, New Cottages, Dupplin,
Perth.

1896 ... KETTLES, Robert, Assistant Forester, Craigend, Perth.

1894 ... KIDD, Wm., Forester, Harewood, Leeds.

1908 ... *KIMMETT, John, Forester, The Lodge, Glenstriven, Toward, Argyllshire.

Date of Election.

1900 ... KING, David, Nurseryman, Osborne Nurseries, Murrayfield.

1910 ... KING, William, Gardener, Victoria Park, Whiteinch, Glasgow.

1906 ... *KINLOCH, Charles Y., of Gourdie, by Murthly.

1903 ... *KINNAIRD, The Master of, 10 St James Square, London.

1898 ... *KINROSS, John, Architect, 2 Abercromby Place, Edinburgh.

1902 ... *KIPPEN, William James, Advocate, B.A., LL.B., Westerton, Balloch, Dumbartonshire.

1910 ... KIRKPATRICK, James, Forester, Balhary, Meigle.

1898 ... KYLLACHY, The Hon. Lord, of Kyllachy, 6 Randolph Crescent, Edinburgh.

1911 ... LAIDLER, George, Strabane, Brodick.

1911 ... LAIRD, Eric P., of R. B. Laird, Dickson & Sons, Ltd., Nurserymen, 17 Frederick Street, Edinburgh.

1912 ... *Laird, James M'Lean Dunn, Assistant Forester, The Cottages, Dupplin, Perthshire.*

1911 ... LAIRD, William Pringle, Nurseryman, 20 High Street, Dundee.

1901 m *LAMB, Alexander, Overseer, Freeland, Forgandenny.

1910 ... *LAMB, Everard Joseph, of Scotby House, Carlisle.

1894 ... *LAMINGTON, The Lord, G.C.M.G., Lamington, Lanarkshire.

1899 ... LAMOND, Alexander, Forester, Freeland, Forgandenny.

1905 ... *LAMONT, Sir Norman, Bt. of Knockdow, Toward, Argyllshire.

1911 ... LANGE, Leopold Peter Harding, Superintendent of Plantations, c/o Conservator of Forests, Pretoria, Transvaal.

1906 ... *LANGLANDS, James H., Cunmont House, by Dundee.

1896 ... *LANSDOWNE, The Marquess of, K.G., 54 Berkeley Square, London, S.W.

1913 ... *LATTA, Robert M'Millan, Factor, Dougalston, Milngavie.

1906 p *LAUDER, Alexander, D.Sc., F.I.C., Edinburgh and East of Scotland College of Agriculture, 13 George Square, Edinburgh.

1901 ... LAUDER, William, Steward, Summerhill House, Enfield, Co. Meath.

1897 ... LAURISTON, John, Forester, Newbridge Green, Upton-on-Severn, Worcestershire.

1913 m LAW, Fred. W., M.A., B.Sc. (Agr.) Student, 13 Beaconsfield Place, Aberdeen.

1912 ... LAWSON, A. Anstruther, Ph.D., D.Sc., Lecturer in Botany, University of Glasgow.

1906 ... LAWSON, William, Factor, Mereworth Estates Office, Maidstone, Kent.

1902 ... *LEARMONT, John, Nurseryman, Larchfield Nurseries, Dumfries.

1911 ... *LEATHER, Major Gerard F. T., Middleton Hall, Belford, Northumberland.

1904 ... LEES, D., of Pitscottie, Cupar, Fife.

1905 ... LEES, Ernest A. G., Factor, Durris Estate, by Aberdeen.

1909 ... LE FANU, Victor Charles, B.A., F.S.I., Estate Office, Bray, Co. Wicklow.

Date of
Election.

1909 ... *LEGAT, Charles Edward, B.Sc.(Agric.), Chief Conservator of Forests, Pretoria, South Africa.

1880 ... LEISHMAN, John, Manager, Cavers Estate, Hawick, Roxburgh-shire.

1909 ... LEITH, The Lord, of Fyvie, Fyvie Castle, Aberdeenshire.

1911 ... LESCHALLAS, Major John Henry Pigé, Glenfinart, Ardentinny.

1908 ... LESLIE, Archibald Stewart, W.S., 33 Queen Street, Edin-burgh.

1868 ... *LESLIE, Charles P., of Castle-Leslie, Glaslough, Ireland.

1914 ... *LESLIE, Peter, M.A., B.Sc. (Agr.), Marischal College, Aberdeen.

1893 Cmp*LEVEN, George, Forester, Bowmont Forest, Roxburgh.

1913 ... LEVEN, William, Assistant Forester, Old Scone, Perth.

1881 ... *LEYLAND, Christopher, Haggerston Castle, Beal, Northumberland.

1907 ... LINDSAY, Hugh, Head Forester, Torwoodlee Estate, Galashiels.

1909 ... *LINDSAY, John, Under Forester, Station Lodge, Brodie.

1907 ... LINDSAY, William, of Messrs J. & H. Lindsay, Ltd., Tourist Agents, 18 St Andrew Street, Edinburgh.

1914 ... *LINLITHGOW, The Marquess of, Hopetoun House, South Queens-ferry.

1909 ... LITTLE, Thomas, Assistant Forester, Burnside Cottage, Canonbie.

1913 ... LIVSEY, Edward, Under Forester, Leases Farm, Well, Bedale.

1913 ... LODGE, Charles William, Assistant Forester, Assloss House, The Dean, Kilmarnock.

1905 ... LOGAN, David, Factor, Saltoun, Pencaitland.

1908 ... *LOGAN, Douglas Campbell, Factor, Portbane, Kenmore, Aberfeldy.

1914 ... LOGAN, Rev. Innes, United Free Manse, Braemar.

1908 ... LOGUE, Hugh, Forester, Knockdow, Toward, Argyllshire.

1883 ... *LONEY, Peter, Estate Agent, 6 Carlton Street, Edinburgh.

1909 ... LONGMUIR, James, Assistant Forester, 12 Houghton Village, King's Lynn, Norfolk.

1911 ... LONGMUIR, James, jun., Forester, School House, Houghton, King's Lynn, Norfolk.

1898 Cp*LOVAT, The Lord, C.B., D.S.O., Beaufort Castle, Beauly, Inverness.

1880 ... *Love, J. W., c/o Mrs Boyce, Byron Street, St Kilda, Victoria, South Australia.

1875 ... *LOVELACE, The Earl of, East Horsley Towers, Woking, Surrey.

1898 ... Low, James, Forester, Ballindalloch, Strathspey.

1900 ... *Low, William, B.Sc., of Balmakewan, Marykirk, Kincardine-shire.

1912 ... *Low, William, of Blebo, Cupar, Fife.

1910 m LOWE, Alex., Sydney Place, Lockerbie.

1912 ... LUKE, Nicol, Forester, Cairndow, via Inveraray.

1908 ... *LUMSDEN, George James, Aithernie, Lundin Links, Fife.

1891 ... *LUMSDEN, Hugh Gordon, of Clova, Lumsden, Aberdeenshire.

1900 ... *LUMSDEN, Robert, jun., 34 North Bridge, Edinburgh.

1908 ... LUNN, George, Forester, Invercauld, Ballater.

1914 ... LUTTRELL, Alexander Fownes, Dunster Castle, Dunster, Somerset.

Date of
Election.

1900 ... *LYELL Lord, of Kinnordy, Kirriemuir.

1909 ... *LYLE, Alexander Park, of Glendelvine, Murthly.

1914 ... LYON, Charles, Boxmaker, Aberdeen.

1907 ... *M'AINSH, Duncan, Wood Merchant, Crieff.

1911 ... M'ANDREW, Hamilton, Merchant, 7 Church Road, Ibrox, Govan.

1906 *m* MACALPINE-LENY, Major R. L., of Dalswinton, Ruanbeg, Kildare, Ireland.

1909 ... *MACARTHUR, Alaster, Bank Agent, Inveraray.

1907 ... *M'BAIN, William, Forester, Estates Office, Drumnadrochit.

1892 *C* *MACBEAN, Simon, Land Steward, Estate Office, Needwood Forest, Sudbery, Derby.

1896 *pm* *M'BEATH, David K., Factor, Benmore Estates Office, Kilmun.

1908 ... M'CALLUM, Alexander, Forester, Park Cottage, Kippindavie, Dunblane.

1908 ... M'CALLUM, D., Assistant Forester, The Groan Cottages, Logiealmond, Perth.

1894 ... M'CALLUM, Edward, Overseer, Kerse Estate, Falkirk.

1898 *p* M'CALLUM, James, Forester, Canford, Wimborne, Dorset.

1901 ...* M'CALLUM, Thomas W., Retired Ground Officer, Dailly, Ayrshire.

1911 ... *M'Caw, Daniel, Forester, Thoresby Park, Ollerton, Notts.*

1904 ... M'CLELLAN, Frank C., Zanzibar Government Service, Pemba, *via* Zanzibar, East Africa.

1870 ... *M'CORQUODALE, D. A., Maryville, Carnoustie, Forfarshire.

1893 ... M'COUBRIE, M. S., Land Steward, Tullamore, King's County, Ireland.

1912 ... M'CUTCHEON, Robert, Forester, Whittingehame, Prestonkirk.

1914 ... MACDONALD, Allan M., Apprentice Forester, Benmore, Kilmun.

1904 ... MACDONALD, Alexander, Factor, Meggernie, Aberfeldy.

1912 ... MACDONALD, Arthur J., Assistant Forester, Chatsworth Institute, Edensor, nr. Bakewell, Derbyshire.

1912 ... *M'Donald, Donald, Foreman Forester, Garth, Balnald, Fortingal, Aberfeldy.*

1914 ... MACDONALD, Donald R., Assistant Forester, Pitcairngreen, Almondbank, by Perth.

1901 ... MACDONALD, Mrs Eleanor E., The Manse, Swinton.

1914 ... M'DONALD, Frank Gordon M'Leod, Assistant Forester, Benmore Estates Office, Kilmun.

1893 *Cp* MACDONALD, George U., Overseer, Haystoun Estate, Woodbine Cottage, Peebles.

1908 ... MACDONALD, The Hon. Godfrey Evan Hugh, Factor, Macdonald Estates Office, Ostaig, by Broadford.

1900 ... *MACDONALD, Harry L., of Dunach, Oban.

1894 ... *MACDONALD, James, Forester, Kinnaird Castle, Brechin.

1903 ... *MACDONALD, James Farquharson, S.S.C. and N.P., Kilmuir, Linlithgow.

1895 ... MACDONALD, John, Forester, Skibo, Dornoch.

1908 ... M'DONALD, John, Forester, Ardgoil Estate, Lochgoilhead.

Date of
Election.

1908 ... MACDONALD, John Ronald M., of Largie, M.A., D.L., J.P., Largie Castle, Tayinloan, Kintyre.

1910 ... MACDONALD, John, Assistant Forester, Rose Cottage, Achnacarry, Spean Bridge.

1913 ... MACDONALD, William, Assistant Forester, New Cottages, Dupplin, Perth.

1907 ... *MACDONALD, T. Martin, of Barguillean, Taynuilt.

1906 ... MACDONALD, William Kid, Windmill House, Arbroath.

1904 ... M'DONALD, William Yeats, of Auquharney, Hatton, Aberdeenshire.

1913 ... M'DOUGALL, Hugh, Forester, Beau-Desert, Rugeley, Staffs.

1895 mp *MACDOUGALL, Professor Robert Stewart, M.A., D.Sc., 9 Dryden Place, Edinburgh.

1912 ... *M'Dougall, William Cumming, Assistant Forester, Budly, Ollerton, Newark.*

1884 ... *MACDUFF, Alex., of Bonhard, Perth.

1906 ... M'EWAN, James, Foreman Forester, Foresters' Bothy, Cothall, Altyre, Forres.

1909 m M'EWAN, John, Assistant Forester, Castle Lachlan, Stralachlan, Greenock.

1908 ... M'EWAN, W., Assistant Forester, Innerbuist Cottage, Stormontfield, Perth.

1909 ... *MacEwan, William, Assistant Forester, Garscube Estate, by Glasgow.*

1904 ... M'EWAN, Wm., Forester, Allangrange, Munlochy, Ross-shire.

1901 ... M'EWEN, Alexander, Overseer, Castle Lachlan, Stralachlan, Greenock.

1898 ... MACFADYEN, Donald, Assistant Forester, Drumlanrig, Thornhill.

1907 ... *MACFARLANE, Archibald, Timber Merchant, Harbour Saw-mills, Paisley.

1910 ... MACFARQUHAR, Donald, Forester, Port Glas, Kenmore, Aberfeldy.

1904 ... *MACFIE, John William, of Rowton Hall, Chester.

1901 ... *M'GARYA, Gilbert Ramsay, Factor, Rosehaugh Estate, Ross-shire.

1901 ... M'GHIE, John, Overseer, Kelburne Estate, Fairlie.

1901 ... *M'GIBBON, Donald, Forester, Rossie Estate, Inchture.

1904 ... M'GIBBON, R., Forester, Wentworth, Rotherham.

1908 ... M'GLASHAN, James, Forester, Belladrum, by Beauly.

1913 m M'GLASHAN, John, Forester, Hollow Lane, Wotton Dorking, Surrey.

1912 ... M'GLASHAN, Tom, Assistant Forester, Kingswood, Murthly.

1902 ... *MACGREGOR, Alasdair Ronald, Edinchip, Lochearnhead.

1902 m *M'GREGOR, Alexander, Forester, Abbeyleix, Queen's Co.

1908 ... *MACGREGOR, Alexander, Iron Merchant, Ravenswood, Dalmuir, Dumbartonshire.

1896 ... M'GREGOR, Angus, Forester, Craigton, Butterstone, Dunkeld.

1899 ... M'GREGOR, Archibald, Forest Office, Forestry Department, Nairobi, B.E.A.

1906 ... *MACGREGOR, Evan Malcolm, Factor, Ard Choille, Perth.

Date of
Election.

1912	...	MacGREGOR, James Gow, Land Steward, Duchal Estate, Kilmacolm.
1910	...	M'GREGOR, John, Assistant Forester, Brucefield, Clackmannan.
1910	...	M'GREGOR, John, Wood Merchant, Tam's Brig Saw-mills, Ayr.
1913	...	*MacGREGOR, Neil, Forester, Bridge of Dye, Banchory, Kincardineshire.
1914	...	M'HARDY, Dr James, Bellfield, Banchory.
1905	m	M'HARDY, James, Forester, Forglen, Turiff, Aberdeenshire.
1904	m	M'HARDY, William, Forester, Chancefield, Falkland, Fife.
1901	C	M'HATTIE, John W., City Gardener, City Chambers, Edinburgh.
1894	...	M'ILWRAITH, Wm., Forester, Hall Barn Estate, Beaconsfield, Bucks.
1907	...	M'INNES, William, Assistant Forester, Advie, Strathspey.
1905	...	M'INTOSH, Alexander, Foreman Forester, East Barkwith, Lincolnshire.
1911	...	M'INTOSH, Donald J., Assistant Forester, Faskally Cottage, Pitlochry.
1895	...	*Macintosh, D. L., The Gardens, Stronvar, Lochearnhead.
1879	...	*M'INTOSH, Professor W. C., 2 Abbotsford Crescent, St Andrews.
1904	...	M'INTOSH, Robert, Forester, Coppice, Rathdrum, Co. Wicklow.
1885	...	*MacINTOSH, William, Fife Estates Office, Banff.
1901	...	MACINTOSH, William, Forester, New Chapel, Boncath R.S.O., South Wales.
1907	...	M'INTYRE, Charles, Forester, Inver, Dunkeld.
1912	...	MACINTYRE, Charles, Assistant Forester, Tomnaharrich, Fort William.
1914	...	MACINTYRE, Daniel, Assistant Forester, Welldale, Douglas, Lanarkshire.
1914	...	M'INTYRE, Hugh, Assistant Forester, Dalzell Home Farm, Motherwell.
1914	...	MACINTYRE, John, Assistant Forester, Raith Estate, Kirkcaldy.
1908	...	MACINTYRE, Peter Brown, Findon Mains, Conon Bridge.
1911	...	M'INTYRE, Thomas Walker, Sorn Castle, Ayrshire.
1892	...	M'KAY, Allan, c/o Park & Co., Ltd., Timber Merchants, Fraserburgh.
1910	...	MACKAY, James Waite, Estate Office, Jervaulx Abbey, Middleham, Yorks.
1865	...	MACKAY, John, Haughhead, Earlston.
1908	...	M'KAY, Murdo, Forester, Castlecomer, Co. Kilkenny.
1887	...	*MACKAY, Peter, Forester and Overseer, Bargany Mains, Dailly, Ayrshire.
1907	...	MACKAY, William, Factor, Chisholm Estates, 19 Union Street, Inverness.
1891	..	MACKENDRICK, James, Forester, Estate Office, Pallas, Loughrea, Co. Galway.
1908	...	MACKENZIE, A., Overseer, Old Place of Mochrum, Kirkcowan, Wigtownshire.

1908 ... MACKENZIE, Lient.-Col. A. F., of Ord, Ord House, Muir of Ord.

1867 ... MACKENZIE, Alex., Warriston Nursery, Inverleith Row, Edinburgh.

1909 ... MACKENZIE, Alex. James, Factor, 62 Academy Street, Inverness.

1907 ... MACKENZIE, Sir Arthur, Bart. of Coul, Strathpeffer.

1901 ... MACKENZIE, Charles, Factor, Clunes, Achnacarry, Spean Bridge.

1909 ... MACKENZIE, Charles J. S., Assistant Forester, Caberfeidh, Carr Bridge.

1908 ... M'KENZIE, Colin, Head Forester, Didlington Hall, Stoke, Ferry, Norfolk.

1901 ... M'KENZIE, Daniel, Forester, Wynyard Estate, Stockton-on-Tees.

1904 ... MACKENZIE, Major E. Walter Blunt, Castle Leod, Strathpeffer.

1908 ... MACKENZIE, Evan North Barton, Kilcoy Castle, Killearnan.

1908 ... MACKENZIE-GILLANDERS, Captain E. B., of Highfield, Muir of Ord.

1913 ... M'KENZIE, George, Estate Overseer, Donamon Castle, Co. Roscommon, Ireland.

1893 ... *MACKENZIE, James, Forester, Cullen House, Cullen.

1899 ... M'KENZIE, James, Wood Merchant, Carr Bridge, Inverness-shire.

1897 ... MACKENZIE, John, Forester, Dalueich Cottage, Ardross, Alness, Ross-shire.

1907 ... MACKENZIE, John, jun., Factor, Dunvegan, Skye.

1913 ... M'KENZIE, Kenneth D., Assistant Forester, New Cottages, Dupplin, Perth.

1900 Cp *MACKENZIE, Sir Kenneth John, Bart. of Gairloch, 10 Moiay Place, Edinburgh, *Past President*.

1908 ... MACKENZIE, Nigel Banks, Factor, Camusmor, Onich.

1908 ... MACKENZIE, Nigel Blair, Factor, Fort William.

1913 ... MACKENZIE, Robert, Assistant Forester, The Village, Dallas, Forres.

1913 ... MACKENZIE, Simon John, Assistant Forester, Chatsworth Institute, Edensor, nr. Bakewell, Derbyshire.

1907 ... MACKENZIE, Colonel Stewart, of Seaforth, Brahan Castle, Dingwall.

1911 ... MACKENZIE, Thomas, Factor, Craigard, Invergarry.

1907 ... MACKENZIE, W. Dalziel, Fawley Court, Henley-on-Thames.

1896 p MACKENZIE, Wm., Forester, Novar, Evanton, Ross-shire.

1905 ... *M'KERCHAR, John, Bulb, Plant and Seed Merchant, 35 Giesbach Road, Upper Holloway, London, N.

1897 ... *M'Kerrow, Robert, Manager, Carton, Maynooth, Co. Kildare.

1907 ... MACKESSACK, George Ross, of Ardgye, Elgin.

1909 ... M'KIE, Henry B., Factor, Freeland, Erskine, Bishopton.

1898 ... *MACKINNON, A., The Gardens, Scone Palace, Perth.

1883 C MACKINNON, George, Cawdor Estate, Bishopbriggs.

1912 ... MACKINTOSH Patrick Turner, Solicitor, 5 Albyn Place, Edinburgh.

Date of
Election.

1878 ... MACKINTOSH, The, of Mackintosh, Moy Hall, Inverness.

1905 .. *MACKINTOSH, W. E., Yr. of Kyllachy, 28 Royal Circus, Edinburgh.

1914 ... MACKINTOSH, William, Assistant Forester, c/o James Mackintosh, Thornbridge, Bakewell, Derby.

1912 ... *MACKINTOSH, William R., Assistant Forester, Dyke, Forres.

1895 C *MACLACHLAN, John, of Maclachlan, Castle Lachlan, Argyll.

1904 ... MACLAGGAN, George C. R., Forester, Hopetoun, S. Queensferry.

1908 ... M'LAREN, James, Chopwellwood House, Rowlands Gill, Co. Durham.

1879 ... *M'LAREN, John, 12 Findhorn Place, Edinburgh.

1909 m MacLARTY, Alexander Sinclair, Forester, Glasserton, Whithorn, Wigtownshire.

1898 ... *Maclean, Archibald Douglas, J.P., Harmony, Balerno.

1908 ... M'LEAN, Donald, 62 Craigmillar Park, Edinburgh.

1906 ... M'LEAN, James Smith, Forester, Douglas Castle, Lanarkshire.

1902 ... MACLEAN, Peter, Forester, Invergarry.

1912 ... M'LENNAN, Donald, Assistant Forester, Sand House, Maidens.

1912 ... MACLEOD, Donald, Assistant Forester, Raith Estate, Kirkcaldy.

1901 ... M'LEOD, Peter, Nurseryman, Perth.

1895 ... MACMILLAN, John D., Steward, Margam Park, Port Talbot, Wales.

1910 ... M'MORRAN, Peter, Assistant Forester, Dalzell, Motherwell.

1904 ... *M'NAB, David Borrie, Solicitor, Clydesdale Bank, Bothwell.

1909 ... M'NAIR, Gregor, Overseer, Conaglen, Ardgour.

1913 ... M'NAUGHTON, Donald, Assistant Forester, New Cottages, Dupplin, Perth.

1911 ... *M'NEILE, Major John, Kippilaw, St Boswells.

1912 ... MacNIVEN, James, Forester, Bredisholm, Baillieston.

1910 m M'PHERSON, Alexander, Tayness, Kilmartin, Lochgilphead.

1914 ... MACPHERSON, Donald, B.Sc., Assistant, College of Agriculture, 5 London Street, Edinburgh.

1909 ... MACPHERSON, Duncan, Forester, Consall Hall, Stoke-on-Trent, Staffordshire.

1890 mp M'RAE, Alexander, Forester, Dundrum, Co. Tipperary.

1899 ... *MACRAE-GILSTRAP, Major John, of Ballimore, Otter Ferry, Argyllshire.

1900 ... M'RAE, Henry, Assistant Forester, Ufton, Southam, Rugby.

1908 ... MACRAE, Sir Colin G., W.S., 45 Moray Place, Edinburgh.

1906 p MACRAE, John, Forester, Highfield, Muir of Ord, Ross-shire.

1907 ... M'RAW, Donald, Manager, Strathgarve, Garve R.S.O.

1879 ... *MACRITCHIE, David, C.A., 4 Archibald Place, Edinburgh.

1895 m M'TAVISH, John, Assistant Forester, The Glen, Skelbo, Sutherland.

1905 ... M'VINNIE, Samuel, Forester, Skeagarvie, Rossmore Park, Monaghan.

1905 ... *MAITLAND, A. D. Steel, of Sauchie, etc., Sauchieburn, Stirling.

1880 ... *MALCOLM, Lieut.-Col. E. D., R.E., of Poltalloch, Kilmartin.

Date of
Election.

1895 ... *MANN, Charles, Merchant, Lumsden, Aberdeenshire.

1909 ... *MANN, James, of Castlecraig, Dolphinton.

1911 ... MANNERS, Charles Robert, Civil Engineer and Estate Factor, 12 Lombard Street, Inverness.

1898 *Cm* *MANSFIELD, The Earl of, Scone Palace, Perth.

1896 ... MAR AND KELLIE, The Earl of, Alloa House, Alloa.

1895 ... *MARGERISON, Samuel, English Timber Merchant, Calverley, near Leeds.

1909 ... MARSDEN, Reginald Edward, Director, Burma Forest School, Pyinmana, Burma, India.

1901 ... *MARSHALL, Archd. M'Lean, Chitcombe, Breda, Sussex.

1905 ... *MARSHALL, Henry Brown, of Racban, Broughton.

1913 ... MARSHALL, James A. G., Rubber Planter, Monk Coniston, Lancs, R.S.O.

1899 ... MARSHALL, John, Timber Merchant, etc., Maybole.

1893 ... MARSHALL, J. Z., Timber Merchant, 2 Dean Terrace, Bo'ness.

1907 ... MARSHALL, William, Assistant Forester, Dell Nursery, Nethy Bridge.

1910 *p* MARTIN, Lieut-Col. Martin, Upper Ostaig, by Broadford, Isle of Skye.

1876 ... *MARTIN, James, Forester, Knipton, Grantham, Lincolnshire.

1911 ... MARTIN, Sir T. Carlaw, LL.D., Director, Royal Scottish Museum, Edinburgh.

1909 ... MASSIE, George Duncan, Solicitor (*Hon. Secretary, Aberdeen Branch*), 147 Union Street, Aberdeen.

1884 *C* *MASSIE, W. H., of Dicksons & Co., 1 Waterloo Place, Edinburgh.

1907 ... MASSON, William, Forester, Meikleour, Perth.

1910 ... MASTERTON, James, Hedger and Assistant Forester, Kennet Cottages, Alloa.

1893 *C* MATHER, R. V., of Laing & Mather, Nurserymen, Kelso.

1901 ... *MATTHEWS, Robert, Land Steward, Duncrub Park, Dunning.

1909 ... MAUDE, James, Timber Merchant, Hebden Bridge, Yorks.

1894 ... *MAUGHAN, John, Estate Agent, Jervaulx Abbey, Middleham R.S.O., Yorks.

1907 ... MAXTONE, James, Overseer, Strathallan, Machany, Perthshire.

1904 ... *MAXWELL, Aymer, Yr. of Monreith, Port William, Wigtownshire.

1891 ... MAXWELL, James, Forester and Overseer, Ruglen, Maybole.

1893 *CMmp* *MAXWELL, Sir John Stirling-, Bart. of Pollok, Pollokshaws, *Honorary Secretary and Past President.*

1886 *Cp* MAXWELL, The Right Hon. Sir Herbert E., Bart. of Monreith, Port William, Wigtownshire, *Past President.*

1908 *p* MAXWELL, Wellwood, of Kirkennan, Dalbeattie.

1908 ... MAXWELL, William James, Factor, Terregles Banks, Dumfries.

1905 *m* MAXWELL, William Jardine Herries, of Munches, Dalbeattie.

1907 ... MEACHER, Sydney George, Land Agent, Marlee, Blairgowrie.

1906 ... MELDRUM, Thomas C., Nurseryman, Forfar.

Date of
Election.

1914 ... MELLES, Joseph William, of Gruline, Aros, Isle of Mull.

1899 ... MELVILLE, David, The Gardens, Dunrobin Castle, Golspie.

1911 ... MELVIN, David, Foreman Forester, Stobhall Estate, Gillowhill, Coupar-Angus.

1914 ... MENZIES, Allan C., Assistant Forester, Foresters' Bothy, Grand-tully.

1901 ... MENZIES, James, Forester, Caledon Estate, Co. Tyrone.

1908 ... *MENZIES, William Dudgeon Graham, J.P., Hallyburton, Coupar-Angus.

1880 ... *MESHAM, Captain, Pontryffydd, Bodvari, Rhyl, Denbighshire.

1877 ... METHVEN, Henry, of Thomas Methven & Sons, 6 Frederick Street, Edinburgh.

1892 ... METHVEN, John, Viewforth, Kennoway, Fife.

1911 ... MICHIE, Henry M., Logan Estates Office, Chapel Rossan, Stran-raer.

1881 *Cmp* *MICHIE, John, M.V.O., Factor, Balmoral, Ballater.

1893 ... MICHIE, William, Forester, Welbeck, Worksop, Notts.

1893 ... *MIDDLEMASS, Archibald, Forester, Tulliallan, Kincardine-on-Forth.

1905 ... MIDDLETON, James, Factor, Braehead House, Kilmarnock.

1910 ... MIDDLETON, James, Assistant Forester, Blythswood, Renfrew.

1905 ... *MILLAR, John, Timber Merchant, Greenhaugh Saw-mills, Govan.

1908 ... *MILLER, Robert E., Bonnycraig, Peebles.

1914 ... MILLER, Thomas, Assistant Forester, Crossgates Dupplin, Perth.

1910 ... *Milli*gan, *Alexander, Head Forester, 11 St James Square, Biggar, Lanarkshire.*

1913 ... MILLIGAN, David M. M., of Findrack, 20 Albyn Place, Aberdeen.

1910 ... MILLIGAN, J. A., Forester, Pippingford Park, Nutley, Sussex.

1899 ... MILNE, Alexander, Factor, Urie Estate Office, Stonehaven.

1902 ... MILNE, Alexander, Forester, Charboro' Park, Wareham, Dorset.

1903 ... MILNE, Colonel George, of Logie, Aberdeenshire.

1904 ... MILNE, Frederick, Assistant Forester, Nursery Cottage, Tarbrax, by Forfar.

1895 ... MILNE, James, Land Steward, Carstairs House, Carstairs.

1906 ... *MILNE, John, Forester, Bicton Estate, East Budleigh, Devon.

1899 ... *Milne, Ritchie, Assistant, Annandale Estate Office, Hillside, Moffat.*

1898 ... *MILNE, Robert P., Spittal Mains, Berwick-on Tweed.

1890 ... MILNE, William, Farmer, Foulden, Berwick-ou-Tweed.

1902 ... MILNE, William, Forester, Huntly Hill, Stracathro, Brechin.

1906 ... MILNE, William, Nurseryman (Wm. Fell & Co., Ltd.), Hexham.

1901 ... *Milne-Home, David William, of Wedderburn, Caldra, Duns.*

1897 *Cp* *MILNE-HOME, J. Hepburn, Irvine House, Canonbie.

1914 ... *MILSOM, Isaac, South Saskatoon Development, Box 60 Nutana, Saskatoon, Saskatchewan, Canada.

Date of
Election.

1914   *m* *MINTO, The Right Hon. The Earl of, Minto House, Hawick.

1909   ... *MIRRIELEES, Frederick Donald, B.A.Oxon., Goddards, Abinger Common, Dorking.

1904   *Cm* MITCHELL, Alexander, Forester, Rosebery, Gorebridge.

1913   ... MITCHELL, Andrew James, Assistant Factor and Architect, 12 Golden Square, Aberdeen.

1912   ... MITCHELL, Andrew W., 8 Queen's Terrace, Aberdeen.

1912   ... MITCHELL, Charles, of Pallinsburn, Cornhill-on-Tweed.

1898   ... MITCHELL, David, Forester, Drumtochty, Fordoun.

1882   *Mp* *MITCHELL, Francis, Forester, Woburn, Beds.

1902   ... *MITCHELL, John, jun., Timber Merchant, Leith Walk Saw-mills, Leith.

1904   ... MITCHELL, John Irvine, M.A., Teacher, 4 Craighouse Terrace, Edinburgh.

1901   ... MITCHELL, William Geddes, Estate Agent, Doneraile, Co. Cork.

1903   *mp* *MOERAN, Archibald E., Land Agent, etc., Lissadell, Stillorgan Park, Co. Dublin.

1914   ... MOFFAT, George, Assistant Forester, Midhope Castle, Hopetoun, South Queensferry.

1902   ... MOFFAT, John, Head Forester, Boiden, Arden, N.B.

1909   ... MOFFAT, William, Forester, Castle Wemyss, Wemyss Bay.

1908   ... *MOISER, Cyril, P.A.S.I., Heworth Grange, York.

1895   ... *MONCREIFFE, Sir Robert D., Bart. of Moncreiffe, Perth.

1906   ... *MOON, John Laurence, Forest Ranger, Forestry Department, Nairobi, British East Africa.

1903   *m* MORAY, The Earl of, Darnaway Castle, Forres.

1897   ... *MORGAN, Alex., Timber Merchant, Crieff, Perthshire.

1899   ... *MORGAN, Andrew, Assistant Factor, Glamis.

1913   ... MORGAN, John, Assistant Forester, The Dean, Kilmarnock.

1895   ... *MORGAN, Malcolm, Timber Merchant, Crieff, Perthshire.

1911   ... MORGAN, W. Dunlop, Forestry Student, 5 Hillside Street, Edinburgh.

1913   ... MORISON, A. E. F., of Bognie, Mountblairy, Turriff.

1907   ... MORRISON, Andrew, Estate Manager, Brodie Mains, Forres.

1911   ... MORRISON, David, Assistant Forester, Main Street, Sorn.

1895   ... MORRISON, Hew, LL.D., Librarian, Edinburgh Public Library.

1908   ... *MORRISON, Hugh, Little Ridge, Tisbury, Wilts.

1911   ... MORRISON, James, Factor for Forglen, 40 Low Street, Banff.

1908   ... MORRISON, John, Factor, Rhives, Golspie.

1903   ... MORRISON, William, Manufacturer, 61 Grant Street, St George Road, Glasgow.

1905   ... MORTON, Andrew, Forester, Stockstruther, Roxburgh.

1914   ... MORTON, James, Manager, Fordell Collieries and Works, Crossgates, Fife.

1905   ... *MOTHERWELL, A. B., Writer, Airdrie.

1908   ... *MOUBRAY, John J., Naemoor, Rumbling Bridge.

1907   ... MOULTRIE, James, Foreman Forester, Denside, Durris, Drumoak, Aberdeenshire.

Date of
Election.

1908 ... Mowat, George, Forester, Carmichael, Thankerton, Lanarkshire.

1906 ... Mowat, John, Overseer, Hazelhead Estate. Aberdeen.

1913 ... Mowat, William, Assistant Forester, Innerbuist Cottage, Stormontfield, Perth.

1890 ... Muirhead, George, F.R.S.E., Commissioner, Speybank, Fochabers.

1912 ... *Muirhead, Roland Eugene, Winona, Bridge of Weir.

1901 ... Mullin, John, Forester, Eglinton Castle, Irvine.

1904 ... Munro, Alexander, Overseer, Iuvereshie, Kincraig.

1903 C Munro, Alexander J., 48 Castle Street, Edinburgh.

1912 ... Munro, Donald, Forester, Coul, Strathpeffer, Ross-shire.

1895 ... Munro, Donald. Forester, Holkham Hall, Norfolk.

1906 p Munro, Donald, Wood Merchant, Ravenswood, Banchory.

1911 ... Munro, Duncan H. Campbell, of Kenlochlaich, Appin, Argyll.

1908 ... *Munro, George, M.B.C.M., Kergord, Weisdale, Shetland.

1905 ... Munro, Sir Hector, Bart. of Foulis Castle, Evanton, Ross-shire.

1911 ... *Munro, Hector, Assistant Forester. Cruachan, Kilchrenan, Taynuilt.*

1909 m Munro, Hugh R., Assistant Forester, The Park, Great Witley, Worcester.

1902 ... *Munro, Sir Hugh Thomas, of Liudertis, Kirriemuir.

1910 ... Munro, James Watson, B.Sc., 391 Great Western Road, Aberdeen.

1907 ... Munro, John, Land Steward and Forester, The Lodge, Tarland, Aberdeenshire.

1911 ... Munro, William, Forester, Forest Department, Nairobi, British East Africa.

1909 ... Munro, William, Factor, Glenferness Estate Office, Nairn.

1909 ... *Murray, Major Alastair Bruce, of Polmaise, Stirling.

1892 Cmp *Murray, Alexander, Forester, Murtbly, Perthshire.

1900 ... Murray, George J. B., Forester, Holylee, Walkerburn.

1904 mp Murray, John M., Assistant Forester. Kingswood, Murthly.

1900 ... Murray, William, of Murraythwaite, Ecclefechan, Dumfriesshire.

1896 ... *Murray. William Hugh, W.S., 48 Castle Street, Edinburgh.

1899 ... *Nairn, Sir Michael B., Bart. of Rankeillour, Manufacturer, Kirkcaldy.

1912 ... *Nairn, Michael, of Pitcarmick, Dysart House, Dysart, Fife.

1904 ... Nairn, Robert, Forester, Rowallan, Kilmarnock.

1907 m Nash, William, Forester, Furnace Road, Muirkirk.

1905 ... *Nasmyth, Norman, of Glenfarg, Glenfarg Lodge, Abernethy.

1909 ... *Naylor, John Murray, Laighton Hall, Welshpool.

1910 ... Neilson, Walter Montgomerie, of Barcuple, Ringford.

1909 ... *Neish, Edward William, Sheriff Substitute, Dundee.

1914 ... Nelson, John Ross, Assistant Forester, North Stables, Kelburn, Fairlie.

1893 ... Nelson, Robert, Assistant Forester, Hannahgate Cottage, Kinmount Estate, Cummertrees, Dumfriesshire.

Date of
Election

1908 ... *NELSON, Thomas Arthur, of Achnacloich, Connel, Argyllshire.

1914 ... NEWLANDS, John, Assistant Forester, Cluny Square, Cardenden.

1910 ... NEWTON, James Whittet, B.Sc., Assistant Conservator of Forests, Londiani, British East Africa.

1895 ... NICOL, James, Forester, Aird's Mill, Muirkirk, Ayrshire.

1912 ... *NICOL, Randall James, of Ballogie, Aboyne, Aberdeenshire.

1906 ... NICOL, William, Forester, Cluny Castle, Ordhead, Aberdeenshire.

1909 ... NICOLL, William, Foreman Forester, Deer Park, Novar, Evanton, Ross-shire.

1901 ... NICOLL, William Peter, Bailiff to H.R.H. The Duchess of Albany, The Farm, Claremont, Esher, Surrey.

1912 ... NIELSEN, P., Seedsman, Jaglvej, 125th, Copenhagen, L.

1893 p *NISBET, J., D.Œc., Royal Societies' Club, 63 St James Street, London, S.W.

1902 ... *Nisbet, Robert C., Farmer, Kingsknowe, Slateford.

1899 ... *NOBBS, Eric Arthur, B.Sc., Ph.D., Department of Agriculture, Salisbury, Rhodesia.

1899 ... NOBLE, Charles, Forester, Donibristle, Aberdour.

1904 ... NOBLE, Hugh C., Newhall Estate Office, Balblair, Invergordon.

1912 ... NORRIS, Henry E. Du C., Agent, Basildon Park, Reading.

1911 ... *OGILVIE, Fergus Menteith, of Barcaldine, Ledaig, Argyllshire.

1909 ... *OGILVIE, George Hamilton, Westlands, Broughty Ferry.

1911 ... OGILVIE, John, M.A., Solicitor, 13 Albert Square, Dundee.

1910 ... OGILVY, Mrs Mary Georgiana Constance N. Hamilton, of Biel, Prestonkirk.

1908 ... OGSTON, Alexander Milne, of Ardoe, near Aberdeen.

1908 ... *OGSTON, James, of Kildrummy, Kildrummy, Aberdeenshire.

1894 ... *ORKNEY, William C , Surveyor's Office, Montrose Royal Asylum.

1899 ... *Orr-Ewing, Sir Archibald Ernest, Bart., Ballikinrain Castle, Balfron.

1906 ... *ORR, George W., Hilston Park, Monmouth.

1907 ... Oswald, Major Julian, Portmore House, Church Street, Weybridge.

1902 ... OSWALD, Richard Alexander, of Auchincruive, Ayr.

1875 ... PAGE, Andrew Duncan, Land Steward, Culzean Home Farm, Ayr.

1911 ... PARK, James, Assistant Forester, Tower Cottage, Durris, Drumoak.

1908 ... PARK, Robert, Contractor, Hamilton Street, Motherwell.

1908 ... PATERSON, Alexander, Forester, Clifton Park, Kelso.

1900 ... PATERSON, George, Timber Merchant, Cliff House, Cults, Aberdeen.

1913 ... PATERSON, William George Rogerson, B.Sc., N.D.A. (Hons.), Principal of West of Scotland Agricultural College, 6 Blythswood Square, Glasgow.

1879 ... *PATON, Hugh, Nurseryman, Kilmarnock, Ayrshire.

1898 ... *PATON, Robert Johnston, Nurseryman, Kilmarnock.

1902 ... *PATON, Tom W., Nurseryman, Kilmarnock.

1914 ... PATTERSON, George, Forester, Scotston, Duns.

1908 ... PEARSON, Andrew, Commissioner, Johnston, Laurencekirk.

1897 ... PEARSON, James, Forester, Sessay, Thirsk, Yorks.

1899 *mp* PEARSON, James, Factor, Altyre Estates Office, Forres, N.B.

1912 *m* PEFFERS, William, Sawmaker, Dovecote Street, Hawick.

1908 ... *PENTLAND, The Lord, Governor of Bengal, India.

1900 *m* *PERRINS, C. W. Dyson, of Ardross, Ardross Castle, Alness.

1904 ... PETERS, William, Assistant Forester, North Lodge, Balbirnie,
Markinch, Fifeshire.

1914 ... PETLEY, Charles, Land Agent, etc., Staple, Canterbury.

1897 ... *PHILIP, Alexander, Solicitor, Brechin, Forfarshire.

1895 ... *PHILIP, William Watt, Factor, Estate Office, Gigha, Argyllshire.

1912 ... PHILIPS, Charles, Assistant Forester, Balvaird, Kirkoswald.

1908 ... PHILLIPS, John, Nurseryman, Granton Road, Edinburgh.

1896 ... *PHILP, Henry, jun., Timber Merchant, Campbell Street,
Dunfermline.

1896 .. *PHILP, John, Timber Merchant, Campbell Street, Dunfermline.

1910 ... *PIKE, James Lyford-, B.Sc.(Agr.) and B.Sc. (Forestry), Rosetta,
Kirkbrae, Liberton.

1896 ... *PITMAN, Archibald Robert Craufurd, W.S., 48 Castle Street,
Edinburgh.

1910 ... PLENDERLEITH, Mungo Sinclair, Fire Insurance Superintendent,
102 St Vincent Street, Glasgow.

1914 ... PLENDERLEITH, William, Assistant Forester, Mill Cottage, Stobo,
Peeblesshire.

1902 ... PLUMMER, C. H. Scott, of Sunderland Hall, Selkirk.

1912 ... *PONSONBY, Thomas Brabazon, J.P., and D.L., Kilcooley
Abbey, Thurles, Ireland.

1897 ... POOLE, Wm., Corn Exchange Buildings, Edinburgh.

1902 ... POPERT, E. P., 49 Britannia Square, Worcester.

1908 ... PORTEOUS, James, Solicitor and Factor, Coldstream.

1899 ... PORTEOUS, Colonel James, of Turfhills, Kinross.

1911 ... PORTEOUS, George, Overseer, Edmonstone Estate, Midlothian.

1912 ... PORTER, Donald Fraser, Waygateshaw, Carluke.

1910 ... PRENTICE, Andrew, Forester, Bank House, Worsley, near
Manchester.

1896 ... PRENTICE, George, Strathore, Thornton.

1898 *Cm* *PRICE, W. M., Factor, Minto, Hawick.

1913 ... PRIMROSE, Sir John Ure, Bart., LL.D., Glasgow.

1908 ... PRINGLE, James Lewis, of Torwoodlee, J.P., D.L., B.A.,
Torwoodlee, Galashiels.

1908 ... PRITCHARD, Henry A., Professor of Estate Management and
Forestry, Royal Agricultural College, Cirencester.

1908 ... PROCTOR, John, Forester, West Grange, East Grange Station,
Dunfermline.

1908 *m* *PURVIS, Colonel Alexander, St Andrews.

1907 ... *Purvis, George, Forester, Cowden Estate, Dollar.*

Date of
Election.

1907 ... RAE, Frederick S., Tangkah Rubber Estates, Jasin, Malacca, Straits Settlement.

1907 *m* RAE, Lewis, Foreman Forester, New Cottage, Dupplin, by Perth.

1876 *C* *RAE, William A., Factor, Murthly Castle, Perthshire.

1901 *p* *RAFFAN, Alexander, Forester, Bonskeid, Pitlochry.

1899 *p Rafn, Johannes, Tree-Seed Merchant, Skovfrókontoret, Copenhagen, F.*

1913 ... *RALPH, James Mackenzie, Bank Clerk, Lisnacree, Corstorphine.

1902 ... RALPH, William, I.S.O., Forrester Road, Corstorphine.

1897 ... RALSTON, A. Agnew, Factor, Philipstoun House, West Lothian.

1907 ... RALSTON, Charles W., Chamberlain on Dukedom of Queensberry, Dabton, Thornhill, Dumfriesshire.

1908 ... *RALSTON, Claude, Factor, Estates Office, Glamis.

1908 ... *RALSTON, Gavin, Factor, Glamis.

1910 ... *RAMSAY, Professor George Gilbert, LL.D., Drumire, Blairgowrie.

1911 ... RANKINE, Professor John, of Bassendean, 23 Ainslie Place, Edinburgh.

1870 ... RATTRAY, Thos., Forester, Westonbirt House, Tetbury, Gloucestershire.

1909 ... RATTRAY, William, Wood Merchant, Tullylumb Terrace, Perth.

1908 ... REDPATH, John, Forester, Paxton, Berwick-on-Tweed.

1905 ... REID, Alexander T., Milldeans, Star, Markinch.

1914 ... REID, George, Manager, Creosoting Works, Bay View, Methil.

1901 ... REID, Hugh, Forester, Ashton Court, Long Ashton, near Bristol.

1909 ... REID, James, jun., Probationer, Royal Botanic Garden, Edinburgh.

1894 ... REID, James S., Forester, Balbirnie, Markinch, Fife.

1913 ... REID, James T. M., Assistant Forester, c/o Mrs Maxwell, Balboughty, nr. Perth.

1911 ... REID, John, Assistant Forester, Cochnó Estate, Duntocher, Dumbartonshire.

1905 ... REID, Robert, Overseer, Kincairney, Dunkeld.

1903 ... REID, Robert Matelé, Thomanean, Milnathort.

1910 ... REIS, Gordon Stanley, B.Sc., Naga Timbool Estate, Post Bangoen Poerba, East Coast Sumatra, Dutch East Indies.

1914 ... RENEY, William, Assistant Forester, Donamon Castle, Roscommon, Ireland.

1901 ... RENNIE, Joseph, Overseer, Hillend, Possil, Maryhill.

1908 ... *RENSHAW, Charles Stephen Bine, B.A., Barochan, Houston.

1912 ... RENTON, James, F.S.I., Factor, Sunbank, Perth.

1914 ... REYNOLDS, Thomas Lewis, Assistant Forester, Darnhall, Eddleston, Peebles.

1910 ... RICHARD, James, Forester, Balnamoon, Brechin.

1873 *Cp* *RICHARDSON, Adam D., 6 Dalkeith Street, Joppa.

1914 ... RICHMOND AND GORDON, The Duke of, K.G., Gordon Castle, Fochabers.

1907 ... RILLIE, Joseph, Assistant Forester, Acklam, Middlesbrough.

1892 ... RITCHIE, Alexander, Overseer, Brucehill, Cardross Estate, Port of Menteith.

1908 ... *RITCHIE, Charles Ronald, W.S., 37 Royal Terrace, Edinburgh.

1913 ... RITCHIE, Matthew Aitken, Assistant Forester, Owood, Woodhall Estate, Holytown.

1898 ... RITCHIE, Wm., Assistant Forester, New Inn Cottage, Stanley.

1906 ... RITCHIE, Wm. H., of Dunnottar House, Stonehaven.

1912 ... ROBB, Henry Grant, Forester, The Nursery, Knowsley, Prescot, Lancs.

1909 ... *ROBERTS, Alex. Fowler, of Fairnilee, Clovenfords, Galashiels.

1914 ... ROBERTS, John, Local Agent, Crown Lodge, Tintern, Monmouth.

1909 ... ROBERTSON, Alexander, Factor, Polmaise, Stirling.

1897 ... *ROBERTSON, A. Barnett, Forester, The Dean, Kilmarnock, Ayrshire.

1914 ... *ROBERTSON, Andrew Forsyth, Forest Assistant, Messrs Steel Bros. & Co., Ltd., Rangoon.

1897 ... ROBERTSON, Andrew N., Forester, The Pines, Graffham, Petworth, Sussex.

1911 ... ROBERTSON, Andrew, Assistant Forester, Dean Road, Kilmarnock.

1899 ... ROBERTSON, Charles, Forester, Colstoun Old Mill, Gifford.

1911 ... ROBERTSON, Colin Halkett, Tebraw Rubber Estates, Johore, *via* Singapore.

1879 *mp* *ROBERTSON, Donald, Forester, Dunrobin, Golspie.

1907 ... *ROBERTSON, Edward Hercules, B.A., Advocate, Burnside, Forfar.

1896 ... ROBERTSON, George, Forester, Monreith Estate Office, Port William.

1908 ... ROBERTSON, George, Foreman Forester, Budby, Ollerton, Newark, Notts.

1910 ... *ROBERTSON, Henry Tod, Coalmaster, Meadowbank, Airdrie.

1900 ... ROBERTSON, James, Forester, Wortley Hall, Wortley, Sheffield.

1904 ... ROBERTSON, James, Forester, Cavens, Kirkbean, Dumfries.

1905 ... *ROBERTSON, James Morton, of Portmore, Portmore House, Eddleston.

1905 ... ROBERTSON, James W., Head Gardener, Letham Grange and Fern, Arbroath.

1907 ... ROBERTSON, J. P., Forester, Edensor, Bakewell.

1905 ... *ROBERTSON, John, Factor, Panmure Estates Office, Carnoustie.

1896 ... ROBERTSON, John, Forester, Rynagoup, Dallas, Forres.

1909 ... *ROBERTSON, John A., c/o Donald Robertson, Dunrobin, Golspie.

1895 ... ROBERTSON, Thomas, Forester, c/o Mrs Shaw, 5 Glenogle Road, Edinburgh.

1910 ... ROBERTSONWHITE, John Peregine, M.A., LL.B., Advocate in Aberdeen, 80 Union Street, Aberdeen.

1912 ... *ROBERTSON, William Hope, W.S., 8 Eton Terrace, Edinburgh.

1912 ... ROBINSON, George, Forestry Inspector, Department of Agriculture, Dublin.

1910 ... ROBINSON, R. G., Department of Lands, State Forests Branch, Tapanui, Otago, N.Z.

1912 ... ROBINSON, R. L., Board of Agriculture, 4 Whitehall Place, London, S.W.

1890 ... *ROBINSON, William, Gravetye Manor, East Grinstead, Sussex.

1899 ... ROBSON, Alex., of Smith & Son, 18 Market Street, Aberdeen.

1897 ... *ROBSON, Charles Durie, 66 Queen Street, Edinburgh.

1900 ... ROBSON, John, Forester, Sawmill Cottage, Baronscourt, Newtown Stewart, Ireland.

1893 *mp* RODGER, James, Forester, 82 Leinster Street, Athy, Co. Kildare.

1908 ... ROGERS, E. Percy, Estate Office, Stanage Park, Brampton Byran, Herefordshire.

1883 ... *ROLLO, The Master of, Duncrub Park, Dunning, Perthshire.

1872 ... *ROSEBERY, The Earl of, K.G., K.T., Dalmeny Park, Edinburgh.

1913 ... ROSE, William Duncan Ogilvie, M.A., Student, 11 Braidburn Crescent, Edinburgh.

1914 ... ROSS, Charles, Assistant Forester, Kilmadock, Doune Lodge, Doune.

1898 ... ROSS, Charles D. M., Factor, Abercairney, Crieff.

1914 ... ROSS, John, Forester, Esslemont, Ellon.

1905 ... ROSS, John S., Factor's Clerk, Monreith Estate Office, Wigtownshire.

1913 ... ROSSE, The Earl of, Birr Castle, Birr.

1906 *m* *ROXBURGHE, The Duke of, K.T., Floors Castle, Kelso.

1903 ... RULE, John, Forester, Huntly.

1908 ... *RUSSELL, David, Silverburn, Leven.

1893 ... RUTHERFORD, James A., Land Agent, Highclere Park, Newbury, Berks.

1870 ... RUTHERFORD, John, Forester, Linthaugh, Jedburgh, Roxburghshire.

1904 ... RUTHERFURD, Henry, Barrister-at-Law, Fairnington, Roxburgh.

1894 ... *SAMSON, David T., Factor, Seafield Estates Office, Cullen.

1875 ... SANG, Edmund, of E. Sang & Sons, Nurserymen, Kirkcaldy.

1906 ... *SANG, J. H., LL.B., W.S., Westbrook, Balerno.

1911 ... SCOTT, Alexander, Head Forester, Corsock, Dalbeattie.

1914 ... SCOTT, A. MacCallum, M.P., 35 Cyril Mansions, Battersea, London, S.W.

1911 ... SCOTT, Crawford Allen, Factor, Killermont and Garscadden Estates Office, Bearsden.

1867 *C* *SCOTT, Daniel, Wood Manager, Darnaway, Forres.

1892 ... SCOTT, David, Overseer, Dumfries House, Cumnock, Ayrshire. •

1901 *Cp* SCOTT, Frank, Forester, Jeaniebank, near Perth.

1911 ... SCOTT, George Ritchie, Farmer, Oxgang, Colinton.

1881 ... SCOTT, James, Forester, Wollaton Hall, Nottingham.

1907 ... *SCOTT, James Cospatrick, P.A.S.I., Yarrow Cottage, Poynder Place, Kelso.

1903 ... SCOTT, John, Forester, Annfield, Hartrigge, Jedburgh.

1908 ... SCOTT, John A., Forester, The Gardens, Knockbrex, Kirkcudbright.

Date of
Election.

1906 ... *SCOIT, John Henry Francis Kinnaird, of Gala, Gala House, Galashiels.

1913 ... SCOTT, William Lightbody, Assistant Forester, Braehead, Douglas, Lanarkshire.

1902 ... *SCRIMGEOUR, James, Horticulturist, Glasnevin College, Dublin.

1890 *C* SCRIMGEOUR, John, Overseer, Doune Lodge, Doune.

1913 ... SELLAR, Robert Hunter Nicol, Agricultural Engineer, Huntly.

1912 ... SHAND, Ebenezer, Apprentice Forester, Haddo House, Aberdeen.

1897 *m* SHARPE, Thomas, Head Forester, Gordon Castle, Fochabers.

1904 ... SHAW, John, Factor, Kilmahew Estate Office, Cardross.

1913 ... SHAW, John, Forester, East Lodge, Castlemilk, Rutherglen.

1896 *mp* *SHAW-STEWART, Sir Hugh, Bart., of Ardgowan, Greenock.

1904 ... *SHELLEY, Sir John Courtown Edward, Bart, Avington, Alresford, Hants.

1898 ... *SHEPPARD, Rev. H. A. Graham-, of Rednock, Ruskie, by Stirling.

1907 ... *SHIACH, Gordon Reid, L.D.S., etc., Ardgilzean, Elgin.

1903 ... *SHIEL, James, Overseer, Abbey St Bathans, Grant's House.

1911 ... SIM, Ernest James, Factor, Airthrey Estate Office, Bridge of Allan.

1911 ... SIM, James, District Forest Officer, King Williamstown, Cape Colony.

1905 ... SIM, John, Forester, Fernybrae, Cornhill, Banffshire.

1913 ... *SIME, Frank, Timber Merchant, Beauly.

1910 ... SIMPSON, Robert, Under Forester, Airth Estate, Larbert.

1912 ... SINCLAIR, John, Forester, Bluehouse, Bridgend, Islay.

1909 ... SINCLAIR, Magnus H., Seedsman, 156A Union Street, Aberdeen.

1906 *p* SINCLAIR, Robert, Board of Agriculture, Castletown, Caithness.

1908 ... SINCLAIR, The Lord, 55 Onslow Square, London, S.W.

1909 ... SINGER, George, Forester, Kilcoy Estate Office, Munlochy.

1900 *m* SINGER, John G., Forester, Whitestone Cottage, Maybole.

1914 ... SKIMMING, John, Foreman Forester, Glasserton Lodge, Monreith, Port William.

1908 ... SKIMMING, Robert, Timber Merchant, Kirkinner.

1868 *CMp* SLATER, Andrew, War Department Estates Office, Tynemouth House, Rothbury, Northumberland.

1902 .. SMART, John, Merchant, 18 Leith Street, Edinburgh.

1893 ... *SMITH, Charles G., Factor, Haddo House, Aberdeen.

1906 ... SMITH, Douglas, P.A.S.I., Land Agent, Estate Office, Thwaite, Erpingham, Norwich.

1912 ... SMITH, F., Forester, Craigmyle Estate, Torphins, Aberdeenshire.

1911 ... *SMITH, George, Factor, Mount Hamilton, by Ayr.

1911 ... SMITH, Herbert, Assistant Forester, Home Farm, Wishaw Estate, Wishaw, Lanarkshire.

1914 ... SMITH, H. Sydney, Hop Factor, 10 St Leonard's Terrace, Chelsea, S.W.

1911 ... SMITH, James, Assistant Forester, Thoresby Park, Ollerton, Notts.

1901 ... *SMITH, James, Forester, 1 Oxmantown Mall, Birr, King's County.

1908 ... SMITH, James, Nurseryman, Darley Dale Nurseries, near Matlock.

1908 ... SMITH, James, Assistant, Town Clerk's Office, Arbroath.

1906 ... SMITH, James Fraser, F.R.H.S., late Gardener, Barons Hotel, Auchnagatt.

1895 *m* SMITH, John, Cabinetmaker, 1 Eastgate, Peebles.

1907 ... *SMITH, J. Grant, Factor, Seafield Estates Office, Grantown-on-Spey.

1914 ... SMITH, John Taylor, Clerk, Board of Agriculture for Scotland, 29 St Andrew Square, Edinburgh.

1901 ... SMITH, Matthew, Manager for Dyer & Co., Peebles.

1908 ... SMITH, Robert, Factor, Cranstoun Riddell, Dalkeith.

1895 ... *SMITH, Thomas, Overseer, The Nursery, Tring Park, Wiggington, Tring, Herts.

1896 ... SMITH, William, Forester, Camperdown, Lochee.

1899 ... SMITH, William, Overseer, Rothes Estate Office, Leslie, Fife.

1896 *p* *SMITH, William G., B.Sc., Ph.D., Lecturer on Biology, Edinburgh and East of Scotland College of Agriculture, George Square, Edinburgh.

1907 ... *SMITHSON, Harry S. C., of Inverernie, Daviot, Highland R.S.O.

1910 ... SMYLY, John George, B.A., Consulting Forester and Land Agent, 22 Earlsfort Terrace, Dublin.

1882 ... *SMYTHE, David M., of Methven Castle, Perth.

1907 ... SOMERSET, The Duke of, Maiden Bradley, Bath; 35 Grosvenor Square, W.

1906 ... SOMERVILLE, Hugh Christopher, 2 Fairhaven, Dalkeith.

1906 ... *SOMERVILLE, Robert Anderson, Eastwoodbrae, Dalkeith.

1889 *Cmp* *SOMERVILLE, Dr William, M.A., D.Sc., D.Œc., F.R.S.E., Professor of Rural Economy, Oxford.

1904 ... SOUTAR, William, Forester, The Farm, Titsey Place, Limpsfield, Surrey.

1914 ... *SPEIRS, Alexander Archibald Hagart, of Elderslie, Houston House, Renfrewshire.

1912 ... *SPEIRS, Robert Robson, Structural Engineer, Maxholme, Bearsden.

1910 ... SPENCE, James George, Forester, West Lodge, Vogrie, Gorebridge.

1898 ... SPENCE, William, Forester, Strathenery, Leslie.

1899 *Cmp* *SPIERS, Adam, Timber Merchant, Warriston Saw-mills, Edinburgh.

1914 ... SPIERS, Thomson B., Assistant in Timber Yard, 4 Warriston Crescent, Edinburgh.

1914 ... SPRAGGAN, David, Forest Apprentice, Benmore, Kilmun.

1883 ... *SPROT, Major Alexander, of Garnkirk, Chryston, Glasgow.

1911 *m* *SPROT, Captain Mark, of Riddell, Lilliesleaf, Roxburghshire.

1909 ... *STAIR, The Earl of, Lochinch, Castle Kennedy.

1899 ..... *STALKER, Wm. J., Nurseryman, Nairn.

1914 ... STARK, Thomas, Head Forester, Holker, Cark-in-Cartmel, Lancs.

1910 *p* *STEBBING, Edward Percy, Indian Forest Service, Lecturer in Forestry, Edinburgh University.

1911 ... STEPHEN, George, Forester, Castle Grant, Grantown.

Date of
Election.

1907 ... STEPHEN, John, Forester, Balliemore, Nethy Bridge.

1901 ... STEWART, Alistair D., Kinfauns Estates Office, Rockdale, Perth.

1897 ... *STEWART, Charles, Forester, Nursery Cottage, Durris, Drumoak, Aberdeenshire.

1908 ... *STEWART, Charles, Achara, Duror of Appin, Argyll.

1907 *m* STEWART, David, Forester, Baunreagh Forestry Station, Mountrath, Queen's Co.

1909 ... STEWART, Sir David, of Banchory-Devenick, Banchory House, Banchory, Devenick.

1910 ... STEWART, Donald, Forester, The Lodge, Inverlochy Castle, Fort William.

1899 ... *STEWART, Duncan D., Factor, Ardenlea, Pitlochry.

1901 ... STEWART, James, Forester, Letham and Fern Estates, Fern, near Brechin.

1914 ... STEWART, James, Foreman Forester, Barcaldine, Ledaig.

1903 ... STEWART, John, Forester, Coltness Estate, Wishaw.

1892 ... *STEWART, Sir Mark J. M'Taggart, Bart. of Southwick, Kirkcudbrightshire.

1903 .. STEWART, Colouel R. K., of Murdostoun, Murdostoun Castle, Lanarkshire.

1914 ... STEWART, Peter, Assistant Forester, Benmore, Kilmun.

1876 ... STEWART, Robert, Forester, Stonefield, Sunnyside, Tarbert, Lochfyne.

1910 ... STEWART, William, of Shambellie, Kirkcudbrightshire.

1904 *Cmp* *STIRLING, Captain Archibald, of Keir, Dunblane, *President*.

1907 *m* STIRLING, John Alexander, of Kippendavie, 4 Connaught Square, London, W.

1911 ... *STIRLING, Thomas Willing, of Muiravonside, Linlithgow.

1908 ... *STIRLING, William, D.L., J.P., of Fairburn, Muir of Ord.

1909 ... *STODART, Charles, Farmer, Wintonhill, Pencaitland.

1906 ... STODDART, James, jun., Joiner, Macondach, Bonnyrigg.

1893 ... STORIE, W., Whitway House, Newbury, Berks.

1914 ... STRACHAN, Adam, Assistant Forester, West Lodge, Ballechin, Ballinluig.

1913 ... *STRATHARN, Tom Dalrymple, Land Agent, P.A S.I., Grimeshill Estate Office, Middleton, Kirkby Lonsdale, Westmoreland.

1908 ... STRATHEDEN and CAMPBELL, The Lord, Hartrigge, Jedburgh.

1908 .. *STRATHMORE AND KINGHORNE, The Earl of, Glamis Castle, Glamis.

1908 ... STUART, Alexander, Lee and Carnwath Estates Office, Cartland, Lanark.

1910 ... STUART, George Morrison, Gardener, The Gardens, Forglen, Turriff.

1912 ... *STUART, Henry, Land Steward, Knoydart, Mallaig, Inverness shire.

1911 ... STUART, Henry Campbell, Factor, Glen Caladh, Tighnabruaich.

1908 *m* STUART, Lord Ninian Edward Crichton, M.P., House of Falkland, Fife.

42

1902 ... STUNT, Walter Charles, Lorenden, Ospringe, Kent.

1907 ... SUTHERLAND, George, Assistant Forester and Saw-miller, Bowmont Forest, Roxburgh.

1914 ... *SUTHERLAND, The Duke of, Dunrobin Castle, Golspie.

1892 m *SUTHERLAND, John D., Member of Board of Agriculture, 29 St Andrew Square, Edinburgh.

1912 ... TAIT, Adam, of Wooplaw, Darnick, Braid Avenue, Edinburgh.

1900 ... *TAIT, James, Westshiel, Penicuik.

1914 ... TAIT, Thomas, Paper Manufacturer, Inverurie Mills, Inverurie.

1914 ... TAYLOR, Alexander Cuthill, Factor, Kildary House, Kildary, Ross-shire.

1902 ... TAYLOR, John, Forester, Orchill Estate, by Braco, Perthshire.

1904 ... TAYLOR, Robert, Assistant Forester, Mosside Cottage, Almond-bank, Perth.

1905 ... TAYLOR, Robert, Forester, West Saline, Saline, Oakley.

1897 ... TAYLOR, William, Forester, Sandside, Kirkcudbright.

1905 ... TELFER, John, Forester, Basildon Park, Reading, Berks.

1914 ... TENNANT, F. J., of Innes, Innes House, Elgin.

1911 ... *TENNANT, H. J., M.P., 33 Bruton Street, London, W.

1877 ... *TERRIS, James, Factor, Dullomuir, Blairadam, Kinross-shire.

1911 ... *Thomas, David Gwilym, Forestry Student, 44 Lauriston Place, Edinburgh.*

1908 ... THOMPSON, Archibald, Overseer, Auchindarroch, Lochgilphead.

1904 ... THOMPSON, Dugald, Forester, Kinnordy, Kirriemuir.

1911 ... *THOMSON, Alexander, of Burgie, Forres.

1893 C THOMSON, David W., Nurseryman, 113 George Street, Edinburgh.

1913 ... THOMSON, Herdman, Nurseryman, 113 George Street, Edinburgh.

1911 ... THOMSON, John, Forester, Kailzie, Peebles.

1902 p *THOMSON, Peter Murray, S.S.C., Cockbridge, Mealsgate, Gumb.

1903 ... THOMSON, Robert, Foreman Forester, 57 Park Hill, Ampthill, Bedfordshire.

1901 ... *THOMSON, Spencer Campbell, of Eilean Shona, 10 Eglinton Crescent, Edinburgh.

1908 ... *THORBURN, Michael Grieve, D.L., etc., of Glenormiston, Inner-leithen.

1911 ... THOW, William Keir, Foreman Forester, Beaufort Estate, Kiltarlity, Beauly.

1904 ... THREIPLAND, Captain W. Murray, Dryburgh Abbey, St Boswells.

1913 ... TIBBLE, Ernest Frank, Assistant Forester, Bridgend, Inverkip.

1906 ... TINDAL, Robert, Forester, Bellspool Cottages, Stobo.

1901 ... TIVENDALE, William D., Head Forester to Duke of Portland, Burnhouse, Galston.

1871 ... *TOMLINSON, Wilson, Forester, Clumber Park, Worksop, Notts.

1912 ... *TORRANCE, James Watt, Timber Merchant, 11 Dundonald Road, Glasgow.

1906 ... *TRAIL, James W. H., A.M., M.D., F.R.S., Professor of Botany, Aberdeen University, 71 High Street, Old Aberdeen.

1914 ... TROUP, Robert Scott, Indian Forest Service, Dehra Dun U.P.,
India.

1903 ... *TULLIBARDINE, The Marquis of, D.S.O., Blair Castle, Blair
Atholl.

1903 ... TURNBULL, John, Forester, Forester's Lodge, Arbigland,
Dumfries.

1910 ... TWEEDIE, Alexander, Forester, etc., Springfield, Kerry, Mon.

1883 ... UNDERWOOD, Henry E., Fornham, St Martin, Bury St Edmunds,
Suffolk.

1903 ... *UNWIN, Arthur Harold, D.Œc., Town House, Haslemere, Surrey.

1908 ... *URQUHART, Angus, Assistant Nursery and Seedsman, Inverness.

1907 ... URQUHART, Colonel Robert, Town Clerk, Forres.

1908 ... *USHER, Sir Robert, Bart. of Norton and Wells, Norton, Ratho
Station, Midlothian.

1908 ... VEITCH, Andrew, Seedsman and Nurseryman, Melrose.

1912 ... *VEITCH, Archibald, Chatlapore Tea Estate, Shamshernagar,
P.O., So. Sylhet, India.

1911 ... VEITCH, Robert, B.Sc., 7 Queen's Crescent, Edinburgh.

1912 ... *VESCI, The Viscount de, D.L., Abbeyleix, Ireland.

1911 ... WADDINGHAM, James Hart, Elsham, Grimsby.

1908 ... WALDRON, Major Patrick John, East Haugh, Pitlochry.

1911 ... WALKER, Austine Harrington, Chemical Manufacturer, Richmond
House, Dullatur, Dumbartonshire.

1903 ... WALKER, Captain George Lawrie, of Crawfordton, Thornhill.

1894 ... WALKER, Henry H., Factor, Monreith, Port William, Wigtownshire.

1878 ... *WALKER, Colonel I. Campbell, Newlands, Camberley, Surrey.

1907 ... *WALKER, James, Wood Merchant, Inverness.

1906 ... *WALKER, John Steven, Yard Foreman, Saw-mills, Hurlford,
Ayrshire.

1906 ... *WALKER, Robert Williamson, C.E., Factor and Land Surveyor,
3 Golden Square, Aberdeen.

1903 ... *Wallace, Andrew, Saw-miller, 5 North Street, Freuchie.*

1912 ... WALLACE, Andrew, Foreman Forester, Foresters' Cottages,
Altyre, Forres.

1893 m WALLACE, David P., Forester, The Saw-mills, Filleigh, South
Molton, N. Devon.

1912 ... WALLACE, John, Land Steward, Dunnikier Estate, Kirkcaldy.

1897 ... *WALLACE, John A. A., of Lochryan, Cairnryan, Stranraer.

1905 ... *WALLACE, Thomas Douglas, F.S.I., Hamilton Palace, Hamilton.

1899 ... WANDESFORDE, R. H., Prior of Castlecomer, Co. Kilkenny.

1909 ... WARING, Captain Walter, M.P., of Lennel, Coldstream.

1900 ... *WARWICK, Charles, Smiley Estate Office, Ailsa, Larne.

1901 ... WASON, Right Hon. Eugene, M.P., P.C., of Blair, Dailly, Ayrshire: 8 Sussex Gardens, Hyde Park, London.

1913 ... WATSON, Alexander S., Assistant Forester, New Cottages, Duppliu, Perth.

1914 ... WATSON, Harry, Assistant Forester, Whitemire, Darnaway, Forres.

1901 ... WATSON, James, Manager, Moy Hall, Inverness-shire.

1893 ... *WATSON, John T., 6 Bruntsfield Gardens, Edinburgh.

1912   *p* WATT, Hugh Boyd, Secretary and Insurance Broker, 12 Great James Street, Bedford Row, London, W.C.

1872 ... WATT, James, J.P., of Little & Ballantyne, Nurserymen, Carlisle.

1893 ... WATT, James W., Knowefield Nurseries, Carlisle.

1911 ... WATT, Sidney, Forester, Pearsie, Kirriemuir.

1911   *m* WATT, William, Assistant Forester, Redstone, Darnaway.

1914 ... WATT, William R., Foreman Forester, Rose Cottage, Achnacarry, Spean Bridge.

1906 ... WEBSTER, Charles, Gardener and Forester, The Gardens, Gordon Castle, Fochabers.

1911 ... *WEBSTER, Sir Francis, Ashbrook, Arbroath.

1908 ... *WEDDERBURN, Ernest Maclagan, LL.B., W.S., F.R.S.E., Factor, 2 Glenfinlas Street, Edinburgh.

1911 ... WEIR, Andrew, Forestry Student, Doonhome, Colinton.

1891 ... *WELSH, James, of Dicksons & Co., 1 Waterloo Place, Edinburgh.

1913 ... WENSLEY, A., Forester, Grimsbury Castle, Hermitage, near Newbury, Berks.

1904 ... WENTWORTH-FITZWILLIAM, George Charles, of Milton, Peterborough.

1902   *mp* WHELLENS, W. Henry, Forester, Thoresby, Ollerton, Notts.

1898 ... *WHITE, J. Martin, Balruddery, near Dundee.

1895 ... WHITE, William, Farmer, Gortonlee, Lasswade.

1884   *C* *WHITTON, James, Superintendent of Parks, 249 George Street, Glasgow.

1914 ... WHYTE, James, Assistant Forester, Donamon Castle, Roscommon, Ireland.

1899 ... *WHYTE, John D. B., Factor, Estate Office, Elveden, Suffolk.

1895 ... WIGHT, Alexander, Overseer, Thurston, Temple Mains, Innerwick.

1869   *p* *WILD, Albert Edward (Conservator of Forests, Darjeeling, India), c/o Henry S. King & Co., 65 Cornhill, London, E.C.

1883 ... WILKIE, Charles, Forester, Lennoxlove, Haddington.

1891 ... WILKIE, G., Architect, Hayfield, Peebles.

1902 ... WILKINSON, John, Factor, The Grange, Kirkcudbright.

1913 ... *WILLANS, John Bancroft, Dalforgan, Kerry, Newton, Montgomeryshire.

1908 ... WILLIAMSON, James A., A.R.I.B.A., Public Works Office, City Chambers, Edinburgh.

1895 ... WILLIAMSON, John, Bank Agent, Loanhead, Midlothian.

1907 ... *WILLIAMSON, John, Joiner and Builder, Grangemouth.

1913 ... WILMOT, Sir Sainthill Eardley-, K.C.I.E., The Warren, Bramley, Guildford.

1913 ... WILSON, Adam, Timber Merchant, Dailly, Ayrshire.

1907   *p* WILSON, Adam Frank, C.D.A.(Edin.), 164 Braid Road, Edinburgh.

1913 ...   WILSON, Albert, Forester, Derwent Valley Water Board, Cliff View, Thornhill Hope, via Sheffield.

1907 ...   WILSON, Andrew Robertson, M.A., M.D., Hopewell, Tarland, Aboyne ; and Cairnmore, Liscard, Cheshire.

1898 ...   *WILSON, David, Timber Merchant, Troon, Ayrshire.

1889 ...   *WILSON, David, jun., of Carbeth, Killearn, Glasgow.

1908 ...   WILSON, Edward Arthur, Rockingham, Edgbaston Park Road, Birmingham.

1907 ...   WILSON, Ian Hall, Saw-mill Manager, Brodie Cottage, Brodie.

1900 ...   WILSON, James, jun., Nurseryman, St Andrews.

1907 ...   WILSON, James G., Assistant, 24 St Andrew Square, Edinburgh.

1910 ...   *Wilson, John, Estate Steward, Brand's Mill, Dunbar.*

1902 ...   WILSON, Sir John, Bart. of Airdrie.

1901 ...   WILSON, John Currie, Factor, Tulliallan Estate Office, Kincardine-on-Forth.

1912 ...   WILSON, John, Estate Agent, Egton Bridge, Yorks.

1914 ...   WILSON, Robert, Assistant Forester, Killincraig, Largs.

1912 ...   *Wilson, Thomas, Assistant Forester, Matlock House, Baslow, Derbyshire.*

1903 ...   WILSON, Thomas, Head Gardener, Glamis Castle, Glamis.

1899 ...   WILSON, William, Timber Merchant, Auchenleck, Ayrshire.

1912 ...   WINTON, Thomas, jun., Timber Merchant, 52 Seafield Road, Dundee.

1893 ...   WISEMAN, Edward, Nurseryman, Elgin.

1895 ...   WISEMAN, William, Nurseryman, Forres.

1906 ...   WOLFE, George, sen., J.P., Shovel Manufacturer, Millburn, Bathgate.

1909 ...   WOOD, James, of Wallhouse, Torphichen.

1907 ...   WOOD, Thomas, Forester, West Lodge, Durie, Leven, Fife.

1914 ...   WOOF, Robert Stephenson, F.S.I., Land Agent, Lowther, Penrith.

1904 ...   WORSFOLD, Edward Mowll, Land Agent, Market Square, Dover.

1904 ...   *Wotherspoon, George, Factor, Cromartie Estate Office, Kildary, Ross-shire.*

1909 ...   WRIGHT, John Moncrieff, of Kinmonth, Bridge of Earn.

1904 ...   WRIGHT, Sir Robert Patrick, F.H.A.S., F.R.S.E., Chairman, Board of Agriculture, 29 St Andrew Square.

1868 ...   WYLLIE, George, Ballogie, Aboyne, Aberdeenshire.

1906 ...   WYLLIE, William, Seedsman, 18 Market Street, Aberdeen.

1908 ...   *YEAMAN, Alexander, W.S., 32 Charlotte Square, Edinburgh.

1904 ...   *YOOL, Thomas, Factor, Ballindalloch Estates Office, Ballindalloch.

1905 ...   YOUNG, John, Hedger, West Lodge, Corehouse, Lanark.

1907 ...   YOUNG, John U., 37 Edgemont Gardens, Langside, Glasgow.

1909 ... YOUNG, Peter, Assistant Forester, Lochend Cottage, Chapelhill,
Methven.

1910 ... YOUNG, R. M., Nursery Manager, Cathcart Nurseries, Newlands,
Glasgow.

1910 ... YOUNG, William George, Estate Cleık, Craigielaw, Longniddry.

1910 *m* YOUNGER, Harry George, of Benmore, 21 Grosvenor Crescent,
Edinburgh.

1912 *m* YOUNGER, James, of Mount Melville, St Andrews.

1899 ... *YULE, Miss Amy Frances, Tarradale House, Muir of Ord.

1911 .... YOUNG, James Weir, P.A.S.I., Land Surveyor, Kinneil Estate
Office, Bo'ness.

INDEX.

VOLS. I. TO XXVIII.

INDEX

To ADDRESSES, ESSAYS, REPORTS, ETC.,

PUBLISHED IN THE

TRANSACTIONS OF THE ROYAL SCOTTISH ARBORICULTURAL SOCIETY,

Vols. I. to XXVIII.

Indicates illustrated Articles.

ABERDEEN. See Exhibitions.

Aberdeen Branch of Arboricultural Society, xix. 362. See Excursions.

Aberdeen University, Course for Foresters at, xxiv. 217.

Aberdeenshire, Arboriculture in. W. Gilchrist, vii. 235.

Abies:—*Anatomy of Leaf as a Means of Determining Species of—W. R. M'Nab, viii. 93. List of Species, viii. 108. *A. nobilis* for Planting up Blanks in Woods—D. Stewart, xxiii. 103. See Douglas Fir.

*Absorption, Creosoting of Timber by. J. Balden, xx. 62.

Acetone, Notes *re*—W. D. A. Bost, xxviii. 271.

Achnacarry, Afforestation at, xxv. 58.

Adam, W. P.: Address, 1877, (Progress of Society; Planting at Blairadam; Establishing Forest School), viii. 193. Address, 1879, (Application for Royal Charter; Progress of Society; Need for Forest School; Planting at Blairadam), ix. 107. See x. 76.

Addresses :— See Adam, W. P. (1877-79); Bailey, F. (1899); Balfour, I. B. (1891-93); Balfour, J. H. (1875); Brown, J. (1855); Cleghorn, H. (1872-74, 1883-86); Dickson, A. (1882); Dunn, M. (1888); Ferguson, R. C. Munro (1895-97); Fothringham, W. Steuart (1904); Hutchison, R. (1867-71, 1880); Lothian, Marquis of (1881); M'Corquodale, W. (1889); Mackenzie. D. F. (1890); Mackenzie, Sir K. J. (1907); Mansfield, Earl of (1900); Methven, J. (1894); Milne, A. (1900); Thomson, W. (1855). Also, Schlich, W.

*Advance Growth, Relation of Light-Intensity to, in Oak and Beech Forests. G. P. Gordon, xxvi. 147.

Advice, Technical, for Private Owners, xxvii. 29.

Advisory Committee on Forestry for Scotland, xxvii. 29.

*Afforestable Lands and Woods in Scotland, Inspection of, xxviii. 154.

Afforestation :— Lord Lovat, xxii. 156; R. C. Munro Ferguson, xxii. 169. And Local Taxation—K. Mackenzie, xxiii. 3. At Talla, xxvii. 104; at Vyrnwy, xxvii. 236. Comparison between the Yields from, and Pasture Lands—Alex. Lauder, xxvii. 113. Deputation from Society to Chancellor of Exchequer, on National, xxii. 200. Deputation from Irish Forestry Society to Chief Secretary for Ireland, xix. 327. Duty of State as regards, xxiii. 1. In Great Britain and Ireland—J. Nisbet, xxii. 139. In Highlands and Islands of Scotland—W. A. Mackenzie, xiii. 318. In Italy, xvii. 321. In Scotland : Forest Survey of Glen Mor—Lord Lovat and Capt. Stirling of Keir, xxv. In the Black Country, xvii. 336. Of Catchment Areas, xxiii. 22 ; F. Bailey, xx. 106 ; G. Baxter, xxiv. 191 ; J. Parry, xvii. 223 ; W. G. Smith, xvii. 86. Of Waste Lands in Denmark, Holland, France, etc., xxii. 207. Report of Royal Commission on—J. Stirling-Maxwell, xxii. 186 ; J. F. Annand, xxii. 188. Royal Commission on : their German and English Critics, etc.— B. Ribbentrop, xxii. 180. State, in Scotland—F. Bailey, xxi. 27. State in Relation to—A. S. Hodderwick, xxiv. 150. Waste Land for —A. C. Forbes, xx. 142. When it comes—J. Fleming, xxiii. 124. See Re-afforestation, and Notes and Queries.

Afforestation Conference, 1907, xxi. 60.

Africa:—*Arboricultural Notes from Portuguese E.—J. A. Alexander, xx. 194. Department of Woods and Forests for West, xvii. 160. Forests in South—J. C. Brown, ix. 45. Forests of British E., xxiii. 113.

Agaricus, xvii. 154.

Age of Trees, viii. 84.

Ageing, Rapid, of Wood, xvii. 291.

Agnew, A. N.: Visit to Forests of Bavaria, 1909, xxiii. 72.

Agricultural College, W. of Scotland, Forestry at. W. F. A. H., xxi. 230.

Agricultural Credit, Co-operative, in Germany and Switzerland, xvii. 331.

Agriculture:—Relation of Forestry to, and Other Industries, xxvii. 121.

Agriculture, Board of:—Deputation to President of, xiv. 192. Deputation to, on Development of Forestry in Scotland, xxvi. 202; xxvii. 104. Letter to—A. Stirling, xxvii. 143. Leaflet by, on Large Brown Pine Weevil, xxviii. 118. President of, on Forestry, xvii. 323. Report of Deputation to President of (1901), xvi. 479. Report of Departmental Committee on Forestry to President of (1902), xvii. 1.

Aitken, A. P.: Leaf-Mould, xv. 70.

Albert or Hemlock Spruce at Loganbank. F. B., xxi. 109.

Alcohol from Sawdust, xix. 362.

Alder Sawfly, Birch and. J. Boyd, xix. 207.

Aldourie, Afforestation at, xxv. 53.

Alexander, J.: Rearing newer Coniferæ from Seed, Cuttings or Grafts, vii. 84.

Alexander, J. A.: *Arboricultural Notes from Portuguese E. Africa, xx. 194.

*Alice Holt Forest, Working-Plan for. W. Schlich and W. F. Perree, xix. 83.

America:—India-rubber Trees of South—J. Ferguson, x. 108. Insect Depredations in Forests of North, xxiv. 222. Timber Supply of United States—W. Harrower. x. 83. Timber Trees introduced from Eastern Seaboard of North—

J. E. Brown, v. 124. Tree Planting at San Jorge, Uruguay—C. E. Hall, xiii. 220. Trees of Western —F. R. S. Balfour, xxi. 121.

American Forestry Congress, xviii. 229.

American, North, and Japanese, Trees suitable for British Woodlands. H. J. Elwes, xix. 76.

Amery, C. F.: Forests of India, viii. 213.

Animals, etc., injurious to Forest Trees. G. Brown, xvii. 277. See also xix. 104.

Annand, J. F.: Erosion and Afforestation Royal Commission Report, xxii. 188; Forestry Exhibition at Highland and Agricultural Society's Show at Peebles, 1906, xx. 87; Forestry in Finland, xvii. 243; *Forestry in the Schwarzwald, xxi. 159; Formation of Plantations, xiii. 268; *Uses of Demonstration Forest, xxvii. 54; White American Spruce as Wind-Mantle, xvi. 473.

Annual Increment:— In girth of Douglas Fir, xxvi. 232. Of Spruce and Scots Pine — J. H. Milne-Home, xxiv. 52; xxvi. 160; xxvii. 34.

Ants, White, Protection of Timber against, xxiii. 227.

Aphis. W. Schlich, xii. 423.

Appeal for Literary Contributions. F. Bailey, xix. 353; xxvi. 234.

Appin Woods. F. B., xxii. 108.

Appointments. See Forestry Appointments, and Notes and Queries.

Apprentices and Under - Foresters, Improving Social and Moral Condition of, etc. C. Y. Michie, v. 61; P. M'Laren, v. 73.

Arable Land :—Arboriculture and— R. M. Ferguson, xxi. 222. Diseased Scots Pines on, xx. 248.

Arboretum :--At Cluny Castle, Aberdeenshire—W. Gilchrist, vii. 19. Inverleith—J. H. Balfour, viii. 1. Formation of—W. H. Whellens, xxvii. 79.

Arboricultural Adornment of Towns. R. C. Munro Ferguson, xvi. 388.

Arboricultural Features of Buteshire. J. Kay, vii. 60.

*Arboricultural Notes from Portuguese E. Africa. J. A. Alexander, xx. 194.

Arboricultural Societies :— Brechin, xviii. 237. Local—R. Philip, i. 38. Scottish, Origin and History

of, etc., vii., 115; viii. 195; ix.
108; xi. 114 (1854-84); xii. 189,
375; xv. 82; xvi. 178; xviii. 1,
5 (1854-1904). Jubilee Dinner of
Scottish, xviii. 31. Diamond
Jubilee Conference and Dinner,
xxviii. 179. See also Notes and
Queries.

Arboriculture:—And Arable Land—
R. M. Ferguson, xxi. 222. In
Aberdeenshire—W. Gilchrist, vii.
235. In Counties of Dumfries,
Kirkcudbright and Wigtown—A.
Pitcaithley, xiii. 293. In Hampshire—A. Peebles, viii. 25; J.
Smith, xi. 511. In Ireland—C. S
France, v. 168. In Kent—J. Duff,
viii. 153. In New Forest, Hants,
History of—G. Lascelles, xiv. 15.
In North Lancashire—G. Dodds,
xi. 188. In Yorkshire—D. Tait,
vii. 137. Influence of—A. Gilchrist, v. 102. Literature of
Scottish—R. Hutchison, vii. 211.
Philosophy of—J. G. Macvicar, iv.
138. Practical—A. Gilchrist, vi.
82; W. Gilchrist, vi. 6; W. Thomson, vi. 51. Rise and Progress of,
vii. 199.

Arbor-vitæ, Giant. A. D. Webster,
xii. 341.

*Arbours, Rustic, etc. C. Y. Michie,
iv. 115.

Ardgoil Estate. W. F. A. H., xxi.
223 xxvii. 105.

Ardross Woods, Working-Plan:—F.
B., xxi. 230. And Larch Canker
—A. D. Richardson, xxii. 64.

Area of Woodlands in Great Britain,
xix. 347.

Argyll:—Excursion to, 1905—A. D.
Richardson, xix. 180. Foresters'
and Gardeners' Society of, xxi. 235.
Woodlands of, xxvii. 104.

*Argyresthia laevigatella, xxi. 195.

Armstrong College, Forestry Instruction at, xx. 112.

Arran, Island of, as Field for Planting. W. A. Mackenzie, xiii. 341.

Arseniate of Soda, Experiment with,
for Protection against Pine Weevil.
T. Neilson, xix 207.

Artificial Manures in Forestry. A.
W. Borthwick, xix. 245.

Artificially Coloured Wood, xix. 215.

Ash:—And its Cultivation—J. Nisbet, xvi. 128. Hungarian, xix.
209.

*Ash Bark Beetle. A. M'Intosh, x.
235.

Atholl, John, Duke of, his Larch

Plantations, etc. J. Booth, xvii.
232.

Auchendaul, Afforestation at, xxv.
59.

Auchincruive, Ayrshire, Trees at.
G. Leven, xix. 212.

Australia:—Forests in Western, xx.
130. Forest Resources of—E. T.
Scammell, xvii. 249 Natural Forests of South—G. M'Ewin, x. 33.
Supply of Timber of—Krichauff,
viii. 110.

Austrian Firs, vii. 52.

Ayrshire, Excursions to (1901), xvi.
507; (1905), xix. 180.

BAILEY, F.: Address, 1899, (Need
for State Forest; Working-Plans
for Woods; Raith Working-Plan;
Timber Resources of Canada and
the United States), xvi. 1; Afforestation of Talla Water-Catchment
Area, xx. 106; Anticipated Curtailment of Timber Supplies from
Sweden, xix. 337; Bo'ness Pit-
Wood Trade, xvi. 9; Damage to
Woods, etc., by Sparks from Railway Engines, xvi. 289; Example
Plots or Forest Gardens, xix. 317;
Forest Nurseries and Gardens, xxi.
54; Forest of Dean (Mr Hill on),
xv. 292; *Forest Tour among
Dunes of Gascony, xi. 291; Forestry at Edinburgh University,
xvii. 206; Forestry Committee
(1902) and Training in Forestry,
xxi. 102; Forestry in France, xi.
221; Forestry in Hungary, xii. 1;
Forests at Mirwart (Dr Schlich's),
xvi. 241; Forests of Norway, xvi.
458; Indian Forest School, xi.
155; Introduction to Course of
Forestry Lectures, Edinburgh University (1891-92), xiii. 174; Note
on Modern Works on Forestry in
English Language, xv. App; State
Afforestation in Scotland, xxi. 27;
*Supply of Telegraph Poles to Post
Office, xix. 343; Tables for Conversion of Measurements, xii. 351;
Teredo navalis and other Sea-
Worms, xxiii. 196; Underplanting, xxi. 198. *Obituary, xxvii. 244.

Bailey, F., and Fisher, Prof.: *State
and other Forests of France visited
by Society in 1904, and Forests of
St Amand and Raismes (Valenciennes), xviii. 74.

Bailey, F., and Macdonald, G. U.:
-*Plan for Pit-Wood Working
Circle at Raith, xv. 223.

Bailey, F., Meiklejohn, J. J. R., White, J. D. B., and Mackenzie, W. : *Plan of Management of Woods at Novar, xvi. 25.

Bailey, L. W., and Jack, E. : Woods of New Brunswick, xi. 9.

Baillie, W. : * Instrument for Measuring Heights of Trees, v. 171.

Balden, J. : *Creosoting of Timber by Absorption, xx. 62.

Balfour, F. R. S. : Creosoting Tree Stumps against Pine Weevil, xxviii. 270· Trees of California, xxii. 213 ; Trees of Western America, xxi. 121.

Balfour, I. B.: Address, 1891, (Forest School : Review of Past and Outline of Future Efforts to Establish, etc.), xiii. 163 ; Address, 1892, (University Forest Education ; Teaching of Practical Foresters), xiii. 301 ; Address, 1893, (Restrictions on Home-Grown Timber ; Forestry Classes at Botanic Gardens and Edinburgh University ; Need for Forest School, etc.), xiv. 1 : Forestry in Britain : Address to Biological Section of British Association, Oxford, 1894, xiv. 55 ; *Report on Tree-Pruning in St James' Park and Piccadilly, xxvi. 31. See Reports by Hon. Scientists. See also xi. 1.

Balfour, J. H. : Address, 1875, (Trees and Climate ; Forest Conservancy ; Education of Foresters ; Arboretum at Inverleith ; Forest Literature ; Disease, etc., in Forest Trees), viii. 1.

Barclay, D. : Plantations on Estate of Sorn, Ayr, xi. 29.

Bark : — Curing of Coppice — J. M'Leod, i. 103. Peeling, Commercial Aspect of—A. T. Williamson, xii. 443. Peeling and Harvesting of. Native—R. Ross, ix. 58. Preparation of Oak, for Sale—W. Thomson, i. 25. Prices of Oak (1856), i. 101. Prices (1869), vi. 144.

Barrie, J. : *Old and Remarkable Trees on Rolle Estate, Devon, xii. 242.

Barry, J. W. : *Measurements of Trees for Cubic Contents, x. 21.

*Basic Slag on Seed-Beds. J. Boyd, xxi. 229.

Basses Pyrénées, Forests of. G. Cadell, xvii. 104.

Bavaria :—*Excursion to, 1909, xxiii.

80. Visit to Forests of, 1909— A. N. Agnew, xxiii. 72.

Bavarian and Saxon Forests, Visit to Some, 1904. J. J. R. Meiklejohn, xviii. 150.

Baxter, G. : Afforestation of Water-Catchment Areas, xxiv. 191.

Baxter, R.: Best Woods for Charcoal, and Process of Charring, viii. 246. Obituary—J. Whytock, xix. 244.

Bayne, L. : Distances at which Forest Trees should be Planted, viii. 77 ; Draining of Plantations, vii. 250 ; Most profitable Felling Ages of Timber Trees, vii. 175 ; Hardwood Plantations, ix. 158.

Beare, T. Hudson : *Timber : Its Strength and How to Test it, xix. 1.

*Beauly, Natural Regeneration . of Scots Pine at, etc. G. Brown, xix. 17.

Bedfordshire, Excursion to, xvii. 301.

Beech :—*And Oak Forests in Denmark—W. G. Smith, xxviii. 241. *And Oak High Forest in France—Prof. Fisher, xviii. 90. Disease in Hedges of — R. Hutchison, ix. 217. Forests, xxvi 147. *Forests of Hesse Nassau— G. Cadell, xiii. 57. Hedges, Planting and Management of—J. Kay, iv. 187. Influence of Thinning on Growth of—A. C. Forbes, xvi. 116. In Scotland, xxiii. 103. On Chiltern Hills, xviii. 225. "Slime-Flux" on, xx. 122.

*Beech Felt Scale. G. Leven, xx. 245.

Beetles :—*Ash Bark—A. M'Intosh, x. 235. Battle with—J. Clark, xvi. 274. Rooks feeding on Pine —J. Boyd, xix. 206. Which infest Coniferæ—R. Hutchison, vii. 123 ; W. Tivendale, vii. 80. See Reports by Hon. Scientists.

*Belgian Forestry in Some of its Aspects. A. T. Gillanders, xix. 139.

*Belgian System of Planting on Turfs. J. Stirling-Maxwell, xxiii. 153.

Belgium, Afforestation of Waste Lands in, xxii. 207.

Bellême, Forest of. Prof. Fisher, xviii. 100.

Bibliography of Forestry. H. B. Watt, xxvi. 230.

Biltmore Forest School, U.S.A.. xxiv. 108 ; xxvi. 98.

Biological Utilisation, etc , of Soil. M. Hardy, xvii. 110.

Birch and Alder Saw-Fly. J. Boyd, xix. 207.

Birch :—Seed, Management of—W. Somerville, xv. 319. Woods, Glen Mor—J. Nisbet, xxv. 70.

Black Country, Re-afforesting, xvii. 336.

*Blackmoor Woods, Working-Plan for. J. Nisbet, xvi. 193.

Blasting, Scientific Tree-Butt, xviii. 225.

Blight. W. Schlich, xii. 423.

*Blister in Larch Plantations. R. Coupar, x. 119.

Boden, F. : Larch in German Forests, xvii. 47.

Bo'ness Pit-Wood Trade. F. Bailey, xvi. 9.

Book-Keeping for Foresters, etc., D. F. Mackenzie, ix. 183 ; W. Thomson, i. 129.

Book Notices, etc. :—

Annand, J. F.: Farming and Forestry: Cultivation of Trees for Shelter and for Timber, xxvi. 239.

Baker, H. Clinton : Illustrations of Conifers, vol. i., xxii. 239 ; vol. ii., xxiii. 235 ; vol. iii. xxvii. 240 (F. R. S. Balfour).

Boulger, G. S.: Wood: Natural History and Industrial Applications of Timbers of Commerce, xvii. 163 (A. D. R.).

Brown, Dr J.: The Forester, xiv. 89.

Charpentier, P. : Timber: Study of Wood in all its Aspects, Commercial and Botanical, etc. Trans. by J. Kennell, xvii. 166 (A. D. R.).

Cooke, Arthur O.: The Forest of Dean, xxviii. 120.

Cooper, C. S., and Westell, W. Percival : Trees and Shrubs of British Isles, Native and Acclimatised, xxiii. 119.

Cox, Dr J. Charles : The Royal Forests of England, xix. 238 (J. Nisbet).

Curtis, C. E.: Elementary Forestry, xix. 229 (J. Nisbet).

Davies, J.: Building Timbers and Architects' Specifications, part of Haworth's " Timber Measurer," xxvi 118 (J. F. A.).

Evelyn, J.: Sylva : a Discourse on Forest Trees, with Essay on Life and Works of Author by J. Nisbet, xxii. 115 (W. S.).

Fernow, Bernhard E. : History of Forestry, xxvii. 115 (F. S.). The Care of Trees in Lawn, Street, and Park : with a List of Trees and Shrubs for Decorative Use, xxvii. 119 (I. B. B.). Forest Conditions of Nova Scotia, xxvii. 242 (R. G.).

Fisher, W. R. : Working-Plan Report on Keir Woods, with Notes on Quoigs and Ardchullary, xxiii. 115 (J. F. A.).

Forbes, A. C. : Development of British Forestry, xxvi. 102 (J. F. A.). English Estate Forestry, xviii. 239 (A. T. G.).

Gamble, J. S. : Manual of Indian Timbers, xvii. 167.

Gerschel, J.: Vocabulaire Forestier : Français—Anglais — Allemand, xix. 235 (A. D. R.).

Giersberg, Dr Fr. : Künstliche Düngung im Forstlichen Betriebe, xix. 365 (A. W. B.).

Gillanders, A. T. : Forest Entomology, xxi. 238.

Government Publications :—Minutes of Evidence, Departmental Committee on Forestry, xvii. 342. Report on Instruction in Forestry, etc., in Germany, by F. Rose, xvii. 342. Report from Representatives abroad respecting Forest Laws, xvii. 342.

Graves, H. S. : Forest Mensuration, xx. 135 ; xxi. 117.

Gregson, Margaret M. : The Story of Our Trees, xxvii. 118.

Groom, P.: Trees and their Life-Histories, xxi. 239.

Hall, A. D. : The Soil : Introduction to Scientific Study of Growth of Crops, xxiii. 236 (A. L.). Fertilisers and Manures, xxiii. 236 (A. L.).

Hanson, C. O. : Forestry for Woodmen, xxvi. 108 (E. P. Stebbing).

Hayford, C.: Gold Coast Land Tenure, and the Forest Bill, 1911, xxvi. 236 (R. G.).

Heath, F. G. : Tree Lore, xxvi. 236.

Henderson, R. : The Estate Manager, xxiv. 234 (J. F. A.).

Henry, Prof. E. : Diseases of the Sweet Chestnut, xxiv. 237 (F. B.). Les Sols Forestiers, xxiii. 237 (R. A. Berry). Sur une théorie nouvelle de la captation de l'azote atmosphérique par les plantes, xxiv. 236 (R. A. Berry).

Hubbard, E. : *Utilisation of Wood Waste.* Trans. by M. J. Sach, xvii. 168.

Hurst, C. : *The Book of the English Oak,* xxvi. 108.

Hutchins, D. E. : *Report* on *Cyprus Forestry,* xxvi. 114 (M. M.).

Irving, H. : *How to Know the Trees,* xxiv. 237.

Jackson, A. Bruce : *Syon House Trees and Shrubs,* xxiv. 236 ; *Albury Park Trees and Shrubs,* xxxviii. 120.

Johns, Rev. C. A. : *British Trees, including finer Shrubs for Garden and Woodland.* Ed. by E. T. Cook and W. Dallimore, xxvi. 240. *The Forest Trees of Britain,* xxvii. 117.

Kensington, W. C. : *Forestry in New Zealand,* xxiii. 120.

Kent, A. H. : *Veitch's Manual of the Coniferæ,* xvi. 335 (J. A. T).

List of Seeds of Hardy Herbaceous Plants and of Trees and Shrubs, xxvi. 117.

Maw, P. T. : *Practice of Forestry, concerning also the Financial Aspect of Afforestation,* xxiii. 116 (J. F. A).

Mayr, Dr H. : *Fremdlandische Wald- und-Parkbäume für Europa,* xix. 363 (A. W. B.).

Mosley, Charles : *The Oak ; Its Natural History, Antiquity, and Folk-lore,* xxvii. 120.

Neudammer Förster - Lehrbuch. By several authors, xxii. 118, (F. S.).

New Forestry Books, xxi. 235 ; xxvi. 100 ; American, xx. 135.

Newstead, R. : *Food of some British Birds,* xxiii. 119.

Nisbet, Dr J. : *Elements of British Forestry,* xxvi. 104 (E. P. Stebbing). *Our Forests and Woodlands,* xvi. 329, (W. S.) ; xxiii. 114. *The Forester: Practical Treatise on British Forestry and Arboriculture for Landowners, Land Agents and Foresters,* xix. 219 (A. W. B., J. F. A., and G. L.).

Note on Modern Works on Forestry —F. Bailey, xv. App.

Quarterly Journal of Forestry pub. for R. Engl. Arbor. Soc., vol. i , No. 4, xxi. 120.

Robinson, W. : *Flora and Sylva,* xxvii. 118.

Sargent, C. S. : *Manual of Trees of N. America,* (*exclusive of Mexico*), xix. 236 (A. D. R.).

Schlich, Dr W. : *Manual of Forestry*—Vol. i., "Forest Policy in the British Empire," xx. 135. Vol. ii., "Sylviculture," xviii. 243 ; xxiv. 232 (E. P. S). Vol. iii., "Forest Management," xviii. 243 ; xxiv. 226 (C.——). Vol. iv., "Forest Protection," xxi. 120. Vol. v., "Forest Utilisation." By W. R. Fisher, xxii. 119, 240.

Schwappach, Dr A. : *Forestry.* Trans. by F. Story and E. A. Nobbs, xviii. 243 (A. D. R.). *Wald und Forstwirtschaft,* xxii. 118 (W. F. A. H.).

Simpson, J. : *British Woods and their Owners,* xxiii. 118 (A. C. F.). *The Estate Nursery,* xix. 234 (J. F. A.).

The New Forestry, or the Continental System adapted to British Woodlands and Game Preservation, xvi. 329 (W. S.) ; xix. 231 (J. F. A.).

Stebbing, E. B. : *Departmental Notes on Insects that affect Forestry in India,* Part iii., xx. 135 (R. S. M.).

Step, E. : *Wayside and Woodland Trees : Pocket Guide to British Sylva,* xxvi. 236.

Stone, H. : *Timbers of Commerce and their Identification,* xviii. 242 (A. D. R).

Thomson, R. : *Gardener's Assistant,* xvii. 341 (A. D. R.).

Unwin, A. Harold : *Future Forest Trees—Importance of German Experiments in Introduction of N. American Trees,* xix. 232 (A. D. R.).

Ward, Dr H. Marshall : *Trees : Handbook of Forest Botany for Woodlands and Laboratory.* Vol. i., "Buds and Twigs" ; Vol. ii., "Leaves," xviii. 241 (A. D. R.). Vol iii , "Flowers and Inflorescences," xx. 133 (A. D. R.). Vol. v., "Form and Habit," xxiii. 114.

Webster, A. D. : *Town Planting, and the Trees, Shrubs, etc., best adapted for resisting Smoke,* xxvi. 110 (J. W. G.). *Webster's Practical Forestry : Popular Handbook on Rearing and Growth of Trees for Profit or Ornament,* xix. 240 (A. D. R.).

Webster's Foresters' Diary, etc., xvii. 167, 342 ; xxi. 240 ; xxiii. 120 ; xxiv. 236 ; xxvi. 114. See vii. 202 ; viii. 9 ; x. 180. See also Literature.

Woodward, J., Jun. : *Planter's Note Book*, xxvii. 241 (S. J. G.).

Booth, J. : John, Duke of Atholl, his Larch Plantations and the Larch Disease, xvii. 232. Obituary, xxii. 120.

Boppe, L. : Report on Visit to Scottish and English Forests (1881), xi. 196. Obituary, xx. 258 : xxi. 114.

Bordeaux Mixture, xxiii. 232.

Border District, Excursion to, 1911. G. Leven, xxvi. 72.

*Boring-Machine, Report on. J. Craig, iii. 101.

Borthwick, A. W. : Artificial Manures in Forestry, xix. 245 ; "From the Ice Age to the Present," xx. 253 ; Larch Disease, xvii. 37 ; Pathological Specimens for Exhibition, xvii. 155 ; Forestry at Home and Abroad, xxviii. 56. See Reports by Hon. Scientists.

Borthwick, A. W., and Wilson, Malcolm : *New Disease on Larch in Scotland, xxvii. 198.

Bost, W. D. Ashton : Notes *re* Acetone, xxviii. 271.

Botanical Geography, etc., of Soil. M. Hardy, xvii. 110.

Botanical Survey of Scotland. A. W. B., xx. 122.

Botrytis cinerea, xxiv. 221.

Boulger, G. S. : British Elms, ix. 27 ; Economic Forestry, xi. 382.

Boyd, J. : *Basic Slag on Seed-Beds, xxi. 229 ; Birch and Alder Saw-Fly, xix. 207 ; Cultivation of Hardwoods, xxi. 44, 150 ; Injurious Effects of Smoke on Trees, xvii. 122 ; Rooks feeding on Pine Beetles, xix. 206.

Bradshott Woods, Working-Plan for. J. Nisbet, xvi. 193.

Brahan, Ross, Plantations, etc., on Estate of. A. Pitcaithley, xi. 501.

Branches, etc., Economic Uses of. J. Johnston, v. 55.

Branches of Society : — Aberdeen, Excursions of—Drumtochty (1906), xx. 238 ; Durris (1907), xxi. 215 ; Forglen and Hatton (1908), xxii. 211 ; Strathbogie (1906), xx. 241. Northern, Excursions of—Lovat Estates (1907), xxi. 205.

Brandis, D. : Distribution of Forests in India, vii. 88 ; Dr Cleghorn's Services to Indian Forestry, xii. 87 ; Progress of Forestry in India, x. 247 ; Proposed School of Forestry, xii. 65 ; Pure and Mixed Forests, xvi. 13. Obituary—W. Schlich, xxi. 112.

Brechin Arboricultural Society, xviii. 237.

Bridges :—On Estates—A. Paterson, iii. 23. Rustic, etc , Construction of—C. Y. Michie, iv. 115.

British Empire, Forest Policy in. J. S. G., xx. 12.

British Forestry, xxii. 97.

Broad-leaved Forests, Coniferous *versus*. F. B., xxii. 109.

Brodie of Brodie. Forestry Exhibition at Inverness, xxvi. 84.

Broilliard, C. : Thinnings, xvi. 100 ; Thinnings in Planted Spruce, xvii. 129. Obituary — A. G. H.-H., xxiv. 119.

Brown, G. : Diseases, Insects, and Animals injurious to Forest Trees, xvii 277 ; *Natural Regeneration in General, with details regarding Scots Pine at Beauly, Inverness-shire, xix. 17 ; Sections of Larch Timber, showing effects of different Soils on Growth, xxvi. 218.

Brown, J. : Address, 1855 (Objects in View in forming Arboricultural Society), i. 1. See xi. 288.

Brown, J. C. : Forests in South Africa, ix. 45 ; On Forest Schools, viii. 225 ; Manufacture of Lucifer Matches in Sweden, x. 223.

Brown, J. E. : Extensive Planting, vi. 216 ; Timber Trees introduced from Eastern N. America, v. 124.

Brown, R. E. : Do Woods pay ? iv. 159 ; *Plantation Roads and Walks, iii. 8 ; Reading-rooms and Libraries for Working-men on Landed Estates, iii. 13 : Wass Pinetum, iv. 164.

Brown, W. : Clearing a Crop of Wood—Field for Foresters—Nature as a Forester—Sawdust—Trees in the Highlands—*Woods and Railways, vi. 192 ; Trees and Climate, v. 12.

Buchan, A. : Meteorological Observations at Carnwath, vii. 285 ; viii. 168, 257 ; ix. 186.

Bucks, Excursion to, xvii. 301.

Bug, Larch :—W. Harrower, ix. 246 ; W. Schlich, xii. 423.

Burdon, E. R. : Research Work and Educational Methods, xxvii. 60.

*Buteshire, Geological and Arbori-cultural Features of, etc. J. Kay, vii. 60.

CADELL, G. : *Beech Forests of Hesse Nassau, xiii. 57 ; Forest Adminis-tration in Switzerland, xii. 78 ; Forests of Basses Pyrenées, xvii. 104 ; *Preparation of Wood Specimens for Exhibition, xiii. 310.

Cadell, H. M. : Sitka Spruce and other Trees in Linlithgowshire and Stirlingshire, xxiii. 158.

Cairngorm Mountains, Altitude of Forest Trees on. H. B. Watt, xvii. 266.

California, Trees of. F. R. S. Balfour, xxii. 213.

Californian Hemlock Spruce, Nursery Treatment of. J. M. Murray, xxi. 41.

Cambridge University : — Chair of Forestry at, xxi. 232. Report of Forestry Committee (1911), xxvi. 100.

Cambridge School of Forestry :— Timber Research work at, xxviii. 105.

Campbell, J. A. : Tap-Root of Larch, xvi. 323.

Canada :—Forest Fires in, xxiii. 105. Forestry in, xxiv. 225. Pulp Industry of, xxiii. 108.

Canadian Forestry Association, xvii. 329.

Canadian Forests, xxvi. 97.

Canadian Timber and Wood-Pulp, Enhanced Value of, xxiv. 99.

Canker :—In Japanese Larch—A. W. Borthwick, xix. 195 ; in Trees, Treatment of, xvii. 157 ; *Larch and Spruce—G. Massee, xvii. 25 ; Larch, Experimental Study of, xxi. 234.

Cape of Good Hope, xvi. 527.

Carabus, xvii. 346.

Carlsbad, Town-Woods of. J. Nisbet, xix. 150.

Carnarvonshire, Trees and Shrubs of. A. D. Webster, xi. 481.

Carnwath, Meteorological Observa-tions at, vii. 285 ; viii. 168, 257 ; ix. 186.

Castle Hill Woodlands, Working-Plan of, 1905 to 1919. F. Story, xx. 36.

Catchment Areas See Afforestation.

Cecidomyia, *xviii. 210 ; xix. 198.

Cedar of Lebanon :—R. Hutchison, xiii. 200. A Gigantic—J. Nisbet, xix. 212.

Cedrus atlantica. H. Fraser, v. 86.

*Celles, State Forest of. Prof. Fisher, xviii. 82.

*Chafer Infestation, Account of. F. Moon, xviii. 201.

*Champenoux, State Forest of. M. Larzillière, xviii. 74.

Chancellor of Exchequer, Deputation to, 1906. W. Steuart Fothring-ham, xix. 323.

Charcoal, Best Woods for, etc. R. Baxter, viii. 246.

Charcoal-Producing Plants. C. Y. Michie, vi. 319.

Chermes. See Larch Bug.

Chiltern Hills Beech, xviii. 225.

Chips, etc., Economic Uses of. J. Johnston, v. 55.

Chloride of Barium, Impregnation of Railway Sleepers with, etc., xvii. 340.

Choice of Trees for Planting. A. G. Hobart-Hampden, xxvi. 233.

Chopwell Woods. Note on Working-Plan for. W. S., xxii. 61.

Christison, D. : Tree-Girth Measure-ments, xvi. 529.

Christison, Sir R. : On Tree Measure-ments, viii. 262. See x. 82.

Cinchona Trees, Cultivation of. J. Ferguson, ix. 251.

Cirencester :—Address at Inaugura-tion of Chair of Forestry, etc., at R. Agr. College of—W. Schlich, xvii. 185 ; Forestry at, xvii. 321.

Cities, Trees in, xxiv. 93.

Civil Engineers on British Forestry, xvii. 156.

Clark, J. : Battle with Beetles, xvi. 274 ; Extraction of Tree-Stumps, xvi. 321.

Cleghorn, H. : Address, 1872, (Forest Conservancy ; Differences in Man-agement of British and Indian Forests), vii. 1 ; Address, 1873, (Points in History of Society : Transactions ; Fuel ; Forests and Climate ; Injurious Insects, etc.), vii. 115 ; Address, 1874, (Rise and Progress of Arboriculture ; Forest Literature ; Forests in N. America, France, British India), vii. 199 ; Address, 1883, (Progress of Forestry in Britain, Australia and America ; Forest Literature ; Edinburgh Forestry Exhibition), x. 179 ; *Address, 1884, (Edin. For. Ex-hibition, Plan of, etc.), xi. 1 ; Address, 1885. (Edin. Exhibition ; Need for British Forestry School), xi. 115 ; Address, 1886, (Establishing Forest School; Colonial and Indian Exhibition, London), xi. 287; Distribution of Timber Trees in India, and Forest Conservancy, v. 91; Management of European Forests, v. 94; Royal Forest School at Vallombrosa, viii. 182. His Services to Indian Forestry (D. Brandis), xii. 87. Presentation to, xii. 198.

Clerus, xvii. 345.

Climate:—And Trees—W. Brown, v. 12. Influence of Forests on, xviii. 231. See vii. 118; viii. 2.

Cluny Castle, Arboretum at. W. Gilchrist, vii. 119.

Clutton, R. W.: Self-Sown Oak Woods of Sussex, vii. 194.

Coccus, xvii. 154.

Cockchafer:—R. S. MacDougall, xvii. 345; *xviii. 208. Combating Attack in Nursery—W. Mackenzie, xx. 119.

*Cockle Park, Experimental Plots at, xviii. 219.

*Colorado Variety of Douglas Fir. A. D. Richardson, xviii. 194.

Committee, Departmental, on Forestry:—Late Mr Hanbury on, xvii. 322. Note upon Dr Nisbet's Criticism of Report of, in Preface to *The Forester*—R. C. Munro Ferguson, xix. 199; Dr Nisbet's Reply, xix. 200. Report of (1902), xvii. 1. Report of (Scotland), xxvi. 121. See xxi. 102.

Committee, Irish Forestry, xxi. 106. Report of, 1908—J. S. Gamble, xxii. 26.

Committee of House of Commons, Select, on Forestry:—Report of (1885), xi. 119; (1886), xi. 315; (1887), xii. 104. See xii. 191.

Company, Limited Liability Timber Estate. W. Somerville, xiv. 100.

Competition, Nursery and Plantation, xxvii. 85; xxviii. 110.

*Compiègne, Forest of. Prof. Fisher, xviii. 107.

Conference:—Afforestation (1907), xxi. 60. On Forestry Education, xviii. 51. Timber Trade—G. U. Macdonald, xxiii. 51.

Congress:—American Forestry, xviii. 229. International Forest, at Paris, xxvii. 112. International, of Silviculture—J. S. Gamble, xvi. 262.

Conifer Disease, A, xix. 360.

Conifer Woods, Glen Mor. J. Nisbet, xxv. 73.

Coniferæ:—At Powerscourt, Co. Wicklow—C. S. France, v. 83. Beetles which infest—R. Hutchison, vii. 123; W. Tivendale, vii. 80. Comparative Value of Exotic, as Ornamental or Timber Trees—A. D. Webster, xii. 246; T. Wilkie, xii. 206. Effects of Geological Position on—Earl of Ducie, i. 41. Evergreens and, introduced from Japan—R. Hutchison, v. 6. Exotic, in Britain, xxiv. 220. Hardwoods and, best adapted to resist attacks of Hares and Rabbits —J. Craig, vi. 233. Introduction and Cultivation of Newer, etc.— R. Hutchison, iii. 44. Leaf-Shedding of, xxiv. 221. *New and Rare, at Penrhyn Castle, N. Wales —A. D. Webster, xi. 55. Pruning of Rarer—R. Hutchison, iv. 170. Raising Exotic, from Seed—J. Ferguson, xxvi. 46. Rearing Newer, from Seed, Cuttings, or Grafts—J. Alexander, vii. 84. Remarkable, in Great Britain— J. N., xx. 126. Returns of Growth and Condition of Newer, in 118 Stations in United Kingdom, iii. 58. Seeds of N. American, xxiii. 231.

Coniferous Plantation, Young, Damage to, by Water-Voles. F. Moon, xxi. 105.

Coniferous Timbers:—Our Imported —A. D. Richardson, xvii. 238. *Economic Disposal of — D. K. M'Beath, xxviii. 251.

Coniferous v. Broad-leaved Forests. F. B., xxii. 109.

Continental Forestry, Notes on. J. Nisbet (1904), xviii. 161; (1905), xix. 161; (1906), xx. 64.

Continental Forests, Study of. F. B., xx. 249.

Continental Notes:—France—A. G. Hobart-Hampden, xxi. 73; xxii. 46 (Errata, xxii. 236); xxiii. 57; xxiv. 56; xxvi. 48; xxvii. 41; xxviii. 60. Germany—B. Ribbentrop, xxi. 180; *xxii. 227; *xxiii. 38; xxiii. 204; *xxiv. 194; xxvi. 204; *xxvii. 212.

Contributions, Appeal for Literary. F. Bailey, xix. 353; xxvi. 234.

Conversion of Stored Coppice into Highwood, etc. H. J. Marshall, xix. 99.

Co-operative Society, Landowners' Forestry. J. Stirling - Maxwell, xxiv. 104; xxviii. 231.

Co-operative Timber-Growing, Profitable. R. Galloway, xix. 291.

Coppice :— Conversion of Stored, into Highwood, etc.—-H. J. Marshall, xix. 99. Management of Oak, etc. —J M'Leod, i. 103 ; J. Whyte, i. 215 ; T. Wilkie, ix. 270.

Coppice-Bark, Curing of, etc. J. M'Leod, i. 103.

Coppice Land, Conversion of. W. M'Corquodale, iv. 47.

Coppice-Woods, Decline in Value of. W. Storie, xix. 203.

Corsican Fir. See Firs.

Corsican Pine. See Pine.

*Cottage, Forester's. R. B. Keay, xii. 288 ; W. MacIntosh, xi. 364 ; A. Pitcaithley, xi. 506.

Coupar, R. : *Blister in Larch Plantations, x. 119.

Coverts. See Game.

Cowley-Brown, F. L. C. : Demonstration Forests for Scotland, xxii. 20 ; Visit to French Private Forest, xxvi. 172.

Craig, J. : *Boring - Machine, iii. 101 ; Coniferæ and Hardwoods best adapted to resist Attacks of Hares and Rabbits, vi. 233 ; Is Grease injurious to Trees? vi. 236.

Credit, Agricultural, Co-operative, in Germany and Switzerland, xvii. 331.

Creosote for Timber - Preserving, Water in, xix. 211.

Creosote Oil, Use of, in United States. W. B. Havelock, xx. 256.

Creosoted Timber, xx. 128.

Creosoting :—Notes on—A. T. Gillanders, xxiii. 172. Of Home-Grown Timber—W. B. Havelock, xx. 58. Timber—G. Leven, xvii. 93. Timber by Absorption—J. Balden, xx. 62. Tree Stumps against Pine Weevil—F. R. S. Balfour, xxviii. 270. See Notes and Queries.

Crossbills, Damage by. J. J. R. Meiklejohn, xvi. 318.

Crozier, J. D. : *Douglas Fir as Commercial Timber Tree, xxi. 31 ; *Sitka Spruce as Tree for Hill-Planting and General Afforestation, xxiii. 7.

*Cryptococcus, xx. 245.

Cryptogamic Plants Injurious to Forest Trees. M. Dunn, viii. 250.

Cryptomyces, xviii. 212.

Cullachy, Afforestation at, xxv. 57.

Cultivation :— Of Hardwoods — J.

Boyd, xxi. 44, 150. Of Willows, xxiii. 191.

Cupar. See Exhibitions.

Cutting Timber by Axe or Saw, Comparative Advantages of. T. Hogg, vi. 227 ; J. Milne, vi. 224.

DAMAGE to Woods, etc. :—By Pine Weevil—E. S. Grant, xx. 53. By Shale Industry, xvi. 470. By Sparks from Railway Engines— F. Bailey, xvi. 289, 524. See Notes and Queries. See also xxii. 15, 221.

Darling, J. : Preparation of Ground for Planting, i. 96 ; Thinning Plantations, i. 210.

Davidson, J. : Profitableness of Rearing Underwood, iv. 21.

Dawson, W. : Excursion to Deeside (1913), xxvii. 67 ; The State and Private Woodlands, xxiv. 121 ; Working-Plan, Glen Mor, xxv. 60.

Dean, Forest of. See Forest of Dean.

Death Duties :—And Timber-Planting—D. F. Mackenzie, xvi. 321. As affecting Woodlands, Note on— R. Galloway, xxiii. 133. On Woods—R. Galloway, xxvii. 36.

Deciduous Trees, for Landscape Forestry. J. Methven, xii. 94.

Deer Forests :—Glen Mor, xxv. 15. Planting of—D. F. Mackenzie, ix. 53 ; and Sporting Lands in Scotland, xxvii. 237.

*Deeside : Excursion to (1913). W. Dawson, xxvii. 67.

*Demonstration Forest, Some Uses of. J. F. Annand, xxvii 54.

Demonstration Forests for Scotland, F. L. C. Cowley-Brown, xxii. 20. See also xx. 113.

Denbighshire : — Experimental Station—F. B., xx. 254. Scheme for Experimental Station—A. D. R., xx. 108.

Dendrometer, Mackenzie's, x. 241.

Denmark :—Afforestation of Waste Lands in, xxii. 207. *Oak and Beech Forests in—W. G. Smith, xxviii. 241. Tour of R. E. A. Soc. in, 1908—F. Story, xxii. 56.

Department of Woods, Appointments by, xxi. 110.

Departmental Committee on Forestry. See Committee.

Deputations :— To Chancellor of Exchequer (1906)—W. Steuart Fothringham, xix. 323. To Chancellor of Exchequer (1909, re National Afforestation), xxii. 200.

To President of Board of Agriculture (1894), xiv. 192 ; (1901), xvi. 479 ; (1912, rc Development of Forestry in Scotland), xxvi. 202. From Irish Forestry Society to Chief Secretary for Ireland (rc State Afforestation), xix. 327. To Secretary for Scotland, xxviii. 1.

Derby, Forestry Exhibition at Royal Show, 1906, and Some of its Lessons, xx. 91.

Development Act and Forestry. R. C. Munro Ferguson, xxiii. 140.

Development and Road Improvement Funds Act (1909), xxiii. 231.

Development Commission and Forestry, xxvi. 3 ; xxvii. 1 ; xxvii. 28 ; xxviii. 14.

Development, Forestry :— England and Wales, xxvi. 156 ; xxvii. 147. Scotland : Deputation to Board of Agriculture, xxvi. 202

Development Fund Grants:—Ireland, xxiv. 108. Position of Scottish Forestry in Regard to, xxviii. 138. Scotland, xxvi. 1, 215.

Dewar, D. : Extraction of Tree-Stumps. xvi. 321. Obituary—J. Gossip, xvi. 336.

Dickson, A. : Address, 1882 (Forest Schools). x. 81.

Diploma in Forestry at Oxford. F. B., xix. 354.

Diplosis, xv. 314.

Disease :—*Conifer, xix. 360. In Beech Hedges—R. Hutchison, ix. 217. Larch—J. Booth, xvii. 232 ; A. W. Borthwick, xvii. 397 ; W. M'Corquodale, ii. 43 ; D. F. Mackenzie, viii. 140 ; F. Story, xvii. 333 ; In Ireland, xxii. 113 : Investigation by Engl. Arbor. Soc., xvii. 43 ; M'Intosh's book on, ii. 31 ; *New, on Larch in Scotland— A. W. Borthwick and Malcolm Wilson, xxvii. 198 ; Novar System of Combating, xix. 339 ; Note on Novar System, etc —J. Nisbet, xx. 39 ; *R. Hartig on, xvii. 19 ; Report by Sub-Committee, xviii. 213. Of Forest Trees—G. Brown, xvii. 277 ; C. Y. Michie, iv. 51 ; See also viii. 13. On *Pinus Laricio* and *P. sylvestris* — H. Maxwell, xx. 117. *Root, in Scots Pine on Farm Lands—B. Ribbentrop, xxi. 143. Spread of Fungus, by Hybernating Mycelium—A. W. B., xx. 122. See Blister, Canker, Dry Rot,

Failures, and Reports by Hon. Scientists.

Diseased Scots Pines on Land formerly Arable, xx. 248.

Distillation of Wood, xxvi. 99.

Dochfour, Afforestation at, xxv. 54.

Dodds, G. : Arboriculture in N. Lancashire, xi. 188 ; Plantations on Estate of Wentworth, Yorks, xii. 156.

Dorset, Corsican Pine in. J. M'Callum, xxiv. 45.

Douglas Fir. See Firs.

Drainage. L. Bayne. vii. 250 ; J. Rutherford, i. 12 ; D. Tait, x. 172.

Driftwood and Insect Attacks. A. Mitchell, xiv. 191 ; xv. 197.

Drought, Resistance of Young Trees to, xx. 247.

Dry-Rot in Larch and Spruce Fir. J. M'Neill, ii. 7.

Dry Seasons of 1868, '69 and '70, Effects of, on Forest Trees, etc. R. Hutchison, vi. 281.

Ducie, Earl of : Effects of Geological Position on Certain Coniferæ, i. 41.

Duff, J. : Arboriculture in Kent, viii. 153 ; Forest Travel in Europe, x. 144 ; Old and Remarkable Trees at Bayham Abbey and Wilderness Park, Kent, viii. 147.

Dumfries, Kirkcudbright and Wigtown, Arboriculture in. A. Pitcaithley, xiii. 293.

Dumfries. See Exhibitions.

*Dunes of Gascony, Forest Tour among. F. Bailey, xi. 291.

Dunkeld, Murthly, and Scone, Excursion to, 1904, xviii. 61.

Dunn, M. : Address, 1888, (Origin and Progress of Society ; Report of Forestry Committee of House of Commons ; Proposed Forest Board ; Openings for Foresters ; Forest Literature ; "Cleghorn Forest Library"), xii. 189 ; Cryptogamic Plants Injurious to Forest Trees, viii. 250 ; Forestry in Scotland in Reign of Queen Victoria, xv. 109 ; Insects Injurious to Forest Trees, etc , viii. 173. *The Late—W. M Gilbert, xvi. 132.

Durham, Excursion to, 1906. A. D. Richardson, xx. 81.

Durris Estate, Douglas Fir on. A. Yeats, xvi. 185. See Excursions.

Dynamite and Tonite, Use of, in Forestry. D. F. Mackenzie, viii. 241.

EARDLEY-WILMOT, S. H. : Indian

State Forestry, xxiii. 217.
*Early Tree-Planting in Scotland :
Historical Notes. H. B. Watt,
xxvi. 12.
Eberswalde :—*Forest School at—A.
C. Forbes, xiii. 234. Session at—
A. F. Wilson, xx. 201.
Economic, and Landscape, Planting.
C. S. France, xii. 322.
Economic Aspects, Forestry in some
of its. W. Somerville, xxii. 121.
*Economic Disposal of Coniferous
Timber. D. K. M'Beath, xxviii.
251.
Economic Forestry. G. S. Boulger,
xi. 382.
Edinburgh. See Exhibitions.
Edinburgh, County of, Excursion in
(1908), xxii. 71.
Edinburgh University :—Forestry at,
F. Bailey, xvii. 206 ; *Practical
Course at Raith, xxiv. 208· See
Notes and Queries.
Education :—Forestry—W. Schlich,
xv. 89 ; E. P. Stebbing, xxiv. 24 ;
Forestry in Great Britain, xxiii.
141. Of Foresters—W. M'Corquo-
dale, ix. 100.
Educational Excursions. F. B., xx.
250.
Educational Methods—E. R. Burdon,
xxvii. 60.
Edwards, A. W. B. : Attack by Large
Larch Saw-Fly, xxiv. 42 ; *Plant-
ing at High Altitudes and in
Exposed Situations, etc., xxvi. 37.
Electricity, Felling Trees by, xxiv.
109.
Electrolysis, Wood Preservation by,
xx. 128.
Elm :—British—G. S. Boulger, ix.
27. English, in Scotland—H.
Maxwell, xx. 244. Seedlings, Mr
Henry's Investigation of—A. D.
Richardson, xxiv. 186.
Elwes, H. J. : Some Japanese and N.
American Trees suitable for British
Woodlands, xix. 76.
Entomological Specimens, Collection
and Preservation of. E. P.
Stebbing, xvii. 135.
Erosion and Afforestation Royal
Commission Report. J. F. Annand,
xxii. 188.
Essays on Experimental Forest Area.
See Forest Area.
Estate, Conducted Experiments in
Silviculture, etc. F. B., xx. 102.
Estate Duty on Timber under Finance
Act of 1910, xxvi. 95.
Estate Forest Museums :—F. B., xx.

110. Murthly—A. Murray, xxii.
237.
Europe, Forest Travel in. J. Duff,
x. 144.
European and Japanese Larch. K.
Mackenzie, xxvi. 229.
European Forests, Management of.
H. Cleghorn, v. 94.
Evergreens, Coniferæ and, introduced
from Japan. R. Hutchison, v. 6.
Evergreen Shrubs, Transplanting.
R. Hutchison, iv. 3.
Example Plots or Forest Gardens.
F. Bailey, xix. 317.
Excursions :—Argyll, Ayr and Ren-
frew (1905), A. D. Richardson,
xix. 180 ; Ayr (1901), xvi. 507.
*Bavaria (1909), xxiii. 80. *Beau-
fort, Dunrobin, Dornoch and Skibo
(1899), xvi. 138. Bedford, Hert-
ford and Buckingham (1903), xvii.
301. Border District (1911)—G.
Leven, xxvi. 72. Clandeboye.
Barons-Court and Castlewellan,
Ulster (1900), xvi. 294. *Deeside
(1913)—Wm. Dawson, xxvii. 67.
Dunkeld, Murthly and Scone
(1904)—A. Murray, xviii. 61.
Edinburgh and Fife, Counties of
(1908), xxii. 71. France (1904),
xviii. 68 ; Report on—G. U.
Macdonald, xviii. 118. Germany
(1895)—R. Galloway, xiv. 195 ;
D. Robertson, xiv. 180 ; A.
Slater, xiv. 163. Lochaber (1910)
—J. Stirling-Maxwell, xxiv.
73. Northumberland and Durham (1906)—A. D. Richardson,
xx. 81. *Speyside (1907), xxi. 95.
Sweden (1902), xvii. 146 ; Reports
on Swedish—G. U. Macdonald,
xvii. 56 ; F. Story, xvii. 68.
*Switzerland (1913)—G. P. Gordon,
xxviii. 83. See also xxviii. 119.
See Branches of Society.
Excursions, How to make the most
of the, x. 185. See Notes and
Queries.
*Exhibition, Preparation of Wood
Specimens for. G. Cadell, xiii.
310.
Exhibitions, Forestry :—At Highland
and Agricultural Shows—Inverness
(1901), xvi. 475 ; Aberdeen (1902),
xvii. 149 ; Dumfries (1903), xvii.
314 ; Perth (1904), xviii. 65 ;
Glasgow (1905)—A. D. Richardson,
xix. 190 ; Peebles (1906)—J. F.
Annand, xx. 87 ; Prestonfield,
Edinburgh (1907), xxi. 90 ; Aber-
deen (1908), xxii. 89 ; Stirling

(1909), xxiii. 101; Dumfries (1910), xxiv. 102; Inverness (1911), xxvi. 84; Cupar (1912), xxvii. 102; Paisley (1913)—G. P. Gordon, xxviii. 97.
At Royal Show, Derby (1906), xx. 91.
At Scottish National Exhibition, Edinburgh (1908), xxi. 217; A. M'Rae, xxii. 77; Glasgow (1911), xxvi. 85.
At Shows of R. Agric. Soc. of England, Lincoln (1907), xxi. 83; Newcastle-upon-Tyne, xxii. 92.
At Anglo-American Exposition, Shepherd's Bush (1914), xxviii. 119.
At Paris (1900), xvi. 339; Nurnberg (1906), xx. 233; St Louis, xviii. 223.
International, Edinburgh (1884), *xi. 68, 562. See also x. 183; xi. 1, 115. Edinburgh (1886), xii. 181.
Exotic Conifers:—In Britain, xxiv. 220. Raising from Seed—J. Ferguson, xxvi. 46.
Experimental Forest Area. See Forest Area.
Experimental Plots:—At Cockle Park, xviii. 219. At Novar—C. Marriott, xx. 101.
Experimental Station, Denbighshire. F. B., xx. 254; A. D. R., xx. 108.
Experimental Study of Larch Canker, xxi. 234.
Experiments:—Estate—Conducted, in Silviculture, etc.—F. B., xx. 102. On Relative Value of Timber Preservatives, xxi. 201. *Seed, with *Pinus sylvestris*—F. Story, xxiii. 168. Sylvicultural, at Novar —R. C. Munro Ferguson, xx. 98. *With Tree Seeds—W. Somerville, xv. 133.
Explosives, Use of, in Forestry— A. Lauder, xxvii. 210.
Exports of Timber from United Kingdom (1905), xix. 218.
Exposed Situations, Planting at. A. W. B. Edwards, xxvi. 37.

FAILURES of Larch—W. Gorrie, viii. 61. See ix. 234. See also Disease.
Farms, Leasehold Timber. A. T. Williamson, xii. 418.
Feaks, M.; Forestry Section in Scottish National Exhibition, Glasgow (1911), xxvi. 85.

Federated Malay States, xxiv. 223.
Felling:—Timber—J. M'Neill, ii. 17; Trees, by Electricity, xxiv. 109; by Machinery, xxiii. 232. Timber-Trees, Most profitable Age for—L. Bayne, vii. 175; W. Gilchrist, v. 131; D. F. Mackenzie, viii. 70. See also viii. 203.
*Felt Scale, Beech. G. Leven, xx. 245.
Fences:—Deterioration of Wire—J. Kay, xv. 317. Filling of Gaps in Live, etc.—W. Gilchrist, iv. 154. * Implement for Straightening Bends in Standards of Wire—A. Gilchrist, iv. 205. *Machine for Mending Broken Strands in Wire —A. Simpson, xiii. 359. *New Straining Pillar for Wire—J. Kay, x. 32. *Plantation—W. Thomson, i. 69. Rearing and Maintaining Live — R. Hutchison, iii. 15. *Straining Pillars for Wire—C. Y. Michie, v. 75.
Fencing:—Cost of—F. B., xxi. 233. Effects of Sulphur on Iron—T. Wilkie, viii. 165. Preserving Posts and Rails for—D. Hamilton, vi. 230. *Two New Modes of— T. Wilkie, viii. 171. *Wire, with Wrought-Iron Standards in Stone Blocks—J. Kay, v. 79.
Ferguson, J.: Cultivation of Cinchona Trees, ix. 251; India-rubber Trees of S. America, x. 108; Raising Exotic Conifers from Seed, xxvi. 46; Teak Plantations at Nelambur, Madras, ix. 114.
Ferguson, R. C. Munro: Address, 1895, (Forestry for Profit; Forestry and the State, etc.), xiv. 91; Address, 1897, (Need for Forest School and Experimental Area, etc.), xv. 81; Afforestation, xxii. 169; Arboricultural Adornment of Towns, xvi. 388; Arboriculture and Arable Land, xxi. 222; Criticisms upon "Scheme for Establishing National Industry of Forestry," xxii. 8; Development Act and Forestry, xxiii. 140; First Steps at Inverliever, xxi. 104; Inverliever State Forest, xxi. 22; Letter (Scottish Rating Bill, etc.) to General Meeting (1896), xv. 1; Note upon Dr Nisbet's Criticism of Report of Departmental Committee on Forestry in Preface to *The Forester*, xix. 199; Note on Raith and Novar Working-Plans, xvi. 96; Sylvicultural Experiments at Novar,

xx. 98 ; Training in Sylviculture, xx. 24 ; Training of Foresters, xvi. 444. Hon. Sec., 1898-1914, xxviii. 226.

Fife, Excursion in, 1908, xxii. 71.

Finance Act, 1910, Estate Duty on Timber under, xxvi. 95.

Financial Aspect of Forestry. P. T. Maw, xxiii. 17.

Finland, Forestry in. J. F. Annand, xvii. 243.

Finlayson, A.: Larch Plantation on Monument Hill, Monteviot, xxvi. 80.

Fireproofing of Wood, xvii. 291.

*Fire Protection Lines in Scots Fir Forests (Dr Kienitz). A. C. Forbes, xvii. 198.

Fires, Forest, xvii. 316 ; in Canada, xxiii. 105.

Firs :—

Corsican, Austrian, and Douglas, as Timber-Trees—R. Hutchison, vii. 52.

Douglas:—A. D. Webster, xi. 165 ; W. H. Whellens, xxiv. 47 ; *and Thuja Gigantea in Mixture—D. K. M'Beath, xxviii. 107 ; *As Commercial Timber-Tree—J. D. Crozier, xxi. 31 ; * Colorado, Variety of—A. D. Richardson, xviii. 194 ; In Scotland—W. Schlich, xii. 226 ; Investigation into Annual Increment in Girth of, xxvi. 232 ; *Megastigmus spermotrophus as Enemy of—R. S. MacDougall, xix. 52; Timber, Uses of—Frank Scott, xxvii. 106 ; On Durris Estate — R. Yeats, xvi. 185 ; Plantation at Taymount—A. D. Richardson, xviii. 200 ; Frank Scott, xxvii. 77 ; W. Somerville, xvii. 269 ; Silvicultural Treatment of—W. Steuart Fothringham, xxviii. 248 ; See xx. 104, and Notes and Queries.

Menzies, xvi. 528.

Mixed Plantations—W. Gilchrist, iii. 2.

Silver:—F. B., xxii. 106 ; Common —C. Y. Michie, v. 138 ; Self-Sowing of—W. Gilchrist, vii. 180 ; Timber of, xvii. 158.

Scots :—Cultivation and Varieties of—W. Gilchrist, vi. 304 ; Durability of Highland, xxiv. 106 ; Fire Protection Lines in Forests of (Dr Kienitz)—A. C. Forbes, xvii. 198 ; Forests of, in N. Germany—A. C. Forbes, xiii.

187 ; Has it deteriorated ?—J. M'Laren and W. M'Corquodale, ix. 176 ; Planting of, after old Crops of Scots—W. M'Corquodale, ii. 48 ; Returns of Prices, at Abernethy—W. Gouk, i. 102.

Fisher, W. R. : *Beech and Oak High Forest in France, xviii. 90 ; Oak in Coppice - with - Standards in North of France, xviii. 109 ; State Forests of *Celles, Gérardmer, *Retz, Bellême, *Compiègne, St Amand, and Raismes (Valenciennes), xviii. 82 et seq. Obituary —A. S., xxiv. 118.

Fleming, Sir J. : When Afforestation comes, xxiii. 124.

Flett, J. S. : Geology and Forestry, xv. 73.

Fluids, Movement of, in Stems. W. R. M'Nab, viii. 203.

Foliage :—*Of Pines, etc., Blending of, for Landscape Effect—C. Y. Michie, iv. 73. Lime-Sulphur Wash for, xxiv. 223.

Forbes, A. C. : Establishing Experimental Forest Area in Scotland, xv. 155 ; *Fire Protection Lines in Scots Fir Forests (Kienitz), xvii. 198 ; *Forest School at Eberswalde, xiii. 234 ; Formation of Plantations, xiii. 91 ; Growing Timber of High Commercial Value, xiv. 122 ; Influence of Thinning on Growth of Beech, xvi. 116 ; Insect Notes from Wiltshire, xiv. 189 ; Is British Forestry Progressive ? xv. 44 ; Scots Fir Forests in N. Germany, xiii. 187 ; Season and Growth of Trees, xv. 75 ; Sitka Spruce in Ireland, xxviii. 264 ; Waste Land for Afforestation, xx. 142.

Fords, etc., on Estates. A. Paterson, iii. 23.

Forest Administration in Switzerland. G. Cadell, xii. 78.

Forest Area, Experimental :—Essays on Establishing, in Scotland— A. C. Forbes, xv. 155 ; D. F. Mackenzie, xv. 179. Report by Judges on Essays on, xv. 148. See also Forestry Area.

Forest Conservancy :—Indian Famine Commission (Extract from Report of), ix. 273. Progress of (India)— H. Cleghorn, v. 91. See vii. 1 ; viii. 3. See also Notes and Queries.

Forest Labour, Returns of Prices (1857), i. 219.

Forest Museums. See Museums.

Forest Nurseries and Gardens. F. Bailey, xxi. 54. See xix. 317.

Forest Nursery Station, Indian Head, Sask. J. Kay, xxiii. 67 ; xxiv. 67.

Forest of Dean : —Forestry Instruction at, xvii. 324. Mr Hill on— F. Bailey, xv. 292. State School of Forestry in, xx. 112, 251 ; xxiv. 217.

Forest Operations in Co. Galway. W. Schlich, xvi. 249.

Forest Pests. R. S. MacDougall, xxviii. 267.

Forest Policy in British Empire. J. S G., xx. 12.

Forest Produce : —Disposing of— A. Peebles, vii. 159. Preparation of, for Sale—W. Thomson, vi. 275. Returns of Prices (1857), i. 219 ; (1859), ii. 41.

Forest Resources : —Of Australia— E. T. Scammell, xvii. 249 Of United Kingdom—H. Maxwell, xxii. 1.

Forest Schools : —Biltmore, U.S.A , xxiv. 108 ; xxvi. 98. Dean Forest, xx. 112, 251 ; xxiv. 217. *Eberswalde—A. C. Forbes, xiii. 234 ; A. F. Wilson, xx. 201. Indian— F. Bailey xi. 155. Ou—J. C. Brown, viii. 225. Proposed—D. Brandis, xii. 65. Research at Indian, xx. 115. S. African— F. B., xix. 356. Vallombrosa—H. Cleghorn, viii. 182. Yale—F. B., xx. 251. See also (on Establishing, in Scotland, etc.), viii. 200 ; ix. 109 ; x. 77, 81 ; xi. 17, 288 ; xiii. 165 ; xiv. 11 ; xvi. 2.

Forest Seeds, Testing of, xxvii. 239.

Forest Service, Imperial, of India, Training of Probationers for, etc. J. Nisbet, xix. 107 ; xxi. 191 ; xxiv. 212.

Forest Soils, Accumulation of Nitrogen in. A. Lauder, xx. 186.

Forest Survey, Collection and Utilisation of Information for, xxvii. 112.

*Forest Tramway. F. Moon, xxi. 71.

Forest Travel in Europe. J. Duff, x. 144.

Forest Trees : —Altitude of, on Cairngorm Mountains — H. B. Watt, xvii. 266. Ornamental and, of Recent Introduction—J. M'Laren, x. 209. Collection, etc., of Seeds of—J. M'Lean, x. 156. Cryptogamic Plants Injurious to, etc.—

M. Dunn, viii. 250. Distances at which they should be planted—L. Bayne, viii. 77. Distribution of Certain, in Scotland, as shown by Post - Glacial Deposits— W. N. Niven, xvii. 97. Effects of Dry Seasons of 1868, '69 and '70 on —R. Hutchison, vi. 281. Insects Injurious to, etc.—M. Dunn, viii. 173. Natural and Artificial Systems ot Rearing—A. E. Wild, v. 88. Pruning—C Y. Michie, v. 34 ; R. Philip, i. 20 ; ii. 11. Thinning and General Management of—"Justitia," ii. 3. *Transplanting—C. Y. Michie, v. 20. Soils best suited to different—W. Gilchrist, vi. 296. See Disease.

Forest Work. G. U. Macdonald, xvi. 451.

Forester, Nature as a. W. Brown, vi. 198.

Forester, The, Note on Review of. J. N., xix. 362.

Forester's Cottage. See Cottage.

Foresters : —A Field for—W. Brown, vi. 202. Education of — W. M'Corquodale, ix. 100. Four Weeks' Course for, at Aberdeen University, xxiv. 217. Register for—J. Kay, v. 155 ; C. Y. Michie, v. 158. Society's Register of, etc. —R. Galloway, xix. 350. Training of—R C. Munro Ferguson, xvi. 444 ; J. Parry, xix. 320. See also i. 8 ; viii. 1 ; xvi. 157.

Foresters' and Gardeners' Society of Argyll, xxi. 235.

Forestry : — And Geology—J. S. Flett, xv. 73. Artificial Manures in—A. W. Borthwick, xix. 245. At Anglo-American Exposition, xxviii. 119. At Home and Abroad —A. W. Borthwick, xxviii. 56. At University of Edinburgh, xvii. 206 ; xxiv. 208 ; see Notes and Queries. At University of Oxford, xxvi. 225. At University of Tokio, xviii. 232. *Belgian, in some of its Aspects—A. T. Gillanders, xix. 139. Bibliography of — H. B. Watt, xxvi. 230. British, xxii. 97. British, and its Future Prospects—J. Nisbet, xvi. 161. British, is it Progressive ?—A. C. Forbes, xv. 44. *Century of (1806 to 1906) on Estate of Learney, Aberdeenshire—F. N. Innes, xx. 168. Chair of, at Cambridge, xi. 232. Civil Engineers on British, xvii. 156. Continental, Notes on

(1904)—J. Nisbet, xviii. 161;
(1905), xix. 161; (1906), xx. 64.
Deciduous Trees for Landscape—
J. Methven, xii. 94. Development
Act, and—R. C. Munro Ferguson,
xxiii. 140. Development Commission and, xxvi. 3; xxvii. 1;
xxvii. 28; xxviii. 14. Degree in,
at Edinburgh University—F. B.,
xx. 248. Diploma in, at Oxford—
F. B., xix. 354. Economic—G.
S. Boulger, xi. 382. Encouragement of Private—A. Schwappach,
xx. 212. Estate, Conducted Ex-
periments in Sylviculture and
other Branches of—F. B., xx. 102.
Financial Aspect of—P. T. Maw,
xxiii. 17. German—F. Story,
xviii. 138. Heredity and—W.
Somerville, xxi. 1. History of, in
Great Britain (1854-1904) — J.
Nisbet, xviii. 20. Immediate Needs
of, in Scotland—J. Stirling-Max-
well, xxiii. 121. In Britain:
Address to Biological Section of
British Assoc., Oxford, 1894—
I. B. Balfour, xiv. 55. In Britain
—A. Schwappach, xvii. 169. In
Finland—J. F. Annand, xvii. 243.
In France—F. Bailey, xi. 221. In
Hungary—F. Bailey, xii. 1. In
Japan, xxiv. 96. In Kent and
Sussex — D. A. Glen, xvi. 414.
In Nurnberg Exhibition, xx. 233.
*In the Schwarzwald — J. F.
Annand, xxi. 159. In Scotland in
Reign of Queen Victoria—M. Dunn,
xv. 109. In Scotland, Discussion
on, xxviii. 121. In Some of Its
Economic Aspects—W. Somerville,
xxii. 121. Indian, in 1905—J.
Nisbet, xix. 128; in 1906, xx. 219.
Indian, Dr Cleghorn's Services to—
D. Brandis, xii. 87. Indian State
—S. H. Eardley-Wilmot, xxiii.
217. Influences affecting British—
W. Somerville, xii. 403. Irish,
xxii. 26. Instruction in Ireland,
xxvi. 158. Lectures, Introduction
to Course of, at Edinburgh University (1891-92)— F. Bailey, xiii.
174. Modern English Works on—
F. Bailey, xv., App. Parliament
and, xviii. 221. Place of, in the
Economic Development of Scotland — Sir J. Stirling-Maxwell,
xxvii. 161. Position of Scottish,
in Regard to the Development
Fund, xxviii. 138. President of
Board of Agriculture on, xvii. 323.
Progress of, in India—D. Brandis,

x. 247. Progress of, in Scotland—
R. Hutchison, ix. 1. Relation of,
to Agriculture and Other Industries, xxvii. 121. Reports on—
see Committee, and Agriculture,
Board of. Scheme for Establishing
National Industry of, xxi. 135;
Criticisms of Scheme—R. Munro
Ferguson, xxii. 8; Reply to Criticisms, xxii. 13. State in Relation
to—W. Schlich, xxii. 130. Steam
Power in—D. F. Mackenzie, vii.
269. Swedish, Recent Developments in—E. Nilson, xix. 136.
*Tools used in—A. Slater, ix. 130.
Use of Dynamite and Tonite in—
D. F. Mackenzie, viii. 241. Use
of Explosives in — A. Lauder,
xxvii. 210. See Book Notices,
Exhibitions, Literature, and Notes
and Queries.

Forestry Appointments, xx. 131. See
Notes and Queries.

Forestry Area, Experimental, in
Wales. Fraser Story, xxvii. 19.

Forestry Association, Canadian, xvii.
329.

Forestry Congress, American, xviii.
229.

Forestry Education :—W. Schlich,
xv. 89; E. P. Stebbing, xxiv. 24.
Conference on, xviii. 51. In Great
Britain, xxiii. 141. See Notes and
Queries.

Forestry Laws, Sweden's New, xviii.
227.

Forestry Problem, Our—W. Schlich,
xvii. 213.

Forestry Society, Irish, xix. 327.

Forestry Station, Irish, xx. 111.

Forests :—And Rainfall—R. C. Moss-
man, xx. 188; see also vii. 115,
285; xviii. 231. Bavarian and
Saxon, Visit to Some (1904)—J. J. R.
Meiklejohn, xviii. 150. *Beech,
of Hesse-Nassau—G. Cadell, xiii.
57. Canadian, xxvi. 97. Demon-
stration, for Scotland, xx. 113;
F. L. C. Cowley-Brown, xxii. 20.
Distribution of, in India — D.
Brandis, vii. 88. Dr Schlich's, at
Mirwart — F. Bailey, xvi. 241.
French Private, Visit to — F.
Cowley-Brown, xxvi. 172. *German
—F. Story, xvi. 424; A. T.
Gillanders, xxviii. 100. Importance
of, in Military Defence—M. Martin,
xxiii. 223. Inverliever State—R.
C. Munro Ferguson, xxi. 22. Larch
in German—F. Boden, xvii. 47.
Management of European — H.

Cleghorn, v. 94. Natural Reproduction of—J. M'Lean, xi. 36. *Oak and Beech in Denmark—W. G. Smith, xxviii. 241. Of Basses Pyrenées—G. Cadell, xvii. 104. Of Bavaria, Visit to (1909)—A. N. Agnew, xxiii. 72. Of India—C. F. Amery, viii. 213; Sir R. Temple, x. 1. Of Norway—F. Bailey, xvi. 458. Of Poland, xviii. 227. Of Scotland—A. Schwappach, xv. 11. Of S. Africa—J. C. Brown, ix. 45. Of S. Australia—G. M'Ewin, x. 33. Of United States, xviii. 229. Planting of Deer—D. F. Mackenzie, ix. 53. Pure and Mixed—D. Brandis, xvi. 13. Remains of Ancient, in Scottish Peat-Mosses—M. I. N., xxii. 113. *Saxon State—A. D. Hopkinson, xxvii. 174; *xxviii. 28. Scots Fir, in N. Germany—A. C. Forbes, xiii. 187. Scottish and English, Report on Visit to (1881)—M. Boppe, xi. 196. *State, and other, of France—Col. F. Bailey, and Prof. Fisher, xviii. 74. State, of Prussia (including Hanover)—W. Somerville, xiv. 140. State Model, for Scotland, xv. 201, 221. Study of Continental—F. B., xx. 249. Swiss, Recent Publications on—W. G. Smith, xxvii. 202. Thuringian, Visit to—J. Michie, xiv. 105. *Working-Plan for Alice Holt—W. Schlich and W. F. Perree, xix. 83. See Notes and Queries.

Forglen, Excursion to, xxii. 211.

Fort Augustus Block, Detailed Survey of, xxv. 12.

Fothringham, W. Steuart: Address at Jubilee Meeting, 1904, (History of Society), xviii. 1; Deputation to Chancellor of Exchequer (1906), xix. 323: Protection of Scots Pine against Black Game, xxviii. 117; Silvicultural Treatment of Douglas Fir, xxviii. 248.

France:—Afforestation of Waste Lands, xxii. 207. Continental Notes—A. G. Hobart Hampden, xxi. 73; xxii. 46; xxiii. 57; xxiv. 56; xxvi. 48: xxvii. 41; xxviii. 60. Forestry in—F. Bailey, xi. 221. *State and other Forests of—Col. Bailey and Prof. Fisher, xviii. 74. See Excursions.

France, C S.: Coniferæ at Powerscourt, v. 83; Excursion of Aberdeen Branch of Society to Forglen and

Hatton, xxii. 211; Landscape and Economic Planting, xii. 322; State of Arboriculture in Ireland, v. 168.

Fraser, A.: Systematic Destruction of Squirrels, xx. 119.

Fraser, H.: *Cedrus atlantica*, v. 86.

Fraser, P. N.: Obituary—A. D. R., xix. 241.

Fraxinus excelsior. J. Nisbet, xvi. 128.

French Private Forest, Visit to. F. Cowley-Brown, xxvi. 172.

"From the Ice Age to the Present." A. W. Borthwick, xx. 253.

Frost:—Effects of, on *Larix europœa*, and *L. leptolepis*—D. Stewart, xxiii. 103. Protection of Young Spruce from—G. U. Macdonald, xix. 287; W. Hall, xxvii. 51.

Fruit Trees, Action of Grass on. A. Lauder, xxvii. 110.

Fuel in the Highlands. W. Brown, vi. 192. See vii. 120.

Fungus:—*A Tree-Strangling, xix. 358. Larch Disease—F. B., xxiii. 230.

Fungus Diseases, Spread of, by Hybernating Mycelium. A. W. B., xx. 122.

GALES, Some Lessons from the Recent. Sir Hugh Shaw-Stewart, xxvii. 172.

Galloway, R.: *xxviii. 229. Death Duties as affecting Woodlands, xxiii. 133; Do. on Woods, xxvii. 36; Law relating to Trees, Woods, etc., in Scotland, xix. 332; Profitable Co-operative Timber-Growing, xix. 291; Report of Excursion to Germany (1895), xiv. 195; Society's Register of Foresters and other Estate men, xix. 350.

*Galls on Willow. R. S. MacDougall, xviii. 208.

Galway County, Forest Operations in. W. Schlich, xvi. 249.

Gamble, J. S.: Forestry Exhibition at Paris, xvi. 339; International Congress of Sylviculture, xvi, 262; Report of Departmental Committee on Irish Forestry (1908), xxii. 26.

Game:—Black, Protection of Scots Pine against—W. Steuart Fothringham, xxviii. 117. Coverts—A. Gilchrist, iv. 103; W. Gilchrist, iv. 29, 91; A. M'Rae, xv. 54; A. D. Webster, xi. 213; T. Wilkie, xii. 371. Rearing of Woods where, preserved—A. Gilchrist, iv. 177.

*Gascony, Forest Tour among Dunes of. F. Bailey, xi. 291.

h

Gases, Wood damaged by. A. Slater, vii. 184.

Gayer, Karl: International Memorial to, xxvii. 114.

Geikie, J.: Soil: its Origin and Nature, xx. 178; xxi. 16, 131.

Geological and Arboricultural Features of Buteshire, etc. J. Kay, vii. 60

Geological Position, Effects of, on certain Coniferæ. Earl of Ducie, i. 41.

Geology and Forestry, J. S. Flett, xv. 73.

Gérardmer, Communal and State Forests of. Prof. Fisher, xviii. 86.

German Forestry. F. Story, xviii. 138.

German Forests, Visit to:—*F. Story, xvi. 424; by R. E. Arbor. Soc.—A. T. Gillanders, xxviii. 100.

Germany:—Afforestation of Waste Lands, xxii. 207. Continental Notes—B. Ribbentrop, xxi. 180; *xxii. 227; *xxiii. 38, 204; *xxiv. 194; *xxvi. 204; *xxvii. 212. Co-operative Agricultural Credit in, xvii. 331. Douglas Firin—M. I. N., xxii. 112. Excursion to (1895)—A. Slater, xiv. 163; Reports on—R. Galloway, xiv. 195; D. Robertson, xiv. 180. Scots Fir Forests in North—A. C. Forbes, xiii. 187. Visit to, etc. (1905), J. J. R. Meiklejohn, xix. 303.

Gilbert, W. M.: *The late Malcolm Dunn, xvi. 132.

Gilchrist, A.: *Implement for Straightening Bends in Standards of Wire Fences, iv. 205; Influence of Arboriculture, v. 102; Practical Arboriculture, vi, 82; Pruning, vii. 40; Rearing of Woods where Game is Preserved, iv. 177; Trees for Margins of Plantations, iv. 24; *Trees Grown on "Undrained Moorband Pan," vi. 334. Under-cover for Game, iv. 103.

Gilchrist, W.: Arboretum at Cluny Castle, vii. 19; Arboriculture in Aberdeenshire, vii. 235; Cultivation and Varieties of Scots Fir, vi. 304; Disposing of Home-grown Timber, vii. 146; Most profitable Felling Ages of Timber Trees, v. 131; Planting of Mixed Fir Plantations, iii. 2; Practical Arboriculture, vi. 6; Self-Sowing of Silver Fir, vii. 180; Soils best suited to Forest Trees, vi. 296; Thinning Plantations, v. 43; Transplanting

Thorn Hedges, etc., iv. 154; Trees, etc., for Planting near Sea, v. 143; Underwood for Game Cover, iv. 29, 91.

Gillanders, A. T.: *Belgian Forestry, xix. 139; Creosoting, xxiii. 172; *Pruning, xi. 49; Visit by R. E. Arbor. Soc. to German Forests, xxviii. 100.

Gipsy Moth, xv. 195.

Glasgow. See Exhibitions.

Glen, D. A.; Forestry in Kent and Sussex, xvi. 414; Formation of Plantations, xi. 173.

Glencorse Smoke Case. M. I. Newbigin, xxii. 221. See also xxii. 15.

Glen Mor, Forest Survey of. Lord Lovat and Captain Stirling of Keir, xxv.

Glen Urquhart, Afforestation at, xxv. 55

Goës, xv. 308.

Gordon, G. P.: *Excursion to Switzerland (1913), xxviii. 83; Forestry Exhibition at H. and A. Society's Show at Paisley (1913), xxviii. 97; Primitive Woodland and Plantation Types in Scotland, xxiv. 153; *Relation of Light Intensity to Advance Growth in Oak and Beech Forests, xxvi. 147; *Vegetation Types at High Altitudes, xxviii. 46.

Gorrie, A.: Plantations on Estate of Raynham, Norfolk, xiii. 331; Planting of Sandhills at Holkham, Norfolk, xiii. 350.

Gorrie, W.: Failures of Larch, viii. 61; How to Measure Annual Growth of Trees, ix. 103; Planting in Groups or Mixed Plantations, vii. 274.

Gossip, J.: Obituary Notice of the late Daniel Dewar, xvi. 336.

Gouk, W.: Prices of Scots Fir at Abernethy, i. 102.

Grandeau, Prof. Louis, Work of. A. Lauder, xxvi. 223.

Grandtully, Plantations at. D. F. Mackenzie, ix. 82.

Grant, A. M'D: Formation of Plantations, x. 204; Rearing and Management of Hardwood Plantations, xi. 373.

Grant, Donald:*Formation of Plantations on Deep Peat, xxviii. 72.

Grant, E. S.: Prevention of Damage by Pine Weevil, xx. 53.

Grants, Development, xxiv. 1, 108, 215; xxvi. 156.

Grass, Action of, on Fruit Trees—A. Lauder, xxvii. 110.

Grease, Is it Injurious to Trees? J. Craig, vi. 236.

Great Britain:—Afforestation, etc., in—J. Nisbet, xxii. 139. Production of Timber in, xxvii. 108.

Growth: — Advance, Relation of Light-Intensity to, etc.—G. P. Gordon, xxvi, 147. Tree, Light in Relation to—A. W. B., xxvi. 181.

HAILSTORM, Effects of, on Growing Timber. H. C. Sampson, xvi. 467.

Hall, C. E. : Tree Planting at San Jorge, Uruquay, xiii. 220.

Hall, T : Notes of Silvicultural Interest, xxi. 176 ; *xxii. 67 ; Planting with Mattock, xxiii. 104.

Hall, W. : Protecting Young Spruce from Frost, xxvii. 51. Raising and Management of Thorn Hedges, xxvi. 165 ; Silvicultural Notes, xxii. 104.

Hamilton, D. : Preserving Timber, vi. 230.

Hampshire:—Arboriculture in – A. Peebles, viii. 25 ; J. Smith, xi. 511. History of Arboriculture of New Forest—G. Lascelles, xiv. 15. Ligneous Plants of—J. Smith, xii. 356. Profits from Timber-growing in —W. Storie, xix. 205.

Hampton Court, Old and Remarkable Trees at. T. Hogg, ix. 145.

Hanbury, Right Hon. R. W., on Departmental Committee's Report, xvii. 322.

Hardwood Plantations. See Plantations.

Hardwoods : — Coniferæ and, best adapted to resist attacks of Hares and Rabbits—J. Craig, vi. 233 ; Cultivation of—J. Boyd, xxi. 44, 150. Table of, giving Soils, Subsoils, and Situations for, iv. 37. See Coniferæ.

Hardy, M. : Botanical Geography and Biological Utilisation of Soil, xvii. 110 ; Humus as Geographical Agency, xvii. 256.

Hares and Rabbits. See Hardwoods.

Harrower, W. : Larch Bug, ix. 246 ; Seasoning Timber, x. 199 ; Timber Supply of United States, x. 83 ; Tree-planting as Investment in Ireland, x. 55.

*Hartig, R., on Larch Disease, xvii. 19.

Hatton, Excursion to, xxii. 211.

Havelock, W. B. : A " Big Tree's "

Centuries of Life, xx. 129. Creosoting of Home-grown Timber, xx. 58. Two Exceptional Trees, xxi. 110.

*Haye, State Forest of. M. Larzillière, xviii. 78.

Heather Moorland, Origin and Development of. W. G. Smith, xvii. 117.

Hedderwick, A. S. : State in Relation to Afforestation, xxiv. 150.

Hedgerow and Field Timber. A. D. Webster, xi. 550.

Hedgerow Timber Trees. R. Philip, iii. 40.

Hedges :—Beech and Thorn—J. Kay, iv. 187. Disease in Beech R. Hutchison, ix. 217. Plants for Gaps in Old—R. Hutchison, iii. 15. Thorn—W. Hall, xxvi. 165 ; W. H. Whellens, xxvi. 61. Transplanting of Old Thorn, etc.—W. Gilchrist, iv. 154.

Heights of Trees, *Instrument for Measuring. W. Baillie, v. 171 ; J. Kay, v. 170.

Hemlock Spruce ; — Nursery Treatment of—J. M. Murray, xxi. 41. At Loganbank—F. B., xxi. 109.

Henry's Investigation of Elm Seedlings. A. D. Richardson, xxiv. 186.

Heredity and Forestry. W. Somerville, xxi. 1.

Hertfordshire, Excursion to, xvii. 301.

*Hesse Nassau, Beech Forests of. G. Cadell, xiii. 57.

Hickory becoming Scarce, xix. 211.

High Altitudes :—Planting at—A. W. B. Edwards, xxvi. 37. *Vegetation Types at—G. P. Gordon, xxviii. 46.

Highclere, Woods and Plantations of. A. Peebles, vi. 245.

Highland and Agricultural Society's Shows, Forestry at. See Exhibitions.

Highlands :—And Islands of Scotland, Afforestation in — W. A. Mackenzie, xiii. 318. Trees in— W. Brown, vi. 192.

Highwood, Conversion of Stored Coppice into, etc.—H. J. Marshall, xix. 99.

Hill, Mr, on Forest of Dean. F. Bailey, xv. 292.

Hill Pasture Land, Belts of Plantations on. T. Wilkie, xii. 337.

*Hill Planting, Sitka Spruce for, etc., J. D. Crozier, xxiii. 7.

Hobart - Hampden, A. G. : Continental Notes—France, xxi. 73 ; xxii. 46 ; xxiii. 57 ; xxiv. 56 ; xxvi. 48 ; xxvii. 41 ; xxviii. 60.

Hogg, T. : Cutting Timber by Axe or Saw, vi. 227 ; Old and Remarkable Trees at Hampton Court, ix. 145.

Holkham, Norfolk, Planting of Sandhills at. A. Gorrie, xiii. 350.

Holland, etc., Afforestation of Waste Lands, xxii. 207.

Home-Grown Timber, Manufacture of—A. T. Williamson, xiii. 151.

Home Nurseries, Expediency of Establishing. J. G. Thomson, iv. 15.

Home Timber Trade Outlook. D. Munro, xxiv. 139.

Hopkinson, A. D. : *State Forests of Saxony, xxvii. 174 ; *xxviii. 28.

*Houston Pinetum. W. Tivendale, vii. 38.

Humus as Geographical Agency. M. Hardy, xvii. 256.

Hungarian Ash, xix. 209.

Hungary, Forestry in. F. Bailey, xii. 1.

Hutchison, R. : Address, 1867, (Growth and Prospects of Society), iv. 167; Address, 1868, (Meeting of Brit. Assoc. at Norwich ; Need for Scientific Investigation and Accurate Observation in Forestry), v. 3 ; Address, 1869, (Importance of Arboriculture as a Science ; Influence of Woods on Climate), v. 99 ; Address, 1870, (Importance of Careful and Accurate Observation ; Formation of Field-Clubs ; Local Museums), vi. 1 ; Address, 1871, (Advantages of belonging to Society ; Importance of Cultivating Moral and Spiritual Faculties ; Theories of Creation ; Circulation of Sap in Trees), vi. 239 ; Address, 1880, (Progress of Arboriculture at Home and Abroad ; Flow of Sap in Trees), ix. 191 ; *Altitude and Appearance of *Wellingtonia gigantea*, vii. 190 ; Beetles, etc., which infest Coniferæ, vii. 123 ; Cedar of Lebanon, etc., xiii. 200 ; Coniferæ and Evergreens introduced from Japan, v. 6. Conservation of Old and Remarkable Trees in Britain, vii. 259 ; Corsican, Austrian and Douglas Firs as Timber Trees, vii. 52 ; Disease in Beech Hedges, ix. 217 ; Economic Uses, etc., of Timber Grown in Scotland, v. 109 ; Effects of Dry Seasons of 1868, '69 and '70 on Trees and Shrubs, vi. 281 ; Introduction and Cultivation of Newer Coniferæ, etc., iii. 44 ; Literature of Scottish Arboriculture, vii. 211 ; *Old and Remarkable Yew Trees in Scotland, xii. 379 ; Progress of Forestry in Scotland, ix. 1 ; Pruning Rarer Coniferæ, iv. 170 ; Rainfall in Wooded and Unwooded Countries, vii. 10 ; Rearing and Maintaining Live Fences, etc., iii. 15 ; Rise and Fall in Value of Timber grown in Scotland, etc., vi. 138 ; Timber Trees Suitable to different Soils, etc., in Scotland, iv. 31 ; Transplanting Pines and Evergreen Shrubs, iv. 3 ; Trees for Shelter in Islands of Scotland, ix. 140.

Hutton, J. : Planting Sandhills, viii. 19 ; Woods and Plantations of Mackintosh Estate, Brae Lochaber, viii. 233.

Hyalopus, xix. 195.

Hybernating Mycelium, Spread of Fungus Diseases by. A. W. B., xx. 122.

Hylesinus, xv. 65, 193 ; xvi. 152 ; xvii. 345.

Hylobius, xvi. 154 ; xxiii. 180. See Weevil.

" ICE Age, from the, to the Present." A. W. Borthwick, xx. 253.

Imported Coniferous Timbers, Our. A. D. Richardson, xvii. 238.

Imports :—Timber into United Kingdom (1903-04), xviii. 238 ; (1905), xix. 218. Timber and other Classes of Woods (1909-10), xxiv. 219.

Impregnation :—Of Railway Sleepers with Chloride of Barium, xvii. 340. Of Timber—D. M'Laren, xvi. 525.

Inchnacardoch, Glendoe, and Dell, Afforestation at, xxv. 56.

Increment, Annual, of Spruce and Scots Pine. J. H. Milne-Home, xxiv. 52 ; xxvi. 160 ; xxvii. 34.

India :—Chief Timber-Trees of—J. Nisbet, xix. 111. Distribution of Forests—D. Brandis, vii. 88. Distribution of Timber Trees, and Forest Conservancy—H. Cleghorn, v. 91. Lecture on Forests of—Sir R. Temple, x. 1. Progress in, in Preparation of Working-Plans, xxvi. 98. Progress of Forestry in —D. Brandis, x. 247. Report on

Forests of—C. F. Amery, viii. 213.
Teak Plantations at Nelambur,
Madras—J. Ferguson, ix. 114.
Indian Departmental Literature,
Publication of, xxi. 108.
Indian Famine Commission : Forest
Conservancy, ix. 273.
Indian Forestry : — Dr Cleghorn's
Services to—D. Brandis, xii. 87.
Notes on, (1905)—J. Nisbet, xix.
128 ; (1906), xx. 219. State—
S. H. Eardley-Wilmot, xxiii. 217.
See also vii. 5.
Indian Forest School. See Forest
Schools.
Indian Forest Service. See Forest
Service.
Indian Head, Sask., Forest Nursery
Station, xxiii. 67 ; xxiv. 67.
India-Rubber Trees of S. America.
J. Ferguson. x. 108.
*Infestation : — Chafer — F. Moon,
xviii. 201. Pine Weevil—D. Mac-
donald, xxiii. 180.
Influence of Forests on Climate, etc.:
Meteorological Observations at
Carnwath. A. Buchan, vii. 285.
Injurious Animals. See Animals.
Innes, Lieut.-Col. F. N. : *Century
of Forestry (1806-1906) on Estate
of Learney, xx. 168. Obituary,
xx. 257.
Inquiry, Larch Disease: Report by
Sub-Committee, xviii. 213.
Insects : — Depredations in N.
American Forests, xxiv. 222.
Forest, How to Combat — W.
Somerville, xiii. 5. Injurious to
Forest Trees—G. Brown, xvii. 277 ;
M. Dunn, viii. 173. Notes from
Wiltshire—A. C. Forbes, xiv. 189.
See vii. 120 ; xiv. 191 ; xvii. 135.
See also Reports by Hon. Scientists.
International Exhibitions. See Ex-
hibitions.
Introductory Remarks, ii. 1 ; iii. 1 ;
iv. 1 ; v. 1.
Invergarry, Afforestation at, xxv. 57 ;
xxviii. 270.
Inverliever Estate : — Afforestation,
xxiii. 106. Forestry Appointment
at, xxi. 232. State Forest—R. C.
Munro Ferguson, xxi. 22. See
Notes and Queries.
Invermoriston, Afforestation at, xxv.
55.
Inverness, Forestry Exhibition at.
Brodie of Brodie, xxvi. 43.
Investigation by Engl. Arbor. Soc.—
Larch Disease, xvii. 43.
Ireland : — Afforestation, etc. — J.

Nisbet, xxii. 139. Arboricultural
Society for, xvi. 526. Arbori-
culture in—C. S. France, v. 168.
Forest Operations in Co. Galway—
W. Schlich, xvi. 249. Forestry
Instruction in, xxvi. 158. Grant
to, from Development Fund, xxiv.
108. Larch Disease in, xxii. 113.
Rural Employment in, and Re-
afforestation, xxi. 107. Sitka
Spruce in—A. C. Forbes, xxviii.
264. Tree-Planting as Investment
in—W. Harrower, x. 55.
Irish Department of Agriculture,
Forestry Operations under, 1909.
A. C. F., xxiii. 229.
Irish Forestry : — Committee, xxi.
106. Report of Departmental
Committee on, 1908—J. S. Gamble,
xxii. 26.
Irish Forestry Society, xix. 327.
Irish Forestry Station, xx. 111.
Ironstone, Wood damaged by Gases
from Calcining. A. Slater, vii. 184.
Isle of Man Arboricultural Society,
xx. 254.
Italy, Re-afforestation in, xvii 321 ;
xxii. 110.

Jack, E., and Bailey, L. W. :
Woods of New Brunswick, xi. 9.
Japan : — Coniferæ and Evergreens
introduced from—R. Hutchison, v.
6. Forestry in, xix. 214 ; xxiv. 96.
Larix leptolepis in— K. Kumé, xx.
28. Uses of Wood in, xviii. 231.
Japanese and N. American Trees
suitable for British Woodlands.
H. J. Elwes, xix. 76.
Japanese Larch. See Larch.
Japanese Oak, xxiii. 105.
Jarrah and Karri, xviii. 226.
Johnston, J. : Economic Uses of
Chips, Branches and Roots of
Trees, v. 55.
Jolyet, A. : Obituary Notice of M.
Boppe, xxi. 114.
Jubilee of Society :—Address, xviii.
1. Dinner, xviii. 31.
"Justitia" : Thinning and General
Management of Forest Trees, ii. 3.

Karri, Jarrah and, xviii. 226.
Kay, J. : Beech and Thorn Hedges,
iv. 187 : Deterioration of Wire
Fences, xv. 317 ; *Geological and
Arboricultural Features of Bute-
shire, vii. 60 ; *Instrument for
Measuring Heights of Trees, v.
170 ; *Measuring and Protracting
Angles or Boundary Lines of

Plantations, etc., vi. 338; *New Straining Pillar for Wire Fences, x. 32; *Old and Remarkable Trees in Island of Bute, ix. 73; Register for Foresters, v. 155; *Transplanting Machine, vii. 186; *Wire-Fencing, with Wrought Iron Standards in Stone Blocks, v. 79. Retirement of, xxiv. 225.

Kay, J.: Forest Nursery Station at Indian Head, xxiii. 67; xxiv. 67.

Keay, R. B.: *Plan for Forester's Cottage, xii. 288.

Kent:—Arboriculture in—J. Duff, viii. 153. Forestry in — D. A. Glen, xvi. 414.

Kiao-chau, Forestry in, xix. 361.

Kienitz, Dr: *Fire Protection Lines in Scots Fir Forests, xvii. 198.

Kirkcudbright, etc., Arboriculture in. A. Pitcaithley, xiii. 293.

Krichauff, Mr: Timber Supply of Australia, viii. 110.

Kumé, K.: *Larix leptolepis* in Japan, xx. 28.

LAIRD, D. P.: Obituary—A. D. R., xix. 241.

Lancashire, North, Arboriculture in. G. Dodds, xi. 188.

Landowners' Forestry Co-operative Society. J. Stirling - Maxwell, xxiv. 104; xxviii. 231.

Landscape and Economic Planting. C. S. France, xii. 322.

Landscape Effect: — Blending of Foliage of Pines, etc., for—C. Y. Michie, iv. 73. Planting in Groups, etc., for—W. Corrie, vii. 274.

Landscape Forestry, Deciduous Trees for. J. Methven, xii. 94.

Landscape Gardening, Philosophy of. J. G. Macvicar, iv. 138.

Langhammer, Visit of Mr, xxiii. 231.

Larch:—*And Spruce Fir Canker—G. Massee, xvii. 25. *Blister in Plantations of—R. Coupar, x. 119. Canker, Ardross Working-Plan and — A. D. Richardson, xxii. 64. Canker, Experimental Study of, xxi. 234. Deterioration of — J. M'Gregor, ix. 234. *Development of Crop—A. Murray, xx. 8. Dry Rot in—J. M'Neill, ii. 7. *European and Japanese—K. Mackenzie, xxvi. 229. Failures of—W. Corrie, viii. 61. In German Forests—F. Boden, xvii. 47. Japanese, xvii. 337; Japanese—Geo. Leven, xxviii. 259. Japanese *v.* European—

W. H. Whellens, xxiii. 105. New Disease on. in Scotland—A. W. Borthwick and Malcolm Wilson, xxvii. 198. Plantation on Monument Hill, Monteviot—A. Finlayson, xxvi. 80. Plantations of John, Duke of Atholl, and Larch Disease — J. Booth. xvii. 232. Seed—G. F. Scott-Elliot, xxiv. 179. Tap-Root of—J. A. Campbell, xvi. 323. Timber, Sections of, showing Effects of different Soils on Growth —G. Brown, xxvi. 218. Underplanted Plantations at Novar—W. Mackenzie, xxiii. 35. Woods in Scotland — E. Nilson, xvi. 123. See Disease, *Larix*, and Notes and Queries.

Larch Bug:—W. Harrower, ix. 246; W. Schlich. xii. 423.

Larch Saw - Fly: — xxiv. 218; A. Raffan, xxvi. 220. Large, xxiii. 186; R S. MacDougall, xx. *43, 96. Large, Attack by—A. W. B. Edwards, xxiv. 42.

*Larch Shoot Moth. R. S. MacDougall, xxi. 195.

Larix: Europœa and *L. leptolepis*, Effects of Frost on, Compared—D. Stewart, xxiii. 103. *Leptolepis*, in Japan—K. Kumé, xx. 28. *Occidentalis*, xxiv. 107.

Larzillière, M.: *State Forest of Champenoux, xviii. 74: *State Forest of Haye, xviii. 78.

Lascelles, G.: History of Arboriculture of New Forest, xiv. 15.

Lathrœa, xix. 195.

Lauder, A.: Action of Grass on Fruit Trees, xxvii. 110; Accumulation of Nitrogen in Forest Soils, xx. 186; Comparison between the yields from Afforestation and Pasture Lands, xxvii. 113; Loganburn Smoke Case, xxii. 15; Oleoresins of some Western Pines. xxviii. 267; Use of Explosives in Forestry, xxvii. 210; Utilisation of Nitrogen of Air, xx. 183; Work of Prof. Louis Grandeau. xxvi. 222.

Law relating to Trees, Woods, etc., in Scotland. R. Galloway, xix. 332.

Leaf-Mould. A. P. Aitken, xv. 70.

Leaf-Shedding of Conifers, due to *Botrytis cinerea*, xxiv. 221.

*Learney. Forestry on Estate of, 1806 to 1906. F. N. Innes, xx. 168.

Lebanon, Cedar of:—R. Hutchison, xiii. 200. A Gigantic — J. Nisbet, xix. 212.

Lectures, Forestry:—Influences affecting British Forestry—W. Somerville, xii. 403. Introduction to Course of, at Edin. Univ. (1891-92), F. Bailey, xiii. 174.

Letter (Scottish Rating Bill, etc.), from President (R. C. Munro Ferguson) to General Meeting, 1896, xv. 1.

Leven, G. :—*Beech Felt Scale, xx. 245 ; *Creosoting Timber, xvii. 93 ; Excursion to Border Districts (1911), xxvi. 72 ; Japanese Larch, xxviii. 259 ; *Phoma pithya*, xv. 319 ; Trees at Auchincruive, Ayrshire, xix. 212.

*Lever Appliance. J. Rodger, xvi. 189.

Libraries and Reading - rooms for Working-men on Landed Estates. R. E. Brown, iii. 13.

Light in Relation to Tree-Growth— A. W. B., xxvi. 181.

Light - Intensity, Relation of, to Advance Growth in Oak and Beech Forests. G. P. Gordon, xxvi. 147.

Light and Shade, Effects of, on Trees. J. K., xxvii. 105

Ligneous Plants of Hampshire. J. Smith, xii. 356.

Lime, Experiment with, etc., for Protection against Pine Weevil— T. Neilson, xix. 207.

Lime - Sulphur, Wash for Foliage, xxiv. 223.

Lime Trees, Attack of, by Larvæ of Winter Moth, xxiv. 107.

Limited Liability Company to acquire Timber Estate. W. Somerville, xiv 100.

Lincoln. See Exhibitions.

Linlithgowshire, Sitka Spruce, etc., in. H. M. Cadell, xxiii. 158.

Liparis, xv. 195.

Literature :—British Forestry, xiv. 89. (See also viii. 9 ; x. 180 ; xv. App.). Of Scottish Arboriculture —R. Hutchison, vii. 211. Publication of Indian Departmental, xxi. 108. See Book Notices.

Load of Timber, What is a? xix. 216.

Local Arboricultural Societies. R. Philip, i. 38.

Local Taxation, Afforestation and K. Mackenzie, xxiii. 3.

Lochaber, Excursion to (1910). J. Stirling-Maxwell, xxiv. 73.

Loganbank. Albert Spruce at. F. B. xxi. 109.

Loganburn (Glencorse) Smoke Case.

A. Lauder, xxii. 15 ; M. I. Newbigin, xxii. 221.

Lophodermium, xvii. 343.

Lophyrus, xx. 96.

Lothian, Marquis of : Address, 1881 (Application for Royal Charter ; School of Forestry ; Progressive Change in Climate of Scotland ; Vitality of Seeds), x. 75.

Lovat Estates, Visit to, by N. Branch of R. S. A. S., xxi. 205.

Lovat, Lord: Afforestation, xxii. 156.

Lovat, Lord, and Stirling of Keir, Capt. : Forest Survey of Glen Mor, xxv.

Lucifer Matches, Manufacture of, in Sweden. J. C. Brown, x. 223.

M'BEATH, D. K. :*Economic Disposal of Coniferous Timber, xxviii. 251. *Thuja Gigantea* and Douglas Fir in Mixture, xxviii. 107.

M'Callum, J. : Corsican Pine in Dorset, xxiv. 45 ; *Witch's Broom on *Pseudotsuga Douglasii*, xxviii. 116 ; Tree-growth in 1913, xxviii. 118.

M'Corquodale, W. : Address, 1889, (Origin of Society ; Chair of Forestry in Edin Unvi. ; Afforestation), xii. 375 ; Conversion of Coppice Land, iv. 47 ; Diseases of Larch (*Larix europæa*), ii. 43 ; Education of Foresters, ix. 100 ; Has Scotch Fir deteriorated? ix. 176 ; Judicious Pruning, x. 166 ; Planting with Scotch Fir after Crops of old Scotch Fir, ii. 48. See xiii. 163.

Macdonald, D. : Infestation by Pine Weevil, xxiii. 180.

Macdonald, D. M. : Laying-out of Mixed Plantation, and Maintenance for first twenty-five years, xix. 32.

Macdonald, G. U. : Forest Work, xvi. 451 ; Notes for Planters, xvii. 287 ; Planting Waste Land for Profit, xviii. 183 ; Prices and Supplies in the Timber Trade, xxviii. 270 ; Protection of Young Spruce from Frost, xix. 287 ; Excursion to France (1904), xviii. 118 ; Excursion to Sweden (1902), xvii. 56 ; Timber Trade Conference, xxiii. 51. See also Plan.

MacDougall. R. S. : Genus *Pissodes*, xv. 25 ; *Larch Shoot Moth, xxi. 195 ; *Large Larch Saw-fly, xx. 43 ; *Megastigmus spermotrophus* as Enemy of Douglas Fir, xix. 52. See Reports by Hon. Scientists.

M'Ewin, G. : Natural Forests of S. Australia, x. 33.

M'Glashen's Transplanting Apparatus, iii. 102.

M'Gregor, J. : Deterioration of Larch, ix. 234.

M'Intosh, A. : *Ash-Bark Beetle, x. 235.

MacIntosh, W. : *Forester's Cottage, xi. 364.

M'Intosh's Work on Disease of Larch, Remarks on, ii. 31.

Mackenzie, D. F. : Address, 1890, ("Waste Land" in Scotland), xiii. 1 ; Book-Keeping for Foresters, ix. 183 ; Clearing Land for Planting, viii. 136 ; Comparative Value of Timber Trees grown in Britain, x. 231 ; Death Duties and Timber Planting, xvi. 321 ; Disease of Larch, viii. 140 ; Disposing of Home-grown Timber, viii. 88 ; Establishing Experimental Forest Area in Scotland, xv. 179 ; Financial Results of Cultivation of Timber, xvi. 494 ; Forestry Section of H. and A. Show at Inverness (1901), xvi. 475 ; Most Profitable Felling Age of Timber-Trees, viii. 70 ; Physiology and Structure of Trees and Shrubs, xiv. 114 ; Plantations at Murthly, Grandtully, etc., ix. 82 ; Planting Deer Forests, ix. 53 ; *Preserving Timber, xiv. 78 ; Prices of Home - grown Timber (1901), xvi. 504 ; Scottish Timber and its Uses, x. 189 ; *Sections of Woods grown in Britain, xiv. 39 ; Use of Dynamite and Tonite in Forestry, viii. 241 ; Use of Steam Power in Forestry, vii. 269. *Obituary, xxiv. 114.

Mackenzie's Dendrometer, x. 241.

Mackenzie, Sir K. J. : Address, 1907, (Retaining Population in Country Districts : Rabbits, etc.), xx. 137 ; Afforestation and Local Taxation, xxiii. 3 ; European and Japanese Larch, xxvi. 229.

Mackenzie, W. : *A Fine Larch, xix. 208 ; Combating Cockchafer Attack in Nursery, xx. 119 ; *Novar Estate, Plan of Management, xvi. 25; Underplanted Larch Plantations at Novar, xxiii. 35.

Mackenzie, W. A. : Afforestation in Highlands and Islands of Scotland, xiii. 318 ; Arran as Field for Planting, xiii. 341.

Mackinnon, W. : Obituary Notice of, xx. 136.

Mackintosh Estate in Brae Lochaber, Woods, etc., on. J. Hutton, viii. 233.

M'Laren, D. : Impregnation of Timber, xvi. 525.

M'Laren, J. : Corsican Pine, v. 52 ; Forest and Ornamental Trees of Recent Introduction, x. 209 ; Has Scotch Fir deteriorated ? ix. 176.

M'Laren, P. : Improving Social and Moral Condition, etc., of Under Foresters and Apprentices, v. 73.

M'Lean, J. : Collection, Preparation, etc., of Forest Tree Seeds, x. 156 ; Natural Reproduction of Forests, xi. 36.

M'Leod, J. : Management of Oak-Coppice and curing of Coppice-Bark, i. 103.

M'Nab, W. R. : Anatomy of Leaf as a means of determining Species of Abies, viii. 93 ; Movements of Fluids in Stems, in Relation to Felling and Seasoning of Timber, viii. 203. See ix. 109.

M'Neill, J. : Dry-Rot in Larch and Spruce Fir, ii. 7 ; Felling of Timber, ii. 17.

M'Pherson, J. : Manufacturing Timber, xvi. 448.

M'Rae, A. : *Detailed Report on Forestry Section in Scot. Nat. Exhibition, Edin. (1908), xxii. 77. Undercover for Game, xv. 54.

Macrae, J. : Attack by Weevil Strophosomus Coryli, xxiii. 185.

Macvicar, Rev. J. G. : Philosophy of Arboriculture and Landscape Gardening, iv. 138.

Mahogany, xxiv. 224.

Malay States, Federated, xxiv. 223.

Management :—Beech and Thorn Hedges—J. Kay, iv. 187. Birch Seed —W. Somerville, xv. 319. European Forests—H. Cleghorn, v. 94. Forest Trees — "Jnstitia," ii. 3. Oak-Coppice—J. M'Leod, i. 103 ; J. Whyte, i. 215. See Plantations.

Mansfield, Earl of : Address, 1900, (Practical Training of Foresters), xvi. 157.

Manufacture :—Home Grown Timber —A. T. Williamson, xiii. 151. Timber—J. M'Pherson, xvi. 448.

Manures, Artificial, in Forestry. A. W. Borthwick, xix. 245.

Maps, Ordnance Survey, of United Kingdom, xx. 256.

Marriott, C. : Experimental Plots at Novar, xx. 101.

Marshall, H. J. : Conversion of Stored Coppice into Highwood, and how I became converted to the latter System of Sylviculture, xix. 99.

Martin, M. : Importance of Forests in Military Defence, xxiii. 223.

Massee, G. : *Lareh and Spruce Fir Canker, xvii. 25.

Matches, Lucifer, Manufacture of, in Sweden. J. C. Brown, x. 223.

Mattock, Planting with the. T. Hall, xxiii. 104.

Maw, P. T. : Financial Aspect of Forestry, xxiii. 17.

Maxwell, H. : English Elm in Scotland, xx. 244 ; Forest Resources of United Kingdom, xxii. 1 ; Is *Rhododendron barbatum* Insectivorous ? xx. 118 ; Larch Disease on *Pinus Laricio* and *P. Sylvestris*, xx. 117 ; On Neglected Woodlands, xix. 357.

Maxwell, W. : *Different Methods of Planting, xxvi. 59.

Mayr, Prof. H. : Obituary— A. W. B., xxiv. 239.

Measurement: *Angles or Boundary Lines of Plantations, etc.—J. Kay, vi. 338. Annual Growth of Living Trees — W. Gorrie, ix. 103. *Heights of Trees, Instrument for —W. Baillie, v. 171 ; J. Kay, v. 170. Tables for Conversion of— F. Bailey, xii. 351. Tree—R. Christison, viii. 262. Trees, for Cubic Contents—J. W. Barry, x. 21. Tree-girth — D. Christison, xvi. 529.

*Megastigmus spermotrophus, as Enemy of Douglas Fir. R. S. MacDougall, xix. 52.

Meiklejohn, J. J. R. : Damage to Pine Woods by Crossbills, xvi. 318 ; Visit to some Bavarian and Saxon Forests (1904), xviii. 150 ; Visit to Switzerland and Germany (1905), xix. 303. See Plan.

Melolontha, xvii. 345 ; *xviii. 208.

Memorial, International, to Karl Gayer, xxvii. 114.

Menzies Fir, xvi. 528.

Meteorological Observations : — At Carnwath—A. Buchan, vii. 285 ; viii. 168, 257 ; ix. 186. Near Carnwath—W. Currie, vii. 290. See Reports by Hon. Scientists.

Methven, J. : Address, 1894, (Planting of Waste Lands in Scotland ; Forest Schools of Europe, India, etc.), xiv. 49 ; Deciduous Trees for Landscape Forestry, xii. 94. Obituary, xxvii. 248.

Mexican Forestry, xix. 214.

Michie, C. Y. : *Blending of Foliage of Pines, etc., for Landscape Effect, iv. 73 ; Charcoal - Producing Plants, vi. 319 ; Culture and Uses of Silver Fir, v. 138 ; Diseases of Forest Trees, iv. 51 ; Economic Uses and Comparative Values of Timber, v. 114. Improving Social and Moral Condition, etc., of Under Foresters and Apprentices, v. 61 ; Pruning of Forests Trees, v. 34 ; Register for Foresters, v. 155 ; *Rustic Bridges, Arbours, etc., iv. 115 ; *Straining - Pillars for Wire Fences, v. 75 ; *Transplanting of Forest Trees, v. 20 ; Trees and Underwood for Planting near Sea, v. 150.

Michie, J. : Visit to the Thuringian Forest, xiv. 105.

Midland Re-afforesting Association. A. D. R., xx. 107.

Military Defence, Importance of Forests in. M. Martin, xxiii. 223.

Milne, A. : Address, 1900, (Past and Present Work of Society ; National Forest System ; Forestry Education and Forest Management in Germany, France, and British India), xvi. 178.

Milne, J. : Comparative Advantages of Cutting Timber by Axe or Saw, vi. 224.

Milne-Home, J. H. : Annual Increment of Spruce and Scots Pine, xxiv. 52 ; xxvi. 160 ; xxvii. 34.

Milroy, T. R. : Rearing and Management of Hardwood Plantations, x. 47.

Mirwart, Visit to Dr Schlich's Forests at. F. Bailey, xvi. 241.

Mitchell, A. : Driftwood and Insect Attacks, xiv. 191 ; xv. 197 ; *Pissodes notatus*, xv. 199.

Mitchell, F. : Old and Remarkable Trees on Earl Spencer's Estates in Northamptonshire, xiii. 83.

Moeran, A. E. : Growing Timber for Profit in United Kingdom, xix. 25.

Moisture, Effect of, on Wood, xxiv. 111.

Monument Hill, Monteviot, Larch Plantation on. A. Finlayson, xxvi 80.

Moon, F. : *Attack by Sawfly Larvæ, xxi. 52 ; *Chafer Infestation, xviii. 201 ; Damage to Coniferous Planta-

tion by Water-Voles, xxi. 105.
*Forest Tramway, xxi. 71.
*"Moorband Pan," Trees grown on Undrained. A. Gilchrist, vi. 334.
Moorlands : — Origin and Development of Heather—W. G. Smith, xvii. 117. *Planting of High—J. Stirling-Maxwell, xx. 1.
Moss Land, Planting on. J. Thomson, i. 120.
Mossman, R. C. : Forests and Rainfall, xx. 188. See Reports by Hon. Scientists.
*Moth, Larch Shoot. R. S. MacDougall, xxi. 195.
Mountain Pine, J. Stirling-Maxwell, xxi. 10.
Munro, D. : Home Timber Trade Outlook, xxiv. 139.
Murray, A. : *Development of Larch Crop, xx. 8 ; Excursion to Dunkeld, Murthly and Scone (1904), xviii. 61 ; Forestry Exhibition at Perth (1904), xviii. 65 ; Forestry Museum, Murthly Estate, xxii. 237 ; *Notes of Silvicultural Interest, xxvii. 206.
Murray, J. M. : Laying-out of Mixed Plantation and Maintenance for first Twenty-five Years, xix. 44 ; Nursery Treatment of Western or Californian Hemlock Spruce, xxi. 41.
Murthly Estate : Excursion to (1904), xviii. 61 ; Forest Museum — A. Murray, xxii. 237 ; Lecturers at, xxiii. 112 ; Plantations at—D. F. Mackenzie, ix. 82.
Museums, Estate Forest :—F. B., xx. 110 ; Murthly, xxii. 237.
Myrtle-Wood, Tasmanian, xix. 210.

NANCY Professor, Death of a, xxiii. 112.
National Industry of Forestry, Scheme for Establishing, xxi. 135. Criticisms on Scheme—R. Munro Ferguson, xxii. 8. Reply to Criticisms, xxii. 13.
Natural Regeneration :—Of Forests —J. M'Lean, xi. 36 ; *In General, with Special Details regarding Scots Pine at Beauly—G. Brown, xix. 17. Of Silver Fir—W. Gilchrist, vii. 180. *Of Woods—W. Somerville, xiii. 63.
Nature as a Forester. W. Brown, vi. 192.
Nectria on Larch, xvii. 344.
Neilson, T. : Experiments with Lime and Arseniate of Soda for Protection against Pine Weevil, xix. 207.

*Nematus Erichsoni, xx. 96. See Larch Sawfly.
Newbigin, M. I. : Glencorse Smoke Case, xxii. 221.
New Brunswick, Woods of. L. W. Bailey and E. Jack, xi. 9.
Newcastle-upon-Tyne. See Exhibitions.
New Forest, Hants, History of Arboriculture of — G. Lascelles, xiv. 15.
Newstead, Melrose, Vegetable Remains at, xxiii. 31.
New Zealand, Timber Resources of, xxiii. 233.
Nilson, E. : Larch Woods in Scotland, xvi. 123 ; Recent Developments in Swedish Forestry, xix. 136 ; Timber Supply from Sweden, xx. 252.
Nisbet, J. : Afforestation and Timber —Planting in Great Britain and Ireland, xxii. 139 ; A Gigantic Cedar of Lebanon, xix. 212 ; Ash and its Cultivation, xvi. 128 ; British Forestry and its Future Prospects, xvi. 161 . Chief Timber-Trees of India, xix. 111 ; Destruction of Rabbits Injurious to Woodlands and Fields, xix. 104 ; History of Forestry in Britain (1854-1904), xviii. 20 ; Notes on Continental Forestry (1904), xviii. 161 ; (1905), xix. 161 ; (1906), xx. 64 ; Notes on Indian Forestry (1905), xix. 128 ; (1906), xx. 219 ; Planting Waste Land for Profit, xix. 259 ; Rate of Growth of Mature Timber-Crops in E. Perthshire, xix. 70 ; Reply to Mr Munro Ferguson's Note upon Dr Nisbet's Criticism of Report of Departmental Committee on Forestry, in Preface to The Forester, xix. 200 ; "The Novar System of Combating Larch Disease," xx. 39 ; "The Railway Fires Act, 1905," xix. 73 ; Training, etc., of Probationers for Indian Forest Service, xix. 107 ; xxi. 191 ; Town-Woods of Carlsbad, Bohemia, xix. 150 ; Utilisation of Existing Woodland Produce, Glen Mor, xxv. 69 ; Working-Plan for British Woodlands, xx. 30 ; *Working-Plan for Earl of Selborne's Blackmoor, Bradshott and Temple Woods, Hants, xvi. 193.
Nitrogen : — In Forest Soils, Accumulation of—A. Lauder, xx. 186. Of Air, Utilisation of—A. Lauder, xx. 183.

Niven, W. N.: Distribution of Certain Forest Trees in Scotland, as shown by Post-Glacial Deposits, xvii. 97.

Nomenclature, Tree. F. B., xvi. 319.

Norfolk, Planting of Sandhills at Holkham. A. Gorrie, xiii. 350.

Northumberland, Excursion to, 1906. A. D. Richardson, xx. 81.

Norway, Forests of. F. Bailey, xvi. 458.

Norwich, Forestry at Roy. Agric. Show, xxiv. 220.

*Notching, Pitting rer*sus*, xxiii. 111.

Notes and Queries :—
A "Big Tree's" Centuries of Life—W. B. Havelock, xx. 129. Aberdeen Branch of Society, xix. 362. Aberdeen University, Four Weeks' Course for Foresters at, xxiv. 217. Afforestation :—At Vyrnwy, xxvii. 236 ; Of Catchment Areas of Water Supplies, xvii. 327 ; Of Inverliever Estate, xxiii. 106 ; Of Reclaimed Lands, xxi. 229 ; Of Surplus Lands—W. Schlich, xxi. 225 ; Of Talla Water-Catchment Area, F. B., xx. 106 ; xxvii. 104. Albert or Hemlock Spruce at Loganbank—F. B., xxi. 109. Alcohol from Sawdust, xix. 362. All Russian Timber Society, xvii. 336. American Forestry Congress. xviii. 229. Appeal for Literary Contributions, xix. 353 ; xxvi. 234. Appin Woods—F. B., xxii. 108. Arboriculture and Arable Land—R. M. Ferguson, xxi. 222. Arboricultural Society :—for Ireland, xvi. 526 ; Isle of Man, xx. 254 ; Royal English, xix. 217. Ardgoil Estate—W. F. A. H., xxi. 223 ; xxvii. 105. Argyllshire, Woodlands of, xxvii. 104. Ash, Hungarian, xix. 209. Artificially Coloured Wood, xix. 215. Attack of Lime Trees by Larvæ of Winter Moth, xxiv. 107.
*Basic Slag on Seed-Beds—J. Boyd, xxi. 229. *Beech Felt Scale, Note on—G. Leven. xx. 245. Beech Tree in Scotland, xxiii. 103. Bibliography of Forestry—H. B. Watt, xxvi. 230. Biltmore Forest School, U.S.A., xxiv. 108 ; xxvi. 98. Birch and Alder Saw-Fly—J. Boyd, xix. 207. Blasting, Scientific Tree-Butt, xviii. 225. Board of

Agriculture Leaflet on the Large Brown Pine Weevil, xxviii. 118. Books, Some Recent Forestry, xxi. 235 ; New Forestry, xxvi. 100. Bordeaux Mixture, xxiii. 232. Botanical Survey of Scotland—A. W. B., xx. 122. Brechin Arboricultural Society, xviii. 237.

Canadian Forestry Association, xvii. 329. Canadian Forests, xxvi. 97. Cape of Good Hope, xvi. 527. Cedar of Lebanon, A Gigantic—J. Nisbet, xix. 212. Chair of Forestry at Cambridge, xxi. 232. Chiltern Hills Beech, xviii. 225. Chloride of Barium for Impregnation of Railway Sleepers, xvii. 340. Choice of Trees for Planting — A. G. Hobart-Hampden, xxvi. 233. Civil Engineers on British Forestry, xvii. 156. Climate, Influence of Forests on, xviii. 231. Collection and Utilisation of Information for a Forest Survey, xxvii. 112. Combating Cockchafer Attack in Nursery—W. Mackenzie, xx. 119. Comparison between the yields from Afforestation and Pasture Lands—Alex. Lauder, xxvii. 113. *Conifer Disease, A, xix. 360. Conifers in Great Britain, Remarkable — J. N., xx. 126. Coniferous *versus* Broad-Leaved Forests — F. B., xxii. 109. Continental Forests, The Study of—F. B., xx. 249. Co-operative Agricultural Credit in Germany and Switzerland, xvii. 331. Coppice-Woods, Decline in Value of—W. Storie, xix. 203. Creosote Oil, Use of in United States—W. B. Havelock, xx. 256. Creosoted Timber, xx. 128. Creosoting of Spruce, Larch, Oak and Scots Pine—M. F. Roberts. xviii. 224. Creosoting Tree Stumps against Pine Weevil—F. R. S. Balfour, xxviii. 270.

Damage :—by Squirrels, xvii. 161 ; to Pine Woods by Crossbills—J. J. R. Meiklejohn, xvi. 318 ; to Young Coniferous Plantation by Water-Voles — F. Moon, xxi. 105. Dean Forest School of Forestry, xx. 112. Death Duties and Timber - Planting—D. F. Mackenzie, xvi. 321. Deer

Forests and Sporting Lands in Scotland, xxvii. 237. Demonstration Forest for Scotland, xx. 113. Denbighshire Scheme for Experimental Station—A. D. R., xx. 108. Deputation to President of Board of Agriculture, xiv. 192. Deterioration of Wire Fences—J. Kay, xv. 317. Development and Road Improvement Funds Act (1909), xxiii. 231. Diploma in Forestry at Oxford —F. B., xix. 354. Diseased Scots Pine on Land formerly Arable, xx. 248. Distillation of Wood, xxvi. 99. Douglas Fir :—J. M., xvi. 326 ; xvii. 160 ; in Germany—M. I. N., xxii. 112. Driftwood and Insect Attacks—A. Mitchell, xiv. 191 ; xv. 197. Durability of Highland Scots Fir, xxiv. 106.

Edinburgh University : — Degree in Forestry at—F. B., xx. 248 ; Forestry at (1904-05), xviii. 233 ; xxi. 232 ; Forestry Class, xvi. 528 ; xviii. 234. Effects of Frost on *Larix europœa* and *L. leptolepis* compared—D. Stewart, xxiii. 103. Effects of Light and Shade on Tree-Growth—J. K., xxvii. 105. Effect of Moisture on Wood, xxiv. 111. English Elm in Scotland—H. Maxwell, xx. 244. Estate-conducted Experiments in Sylviculture, etc.— F. B., xx. 102. Estate Duty on Timber under Finance Act of 1910, xxvi. 95. Estate Forest Museums — F. B., xx. 110. *European and Japanese Larch— K. Mackenzie, xxvi. 229. Excursions, Educational — F. B., xx. 250. Excursion to Switzerland (1913), xxviii. 119. Experiment with Lime and Arseniate of Soda for Protection against Pine Weevil—T. Neilson, xix. 207. Experimental Plots :—*at Cockle Park, xviii. 219 ; at Novar—C. Marriott, xx. 101. Experimental Station, Denbighshire—F. B., xx. 254. Experimental Study of Larch Canker, xxi. 234. Exotic Conifers in Britain, xxiv. 220. Exports from United Kingdom (1905), xix. 218. Extraction of Tree-Stumps — J. Clark, D. Dewar, and D. F. Robertson, xvi. 320.

Federated Malay States, xxiv. 223. Felling Trees by Electricity, xxiv. 109. Fencing, Cost of— F. B., xxi. 233. Foreign Plants —Japanese Larch, xvii. 337. Forest Conservation in United States, xxi. 227 ; xxiv. 225. Forest Fires, xvii. 316 ; in Canada, xxiii. 105. Forest Pests—R. S. MacDougall, xxviii. 267. Forest School, Yale—F. B., xx. 251. Forest Terminology, xxvi. 97, 229. Foresters' and Gardeners' Society of Argyll, xxi. 235. Forestry and the Anglo-American Exposition, xxviii. 119. Forestry Appointments :—xviii. 234 ; xix. 217 ; xxii. 114 ; xxiii. 232 ; xxvi. 232 ; at Inverliever, xxi. 232 ; by Department of Woods, xxi. 110 ; by General Post Office—F. B., xx. 113 ; obtained by Students of Edin. Univ. Forestry Class, xviii. 235. Forestry :—at Cirencester, xvii. 321 ; at R. Agric. Show, Norwich, xxiv. 220 ; at W. of Scotland Agric. College—W. F. A. H., xxi. 230 ; in Canada, xxiv. 225 ; in Japan, xix. 214 ; in Kiaochau, xix. 361 ; Mexican, xix. 214 ; Prize Essays on, xvii. 338 ; School of, for Wales, xvii. 339 ; Teaching of, in the Provinces, xvi. 528 ; xvii. 337 ; xviii. 233. Forestry Committee (1902) and Training in Forestry—F. Bailey, xxi. 102. Forestry Education at Imperial University of Tokio, xviii. 232. Forestry Exhibition, British (Willesden, 1904), xvii. 338. Forestry Instruction :—at Armstrong College, xx. 112 ; at Forest of Dean, xvii. 324. Forestry Lectureships, Appointments to, etc. (1904), xviii. 234 ; xix. 217 ; (1913) xxvii. 110 ; xxvii. 239 ; xxviii. 116. Forestry Museum : Murthly Estate —A. Murray, xxii. 237. Forestry Operations, under Irish Department of Agriculture (1909)—A. C. F., xxiii. 229. Forests :— and Forestry Problems, in Sierra Leone, xxvi. 98 ; in W. Australia, xx. 130 ; of British E. Africa Protectorate, xxiii. 113 ; of Central Vosges Mountains, xxiii. 113. "From the Ice-Age to the Present"—A. W. Borthwick,

xx. 253. Fruit Trees (See Grass).

Geology and Forestry—J. S. Flett, xv. 73. Grants from Development Fund, xxiv. 215 ; to Ireland, xxiv. 108. Grass, Action of, on Fruit Trees—Alex. Lauder, xxvii. 110.

Hickory becoming Scarce, xix. 211. Imports of Timber into United Kingdom (1903-04), xviii. 238 ; (1905), xix. 218 ; (1909-10), xxiv. 219. Impregnation of Timber—D. M'Laren, xvi. 525. India, Progress in, in Preparation of Working-Plans, xxvi. 98. Indian Departmental Literature, Publication of, xxi. 108. Insect Depredations in N. American Forests, xxiv. 222. Insect Notes from Wiltshire—A. C. Forbes, xiv. 189. International Forest Congress at Paris, xxvii. 112. Inverliever : — First Steps at —R. C. Munro Ferguson, xxi. 104 ; Plantations at, xxi. 111 ; Progress at, xxiv. 105 ; Rainfall at, xxiv. 220. Investigation into Current Annual Increment in Girth of Douglas Fir, xxvi. 232. Ireland, Rural Employment in, and Re-afforestation, xxi. 107. Irish Forestry Committee, An, xxi. 106. Irish Forestry Station, xx. 111.

Japan, Uses of Wood in, xviii. 231. Japanese Larch — H. Shaw-Stewart, xxviii. 271. Japanese Larch v. European — W. H. Whellens, xxiii. 105. Japanese Oak, xxiii. 105. Jarrah and Karri, xviii. 226.

Landowners' Forestry Co-operative Society—J. Stirling-Maxwell, xxiv. 104. Larch :—*A Fine— W. Mackenzie, xix. 208 ; A New, xxiv. 112 ; and the Moth, xvii. 334 ; New Danger for, · xvii. 158 ; on Sakhalin, xvii. 159 ; Russian, xix. 209. Larch Disease :—in Ireland, xxii. 113 ; on Pinus Laricio and P. sylvestris —H. Maxwell, xx. 117. Larch Disease Fungus—F. B., xxiii. 230. Larch, Japanese, and Larch Disease—F. Story, xvii. 333. Larch Saw-fly, xxiv. 218. Larix occidentalis, xxiv. 107. Late Mr Hanbury on Report of Departmental Committee, xvii. 322. Leaf-Mould—A. P. Aitken,

xv. 70. Leaf-Shedding of Conifers, due to Botrytis cinerea, xxiv. 221. Lecturers at Murthly, xxiii. 112. Lime-Sulphur Wash for Foliage, xxiv. 223.

Mahogany, xxiv. 224. Management of Birch Seed—W. Somerville, xv. 319. Menzies Fir, xvi. 528. Midland Re-afforesting Association—A. D. R., xx. 107. Mr Langhammer's Visit, xxiii. 231. Memorial, International, to Karl Gayer, xxvii. 114.

Nancy Professor, Death of a, xxiii. 112. New Forestry Books, xxvi. 100. Nomenclature of Trees— F. B., xvi. 319. Notes re Acetone —W. D. A. Bost, xxviii. 272.

Oleoresins of some Western Pines —A. Lauder, xxviii. 267. Ordnance Survey Maps of United Kingdom, xx. 256.

Parliament and Forestry, xviii. 221. Pathological Specimens for Exhibition—A. W. Borthwick, xvii. 155. Phoma pithya —G. Leven, xv. 319. Pissodes notatus—A. Mitchell, xv. 199. *Pitting v. Notching, xxiii. 11. Pitwood, Scarcity of, xxviii. 266. Planting with Mattock—T. Hall, xxiv. 104. Poland, Forests of, xviii. 227. Preservative against Wood Splitting, xxiv. 110. Preserving Sleepers from Decay, xxiii. 234. President of Board of Agriculture on Forestry, xvii. 323. Prices and Supplies in Timber Trade—G. U. Macdonald, xxviii. 268. Prices of Home-Grown Timber—J. M., xvi. 327. Protection of Scots Pine against Black Game—W. Steuart Fothringham, xxviii. 117. Pulp Industry of Canada, xxiii. 108.

Rabbits, xxiv. 109. Railway Fires Act, 1905 — F. B., xxii. 111. Railway Rates, xvii. 318. Railway Sleepers from Irish-Grown Timber, xviii. 225. Rate of Growth of Pseudotsuga Douglasii in Woods of Saxony—communicated by J. Booth, xx. 104. Rating of Woodlands and Railway Rates on Timber — R. Galloway, xxvi. 96. Re-afforesting the Black Country, xvii. 336. Re-afforestation :—in Italy, xvii. 321 ; xxii. 110 ; in Scotland, xx. 254. Remains of Ancient Forests in Scottish Peat-Mosses —

M. I. N., xxii. 113. Report of Excursion to Germany (1895)— R. Galloway, xiv. 195. Research at Indian Forest School, xx. 115. Resistance of Young Trees to Drought, xx. 247. Retirement :—of Mr Grant Thomson —R. M. F., xxiv. 113 ; *of Mr James Kay—A. D. R., xxiv. 225. *Rhododendron barbatum*, is it Insectivorous?—H. Maxwell, xx. 118. Rooks feeding on Pine Beetles — J. Boyd, xix. 206. Royal Botanic Garden, Edinburgh, Proposed Guild, xxvii. 239. Ruping Process of Creosoting Timber, xxvii. 235. Russia, Timber Resources of European, xviii. 228. Russia's Timber Trade with United Kingdom, xviii. 228.

St Louis Exhibition (Society's Exhibit), xviii. 223. School of Forestry in Forest of Dean, xx. 251 ; xxiv. 217 ; Scots Pine, A Large, xxvi. 231. Scottish Peat Mosses, History of—A. W. B., xx. 125. Scottish Tree Seeds for Norway and Sweden, xvi. 526. Season and Growth of Trees—A. C. Forbes, xv. 75. Seeds of N. American Conifers, xxiii. 231 ; xxiv. 108. Silver Fir—F. B., xxii. 106. *Sirex juvencus* and *S. gigas*—W. Somerville, xv. 200. Sir Herbert Maxwell on Neglected Woodlands, xix. 357. Sir Walter Scott on Thinning, xxii. 114. Sir William Schlich, K. C. I. E., xxiii. 105. "Slime-Flux" on Beech-Trees, xx. 122. South African School of Forestry—F. B., xix. 356. Sparks from Engines, xvi. 524 ; Prevention of, xvii. 326. Spread of Fungus Diseases by means of Hybernating Mycelium —A. W. B., xx. 122. Suggested Use of *Abies nobilis* for Planting up Blanks in Old and Young Woods— D. Stewart, xxiii. 103. Survivor of Rannoch Black Wood —F. B., xvi. 320. Sweden, xvii. 339. Sweden's New Forestry Laws, xviii. 227. Sylvicultural Experiments at Novar —R. C. Munro Ferguson, xx. 98. Sylvicultural Notes—W. Hall, xxii. 104. Systematic Destruction of Squirrels—A. Fraser, xx. 119.

Tap-Root of Larch—J. A. Campbell, xvi. 323. Tasmanian Wood, A New, xix. 210. Testing of Forest Seeds, xxvii. 239. *The Forester*, Note upon Dr Nisbet's Criticism of Report of Departmental Committee on Forestry in Preface to— R. C. Munro Ferguson, xix. 199 ; Reply thereto — J. Nisbet, xix. 200. *The Forester*, Note on Review of — J. Nisbet, xix. 362. Timber :—Douglas Fir — Frank Scott, xxvii. 106 ; A New—A. D. R., xx. 127 ; of Silver Fir and Spruce, xvii. 158 ; Preservation, Seasoning and Strengthening of, xvii. 325 ; Prices of, in S. of England (1904-05)—W. Storie, xix. 204 ; Production of, in Great Britain, xxvii. 108. Seasoning of, xix. 215 ; Weight of, xix. 217 ; What is a Load of ? xix. 216. Timber - Growing, Profits from, in Hampshire—W. Storie, xix. 205. Timber Imports and Exports—F. B., xvi. 327. Timber Resources of New Zealand, xxiii. 233. Timber-Supply : — From Sweden — E. Nilson, xx. 252 ; of United States, xxiv. 221. Timber-Trade of E. Siberia, xxiii. 110. Treatment of Canker in Trees, xvii. 157. Tree - Felling by Machinery, xxiii. 232. Tree-Girth Measurements—D. Christison, xvi. 529. Tree-Growth in 1913—J. M'Callum, xxviii. 118. *Tree-Strangling Fungus, A, xix. 358. Trees at Auchincruive, Ayrshire—G. Leven, xix. 212. Trees, Two Exceptional—W. B. Havelock, xxi. 110. Tupelo Wood, xix. 210.

" Unemployed " :—Problem of the, xvii. 161 ; Value of Work done by, xxiii. 107. United States, Forests of, xviii. 229. University of Cambridge, xxvi. 100. Visits of Foreign Professors to Scotland, xxiv. 107.

Water in Creosote for Timber Preserving, xix. 211. West Africa, Department of Woods and Forests for, xvii. 160. Willow Timber, Value of—A. D. R., xx. 127. *Witch's Broom on *Pseudotsuga Douglasii*—J. M'Callum, xxviii. 116. Wood: Its Botanical and Technical Aspect, xxi. 233.

Wood Paving, British Oak for, xviii. 226. Wood Preservation by Electrolysis, xx. 128. Wood-Pulp, xxiii. 233. Woods, Systematic Management of, xvii. 338. Working-Plan for Ardross Woods—F. B., xxi. 230.

Novar: — Experimental Plots at— C. Marriott, xx. 101. Sylvicultural Experiments at — R. C. Munro Ferguson, xx. 98. Underplanted Larch Plantations at — W. Mackenzie, xxiii. 35.

Novar and Raith Working-Plans— R. C. Munro Ferguson, xvi. 96.

Novar System of Combating Larch Disease, xix. 339 ; Note on—J. Nisbet, xx. 39.

Novar Woods, Scheme of Management. F. Bailey, J. J. R. Meiklejohn, J. D. B. Whyte, and W. Mackenzie, xvi. 25.

Nürnberg, Forestry in Exhibition at (1906), xx. 233.

Nurseries:—and Gardens, Forest—F. Bailey, xxi. 54. Forest, at Indian Head, Sask., xxiii. 67 ; xxiv. 67. Home, Expediency of Establishing —J. G. Thomson, iv. 15.

Nursery and Plantation Competition, xxvii. 85 ; xxviii. 110.

Nursery Treatment of Western or Californian Hemlock Spruce. J. M. Murray, xxi. 41.

Oak: — *And Beech Forests in Denmark—W. G. Smith, xxviii. 241. British—J. Smith, xiii. 21. British, for Wood-paving, xviii. 226. In Coppice-with-Standards in North of France—Prof. Fisher, xviii. 109. In Scotland – I. B Balfour, xvi. 315. Japanese, xxiii. 105.

Oak Bark. See Bark.

Oak Coppice. See Coppice.

Oak Tortrix or Leaf-Roller. R. S. MacDougall, xix. 196.

Oak Woods: — Of Glen Mor — J. Nisbet, xxv. 71. Self-Sown, of Sussex—R. W. Clutton, vii. 194. See xxvi. 147.

Obituary Notices:—*Lieut. Col. F. Bailey, xxvii. 244. Baxter, R. (J. Whytock), xix. 244. Booth, J., xxii. 120. Boppe, L. (A. Jolyet and F. B.), xx. 258 ; xxi. 114, 116. Brandis, Sir D. (W. Schlich), xxi. 112. Broilliard, C. (A. G. H.-H.), xxiv. 119. Dewar D., (J. A. Gossip), xvi. 336. Dunn,

M. (W. M. Gilbert), xvi. 132. Fisher, W. R. (A. S.), xxiv. 118. Fraser, P. N. (A. D. R.), xix. 241. Innes, Lieut.-Col. F. N. (S. J. G.), xx. 257. Laird, D. P. (A. D. R.), xix. 241. *Mackenzie, D. F., xxiv. 114. Mackinnon, W. (A. D. R.), xx. 136. Mansfield, Earl of (R. M. F.), xix. 367. Mayr, Prof. H. (A. W. B.),xxiv. 239 ; *xxvi. 120. Methven, John, xxvii. 248. Pitcaithley, A. (A. D. R.), xix. 242. Ramsden, Sir John, Bart., xxviii. 272. Robertson, J., xxiv. 117. Seafield, Caroline, Countess of (W. T.), xxvi. 119. Thomson, J. G., xxvii. 247.

Official Notifications : — Board of Agriculture for Scotland ; Forestry Development ; Grant from Development Fund ; Forestry Instruction in Ireland, xxvi 156 Statement by Development Commission ; Advisory Committee on Forestry ; Technical Advice for Private Owners, xxvii. 28.

Oleoresins of some Western Pines— A. Lauder, xxviii. 267.

Ordnance Survey Maps of United Kingdom, xx. 256.

Ornamental Trees, Comparative Value of Exotic Coniferæ as. T. Wilkie, xii. 206 ; A. D. Webster, xii. 246.

Osiers, Cultivation of. R. Sinclair, xxi. 50.

Oxford University : — Diploma in Forestry at—F. B., xix. 354. Forestry at, xxvi. 225.

Paisley. See Exhibitions.

Paris : — Forestry Exhibition at (1900)—J. S. Gamble, xvi. 339. International Forest Congress at, xxvii. 112.

Parliament and Forestry, xviii. 221.

Parry, J. : Afforestation of Waterworks' Catchment Areas, xvii. 223 ; Training of Foresters, xix. 320.

Pasture Lands, Comparison between the yields from, and Afforestation —Alex. Lauder, xxvii. 113.

Paterson, A. : Roads, Bridges, Fords and Walks on Estates, iii. 23 ; Transplanting by M'Glashen's Apparatus, iii. 102.

Pathological Specimens for Exhibition. A. W. Borthwick, xvii. 155.

Pear Midge, xv. 314.

Pearson, J. : Valuation of Woods, etc., for Transfer, xvi. 398.

*Peat, Formation of Plantations on, —Donald Grant, xxviii. 72.

Peat-Mosses :—Remains of Ancient Forests in Scottish — M. I. N., xxii. 113. Scottish, History of— A. W. B., xx. 125.

Peebles. See Exhibitions.

Peebles, A. : Arboriculture in Hampshire, viii. 25 ; Disposing of Produce of Woods and Plantations, vii. 159 ; Woods and Plantations of Highclere, Hants, vi. 245.

Penrhyn, N. Wales :—*Coniferæ at— A. D. Webster, xi. 55. Plantations on Estate of—A. D. Webster, xii. 165.

Pentland, Lord, Correspondence with, in regard to Small Landholders' (Scotland) Bill, and Department of Forestry, xxvi. 1.

Peridermium, xvii. 344.

Perth. See Exhibitions.

Perthshire, E., Rate of Growth of Mature Timber-Crops in— J. Nisbet, xix. 70.

Peziza, *xvii. 19 ; xvii. 344.

Philip, R. : Hedgerow Timber Trees, iii 40 ; Local Arboricultural Societies, i. 38 ; Planting, i. 86 ; Preparation of Waste Land for Planting, ii. 21 ; Pruning Forest Trees, i. 20 ; ii. 11 ; Thinning Plantations, i. 43.

Philosophy of Arboriculture and Landscape Gardening. J. G. Macvicar, iv. 138.

Phoma :—W. Somerville, xv. 191 ; G. Leven, xv. 319.

Physiology and Structure of Trees and Shrubs. D. F. Mackenzie, xiv. 114.

*Piccadilly, etc., Tree-Pruning in. I. B. Balfour, xxvi. 31.

Picea :—Alba, as Wind-Mantle, xvi. 473. Nordmanniana — A. D. Webster, ix. 94. Pectinata − C. Y. Michie, v. 138 ; see Silver Fir.

Pine :—*Blending of Foliage of, etc., for Landscape Effect—C. Y. Michie, iv. 73. Corsican—J. M'Laren, v. 52 ; A. D. Webster, xi. 181. Corsican in Dorset—J. M'Callum, xxiv. 45. Scots, A Large, xxvi. 231. Scots, Annual Increment of, xxiv. 52 ; xxvi. 160 ; xxvii. 34. Scots, Diseased, on Land formerly Arable, xx. 248. *Scots, Natural Regeneration of, at Beauly, etc.—G. Brown, xix. 17. Scots. Protection of, against Black Game — W.

Steuart Fothringham, xxviii. 117. *Scots, Root Disease in, on Farm Lands—B. Ribbentrop, xxi. 143. *The Mountain—J. Stirling-Maxwell, xxi. 10. Transplanting, etc.—R. Hutchison, iv. 3. Diseases of Pine, see xvii. 343.

Pine Beetle, xv. 65.

Pines, Western, Oleoresins of. A. Lauder, xxviii. 267.

Pinetum : — *Houston — W. Tivendale, vii. 38. Wass—R. Brown, iv. 164.

Pine Weevil. See Weevil, and Reports by Hon. Scientists.

Pine Weevil, Large Brown — Board of Agri. Leaflet on, xxviii. 118.

Pinus Laricio :− J. M'Laren, v. 52. And P. sylvestris, Larch Disease on—H. Maxwell, xx. 117. See Pine.

Pinus Sylvestris :—Experiments with Seed—F. Story, xxiii. 168. Larch Disease on, etc., xx. 117.

Pirrie, A. : Early Management of Plantations, i. 207.

Pissodes : — A. Mitchell, xv. 199. The Genus—R. S. MacDougall, xv. 25. See Reports by Hon. Scientists.

Pitcaithley, A. : Arboriculture in Dumfries, Kirkcudbright, and Wigtown, xiii. 293 ; *Forester's Cottage, xi. 506 ; Plantations, etc., at Brahan, Ross, xi. 501. Obituary —A. D. R., xix. 242.

*Pitting v. Notching, xxiii. 111.

Pit-wood, Scarcity of, xxviii. 266.

Pit-wood Timber, Advantages of Growing — W. M. Stewart, xix. 282.

Pit-wood Trade, Bo'ness. F. Bailey, xvi. 9.

*Pit-wood Working Circle, Raith, Plan for, xv. 223.

Plans, Working :—*Alice Holt Forest, —W. Schlich and W. F. Perree, xix. 83. Ardross Woods—F. B., xxi. 230. Ardross, and Larch Canker—A. D. Richardson, xxii. 64. *Blackmoor, Bradshott, and Temple Woods, Hants—J. Nisbet, xvi. 193. Castle Hill Woodlands, 1905 to 1919—F. Story, xx. 36. Chopwell Woods—W. S., xxii. 61. Glen Mor—W. Dawson, xxv. 60. Note on Raith and Novar—R. C. Munro Ferguson, xvi. 96. *Novar Woods—F. Bailey, J. J. R. Meiklejohn, J. D. B. Whyte, and W. Mackenzie, xvi. 25. Preparing, for British Woodlands—J. Nisbet,

xx. 30. Progress, in India, in Preparation of, xxvi. 98. *Raith Pit-wood Working Circle — F. Bailey, G. U. Macdonald, xv. 223. See also xvi. 4.

Plantations : — Belts of, on Hill Pasture Land—T. Wilkie, xii. 337. Disposing of Produce—A. Peebles, vii. 159. Draining—L. Bayne, vii. 250. Early Management of—A. Pirrie, i. 207. *Enclosing—A. Slater, ix. 199. *Fences — W. Thomson, i. 69. Formation of—J. F. Annand, xiii. 268 ; A. C. Forbes, xiii. 91. D. A. Glen, xi. 173 ; A. M'D. Grant, x. 204 ; J. Rodger, xiv. 133 ; *on Deep Peat —Donald Grant, xxviii. 72. John, Duke of Atholl, his Larch Plantations, and the Larch Disease—J. Booth, xvii. 232. Laying out of Mixed, and Maintenance for first Twenty-tive Years—D. M. Macdonald, xix. 32. J. M. Murray, xix. 44. Planting of Mixed Fir—W. Gilchrist, iii. 2. Preparation of Produce for Sale—W. Thomson, vi. 275. Primitive Types in Scotland—G. P. Gordon, xxiv. 153. Rearing and Management of Hardwood—L. Bayne, ix. 158 ; A. M'D. Grant, xi. 373 ; T. R. Milroy, x. 47 ; A. Slater, x. 61 ; D. Tait, ix. 225 ; T. Wilkie, ix. 152, 242. Reclamation of Neglected —J. Thomson, i. 114 ; W. Thomson, vi. 205 ; J. Whyte, i. 110. *Roads and Walks—R. E. Brown, iii. 8. Teak, at Nelambur, Madras—J. Ferguson, ix. 114. Thinning—J. Darling, i. 210 ; W. Gilchrist, v. 43 ; R. Philip, i. 43. Trees for Exposed Margins of—A. Gilchrist, iv. 24. Underplanted Larch, at Novar—W. Mackenzie, xxiii. 35. Valuation of, tor Transfer — J. Pearson, xvi. 398.

Plantations, etc., on Estates of :— Brahan, Ross—A. Pitcaithley, xi. 501. Highclere, Hants — A. Peebles, vi. 245. Inverliever, xxi. 111. Mackintosh, Brae Lochaber —J. Hutton, viii. 233. Murthly, Grandtully, etc., Perthshire—D. F. Mackenzie, ix. 82. Penrhyn, N. Wales—A. D. Webster, *xi. 55 ; xii. 165. Raynham, Norfolk—A. Gorrie, xiii. 331. Sorn, Ayr—D. Barclay, xi. 29. Wentworth, York shire — G. Dodds, xii. 156.

Planters, Notes for. G. U. Macdonald, xvii. 287.

Planting : — As an Investment in Ireland — W. Harrower, x. 55. *At High Altitudes and in Exposed Situations, etc.—A. W. B. Edwards, xxvi. 37. Beech and Thorn Hedges—J. Kay, iv. 187. Best Size of Plants for, etc.— A. Slater, x. 39. Clearing Land for—D. F. Mackenzie, viii. 136. Deer Forests with Timber Trees for Shelter — D. F. Mackenzie, ix. 53. *Different Methods of—W. Maxwell, xxvi. 59. Distances at which Forest Trees should be Planted—L. Bayne, viii. 77. Exposed Margins of Plantations, Trees for — A. Gilchrist, iv. 24. Extensive — J. Brown, vi. 216. For Shelter—H. Shaw-Stewart, xxiv. 178. *Historical Notes of Early, in Scotland—H. B. Watt, xxvi. 12. In Groups. or Mixed Plantations—W. Gorrie, vii. 274. In Towns, Trees and Shrubs for— A. D. Webster, xiii. 123. Island of Arran as Field for — W. A. Mackenzie, xiii. 341. Landscape and Economic—C. S. France, xii. 322. Mixed Fir Plantations—W. Gilchrist, iii. 2. *Of High Moorlands—J. Stirling-Maxwell, xx. 1. On — W. Thomson, i. 75 ; R. Philip, i. 86. On Moss Land—J. Thomson, i. 120. *On Turfs, Belgian System of — J. Stirling-Maxwell, xxiii. 153. Preparation of Ground for—J. Darling, i. 96. Preparation of Waste Land for—R. Philip, ii. 21. Sandhills — A. Gorrie, xiii. 350 ; J. Hutton, viii. 19. Scotch Fir after Old Scotch Fir — W. M'Corquodale, ii. 48. Tree, at San Jorge, Uruguay — C. E. Hall, xiii. 220. Trees and Underwood for Sea - coasts — W. Gilchrist, v. 143 ; C. Y. Michie, v. 150. Underwood as Cover for Game—A. Gilchrist, iv. 103 ; W. Gilchrist, ix. 29, 91. Waste Land for Profit—G. U. Macdonald, xviii. 183 ; J. Nisbet, xix. 259. With the Mattock—T. Hall, xxiii. 104.

Plants :—Charcoal-Producing—C. Y. Michie, vi. 319. Ligneous, of Hampshire—J. Smith, xii. 356.

Poland, Forests of, xviii. 227.

Poplars, Black and Ontario—I. B. Balfour, xvi. 314.

*Portuguese E. Africa, Arboricultural

Notes from. J. A. Alexander, xx. 194.

Post Office : — Appointments by — F. B., xx. 113. Supply of Telegraph Poles to—F. Bailey, xix. 343.

Powerscourt, Coniferæ at — C. S. France, v. 83.

Preparation :—Of Ground for Planting—J. Darling, i. 96. Of Waste Land for Planting—R. Philip, ii. 21.

Presentation to Dr Cleghorn, xii. 198.

Preservative :—Against Wood-Splitting, xxiv. 110. Timber, Experiments on Relative Value of, xxi. 201.

Preserving :—Sleepers from Decay, xxiii. 234. Wood by Electrolysis, xx. 128. See Timber, and Creosoting.

Prestonfield, Edinburgh. See Exhibitions.

Primitive Woodland and Plantation Types in Scotland. G. P. Gordon, xxiv. 153.

Private Forestry, Encouragement of. A. Schwappach, xx. 212.

Probationers for Indian Forest Service, xix. 107 ; xxi. 191 ; xxiv. 212.

Produce, Forest :—*Disposing of—A. Peebles, vii. 159. Preparation of, for Sale — W. Thomson, vi. 275.

Pruning :—Different Methods of—A. Gilchrist, vii. 40. Forest Trees— C. Y. Michie, v. 34 ; R. Philip, i. 20 ; ii. 11. In Relation to Production of Timber—J. B. Smyth, viii. 54. *Its Ornament and Utility—A. T. Gillanders, xi. 49. Judicious—W. M'Corquodale, x. 166. Rarer Coniferæ—R. Hutchison, iv. 170. *Trees in St James's Park and Piccadilly, London — I. B. Balfour, xxvi. 31.

Prussia :—*Investigations in Regard to Quality of Timber—W. Somerville, xv. 279. State Forests of— W. Somerville, xiv. 140.

Pseudotsuga :—List of Species, viii. 108. Douglasii, Rate of Growth of, in Woods of Saxony—communicated by J. Booth, xx. 104. *Witch's Broom on—J. M'Callum, xxviii. 116. See Douglas Fir.

Pulp Industry of Canada, xxiii. 108. See Wood-Pulp.

Pyrenées, Basses, Forests of. G. Cadell, xvii. 104.

Rabbits :—xxiv. 109. Injurious to Woodlands and Fields, Destruction of—J. Nisbet, xix. 104. See xx. 140.

Raffan, A. : Larch Sawfly, xxvi. 220.

Rafn, J. : Tree Seed-Testing, xvi. 277, 407.

Railway and Canal Traffic Act, 1888. A. T. Williamson, xii. 425.

Railway Fires Act, 1905. J. Nisbet, xix. 73 ; F. B., xxii. 111.

Railway Rates on Timber, xvii. 318 ; R. Galloway, xxvi. 96.

Railway Sleepers : — From Home-Grown and Foreign Timber, xxvii. 188. From Irish-Grown Timber, xviii. 225. Impregnation of, with Chloride of Barium, xvii. 340. Preserving from Decay, xxiii. 234.

*Railways, Woods and. W. Brown, vi. 192.

Rainfall : — At Inverliever (1910), xxiv. 220. Forests and—R. C. Mossman, xx. 188. In Wooded and Unwooded Countries — R. Hutchison, vii. 10. See vii. 114, 285. See also Climate, and Reports by Hon. Scientists.

Raismes, Valenciennes, Forest of. Prof. Fisher, xviii. 109.

Raith :—And Novar Working-Plans —R. C. Munro Ferguson, xvi. 96. *Practical Course in Forestry at (1910), xxiv. 208. *Working-Plan for Pit-wood Working Circle—F. Bailey and G. U. Macdonald, xv. 223.

Ramsden, Sir John, Bart., Obituary, xxviii. 272.

Rannoch Black Wood, Survivor of. F. B., xvi. 320.

Rate of Growth :—Of Mature Timber-Crops in E. Perthshire—J. Nisbet, xix. 70. Of Pseudotsuga Douglasii in Woods of Saxony, xx. 104.

Rating Act (1874), xxiii. 137.

Rating of Woodlands. R. Galloway, xxvi. 96.

Raynham, Norfolk, Plantations on Estate of. A. Gorrie, xiii. 331.

Reading - rooms and Libraries for Working-men on Landed Estates. R. E. Brown, iii. 13.

Re-afforestation :—In Ireland, xxi. 107. See Afforestation, and Notes and Queries.

Re-afforesting Association, Midland. A. D. R., xx. 107.

Reclaimed Lands, Afforestation of, xxi. 229.

Reclamation of Neglected Plantations. J. Thomson, i. 114 ; W. Thomson, vi. 205 ; J. Whyte, i. 110.

Regeneration of Forests, Natural. See Natural Regeneration.

Register for Foresters :—Establishing —J. Kay, v. 155 ; C. Y. Michie, v. 158. The Society's—R. Galloway, xix. 350.

Remains :—Of Ancient Forests in Scottish Peat-Mosses—M. I. N., xxii. 113. Vegetable, at Newstead, Melrose, xxiii. 31.

Renfrew, Excursion to, 1905. A. D. Richardson, xix. 180.

Reports by Honorary Scientists :—
Prof. I. B. Balfour (Botanist) :— Black and Ontario Poplars, xvi. 314. Oak in Scotland, xvi. 315. Dr A. W. Borthwick (Cryptogamist) : — *Agaricus melleus*, xvii. 154. Canker in Japanese Larch, xix. 195 ; xx. 96. *Coccus fagi*, xvii. 154. *Cryptomyces maximus*, xviii. 212. *Hyalopus populi*, xix 195. *Lophodermium Pinastri*, xvii. 343. *Lathræa squamaria*, xix. 195. *Nectria* on Larch, xvii. 344. *Peridermium pini*, xvii. 344. *Peziza Wilkommii*, xvii. 344. *Sphærella taxi*, xvii. 154. *Trametes radiciperda*, xvii. 153.

Prof. W. Somerville (Cryptogamist) : — *Phoma pithya* on Douglas Fir, xv. 191. *Roestelia lacerata* ("Cluster-Cup") on Hawthorn, xv. 306. *Trametes radiciperda* on Larch, xv. 190.

Dr R. S. MacDougall (Entomologist) : — *Aphis abietina*, xxviii. 267. *Carabus*, xvii. 346. *Cecidomyia heterobia* (Galls on Willow) *xviii. 210 ; xix. 198. *Clerus formicarius*, xvii. 345. *Diplosis pyrivora* (Pear Midge), xv. 314. *Goes tigrina*, xv. 308. *Hylesinus palliatus*, xvi. 152. *Hylesinus piniperda* (Pine Beetle), xv. 65, 193 ; xvii. 345. *Hylobius abietis* (Large Pine Weevil), xvi. 154. *Liparis dispar* (Gipsy Moth), xv. 195. List of Insects and Trees on which they are found, xv. 307. *Lophyrus pini* and *L. rufus*, xx. 96. *Melolontha vulgaris* (Cockchafer), xvii. 345 ; *xviii. 208. *Nematus Erichsoni* (Large Larch Sawfly), xx. 96 : xxviii. 267. *Orchestes querci*, xvii.

345. *Pissodes notatus* (Small Brown Weevil), xv. 192, 308. *Pissodes pini*, xv. 311. *Retinia buoliana* (Pine Shoot Twister), xx. 97. *Retinia resinella*, xvii. 346. *Rhagium bifasciatum*, xvii. 346. *Rhizophagus depressus*, xvii. 345. *Rhyssa persuasoria*, xv. 312 ; xvii. 345. *Sciurus vulgaris* (Squirrel), xv. 68. *Sirex gigas* (Giant Wood Wasp) and *S. juvencus* (Steel - blue Wood - Wasp), xv. 194, 311. *Tortrix curtisella*, xix. 198. *Tortrix viridana* (Oak *Tortrix* or Leaf-Roller), xix. 196.

R. C. Mossman, F.R.S.E. (Meteorologist) :—Meteorology of Scotland for year ending Sept. 30, 1896, xv. 61 ; 1897, xv. 186 ; 1898, xv. 301 ; 1899, xvi. 146 ; 1900, xvi. 306.

Reports on Forestry. See Committee and Agriculture, Board of.

Research at Indian Forest School, xx. 115.

Research Work and Educational Methods. E. R Burdon, xxvii. 60.

Research Work, Timber, at the Cambridge School of Forestry, xxviii. 105.

Retinia, xvii. 346 ; xx. 97.

Retirements :—Mr Grant Thomson— R. M. F., xxiv. 113 ; Mr J. Kay— A. D. R., xxiv. 225.

Returns of Prices :—Forest Produce (1859), ii. 41. Scots Fir at Abernethy—W. Gouk, i. 102. Timber and Oak Bark (1856), i. 101. Timber and other Forest Produce and Forest Labour (1857), i. 219. Timber, Bark, etc. (1869), vi. 144. Timber, Home-Grown (1901)—D. F. Mackenzie, xvi. 504. Timber-Trees in Scotland (1869)—W. Gilchrist, v. 136.

*Retz, Forests of. Prof. Fisher, xviii. 90.

Reuss, Prof. : Report on Forestry Exhibition, Edinburgh (1884), xi. 562.

Review of *The Forester*. Note on. J. N., xix. 362.

Reviews of Books. See Book Notices. *Rhagium*, xvii. 346. *Rhizophagus*, xvii. 345. *Rhododendron barbatum*, is it Insectivorous? H. Maxwell, xx. 118. *Rhyssa*. xv. 312 ; xvii. 345. Ribbentrop, B. : Continental Notes— Germany. xxi. 180 ; xxii. 227 ; xxiii. *38, 204 ; *xxiv. 194 ; *xxvi.

204 ; *xxvii. 212 ; *Root Disease in Scots Pine on Farm Lands, xxi. 143; Royal Commission on Afforestation : their German and English Critics, and Remarks thereon, xxii. 180.

Richardson, A. D. : Ardross Working-Plan and Larch Canker, xxii. 64 ; *Colorado Variety of Douglas Fir, xviii. 194 ; *Douglas Fir Plantation at Taymount, xviii. 200 ; Excursion to Argyll, Ayr and Renfrew (1905), xix. 180 ; Excursion to Northumberland and Durham (1906), xx. 81. Forestry Exhibition at H. and A. Society's Show at Glasgow (1905), xix. 190. Mr Henry's Investigation of Elm Seedlings, xxiv. 186. Our Imported Coniferous Timber, xvii. 238.

Roads, etc. : — On Estates — A. Paterson, iii. 23. *Plantation— R. E. Brown, iii. 8.

Roberts, M. F. : Letter on Creosoting of Spruce, Larch, Oak and Scots Pine, xviii. 224.

Robertson, D. : Report on Excursion to Germany (1895), xiv. 180.

Robertson, D. F. : Extraction of Tree-Stumps, xvi. 320.

Robertson, J. : Obituary Notice, xxiv. 117.

Rodger, J. : Formation of Plantations, xiv. 133 ; Lever Appliance, xvi. 189.

Roestelia, xv. 306.

Roman Military Station at Newstead, Melrose, Vegetable Remains from Site of, xxiii. 31.

Rooks feeding on Pine Beetles—J. Boyd, xix. 206.

*Root Disease in Scots Pine on Farm Lands. B. Ribbentrop, xxi. 143.

Roots, etc., Economic Uses of. J. Johnston, v. 55.

Ross, R. : Peeling and Harvesting of Native Barks, ix. 58.

Royal Agricultural Society of England :— Tour in Denmark (1908)—F. Story, xxii. 56. See Exhibitions.

Royal Botanic Garden, Edinburgh, Proposed Guild, xxvii. 239.

Royal Commission on Afforestation : their German and English Critics, etc. B. Ribbentrop, xxii. 180. Report of—J. Stirling-Maxwell, xxii. 186 ; J. F. Annand, xxii. 188.

Royal English Arbori. Soc., Visit to German Forests—A. T. Gillanders, xxviii. 100.

Rural Employment in Ireland, etc., xxi. 107.

Russia : — Timber Resources of European, xviii. 228. Timber Trade with United Kingdom, xviii. 228. Wood Business on Rivers Dnieper and Beregina, x. 243.

Russian Larch, xix. 209.

Russian Timber Society, xvii. 336.

*Rustic Bridges, Arbours, etc., Construction of. C. Y. Michie, iv. 115.

Rutherford, J. : Drainage, i. 12 ; Thinning, i. 54.

St Amand, Valenciennes, Forest of. Prof. Fisher, xviii. 109.

*St James's Park, etc., Tree-Pruning in. I. B. Balfour, xxvi. 31.

St Louis Exhibition (Society's Exhibit at), xviii. 223.

Sakhalin, Larch on, xvii. 159.

Sampson, H. C. : Effects of Hailstorm on Growing Timber, xvi. 467.

Sandhills :—Experiments in Planting —J. Hutton, viii. 19. Planting of, at Holkham, Norfolk — A. Gorrie, xiii. 350.

San Jorge. Uruguay, Tree-Planting at. C. E. Hall, xiii. 220.

Saskatchewan, Forest Nursery Station at Indian Head, xxiii. 67 ; xxiv. 67.

Sawdust : — W. Brown, vi. 192. Alcohol from, xix. 362.

Sawfly : — *Attack by Larvæ — F. Moon, xxi. 52. Birch and Alder —J. Boyd, xix. 207. Larch, xxiv. 218 ; A. Raffan, xxvi. 220. Large Larch, xxiii. 186 ; *R. S. Mac-Dougall, xx. 43 ; Attack by — A. W. B. Edwards, xxiv. 42. See xx. 96.

Saxony :—Rate of Growth of *Pseudotsuga Douglasii* in Woods of, xx. 104. *State Forests of—A D. Hopkinson, xxvii. 174 ; *xxviii. 28.

Scammell, E. T. : Forest Resources of Australia, xvii. 249.

Schlich, W : Address at Inauguration of Chair of Forestry, etc., at Royal Agricultural College, Cirencester (Timber Supplies ; Economic Forestry ; Dangers to Forest Trees, etc.), xvii. 185 ; *Douglas Fir in Scotland, xii. 226 ; Forest Operations in Co. Galway, xvi. 249 ; Forestry Education, xv. 89. Larch Bug, "Aphis," or "Blight," xii. 423 ; Letter on Afforestation of

Surplus Lands, xxi. 225 ; Obituary Notice of Sir D. Brandis, xxi. 112 ; Our Forestry Problem, xvii. 213 ; Outlook of World's Timber Supply, xvi. 355 ; State in Relation to Forestry, xxii. 130 ; *Working-Plan for Alice Holt Forest, xix. 83. His Forests at Mirwart (Col. Bailey), xvi. 241. See xxiii. 105.

Schools, Forest. See Forest Schools.

Schwappach, A. : Encouragement of Private Forestry, xx. 212 ; Forestry in Britain, xvii. 169 ; Importance of Density in Sylviculture, xv. 3 ; Report on Visit to Forests of Scotland (1896), xv. 11.

*Schwarzwald, Forestry in the. J. F. Annand, xxi. 159.

Sciurus, xv. 68.

Scone, Excursion to (1904), xviii. 61.

Scotland : — Afforestation in Highlands and Islands of—W. A. Mackenzie, xiii. 318. Botanical Survey of—A. W. B., xx. 122. Demonstration Forests for — xx. 113 ; F. L. C. Cowley-Brown, xxii. 20. Development of Forestry in : Deputation to Board of Agriculture, xxvi. 202 ; Discussion on, xxviii. 121. Distribution of Certain Forest Trees in, as shown by Post-Glacial Deposits—W. N. Niven, xvii. 97. Douglas Fir in — W. Schlich, xii. 226. English Elm in —H. Maxwell, xx. 244. Forestry in, in Reign of Queen Victoria—M. Dunn, xv. 109. Historical Notes of Early Tree-Planting in, xxvi. 12. Immediate Needs of Forestry in— J. Stirling-Maxwell, xxiii. 121. Primitive Woodland and Plantation Types in, xxiv. 153. Reforestation in, xx. 254. State Afforestation in—F. Bailey, xxi. 27. Visit to Forests of (1896)—A. Schwappach xv. 11.

Scots Fir. See Firs.

Scots Pine. See Pine.

Scott-Elliot, G. F. : Larch Seed, xxiv. 179.

Scott, Frank : Douglas Fir Plantation at Taymount, xxvii. 77 ; Uses of Douglas Fir Timber, xxvii. 106.

Scott, Sir Walter, on Thinning, xxii. 114.

Scottish Arboricultural Society (1854-1884), xi. 114.

Scottish Arboriculture, Literature of. R. Hutchison, vii. 211.

Scottish National Exhibition, Glasgow (1911), Forestry at. M. Feaks, xxvi. 85.

Sea, Trees and Underwood best suited for Planting near. W. Gilchrist, v. 143 ; C. Y. Michie, v. 150.

Sea - Worms, Teredo navalis, and other. F. Bailey, xxiii. 196.

Season and Growth of Trees. A. C. Forbes, xv. 75.

Seasoning, etc., of Timber. See Timber.

Secretary for Scotland, Deputation to, 1913, xxviii. 1.

*Sections of Woods Grown in Britain. D. F. Mackenzie, xiv. 39.

Seed :—Collection, Preparation, etc., of Forest Tree—J. M'Lean, x. 156. *Experiments with Tree — W. Somerville, xv. 133. Larch—G. F. Scott-Elliot, xxiv. 179. Of N. American Conifers, xxiii. 231 ; xxiv. 108. Raising Exotic Conifers from, xxvi. 46. Scottish Tree, for Norway and Sweden, xvi. 526. Testing Tree—J. Rafn, xvi. 277, 407.

*Seed-beds, Basic Slag on. J. Boyd, xxi. 229.

*Seed Experiments with Pinus sylvestris. F. Story, xxiii. 168.

Seeds, Forest, Testing of, xxvii. 239.

*Selborne's, Earl of, Hampshire Woods, Working - Plan for. J. Nisbet, xvi. 193.

Self-Sown Oak Woods of Sussex. R. W. Clutton, vii. 194.

Shale Industry, Damage to Trees by, xvi. 470.

Shaw-Stewart, Sir H. : Japanese Larch, xxviii. 270 ; Planting for Shelter, xxiv. 178 ; Some Lessons from the Recent Gales, xxvii. 172.

Sheep Farms, Glen Mor, xxv. 13.

Shelter :—Planting for — H. Shaw-Stewart, xxiv. 178. Trees for, in Islands of Scotland—R. Hutchison, ix. 140. See xxvi. 37.

Shootings : Fort Augustus Block, Glen Mor, xxv. 19.

Siberia, E., Timber Trade of, xxiii. 110.

Sierra Leone, Forests and Forestry Problems in, xxvi. 98.

Silver Fir. See Firs.

Silvicultural :—*Notes of Interest— A. Murray xxvii. 206 ; Treatment of Douglas Fir — W. Steuart Fothringham, xxviii. 248.

Simpson, A. : *Machine for Mending Broken Strands in Wire Fences, xiii. 359.

Sinclair, R. : Cultivation of Osiers, xxi. 50.

Sirex, xv. 194, 311. See Notes and Queries.

Sitka Spruce :—And other Trees, in Linlithgowshire and Stirlingshire— H. M. Cadell, xxiii. 158. *As Tree for Hill Planting and General Afforestation — J. D. Crozier, xxiii. 7. In Ireland—A. C. Forbes, xxviii. 264.

Slater, A. : *Enclosing Plantations, ix. 199 ; Rearing and Management of Hardwood Plantations, x. 61 ; Size of Plants and Methods of Planting, to produce best results, x. 39 ; Some Aspects of Excursion to Germany (1895), xiv. 163 ; *Tools used in Forestry, ix. 130 ; Wood damaged by Gases from Calcining Ironstone, vii. 184.

Sleepers, Railway :—From Home-Grown and Foreign Timber, xxvii. 188. Impregnation of, with Chloride of Barium, xvii. 340. Preserving from Decay, xxiii. 234.

"Slime-Flux" on Beech Trees, xx. 122.

Small Landholders (Scotland) Bill, Correspondence with Lord Pentland in regard to, xxvi. 1.

Small-Wood, Utilisation of. A. T. Williamson, xiii. 145.

Smith, J. : Arboriculture in Hampshire, xi. 511 ; British Oaks, xiii. 21 ; Ligneous Plants of Hampshire, xii. 356.

Smith, W. G. : Afforestation of Waterworks' Gathering-Grounds, xvii. 86 ; *Oak and Beech Forests in Denmark, xxviii. 241 ; Origin and Development of Heather Moorland, xvii. 117 ; Recent Publications on Swiss Forests, xxvii. 202 ; Vegetation of Woodlands, xxiv. 6, 131 ; Woods of Somerset, xx. 216.

Smoke Case, Glencorse (or Loganburn). A. Lauder, xxii. 15 ; M. I. Newbigin, xxii. 221.

Smoke, Injurious Effects of, on Trees. J. Boyd, xvii. 122.

Smyth, J. B. : Pruning in Relation to Production of Timber, viii. 54.

Soil :—Botanical Geography and Biological Utilisation of—M. Hardy, xvii. 110. Its Origin and Nature —J. Geikie, xx. 178 ; xxi. 16, 131.

Soils :—Accumulation of Nitrogen in Forest—A. Lauder, xx. 186. Best suited for different kinds of Forest Trees, as indicated by Plants growing naturally upon them—W. Gilchrist, vi. 296. Best suited for Particular Trees, etc.—R. Hutchison, iv. 31 ; Returns of, iv. 39. Trees best adapted for various— A. D. Webster, xiii. 254.

Somerset, Woods of. W. G. Smith, xx. 216.

Somerville, W. : Douglas Fir Plantation at Taymount, xvii. 269 ; *Experiments with Tree Seeds, xv. 133 ; Forestry in some of its Economic Aspects, xxii. 121 ; Heredity and Forestry, xxi. 1 ; How to Combat Injurious Forest Insects, xiii. 5 ; Influences affecting British Forestry, xii. 403 ; *Investigations in Prussia regarding Quality of Timber, xv. 279 ; Limited Liability Company to acquire Timber Estate, xiv. 100 ; Management of Birch Seed, xv. 319 ; *Natural Regeneration of Woods, xiii. 63 ; State Forests of Prussia, etc., xiv. 140. See Reports by Hon. Scientists.

Sorn, Ayr, Plantations on Estate of. D. Barclay, xi. 29.

South Africa, Forests in. J. C. Brown, ix. 45.

South African School of Forestry. F. B., xix. 356.

South America, Cultivation of India-Rubber Trees of. J. Ferguson, x. 108.

Sparks from Railway Engines :— Damage to Woods, etc., by—F. Bailey, xvi. 289. Prevention of, xvi. 524 ; xvii. 326.

Speyside, Excursion to (1907), xxi. 95.

Sphærella, xvii. 154.

Spiers, A. : Home Timber-Trade in E. of Scotland, xix. 66.

Spruce : — Albert or Hemlock, at Loganbank — F. B., xxi. 109. Annual Increment of, xxiv. 52 ; xxvi. 160 ; xxvii. 34. *Canker— G. Massee, xvii. 25. Dry Rot in —J. M'Neill, ii. 7. Protection of Young, from Frost—William Hall, xxvii. 51—G. U. Macdonald, xix. 287. Thinnings in Planted—M. Broilliard, xvii. 129. Timber of, xvii. 158. Western or Californian Hemlock—J. M. Murray, xxi. 41. White American as Wind-Mantle —J. F. Annand, xvi. 473. See Sitka Spruce.

Squirrels :—Damage by, xvii. 161.

Systematic Destruction of — A. Fraser, xx. 119. See xv. 68.

State:—And Afforestation, xxv. 83. And Private Woodlands — W. Dawson, xxiv. 121. Duty of, as regards Afforestation, xxiii. 1. In Relation to Afforestation—A. S. Hedderwick, xxiv. 150. In Relation to Forestry—W. Schlich, xxii. 130.

State Afforestation:—Deputation to Chief Secretary for Ireland, xix. 327. In Scotland—F. Bailey, xxi. 27.

State Forestry, Indian. S. H. Eardley-Wilmot, xxiii. 217.

State Forests:—Inverliever—R. C. Munro Ferguson, xxi. 22. Model, for Scotland, xv. 201, 221. *Saxony —A. D. Hopkinson, xxvii 174; xxviii. 28.

State School of Forestry in Forest of Dean. xxiv. 217.

Steam Power, Use of, in Forestry. D. F. Mackenzie, vii. 269.

Stebbing, E. P.: Collection and Preservation of Entomological Specimens, etc., xvii. 135; Forestry Education: Its Importance and Requirements, xxiv. 24.

Stewart, D.: Abies nobilis for Planting up Blanks in Old and in Young Woods, xxiii. 103; Effects of Frost on Plants of Larix europœa, and L. leptolepis compared, xxiii. 103.

Stewart, W. Maitland: Advantages of Growing Pit-wood Timber, xix. 282.

Stirling. See Exhibitions.

Stirling-Maxwell, Sir J.: *Belgian System of Planting on Turfs, xxiii. 153; Excursion to Lochaber (1910), xxiv. 73; Immediate Needs of Forestry in Scotland, xxiii. 121; Landowners' Forestry Co-operative Society, xxiv. 104, xxviii. 231; Place of Forestry in the Economic Development of Scotland, xxvii. 161; *Planting of High Moorlands, xx. 1: Report of Royal Commission on Afforestation, xxii. 186; *The Mountain Pine, xxi. 10.

Stirling of Keir, Capt.: Letter to Board of Agriculture. xxvii. 143.

Stirling of Keir, Capt., and Lovat, Lord: Forest Survey of Glen Mor, xxv.

Stirlingshire, Sitka Spruce, etc., in. H. M. Cadell, xxiii. 158.

Stocking of Ground, Glen Mor, xxv. 53.

Storie, W.: Decline in Value of Coppice Woods, xix. 203: Prices of Timber in South of England (1904-05). xix. 204: Profits from Timber-Growing in Hampshire, xix. 205.

Story, F.: Excursion to Sweden (1902), xvii. 68; Experimental Forestry Area in Wales, xxvii. 19; German Forestry, xviii. 138; Japanese Larch and Larch Disease, xvii. 333; R. E. A. Society's Tour in Denmark (1908), xxii. 56: *Seed Experiments with Pinus sylvestris. xxiii. 168: The Zürich Woods, xxii. 34; *Visit to German Forests, xvi. 424; Working-Plan (1905-1919) of Castle Hill Woodlands. xx. 36.

*Straining Pillars for Wire Fences. J. Kay, x. 32: C. Y. Michie, v. 75.

Strophosomus Coryli, Attack by. J. Macrae, xxiii. 185.

Stumps, Tree, Extraction of, xvi. 320.

Sulphur, Effects of, on Iron Fencing. T. Wilkie, viii. 165.

Surplus Lands, Afforestation of. W. Schlich, xxi. 225.

Survey, Botanical, of Scotland. A. W. B., xx. 122.

Sussex:—Forestry in—D. A. Glen, xvi. 414. Self-Sown Oak Woods of—R. W. Clutton, vii. 194.

Sweden:—Anticipated Curtailment of Timber Supplies from—F. Bailey, xix. 337. Finspong Forest, xvii. 339. Manufacture of Matches in— J. C. Brown, x. 223. New Forestry Laws, xviii. 227. Timber-Supply from—E. Nilson, xx. 252. See Excursions.

Swedish Forestry, Some Recent Developments in. E. Nilson, xix. 136.

Swiss Forests. Recent Publications on. W. G. Smith, xxvii. 202.

Switzerland:—And Germany, Visit to (1905)—J. J. R. Meiklejohn, xix. 303. Co-operative Agricultural Credit in, xvii. 331. Forest Administration in Canton Vaud—G. Cadell, xii. 78. See Excursions.

Sylvicultural Experiments at Novar. R. C. Munro Ferguson, xx. 93.

Sylvicultural Notes: F. Hall, xxi. 176; *xxii. 67: W. Hall, xxii. 104.

Sylviculture: — Estate — Conducted Experiments in, etc.—F. B., xx

102. Importance of Density in—A. Schwappach, xv. 3. International Congress of—J. S. Gamble, xvi. 262. Training in— R. C. Munro Ferguson, xx. 24.

TABLE for Conversion of Measurements. F. Bailey, xii. 351.

Tait, D. : Arboriculture in Yorkshire, vii. 137 ; Comparative Value of Timber - Trees grown in Britain, xii. 431 ; Disposing of Home-Grown Timber, vii. 72 ; Drainage, x. 172 ; Hardwood Plantations, ix. 225.

Talla Water-Catchment Area, Afforestation of. F. Bailey, xx. 106 ; xxvii. 104.

Tap-Root of Larch. J. A. Campbell, xvi. 323.

Tasmanian Wood, A New, xix. 210.

Taxation, Local, Afforestation and. K. Mackenzie, xxiii. 3.

Taxus baccata. See Yew Trees.

Taymount, Douglas Fir Plantation at. *A. D. Richardson, xviii. 200 ; Scott, Frank, xxvii. 77 ; W. Somerville, xvii. 269.

Teak Plantations at Nelambur, Madras. J. Ferguson, ix. 114.

*Telegraph Poles, Supply of, to Post Office. F. Bailey, xix. 343.

Temple, Sir R. : Lecture on Forests of India, x. 1.

*Temple Woods, Working-Plan for, xvi. 193.

Tenure :—Of Holdings, Glen Mor, xxv. 32. Of Land under Afforestation : Five Different Systems, xxv. 83.

Teredo navalis and other Sea-Worms. F. Bailey, xxiii. 196.

Terminology, Forest, xxvi. 97, 229.

Thinning :—M. Broilliard, xvi. 100 ; J. Darling, i. 210 ; W. Gilchrist, v. 43 ; "Justitia," ii. 3 ; R. Philip, i. 43 ; J. Rutherford, i. 54 ; W. Thomson, i. 64. Influence of, on Growth of Beech—A. C. Forbes, xvi. 116. In Planted Spruce—M. Broilliard, xvii. 129. Sir Walter Scott on, xxii. 114.

Thomson, G. : Retirement of, xxiv. 113.

Thomson, J. : Planting on Moss Land, i. 120 ; Reclamation of Neglected Plantations, i. 114.

Thomson, J. G. : Expediency of Establishing Home Nurseries, iv. 15. Obituary, xxvii. 247.

Thomson, P. Murray : *The Utilisation of Disused Pit-banks, xxvii. 30.

Thomson, W. : Address, 1855 (Qualifications necessary for Foresters), i. 8 ; Book-keeping for the Forest, i. 129 ; On Planting, i. 75 ; *Plantation Fences, i. 69 ; Practical Arboriculture, vi. 51 ; Preparation of Oak Bark for Sale, i. 25 ; Preparation of Produce of Plantations for Sale, vi. 275 ; Reclamation of Neglected Plantations, vi. 205 ; Thinning, i. 64. See viii. 1.

Thorn Hedges. W. Hall, xxvi. 165 ; J. Kay. iv. 187 ; W. H. Whellens, xxvi. 61.

Thuja gigantea :—A. D. Webster, xii. 341—*And Douglas Fir in Mixture. D. K. M'Beath, xxviii. 107.

Thuringian Forest, Visit to the. J. Michie, xiv. 105.

Timber :—And Death Duties—D. F. Mackenzie, xvi. 321. A new—A. D. R., xx. 127. *Coniferous, Economic Disposal of—D. K. M'Beath, xxviii. 251. Creosoted, xx. 128. Creosoting—*G. Leven, xvii. 93 ; by Absorption — J. Balden, xx. 62 ; of Home-Grown—W. B. Havelock, xx. 58 ; by Rüping Process, xxvii. 235. Cutting by Axe or Saw—T. Hogg, vi. 227 ; J. Milne, vi. 224. Douglas Fir, Uses of — Frank Scott, xxvii. 106. Disposing of Home-Grown—W. Gilchrist, vii. 146 ; D. F. Mackenzie, viii. 88 ; D. Tait, vii. 72. Economic Uses, and Comparative Values of — R. Hutchison, v. 109 ; C. Y. Michie, v. 114. Effects of Hailstorm on Growing—H. C. Sampson, xvi. 467. Enhanced Value of Canadian, xxiv. 99. Estate Duty on, under Finance Act of 1910, xxvi. £5. Exports from United Kingdom, xvi. 327 ; (1905), xix. 218. Felling of—J. M'Neill, ii. 17. Financial Results of Cultivation of—D. F. Mackenzie, xvi. 494. Growing for Profit in United Kingdom—A. E. Moeran, xix. 25. Growing Pit-Wood—W. M. Stewart, xix. 282. Hedgerow and Field—A. D. Webster, xi. 550. Imports into United Kingdom—F. B., xvi. 327 ; (1903-04), xviii. 238 ; (1905), xix. 218 ; (1909-10), xxiv. 219. Impregnation of—D. M'Laren, xvi. 525. *Its Strength and How to Test it—T. Hudson Beare, xix. 1.

*Manufacture of Home-Grown—
A. T. Williamson, xiii. 151.
Manufacturing — J. M'Pherson,
xvi. 448. Movements of Fluids in
Stems, in Relation to Felling and
Seasoning of—W. R. M'Nab, viii.
203. Of High Commercial Value,
Growing of—A. C. Forbes, xiv.
122. Of Silver Fir and Spruce,
xvii. 158. Our Imported Coniferous—A. D. Richardson, xvii.
238. Preservation, Seasoning and
Strengthening of, xvii. 325. Preserving— D. Hamilton, vi. 230 ;
*D. F. Mackenzie, xiv. 78. Prices
(1856), i. 101 ; (1857), i. 219 ;
(1869), vi. 144 ; Prices of Home,
xxvii. 222; Of Home-Grown (1901),
xvi. 504 ; J. M., xvi. 327 ; in
South of England (1904-05)—W.
Storie, xix. 204. Production of, in
Great Britain, xxvii. 108. Profits
from Growing of, in Hampshire—
W. Storie, xix. 205. Protection of,
against White Ants, xxiii. 227.
Pruning in Relation to Production of—J. B. Smyth, viii. 54.
*Prussian, Investigation regarding
Quality of—W. Somerville, xv.
279. Rate of Growth of Mature
Crops in E. Perthshire—J. Nisbet,
xix. 70. Rise and Fall in Value
of, in Scotland, etc. (1857-69)—R.
Hutchison, vi. 138. Research Work
at the Cambridge School of
Forestry, xxviii. 105 Scottish, and
its Uses—D. F. Mackenzie, x. 189 ;
Seasoning, xix. 215 ; W. Harrower,
x. 199 ; T. Wilkie, viii. 190.
Sections of Larch, showing Effects
of different Soils on Growth — G.
Brown, xxvi. 218. Treatment of
Crops to Middle Age, especially
Mixed Woods — "T.," xx. 21.
Value of Willow—A. D. R., xx.
127. Water in Creosote for Pre-
serving, xix. 211. Weight of, xix.
217. What is a Load of? xix. 216.
Wood, Plan to meet needs for,
xxviii. 78.
Timber Estate, Limited Liability
Company for acquiring. W.
Somerville, xiv. 100.
Timber Farms, Creation of Leasehold.
A. T. Williamson, xii. 418.
Timber-Growing, Profitable Co-opera-
tive. R. Galloway, xix. 291.
Timber-Planting, etc., in Great Brit.
and Ireland. J. Nisbet, xxii. 139.
Timber Preservatives, Experiments
on Relative Values of, xxi. 201.

Timber Resources :—Of Canada, xvi.
6. Of European Russia, xviii.
228. Of New Zealand, xxiii. 233.
Of United States, xvi. 6.
Timber Society, All Russian, xvii.
336.
Timber Supplies :—From Abroad—
A. T. Williamson, xiii. 353. From
Sweden — E. Nilson, xx. 252 ;
Anticipated Curtailment of — F.
Bailey, xix. 337. Of Australia—
Krichauff, viii. 110. Of United
States, xxiv. 221 ; W. Harrower,
x. 83. World's, Insufficiency of,
xvi. 384 ; Outlook of—W. Schlich,
xvi. 355. See xvii. 187.
Timber Trade :—Conference—G. U.
Macdonald, xxiii. 51. Home, in
E. of Scotland—A. Spiers, xix. 66.
Home, Outlook—D. Munro, xxiv.
139. Of E. Siberia, xxiii. 110.
Prices and Supplies — G. U.
Macdonald, xxviii. 270. Russia's,
with United Kingdom, xviii. 228.
Timber Trees :—Comparative Value
of Exotic Coniferæ as — A. D.
Webster, xii. 246 ; T. Wilkie, xii.
206. Comparative Value of,
Grown in Britain — D. F. Mac-
kenzie, x. 231 ; D. Tait, xii. 431.
*Douglas Firs as Commercial—J.
D. Crozier, xxi. 31. Hedgerow—R.
Philip, iii. 40. Introduced from
Eastern N. America—J. E. Brown,
v. 124. Most Profitable Felling
Age of—L. Bayne, vii. 175 ; W.
Gilchrist, v. 131 ; D. F. Mackenzie,
viii. 70. Of India—J. Nisbet, xix.
111 ; Distribution of, etc. — H.
Cleghorn, v. 91. Suitable to
different Soils, in Scotland, etc.—
R. Hutchison, iv. 31.
Tivendale, W. : Beetles which affect
Coniferæ, vii. 80 ; *Houston
Pinetum, vii. 38.
Tokio, Forestry Education at Imperial
University of, xviii. 232.
Tonite, Dynamite and, Use of, in
Forestry. D. F. Mackenzie, viii. 241.
*Tour of Inspection of Woods and
Afforestable Lands in Scotland,
Report on, xxviii. 154.
*Tools used in Forestry. A. Slater,
ix. 130.
Tortrix, xix. 196, 198.
Towns : Arboricultural Adornment
of—R. C. Munro Ferguson, xvi.
388. Trees and Shrubs for—A. D.
Webster, xiii. 123.
Town-Woods of Carlsbad (Bohemia).
J. Nisbet, xix. 150.

Traffic Act, Railway and Canal, 1888.
A. T. Williamson, xii. 425.
Training :—In Forestry, xxi. 102.
In Sylviculture — R. C. Munro
Ferguson, xx. 24. Of Foresters—
R. C. Munro Ferguson, xvi. 444 ;
J. Parry, xix. 320. Of Probationers
for Indian Forest Service — J.
Nisbet, xix. 107 ; xxi. 191.
Trametes, xvii. 153.
*Tramway, Forest. F. Moon, xxi.
Transplanting : — *Forest Trees —
C. Y. Michie, v. 20. *Machine—
J. Kay, vii. 186. M'Glashen's
Apparatus. iii. 102. Old Thorn
Hedges—W. Gilchrist, iv. 154.
Pines and Evergreen Shrubs—R.
Hutchison, iv. 3.
Tree-Growth in 1913. J. M'Callum,
xxviii. 118.
Trees :—A " Big Tree's " Centuries
of Life—W. B. Havelock, xx. 129.
Age of, viii. 84. And Climate—
W. Brown, v. 12 ; See vii. 118 ;
viii. 1. And Shrubs for Towns—
A. D. Webster, xiii. 123. And
Shrubs of Carnarvonshire—A. D.
Webster, xi. 481. Best adapted
for various Soils—A. D. Webster,
xiii. 254. Choice of, for Planting
—A. G. Hobart-Hampden, xxvi.
233. Damage to, by Shale In-
dustry, xvi. 470. Deciduous, for
Landscape Forestry—J. Methven,
xii. 94. *Experiments with Seeds
—W. Somerville, xv. 133. Felling
by Electricity, xxiv. 109. Forest
and Ornamental, of Recent Intro-
duction — J. M'Laren, x. 209.
Forest, Collection, etc., of Seeds—
J. M'Lean, x. 156. For Exposed
Margins of Plantations—A. Gil-
christ, iv. 24. *For High Altitudes
and Exposed Situations, xxvi. 37.
For Planting within Influence of
Sea—W. Gilchrist, v. 143 ; C. Y.
Michie, v. 150 For Shelter, in
Islands of Scotland—R. Hutchison,
ix. 140. *Grown on " Undrained
Moorband Pan "—A. Gilchrist, vi.
334. *Historical Notes of Early
Planting in Scotland—H. B. Watt,
xxvi. 12. How to Measure Annual
Growth of—W. Gorrie, ix. 103.
India-Rubber, of S. America—J.
Ferguson, x. 108. In Cities, xxiv.
93. In the Highlands—W. Brown,
vi. 192. Effects of Light and Shade
on—J. K., xxvii. 105. Injurious
Effects of Smoke on—J. Boyd, xvii.
122. *Instrument for Measuring

Heights of—W. Baillie, v. 171 ;
J. Kay, v. 170. Is Grease injurious
to ?—J. Craig, vi. 236. Japanese
and N. American, suitable for
British Woodlands—H. J. Elwes,
xix. 76. Measurements — R.
Christison, viii. 262 ; *for Cubic
Contents—J. W. Barry, x. 21.
Nomenclature—F. B., xvi. 319.
Of California—F. R. S. Balfour,
xxii. 213. Of Western America—
F. R. S. Balfour, xxi. 121. Plant-
ing, as Investment in Ireland—W.
Harrower, x. 55. *Pruning, in St
James's Park and Piccadilly—I. B.
Balfour, xxvi. 31. Resistance of
Young, to Drought, xx. 247.
Season and Growth of — A. C.
Forbes, xv. 75. Seed—Testing—
J. Rafn, xvi. 277, 407. Structure,
etc., of—D. F. Mackenzie, xiv.
114. Woods, Plantations, etc.,
Law Relating to, in Scotland—R.
Galloway, xix. 332. See Notes
and Queries, and *infra*.
Trees, Old and Remarkable :—*At
Ardkinglas, Argyleshire—T.
Wilkie, ix. 169. At Bayham
Abbey and Wilderness Park, Kent—
J. Duff, viii. 147. *At Gordon
Castle, Banffshire—J. Webster, ix.
63. At Hampton Court, Leo-
minster—T. Hogg, ix. 145. At
Holwood, Kent—A. D. Webster,
xii. 301. Conservation of, in
Britain—R. Hutchison, vii. 259.
*In Island of Bute—J. Kay, ix.
73. On Earl Spencer's Estates in
Northamptonshire — F. Mitchell,
xiii. 83. *Ou Rolle Estate, Devon
—J. Barrie, xii. 242. *Yew, in
Scotland—R. Hutchison, xii. 379.
Tree-Butt Blasting, Scientific, xviii.
225.
Tree Stumps, Creosoting against
Pine Weevil—F. R. S. Balfour,
xxviii. 270.
Tupelo Wood, xix. 210.
*Turfs, Belgian System of Planting
on. J. Stirling - Maxwell, xxiii.
153.
Turnery, Utilisation of Small-Wood
for. A. T. Williamson. xiii. 145.

UNDER-FORESTERS, Improving Social
and Moral Condition of, etc. P.
M'Laren, v. 73 ; C. Y. Michie, v.
61.
Underplanted Larch Plantations at
Novar. W. Mackenzie, xxiii. 35.
Underplanting. F. Bailey, xxi. 198.

Underwood :—For Planting near Sea —W. Gilchrist, v. 143; C. Y. Michie, v. 150. Profitableness of Rearing—J. Davidson, iv. 21. See Game.

Unemployed :—Problem of, xvii. 161. Value of Work done by, xxiii. 107.

United Kingdom, Forest Resources of. H. Maxwell, xxii. 1.

United States :—Forest Conservation in, xxi. 227 ; xxiv. 225. Forests of, xviii. 229. Timber Supply of, xxiv. 221 ; W. Harrower, x. 83.

Uses, Economic:—Of Chips, Branches, and Roots of Trees—J. Johnston, v. 55. Of Timber Grown in Scotland—R. Hutchison, v. 109 ; C. Y. Michie, v. 114. Of Wood in Japan, xviii. 231.

Uses, Some, of Demonstration Forest. J. F. Annand, xxvii. 54.

*Utilisation:—Of Disused Pit-banks —P. Murray Thomson, xxvii. 30. Of Nitrogen of Air—A. Lauder, xx. 183.

Vallombrosa, Royal Forest School at. H. Cleghorn, viii. 182.

Valuation of Wood for Transfer. J. Pearson, vii. 398.

Value, Comparative, of Timber grown in Scotland. R. Hutchison, v. 109 ; C. Y. Michie, v. 114.

Vaud, Switzerland, Forest Administration in. G. Cadell, xii. 78.

Vegetable Remains from Site of Roman Military Station at Newstead, Melrose, xxiii. 31.

Vegetation of Woodlands. W. G. Smith, xxiv. 6, 131.

*Vegetation Types at High Altitudes. G. P. Gordon, xxviii. 46.

Visits of Foreign Professors to Scotland, xxiv. 107.

Visit by R. E. Arbor. Soc. to German Forests. A. T. Gillanders, xxviii. 100.

Vosges Mountains, Forests of Central, xxiii. 113.

Vyrnwy, Afforestation at, xxvii. 236.

Wales : — Experimental Forestry Area in—Fraser Story, xxvii. 19. School of Forestry for, xvii. 339.

Walks, on Estates, etc. R. E. Brown, iii. 8 ; A. Paterson, iii. 23.

Wass Pinetum. R. Brown, iv. 164.

Waste Land :—Afforestation of, xxii. 207. Planting for Profit—G. U. Macdonald, xviii. 183 ; J. Nisbet, xix. 259. Preparation of — R.

Philip, ii. 21. Value of, for Afforestation—A. C. Forbes, xx. 142. See xiii. 1 ; xiv. 51.

Water-Catchment Areas:—Afforestation of, G. Baxter, xxiv. 191. Afforestation of Talla—F. Bailey, xx. 106.

Water-Voles, Damage by. F. Moon, xxi. 105.

Waterworks' Catchment Areas, Afforestation of, xvii. 327 ; J. Parry, xvii. 223 ; W. G. Smith, xvii. 86.

Watt, H. B. : Altitude of Forest Trees on Cairngorm Mountains, xvii. 266 ; Bibliography of Forestry, xxvi. 230 ; *Early Tree-Planting in Scotland, xxvi. 12.

Webster, A. D. : Comparative Value of Exotic Coniferæ as Ornamental or Timber Trees in Britain, xii. 246 ; *Coniferæ at Penrhyn Castle, N. Wales, xi. 55 ; Corsican Pine, xi. 181 ; Culture, etc., of Picea Nordmanniana, ix. 94 ; Douglas Fir, xi. 165 ; Game Coverts, xi. 213 : Giant Arbor-Vitæ, xii. 341. Hedgerow and Field Timber, xi. 550 ; Old and Remarkable Trees at Holwood, Kent, xii. 301. Plantations on Penrhyn Estate, N. Wales, xii. 165. Trees and Shrubs for Planting in Towns, xiii. 123 ; Trees and Shrubs of Carnarvonshire, xi. 481 : Trees best adapted for Various Soils, xiii. 254.

Webster, J. : *Old and Remarkable Trees at Gordon Castle, ix. 63.

Weevil :—Creosoting Tree Stumps against Pine—F. R. S. Balfour, xxviii. 270. Experiments with Lime, etc., for Protection against Pine—T. Neilson, xix. 207. Infestation by Pine—D. Macdonald, xxiii. 180. Large Brown Pine, Leaflet on, xxviii. 118. Prevention of Damage by Pine—E. S. Grant, xx. 53. Strophosomus Coryli, Attack by—J. Macrae, xxiii. 185. See Reports by Hon. Scientists.

Weight of Timber, xix. 217.

*Wellingtonia gigantea, Altitude, etc., of. R. Hutchison, vii. 190.

Wentworth, Yorkshire, Plantations on Estate of. G. Dodds, xii. 156.

Western Hemlock Spruce, Nursery Treatment of. J. M. Murray, xxi. 41.

Whellens, W. H. : Arboretum, Formation of, xxvii. 79 ; Douglas Fir, xxiv. 47 : Japanese Larch r.

European Larch, xxiii. 105 ; Thorn Hedges, xxvi. 61.

When Afforestation comes. J. Fleming, xxiii. 124.

Whyte, J. : Oak Coppice Woods, and Coppice Bark, i. 215 ; Reclamation of Neglected Plantations, i. 110.

Whyte, J. D. B. : *Novar Estate, Plan of Management, xvi. 25.

Whytock, J. : Obituary Notice of Mr R. Baxter, xix. 244.

Wigtown, etc. Arboriculture in. A. Pitcaithley, xiii. 293.

Wild, A. E. : Natural and Artificial Rearing of Forest Trees, v. 88.

Wilkie, T. : Belts of Plantations on Hill Pasture Land, xii. 337 ; Comparative Value of Exotic Coniferæ as Ornamental or Timber Trees, xii. 206 ; Deleterious Effects of Sulphur on Iron Fencing, viii. 165 ; Hardwood Plantations, ix. 152. 242 ; Oak Coppice, ix. 270 ; *Old and Remarkable Trees at Ardkinglas, Argyleshire, ix. 169. Seasoning Timber, viii. 190 ; *Two new Modes of Fencing, viii. 171 ; Underwood for Game Coverts, in High Forest, xii. 371.

Williamson, A. T. : Bark-Peeling, Commercial Aspect of, xii. 443 ; Leasehold Timber Farms, xii. 418 ; *Manufacture of Home - grown Timber, xiii. 151 ; Railway and Canal Traffic Act (1888), xii. 425 ; Timber Supplies from Abroad, xiii. 353 ; Utilisation of Small-Wood for Turnery, etc., xiii. 145.

Willow :—Cultivation of, xxiii. 191. *Galls on—R. S. MacDougall, xviii. 208.

Willow Timber, Value of. A. D. R., xx. 127.

Wilson, A. F. : Session at Eberswalde Forest Academy, xx. 201.

Wilson, Malcolm, and A. W. Borthwick : New Disease on Larch in Scotland, xxvii. 198.

Wind - Mantle, White American Spruce as. J. F. Annand, xvi. 473.

Winter Moth, Attack of Lime Trees by Larvæ of, xxiv. 107.

Wire Fences. See Fences and Fencing.

*Witch's Broom on *Pseudotsuga Douglasii*. J. M'Callum, xxviii. 116.

Wood : — A new Tasmanian, xix. 210. Artificially Coloured, xix. 215. Best kinds for Charcoal, etc.

—R. Baxter, viii. 246. Business in Russia, x. 243. Clearing Crop of, earlier than usual—W. Brown, vi. 192. Distillation of, xxvi. 99. Effect of Moisture on, xxiv. 111. Imports of Manufactured (1909-10), xxiv. 219. Preservation by Electrolysis, xx. 128. Preservative against Splitting, xxiv. 110. Rapid Ageing and Fireproofing of, xvii. 291. *Sections of, grown in Britain— D. F. Mackenzie, xiv. 39. *Specimens for Exhibition—G. Cadell, xiii. 310. Tupelo, xix. 210. Uses of, in Japan, xviii. 231.

Woodlands :—And Fields, Destruction of Rabbits Injurious to—J. Nisbet, xix. 104. Area of, in Great Britain, xix. 347. British, Some Japanese and N. American Trees Suitable for—H. J. Elwes, xix. 76. British Working-Plans for—J. Nisbet, xx. 30. Castle Hill, Working-Plan of—F. Story, xx. 36. Death Duties as affecting —R. Galloway, xxiii. 133. Primitive Types in Scotland—G. P. Gordon, xxiv. 153. Rating of, xxvi. 96. Sir Herbert Maxwell on Neglected, xix. 357. The State and Private—W. Dawson, xxiv. 121. Vegetation of—W. G. Smith, xxiv. 6, 131.

Wood-Paving, British Oak for, xviii. 226.

Wood-Pulp, xxiii. 233 ; Enhanced Value of Canadian, xxiv. 99. See Pulp.

Woods : — *And Afforestable Lands in Scotland, Report of Inspection of, xxviii. 154. *And Railways— W. Brown, vi. 192. Damage to, by Gases from Calcining Ironstone —A. Slater, vii. 184. Death Duties on, xxvii. 36. Disposing of Produce—A. Peebles, vii. 159. Do they Pay ?—R. Brown, iv. 159. *Natural Regeneration of—W. Somerville, xiii. 63. Of Highclere, Hants—A. Peebles, vi. 245. Of New Brunswick—L. W. Bailey and E. Jack, xi. 9. Of Somerset— W. G. Smith, xx. 216. Of Zürich —F. Story, xxii. 34. Rainfall in Wooded and Unwooded Countries — R. Hutchison, vii. 10. Rearing of, profitably, where game is preserved—A. Gilchrist, iv. 177. Self-Sown Oak of Sussex — R. W. Clutton, vii. 194. Systematic Management of, xvii. 338. Town-

Woods of Carlsbad—J. Nisbet,
xix. 150. Treatment of Mixed,
etc.—"T.," xx. 21· Valuation of,
for Transfer—J. Peaison, xvi. 398.
See Plantations.
Wood Timber, Plan to meet needs
for, xxviii. 78
Working-Plan. See Plan.
Workmen's Dwellings, Glen Mor,
xxv. 32.
Wood-Wasps, xv. 194, 311.
World's Timber Supply :—Insuffici-
ency of, xvi. 384. Outlook—W.
Schlich, xvi. 355. See xvii. 187.

YALE Forest School. F. B., xx. 251.
Yeats, A. : Douglas Fir on Durris
Estate, xvi. 185.
*Yew Trees, Old and Remarkable, in
Scotland. R. Hutchison, xii. 379.
Yorkshire. Arboriculture in. D.
Tait, vii. 137.

ZÜRICH Woods. F. Story, xxii. 34.